Elements
of Argument

NINTH EDITION

Elements of Argument

A Text and Reader

Annette T. Rottenberg

Donna Haisty Winchell

CLEMSON UNIVERSITY

Bedford/St. Martin's

Boston ◆ New York

For Bedford/St. Martin's

Senior Developmental Editor: John E. Sullivan III
Production Editors: Kendra LeFleur and Karen Stocz
Production Supervisor: Jennifer Peterson
Senior Marketing Manager: Karita dos Santos
Editorial Assistant: Alicia Young
Copyeditor: Lisa Wehrle
Text Design: Claire Seng-Niemoeller
Cover Design: Sara Gates
Cover Art: Soonae Tark, *Kiss #2*, 2006, acrylic on paper, 29.5 x 21.5 inches
Composition: Achorn International, Inc.
Printing and Binding: RR Donnelley & Sons

President: Joan E. Feinberg
Editorial Director: Denise B. Wydra
Editor in Chief: Karen S. Henry
Director of Marketing: Karen Melton Soeltz
Director of Editing, Design, and Production: Marcia Cohen
Assistant Director of Editing, Design, and Production: Elise S. Kaiser
Managing Editor: Elizabeth M. Schaaf

Library of Congress Control Number: 2008925885

Manufactured in the United States of America.

3   2   1   0   9   8

f   e   d   c   b   a

For information, write: Bedford/St. Martin's, 75 Arlington Street, Boston, MA 02116 (617-399-4000)

ISBN-10: 0–312–48047–4
ISBN-13: 978–0–312–48047–9

Acknowledgments

ACLU. "What is the U.S.A. Patriot Act?" From the *ACLU Online Newsletter.* Reprinted by permission of the American Civil Liberties Union.

Acknowledgments and copyrights are continued at the back of the book on pages 799–804, which constitute an extension of the copyright page. It is a violation of the law to reproduce these selections by any means whatsoever without the written permission of the copyright holder.

Preface for Instructors

PURPOSE

Argumentation as the basis of a composition course should need no defense, especially at a time of renewed pedagogical interest in critical thinking. A course in argumentation encourages practice in close analysis, use of supporting materials, and logical organization. It encompasses all the modes of development around which composition courses are often built. It teaches students to read and to listen with more than ordinary care. Not least, argument can engage the interest of students who have been indifferent or even hostile to required writing courses. Because the subject matter of argument can be found in every human activity—from the most trivial to the most elevated—both students and teachers can choose the materials that appeal to them.

Composition courses using the materials of argument are, of course, not new. But the traditional methods of teaching argument through mastery of the formal processes of reasoning cannot account for the complexity of arguments in practice. Even more relevant to our purposes as teachers of composition is the tenuous relationship between learning about induction and deduction, however helpful in analysis, and the actual process of student composition. The challenge has been to find a method of teaching argument that assists students in defending their claims as directly and efficiently as possible, a method that reflects the way people actually go about organizing and developing claims outside the classroom.

One such method, first adapted to classroom instruction by teachers of rhetoric and speech, uses a model of argument advanced by Stephen Toulmin in *The Uses of Argument*. Toulmin was interested in producing a description of the real process of argument. His model was the law. "Arguments," he said, "can be compared with lawsuits, and the claims we make and argue for in extra-legal contexts with claims made in the courts."[1] Toulmin's model of argument was based on three principal elements: claim, evidence, and warrant. These elements answered the questions, "What are you trying to prove?" "What have you got to go on?"

[1] Stephen Toulmin, *The Uses of Argument* (Cambridge: Cambridge UP, 1958), p. 7.

"How did you get from evidence to claim?" Needless to say, Toulmin's model of argument does not guarantee a classroom of skilled arguers, but his questions about the parts of an argument and their relationship are precisely the ones that students must ask and answer in writing their own essays and analyzing those of others. They lead students naturally into the formulation and development of their claims.

In this text we have adapted—and greatly simplified—some of Toulmin's concepts and terminology for first-year students. We have also introduced two elements of argument with which Toulmin is not directly concerned. Most rhetoricians consider them indispensable, however, to discussion of what actually happens in the defense or rejection of a claim. One is motivational appeals—warrants based on appeals to the needs and values of an audience, designed to evoke emotional responses. A distinction between logic and emotion may be useful as an analytical tool, but in producing or attacking arguments human beings find it difficult, if not impossible, to make such a separation. In this text, therefore, persuasion through appeals to needs and values is treated as a legitimate element in the argumentative process.

We have also stressed the significance of audience as a practical matter. In the rhetorical or audience-centered approach to argument, to which we subscribe in this text, success is defined as acceptance of the claim by an audience. Arguers in the real world recognize intuitively that their primary goal is not to demonstrate the purity of their logic but to win the adherence of their audiences. To gain this adherence, students need to be reminded of the necessity for establishing themselves as credible sources for their readers.

We hope *Elements of Argument* will lead students to discover not only the practical and intellectual rewards of learning how to argue but the real excitement of engaging in civilized debate.

ORGANIZATION

In Part One, after four introductory chapters, a chapter each is devoted to the chief elements of argument—the definitions that lay a foundation for shared understanding, the claims that students make in their arguments, the support they must supply for their claims, and the warrants that underlie their arguments. Popular fallacies as well as induction and deduction are treated in Chapter 9; because fallacies represent errors of reasoning, a knowledge of induction and deduction can make clear how and why fallacies occur. Chapter 10 deals with the power of word choice in arguing effectively.

We have provided examples, readings, discussion questions, and writing suggestions that are, we hope, both practical and stimulating. The examples include essays, articles, speeches, news reports, editorial opinions, letters to the editor, excerpts from online sources, cartoons, and advertisements. They reflect the liveliness and complexity of argumentation that exercises with no realistic context often suppress.

The selections and advertisements in Part One support in several ways the discussions of argumentation. First, they illustrate the elements of argument; in each chapter, one or more essays have been analyzed to emphasize the principles of argument explained in the chapter. Second, they are a mix of pieces drawn from current publications as well as classic essays and cover as many different subjects as possible to convince students that argument is a pervasive force in the world they read about and live in. Third, some of the essays are obviously flawed and thus enable students to identify the kinds of weaknesses they should avoid in their own essays.

Part Two takes up the process of writing, researching, and presenting arguments. Chapters 11 and 12 explain how to find a topic, define the issues that it embraces, organize the information, and draft and revise an argument. They introduce students to the business of finding sources and using and documenting those sources effectively in research papers. Part Two includes two annotated student research papers: one that employs the Modern Language Association (MLA) documentation system, the other that represents research in the social and natural sciences and uses a modified American Psychological Association (APA) documentation style. Chapter 13 provides guidelines for presenting arguments orally.

Part Three, "Multiple Viewpoints," exhibits arguers in action, using informal and formal language, often debating head-on. The topics of its selections and cartoons capture everyday headlines, and despite their immediacy, they are likely to arouse passions and remain controversial for a long time. Whether as matters of national policy or personal choice, these topics call for decisions based on familiarity with competing views.

NEW TO THIS EDITION

Although the principles and concerns of the book have not changed, the new material in this edition should enhance the versatility of the text, deepen students' awareness of how pervasive argument is, and increase their ability to think critically and communicate persuasively. There are many new selections on current topics; half of the readings are new. In addition, we have revised many of the Writer's Guides and have added a new Writer's Guide on annotating a text. We have also added more help for understanding and working with the elements of argument: "Practice" assignments within each chapter ask students to apply what they've learned right away, and end-of-chapter assignments now include both discussion and writing prompts to help students move from informal to written response. New "sentence forms" templates help students understand the structure of summary and response in argument as they construct arguments of their own. And because working with visual texts has become increasingly important, all of Chapter 3, "Reading Visual Texts Critically," is devoted to that topic. It includes seven new visuals (photographs, advertisements, and Web pages) for illustration and analysis.

There's now also more help for researching and writing argumentative papers. A new Chapter 4, "Writing about Argument," includes more help with summary, paraphrase, quoting, documenting sources, and avoiding plagiarism. In Part Two, we've included new sample MLA and APA papers to provide updated models for students. We've also added new "source maps" diagrams to Part Two—a feature popular in many of our grammar handbooks—to help show students how citations spring from sources, illustrating both the mechanics and practical realities of citation.

In Part Three, new pro-con debates focus on the issues of governmental seizure of private property and the risks of citizen journalism. New Multiple Viewpoints chapters explore immigration, academic integrity, and medical ethics. So that instructors can more easily assign time-tested essays in the context of instruction on argument, the classic selections previously found at the end of the book have been integrated throughout. Finally, to keep the size of the book as brief as possible, the literature appendix has been moved to the book's Web site. You can find it at bedfordstmartins .com/rottenberg.

ANCILLARIES

The instructor's manual, *Resources for Teaching ELEMENTS OF ARGUMENT,* provides additional suggestions for using the book as well as for finding and using the enormous variety of materials available in a course on argument.

A companion Web site at bedfordstmartins.com/rottenberg includes annotated links for students and instructors looking for further information on controversial topics, debates, and rhetorical theory. It also includes exercises for students on fallacies and warrants.

Mixed media and everyday arguments can be both more accessible and more challenging for students to examine. The i•claim CD-ROM offers a new way to visualize argument. It features six tutorials and an illustrated glossary. The i•claim CD-ROM can be packaged for free with *Elements of Argument*. To see a sample tutorial, visit bedfordstmartins.com/iclaim. For ordering information, contact your local sales representative or e-mail us at sales_support@bfwpub.com.

Also available is *Teaching Argument in the Composition Course*, by Timothy Barnett. It offers a range of perspectives, from Aristotle to the present day, on argument and on teaching argument. The twenty-eight readings—many of them classic works in the field—present essential insights and practical information. For ordering information, contact your local sales representative or e-mail us at sales_support@bfwpub.com.

ALSO AVAILABLE

A briefer edition, *The Structure of Argument*, Sixth Edition, is available for instructors who prefer a shorter text with fewer readings. It presents only Parts One and Two.

ACKNOWLEDGMENTS

This book has profited by the critiques and suggestions of reviewers and instructors who responded to a questionnaire. We appreciate the thoughtful consideration given to previous editions by Nancy E. Adams, Timothy C. Alderman, Yvonne Alexander, John V. Andersen, Lucile G. Appert, William Arfin, Alison K. Armstrong, Karen Arnold, Angel M. Arzán, Mark Edward Askren, Michael Austin, David B. Axelrod, Jacquelyn A. Babush, Peter Banland, Carol A. Barnes, Tim Barnett, Marilyn Barry, Marci Bartolotta, Bonnie C. Bedford, Frank Beesley, Don Beggs, Martine Bellen, Bruce Bennett, Maureen Dehler Bennett, Chester Benson, Robert H. Bentley, Scott Bentley, Arthur E. Bervin, Patricia Bizzell, Don Black, Kathleen Black, Stanley S. Blair, Laurel Boyd, Mary Virginia Brackett, Robert J. Branda, Dianne Brehmer, Alan Brown, Megan Brown, Paul L. Brown, Bill Buck, W. K. Buckley, Alison A. Bulsterbaum, Clarence Bussinger, Deborah N. Byrd, Gary T. Cage, Ruth A. Cameron, Rita Carey, Barbara R. Carlson, Eric W. Cash, Donna R. Chaney, Gail Chapman, Linda D. Chinn, Roland Christian, Gina Claywell, John O. Clemonts, Paul D. Cockeram, Tammy S. Cole, John Conway, Thomas S. Costello, Martha J. Craig, David J. Cranmer, Edward Crothers, Jennifer Cunningham, Sara Cutting, Jo Ann Dadisman, Sandra Dahlberg, Mimi Dane, Judy Davidson, Cynthia C. Davis, Philip E. Davis, Stephanie Demma, Loretta Denner, Cecile de Rocher, Julia Dietrich, Marcia B. Dinnech, Felicia A. Dixon, Jane T. Dodge, Ellen Donovan, L. Leon Duke, P. Dunsmore, Bernard Earley, Carolyn Embree, Carolyn L. Engdahl, Gwyn Enright, Stephen Ersinghaus, David Estes, Kristina Faber, Lester Faigley, Faridoun Farroth, B. R. Fein, Delia Fisher, Philip L. Fishman, Catherine Fitzgerald, Evelyn Flores, David D. Fong, Donald Forand, Mary A. Fortner, Alice R. France, Leslye Friedberg, Sondra Frisch, Richard Fulkerson, Maureen Furniss, Diane Gabbard, Donald J. Gadow, Eric Gardner, Frieda Gardner, Gail Garloch, Darcey Garretson, Victoria Gaydosik, E. R. Gelber-Beechler, Scott Giantralley,

Michael Patrick Gillespie, Paula Gillespie, Wallace Gober, Sara Gogol, Stuart Goodman, Joseph Gredler, Lucie Greenberg, Mildred Buza Gronek, Marilyn Hagans, Linda L. Hagge, Lee T. Hamilton, Carolyn Han, Phillip J. Hanse, Pat Hardré, Susan Harland, A. Leslie Harris, Carolyn G. Hartz, Theresia A. Hartz, Fredrik Hausmann, Michael Havens, William Hayes, Ursula K. Heise, Anne Helms, Tena Lea Helton, Peter C. Herman, Diane Price Herndl, Heidi Hobbs, William S. Hochman, Sharon E. Hockensmith, Andrew J. Hoffman, Joyce Hooker, Richard S. Hootman, Laura Hope-Aleman, Clarence Hundley, Patrick Hunter, Richard Ice, Mary Griffith Jackson, Ann S. Jagoe, Katherine James, Missy James, Ruth Jeffries, Owen Jenkins, Ruth Y. Jenkins, Iris Jennings, Linda Johnson, Richard M. Johnson, Janet Jubnke, E. C. Juckett, Catherine Kaikowska, George T. Karnezis, Richard Katula, Mary Jane Kearny, Joanne Keel, Patricia Kellogg-Dennis, N. Kesinger, Susan Kincaid, Joanne Kirkland, Judith Kirscht, Nancy Klug, John H. Knight, Paul D. Knoke, Frances Kritzer, George W. Kuntzman, Barbara Ladd, Jocelyn Ladner, M. Beardsley Land, Marlene J. Lang, Lisa Lebduska, Sara R. Lee, William Levine, Mary Levitt, Diana M. Liddle, Jack Longmate, Cynthia Lowenthal, Marjorie Lynn, Marcia MacLennan, Chantelle MacPhee, Nancy McGee, Patrick McGuire, Ray McKerrow, Michael McKoski, Pamela J. McLagen, Suzanne McLaughlin, Dennis McMillan, Donald McQuade, Christina M. McVay, D'Ann Madewell, Beth Madison, Susan Maloney, Dan M. Manolescu, Barbara A. Manrigue, Joyce Marks, Quentin E. Martin, Michael Matzinger, Charles May, Alan Merickel, Jean-Pierre Meterean, Ekra Miezan, Carolyn R. Miller, Lisa K. Miller, Logan D. Moon, Dennis D. Moore, Dan Morgan, Karen L. Morris, Curt Mortenson, Philip A. Mottola, Thomas Mullen, Charlotte A. Myers, Joan Naake, Michael B. Naas, Joseph Nassar, Byron Nelson, Elizabeth A. Nist, Jody Noerdlinger, Paralee F. Norman, Dr. Mary Jean Northcutt, Thomas O'Brien, James F. O'Neil, Mary O'Riordan, Arlene Okerland, Renee Olander, Elizabeth Oldfield, Amy Olsen, Richard D. Olson, Steven Olson, Lori Jo Oswald, Sushil K. Oswald, Roy Kenneth Pace II, Gary Pak, Linda J. Palumbo, Edna Parker, Jo Patterson, Laurine Paule, Leland S. Person, Betty Peters, Kelly S. Petersen, Nancy L. Peterson, Susan T. Peterson, Steve Phelan, Gail W. Pieper, Gloria Platzner, Mildred Postar, Ralph David Powell, Jr., Rossana Pronesti, Teresa Marie Purvis, Mark Razor, Barbara E. Rees, Karen L. Regal, Pat Regel, Charles Reinhart, Thomas C. Renzi, Janice M. Reynolds, Douglas F. Rice, G. A. Richardson, Beverly A. Ricks, James M. Ritter, Katherine M. Rogers, Marilyn Mathias Root, Judith Klinger Rose, Cathy Rosenfeld, Robert A. Rubin, Norma L. Rudinsky, Lori Ruediger, Cheryl W. Ruggiero, Richard Ruppel, Victoria Anne Sager, Joseph L. Sanders, Irene Schiller, Suzette Schlapkohl, Sybil Schlesinger, Richard Schneider, Eileen Schwartz, Esther L. Schwartz, Eugene Senff, Jeffrey Seyall, Ron Severson, Lucy Sheehey, William E. Sheidley, Sallye J. Sheppeard, Sally Bishop Shigley, John Shout, Craig L. Shurtleff, Dr. Barbara L. Siek, Thomas Simmons, Michael Simms, Jacqueline Simon,

Richard Singletary, Roger L. Slakey, Thomas S. Sloane, Beth Slusser, Denzell Smith, Rebecca Smith, Margaret Smolik, James R. Sodon, Katherine Sotol, Donald L. Soucy, Minoo Southgate, Linda Spain, Richard Spilman, Sarah J. Stafford, Jim Stegman, Martha L. Stephens, Arlo Stoltenberg, Elissa L. Stuchlik, Judy Szaho, Andrew Tadie, Fernanda G. Tate-Owens, R. Terhorst, Marguerite B. Thompson, Arline R. Thorn, Mary Ann Trevathan, Sandia Tuttle, Whitney G. Vanderwerff, Jennie VerSteeg, Les Wade, David L. Wagner, Jeanne Walker, James Wallace, Linda D. Warwick, Carol Adams Watson, Roger D. Watson, Karen Webb, Raymond E. Whelan, Betty E. White, Julia Whitsitt, Toby Widdicombe, Mary Louise Willey, Heywood Williams, Matthew C. Wolfe, Alfred Wong, Bonnie B. Zitz, and Laura Zlogar.

In addition, we would like to thank those instructors who completed a questionnaire for the Eighth Edition: Effrossini Piliouni Albrecht, Kathleen Allison, Jim Bonnett, Nick Boone, Eleanor Bunting, Harry Costigan, Karen Craig, David Hulm, Jennifer Kirchoff, Beth Madison, Jim Matthews, Kathryn McCormick, John McKinnis, Patrick McMahon, Amy Minervini, Dana Nkana, Nancy Raftery, Marlisa Santos, Martha Smith, James Sodon, Deborah Steward, Andrea Van Vorhis, and Joseph Walker.

We are also grateful to Kate Kiefer and Meg Morgan for their in-depth reviews.

We would like to thank those instructors who completed a questionnaire for the Ninth Edition: Corinne Andersen, Peace College; Martha Bachman, Camden County College; Carol Bone, Washtenaw Community College; Carol Brown, South Puget Sound Community College; Diane N. Chapin, Montgomery College; Elizabeth Cater Childs, Auburn University; William Curl, University of Wisconsin–Fox Valley; Joe Davis III, North Iowa Area Community College; Kathy Dechter, Columbia Basin College; Genesis M. Downey, Owens Community College; Stephanie Gordon, University of Colorado–Colorado Springs; Kerry Moquett, Humphreys College; Joan Naake, Montgomery College–Germantown; Susan Reddington, Cabrillo College; Craig L. Shurtleff, Illinois Central College; James R. Sodon, St. Louis Community College; and Will Zhang, Des Moines Area Community College.

We are also grateful for the work of those reviewers who chose to remain anonymous.

We are also thankful to the following instructors for their in-depth reviews: Robert Arnold, University of North Carolina–Charlotte; Shanti Bruce, Nova Southeastern University; Jeffrey Hotz, Montgomery College; Kathy Mennen, Washtenaw Community College; Susan Miller, University of Utah; and Marti Singer, Georgia State University.

We appreciate the contributions that Gail Stygall of the University of Washington made to a previous edition of the instructor's manual, which have been retained in this edition. We also thank once again Fred Kemp of Texas Tech University, who drafted the section on responding online;

Barbara Fister of Gustavus Adolphus College, who revised the discussion of information technologies; and Tim Barnett of Northeastern Illinois University, who enlarged and updated the sections on critical reading, evaluating electronic sources, note taking, and summarizing, and for drafting the sample analysis of a Web site. All of their contributions have been retained in this edition.

We are grateful to those at Bedford/St. Martin's who have helped in numerous ways large and small: Joan Feinberg, Elizabeth Schaaf, Denise Wydra, Karen Henry, Steve Scipione, Sandy Schechter, Alicia Young, Naomi Kornhauser, Kendra LeFleur, Karen Stocz, Rebecca Merrill, Sue Brekka, Lisa Wehrle and, most especially, John Sullivan.

Brief Contents

Contents

6. Defending Claims 157

8. Analyzing Warrants   272

9. Avoiding Flawed Logic 322

important. They claim, "It is impossible either in speech or in writing to put two facts together without giving some slight emphasis or slant."

SAMPLE ANNOTATED ESSAY

President's Address to the Nation, September 11, 2006   *393*
GEORGE W. BUSH

Five years after the terrorist attacks of 2001, President George W. Bush talks of "the nature of the threat still before us, what we are doing to protect our nation, and the building of a more hopeful Middle East. . . ."

Writer's Guide: Choosing Your Words Carefully   400

READINGS FOR ANALYSIS

Americans Entitled to Cheap Gas—Right?   *401*
JOAN RYAN

A journalist takes a sarcastic look at Americans' assumption that they deserve the best of everything—no matter what it costs.

Shotgun Weddings   *403*
KATHA POLLITT

A journalist claims that marriage is all a matter of economics.

Politics and the English Language   *406*
GEORGE ORWELL

In this 1946 essay, the author of *1984* suggests why the hand that pens a stale metaphor should not be trusted with the reins of government.

DEBATE: DOES THE GOVERNMENT HAVE THE RIGHT TO REGULATE GUNS?

The Right to Bear Arms   *417*
WARREN E. BURGER

A former chief justice of the United States examines the historical roots of the Second Amendment in order to construct an appeal for gun control.

A God-Given Natural Right   *420*
ROGER D. McGRATH

A history professor and Captain in the Naval Detachment of the California State Military Reserve argues that the Bill of Rights does not have to grant the right to bear arms but rather that it assumes that right already exists.

Part Two

Researching, Writing, and Presenting Arguments 429

11. Planning and Researching an Argumentative Paper 431

12. Writing an Argumentative Paper 474

Part Three

Multiple Viewpoints   533

14. How Far Will We Go to Change Our Body Image?   535

15. Is Academic Integrity on Our College Campuses under Assault?   566

16. Have We Become Too Reliant on Standardized Testing? 595

17. What Is the Role of Sex and Violence in Popular Culture? 636

18. Are Limits on Freedom of Speech Ever Justified?   672

to exclude others may seem intolerant," he writes, "but such a right is indispensable to private groups seeking to define themselves, to chart their own moral course, and to work together for common ends."

19. Why and How Should Immigration Be Controlled?   703

The Miami bureau chief for *Newsweek* describes the rush to citizenship being made by legal immigrants who have become nervous as a result of the immigration debates.

According to this *Time* reporter, one negative result of the recent debates over immigration has been a resurgence of interest in white supremacist organizations.

20. In the World of Medicine, Who Decides What Is Ethical? 735

A specialist on health issues reveals the inequities in who is put on the waiting list for organ transplants. The criteria too often include the patient's ability to pay.

A physician explains that the harvesting of organs raises the thorny question of what the difference is between the dead and the nearly dead.

A specialist in health law and bioethics examines the controversy surrounding whether cancer patients should have the right to try experimental drugs as a last resort.

According to a *Time* editor, there were no easy answers when parents asked that their brain-damaged daughter have her growth and development artificially stunted to make her smaller and more manageable.

A physician and professor of bioethics examines the question of what should be done with "left over" frozen embryos.

A writer on health issues argues that in an emergency, doctors should put aside their personal beliefs if necessary to do what is best for the patient — but too often they don't.

ALBERTO R. GONZALES

A former attorney general argues that the rule of law is not enough to deal with enemy combatants but rather that military commissions must be used in their trials to overcome limitations of the civilian justice system.

Panel Hears about Falsehoods in Two Wartime Incidents   792

MICHAEL LUO

A reporter uses the cases of Jessica Lynch and Pat Tillman to illustrate the tendency of those in charge to give the public the heroes they want in time of war, even when it means twisting the truth.

What Abu Ghraib Taught Me   794

BARBARA EHRENREICH

A disillusioned feminist laments the fact that women were involved in the mistreatment of prisoners at Abu Ghraib.

Thinking and Writing about the Effect of Terrorism on the American Idea of Justice   797

Elements
of Argument

Understanding Argument

CHAPTER 1

Understanding the Structure of Argument

THE NATURE OF ARGUMENT

Television news used to mean thirty minutes of local news followed by thirty minutes of national news in the early evening with a late-night local edition incorporating late-breaking news. A triumph like the first moon walk or a tragedy like the assassination of John F. Kennedy in 1963 or that of Martin Luther King Jr. in 1968 justified breaking into regularly scheduled programming, whatever the hour. An event as momentous as a royal wedding or the death of a president or former president, then as now, was the rare occasion for several days of televised coverage. Those were the days before the advent of twenty-four-hour news stations that today are a staple of American life. Now, the latest news is instantly as close as our remote controls.

News shows were originally designed to present, in brief, the facts of what was happening around the country and around the world. The need to broadcast day in and day out, however, has increasingly led to a need to fill time by talking about rather than presenting the news. Analysis of the news is crucial to understanding the events that shape our world, and hearing different perspectives can help enlighten the listening and reading public. Any subject, however, can become the subject of debate if at least two people have different opinions on it, and television networks seem never to be at a loss to find at least one advocate for any position. The early twenty-first century has found viewers increasingly questioning attempts by commentators to make a controversy out of everything, from the way a murder investigation was handled to the bad behavior of celebrities. They are sometimes left wondering what truly is worth arguing about.

Many controversial questions, some of them as old as human civilization itself, will not be settled nor will they vanish despite the energy we devote to settling them. Unresolved, they are submerged for a while and then reappear, sometimes in another form, sometimes virtually unchanged. Capital punishment is one such stubborn problem; abortion is another. Other issues of major concern today are different from the issues that writers focused on as recently as five or ten years ago. Today we are concerned about terrorism, stem-cell research, immigration, and the ethics of cloning, to name only a few. Whatever issues are of most immediate or most long-lasting concern, we value the argumentative process because it is indispensable to the preservation of a free society, even though that freedom may sometimes be abused. Clearly, if all of us agreed about everything, if harmony prevailed everywhere, the need for argument would disappear. But given what we know about the contentious nature of human beings and their conflicting interests, we should not be surprised to find ourselves drawn into the controversies that swirl around us daily.

Arguments are implicit dialogues. Thus the argumentative process is inherently dramatic; a good argument can create the kinds of tensions generated at sporting events. Who will win? What are the factors that enable a winner to emerge? One of the most popular and enduring situations on television is the courtroom debate, in which two lawyers confront each other before an audience of judge and jury that must render a heart-stopping verdict. Tensions are high because a life is in the balance. An occasional real court case will thus capture the attention of the nation, and in the real world, presidential debates have the power to make or break a candidate.

Of course, not all arguments end in clear victories for one side or another. Nor should they. In a democratic society of competing interests and values, a compromise between two or more extreme points of view may be the only viable solution to a vexing problem. Although formal debates under the auspices of a debating society, such as those take place on many college campuses, usually end in winners and losers, real-life problems—both public and private—are often resolved through negotiation. Courtroom battles may result in compromise, and the law itself allows for exemptions and extenuating circumstances. Elsewhere in this book we speak of the importance of tradeoffs in social and political transactions, giving up one thing in return for another.

Keep in mind, however, that some compromises will not be morally defensible. In searching for a middle ground, the thoughtful arguer must determine that the consequences of a negotiated solution will contribute to the common good, not merely advance personal interests. (At the beginning of Chapter 4, you will find instructions for writing arguments in which you look for common ground.)

Consider how the writing of arguments that you will do in this course differs from simply reporting the facts about a subject. It is the difference between the articles that appear on the front page of the newspaper and those on the editorial page. The following piece from 2006 is a newspaper account of plans to test a new method of screening airline passengers. The author's purpose is not to take a stand but to provide information — information that could affect you in the near future.

X-ray Tests Both Security, Privacy

THOMAS FRANK

S cientists have struggled for four years to build what seemed impossible: an airport X-ray machine that can look through clothing to spot hidden weapons without producing explicit photos of a passenger's body.

The Transportation Security Administration (TSA) will start testing such a device next month in Phoenix. It is the first new passenger-screening machine deployed since mid-2004.

The technology has never been used for security screening. One privacy advocate, doubting TSA assurances, fears that the machine will produce graphic images of passengers that could end up on the Internet.

"People really need to understand that the TSA is putting in place technology that does in fact do a digital strip search and stores those images at least temporarily," said Marc Rotenberg, executive director of the Electronic Privacy Information Center.

"The TSA, however, says the images are cartoonlike sketches that show 5 only outlines of each passenger and are never stored. "There's a privacy-security balance," spokeswoman Ellen Howe said. "We can see what we need to see without seeing what we don't need to see."

The technology, called backscatter X-ray, shoots low-intensity X-ray beams that penetrate clothing and bounce off a person's skin, or scatter backward. Sensors detect backscatter X-rays to create an image of the person's body and items being carried, such as watches, keys, and weapons.

Unlike traditional X-rays, which go through the body and involve more radiation, backscatter X-rays can't see inside a person.

A 2003 report by the National Council on Radiation Protection and Measurements, which Congress created to develop radiation guidelines, said someone would need 2,500 backscatter scans a year before reaching the limits of safe radiation exposure.

Frank Cerra, a physicist with the National Institute of Standards and Technology who co-wrote the report, said a backscatter scan gives off "very, very minimal" radiation. "It's like being out in the sun for 15 to 20 minutes."

The TSA has studied backscatter X-rays since shortly after the Septem- 10 ber 11 attacks because the technology has the potential to be better at finding weapons than metal detectors and screeners.

Thomas Frank is the aviation security correspondent for *USA Today*, where this article appeared on December 27, 2006.

"They're foolproof when it comes to finding metal guns and metal knives," said Clark Kent Ervin, the former Homeland Security Department inspector general who recommended backscatter after his investigations found screeners repeatedly missed hidden weapons.

"A big reason why our tests were so successful in getting guns and knives through is because there was a reluctance on screeners' parts to search people" if a metal detector sounded an alarm, Ervin said.

The technology is less foolproof at finding plastic explosives because of the modifications made to protect passenger privacy.

The backscatter machine to be tested in Phoenix is programmed to erase anatomical details. This "edge detection" technology looks for changes in density or molecular structure on the person and draws outlines around those areas.

A metal object, far more dense than human tissue, is highlighted by a   15
heavy black line. But body contours, if they register at all, appear as faint gray lines because "they don't have edges," said Daniel Strom, a scientist at Pacific Northwest National Laboratory. "It only shows anomalies, like metal and ceramics."

Robert Gould, a radiologist at the University of California, San Francisco who reviewed images from the backscatter machine TSA will test, said the machine also erases detail within highlighted areas. "They suppress all the information within the boundaries they detect."

The modifications could create problems in detecting some plastic explosives that have a density similar to human tissue, said Andrew Karam, a physicist and fellow at the Center for Advanced Defense Studies, a national-security think tank.

"I can smooth (plastic explosives) out like spackle so there really is not a sharp edge. That's something I think is going to be really hard to find," Karam said.

These backscatter X-rays "will find obvious stuff," Karam added.

"I don't know if it will find anything else."   20

The manufacturer, American Science and Engineering of suburban Boston, says its $100,000 backscatter machine finds many weapons missed by screeners and metal detectors.

The modifications made for the TSA "trade off detection for a level of privacy," Richard Mastronardi, a company vice president, told an aviation security conference in November. When the machine is programmed to maximize privacy protection, "you start to lose the ability to see" plastic explosives.

Karam said backscatter X-rays still have merit. "The object is not to prevent everything that can conceivably happen," he said. "The object is to make it difficult."

Although the purpose of Frank's article is to report the news, he brings in statements from others that make clear some of the conversation that is

already going on regarding backscatter screening and some of the controversy it is already arousing. The piece presents the opinions of individuals
who approach the controversy from different perspectives, yet it maintains
the author's own subjectivity. You would expect Marc Rotenberg, executive
director of the Electronic Privacy Information Center, to oppose the x-raying
of airline passengers. You would expect those working for American Science
and Engineering, the manufacturer of the x-ray machines, to defend their
usefulness. And you would expect Frank, as a news reporter, to present
the opposing views fairly.

Now consider the purpose of the following column written by Joe
Sharkey on the same subject. What was Sharkey's purpose in writing? Is his
purpose the same as Frank's? How does the tone of the two pieces differ?

Airport Screeners Could See X-rated X-rays

JOE SHARKEY

I am looking at a copy of an ad that ran in the back of comic books in the
1950s and early 1960s.

"X-Ray Specs! See Thru Clothing!" blares the copy, which is illustrated
with a cartoon of a drooling geek wearing the amazing toy goggles and leer-
ing at a shapely woman.

Now, any kid with half a brain knew that X-Ray Specs were a novelty
gag that didn't really work. But time marches on and technology makes the
impossible possible. Stand by, air travelers, because the Homeland Security Department is preparing to install and test high-tech machines at airport
checkpoints that will, as the comic-book ads promised, "See Thru Clothing!"

Get ready for electronic portals known as backscatters, expected to be
tested at a handful of airports this year, that use X-ray imaging technology
to allow a screener to scan a body. And yes, the body image is detailed. Let's
not be coy here, ladies and gentlemen:

"Well, you'll see basically everything," said Bill Scannell, a privacy ad- 5
vocate and technology consultant. "It shows nipples. It shows the clear outline of genitals."

The Homeland Security Department's justification for the electronic
strip searches has a certain logic. In field test after field test, it found that
federal airport screeners using metal-detecting magnetometers did a miserable job identifying weapons concealed in carry-on bags or on the bodies
of undercover agents.

Joe Sharkey is a columnist writing frequently about business travel for the *New York Times*.

In a clumsy response late last year, the department instituted intrusive pat-downs at checkpoints after two planes in Russia blew up from nonmetallic explosives that had apparently been smuggled into the aircraft by female Chechen terrorists. But it reduced the pat-downs after passengers erupted in outrage at the groping last December.

"The use of these more thorough examination procedures has been protested by passengers and interest groups, and have already been refined" by the Transportation Security Administration, Richard Skinner, the acting inspector general of the Homeland Security Department, told a Senate committee in January. Skinner said then that the TSA was ramping up tests of new technologies like backscatter imaging.

Last month, Michael Chertoff, the Homeland Security secretary, told a Senate subcommittee that "technology is really what we ultimately have to use in order to get to the next level" in security.

The technology is available, he said. "It's a question of the decision to deploy it and to try to balance that with legitimate privacy concerns," he added. "We haven't put it out yet because people are still hand-wringing about it." 10

Steve Elson isn't exactly hand-wringing. Let's just say he is mighty skeptical. A former Federal Aviation Administration investigator, Elson led the agency's red team of undercover agents who poked around airports looking for—and finding—holes in security.

"Backscatting has been around for years," he said. "They started talking about this stuff back during the protests when they were grabbing women. Under the right circumstances, the technology has some efficacy and can work. That is, provided we're willing to pay the price in a further loss of personal privacy."

He isn't. "I have a beautiful 29-year-old daughter and a beautiful wife, and I don't want some screeners to be looking at them through their clothes, plain and simple," he said.

Like many security experts, Elson argues for a sensible balance between risk management and risk reduction. On numerous occasions since the 2001 terrorist attacks, he has led reporters on test runs at airports, showing how easy it is to penetrate security throughout the airport.

Thwarting body-scanning technology would be simple, he argues. Because of concerns about radiation, body scanners are designed not to penetrate the skin. All that's needed is someone heavily overweight to go through the system, he said. I won't quote him directly on the details; suffice it to say he posits that a weapon or explosives pack could be tucked into flabby body folds that won't be penetrated by the scanner. 15

Homeland Security has not identified the airports that will test backscatters. More than a dozen have been selected to test various new technologies.

One maker of backscatters is Rapiscan Security Products, a unit of OSI Systems. "Since the Russian plane tragedy, which is suspected due to suicide bombers, the interest has heightened for these needs, especially for the body scanner," Deepak Chopra, the chief executive of OSI Systems, recently told analysts.

Scannell, the privacy advocate, scorns that reasoning as alarmist nonsense. He does see one virtue, though, for some airport screeners if backscatting technology becomes the norm.

"They'll be paid to go to a peep show," he said. "They won't even need to bring any change."

Today, of course, the conversation about any controversial issue can go far beyond televised or printed news. If the latest news is as close as your remote control, it is also as close as your computer mouse or even your cell phone. The Internet provides everyone a voice on almost any subject.

Sharkey's piece, which appeared in the *New York Times* in May 2005, was the subject of hundreds of blog postings. The vast majority found the whole idea of being x-rayed at airports distasteful and a threat to privacy. Some writers said they would never fly again if the screening techniques were implemented. One of the few dissenting voices was that of Chris Kapper. Note that, unlike Frank, he clearly states his opinion about the new x-ray technique.

Freedom to Live Trumps All!

CHRIS KAPPER

I have read many different comments to this story.

The opinions against the technology seem to boil down to this:

1. It is offensive to be viewed naked.
2. Being viewed naked is an affront to personal freedom.
3. This is a slippery slope and once allowed here it will be allowed everywhere until there are virtually no personal freedoms left.

The opinions for the technology seem to boil down to this:

1. Who cares if one is viewed naked?
2. It is better to be seen naked and alive than be dead.
3. This will make the airplanes safer.
4. This is a less obtrusive way to search passengers.

Chris Kapper posted this response to Joe Sharkey's article, "Airport Screeners Could See X-rated X-rays," on CNET's TalkBack, on May 27, 2005.

I have to agree—for the most part—with the latter. Here is why:

1. In the demonstration I saw, the screeners could not see the people—all they could see were the images. Therefore, they never saw a person walk up, through, and then leave. The point is that if their own mother walked through, they would have no idea since you can't tell who it is.

2. Nobody else can see your image other than the security operator. That includes other passengers and employees of the airports.

3. This is much less obtrusive than removing shoes, clothing, and emptying out all of your pockets—in front of everyone.

4. The fundamental liberty is the right to life. One's right to live trumps others' rights.

5. It is not only the liberty of the passengers and crew that must be considered here. It is their lives as well as the lives of all the people on the ground as that airplane flies over. Additionally, it is the nation's and even the world's economy and peace that must be considered. Remember what 9/11 did to the economy and the peace in the world?

6. Air travel is not a required means of travel. You can use other public transportation. You can travel by car or even by boat. Air travel is a convenience—and a choice. When you buy your ticket, you agree to be bound by their rules and policies.

7. For the person who quoted Benjamin Franklin—"They who would give up an essential liberty for temporary security, deserve neither liberty or security." IMHO, this technology does not cause you to give up any ESSENTIAL liberty and there is nothing TEMPORARY about DEATH!

Most of the arguments in this book will deal with matters of public controversy, an area traditionally associated with the study of argument. As the word *public* suggests, these matters concern us as members of a community. In the arguments you will read in this book, human beings are engaged in explaining and defending their own actions and beliefs and opposing those of others. They do this for at least two reasons: to justify what they do and think both to themselves and to their opponents and, in the process, to solve problems and make decisions, especially those dependent on a consensus among conflicting views.

PRACTICE

1. Locate in Frank's article the one sentence that you believe best summarizes the thesis or main idea that he is trying to support. Do the same for Kapper's posting.

2. An author's tone reveals his attitude toward his subject. Describe the tone in Sharkey's piece. Give specific examples of words or phrases that contribute to that tone.

3. Locate online or in newspapers two articles on the same subject, one that is objective and one that is subjective. Be prepared to explain the difference.

4. As you read through articles that you and your classmates located for #3, what can you conclude about how the purpose in the objective articles is different from that in the subjective ones?

WHY STUDY ARGUMENT?

If you can listen to arguments daily courtesy of CNN or Fox News, and all you have to do to enter the dialogue is to open Internet Explorer or Firefox, why *study* argument? Since you've engaged in some form of the argumentative process all your life, is there anything to be learned that experience hasn't taught you? We think there is. If you've ever felt frustration in trying to decide what is wrong with an argument, either your own or someone else's, you might have wondered if there were rules to help in the analysis. If you've ever been dissatisfied with your attempt to prove a case, you might have wondered how good arguers, the ones who succeed in persuading people, construct their cases. Good arguers do, in fact, know and follow rules. Studying and practicing these rules can provide you with some of the same skills.

You will find yourself using these skills in a variety of situations, not only in arguing important public issues. You will use them, for example, in your academic career. Whatever your major field of study—the humanities, the social sciences, the physical sciences, business, education—you will be required to defend views about materials you have read and studied.

HUMANITIES Why have some of the greatest novels resisted translation into great films?

SOCIAL SCIENCE What is the evidence that upward social mobility continues to be a positive force in American life?

PHYSICAL SCIENCE What effect will global warming have on agriculture in North America?

BUSINESS Is a 401(k) the best way of investing for retirement?

EDUCATION Are standardized tests exerting too much control over the public school curriculum?

The conventions or rules for reporting results might differ from one field of study to another, but for the most part, the rules for defining terms, evaluating evidence, and arriving at conclusions cross disciplinary lines. In a variety of professions, you will encounter situations at work that will require analytical and argumentative skills. Almost everywhere—in the smallest businesses as well as the largest corporations—a worker who can articulate his or her views clearly and forcefully has an important advantage in gaining access to positions of greater interest and challenge.

You may not anticipate doing the kind of writing or speaking at your job that you will practice in your academic work. It is probably true that in some careers, writing constitutes a negligible part of a person's duties. But outside the office, the studio, the lab, and the salesroom, you will be called on to exhibit argumentative skills as a citizen, as a member of a community, and as a consumer of leisure. In these capacities, you can contribute to decision making if you are knowledgeable and prepared. By writing or speaking to the appropriate authorities, you can argue for a change in the grading policy at your school, against a change in automobile insurance rates, or for the reelection of a city council member.

A course in argumentation offers another invaluable dividend: It can help you to cope with the bewildering confusion of voices in the world around you. It can give you tools for distinguishing between what is true and what is false, what is valid and what is invalid, in the claims of politicians, promoters of causes, newscasters, advertisers, salespeople, teachers, parents and siblings, employers and employees, neighbors, friends, and lovers, any of whom may be engaged at some time in attempting to persuade you to accept a belief or adopt a course of action. It can even offer strategies for working through a personal dilemma. Most of us are painfully aware of opportunities we lost because we were uncertain of how to proceed, even in matters that affected us deeply.

So far we have treated argument as an essentially pragmatic activity that benefits the individual. But choosing argument over force or evasion has clear moral benefits for society as well. We can, in fact, defend the study of argumentation for the same reasons that we defend universal education despite its high cost and sometimes controversial results. In a democracy, widespread literacy ultimately benefits all members of a society, not only those who are the immediate beneficiaries of education, because only an informed citizenry can make responsible choices. Distinguished rhetorician Wayne C. Booth explains that "democracy depends on a citizenry that can reason for themselves, on men who know whether a case has been proved, or at least made probable."[1]

It is not too much to say that argument is a civilizing influence, the very basis of democratic order. In repressive regimes, coercion, which may express itself in a number of reprehensible forms—censorship, imprisonment, exile, torture, or execution—is a favored means of removing opposition to establishment "truth." In free societies, arguments and debate remain the preeminent means of arriving at consensus.

---

[1] Wayne C. Booth, "Boring from Within: The Art of the Freshman Essay," adapted from a speech delivered to the Illinois Council of College Teachers of English in May 1963.

Of course, rational discourse in a democracy can and does break down. Confrontations with police at abortion clinics, shouting and heckling at a meeting to prevent a speaker from being heard, student protests against university policies—such actions have become common in recent years. The demands of the demonstrators are often passionately and sincerely held, and the protestors sometimes succeed through force or intimidation in influencing policy changes. When this happens, however, we cannot be sure that the changes are justified. History and experience teach us that reason, to a far greater degree than other methods of persuasion, ultimately determines the rightness or wrongness of our actions.

THE TERMS OF ARGUMENT

A distinction is sometimes made between argument and persuasion. Argument, according to most authorities, gives primary importance to logical appeals. Persuasion introduces the element of ethical and emotional appeals. The difference is one of emphasis. In real-life arguments about social policy, the distinction is hard to measure. In this book, we use the term *argument* to represent forms of discourse that attempt to persuade readers or listeners to accept a claim, whether acceptance is based on logical or on emotional appeals or, as is usually the case, on both. The following is our brief definition of the term: An argument is a statement or statements offering support for a claim.

An argument is composed of at least three parts: the claim, the support, and the warrant.[2]

■ The Claim

The claim (also called a proposition) answers the question "What are you trying to prove?" It will generally appear as the thesis statement of your essay, although in some arguments, it may not be stated directly. There are three principal kinds of claim (discussed more fully in Chapter 6): claims of fact, of value, and of policy. *Claims of fact* assert that a condition has existed, exists, or will exist and are based on facts or data that the audience will accept as being objectively verifiable.

- The diagnosis of autism is now far more common than it was twenty years ago.

---

[2]Some of the terms and analyses used in this text are adapted from Stephen Toulmin's *The Uses of Argument* (Cambridge: Cambridge University Press, 1958).

- Fast foods are contributing significantly to today's epidemic of child-hood obesity.
- Global warming will affect the coastlines of all continents.

All these claims must be supported by data. Although the last example is an inference or an educated guess about the future, a reader will probably find the prediction credible if the data seem authoritative.

Claims of value attempt to prove that some things are more or less desirable than others. They express approval or disapproval of standards of taste and morality. Advertisements and reviews of cultural events are one common source of value claims, but such claims emerge whenever people argue about what is good or bad, beautiful or ugly.

- Mel Gibson's *Apocalypto* is marred by its excessive violence.
- Abortion is wrong under any circumstances.
- The right to privacy is more important than the need to increase security at airports.

Claims of policy assert that specific policies should be instituted as solutions to problems. The expression *should*, *must*, or *ought to* usually appears in the statement.

- The electoral college should be replaced by popular vote as the means of electing a president.
- Attempts at making air travel more secure must not put in jeopardy the passengers' right to privacy.
- Backscatter x-raying ought to be implemented at every American airport as soon as possible as a means of detecting concealed weapons.

Policy claims call for analysis of both fact and value. (A full discussion of claims follows in Chapter 6.)

PRACTICE

1. Classify each of the following as a claim of fact, value, or policy.
   a. Solar power could supply 20 percent of the energy needs now satisfied by fossil and nuclear power.
   b. Violence on television produces violent behavior in children who watch more than four hours a day.
   c. Both intelligent design and evolutionary theory should be taught in the public schools.
   d. Some forms of cancer are caused by viruses.
   e. Dogs are smarter than cats.
   f. The money that our government spends on the space program would be better spent solving domestic problems like unemployment and homelessness.
   g. Wherever the number of illegal aliens increases, the crime rate also increases.

h. Movie sequels are generally inferior to their originals.

i. Tom Hanks is a more versatile actor than Tom Cruise.

j. Adopted children who are of a different race than their adoptive parents should be raised with an understanding of the culture of their biological parents.

k. Average yearly temperatures in North America are already being affected by global warming.

l. Human activity is the primary cause of global warming.

2. Classify Frank's claim in "X-ray Tests Both Security, Privacy" as a claim of fact, value, or policy. Do the same for Chris Kapper's in his posting "Freedom to Live Trumps All!"

3. Argue that Sharkey, in his "Airport Screeners Could See X-rated X-rays," is supporting a claim of fact or that he is supporting a claim of value.

■ The Support

Support consists of the materials used by the arguer to convince an audience that his or her claim is sound. These materials include evidence and motivational appeals. The *evidence* or data consist of facts, statistics, and testimony from experts. The *motivational appeals* are the ones that the arguer makes to the values and attitudes of the audience to win support for the claim. The word *motivational* points out that these appeals are the reasons that move an audience to accept a belief or adopt a course of action. (See chapter 7 for a detailed discussion of support.)

■ The Warrant

Certain assumptions underlie all the claims we make. In argument, the term *warrant* is used for such an assumption, a belief or principle that is taken for granted. It may be stated or unstated. If the arguer believes that the audience shares her assumption, she may believe it unnecessary to express it. But if she thinks that the audience is doubtful or hostile, she may decide to state the assumption to emphasize its importance or argue for its validity. The warrant, stated or not, allows the reader to make the same connection between the support and the claim that the author does.

This is how the warrant works. Before he posted on the blog about the proposed x-raying of airline passengers, Kapper had read earlier postings discussing the issue. He considered the arguments he had heard in favor of and against the x-ray technique and actually went so far as to summarize them in his posting. The conclusion he reached, which became the claim of his piece of writing, was that he agrees for the most part with those who argue in favor of the new screening technique. In outline form, a portion of his argument looks like this:

CLAIM: Backscatter screening should be implemented in America's airports.

SUPPORT: Backscatter screening will make planes safer.

WARRANT: Any screening technique that will make planes safer
should be implemented.

The following example demonstrates how a different kind of warrant, based on values, can also lead an audience to accept a claim.

CLAIM: Backscatter screening should be implemented in
America's airports.

SUPPORT: Being seen naked by a security screener is better than
dying.

WARRANT: Being safe is worth a small loss of privacy.

Kapper's title shows how strongly he feels about this warrant: "Freedom to Live Trumps All!"

Let us suppose that the reader agrees with the supporting statement, that being seen naked by a security screener is better than dying. But to accept the claim, the reader must also agree with the principle expressed in the warrant, that being safe is worth a small loss of privacy. He or she can then agree that backscatter screening should be implemented. Notice that this warrant, like all warrants, certifies that the relationship between the support and the claim is sound.

One more important characteristic of the warrant deserves mention. In many cases, the warrant is a more general statement of belief than the

Writer's Guide: Learning the Key Terms

Claim — the proposition that the author is trying to prove. The claim may appear as the thesis statement of an essay but may be implied rather than stated directly.

- *Claims of fact* assert that a condition has existed, exists, or will exist and are based on facts or data that the audience will accept as being objectively verifiable.

- *Claims of value* attempt to prove that some things are more or less desirable than others; they express approval or disapproval of standards of taste and morality.

- *Claims of policy* assert that specific plans or courses of action should be instituted as solutions to problems.

Support — the materials used by the arguer to convince an audience that his or her claim is sound; those materials include evidence and motivational appeals.

Warrant — an inference or assumption; a belief or principle that is taken for granted in an argument.

claim. It can, therefore, support many claims, not only the one in a particular argument. For example, the warrant you have just read—being safe is worth a small loss of privacy—is a broad assumption or belief that we take for granted and that can underlie claims about many other practices in American society. (For more on warrants, see Chapter 8.)

PRACTICE

1. Report on an argument you have heard or read recently. Identify the parts of that argument—claim, support, warrant—as they are defined in this chapter. What were the strengths and weaknesses of the argument?

2. Choose one of the more controversial claims from the list on pages 13–14. Explain why it is controversial. Would it be difficult to support? Impossible? Are the warrants unacceptable to many people? If there has been a change in recent years in public acceptance of the claim, offer what you think may be an explanation for the change.

THE AUDIENCE

All arguments are composed with an audience in mind. We have already pointed out that an argument is an implicit dialogue or exchange. Often the writer of an argument about a public issue is responding to another writer or speaker who has made a claim that needs to be supported or opposed. Even when our audience is unknown, we write to persuade the unconvinced, to acquaint them with good reasons for changing their minds. In writing your own arguments, you should assume that there is a reader who may not agree with you. Throughout this book, we will continue to refer to ways of reaching such a reader.

Speakers are usually better informed than writers about their audience. Some writers, however, are familiar with the specific persons or groups who will read their arguments; advertising copywriters are a conspicuous example. They discover their audiences through sophisticated polling and marketing techniques and direct their messages to a well-targeted group of prospective buyers. Other professionals may be required to submit reports to persuade a specific and clearly defined audience of certain beliefs or courses of action: An engineer may be asked by an environmental interest group to defend his plans for the building of a sewage treatment plant; or a town planner may be called on to tell the town council why she believes that rent control may not work; or a sales manager may find it necessary to explain to his superior why a new product should be launched in the Midwest rather than the South.

In such cases, the writer asks some or all of the following questions about the audience:

- Why has the audience requested this report? What do they want to get out of it?
- How much do they already know about the subject?
- Are they divided or agreed on the subject?
- What is their emotional involvement with the issues?

Providing abundant evidence and making logical connections between the parts of an argument may not be enough to win agreement from an audience. In fact, success in convincing an audience is almost always inseparable from the writer's credibility or the audience's belief in the writer's trustworthiness. Aristotle, the Greek philosopher who wrote a treatise on argument that has influenced its study and practice for more than two thousand years, considered credibility—what he called *ethos*—the most important element in the arguer's ability to persuade the audience to accept his or her claim.

Aristotle named intelligence, character, and goodwill as the attributes that produce credibility. Today we might describe these qualities somewhat differently, but the criteria for judging a writer's credibility remain essentially the same. First, the writer must convince the audience that he is knowledgeable, that he is as well informed as possible about the subject. Second, he must persuade his audience that he is not only truthful in the presentation of his evidence but also morally upright and dependable. Third, he must show that, as an arguer with good intentions, he has considered the interests and needs of others as well as his own.

As an example in which the credibility of the arguer is at stake, consider a wealthy Sierra Club member who lives on ten acres of a magnificent oceanside estate and who appears before a community planning board to argue against future development of the area. The board, acting in the interests of all the citizens of the community, will ask themselves: Has the arguer proved that his information about environmental impact is complete and accurate? Has he demonstrated that he sincerely desires to preserve the wilderness, not merely his own privacy and space? And has he made clear that he has considered the needs and desires of those who might want to live in a housing development by the ocean? If the answers to all of these questions are yes, then the board will hear the arguer with respect, and the arguer will have begun to establish his credibility.

A reputation for intelligence, character, and goodwill is not often earned overnight. And it can be lost more quickly than it is gained. Once a writer or speaker has betrayed an audience's belief in her character or judgment, she may find it difficult to persuade an audience to accept subsequent claims, no matter how sound her data and reasoning are.

Political life is full of examples of lost and squandered credibility. After it was discovered that President Lyndon Johnson had deceived the American public about U.S. conduct in the Vietnam War, he could not regain his popularity. After President Gerald Ford pardoned former President Richard Nixon for his complicity in the cover up of the bugging and burglary of the Democratic National Committee headquarters at the Watergate office complex, Ford was no longer a serious candidate for re-election. After proof emerged that President Bill Clinton had lied to a grand jury and the public about his sexual relationship with a young White House intern, public approval of his political record remained high, but approval of his moral character declined and threatened to diminish his influence.

We can see the practical consequences when an audience realizes that an arguer has been guilty of a deception — misusing facts and authority, suppressing evidence, distorting statistics, violating the rules of logic. But suppose the arguer is successful in concealing his or her manipulation of the data and can persuade an uninformed audience to take the action or adopt the idea that he or she recommends. Even supposing that the argument promotes a "good" cause, is the arguer justified in using evasive or misleading tactics?

The answer is no. To encourage another person to make a decision on the basis of incomplete or dishonestly used data is profoundly unethical. It indicates lack of respect for the rights of others — their right to know at least as much as you do about the subject, to be allowed to judge and compare, to disagree with you if they challenge your interests or find holes in the logic of your argument. If the moral implications are still not clear, try to imagine yourself not as the perpetrator of the lie but as the victim.

There is also a danger in measuring success wholly by the degree to which audiences accept our arguments. Both as writers and readers, we must be able to respect the claim, or proposition, and what it tries to demonstrate. The English philosopher Stephen Toulmin has said, "To conclude that a proposition is true, it is not enough to know that this [person] or that finds it 'credible'; the proposition itself must be worthy of credence."[3]

No matter what the subject, there are certain basic steps that a writer can take to ensure that not only the proposition, or claim, but the whole argument is worthy of credence. You are not yet an expert in many of the subjects you will deal with in assignments, although you are knowledgeable about many other things, including your cultural and social activities. But there are several ways in which you can develop confidence by your discussion of topics derived from academic disciplines, such as political science, psychology, economics, sociology, and art, on which most assignments will be based. The following steps that every writer of argumentative texts should follow will be the basis for Chapters 5–10.

[3] *An Examination of the Place of Reason in Ethics* (Cambridge: Cambridge University Press, 1964), p. 71.

■ Defining Key Terms (Chapter 5)

Many of the controversial questions you will read or write about are primarily arguments of definition. Such terms as *abortion, pornography, racism, poverty, freedom of speech*, and *terrorism* must be defined before useful solutions to the problems they represent can be formulated. Even if the primary purpose of your essay is not definition, you can successfully communicate with an audience only if that audience understands how you are using key terms.

■ Choosing an Appropriate Claim (Chapter 6)

It must be clear to the individual or group that constitutes your audience what change in thought or what action you hope to achieve by presenting your case. If you are seeking a change in your reader's thinking on a subject, you will have a much greater chance of accomplishing your goal if you consider the audience's current thinking on the subject and are realistic about the extent to which you might hope to change that thinking. If there is something you want your audience to do, that action must be realistically within the power of that audience.

■ Choosing and Documenting Appropriate Sources (Chapter 7)

You must present evidence of careful research, demonstrating that you have been conscientious in finding the best authorities, giving credit, and attempting to arrive at the truth.

■ Analyzing Assumptions (Chapter 8)

You must consider the warrant or assumption on which your argument is based. A warrant need not be expressed if it is so widely accepted that you can assume any reasonable audience will not need proof of its validity. You must be prepared to defend any other warrant.

■ Analyzing Logical Errors (Chapter 9)

Understanding the ways in which inductive and deductive reasoning processes work can help you to determine the truth and validity of your arguments, as well as other arguments, and to identify and correct faulty reasoning.

■ Editing for Appropriate Language (Chapter 10)

Another important resource is the careful use of language, not only to define terms and express personal style but also to reflect clarity of thought, to avoid the clichés and outworn slogans that frequently substitute for fresh ideas, and to avoid word choices that would make your audience unwilling to consider your ideas.

Now let's turn to an example of argumentative writing and the analysis that follows it. Some of the terms introduced in this chapter appear in boldface in the analysis.

SAMPLE ANALYSIS

Will the Politics of Teen Sex Stop a Cancer Vaccine?

ADVOCATES FOR YOUTH

There's a Vaccine That Could Prevent Cervical Cancer?

After a decade of development, two drug companies—Merck and Glaxo-SmithKline—are close to marketing the first ever cancer vaccines that show 100 percent efficacy in combating the most dangerous strains of the human papilloma virus (HPV), the cause of almost all cervical cancers,[1] the second most common type of cancer among women worldwide, and the leading cause of cancer death among women in the developing world.[2]

Since genital HPV is a sexually transmitted disease (STD), to be effective, the vaccine must be administered to young women in their early teen years—*before* they initiate sex. Research and clinical trials continue to find the vaccine safe.

The policy question? With 10,000 American women contracting cervical cancer each year and 4,000 deaths from the disease annually, will *all* women, including young women, have access to a vaccine that could save their lives? The initial reaction of some religious conservatives to the HPV vaccine is disturbing because it appears to place the promotion of abstinence-only programs above the prevention of a killer disease. Yet, research and basic common sense state this is not an "either/or" issue. It's possible to promote abstinence, educate young people about contraception, and prevent cervical cancer without these objectives getting in the way of each other. It's not just the smart thing to do—it's the right thing to do.

Who Would Possibly Object?

Again, some religious conservatives object—religious conservatives who, in tandem with the Bush administration, have spent over $1.1 billion in federal and state taxpayers' dollars on programs that promote abstinence until marriage as the only acceptable behavior for Americans and the only way to prevent pregnancy, HIV, and other sexually transmitted diseases.

Groups that promote an abstinence-only-until-marriage approach to 5 sex education intensely market the threat of HPV as a reason for promoting abstinence only. They claim a vaccine will promote promiscuity by lessening people's fears regarding HPV and cervical cancer.

"Our concern is that this vaccine will be marketed to a segment of the population that should be getting a message about abstinence," said Tony Perkins of the Family Research Council. He would not inoculate his own daughter, because she would be more inclined to have sex outside marriage. "It sends the wrong message." (Tony Perkins, President of the Family Research Council)[3]

> I personally object to vaccinating children against a disease that is
> 100 percent preventable with proper sexual behavior. ✔
> —Leslie Unruh, Executive Director of the National Abstinence Clearinghouse[4]

Who Will Make the Decision?

The Advisory Committee on Immunization Practices (ACIP) will make the decision. Attached to the Centers for Disease Control and Prevention (CDC), ACIP sets the nation's list of recommended immunizations—setting the standard for doctors and insurers and for public funding of vaccinations. ACIP's ruling is not binding; but most states look to its recommendations to mandate which vaccines children must get before entering school.[3]

Will Ideology or Science
Dictate the Decision?

Consider that the Bush administration has already appointed one ACIP member (Reginald Finger) from the ranks of the religious right. Until September 2005, Mr. Finger was the medical issues analyst at Focus on the Family,[3] an ultra-conservative religious organization founded by James Dobson.

The precedents set by this administration for medical decisions are also 10 troubling. The FDA, in a highly criticized move, chose to placate religious conservatives by refusing non-prescription status for emergency contraception (EC), despite the fact that the FDA's own scientific advisory committee voted overwhelmingly to make EC available without a doctor's prescription.

This political decision prompted an editorial in the *New England Journal of Medicine* which stated:

> The recent actions of the FDA leadership have made a mockery of the process of evaluating scientific evidence, disillusioned many of the participating scientists both inside and outside the agency, squandered the public trust, and tarnished the agency's image. American women and the dedicated professionals at the FDA deserve better.[8]

The Myth That Prevention Causes Adolescent Promiscuity

Supporters of abstinence-only-until-marriage programs have long claimed that sex education, which includes information about condoms and birth control, encourages teens to have sex—a claim rebutted by scientific research:

> Current research indicates that encouraging abstinence and urging better use of contraception are compatible goals. Evidence shows that sexuality education that discusses contraception does not increase sexual activity, and programs that emphasize abstinence as the safest and best approach, while also teaching about contraceptives for sexually active youth, do not decrease contraceptive use. — American Academy of Pediatrics[9]

This myth was again promulgated by the FDA, which claimed that making EC available without prescription would fuel risky teen behavior, a claim that was also explicitly rejected by leading medical authorities:

> An increase in awareness and availability of emergency contraception to teens does not change reported rates of sexual activity or increase the frequency of unprotected intercourse among adolescents. — American Academy of Pediatrics[10]
>
> Data demonstrating that ready access to Plan B by adolescents as young as 15 did not lead to increased irresponsible sexual behavior were available in December 2003 and had been reviewed by the advisory committee. Moreover, the agency was conspicuously unable, then or later, to cite any data to support different safety or efficacy profiles in different age groups—a damning indictment of the basis for the disapproval. — *New England Journal of Medicine*[8]

Clearly, prevention does not cause risky sexual behavior. A vaccine to prevent cervical cancer will not cause promiscuity any more than an umbrella will cause rain or a seat belt will cause an accident.

Why Do Some Conservatives Seem to Need HPV?

In recent years, religious conservatives have become increasingly reliant on HPV as a tool to attack condoms. They have denigrated condom use as "Russian roulette," relying on false claims that condoms fail to provide any protection for HPV.

Among their conservative allies in Congress, Senator Tom Coburn has in the past introduced legislation to require condom labeling, stressing the risk of HPV infection and warning that condoms offer "little or no protection" against the virus—a claim disputed by current research. Moreover, he has many conservative friends on the Hill who share his views on the efficacy, or lack thereof, of condoms:

We need to yell it to the top of the rooftops that these condoms we're sending down to you don't protect you. . . . [You] have a false sense of security. So I think we're sending the wrong message when we use taxpayer dollars to give condoms out to these kids and we don't tell them, 'By the way, you'll probably be dead at age 24 by cervical cancer. But we're giving you condoms, so go do your thing.' To me, abstinence is the only way." — Representative Jo Ann Davis, R-Virginia[11]

What Will Happen?

The administration has shown significant deference to religious conservatives when it comes to issues involving sexual and reproductive health.

From stem-cell research to sex education, from a diminished emphasis on condoms to denying non-prescription status to EC, evidence-based prevention has taken a back seat to ideology and politics.

With respect to HPV and the cervical cancer vaccine, the religious conservative movement could persuade its base to avoid vaccination; it could work to prevent mass inoculation of young people by trying to block the vaccines' acceptance by regulators; or it could attack the vaccines' funding at federal and state levels.

Not all religious conservatives are on record opposing the HPV vaccine. Some, such as Dr. Gene Rudd of the Christian Medical Association, have hailed the vaccine as an important medical breakthrough. Yet, even Dr. Rudd argues that the vaccine should not be mandatory. Nonetheless, if Dr. Rudd and others like him can convince their constituents that this vaccine is a positive development, public health will be the beneficiary. 20

Does "Saving Souls" Trump Saving Lives?

Clearly, there must be public consensus that no woman in this country should be denied the opportunity to avoid cervical cancer. Vaccinating young people, before they are sexually active, affords the best opportunity to use this medical breakthrough to do just that.

Cancer is a public health challenge that needs to be conquered; it is not an appropriate venue for political or ideological debate.

NOTE: About 67 percent of young people are sexually active by age 18[5]; roughly 90 percent of Americans are not virgins on their wedding nights[6]; and experts estimate that up to 70 percent of all sexually active adults worldwide have been exposed to HPV.[7]

REFERENCES

1. Walboomers JMM, Jacobs MV, Manos MM, Bosch FX, Kummer JA et al., Human papilloma virus is a necessary cause of invasive cervical cancer worldwide, *Journal of Pathology* 1999; 189:12–19.

2. National Cervical Cancer Coalition, *What Is the National Cervical Cancer Coalition (NCCC)?* http://www.nccc-online.org/; accessed 10/27/2005.

3. *Fortune Magazine*, October 17, 2005, Guyon J, Cancer and the culture wars: the coming storm over a cancer vaccine.

4. *AIDS Treatment Update*, October 24, 2005, Bernard EJ, An HPV vaccine, what it might really mean, Aidsmap; http://www.nam.org.uk/en/news/3429199D-5FE5-4795-B0E6-CD957617C160.asp; accessed 10/27/2005.

5. National Center for Health Statistics, Teenagers in the United States: sexual activity, contraceptive use, and childbearing, 2002. *Vital and Health Statistics* [Series 23, No. 24] December 25.

6. Michael RT, Gagnon JH, Laumann ED, Kolata G, *Sex in America: A Definitive Survey*, Boston: Little Brown, 1994.

7. Marr L, *Sexually Transmitted Diseases: A Physician Tells You What You Need to Know*, Baltimore, MD: Johns Hopkins University Press, 1998.

8. *New England Journal of Medicine*, editorial, September 22, 2005.

9. American Academy of Pediatrics (August 2005), Adolescent pregnancy: current trends and issues, *Pediatrics*.

10. American Academy of Pediatrics (October, 2005), Policy statement, emergency contraception, *Pediatrics*.

11. Representative Jo Ann Davis (R-VA), Subcommittee on Criminal Justice, Drug Policy and Human Resources of the House Government Reform Committee, *U.S. Representative Mark Souder (R-IN) Holds Hearing on Cervical Cancer and HPV*, March 11, 2004 [Committee Hearing].

■ Analysis

The author of the article, an anonymous writer for the organization Advocates of Youth, takes time in the first two paragraphs to make clear what the human papilloma virus is and why a vaccine against it must be administered while girls are young. To the extent that it is necessary, he is **defining** a key term. He also emphasizes the magnitude of this new development in cancer prevention when he cites statistics on how serious a threat to women HPV is. He then goes on in paragraph 3 to explain why the development of "the first ever cancer vaccines that show 100 percent efficacy in combating the most dangerous strains of the human papilloma virus (HPV), the cause of almost all cervical cancers" is even controversial. At the end of the third paragraph, he states his thesis, a **claim of value**: "It's possible to promote abstinence, educate young people about contraception, and prevent cervical cancer without these objectives getting in the way of each other. It's not just the smart thing to do—it's the right thing to do." The references in his opening paragraphs to promoting abstinence and educating young people look ahead to his further discussion of why he finds "disturbing" the objection to the vaccine expressed by some religious conservatives. He labels correctly as an either/or fallacy the tendency on the part of these conservatives to view the current situation as a choice between promoting abstinence-only programs and stopping a killer disease.

The headings in the essay help readers to follow the writer's argument from one main point to another. What religious conservatives fear is that with the threat of HPV gone, American youth will become more promiscuous. Like anyone trying to construct a strong argument, the writer shows an awareness of what his opponents' position is before attempting to undermine that position. He does so through the type of **support** he offers. He wants to establish that religious conservatives have backed abstinence-only programs, so he cites the $1.1 billion federal and state dollars that they "in tandem with the Bush administration" have spent on abstinence-only programs. To establish his opponents' position, he also quotes conservatives who do not support vaccination against a disease that is preventable through abstinence, establishing their conservative affiliations by providing their titles.

The author is guilty of his own either/or fallacy when he calls his fourth section "Will Ideology or Science Dictate the Decision?" In this instance, though, his support for his claim comes in the form of examples of how conservatives are affecting policy decisions. He attacks these conservatives indirectly when he quotes from the highly respected *New England Journal of Medicine*. He is still showing the flaws in his opponents' line of reasoning but also the political clout they have.

The author also supports his claim of value by offering scientific research in rebuttal of his opponents' claim of policy, which is that the HPV vaccine should not be given to our teenagers since infection is 100 percent preventable when young people abstain from sex. His quotations from the American Academy of Pediatrics and from the *New England Journal of Medicine* help dispel what he terms the "myth" that knowledge of contraceptives will lead teens into risky sexual behavior — or into sexual behavior of any kind. He also points out that those who, like Senator Tom Coburn and Representative Jo Ann Davis, argue that condoms do not protect against HPV do so in light of current research to the contrary. His argument here would have been stronger if he had cited supporting research.

The author concludes that religious conservatives clearly have political power in the areas of sexual and reproductive health. This is a power that they could use to support HPV vaccination. The piece ends with a section with the catchy title "Does 'Saving Souls' Trump Saving Lives?" The quotation marks around "Saving Souls" suggest that the writer questions whether it is the saving of souls that motivates religious conservatives or perhaps whether using the threat of the HPV virus as a means of scaring teenagers out of having sex is a legitimate means of trying to save their souls.

At the end the writer sums up his reservations about the politicization of health care: "From stem-cell research to sex education, from a diminished emphasis on condoms to denying non-prescription status to EC, evidence-based prevention has taken a back seat to ideology and politics." He then restates his claim of value: "Cancer is a public health challenge that needs to be conquered; it is not an appropriate venue for political or ideological debate."

What is the **warrant** underlying this argument? What assumption or assumptions are behind the author's argument? One could be worded in this form:

CLAIM: It is wrong to let politics or ideology stand in the way of administering the HPV vaccine.

SUPPORT: The HPV vaccine, if given early enough, will save lives.

WARRANT: It is wrong to let politics or ideology stand in the way of administering a medication that will save lives.

This warrant, like many, because it is a broad statement, could underlie a number of different arguments.

A few more points need to be made about this particular argument. Unlike others in this chapter, it is a documented essay. The notes at the end identify the sources from which the author drew his information. Often on the Internet and almost always in journalist writing, sources are referred to, but not cited in their entirety. In academic and scholarly writing, however, you should always completely identify your sources. Later chapters will provide more examples of documented essays and guidelines for documentation.

Keep in mind also the **audience** for which this essay was intended. It appeared originally on the Web site of Advocates for Youth. The organization sums up its mission in this way:

> Advocates for Youth is dedicated to creating programs and advocating for policies that help young people make informed and responsible decisions about their reproductive and sexual health. Advocates provides information, training, and strategic assistance to youth-serving organizations, policy makers, youth activists, and the media in the United States and the developing world.

The writer is addressing primarily those who already share his concern about the health of today's youth and about educating youth regarding their reproductive and sexual health. His is a voice of moderation compared to those who advocate abstinence as the only approach to sexuality. Even in his **language**, he wisely uses moderation, presenting himself as reasonable and knowledgeable yet not attacking those with whom he does not agree. His note at the end of the essay acknowledges a reality that he believes Americans must confront: the fact that most youth will not abstain from sex no matter what they are taught.

PRACTICE

Using the analysis of "Will the Politics of Teen Sex Stop a Cancer Vaccine?" as a model, apply to the following essay the terms of argument introduced in this chapter.

Why U.S. Health Care Costs Aren't Too High

CHARLES R. MORRIS

There is nearly a consensus that American health care is careening toward fiscal catastrophe. Reasonable estimates of unfunded health care liabilities are sky-high. But the belief that health care costs threaten to wreck the U.S. economy is misguided.

In the first place, procedure by procedure, those costs are quite probably falling. It is spending that is rising, which is not the same thing at all. The advent of minimally invasive techniques means that, for example, the cost of a gallbladder operation has dropped substantially, and the patient can usually return to work the next day instead of sitting at home for a week. But because many more people are now willing to undergo the surgery, total spending is up. It's the same story with all kinds of medical care, from hip replacement to the treatment of depression. In other industries, falling prices and added features have similarly led to big increases in spending—on PCs, cell phones, and video games, for example—but we call that a productivity triumph, not a "cost" problem.

Three-quarters of health care spending goes toward people who are very sick. Yes, interventions are sometimes overdone, but doctors don't know in advance which of their patients are going to die, and the great majority of very sick patients recover. Over the past thirty years, the death rate from heart attacks has plummeted, so millions of heart attack survivors are now going to work or playing with their grandchildren. And, of course, successful health care always breeds more spending: The people who used to die of heart attacks now live on to consume expensive medications, visit specialists, and contract cancer or Alzheimer's. Does that mean we should stop saving heart attack victims?

Besides, one person's spending is always someone else's revenue. Explain to GE Healthcare ($15 billion in revenues, 45,000 employees, sales in 100 countries) why rising health care spending is a bad thing. The profile of Medtronics—in the areas of growth, profitability, and R&D spending—closely tracks that of Intel ten years ago. Modern operating rooms boast millions of dollars' worth of equipment, and the vendors include global corporate giants and tiny start-ups.

Health care is now, by most measures, America's largest industry and 5 biggest private employer, as well as a major source of competitive advantage for the United States. Health care's growing share of GDP, moreover, is entirely in keeping with historical trends. A hundred and fifty years ago, agriculture accounted for about half of GDP; it accounts for only 3%

Charles R. Morris has written widely on topics such as Catholicism, IBM, and economics. This article appeared in the February 2007 *Harvard Business Review*.

now. Fifty years ago, a third of the workforce was in manufacturing, but only 10% is now, although real American manufacturing output is currently far higher. Simple economics is driving health care's expansion: As a society grows richer, the marginal value of one more toy inevitably pales in comparison with another year of life in which to enjoy all one's toys.

Without a truly radical adjustment in health care spending patterns, which there is no reason to expect, demographics alone will drive health care's share of GDP—now 16%—to as high as 25% to 30% over the next couple of decades. In purely economic terms, that would not be a bad thing. Indeed, in terms of trade balances and international competitiveness, it might be a positive development. And even at very modest levels of overall economic growth, people could still increase their spending on cosmetics, video games, and other fun things, although perhaps a tad more slowly than they do now. In short, at least for the foreseeable future, health care in the United States is an economic, a societal, and an affordable good.

To be sure, there are serious problems of waste in health care, just as there are in investment banking, the media, and most other industries. Better oversight may be the answer, but it will be the work of decades. In the meantime, the challenge is one of financing, not affordability. The current primary financing mechanisms—employer-based insurance and Medicare—are clearly breaking down. And privatization is an unrealistic solution: While it may, barely, be feasible to privatize old-age pensions (the savings shortfall is far smaller in pensions than it is in health care), privatizing both pensions and health care is a pipe dream.

Instead, in time-honored fashion, a succession of presidents and Congresses will respond to the challenge with a mix of cuts and patches. Spending will keep on rising, and it will continue to shift toward government accounts. Taxes will go up after a lag, and everyone will lie about it. Over time, some highly imperfect but tolerable new accommodation will emerge. Elegant it won't be. That's just the way we do things.

ASSIGNMENTS FOR UNDERSTANDING THE STRUCTURE OF ARGUMENT

READING AND DISCUSSION QUESTIONS

1. Consider at what point news stations cross the line between reporting the news and analyzing the news. Think of some examples from recent news stories that illustrate the argumentative nature of today's news coverage.

2. Do you believe that presidential debates are good examples of argumentation? Explain.

3. What are some of the controversial issues in the field of your major or a major that you are considering? Analyze one or more of them using the terms of argumentation introduced in this chapter.

4. When you write essays and reports for your classes, how do you establish your credibility? On the other hand, how do students lose their credibility with the instructors who read their work?

WRITING SUGGESTIONS

5. Write an essay in which you support your opinion about whether backscatter screening should be implemented at America's airports.

6. Write an essay in which you argue whether or not you believe that the HPV vaccination should be added to the list of vaccinations recommended by the Advisory Committee on Immunization Practices.

CHAPTER 2

Reading and Listening Critically

Most of us learn how to read, to listen to, to write—and, with the increased use of computer technology, to view—arguments by attending critically to the arguments of those who have already mastered the important elements as well as those who have not. As we acquire skill in analyzing arguments, we learn to uncover the clues that reveal meaning and to become sensitive to the kinds of claims and support, language and visuals that experienced writers use in persuading their audiences.

A full response to any argument means more than understanding the message. It also means evaluating, deciding whether the message is successful, and then determining how it succeeds or fails in persuading us. In making these judgments about the arguments of others, we learn how to deliver our own. We try to avoid what we perceive to be flaws in another's arguments, and we adapt the strategies that produce clear, honest, forceful arguments.

RESPONDING AS A CRITICAL READER

Critical reading is essential for mastery of most college subjects, but its importance for reading and writing about argument, where meaning is often complex and multilayered, cannot be overestimated. Reading arguments critically requires you to at least temporarily suspend notions of absolute "right" and "wrong" and to intellectually inhabit gray areas that do not allow for simple "yes" and "no" answers. Of course, even in these areas, significant decisions about such things as ethics, values, politics, and the law must be made, and in studying argument you shouldn't fall into the trap of simple relativism: the idea that all answers to a given problem are equally correct at all times. We must make decisions about arguments with the understanding that reasonable people can disagree on the validity of ideas. Read others' arguments carefully and consider how their ideas can contribute to or complicate your own. Also recognize that what appears to be a final solution will always be open to further negotiation as new participants, new historical circumstances, and new ideologies become involved in the debate.

The ability to read arguments critically is essential to advanced academic work—even in science and math—since it requires the debate of multifaceted issues rather than the memorization of facts. Just as important, learning to read arguments critically helps you develop the ability to *write* effective arguments, a process valued at the university, in the professional world, and in public life.

PREREADING STRATEGIES

Whether reading to comprehend or to evaluate any text, do the following:

1. Take prereading activities seriously. Clearly, the more information you have about an author and a subject, the easier and more productive your reading will be. However, you should learn to read in a way that allows you to discover not just meaning in the text itself but information about the author's point of view and background, the audience the author is writing for, and the author's motives and ideology. Such understanding comes from close analysis of texts but also from background reading on the author or the subject (a task made significantly easier by the Internet) and discussion with your classmates and instructors on the material.

2. Work hard to understand the kind of text you are reading. Was it published recently? Was it written for a specific or a general audience? Is it a textbook and therefore likely to cover the basic points of an issue but not to take a strong stance on anything? Does it come from a journal that publishes primarily conservative or liberal writers?

3. Imagine the initial context in which the author was writing, the problem the author was trying to deal with. What values and ideals are shared by the author and the audience most likely to agree with the argument? How might these values and ideals help make sense of the context?

4. Pay attention to the title, as it may state the purpose of the argument in specific terms.

PRACTICE

Apply the Prereading Strategies to this famous document from America's past.

The Declaration of Independence

THOMAS JEFFERSON

When in the course of human events, it becomes necessary for one people to dissolve the political bands which have connected them with another, and to assume among the Powers of the earth, the separate and equal station to which the Laws of Nature and Nature's God entitle them, a decent respect to the opinions of mankind requires that they should declare the causes which impel them to the separation.

We hold these truths to be self-evident, that all men are created equal, that they are endowed by their Creator with certain unalienable Rights, that among these are Life, Liberty and the pursuit of Happiness.

That to secure these rights, Governments are instituted among Men, deriving their just powers from the consent of the governed.

That whenever any Form of Government becomes destructive of these ends, it is the Right of the People to alter or to abolish it, and to institute a new Government laying its foundation on such principles and organizing its powers in such form, as to them shall seem most likely to effect their Safety and Happiness. Prudence, indeed, will dictate that Governments long established should not be changed for light and transient causes; and accordingly all experience hath shown that mankind are more disposed to suffer, while evils are sufferable, than to right themselves by abolishing the forms to which they are accustomed. But when a long train of abuses and usurpations pursuing invariably the same Object evinces a design to reduce them under absolute Despotism, it is their right, it is their duty, to throw off such government, and to provide new Guards for their future security.

Such has been the patient sufferance of these Colonies; and such is now the necessity which constrains them to alter their former Systems of Government. The history of the present King of Great Britain is a history of repeated injuries and usurpations, all having in direct object the establishment of an absolute Tyranny over these States. To prove this, let Facts be submitted to a candid world.

He has refused his Assent to Laws, the most wholesome and necessary for the public good.

He has forbidden his Governors to pass Laws of immediate and pressing importance, unless suspended in their operation till his Assent should be obtained; and when so suspended, he has utterly neglected to attend to them.

He has refused to pass other Laws for the accommodation of large districts of people, unless those people would relinquish the right of Representation in the Legislature, a right inestimable to them and formidable to tyrants only.

Thomas Jefferson (1743–1826) served as governor of Virginia, minister to France, secretary of state, vice president under John Adams, and president from 1801 to 1809.

He has called together legislative bodies at places unusual, uncomfortable, and distant from the depository of their Public Records, for the sole purpose of fatiguing them into compliance with his measures.

He has dissolved Representative Houses repeatedly, for opposing with manly firmness his invasions on the rights of the people.

He has refused for a long time, after such dissolutions, to cause others to be elected; whereby the Legislative Powers, incapable of Annihilation, have returned to the People at large for their exercise; the State remaining in the mean time exposed to all the danger of invasion from without, and convulsions within.

He has endeavored to prevent the population of these States; for that purpose obstructing the Laws of Naturalization of Foreigners; refusing to pass others to encourage their migration hither, and raising the conditions of new Appropriations of Lands.

He has obstructed the Administration of Justice, by refusing his Assent to Laws for establishing Judiciary Powers.

He has made Judges dependent on his Will alone, for the tenure of their offices, and the amount and payment of their salaries.

He has erected a multitude of New Offices, and sent hither swarms of Officers to harass our People, and eat out their substance.

He has kept among us, in time of peace, Standing Armies without the consent of our Legislature.

He has affected to render the Military independent of and superior to the Civil Power.

He has combined with others to subject us to jurisdictions foreign to our constitution, and unacknowledged by our laws; giving his Assent to their acts of pretended Legislation:

For quartering large bodies of armed troops among us:

For protecting them, by a mock Trial, from Punishment for any Murders which they should commit on the Inhabitants of these States:

For cutting off our Trade with all parts of the world:

For imposing Taxes on us without our Consent:

For depriving us in many cases, of the benefits of Trial by Jury:

For transporting us beyond Seas to be tried for pretended offenses:

For abolishing the free System of English Laws in a Neighbouring Province, establishing therein an Arbitrary government, and enlarging its boundaries so as to render it at once an example and fit instrument for introducing the same absolute rule into these Colonies:

For taking away our Charters, abolishing our most valuable Laws, and altering fundamentally the Forms of our Governments:

For suspending our own legislatures, and declaring themselves invested with Power to legislate for us in all cases whatsoever.

He has abdicated Government here, by declaring us out of his Protection and waging War against us.

He has plundered our seas, ravaged our Coasts, burnt our towns and destroyed the Lives of our people.

He is at this time transporting large Armies of foreign Mercenaries to compleat the works of death, desolation and tyranny, already begun with circumstances of Cruelty & perfidy scarcely paralleled in the most barbarous ages, and totally unworthy the Head of a civilized nation.

He has constrained our fellow Citizens taken Captive on the high Seas to bear Arms against their Country, to become the executioners of their friends and Brethren, or to fall themselves by their Hands.

He has excited domestic insurrections amongst us, and has endeavored to bring on the inhabitants of our frontiers, the merciless Indian Savages, whose known rule of warfare is an undistinguished destruction of all ages, sexes, and conditions.

In every stage of these Oppressions We Have Petitioned for Redress in the most humble terms. Our repeated petitions have been answered only by repeated injury. A Prince, whose character is thus marked by every act which may define a Tyrant, is unfit to be the ruler of a free People.

Not have We been wanting in attention to our British brethren. We have warned them from time to time of attempts by their legislature to extend an unwarrantable jurisdiction over us. We have reminded them of the circumstances of our emigration and settlement here. We have appealed to their native justice and magnanimity and we have conjured them by the ties of our common kindred to disavow these usurpations, which would inevitably interrupt our connections and correspondence. They too have been deaf to the voice of justice and of consanguinity. We must, therefore, acquiesce in the necessity, which denounces our Separation, and hold them, as we hold the rest of mankind, Enemies in War, in Peace Friends.

We, therefore, the Representatives of the United States of America, in General Congress, Assembled, appealing to the Supreme Judge of the world for the rectitude of our intentions, do, in the Name, and by Authority of the good People of these Colonies, solemnly publish and declare, That these United Colonies are, and of Right ought to be, Free and Independent States; that they are Absolved from all Allegiance to the British Crown, and that all political connection between them and the State of Great Britain, is and ought to be totally dissolved; and that as Free and Independent States, they have full power to levy War, conclude Peace, contract Alliances, establish Commerce, and to do all other Acts and Things which Independent States may of right do. And for the support of this Declaration, with a firm reliance on the protection of Divine Providence, we mutually pledge to each other our lives, our Fortunes and our sacred Honor.

COMPREHENDING ARGUMENTS

The first step in the critical reading process is comprehension—understanding what an author is trying to prove. Comprehending academic arguments can be difficult because they are often complex and often challenge accepted notions. Academic writing also sometimes assumes that readers already have a great deal of knowledge about a subject and therefore can require further research for comprehension.

Readers sometimes fail to comprehend a text they disagree with or that is new to them, especially in dealing with essays or books making controversial, value-laden arguments. Some research even shows that readers will sometimes remember only those parts of texts that match their points of view.[1] The study of argument does not require you to accept points of view you find morally or otherwise reprehensible, but to engage with these views, no matter how strange or repugnant they might seem, on your own terms.

To comprehend difficult texts you should understand that reading and writing are linked processes, and use writing to help your reading. This can mean writing comments in the margins of the book or essay itself or in a separate notebook; highlighting passages in the text that seem particularly important; or freewriting about the author's essential ideas after you finish reading. For complex arguments, write down the methods the author uses to make the argument: Did the text make use of historical evidence or rely on the voice of experts? Were emotional appeals made to try to convince readers, or did the text rely on scientific or logical forms of evidence? Did the author use analogies or comparisons to help readers understand the argument? Was some combination of these or other strategies used? Writing down the author's methods for argumentation can make even the most complex arguments understandable.

STRATEGIES FOR COMPREHENDING ARGUMENTS

1. Skim the article or book for the main idea and overall structure. At this stage, avoid concentrating on details.

   a. Make a skeleton outline of the text in your mind or on paper. From this outline and the text itself, consider the relationship between the beginning, middle, and end of the argument. How has the author divided these sections? Are there subheadings in the body of the text? If you are reading a book, how are the chapters broken up? What appears to be the logic of the author's organization?

   b. From your overview, what is the central claim or argument of the essay? What is the main argument against the author's central claim and how would the author respond to it?

2. Remember that the claim is usually in one of the first two or three paragraphs (if it is an essay) or in the first chapter (if it is a book). The beginning of an argument can have other purposes, however; it may describe the position that the author will oppose or provide background for the whole argument.

3. Pay attention to topic sentences. The topic sentence is usually but not always the first sentence of a paragraph. It is the general statement that controls the details and examples in the paragraph.

---

[1]See, for example, Patrick J. Slattery, "The Argumentative, Multiple-Source Paper: College Students Reading, Thinking, and Writing about Multiple Points of View," *Journal of Teaching Writing* 10, Fall/Winter 1991, pp. 181–99.

4. Don't overlook language signposts, especially transitional words and phrases that tell you whether the writer will change direction or offer support for a previous point — words and phrases like *but, however, nevertheless, yet, moreover, for example, at first glance, more important, the first reason,* and so on.

5. When it comes to vocabulary, you can either guess the meaning of an unfamiliar word from the context and go on or look it up immediately. The first method makes for more rapid reading and is sometimes recommended by teachers, but guessing can be risky. Keep a good dictionary handy. If a word you don't understand seems crucial to meaning, look it up before going on.

6. If you use a colored marker to highlight main points, use it sparingly. Marking passages in color is meant to direct you to the major ideas and reduce the necessity for rereading the whole passage when you review. Look over the marked passages after reading and do a five-minute freewrite to sum up the central parts of the argument.

7. Once you are done reading, think again about the original context the text was written in: Why did the author write it and for whom? Why might an editor have published it in a book or journal, and why did your instructor assign it for you to read?

SAMPLE ANNOTATED ESSAY

Sex And The Cinema

EDWARD JAY EPSTEIN

Background for the argument — contrast with early days

Ⅰn the early days of Hollywood, nudity—or the illusion of it—was considered such an asset that director Cecil B. DeMille famously made bathing scenes an obligatory ingredient of his biblical epics. Nowadays, nudity is a decided liability when it comes to the commercial success of the movie. In 2004, none of the six major studios' top 25 grossing films, led by *Spider-Man 2, Shrek 2, Harry Potter and the Prisoner of Azkaban*, and *The Incredibles*, contained any sexually oriented nudity; only one had a restrictive R rating—Warner Bros.' *Troy*—and that was mainly due to the film's gory violence, not its sexual content. The absence

Examples of Top 25 movies with no sex

Claim

This essay appeared on August 15, 2005, in *Slate*, a daily online magazine affiliated with the *Washington Post*.

Claudette Colbert in *The Sign of the Cross* (1932), directed by Cecil B. DeMille

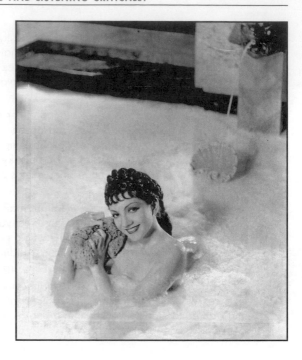

of sex—at least graphic sex—is key to the success of Hollywood's moneymaking movies. Directors may consider a sex scene artistically integral to their movie, but studios, which almost always have the right to exercise the final cut, also have to consider three factors.

Three factors to consider

I

First, there is the rating system. For a film to play in movie theaters belonging to the National Association of Theater Owners—which includes all the multiplexes in America—it first needs to obtain a rating from a board organized by the Motion Picture Association of America—the trade association of the six major studios. All the expenses for rating movies are paid to the MPAA by the studio out of a percentage deducted from box-office receipts. As it presently works, a movie that contains sexually oriented nudity gets either an NC-17 or an R rating, depending on how graphically sex is depicted. The NC-17 rating, which forbids theaters from admitting children under the age of 18, is the equivalent of a death sentence as far as the studios are concerned. In fact, since the

Topic sentence: NC-17 = box-office failure

financial disaster of Paul Verhoeven's NC-17 *Showgirls* in 1995, no studio has attempted a wide release of a NC-17 film. As one Paramount executive suggested, because of their sexually related nudity, movies such as Louis Malle's *Pretty Baby*, Bernardo Bertolucci's *Last Tango in Paris*, and Stanley Kubrick's *A Clockwork Orange* would not even be considered by a major studio today. So far this year there has been only one limited release of an NC-17 film by a studio: the documentary *Inside Deep Throat*, which yielded Universal less from the box-office — $330,000 — than it cost to wrangle media stars and others to free screenings and dinners to promote it.

Old movies with sex that wouldn't be made today

If a movie contains less explicit nudity, it earns an R rating, which merely prohibits youth unaccompanied by an adult. Even though this option means that some number of multiplex employees — who might otherwise be selling popcorn — are required to check the identity documents of the teenage audience, theaters accept R rated films, especially when, as was the case with *Troy*, the R is for the sort of graphic violence that is also the principal attraction. But even if an R doesn't prevent studios from staging a wide opening of a movie at the multiplexes, it complicates the movie's all-important marketing drive. For one thing, if a film receives an R rating, many television stations and cable networks, particularly teenage-oriented ones, are not allowed to accept TV ads for the movies. In addition, an R rating — especially for sexual content — will preclude any of the fast-food chains, beverage companies, or toy manufacturers that act as the studios' merchandise tie-in partners from backing the movie with tens of millions of dollars in free advertising. As a result, it becomes much more expensive to alert and herd audiences to R rated films.

Topic sentence
—Many stations and networks can't show ads for R movies.
—Food and toy companies won't back R movies.

II

Second, there is the Wal-Mart consideration. In 2004, the six studios took in $20.9 billion from home-video sales, according to the studios' own internal numbers. Wal-Mart, including its Sam's Club stores, accounted for over one-quarter of those sales, which means that Wal-Mart wrote more than $5 billion in checks to the studios in 2004. Such enormous buying power comes dangerously close to constituting what the Justice Department calls a monopsony—control of a market by a single buyer—and it allows the giant retailer to effectively dictate the terms of trade. Internet mythology aside, Wal-Mart doesn't use its clout to advance any political agenda or social engineering objective, according to a studio executive involved in the process; it is "strictly business." Wal-Mart uses DVDs, especially the weekly released hits, to lure in customers who, while they pass through the store, may buy more profitable items, such as toys, clothing, or electronics.

New DVDs = more customers, who buy other products

Wal-Mart's main concern with the content of the DVDs is that they not offend important customers—especially mothers—by containing material that may be inappropriate for children. It guards against this risk with a "decency policy" that consigns DVDs containing sexually related nudity to "adult sections" of the store, which greatly reduces their sales. (Wal-Mart is less concerned with vulgar behavior and language.) These guidelines, in turn, put studios under tremendous pressure to sanitize their films of sexual content. The Wal-Mart buyer would merely have to order for their stores the "in-flight entertainment" version of DVDs, from which studios expunge nudity and other sexually explicit scenes for airline passengers (censorship that almost all directors quietly accept). In light of such leverage, studios have to weigh the Wal-Mart factor with great care.

Wal-Mart's "decency policy" forces studios to avoid sexual content

Topic sentence

Finally, movies with nudity are a problem for the studios' other main moneymaker: television. As became abundantly clear in the controversy surrounding Janet Jackson's wardrobe malfunction at Superbowl XXXVIII, broadcast television is a government-regulated enterprise. When the government grants a free license to a station to broadcast over the public airwaves, it does so under the condition that it conform to the rules enforced by the Federal Communications Commission. Among those rules is the standard of "public decency," which among other things specifically prohibits salacious nudity—which is why CBS had to pay a fine for Ms. Jackson's brief exposure. Because the FCC regulates broadcast television (though not cable television), television stations run similar

III Topic sentence

Movies on TV must meet standards of "public decency"

5

risks—and embarrassments—if they show movies that include even partial nudity. So, before a studio can license such a movie to a broadcast network, it first has to cut out all the nudity and other scenes that run afoul of the decency standard. Aside from the expense involved, it requires the hassle of obtaining the director's permission, which is contractually required by the Directors Guild of America. The same is true in studio sales to foreign television companies, which have their own government censorship. Since graphic sex in movies is a triple liability, the studios can be expected to increasingly find that the artistic gain that comes from including it does not compensate for the financial pain and greenlight fewer and fewer movies that present this problem. We may live in an anything-goes age, but if a studio wants to make money, it has to limit how much of "anything"—at least anything sexually explicit—it shows on the big screen. As one studio executive with an MBA lamented, "We may have to leave sex to the independents."

Conclusion restates claim

PRACTICE

1. Choose an editorial of at least two paragraphs from your school paper or another newspaper on a controversial subject that interests you. The title will probably reveal the subject. Annotate the editorial as you read, using the annotations on "Sex and the Cinema" as a model. Then read the article again. You should discover that annotating the article caused you to read more carefully, more critically, with greater comprehension and a more focused response.

2. Summarize the claim of the editorial in one sentence. Has the author proved his or her point?

EVALUATING ARGUMENTS

The second step in the critical reading of arguments involves evaluation—careful judgment of the extent to which the author has succeeded in making a point—which can be difficult because some readers who do not thoroughly engage with an author's point of view may immediately label an argument they disagree with as "wrong," and some readers believe they are incapable of evaluating the work of a published, "expert" author because they do not feel expert enough to make such judgments.

Evaluating arguments means moving beyond comprehending the context the author was writing within and starting to question it. One way to do this is to envision audiences the text was probably *not* written for, by considering, for example, whether an essay written for an academic audience takes into account the world outside the university. In addition, why is the problem significant to the author? For whom would it not be significant, and why?

When you evaluate an argument, imagine at least two kinds of audience for the text. Decide whose views would conflict most with the author's, and why. What ideology or values underlie the point of view most diametrically opposed to the author's argument? Then imagine yourself as a friend of the writer who simply wants him or her to succeed in clarifying and developing the argument. You could ask what additional methods the author should use to make the argument more effective or how the writer could more fully address opposing points of view. Are there any significant questions or issues the author has left unaddressed? How could he or she build on the strengths of the argument and downplay the weaknesses?

At this point, consider how you personally respond to the argument presented in the text, and your own response in light of the questions you've asked. Critically evaluating an argument means not simply reading a text and agreeing or disagreeing with it, but doing serious analytical work that addresses multiple viewpoints before deciding on the effectiveness of an argument.

STRATEGIES FOR EVALUATING ARGUMENTS

1. As you read the argument, don't be timid about asking questions of the text. No author is infallible, and some are not always clear. Disagree with the author if you feel confident of the support for your view, but first read the whole argument to see if your questions have been answered. If not, this may be a signal to read the article again. Be cautious about concluding that the author hasn't proved his or her point.

2. Reading an assigned work is usually a solitary activity, but what follows a reading should be shared. Talk about the material with classmates or others who have read it, especially those who have responded to the text differently than you did. Consider their points of view. You probably know that discussion of a book or a movie strengthens both your memory of details and your understanding of the whole. And defending or modifying your evaluation will mean going back to the text and finding clues that you may have overlooked. Not least, it can be fun to discuss even something you didn't enjoy.

3. Consider the strengths of the argument and examine the useful methods of argumentation, the points that are successfully made (and those which help the reader to better understand the argument), and what makes sense about the author's argument.

4. Consider the weaknesses of the argument and locate instances of faulty reasoning, unsupported statements, and the limitations of the author's assumptions about the world (the warrants that underlie the argument).

5. Consider how effective the title of the reading is and whether it accurately sums up a critical point of the essay. Come up with an alternative title that would suit the reading better, and be prepared to defend this alternative title.

6. Evaluate the organizational structure of the essay. The author should lead you from idea to idea in a logical progression, and each section should relate to the ones before and after it and to the central argument in significant ways. Determine whether the writer could have organized things more clearly, logically, or efficiently.

7. Look at how the author follows through on the main claim, or thesis, of the argument. The author should stick with this thesis and not waver throughout the text. If the thesis does waver, there could be a reason for the shift in the argument, or perhaps the author is being inconsistent. The conclusion should drive home the central argument.

8. Evaluate the vocabulary and style the author uses. Is it too simple or too complicated? The vocabulary and sentence structure the author uses could relate to the audience the author was initially writing for.

SAMPLE ANALYSIS

The Gettysburg Address

ABRAHAM LINCOLN

Four score and seven years ago our fathers brought forth on this continent, a new nation, conceived in Liberty, and dedicated to the proposition that all men are created equal.

Now we are engaged in a great civil war, testing whether that nation, or any nation so conceived and so dedicated, can long endure. We are met on a great battle-field of that war. We have come to dedicate a portion of that field, as a final resting place for those who here gave their lives that that nation might live. It is altogether fitting and proper that we should do this.

But, in a larger sense, we can not dedicate—we can not consecrate— we can not hallow—this ground. The brave men, living and dead, who struggled here, have consecrated it, far above our poor power to add or

---

Abraham Lincoln (1809–1865), the sixteenth president of the United States, delivered this speech at Gettysburg, Pennsylvania, on November 19, 1863.

detract. The world will little note, nor long remember what we say here, but it can never forget what they did here. It is for us the living, rather, to be dedicated here to the unfinished work which they who fought here have thus far so nobly advanced. It is rather for us to be here dedicated to the great task remaining before us—that from these honored dead we take increased devotion to that cause for which they gave the last full measure of devotion—that we here highly resolve that these dead shall not have died in vain—that this nation, under God, shall have a new birth of freedom— and that government of the people, by the people, for the people, shall not perish from the earth.

The following evaluation is by Charles Adams, whose stand on the Civil War is clear from the title of the book from which the excerpt is taken: *When in the Course of Human Events: Arguing the Case for Southern Secession* (2000). Lincoln made his famous short speech in 1863 as a memorial to the thousands who had died at Gettysburg, but in doing so, he was also making an argument. The text in quotation marks is from the address itself. The rest is Adams's evaluation of it. As you read, consider what argument Lincoln is making but also whether or not you agree with Adams's evaluation.

Lincoln's Logic

CHARLES ADAMS

> Lincoln has become one of our national deities and a realistic examination of him is thus no longer possible.   —H. L. Mencken, 1931

At the Gettysburg Cemetery

Lincoln's mental processes and his logic have fascinated me ever since my university days. In a class in logic, we studied his Gettysburg Address. The analysis showed that this famous speech didn't fit the real world. It was good poetry, perhaps, but was it good thinking? It's chiseled in stone in the Lincoln Memorial in Washington, and it ranks in the minds of most

---

Charles Adams, a leading scholar on the history of taxation, is the author of *Fight, Flight, Fraud* (1982); *Those Dirty Rotten Taxes* (1998); and *For Good and Evil* (2nd Ed., 2001). His essay comes from *When in the Course of Human Events: Arguing the Case for Southern Secession* (2000).

Americans with the Declaration of Independence and the Constitution. This oration was given to dedicate the cemetery at Gettysburg, where tens of thousands of young men died in a battle that was probably the turning point of the war. The address is reminiscent of the funeral oration of Pericles of Athens in the fifth century B.C. But Pericles's oration seemed to fit the real world of his day and the virtues of Athenian democracy. Lincoln's address did not fit the world of his day. It reflected his logic, which was based on a number of errors and falsehoods. That it has survived with such reverence is one of the most bizarre aspects of the war.

"Four Score and Seven Years Ago"

By simple arithmetic that would be 1776, when the Revolutionary War started and the Declaration of Independence was signed. That declaration was written with "decent respect for the opinions of mankind," to explain the reasons for the separation of the thirteen colonies from Great Britain. It contained no endowment of governmental power and created no government. The government came later in 1781 with the Articles of Confederation. The articles stated that this confederation was established by "sovereign states," like many of the leagues of states throughout history. To be accurate, Lincoln should have said "four score and two years ago," or better still, "three score and fourteen years ago." Even the Northern newspapers winced. The *New York World* sharply criticized this historical folly. "*This* United States" was not created by the Declaration of Independence but "the result of the ratification of a compact known as the Constitution," a compact that said nothing about equality. Others accused Lincoln of "gross ignorance or willful misstatement." Yet today, that gross ignorance is chiseled in stone as if it were some great truth like scripture, instead of a willful misstatement.

"Our Fathers Brought Forth on This Continent, a New Nation"

The federal compact among the former thirteen colonies, the new "sovereign states," as expressed in the Articles of Confederation in 1781, was not a nation as that term was then and is normally used. That was recently explained by Carl N. Degler, professor of American history at Stanford University, in a memorial lecture given at Gettysburg College in 1990: "The Civil War, in short, was not a struggle to save a failed union, but to create a nation that until then had not come into being."

Thus Lincoln's "new nation" really came into being by force of arms in the war between the states. Lincoln, according to Professor Degler, had a lot in common with Germany's Otto von Bismarck, who built a united Germany in the nineteenth century and believed that "blood and iron" were the main force for national policy. When it came to blood, Lincoln surpassed them all. The slaughter of Confederate men only matched, on a proportionate basis, the losses incurred by the Russians and the Germans in World War II.

In Lincoln's first inaugural address he used the word "Union" twenty
times but "nation" not at all. But once the South seceded, the term began to
disappear, and by the time of the Gettysburg Address, it was the American
"nation" that was used, and the word "Union" had disappeared completely.

Thus the call from Northern peace Democrats—"the constitution as
it is; the Union as it was"—seems to make sense, but as Lincoln took over
control of the federal government, he soon wanted no part of it. Although he tried to trace the "new nation" back to 1776, he had to ignore
history and the intention and words of the Founders, and create a new
"gospel according to Lincoln" on the American commonwealth. Lincoln's new nation had no constitutional basis—no peaceful legal process.
It was created by war, by "blood and iron," like Bismarck's Germany, and
has survived to this day. In a sense, Lincoln did more to create America
than did the Founding Fathers. It is Lincoln who is the father of our present country, not George Washington. Lincoln's Gettysburg reference to
the Founders creating a new nation was not true. Just as Julius Caesar created an imperial order out of a republic, so Lincoln created a nation out
of a compact among states, and both used their military forces to do so.

"Conceived in Liberty"

A leading man of letters in Britain during the American Revolution,
Samuel Johnson, replied to the Americans' claims of tyranny in his book
Taxation Not Tyranny (1775). He said, "How is it that we hear the loudest
yelps for liberty among the drivers of negroes?"

The British are still chiding us for the absurdity of the Declaration of
Independence. Some years ago, while I was living in a British colony, we
Americans got together on the Fourth of July for a barbecue. One of my
older English friends asked me what the celebration was all about. I took
the bait and told him it was to celebrate the signing of the Declaration of
Independence. He replied, "Wasn't that document kind of a farce? All
that verbiage about equality of all men and liberty when over a million
black people were in bondage for life, and their children and children's
children?" Of course I had no answer, for the term "all men" meant all
white men. And to make matters worse, it really meant "white guys," as
white women weren't much better off. What is not known is that when
Lincoln issued his Emancipation Proclamation, many of the early
women's rights groups asked, How about us too? Thus the declaration
that Lincoln refers to in his address, of four score and seven years ago, was
not conceived in liberty *nor* was it dedicated to the proposition that all
men were created equal. So much for logic and reality.

Lincoln's logic at Gettysburg, as elsewhere, reveals a trial lawyer with a
tool of his craft—using the best logic he can muster to support his client's
(the North's) case, however bad that case may be. It is also, of course, the
craft of a politician, which may explain why so many politicians are lawyers.

"Today We Are Engaged in a Great Civil War"

Actually, it wasn't a civil war as that term was then, and is now, defined. 10
A civil war is a war that breaks out in a nation between opposing groups
for control of the state, for example, in Russia in 1917 with the Red
against the Whites or in China in the 1940s.

The War of Rebellion, as the war was called in the North, was really a
war for Southern independence. The Southern states had withdrawn from
the Union by democratic process—the same process they had followed to
join the Union initially. The Northern federation went to war to prevent
their secession from the Union just as Britain went to war in 1776 to prevent the colonies from seceding from the British nation. It was the fun-
damentals of the Revolutionary War, eighty-five years before. It was, if
you get down to the nuts and bolts of it, a war of conquest by the North
to destroy the Confederacy and to establish a new political leadership
over the conquered territories. Illiterate slaves were given the vote, and
the rest of the Southern society, the ruling groups, were not permitted to
vote. The poor, illiterate blacks were then told by Northern occupation
forces to vote as directed, and they did so, infuriating the conquered
people and creating a zeal for white supremacy that is only in our time
losing its grip on Southern society.

"Testing Whether That Nation . . . Can Long Endure"

That comment seems to presuppose that the South was out to conquer the
Northern federation. That is as absurd as saying that the revolting colonies
in 1776 were out to destroy the British nation. The thirteen colonies' withdrawal from the British Empire in 1776 was the same as the attempt of the
Southern states to withdraw in 1861 from the 1789 federation. In reality,
the 1789 federation was not in any danger. It would have endured with secession. Unlike Grant, Lee was not out to conquer the North. In reality,
this logic was as absurd as the rest of Lincoln's funeral oration.

"A Final Resting Place for Those Who Here Gave Their Lives That That Nation Might Live"

Again, "that nation" was not in danger of dying—that was not Southern
Confederate policy and Lincoln knew it. But again, he was only being a
good lawyer, arguing his client's case as best he could, and with no rebuttal he was an easy winner.

"And That Government of the People, by the People and for the People Shall Not Perish from the Earth"

Why did Lincoln even suggest that secession by the Southern states
would mean that democracy would perish from the earth—in America or
elsewhere? That was perfect nonsense, and Lincoln knew it, but again,
there was no one to rebut his argument.

Lincoln's repeated assertion that secession would amount to a fail- 15
ure of the American experiment with democracy and liberty "just is plain
nonsense," wrote Professor Hummel in his refreshing book on the Civil
War, *Emancipating Slaves, Enslaving Free Men.*[2] The London *Times* seems to
have best understood what was going on in America with the Northern
invasion to prevent secession: "If Northerners . . . had peaceably allowed
the seceders to depart, the result might fairly have been quoted as illustrating the advantages of Democracy, but when Republicans put empire
above liberty, and resorted to political oppression and war . . . . It was clear
that nature at Washington was precisely the same as nature at St. Petersburg. . . . Democracy broke down . . . when it was upheld, like any other
Empire, by force of arms."[3]

By 1860 democracy was strongly entrenched throughout Western civilization, and certainly in the American states. The democratic process
had emerged decades before in Europe — in Britain, France, the Netherlands, Switzerland, and so on. The war in America for Southern independence was in no way a danger to the concept of government "of the
people." Strange as it may seem, as it turned out, it was Lincoln who was
out to destroy governments of the people in the eleven Southern states.
The declaration's assertion that governments derive their "just powers
from the consent of the governed" was not an acceptable idea in Lincoln's mind so far as the South was concerned. Like a good lawyer he ignored it.

What makes Lincoln's ending so outrageous is that he didn't believe
in the self-determination of peoples, as British writers noted in 1861 and
a hundred years later in 1961.

Ordinances of secession had been adopted in the Southern states,
often with huge majorities. Their right to govern by consent was not acceptable to Lincoln's thinking — that would undermine his client's case.
Yet it was Lincoln who ended up destroying the Union as it was and substituting an all-powerful national government in which the states were
relegated to not much more than county status. There emerged the "imperial presidency" that is with us to this day, in which presidents can go
to war, without congressional approval, spend money without congressional approval; in fact, they can rule by decree like the consuls of Rome.
In other Western democracies, this is not so. Their chief executive must
have the permission and approval of their legislature to do such things.
Thus Lincoln did more to destroy the Union than preserve it. Is not this
irony at its best?

---

[2] Jeffrey Hummel, *Emancipating Slaves, Enslaving Free Men* (Chicago: Open Court
1997), p. 352.
[3] *Times* editorial, September 13, 1862, p. 8, cited in *Emancipating Slaves*, p. 352.

PRACTICE

1. Return to "Sex and the Cinema" and reread it in light of the Strategies for Evaluating Arguments.

2. What is your evaluation of Adams's essay, "Lincoln's Logic"?

RESPONDING AS A WRITER

Notice the difference between the annotations a student made in response to the following essay and those another student made earlier in response to "Sex and the Cinema" (p. 37). In the earlier example, the student was making marginal notes primarily on the ideas presented in the essay. Here the annotations focus on how the essay is written. In other words, the student is looking at the piece from a writer's perspective.

The essay is a claim of value in which, as the title suggests, the author claims that competitive sports are destructive. In arguments about values, the author may or may not suggest a solution to the problem caused by the belief or behavior. If so, the solution will be implicit—that is, unexpressed or undeveloped—as is the case here, and the emphasis will remain on support for the claim.

Keep in mind that an essay of this length can never do justice to a complicated and highly debatable subject. It will probably lack sufficient evidence, as this one does, to answer all the questions and objections of readers who enjoy and approve of competitive games. What it can do is provoke thought and initiate an intelligent discussion.

SAMPLE ANNOTATED ESSAY

No-Win Situations

ALFIE KOHN

Intro: personal experience

I learned my first game at a birthday party. You remember it: X players scramble for X-minus-one chairs each time the music stops. In every round a child is eliminated until at the end only

---

This article by Alfie Kohn, author of *No Contest: The Case against Competition* (1986) and *The Homework Myth: Why Our Kids Get Too Much of a Bad Thing* (2006), appeared in *Women's Sports and Fitness Magazine* (July–August 1990).

one is left triumphantly seated while everyone else is standing on the sidelines, excluded from play, unhappy . . . losers.

This is how we learn to have a good time in America.

Competition

Several years ago I wrote a book called *No Contest*, which, based on the findings of several hundred studies, argued that competition undermines self-esteem, poisons relationships, and holds us back from doing our best. I was mostly interested in the win/lose arrangement that defines our work-places and classrooms, but I found myself nagged by the following question: If competition is so destructive and counterproductive during the week, why do we take for granted that it sud-denly becomes benign and even desirable on the weekend?

Warrant

This is a particularly unsettling line of inquiry for athletes or parents. Most of us, after all, as-sume that competitive sports teach all sorts of useful lessons and, indeed, that games by defini-tion must produce a winner and a loser. But I've come to believe that recreation at its best does not require people to try to triumph over others. Quite to the contrary.

Claim or thesis statement

Terry Orlick, a sports psychologist at the Uni-   5
versity of Ottawa, took a look at musical chairs and proposed that we keep the basic format of re-moving chairs but change the goal; the point be-comes to fit everyone on a diminishing number of seats. At the end, a group of giggling children tries to figure out how to squish onto a single chair. Everybody plays to the end; everybody has a good time.

Support: expert opinion, alternatives to competitive games

Orlick and others have devised or collected hundreds of such games for children and adults alike. The underlying theory is simple: All games involve achieving a goal despite the presence of an obstacle, but nowhere is it written that the ob-stacle has to be someone else. The idea can be for each person on the field to make a specified con-tribution to the goal, or for all the players to reach a certain score, or for everyone to work with her partners against a time limit.

Note the significance of an "opponent" becoming a "partner." The entire dynamic of the game shifts, and one's attitude toward the other players changes with it. Even the friendliest game of tennis can't help but be affected by the game's inherent structure, which demands that each person try to hit the ball where the other can't get to it. You may not be a malicious person, but to play tennis means that you try to make the other person fail.

Refuting the opposing view

I've become convinced that not a single one of the advantages attributed to sports actually requires competition. Running, climbing, biking, swimming, aerobics—all offer a fine workout without any need to try to outdo someone else. Some people point to the camaraderie that results from teamwork, but that's precisely the benefit of cooperative activity, whose very essence is that *everyone* on the field is working together for a common goal. By contrast, the distinguishing feature of team competition is that a given player works with and is encouraged to feel warmly toward only half of those present. Worse, a we-versus-they dynamic is set up, which George Orwell once called "war minus the shooting."

No advantages in competition

1)

2)

The dependence on sports to provide a sense of accomplishment or to test one's wits is similarly misplaced. One can aim instead at an objective standard (How far did I throw? How many miles did we cover?) or attempt to do better than last week. Such individual and group striving—like cooperative games—provides satisfaction and challenge without competition.

If large numbers of people insist that we can't do without win/lose activities, the first question to ask is whether they've ever tasted the alternative. When Orlick taught a group of children non-competitive games, two-thirds of the boys and all of the girls preferred them to the kind that require opponents. If our culture's idea of fun requires beating someone else, it may just be because we don't know any other way.

10

It may also be because we overlook the psychological costs of competition. Most people lose in most competitive encounters, and it's obvious why that causes self-doubt. But even winning

3)

doesn't build character. It just lets us gloat temporarily. Studies have shown that feelings of self-worth become dependent on external sources of evaluation as a result of competition. Your value is defined by what you've done and who you've beaten. The whole affair soon becomes a vicious circle: The more you compete, the more you *need* to compete to feel good about yourself. It's like drinking salt water when you're thirsty. This process is bad enough for us; it's a disaster for our children.

4) While this is going on, competition is having an equally toxic effect on our relationships. By definition, not everyone can win a contest. That means that each child inevitably comes to regard others as obstacles to his or her own success. Competition leads children to envy winners, to dismiss losers (there's no nastier epithet in our language than "loser!"), and to be suspicious of just about everyone. Competition makes it difficult to regard others as potential friends or collaborators; even if you're not my rival today, you could be tomorrow.

This is not to say that competitors will always detest one another. But trying to outdo someone is not conducive to trust—indeed it would be irrational to trust a person who gains from your failure. At best, competition leads one to look at others through narrowed eyes; at worst, it invites outright aggression.

Changing the Structure of Sports

Conclusion

But no matter how many bad feelings erupt during competition, we have a marvelous talent for blaming the individuals rather than focusing on the structure of the game itself, a structure that makes my success depend on your failure. Cheating may just represent the logical conclusion of this arrangement rather than an aberration. And sportsmanship is nothing more than an artificial way to try to limit the damage of competition. If we weren't set against each other on the court or the track, we wouldn't need to keep urging people to be good sports; they might well be working *with* each other in the first place.

New idea that confirms his claim

As radical or surprising as it may sound, the 15
problem isn't just that we compete the wrong
way or that we push winning on our children too
early. The problem is competition itself. What we
need to be teaching our daughters and sons is
that it's possible to have a good time—a better
time—without turning the playing field into a
battlefield.

■ Analysis

The pattern of organization in this essay is primarily a *defense of the main idea*—that competitive sports are psychologically unhealthy. But because the author knows that competitive sports are hugely popular, not only in the United States but in many other parts of the world, he must also try to *refute the opposing view*—that competition is rewarding and enjoyable. In doing so, Kohn fails to make clear distinctions between competitive sports for children, who may find it difficult to accept defeat, and for adults, who understand the consequences of any competitive game and are psychologically equipped to deal with them. Readers may therefore share Kohn's misgivings about competition for children but doubt that his criteria apply equally to adults.

The *claim*, expressed as the *thesis statement* of the essay, appears at the end of paragraph 4: "recreation at its best does not require people to try to triumph over others. Quite to the contrary." The three-paragraph introduction recounts a relevant personal experience as well as the reasons that prompted Kohn to write his essay. Because we are all interested in stories, the recital of a personal experience is a popular device for introducing almost any subject.

The rest of the essay, until the last two paragraphs, is devoted to summarizing the benefits of cooperative play and the disadvantages of competitive sport. The emphasis is overwhelmingly on the disadvantages as stated in the third paragraph: "competition undermines self-esteem, poisons relationships, and holds us back from doing our best." This is the *warrant*, the assumption that underlies the claim. In fact, here Kohn is referring to a larger study that he wrote about competition in workplaces and classrooms. We must accept this broad generalization, which applies to many human activities, before we can agree that the claim about competition in sports is valid.

Kohn relies for support on examples from common experience and on the work of Terry Orlick, a sports psychologist. The examples from experience are ones that most of us will recognize. Here we are in a position to judge for ourselves, without the mediation of an expert, whether the influence of competition in sports is as hurtful as Kohn insists. Orlick's research suggests a solution—adaptations of familiar games that will provide enjoyment but avoid competition. On the other hand, the results from studies by one psychologist whose work we aren't able to verify and the mention of "studies" in paragraph 3 without further attribution are probably not enough to answer all the arguments in favor of competition. Critics may also ask if Kohn has offered support for one of his contentions—that competition "holds us back from doing our best" (para. 3). (Support for this may appear in one of Kohn's books.)

The last two paragraphs sum up his argument that "the problem is competition itself" (para. 15)—the structure of the game rather than the people who play. Notice that this summary does not merely repeat the main idea. Like many thoughtful summaries, it also offers a new idea about good sportsmanship that confirms his conclusion.

The language is clear and direct. Kohn's article, which appeared in a women's sports magazine, is meant for the educated general reader, not the expert. This is also the audience for whom most student papers are written. But the written essay need not be unduly formal. Kohn uses contractions and the personal pronouns *I* and *you* to establish a conversational context. One of the particular strengths of his style is the skillful use of transitional expressions, words like *this* and *also* and clauses like *This is not to say that* and *Note the significance of* to make connections between paragraphs and new ideas.

The tone is temperate despite the author's strong feelings about the subject. Other authors, supporting the same argument, have used language that borders on the abusive about coaches and trainers of children's games. But a less inflammatory voice is far more effective with an audience that may be neutral or antagonistic.

You will find it helpful to look back over the essay to see how the examples we've cited and others work to fulfill the writer's purpose.

Writer's Guide: Annotating a Text

One purpose of annotating a text is to comprehend it more fully. Another is to prepare to write about it.

1. If you use a highlighter as you read a text, use it sparingly. Highlighting too much of a text is not very useful when it comes time to review what you have marked. You might consider a more targeted approach to highlighting, focusing only on thesis statement and topic sentences in an essay, for example, or on conclusions in a report.

2. More useful than highlighting is making marginal notes, perhaps underlining the portion of the text that each note refers to. With underlining as with highlighting, however, increased quantity equals decreased usefulness. Some of the most useful marginal notes will be those that summarize key

ideas in your own words. Such paraphrases force you to understand the text well enough to reword its ideas, and reading the marginal notes is a quick way to review the text when you do not have time to reread all of it.

3. If you are making notes both on what a piece of writing says and how it says it, you may want to place marginal notes about content on one side of the text and those about rhetorical strategies on the other. Notations about how a piece is written can focus on structural devices such as topic sentences, transitional words or phrases, and the repetition of ideas or sentence structure but also on rhetorical concerns such as identifying the claim, support, and warrant; the tone; and the types of appeal.

4. As you annotate a text, you may also want to make note of questions you still have after having read the text. These questions may be the basis for class discussion.

5. You may also find it useful to note similarities that you see between the text you are reading and others you have read or between the text and your own experience.

PRACTICE

Using the annotations on Kohn's "No-Win Situations" as a model, respond to the following essay not primarily in terms of its ideas but in terms of the way it is written.

"Freak dancing": If Only It Stopped There

DESDA MOSS

With prom season approaching, some adults who haven't been to a school dance since the Hustle was the hot craze might need a lesson to prepare them for what's happening in gymnasiums across the nation.

It goes by many names and has been a growing trend in recent years. Some call it "freak dancing." Some call it grinding. Some call it booty dancing. Parents who see it for the first time generally call it, well, disgusting, and find it more than a little disturbing. (I won't explore the Freudian reasons why seeing kids in braces simulating sex is disturbing to grown-ups; check your local listings for *Dr. Phil.*) A friend of mine who recently attended a "sweet 16" birthday party observed partygoers engaging in moves that would make a lap dancer blush.

Desda Moss is a freelance writer in Virginia. This article appeared on April 7, 2005, on USA Today.com.

To be sure, dancing has always been risky business—from the forbidden passions of the Lambada to the hip-shaking roots of rock 'n' roll—every generation seems to have created a hormone-driven dance du jour. But with modesty and subtlety in short supply in our hypersexualized society, today's teens seem to be testing the limits of decency with unprecedented vigor. In some communities, schools have banned overtly suggestive dancing altogether.

As expected, that has set off a new round of intergenerational snipping, with parents and other authority figures being accused of overreacting and trouncing on the right of free expression. After all, some contend, it's only dancing. Others point out that what teens today are doing is no different from the slow dragging their middle-aged parents did in their day under the glow of blue lights in the basement.

I spent my teen years watching *Soul Train*, following every dance   5 move and hoping to duplicate them after practicing for hours in my living room. Often, my dad would watch the show with me and offer comments. "Looks like maggots in a bucket," he'd say.

His own style was more one of restrained grace. His footwork was a study in cool, minimalist movement. It was only the look of pure bliss that revealed he was in the zone.

My late father didn't live to see the freak dancing trend hold. But should anyone be inclined to get their knickers in a twist over this latest form of teen rebellion, I would advise them to consider the findings of a new study in this month's edition of *Pediatrics*. It suggests we have bigger issues to deal with than mere simulated sex. It found that about one in five ninth-graders surveyed (we're talking 14-year-olds) reported they'd had oral sex. Almost a third said they'd like to try it within the next six months. Finally, this: 13 percent of the participants reported that they'd had intercourse.

Now that's something to freak about.

RESPONDING AS A CRITICAL LISTENER

Of course, not all public arguments are written. Oral arguments on radio and television now enjoy widespread popularity and influence. In fact, their proliferation means that we listen far more than we talk, read, or write. Today the art of listening has become an indispensable tool for learning about the world we live in. One informed critic predicts that the dissemination of information and opinions through the electronic media will "enable more and more Americans to participate directly in making the laws and policies by which they are governed."[4]

---

[4]Lawrence K. Grossman, *The Electronic Republic: Reshaping Democracy in the Information Age* (New York: Viking, 1995).

Because we are interested primarily in arguments about public issues — those that involve democratic decision making — we will not be concerned with the afternoon television talk shows that are largely devoted to personal problems. (Occasionally, however, *Oprah* introduces topics of broad social significance.) More relevant to the kinds of written arguments you will read and write about in this course are the television and radio shows that also examine social and political problems. The most intelligent and responsible programs usually consist of a panel of experts — politicians, journalists, scholars — led by a neutral moderator (or one who, at least, allows guests to express their views). Some of these programs are decades old; others are more recent — *Meet the Press, Face the Nation, Hardball with Chris Matthews, The McLaughlin Group, The NewsHour with Jim Lehrer.* An outstanding radio show, *Talk of the Nation* on National Public Radio, invites listeners, who are generally informed and articulate, to call in and ask questions of, or comment on remarks made by, experts on the topic of the day.

Several enormously popular radio talk shows are hosted by people with strong, sometimes extreme ideological positions. They may use offensive language and insult their listeners in a crude form of theater. Among the most influential shows are those of Don Imus and Howard Stern. In addition, elections and political crises bring speeches and debates on radio and television by representatives of a variety of views. Some are long and formal, written texts that are simply read aloud, but others are short and impromptu.

Whatever the merits or shortcomings of individual programs, significant general differences exist between arguments on radio and television and arguments in the print media. These differences include the degree of organization and development and the risk of personal attacks.

First (excluding for the moment the long, prepared speeches), contributions to a panel discussion must be delivered in fragments, usually no longer than a single paragraph, weakened by time constraints, interruptions, overlapping speech, memory gaps, and real or feigned displays of derision, impatience, and disbelief by critical panelists. Even on the best programs, the result is a lack of both coherence — or connections between ideas — and solid evidence that requires development. Too often we are treated to conclusions with little indication of how they were arrived at.

The following brief passage appeared in a newspaper review of "Resolved: The flat tax is better than the income tax," a debate on *Firing Line* by an impressive array of experts. It illustrates some of the difficulties that accompany programs attempting to capture the truth of a complicated issue on television or radio.

> "It is absolutely true," says a proponent. "It is factually untrue," counters an opponent. "It's factually correct," responds a proponent. "I did my math right," says a proponent. "You didn't do your math right," says an opponent. At one point in a discussion of interest income, one of the experts says, "Oh, excuse me, I think I got it backward."

No wonder the television critic called the exchange "disjointed and at times perplexing."[5]

In the sensational talk shows the participants rely on personal experience and vivid anecdotes, which may not be sufficiently typical to prove anything.

Second, listeners and viewers of all spoken arguments are in danger of evaluating them according to criteria that are largely absent from evaluation of written texts. It is true that writers may adopt a persona or a literary disguise, which the tone of the essay will reflect. But many read-

---

STRATEGIES FOR CRITICAL LISTENING

Listening is hearing with attention, a natural and immensely important human activity, which, unfortunately, many people don't do very well. The good news is that listening is a skill that can be learned and, unlike some other skills, practiced every day without big investments of money and effort.

Here are some of the characteristics of critical listening most appropriate to understanding and responding to arguments.

1. Above all, listening to arguments requires concentration. If you are distracted, you cannot go back as you do with the written word to clarify a point or recover a connection. Devices such as flow sheets and outlines can be useful aids to concentration. In following a debate, for example, judges and other listeners often use flow sheets — distant cousins of baseball scorecards — to record the major points on each side and their rebuttals. For roundtable discussions or debates you can make your own simple flow chart to fill out as you listen, with columns for claims, different kinds of support, and warrants. Leave spaces in the margin for your questions and comments about the soundness of the proof. An outline is more useful for longer presentations, such as lectures. As you listen, try to avoid being distracted by facts alone. Look for the overall pattern of the speech.

2. Listeners often concentrate on the wrong things in the spoken argument. We have already noted the distractions of appearance and delivery. Research shows that listeners are likely to give greater attention to the dramatic elements of speeches than to the logical ones. But you can enjoy the sound, the appearance, and the drama of a spoken argument without allowing these elements to overwhelm what is essential to the development of a claim.

3. Good listeners try not to allow their prejudices to prevent careful evaluation of the argument. This doesn't mean accepting everything or even most of what you hear. It means trying to avoid premature judgments about what is actually said. This precaution is especially relevant when the speakers and their views are well known and the listener has already formed an opinion about them, favorable or unfavorable.

---

[5]Walter Goodman, "The Joys of the Flat Tax, Excluding the Equations," *New York Times*, December 21, 1995, sec. C, p. 14.

ers will not be able to identify it or recognize their own response to it. Listeners and viewers, however, can hardly avoid being affected by characteristics that are clearly definable: a speaker's voice, delivery, bodily mannerisms, dress, and physical appearance. In addition, listeners may be adversely influenced by clumsy speech containing more slang, colloquialisms, and grammar and usage errors than written texts that have had the benefit of revision.

But if listeners allow consideration of physical attributes to influence their judgment of what the speaker is trying to prove, they are guilty of an ad hominem fallacy—that is, an evaluation of the speaker rather than the argument. This is true whether the evaluation is favorable or unfavorable. (See p. 341 for a discussion of this fallacy.)

Talk shows may indeed be disjointed and perplexing, but millions of us find them both instructive and entertaining. Over time we are exposed to an astonishing variety of opinions from every corner of American life, and we also acquire information from experts who might not otherwise be available to us. Then there is the appeal of hearing the voices, seeing the faces of people engaged in earnest, sometimes passionate, discourse—a short, unrehearsed drama in which we also play a part as active listeners in a far-flung audience.

ASSIGNMENTS FOR READING AND LISTENING CRITICALLY

READING AND DISCUSSION QUESTIONS

1. Consider the claim that Desda Moss is supporting in "'Freak Dancing': If Only It Stopped There." How valid do you consider that claim to be, and why?

2. Listen to a recording of Martin Luther King Jr.'s "I Have a Dream" and discuss how the language of the speech adds power to the ideas.

3. Watch (and *listen to*) one of the afternoon television talk shows like *Oprah* in which guests discuss a controversial social problem. (The *TV Guide*, daily newspapers, and online listings often list the subject. Past topics on *Oprah* include when parents abduct their children, when children kill children, and when surgery changes patients' lives.) Analyze the discussion, considering the major claims, the most important evidence, and the declared or hidden warrants. How much did the oral format contribute to success or failure of the arguments?

4. Watch one episode of either the *Daily Show with Jon Stewart* or the *Colbert Report* and discuss how the show, successfully or not, tries to use humor to make serious points about political and/or social issues.

WRITING SUGGESTIONS

5. Write an essay responding as a writer to "Sex and the Cinema." You may choose to support an evaluative claim that analyzes how effective the essay is or one that objectively analyzes how the essay is written.

6. Write an essay evaluating "'Freak Dancing': If Only It Stopped There."

7. Write a critical response to the Declaration of Independence.

8. Do you agree with Alfie Kohn in "No-Win Situations" that games and sports should not be so competitive? Write an essay explaining why or why not.

9. Choose an editorial from your school newspaper or a local newspaper and write an evaluation of it.

10. Listen to one of the television talk shows that feature experts on social and political issues. Choose a show such as the *O'Reilly Factor, Hannity and Colmes,* or *The McLaughlin Group.* Write a review, telling how much you learned about the subject(s) of discussion. Be specific about the features of the show that were either helpful or unhelpful to your understanding.

11. Given Charles Adams's criticism of Lincoln's "Gettysburg Address" what could you say in its defense? Explain in an essay why this short speech has become a classic when so many others have not.

CHAPTER 3

Reading Visual Texts Critically

RESPONDING TO A VISUAL ARGUMENT

Man has been communicating by pictures longer than he has been using words. With the development of photography in this century we are using pictures as a means of communication to such an extent that in some areas they overshadow verbal language.[1]

Paul Wendt wrote these words long before the digital age. Now we can snap pictures with our cell phones and send them to the other side of the world. Most elementary school children know how to use *Google* or another search engine to find pictures of almost anything imaginable, and by middle school they know how to go to *YouTube* to see thousands of amateur videos or to submit their own.

Wendt was writing, however, about the persuasive power of pictures, or pictures as argument. The nation saw the power of the visual in the 2008 presidential campaign when questions for the candidates came for the first time in the form of video clips submitted via *YouTube*—and campaigns may never be the same. Questions were not merely read by a moderator or asked by a panel of journalists. They didn't come in the form of disembodied voices over a telephone line. They came from real people who were visible on the screen to the candidates and to the whole country. Two women looked straight into the camera and asked the candidates if they would let them get married to each other. A snowman asked about global warming and what it would mean to his son's future. A young man asked what they could do

[1] Paul Wendt, "The Language of Pictures," in S. I. Hayakawa, ed., *The Use and Misuse of Language* (Greenwich, Conn.: Fawcett, 1962), p. 175.

61

to protect his "baby" and held up an assault rifle. The visual images did not replace the verbal language, but complemented it. They were an integral part of the argument.

You've probably seen similarly powerful still images in photographic journalism: soldiers in battle, destruction by weather disasters, beautiful natural landscapes, inhumane living conditions, the great mushroom cloud of early atomic explosions. These photographs and thousands of others encapsulate arguments of fact, value, and policy. We often don't need to read their captions to understand what they tell us: *The tornado devastated the town. The Grand Canyon is our most stupendous national monument. We must not allow human beings to live like this.*

An exception would be a pair of pictures that gained wide circulation in the aftermath of Hurricane Katrina in 2005. They seemed innocuous enough when seen without commentary, except to show the extent of the flooding. One shows a young black man wading through the chest-deep floodwaters carrying a black garbage bag. Another shows a young white man also wading through chest-deep water, wearing a backpack and accompanied by a young white woman wearing a backpack and dragging a bag. The text accompanying the pictures, however, shows the bias of those who described the pictures. Next to the picture of the black youth are these words: "A young man walks through chest deep water after looting a grocery store in New Orleans on Tuesday, August 30, 2005." Notice the difference in the words accompanying the other picture: "Two residents wade through chest deep flood water after finding bread and soda from a local grocery store after Hurricane Katrina came through the area in New Orleans, Louisiana." The wording produced such a response that *Yahoo!* offered this statement:

> News photos are an especially popular section of Yahoo! News. In part, this is because we present thousands of news photos from some of the leading news services, including The Associated Press, Reuters, and Agence France Press. To make this volume of photos available in a timely manner, we present the photos and their captions as written, edited and distributed by the news services with no additional editing at Yahoo! News.
>
> In recent days, a number of readers of Yahoo! News have commented on differences in the language in two Hurricane Katrina-related photo captions (from two news services). Since the controversy began, the supplier of one of the photos has asked all its clients to remove the photo from their databases. Yahoo! News has complied with the AFP request. . . . Yahoo! News regrets that these photos and captions, viewed together, may have suggested a racial bias on our part. We remain committed to bringing our readers the full collection of photos as transmitted by our wire service partners.[2]

Other images provided additional glimpses into the aftermath of Katrina. The photograph of Milvertha Hendricks was striking enough that

---

[2]The Yahoo! News statement can be found at http://news.yahoo.com/page/photostatement.

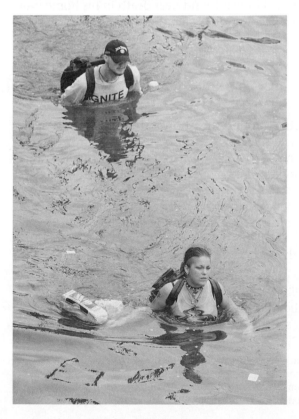

"Looting" and "finding"

David Dante Troutt, Charles Ogletree, and Derrick Bell used a color version of it for the cover photo of their book, *After the Storm: Black Intellectuals Explore the Meaning of Hurricane Katrina.*

PRACTICE

1. Look closely at the photograph of a flag-draped woman taken following Hurricane Katrina. Who is pictured? What sort of expression does she have on her face? Then consider why the elderly woman might have a blanket that looks like an American flag draped over her. What do you know about the rescue of Katrina victims that might be relevant to how you "read" the picture as an argument? Under the circumstances, how might the flag blanket be seen as symbolic? What claim might you infer from the picture?

2. Now compare the picture to the next photo, "At the Time of the Louisville Flood," taken in 1937 by Margaret Bourke-White. Do you see any similarity in the message being conveyed by each? Explain.

3. Finally, look at the third picture and decide if you feel it conveys a similar or a very different message.

Edgar Hollingsworth, the seventy-four-year-old man shown being rescued in the third picture, snapped by Bruce Chambers of the *Orange County Register*, survived the hurricane but was found near death in his home fourteen days after the storm. He died four days later in the hospital.

The reactions this third picture has elicited provide an excellent illustration of varied responses to the same visual image. Not every viewer will "read" a picture in the same way. Not every viewer will see it as support for the same argument. These are some of the responses that the picture of Hollingsworth's rescue has produced:

• A typical headline accompanying the photo called the discovery of Hollingsworth a "miracle rescue." According to a report from Post-Gazette.com, "The rescue was a bright spot on a day in which the owners of a nursing home were charged in the deaths of dozens of patients killed by hurricane floodwaters, the death toll in Louisiana jumped to 423 and the New Orleans mayor warned that the city is broke."[3] And according to Keith Sharon of the *Orange County Register*, "The rescue pumped up the spirits of [California] Task Force 5, which has been mostly marking the locations of dead bodies for the last week."[4]

• *USA Today* termed the photo "iconic."[5] Marcia Prouse, director of photography at the *Orange County Register*, had a similar view: "This man's story needs to be told. He's an important symbol of the hurricane. . . . It's anybody's father or grandfather."[6]

[3] See http://www.post-gazette.com/pg/05257/570999.stm.
[4] See http://www.ocregister.com/blog/rescue/.
[5] See http://www.usatoday.com/news/nation/2005-11-10-hollingsworth-katrina_x.htm.
[6] See http://www.editorandpublisher.com/eandp/news/article_display.jsp?vnu_content_id=1001137369.

Eric Gay, "Milvertha Hendricks, 84, waiting in the rain outside the New Orleans Convention Center on September 1, 2005"

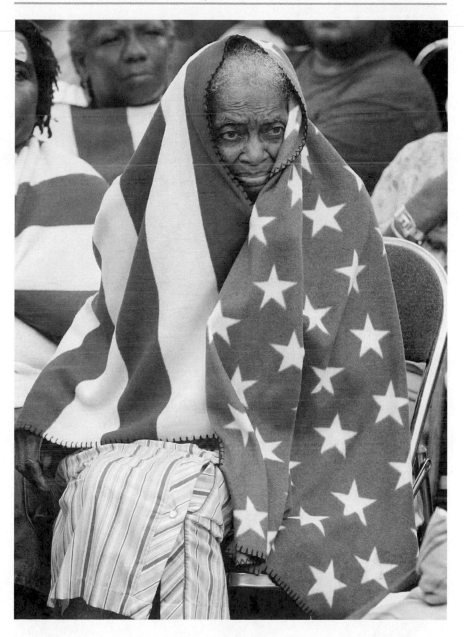

- Chambers's picture has become known through Internet chat as the *Katrina Pietá*. The *Pietá* alluded to is Michelangelo's famous sculpture of Mary holding the body of Christ after his crucifixion. The way that the National Guardsman is holding Hollingsworth is reminiscent

Margaret Bourke-White, "At the Time of the Louisville Flood" (1937)

Bruce Chambers, "Edgar Hollingsworth rescued from his home after Hurricane Katrina" (2005)

of Mary's pose, and the link to the loving mother of Jesus leads to a positive interpretation of the scene.

- For some, the sight of two white aid workers and one Hispanic one aiding a black man provides a sharp contrast to other images that stress the racial tension that grew out of Katrina's aftermath.

- Others were enraged by rules that could have kept the rescue team from entering Hollingsworth's home to rescue him. Keith Sharon wrote, "In the past few days, the Federal Emergency Management Agency has ordered searchers not to break into homes. They are supposed to look in through a window and knock on the door. If no one cries out for help, they are supposed to move on. If they see a body, they are supposed to log the address and move on." The rescue team went against orders in breaking down the door to reach Hollingsworth. Sharon added that earlier "they had been frustrated when FEMA delayed their deployment for four days, housing them in the Hyatt Regency in Dallas."[7] The Sharon quotes are referenced on DailyKOS.com, under the title "American Shame: The Edgar Hollingsworth Story."[8]

Just as readers bring to an argument their biases and their own personal store of experiences, so do viewers bring the same to a visual argument.

Photographs, of course, function everywhere as instruments of persuasion. Animal-rights groups show pictures of brutally mistreated dogs and cats; children's rights advocates publish pictures of sick and starving children in desolate refugee camps. On a very different scale, alluring photographs from advertisers—travel agencies, restaurants, sporting goods manufacturers, clothiers, jewelers, movie studios—promise to fulfill our dreams of pleasure.

But photographs are not the only visual images we respond to. We are also susceptible to other kinds of illustrations and to signs and symbols which over the years have acquired connotations, or suggestive significance. The flag or bald eagle, the shamrock, the crown, the cross, the hammer and sickle, and the swastika can all rouse strong feelings for or against the ideas they represent. These symbols may be defined as abbreviated claims of value. They summarize the moral, religious, and political principles by which groups of people live and often die. In commercial advertisements we recognize symbols that aren't likely to enlist our deepest loyalties but, nevertheless, have impact on our daily lives: the apple with a bite in it, the golden arches, the Prudential rock, the Nike swoosh, and a thousand others.

---

[7] Keith Sharon, "Survivor Rescued 16 Days after the Hurricane," *Orange County Register*, September 14, 2005.

[8] See www.dailykos.com/story/2005/9/14/12516/3649.

In fact, a closer look at commercial and political advertising, which is heavily dependent on visual argument and is something we are all familiar with, provides a useful introduction to this complex subject. We know that advertisements, with or without pictures, are short arguments, often lacking fully developed support, whose claims of policy urge us to take an action: Buy this product or service; vote for this candidate or issue. The claim may not be directly expressed, but it will be clearly implicit. In print, on television, or on the Internet, the visual representation of objects, carefully chosen to appeal to a particular audience, can be as important as, if not more important than, any verbal text.

PRACTICE

Analyze the argument being made by the advertisement on page 69. Consider these questions:

1. Why is the gun so much larger than the printed message below it?
2. What claim of policy is this ad making?
3. Would that claim be as successful if the note were excluded? Why, or why not?
4. Would additional facts about guns make the ad more effective?
5. What is the basis of the emotional appeal? Is there more than one?
6. Does the ad go too far in exploiting our emotions?

In a political advertisement we often see a picture of the candidate surrounded by a smiling family. The visual image is by now a cliché, suggesting traditional values — love and security, the importance of home and children. Even if we know little or nothing about his or her platform, we are expected to make a sympathetic connection with the candidate.

In a commercial advertisement the image may be a picture of a real or fictitious person to whom we will react favorably. Consider the picture on a jar of spaghetti sauce. As a famous designer remarked, "When you think about it, sauce is mostly sauce. It's the label that makes the difference."[9] And what, according to the designer, does the cheerful face of Paul Newman on jars of his spaghetti sauce suggest to the prospective buyer? "Paul Newman. Paul Newman. Paul Newman. Blue eyes. All the money goes to charity. It's humanitarian, funny, and sexy. Selling this is like falling off a log." Not a word about the quality of the sauce.

Even colleges, which are also selling a product, must think of appropriate images to attract their prospective customers — students. Today the fact that more women than men are enrolled in college has caused some schools to rethink their images. One college official explained:

---

[9] Tibor Kalman, "Message: Sweet-Talking Spaghetti Sauce," *New York Times Magazine*, December 13, 1998, p. 81.

A gun in the home is much more likely to
kill a family member than to kill an intruder.

CEASE ⌂ FIRE

Think about your family before you think about getting a handgun.

Cease Fire, Inc. P.O. Box 33424, Washington, D.C. 20033-0424.

We're having our recruiting literature redesigned, and we've been thinking about what's a feminine look and what's a masculine look. We have a picture of a library with a lot of stained glass, and people said that was kind of a feminine cover. Now we're using a picture of the quadrangle.[10]

In addition to the emblem itself, the designer pays careful attention to a number of other elements in the ad: colors, light and shadow, foreground and background, relative sizes of pictures and text, and placement of objects on the page or screen. Each of these contributes to the total effect, although we may be unaware of how the effect has been achieved. (In the ad that follows, you will be able to examine some of the psychological and aesthetic devices at work.)

When there is no verbal text, visual images are less subject to analysis and interpretation. For one thing, if we are familiar with the objects in the picture, we see the whole image at once, and it registers immediately. The verbal message is linear and takes far longer to be absorbed. Pictures, therefore, appear to need less translation. Advertisers and other arguers depend on this characteristic to provide quick and friendly acceptance of their claims, although the image may, in fact, be deceptive.

This expectation of easy understanding poses a danger with another visual ally of the arguer—the graph or chart. Graphics give us factual information at a glance. In addition to the relative ease with which they can be read, they are "at their best . . . instruments for reasoning about quantitative information. . . . Of all methods for analyzing and communicating statistical information, well-designed data graphics are usually the simplest and at the same time the most powerful."[11]

Nevertheless, they may mislead the quick reader. Graphics can lie. "The lies are told about the major issues of public policy—the government budget, medical care, prices, and fuel economy standards, for example. The lies are systematic and quite predictable, nearly always exaggerating the rate of recent change."[12]

Visual images, then, for all their apparent immediacy and directness, need to be read with at least the same attention we give to the verbal message if we are to understand the arguments they represent.

Consider these questions as you analyze images:

1. What does the arguer want me to do or believe? How important is the visual image in persuading me to comply?

2. Has the visual image been accompanied by sufficient text to answer questions I may have about the claim?

---

[10] *New York Times,* December 6, 1998, p. 38.

[11] Edward R. Tufte, *The Visual Display of Quantitative Information* (Cheshire, Conn.: Graphics Press, 1983), introduction.

[12] Tufte, *The Visual Display,* p. 76.

3. Are the visual elements more prominent than the text? If so, why?

4. Is the visual image representative of a large group, or is it an exception that cannot support the claim?

5. Does the arrangement of elements in the message tell me what the arguer considers most important? If so, what is the significance of this choice?

6. Can the validity of this chart or graph be verified?

7. Does the visual image lead me to entertain unrealistic expectations? (Can using this shampoo make hair look like that shining cascade on the television screen? Does the picture of the candidate for governor, shown answering questions in a classroom of eager, smiling youngsters, mean that he has a viable plan for educational reform?)

■ Sample Analysis of an Advertisement

We have pointed out that a commercial advertisement is a short argument that makes an obvious policy claim, which may or may not be explicit: *You should buy this product.* Depending on the medium—television, print, radio, or Internet—an ad may convey its message through language, picture, or sound.

Here is how one analyst of advertising sums up the goals of the advertiser: (1) attract attention, (2) arouse interest, (3) stimulate desire, (4) create conviction, and (5) get action.[13] Needless to say, not every ad successfully fulfills all these objectives. If you examine the ad reproduced on page 72, you can see how the advertiser brings language and visual image together in an attempt to support the claim.

The image in the ad appeals to our common knowledge as Americans. We have probably all heard the story of how George Washington, as a boy, chopped down a cherry tree. The clothes that the young boy in the ad is wearing—particularly the tricorner hat—along with the architecture, suggest a colonial setting. The hatchet hidden behind the boy's back combined with the exclamation "Oops!" calls to mind the specific story about Washington. Upon hearing the story, you may have envisioned a much smaller tree and less substantial damage, but it is critical to the ad's effect that in this rendering of the story of our first president's youth, the tree has fallen on someone's house, possibly the Washingtons'. The ad appears to have been reproduced on parchment, another detail that helps to place the incident historically, and each corner is subtly decorated with a cherry.

What has made the cherry tree story a classic for teaching morals is what the young Washington is said to have done after he chopped down the tree. All of us are familiar with the words "I can not tell a lie," Washington's response when questioned about what he had done. It was a fitting

---

[13] J. V. Lund, *Newspaper Advertising* (New York: Prentice-Hall, 1947), p. 83.

reply for a man who would later be chosen to lead the new nation. The largest text on the page—and the text most likely therefore to catch the attention of a reader casually flipping through *Newsweek*—is a play on this famous quote that changes *I* to *we*. The identification with Washington and his famous words is particularly critical for a company whose name may not be a household word. The designers of the ad, having captured the attention of the reader with the image and the quote, go on in the smaller text to build on the foundation they have established.

Like most ads, this one is a claim of policy asking the audience to buy a product. In this case the product is Encompass Insurance. One of the frustrations of dealing with an insurance company is that not every possible type of loss is covered by the standard policy. Unfortunately, the homeowner often does not find this out until the damage has already been done. The ad is designed to sell the company's *Elite* policy, which "covers many of life's unexpected perils," unlike most insurance companies, which "only cover things that are specifically listed in your policy." The text continues, "It covers pretty much everything that befalls your household, even if something like 'damage caused by child chopping down cherry tree' isn't specifically listed." Two examples of the sorts of damage that the company might cover are Worker's Compensation for an employee in your household and the recovery of lost computer data.

The support for the claim is not specific. The writer carefully avoided absolute statements, using instead such qualifiers as *many, pretty much,* and *most everything.* The last two are colloquial expressions that are designed to suggest that those who work for Encompass are simple folks with whom the average reader could identify. And if you want any more specifics about what the policy actually says—after all, the legal document that is an insurance policy can hardly use such qualifiers—you can call toll-free or visit the company's Web site.

The underlying warrant is that it is better to buy an insurance policy that covers you against damages that are not specifically listed on the policy than one that does not. A person in the market for insurance would certainly want to read the fine print and know the cost of the insurance compared to that offered by other companies before accepting the warrant and thus the claim.

The colloquial language and even the name of the policy—The Encompass Universal Security Policy—Elite—are designed to appeal to the reader's need to feel secure. The word choice also adds a subtle humor, from the cartoonlike "Oops!" to the final echo of the Pledge of Allegiance: "Liberty, Justice, and Really Good Insurance."

■ Sample Analysis of a Web Site

The Internet provides an important forum for individuals and organizations to make arguments. Through the Internet, anyone with access to a networked computer can potentially publish his or her ideas. While this ease of publication is exciting, it also means writers hoping to obtain reliable information from the Web need to read Web sites critically (see Prereading Strategies on page 32 for further insight into this issue).

With new genres being created daily, some researchers have noted five major types of Web pages:[14]

---

[14] See, for example, the Widener University Wolfgram Memorial Library Web site at http://www2.widener.edu/Wolfgram-Memorial-Library/webevaluation/webeval.htm.

1. *Advocacy Web Pages:* Advocacy pages are typically created by not-for-profit organizations wishing to influence public opinion, and the URL for the site is likely to contain the domain suffix *.org* (organization).

2. *Business/Marketing Web Pages:* The majority of businesses in the United States have a Web presence today, and most business pages are either advertising or provide online opportunities to purchase goods and services. The addresses for such sites typically contain the domain suffix *.com* (for commercial).

3. *News Web Pages:* News pages provide current information on local, national, and international events. The addresses for news sites also contain the abbreviation *.com,* reflecting the fact that the news industry is also a business.

4. *Informational Web Pages:* Informational pages provide data such as that found in dictionaries or atlases. The addresses for these sites sometimes include *.edu* (university), *.k12* (primary or secondary school), or *.gov* (government) because they are often sponsored by academic institutions or government agencies.

5. *Personal Web Pages:* Personal pages are created by individuals, and can be intimate, entertaining, informative, bizarre, or some combination of these things. While the addresses for personal sites can end in *.com, .edu, .k12, .org,* or *.gov,* the presence of a tilde (~) in the address suggests that the page represents an individual.

On page 75 is a copy of the home page for *The Hunger Site.* At first glance, the site appears to be a combination informational page (because it presents facts about world hunger) and business/marketing page (because it advertises a variety of products). It is in fact both of these things as well as a site for philanthropy (since advertisers' money pays for the food).

The significance of charitable giving to the site's mission is suggested by several things. Most directly, a viewer's eye is immediately drawn to the text at the top of the page that exclaims, "Click to Give FREE Food!" and to a gold icon reading "Click Here to Give—it's FREE." The icon appears in the upper right portion of the ad and draws the eye with its color and placement. It also presents an appealing prospect to readers: that they can be generous by supporting a significant cause and do so without spending money (the food is "free"). When you click on the icon, *The Hunger Site* donates 1.1 cups of food (or the financial equivalent) to the hungry. The large picture at the bottom of the opening screen of the site changes over time but through text and images emphasizes the need to fight hunger worldwide.

The emphasis on giving is furthered by the three links to the left of the gold icon: "1. You click daily. 2. Sponsors pay for cups of food. 3. Shop our store and give more." Two buttons below the icon and this list give the reader the chance to register, and in doing so to provide more food to the hungry, and to e-mail friends an electronic card with prewritten statis-

The Hunger Site Home Page

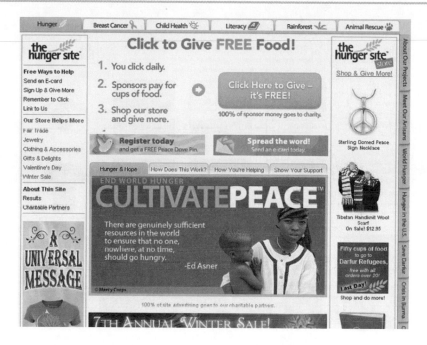

tics and other information provided by *The Hunger Site*. In this way, viewers become coauthors with the authors of the site in writing the card's text.

Down the left side of the home page are similar links: "Free Ways to Help," "Our Store Helps More," and "About This Site." Clicking on any of the list of items sold online through the site gives the reader more opportunities to provide food for others, opportunities linked to purchasing products. Buying a T-shirt, for instance, will mean an additional twenty-five cups of food provided by the merchant. Some of the less traditional "products" are items like shoes for children in another country or schooling for girls in a traditionally male-dominated region.

It is this connection that links *The Hunger Site* to business interests, interests highlighted by the *.com* in the site's URL. Though donations can be given without spending money, the site also links consumer needs and desires to philanthropy by providing visitors the opportunity to support the hungry by purchasing a wide variety of goods—from clothing to flowers to seasonal gifts and decorations. Consumer givers, then, can feel good that the money they are spending is contributing to a valuable cause. In this way, viewers feel inspired to shop more, meaning that *The Hunger Site* has the potential to bind together corporate interests, consumer interests, and international benevolence.

In many ways, then, *The Hunger Site* reads like a traditional advertisement. It appeals to customers because it represents an easy way to do something

The Hunger Site Thank You Page

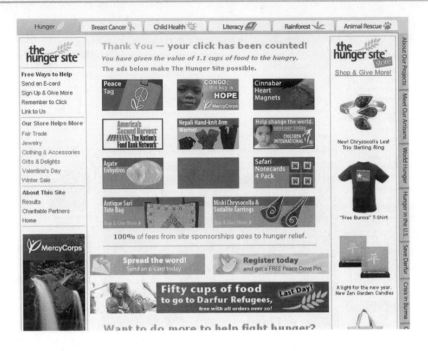

socially responsible. To develop customer loyalty, businesses and organizations strive for "brand recognition," and *The Hunger Site* is no exception. It uses a golden strand of wheat as its logo. Gold, symbolizing both wheat and true value, is the color of the icon that allows browsers to contribute food with a single click.

Distinguishing *The Hunger Site* from traditional print text is its embeddedness in a "web" of other pages. Through tabs down the right side of the page, *The Hunger Site* links directly to pages that provide additional information about the site as well as sales and charitable giving opportunities. Some pages are official parts of *The Hunger Site;* others such as *Save Darfur,* which receives donations from *The Hunger Site,* are separate sites.

One aim of a comprehensive Web site is to provide answers to questions about the site. Unlike a print advertisement, *The Hunger Site* has enough space to provide, for example, information about *The Hunger Site*'s projects and artisans. Readers interested in more information on *The Hunger Site* can do a general search of the Web to determine the legitimacy of the site.

Although it consists of multiple pages, *The Hunger Site* is also different from printed articles and books because it does not follow any traditional sense of order. Readers typically start on the site's home page, but from there they can go in multiple directions, each one equally logical. The authors of *The Hunger Site* have not determined a set path for readers to follow: Viewers can find information about world hunger, about hunger in the United States, about the amount of food given each day and each year, about ways of providing food to the hungry, and about bargains on a range of international products. The reader is in control of the direction to be taken in the text, and the possible directions are numerous and cater to multiple needs.

RESPONDING ONLINE

You have learned that writers need the responses of readers and other writers to improve their writing. Electronic networks now allow your writing to be distributed almost instantaneously to dozens or even thousands of readers with virtually no copying or mailing costs. Readers can respond to you just as quickly and cheaply. Even though there can be pitfalls and problems with communicating online, the overall ease of use encourages writers to seek, and readers to provide, editorial feedback.

■ Guidelines for Responding Online

You know that in face-to-face conversation the words themselves constitute only a part of your message. Much of what you say is communicated through your body language and tone of voice. Written words provide a much narrower channel of communication, which is why you must be more careful when you write to others than when you speak directly to them. Electronic writing, however, especially through e-mail, fosters a casualness and immediacy that often fools writers into assuming they are talking privately rather than writing publicly. Online you may find yourself writing quickly, carelessly, and intimately; without the help of your tone and body language, you may end up being seriously misunderstood. Words written hastily are often read much differently than intended; this is especially true when the writer attempts an ironic or sarcastic tone. For example, if a classmate walks up to you with a critical comment about one of your sentences and you respond by saying "I didn't realize you were so smart," the words, if unaccompanied by a placating smile and a pleasant, jocular tone, may come across as sarcastic or hostile. In e-writing, the same words appear without the mitigating body language and may be perceived as harsh, possibly insulting. You must keep this danger in mind as you respond online or risk alienating your reader.

Keep in mind, too, that e-mail may be read not only by your addressee but also by anyone with whom the addressee chooses to share your message. An intemperate or indiscreet message may be forwarded to other classmates or your instructor, or, depending on the limits of the system, to many other readers whom you do not know.

Experienced online communicators advocate a set of network etiquette guidelines. Here are some generally accepted rules:

- Keep your sentences short and uncomplicated.

- Separate blocks of text—which should be no more than four or five lines long—by blank lines. For those rare occasions when a comment requires more than ten or fifteen consecutive lines of text, use subheadings on separate lines to guide your reader.

- Refer specifically to the text to which you are responding. You may want to quote directly from it, cutting and pasting phrases or sentences from the document to help show exactly what you are responding to.

- Greet the person(s) to whom you are writing politely and by name.

- Be wary about attempting to be funny. Humor, as just explained, often requires a context, tone of voice, and body language to emphasize that it is not to be taken seriously. Writing witty comments that are sure to be taken humorously calls for skill and care, and e-mail messages usually are written too quickly for either.

- Avoid profanity or invective, and be wary of brusque or abrupt statements. Consider how you would feel if someone wrote to you that way.

- Avoid discussion of politics or religion unless that is the specific topic of your message.

- Do not ridicule public figures. Your reader may not share your opinions of, say, Senator Edward Kennedy or Stephen Colbert.

- Frame all comments in a helpful, not critical, tone. For instance, rather than beginning a critique with "I found a number of problems in your text," you may want to start out more like this: "You have some good ideas in this paper, and with a few changes I think it will do well."

ASSIGNMENTS FOR READING VISUAL TEXTS CRITICALLY

READING AND DISCUSSION QUESTIONS

1. Steven Johnson, author of *The Ghost Map*, writes, "It has become a cliché to say that we now live in a society where image is valued over substance, where our desires are continually stoked by the illusory fuel of marketing messages." Do you believe that we live in the society Johnson describes? Explain.

2. Locate an advertisement that you find interesting visually as well as verbally. Using as a model the analysis of the ad for Encompass Insurance (p. 72), what sorts of observations can you make about your ad?

3. Exchange ads with a classmate and discuss whether the two of you respond in the same way to each ad.

4. Research *The Hunger Site* and decide for yourself how effective it is in getting food to those in need.

WRITING SUGGESTIONS

5. Choose an advertisement taking into consideration both the visual and the verbal. Turn your obsevations into the thesis of an essay explaining the ad's argument.

6. Find a picture that you believe makes a political statement and write an analysis making clear what you believe that statement is.

7. Find two pictures that present either complementary or conflicting arguments. Write an essay explaining the arguments.

8. Write an essay explaining what visual images represent your school and why.

9. Virtually every charity these days has a Web site. Choose one of these sites to analyze, using as a model the analysis of *The Hunger Site*.

10. Analyze your school's Web site and explain in an essay the image or images of your school that the site presents. Do you believe that the site presents an accurate image of the school? In other words, is the argument that it makes about the school an appropriate one? Explain.

CHAPTER 4

Writing about Argument

Anytime the press cover a major speech, whether by the president, the chairman of the Federal Reserve, or the accused party in the most recent sex scandal, their next step is an analysis of every detail of the speaker's words and manner. People not only like to listen to arguments but they also like to argue about them. Political pundit Bill O'Reilly even has an analyst come in regularly to critique the body language of political and media headliners.

An understanding of the elements of argument provides you not only with the ability to write your own arguments but also with the vocabulary to write about those of others. When you write an essay about an argument that you have read, listened to, or seen, you have two major options. You may choose to make a factual, nonjudgmental statement about the argument, or you may choose to evaluate it.

WRITING THE CLAIM

If you examined the most recent McDonald's commercial and wrote an essay explaining what tactics were used to try to persuade consumers to eat at McDonalds's or to try McDonald's newest sandwich, you would be supporting a factual claim, or a claim of fact. On the other hand, if you evaluated the ad's effectiveness in attracting adult consumers, you would be supporting an evaluative claim, or a claim of value. It's the difference between *explaining* Geico's use of a talking gecko in its ads and *praising* that marketing decision. What this means, of course, is that what you write about a commercial or any other type of argument that you see or read will itself have a claim of fact or a claim of value as its thesis.

What about a claim of policy, the third type of claim introduced in Chapter 1? In writing about an argument, it would be rare to have a thesis that expressed what should or should not be done. Claims of policy are future oriented. They do not look back and express what should have been done in the past, but instead look forward to what should be done in the future. You might write an essay about what McDonald's should do in its future ads, but you would not really be writing about an existing argument, although you might use current ads as examples.

Think how claims of fact and claims of value might serve as thesis statements for essays *about* written arguments. In Chapter 2, Charles Adams's essay "Lincoln's Logic" is a criticism of Lincoln's Gettysburg Address and thus supports a claim of value:

> Lincoln's address did not fit the world of his day. It reflected his logic, which was based on a number of errors and falsehoods.

An objective analysis of the speech, based on a claim of fact, might explain the oration in the context of its time or Lincoln's use of poetic language.

In Chapter 2, you also read the Declaration of Independence. Consider how your thesis would look different if you were making a *statement* about the document than if you were making a *judgment*:

CLAIMS OF FACT: The Declaration of Independence bases its claim on two kinds of support: factual evidence and appeals to the values of its audience.

As a logical pattern of argument, the Declaration of Independence is largely deductive.

CLAIMS OF VALUE: Jefferson's clear, elegant, formal prose remains a masterpiece of English prose and persuades us that we are reading an important document.

The document's impact is lessened for modern readers because several significant terms are not defined.

In these examples based on the Gettysburg Address and the Declaration of Independence, we were looking at one document at a time and thus at a single argument. At times you will want to compare two (or more) arguments, synthesizing their ideas. Again, there are two basic types of thesis that you might choose to support, those that *objectively analyze* the points of comparison or contrast between the two and those that *evaluate* the two in relationship to each other. If you wrote claims about how the two pieces compare, they might look like these:

CLAIMS OF FACT: Where Jefferson based his argument primarily on logical appeal, Lincoln depended primarily on emotional appeal.

Because Lincoln's purpose was to dedicate a cemetery, he left implicit most of his references to the political situation that was on the minds of his listeners. Because Jefferson knew he was justifying rebellion for King George III but also for the future, he spelled out explicitly why the colonies were breaking with England.

CLAIMS OF VALUE: Lincoln's address is a period piece that recalls a dark chapter in American history, but Jefferson's Declaration has had a much greater impact as an inspiration for other reform movements worldwide.

Different as the two historical documents are, both the Gettysburg Address and the Declaration of Independence were effective in achieving their respective purposes.

PRACTICE

1. Read the following essay and then write two different thesis statements that you could support about it, one a claim of fact and the other a claim of value.

Let's Have No More Monkey Trials

CHARLES KRAUTHAMMER

The half-century campaign to eradicate any vestige of religion from public life has run its course. The backlash from a nation fed up with the A.C.L.U. kicking crèches out of municipal Christmas displays has created a new balance. State-supported universities may subsidize the activities of student religious groups. Monuments inscribed with the Ten Commandments are permitted on government grounds. The Federal Government is engaged in a major antipoverty initiative that gives money to churches. Religion is back out of the closet.

But nothing could do more to undermine this most salutary restoration than the new and gratuitous attempts to invade science, and most particularly evolution, with religion. Have we learned nothing? In Kansas, conservative school-board members are attempting to rewrite statewide standards for teaching evolution to make sure that creationism's modern stepchild, intelligent design, infiltrates the curriculum. Similar anti-Darwinian mandates are already in place in Ohio and are being fought over in 20 states. And then, as if to second the evangelical push for this tarted-up version of creationism, out of the blue appears a declaration from Christoph Cardinal

Charles Krauthammer, winner of the 1987 Pulitzer Prize for distinguished commentary, writes a nationally syndicated column for the *Washington Post* Writers Group. He also writes for *Time* magazine, the *Weekly Standard*, the *New Republic*, and the *National Interest*. This piece appeared in *Time* on August 1, 2005.

Schönborn of Vienna, a man very close to the Pope, asserting that the supposed acceptance of evolution by John Paul II is mistaken. In fact, he says, the Roman Catholic Church rejects "neo-Darwinism" with the declaration that an "unguided evolutionary process—one that falls outside the bounds of divine providence—simply cannot exist."

Cannot? On what scientific evidence? Evolution is one of the most powerful and elegant theories in all of human science and the bedrock of all modern biology. Schönborn's proclamation that it cannot exist unguided—that it is driven by an intelligent designer pushing and pulling and planning and shaping the process along the way—is a perfectly legitimate statement of faith. If he and the Evangelicals just stopped there and asked that intelligent design be included in a religion curriculum, I would support them. The scandal is to teach this as science—to pretend, as does Schönborn, that his statement of faith is a defense of science. "The Catholic Church," he says, "will again defend human reason" against "scientific theories that try to explain away the appearance of design as the result of 'chance and necessity,'" which "are not scientific at all." Well, if you believe that science is reason and that reason begins with recognizing the existence of an immanent providence, then this is science. But, of course, it is not. This is faith disguised as science. Science begins not with first principles but with observation and experimentation.

In this slippery slide from "reason" to science, Schönborn is a direct descendant of the early 17th century Dutch clergyman and astronomer David Fabricius, who could not accept Johannes Kepler's discovery of elliptical planetary orbits. Why? Because the circle is so pure and perfect that reason must reject anything less. "With your ellipse," Fabricius wrote Kepler, "you abolish the circularity and uniformity of the motions, which appears to me increasingly absurd the more profoundly I think about it." No matter that, using Tycho Brahe's most exhaustive astronomical observations in history, Kepler had empirically demonstrated that the planets orbit elliptically.

This conflict between faith and science had mercifully abated over the   5
past four centuries as each grew to permit the other its own independent sphere. What we are witnessing now is a frontier violation by the forces of religion. This new attack claims that because there are gaps in evolution, they therefore must be filled by a divine intelligent designer.

How many times do we have to rerun the Scopes "monkey trial"? There are gaps in science everywhere. Are we to fill them all with divinity? There were gaps in Newton's universe. They were ultimately filled by Einstein's revisions. There are gaps in Einstein's universe, great chasms between it and quantum theory. Perhaps they are filled by God. Perhaps not. But it is certainly not science to merely declare it so.

To teach faith as science is to undermine the very idea of science, which is the acquisition of new knowledge through hypothesis, experimentation, and evidence. To teach it as science is to encourage the supercilious caricature of America as a nation in the thrall of religious authority. To teach it as science is to discredit the welcome recent advances in permitting the public expression of religion. Faith can and should be proclaimed from every mountaintop and city square. But it has no place in science class. To impose it on the teaching of evolution is not just to invite ridicule but to earn it.

2. Share your possible thesis statements with your classmates and discuss how an essay with each might be organized.

PLANNING THE STRUCTURE

When your purpose in writing about an argument is to support a factual claim, you will most likely use a very simple and direct form of organization called defending the main idea. In all forms of organization, you need to defend your main idea, or claim, with support; in this case, the support will come from the argument or arguments you are writing about.

At times, your claim may set up the organization of your essay, as was the case with the first example about the Declaration of Independence:

> The Declaration of Independence bases its claim on two kinds of support: factual evidence and appeals to the values of its audience.

The body of an essay with this thesis would most likely have two main divisions, one about factual evidence, providing examples, and the other about appeals to values, also providing examples. The other thesis about the Declaration of Independence does not suggest such an obvious structure. An essay based on that thesis would need to explain how the Declaration is an example of deductive reasoning, most likely by first establishing what generalization the document is based on and then what specifics Jefferson uses to prove that the colonists' situation fits that generalization.

Remember that when you compare or contrast two arguments, there will be two basic patterns to choose from for structuring the essay. One, often called *point-by-point* comparison, discusses each point about Subject A and Subject B together before moving on to the second point, where again both subjects are discussed:

    I.   Introduction
    II. Context
        A. Jefferson
        B. Lincoln
    III. Implicitness/explicitness
        A. Jefferson
        B. Lincoln
    IV. Language
        A. Jefferson
        B. Lincoln
    V. Conclusion

The second, often called *parallel order* comparison, focuses in roughly half the essay on Subject A and then in the other half on Subject B. The points made in each half should be parallel and should be presented in the same order:

SAMPLE ESSAYS WITH ANALYSIS

The two essays below are an argument written by Alan Dershowitz shortly after the terrorist attacks of September 11, 2001, and an evaluation of it written by Seth Finkelstein approximately three months later. Notice what Finkelstein says about Dershowitz's article but also how each author organizes his essay.

Is There a Torturous Road to Justice?

ALAN M. DERSHOWITZ

The FBI's frustration over its inability to get material witnesses to talk has raised a disturbing question rarely debated in this country: When, if ever, is it justified to resort to unconventional techniques such as truth serum, moderate physical pressure, and outright torture?

The constitutional answer to this question may surprise people who are not familiar with the current U.S. Supreme Court interpretation of the 5th Amendment privilege against self-incrimination: Any interrogation technique, including the use of truth serum or even torture, is not prohibited. All that is prohibited is the introduction into evidence of the fruits of such techniques in a criminal trial against the person on whom the techniques were used. But the evidence could be used against that suspect

Alan M. Dershowitz is the Felix Frankfurter Professor of Law at Harvard Law School and a civil liberties attorney who defends the indigent as well as the famous. One of his many works of fiction and nonfiction is *The Case for Peace: How the Arab-Israeli Conflict Can Be Resolved* (2005). His article appeared in *Commentary* on November 8, 2001.

in a non-criminal case—such as a deportation hearing—or against some-one else.

If a suspect is given "use immunity"—a judicial decree announcing in advance that nothing the defendant says (or its fruits) can be used against him in a criminal case—he can be compelled to answer all proper questions. The issue then becomes what sorts of pressures can constitutionally be used to implement that compulsion. We know that he can be imprisoned until he talks. But what if imprisonment is insufficient to compel him to do what he has a legal obligation to do? Can other techniques of compulsion be attempted?

Let's start with truth serum. What right would be violated if an immunized suspect who refused to comply with his legal obligation to answer questions truthfully were compelled to submit to an injection that made him do so?

Not his privilege against self-incrimination, since he has no such priv- 5 ilege now that he has been given immunity.

What about his right of bodily integrity? The involuntariness of the injection itself does not pose a constitutional barrier. No less a civil libertarian than Justice William J. Brennan rendered a decision that permitted an allegedly drunken driver to be involuntarily injected to remove blood for alcohol testing. Certainly there can be no constitutional distinction between an injection that removes a liquid and one that injects a liquid.

What about the nature of the substance injected? If it is relatively benign and creates no significant health risk, the only issue would be that it compels the recipient to do something he doesn't want to do. But he has a legal obligation to do precisely what the serum compels him to do: answer all questions truthfully.

What if the truth serum doesn't work? Could the judge issue a "torture warrant," authorizing the FBI to employ specified forms of non-lethal physical pressure to compel the immunized suspect to talk?

Here we run into another provision of the Constitution—the due process clause, which may include a general "shock the conscience" test. And torture in general certainly shocks the conscience of most civilized nations.

But what if it were limited to the rare "ticking bomb" case—the situ- 10 ation in which a captured terrorist who knows of an imminent large-scale threat refuses to disclose it?

Would torturing one guilty terrorist to prevent the deaths of a thousand innocent civilians shock the conscience of all decent people?

To prove that it would not, consider a situation in which a kidnapped child had been buried in a box with two hours of oxygen. The kidnapper refuses to disclose its location. Should we not consider torture in that situation?

All of that said, the argument for allowing torture as an approved technique, even in a narrowly specified range of cases, is very troubling.

We know from experience that law enforcement personnel who are given limited authority to torture will expand its use. The cases that have generated the current debate over torture illustrate this problem. And, concerning the arrests made following the September 11 attacks, there is no reason to believe that the detainees know about specific future terrorist targets. Yet there have been calls to torture these detainees.

I have no doubt that if an actual ticking bomb situation were to arise, our law enforcement authorities would torture. The real debate is whether such torture should take place outside of our legal system or within it. The answer to this seems clear: If we are to have torture, it should be authorized by the law.

Judges should have to issue a "torture warrant" in each case. Thus we would not be winking an eye of quiet approval at torture while publicly condemning it.

Democracy requires accountability and transparency, especially when extraordinary steps are taken. Most important, it requires compliance with the rule of law. And such compliance is impossible when an extraordinary technique, such as torture, operates outside of the law.

Alan Dershowitz's Tortuous Torturous Argument

SETH FINKELSTEIN

It's torture. Literally. That is, whether or not the United States government should use torture as a method of interrogation for suspected terrorists is now a subject of debate.

Surprisingly, long-time civil-libertarian Alan Dershowitz has been writing unexpectedly in favor of the legal basis for torture. On November 8, 2001, in a commentary for *Los Angeles Times* "Is There a Tortuous Road to Justice?" he discusses a proposal for a "torture warrant."

Much of the reaction to Alan Dershowitz's advocacy has blurred over a subtle point. Given that torture is such an incendiary subject, he's been accused of advocating torture itself ("Dershowitz: Make Torture an Option" reads a headline on cbsnews.com). However, a careful reading of his commentary makes it clear that he isn't putting forth an argument in favor of torture *per se*. Rather, he postulates it will occur (*"I have no doubt that if an actual ticking bomb situation were to arise, our law enforcement authorities would torture."*). His point is then almost tangential from that perspective, a professorial concern with the due process of torture! To wit:

Seth Finkelstein is a computer programmer, system administrator, and consultant programmer who has worked extensively doing anti-censorware research. He is the winner of an EFF Pioneer Award. This article was posted to the Ethical Spectacle Web site February 2002.

The real debate is whether such torture should take place outside of our legal system or within it. The answer to this seems clear: If we are to have torture, it should be authorized by the law.

In this piece, I will not take up the arguments against torture. That's been done far better elsewhere, by other civil-libertarians such as Harvey Silverglate, or Amnesty International. Rather, I stand in awe of Dershowitz's focus on legal authorization of torture as the *"real debate."* All the moral and practical questions are swept away by his assumption of inevitability. We are left only to consider how to deal with what, if any, judicial procedures should surround torture.

He goes on to assert: 5

Democracy requires accountability and transparency, especially when extraordinary steps are taken. Most important, it requires compliance with the rule of law. And such compliance is impossible when an extraordinary technique, such as torture, operates outside of the law.

While this sounds stirring, on reflection, the meaning of the call for "accountability and transparency" is not at all clear to me. If torture is illegal, then by definition it's operating outside the law. So if a torture warrant is created, obviously torture *with warrant* would be within the law. But there seems to be a tail-wagging-the-dog situation here. Torture doesn't comply with the rule of law because it's against the law. If the law is changed so that torture is permitted (*with warrant*), then it's only become compliant with the rule of law because that rule has been changed to accept it.

What is the *purpose* of the torture warrant? Is it an anti-hypocrisy measure, to force us, as a society, to confront what we are doing? To have a public record of the event, that the defense attorney can use in a trial? To allow the torture to be supervised, with proper medical monitoring, to guard against it becoming life-threatening? To officially provide for doctors to treat the torturee during and after the ordeal?

Perhaps the idea is the simple belief that we can have legal torture, which is bad, but illegal torture would be worse. However, the obvious rebuttal is that we would end up having both legal and illegal torture, feeding off each other. Dershowitz even explicitly takes this into account (*"We know from experience that law enforcement personnel who are given limited authority to torture will expand its use."*).

So, in the face [of] this expansion of authority to torture, what is gained by making it "accountable"? The anti-hypocrisy basis seems to be Dershowitz's rationale, as he justified the above by saying:

Judges should have to issue a "torture warrant" in each case. Thus we would not be winking an eye of quiet approval at torture while publicly condemning it.

Overall, Dershowitz's reasoning seems shockingly convoluted. We end 10 up resolving the conflict between torture and the rule of law by changing the rule of law to accommodate torture. Then an admitted following expansion in torture (both from legal and illegal sources) is brushed aside with the argument that the legal torture would somehow possess accountability and transparency (accountable for what? transparent how?). Suppose Dershowitz is correct that there will be illegal torture under desperate circumstances, and without issuing a torture warrant, as a society we will be "winking an eye" to it. Is he really arguing that it's better to have more torture (due to the admitted effects of the tendency [to] "expand its use"), but at least some of the torture will then be *authorized* torture? That is, judicial process is regarded as so sacred that it's worth **torturing more people** in order to preserve it in the merest formal sense? That's both tortuous and torturous.

■ Analysis

The short article by Dershowitz has a very clear structure. In his first paragraph, he asks a question that sets up a list of three techniques that he believes could be used to get information from suspected terrorists: truth serum, moderate physical pressure, and outright torture. He leaves his mention of these techniques in the form of a question, questioning in turn each of the three techniques as he builds toward his claim, which comes at the end of the essay: "Most important, [democracy] requires compliance with the rule of law. And such compliance is impossible when an extraordinary technique, such as torture, operates outside of the law." He makes the surprising point that such forms of interrogation are not against the law, although it is against the law to use information so gained against the suspect in a criminal trial against him.

Dershowitz goes methodically through the three proposed techniques. In each case, he counters opposition based on the assumption that what he is proposing is illegal. He tries to achieve middle ground with skeptical readers when he writes, "All of that said, the argument for allowing torture as an approved technique, even in a narrowly specified range of cases, is very troubling." What troubles him more, ultimately, is that he feels sure that if law enforcement personnel were given limited authority to torture, they would not be bound by narrow guidelines, especially if faced with a "ticking bomb" situation. The only question for Dershowitz is whether the torture should take place within the law or outside of it. His specific proposal is that judges be given the right to issue "torture warrants" in specific cases.

Dershowitz's argument follows a common overall structure: He presents a problem and then possible solutions to it.

Finkelstein's piece is a response to and an evaluation of Dershowitz's article and an example of the type of writing discussed in this chapter. His is clearly a claim of value where Dershowitz's is a claim of policy. To describe Dershowitz's writing, Finkelstein uses such words as *convoluted* and, in the title, *tortuous*, which means full of twists and turns. (*Torturous* is the adjective form of *torture*.) For him, it's torture to think that "whether or not the

United States government should use torture as a method of interrogation for suspected terrorists is now a subject of debate." He mocks Dershowitz for being concerned with "the due process of torture" and for brushing aside all arguments against torture by assuming it will happen anyway, a logical fallacy called "begging the question" (see p. 343). He follows good form in quoting Dershowitz to make his points.

Much of the second half of Finkelstein's argument is devoted to questioning the purpose of making torture legal, even in a narrow range of circumstances approved by a judge. Finkelstein uses Dershowitz's own words to establish that illegal torture will go on even with the existence of legal torture and asks what the advantage is to having both illegal and legal torture.

USING SENTENCE FORMS TO CONSTRUCT AN ARGUMENT

When you present an argument, it may be important to clearly explain how a previous writer has approached a situation—and then explain how your view differs. There's no point repeating exactly what an author writes and then end by saying "and I agree with everything." Instead, academic writing means explaining current thinking on a topic and showing how it is different from what you believe. Sometimes the points of difference are large, sometimes small. But in writing for college, it is crucial that you explain your own understanding of a situation *and* express your own point of view.

It is easier to think about how you might summarize the argument of others and present your own if you have a model from which to work. This kind of model is called a sentence form, and it can help you to organize a presentation of another's views and your response to them.

Here is a basic sentence form for this kind of work.

PRESENTING ANOTHER'S VIEW AND RESPONDING TO IT

In his/her essay _____, X writes that _____.
However, I think that _____.

Writing in college means taking part in an ongoing conversation. You need to be respectful of what others say and write, and you need to account for their positions accurately. You'll want to be sure to clearly summarize the author's presentation. We have more to say about summary shortly, but, briefly put, in writing arguments, you must show the author's point before you explain how your ideas differ. You'll need to be able to sum up in a neutral, fair way what the writer says. Then, when you respond, you can agree on some points, but you'll need to focus on the points of disagreement.

Where you agree with some of what a writer says, but not all of it, you must distinguish between the parts you think are correct and those parts that are not. A sentence form for that kind of response might look like this:

AGREEING IN PART

X argues that _____. While I agree that _____ and
_____ are valid points, I do not agree that _____.
Instead, I would argue that _____.

At times you'll need to correct a distortion or misstatement of fact. Statistics, for instance, can be and often are manipulated to present the arguer's viewpoint in the best light. You may wish to propose an alternative interpretation or set the statistics in a different context, one more accurate and favorable to your own point of view. Of course, you'll want to be certain that you do not distort statistics. (For more on the importance of using statistics fairly, see the full discussion on pages 222–23.) Here's a sentence form for correcting factual information in an argument.

CORRECTING A FACTUAL MISTAKE

While X claims _____, it is actually true that _____.

More often, rather than correcting clear mistakes of fact, you'll need to refine the argument of a writer. You may find that much of the argument makes sense to you, but that the writer does not sufficiently anticipate important objections. In those cases, a sentence form such as the following can help you refine the argument to make a stronger conclusion.

REFINING ANOTHER'S ARGUMENT

While X claims _____ and _____, he/she fails to
consider the important point _____. Therefore, a more accurate
conclusion is _____.

At times you'll need to distinguish between the views of two different writers and then weigh in with your own assessment of the situation. When two authors write on the same topic, they will most likely share similar views on some of the points. They will, however, disagree on other points. Similarly, you may find that you agree with some of what each writer has to say, but disagree with some other parts. Your job is to identify the points of contrast between the two authors and then explain how your own position differs from one or both. In those cases, you may find the following sentence form helpful.

EXPLAINING CONTRASTING VIEWS AND ADDING YOUR POSITION

On the topic of _____, X claims that _____. In
contrast, Y argues that _____. However, I believe that
_____.

While these sentence forms seem rather simple—perhaps even simplistic—keep in mind that good writers use them all the time. Once you have tried them out a few times, you'll begin to use them automatically, perhaps without even realizing it. They are powerful tools for incorporating others' views into your own work and then helping you to make careful distinctions about various parts of arguments—a crucial skill in thinking and writing critically.

PROVIDING SUPPORT

In writing about any argument, you will need to understand the argument and to make it clear to your readers that you do. You cannot write a clear explanation or a fair evaluation if you do not have a clear understanding of your subject. You will need to look closely at the piece to recall what specific words or ideas led you to the thesis statement that you have chosen to support.

Your support for your thesis will come from the text or texts you are writing about in the form of summary, paraphrase, or quotations. The ability to summarize, paraphrase, and quote material from your source is necessary in writing about arguments, but it is also essential in writing your own arguments, especially those that require research.

■ Summarizing

A summary involves shortening the original passage as well as putting it into your own words. It gives the gist of the passage, including the important points, while leaving out details. What makes summarizing difficult is that it requires you to capture often long and complex texts in just a few lines or a short paragraph. To summarize well, you need to imagine yourself as the author of the piece you are summarizing and be true to the ideas the author is expressing, even when those ideas conflict with your point of view. You must then move smoothly from being a careful reader to being a writer who, in your own words, recreates another's thoughts.

We summarize for many reasons: to let our boss know the basics of what we have been doing or to tell a friend why she should or should not see a movie. In your classes you are often asked to summarize articles or books, and even when this is not an explicit part of an assignment, the ability to summarize is usually expected. That is, when you are instructed to analyze an essay or to compare and contrast two novels, central to this work is the ability to carefully comprehend and recreate authors' ideas. Summarizing is the cornerstone on which all other critical reading and writing tasks are built.

When you are asked to write a research paper, the ability to summarize effectively is especially critical, because some sources, though useful for your argument, will simply be too long to include in your text. It is up to you, then, to summarize those points and ideas that are most critical for your argument either because they support that argument or because they represent a counter point of view.

For instance, Charles Krauthammer's main idea in the first paragraph of his "Let's Have No More Monkey Trials" might be summarized in this way:

> According to Krauthammer (2005), after fifty years of attempts to separate religion from public life on the local, state, and federal levels, religion is making a comeback (p. 46).

The statement is not a direct quotation, so it would not be in quotation marks in an essay about the article. The example shows the American Psychological Association (APA) style of documentation used to acknowledge that the idea comes from an article by Krauthammer published in 2005. Returning to the original source makes it clear that the passage is far too long to quote in full in a short essay, but it is easily summarized without losing Krauthammer's idea. The summary illustrates APA style for documenting the use of a source that is named in the writer's sentence. In other examples in this chapter, you will see more illustrations of the use of both APA and Modern Language Association (MLA) styles of documentation, which are explained in more detail in the Writer's Guides in this chapter and in Chapter 11.

When summarizing long or difficult texts, try some of the following strategies to help you comprehend the essential points of the text.

1. Before you summarize, analyze the text using the strategies given in the section on "Responding as a Critical Reader" in Chapter 2 (p. 31). For example, you should always utilize prereading strategies by looking over the text as a whole before you read it carefully. Such work will often yield clues about the central idea of the text from the title, the subheadings, and the introduction. Also, use your pen once you begin to read the text so that you link the acts of reading and writing. Underline important ideas, ask questions in the margins about difficult or significant ideas, and highlight topic sentences. Take a few minutes after reading the text to jot down the essential ideas and any questions you have about the reading.

2. Reread the introduction and conclusion after you have read the essay once or twice. These two sections should complement each other and offer clues to the most significant issues of the text. An introduction or conclusion is often more than one paragraph; therefore, it is important that you read the first and last few paragraphs of an essay to understand what the author is trying to impress upon the reader. If you are summarizing a book, look especially at the preface, the first and last chapters, and any reviewers' comments. These sections will not tell you everything you need to know to summarize an entire book, but they will help you decide which points matter.

3. For a difficult essay, you may want to list all the subheadings (if they are used) or the topic sentence of each paragraph. These significant guideposts will map the piece as a whole: What do they tell

you about the central ideas and the main argument the author is making? After reviewing the subheads or topic sentences, can you reread the essay and engage more easily with its finer points? For a book, you can do the same thing with chapter headings to break down the essential ideas. Remember that when you summarize, you must put another's words into your own (and cite the original text as well), so do not simply let a list of the subheadings or chapter titles stand as your summary. They likely won't make sense when put together in paragraph form, but they will provide you with valuable ideas regarding the central points of the text.

4. Remember that summarizing requires attention to overall meanings and not to specific details. Therefore, avoid including many specific examples or concrete details from the text you are summarizing and try to let your reader know what these examples and details add up to. Some of the specificity and excitement of the original text will be lost, but when summarizing, the goal is to let the reader know the essential meaning of the original text in a clear, straightforward way. Of course, if you need to respond, as part of your argument, to specifics in the essay, you should do so, but you will most likely do so in the form of a paraphrase or a direct quotation.

There are two types of summaries, rhetorical and referential. The two share some characteristics. Both types should

- Be objective instead of expressing opinions.
- Identify the author and the work.
- Use present tense.
- Summarize the main points of the whole work or passage, not just part of it.

A *rhetorical* summary summarizes the text in terms of rhetorical choices the author made. An example:

> In "Let's Have No More Monkey Trials," Charles Krauthammer celebrates the end of the separation of religion from public life at the local, state, and federal levels but argues that the progress made will be undermined by those trying to replace the teaching of evolution with the teaching of intelligent design, a new form of creationism. He notes that Christoph Cardinal Schönborn of Vienna . . .

The other type of summary, a *referential* summary, focuses on ideas rather than on the author's actions and decisions.

> According to Charles Krauthammer in his article "Let's Have No More Monkey Trials," a fifty-year trend toward removing religion from public life is now being reversed. This positive movement, however, is threatened by those who are trying to replace the teaching of evolution with the teaching of intelligent design, a new form of creationism. Christoph Cardinal Schönborn of Vienna has asserted that . . .

■ Paraphrasing

Paraphrasing involves restating the content of an original source in your own words. It differs from summarizing in that a paraphrase is roughly the same length as the passage it paraphrases instead of a condensation of a longer passage. You will use paraphrasing when you want to capture the idea but there is nothing about the wording that makes repeating it necessary. You may also use it when the idea can be made clearer by rephrasing it or when the style is markedly different from your own. Here is an example drawn from a student paper presented in its entirely in Chapter 12:

> Randolph Warren, a victim of the thalidomide disaster himself and founder and executive director of the Thalidomide Victims Association of Canada, reports that it is estimated 10,000 to 12,000 deformed babies were born to mothers who took thalidomide. (40)

There is no single sentence on page 40 of the Warren article that both provides the estimate of number of affected babies and identifies Warren as one of them. Both the ideas were important, but neither of them was worded in such a unique way that a direct quote was needed. Therefore, a paraphrase was the logical choice. In this case, the writer correctly documents the paraphrase using Modern Language Association (MLA) style.

■ Quoting

You may want to quote passages or phrases from your sources if they express an idea in words more effective than your own. In reading a source, you may come across a statement that provides succinct, irrefutable evidence for an issue you wish to support. If the author of this statement is a professional in his or her field, someone with a great deal of authority on the subject, it would be appropriate to quote that author. A student research paper in Chapter 12 is Jessica Smith-Garcia's about women in combat. Suppose, during the course of Jessica's research for her paper, she found several sources that agree that women in the military who are denied combat experience are, as a result, essentially being denied a chance at promotion to the highest ranks. Others argue that such considerations should not be a deciding factor in assigning women to combat. To represent the latter of these two positions, Jessica chose to use a quotation from an authority in the field, using APA style:

> Elaine Donnelly, president of the Center for Military Readiness, says, "Equal opportunity is important, but the armed forces exist to defend the country. If there is a conflict between career opportunities and military necessity, the needs of the military must come first" (as qtd. in "Women in the Military," 2000).

It is especially important in argumentative writing to establish a source's authority on the subject under discussion. The most common way of doing this is to use that person's name and position of authority to introduce the quotation, as in the previous example. It is correct in both MLA and APA styles to provide the author's name in parentheses at the end of the quoted material, but that type of documentation precludes lending to the quote the weight of its having come from an authority. It is likely that those readers not in the military—and even some who are—will not know who Donnelly is just by seeing her name in parentheses. Your writing will always have more power if you establish the authority of each author from whose work you quote, paraphrase, or summarize. To establish authority, you may refer to the person's position, institutional affiliation, publications, or some other similar "claim to fame."

Another example, also using APA style:

> According to the late Ulysses S. Seal III (1982), founder of the Conservation Breeding Specialist Group and of a "computer dating service" for mateless animals, "None of these [zoo] budgets is allocated specifically for species preservation. Zoos have been established primarily as recreational institutions and are only secondarily programs in conservation, education, and research." (p. 74)

Notice that once the name of the author being cited has been mentioned in the writer's own text, it does not have to be repeated in the parentheses.

Writer's Guide: Incorporating Quotations into Your Text

1. The most effective way to lead into the first quotation from a source is to use the author's full name and his or her claim to authority — a few words identifying the person by title, institutional affiliation, or publications. Remember that for readers who are not specialists, the name of an author you are quoting may have little meaning, and relegating the last name to a parenthesis at the end of the quotation does not use that author's authority to strengthen your argument. Once you have used the full name, any future references may use only the last name of the author. If the author's name, full or last only, is used in your lead-in to the quote, you do not have to repeat it in the parentheses that complete the documentation. One additional advantage of mentioning the author or authors is that a reader can tell where your ideas leave off and those from your source begin.

2. There are three primary means of linking a supporting quotation to your own text. Remember that in each case, the full citation for the source will be listed alphabetically by the author's name in the list of works cited at the end of the paper, or by title if no author is given. The number in parentheses is the page of that source on which the quotation appears. The details of what appears in parentheses will be covered later in the discussion of APA (American Psychological Association) and MLA (Modern Language Association) documentation styles.

- You may choose to make a brief quotation a grammatical part of your own sentence. In that case, you do not separate the quotation from your sentence with a comma, unless there is another reason for the comma, and you do not capitalize the first word of the quotation, unless there is another reason for doing so. In this sort of situation, there may be times when you have to change the tense of a verb, in brackets, to make the quotation fit smoothly into your text or when you need to make other small changes, always in brackets.

  ### Examples:
  ### APA style

  James Rachels (1976), University Professor of Philosophy at the University of Alabama at Birmingham and author of several books on moral philosophy, explains that animals' right to liberty derives from "a more basic right not to have one's interests needlessly harmed" (p. 210).

  ### MLA style

  James Rachels, University Professor of Philosophy at the University of Alabama at Birmingham and author of several books on moral philosophy, explains that animals' right to liberty derives from "a more basic right not to have one's interests needlessly harmed" (210).

- You may use a traditional speech tag such as "he says" or "she writes." This is the most common way of introducing a quotation. Be sure to put a comma after the tag and to begin the quotation with a capital letter. At the end of the quotation, close the quotation, add the page number and any other necessary information in parentheses, and then add the period.

  ### Examples:
  ### APA style

  James Rachels (1976), University Professor of Philosophy at the University of Alabama at Birmingham and author of several books on moral philosophy, writes, "The right to liberty — the right to be free of external constraints on one's actions — may then be seen as derived from a more basic right not to have one's interests needlessly harmed" (p. 210).

  ### MLA style

  James Rachels, University Professor of Philosophy at the University of Alabama at Birmingham and author of several books on moral philosophy, writes, "The right to liberty — the right to be free of external constraints on one's actions — may then be seen as derived from a more basic right not to have one's interests needlessly harmed" (210).

Students are sometimes at a loss as to what sorts of verbs to use in these tag statements. Try using different terms from this list or others like them. Remember that in writing about a printed or electronic text, it is customary to write in present tense unless there is a compelling reason to use past tense.

argues	concludes
asks	continues
asserts	counters

declares	questions
explains	replies
implores	responds
insists	states
proclaims	suggests

- You may vary the way you introduce quotations by at times using a colon to separate the quotation from a *complete sentence* that introduces it.

  ### Examples:

  ### APA style

  For example, the Zurich Zoo's Dr. Heini Hediger (1985) protests that it is absurd to attribute human qualities to animals at all, but he nevertheless resorts to a human analogy: "Wild animals in the zoo rather resemble estate owners. Far from desiring to escape and regain their freedom, they are only bent on defending the space they inhabit and keeping it safe from invasion" (p. 9).

  ### MLA style

  The late Ulysses S. Seal III, founder of the Conservation Breeding Specialist Group and of a "computer dating service" for mateless animals, acknowledges the subordinate position species preservation plays in budgeting decisions: "Zoos have been established primarily as recreational institutions and are only secondarily developing programs in conservation, education, and research" (74).

3. Long quotations are handled differently from shorter ones. In APA style, a quotation of more than forty words, and in MLA style, a quotation of more than four lines, is set off as a block quotation. That means that the writer must doublespace before and after the quotation — as well as doublespacing the quotation itself — and indent the whole quotation ten spaces from the left margin. The passage is not placed in quotation marks because the placement on the page indicates that it is a quotation. With block quotations, the parentheses used to provide documentation at the end of the passage are placed after, rather than before, the period. Block quotations should be used sparingly.

4. Avoid "floating" quotations. That is, do not jump from a sentence of your own text into a quotation with no connection between the two. Introduce every direct quotation.

5. Avoid back-to-back quotations. There should always be some of your own ideas to justify including a quotation, so some of your own text should always intervene between quoted passages.

PRACTICE

Write a summary of Alan Dershowitz's "Is There a Torturous Road to Justice?" using either the rhetorical method, which explains what the author is doing in the piece, or using the referential method, which focuses instead on the ideas.

Be sure to remain objective. Include at least one direct quotation in your summary. Identify the author and the title in your first sentence and provide in parentheses the page number for the quotation(s).

DOCUMENTING YOUR SOURCES

Chapter 12 will provide additional information about documenting sources, but you should start now documenting your use of others' work, even when the only sources you use are essays from this textbook. The single most important thing to remember is why you need to inform your reader about your use of sources. Once it is clear from your writing that an idea or some language came from a source and thus is not your own original thought or language, full documentation provides the reader with a means of identifying and, if necessary, locating your source. If you do not indicate your source, your reader will naturally assume that the ideas and the language are yours. It is careless to forget to give credit to your sources. It is dishonest to intentionally take credit for what is not your own intellectual property.

The following Writer's Guide provides the general guidelines for documenting your use of sources.

Writer's Guide: Documenting Use of Summary, Paraphrase, and Quotation

1. One of the most common mistakes that student writers make is to think that material needs to be documented only if they use another author's words. In fact, you must give credit for any *ideas* you get from others, not only for wording you get from them.

2. You must identify the author and the location of ideas that you summarize. A *summary* is the condensing of a longer passage into a shorter one, using your own words. You will use summary often in your academic writing when you want to report briefly on an idea covered at greater length in your source.

3. You must identify the author and the location of ideas that you paraphrase. A *paraphrase* is a rewording of another author's idea into your own words. A paraphrased passage is roughly the same length as the original.

4. You must identify the author and the location of language that you quote. A *quotation* is the copying of the exact wording of your source and is placed in quotation marks. Remember that *exact* means just that. You cannot change anything inside quotation marks, with these exceptions: (a) If there is a portion of the quotation that is not relevant to the point that you are making and *that can be omitted without distorting the author's meaning,*

you may indicate an omission of a portion of the quotation with an ellipsis (. . .). If there is a sentence break within the portion you are omitting, add a fourth period to the ellipsis to so indicate. (b) If you need to make a very slight change in the quote to make the quote fit grammatically into your own text or to avoid confusion and if the change does not distort the author's meaning, you may make that slight change and place the changed portion in square brackets ([ ]). This method is used primarily to change the tense of a quoted passage to match that of your text or to identify a person identified in the quotation only by a pronoun.

5. Both the MLA and the APA systems make use of in-text or parenthetical documentation. That means that while a complete bibliographical listing for each work summarized, paraphrased, or quoted in your text is included in a Works Cited or References list at the end of your paper, each is also identified exactly at the point in the text where you use the source. If you are using the MLA system of documentation, the system most commonly used in the humanities, immediately following the sentence in which you use material from a source, you need to add in parentheses the author's name and the page number on which the material you are using appeared in the original source. However, since the credibility of your sources is critical in argumentative writing, it is even better to name the source in your own sentence and to identify the position or experience that makes that person a reliable source for the subject being discussed. In that case, you do not need to repeat the author's name in the parentheses. In fact, any time the author's name is clear from the context, you do not need to repeat it in the parentheses.

Acceptable: The mall has been called "a common experience for the majority of American youth" (Kowinski 3).

Better: According to William Severini Kowinski, author of *The Malling of America*, "The mall is a common experience for the majority of American youth" (3).

In the APA system, the system most commonly use in the social sciences, in-text or parenthetical documentation is handled a bit differently because the citation includes the year of publication. The most basic forms are these:

The mall has been called "a common experience for the majority of American youth" (Kowinski, 1985, p. 3).

Kowinski (1985) writes, "The mall is a common experience for the majority of American youth (p. 3).

6. Remember that these examples show only the most basic forms for documenting your sources. Some works will have more than one author. Sometimes you will be using more than one work by the same author. Usually Web sites do not have page numbers. Long quotations need to be handled differently from short ones. For all questions about documenting your use of sources not covered here, see Chapter 12.

Note: If you are writing about an essay in this book, you have a slightly more complicated situation than if you were looking at the essay in its original place of publication. Unless your instructor indicates otherwise, use the page numbers on which the essay appears in this textbook when summarizing, paraphrasing, or quoting from it instead of going back to the page numbers of the original. Also, unless your instructor indicates otherwise, use this model for listing in your Works Cited page an essay reprinted here:

Kowinski, William Severini. "Kids in the Mall: Growing Up Controlled." New York: Morrow, 1985. Rpt. in *Elements of Argument: A Text and Reader.* Annette T. Rottenberg and Donna Haisty Winchell. 9th ed. Boston: Bedford/St. Martin's, 2009. 171–176.

AVOIDING PLAGIARISM

Plagiarism is the use of someone else's words or ideas without adequate acknowledgment—that is, presenting such words or ideas as your own. Putting something into your own words is not in itself a defense against plagiarism; the source of the ideas must be identified as well. Giving credit to the sources you use serves three important purposes: (1) it reflects your own honesty and seriousness as a researcher; (2) it enables the reader to find the source of the reference and read further, sometimes to verify that the source has been correctly used; and (3) it adds the authority of experts to your argument. Plagiarism is nothing less than cheating, and it is an offense that deserves serious punishment. You can avoid accidentally slipping into plagiarism if you are careful in researching and writing your papers.

Taking care to document sources is an obvious way to avoid plagiarism. You should also be careful in taking notes and, when writing your paper, indicating where your ideas end and someone else's begin. When taking notes, make sure either to quote word for word or to paraphrase—one or the other, not both. If you quote, enclose any language that you borrow from other sources in quotation marks. That way, when you look back at your notes days or weeks later, you won't mistakenly assume that the language is your own. If you know that you aren't going to use a particular writer's exact words, then take the time to summarize that person's ideas right away. That will save you time and trouble later.

When using someone else's ideas in your paper, always let the reader know where that person's ideas begin and end. Here is an example from a student paper that uses APA style:

When zoo animals do mate successfully, the offspring is often weakened by inbreeding. According to geneticists, this is because a population of 150 breeder animals is necessary in order to "assure the more or less permanent survival of a species in captivity." (Ehrlich & Ehrlich, 1981, p. 211).

The phrase "according to geneticists" indicates that the material to follow comes from another source, cited parenthetically at the end of the borrowed material. If the student had not included the phrase "according to geneticists," it might look as if she only borrowed the passage in quotation marks, and not the information that precedes that passage.

READINGS FOR ANALYSIS

Should We Fight Terror with Torture?

ALAN M. DERSHOWITZ

The great American justice Oliver Wendell Holmes Jr. once remarked that "it is revolting to have no better reason for a rule of law than that it was laid down in the time of Henry IV. It is still more revolting if the grounds upon which it was laid down have vanished long since, and the rule simply persists from blind imitation of the past." The rules of law regulating how civilized societies protect their citizens from aggression were not laid down as far back as the time of Henry IV. They were enacted, in significant part, following the two awful wars of the 20th century in which massive numbers of civilians were targeted for death and murdered in cold blood. The human-rights revolution of the mid-20th century was largely a reaction to the human wrongs of the Holocaust.

The period between the end of the Second World War and now has seen more profound changes in the nature of warfare than occurred from the time of Henry IV to the beginning of the First World War. Weapons of mass destruction in the hands of suicide terrorists with no fear of death and no home address have rendered useless the deterrent threat of massive retaliation. This threat has been the staple of military policy since the days of the Bible. Because suicide terrorists cannot be deterred, they must be pre-empted and prevented from carrying out their threats against civilians before they occur. This change in tactics requires significant changes in the laws of war—laws that have long been premised on the deterrent model.

Consider, for example, the United Nations Charter, drafted in the aftermath of Germany's aggressive war between 1939 and 1945. Article 51 confirms "the inherent right of individual or collective [to] self-defense if an armed attack occurs against a member." The use of the word "occurs" would seem to require a nation, seeking to act in compliance with the charter, to wait until it is actually attacked before it responds in self-defense. But what

For information on Alan M. Dershowitz, see the footnote on p. 85.

should a democratic nation do if it becomes aware of an imminent threat of attack by a group of suicide terrorists in a distant part of the world? Surely it should not simply wait until an "armed attack occurs" and then engage in retaliatory self-defense. First, there is often no known entity to attack, since the suicide terrorists have died and the leaders who sent them have gone into hiding among civilians and may well be preparing renewed terrorist attacks. Second, there is no good reason for a democracy to have to absorb a first blow against its civilian population, especially if that blow can be catastrophic. Third, there is little possibility that potentially catastrophic first blows can be deterred by the threat of retaliation against a phantom enemy who welcomes martyrdom.

Despite these new realities, the old UN charter has not been changed, though it is currently in the process of being "redefined." A "High Level Panel on Threats, Challenge, and Change" has recommended that despite the "restrictive" language of Article 51, a nation should be free to take proportional military action against an "imminent" attack if no other means are available. But it also proposed that if a threat, though catastrophic and highly likely, is not imminent, a nation may not resort to preventive self-help. Instead it must seek the approval of the Security Council. In other words, pre-emptive self-defense against imminent threat is consistent with Article 51, but preventive self-defense against more distant, though equally certain, threats requires approval by the Security Council. While this distinction makes sense in theory, it fails to recognize that the Security Council is a highly politicized body, with veto-power in the hands of nations that have long supported terrorism, at least on a selective basis. No nation, facing a highly likely catastrophic threat—even if it is not imminent—will rely on the whim of other nations with agendas different from its own. As the former U.S. Secretary of State Dean Acheson once, aptly, put it, "The survival of states is not a matter of law." States will do what they deem necessary, not only to ensure their own survival, but also to protect the lives of their citizens from catastrophic threats.

Consider, for example, the developing Iranian nuclear threat. The Iran- 5 ian leadership has threatened to attack Israel and American targets. If Iran gets close to having a deliverable nuclear weapon, and if one of its target nations has the capacity to destroy its nuclear program the way Israel destroyed the Iraqi reactor back in 1981—with one air-strike and a single casualty— it should have the legal right to do so. This would be especially so if the Security Council refused to do anything to stop Iran because of self-serving Russian or Chinese vetoes. We are not yet at that decision point, and it is unlikely that the Iranian nuclear threat can be ended by surgical air strikes, but international law should authorize preventive self-defense if the threat is cataclysmic and relatively certain, even if not imminent, and if it can be abated with few civilian casualties.

In any event, the UN report "sees no need to amend Article 51" since it can be reinterpreted to permit states to take pre-emptive action against imminent threat, but not to take preventive action against longer-term threats. Even the recommended reinterpretation does not have the force of law. It is merely the opinion of a high-level panel which has received no formal approval by the United Nations. It would be far better to change Article 51 [yet] there is an apparent allergy to changing old laws, whether they go back to Henry IV or to the post–World War II period, [to] reflect the new realities.

The laws of pre-emptive and preventive self-defense are but one example of the legal sclerosis from which we are suffering in the war against terrorism. The human-rights rules that were enacted to protect civilians are now being turned on their heads by self-proclaimed human-rights groups. Instead of being a shield for innocent civilians, they are being used as a sword by terrorists against civilians. Terrorists deliberately hide among civilians, most often civilians who support them. In order to prevent the terrorists from carrying out their threats, democratic nations must often take actions that endanger some civilians. For example, when coalition forces targeted Abu Musab al-Zarqawi and his "spiritual adviser," Abu Abdul-Rahman, they inadvertently killed several civilians, including a child. This was not the first time that targeting terrorists has resulted in collateral casualities. When the U.S. targeted Abu Ali, known as Qaed Salim Sinan al-Harethi, in Yemen in 2002, they also killed five other people, at least some of whom were probably al-Qa'ida members or supporters. Israel, as well, has caused the deaths of civilians in its efforts to pre-empt terrorist attacks by targeting "ticking bomb" terrorists as well as terrorist commanders who were the equivalents of Zarqawi and Rahman.

Human-rights organizations often fail to distinguish between civilian deaths accidentally caused by democracies despite their best efforts to avoid them, and civilian deaths deliberately caused by terrorists who seek to maximize civilian casualties by constructing anti-personnel bombs, designed to kill as many innocent people as possible, and by specifically targeting crowded buses and other soft targets. These human-rights organizations blink at the reality that terrorists seek not only to maximize civilian deaths among their enemies, but also seek to maximize civilian deaths caused by their enemies, even if the victims are their own supporters. As one European diplomat told the *New York Times*, the terrorists understand the "harsh arithmetic of pain." Enemy "casualties play in their favor" and casualties inflicted on their own people by the enemy "play in their favor."

By condemning all targeted killing of terrorists, human-rights groups actually increase the risks to civilians. The law should permit the targeting of individuals who are actively engaged in terrorist planning and actions, so long as it is highly likely that the target is an actual terrorist, that the number of likely civilian deaths is proportional to the likely civilian deaths that would have been caused by the targeted terrorists, and that there is no other alternative—such as arrest—that is feasible under the circumstances. The law should also cast the blame for unintended civilian deaths caused by democracies on the terrorists who deliberately hide among civilians using them as "shields." The domestic law of most democratic nations does precisely that. If a bank robber takes a teller hostage and uses him as a shield against the police, and if the police, in an effort to shoot the robber who is firing from behind his shield, kills the shield, it is the robber who is guilty of murder, even though it was the policeman who fired the fatal shot. The same should be the case in international law.

Next, consider the problem of what to do with captured "prisoners" who are believed to be terrorists. This vague category of detainees is comprised of several different sub-groups. There are those who were captured in the course of military action in a foreign country. The United States and its allies captured Taliban "soldiers" and those fighting alongside them in Afghanistan. A few wore ersatz uniforms; most did not. Some were just in the wrong place at the wrong time. Then there were admitted members of al-Qa'ida, ranging from Khalid Sheikh Mohammed, the alleged number two or three man in the organization, to Zacarias Moussaoui, a terrorist wannabe who may or may not have been the "20th" September 11 hijacker. Some of the detainees are believed to have valuable real-time information that could save lives. Others are simply terrorist pawns willing to do whatever they are told, even if it entails suicide. Inevitably, some, probably, are completely innocent and not dangerous.

The problem is that the current laws regulating the detention of combatants are near useless when it comes to this motley array of detainees. These detainees simply do not fit into the old, anachronistic categories. Most are not classic prisoners of war. They were not part of a uniformed army under the command of a nation. But neither do they fit into the classic definition of "unlawful combatants." They are not spies or saboteurs, as those terms have been understood in the context of conventional warfare. Nor are many of them simple "criminals," subject to ordinary trials under the domestic law of crimes. They comprise a new category—or set of categories—unto themselves. They cannot be held as POWs until the end of the war, because this is a war that will never end. They cannot simply be released, because many of them would quickly volunteer to engage in suicide terrorist missions against their former captors, as some already have done. Most cannot be tried as criminals, because their actions took place outside the jurisdiction of the detaining nation. Those who have valuable, real-time information will be interrogated, and—short of the absolute law against "torture"—there are few, if any, rules governing the nature of permissible interrogation when the object is not to elicit "incrimination confessions" for purposes of criminal prosecution, but rather to obtain "preventive intelligence" for the purpose of pre-empting future terrorist attacks.

Should the same rules that govern the interrogation of ordinary criminal suspects be applicable? Or should more latitude be afforded to interrogators in the preventive context? Should sleep deprivation be authorized? Loud music? Alternating heat and cold? Uncomfortable and/or painful seating? What about truth serum? False threats? We know that the United States has used "water boarding"—a technique that produces a near-drowning experience but no physical after-effects—on Khalid Sheikh Mohammed, a high-ranking al-Qa'ida detainee. Is that categorized as torture? I certainly think so, but the United States government apparently does not. We need rules even for such unpleasant practices.

There is today a vast "black hole" in the law. It is this hole that accounts for Guantanamo, extraordinary renditions and other phantom places and actions about which we know nothing. As a lifelong civil libertarian, I strongly oppose such gaps in the law. The rule of law requires that all governmental action be subject to legal constraints. The refusal to change old laws that do not fit new situations is bad for human rights and dangerous to democratic accountability.

Nor does it help the situation when Amnesty International and other human-rights groups exaggerate the problems and cast all the blame on democracies that are seeking—sometimes by questionable means—to keep their citizens safe from terrorists. Anne Fitzgerald of Amnesty recently compared the alleged terrorists being detained by the U.S. and its allies to the "disappeared" in Argentina during the Junta. The comparison is obscene. The disappeared in Argentina were mostly political opponents of the Junta, many of whom were tortured to death and dropped into the ocean from aircraft. Credible sources estimate that as many as 30,000 people may have been killed. Pregnant women had their babies ripped from their wombs so they could be adopted by childless friends of the Junta. There is no evidence of anything even close to this being done by the United States today in its sometimes excessive efforts to prevent terrorism. The problems are bad enough without the need to exaggerate them for political and ideological purposes.

Human-rights groups undercut the real interests of human rights when 15 they exaggerate the faults of democracies and minimize the faults of terrorists. Most democracies seek to operate within the rule of laws, and laws must realistically reflect the desirable balance between the legitimate needs of security and the equally legitimate claims of human rights. Striking this balance is a daunting task, and it is in the nature of such balances that few are ever satisfied that it has been properly struck. It is far easier to stick with the comfortable old ways, even if it produces hypocrisy and gaping holes in the law.

Laws must change with the times. They must adapt to new challenges. That has been the genius of the common law. Ironically, it is generally the left that seeks change in the laws, while the right is satisfied with Henry IV. Today it is many on the left who resist any changes in the law of war or human rights. They deny the reality that the war against terrorism is any way different from conventional wars of the past, or that the old laws must be adapted to the new threats. The result is often an unreasonable debate of extremes: the hard left insists that the old laws should not be tampered with in the least; the hard right insists that the old laws are entirely inapplicable to the new threats, and that democratic governments should be entirely free to do whatever it takes to combat terrorism, without regard to anachronistic laws. Both extremes are dangerous. What is needed is a new set of laws, based on the principles of the old laws of war and human rights—the protection of civilians—but adapted to the new threats against civilian victims of terrorism.

The President of the supreme court of Israel, Aharon Barak, in deciding that torture could not be justified even for purposes of securing information that might prevent terrorism, wrote the following lines: "[It] is the destiny of democracy that not all means are acceptable to it, and not all practices employed by its enemies are open before it. Although a democracy must often fight with one hand tied behind its back, it nonetheless has the upper hand. Preserving the Rule of Law and recognition of an individual's liberty constitutes an important component in its understanding of security. At the end of the day, they [add to] its strength. . . ."

But, while it may well be necessary for democracies to fight terrorists with one hand tied behind their backs, it is neither necessary nor desirable for a democracy to fight with two hands tied behind its back, especially when the ropes that bind the second hand are anachronistic laws that can be changed without compromising legitimate human rights. The laws must be changed to permit democracies to fight fairly and effectively against those who threaten its citizens. To paraphrase Robert Jackson, who served as the United States chief prosecutor at Nuremberg—the law must not be "a suicide pact."

READING AND DISCUSSION QUESTIONS

1. Why does Dershowitz believe that the deterrent model of war is no longer a realistic model to use? What, specifically, in Article 51 of the United Nations Charter is it that he sees as no longer realistic?

2. Why does he believe even the "redefinition" of Article 51 is not enough?

3. Dershowitz quotes a European diplomat who uses the term "harsh arithmetic of pain." What does that term mean, applied to terrorism?

4. What is Dershowitz's view of civilian casualties?

5. Why are prisoners of war in the war on terrorism different from other prisoners before them?

6. What is Dershowitz's claim in the essay? Where is it most clearly stated?

7. What title could the essay be given that is more relevant to what the essay actually says?

WRITING SUGGESTIONS

8. In his much briefer article earlier in the chapter, Dershowitz argues in favor of very special techniques for eliciting information from suspected terrorists. Write an argument supporting whether or not that claim is more convincing once it is placed in the context of this more fully developed piece.

9. Write an essay explaining two or more of the techniques that Dershowitz uses in supporting his argument.

10. Write an essay evaluating how successful Dershowitz is in defending his claim.

Parents Need Help: Restricting Access to Video Games

BARBARA DAFOE WHITEHEAD

A century ago, Jane Addams and other progressive reformers in Chicago responded to the dangers of the industrial age by creating laws and institutions that would protect children from the unwholesome lures of the city streets. Her work is rightly honored. A similar, and equally important, struggle is being waged in Illinois today. On the surface, it's about the sale of video games to kids. It's also a debate about a deeper question: To what degree does the responsibility for teaching good values to children fall solely on parents? Should some of that responsibility be shared by the state?

Those who make and sell video games say parents alone should bear the responsibility. On the other side is Illinois Governor Rod Blagojevich. He's trying to outlaw the sale of excessively violent or sexually explicit video games to children under eighteen. In his effort to restrict such sales he's making the argument that raising children is a shared responsibility: "Parenting is hard work and the state has a compelling interest in helping parents raise their children to be upstanding men and women."

The governor firmly believes that parents have the primary responsibility for teaching their children right from wrong. He believes just as firmly that parents should not have their efforts subverted by the avalanche of "amusements" that tell kids it is fun to blow people up. "Too many of the video games marketed to our children teach them all of the wrong lessons and all of the wrong values," Blagojevich writes in a "letter to Illinois parents" posted on the state's informational Web site (www.safegamesIllinois .com). "These games use violence, rage, and sexual aggression as play. That is not acceptable. When kids play, they should play like children, not like gangland assassins."

The governor's reference to gangland assassins is not an overstatement. One video game, the top-selling, industry-award-winning Grand Theft Auto: San Andreas, features gang warfare and the killing of prostitutes. Another, released on the forty-first anniversary of the Kennedy assassination, gets players to step into the shoes of Lee Harvey Oswald and to aim at the president's head as his motorcade rolls by. "Content descriptors" for video games also suggest how lurid the violence can be. These games include depictions of "blood and gore (mutilation of body parts)," "intense violence (human injury or death)," and "sexual violence (depictions of rape and other sexual acts)."

Barbara Dafoe Whitehead is codirector of the National Marriage Project at Rutgers University and the author of *The Divorce Culture: Rethinking Our Commitments to Marriage and Family* (1998) and *Why There Are No Good Men Left: The Romantic Plight of the New Single Woman* (2003). The column appeared in *Commonweal* on January 28, 2005.

No sooner had Blagojevich unveiled his proposal than he faced power- 5 ful organized opposition from the entertainment industry. The Illinois Retail Merchants Association, the National Association of Theater Owners, the Entertainment Software Rating Board, and the Motion Picture Association of America took strong exception to the legislation. Imposing a curb on the free market is not the way to protect kids, these critics argued. Instead, parents should screen what their kids are buying and playing. As one lobbyist put it: "Retailers can't be held accountable for lack of oversight by parents."

This is a distortion of the governor's position, and of the problem. No one denies that parents have the primary responsibility for monitoring their kids. Blagojevich points out, though, that the sophisticated technology of video games makes that very hard to do. Consequently, it's up to the state to step in on the side of parents and children to help them cope.

The industry argument would be plausible if it were still 1955. Back then, it was easier for parents to exercise strict oversight. The big, boxy home entertainment technologies of that era—radio, television, and record players—produced images and sounds that parents could see and hear. They came with OFF buttons for parents to push and plugs for parents to pull. All that has changed. The new entertainment technologies include a dizzying and ever-multiplying array of small, portable, individual, kid-friendly devices that defy close parental supervision. It was easy for parents to check on a half-hour TV show. It's much harder to review a video game. The games feature successive levels of difficulty; players must qualify at a lower level before earning the right to move to a higher level. So it takes time and practice before acquiring the skill to progress to the highest level of the game—which may also be its highest level of violence. To ensure that a video game isn't excessively violent, a parent would have to be looking over a child's shoulder until the highest level of play was finally revealed. This could take days.

Moreover, it isn't as if parents and the video-game industry meet each other on a level playing field. This is a multibillion-dollar industry that spends all its time and money devising ever more ingenious ways to market to kids over the heads of their parents and to deliberately undermine the ability of parents to regulate what their children are seeing. And in a tactic called "age compression," the marketers target their appeals to ever-younger kids. Like the youth sex revolution, the youth marketing revolution has migrated down the age scale. Even four-year-olds know what is cool.

To be sure, the industry's Entertainment Software Rating Board has voluntarily established its own ratings system. The trouble is: It isn't enforced. A study by the Federal Trade Commission found that early teens were able to buy games rated M (Mature 17+) 69 percent of the time.

It is telling that the makers and sellers of video games have responded 10 so quickly and vigorously to Governor Blagojevich's very modest proposal. Clearly the corporate sector finds it in its interest to prompt kids to engage in fantasy rape, beheadings, and mass murder. And why should we expect otherwise? Its interest is the bottom line. Violence sells. But isn't it in the compelling interest of the community to curb such violent play?

READING AND DISCUSSION QUESTIONS

1. Do you believe that video games are getting too violent and sexually explicit?
2. Is Whitehead right that the rating system for video games is not enforced? What might be done to make it work?
3. What is your position as to who should bear the responsibility of keeping violent and sexually explicit video games away from children? Or is there a need to keep them away?
4. Why are our children and teens attracted to games that are so violent?
5. How do you respond to Whitehead's statement that the video-game industry "spends all its time and money devising ever more ingenious ways to market to kids over the heads of their parents and to deliberately undermine the ability of parents to regulate what their children are seeing"?
6. To what extent are the choices children and teens make when it comes to video games in keeping with choices they make in choosing movies and television shows? Is there a difference in the level of control parents and the businesses involved have?

WRITING SUGGESTIONS

7. Write an essay explaining how Whitehead's bias is revealed not only in her statements about the governor and the video-game industry but also in the language she uses in discussing them.
8. How convincing is Whitehead in arguing that, as her title says, parents need help?
9. What warrants, or underlying assumptions, are behind Whitehead's argument?

Warfare: An Invention — Not a Biological Necessity

MARGARET MEAD

Is war a biological necessity, a sociological inevitability, or just a bad invention? Those who argue for the first view endow man with such pugnacious instincts that some outlet in aggressive behaviour is necessary if man is to reach full human stature. It was this point of view which lay behind William

---

Margaret Mead (1901–1978), the first American anthropologist to study childhood, adolescence, and gender, focused her work on culture rather than biology or race as the primary focus in determining variations in human behavior and personality. Her findings are detailed in hundreds of articles and numerous bestselling books, such as *Coming of Age in Samoa* (1928), *Growing Up in New Guinea* (1930), and *Sex and Temperament* (1935). This article, in which Mead argues that warfare is a cultural invention and not a biological necessity, was published in *Asia* in 1940.

James's famous essay, "The Moral Equivalent of War," in which he tried to retain the warlike virtues and channel them in new directions. A similar point of view has lain behind the Soviet Union's attempt to make competition between groups rather than between individuals. A basic, competitive, aggressive, warring human nature is assumed, and those who wish to outlaw war or outlaw competitiveness merely try to find new and less socially destructive ways in which these biologically given aspects of man's nature can find expression. Then there are those who take the second view: warfare is the inevitable concomitant of the development of the state, the struggle for land and natural resources, of class societies springing not from the nature of man, but, from the nature of history. War is nevertheless inevitable unless we change our social system and outlaw classes, the struggle for power, and possessions; and in the event of our success warfare would disappear, as a symptom vanishes when the disease is cured.

One may hold a sort of compromise position between these two extremes; one may claim that all aggression springs from the frustration of man's biologically determined drives and that, since all forms of culture are frustrating, it is certain each new generation will be aggressive and the aggression will find its natural and inevitable expression in race war, class war, nationalistic war, and so on.

All three of these positions are very popular today among those who think seriously about the problems of war and its possible prevention, but I wish to urge another point of view, less defeatist, perhaps, than the first and third and more accurate than the second: that is, that warfare, by which I mean recognized conflict between two groups as groups, in which each group puts an army (even if the army is only fifteen pygmies) into the field to fight and kill, if possible, some of the members of the army of the other group—that warfare of this sort is an invention like any other of the inventions in terms of which we order our lives, such as writing, marriage, cooking our food instead of eating it raw, trial by jury, or burial of the dead, and so on. Some of this list anyone will grant are inventions: trial by jury is confined to very limited portions of the globe; we know that there are tribes that do not bury their dead but instead expose or cremate them; and we know that only part of the human race has had the knowledge of writing as its cultural inheritance. But, whenever a way of doing things is found universally, such as the use of fire or the practice of some form of marriage, we tend to think at once that it is not an invention at all but an attribute of humanity itself. And yet even such universals as marriage and the use of fire are inventions like the rest, very basic ones, inventions which were, perhaps, necessary if human history was to take the turn that it has taken, but nevertheless inventions. At some point in his social development man was undoubtedly without the institution of marriage or the knowledge of the use of fire.

The case for warfare is much clearer because there are peoples even today who have no warfare. Of these the Eskimos are perhaps the most conspicuous examples, but the Lepchas of Sikkim described by Geoffrey Gorer in

Himalayan Village are as good. Neither of these peoples understands war, not even defensive warfare. The idea of warfare is lacking, and this idea is as essential to really carrying on war as an alphabet or a syllabary is to writing. But, whereas the Lepchas are a gentle, unquarrelsome people, and the advocates of other points of view might argue that they are not full human beings or that they had never been frustrated and so had no aggression to expand in warfare, the Eskimo case gives no such possibility of interpretation. The Eskimos are not a mild and meek people; many of them are turbulent and troublesome. Fights, theft of wives, murder, cannibalism, occur among them—all outbursts of passionate men goaded by desire or intolerable circumstance. Here are men faced with hunger, men faced with loss of their wives, men faced with the threat of extermination by other men, and here are orphan children, growing up miserably with no one to care for them, mocked and neglected by those about them. The personality necessary for war, the circumstances necessary to goad men to desperation are present, but there is no war. When a travelling Eskimo entered a settlement, he might have to fight the strongest man in the settlement to establish his position among them, but this was a test of strength and bravery, not war. The idea of warfare, of one group organizing against another group to maim and wound and kill them was absent. And, without that idea, passions might rage but there was no war.

But, it may be argued, is not this because the Eskimos have such a low 5 and undeveloped form of social organization? They own no land, they move from place to place, camping, it is true, season after season on the same site, but this is not something to fight for as the modern nations of the world fight for land and raw materials. They have no permanent possessions that can be looted, no towns that can be burned. They have no social classes to produce stress and strains within the society which might force it to go to war outside. Does not the absence of war among the Eskimos, while disproving the biological necessity of war, just go to confirm the point that it is the state of development of the society which accounts for war and nothing else?

We find the answer among the pygmy peoples of the Andaman Islands in the Bay of Bengal. The Andamans also represent an exceedingly low level of society; they are a hunting and food-gathering people; they live in tiny hordes without any class stratification; their houses are simpler than the snow houses of the Eskimo. But they knew about warfare. The army might contain only fifteen determined pygmies marching in a straight line, but it was the real thing none the less. Tiny army met tiny army in open battle, blows were exchanged, casualties suffered, and the state of warfare could only be concluded by a peacemaking ceremony.

Similarly, among the Australian aborigines, who built no permanent dwellings but wandered from water hole to water hole over their almost desert country, warfare—and rules of "international law"—were highly developed. The student of social evolution will seek in vain for his obvious causes of war, struggle for lands, struggle for power of one group over another, expansion of population, need to divert the minds of a populace restive under tyranny, or even the ambition of a successful leader to enhance his own prestige. All are absent, but warfare as a practice remained, and men engaged in it and killed one another in the course of a war because killing is what is done in wars.

From instances like these it becomes apparent that an inquiry into the causes of war misses the fundamental point as completely as does an insistence upon the biological necessity of war. If a people have an idea of going to war and the idea that war is the way in which certain situations, defined within their society, are to be handled, they will sometimes go to war. If they are a mild and unaggressive people, like the Pueblo Indians, they may limit themselves to defensive warfare, but they will be forced to think in terms of war because there are peoples near them who have warfare as a pattern, and offensive, raiding, pillaging warfare at that. When the pattern of warfare is known, people like the Pueblo Indians will defend themselves, taking advantage of their natural defenses, the mesa village site, and people like the Lepchas, having no natural defenses and no idea of warfare, will merely submit to the invader. But the essential point remains the same. There is a way of behaving which is known to a given people and labeled as an appropriate form of behavior; a bold and warlike people like the Sioux or the Maori may label warfare as desirable as well as possible, a mild people like the Pueblo Indians may label warfare as undesirable, but to the minds of both peoples the possibility of warfare is present. Their thoughts, their hopes, their plans are oriented about this idea—that warfare may be selected as the way to meet some situation.

So simple peoples and civilized peoples, mild peoples and violent, assertive peoples, will all go to war if they have the invention, just as those peoples who have the custom of dueling will have duels and peoples who have the pattern of vendetta will indulge in vendetta. And, conversely, peoples who do not know of dueling will not fight duels, even though their wives are seduced and their daughters ravished; they may on occasion commit murder but they will not fight duels. Cultures which lack the idea of the vendetta will not meet every quarrel in this way. A people can use only the forms it has. So the Balinese have their special way of dealing with a quarrel between two individuals: if the two feel that the causes of quarrel are heavy, they may go and register their quarrel in the temple before the gods, and, making offerings, they may swear never to have anything to do with each other again. . . . But in other societies, although individuals might feel as full of animosity and as unwilling to have any further contact as do the Balinese, they cannot register their quarrel with the gods and go on quietly about their business because registering quarrels with the gods is not an invention of which they know.

Yet, if it be granted that warfare is, after all, an invention, it may never- 10 theless be an invention that lends itself to certain types of personality, to the exigent needs of autocrats, to the expansionist desires of crowded peoples, to the desire for plunder and rape and loot which is engendered by a dull and frustrating life. What, then, can we say of this congruence between warfare and its uses? If it is a form which fits so well, is not this congruence the essential point? But even here the primitive material causes us to wonder, because there are tribes who go to war merely for glory, having no quarrel with the enemy, suffering from no tyrant within their boundaries, anxious neither for land nor loot nor women, but merely anxious to win prestige which within that tribe has been declared obtainable only by war and without which no young man can hope to win his sweetheart's smile of approval. But if, as was the case with the Bush Negroes of Dutch Guiana, it is artistic ability which is necessary to win a girl's approval, the same young man would have to be carving rather than going out on a war party.

In many parts of the world, war is a game in which the individual can win counters—counters which bring him prestige in the eyes of his own sex or of the opposite sex; he plays for these counters as he might, in our society, strive for a tennis championship. Warfare is a frame for such prestige-seeking merely because it calls for the display of certain skills and certain virtues; all of these skills—riding straight, shooting straight, dodging the missiles of the enemy and sending one's own straight to the mark— can be equally well exercised in some other framework and, equally, the virtues endurance, bravery, loyalty, steadfastness—can be displayed in other contexts. The tie-up between proving oneself a man and proving this by a success in organized killing is due to a definition which many societies have made of manliness. And often, even in those societies which counted success in warfare a proof of human worth, strange turns were given to the idea, as when the plains Indians gave their highest awards to the man who touched a live enemy rather than to the man who brought in a scalp—from a dead enemy—because the latter was less risky. Warfare is just an invention known to the majority of human societies by which they permit their young men either to accumulate prestige or avenge their honor or acquire loot or wives or slaves or sago lands or cattle or appease the blood lust of their gods or the restless souls of the recently dead. It is just an invention, older and more widespread than the jury system, but none the less an invention.

But, once we have said this, have we said anything at all? Despite a few stances, dear to the instances of controversialist, of the loss of the useful arts, once an invention is made which proves congruent with human needs or social forms, it tends to persist. Grant that war is an invention, that it is not a biological necessity nor the outcome of certain special types of social forms, still once the invention is made, what are we to do about it? The Indian who had been subsisting on the buffalo for generations because with his primitive weapons he could slaughter only a limited number of buffalo did not return to his primitive weapons when he saw that the white man's more efficient weapons were exterminating the buffalo. A desire for the white man's cloth may mortgage the South Sea Islander to the white man's plantation, but he does not return to making bark cloth, which would have left him free. Once an invention is known and accepted, men do not easily relinquish it. The skilled workers may smash the first steam looms which they feel are to be their undoing, but they accept them in the end, and no movement which has insisted upon the mere abandonment of usable inventions has ever had much success. Warfare is here, as part of our thought; the deeds of warriors are immortalized in the words of our poets, the toys of our children are modeled upon the weapons of the soldier, the frame of reference within which our statesmen and our diplomats work always contains war. If we know that it is not inevitable, that it is due to historical accident that warfare is one of the ways in which we think of behaving, are we given any hope by that? What hope is there of persuading nations to abandon war, nations so thoroughly imbued with the idea that to resort to war is, if not actually desirable and noble, at least inevitable whenever certain defined circumstances arise?

In answer to this question I think we might turn to the history of other social inventions, and inventions which must once have seemed as finally entrenched as warfare. Take the methods of trial which preceded the jury system: ordeal and trial by combat. Unfair, capricious, alien as they are to our feeling today, they were once the only methods open to individuals accused of some offense. The invention of trial by jury gradually replaced these methods until only witches, and finally not even witches, had to resort to the ordeal. And for a long time the jury system seemed the best and finest method of settling legal disputes, but today new inventions, trial before judges only or before commissions, are replacing the jury system. In each case the old method was replaced by a new social invention. The ordeal did not go out because people thought it unjust or wrong; it went out because a method more congruent with the institutions and feelings of the period was invented. And, if we despair over the way in which war seems such an ingrained habit of most of the human race, we can take comfort from the fact that a poor invention will usually give place to a better invention.

For this, two conditions, at least, are necessary. The people must recognize the defects of the old invention, and someone must make a new one. Propaganda against warfare, documentation of its terrible cost in human suffering and social waste, these prepare the ground by teaching people to feel that warfare is a defective social institution. There is further needed a belief that social invention is possible and the invention of new methods which will render warfare as out of date as the tractor is making the plough, or the motor car the horse and buggy. A form of behavior becomes out of date only when something else takes its place, and, in order to invent forms of behavior which will make war obsolete, it is a first requirement to believe that an invention is possible.

READING AND DISCUSSION QUESTIONS

1. What theories does Mead refute before explaining her own?
2. To what other inventions does Mead compare war?
3. What conclusions does she draw from her observations about Eskimos?

4. She ponders if it does any good to recognize war as an invention. How does she answer her own question?

5. What solution to the problem of warfare does Mead propose? Do you find any flaws in her proposal? Explain your agreement or disagreement with the plausibility of her solution.

6. In an article entitled "Where Have All the Young Men Gone? The Perfect Substitute for War," the author, Paul Auster, marvels at the significance of a gathering in 1998 of more than a million people to celebrate France's victory in the World Cup of soccer. "The vast majority of Europeans," he writes, "have found a way to hate one another without hacking one another to pieces."[1] Do you agree that sports are an outlet for hostility that once would have found an outlet in battle? Explain.

WRITING SUGGESTIONS

7. Mead uses a common organizational strategy—refuting the opposing view. In this essay she refutes several theories about the origins of warfare. Summarize these theories. Where does she state her own thesis?

8. Mead supports her argument with examples and analogies. Are they all equally convincing? To what extent does the success of her essay depend on her use of examples?

DEBATE: How Serious Is the Problem of Online Predators?

MySpace and Sex Offenders: What's the Problem?

BOB SULLIVAN

In October, Wired News reporter Kevin Poulsen ran a simple experiment that produced some disturbing results. He wrote a computer program that matched databases of registered sex offenders with MySpace profiles and found hundreds of matches.

On Poulsen's list: A thrice-convicted sex offender who had recently finished a nine-year jail term for sexually abusing two young boys. It turned out he was using MySpace to approach and proposition young boys. The offender was soon arrested again.

---

[1] *New York Times Magazine*, April 4, 1999, p. 144.

Bob Sullivan covers Internet scams and consumer fraud for MSNBC.com and has received numerous awards for that work. In 2004 he published *Your Evil Twin: Behind the Identity Theft Epidemic*. He posted this essay to his blog on May 29, 2007.

Two months after Poulsen's story was published, MySpace announced it had hired an outside company, Sentinel Tech Holding Corp., to compare registered sex offenders rolls with MySpace profiles and root out sex criminals from the site. Until earlier this month, though, it appeared little progress had been made.

Then, a public spat erupted between a group of state attorneys general and MySpace, with the AGs demanding to know how many offenders the review had uncovered. After about a week of public jousting, MySpace said it had removed 7,000 profiles that might have belonged to registered sex offenders.

The controversy has raised questions about MySpace's diligence in try- 5 ing to keep predators off its service and its ability to work with some law enforcement officials.

That so many registered offenders were attracted to MySpace, largely a haunt for young Web users, is disturbing to Connecticut Attorney General Richard Blumenthal.

"It is a very, very frightening number when you consider they . . . are using their real names," he said. "One would think a convicted sex offender would use an alias. This number is just the most visible tip of the predatory problem on MySpace and other social networking sites."

Why did this rather public controversy over sex offender MySpace pages erupt this month? Curiously, it began when MySpace—often criticized for inaction on child safety issues—took a strong action against registered sex offenders.

Sentinel Starts

The initial spark flew on May 2, when MySpace unceremoniously turned on the product developed by Sentinel and began removing profiles from the site.

Within days, the group of attorney general offices already eyeing My- 10 Space policies found out about the deletions and became concerned that evidence of crimes might be destroyed.

"We were rather concerned that we were hearing back channel information about profiles being removed and deleted without us receiving that information," said Nils Frederiksen, a spokesman for Pennsylvania Attorney General Tom Corbett. "We need to know which Pennsylvania residents have been identified because of possible terms and conditions of their release that may have been violated."

Some probation agreements prevent sex offenders from using computers at all; others prevent them from any contact with minors. The offenders' MySpace profiles may have included clear evidence that such provisions were being violated, Frederiksen said.

"Along the way we were hearing that this was a work in progress, that it wasn't ready," he said. "Then in the spring we found out they'd already deleted profiles. That was what motivated the public call to action."

On May 15, eight attorneys general sent a letter to MySpace demanding more information about registered offenders on the site. The next day, MySpace refused to provide the data, saying it could only do so if compelled by a court order. Several states began seeking court orders to obtain the data, but five days later MySpace announced that an agreement had been reached to share the information.

A Misunderstanding

To MySpace officials, it was all a misunderstanding. The new system was still 15 being tested when the suspect profiles began being removed, so the company believed there was no need, at that point, to notify attorneys general who were already working with the company, said one MySpace official, who agreed to discuss the matter on condition he not be identified.

And the profile removal process was designed to preserve any evidence law enforcement might subsequently need, the company said.

"In addition to immediately removing registered sex offenders from MySpace, our plans have always been to provide the information collected by Sentinel . . . to law enforcement, including the attorneys general," Mike Angus, executive vice president and general counsel for Fox Interactive Media, which owns MySpace, said in a statement.

But the spat likely signals more than concern about deletion of evidence. There is obvious sentiment among law enforcement agencies that MySpace was acting too slowly to remove known sex offenders from the site.

"We were disappointed it's taken a year to get to this point," Frederiksen said. His office had approached MySpace about the sex offender issue even before the Wired story was published. "We would like to see things move forward in a faster pace."

No National Sex Offender Registry

But company officials say government sex offender registries are to blame 20 for the hold-up.

Because most registries are maintained by state offices and there is no national database, Sentinel had to build a tool that collected information on 600,000 offenders from more than 50 sources, the company said. Because the data couldn't be downloaded from registry Web sites, collecting the data was a complicated project. Building the tool took about 6 months, the official said.

Still, some officials in the various attorney general offices suggested MySpace had another motivation for moving slowly and deleting profiles without informing public officials: quietly removing the offender profiles without drawing attention to the number of convicted sex criminals who lurk on the site.

"In fairness to MySpace, it did take the step of hiring Sentinel . . . but they are ambivalent about releasing the results," Blumenthal said. "Perhaps they feel it may reflect badly on this site and other sites."

In his October story, Poulsen concluded that matching sex offender registries to MySpace profiles was hardly the most effective tool for improving the site's safety. After all, would-be predators could easily foil such filters by registering with fake names and other information. Blumenthal and other attorneys general are pushing for additional measures, such as mandatory age verification to keep kids off the site altogether.

But the presence of 7,000 registered offenders on the site—and the time 25 span required to remove them—raises inevitable questions about MySpace's ability to keep its neighborhood safe.

"The measures taken by MySpace have been baby steps when giant strides are needed," Blumenthal said.

MySpace Not Responsible for Predators

KEVIN ALEXANDER

There is no way to stop a determined predator. There is no way to stop a determined victim.

On June 19, a 14-year-old girl and her mother filed a lawsuit against MySpace. The suit claims that MySpace's lack of age verification allowed a 19-year-old man, Pete Solis, to lie about his age and contact the girl. Solis convinced the 14-year-old to meet him outside of cyberspace, where he took her to dinner and a movie and then allegedly raped her.

The family's lawyer, Adam Loewy, said the family is seeking $30 million worth of damages, citing MySpace's security features as "utterly ineffective." He also dropped this bombshell: "MySpace is more concerned with making money than protecting children online." Get out of town, Mr. Loewy. MySpace is a business, and one that has never advertised itself as an online baby-sitting service. Making money is its reason for existence.

If the rape allegations are true, then this is a tragedy. Nearly all actions taken by predators are tragedies, but this lawsuit is frivolous, and potentially damaging to the nature of the Internet.

This kind of thing happens cyclically. Video games, music, and tele- 5 vision have all been blamed for the actions of a few naive or demented people. Corporations and organizations are demonized, lawsuits are filed, most are thrown out, and the parents of the offender or victim sneak off the radar. That's what is happening here. Any police officer will tell you that nearly all youth crimes happen because some moron forgot to be a parent.

Kevin Alexander was a student at Texas A&M when he wrote this for the independent student newspaper the *Battalion* in June 2006.

This girl's mother failed here several times. She didn't convince her daughter of the dangers of cyberspace; she didn't monitor her Internet usage well enough, she let her 14-year-old daughter physically meet a 19-year-old man, and she's now sending the wrong message by deflecting the responsibility onto a Web site that has no control over sociopaths.

The girl, as traumatic as her experience was, should be held responsible, too. At 14 years of age, she's capable of calculating risk and other higher brain functions. She ignored the danger of dealing with someone she didn't know. She gave away personal information and she consented to physically meet Solis. She could've prevented being a victim, but she was determined to ignore all the apparent risks, and she paid for it.

There are more than 80 million users on MySpace. So far, only three cases of molestation have hit the courts. They are anomalies, and they are impossible to extinguish completely. Teenage socialization is oftentimes chaotic, and predators are unbalanced equations.

Fortunately, MySpace has foreseen this, and has attempted to protect itself. When creating an account, users must sign a waiver that states, "MySpace .com is not responsible for the conduct, whether online or offline, of any user of the MySpace Services." The 14-year-old signed this agreement, and thus signed away her protection under naiveté. This should be enough to get the suit thrown out, but it's big trouble for the Internet if it isn't.

The Internet is a gigantic medium for everything. If this lawsuit goes 10 through, then any Web site that deals with any sort of exchange, be it monetary, information, or services, is at risk for lawsuit. If someone does something stupid while on the Internet, then that person can sue the Net. There are tons of predators out there, and there are tons of waiting victims. It's unknown as of now which ones are more dangerous.

DISCUSSION QUESTIONS

1. To what extent are those who are responsible for MySpace to be applauded for their attempts to make their site safer? What do you believe has been wrong with their attempts?

2. Do you believe that deleting profiles of sex offenders is the best way to solve the problem of online predators? Why, or why not?

3. What is your opinion of the state's use of MySpace profiles to catch predators violating their parole?

4. Are you convinced that there really is danger in using MySpace? Explain.

5. What is Sullivan's thesis?

6. In Alexander's article, how culpable do you believe the teenaged girl is in what happened to her? Do you think that many girls her age actually meet men they have communicated with online?

7. How much responsibility do you believe her mother has to bear for what happened?

8. Respond to this statement by Adam Loewy, the lawyer: " 'MySpace is more concerned with making money than protecting children online.' "

9. How would you state Alexander's thesis?

10. Research what happened to the lawsuit filed by the girl's family.

11. Explain which you believe to be a stronger argument—Sullivan's or Alexander's—and why.

ASSIGNMENTS FOR WRITING ABOUT ARGUMENT

READING AND DISCUSSION QUESTIONS

1. Choose an editorial from your campus or local newspaper and evaluate it. How successful an argument does it make?

2. In his essay, "Should We Fight Terror with Torture?," Alan Dershowitz argues for new rules of war. In her essay, "War: An Invention—Not a Biological Necessity," Margaret Mead argues for a new perception of why human beings go to war. How are Mead's ideas from 1940 relevant to Dershowitz's from 2001?

3. Evaluate the argument that Charles Krauthammer makes in his essay, "Let's Have No More Monkey Trials."

4. Barbara Dafoe Whitehead argues that parents need help from the state in controlling their children's leisure activities. Charles Krauthammer argues that parents should not interfere with the way the state says that science should be taught in public schools. Who provides a more convincing argument?

WRITING SUGGESTIONS

5. Choose an editorial from your campus or local newspaper and write an objective analysis of it. Your thesis statement will be a claim of fact.

6. Locate two editorials or two articles that take different stands on the same controversial issue. Write an analysis in which you objectively compare the two as examples of argumentation.

7. Locate two editorials or two articles that take different stands on the same controversial issue. Write an essay in which you argue which of the two is a more effective argument and why.

8. Explain in an essay which of the two essays about MySpace presents a stronger argument, Kevin Alexander's or Bob Sullivan's.

CHAPTER 5

Defining Key Terms

THE PURPOSES OF DEFINITION

Before we examine the other elements of argument, we need to consider definition, a component you may have to deal with early in writing an essay. Definition may be used in two ways: to clarify the meanings of vague or ambiguous terms or as a method of development for the whole essay. In some arguments your claims will contain words that need explanation before you can proceed with any discussion. But you may also want to devote an entire essay to the elaboration of a broad concept or experience that cannot be adequately defined in a shorter space.

The Roman statesman Cicero said, "Every rational discussion of anything whatsoever should begin with a definition in order to make clear what is the subject of dispute." Arguments often revolve around definitions of crucial terms. For example, how does one define *democracy*? Does a democracy guarantee freedom of the press, freedom of worship, freedom of assembly, and freedom of movement? In the United States, we would argue that such freedoms are essential to any definition of *democracy*. But countries in which these freedoms are nonexistent also represent themselves as democracies or governments of the people. In the words of Senator Daniel P. Moynihan, "For years now the most brutal totalitarian regimes have called themselves 'people's' or 'democratic' republics." Rulers in such governments are aware that defining their regimes as democratic may win the approval of people who would otherwise condemn them. In his formidable attack on totalitarianism in *1984*, George Orwell coined the slogans "War Is Peace" and "Slavery Is Freedom," phrases that represent the corrupt use of definition to distort reality.

But even where there is no intention to deceive, the snares of definition are difficult to avoid. How do you define *abortion*? Is it "termination of pregnancy"? Or is it "murder of an unborn child"? During a celebrated trial in 1975 of a physician who performed an abortion and was accused of manslaughter, the prosecution often used the word *baby* to refer to the fetus, but the defense referred to "the products of conception." These definitions of *fetus* reflected the differing judgments of those on opposite sides. Not only do judgments create definitions; definitions influence judgments. In the abortion trial, the definitions of *fetus* used by both sides were meant to promote either approval or disapproval of the doctor's action.

Definitions can indeed change the nature of an event or a "fact." How many farms are there in the state of New York? The answer to the question depends on the definition of *farm*. In 1979 the *New York Times* reported:

> Because of a change in the official definition of the word "farm," New York lost 20 percent of its farms on January 1, with numbers dropping from 56,000 to 45,000. . . .
> Before the change, a farm was defined as "any place from which $250 or more of agricultural products is sold" yearly or "any place of 10 acres or more from which $50 or more of agricultural products is sold" yearly. Now a farm is "any place from which $1,000 or more of agricultural products is sold" in a year.[1]

A change in the definition of *poverty* can have similar results. An article in the *New York Times*, whose headline reads, "A Revised Definition of Poverty May Raise Number of U.S. Poor," makes this clear:

> The official definition of *poverty* used by the Federal Government for three decades is based simply on cash income before taxes. But in a report to be issued on Wednesday, a panel of experts convened by the [National] Academy of Sciences three years ago at the behest of Congress says the Government should move toward a concept of poverty based on disposable income, the amount left after a family pays taxes and essential expenses.[2]

The differences are wholly a matter of definition. But such differences can have serious consequences for those being defined, most of all in the disposition of billions of federal dollars in aid of various kinds. In 1992 the Census Bureau classified 14.5 percent of Americans as poor. Under the new guidelines, at least 15 or 16 percent would be poor, and, under some measures recommended by a government panel, 18 percent would be so defined.

In fact, local and federal courts almost every day redefine traditional concepts that can have a direct impact on our everyday lives. The definition of *family*, for example, has undergone significant changes that acknowledge the existence of new relationships. In January 1990 the New Jersey

[1]*New York Times*, March 4, 1979, sec. 1, p. 40.
[2]*New York Times*, April 10, 1995, sec. A, p. 1.

Supreme Court ruled that a family may be defined as "one or more persons occupying a dwelling unit as a single nonprofit housekeeping unit, who are living together as a stable and permanent living unit, being a traditional family unit or the *functional equivalent* thereof" (italics for emphasis added). This meant that ten Glassboro State College students, unrelated by blood, could continue to occupy a single-family house despite the objection of the borough of Glassboro.[3] Even the legal definition of *maternity* has shifted. Who is the mother—the woman who contributes the egg or the woman (the surrogate) who bears the child? Several states, acknowledging the changes brought by medical technology, now recognize a difference between the birth mother and the legal mother.

DEFINING THE TERMS IN YOUR ARGUMENT

In some of your arguments you will introduce terms that require definition. We've pointed out that a definition of *poverty* is crucial to any debate on the existence of poverty in the United States. The same may be true in a debate about the legality of euthanasia, or mercy killing. Are the arguers referring to passive euthanasia (the withdrawal of life-support systems) or to active euthanasia (the direct administration of drugs to hasten death)?

It is not uncommon, in fact, for arguments about controversial questions to turn into arguments about the definition of terms. If, for example, you wanted to argue in favor of the regulation of religious cults, you would first have to define *cult*. In so doing, you might discover that it is not easy to distinguish clearly between conventional religions and cults. Then you would have to define *regulation*, spelling out the legal restrictions you favored so as to make them apply only to cults, not to established religions. An argument on the subject might end almost before it began if writer and reader could not agree on definitions of these terms. While clear definitions do not guarantee agreement, they do ensure that all parties understand the nature of the argument.

■ Defining Vague and Ambiguous Terms

You will need to define other terms in addition to those in your claim. If you use words and phrases that have two or more meanings, they may appear vague and ambiguous to your reader. In arguments of value and policy abstract terms such as *freedom, justice, patriotism*, and *equality* require clarification. Despite their abstract nature, however, they are among the most important in the language because they represent the ideals that shape our laws. When conflicts arise, the courts must define these terms to establish the legality of certain practices. Is the Ku Klux Klan permitted to make dis-

---

[3] *New York Times*, February 1, 1990, sec. B, p. 5.

paraging public statements about ethnic and racial groups? That depends on the court's definition of *free speech*. Can execution for some crimes be considered cruel and unusual punishment? That, too, depends on the court's definition of *cruel and unusual punishment*. In addition, such terms as *happiness, mental health, success,* and *creativity* often defy precise definition because they reflect the differing values within a society or a culture.

The definition of *success*, for example, varies not only among social groups but also among individuals within the group. One scientist has postulated five signs by which to measure success: wealth (including health), security (confidence in retaining the wealth), reputation, performance, and contentment.[4] Consider whether all of these are necessary to your own definition of *success*. If not, which may be omitted? Do you think others should be added? Notice that one of the signs—reputation—is defined by the community; another—contentment—can be measured only by the individual. The assessment of performance probably owes something to both the group and the individual.

Christopher Atkins, an actor, gave an interviewer an example of an externalized definition of success—that is, a definition based on the standards imposed by other people:

> Success to me is judged through the eyes of others. I mean, if you're walking around saying, "I own a green Porsche," you might meet somebody who says, "Hey, that's no big deal. I own a green Porsche and a house." So all of a sudden, you don't feel so successful. Really, it's in the eyes of others.[5]

So difficult is the formulation of a universally accepted measure for success that some scholars regard the concept as meaningless. Nevertheless, we continue to use the word as if it represented a definable concept because the idea of success, however defined, is important for the identity and development of the individual and the group. It is clear, however, that when crossing subcultural boundaries, even within a small group, we need to be aware of differences in the use of the word. If contentment—that is, the satisfaction of achieving a small personal goal—is enough, then a person making a minimal salary but doing work that he or she loves may be a success. But you should not expect all your readers to agree that these criteria are enough to define *success*.

In arguing about aesthetic matters, whose vocabulary is almost always abstract, the criteria for judgment must be revealed, either directly or indirectly, and then the abstract terms that represent the criteria must be defined. If you want to say that a film is distinguished by great acting, have you made clear what you mean by *great*? That we do not always understand or agree on the definition of *great* is apparent, say, on the morning after the Oscar winners have been announced.

---

[4] Gwynn Nettler, *Social Concerns* (New York: McGraw-Hill, 1976), pp. 196–97.
[5] *New York Times*, August 6, 1982, sec. 3, p. 8.

Even subjects that you feel sure you can identify may offer surprising insights when you rethink them for an extended definition. One critic, defining *rock music,* argued that the distinguishing characteristic of rock music was noise—not beat, not harmonies, not lyrics, not vocal style, but noise, "nasty, discordant, irritating noise—or, to its practitioners, unfettered, liberating, expressive noise."[6] In producing this definition, the author had to give a number of examples to prove that he was justified in rejecting the most familiar criteria.

Consider the definition of *race,* around which so much of American history has revolved, often with tragic consequences. Until recently, the only categories listed in the census were white, black, Asian-Pacific, and Native American, "with the Hispanic population straddling them all." But rapidly increasing intermarriage and ethnic identity caused a number of political and ethnic groups to demand changes in the classifications of the Census Bureau. Some Arab Americans, for example, prefer to be counted as "Middle Eastern" rather than white. Children of black-white unions are defined as black 60 percent of the time, while children of Asian-white unions are described as Asian 42 percent of the time. Research is now being conducted to discover how people feel about the terms being used to define them. As one anthropologist pointed out, "Socially and politically assigned attributes have a lot to do with access to economic resources."[7]

PRACTICE

1. Use one or more cases to illustrate how, in a court of law, guilt or innocence can hinge on a matter of definition.

2. Choose two terms that are sometimes confused and define them to make their differences clear. Some examples are *active euthanasia* and *passive euthanasia, psychologist* and *psychiatrist, manslaughter* and *murder, envy* and *jealousy, sympathy* and *pity,* and *liberal* and *radical.*

3. Many recent controversial movements and causes are identified by terms that have come to mean different things to different people. Define the following terms, considering any positive or negative connotations of each. Also consider whether there is a term with a similar meaning that has more positive or more negative connotations.

   a. abortion

   b. war on terror

   c. affirmative action

   d. assisted suicide

   e. the Patriot Act

   f. undocumented workers

[6]Jon Pareles, "Noise Evokes Modern Chaos for a Band," *New York Times,* March 9, 1986, sec. H, p. 26.

[7]*Wall Street Journal,* September 9, 1995, sec. B, p. 1.

METHODS FOR DEFINING TERMS

Reading a dictionary definition is the simplest and most obvious way to learn the basic definition of a term. An unabridged dictionary is the best source because it usually gives examples of the way a word can be used in a sentence; that is, it furnishes the proper context.

In many cases, the dictionary definition alone is not sufficient. It may be too broad or too narrow for your purpose. Suppose, in an argument about pornography, you wanted to define the word *obscene*. *Webster's New International Dictionary* (third edition, unabridged) gives the definition of *obscene* as "offensive to taste; foul; loathsome; disgusting." But these synonyms do not tell you what qualities make an object or an event or an action "foul," "loathsome," and "disgusting." In 1973 the Supreme Court, attempting to narrow the definition of *obscenity*, ruled that obscenity was to be determined by the community in accordance with local standards. One person's obscenity, as numerous cases have demonstrated, may be another person's art. The celebrated trials in the early twentieth century about the distribution of novels regarded as pornographic—D. H. Lawrence's *Lady Chatterley's Lover* and James Joyce's *Ulysses*—emphasized the problems of defining obscenity.

Another dictionary definition may strike you as too narrow. *Patriotism*, for example, is defined in one dictionary as "love and loyal or zealous support of one's country, especially in all matters involving other countries." Some readers may want to include an unwillingness to support government policies they consider wrong.

These limitations are the reason that opening an essay with a dictionary definition is often not a very effective strategy, although it is a strategy often used by beginning writers. In order to initiate the effective discussion of a key term, you should be able to define it in your own words.

■ Stipulation

In stipulating the meaning of a term, the writer asks the reader to accept a definition that may be different from the conventional one. He or she does this to limit or control the argument. Someone has said, "Part of the task of keeping definitions in our civilization clear and pure is to keep a firm democratic rein on those with the power, or craving the power, to stipulate meaning." Perhaps this writer was thinking of a term like *national security*, which can be defined by a nation's leaders in such a way as to sanction persecution of citizens and reckless military adventures. Likewise, a term such as *liberation* can be appropriated by terrorist groups whose activities often lead to oppression rather than liberation.

Religion is usually defined as a belief in a supernatural power to be obeyed and worshiped. But in an article entitled "Civil Religion in America," a sociologist offers a different meaning:

> While some have argued that Christianity is the national faith, and others that church and synagogue celebrate only the generalized religion of "the American way of life," few have realized that there actually exists alongside of and rather clearly differentiated from the churches an elaborate and well-institutionalized civil religion in America. This article argues not only that there is such a thing, but also that this religion . . . has its own seriousness and integrity and requires the same care in understanding that any other religion does.[8]

When the author adds, "This religion—there seems no other word for it—was neither sectarian nor in any specific sense Christian," he emphasizes that he is distinguishing his definition of religion from definitions that associate religion and church.

Even the word *violence*, which the dictionary defines as "physical force used so as to injure or damage" and whose meaning seems so clear and uncompromising, can be manipulated to produce a definition different from the one normally understood by most people. Some pacifists refer to conditions in which "people are deprived of choices in a systematic way" as "institutionalized quiet violence." Even where no physical force is employed, this lack of choice in schools, in the workplace, in the black ghettos is defined as violence.[9]

In *Through the Looking-Glass* Alice asked Humpty Dumpty "whether you can make words mean so many different things."

> "When *I* use a word," Humpty Dumpty said scornfully, "it means just what I choose it to mean—neither more nor less."[10]

A writer, however, is not free to invent definitions that no one will recognize or that create rather than solve problems between writer and reader.

■ Negation

To avoid confusion it is sometimes helpful to tell the reader what a term is *not*. In discussing euthanasia, a writer might say, "By euthanasia I do not mean active intervention to hasten the death of the patient."

A negative definition may be more extensive, depending on the complexity of the term and the writer's ingenuity. The critic of rock music quoted earlier in this chapter arrived at his definition of *noise* by rejecting attributes that seemed misleading. The former Communist party member Whittaker Chambers, in a foreword to a book on the spy trial of Alger Hiss, defined *communism* this way:

---

[8]Robert N. Bellah, "Civil Religion in America," *Daedalus*, Winter 1967, p. 1.

[9]Newton Garver, "What Violence Is," in James Rachels, ed., *Moral Choices* (New York: Harper and Row, 1971), pp. 248–49.

[10]Lewis Carroll, *Alice in Wonderland and Through the Looking-Glass* (New York: Grosset and Dunlap, 1948), p. 238.

First, let me try to say what Communism is not. It is not simply a vicious plot hatched by wicked men in a subcellar. It is not just the writings of Marx and Lenin, dialectical materialism, the Politburo, the labor theory of value, the theory of the general strike, the Red Army secret police, labor camps, underground conspiracy, the dictatorship of the proletariat, the technique of the coup d'état. It is not even those chanting, bannered millions that stream periodically, like disorganized armies, through the heart of the world's capitals: Moscow, New York, Tokyo, Paris, Rome. These are expressions, but they are not what Communism is about.[11]

This, of course, is only part of the definition. Any writer beginning a definition in the negative must go on to define what the term *is*.

■ Examples

One of the most effective ways of defining terms in an argument is to use examples. Both real and hypothetical examples can bring life to abstract and ambiguous terms. The writer in the following passage defines *preferred categories* (classes of people who are meant to benefit from affirmative action policies) by invoking specific cases:

The absence of definitions points up one of the problems with preferred categories. . . . These preferred categories take no account of family wealth or educational advantages. A black whose father is a judge or physician deserves preferential treatment over any nonminority applicant. The latter might have fought his way out of the grinding poverty of Appalachia, or might be the first member of an Italian American or a Polish American family to complete high school. But no matter.[12]

Insanity is a word that has been used and misused to describe a variety of conditions. Even psychiatrists are in dispute about its meaning. In the following anecdote, examples narrow and refine the definition.

Dr. Zilboorg says that present-day psychiatry does not possess any satisfactory definition of mental illness or neurosis. To illustrate, he told a story: A psychiatrist was recently asked for a definition of a "well-adjusted person" (not even slightly peculiar). The definition: "A person who feels in harmony with himself and who is not in conflict with his environment." It sounded fine, but up popped a heckler. "Would you then consider an anti-Nazi working in the underground against Hitler a maladjusted person?" "Well," the psychiatrist hemmed, "I withdraw the latter part of my definition." Dr. Zilboorg withdrew the first half for him. Many persons in perfect harmony with themselves, he pointed out, are in "distinctly pathological states."[13]

---

[11]*Witness* (New York: Random House, 1952), p. 8.
[12]Anthony Lombardo, "Quotas Work Both Ways," *U.S. Catholic*, February 1974, p. 39.
[13]Quoted in *The Art of Making Sense*, p. 48.

■ Extended Definition

When we speak of an extended definition, we usually refer not only to length but also to the variety of methods for developing the definition. Let's take the word *materialism*. A dictionary entry offers the following sentence fragments as definitions: "1. the doctrine that comfort, pleasure, and wealth are the only or highest goals or values. 2. the tendency to be more concerned with material than the spiritual goals or values." But the term *materialism* has acquired so many additional meanings, especially emotional ones, that an extended definition serves a useful purpose in clarifying the many different ideas surrounding our understanding of the term.

Below is a much longer definition of *materialism*, which appears at the beginning of an essay entitled "People and Things: Reflections on Materialism."[14]

> There are two contemporary usages of the term *materialism*, and it is important to distinguish between them. On the one hand we can talk about *instrumental materialism*, or the use of material objects to make life longer, safer, more enjoyable. By instrumental, we mean that objects act as essential means for discovering and furthering personal values and goals of life, so that the objects are instruments used to realize and further those goals. There is little negative connotation attached to this meaning of the word, since one would think that it is perfectly sensible to use things for such purposes. While it is true that the United States is the epitome of materialism in this sense, it is also true that most people in every society aspire to reach our level of instrumental materialism.
>
> On the other hand the term has a more negative connotation, which might be conveyed by the phrase *terminal materialism*. This is the sense critics use when they apply the term to Americans. What they mean is that we not only use our material resources as instruments to make life more manageable, but that we reduce our ultimate goals to the possession of things. They believe that we don't just use our cars to get from place to place, but that we consider the ownership of expensive cars one of the central values in life. Terminal materialism means that the object is valued only because it indicates an end in itself, a possession. In instrumental materialism there is a sense of directionality, in which a person's goals may be furthered through the interactions with the object. A book, for example, can reveal new possibilities or widen a person's view of the world, or an old photograph can be cherished because it embodies a relationship. But in terminal materialism, there is no sense of reciprocal interaction in the relation between the object and the end. The end is valued as final, not as itself a means to further ends. And quite often it is only the status label or image associated with the object that is valued, rather than the actual object.

In the essay from which this passage is taken, the authors distinguish between two kinds of materialism and provide an extended explanation, using contrast and examples as methods of development. They are aware

[14]Mihaly Csikszentmihalyi and Eugene Rochberg-Halton, "People and Things: Reflections on Materialism," *University of Chicago Magazine*, Spring 1978, pp. 7–8.

that the common perception of materialism — the love of things for their own sake — is a negative one. But this view, according to the authors, doesn't fully account for the attitudes of many Americans toward the things they own. There is, in fact, another more positive meaning that the authors call *instrumental materialism*. You will recognize that the authors are *stipulating* a meaning with which their readers might not be familiar. In their essay they distinguish between *terminal materialism*, in which "the object is valued only because it indicates an end in itself," and *instrumental materialism*, "the use of material objects to make life longer, safer, more enjoyable." Since *instrumental materialism* is the less familiar definition, the essay provides a great number of examples that show how people of three different generations value photographs, furniture, musical instruments, plants, and other objects for their memories and personal associations rather than as proof of the owners' ability to acquire the objects or win the approval of others.

THE DEFINITION ESSAY

The argumentative essay can take the form of an extended definition. An example of such an essay is the one from which we've just quoted, as well as the essays at the end of this chapter. The definition essay is appropriate when the idea under consideration is so controversial or so heavy with historical connotations that even a paragraph or two cannot make clear exactly what the arguer wants his or her readers to understand. For example, if you were preparing a definition of *patriotism*, you would probably use a number of methods to develop your definition: personal narrative, examples, stipulation, comparison and contrast, and cause-and-effect analysis.

Writer's Guide: Writing a Definition Essay

The following important steps should be taken when you write an essay of definition.

1. Choose a term that needs definition because it is controversial or ambiguous, or because you want to offer a personal definition that differs from the accepted interpretation. Explain why an extended definition is necessary. Or choose an experience that lends itself to treatment in an extended definition. One student defined *culture shock* as she had experienced it while studying abroad in Hawaii among students of a different ethnic background.

2. Decide on the thesis — the point of view you wish to develop about the term you are defining. If you want to define *heroism*, for example, you may choose to develop the idea that this quality depends on motivation and awareness of danger rather than on the specific act performed by the hero.

3. Distinguish wherever possible between the term you are defining and other terms with which it might be confused. If you are defining *love*, can you make a clear distinction between the different kinds of emotional attachments contained in the word?

4. Try to think of several methods of developing the definition — using examples, comparison and contrast, analogy, cause-and-effect analysis. However, you may discover that one method alone — say, use of examples — will suffice to narrow and refine your definition.

5. Arrange your supporting material in an order that gives emphasis to the most important ideas.

SAMPLE ANNOTATED ESSAY

The Definition of Terrorism

BRIAN WHITAKER

Decide for yourself whether to believe this, but according to a new report there were only 16 cases of international terrorism in the Middle East last year.

That is the lowest number for any region in the world apart from North America (where there were none at all). Europe had 30 cases—almost twice as many as the Middle East—and Latin America came top with 193.

The figures come from the U.S. state department's annual review of global terrorism, which has just been published on the internet. Worldwide, the report says confidently, "there were 423 international terrorist attacks in 2000, an increase of 8% from the 392 attacks recorded during 1999."

No doubt a lot of painstaking effort went into counting them, but the statistics are fundamentally meaningless because, as the report points

Statistics on terrorism from before 9/11

This article was published May 7, 2001, in *Guardian Unlimited*, the daily online version of the British newspaper the *Guardian*. Whitaker is an editor on Comment Is Free, the *Guardian*'s Web expansion.

Problems with attempts to define terrorism

out, "no one definition of terrorism has gained universal acceptance."

That is an understatement. While most people 5 agree that terrorism exists, few can agree on what it is. A recent book discussing attempts by the UN and other international bodies to define terrorism runs to three volumes and 1,866 pages without reaching any firm conclusion.

U.S. State Department's definition

Using the definition preferred by the state department, terrorism is: "Premeditated, politically motivated violence perpetrated against noncombatant* targets by subnational groups or clandestine agents, usually intended to influence an audience." (The asterisk is important, as we shall see later.)

Definition of "international" terrorism

"International" terrorism—the subject of the American report—is defined as "terrorism involving citizens or the territory of more than one country."

Main point of agreement is motivation

The key point about terrorism, on which almost everyone agrees, is that it's politically motivated. This is what distinguishes it from, say, murder or football hooliganism. But this also causes a problem for those who compile statistics because the motive is not always clear—especially if no one has claimed responsibility.

Example of incidents with no known motivation

So the American report states—correctly—that there were no confirmed terrorist incidents in Saudi Arabia last year. There were, nevertheless, three unexplained bombings and one shooting incident, all directed against foreigners.

Another part of the definition

Another essential ingredient (you might think) 10 is that terrorism is calculated to terrorize the public or a particular section of it. The American definition does not mention spreading terror at all, because that would exclude attacks against property. It is, after all, impossible to frighten an inanimate object.

Among last year's attacks, 152 were directed against a pipeline in Colombia which is owned by multinational oil companies. Such attacks are of concern to the United States and so a definition is required which allows them to be counted.

Questions about which examples meet the criteria

For those who accept that terrorism is about terrorizing people, other questions arise. Does it include threats, as well as actual violence? A few years ago, for example, the Islamic Army in Yemen warned foreigners to leave the country if they valued their lives but did not actually carry out its threat.

More recently, a group of Israeli peace activists were arrested for driving around in a loudspeaker van, announcing a curfew of the kind that is imposed on Palestinians. Terrifying for any Israelis who believed it, but was it terrorism?

Another characteristic

Another characteristic of terrorism, according to some people, is that targets must be random — the intention being to make everyone fear they might be the next victim. Some of the Hamas suicide bombings appear to follow this principle but when attacks are aimed at predictable targets (such as the military) they are less likely to terrorize the public at large.

What terrorism is not

Definitions usually try to distinguish between 15 terrorism and warfare. In general this means that attacks on soldiers are warfare and those against civilians are terrorism, but the dividing lines quickly become blurred.

The state department regards attacks against "noncombatant* targets" as terrorism. But follow the asterisk to the small print and you find that "noncombatants" includes both civilians and military personnel who are unarmed or off duty at the time. Several examples are given, such as the 1986 disco bombing in Berlin, which killed two servicemen.

Examples

The most lethal bombing in the Middle East last year was the suicide attack on USS *Cole* in Aden harbor which killed 17 American sailors and injured 39 more.

Unanswered questions

As the ship was armed and its crew on duty at the time, why is this classified as terrorism? Look again at the small print, which adds: "We also consider as acts of terrorism attacks on military installations or on armed military personnel when a state of military hostilities does not exist at the site, such as bombings against U.S. bases."

A similar question arises with Palestinian attacks on quasi-military targets such as Israeli settlements. Many settlers are armed (with weapons supplied by the army) and the settlements themselves — though they contain civilians — might be considered military targets because they are there to consolidate a military occupation.

If, under the state department rules, Palestinian 20
mortar attacks on settlements count as terrorism, it
would be reasonable to expect Israeli rocket attacks
on Palestinian communities to be treated in the
same way—but they are not. In the American definition, terrorism can never be inflicted by a state.

Israeli treatment of the Palestinians is classified
as a human rights issue (for which the Israelis get
a rap over the knuckles) in a separate state department report.

Denying that states can commit terrorism is
generally useful, because it gets the U.S. and its allies off the hook in a variety of situations. The disadvantage is that it might also get hostile states
off the hook—which is why there has to be a list
of states that are said to "sponsor" terrorism while
not actually committing it themselves.

Interestingly, the American definition of terrorism is a reversal of the word's original meaning,
given in the Oxford English Dictionary as "government by intimidation." Today it usually refers
to intimidation of governments.

The first recorded use of "terrorism" and "terrorist" was in 1795, relating to the Reign of Terror instituted by the French government. Of course, the
Jacobins, who led the government at the time,
were also revolutionaries and gradually "terrorism" came to be applied to violent revolutionary
activity in general. But the use of "terrorist" in an
anti-government sense is not recorded until 1866
(referring to Ireland) and 1883 (referring to Russia).

In the absence of an agreed meaning, making 25
laws against terrorism is especially difficult. The
latest British anti-terrorism law gets round the problem by listing 21 international terrorist organizations by name. Membership of these is illegal in
the UK.

There are six Islamic groups, four anti-Israel
groups, eight separatist groups, and three opposition groups. The list includes Hizbullah, which
though armed, is a legal political party in Lebanon,
with elected members of parliament.

Among the separatist groups, the Kurdistan
Workers Party—active in Turkey—is banned, but
not the KDP or PUK, which are Kurdish organizations active in Iraq. Among opposition groups,

*Limitations of
American definition*

*The term's original
meaning*

Its history

*The difficulty of
making laws against
terrorism*

the Iranian People's Mujahedeen is banned, but not its Iraqi equivalent, the INC, which happens to be financed by the United States.

Issuing such a list does at least highlight the anomalies and inconsistencies behind anti-terrorism laws. It also points toward a simpler—and perhaps more honest—definition: terrorism is violence committed by those we disapprove of.

*This author's
stipulated definition*

■ Analysis

In the United States, terrorism has received unprecedented attention since the tragic events of September 11, 2001. You may have been surprised to learn that Whitaker's essay was written in May of that year, before planes crashing into the World Trade Center, the Pentagon, and a field in Pennsylvania forever gave the term new meaning for Americans. Just as the problem of terrorism has not yet been solved, however, the problem of defining terrorism remains unsolved as well. It is still true that "no one definition of terrorism has gained universal acceptance."

The essay starts on an unusual note: "Decide for yourself whether to believe this," referring to the low number of cases of international terrorism reported in the Middle East for 2000. That statement suggests that readers should approach the numbers with skepticism. Although the specific numbers cited in the essay are at first attributed only to "a new report," Whitaker goes on to indicate that his statistical support comes from the U.S. State Department. He acknowledges that "a lot of painstaking effort" went into counting the instances of terrorism, but goes on to declare the numbers "fundamentally meaningless" because of the lack of an agreed-upon definition of the term.

In paragraphs 6 and 7, Whitaker provides the State Department's definitions of terrorism and international terrorism. He then goes on to use a combination of types of support to back up his claim, as is common in writing an extended definition. In paragraphs 8, 10, and 14, he introduces three characteristics of terrorism—that it is politically motivated, that it "is calculated to terrorize the public or a particular section of it," and that its targets must be random. Throughout the body of the essay, he includes examples to illustrate his key points. In paragraph 15, Whitaker employs another technique used often in extended definition: He tells what terrorism is not.

The last third of the essay deals in part with unanswered questions and the limitations of the State Department's definition, illustrating the complications involved in defining terrorism and in passing laws against it.

Only at the end does Whitaker stipulate his own definition of terrorism. He is not providing a technical definition or one that he believes will gain universal acceptance. What he offers is his honest assessment of what Americans really perceive terrorism to be: "violence committed by those we disapprove of."

Race by the Numbers

ORLANDO PATTERSON

In recent weeks, reporting and commentary that misinterpret early census results have been persistently misinforming the nation about its ethnic and racial composition. The misinformation is dangerous, since it fuels fears of decline and displacement among some whites, anxieties that are not only divisive but groundless. The Center for Immigration Studies, for example, a think tank in Washington, recently warned that by the middle of the century non-Hispanic whites will cease to be a majority and that "each group in the new minority-majority country has longstanding grievances against whites."

Many articles have echoed the view that whites are fast becoming a minority in many areas of the country, largely because of the growth of the Hispanic population. The *New York Times* reported that seventy-one of the top 100 cities had lost white residents and made clear only in the third paragraph of the article that it is really "non-Hispanic whites" who are now a minority in these cities. Similarly, the *Miami Herald* reported that 20 cities and unincorporated communities in Miami-Dade county "went from majority to minority white, non-Hispanic." Left without commentary was the fact that the total white population—including Hispanic whites—of Miami, for example, is actually a shade under 70 percent.

These articles and too many others have failed to take account of the fact that nearly half of the Hispanic population is white in every social sense of this term; 48 percent of so-called Hispanics classified themselves as solely white, giving only one race to the census taker. Although all reports routinely note that "Hispanics can be of any race," they almost always go on to neglect this critical fact, treating Hispanics as if they were, in fact, a sociological race comparable to "whites" and "blacks."

Orlando Patterson is a professor of sociology at Harvard and the author of *Rituals of Blood* (1998), the second volume of a trilogy on race relations, as well as *Slavery and Social Death: A Comparative Study* (2007). This article appeared in the *New York Times* on May 8, 2001.

In any case, the suggestion that the white population of America is fast on the way to becoming a minority is a gross distortion. Even if we view only the non-Hispanic white population, whites remain a robust 69.1 percent of the total population of the nation. If we include Hispanic whites, as we should, whites constitute 75.14 percent of the total population, down by only 5 percent from the 1990 census. And this does not take account of the 6.8 million people who identified in the census with "two or more races," 80 percent of whom listed white as one of these races.

Even with the most liberal of assumptions, there is no possibility that   5
whites will become a minority in this nation in this century. The most recent census projections indicate that whites will constitute 74.8 percent of the total population in 2050, and that non-Hispanic whites will still be 52.8 percent of the total. And when we make certain realistic sociological assumptions about which groups the future progeny of Hispanic whites, mixed couples, and descendants of people now acknowledging two or more races are likely to identify with, there is every reason to believe that the non-Hispanic white population will remain a substantial majority—and possibly even grow as a portion of the population.

Recent studies indicate that second-generation Hispanic whites are intermarrying and assimilating mainstream language and cultural patterns at a faster rate than second-generation European migrants of the late nineteenth and early twentieth centuries.

The misleading reports of white proportional decline are likely not only to sustain the racist fears of white supremacist groups but also to affect the views of ordinary white, nonextremist Americans. A false assumption that whites are becoming a minority in the nation their ancestors conquered and developed may be adding to the deep resentment of poor or struggling whites toward affirmative action and other policies aimed at righting the wrongs of discrimination.

How do we account for this persistent pattern of misinformation? Apart from the intellectually lazy journalistic tendency to overemphasize race, two influences are playing into the discussion.

One is the policy of the Census Bureau itself. Though on the one hand, the census has taken the progressive step of allowing citizens to classify themselves in as many racial ways as they wish, breaking up the traditional notion of races as immutable categories, on the other hand it is up to its age-old mischief of making and unmaking racial groups. As it makes a new social category out of the sociologically meaningless collection of peoples from Latin America and Spain, it is quietly abetting the process of demoting and removing white Hispanics from the "true" white race—native-born non-Hispanic whites.

There is a long history of such reclassification by federal agencies. In the   10
early decades of the twentieth century, the Irish, Italians, and Jews were

classified as separate races by the federal immigration office, and the practice was discontinued only after long and vehement protests from Jewish leaders. In 1930 Mexicans were classified as a separate race by the Census Bureau—which reclassified them as white in 1940, after protests. Between then and the 1960s, people from Latin America were routinely classified as whites; then, when vast numbers of poor immigrants began coming from Latin America, the Hispanic category emerged.

The first stage of racial classification, now nearly successfully completed for Hispanics, is naming and nailing them all together while disingenuously admitting that they can be "of any race." Next, the repeated naming and sociological classification of different groups under a single category inevitably leads to the gradual perception and reconstruction of the group as another race. Much the same process of racialization is taking place with that other enormous sociological nongroup, Asian Americans.

The other influence on perceptions of who is "white" originates among the so-called Hispanics. For political and economic reasons, including the benefits of affirmative action programs, the leadership of many Hispanic groups pursues a liberal, coalition-based agenda with African Americans and presses hard for a separate, unified Latino classification. This strategy is highly influential even though nearly half of Hispanics consider themselves white.

For African Americans, the nation's major disadvantaged minority, these tendencies are problematic, although African American leaders are too shortsighted to notice. Latino coalition strategies, by vastly increasing the number of people entitled to affirmative action, have been a major factor in the loss of political support for it. And any fear of a "white" group that it might lose status tends to reinforce stigmatization of those Americans who will never be "white."

In this volatile transitional situation, where the best and worst are equally possible in our racial relations and attitudes, the very worst thing that journalists, analysts and commentators can do is to misinform the white majority that it is losing its majority status—something that recent surveys indicate it is already all too inclined to believe. We should stop obsessing on race in interpreting the census results. But if we must compulsively racialize the data, let's at least keep the facts straight and the interpretations honest.

READING AND DISCUSSION QUESTIONS

1. Where does Patterson state his claim?
2. What subtitles can you provide for the different parts of his argument? The topic sentences in several paragraphs offer clues to the organization.
3. According to Patterson, how is the matter of definition relevant to statistics about race?

4. Patterson's claim is strongly supported by statistics, history, and political analysis. Do you think these different kinds of support are equally persuasive? Which one is most susceptible to challenge? Why?

5. What is Patterson's objection to the definitions of *Hispanic* and *non-Hispanic* that are published by the Census Bureau and other agencies?

WRITING SUGGESTIONS

6. Narrate an experience you have had in which you felt you were either aided or hindered by the fact that you were defined as a member of a specific group. It could be a group such as those defined by gender, race, religious affiliation, or membership on a team or in a club.

7. Would adoption at the state level of a policy prohibiting classifying people by race, color, ethnicity, or national origin be beneficial or pernicious for the individual and for society? In other words, what is good or bad about classifying people?

8. Find a subject in which definition is critical to how statistics are interpreted and which can be argued successfully in a 750- to 1,000-word paper. Your essay should provide proof for a claim. (Patterson uses numbers to prove that whites need not fear that their numbers are declining.) Other subjects that depend on statistical support can be found throughout this book.

Family a Symbol of Love and Life, but Not Politics

ERIC ZORN

*F*amily is one of our loveliest words. It speaks of a warm, enveloping, comforting, inspiring connection—a love relationship, a commitment, a safe harbor, a common enterprise.

Sometimes, sure, it's a messy and maddening entanglement. But even when it's imperfect, family is the foundation of identity and the cornerstone of success.

To many people—people of all faiths, orientations, and political beliefs—"family" is the word that expresses that which they hold most dear.

Not money. Not possessions. Not fame. Not career. Not country. Not friendship. Not romance. Not even freedom.

Eric Zorn is a columnist for the *Chicago Tribune*, where this essay was first published on May 23, 2004, and coauthor of *Murder of Innocence* (1990).

Family. 5

So it's time we took it back.

Sorry, Family PAC and Illinois Family Institute.

You, too, Focus on the Family, Family Research Council, Family Foundation, Pro-Family Network, American Family Association, and Culture and Family Institute.

Set that word down and back away slowly. It belongs to all of us.

You and other conservative organizations have monopolized it for 10 too long, turned it into shorthand for a social and political outlook that excludes rather than includes, and hectors those who don't, can't, or won't conform to your notions of morality.

"Family values" has come to mean the promotion of abstinence-only sex education, religion in the public sphere, education vouchers, traditional gender roles, and censorship. It's come to mean opposition to abortion rights and, particularly these days, resistance to the extension of full civil rights to gays and lesbians.

In covering the landmark beginning of legal gay marriages in Massachusetts last week, virtually every news organization featured the fulminations of officials from the Massachusetts Family Institute ("The piece of paper that says 'marriage' has been redefined and devalued!"), while Peter LaBarbera, executive director of the Illinois Family Institute ("A man marrying another man is a far cry from Rosa Parks!"), has become the go-to guy for local journalists seeking quotes from opponents of gay marriage.

The irony is that gay weddings mark an endorsement of family — of the power of that formal and lasting bond.

When two people get married, they are saying to society, "Yes! We believe in the fundamental importance of this institution in building and maintaining family ties. We want to join it and affirm that belief to the world."

And when a culture expands its definition of marriage to include the 15 expressions of lifelong commitment between two people of the same sex, it strengthens families by advancing the acceptance and tolerance of gay people.

Not every parent is as accepting of his gay child as Chicago Alderman Richard Mell, whose personal and political support for his daughter, who is a lesbian, has become a local legend. But the more our society loses its judgmental attitude about who loves whom and what sorts of unions are most normal, the closer we get to the day when extended families no longer are ripped apart by homosexuality.

I could argue that strengthening families is why we need to provide quality day care for working parents, why we need to work hard to maintain strict government neutrality in matters of faith, and why we should offer nonideological sex education to children and reproductive choice to women.

I could make the case that it reflects good family values to shift more of the tax burden to the rich, to support stem cell medical research and universal health care, to devote our energies to boosting public education, and to protect our natural environment against industrial polluters.

I could, but I won't.

"Family" is too important to too many of us to drag its name through 20 the muck of our bitter sociopolitical debates, let alone to yield it to one side or the other in the culture wars.

No one owns it. The left doesn't own peace and compassion, the right doesn't own the flag or the family.

The word "family" resonates profoundly in all of us—married, single, gay, straight, adopted, "biological," living alone or in crowded households bursting with the exuberant chaos of children. To have family, to be family with others, is to be fully human.

Mom always taught me to share. So, shall we?

READING AND DISCUSSION QUESTIONS

1. Where does Zorn most directly define the word *family*?
2. What does he mean when he says that we need to take family back? From whom?
3. How has the definition of the word *family* been politicized?
4. How do gay marriages expand the definition of family, according to Zorn?
5. What strategy is Zorn using when he tells his readers what he could argue, but won't?
6. What claim is Zorn supporting in the essay?

WRITING SUGGESTIONS

7. Even if you do not support same-sex marriage, do you believe that the definition of marriage is changing? Explain.
8. Explain whether or not you agree with this statement by Zorn: "And when a culture expands its definition of marriage to include the expressions of lifelong commitment between two people of the same sex, it strengthens families by advancing the acceptance and tolerance of gay people."

Don't Torture English to Soft-Pedal Abuse

GEOFFREY NUNBERG

"Torture is torture is torture," Secretary of State Colin Powell said this week in an interview on *Fox News Sunday* with Chris Wallace.

That depends on what papers you read. The media in France, Italy, and Germany have been routinely using the word "torture" in the headings of their stories on the abuses in the Abu Ghraib prison.[1] And so have the British papers, not just the left-wing *Guardian* ("Torture at Abu Ghraib") but the right-wing *Express* ("Outrage at U.S. Torture of Prisoners") and Rupert Murdoch's *Times* ("Inside Baghdad's Torture Jail").

But the American press has been more circumspect, sticking with vaguer terms such as "abuse" and "mistreatment." In that, they may have been taking a cue from Defense Secretary Donald Rumsfeld. Asked about torture in the prison, he said, "What has been charged so far is abuse, which is different from torture. I'm not going to address the 'torture' word."

Some on the right have depicted the abuses even more mildly than that. In an opinion piece in the Los Angeles *Times*, Midge Decter called the treatment of detainees a "nasty hazing." Rush Limbaugh said it was "no different than what happens at the Skull and Bones initiation." On a San Francisco radio station, shock jocks were describing the prison as "Abu Grab-Ass" and talking about the treatment in a ribald way that made it sound like *Animal House III — Bluto Bonks Baghdad.*

Some American media have avoided "the 'torture' word" because 5 they want to play down the abuse of prisoners. Others are nervous about provoking attacks from the moral equivalence police: "Are you suggesting we're as bad as they are?"

But to a lot of Americans, *torture* and *torturer* don't seem quite the right words for the scenes in those photos. Torture may be familiar in the modern world, but it's also remote; we only see it up close in the movies. *Torture* suggests an aestheticized ritual. It doesn't seem odd that the torture scenes in *Battle of Algiers* should have a Bach chorale in the background.

---

[1] In April 2004, news broke in *The New Yorker* and on *60 Minutes* that presented in a particularly bad light a handful of American soldiers on duty at the Abu Ghraib prison in Iraq. In photos on the Internet, which were shown repeatedly on televised news and in print around the world, the young men and women were shown standing by smiling while forcing Iraqi detainees at the prison to strike a series of humiliating poses. Some of the American soldiers are now in prison themselves as a result of their actions.

Geoffrey Nunberg is a consulting professor in Stanford University's Department of Linguistics, the author of the books *Going Nucular* (2004) and *Talking Right* (2007), and a featured radio commentator. This essay was adapted from a piece he did on NPR's *Fresh Air*, which appeared in *Newsday* in May 2004.

In the movies, the torturer's cruelty is ironically counterpoised by a cosmopolitan and often effete manner—Laurence Olivier in *Marathon Man*, Gert Frobe in *Goldfinger*, or the Mohammed Khan character in *Lives of a Bengal Lancer* telling Gary Cooper, "We have ways of making men talk."

There are no middle-class middle-American torturers in our gallery, much less torturers with the pudding faces of those GIs who could have been working at McDonald's a year ago. And the humiliations they were inflicting didn't seem to have much in common with the rituals of pain and submission that *torture* brings to mind. The GIs went down another road, even if it fell off just as sharply.

That's what creates the sense of incongruity we feel when we see those photos. Those may have been far from Delta House high jinks, but you wouldn't know it from the clowning poses the GIs were striking.

True, "hazing" is a shamefully dishonest name for this. Leaving aside   10 the severity of the abuses, the prisoners weren't in a position to resign from the club, nor were they about to be given membership pins when pledge week was over. You may as well say that the Los Angeles police were hazing Rodney King.

But what went on in Abu Ghraib has at least this in common with hazing: It's the sort of thing that any adolescent with a normal libido might be capable of—or worse, if the circumstances permit. As the Stanford psychologist Phil Zimbardo showed in a famous experiment more than thirty years ago, it doesn't take a lot to transform a group of well-mannered college students into sadistic prison guards, provided someone in authority seems to be giving them the nod.

Granted, what the Americans did in Abu Ghraib isn't remotely comparable to what went on there during Saddam Hussein's regime.

But it was torture, not just by the definitions of the Geneva Conventions, but by any ordinary standards of decency. Torture is torture is torture, as Secretary Powell put it—it isn't a place to be drawing fine semantic distinctions.

And it would be a good thing to acknowledge that "torture" is not quite as exotic an activity as the movies make it out to be. Looking at the unsettlingly familiar faces of the American soldiers in the Abu Ghraib photos, you realize that what can be most disturbing isn't the brutality that is inhuman so much as the brutality that is all too.

READING AND DISCUSSION QUESTIONS

1. Nunberg argues that the media control, to a certain extent at least, how the public perceive events. Besides the treatment of prisoners at Abu Ghraib prison in Iraq, how have the media exerted control over public perceptions?

2. What is Nunberg referring to when he makes this statement: "Others are nervous about provoking attacks from the moral equivalence police: 'Are you suggesting we're as bad as they are?'"

3. What is it that creates the sense of incongruity in the pictures from Abu Ghraib to which Nunberg refers?

4. In what sense was what went on at Abu Ghraib similar to hazing, although Nunberg calls hazing "a shamefully dishonest name for this"?

5. Explain what you believe Nunberg means by his last sentence.

WRITING SUGGESTIONS

6. Choose an event other than the Abu Ghraib scandal that was widely publicized and explain to what extent you believe the media controlled public perceptions of the event.

7. Write an essay in which you explain how governments sometimes hide the full truth behind euphemisms and other careful word choices. You may want to compare your ideas about language use with those expressed by George Orwell in his classic 1946 essay "Politics and the English Language."

DEBATE: Is the definition of marriage changing?

Gay Marriage Shows Why We Need to Separate Church and State

HOWARD MOODY

If members of the church that I served for more than three decades were told I would be writing an article in defense of marriage, they wouldn't believe it. My reputation was that when people came to me for counsel about getting married, I tried to talk them out of it. More about that later.

We are now in the midst of a national debate on the nature of marriage, and it promises to be as emotional and polemical as the issues of abortion and homosexuality have been over the past century. What all these debates have in common is that they involved both the laws of the state and the theology of the church. The purpose of this writing is to suggest that the gay-marriage debate is less about the legitimacy of the loving relationship of a same-sex couple than about the relationship of church and state and how they define marriage.

In Western civilization, the faith and beliefs of Christendom played a major role in shaping the laws regarding social relations and moral behavior. Having been nurtured in the Christian faith from childhood and having served a lifetime as an ordained Baptist minister, I feel obligated

---

Reverend Howard Moody is minister emeritus of Judson Memorial Church in New York City. This article was published in July 2004 in the *Nation*.

first to address the religious controversy concerning the nature of marriage. If we look at the history of religious institutions regarding marriage we will find not much unanimity but amazing diversity—it is really a mixed bag. Those who base their position on "tradition" or "what the Bible says" will find anything but clarity. It depends on which "tradition" in what age reading from whose holy scriptures.

In the early tradition of the Jewish people, there were multiple wives and not all of them equal. Remember the story of Abraham's wives, Sara and Hagar. Sara couldn't get pregnant, so Hagar presented Abraham with a son. When Sara got angry with Hagar, she forced Abraham to send Hagar and her son Ishmael into the wilderness. In case Christians feel superior about their "tradition" of marriage, I would remind them that their scriptural basis is not as clear about marriage as we might hope. We have Saint Paul's conflicting and condescending words about the institution: "It's better not to marry." Karl Barth called this passage the Magna Carta of the single person. (Maybe we should have taken Saint Paul's advice more seriously. It might have prevented an earlier generation of parents from harassing, cajoling, and prodding our young until they were married.) In certain religious branches, the church doesn't recognize the licensed legality of marriage but requires that persons meet certain religious qualifications before the marriage is recognized by the church. For members of the Roman Catholic Church, a "legal divorce" and the right to remarry may not be recognized unless the first marriage has been declared null and void by a decree of the church. It is clear that there is no single religious view of marriage and that history has witnessed some monumental changes in the way "husband and wife" are seen in the relationship of marriage.

In my faith-based understanding, if freedom of choice means any- 5 thing to individuals (male or female), it means they have several options. They can be single and celibate without being thought of as strange or psychologically unbalanced. They can be single and sexually active without being labeled loose or immoral. Women can be single with child without being thought of as unfit or inadequate. If these choices had been real options, the divorce rate may never have reached nearly 50 percent.

The other, equally significant choice for people to make is that of lifetime commitment to each other and to seal that desire in the vows of a wedding ceremony. That understanding of marriage came out of my community of faith. In my years of ministry I ran a tight ship in regard to the performance of weddings. It wasn't because I didn't believe in marriage (I've been married for sixty years and have two wonderful offspring) but rather my unease about the way marriage was used to force people to marry so they wouldn't be "living in sin."

The failure of the institution can be seen in divorce statistics. I wanted people to know how challenging the promise of those vows was and not to feel this was something they had to do. My first question in premarital counseling was, "Why do you want to get married and spoil a beautiful friendship?" That question often elicited a thoughtful and emotional answer. Though I was miserly in the number of weddings I performed, I always made exceptions when there were couples who had difficulty finding clergy who would officiate. Their difficulty was because they weren't of the same religion, or they had made marital mistakes, or what they couldn't believe. Most of them were "ecclesiastical outlaws," barred from certain sacraments in the church of their choice.

The church I served had a number of gay and lesbian couples who had been together for many years, but none of them had asked for public weddings or blessings on their relationship. (There was one commitment ceremony for a gay couple at the end of my tenure.) It was as though they didn't need a piece of paper or a ritual to symbolize their lifelong commitment. They knew if they wanted a religious ceremony, their ministers would officiate and our religious community would joyfully witness.

It was my hope that since the institution of marriage had been used to exclude and demean members of the homosexual community, our church, which was open and affirming, would create with gays and lesbians a new kind of ceremony. It would be an occasion that symbolized, between two people of the same gender, a covenant of intimacy of two people to journey together, breaking new ground in human relationships—an alternative to marriage as we have known it.

However, I can understand why homosexuals want "to be married" 10 in the old-fashioned "heterosexual way." After all, most gays and lesbians were born of married parents, raised in a family of siblings; many were nourished in churches and synagogues, taught about a living God before Whom all Her creatures were equally loved. Why wouldn't they conceive their loving relationships in terms of marriage and family and desire that they be confirmed and understood as such? It follows that if these gays and lesbians see their relationship as faith-based, they would want a religious ceremony that seals their intentions to become lifelong partners, lovers and friends, that they would want to be "married."

Even though most religious denominations deny this ceremony to homosexual couples, more and more clergy are, silently and publicly, officiating at religious rituals in which gays and lesbians declare their vows before God and a faith community. One Catholic priest who defied his church's ban said: "We can bless a dog, we can bless a boat, but we can't say a prayer over two people who love each other. You don't have to call it marriage, you can call it a deep and abiding friendship, but you can bless it."

We have the right to engage in "religious disobedience" to the regulations of the judicatory that granted us the privilege to officiate at wedding ceremonies, and suffer the consequences. However, when it comes to civil law, it is my contention that the church and its clergy are on much shakier ground in defying the law.

In order to fully understand the conflict that has arisen in this debate over the nature of marriage, it is important to understand the difference between the religious definition of marriage and the state's secular and civil definition. The government's interest is in a legal definition of marriage—a social and voluntary contract between a man and woman in order to protect money, property, and children. Marriage is a civil union without benefit of clergy or religious definition. The state is not interested in why two people are "tying the knot," whether it's to gain money, secure a dynasty, or raise children. It may be hard for those of us who have a religious or romantic view of marriage to realize that loveless marriages are not that rare. Before the Pill, pregnancy was a frequent motive for getting married. The state doesn't care what the commitment of two people is, whether it's for life or as long as both of you love, whether it's sexually monogamous or an open marriage. There is nothing spiritual, mystical, or romantic about the state's license to marry—it's a legal contract.

Thus, George W. Bush is right when he says that "marriage is a sacred institution" when speaking as a Christian, as a member of his Methodist church. But as president of the United States and leader of all Americans, believers and unbelievers, he is wrong. What will surface in this debate as litigation and court decisions multiply is the history of the conflict between the church and the state in defining the nature of marriage. That history will become significant as we move toward a decision on who may be married.

After Christianity became the state religion of the Roman empire in A.D. 325, the church maintained absolute control over the regulation of marriage for some 1,000 years. Beginning in the sixteenth century, English kings (especially Henry VIII, who found the inability to get rid of a wife extremely oppressive) and other monarchs in Europe began to wrest control from the church over marital regulations. Ever since, kings, presidents, and rulers of all kinds have seen how important the control of marriage is to the regulation of social order. In this nation, the government has always been in charge of marriage.

That is why it was not a San Francisco mayor licensing same-sex couples that really threatened the president's religious understanding of marriage but rather the Supreme Judicial Court of Massachusetts, declaring marriage between same-sex couples a constitutional right, that demanded a call for constitutional amendment. I didn't understand how important that was until I read an op-ed piece in the *Boston Globe* by Peter Gomes, professor of Christian morals and the minister of Memorial Church at Harvard University, that reminds us of a seminal piece of our history:

> The Dutch made civil marriage the law of the land in 1590, and the first marriage in New England, that of Edward Winslow to the widow Susannah White, was performed on May 12, 1621, in Plymouth by Governor William Bradford, in exercise of his office as magistrate.

There would be no clergyman in Plymouth until the arrival of the Reverend Ralph Smith in 1629, but even then marriage would continue to be a civil affair, as these first Puritans opposed the English custom of clerical marriage as unscriptural. Not until 1692, when Plymouth Colony was merged into that of Massachusetts Bay, were the clergy authorized by the new province to solemnize marriages. To this day in the Commonwealth the clergy, including those of the archdiocese, solemnize marriage legally as agents of the Commonwealth and by its civil authority. Chapter 207 of the General Laws of Massachusetts tells us who may perform such ceremonies.

Now even though it is the civil authority of the state that defines the rights and responsibilities of marriage and therefore who can be married, the state is no more infallible than the church in its judgments. It wasn't until the mid-twentieth century that the Supreme Court declared anti-miscegenation laws unconstitutional. Even after that decision, many mainline churches, where I started my ministry, unofficially discouraged interracial marriages, and many of my colleagues were forbidden to perform such weddings.

The civil law view of marriage has as much historical diversity as the church's own experience because, in part, the church continued to influence the civil law. Although it was the Bible that made "the husband the head of his wife," it was common law that "turned the married pair legally into one person—the husband," as Nancy Cott documents in her book *Public Vows: A History of Marriage and the Nation* (an indispensable resource for anyone seeking to understand the changing nature of marriage in the nation's history). She suggests that "the legal doctrine of marital unity was called coverture . . . [which] meant that the wife could not use legal avenues such as suits or contracts, own assets, or execute legal documents without her husband's collaboration." This view of the wife would not hold water in any court in the land today.

As a matter of fact, even in the religious understanding of President Bush and his followers, allowing same-sex couples the right to marry seems a logical conclusion. If marriage is "the most fundamental institution of civilization" and a major contributor to the social order in our society, why would anyone want to shut out homosexuals from the "glorious attributes" of this "sacred institution"? Obviously, the only reason one can discern is that the opponents believe that gay and lesbian people are not worthy of the benefits and spiritual blessings of "marriage."

At the heart of the controversy raging over same-sex marriage is the 20 religious and constitutional principle of the separation of church and state. All of us can probably agree that there was never a solid wall of separation, riddled as it is with breaches. The evidence of that is seen in the ambiguity of tax-free religious institutions, "in God we trust" printed on our money and "under God" in the Pledge of Allegiance to our country.

All of us clergy, who are granted permission by the state to officiate at legal marriage ceremonies, have already compromised the "solid wall" by signing the license issued by the state. I would like to believe that my authority to perform religious ceremonies does not come from the state but derives from the vows of ordination and my commitment to God. I refuse to repeat the words, "by the authority invested in me by the State of New York, I pronounce you husband and wife," but by signing the license, I've become the state's "handmaiden."

It seems fitting therefore that we religious folk should now seek to sharpen the difference between ecclesiastical law and civil law as we beseech the state to clarify who can be married by civil law. Further evidence that the issue of church and state is part of the gay-marriage controversy is that two Unitarian ministers have been arrested for solemnizing unions between same-sex couples when no state licenses were involved. Ecclesiastical law may punish those clergy who disobey marital regulations, but the state has no right to invade church practices and criminalize clergy under civil law. There should have been a noisy outcry from all churches, synagogues, and mosques at the government's outrageous contravention of the sacred principle of the "free exercise of religion."

I come from a long line of Protestants who believe in a "free church in a free state." In the issue before this nation, the civil law is the determinant of the regulation of marriage, regardless of our religious views, and the Supreme Court will finally decide what the principle of equality means in our Constitution in the third century of our life together as a people. It is likely that the Commonwealth of Massachusetts will probably lead the nation on this matter, as the State of New York led to the Supreme Court decision to allow women reproductive freedom.

So what is marriage? It depends on whom you ask, in what era, in what culture. Like all words or institutions, human definitions, whether religious or secular, change with time and history. When our beloved Constitution was written, blacks, Native Americans, and, to some extent, women were quasi-human beings with no rights or privileges, but today they are recognized as persons with full citizenship rights. The definition of marriage has been changing over the centuries in this nation, and it will change yet again as homosexuals are seen as ordinary human beings.

In time, and I believe that time is now, we Americans will see that all the fears foisted on us by religious zealots were not real. Heterosexual marriage will still flourish with its statistical failures. The only difference will be that some homosexual couples will join them and probably account for about the same number of failed relationships. And we will discover that it did not matter whether the couples were joined in a religious ceremony or a secular and civil occasion for the statement of their intentions.

Will It Be Marriage or Civil Union?

JO ANN CITRON

This fall, while the right was still staggering from the U.S. Supreme Court's decision in *Lawrence v. Texas*, Massachusetts dealt conservatives another body blow when its highest court legalized same-sex marriage. In a 4–3 ruling authored by Chief Justice Margaret Marshall, the Supreme Judicial Court (SJC) held that denying marriage to homosexuals violates the Massachusetts Declaration of Rights, the state constitution. To remedy the violation, the court changed the common-law definition of civil marriage to eliminate its opposite-sex requirement and to compel the issuance of marriage licenses to qualified persons of the same sex. Civil marriage in Massachusetts now means "the voluntary union of two persons as spouses, to the exclusion of all others." The legislature, which was directed to "take such action as it may deem appropriate in light of this opinion," has been running for cover ever since.[1]

A friend recently asked me how important the Massachusetts decision is in the struggle to achieve marriage equality in the United States. I was struck, first of all, by the terms of the question because "marriage equality" is not the same as "marriage." The issue all along has been whether gays will get marriage or some equivalent formality that will make them equal to their heterosexual counterparts. There are those who say that civil union is marriage equality. It's what Vermont said and what many Massachusetts legislators are saying in their desperate search for an escape route from the SJC ruling. It's also what William Eskridge claimed in his 2002 book, *Equality Practice: Civil Union and the Future of Gay Rights*, where he argues that, while there is no principled basis for withholding marriage from gays and lesbians, the gay community should bow to the political will of the majority and move slowly, accepting the equality of civil union now and pressing for marriage later when it becomes more palatable to the majority. Eskridge views *Baker v. State*, the Vermont civil union decision, as the equivalent of *Brown v. Board of Education*, the 1954 landmark civil rights decision that opened the way to racial integration in this country. Marriage activist Evan Wolfson, on the other hand, views *Baker* as the gay rights version of *Plessy v. Ferguson*, the railway carriage case that authorized "separate but equal" status for disfavored minorities.

---

[1] *Goodridge v. Department of Public Health.*

Jo Ann Citron practices alternate family and civil rights law with the firm Altman & Citron and is a member of the Women's Studies Department at Wellesley College. The article was published in the *Gay and Lesbian Review Worldwide* in March–April 2004.

This essay is being written during the 180-day waiting period following the issuance of the decision, a period of either genuine confusion or deliberate obfuscation, depending on the degree of cynicism with which you view the political process. It might be useful at this point to summarize what the court said and how the legislature has responded. The court began by reminding everyone that the Massachusetts marriage statute is a licensing law. Because marriage has always been understood to mean the union of a man and a woman, the statute cannot be construed to authorize issuing a license to two people of the same sex. But to bar gay couples from all the benefits, protections, and obligations that accompany marriage violates the Massachusetts constitution, which means that the current marriage licensing law is unconstitutional. The remedy the court fashioned was to change the common law definition of civil marriage to eliminate its opposite-sex requirement, thereby removing the bar that excludes gay couples from obtaining marriage licenses.

Rather than declare that cities and towns must immediately begin to issue marriage licenses to gays, which would have created chaos, the court granted the legislature 180 days to revise state statutes so as to bring them into line with its ruling and to clean up a complicated domestic relations regulatory scheme that refers to husbands and wives. The court reminded the legislature that it retains "broad discretion to regulate marriage." This means that the Legislature can continue to impose certain restrictions upon persons who wish to marry. The legislature may refuse to authorize granting a marriage license to persons under a certain age, or to siblings, or to a parent and child. It may require a blood test or a birth certificate, or that applicants turn around three times and face north, or anything else that would be constitutional. But, as I read the decision, the legislature may not refuse to grant a license to otherwise qualified gay couples.

The SJC was perfectly clear in stating that the remedy for the consti- 5 tutional violation was the reformulation of the definition of civil marriage. Yet many legislators, together with the current attorney general, want to take a different view of the matter. They have seized upon the "protections, benefits, and obligations" language in the opinion in the hope that, by providing the benefits that marriage yields in our society, they can avoid providing marriage itself. The legislature has asked the SJC to render an advisory opinion about a civil union bill, and the SJC has invited interested parties to submit briefs. Meanwhile, the Massachusetts constitutional convention is scheduled to meet on February 11, 2004, to vote on a Defense of Marriage Act or DOMA that, in its present form, would not only prevent gay marriage but would also outlaw domestic partner benefits. If the legislature passes the DOMA in a second convention, the measure would appear on the ballot in November of 2006 and voters could, by a simple majority, amend the state constitution to make gay marriage, civil union, and domestic partnerships illegal. The political reality is that such a DOMA will probably not garner the necessary votes either in the legislature or among voters; however, a simple DOMA limiting itself to marriage is more likely to succeed, especially in the face of the SJC decision, which presents the right with what it would call a "clear and present danger." This means that gay marriage could become legal in Massachusetts on May 18, 2004, via the SJC decision and illegal in Massachusetts on November 14, 2006, via a voter referendum. No one knows what will happen to gay couples who marry in the interim. Let the courts sort through that one!

Massachusetts has a good track record when it comes to gay families: It permits second-parent adoption; it allows two women to appear as "parent" on a child's birth certificate; it protects the relationship between a child and her nonbiological parent. At the very least, *Goodridge* is going to yield "marriage equality" in some form of civil union. The problem, of course, is that there is no such thing as "marriage equality" for anyone who files federal income tax returns, bequeaths an estate, or travels outside of Massachusetts. When it comes to federal benefits or the tax-free transfer of marital property or the ability to have another state recognize your Massachusetts relationship, marriage is the only status that will do. This is why some are downplaying the SJC decision, pointing out that even if people are able to marry in Massachusetts, their status will not be recognized by the federal government or by any other state with a DOMA. In that respect, marriage is indeed no different from civil union. In fact, it might even be worse for a while. We're beginning to see judges in some states accept the validity of a Vermont civil union. Even in states with a DOMA, it will be possible to find a judge who would give full faith and credit to a civil union because most DOMA laws have nothing to say about civil unions. Not so with marriage. For the time being, a Massachusetts marriage will be even less portable than a Vermont civil union.

But let there be no mistake: Whatever happens in Massachusetts is absolutely critical to how the gay marriage question will be answered in the rest of the United States. What happens here is even more important than what happened in Vermont. Here's why. The next marriage case with a reasonable likelihood of success is working its way through the courts in New Jersey, a state with a history of progressive court decisions. New Jersey will be looking very carefully at the way Vermont and Massachusetts have addressed the marriage question. If the Massachusetts SJC ratifies its decision and mandates the issuance of marriage licenses, New Jersey will look at its predecessor states and see two alternative models, marriage and civil union. New Jersey will choose one or the other. But the SJC could fail to confirm its marriage decision and approve instead some form of civil union. Coupled with the Vermont ruling, this will create a critical mass in favor of civil union, an outcome that will make it far more likely that New Jersey will opt for civil union over marriage. After that, the rest of the states will almost certainly fall into line with civil unions, and that will spell the end of gay marriage, probably forever.

Ironically, it may also mean the end of marriage in its present form, the one that the right is working so hard to preserve. Conservatives Andrew Sullivan and David Brooks have argued that the best way to protect marriage would be to open it to anyone who wants to vow fidelity and is willing to forego an easy exit from a supposedly permanent relationship. Marriage is, after all, a conservative institution, and persons who enter it with the blessing of the state may not leave it without the state's permission. Already, as a result of the marriage cases and their surrounding discourse, the very term "marriage" is being qualified. We now speak of "civil marriage" to distinguish it from the religious ceremonies that are but one of its aspects. Insofar as material benefits are concerned, marriage is a civil institution. Those material benefits can attach just as easily to any civil institution the state cares to identify. This is, after all, the point of wanting to offer gays something called "union" rather than something called "marriage." Nothing but prejudice prevents state and federal governments from offering to partners in a civil union the identical benefits, protections, and obligations that the state now offers to spouses.

William Eskridge is wrong in thinking that civil union is a step on the path towards marriage. Civil union and marriage are not sequential; they are alternatives to one another. There is no reason to think that the country will permit civil union now and confer marriage later. In fact, the reality is likely to be quite the reverse. Because of equal protection considerations, the civil union alternative will have to be available to straights as well as gays. And if my analysis is correct, it will become more widely available to everyone in the coming years. At the moment, there is little incentive for marriage-eligible couples to elect a civil union. But this will change.

It is not difficult to imagine a tacit compromise in which the right is 10 allowed to maintain its stranglehold on marriage in exchange for allowing the material benefits now associated with it to break free and accompany civil union. This is another reason why the Massachusetts decision in favor of marriage is strategically important. As long as even a single state has legalized marriage, civil union becomes more attractive to the right. And the gay community can leverage those few gay marriage licenses into a demand that marriage benefits attach to civil unions.

In my view, this would be a good outcome. I say this as someone who views marriage as a regressive institution that has never been good to women, that insidiously creates insiders and outsiders, and, most importantly, that violates the separation of church and state at the heart of our form of government. The state should not be in the business of attaching material benefits to a religious institution. The right to social security death benefits, the right to favorable tax treatment, the right to take your formalized relationship with you when you travel, should be detached from marriage altogether and should be awarded according to some other equitable system. To the extent that this becomes so, there will eventually be no material difference between the old form of marriage and the new form of civil unions. Traditional marriage will endure as a religious institution. Already there are hundreds of clergy willing to perform marriage ceremonies for gay congregants and thousands of gay couples who have participated in these ceremonies whose benefits are wholly spiritual. Over time, civil union and civil marriage will ultimately come to mean much the same thing. Whether the SJC ratifies its original position or abandons it, *Goodridge* brings us closer to a consensus around civil union. It is time for the gay community to turn its attention to winning for civil union all the rights, benefits, protections, and obligations of marriage. That is the truly revolutionary project.

DISCUSSION QUESTIONS

1. Why is definition a critical element in Moody's argument? Why is it a critical element in Citron's? Do the two of them agree on a definition of marriage?

2. What is Moody's attitude toward same-sex marriage? Why, in his opinion, do more serious problems arise when it comes to the laws of the state than the theology of the church?

3. Why does Moody believe that President Bush was wrong in saying, as president, that "marriage is a sacred institution"? Were you surprised by Moody's explanation of the history of marriage in the United States?

4. When Citron published her essay, the nation was awaiting Massachusetts's decision on the legality of same-sex marriages. What was her biggest fear about the future of the legal standing of same-sex relationships?

5. Analyze Citron's analogy between decisions regarding same-sex unions and two Supreme Court decisions regarding racial integration, *Plessy v. Ferguson* and *Brown v. Board of Education*.

6. What is the author's claim in each of the two essays?

ASSIGNMENTS FOR UNDERSTANDING DEFINITION

READING AND DISCUSSION QUESTIONS

1. Contrast the claims made by Jo Ann Citron in "Will It Be Marriage or Civil Union?" and Howard Moody in "Gay Marriage Shows Why We Need to Separate Church and State."

2. Contrast Citron's claim with that supported by Eric Zorn in "Family a Symbol of Love and Life, but Not Politics."

3. Use Orlando Patterson's "Race by the Numbers" as a starting point to discuss to what extent you believe you either are or are not defined by your racial identity.

WRITING ASSIGNMENTS

4. Using Geoffrey Nunberg's "Don't Torture English to Soft-Pedal Abuse" as a model, choose a term and explain in an essay of 500 words how its meaning has been manipulated for political purposes.

5. Explain in a brief essay to what extent you found Orlando Patterson's argument convincing and why.

6. Write about an important or widely used term whose meaning has changed since you first learned it. Such terms often come from the slang of particular groups: drug users, rock music fans, musicians, athletes, computer programmers, or software developers.

7. Define the differences between necessities, comforts, and luxuries. Consider how they have changed over time.

CHAPTER 6

Defending Claims

Claims, or propositions, represent answers to the question "What are you trying to prove?" Although they are the conclusions of your arguments, they often appear as thesis statements. Claims can be classified as *claims of fact, claims of value,* and *claims of policy.*

CLAIMS OF FACT

Claims of fact assert that a condition has existed, exists, or will exist and that their support consists of factual information   information such as statistics, examples, and testimony that most responsible observers assume can be verified.

Many facts are not matters for argument: Our own senses can confirm them, and other observers will agree about them. We can agree that a certain number of students were in the classroom at a particular time, that lions make a louder sound than kittens, and that apples are sweeter than potatoes.

We can also agree about information that most of us can rarely confirm for ourselves—information in reference books, such as atlases, almanacs, and telephone directories; data from scientific resources about the physical world; and happenings reported in the media. We can agree on the reliability of such information because we trust the observers who report it.

However, the factual map is constantly being redrawn by new data in such fields as history and science that cause us to reevaluate our conclusions. For example, the discovery of the Dead Sea Scrolls in 1947 revealed that some books of the Bible—Isaiah, for one—were far older than we had thought. Recent research has proven that cervical cancer is caused by a virus and that a vaccination given early enough can possibly prevent it.

In your conversations with other students you probably generate claims of fact every day, some of which can be verified without much effort, others of which are more difficult to substantiate.

CLAIM: Most of the students in this class come from towns within fifty miles of Boston.

To prove this the arguer would need only to ask the students in the class where they come from.

CLAIM: More students entering this fall had AP credit for one or more courses than in any past year.

To prove this claim, the arguer would have to have access to entering students' records from the time Advanced Placement was first accepted to the present.

CLAIM: The Red Sox will win the pennant this year.

This claim is different from the others because it is an opinion about what will happen in the future. But it can be verified (in the future) and is therefore classified as a claim of fact.

More complex factual claims about political and scientific matters remain controversial because proof on which all or most observers will agree is difficult or impossible to obtain.

CLAIM: Bilingual programs are less effective than English-only programs in preparing students for higher education.

CLAIM: The only life in the universe exists on this planet.

Not all claims are so neatly stated or make such unambiguous assertions. Because we recognize that there are exceptions to most generalizations, we often qualify our claims with words such as *generally, usually, probably,* and *as a rule.* It would not be true to state flatly, for example, "College graduates earn more than high school graduates." This statement is generally true, but we know that some high school graduates who are electricians or city bus drivers or sanitation workers earn more than college graduates who are schoolteachers or nurses or social workers. In making such a claim, therefore, the writer should qualify it with a word that limits the claim.

To support a claim of fact, the writer needs to produce sufficient and appropriate data—that is, examples, statistics, and testimony from reliable sources. Provided this requirement is met, the task of establishing a factual claim would seem to be relatively straightforward. But as you have probably already discovered in ordinary conversation, finding convincing support for factual claims can pose a number of problems. Whenever you try to establish a claim of fact, you will need to ask at least three questions about the material you plan to use: *What are sufficient and appropriate data? Who are the reliable authorities?* and *Have I made clear whether my statements are facts or inferences?*

■ Sufficient and Appropriate Data

The amount and kind of data for a particular argument depend on the importance and complexity of the subject. The more controversial the subject, the more facts and testimony you will need to supply. Consider the claim "The murder rate in New York City has decreased steadily over the last ten years." If you want to prove the truth of this claim, obviously you will have to provide a larger quantity of data than for a claim that says, "The number of students at Trenton High School increased 10 percent between 2005–2006 and 2006–2007." In examining your facts and opinions, an alert reader will want to know if they are accurate, current, and typical of other facts and opinions that you have not mentioned.

In arguments about more controversial issues, the reader will also look for testimony from more than one authority, although there may be cases where only one or two experts who have achieved a unique breakthrough in their field will be sufficient. These cases would probably occur most frequently in the physical sciences. The Nobel Prize winners James Watson and Francis Crick, who first discovered the structure of the DNA molecule, are an example of such experts. However, in the case of the so-called Hitler diaries that surfaced in 1983, at least a dozen experts—journalists, historians, bibliographers who could verify the age of the paper and the ink— were needed to establish that they were forgeries.

■ Reliable Authorities

Not all those who pronounce themselves experts are trustworthy. Your own experience has probably taught you that you cannot always believe the reports of an event by a single witness. The witness may be poorly trained to make accurate observations—about the size of a crowd, the speed of a vehicle, his distance from an object. Or his own physical conditions— illness, intoxication, disability—may prevent him from seeing or hearing or smelling accurately. The circumstances under which he observes the event—darkness, confusion, noise—may also impair his observation. In addition, the witness may be biased for or against the outcome of the event, as in a hotly contested baseball game, where the observer sees the play that he wants to see. You will find the problems associated with the biases of witnesses to be relevant to your work as a reader and writer of argumentative essays.

You will undoubtedly want to quote authors in some of your arguments. In most cases you will not be familiar with the authors. But there are guidelines for determining their reliability: the rank or title of the experts, the acceptance of their publications by other experts, their association with reputable universities, research centers, or think tanks. For example, for a paper on euthanasia, you might decide to quote from an article by Paul R. McHugh, the Henry Phipps Professor of Psychiatry at the Johns Hopkins University School of Medicine and psychiatrist in chief at the Johns Hopkins Hospital in Baltimore. For a paper on crime by youth groups, you might want to use material supplied by Elizabeth Glazer, chief of Crime Control Strategies in the U.S. Attorney's office for the Southern District of New York, where she previously served as chief of both the Organized Crime Unit and Violent Gang Unit. Most readers of your arguments would agree that these authors have impressive credentials in their fields.

What if several respectable sources are in conflict? What if the experts disagree? After a preliminary investigation of a controversial subject, you may decide that you have sufficient material to support your claim. But if you read further, you may discover that other material presented by equally qualified experts contradicts your original claim. In such circumstances you will find it impossible to make a definitive claim. (On pp. 213–27 in the treatment of support of a claim by evidence, you will find a more elaborate discussion of this vexing problem.)

■ Facts or Inferences

We have defined a fact as a statement that can be verified. An inference is "a statement about the unknown on the basis of the known."[1] The difference between facts and inferences is important to you as the writer of an argument because an inference is an *interpretation*, or an opinion reached after informed evaluation of evidence.

You have probably come across a statement such as the following in a newspaper or magazine: "Excessive television viewing has caused the steady decline in the reading ability of children and teenagers." Presented this way, the statement is clearly intended to be read as a factual claim that has been or can be proved. But it is an inference. The facts, which can be and have been verified, are (1) the reading ability of children and teenagers has declined and (2) the average child views television for six or more hours a day. (Whether this amount of time is "excessive" is also an opinion.) The cause-and-effect relation between the two facts is an interpretation of the investigator, who has examined both the reading scores and the amount of time spent in front of the television set and *inferred* that one is the cause of

---

[1]S. I. Hayakawa, *Language in Thought and Action* (New York: Harcourt, Brace, Jovanovich, 1978), p. 35.

the other. The causes of the decline in reading scores are probably more complex than the original statement indicates. Since we can seldom or never create laboratory conditions for testing the influence of television separate from other influences in the family and the community, any statement about the connection between reading scores and television viewing can only be a guess.

By definition, no inference can ever do more than suggest probabilities. Of course, some inferences are much more reliable than others and afford a high degree of probability. Almost all claims in science are based on inferences, interpretations of data on which most scientists agree. Paleontologists find a few ancient bones from which they make inferences about an animal that might have been alive millions of years ago. We can never be absolutely certain that the reconstruction of the dinosaur in the museum is an exact copy of the animal it is supposed to represent, but the probability is fairly high because no other interpretation works so well to explain all the observable data — the existence of the bones in a particular place, their age, their relation to other fossils, and their resemblance to the bones of existing animals with which the paleontologist is familiar.

Inferences are profoundly important, and most arguments could not proceed very far without them. But an inference is not a fact. The writer of an argument must make it clear when he or she offers an inference, an interpretation, or an opinion that it is not a fact.

Writer's Guide: Defending a Claim of Fact

Here are some guidelines that should help you to defend a factual claim. (We'll say more about support of factual claims in Chapter 7.)

1. Be sure that the claim — what you are trying to prove — is clearly stated, preferably at the beginning of your paper.

2. Define terms that may be controversial or ambiguous. For example, in trying to prove that "radicals" had captured the student government, you would have to define "radicals," distinguishing them from "liberals" or members of other ideological groups, so that your readers would understand exactly what you meant.

3. As far as possible, make sure that your evidence — facts and opinions, or interpretations of the facts — fulfills the appropriate criteria. The data should be sufficient, accurate, recent, typical; the authorities should be reliable.

4. Make clear when conclusions about the data are inferences or interpretations, not facts. For example, you should not write, "The series of lectures

> titled Modern Architecture, sponsored by our fraternity, was poorly attended because the students at this college aren't interested in discussions of art." What proof could you offer that this *was* the reason and that your statement was a *fact*? Perhaps there were other reasons that you hadn't considered.
>
> 5. Emphasize your most important evidence by placing it at the beginning or the end of your paper (the most emphatic positions in an essay) and devoting more space to it.

SAMPLE ANNOTATED ESSAY: CLAIM OF FACT

A Reassuring Scorecard for Affirmative Action

MICHAEL M. WEINSTEIN

Introduction:
a) Review of the attack on affirmative action

Affirmative action — preferential treatment toward women and minority applicants as practiced by employers, university admissions officers, and government contractors — remains under attack thirty-two years after President Johnson ordered federal contractors to seek female and minority employees. Two states have voted to wipe out the use of race- and gender-based preferences by state agencies. Parents have challenged the race-based admissions policies of public schools. Even Joseph Lieberman, the [2000] Democratic candidate for vice president, once opposed policies "based on group preference instead of individual merit."

b) Specific criticism

Some of affirmative action's critics contend that preferential hiring and admissions are always wrong in principle no matter how attractive the consequences. But other critics focus on affirmative action's alleged failings. According to this argument, the policy creates divisive workplaces, breeds cynicism and corruption, and hurts many of the individuals it is supposed to help. That debate should turn on the facts. Instead it has been fueled almost entirely by anecdotes — until now.

Michael M. Weinstein, Ph.D., is director of programs for the Robin Hood Foundation. He was on the editorial board of the *New York Times* when he wrote this October 17, 2000, article.

Refutation:
authoritative source
of new data

In the most recent issue of the *Journal of Economic Literature,* a publication of the American Economic Association, two respected economists provide an eighty-five page review of over two hundred serious scientific studies of affirmative action. Harry Holzer of Georgetown University and David Neumark of Michigan State University ferret out every statistic from the studies to measure the effects of affirmative action. Harsh critics of affirmative action will not find much comfort.

Claim: general benefits
for women and
minorities under
affirmative action

The authors concede the evidence is sometimes murky. Yet they find that affirmative action produces tangible benefits for women, for minority entrepreneurs, students, and workers, and for the overall economy. Employers adopting the policy increase the relative number of women and minority employees by an average of between 10 and 15 percent. Affirmative action has helped boost the percentage of blacks attending college by a factor of three and the percentage of blacks enrolled in medical school by a factor of four since the early 1960s. Between 1982 and 1991 the number of federal contracts going to black-owned businesses rose by 125 percent, even though the total number of federal contracts rose by less than 25 percent during the period.

Support: a) Data
about employment,
education, business

To no one's surprise, the two economists rivet   5
on economic performance. Here, the survey is interesting for what it does *not* find. There is, the authors say, little credible evidence that affirmative action appointees perform badly or diminish the overall performance of the economy.

b) Data about
credentials

Women hired under affirmative action, they say, largely match their male counterparts in credentials and performance. Blacks and Hispanics hired under affirmative action generally lag behind on credentials, such as education, but usually perform about as well as nonminority employees.

c) Data about worker
performance

In a separate study, Mr. Holzer and Mr. Neumark interviewed thousands of supervisors and showed that they ranked most affirmative action hires roughly the same as ordinary hires. The authors find that companies undertaking affirmative action use extensive recruitment and training to bring workers who fall a notch below average on credentials up to the performance level of other workers.

d) Data about student performance

Critics have often pointed to the wide gap between SAT scores of black and white students admitted to selective universities as proof that they are lowering standards for minority students and putting them in settings they cannot handle. But the use of a test gap as a measure of reverse discrimination is misleading. Much of the gap would exist even if admissions were race-blind. Colleges pull applicants from a population that includes many more high-scoring whites than blacks.

A discrimination-free procedure would start by tapping the pool, largely white, of high scorers and then turn to the pool of lower-scoring whites and blacks. The average test scores for whites admitted to the college would thus exceed that of the blacks admitted.

To be sure, some selective universities add to the test gap by giving preference to minority applicants. But, the data shows, black students at elite colleges graduate at greater rates than blacks at less demanding colleges, disproving claims that affirmative action disserves minority students.

e) Data about social benefits

The Holzer-Neumark survey shows that affirmative action in admissions has produced significant social benefits. For example, black doctors choose more often than their white medical school classmates to serve indigent or minority patients in inner cities and rural areas.

Conclusion: Contrary to criticism, evidence justifies affirmative action.

Though favorable, these findings hardly end the debate on affirmative action. The critics who refuse to accept government-sanctioned racial or gender preferences no matter what the benefit will continue to object. Affirmative action can be misused, as when whites running a company create a fiction of black ownership to qualify for credits in seeking government contracts. But the evidence marshaled by the authors largely vindicates affirmative action and should provide the ammunition for rebutting those critics who refuse to take facts into account.

■ Analysis

This article offers evidence that affirmative action provides benefits to women and minorities. A claim of fact often responds to some widely held belief that the author considers to be wrong—in this case, the failure of affirmative action. We need to ask three questions about a claim of fact: Are the data sufficient and appropriate? Are the authorities reliable? Are the distinctions between facts and inferences clear? Within its brief compass, this argument comes close to satisfying these criteria. In addition, its organization is straightforward, with a clearly defined introduction, body, and conclusion.

The first three paragraphs constitute the introduction. First, the author reviews some of the claims of the opposition. At the end of the second paragraph, he makes clear his own emphasis: "That debate should turn on the facts." He then cites his source for the facts—a report in a respected professional journal by two university economists, who have examined the data on affirmative action in over two hundred serious scientific studies. This information reassures the reader that the first two criteria for judging a claim of fact will be met.

The body of the essay contains support for the claim, first in a short summary, then in substantial detail. Much of the data is statistical, a specific form of information that most readers find convincing and relatively easy to assimilate. (Of course, readers must regard the source as trustworthy.) The author has offered some interpretations—in paragraph 8, for example—to clarify what he considers a misunderstanding. Notice also the use of "To be sure," an expression that usually indicates that the writer recognizes an exception to his view. But the argument stands firmly on the facts. The ending is one often used by debaters—a modest challenge to the opposing side.

PRACTICE

As you read the following essay, answer these questions:

1. What is Samuelson's claim?
2. Has Samuelson defined key terms? Are there terms that need to be defined that are not?
3. What type of evidence does he offer? Is the evidence sufficient, accurate, recent, and typical? Are the authorities reliable?
4. Are any inferences presented as inferences rather than as facts?
5. What might Samuelson's rationale have been for organizing the essay as he did?

Picking Sides for the News

ROBERT J. SAMUELSON

We in the news business think we're impartial seekers of truth, but most Americans think otherwise. They view us as sloppy, biased, and self-serving. In 1985, 56 percent of the public felt news organizations usually got their facts straight, says the Pew Research Center. By 2002 that was 35 percent. In 1985 the public thought the media "moral" by 54 to 13 percent; by 2003 opinion was split 40 to 38 percent. Americans think the "media make news rather than just report it," says Pew's Andrew Kohut. The obsession with "scandal in high places" is seen as building audiences rather than advancing the public interest.

Still, the latest Pew survey confirms—with lots of numbers—something disturbing that we all sense: people are increasingly picking their media on the basis of partisanship. If you're Republican and conservative, you listen to talk radio and watch the Fox News Channel. If you're liberal and Democratic, you listen to National Public Radio and watch "NewsHour with Jim Lehrer." It's like picking restaurants: Chinese for some, Italian for others. And everyone can punch up partisan blogs—the fast food of the news business. What's disturbing is that, like restaurants, the news media may increasingly cater to their customers' (partisan) tastes. News slowly becomes more selective and slanted.

Rush Limbaugh has 14.5 million weekly listeners. By Pew, 77 percent are conservative, 16 percent moderate, and 7 percent liberal. Or take Fox's 1.3 million prime-time viewers: 52 percent are conservative, 30 percent moderate, and 13 percent liberal. By contrast, 36 percent of Americans are conservative, 38 percent moderate, and 18 percent liberal. The liberals' media favorites are slightly less lopsided. "NewsHour's" audience is 22 percent conservative, 44 percent moderate, and 27 percent liberal. NPR's audience is 31 percent conservative, 33 percent moderate, and 30 percent liberal. Of course, many news outlets still have broad audiences. Daily newspapers are collectively close to national averages; so is CNN.

But the partisan drift may grow because distrust is spreading. In 1988 Pew found that 58 percent of the public thought there was "no bias" in election coverage. Now that's 38 percent: 22 percent find a Democratic bias, 17 percent a Republican. Almost all major media have suffered confidence declines. Among Republicans, only 12 percent say they believe "all or most" of Newsweek; for Democrats the figure is twice that, 26 percent. In 1985 the overall figure was higher (31 percent), with little partisan gap. Newsweek's numbers typify mainstream media. Only 14 percent of Republicans believe "all or most" of the *New York Times*, versus 31 percent of Democrats.

What's going on? Why should we care?

5

Robert J. Samuelson, a contributing editor of *Newsweek*, has written a column for the *Washington Post* since 1977. This article appeared in *Newsweek* on June 28, 2004.

Up to a point, conservative talk radio and Fox represent a desirable backlash against the perceived "liberal bias" of network news and mainstream media. I've worked in the mainstream press for 35 years. Editors and reporters reflexively deny a liberal bias, even though many ordinary people find it and mainstream newsrooms are politically skewed. Here are the latest Pew figures: 7 percent of national reporters and editors are conservative (a fifth the national rate), and 34 percent are liberal (almost twice the national rate). Most reporters I know believe fiercely in being fair and objective. Still, the debate over "what's news and significant?" is warped. Talk radio and Fox add other views.

But the sorting of audiences by politics also poses dangers—for the media and the country. We journalists think we define news, and from day to day, we do. Over the longer run, that's less true. All news organizations must satisfy their audiences. If they don't, they go out of business. "Media bias is product differentiation," says James T. Hamilton of Duke, whose book "All the News That's Fit to Sell" shows how economic forces powerfully shape news judgments. If liberals and conservatives migrate to rival media camps, both camps may ultimately submit to the same narrow logic: like-minded editors and reporters increasingly feed like-minded customers stories that reinforce their world view.

Economic interests and editorial biases will converge. The New York Times is now a national paper; 49 percent of its daily circulation is outside the New York area, up from 38 percent five years ago. There's home delivery in 275 markets, up from 171 five years ago. But if the Times sells largely to upscale readers (average household income is $90,381, almost twice the national average) with vaguely liberal views, it risks becoming hostage to their sensibilities. No less does Fox risk becoming hostage to its base.

The worthy, if unattainable, ideals of fairness and objectivity will silently erode. Many forces push that way: new technologies (cable, the Internet); the blending of news and entertainment; the breakdown between "hard news" and interpretation; intense competition; changing news habits of the young. The damage will not just be to good journalism. Tom Rosenstiel of the Project for Excellence in Journalism notes that respected national media develop common facts and language that helps hold society together and solve common problems. It will be a sad day when we trust only the media that voice our views.

CLAIMS OF VALUE

Unlike claims of fact, which attempt to prove that something is true and which can be validated by reference to the data, claims of value make a judgment. They express approval or disapproval. They attempt to prove that some action, belief, or condition is right or wrong, good or bad, beautiful or ugly, worthwhile or undesirable.

CLAIM: Democracy is superior to any other form of government.

CLAIM: Killing animals for sport is wrong.

CLAIM: The Sam Rayburn Building in Washington is an aes-
             thetic failure.

Some claims of value are simply expressions of tastes, likes and dislikes, or preferences and prejudices. The Latin proverb *"De gustibus non est
disputandum"* states that we cannot dispute about tastes. Suppose you express a preference for chocolate over vanilla. If your listener should ask
why you prefer this flavor, you cannot refer to an outside authority or
produce data or appeal to her moral sense to convince her that your preference is justified.

Many claims of value, however, can be defended or attacked on the
basis of standards that measure the worth of an action, a belief, or an object. As far as possible, our personal likes and dislikes should be supported
by reference to these standards. Value judgments occur in any area of
human experience, but whatever the area, the analysis will be the same.
We ask the arguer who is defending a claim of value: *What are the standards or criteria for deciding that this action, this belief, or this object is good
or bad, beautiful or ugly, desirable or undesirable? Does the thing you are defending fulfill these criteria?*

There are two general areas in which people often disagree about
matters of value: aesthetics and morality. They are also the areas that offer
the greatest challenge to the writer. What follows is a discussion of some
of the elements of analysis that you should consider in defending a claim
of value in these areas.

Aesthetics is the study of beauty and the fine arts. Controversies over
works of art—the aesthetic value of books, paintings, sculpture, architecture, dance, drama, and movies—rage fiercely among experts and laypeople alike. They may disagree on the standards for judging or, even if
they agree about standards, may disagree about how successfully the art
object under discussion has met these standards.

Consider a discussion about popular music. Hearing someone praise
the singing of Manu Chao, a hugely popular European singer now playing to American crowds, you might ask why he is highly regarded. You
expect Chao's fans to say more than "I like him" or "He's great." You expect them to give reasons to support their claims. They might show you
a short review from a respected newspaper that says, "Mr. Chao's gift is
simplicity. His music owes a considerable amount to Bob Marley . . . but
Mr. Chao has a nasal, regular-guy voice, and instead of the Wailers' brooding, bass-heavy undertow, Mr. Chao's band delivers a lighter bounce. His
tunes have the singing directness of nursery rhymes."[2] Chao's fans accept
these criteria for judging a singer's appeal.

---

[2]Jon Pareles, *New York Times*, July 10, 2001, p. B1.

You may not agree that simplicity, directness, and a regular-guy voice are the most important qualities in a popular singer. But the establishment of standards itself offers material for a discussion or an argument. You may argue about the relevance of the criteria, or you may agree with the criteria but argue about the success of the singer in meeting them. Perhaps you prefer complexity to simplicity. Or even if you choose simplicity, you may not think that Chao has exhibited this quality to good effect.

It is probably not surprising then, that, despite wide differences in taste, professional critics more often than not agree on criteria and whether an art object has met the criteria. For example, almost all movie critics agree that *Citizen Kane* and *Gone with the Wind* are superior films. They also agree that *Plan 9 from Outer Space,* a horror film, is terrible.

Value claims about morality express judgments about the rightness or wrongness of conduct or belief. Here disagreements are as wide and deep as in the arts. The first two examples on page 168 reveal how controversial such claims can be. Although you and your reader may share many values—among them a belief in democracy, a respect for learning, and a desire for peace—you may also disagree, even profoundly, about other values. The subject of divorce, for example, despite its prevalence in our society, can produce a conflict between people who have differing moral standards. Some people may insist on adherence to absolute standards, arguing that the values they hold are based on immutable religious precepts derived from God and biblical scripture. Since marriage is sacred, divorce is always wrong, they say, whether or not the conditions of society change. Other people may argue that values are relative, based on the changing needs of societies in different places and at different times. Since marriage is an institution created by human beings at a particular time in history to serve particular social needs, they may say, it can also be dissolved when other social needs arise. The same conflicts between moral values might occur in discussions of abortion or suicide.

As a writer you cannot always know what system of values your reader holds. Yet it might be possible to find a rule on which almost all readers agree. One such rule was expressed by the eighteenth-century German philosopher Immanuel Kant: "Man and, in general, every rational being exists as an end in itself and not merely as a means to be arbitrarily used by this or that will." Kant's prescription urges us not to subject any creature to a condition that it has not freely chosen. In other words, we cannot use other creatures, as in slavery, for our own purposes. (Some philosophers would extend this rule to the treatment of animals by human beings.) This standard of judgment has, in fact, been invoked in recent years against medical experimentation on human beings in prisons and hospitals without their consent and against the sterilization of poor or mentally retarded women without their consent.

Nevertheless, even where people agree about standards for measuring behavior, a majority preference is not enough to confer moral value. If in a certain neighborhood a majority of heterosexual men decide to harass a

Writer's Guide: Defending a Claim of Value

The following suggestions are a preliminary guide to the defense of a value claim. (We discuss support for value claims further in Chapter 7.)

1. Try to make clear that the values or principles you are defending are important and relatively more significant than other values. Keep in mind that you and your readers may differ about their relative importance. For example, although your readers may agree with you that brilliant photography is important in a film, they may think that a well-written script is even more crucial to its success. And although they may agree that freedom of the press is a mainstay of democracy, they may regard the right to privacy as even more fundamental.

2. Suggest that adherence to the values you are defending will bring about good results in some specific situation or bad results if respect for the values is ignored. You might argue, for example, that a belief in freedom of the press will make citizens better informed and the country stronger while a failure to protect this freedom will strengthen the forces of authoritarianism.

3. Since value terms are abstract, use examples and illustrations to clarify meanings and make distinctions. Comparisons and contrasts are especially helpful. If you use the term *heroism,* can you provide examples to differentiate between *heroism* and *foolhardiness* or *exhibitionism*?

4. Use testimony of others to prove that knowledgeable or highly regarded people share your values.

few gay men and lesbians, that consensus does not make their action right. In formulating value claims, you should be prepared to ask and answer questions about the way in which your value claims and those of others have been arrived at. Lionel Ruby, an American philosopher, sums it up in these words: "The law of rationality tells us that we ought to justify our beliefs by evidence and reasons, instead of asserting them dogmatically."[3]

Of course, you will not always be able to persuade those with whom you argue that your values are superior to theirs and that they should therefore change their attitudes. Nor, on the other hand, would you want to compromise your values or pretend that they were different to win an argument. What you can and should do, however, as Lionel Ruby advises, is give *good reasons* that you think one thing is better than another. If as a child you asked why it was wrong to take your brother's toys, you might have been told by an exasperated parent, "Because I say so." Some adults still give such answers in defending their judgments, but such answers are not arguments and do nothing to win the agreement of others.

---

[3] *The Art of Making Sense* (New York: Lippincott, 1968), p. 271.

Kids in the Mall:
Growing Up Controlled
WILLIAM SEVERINI KOWINSKI

> Butch heaved himself up and loomed over the group. "Like it was different for me," he piped. "My folks used to drop me off at the shopping mall every morning and leave me all day. It was like a big free baby-sitter, you know? One night they never came back for me. Maybe they moved away. Maybe there's some kind of a Bureau of Missing Parents I could check with."
>
> —Richard Peck,
> *Secrets of the Shopping Mall,*
> a novel for teenagers

Introduction:
interesting personal
anecdote

From his sister at Swarthmore, I'd heard about a kid in Florida whose mother picked him up after school every day, drove him straight to the mall, and left him there until it closed — all at his insistence. I'd heard about a boy in Washington who, when his family moved from one suburb to another, pedaled his bicycle five miles every day to get back to his old mall, where he once belonged.

Additional examples of
mall experience

These stories aren't unusual. The mall is a common experience for the majority of American youth; they have probably been going there all their lives. Some ran within their first large open space, saw their first fountain, bought their first toy, and read their first book in a mall. They may have smoked their first cigarette or first joint, or turned them down, had their first kiss or lost their virginity in the mall parking lot. Teenagers in America now spend more time in the mall than anywhere else but home and school. Mostly it is their choice, but some of that mall time is put in as the result of two-paycheck and single-parent

---

William Severini Kowinski is a freelance writer who has been the book review editor and managing arts editor of the *Boston Phoenix*. This excerpt is from his book *The Malling of America: An Inside Look at the Great Consumer Paradise* (1985, revised 2002).

Reasons for the author's interest

households, and the lack of other viable alternatives. But are these kids being harmed by the mall?

I wondered first of all what difference it makes for adolescents to experience so many important moments in the mall. They are, after all, at play in the fields of its little world and they learn its ways; they adapt to it and make it adapt to them. It's here that these kids get their street sense, only it's mall sense. They are learning the ways of a large-scale, artificial environment; its subtleties and flexibilities, its particular pleasures and resonances, and the attitudes it fosters.

The presence of so many teenagers for so much time was not something mall developers planned on. In fact, it came as a big surprise. But kids became a fact of mall life very easily, and the International Council of Shopping Centers found it necessary to commission a study, which they published along with a guide to mall managers on how to handle the teenage incursion.

Expert opinion

The study found that "teenagers in suburban 5 centers are bored and come to the shopping centers mainly as a place to go. Teenagers in suburban centers spent more time fighting, drinking, littering and walking than did their urban counterparts, but presented fewer overall problems." The report observed that "adolescents congregated in groups of two to four and predominantly at locations selected by them rather than management." This probably had something to do with the decision to install game arcades, which allow management to channel these restless adolescents into naturally contained areas away from major traffic points of adult shoppers.

Why the malls encourage adolescent presence

The guide concluded that mall management should tolerate and even encourage the teenage presence because, in the words of the report, "The vast majority support the same set of values as does shopping center management." *The same set of values* means simply that mall kids are already preprogrammed to be consumers and that the mall can put the finishing touches to them as hard-core, lifelong shoppers just like everybody else. That, after all, is what the mall is about. So it shouldn't be surprising that in spending a lot of

Disadvantages:
a) Exposure to high-
consumption society

time there, adolescents find little that challenges the assumption that the goal of life is to make money and buy products, or that just about everything else in life is to be used to serve those ends.

Growing up in a high-consumption society already adds inestimable pressure to kids' lives. Clothes consciousness has invaded the grade schools, and popularity is linked with having the best, newest clothes in the currently acceptable styles. Even what they read has been affected. "Miss [Nancy] Drew wasn't obsessed with her wardrobe," noted the *Wall Street Journal*. "But today the mystery in teen fiction for girls is what outfit the heroine will wear next." Shopping has become a survival skill and there is certainly no better place to learn it than the mall, where its importance is powerfully reinforced and certainly never questioned.

b) Social pressures to
buy

The mall as a university of suburban materialism, where Valley Girls and Boys from coast to coast are educated in consumption, has its other lessons in this era of change in family life and sexual mores and their economic and social ramifications. The plethora of products in the mall, plus the pressure on teens to buy them, may contribute to the phenomenon that psychologist David Elkind calls "the hurried child": kids who are exposed to too much of the adult world too quickly and must respond with a sophistication that belies their still-tender emotional development. Certainly the adult products marketed for children — form-fitting designer jeans, sexy tops for preteen girls — add to the social pressure to look like an adult, along with the home-grown need to understand adult finances (why mothers must work) and adult emotions (when parents divorce).

c) Mall as babysitter

Kids spend so much time at the mall partly because their parents allow it and even encourage it. The mall is safe, doesn't seem to harbor any unsavory activities, and there is adult supervision; it is, after all, a controlled environment. So the temptation, especially for working parents, is to let the mall be their baby-sitter. At least the kids aren't watching TV. But the mall's role as a surrogate mother may be more extensive and more profound.

d) Mall as substitute for home

Karen Lansky, a writer living in Los Angeles, 10 has looked into the subject, and she told me some of her conclusions about the effects on its teenaged denizens of the mall's controlled and controlling environment. "Structure is the dominant idea, since true 'mall rats' lack just that in their home lives," she said, "and adolescents about to make the big leap into growing up crave more structure than our modern society cares to acknowledge." Karen pointed out some of the elements malls supply that kids used to get from their families, like warmth (Strawberry Shortcake dolls and similar cute and cuddly merchandise), old-fashioned mothering ("We do it all for you," the fast-food slogan), and even home cooking (the "homemade" treats at the food court).

e) Encouragement of passivity

The problem in all this, as Karen Lansky sees it, is that while families nurture children by encouraging growth through the assumption of responsibility and then by letting them rest in the bosom of the family from the rigors of growing up, the mall as a structural mother encourages passivity and consumption, as long as the kid doesn't make trouble. Therefore all they learn about becoming adults is how to act and how to consume.

f) Undemanding jobs

Kids are in the mall not only in the passive role of shoppers — they also work there, especially as fast-food outlets infiltrate the mall's enclosure. There they learn how to hold a job and take responsibility, but still within the same value context. When *CBS Reports* went to Oak Park Mall in suburban Kansas City, Kansas, to tape part of their hour-long consideration of malls, "After the Dream

Example

Comes True," they interviewed a teenaged girl who worked in a fast-food outlet there. In a sequence that didn't make the final program, she described the major goal of her present life, which was to perfect the curl on top of the ice-cream cones that were her store's specialty. If she could do that, she would be moved from the lowly soft-drink dispenser to the more prestigious ice-cream division, the curl on top of the status ladder at her restaurant. These are the achievements that are important at the mall.

Other benefits of such jobs may also be overrated, according to Laurence D. Steinberg of the

Details

University of California at Irvine's social ecology department, who did a study on teenage employment. Their jobs, he found, are generally simple, mindlessly repetitive, and boring. They don't really learn anything, and the jobs don't lead anywhere. Teenagers also work primarily with other teenagers; even their supervisors are often just a little older than they are. "Kids need to spend time with adults," Steinberg told me. "Although they get benefits from peer relationships, without parents and other adults it's one-side socialization. They hang out with each other, have age-segregated jobs, and watch TV."

Advantages:
a) Time with other adolescents

Perhaps much of this is not so terrible or even so terribly different. Now that they have so much more to contend with in their lives, adolescents probably need more time to spend with other adolescents without adult impositions, just to sort things out. Though it is more concentrated in the mall (and therefore perhaps a clearer target), the value system there is really the dominant one of the whole society. Attitudes about curiosity, initiative, self-expression, empathy, and disinterested learning aren't necessarily made in the mall; they are mirrored there, perhaps a bit more intensely — as through a glass brightly.

b) Educational opportunities

Besides, the mall is not without its educational 15 opportunities. There are bookstores, where there is at least a short shelf of classics at great prices, and other books from which it is possible to learn more than how to do sit-ups. There are tools, from hammers to VCRs, and products, from clothes to records, that can help the young find and express themselves. There are older people with stories, and places to be alone or to talk one-on-one with a kindred spirit. And there is always the passing show.

Conclusion and claim of value: mall as a controlled environment that teaches a few valuable lessons

The mall itself may very well be an education about the future. I was struck with the realization, as early as my first forays into Greengate, that the mall is only one of a number of enclosed and controlled environments that are part of the lives of today's young. The mall is just an extension, say, of those large suburban schools — only there's Karmelkorn instead of chem lab, the ice rink instead of the gym: It's high school without the impertinence of classes.

Growing up, moving from home to school to the mall—from enclosure to enclosure, transported in cars—is a curiously continuous process, without much in the way of contrast or contact with unenclosed reality. Places must tend to blur into one another. But whatever differences and dangers there are in this, the skills these adolescents are learning may turn out to be useful in their later lives. For we seem to be moving inexorably into an age of preplanned and regulated environments, and this is the world they will inherit.

Still, it might be better if they had more of a choice. One teenaged girl confessed to *CBS Reports* that she sometimes felt she was missing something by hanging out at the mall so much. "But I'm here," she said, "and this is what I have."

■ Analysis

Kowinski has chosen to evaluate one aspect of an extraordinarily successful economic and cultural phenomenon—the commercial mall. He asks whether the influence of the mall on adolescents is good or bad. The answer seems to be a little of both. The good values may be described as exposure to a variety of experiences, a protective structure for adolescents who often live in unstable environments, and immersion in a world that may well serve as an introduction to adulthood. But the bad values, which Kowinski thinks are more influential (as the title suggests), are those of the shoppers' paradise, a society that believes in acquisition and consumption of goods as ultimate goals, and too much control over the choices available to adolescents. The tone of the judgment, however, is moderate and reflects a balanced, even scholarly, attitude. More than other arguments, the treatment of values requires such a voice, one that respects differences of opinion among readers. But serious doesn't mean heavy. His style is formal but highly readable, brightened by interesting examples and precise details. The opening paragraph is a strikingly effective lead.

Some of his observations are personal, but others are derived from studies by professional researchers, from *CBS Reports* to a well-known writer on childhood. These studies give weight and authority to his conclusions. Here and there we detect an appealing sympathy for adolescents who spend time in their controlled mall environments.

Like any thoughtful social commentator, Kowinski casts a wide net. He sees the mall not only as a hangout for teens but as a good deal more, an institution that offers insights into family life and work, the changing urban culture, the nature of contemporary entertainment, even glimpses of a somewhat forbidding future.

PRACTICE

As you read the following essay, answer these questions:

1. What is Ebert's claim?
2. What criteria does Ebert seem to use in judging the film? What values seem to underlie his review?
3. What type of support does he offer to convince his readers that his value judgment is valid? Is the evidence sufficient?
4. Do you find Ebert's argument convincing? Why or why not?

Crash

ROGER EBERT

" C rash" tells interlocking stories of whites, blacks, Latinos, Koreans, Iranians, cops and criminals, the rich and the poor, the powerful and powerless, all defined in one way or another by racism. All are victims of it, and all are guilty of it. Sometimes, yes, they rise above it, although it is never that simple. Their negative impulses may be instinctive, their positive impulses may be dangerous, and who knows what the other person is thinking?

The result is a movie of intense fascination; we understand quickly enough who the characters are and what their lives are like, but we have no idea how they will behave, because so much depends on accident. Most movies enact rituals; we know the form and watch for variations. "Crash" is a movie with free will, and anything can happen. Because we care about the characters, the movie is uncanny in its ability to rope us in and get us involved.

"Crash" was directed by Paul Haggis, whose screenplay for "Million Dollar Baby" led to Academy Awards. It connects stories based on coincidence, serendipity, and luck, as the lives of the characters crash against one another like pinballs. The movie presumes that most people feel prejudice and resentment against members of other groups, and observes the consequences of those feelings.

Roger Ebert has been the film critic of the *Chicago Sun-Times* since 1967 and is the author of more than fifteen books about film. He appeared for years on a televised show about movies, first with the late Gene Siskel and then with Richard Roeper. He won the Pulitzer Prize for criticism in 1975, and his reviews are now syndicated in more than two hundred newspapers in the United States, Canada, England, Japan, and Greece.

One thing that happens, again and again, is that peoples' assumptions prevent them from seeing the actual person standing before them. An Iranian (Shaun Toub) is thought to be an Arab, although Iranians are Persian. Both the Iranian and the white wife of the district attorney (Sandra Bullock) believe a Mexican-American locksmith (Michael Pena) is a gang member and a crook, but he is a family man.

A black cop (Don Cheadle) is having an affair with his Latina partner 5 (Jennifer Esposito), but never gets it straight which country she's from. A cop (Matt Dillon) thinks a light-skinned black woman (Thandie Newton) is white. When a white producer tells a black TV director (Terrence Dashon Howard) that a black character "doesn't sound black enough," it never occurs to him that the director doesn't "sound black," either. For that matter, neither do two young black men (Larenz Tate and Ludacris), who dress and act like college students, but have a surprise for us.

You see how it goes. Along the way, these people say exactly what they are thinking, without the filters of political correctness. The district attorney's wife is so frightened by a street encounter that she has the locks changed, then assumes the locksmith will be back with his "homies" to attack them. The white cop can't get medical care for his dying father, and accuses a black woman at his HMO with taking advantage of preferential racial treatment. The Iranian can't understand what the locksmith is trying to tell him, freaks out, and buys a gun to protect himself. The gun dealer and the Iranian get into a shouting match.

I make this sound almost like episodic TV, but Haggis writes with such directness and such a good ear for everyday speech that the characters seem real and plausible after only a few words. His cast is uniformly strong; the actors sidestep cliches and make their characters particular.

For me, the strongest performance is by Matt Dillon, as the racist cop in anguish over his father. He makes an unnecessary traffic stop when he thinks he sees the black TV director and his light-skinned wife doing something they really shouldn't be doing at the same time they're driving. True enough, but he wouldn't have stopped a black couple or a white couple. He humiliates the woman with an invasive body search, while her husband is forced to stand by powerless, because the cops have the guns—Dillon, and also an unseasoned rookie (Ryan Phillippe), who hates what he's seeing but has to back up his partner.

That traffic stop shows Dillon's cop as vile and hateful. But later we see him trying to care for his sick father, and we understand why he explodes at the HMO worker (whose race is only an excuse for his anger). He victimizes others by exercising his power, and is impotent when it comes to helping his father. Then the plot turns ironically on itself, and both of the cops find themselves, in very different ways, saving the lives of the very same TV director and his wife. Is this just manipulative storytelling? It didn't feel that way to me, because it serves a deeper purpose than mere irony: Haggis is telling parables, in which the characters learn the lessons they have earned by their behavior.

Other cross-cutting Los Angeles stories come to mind, especially Law-   10
rence Kasdan's more optimistic "Grand Canyon" and Robert Altman's more
humanistic "Short Cuts." But "Crash" finds a way of its own. It shows the
way we all leap to conclusions based on race—yes, all of us, of all races, and
however fair-minded we may try to be—and we pay a price for that. If
there is hope in the story, it comes because as the characters crash into one
another, they learn things, mostly about themselves. Almost all of them are
still alive at the end, and are better people because of what has happened
to them. Not happier, not calmer, not even wiser, but better. Then there are
those few who kill or get killed; racism has tragedy built in.

Not many films have the possibility of making their audiences better
people. I don't expect "Crash" to work any miracles, but I believe anyone
seeing it is likely to be moved to have a little more sympathy for people
not like themselves. The movie contains hurt, coldness, and cruelty, but is
it without hope? Not at all. Stand back and consider. All of these people,
superficially so different, share the city and learn that they share similar
fears and hopes. Until several hundred years ago, most people everywhere
on earth never saw anybody who didn't look like them. They were not
racist because, as far as they knew, there was only one race. You may have
to look hard to see it, but "Crash" is a film about progress.

CLAIMS OF POLICY

Claims of policy argue that certain conditions should exist. As the name
suggests, they advocate adoption of policies or courses of action because
problems have arisen that call for solution. Almost always *should* or *ought
to* or *must* is expressed or implied in the claim.

CLAIM: Voluntary prayer should be permitted in public schools.

CLAIM: A dress code should be introduced for all public high schools.

CLAIM: A law should permit sixteen-year-olds and parents to
           "divorce" each other in cases of extreme incompatibility.

CLAIM: Mandatory jail terms should be imposed for drunk driv-
           ing violations.

In defending such claims of policy you may find that you must first
convince your audience that a problem exists. This will require that, as part
of your longer argument, you make a factual claim, offering data to prove
that present conditions are unsatisfactory. You may also find it necessary to
refer to the values that support your claim. Then you will be ready to introduce your policy, to persuade your audience that the solution you propose
will solve the problem.

Writer's Guide: Defending a Claim of Policy

The following steps will help you organize arguments for a claim of policy.

1. Make your proposal clear. The terms in the proposal should be precisely defined.

2. If necessary, establish that there is a need for a change. When changes have been resisted, present reasons that explain this resistance. (It is often wrongly assumed that people cling to cultural practices long after their significance and necessity have eroded. But rational human beings observe practices that serve a purpose. The fact that you and I may see no value or purpose in the activities of another is irrelevant.)

3. Consider the opposing arguments. You may want to state the opposing arguments in a brief paragraph before answering them in the body of your argument.

4. Devote the major part of your essay to proving that your proposal is an answer to the opposing arguments and enumerating its distinct benefits for your readers.

5. Support your proposal with solid data, but don't neglect the moral considerations and the commonsense reasons, which may be even more persuasive.

We will examine a policy claim in which all these parts are at work. The claim can be stated as follows: "The time required for an undergraduate degree should be extended to five years." Immediate agreement with this policy among student readers would certainly not be universal. Some students would not recognize a problem. They would say, "The college curriculum we have now is fine. There's no need for a change. Besides, we don't want to spend more time in school." First, then, the arguer would have to persuade a skeptical audience that there is a problem—that four years of college are no longer enough because the stock of knowledge in almost all fields of study continues to increase. The arguer would provide data to show that students today have many more choices in history, literature, and science than students had in those fields a generation ago. She would also emphasize the value of greater knowledge and more schooling compared to the value of other goods the audience cherishes, such as earlier independence. Finally, the arguer would offer a plan for implementing her policy. Her plan would have to consider initial psychological resistance, revision of the curriculum, costs of more instruction, and costs of lost production in the workforce. Most important, she would point out the benefits for both individuals and society if this policy were adopted.

In this example, we assumed that the reader would disagree that a problem existed. In many cases, however, the reader may agree that there is a problem but disagree with the arguer about the way to solve it. Most of us, no doubt, agree that we want to reduce or eliminate the following problems: misbehavior and vandalism in schools, drunk driving, crime on the streets, child abuse, pornography, pollution. But how should we go about solving those problems? What public policy will give us well-behaved, diligent students who never destroy school property? Safe streets where no one is ever robbed or assaulted? Loving homes·where no child is ever mistreated? Some members of society would choose to introduce rules or laws that punish infractions so severely that wrongdoers would be unwilling or unable to repeat their offenses. Other members of society would prefer policies that attempt to rehabilitate or reeducate offenders through training, therapy, counseling, and new opportunities.

SAMPLE ANNOTATED ESSAY: CLAIM OF POLICY

College Life versus My Moral Code

ELISHA DOV HACK

M any people envy my status as a freshman at Yale College. My classmates and I made it through some fierce competition, and we are excited to have been accepted to one of the best academic and extracurricular programs in American higher education. I have an older brother who attended Yale, and I've heard from him what life at Yale is like.

Background that reveals his respect for Yale and his connection to it through his brother

He spent all his college years living at home because our parents are New Haven residents, and Yale's rules then did not require him to live in the dorms. But Yale's new regulations demand that I spend my freshman and sophomore years living in the college dormitories.

How residency rules have changed

Establishes the problem

I, two other freshmen, and two sophomores have refused to do this because life in the dorms, even on the floors Yale calls "single sex," is contrary

---

Elisha Dov Hack was a member of the Yale College freshman class of 1997. This article appeared on September 9, 1997, in the *New York Times*. The case brought by Hack and four other Jewish students remained in court until all but Hack had graduated. Hack went on to marry before his 2003 graduation in engineering sciences.

to the fundamental principles we have been taught as long as we can remember — the principles of Judaism lived according to the Torah and 3,000-year-old rabbinic teachings. Unless Yale waives its residence requirement, we may have no choice but to sue the university to protect our religious way of life.

Examples of affronts to his religious beliefs

Bingham Hall, on the Yale quadrangle known as the Old Campus, is one of the dorms for incoming students. When I entered it two weeks ago during an orientation tour, I literally saw the handwriting on the wall. A sign titled "Safe Sex" told me where to pick up condoms on campus. Another sign touted 100 ways to make love without having sex, like "take a nap together" and "take a steamy shower together."

Another example of accepted dorm standards

That, I am told, is real life in the dorms. The "freshperson" issue of the *Yale Daily News* sent to entering students contained a "Yale lexicon" defining *sexile* as "banishment from your dorm room because your roommate is having more fun than you." If you live in the dorms, you're expected to be part of the crowd, to accept these standards as the framework for your life.   5

Can we stand up to classmates whose sexual morality differs from ours? We've had years of rigorous religious teaching, and we've watched and learned from our parents. We can hold our own in the intellectual debate that flows naturally from exchanges during and after class. But I'm upset and hurt by this requirement that I live in the dorms.

Challenges whether Yale should make it difficult for students to maintain their morals outside of class

Why is Yale — an institution that professes to be so tolerant and open-minded — making it particularly hard for students like us to maintain our moral standards through difficult college years?

Tries to achieve middle ground by acknowledging that morality has changed but argues that exceptions to the policy are already made

We are not trying to impose our moral standards on our classmates or on Yale. Our parents tell us that things were very different in college dormitories in their day and that in most colleges in the 1950s students who allowed guests of the opposite sex into their dorm rooms were subject to expulsion. We acknowledge that today's morality is not that of the 50s. We are asking only that Yale give us the same permission to live off campus that it gives any lower classman who is married or at least twenty-one years old.

Attacks the opposition by defining immorality as Yale's religion

Yale is proud of the fact that it has no "parietal rules" and that sexual morality is a student's own business. Maybe this is what Dean Richard H. Brodhead meant when he said that "Yale's residential colleges carry . . . a moral meaning." That moral meaning is, basically, "Anything goes." This morality is Yale's own residential religion, which it is proselytizing by force of its regulations.

Floors designated by gender are not the solution

The source of conflict

We cannot, in good conscience, live in a place where women are permitted to stay overnight in men's rooms, and where visiting men can traipse through the common halls on the women's floors— in various stages of undress—in the middle of the night. The dormitories on Yale's Old Campus have floors designated by gender, but there is easy access through open stairwells from one floor to the next.

The moral message Yale's residences convey today 10 is not one that our religion accepts. Nor is it a moral environment in which the five of us can spend our nights, or a moral surrounding that we can call home.

Uses Yale's own advertising against it

Yale sent me a glossy brochure when it welcomed me as an entering student. It said, "Yale retains a deep respect for its early history and for the continuity that its history provides—a continuity based on constant reflection and reappraisal." Yale ought to reflect on and reappraise a policy that compels us to compromise our religious principles.

CLAIM OF POLICY:

A university that espouses a willingness to reflect and reappraise should not compel Hack and the other Jewish students to compromise their principles.

▪ Analysis

Notice that Hack's article originally appeared in the *New York Times*. Most would agree that it is unusual to see a piece written by a college freshman in such a prestigious publication, but the fact that he was accepted at Yale immediately establishes him as a member of an academically elite group, as Hack points out in his second sentence. He meets the possible objection that he does not yet know enough about what life at Yale is like by pointing out that his older brother went there. The crucial difference is that the university's rules have been changed in the interim. Where his older brother lived at home, Hack is required by university policy to live on campus his first two years. Therein lies the problem.

Hack most directly states his objection to Yale's residency requirement in his third paragraph—that life in the dorms "is contrary to the fundamental principles [he and four other Jewish students] have been taught as long as [they] can remember—"the principles of Judaism lived according to the Torah and 3,000-year-old rabbinic teachings." He also captures the intensity of his feelings on the subject by stating that he and the four other students who are in the same position "may have no choice but to sue the university to protect [their] religious way of life."

Hack supports his assertion that life in a Yale dormitory would pose a threat to his moral standards by citing examples of posters on dorm walls that advise safe sex and newspaper articles that joke about premarital sex. Hack feels that his religious training has prepared him to defend his moral principles, but he asks why an institution considered so tolerant cannot also be tolerant of those who want to maintain their conservative practices and beliefs: "Why is Yale—an institution that professes to be so tolerant and open-minded—making it particularly hard for students like us to maintain our moral standards through difficult college years?"

Hack heads off a possible objection to his argument by explaining that he and the other Jewish students are not trying to impose their moral standards on others. They simply don't want to have others' standards imposed on them. Some would argue that an assignment to a dorm that has floors designated by gender should be accommodation enough, but even those have open stairwells between floors. If exceptions are made for students who are married or who are twenty-one, why can an exception not be made for those who object to dorm life for religious reasons?

A characteristic of good arguers is that they know well their opponents' position. Hack acknowledges that he even knows well the language Yale uses in "selling" itself to new students. He quotes the brochure that Yale sent him: "Yale retains a deep respect for its early history and for the continuity that its history provides—a continuity based on constant reflection and reappraisal." His request and claim is that Yale should reappraise a position that compels him to compromise his religious principles.

What happened to the lawsuit to which Hack refers? It was tied up in court until 2001, when all of the students involved except Hack had graduated. The students lost the legal battle at all levels, primarily because their case depended on their proving that having to live in a residence hall constituted discrimination based on religion. The university successfully argued that the residence requirement was not discriminatory. Hack graduated from Yale in 2003. All five students chose to live in apartments during their first two years while paying full housing fees for dorm rooms they never occupied.

Supersize Your Child?

RICHARD HAYES

In the late 1950s, soon after Watson and Crick had discovered DNA's structure, scientists began predicting that someday we'd be able to genetically engineer our children. We'd design them to be healthy, smart, and attractive, with life spans of 200 years, photographic memories, enhanced lung capacity for athletic endurance, and more. Our children would pass these modifications to their own children and add new ones as well. Humanity would take control of its own evolution and kick it into overdrive.

Few people took these speculations very seriously. Could this sort of genetic engineering really be done? Even if it could, would anyone really want to do it? If they did, wouldn't society step in and set limits? In any event, wouldn't it be decades before we'd have to worry about this?

Now it's 2004, and those decades have passed. The era of genetically modified humans is close upon us. Almost every day we read of new breakthroughs: cloning, artificial chromosomes and now high-tech sex selection. Scientists create genetically modified animals on an assembly-line basis. Biotech entrepreneurs discuss the potential market for genetically modified children at investors' conferences. For the most part, society has not stepped in and set limits.

Last year *Science* magazine reported that a variant of the human 5-HTT gene reduces the risk of depression following stressful experiences. Depression can be a devastating condition. Would it be wrong if a couple planning to start a family used in vitro fertilization procedures to have the 5-HTT gene variant inserted into the embryos of their prospective children? Taken as an isolated instance, many people would be hard-pressed to say that it was.

In 1993, University of California at San Francisco biochemist Dr. 5 Cynthia Kenyon discovered a variant of the DAF-2 gene that doubles the two-week life span of nematode worms. The university filed for patents based on knowledge of the metabolic pathway regulated by the human version of the DAF-2 gene. In 1999, Kenyon and others founded Elixir Pharmaceuticals, a biotech firm. In early 2003, Elixir licensed the university's patent rights to Kenyon's discoveries and secured $17 million in private financing. In an earlier interview with *ABC News*, Kenyon said she saw no reason humans might not be able to achieve 200-year life spans.

Richard Hayes is the executive director of the Center for Genetics and Society, a California-based nonprofit organization working for the responsible governance of genetic technologies. This piece was published on the TomPaine.com Web site in February 2004.

"Post-human" Nature

Last June at Yale University, the World Transhumanist Association held its first national conference. The Transhumanists have chapters in more than 20 countries and advocate the breeding of "genetically enriched" forms of "post-human" beings. Other advocates of the new techno-eugenics, such as Princeton University professor Lee Silver, predict that by the end of this century, "All aspects of the economy, the media, the entertainment industry, and the knowledge industry [will be] controlled by members of the GenRich class . . . Naturals [will] work as low-paid service providers or as laborers . . .".

What happens then? Here's Dr. Richard Lynn, emeritus professor at the University of Ulster, who, like Silver, supports human genetic modification: "What is called for here is not genocide, the killing off of the population of incompetent cultures. But we do need to think realistically in terms of the 'phasing out' of such peoples. . . . Evolutionary progress means the extinction of the less competent."

Notice that I've gone, in just four steps, from reducing susceptibility to depression, to extending the human life span, to the creation of a genetic elite, to proposals that genetically inferior people be "phased out."

When first presented with this scenario, people typically respond in one of two ways. Some say, "It's impossible." Others say, "It's inevitable." Notice what these otherwise diametrically different responses have in common: both counsel passivity. If the "post-human future" is impossible, there's no need to try to prevent it. If it's inevitable, such efforts would be in vain.

Will it actually be possible to genetically engineer our children? Most 10 scientists who have studied this question conclude that although the techniques need to be refined, there's no reason to believe it can't be done. Meanwhile, research on stem cells, cloning, artificial chromosomes and more continues to refine those techniques.

Many people believe that to suggest that manipulating genes can affect behavioral and cognitive traits in humans is to indulge discredited ideologies of "genetic determinism." It's true that the crude sociobiology of the 1970s has been discredited, as have simplistic notions that there exist "I.Q. genes" or "gay genes" that determine one's intelligence or sexual orientation. But to say that genes have no influence over traits is equally simplistic. Some genes have minimal influence, others have greater influence. Some have influence in the presence of certain environmental factors but no influence otherwise. Few genes determine anything; most confer propensities.

Deepening Inequality

Suppose scientists found a gene giving male children a 15 percent greater chance of growing one inch taller than they would have grown without that gene, all else equal. If fertility clinics offered to engineer embryos to include this gene, would there be customers? Yes. Couples would say, "In this competitive world, I want to do anything I can that might give my child an edge."

Once we allow children to be designed through embryo modification, where would we stop? If it's acceptable to modify one gene, why not two? If two, why not 20? Or 200? There are some 30,000 genes in the human genome. Each contributes, in smaller or larger proportions, to some propensity. Where would we stop? On what grounds?

Some suggest we allow embryo modification for certified medical conditions and prohibit it for cosmetic or enhancement purposes. It's unlikely that this would succeed. Prozac, Viagra, and Botox were all developed for medical purposes but in the blink of an eye became hugely profitable cosmetic and enhancement consumer products.

Will the use of genetic engineering to redesign our children exacer- 15
bate inequality? Amazingly, the neo-eugenic advocates don't deny that it will. As good libertarians, they celebrate free markets and social Darwinism, and counsel us to accept a rising tide of genetically enhanced inequality as the inevitable result of human ingenuity and desire.

But couldn't this be prevented? Wouldn't society step in? Several years ago, a team of health policy academics examined a range of proposals, including systems of national health insurance making eugenic engineering available to all, or preferentially to the poor, or by lottery. Despite their best efforts, they couldn't identify any realistic set of policies that would prevent the new eugenic technologies, once allowed at all, from generating unprecedented inequality.

And consider the international implications. What happens when some country announces an aggressive program of eugenic engineering explicitly intended to create a new, superior, omni-competent breed of human? What does the rest of the world do then?

We need to take a deep breath and realize what is going on here. The birth of the first genetically modified child would be a watershed moment in human history. It would set off a chain of events that would feed back upon themselves in ways impossible to control.

Unnatural Selection

Everything we experience, everything we know, everything we do is experienced, known and done by a species—homo sapiens—which evolved through natural selection over hundreds of thousands of years. We differ as individuals, but we are a single human species with a shared biology so fundamental to what we are that we are not even conscious of it, or of the manifold ways it unites us. What happens if we begin changing that fundamental shared biology?

Three hundred years ago the scientific and political leaders of that era 20
took as a self-evident fact the division of humanity into "superior" and "inferior" types, designed by Providence respectively as masters and slaves.

Human beings were bred, bought and sold, like cattle or dogs. After three hundred years of struggle and bloodshed we are on the verge—barely—of putting this awful legacy behind us.

Or maybe not. If left uncontrolled, the new human genetic technologies could set us on a trajectory leading to a new Dark Age in which people are once again regarded as little better than cattle or dogs. Here is "bioethicist" Gregory Pence, who has testified in support of human cloning before the U.S. Congress and elsewhere:

> [M]any people love their retrievers and their sunny dispositions around children and adults. Could people be chosen in the same way? Would it be so terrible to allow parents to at least aim for a certain type, in the same way that great breeders . . . try to match a breed of dog to the needs of a family?

The common initial responses to the prospect of the new techno-eugenics—"It's impossible," and "It's inevitable"—are incorrect and unhelpful. The response we need to affirm is at once more realistic and more challenging: The techno-eugenic future certainly is possible, and is certainly not inevitable.

Road to Regulation

In 1997, the Council of Europe negotiated an important international agreement, the Convention on Biomedicine and Human Rights. Thus far, it has been signed by more than two-thirds of the council's 45 member countries. The convention draws the lines on human genetic modification in just the right ways. It allows medical research, including stem cell research, to continue, and does not restrict abortion rights, but it bans genetic modifications that would open the door to high-tech eugenic engineering. Many countries in Asia, Africa, and Latin America have likewise begun to address these issues through legislation.

These efforts are encouraging, but we have a long way to go before such policies are implemented, as they must be, worldwide. In some countries, notably the United States, the politics of the new genetic technologies have become polarized to the point of gridlock. The religious right insists on total bans on nearly all human embryo research, while bio-research interests and the biotech industry insist on nearly total freedom from any meaningful social oversight and accountability.

In other countries, and at the international level, the challenge of a new high-tech, free market eugenics, while worrisome, can seem remote in comparison with the real existing challenges of warfare, hunger, and disease.   25

What is to be done? More than anything, we need to realize the unprecedented nature of the challenges that the new human genetic technologies present. We need to distinguish benign applications of these technologies from pernicious ones, and support the former while opposing the latter. Concerned organizations and individuals need to engage these challenges and make their voices heard worldwide. National and international leaders in politics, the sciences and the arts need to declare that humanity is not going to let itself be split asunder by human genetic technology. The United Nations and other international bodies need to give these issues the highest attention. The hour is late. There is no greater challenge before us.

READING AND DISCUSSION QUESTIONS

1. Hayes alerts us that he is using the organization of his essay to help make his point. Explain where and how he does that. How does he appeal to his readers' need to feel secure? Why might his readers feel their sense of security being threatened?

2. Is Hayes supporting a claim of fact, value, or policy? Where does he state that claim most directly?

3. What types of support does Hayes offer to back up his opinion? How convincing do you find his support to be?

4. Can you identify the warrant underlying Hayes's argument? In order to accept his claim, what assumption of his must you agree with? Does he state his warrant explicitly anywhere in the essay?

WRITING SUGGESTIONS

5. Write an essay in which you either support or argue against Hayes's claim.

6. Write an essay in which you explain your own position on who should set limits on genetic engineering.

7. Choose an invention or scientific development that people once said was impossible and explain how those skeptics were proved wrong.

8. Choose an invention or scientific development and explain how it is now used, for good or ill, for purposes it was never intended to serve.

"Saw" Good at Tying Things in Knots

WESLEY MORRIS

All anybody should want from a horror movie is the steady tightening in the pit of your stomach. While the new sado-masochistic gross-out flick "Saw" often resembles the ghastliest editions yet of "Fear Factor" and "Survivor" and features some of the grodiest direction this side of "Project Greenlight," it does manage at times to knead your tummy like dough, using real suspense for a rolling pin.

Wesley Morris is currently a film critic at the *Boston Globe* and formerly wrote film reviews and essays for the *San Francisco Examiner* and the *San Francisco Sun-Chronicle*. This review appeared on October 24, 2004, in the *Boston Globe*.

Most of it is generated from wondering whether the movie will deliver on the promise of one of its posters, which shows a foot severed from its leg. It's the kind of terror that really has nothing to do with the plot, which, by the time it's been fully carried out, is as twisted as your stomach.

A doctor (Cary Elwes) and a bratty young photographer (Leigh Whannell, the movie's writer) wake up on either side of the sort of big, grimy bathroom you see only in bad horror movies and good music videos. Each man's leg is chained to a pipe, and neither has any idea how he got there or what that male body is doing lying dead between them in its undies. There's a gun in one hand, a tape recorder in the other, and a pool of blood around the head.

After beginning the dopey dialogue (mostly from Elwes, who brings a dinner-theater zest to his predicament), both men discover personal notes that indicate what they have to do: One has to kill the other to survive. And while you wait for Joe Rogan or Jeff Probst to supervise the mayhem, the two men start following the series of clues, which have been left on cassette tapes and elsewhere by a sicko watching on a surveillance camera. The contestants (what else are they?) turn up a pair of hacksaws and immediately start using them in vain on their chains. Silly rabbits, hacksaws are for ankles.

By this point, the movie has likely won your dread. So rather than commence with the cutting, "Saw" takes a break, in order for the doctor to treat the photographer to the hunch he has about who might be behind this stunt. It's in these flashbacks that screenwriter Whannell and director James Wan are exposed as being under the dubious influence of every movie in the modern psychopath-movie liquor cabinet—and "The Usual Suspects," too. 5

Someone has been rounding up people who've been "wasting their lives" and subjecting them to horrific tortures to prove how much they want to live. While the victims demonstrate this, the editing and photography go predictably nuts, running around them and deliriously speeding up their futile escapes. One man tried to crawl through a nest of barbed wire to freedom. Another was slathered in a flammable jelly and asked to crawl across a floor strewn with glass to decipher a code that would free him. He had to do this holding a candle. (He failed.) The sole "winner" was a woman who had to fish a key from a living man's stomach or her head would explode. Frankly, that looks comparatively easy.

Two detectives on the case—Ken Leung and a never nuttier Danny Glover—fingered the good doctor as the culprit. He was innocent of those crimes but guilty of a lesser one that makes a decent alibi. But the movie persists in dredging up more implausible mysteries and domestic drama, namely through some terribly handled scenes between the doctor and his soon-to-be-jeopardized family.

Eventually, it grows frustrating to watch the movie's puzzle assemble itself—even once it does, there are pieces still missing. Why, for instance, does Glover's freaky character love news clippings as much as the average serial killer? And are we really to believe the major curveball in the final scene?

Not really. But as long as "Saw" stays in that big, nasty bathroom, all we need to believe is the knot in our stomachs.

READING AND DISCUSSION QUESTIONS

1. Morris establishes immediately "[a]ll anybody should want from a horror movie." What is it that all viewers should want?

2. The reference in the first paragraph to the way the movie makes a viewer's stomach feel may not seem significant at first glance, but how does Morris follow through on this idea of a "gut-level" response to horror?

3. How does Morris manage to praise the movie in the first paragraph in spite of referring to it as a "sado-masochistics gross-out flick" with "grody" direction?

4. What other weakness does Morris see in the film?

5. What is Morris's ultimate judgment regarding the film? On what criteria does he base that judgment?

6. How effective is the support that Morris offers for his assessment?

WRITING SUGGESTIONS

7. Write an essay in which you explain your own criteria for evaluating horror films. Or choose another genre (romantic comedy, drama, or mockumentry, for example) and write evaluating criteria for it.

8. If you have seen *Saw*, write an essay explaining whether or not you agree with Morris's assessment of the film.

9. Write your own review of a recent movie, being sure to establish the criteria for evaluation on which you base your review. See Ebert's review of *Crash* earlier in this chapter for another example of a movie review.

Letter from Birmingham Jail

MARTIN LUTHER KING JR.

A Call for Unity: A Letter
from Eight White Clergymen

April 12, 1963

We the undersigned clergymen are among those who, in January, issued "An Appeal for Law and Order and Common Sense," in dealing with racial problems in Alabama. We expressed understanding that honest convictions in racial matters could properly be pursued in the courts, but urged that decisions of those courts should in the meantime be peacefully obeyed.

Since that time there had been some evidence of increased forebearance and a willingness to face facts. Responsible citizens have undertaken to work on various problems which cause racial friction and unrest. In Birmingham, recent public events have given indication that we all have opportunity for a new constructive and realistic approach to racial problems.

However, we are now confronted by a series of demonstrations by some of our Negro citizens, directed and led in part by outsiders. We recognize the natural impatience of people who feel that their hopes are slow in being realized. But we are convinced that these demonstrations are unwise and untimely.

We agree rather with certain local Negro leadership which has called for honest and open negotiation of racial issues in our area. And we believe this kind of facing of issues can best be accomplished by citizens of our own metropolitan area, white and Negro, meeting with their knowledge and experience of the local situation. All of us need to face that responsibility and find proper channels for its accomplishment.

Just as we formerly pointed out that "hatred and violence have no 5 sanction in our religious and political traditions," we also point out that such actions as incite to hatred and violence, however technically peaceful those actions may be, have not contributed to the resolution of our local problems. We do not believe that these days of new hope are days when extreme measures are justified in Birmingham.

Martin Luther King Jr. (1929–1968) was a clergyman, author, distinguished civil rights leader, and winner of the Nobel Prize for peace in 1964 for his contributions to racial harmony and his advocacy of nonviolent response to aggression. He was assassinated in 1968. In "Letter from Birmingham Jail," he appears as a historian and philosopher. He wrote the letter from a jail cell on April 16, 1963, after his arrest for participation in a demonstration for civil rights for African Americans. The letter was a reply to eight Alabama clergymen who, in the first letter reprinted here, had condemned demonstrations in the streets. King's essay is from *A Testament of Hope* (1986).

We commend the community as a whole, and the local news media and law enforcement officials in particular, on the calm manner in which these demonstrations have been handled. We urge the public to continue to show restraint should the demonstrations continue, and the law enforcement officials to remain calm and continue to protect our city from violence.

We further strongly urge our own Negro community to withdraw support from these demonstrations, and to unite locally in working peacefully for a better Birmingham. When rights are consistently denied, a cause should be pressed in the courts and in negotiations among local leaders, and not in the streets. We appeal to both our white and Negro citizenry to observe the principles of law and order and common sense.

(Signed)
C.C.J. Carpenter, D.D., L.L.D., Bishop of Alabama; Joseph A. Durick, D.D., Auxiliary Bishop, Diocese of Mobile-Birmingham; Rabbi Milton L. Grafman, Temple Emanu-El, Birmingham, Alabama; Bishop Paul Hardin, Bishop of the Alabama–West Florida Conference of the Methodist Church; Bishop Nolan B. Harmon, Bishop of the North Alabama Conference of the Methodist Church; George M. Murray, D.D., L.L.D., Bishop Coadjutor, Episcopal Diocese of Alabama; Edward V. Ramage, Moderator, Synod of the Alabama Presbyterian Church in the United States; Earl Stallings, Pastor, First Baptist Church, Birmingham.

King's Reply from Birmingham Jail

My dear Fellow Clergymen,

While confined here in the Birmingham city jail, I came across your recent statement calling our present activities "unwise and untimely." Seldom, if ever, do I pause to answer criticism of my work and ideas. If I sought to answer all of the criticisms that cross my desk, my secretaries would be engaged in little else in the course of the day, and I would have no time for constructive work. But since I feel that you are men of genuine good will and your criticisms are sincerely set forth, I would like to answer your statement in what I hope will be patient and reasonable terms.

I think I should give the reason for my being in Birmingham, since you have been influenced by the argument of "outsiders coming in." I have the honor of serving as president of the Southern Christian Leadership Conference, an organization operating in every southern state, with headquarters in Atlanta, Georgia. We have some eighty-five affiliate organizations all across the South — one being the Alabama Christian Movement for Human Rights. Whenever necessary and possible we share staff, educational, and financial resources with our affiliates. Several months ago our local affiliate here in Birmingham invited us to be on call to engage in a nonviolent direct-action program if such were deemed necessary. We readily consented and when the hour came we lived up to our promises. So I am here, along with several members of my staff, because we were invited here. I am here because I have basic organizational ties here.

Beyond this, I am in Birmingham because injustice is here. Just as the eighth-century prophets left their little villages and carried their "thus saith the Lord" far beyond the boundaries of their hometowns; and just as the Apostle Paul left his little village of Tarsus and carried the gospel of Jesus Christ to practically every hamlet and city of the Graeco-Roman world, I too am compelled to carry the gospel of freedom beyond my particular hometown. Like Paul, I must constantly respond to the Macedonian call for aid.

Moreover, I am cognizant of the interrelatedness of all communities and states. I cannot sit idly by in Atlanta and not be concerned about what happens in Birmingham. Injustice anywhere is a threat to justice everywhere. We are caught in an inescapable network of mutuality, tied in a single garment of destiny. Whatever affects one directly affects all indirectly. Never again can we afford to live with the narrow, provincial "outside agitator" idea. Anyone who lives in the United States can never be considered an outsider anywhere in this country.

You deplore the demonstrations that are presently taking place in 5 Birmingham. But I am sorry that your statement did not express a similar concern for the conditions that brought the demonstrations into being. I am sure that each of you would want to go beyond the superficial social analyst who looks merely at effects, and does not grapple with underlying causes. I would not hesitate to say that it is unfortunate that so-called demonstrations are taking place in Birmingham at this time, but I would say in more emphatic terms that it is even more unfortunate that the white power structure of this city left the Negro community with no other alternative.

In any nonviolent campaign there are four basic steps: (1) collection of the facts to determine whether injustices are alive, (2) negotiation, (3) self-purification, and (4) direct action. We have gone through all of these steps in Birmingham. There can be no gainsaying of the fact that racial injustice engulfs this community.

Birmingham is probably the most thoroughly segregated city in the United States. Its ugly record of police brutality is known in every section of this country. Its unjust treatment of Negroes in the courts is a notorious reality. There have been more unsolved bombings of Negro homes and churches in Birmingham than any city in this nation. These are the hard, brutal, and unbelievable facts. On the basis of these conditions Negro leaders sought to negotiate with the city fathers. But the political leaders consistently refused to engage in good faith negotiation.

Then came the opportunity last September to talk with some of the leaders of the economic community. In these negotiating sessions certain promises were made by the merchants—such as the promise to remove the humiliating racial signs from the stores. On the basis of these promises Reverend Shuttlesworth and the leaders of the Alabama Christian Movement for Human Rights agreed to call a moratorium on any type of demonstrations. As the weeks and months unfolded we realized that we were the victims of a broken promise. The signs remained. Like so many experiences of the past we were confronted with blasted hopes, and the dark shadow of a deep disappointment settled upon us. So we had no alternative except that of preparing for direct action, whereby we would present our very bodies as a means of laying our case before the conscience of the local and national community. We were not unmindful of the difficulties involved. So we decided to go through a process of self-purification. We started having workshops on nonviolence and repeatedly asking ourselves the questions, "Are you able to accept blows without retaliating?" "Are you able to endure the ordeals of jail?" We decided to set our direct-action program around the Easter season, realizing that with the exception of Christmas, this was the largest shopping period of the year. Knowing that a strong economic withdrawal program would be the by-product of direct action, we felt that this was the best time to bring pressure on the merchants for the needed changes. Then it occurred to us that the March election was ahead and so we speedily decided to postpone action until after election day. When we discovered that Mr. Connor was in the run-off, we decided again to postpone action so that the demonstrations could not be used to cloud the issues. At this time we agreed to begin our nonviolent witness the day after the run-off.

This reveals that we did not move irresponsibly into direct actions. We too wanted to see Mr. Connor defeated; so we went through postponement after postponement to aid in this community need. After this we felt that direct action could be delayed no longer.

You may well ask, "Why direct action? Why sit-ins, marches, etc.? Isn't negotiation a better path?" You are exactly right in your call for negotiation. Indeed, this is the purpose of direct action. Nonviolent direct action seeks to create such a crisis and establish such creative tension that a community that has constantly refused to negotiate is forced to confront the issue. It seeks so to dramatize the issue that it can no longer be ignored. I just referred to the creation of tension as a part of the work of the nonviolent resister. This may sound rather shocking. But I must confess that I am not afraid of the word tension. I have earnestly worked and preached against violent tension, but there is a type of constructive nonviolent tension that is necessary for growth. Just as Socrates felt that it was necessary to create a tension in the mind so that individuals could rise from the bondage of myths and half-truths to the unfettered realm of creative analysis and objective appraisal, we must see the need of having nonviolent gadflies to create the kind of tension in society that will help men to rise from the dark depths of prejudice and racism to the majestic heights of understanding and brotherhood. So the purpose of the direct action is to create a situation so crisis-packed that it will inevitably open the door to negotiation. We, therefore, concur with you in your call for negotiation. Too long has our beloved Southland been bogged down in the tragic attempt to live in monologue rather than dialogue.

One of the basic points in your statement is that our acts are untimely. Some have asked, "Why didn't you give the new administration time to act?" The only answer that I can give to this inquiry is that the new administration must be prodded about as much as the outgoing one before it acts. We will be sadly mistaken if we feel that the election of Mr. Boutwell will bring the millennium to Birmingham. While Mr. Boutwell is much more articulate and gentle than Mr. Connor, they are both segregationists, dedicated to the task of maintaining the status quo. The hope I see in Mr. Boutwell is that he will be reasonable enough to see the futility of massive resistance to desegregation. But he will not see this without pressure from the devotees of civil rights. My friends, I must say to you that we have not made a single gain in civil rights without determined legal and nonviolent pressure. History is the long and tragic story of the fact that privileged groups seldom give up their privileges voluntarily. Individuals may see the moral light and voluntarily give up their unjust posture; but as Reinhold Niebuhr has reminded us, groups are more immoral than individuals.

We know through painful experience that freedom is never voluntarily given by the oppressor; it must be demanded by the oppressed. Frankly, I have never yet engaged in a direct-action movement that was "well-timed," according to the timetable of those who have not suffered unduly from the disease of segregation. For years now I have heard the words "Wait!" It rings in the ear of every Negro with a piercing familiarity. This "Wait" has almost always meant "Never." It has been a tranquilizing thalidomide, relieving the emotional stress for a moment, only to give birth to an ill-formed infant of frustration. We must come to see with the distinguished jurist of yesterday that "justice too long delayed is justice denied." We have waited for more than 340 years for our constitutional and God-given rights. The nations of Asia and Africa are moving with jetlike speed toward the goal of political independence, and we still creep at horse and buggy pace toward the gaining of a cup of coffee at a lunch counter. I guess it is easy for those who have never felt the stinging darts of segregation to say, "Wait." But when you have seen vicious mobs lynch your mothers and fathers at will and drown your sisters and brothers at whim; when you see hate-filled policemen curse, kick, brutalize, and even kill your black brothers and sisters with impunity; when you see the vast majority of your 20 million Negro brothers smothering in an airtight cage of poverty in the midst of an affluent society; when you suddenly find your tongue twisted and your speech stammering as you seek to explain to your six-year-old daughter why she can't go to the public amusement park that has just been advertised on television, and see tears welling up in her little eyes when she is told that Funtown is closed to colored children, and see the depressing clouds of inferiority begin to form in her little mental sky, and see her begin to distort her little personality by unconsciously developing a bitterness toward white people; when you have to concoct an answer for a five-year-old son asking in agonizing pathos: "Daddy, why do white people treat colored people so mean?"; when you take a cross-country drive and find it necessary to sleep night after night in the uncomfortable corners of your automobile because no motel will accept you; when you are humiliated day in and day out by nagging signs reading "white" and "colored"; when your first name becomes "nigger" and your middle name becomes "boy" (however old you are) and your last name becomes "John," and when your wife and mother are never given the respected title "Mrs."; when you are harried by day and haunted by night by the fact that you are a Negro, living constantly at tiptoe stance never quite knowing what to expect next, and plagued with inner fears and outer resentments; when you are forever fighting a degenerating sense of "nobodiness"; then you will understand why we find it difficult to wait. There comes a time when the cup of endurance runs over, and men are no longer willing to be plunged into an abyss of injustice where they experience the blackness of corroding despair. I hope, sirs, you can understand our legitimate and unavoidable impatience.

You express a great deal of anxiety over our willingness to break laws. This is certainly a legitimate concern. Since we so diligently urge people to obey the Supreme Court's decision of 1954 outlawing segregation in the public schools, it is rather strange and paradoxical to find us consciously breaking laws. One may well ask, "How can you advocate breaking some laws and obeying others?" The answer is found in the fact that there are two types of laws: There are *just* and there are *unjust* laws. I would agree with Saint Augustine that "An unjust law is no law at all."

Now what is the difference between the two? How does one determine when a law is just or unjust? A just law is a man-made code that squares with the moral law or the law of God. An unjust law is a code that is out of harmony with the moral law. To put it in the terms of Saint Thomas Aquinas, an unjust law is a human law that is not rooted in eternal and natural law. Any law that uplifts human personality is just. Any law that degrades human personality is unjust. All segregation statutes are unjust because segregation distorts the soul and damages the personality. It gives the segregator a false sense of superiority, and the segregated a false sense of inferiority. To use the words of Martin Buber, the great Jewish philosopher, segregation substitutes an "I-it" relationship for the "I-thou" relationship, and ends up relegating persons to the status of things. So segregation is not only politically, economically, and sociologically unsound, but it is morally wrong and sinful. Paul Tillich has said that sin is separation. Isn't segregation an existential expression of man's tragic separation, an expression of his awful estrangement, his terrible sinfulness? So I can urge men to disobey segregation ordinances because they are morally wrong.

Let us turn to a more concrete example of just and unjust laws. An 15
unjust law is a code that a majority inflicts on a minority that is not binding on itself. This is difference made legal. On the other hand, a just law
is a code that a majority compels a minority to follow that it is willing to
follow itself. This is sameness made legal.

Let me give another explanation. An unjust law is a code inflicted
upon a minority which that minority had no part in enacting or creating
because they did not have the unhampered right to vote. Who can say
that the legislature of Alabama which set up the segregation laws was democratically elected? Throughout the state of Alabama all types of conniv-
ing methods are used to prevent Negroes from becoming registered voters,
and there are some counties without a single Negro registered to vote despite the fact that the Negro constitutes a majority of the population. Can
any law set up in such a state be considered democratically structured?

These are just a few examples of unjust and just laws. There are some
instances when a law is just on its face and unjust in its application. For
instance, I was arrested Friday on a charge of parading without a permit.
Now there is nothing wrong with an ordinance which requires a permit
for a parade, but when the ordinance is used to preserve segregation and
to deny citizens the First Amendment privilege of peaceful assembly and
peaceful protest, then it becomes unjust.

I hope you can see the distinction I am trying to point out. In no
sense do I advocate evading or defying the law as the rabid segregationist
would do. This would lead to anarchy. One who breaks an unjust law
must do it *openly, lovingly* (not hatefully as the white mothers did in New
Orleans when they were seen on television screaming, "nigger, nigger,
nigger"), and with a willingness to accept the penalty. I submit that an individual who breaks a law that conscience tells him is unjust, and willingly accepts the penalty by staying in jail to arouse the conscience of the
community over its injustice, is in reality expressing the very highest respect for law.

Of course, there is nothing new about this kind of civil disobedience.
It was seen sublimely in the refusal of Shadrach, Meshach, and Abednego
to obey the laws of Nebuchadnezzar because a higher moral law was involved. It was practiced superbly by the early Christians who were willing
to face hungry lions and the excruciating pain of chopping blocks, before
submitting to certain unjust laws of the Roman Empire. To a degree
academic freedom is a reality today because Socrates practiced civil disobedience.

We can never forget that everything Hitler did in Germany was 20
"legal" and everything the Hungarian freedom fighters did in Hungary
was "illegal." It was "illegal" to aid and comfort a Jew in Hitler's Germany.
But I am sure that if I had lived in Germany during that time I would have
aided and comforted my Jewish brothers even though it was illegal. If I
lived in a Communist country today where certain principles dear to the

Christian faith are suppressed, I believe I would openly advocate disobeying these antireligious laws. I must make two honest confessions to you, my Christian and Jewish brothers. First, I must confess that over the last few years I have been gravely disappointed with the white moderate. I have almost reached the regrettable conclusion that the Negro's great stumbling block in the stride toward freedom is not the White Citizen's Councilor or the Ku Klux Klanner, but the white moderate who is more devoted to "order" than to justice; who prefers a negative peace which is the absence of tension to a positive peace which is the presence of justice; who constantly says, "I agree with you in the goal you seek, but I can't agree with your methods of direct action"; who paternalistically feels that he can set the timetable for another man's freedom; who lives by the myth of time and who constantly advises the Negro to wait until a "more convenient season." Shallow understanding from people of good will is more frustrating than absolute misunderstanding from people of ill will. Lukewarm acceptance is much more bewildering than outright rejection.

I had hoped that the white moderate would understand that law and order exist for the purpose of establishing justice, and that when they fail to do this they become dangerously structured dams that block the flow of social progress. I had hoped that the white moderate would understand that the present tension of the South is merely a necessary phase of the transition from an obnoxious negative peace, where the Negro passively accepted his unjust plight, to a substance-filled positive peace, where all men will respect the dignity and worth of human personality. Actually, we who engage in nonviolent direct action are not the creators of tension. We merely bring to the surface the hidden tension that is already alive. We bring it out in the open where it can be seen and dealt with. Like a boil that can never be cured as long as it is covered up but must be opened with all its pus-flowing ugliness to the natural medicines of air and light, injustice must likewise be exposed, with all of the tension its exposing creates, to the light of human conscience and the air of national opinion before it can be cured.

In your statement you asserted that our actions, even though peaceful, must be condemned because they precipitate violence. But can this assertion be logically made? Isn't this like condemning the robbed man because his possession of money precipitated the evil act of robbery? Isn't this like condemning Socrates because his unswerving commitment to truth and his philosophical delvings precipitated the misguided popular mind to make him drink the hemlock? Isn't this like condemning Jesus because His unique God-consciousness and never-ceasing devotion to His will precipitated the evil act of crucifixion? We must come to see, as federal courts have consistently affirmed, that it is immoral to urge an individual to withdraw his efforts to gain his basic constitutional rights because the quest precipitates violence. Society must protect the robbed and punish the robber.

I had also hoped that the white moderate would reject the myth of time. I received a letter this morning from a white brother in Texas which said: "All Christians know that the colored people will receive equal rights eventually, but it is possible that you are in too great of a religious hurry. It has taken Christianity almost two thousand years to accomplish what it has. The teachings of Christ take time to come to earth." All that is said here grows out of a tragic misconception of time. It is the strangely irrational notion that there is something in the very flow of time that will inevitably cure all ills. Actually time is neutral. It can be used either destructively or constructively. I am coming to feel that the people of ill will have used time much more effectively than the people of good will. We will have to repent in this generation not merely for the vitriolic words and actions of the bad people, but for the appalling silence of the good people. We must come to see that human progress never rolls in on wheels of inevitability. It comes through the tireless efforts and persistent work of men willing to be co-workers with God, and without this hard work time itself becomes an ally of the forces of social stagnation. We must use time creatively, and forever realize that the time is always ripe to do right. Now is the time to make real the promise of democracy, and transform our pending national elegy into a creative psalm of brotherhood. Now is the time to lift our national policy from the quicksand of racial injustice to the solid rock of human dignity.

You spoke of our activity in Birmingham as extreme. At first I was rather disappointed that fellow clergymen would see my nonviolent efforts as those of the extremist. I started thinking about the fact that I stand in the middle of two opposing forces in the Negro community. One is a force of complacency made up of Negroes who, as a result of long years of oppression, have been so completely drained of self-respect and a sense of "somebodiness" that they have adjusted to segregation, and of a few Negroes in the middle class who, because of a degree of academic and economic security, and because at points they profit by segregation, have unconsciously become insensitive to the problems of the masses. The other force is one of bitterness and hatred, and comes perilously close to advocating violence. It is expressed in the various black nationalist groups that are springing up over the nation, the largest and best known being Elijah Muhammad's Muslim movement. This movement is nourished by the contemporary frustration over the continued existence of racial discrimination. It is made up of people who have lost faith in America, who have absolutely repudiated Christianity, and who have concluded that the white man is an incurable "devil." I have tried to stand between these two forces, saying that we need not follow the "do-nothingism" of the complacent or the hatred and despair of the black nationalist. There is the more excellent way of love and nonviolent protest. I'm grateful to God that, through the Negro church, the dimension of nonviolence entered our struggle. If this philosophy had not emerged, I am convinced that by now many streets of the South would be flowing with floods of blood. And I am further convinced that if our white brothers dismiss us as "rabble-rousers" and "outside agitators" those of us who are working through the channels of nonviolent direct action and refuse to support our nonviolent efforts, millions of Negroes, out of frustration and despair, will seek solace and security in black nationalist ideologies, a development that will lead inevitably to a frightening racial nightmare.

Oppressed people cannot remain oppressed forever. The urge for freedom will eventually come. This is what happened to the American Negro. Something within has reminded him of his birthright of freedom; something without has reminded him that he can gain it. Consciously and unconsciously, he has been swept in by what the Germans call the *Zeitgeist*, and with his black brothers of Africa, and his brown and yellow brothers of Asia, South America, and the Caribbean, he is moving with a sense of cosmic urgency toward the promised land of racial justice. Recognizing this vital urge that has engulfed the Negro community, one should readily understand public demonstrations. The Negro has many pent-up resentments and latent frustrations. He has to get them out. So let him march sometime; let him have his prayer pilgrimages to the city hall; understand why he must have sit-ins and freedom rides. If his repressed emotions do not come out in these nonviolent ways, they will come out in ominous expressions of violence. This is not a threat; it is a fact of history. So I have not said to my people "get rid of your discontent." But I have tried to say that this normal and healthy discontent can be channelized through the creative outlet of nonviolent direct action. Now this approach is being dismissed as extremist. I must admit that I was initially disappointed in being so categorized.

But as I continued to think about the matter I gradually gained a bit of satisfaction from being considered an extremist. Was not Jesus an extremist in love—"Love your enemies, bless them that curse you, pray for them that despitefully use you." Was not Amos an extremist for justice—"Let justice roll down like waters and righteousness like a mighty stream." Was not Paul an extremist for the gospel of Jesus Christ—"I bear in my body the marks of the Lord Jesus." Was not Martin Luther an extremist—"Here I stand; I can do none other so help me God." Was not John Bunyan an extremist—"I will stay in jail to the end of my days before I make a butchery of my conscience." Was not Abraham Lincoln an extremist—"This nation cannot survive half slave and half free." Was not Thomas Jefferson an extremist—"We hold these truths to be self-evident, that all men are created equal." So the question is not whether we will be extremist but what kind of extremist will we be. Will we be extremists for hate or will we be extremists for love? Will we be extremists for the preservation of injustice—or will we be extremists for the cause of justice? In that dramatic scene on Calvary's hill, three men were crucified. We must not forget that all three were crucified for the same crime—the crime of extremism. Two were extremists for immorality, and thusly fell below their environment. The other, Jesus Christ, was an extremist for love, truth, and goodness, and thereby rose above his environment. So, after all, maybe the South, the nation, and the world are in dire need of creative extremists.

I had hoped that the white moderate would see this. Maybe I was too optimistic. Maybe I expected too much. I guess I should have realized that few members of a race that has oppressed another race can understand or appreciate the deep groans and passionate yearnings of those that have been oppressed and still fewer have the vision to see that injustice must be rooted out by strong, persistent, and determined action. I am thankful, however, that some of our white brothers have grasped the meaning of this social revolution and committed themselves to it. They are still all too small in quantity, but they are big in quality. Some like Ralph McGill, Lillian Smith, Harry Golden, and James Dabbs have written about our struggle in eloquent, prophetic, and understanding terms. Others have marched with us down nameless streets of the South. They have languished in filthy roach-infested jails, suffering the abuse and brutality of angry policemen who see them as "dirty nigger-lovers." They, unlike so many of their moderate brothers and sisters, have recognized the urgency of the moment and sensed the need for powerful "action" antidotes to combat the disease of segregation.

Let me rush on to mention my other disappointment. I have been so greatly disappointed with the white church and its leadership. Of course, there are some notable exceptions. I am not unmindful of the fact that each of you has taken some significant stands on this issue. I commend you, Reverend Stallings, for your Christian stance on this past Sunday, in welcoming Negroes to your worship service on a nonsegregated basis. I commend the Catholic leaders of this state for integrating Springhill College several years ago.

But despite these notable exceptions I must honestly reiterate that I have been disappointed with the church. I do not say that as one of the negative critics who can always find something wrong with the church. I say it as a minister of the gospel, who loves the church; who was nurtured in its bosom; who has been sustained by its spiritual blessings, and who will remain true to it as long as the cord of life shall lengthen.

I had the strange feeling when I was suddenly catapulted into the leadership of the bus protest in Montgomery several years ago that we would have the support of the white church. I felt that the white ministers, priests, and rabbis of the South would be some of our strongest allies. Instead, some have been outright opponents, refusing to understand the freedom movement and misrepresenting its leaders; all too many others have been more cautious than courageous and have remained silent behind the anesthetizing security of the stained-glass windows. 30

In spite of my shattered dreams of the past, I came to Birmingham with the hope that the white religious leadership of this community would see the justice of our cause, and with deep moral concern, serve as the channel through which our just grievances would get to the power structure. I had hoped that each of you would understand. But again I have been disappointed. I have heard numerous religious leaders of the South call upon their worshipers to comply with a desegregation decision because it is the *law,* but I have longed to hear white ministers say, "Follow this decree because integration is morally *right* and the Negro is your brother." In the midst of blatant injustices inflicted upon the Negro, I have watched white churches stand on the sideline and merely mouth pious irrelevancies and sanctimonious trivialities. In the midst of a mighty struggle to rid our nation of racial and economic injustice, I have heard so many ministers say, "Those are social issues with which the gospel has no real concern," and I have watched so many churches commit themselves to a completely otherworldly religion which made a strange distinction between body and soul, the sacred and the secular.

So here we are moving toward the exit of the twentieth century with a religious community largely adjusted to the status quo, standing as a taillight behind other community agencies rather than a headlight leading men to higher levels of justice.

I have traveled the length and breadth of Alabama, Mississippi, and all the other southern states. On sweltering summer days and crisp autumn mornings I have looked at her beautiful churches with their lofty spires pointing heavenward. I have beheld the impressive outlay of her massive religious education buildings. Over and over again I have found myself asking: "What kind of people worship here? Who is their God? Where were their voices when the lips of Governor Barnett dripped with words of interposition and nullification? Where were they when Governor Wallace gave the clarion call for defiance and hatred? Where were their voices of support when tired, bruised, and weary Negro men and women decided to rise from the dark dungeons of complacency to the bright hills of creative protest?"

Yes, these questions are still in my mind. In deep disappointment, I have wept over the laxity of the church. But be assured that my tears have been tears of love. There can be no deep disappointment where there is not deep love. Yes, I love the church; I love her sacred walls. How could I do otherwise? I am in the rather unique position of being the son, the grandson, and the great-grandson of preachers. Yes, I see the church as the body of Christ. But, oh! How we have blemished and scarred that body through social neglect and fear of being nonconformists.

There was a time when the church was very powerful. It was during 35 that period when the early Christians rejoiced when they were deemed worthy to suffer for what they believed. In those days the church was not merely a thermometer that recorded the ideas and principles of popular opinion; it was a thermostat that transformed the mores of society. Wherever the early Christians entered a town the power structure got disturbed and immediately sought to convict them for being "disturbers of the peace" and "outside agitators." But they went on with the conviction that they were "a colony of heaven," and had to obey God rather than man. They were small in number but big in commitment. They were too God-intoxicated to be "astronomically intimidated." They brought an end to such ancient evils as infanticide and gladiatorial contest.

Things are different now. The contemporary church is often a weak, ineffectual voice with an uncertain sound. It is so often the archsupporter of the status quo. Far from being disturbed by the presence of the church, the power structure of the average community is consoled by the church's silent and often vocal sanction of things as they are.

But the judgment of God is upon the church as never before. If the church of today does not recapture the sacrificial spirit of the early church, it will lose its authentic ring, forfeit the loyalty of millions, and be dismissed as an irrelevant social club with no meaning for the twenti-eth century. I am meeting young people every day whose disappointment with the church has risen to outright disgust.

Maybe again, I have been too optimistic. Is organized religion too in-extricably bound to the status quo to save our nation and the world? Maybe I must turn my faith to the inner spiritual church, the church within the church, as the true *ecclesia* and the hope of the world. But again I am thankful to God that some noble souls from the ranks of or-ganized religion have broken loose from the paralyzing chains of con-formity and joined us as active partners in the struggle for freedom. They have left their secure congregations and walked the streets of Albany, Georgia, with us. They have gone through the highways of the South on tortuous rides for freedom. Yes, they have gone to jail with us. Some have been kicked out of their churches, and lost support of their bishops and fellow ministers. But they have gone with the faith that right defeated is stronger than evil triumphant. These men have been the leaven in the lump of the race. Their witness has been the spiritual salt that has pre-served the true meaning of the gospel in these troubled times. They have carved a tunnel of hope through the dark mountain of disappointment.

I hope the church as a whole will meet the challenge of this decisive hour. But even if the church does not come to the aid of justice, I have no despair about the future. I have no fear about the outcome of our struggle in Birmingham, even if our motives are presently misunderstood. We will reach the goal of freedom in Birmingham and all over the nation, because the goal of America is freedom. Abused and scorned though we may be, our destiny is tied up with the destiny of America. Before the Pil-grims landed at Plymouth we were here. Before the pen of Jefferson etched across the pages of history the majestic words of the Declaration of Independence, we were here. For more than two centuries our forepar-ents labored in this country without wages; they made cotton king; and they built the homes of their masters in the midst of brutal injustice and

shameful humiliation—and yet out of a bottomless vitality they continued to thrive and develop. If the inexpressible cruelties of slavery could
not stop us, the opposition we now face will surely fail. We will win our
freedom because the sacred heritage of our nation and the eternal will of
God are embodied in our echoing demands.

I must close now. But before closing I am impelled to mention one 40
other point in your statement that troubled me profoundly. You warmly
commended the Birmingham police force for keeping "order" and "preventing violence." I don't believe you would have so warmly commended
the police force if you had seen its angry violent dogs literally biting six
unarmed, nonviolent Negroes. I don't believe you would so quickly commend the policemen if you would observe their ugly and inhuman treatment of Negroes here in the city jail; if you would watch them push and
curse old Negro women and young Negro girls; if you would see them
slap and kick old Negro men and young boys; if you will observe them,
as they did on two occasions, refuse to give us food because we wanted to
sing our grace together. I'm sorry that I can't join you in your praise for
the police department.

It is true that they have been rather disciplined in their public han-
dling of the demonstrators. In this sense they have been rather publicly
"nonviolent." But for what purpose? To preserve the evil system of segregation. Over the last few years I have consistently preached that nonviolence demands that the means we use must be as pure as the ends we
seek. So I have tried to make it clear that it is wrong to use immoral means
to attain moral ends. But now I must affirm that it is just as wrong, or
even more so, to use moral means to preserve immoral ends. Maybe Mr.
Connor and his policemen have been rather publicly nonviolent, as Chief
Pritchett was in Albany, Georgia, but they have used the moral means of
nonviolence to maintain the immoral end of flagrant racial injustice. T. S.
Eliot has said that there is no greater treason than to do the right deed for
the wrong reason.

I wish you had commended the Negro sit-inners and demonstrators
of Birmingham for their sublime courage, their willingness to suffer, and
their amazing discipline in the midst of the most inhuman provocation.
One day the South will recognize its real heroes. They will be the James
Merediths, courageously and with a majestic sense of purpose facing jeer-
ing and hostile mobs and the agonizing loneliness that characterizes the
life of the pioneer. They will be old, oppressed, battered Negro women,
symbolized in a seventy-two-year-old woman of Montgomery, Alabama,
who rose up with a sense of dignity and with her people decided not to
ride the segregated buses, and responded to one who inquired about her
tiredness with ungrammatical profundity: "My feet is tired, but my soul
is rested." They will be the young high school and college students,
young ministers of the gospel, and a host of their elders courageously and
nonviolently sitting-in at lunch counters and willingly going to jail for

conscience's sake. One day the South will know that when these disinherited children of God sat down at lunch counters they were in reality standing up for the best in the American dream and the most sacred values in our Judeo-Christian heritage, and thusly, carrying our whole nation back to those great wells of democracy which were dug deep by the Founding Fathers in the formulation of the Constitution and the Declaration of Independence.

Never before have I written a letter this long (or should I say a book?). I'm afraid that it is much too long to take your precious time. I can assure you that it would have been much shorter if I had been writing from a comfortable desk, but what else is there to do when you are alone for days in the dull monotony of a narrow jail cell other than write long letters, think strange thoughts, and pray long prayers?

If I have said anything in this letter that is an overstatement of the truth and is indicative of an unreasonable impatience, I beg you to forgive me. If I have said anything in this letter that is an understatement of the truth and is indicative of my having a patience that makes me patient with anything less than brotherhood, I beg God to forgive me.

I hope this letter finds you strong in the faith. I also hope that cir- 45 cumstances will soon make it possible for me to meet each of you, not as an integrationist or a civil rights leader, but as a fellow clergyman and a Christian brother. Let us all hope that the dark clouds of racial prejudice will soon pass away and the deep fog of misunderstanding will be lifted from our fear-drenched communities and in some not too distant tomorrow the radiant stars of love and brotherhood will shine over our great nation with all of their scintillating beauty.

Yours for the cause of Peace and Brotherhood,

Martin Luther King Jr.

READING AND DISCUSSION QUESTIONS

1. What are some of the steps that King and his sympathizers took to try to avoid direct action in Birmingham? Why was Birmingham a logical target for the action, when it came?

2. Explain King's distinction between just and unjust laws. Are there dangers in attempting to make such a distinction?

3. What are some of the most vivid examples of the sort of discrimination that King and his followers hoped to end?

4. Why does King say that the white moderate is a greater threat to African American progress than the outspoken racist? Is his explanation convincing?

5. What other group does King express disappointment with?

6. What claim is King supporting in the letter?

7. King uses figurative language in the letter. Find some particularly vivid passages and evaluate their effectiveness in the context of the letter.

WRITING SUGGESTIONS

8. Write a one-paragraph summary of the letter.
9. Can you think of a law against which defiance would be justified? Explain why the law is unjust and why refusal to obey it would be morally defensible.
10. Write an essay in which you summarize and evaluate King's criticism of the political and religious establishments of his day.

DEBATE: Under what circumstances should the government have the right to seize personal property?

One Year later, Power to Seize Property Ripe for Abuse

USA TODAY

Remember Susette Kelo? The New London, Connecticut, nurse lost a landmark legal fight to save her pink cottage from being seized by city officials, who wanted to hand it over to developers. Just over a year ago, the U.S. Supreme Court ruled against her. It held 5–4 that local governments could condemn private property, not just for a public purpose such as a road or school, but also to give to developers if a locality's economic future is at issue.

As it turned out, that wasn't the end of the story. The house won't be bulldozed after all. Last month, officials agreed to move it to another location so that her land can round out a waterfront development site — a compromise Kelo suggested years ago to little avail.

Meanwhile, the ruling has ignited a nationwide fight between developers rushing to seize a fresh opportunity and an unlikely political coalition that sees the decision as an assault on America's "home-as-castle" mind-set.

Emboldened by the ruling, local governments have threatened or condemned 5,783 properties for private projects in the past year, according to the Institute for Justice, the libertarian law firm that defended Kelo. That's up from an annual average of 2,056 such threats and takings from 1998 to 2002, the Institute said.

This unsigned piece expresses *USA Today*'s editorial stance on eminent domain. It and the opposing view by Donald J. Borut appeared in the July 10, 2006, issue of that newspaper.

Of 117 projects the Institute studied over the past year, most involved   5
taking lower-income homes, apartments and mobile home parks to construct upscale condominiums or retail development, driving the working
poor from their homes.

But the Kelo case also has inspired a political backlash unusual in the
annals of Supreme Court rulings. It has united conservative defenders of
property rights and liberals who say the seizures amount to corporate welfare at the expense of the powerless.

They've scored significant victories:

- Twenty-five states have enacted laws to curb eminent domain
  seizures—something the Supreme Court invited them to do in making
  its ruling.

- The U.S. House of Representatives voted 376–38 last year to bar federal economic development funds to state and local agencies that use
  eminent domain for private commercial development. A similar bill
  is stalled in the Senate.

- On June 23, one year after the Kelo decision, President Bush issued
  an executive order that federal agencies can seize private property
  only for public projects.

Those actions should help ensure that the growing movement to prevent unjustified seizures of private property will gain momentum. In the
words of dissenting Justice Sandra Day O'Connor, "the government now
has the license to transfer property from those with fewer resources to those
with more" as long as there is some purported economic benefit. And that
is wrong.

Supporters of seizures such as the one in New London argue that abuses
are rare and that condemnation is needed to revitalize abandoned or blighted
areas and encourage the growth of jobs. But the truth is that under the court's
ruling almost no one's property is safe unless states impose limits.

Seizures of one person's property to benefit another should be rare and   10
a last resort. The halfway happy ending to Susette Kelo's ordeal should encourage political leaders to do more to stop bulldozers from plowing through
the American dream.

Vital Tool of Last Resort

DONALD J. BORUT

In all the noise that surrounded the decision by the Supreme Court one year ago to continue to allow cities to use eminent domain when considering the economic future of their communities, something vital was left out: the facts.

Without eminent domain to clear title on abandoned and vacant properties—the primary use of eminent domain in this country—rundown buildings and empty lots would attract trash, rodents and trouble. Blighted structures would sit abandoned. If owners didn't want to sell or were holding out for more money, the cities and their taxpayers could do nothing to get rid of them.

Despite what some might claim, this is how eminent domain has been and continues to be used in this country: to revitalize older parts of Philadelphia; to transform an area in Indianapolis once referred to as "Dodge City" into a beautiful, mixed-income neighborhood; to save a historic church in Fitzgerald, Georgia.

Let's take a closer look at the facts:

Since the Supreme Court's *Kelo* ruling, 43 state legislatures reviewed eminent domain laws and made changes to meet the needs of their communities. In a few cases, after numerous public hearings, legislators determined that no change was needed. 5

According to a survey by the National League of Cities, 76% of municipalities had not used eminent domain in the past three years in connection with an economic development project. But where it was invoked, eminent domain was used only as a last resort after all other options were explored.

Of the 5,700-plus properties claimed by the Institute for Justice to involve eminent domain in the past year, many were part of 117 multiphased and publicly scrutinized economic development projects begun well before the *Kelo* decision to eradicate blight—a practice even dissenting Justice Sandra Day O'Connor found appropriate.

Ensuring that owners receive appropriate compensation for their properties is equally important. In cases such as Norwood, Ohio, which was cited by the Institute as an abuse, the majority of owners willingly received twice the assessed fair market value; the "hold-outs" three times their value.

The prudent use of eminent domain has brought hope and opportunity—through good jobs and better housing—to thousands of Americans. That story deserves to be told.

Donald J. Borut is the executive director of the National League of Cities, the nation's oldest and largest national organization representing municipal governments. Before assuming that position in 1990, he was deputy executive director of the International City Management Association, an organization of professional administrators in local governments.

DISCUSSION QUESTIONS

1. Why was the *Kelo* case considered a landmark decision? What have been some of the effects of the ruling, according to the editorial?

2. What claim are the *USA Today* editors supporting? What types of support do these unnamed editors offer for their claim?

3. According to Borut, what is the primary use of eminent domain in this country? What facts does Borut offer in defending his position? Is there any overlap between his facts and those offered in the editorial?

4. What is Borut's claim?

5. Where, if anywhere, do the two arguments share common ground?

6. Which of the two arguments do you find more convincing? Is your opinion influenced by any experience you or someone you know has had with eminent domain? By previous reading or discussion of the subject? Explain.

ASSIGNMENTS FOR DEFENDING CLAIMS

READING AND DISCUSSION QUESTIONS

1. Locate a movie review online or in hard copy that has a clear claim and is based on clear evaluative criteria. Choose a review that is an essay, not just a single paragraph. Bring it to class and share it with your class or group. By looking at a range of different reviews, come to some conclusions about the sort of criteria used in making judgment calls about movies and what sort of claims provide good thesis statements for reviews. What are some other characteristics that all or most good movie reviews share?

2. Consider one or more of your school's policies that you would like to see changed. In your opinion, what exactly is wrong with the policy as it currently exists? What exactly would you recommend be done to improve the situation?

3. Samuelson argues that different news sources slant their news toward different audiences. Do you agree with his argument? Why, or why not? What examples can you provide in support of your opinion?

WRITING ASSIGNMENTS

4. Write an essay explaining whether you believe that the editors of *USA Today* or Borut has the stronger argument regarding eminent domain, and why.

5. Choose a controversial issue in the field in which you are majoring or one in which you might major. Practice differentiating among the three types of claims by writing a claim of fact, a claim of value, and a claim of policy on that issue.

6. Choose one of the three claims you wrote for assignment five above and write an essay supporting it.

CHAPTER 7

Providing Support

TYPES OF SUPPORT: EVIDENCE AND APPEALS TO NEEDS AND VALUES

All the claims you make—whether of fact, of value, or of policy—must be supported. Sometimes you will use your own experience as support for a claim. At other times you may conduct interviews, field research, lab experiments, or surveys to obtain support for your position. For the majority of your assignments, you will most likely turn primarily to print and electronic sources.

Support for a claim represents the answer to the question "What have you got to go on?"[1] There are two basic kinds of support in an argument: evidence and appeals to needs and values.

Evidence, as one dictionary defines it, is "something that tends to prove; ground for belief." When you provide evidence, you use facts, including statistics, and opinions, or interpretations of facts—both your own and those of experts. In the following conversation, the first speaker offers facts and the opinion of an expert to convince the second speaker that robots are exceptional machines.

"You know, robots do a lot more than work on assembly lines in factories."
"Like what?"

[1] Stephen Toulmin, *The Uses of Argument* (Cambridge: Cambridge University Press, 1958), p. 98.

"They shear sheep, pick citrus fruit, and even assist in neurosurgery. And by the end of the century, every house will have a robot slave."

"No kidding. Who says so?"

"An engineer who's the head of the world's largest manufacturer of industrial robots."

A writer often appeals to readers' needs (that is, requirements for physical and psychological survival and well-being) and values (or standards for right and wrong, good and bad). In the following conversation, the first speaker makes an appeal to the universal need for self-esteem and to the principle of helping others, a value the second speaker probably shares.

"I think you ought to come help us at the nursing home. We need an extra hand."

"I'd like to, but I really don't have the time."

"You could give us an hour a week, couldn't you? Think how good you'd feel about helping out, and the residents would be so grateful. Some of them are very lonely."

Although they use the same kinds of support, conversations are less rigorous than arguments addressed to larger audiences in academic or public situations. In the debates on public policy that appear in the media and in the courts, the quality of support can be crucial in settling urgent matters. The following summary of a well-known court case demonstrates the critical use of both evidence and value appeals in the support of opposing claims.

On March 30, 1981, President Ronald Reagan and three other men were shot by John W. Hinckley Jr., a young drifter from a wealthy Colorado family. Hinckley was arrested at the scene of the shooting. In his trial the factual evidence was presented first: Dozens of reliable witnesses had seen the shooting at close range. Hinckley's diaries, letters, and poems revealed that he had planned the shooting to impress actress Jodie Foster. Opinions, consisting of testimony by experts, were introduced by both the defense and the prosecution. This evidence was contradictory. Defense attorneys produced several psychiatrists who defined Hinckley as insane. If this interpretation of his conduct convinced the jury, then Hinckley would be confined to a mental hospital rather than a prison. The prosecution introduced psychiatrists who interpreted Hinckley's motives and actions as those of a man who knew what he was doing and knew it was wrong. They claimed he was *not* insane by legal definition. The fact that experts can make differing conclusions about the meaning of the same information indicates that interpretations are less reliable than other kinds of support.

Finally, the defense made an appeal to the moral values of the jury. Under the law, criminals judged to be insane are not to be punished as harshly as criminals judged to be sane. The laws assume that criminals who cannot be held responsible for their actions are entitled to more compassionate treatment, confinement to a mental hospital rather than prison. The jury accepted the interpretive evidence supporting the claim of the defense, and Hinckley was pronounced not guilty by reason of insanity. Clearly the moral concern for the rights of the insane proved to be decisive.

In your arguments you will advance your claims, not unlike a lawyer, with these same kinds of support. But before you begin, you should ask two questions: Which kind of support should I use in convincing an audience to accept my claim? and How do I decide that each item of support is valid and worthy of acceptance? This chapter presents the different types of evidence and appeals you can use to support your claim and examines the criteria by which you can evaluate the soundness of that support.

EVIDENCE

■ Factual Evidence

In Chapter 6, we defined facts as statements possessing a high degree of public acceptance. In theory, facts can be verified by experience alone. Eating too much will make us sick; we can get from Hopkinton to Boston in a half hour by car; in the Northern Hemisphere it is colder in December than in July. The experience of any individual is limited in both time and space, so we must accept as fact thousands of assertions about the world that we ourselves can never verify. Thus we accept the report that human beings landed on the moon in 1969 because we trust those who can verify it. (Country people in Morocco, however, received the news with disbelief because they had no reason to trust the reporters of the event. They insisted on trusting their senses instead. One man said, "I can see the moon very clearly. If a man were walking around up there, wouldn't I be able to see him?")

Factual evidence appears most frequently as examples and statistics, which are a numerical form of examples.

Examples

Examples are the most familiar kind of factual evidence. In addition to providing support for the truth of a generalization, examples can enliven otherwise dense or monotonous prose.

In the following paragraph the writer supports the claim in the topic sentence by offering a series of specific examples.

> Americans expect the next century to bring some striking political and
> social changes, but people are discerning. Two-thirds believe gay marriages

probably will be legal and over half think that fathers will spend as much time and energy with their kids as mothers. Half of the public also predicts that Social Security will probably die; that view is particularly prevalent among younger Americans. But a majority doubts that cigarette smoking will be illegal or that all racial and gender discrimination will disappear.[2]

Hypothetical examples, which create imaginary situations for the audience and encourage them to visualize what might happen under certain circumstances, can also be effective. The following paragraph illustrates the use of hypothetical examples. (The author is describing megaschools, high schools with more than two thousand students.)

> And in schools that big there is inevitably a critical mass of kids who are neither jocks nor artists nor even nerds, kids who are nothing at all, nonentities in their own lives. . . . The creditable ballplayer who might have made the team in a smaller school is edged out by better athletes. The artist who might have had work hung in a smaller school is supplanted by abler talents. And the disaffected and depressed boy who might have found a niche, or a friend, or a teacher who noticed, falls between the cracks. Sometimes he quietly drops out. Sometimes he quietly passes through. And sometimes he comes to school with a gun.[3]

All claims about vague or abstract terms would be boring or unintelligible without examples to illuminate them. For example, if you claim that a movie contains "unusual sound effects," you will certainly have to describe some of the effects to convince the reader that your generalization can be trusted.

Statistics

Statistics express information in numbers. In the following example statistics have been used to express raw data in numerical form.

> Surveys have shown that almost half of all male high school seniors — and nearly 20 percent of all ninth grade boys — can be called "problem drinkers." . . . Over 5,000 teenagers are killed yearly in auto accidents due to drunken driving.[4]

These grim numbers probably have meaning for you, partly because you already know that alcoholism exists even among young teenagers and partly because your own experience enables you to evaluate the numbers. But if you are unfamiliar with the subject, such numbers may be difficult or impossible to understand. Statistics, therefore, are more effective in

[2] Elizabeth Crowley, "Putting Faith in Technology for Year 3000," *Wall Street Journal*, September 15, 2000, sec. A, p. 10.

[3] Anna Quindlen, "The Problem of the Megaschool," *Newsweek*, March 26, 2001, p. 68.

[4] "The Kinds of Drugs Kids Are Getting Into" (Spring House, Pa.: McNeil Pharmaceutical, n.d.).

comparisons that indicate whether a quantity is relatively large or small and sometimes even whether a reader should interpret the result as gratifying or disappointing. For example, if a novice gambler were told that for every dollar wagered in a state lottery, 50 percent goes back to the players as prizes, would the gambler be able to conclude that the percentage is high or low? Would he be able to choose between playing the state lottery and playing a casino game? Unless he had more information, probably not. But if he were informed that in casino games, the return to the players is over 90 percent and in slot machines and racetracks the return is around 80 percent, the comparison would enable him to evaluate the meaning of the 50 percent return in the state lottery and even to make a decision about where to gamble his money.[5]

Comparative statistics are also useful for measurements over time. For instance, the following statistics show what comparisons based on BMI or body mass index reveal about how Miss America contestants have changed over the years.

> Miss America contestants have become increasing thinner over the past 75 years. In the 1920s, contestants had BMIs in the normal range of 20–25. Since then, pageant winners' body weights have decreased steadily to a level about 12 percent below levels from the mid-1900s. Since 1970, nearly all of the winners have had BMIs below the healthy range, with some as low as 16.9, a BMI that would meet part of the diagnostic criteria for anorexia nervosa.[6]

Diagrams, tables, charts, and graphs can make clear the relations among many sets of numbers. Such charts and diagrams allow readers to grasp the information more easily than if it were presented in paragraph form.

The graphs that constitute Figures 1 and 2 on pages 216 and 217 summarize the information produced by polls about cancer care and cancer costs. The pie charts on page 218 (Figures 3 and 4) clarify coverage of Africa by two popular newsmagazines.

■ Opinions: Interpretations of the Facts

We have seen how opinions of experts influenced the verdict in the trial of John Hinckley. Facts alone were not enough to substantiate the claim that Hinckley was guilty of attempted assassination. Both the defense and the prosecution relied on experts—psychiatrists—to interpret the facts. Opinions or interpretations about the facts are the inferences discussed in Chapter 6. They are an indispensable source of support for your claims.

---

[5] Curt Suphee, "Lotto Baloney," *Harper's,* July 1983, p. 201.
[6] S. Rubenstein and B. Caballero, "Is Miss America an Undernourished Role Model?" *JAMA* (2000), p. 1569. Qtd. in Jillian Croll, "Body Image and Adolescents," *Guidelines for Adolescent Nutrition Services,* J. Stang and M. Story, eds. (2005). June 9, 2007. http://www.epi.umn.edu/let/pubs/adol_book.shtm.

FIGURE 1
Ratings of Health-Care System for Cancer Care

How would you rate the health-care system in America today when it comes to providing cancer care?

Comparison question asked of general public: How would you rate the health-care system in America today?

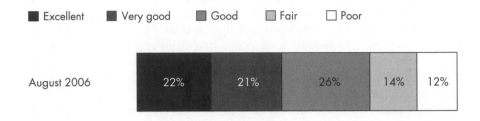

Note: Don't know and refused responses not shown.
Source: USA Today/Kaiser Family Foundation/Harvard School of Public Health, *National Survey of Households Affected by Cancer* (conducted Aug. 1–Sept. 14, 2006); Employee Benefit Research Institute, *Health Confidence Survey* (conducted June 30–Aug. 6, 2005).

Suppose a nightclub for teenagers has opened in your town. That is a fact. What is the significance of it? Is the club's existence good or bad? What consequences will it have for the community? Some parents oppose the idea of a nightclub, fearing that it may allow teenagers to escape from parental control and engage in dangerous activities. Other parents approve of a club, hoping that it will serve as a substitute for unsupervised congregation in the streets. The importance of these interpretations is that they, not the fact itself, help people decide what actions they should take. If the community accepts the interpretation that the club is a source of delinquency, they may decide to revoke the owner's license and close it. As one writer puts it, "The interpretation of data becomes a struggle over power."

Opinions or interpretations of facts generally take four forms: (1) They may suggest the cause for a condition or a causal connection between two sets of data; (2) they may offer predictions about the future; (3) they may suggest solutions to a problem; (4) they may refer to the opinion of experts.

FIGURE 2
Financial Burden of Cancer Care by Insurance Status, Income, and Age

Percent saying the cost of cancer care is a *major* burden on their family...

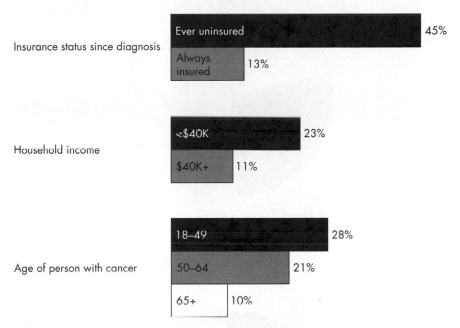

Insurance status since diagnosis

- Ever uninsured — 45%
- Always insured — 13%

Household income

- <$40K — 23%
- $40K+ — 11%

Age of person with cancer

- 18–49 — 28%
- 50–64 — 21%
- 65+ — 10%

Source: USA Today/Kaiser Family Foundation/Harvard School of Public Health, *National Survey of Households Affected by Cancer* (conducted Aug. 1–Sept. 14, 2006).

Causal Connection

Anorexia nervosa is a serious, sometimes fatal, disease characterized by self-starvation. It is found largely among young women. Physicians, psychologists, and social scientists have speculated about the causes, which remain unclear. A leading researcher in the field, Hilde Bruch, believes that food refusal expresses a desire to postpone sexual development. Another authority, Joan Blumberg, believes that one cause may be biological, a nervous dysfunction of the hypothalamus. Still others infer that the causes are cultural, a response to the admiration of the thin female body.[7]

Predictions about the Future

In the fall and winter of 1989 to 1990 extraordinary events shook Eastern Europe, toppling Communist regimes and raising more popular forms of

[7] Phyllis Rose, "Hunger Artists," *Harper's*, July 1988, p. 82.

FIGURE 3

Percentages of Five Story Topics about Africa in *Newsweek*, August 1989 to August 1991

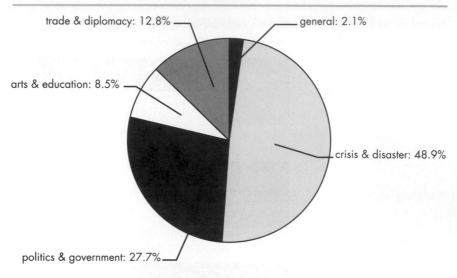

FIGURE 4

Percentages of Five Story Topics about Africa in *Time*, August 1989 to August 1991

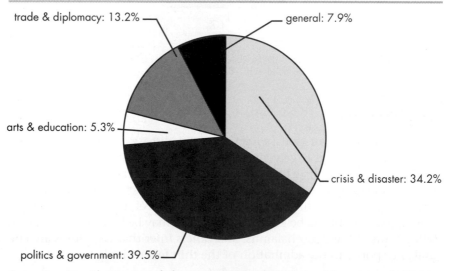

Source: Jerry Domatob, "Coverage of Africa in American Popular Magazines," *Issue: A Journal of Opinion,* 22 (Winter-Spring 1994): 25.

government. Politicians and scholars offered predictions about future changes in the region. One expert, Zbigniew Brzezinski, former national security adviser under President Carter, concluded that the changes for the Soviet Union might be destructive.

It would be a mistake to see the recent decisions as marking a break-through for democracy. Much more likely is a prolonged period of democratizing chaos. One will see the rise in the Soviet Union of increasingly irreconcilable conflicts between varying national political and social aspirations, all united by a shared hatred for the existing Communist nomenklatura. One is also likely to see a flashback of a nationalist type among the Great Russians, fearful of the prospective breakup of the existing Great Russian Empire.[8]

Solutions to Problems

How shall we solve the problems caused by young people in our cities "who commit crimes and create the staggering statistics in teenage pregnancies and the high abortion rate"? The minister emeritus of the Abyssinian Baptist Church in New York City proposes establishment of a national youth academy with fifty campuses on inactive military bases. "It is a 'parenting' institution. . . . It is not a penal institution, not a prep school, not a Job Corps Center, not a Civilian Conservation Camp, but it borrows from them." Although such an institution has not been tried before, the author of the proposal thinks that it would represent an effort "to provide for the academic, moral, and social development of young people, to cause them to become responsible and productive citizens."[9]

Expert Opinion

For many of the subjects you discuss and write about, you will find it necessary to accept and use the opinions of experts. Based on their reading of the facts, experts express opinions on a variety of controversial subjects: whether capital punishment is a deterrent to crime; whether legalization of marijuana will lead to an increase in its use; whether children, if left untaught, will grow up honest and cooperative; whether sex education courses will result in less sexual activity and fewer illegitimate births. The interpretations of the data are often profoundly important because they influence social policy and affect our lives directly and indirectly.

For the problems mentioned above, the opinions of people recognized as authorities are more reliable than those of people who have neither thought about nor done research on the subject. But opinions may also be offered by student writers in areas in which they are knowledgeable. If you were asked, for example, to defend or refute the statement that work has advantages for teenagers, you could call on your own experience and that of your friends to support your claim. You can also draw on your experience to write convincingly about your special interests.

[8]*New York Times,* February 9, 1990, sec. A, p. 13.

[9]Samuel D. Proctor, "To the Rescue: A National Youth Academy," *New York Times,* September 16, 1989, sec. A, p. 27.

One opinion, however, is not as good as another. The value of any opinion depends on the quality of the evidence and the trustworthiness of the person offering it.

PRACTICE

1. Choose either Figure 1, "Ratings of Health-Care System for Cancer Care" (p. 216), or Figure 2, "Financial Burden of Cancer Care by Insurance Status, Income, and Age" (p. 217). Consider the facts presented in the graph you chose. What is one conclusion you can draw based on those facts? Summarize that conclusion in one sentence and make it the topic sentence for a paragraph. Then use facts from the graph as specific support to complete the paragraph.

2. Do the same with Figure 3 and Figure 4 (p. 218), the pie charts about Africa, but this time consider both charts.

3. Write two possible topic sentences supporting conclusions you were able to draw from the information in Figure 1, one a statement of fact and the other a statement of opinion. Do the same with Figure 2.

EVALUATION OF EVIDENCE

Before you begin to write, you must determine whether the facts and opinions you have chosen to support your claim are sound. Can they convince your readers? A distinction between the evaluation of facts and the evaluation of opinions is somewhat artificial because many facts are verified by expert opinion, but for our analysis we discuss them separately.

■ Evaluation of Factual Evidence

As you evaluate factual evidence, you should keep in mind the following questions:

1. Is the evidence up to date? The importance of up-to-date information depends on the subject. If you are defending the claim that suicide is immoral, you will not need to examine new data. For many of the subjects you write about, recent research and scholarship will be important, even decisive, in proving the soundness of your data. "New" does not always mean "best," but in fields where research is ongoing—education, psychology, technology, medicine, and all the natural and physical sciences—you should be sensitive to the dates of the research.

In writing a paper a few years ago warning about the health hazards of air pollution, you would have used data referring only to outdoor pollution produced by automobile and factory emissions. But writing about air pollution today, you would have to take into account new data about indoor pollution, which has become a serious problem as a result of attempts to conserve energy. Because research studies in indoor pollution are continually being updated, recent evidence will probably be more accurate than past research.

2. Is the evidence sufficient? The amount of evidence you need depends on the complexity of the subject and the length of your paper. Given the relative brevity of most of your assignments, you will need to be selective. For the claim that indoor pollution is a serious problem, one example would obviously not be enough. For a 750- to 1,000-word paper, three or four examples would probably be sufficient. The choice of examples should reflect different aspects of the problem: in this case, different sources of indoor pollution — gas stoves, fireplaces, kerosene heaters, insulation — and the consequences for health.

Indoor pollution is a fairly limited subject for which the evidence is clear. But more complex problems require more evidence. A common fault in argument is generalization based on insufficient evidence. In a 1,000-word paper you could not adequately treat the causes of conflict in the Middle East; you could not develop workable proposals for health-care reform; you could not predict the development of education in the next century. In choosing a subject for a brief paper, determine whether you can produce sufficient evidence to convince a reader who may not agree with you. If not, the subject may be too large for a brief paper.

3. Is the evidence relevant? All the evidence should, of course, contribute to the development of your argument. Sometimes the arguer loses sight of the subject and introduces examples that are wide of the claim. In defending a national health-care plan, one student offered examples of the success of health maintenance organizations, but such organizations, although subsidized by the federal government, were not the structure favored by sponsors of a national health-care plan. The examples were interesting but irrelevant.

Also keep in mind that not all readers will agree on what is relevant. Is the unsavory private life of a politician relevant to his or her performance in office? If you want to prove that a politician is unfit to serve because of his or her private activities, you may first have to convince some members of the audience that private activities are relevant to public service.

4. Are the examples representative? This question emphasizes your responsibility to choose examples that are typical of all the examples you do not use. Suppose you offered Vermont's experience to support your claim that same-sex marriage should be legal. Is the experience of Vermont typical of what is happening or may happen in other states? Or is Vermont, a small, mostly rural New England state, different enough from other states to make the example unrepresentative?

5. Are the examples consistent with the experience of the audience? The members of your audience use their own experiences to judge the soundness of your evidence. If your examples are unfamiliar or extreme, they will probably reject your conclusion. Consider the following excerpt from Jacob Neusner's hypothetical commencement speech, which is meant to represent a faculty member's response to student apathy.

> For years we have created an altogether forgiving world, in which whatever slight effort you gave was all that was demanded. When you did not keep appointments, we made new ones. When your work came in beyond the deadline, we pretended not to care.
>
> Worse still, when you were boring, we acted as if you were saying something important. When you were garrulous and talked to hear yourself talk, we listened as if it mattered. When you tossed on our desks writing upon which you had not labored, we read it and even responded, as though you earned a response. When you were dull, we pretended you were smart. When you were predictable, unimaginative, and routine, we listened as if to new and wonderful things. When you demanded free lunch we served it.

If most members of the audience find that such a description doesn't reflect their own attitudes or those of their friends, they will probably question the validity of the claim.

■ Evaluation of Statistics

The questions you must ask about examples also apply to statistics. Are they recent? Are they sufficient? Are they relevant? Are they typical? Are they consistent with the experience of the audience? But there are additional questions directed specifically to evaluation of statistics.

1. Do the statistics come from trustworthy sources? Perhaps you have read newspaper accounts of very old people, some reported to be as old as 135, living in the Caucasus or the Andes, nourished by yogurt and hard work. But these statistics are hearsay; no birth records or other official documents exist to verify them. Now two anthropologists have concluded that the numbers were part of a rural mythology and that the ages of the people were actually within the normal range for human populations elsewhere.[10]

Hearsay statistics should be treated with the same skepticism accorded to gossip or rumor. Sampling a population to gather statistical information is a sophisticated science; you should ask whether the reporter of the statistics is qualified and likely to be free of bias. Among the generally reliable sources are polling organizations such as Gallup, Roper, and Louis Harris and agencies of the U.S. government such as the Census Bureau and the Bureau of Labor Statistics. Other qualified sources are well-known research foundations, university centers, and insurance com-

---

[10] Richard B. Mazess and Sylvia H. Forman, "Longevity and Age Exaggeration in Vilcabamba, Ecuador," *Journal of Gerontology* (1979), pp. 94–98.

panies that prepare actuarial tables. Statistics from underdeveloped countries are less reliable for obvious reasons: lack of funds, lack of trained statisticians, lack of communication and transportation facilities to carry out accurate censuses.

2. Are the terms clearly defined? In an example in Chapter 5, the reference to poverty (p. 123) made clear that any statistics would be meaningless unless we knew exactly how *poverty* was defined by the user. *Unemployment* is another term for which statistics will be difficult to read if the definition varies from one user to another. For example, are seasonal workers employed or unemployed during the off-season? Are part-time workers employed? (In Russia they are unemployed.) Are workers on government projects employed? (During the 1930s they were considered employed by the Germans and unemployed by the Americans.) The more abstract or controversial the term, the greater the necessity for clear definition.

3. Are the comparisons between comparable things? Folk wisdom warns us that we cannot compare apples and oranges. Population statistics for the world's largest city, for example, should indicate the units being compared. Greater London is defined in one way, greater New York in another, and greater Tokyo in still another. The population numbers will mean little unless you can be sure that the same geographical units are being compared.

4. Has any significant information been omitted? *The Plain Truth*, a magazine published by the World-Wide Church of God, advertises itself as follows:

> *The Plain Truth* has now topped 5,000,000 copies per issue. It is now the fastest-growing magazine in the world and one of the widest circulated mass-circulation magazines on earth. Our circulation is now greater than *Newsweek*. New subscribers are coming in at the rate of around 40,000 per week.

What the magazine neglects to mention is that it is *free*. There is no subscription fee, and the magazine is widely distributed in drugstores, supermarkets, and airports. *Newsweek* is sold on newsstands and by subscription. The comparison therefore omits significant information.

■ Evaluation of Opinions

When you evaluate the reliability of opinions in subjects with which you are not familiar, you will be dealing almost exclusively with opinions of experts. Most of the following questions are directed to an evaluation of authoritative sources. But you can also ask these questions of students or of others with opinions based on their own experience and research. Keep them in mind when doing research on the Web.

1. Is the source of the opinion qualified to give an opinion on the subject? The discussion on credibility in Chapter 1 (pp. 17–21) pointed out that certain achievements by the interpreter of the data—publications, acceptance by colleagues—can tell us something about his or her competence. Although these standards are by no means foolproof (people of outstanding reputations have been known to falsify their data), nevertheless they offer assurance that the source is generally trustworthy. The answers to questions you must ask are not hard to find: Is the source qualified by education? Is the source associated with a reputable institution—a university or a research organization? Is the source credited with having made contributions to the field—books, articles, research studies? Suppose that in writing a paper on organ transplants you came across an article by Peter Medawar. He is identified as follows:

> Sir Peter Medawar, British zoologist, winner of the 1960 Nobel Prize in Physiology or Medicine, for proving that the rejection by the body of foreign organs can be overcome; president of the Royal Society; head of the National Institute for Medical Research in London; a world leader in immunology.

These credentials would suggest to almost any reader that Medawar was a reliable source for information about organ transplants.

If the source is not so clearly identified, you should treat the data with caution. Such advice is especially relevant when you are dealing with popular works about such subjects as miracle diets, formulas for instant wealth, and sightings of monsters and UFOs. Do not use such data until you can verify them from other, more authoritative sources.

In addition, you should question the identity of any source listed as "spokesperson" or "reliable source" or "an unidentified authority." The mass media are especially fond of this type of attribution. Sometimes the sources are people in public life who plant stories anonymously or off the record for purposes they prefer to keep hidden.

Even when the identification is clear and genuine, you should ask if the credentials are relevant to the field in which the authority claims expertise. So specialized are areas of scientific study today that scientists in one field may not be competent to make judgments in another. William Shockley is a distinguished engineer, a Nobel Prize winner for his contribution to the invention of the electronic transistor. But when he made the claim, based on his own research, that blacks are genetically inferior to whites, geneticists accused Shockley of venturing into a field where he was unqualified to make judgments. Similarly, advertisers invite stars from the entertainment world to express opinions about products with which they are probably less familiar than members of their audience. All citizens have the right to express their views, but this does not mean that all views are equally credible or worthy of attention.

2. Is the source biased for or against his or her interpretation? Even authorities who satisfy the criteria for expertise may be guilty of bias. Bias arises as a result of economic reward, religious affiliation, political loyalty, and other interests. The expert may not be aware of the bias; even an expert can fall into the trap of ignoring evidence that contradicts his or her own intellectual preferences. A British psychologist has said:

> The search for meaning in data is bound to involve all of us in distortion to greater or lesser degree. . . . Transgression consists not so much in a clear break with professional ethics, as in an unusually high-handed, extreme or self-deceptive attempt to promote one particular view of reality at the expense of all others.[11]

Before accepting the interpretation of an expert, you should ask: Is there some reason why I should suspect the motives of this particular source?

Consider, for example, an advertisement claiming that sweetened breakfast cereals are nutritious. The advertisement, placed by the manufacturer of the cereal, provides impeccable references from scientific sources to support its claims. But since you are aware of the economic interest of the company in promoting sales, you may wonder if they have reproduced only facts that favor their claims. Are there other facts that might prove the opposite? As a careful researcher you would certainly want to look further for data about the advantages and disadvantages of sugar in our diets.

It is harder to determine bias in the research done by scientists and university members even when the research is funded by companies interested in a favorable review of their products. If you discover that a respected biologist who advocates the use of sugar in baby food receives a consultant's fee from a sugar company, should you conclude that the research is slanted and that the scientist has ignored contrary evidence? Not necessarily. The truth may be that the scientist arrived at conclusions about the use of sugar legitimately through experiments that no other scientist would question. But it would probably occur to you that a critical reader might ask about the connection between the results of the research and the payment by a company that profits from the research. In this case you would be wise to read further to find confirmation or rejection of the claim by other scientists.

The most difficult evaluations concern ideological bias. Early in our lives we learn to discount the special interest that makes a small child brag, "My mother (or father) is the greatest!" Later we become aware that the claims of people who are avowed Democrats or Republicans or supply-side economists or Yankee fans or zealous San Franciscans or joggers must be

[11] Liam Hudson, *The Cult of the Fact* (New York: Harper and Row, 1972), p. 125.

examined somewhat more carefully than those of people who have no special commitment to a cause or a place or an activity. This is not to say that all partisan claims lack support. They may, in fact, be based on the best available support. But whenever special interest is apparent, there is always the danger that an argument will reflect this bias.

3. Has the source bolstered the claim with sufficient and appropriate evidence? An author might claim, "Statistics show that watching violence on television leads to violent behavior in children." But if the author gave no further information—neither statistics nor proof that a cause-effect relation exists between televised violence and violence in children, the critical reader would ask, "What are the numbers? Who compiled them?"

Even those who are reputed to be experts in the subjects they discuss must do more than simply allege that a claim is valid or that the data exist. They must provide facts to support their interpretations.

■ When Experts Disagree

Authoritative sources can disagree. Such disagreement is probably most common in the social sciences. They are called the "soft" sciences precisely because a consensus about conclusions in these areas is more difficult to arrive at than in the natural and physical sciences. Consider the controversy over what determines the best interests of the child where both biological and foster parents are engaged in trying to secure custody. Experts are deeply divided on this issue. Dr. Daniel J. Cohen, a child psychologist and director of the Yale Child Study Center, argues that the psychological needs of the child should take precedence. If the child has a stable and loving relationship with foster parents, that is where he should stay. But Bruce Bozer and Bernadine Dohrn of the Children and Family Justice Center at Northwestern University Law School insist that "such a solution may be overly simplistic." The child may suffer in later life when he learns that he has been prevented from returning to biological parents "who fought to get him back."[12]

But even in the natural and physical sciences, where the results of observation and experiment are more conclusive, we encounter heated differences of opinion. A popular argument concerns the extinction of the dinosaurs. Was it the effect of an asteroid striking the earth? Or widespread volcanic activity? Or a cooling of the planet? All these theories have their champions among the experts.

Environmental concerns also produce lively disagreements. Scientists have lined up on both sides of a debate about the importance of protecting the tropical rain forest as a source of biological, especially mammalian, diversity. Dr. Edward O. Wilson, a Harvard biologist, whose books

[12] *New York Times,* September 4, 1994, sec. E, p. 3.

have made us familiar with the term *biodiversity,* says, "The great major-ity of organisms appears to reach maximum diversity in the rain forest. There is no question that the rain forests are the world's headquarters of diversity." But in the journal *Science* another biologist, Dr. Michael Mares, a professor of zoology at the University of Oklahoma, argues that "if one could choose only a single South American habitat in which to preserve the greatest mammalian diversity, it would be the dry lands. . . . The dry lands are very likely far more highly threatened than the largely inacces-sible rain forests."[13] A debate of more immediate relevance concerns pos-sible dangers in genetically modified foods, as distinguished from foods modified by traditional breeding practices. Dr. Louis Pribyl, a U.S. Food and Drug Administration microbiologist, has accused the agency of claiming "that there are no unintended effects that raise the FDA's level of concern. But . . . there are no data to back up this contention." On the other hand, Dr. James Marjanski, the FDA's biotechnology coordinator, maintains that "as long as developers of these foods follow agency guide-lines, genetically engineered foods are as safe as any on the market."[14]

How can you choose between authorities who disagree? If you have applied the tests discussed so far and discovered that one source is less qualified by training and experience or makes claims with little support or appears to be biased in favor of one interpretation, you will have no difficulty in rejecting that person's opinion. If conflicting sources prove to be equally reliable in all respects, then continue reading other authorities to determine whether a greater number of experts support one opinion rather than another. Although numbers alone, even of experts, don't guarantee the truth, nonexperts have little choice but to accept the au-thority of the greater number until evidence to the contrary is forthcom-ing. Finally, if you are unable to decide between competing sources of evidence, you may conclude that the argument must remain unsettled. Such an admission is not a failure; after all, such questions are considered controversial because even the experts cannot agree, and such questions are often the most interesting to consider and argue about.

APPEALS TO NEEDS AND VALUES

Good factual evidence is usually enough to convince an audience that your factual claim is sound. Using examples, statistics, and expert opin-ion, you can prove, for example, that women do not earn as much as men for the same work. But even good evidence may not be enough to con-vince your audience that unequal pay is wrong or that something should

[13] *New York Times,* April 7, 1992, sec. C, p. 4.
[14] *New York Times,* December 1, 1999, sec. A, p. 15.

be done about it. In making value and policy claims, an appeal to the needs and values of your audience is absolutely essential to the success of your argument. If you want to persuade the audience to change their minds or adopt a course of action—in this case, to demand legalization of equal pay for equal work—you will have to show that assent to your claim will bring about what they want and care deeply about.

As a writer, you cannot always know who your audience is; it's impossible, for example, to predict exactly who will read a letter you write to a newspaper. Even in the classroom, you have only partial knowledge of your readers. You may not always know or be able to infer what the goals and principles of your audience are. You may not know how they feel about big government, the draft, private school education, feminism, environmental protection, homosexuality, religion, or any of the other subjects you might write about. If the audience concludes that the things you care about are very different from what they care about, if they cannot identify with your goals and principles, they may treat your argument with indifference, even hostility, and finally reject it. But you can hope that decent and reasonable people will share many of the needs and values that underlie your claims.

■ Appeals to Needs

The most familiar classification of needs was developed by the psychologist Abraham H. Maslow in 1954.[15] These needs, said Maslow, motivate human thought and action. In satisfying our needs, we attain both long- and short-term goals. Because Maslow believed that some needs are more important than others, he arranged them in hierarchical order from the most urgent biological needs to the psychological needs that are related to our roles as members of a society.

PHYSIOLOGICAL NEEDS Basic bodily requirements: food and drink; health; sex

SAFETY NEEDS Security; freedom from harm; order and stability

BELONGINGNESS AND LOVE NEEDS Love within a family and among friends; roots within a group or a community

ESTEEM NEEDS Material success; achievement; power, status, and recognition by others

SELF-ACTUALIZATION NEEDS Fulfillment in realizing one's potential

For most of your arguments you won't have to address the audience's basic physiological needs for nourishment or shelter. The desire for health, however, now receives extraordinary attention. Appeals to buy

---

[15]*Motivation and Personality* (New York: Harper and Row, 1954), pp. 80–92.

health foods, vitamin supplements, drugs, exercise and diet courses, and health books are all around us. Many of the claims are supported by little or no evidence, but readers are so eager to satisfy the need for good health that they often overlook the lack of facts or authoritative opinion. The desire for physical well-being, however, is not so simple as it seems; it is strongly related to our need for self-esteem and love.

Appeals to our needs to feel safe from harm, to be assured of order and stability in our lives are also common. Insurance companies, politicians who promise to rid our streets of crime, and companies that offer security services all appeal to this profound and nearly universal need. (We say "nearly" because some people are apparently attracted to risk and danger.) At this writing those who monitor terrorist activity are attempting both to arouse fear for our safety and to suggest ways of reducing the dangers that make us fearful.

The last three needs in Maslow's hierarchy are the ones you will find most challenging to appeal to in your arguments. It is clear that these needs arise out of human relationships and participation in society. Advertisers make much use of appeals to these needs.

BELONGINGNESS AND LOVE NEEDS

"Whether you are young or old, the need for companionship is universal." (ad for dating service)

"Share the Fun of High School with Your Little Girl!" (ad for a Barbie Doll)

ESTEEM NEEDS

"Enrich your home with the distinction of an Oxford library."

"Apply your expertise to more challenges and more opportunities. Here are outstanding opportunities for challenge, achievement, and growth." (Perkin-Elmer Co.)

SELF-ACTUALIZATION NEEDS

"Be all that you can be." (former U.S. Army slogan)

"Are you demanding enough? Somewhere beyond the cortex is a small voice whose mere whisper can silence an army of arguments. It goes by many names: integrity, excellence, standards. And it stands alone in final judgment as to whether we have demanded enough of ourselves and, by that example, have inspired the best in those around us." (*New York Times*)

Of course, it is not only advertisers who use these appeals. We hear them from family and friends, from teachers, from employers, from editorials and letters to the editor, from people in public life.

■ Appeals to Values

Needs give rise to values. If we feel the need to belong to a group, we learn to value commitment, sacrifice, and sharing. And we then respond to arguments that promise to protect our values. It is hardly surprising that values, the principles by which we judge what is good or bad, beautiful or ugly, worthwhile or undesirable, should exercise a profound influence on our behavior. Virtually all claims, even those that seem to be purely factual, contain expressed or unexpressed judgments. When Michael M. Weinstein in Chapter 6 (pp. 162–64) quotes evidence that affirmative action does not promote unqualified candidates, he does so not because he is doing research for academic reasons but because he hopes to persuade people that affirmative action is good social policy.

For our study of argument, we will speak of groups or systems of values because any single value is usually related to others. People and institutions are often defined by such systems of values. We can distinguish, for example, between those who think of themselves as traditional and those who think of themselves as modern by listing their differing values. One writer contrasts such values in this way:

> Among the values of traditionalism are merit, accomplishment, competition, and success; self-restraint, self-discipline, and the postponement of gratification; the stability of the family; and a belief in certain moral universals. The modernist ethos scorns the pursuit of success; is egalitarian and redistributionist in emphasis; tolerates or encourages sensual gratification; values self-expression as against self-restraint; accepts alternative or deviant forms of the family; and emphasizes ethical relativism.[16]

Systems of values are neither so rigid nor so distinct from one another as this list suggests. Some people who are traditional in their advocacy of competition and success may also accept the modernist values of self-expression and alternative family structures. Values, like needs, are arranged in a hierarchy; that is, some are clearly more important than others to the people who hold them. Moreover, the arrangement may shift over time or as a result of new experiences. In 1962, for example, two speech teachers prepared a list of what they called "Relatively Unchanging Values Shared by Most Americans."[17] Included were "puritan and pioneer standards of morality" and "perennial optimism about the future." More than forty-five years later, an appeal to these values might fall on a number of deaf ears.

You should also be aware of not only changes over time but also different or competing value systems that reflect a multitude of subcultures

---

[16]Joseph Adelson, "What Happened to the Schools," *Commentary,* March 1981, p. 37.
[17]Edward Steele and W. Charles Redding, "The American Value System: Premises for Persuasion," *Western Speech,* 26 (Spring 1962), pp. 83–91.

in the United States. Differences in age, sex, race, ethnic background, social environment, religion, even in the personalities and characters of its members define the groups we belong to. Such terms as *honor, loyalty, justice, patriotism, duty, responsibility, equality, freedom,* and *courage* will be interpreted very differently by different groups.

All of us belong to more than one group, and the values of the several groups may be in conflict. If one group to which you belong—say, peers of your own age and class—is generally uninterested in and even scornful of religion, you may nevertheless hold to the values of your family and continue to place a high value on religious belief.

How can a knowledge of your readers' values enable you to make a more effective appeal? Suppose you want to argue in favor of a sex education program in the middle school you attended. The program you support would not only give students information about contraception and venereal disease but also teach them about the pleasures of sex, the importance of small families, and alternatives to heterosexuality. If the readers of your argument are your classmates or your peers, you can be fairly sure that their agreement will be easier to obtain than that of their parents, especially if their parents think of themselves as conservative. Your peers are more likely to value experimentation, tolerance of alternative sexual practices, freedom, and novelty. Their parents are more likely to value restraint, conformity to conventional sexual practices, obedience to family rules, and foresight in planning for the future.

Knowing that your peers share your values and your goals will mean that you need not spell out the values supporting your claim; they are understood by your readers. Convincing their parents, however, who think that freedom, tolerance, and experimentation have been abused by their children, will be a far more challenging task. In one written piece you have little chance of changing their values, a result that might be achieved only over a longer period of time. So you might first attempt to reduce their hostility by suggesting that, even if a community-wide program were adopted, students would need parental permission to enroll. This might convince some parents that you share their values regarding parental authority and primacy of the family. Second, you might look for other values to which the parents subscribe and to which you can make an appeal. Do they prize maturity, self-reliance, responsibility in their children? If so, you could attempt to prove, with authoritative evidence, that the sex education program would promote these qualities in students who took the course.

But familiarity with the value systems of prospective readers may also lead you to conclude that winning assent to your argument will be impossible. It would probably be fruitless to attempt to persuade a group of lifelong pacifists to endorse the use of nuclear weapons. The beliefs, attitudes, and habits that support their value systems are too fundamental to yield to one or two attempts at persuasion.

EVALUATION OF APPEALS TO NEEDS AND VALUES

If your argument is based on an appeal to the needs and values of your audience, the following questions will help you evaluate the soundness of your appeal.

1. Have the values been clearly defined? If you are appealing to the patriotism of your readers, can you be sure that they agree with your definition? Does patriotism mean "Our country, right or wrong!" or does it mean dissent, even violent dissent, if you think your country is wrong? Because value terms are abstractions, you must make their meaning explicit by placing them in context and providing examples.

2. Are the needs and values to which you appeal prominent in the reader's hierarchy at the time you are writing? An affluent community, fearful of further erosion of quiet and open countryside, might resist an appeal to allow establishment of a high-technology firm, even though the firm would bring increased prosperity to the area.

3. Is the evidence in your argument clearly related to the needs and values to which you appeal? Remember that the reader must see some connection between your evidence and his or her goals. Suppose you were writing an argument to persuade a group of people to vote in an upcoming election. You could provide evidence to prove that only 20 percent of the town voted in the last election. But this evidence would not motivate your audience to vote unless you could provide other evidence to show that their needs were not being served by such a low turnout.

Writer's Guide: Using Effective Support

1. In deciding how much support you need for your claim, it is always a good idea to assume that you are addressing an audience that may be at least slightly hostile to that claim. Those who already agree with you do not need convincing.

2. Keep a mental, if not a written, list of the different types of support you use in an essay. Few essays will use all of the different types of support, but being aware of all the possibilities will prevent you from forgetting to draw on one or more types of support that may advance your argument.

3. In that checklist of types of support, don't forget that there are two main categories: evidence and appeals to needs and values. Appeals to needs and values will generally need the reinforcement that comes from more objective forms of evidence, but the two in combination can often provide the strongest case for your claim. Aristotle explained that in an ideal world, arguers could depend on logic alone, but we live in a world that is far from ideal.

4. Use the following questions about the evaluation of evidence as a check-list to analyze the support you use in your argumentative essays:

Factual evidence:

- Is the evidence up to date?
- Is the evidence sufficient?
- Is the evidence relevant?
- Are the examples representative?
- Are the examples consistent with the experience of the audience?

Statistics:

- Do the statistics come from trustworthy sources?
- Are the terms clearly defined?
- Are the comparisons between comparable things?
- Has any significant information been omitted?

Opinion:

- Is the source of the opinion qualified to give an opinion on the subject?
- Is the source biased for or against his or her interpretation?
- Has the source bolstered the claim with sufficient and appropriate evidence?

5. Also check your essays against the list of questions regarding appeals to needs and values:

- Have the values been clearly defined?
- Are the needs and values to which you appeal prominent in the reader's hierarchy at the time you are writing?
- Is the evidence in your argument clearly related to the needs and values to which you appeal?

PRACTICE

1. Locate two advertisements from magazines or newspapers that appeal to needs or values or both. Be prepared to explain what needs and/or values the ads appeal to.

2. Share your ads with your classmates so that everyone can get an idea of the range of how ads appeal to needs and values.

3. Choose one of the ads your class compiled and write a paragraph analyzing its appeal to needs and/or values.

4. Write an essay in which you compare two ads for the same product or same type of product in terms of the types of appeal that they use.

Single-Sex Education Benefits Men Too

CLAUDIUS E. WATTS III

Introduction: background of the problem

L ast week Virginia Military Institute, an all-male state college, got the good news from a federal judge that it can continue its single-sex program if it opens a leadership program at Mary Baldwin College, a nearby private women's school. But it is likely that the government will appeal the decision. Meanwhile, the Citadel, another such institution in Charleston, S.C., remains under attack. Unwittingly,

The values that the author will defend

so are some fundamental beliefs prevalent in our society: namely, the value of single-sex education, the need for diversity in education, and the freedom of choice in associating with, and not associating with, whomever one chooses.

When Shannon Faulkner received a preliminary injunction to attend day classes with the Citadel's Corps of Cadets, she was depicted as a nineteen-year-old woman fighting for her constitutional rights, while the Citadel was painted as an outdated and chauvinistic Southern school that had to be dragged into the twentieth century.

But the Citadel is not fighting to keep women out of the Corps of Cadets because there is a grandiose level of nineteenth-century machismo

Claim of policy: to preserve single-sex education for men

to protect. Rather, we at the Citadel are trying to preserve an educational environment that molds young men into grown men of good character, honor, and integrity. It is part of a single-sex educational system that has proven itself successful throughout history.

Support: expert opinion, appeal to values

The benefits of single-sex education for men are clear: Says Harvard sociologist David Riesman, not only is single-sex education an optimal means of character development, but it also removes the dis-

---

Lieutenant General Claudius E. Watts III, retired from the U.S. Air Force, is a former president of the Citadel in South Carolina. This selection is from the May 3, 1995, edition of the *Wall Street Journal*.

tractions of the "mating-dating" game so prevalent in society and enables institutions to focus students on values and academics.

In short, the value of separate education is,   5
simply, the fact it is separate.

In October 1992, a federal appeals court ruled that "single-sex education is pedagogically justifiable." Indeed, a cursory glance at some notable statistics bears that out. For instance, the Citadel has the highest retention rate for minority students of any public college in South Carolina: 67 percent of black students graduate in four years, which is more than 2½ times the national average. Additionally, the Citadel's four-year graduation rate for all students is 70 percent, which compares with 48 percent nationally for all other public institutions and 67 percent nationally for private institutions. Moreover, many of the students come from modest backgrounds. Clearly, the Citadel is not the bastion of male privilege that the U.S. Justice Department, in briefs filed by that agency, would have us all believe.

Support: statistics

While the Justice Department continues to reject the court's ruling affirming the values of single-sex education, others continue to argue that because the federal military academies are coeducational, so should the Citadel be. However, it is not the Citadel's primary mission to train officers for the U.S. armed forces. We currently commission approximately 30 percent of our graduates, but only 18 percent actually pursue military careers. At the Citadel, the military model is a means to an end, not the end itself.

Support: facts, statistics

Today there are eighty-four women's colleges scattered throughout the United States, including two that are public. These colleges defend their programs as necessary to help women overcome intangible barriers in male-dominated professions. This argument has merit; women's colleges produce only 4.5 percent of all female college graduates but have produced one-fourth of all women board members of Fortune 500 companies and one-half of the women in Congress. However, the educational benefits of men's colleges are equally clear; and to allow women alone

Support: facts, statistics

Support: causal connection

to benefit from single-sex education seems to perpetuate the very stereotypes that women—including Ms. Faulkner—are trying to correct.

Warrant: men should enjoy the same freedom of choice

If young women want and need to study and learn in single-sex schools, why is it automatically wrong for young men to want and need the same? Where is the fairness in this assumption?

Support: causal connection

"At what point does the insistence that one individual not be deprived of choice spill over into depriving countless individuals of choice?" asks Emory University's Elizabeth Fox Genovese in an article by Jeffrey Rosen published in the February 14 *New Republic*.

Support: appeal to values

Yet so it is at the Citadel. While one student maintains that she is protecting her freedom to associate, we mustn't forget that the Citadel's cadets also have a freedom—the freedom not to associate. While we have read about one female student's rights, what hasn't been addressed are the rights of the 1,900 cadets who chose the Citadel—and the accompanying discipline and drill—because it offered them the single-sex educational experience they wanted. Why do one student's rights supersede all theirs?

Support: predictions about the future

One might be easily tempted to argue on the grounds that Ms. Faulkner is a taxpayer and the Citadel is a tax-supported institution. But if the taxpayer argument holds, the next step is to forbid all public support for institutions that enroll students of only one sex. A draconian measure such as this would surely mean the end of private—as well as public—single-gender colleges.

Backing for warrant: tax-supported education should be equal for men and women

Most private colleges—Columbia and Converse, the two all-female schools in South Carolina, included—could not survive without federal financial aid, tax exemptions, and state tax support in the form of tuition grants. In fact, nearly 900 of Columbia and Converse's female students receive state-funded tuition grants, a student population that is almost half the size of the Corps of Cadets. In essence, South Carolina's two private women's colleges may stand or fall with the Citadel.

Carried to its logical conclusion, then, the effort to coeducate the Citadel might mean the end of all single-sex education—for women as well as men, in private as well as public schools.

10

■ Analysis: Support

In 1993 Shannon Faulkner, a woman, was rejected for admission to the Citadel, an all-male state-supported military academy in South Carolina. In 1995, after a long court battle, she was admitted but resigned after a week of physical and emotional stress. The Court was asked to decide if an education equal to that of the Citadel could be provided for women at a nearby school.

Claudius Watts III tackles a subject that is no longer controversial in regard to women's colleges: the virtues of single-sex education. But in this essay he argues that colleges for men only deserve the same right as women's colleges to exclude the opposite sex.

The author has taken care in the limited space available to cover all the arguments that had emerged in the case of Shannon Faulkner. At the end of the opening paragraph he lays out the three ideas he will develop—the value of single-sex education, the need for diversity in education, and freedom of choice. In paragraphs 3 through 6 he supports his case for the benefits of separate education by first quoting a prominent sociologist and then offering statistics to prove that the male Citadel population is both diverse and successful. In paragraph 7 he refutes a popular analogy—that since the service academies, like West Point and the Naval Academy, admit women, so should the Citadel. The goals of the Citadel, he says, are broader than those of the service academies. But he does more. In paragraph 8 he provides data that women's colleges produce successful graduates. This reinforces his claim that separate education has advantages over coed schooling. Perhaps it also helps to make friends of opponents who might otherwise be hostile to arguments favoring male privileges.

Notice the transition in paragraph 10. This leads the author to the defense of his last point, the far more elusive concept of freedom of choice and the rights of individuals, ideas whose validity cannot be measured in numbers. He introduces this part of his argument by quoting the words of a supporter of single-sex education, a woman professor at Emory University. He makes a strong appeal to the reader's sense of fairness and belief in the rights of the majority, represented here by the male students at the Citadel. There is also an obvious appeal to fear, an implied threat of the danger to women's colleges, in the next-to-last sentence of the essay. Finally, he invokes logic. If single-sex education cannot be defended for males, neither can it be defended for females. He assumes that against logic there can be no real defense.

Some leading advocates for women's rights have, in fact, agreed with General Watts's arguments for that reason. But those who supported both Shannon Faulkner's admission to the Citadel and the sanctity of women's colleges will claim that women, as a disadvantaged group, deserve special consideration, while men do not. (One writer even insisted that the Citadel *needed* women as a civilizing influence.) General Watts's argument, however, went some distance toward reopening the dialogue.

At times, assignments may ask you to analyze or evaluate the evidence and appeals to needs and values offered in support of a claim. At other times, you will have to discover your own support for use in an argument that you are writing. After the following essay about sport utility vehicles and its reading and discussion questions, you will first find an example of an essay of the type you might write if you were asked to evaluate an author's use of support. It is followed by a student essay that illustrates effective use of support.

The True Costs of SUVs

HAL R. VARIAN

Traffic fatalities in the United States fell steadily from 54,600 in 1972 to 34,900 in 1992. But then they started to rise again, and by 2002 there were 38,300 traffic deaths a year.

Our performance compared with other countries has also deteriorated. America's ranking has fallen from first to ninth over the last thirty years, with Australia, Britain, and Canada all having better records.

A big part of the difference between the United States and other countries seems to be the prevalence of sport utility vehicles and pickups on American highways. Sales of light trucks—SUVs, pickups, and minivans—were about a fifth of total automobile sales thirty years ago. Now they account for more than half.

But aren't large vehicles supposed to be safer than small cars? Yes, they are safer for their occupants in collisions, but their design makes them all the more dangerous for anyone they hit.

Michelle White, an economist at the University of California, San 5 Diego, estimates that for each fatality that light-truck drivers avoid for themselves and their passengers, they cause four fatalities involving car occupants, pedestrians, bicyclists, and motorcyclists. "Safety gains for those driving light trucks," Ms. White said, "come at an extremely high cost to others."

Being larger than ordinary vehicles, SUVs and light trucks cause more damage to upper bodies and heads in collisions. Furthermore, their bumpers

A professor in the School of Information Management and Systems at the University of California at Berkeley, Hal R. Varian has written economics textbooks as well as columns for the *New York Times*. This piece appeared in the *Times* as the "Economic Scene" article on December 18, 2003.

do not always align with automobile bumpers, and their body structure is stiffer, transferring more force to other vehicles during impact.

A few weeks ago, the auto industry announced a voluntary plan to deal with some of these design problems. They intend to make side-impact airbags standard to help protect heads and upper bodies better in collisions, and they intend to standardize bumper heights.

These will no doubt be helpful improvements, but do they go far enough?

Recently Ms. White examined the econometrics of traffic accidents in an attempt to measure the benefits and costs of changing the number of light trucks on the road. . . .

Ms. White notes that changing average vehicle size could, in prin- 10
ciple, increase or decrease the cost of accidents.

Suppose the cost of a small vehicle–large vehicle collision is $50, the cost of a small vehicle–small vehicle collision is $45, and the cost of a large vehicle–large vehicle collision is $40.

If all vehicles are small, and there are 10 accidents a year, the total cost of the accidents is $450. But if 10 percent of the small vehicles are replaced by large ones, the average cost of collisions becomes $458.50, since more collisions will be between large and small vehicles. On the other hand, if

The results of an accident in New York involving a sport utility vehicle and a smaller car. Traffic fatalities are on the rise, apparently linked to the increase of SUVs.

G. Paul Burnett/*New York Times*

60 percent of the vehicles on the road are large, the average cost of a collision is only $456, since more collisions are between large vehicles.

Think about a safety-conscious soccer mom choosing a vehicle. If there are mostly small cars in her town, she can reduce the risk to her and her family in the event of a collision by buying an SUV.

The unfortunate side effect is that the large SUV would cause significant damage to smaller cars if she was involved in an accident.

The laudable private incentive to choose a safe vehicle could, perversely, reduce overall safety.   15

In addition, Ms. White finds that people involved in single-vehicle crashes are more likely to be killed or seriously injured if they are in SUVs or light trucks rather than cars. This may be a result of the increased likelihood of rollovers.

On the other hand, suppose everybody in town drives an SUV. Then the soccer mom will definitely want to purchase one for herself, since it would both increase her family's safety and reduce the overall costs of collisions.

In this case, private incentives and social incentives are aligned.

The dynamics involved is the same as that of an arms race: If other families buy bigger vehicles, then you will want to as well, if only in self-defense.

To see where we are in this arms race, Ms. White examined crash data   20
maintained by the National Highway Safety Administration. . . .

Using this data, Ms. White was able to estimate how the probability of fatalities or serious injury varied with the types of vehicles involved in collisions.

For example, in a two-car accident, the probability of a fatality in the car is 38 percent less than in a car–light truck accident. However, in car–light truck accidents, the probability of fatalities in the light truck is 55 percent less than it would be in a truck–truck accident.

If a light truck hits a pedestrian or a cyclist, the probability of fatalities is about 82 percent greater than if a car is involved.

Ms. White then asked what the impact would be of replacing a million light trucks with cars. She considered two models for driver behavior. In the first, she assumed that the former drivers of light trucks would have the same number of accidents as they did when driving trucks. In the second, she assumed that the former drivers of light trucks would have the same accident probabilities as other car drivers.

Using conventional methods for value-of-life calculations, she finds   25
that each light-truck owner who switches to a car saves about $447 in total expected costs of accidents.

Ms. White examines various policies that might persuade drivers to adopt such changes, including changes in liability rules, traffic rules, and insurance rules.

Unfortunately, each of these policies has its problems, so there are no easy solutions.

One interesting way to reduce the arms race problem would be to link automobile liability insurance to gasoline taxes. This means drivers whose cars use more gasoline and those who drive a lot would pay more for their insurance—not unreasonable, since, on average, they impose more costs in accidents.

Aaron Edlin, a professor of economics and law at the University of California, Berkeley, has argued that such "pay at the pump" insurance premiums would have many other benefits (www.bepress.com/aaronedlin/contribution5/). So this type of payment scheme is worth considering for a variety of reasons.

READING AND DISCUSSION QUESTIONS

1. For the purposes of his article, how is Varian defining *light truck?*
2. What relationship does he see between light trucks and the number of traffic fatalities?
3. What type of support does Varian use in the three opening paragraphs? Does he use that type of support anywhere else in the essay?
4. What other types of support does Varian make use of in his essay? What types of support do you find most effective in making his argument? What types do you find least effective?
5. What claim is Varian supporting in the essay?
6. How does Varian document his sources? How does he try to establish that his sources are reliable?

The True Confusion about SUV Costs

BETHANY ROYCE

Hal R. Varian entitled his December 18, 2003, *New York Times* piece on sport utility vehicles "The True Costs of SUVs." A more accurate title might have been "The Confusing Costs of SUVs." While Varian turns to the right type of support for his subject—statistics—his use of that support is more confusing than enlightening.

Varian made a wise choice in appealing to his readers' need to feel safe and secure. His statistics are most appealing when he points out that for twenty years the number of traffic fatalities in our country went down and that parents can feel secure knowing that they can make their children safer by buying light trucks (SUVs, pickups, or minivans) instead of cars. In each

---

Bethany Royce teaches business courses and introductory economics at a two-year college in Florida and writes a consumer advice column for a local newspaper.

case, however, there is a negative side. The number of fatalities started rising again between 1992 and 2002, in part because of the increase in the number of sales of light trucks during that time. And Varian tells us that in making their families safer by buying light trucks, they are increasing the risk of doing more harm to others should they be involved in accidents.

For the rest of his support, Varian draws primarily on research done by Michelle White, whom he identifies only as "an economist at the University of California, San Diego" (238). She may have done excellent work, but the way that Varian explains it is confusing and unconvincing. White tries to predict how the cost of accidents would change depending on the size of the vehicles involved. Instead of using realistic cost estimates, however, she arbitrarily assigns the cost of $50 to a small vehicle–large vehicle collision, the cost of $45 to a small vehicle–small vehicle collision, and the cost of $40 to a large vehicle–large vehicle collision. Varian summarizes what this hypothetical scenario reveals:

> If all vehicles are small, and there are 10 accidents a year, the total cost of the accidents is $450. But if 10 percent of the small vehicles are replaced by large ones, the average cost of collisions becomes $458.50, since more collisions will be between large and small vehicles. On the other hand, if 60 percent of the vehicles on the road are large, the average cost of a collision is only $456, since more collisions are between large vehicles. (239–40)

Average Americans are left wondering what all of this means to them. The hypothetical situation cannot be easily applied to any individual driver and certainly not to any specific accident. How should a reader evaluate the information in attempting to make the decision regarding what size vehicle to buy? The driver who just paid $3000 in car repairs is going to find any of the numbers Varian cites attractive.

There are a lot of "ifs" in Varian's argument. If you live in a town with lots of SUVs, it is safer to drive one yourself. If you live in a town where there are few SUVs, you should drive a car so that you would not be as likely to hurt someone else in a wreck. If you have a single-vehicle accident in an SUV, you are more likely to be killed. If you hit a pedestrian while driving one, you are more likely to kill that person.

There are also few clear conclusions to be drawn from the support   5 that Varian offers. After Ms. White examines "various policies that might persuade drivers to adopt such changes, including changes in liability rules, traffic rules, and insurance rates," the unfortunate conclusion is that "each of these policies has its problems, so there are no easy solutions" (240). The only solution that Varian advances as "worth considering" is one by a colleague of his at the University of California, Berkeley, that would link a vehicle owner's liability insurance to gas taxes (241). Overall the article succeeds more in revealing the complexities involved in the increased use of SUVs than in clarifying any of those complexities.

Safer? Tastier? More Nutritious?
The Dubious Merits of Organic Foods

KRISTEN WEINACKER

Organic foods are attractive to some consumers because of the principles behind them and the farming techniques used to produce them. There is a special respect for organic farmers who strive to maintain the ecological balance and harmony that exist among living things. As these farmers work in partnership with nature, some consumers too feel a certain attachment to the earth (Wolf 1–2). They feel happier knowing that these foods are produced without chemical fertilizers, pesticides, and additives to extend their shelf life (Pickerell; Agricultural Extension Service 5). They feel that they have returned to nature by eating organic foods that are advertised as being healthy for maintaining a vigorous lifestyle. Unfortunately, research has not provided statistical evidence that organic foods are more nutritious than conventionally grown ones.

The debate over the nutritional benefits has raged for decades. Defenders of the nutritional value of organic foods have employed excellent marketing and sales strategies. First, they freely share the philosophy behind their farming and follow up with detailed descriptions of their management techniques. Second, organic farmers skillfully appeal to our common sense. It seems reasonable to believe that organic foods are more nutritious since they are grown without chemical fertilizers and pesticides. Third, since the soil in which these crops are grown is so rich and healthy, it seems plausible that these crops have absorbed and developed better nutrients. As Lynda Brown asserts in her book *Living Organic*, "Organic farmers believe that growing crops organically provides the best possible way to produce healthy food" (26). Brown provides beautifully illustrated and enlarged microscopic photographs to show the more developed structure of organic foods compared to conventional products to convince the consumer to believe that organic foods are more nutritious (27). Fourth, many consumers view the higher price tags on organic foods and assume that they must be more nutritious. Generalizations permeate the whole world of organic foods. These marketing strategies persuade the consumer that organic foods are healthier than conventional foods without providing any factual comparisons.

At the time she wrote this essay, Kristen Weinacker was an undergraduate at Clemson University.

In their book *Is Our Food Safe?* Warren Leon and Caroline Smith Dewaal compare organic and conventionally produced foods. They strongly suggest that consumers buy organic foods to help the environment (68). They believe that organic foods are healthier than conventional ones. However, statistics supporting this belief are not provided. The authors even warn consumers that they need to read product labels because some organic foods may be as unhealthy as conventional ones (68–69). An interesting poll involving 1,041 adults was conducted by ABC News asking, "Why do people buy organic?" Analyst Daniel Merkle concluded that 45% of the American public *believes* that organic products are more nutritious than conventionally grown ones. Also, 57% of the population maintains that organic farming is beneficial for the environment. According to the pollsters, the primary reason why people bought organic foods is the belief that they are healthier because they have less pesticide residue. However, there has never been any link established between the nutritional value of organic foods and the residue found on them. Clever marketing strategies have made the need for concrete data really not of prime importance for the consumer to join the bandwagon promoting organic foods.

This pervasive belief among the American public that organic foods are probably healthier than conventionally grown foods was reiterated in my telephone interview with Mr. Joseph Williamson, an agricultural county extension agent working with Clemson University. When asked if organically grown foods are more nutritious than those grown conventionally, he replied that they probably were for two reasons. First, organic crops tend to grow more slowly. Therefore, the nutrients have more time to build up in the plants. Second, organic plants are usually grown locally. The fruits and vegetables are allowed to stay on the plants for a longer period of time. They ripen more than those picked green and transported across miles. He contends that these conditions promote a better nutrient buildup. Unfortunately, the extension agent acknowledges that statistical evidence is not available to support the claim that organic products are more nutritious.

An article entitled "Effects of Agricultural Methods in Nutritional Quality: A Comparison of Organic with Conventional Crops" reports on conclusions drawn by Dr. Virginia Worthington, a certified nutrition specialist. Worthington examines why it is so difficult to ascertain if organic foods are more nutritious. First, "the difference in terms of health effects is not large enough to be readily apparent." There is no concrete evidence that people are healthier eating organic foods or, conversely, that people become more ill eating conventionally grown produce. Second, Dr. Worthington notes that variables such as sunlight, temperature, and amount of rain are so inconsistent that the nutrients in crops vary yearly. Third, she points out that the nutrient value of products can be changed by the way products are stored and shipped. After reviewing at least thirty studies dealing with the question if organic foods are more nutritious than conventionally grown ones, Dr. Worthington concludes that there is too little data available to substantiate the claim of higher nutritional value in organic foods. She also believes that it is an impossible task to make a direct connection between organic foods and the health of those people who consume them.

After being asked for thirty years about organic foods by her readers and associates, Joan Dye Gusson, writer for *Eating Well* magazine, firmly concludes that there is "little hard proof that organically grown produce is reliably more nutritious." Reviewing seventy years' worth of studies on the subject, Gusson has no doubt that organic foods should be healthier because of the way they are produced and cultivated. Gusson brings up an interesting point about chemical and pesticide residue. She believes that the fact that organic foods have been found to have fewer residues does not make them automatically more nutritious and healthier for the consumer. As scientific technologies advance, Gusson predicts that research will someday discover statistical data that will prove that organic foods have a higher nutritional value compared to conventionally grown ones.

In order to provide the public with more information about the nature of organic foods, the well-known and highly regarded magazine *Consumer Reports* decided to take a closer look at organic foods in their January 1998 magazine, in an article entitled "Organic Foods: Safer? Tastier? More nutritious?" By conducting comparison tests, their researchers discovered that organic foods have less pesticide residue, and that their flavors are just about the same as conventionally grown foods. These scientists came to the conclusion that the "variability within a given crop is greater than the variability between one cropping system and another." *Consumer Reports* contacted Professor Willie Lockeretz from the Tufts University School of Nutrition Science and Policy. He told researchers that "the growing system you use probably does affect nutrition. . . . But it does it in ways so complex you might be studying the problem forever." Keeping in mind these comments made by Dr. Lockeretz, *Consumer Reports* believes it would be an impossible task to compare the nutritional values of organic and conventional foods. Therefore, researchers at *Consumer Reports* decided not to carry out that part of their comparison testing.

Although statistical evidence is not available at this time to support the claim that organic foods are more nutritious than conventionally grown ones, there is a very strong feeling shared by a majority of the general public that they are. We are called back to nature as we observe the love that organic farmers have for the soil and their desire to work in partnership with nature. We are easily lured to the attractive displays of organic foods in the grocery stores. However, we must keep in mind the successful marketing techniques that have been used to convince us that organic foods are more nutritious than conventionally grown ones. Although common sense tells us that organic foods should be more nutritious, research has not provided us with any statistical data to prove this claim.

Works Cited

Agricultural Extension Service. *Organic Vegetable Gardening.* The University of Tennessee. PB 1391.

Brown, Lynda. *Organic Living.* New York: Dorling Kindersley Publishing, Inc., 2000.

Gussow, Joan Dye. "Is Organic Food More Nutritious?" *Eating Well* (May/June 1997). 27 March 2003. <http://www.prnac.net/rodmap-nutrition.html>.

"Effect of Agricultural Methods on Nutritional Quality: A Comparison of Organic with Conventional Crops." *Alternative Therapies* 4 (1998): 58–69. 18 Feb. 2003. <http://www.purefood.org/healthier101101.cfm>.

Leon, Warren, and Caroline Smith DeWaal. *Is Our Food Safe?* New York: Three Rivers Press, 2002.

Merkle, Daniel. "Why Do People Buy Organic?" ABCNews.com. 3 Feb. 2000. 27 March 2003.

"Organic Foods: Safer? Tastier? More Nutritious?" *Consumer Reports.* Jan. 1998. 24 Feb. 2003. <http://www.consumerreports.org/main/detailsv2.jsp?content%3%ecnt_id +18959&f>.

Pickrell, John. "Federal Government Launches Organic Standards." *Science News* 162.17 (Nov. 2002). <http://www.sciencenews.org/20021102/food.asp._17_March 2003>.

Williamson, Joseph. Telephone interview. 28 Feb. 2003.

Wolf, Ray, ed. *Organic Farming: Yesterday's and Tomorrow's Agriculture.* Philadelphia: Rodale Press, 1977.

READINGS FOR ANALYSIS

Connecting the Dots . . . to Terrorism

BERNARD GOLDBERG

M ost of the time television is nothing more than a diversion—proof, as the old quip goes, that we would rather do anything than talk to each other. We'd also rather watch a bad sitcom than read a good book. Bad sitcoms get millions of viewers; good books get thousands. In an "entertainment culture," even the news is entertainment. Certainly too much local news has been pure fluff for some time now, with their Ken and Barbie anchors who have nothing intelligent to say but look great

---

Bernard Goldberg was a reporter and producer for CBS for more than thirty years. He has won seven Emmy awards and was once rated by *TV Guide* as one of the ten most interesting people on television. This chapter is from his 2002 book *Bias: A CBS Insider Exposes How the Media Distort the News*, written after he left the network.

while they're saying it. And because network news is losing viewers every year, executives and producers are trying to figure out ways to hold on to the ones they still have. They think cosmetics will work, so they change the anchor desk or they change the graphics. They get the anchor to stand instead of sit. They feature more "news you can use." They put Chandra Levy[18] on all over the place, hoping they can concoct a ratings cocktail by mixing one part missing intern with ten parts sex scandal.

And then something genuinely big and really important happens that shakes us to our core, and all those producers who couldn't get enough of Chandra are through with her. Only in the fickle world of television news can someone who has disappeared without a trace disappear a second time.

And it's when that history-making story comes along that Americans — no matter what their politics, religion, age, race, or sex — turn to television, not just for information, but also for comfort and for peace of mind. It doesn't happen often, but when it does, television becomes a lot more than just a diversion.

It happened when John Kennedy was assassinated. We all turned to Walter Cronkite and Huntley and Brinkley, not just for facts, but also for reassurance — that despite the terrible tragedy, America was going to be okay.

It happened when *Challenger* blew up. And it happened again on September 11, 2001, when a band of religious lunatics declared war on the United States of America to punish us for not wanting to dwell in the fourteenth century, where they currently reside, and, of course, to show the world that their intense hatred of Israel — *and of Israel's friends* — knows no bounds. On September 11, they not only killed as many innocent Americans as they could in the most dramatic way they knew how, but, as the *Wall Street Journal* put it, they also "wiped out any remaining illusions that America is safe from mass organized violence."

On that day we all turned to television. We turned to Dan Rather and Peter Jennings and Tom Brokaw and the others. And they did a fine job, as they often do when covering tragedy. They showed empathy. They were fair and accurate, and the information they passed along to us wasn't filtered through the usual liberal political and social sensibilities. They gave us the news on that day the way they should give us the news *all the time*, whether the story is about race or feminism or taxes or gay rights or anything else. *For a change, they gave it to us straight.*

On the night of September 11, 2001, Peter Jennings made a point about how, in times of danger and tragedy, television serves the function that campfires used to serve in the old days when Americans migrated westward in covered wagons. Back then, they would sit around the campfire and get the news from other travelers about what they should look

5

---

[18] *Chandra Levy*: A government intern whose disappearance was widely covered in the press in 2001. — EDS.

out for down the road. "Some people pulled the wagons around," Peter said, "and discussed what was going on and tried to understand it." But the campfire was more than just a meeting place where families could pick up important information. The campfire also provided a sense of community, a sense that *we're all in this together*. That's what television was on September 11.

As I listened to Peter tell that story, I thought about another American tragedy that shocked us six years earlier, when Timothy McVeigh — another true believer who cared nothing about killing innocent Americans — blew up the federal building in Oklahoma City. I thought about how it took some of the media elites only a few days before they started to play one of their favorite games — connect the dots. What they found back then — or more accurately, what they convinced themselves they found — was a line stretching from Oklahoma City to the Republican Party to conservatives in general and finally to Rush Limbaugh.

Dan Rather said, "Even after Oklahoma City, you can turn on your radio in any city and still dial up hate talk: extremist, racist, and violent from the hosts and those who call in."

Time senior writer Richard Lacayo put it this way: "In a nation that 10 has entertained and appalled itself for years with hot talk on radio and the campaign trail, the inflamed rhetoric of the '90s is suddenly an unindicted coconspirator in the blast."

Nina Easton wrote in the *Los Angeles Times*, "The Oklahoma City attack on federal workers and their children also alters the once-easy dynamic between charismatic talk show host and adoring audience. Hosts who routinely espouse the same antigovernment themes as the militia movement now must walk a fine line between inspiring their audience — and inciting the most radical among them."

On *Face the Nation*, Bob Schieffer asked this question: "Mr. Panetta, there's been a lot of antigovernment rhetoric, it comes over talk radio, it comes from various quarters. Do you think that that somehow has led these people to commit this act, do they feed on that kind of rhetoric, and what impact do you think it had?"

Carl Rowan, the late columnist, was quoted in a *Washington Post* story saying that, "Unless Gingrich and Dole[19] and the Republicans say 'Am I inflaming a bunch of nuts?' you know we're going to have some more events. I am absolutely certain the harsher rhetoric of the Gingriches and the Doles . . . creates a climate of violence in America."

And David Broder had this to say in the *Washington Post*: "The bombing shows how dangerous it really is to inflame twisted minds with statements that suggest political opponents are enemies. For two years, Rush

[19] *Gingrich and Dole*: Newt Gingrich (b. 1943) was Speaker of the House of Representatives from 1995 to 1999. Robert Dole (b. 1923) was a Senate majority leader and served in the Senate from 1968 to 1996. — EDS.

Limbaugh described this nation as 'America held hostage' to the policies of the liberal Democrats, as if the duly elected president and Congress were equivalent to the regime in Tehran. I think there will be less tolerance and fewer cheers for that kind of rhetoric."

The message was clear: Conservative talk radio and conservative 15 politicians created an antigovernment atmosphere in America that spawned Timothy McVeigh and therefore were at least partially to blame for his terrorism. It's true, of course, that the atmosphere in which we live contributes to everything that happens in our culture. Calling people "kikes" or "niggers" makes it easier to see them as less than human and to treat them as something less than human. But to point fingers at talk radio for somehow encouraging Timothy McVeigh strikes me as a stretch at best; more likely it's just another opportunity for liberal journalists to blame conservatives for one more evil. And if this kind of connecting the dots is fair game, then should we also accuse Americans who spoke out loudly and forcefully against the war in Vietnam—including many journalists—of contributing to the 1972 bombing of the Pentagon and to other sometimes deadly terrorism, perpetuated by fanatics on the Left? According to the media elites' rulebook, when liberals rant it's called free speech; when conservatives rant it's called incitement to terrorism.

As I watched the coverage of the attacks on the Pentagon and the World Trade Center, I wondered why I hadn't seen more stories on television news, long before these zealots flew their hijacked planes into American buildings, about the culture of anti-American hate that permeates so much of the Middle East—stories that might help explain how little Arab children can grow up to become fanatical suicide bombers.

If the media found it so important to discuss the malignant atmosphere created by "hot" conservative talk radio, then why didn't they find it important to delve into this malignant atmosphere that seems to have bred such maniacal killers? Why would journalists, so interested in connecting the dots when they thought they led to Rush Limbaugh, be so uninterested in connecting the dots when there might actually be dots to connect—*from hateful, widely held popular attitudes in much of the Arab world straight to the cockpits of those hijacked jetliners?*

One of the networks put an American Muslim woman on the news who said that no one blamed Christianity when McVeigh killed all those people. Why blame Islam now? The reporter interviewing this woman let her have her say, never bothering to point out that Timothy McVeigh didn't kill all those people in the name of Christianity. Suicide airplane hijackers, on the other hand, are people who actually believe their murderous acts will earn them a one-way ticket to Paradise.

Was what happened on September 11 a subversion of Islam, as pundits and journalists on network and cable TV told us over and over again? Or was it the result of an *honest* reading of the Koran? It's true, of course, that if taken too literally by uncritical minds, just about any holy book can lead to bad things. Still, why are there no Christian suicide bombers, or Jewish suicide bombers, or Hindu suicide bombers, or Buddhist suicide bombers, but no apparent shortage of Muslim suicide bombers? If Islam is "a religion of peace" as so many people from President Bush on down were telling us (and, for what it's worth, I'm prepared to believe that it is), then what exactly is it in the Koran that so appeals to these Islamic fanatics? Don't look for that answer on the network news. A *Lexis-Nexis* search going back to 1991 linking the words "Koran" and "terrorist" produced absolutely nothing that told us what the Koran actually says which *might* encourage a Muslim, no matter how misguided, to commit acts of terrorism.

I understand that even to ask questions about a possible connection 20 between Islam and violence is to tread into politically incorrect terrain. But it seems to me that the media need to go there anyway. And any network that can put thousands of stories on the air about sex and murder should be able to give us a few on the atmosphere that breeds religious zealotry. It might have helped us see what was coming on September 11.

In fact, I learned much more about the atmosphere that breeds suicide bombers from one short article in *Commentary* magazine than I have from watching twenty years of network television news. In its September 2001 issue (which came out before the attack on America), there was an article by Fiamma Nirenstein, an Italian journalist based in Israel, entitled "How Suicide Bombers Are Made." In it, she tells about a "river of hatred" that runs through not just the most radical of Arab nations but also much of what we like to think of as the "moderate" Arab world.

She tells us about a series of articles that ran in the leading government-sponsored newspaper in Egypt, *Al Ahram*, about how Jews supposedly use the blood of Christians to make matzah for Passover.

She tells us about a hit song in Cairo, Damascus, and the West Bank with the catchy title "I Hate Israel."

Why didn't I know this? A computer check soon answered my question. On television, only CNN reported the "I Hate Israel" story. On radio, NPR did a piece. So did the *Christian Science Monitor* and the *Chicago Tribune*. The *Los Angeles Times* ran a short wire service story that said "'I Hate Israel' . . . made an overnight singing sensation of a working-class crooner."

Can you imagine if the big hit song in Israel was "I Hate Palestine" or 25 "I Hate Arabs"? The *New York Times* would have put the story on page one and then run an editorial just to make sure we all got the message—that the song is indecent and contributes to an atmosphere of hate. And since the *Times* sets the agenda for the networks, Dan Rather, Tom Brokaw, and Peter Jennings would have all fallen into line and run big stories on their evening newscasts, too, saying the exact same thing. A week later, Mike Wallace would have landed in Tel Aviv looking absolutely mortified that those Jews would do such a thing.

And that's part of the problem. Despite the liberalism of the media, there is a subtle form of racism at work here. As Fiamma Nirenstein writes, "The Arabs, it is implicitly suggested, are a backward people, not to be held to civilized standards of the West." Of the Israelis, however, the American media expect much more. That is why a song called "I Hate Israel" becomes a big hit, and yet is not a news story. And it is why a series of stories in a government-sponsored newspaper—in a supposedly moderate country—about Jews killing Christians for their blood holds almost no interest for American journalists.

It's true that not long after the twin towers of the World Trade Center came tumbling down, the networks showed us pictures of Palestinians in East Jerusalem honking their horns, firing their guns into the air, and generally having a good old time celebrating the death of so many Americans in New York and Washington. They cheered "God is great" while they handed out candy, which is a tradition in the Arab world when something good happens.

It's not that there's been a total news blackout of anti-American hate in the Middle East—*Nightline* has done some good, intelligent work in this area—it's just that we need more than pictures of happy Palestinians reveling in the death of thousands of Americans. And we need more than what has become a staple of Middle East television news coverage: young children throwing stones at Israeli soldiers—the perfect made-for-television David and Goliath story. What we need are stories that connect the dots, not just back to Afghanistan and its backward and repressive Taliban government, but also between the fanatics in New York and Washington and a cultural environment in the Arab world where even "moderates" hand out candy to celebrate the massacre of Americans.

But here the media—apparently feeling squeamish about stories that put the "underdogs" in a bad light—keep us virtually in the dark. And it's not just little tidbits like "I Hate Israel" and articles about Jews taking Christian blood that I—and almost all Americans—knew nothing about. Here's a quick rundown of what goes on in much of the Middle East as reported by Ms. Nirenstein in *Commentary*—news that is virtually ignored on the big American TV networks:

> In Egypt and Jordan, news sources have repeatedly warned that Israel has distributed drug-laced chewing gum and candy, intended (it is said) to kill children and make women sexually corrupt. . . .
>
> [Palestinian television] recently asserted that, far from being extermination camps, Chelmo, Dachau, and Auschwitz were in fact mere "places of disinfection."
>
> On April 13—observed in Israel as Holocaust Remembrance Day—the official Palestinian newspaper *Al-Hayat al-Jadida* featured a column . . . entitled "The Fable of the Holocaust."

A columnist in Egypt's government-sponsored Al-Akhbar thus expressed his "thanks to Hitler, of blessed memory, who on behalf of the Palestinians took revenge in advance on the most vile criminals on the face of the earth. Still, we do have a complaint against [Hitler], for his revenge on them was not enough."

In addition to these examples, Ms. Nirenstein cites a textbook for Syrian tenth graders which teaches them that "the logic of justice obligates the application of the single verdict [on the Jews] from which there is no escape: namely, that their criminal intentions be turned against them and that they be exterminated." And she notes that in June 2001, two weeks after the fatal collapse of a Jewish wedding hall in Jerusalem, Palestinian television broadcast a sermon by a Muslim imam praying that "this oppressive Knesset [Israel's parliament] will [similarly] collapse over the heads of the Jews."

I did not know any of that because it's simply not the kind of news that we normally get from the Middle East — certainly not from network evening newscasts or from *Dateline, 20/20,* or *48 Hours,* three news magazine programs that are usually too busy peddling the trivial and sensational to bother with more significant stories. And besides, that kind of news makes liberal journalists uneasy. After all, these are the same people who bend over backwards to find "moral equivalence" between Palestinian terrorists who blow up discos in Tel Aviv filled with teenagers, on the one hand, and Israeli commandos who *preemptively* kill terrorist ringleaders *before* they send their suicide bombers into Israel on a mission to kill Jews, on the other.

On September 11, right after the networks showed us the pictures of Palestinians celebrating American deaths, they also showed us Yasser Arafat expressing his condolences and giving blood for the American victims. This, in its way, represented a kind of moral equivalence: while some Palestinians celebrate, the news anchors were suggesting, their leader does not; he is somber and, we're led to believe, absolutely shocked. But we could have done with a little less moral equivalence on the part of the press and a little more tough journalism. Someone should have asked the leader of the Palestinian people if he understood that the cultures that he and other "moderate" Arab leaders preside over "carefully nurture and inculcate resentments and hatreds against America and the non-Arab world," as a *Wall Street Journal* editorial put it. And if that's asking too much of a field reporter covering a seemingly shaken and distraught Arafat in the wake of September 11, then an anchor back in New York should have wondered out loud about that very connection.

But to have asked such a question might have been viewed as anti-Arab (and therefore pro-Israeli), and reporters and anchors would rather be stoned by an angry mob in Ramallah than be seen in that light. So we didn't learn that day if Chairman Arafat quite understood his role in the celebration he so deplored. Nor did we get an explanation on the news about why there were not thousands of other Arabs in the streets—on the West Bank or in Jerusalem or in the "moderate" Arab countries—expressing their *condolences*. Was it because they are afraid to show support for American victims of terrorism? Or was it because they, like the Palestinians we saw with great big smiles, didn't feel that bad about what happened?

If the networks can give us months and months of Chandra and JonBenet and Lorena Bobbitt and Joey Buttafuoco,[20] then they can give us more than they do about the river of hatred that breeds suicide bombers.

But this is where journalists—given their liberal tendency to empathize with, and sometimes even root for, the "underdog"—run into a big problem: if they start to connect those ideological and religious dots, they may not like what they find. 35

American journalists who covered the civil rights struggle recognized the pathology of racism and rightly made no allowance for it. They understood that in order for evil to flourish in places throughout the South, all it took was a few fundamentally bad people—while everybody else sat around making believe it wasn't happening, either because they were afraid or because they just didn't want to get involved.

The Middle East, of course, is a place with a long and troubled history. But it should be obvious that a place that turns "I Hate Israel" into a hit, that runs stories in its most important newspaper about Jews killing Christians for their blood, that faults Hitler *only because he did not kill more Jews*, and that celebrates the murder of thousands of innocent Americans is a place populated by many nasty people. Perhaps it has many good people, too, who just don't want to get involved. The point is, a story about all of this is at least as important as a story about Anne Heche and her sex life, even if sex does better in the ratings than disturbing news about raw, ignorant hatred in the world of Islam.

None of this is an argument that the media are intentionally pro-Arab. Rather, like the U.S. State Department, they are pro "moral equivalence." If they connect the dots with stories on the news about hit songs called "I Hate Israel" and all the rest, the Arab world will accuse the "Jewish-controlled" American media of being sympathetic to "Israeli oppression." If journalists—who were so willing to connect the dots when there was a belief that they led to Rush Limbaugh—connected *these* dots, they might find that there are a lot fewer moderates in those moderate places than they keep telling us about.

---

[20]JonBenet and Lorena Bobbitt and Joey Buttafucco: JonBenet Ramsey was a six-year-old beauty pageant contestant found murdered in the basement of her home in Boulder, Colorado, the day after Christmas 1996, whose case has never been solved. Lorena Bobbit cut off her husband's penis in 1993 allegedly because of long-term abuse. Joey Buttafuoco's under-aged lover, Amy Fisher, shot his wife in the face in 1992.

So they look the other way, which, as Ms. Nirenstein tells us, is not that easy. One has to turn "a determinedly blind eye to this river of hatred . . . [and] to be persuaded that, after all, 'everybody' in the Middle East really wants the same thing."

Obviously, there are legitimate issues about which there are differing 40 viewpoints in the Middle East: Should Israel blow up the houses that belong to the families of terrorists? Should Israel allow the construction of new settlements on the West Bank? These are two that come quickly to mind.

But moral equivalence and the quest for evenhanded journalism should not stop the media from telling us more—much more in my view—about the kind of backwardness and hatred that is alive and well, *not just in places like Kabul and Baghdad*, but in "moderate" cities and villages all over the Arab world. Even if it means going against their liberal sensibilities and reporting that sometimes even the underdog can be evil.

READING AND DISCUSSION QUESTIONS

1. How does Goldberg support his claim that television draws Americans together in times of crisis?

2. How does he believe the news is different during times of crisis from how it usually is?

3. Explain the title that Goldberg chose for this piece. What does he claim the "media elites" have "connected the dots" to find?

4. What does Goldberg believe the news media are *not* telling Americans? What sort of support does he offer for that part of his argument?

5. What type or types of support that Goldberg uses do you find most effective? Why?

WRITING SUGGESTIONS

6. Analyze the types of support that Goldberg makes use of in his essay.

7. Evaluate the effectiveness of the major types of support that he uses in his essay.

8. Attack or defend the claim that Goldberg is advancing in his essay.

9. What is your personal opinion of the media coverage of the tragedies of September 11?

10. Do you believe that your education has exposed you to recent history as well as the more distant past? Explain.

A New Look, an Old Battle

ANNA QUINDLEN

Public personification has always been the struggle on both sides of the abortion battle lines. That is why the people outside clinics on Saturday mornings carry signs with photographs of infants rather than of zygotes, why they wear lapel pins fashioned in the image of tiny feet and shout, "Don't kill your baby," rather than, more accurately, "Don't destroy your embryo." Those who support the legal right to an abortion have always been somewhat at a loss in the face of all this. From time to time women have come forward to speak about their decision to have an abortion, but when they are prominent, it seems a bit like grandstanding, and when they are not, it seems a terrible invasion of privacy when privacy is the point in the first place. Easier to marshal the act of presumptive ventriloquism practiced by the opponents, pretending to speak for those unborn unknown to them by circumstance or story.

But the battle of personification will assume a different and more sympathetic visage in the years to come. Perhaps the change in the weather was best illustrated when conservative Sen. Strom Thurmond invoked his own daughter to explain a position opposed by the antiabortion forces. The senator's daughter has diabetes. The actor Michael J. Fox has Parkinson's disease. Christopher Reeve is in a wheelchair because of a spinal-cord injury, Ronald Reagan locked in his own devolving mind by Alzheimer's. In the faces of the publicly and personally beloved lies enormous danger for the life-begins-at-conception lobby.

The catalytic issue is research on stem cells. These are versatile building blocks that may be coaxed into becoming any other cell type; they could therefore hold the key to endless mysteries of human biology, as well as someday help provide a cure for ailments as diverse as diabetes, Parkinson's, spinal-cord degeneration, and Alzheimer's. By some estimates, more than 100 million Americans have diseases that scientists suspect could be affected by research on stem cells. Scientists hope that the astonishing potential of this research will persuade the federal government to help fund it and allow the National Institutes of Health to help oversee it. This is not political, researchers insist. It is about science, not abortion.

And they are correct. Stem-cell research is typically done by using frozen embryos left over from in vitro fertilization. If these embryos were placed in the womb, they might eventually implant, become a fetus, then a child. Unused, they are the earliest undifferentiated collection of cells

---

Anna Quindlen is a Pulitzer Prize–winning journalist and best-selling novelist. This piece appeared in the April 9, 2001, issue of *Newsweek* magazine.

made by the joining of the egg and sperm, no larger than the period at the end of this sentence. One of the oft-used slogans of the anti-abortion movement is "abortion stops a beating heart." There is no heart in this preimplantation embryo, but there are stem cells that, in the hands of scientists, might lead to extraordinary work affecting everything from cancer to heart disease.

All of which leaves the anti-abortion movement trying desperately to   5 hold its hard line, and failing. Judie Brown of the American Life League can refer to these embryos as "the tiniest person," and the National Right to Life organization can publish papers that refer to stem-cell research as the "destruction of life." But ordinary people with family members losing their mobility or their grasp on reality will be able to be more thoughtful and reasonable about the issues involved.

The anti-abortion activists know this, because they have already seen the defections. Some senators have abandoned them to support fetal-tissue research, less promising than stem-cell work but still with significant potential for treating various ailments. Elected officials who had voted against abortion rights found themselves able to support procedures that used tissue from aborted fetuses; perhaps they were men who had fathers with heart disease, who had mothers with arthritis and whose hearts resonated with the possibilities for alleviating pain and prolonging life. Senator Thurmond was one, Senator McCain another. Former senator Connie Mack of Florida recently sent a letter to the president, who must decide the future role of the federal government in this area, describing himself "as a conservative pro-life now former member" of Congress, and adding that there "were those of us identified as such who supported embryonic stem-cell research."

When a recent test of fetal tissue in patients with Parkinson's had disastrous side effects, the National Right to Life Web site ran an almost gloating report: "horrific," "rips to shreds," "media cheerleaders," "defy description." The tone is a reflection of fear. It's the fear that the use of fetal tissue to produce cures for debilitating ailments might somehow launder the process of terminating a pregnancy, a positive result from what many people still see as a negative act. And it's the fear that thinking—really thinking—about the use of the earliest embryo for life-saving research might bring a certain long-overdue relativism to discussions of abortion across the board.

The majority of Americans have always been able to apply that relativism to these issues. They are more likely to accept early abortions than later ones. They are more tolerant of a single abortion under exigent circumstances than multiple abortions. Some who disapprove of abortion in theory have discovered that they can accept it in fact if a daughter or a girlfriend is pregnant.

And some who believe that life begins at conception may look into the vacant eyes of an adored parent with Alzheimer's or picture a paralyzed child walking again, and take a closer look at what an embryo really is, at what stem-cell research really does, and then consider the true cost of a cure. That is what Senator Thurmond obviously did when he looked at his daughter and broke ranks with the true believers. It may be an oversimplification to say that real live loved ones trump the imagined unborn, that a cluster of undifferentiated cells due to be discarded anyway is a small price to pay for the health and welfare of millions. Or perhaps it is only a simple commonsensical truth.

READING AND DISCUSSION QUESTIONS

1. Understanding Quindlen's argument requires an understanding of the terms she uses. In her introductory paragraph, she refers to "public personification," "grandstanding," and "presumptive ventriloquism." Explain these terms in the context of her argument.

2. Why are anti-abortion activists opposed to the use of stem-cell research? How does Quindlen defend her own position?

3. What does Quindlen mean when she says that stem-cell research "might bring a certain long-overdue relativism to discussions of abortion" (para. 7)? (The meaning of *relativism* is the key.)

4. Although this essay clearly suggests a policy, it is primarily a claim of value: Stem-cell research is vital because it will contribute to the life and health of our loved ones. Point out places in the essay where Quindlen makes an emotional appeal to our compassion.

WRITING SUGGESTIONS

5. The debate about stem-cell research in the Congress, the media, and the medical and scientific professions, expanded after a speech by President Bush on August 9, 2001, in which he agreed to permit limited research on stem cells. Look up some of the news stories, editorials, and letters to the editors that followed his speech, and summarize the opposition to the president's proposal.

6. Quindlen explores the possible influence of stem-cell research on increased acceptance of abortion. Write an essay that argues for or against the right of a woman to an abortion. If you have reservations, make clear what circumstances would govern your judgment.

Marriage-Plus

THEODORA OOMS

The public has been concerned about "family breakdown" for a long time, but it was not until the passage of welfare reform in 1996 that the federal government decided to get into the business of promoting marriage. Although it was little noticed at the time, three of the four purposes of the welfare legislation refer directly or indirectly to marriage and family formation. The law exhorts states to promote "job preparation, work and marriage," to "prevent and reduce the incidence of out-of-wedlock pregnancies," and to "encourage the formation and maintenance of two-parent families."

The Bush administration, as it contemplates this year's extension of welfare legislation, plans to make marriage even more central. The administration's reauthorization proposal, announced February 27, includes $300 million for demonstration grants to focus on promoting healthy marriages and reducing out-of-wedlock births.[21] Meanwhile, Oklahoma Governor Frank Keating has launched a $10 million, multisector marriage initiative, and other smaller-scale government-sponsored initiatives have been enacted in Arizona, Florida, Louisiana, Michigan, and Utah. The federal government is primarily concerned with reducing out-of-wedlock births, which it views as a principal cause of welfare dependency and a host of other social problems. By contrast, state marriage initiatives are most concerned about the effects of high divorce rates and father absence on children.[22]

This new emphasis on marriage as a panacea for social problems is troubling to many liberals. For one thing, it risks being dismissive of children who happen to find themselves in single-parent families. It also can be seen as disparaging single mothers and ignoring the fact that many women have left abusive marriages for good reasons.

That said, it's hard to dismiss an overwhelming consensus of social-science research findings that children tend to be better off, financially and emotionally, when their parents are married to each other. Around 50 percent of all first marriages are expected to end in divorce, and 60 percent of all divorces involve children. One-third of all births are out of

[21] See *Working Toward Independence: The President's Plan to Strengthen Welfare Reform*, February 2002. http://www.whitehouse.gov/news/releases/2002/02/welfare-reform-announcement-book.pdf.

[22] Theodora Ooms, "The Role of the Federal Government in Strengthening Marriage," in *Virginia Journal of Social Policy and the Law*, Fall 2002. To be posted on www.clasp.org.

Theodora Ooms is a senior policy analyst at the Center for Law and Social Policy. Her article is an annotated version of one that originally appeared in a special issue of *The American Prospect* on "The Politics of the American Family," April 8, 2002.

wedlock, nearly 40 percent of children do not live with their biological fathers, and too many nonresident fathers neither support nor see their children on a regular basis.

Children living with single mothers are five times as likely to be poor 5 as those in two-parent families. Growing up in a single-parent family also roughly doubles the risk that a child will drop out of school, have difficulty finding a job, or become a teen parent. About half of these effects appear to be attributable to the reduced income available to single parents, but the other half is due to non-economic factors.[23] It's not just the presence of two adults in the home that helps children, as some argue. Children living with cohabiting partners and in stepfamilies generally do less well than those living with both married biological parents.[24]

Marriage also brings benefits to husbands and wives. Married adults are more productive on the job, earn more, save more, have better physical and mental health, and live longer, according to an extensive review of research, conducted by scholar Linda Waite. Although Waite admits that these findings partly reflect the selection of better-adjusted people into marriage, she finds that when people marry, they act in more health promoting and productive ways.[25]

Conservatives are prone to exaggerate these research findings and underplay the importance of economics. If married people are more likely (other things being equal) to produce thriving children, other things are not, in fact, equal. It's not just the case that single mothers find themselves poor because they are unmarried; they find themselves unmarried because they are poor. Successful marriages are more difficult when husbands and wives are poorly educated, lack access to jobs that pay decently, and cannot afford decent child care. Economic hardship and other problems associated with poverty can wreak havoc on couples' relationships.

The controversy mostly isn't about research, however, but about values.[26] Most people regard decisions to marry, divorce, and bear children

---

[23] Sara McLanahan and Julien Teitler, "The Consequences of Father Absence," in *Parenting and Child Development in "Non-Traditional" Families*, ed. Michael E. Lamb (Mahwah, NJ: Lawrence Erlbaum, 1998). Also see Sara McLanahan and Gary Sanderfur, *Growing Up with a Single Parent: What Hurts, What Helps* (Cambridge, MA: Harvard UP, 1994).

[24] See McLanahan and Teitler; Susan L. Brown, "Child Well-Being in Cohabiting Unions" and Wendy D. Manning, "The Implications of Cohabitation for Children's Well-Being," in *Just Living Together: Implications of Cohabitation for Children, Families and Social Policy*, eds. Alan Booth and Ann C. Crouter (Mahwah, NJ: Lawrence Erlbaum, 2002).

[25] Linda J. Waite and Maggie Gallagher, *The Case for Marriage: Why Married People Are Happier, Healthier and Better Off Financially* (New York: Doubleday, 2000).

[26] Theodora Ooms, *Toward More Perfect Unions: Putting Marriage on the Public Agenda* (Washington, DC: Family Impact Seminar, 1998). Available from tooms@clasp.org.

as intensely private. Any policy proposals that hint at coercing people to marry, reinforcing Victorian conceptions of gender roles, or limiting the right to end bad marriages are viewed as counter to American values of individual autonomy and privacy. Some worry about the existence of hidden agendas that threaten to put women back into the kitchen, ignore domestic violence, and eliminate public assistance for low-income families. Others fear that holding out marriage as the ideal blames single parents, many of whom do a terrific job under difficult circumstances. Use of the term "illegitimate" is especially offensive because it stigmatizes children (and, in fact, is legally inaccurate, as children born outside of marriage now have virtually the same legal rights as those born within marriage).[27] And some worry that the pro-marriage agenda discriminates against ethnic and sexual minorities and their children, particularly gays and lesbians.

There are also more pragmatic concerns. Skeptics of the pro-marriage agenda observe that the decline in marriage is worldwide, a result of overwhelming social and economic forces that cannot be reversed. In their view, attempts to change family formation behavior are largely futile; we should instead just accept and help support the increasing diversity of family forms. For others, the concern is less about the value of promoting marriage and more about whether government, rather than individuals, communities, or faith institutions, should lead the charge.

Finally, marriage per se is too simplistic a solution to the complex problems of the poor. Marrying a low-income, unmarried mother to her child's father will not magically raise the family out of poverty when the parents often have no skills, no jobs, terrible housing, and may be struggling with depression, substance abuse, or domestic violence. Advocates also worry that funds spent on untested marriage-promotion activities will be taken away from programs that provide desperately needed services for single parents, such as child care.

In response to some of these concerns—as well as research showing that serious parental conflict harms children—some marriage advocates respond that marriage per se should not be the goal but rather voluntary, "healthy" marriages.[28] They also agree that protections should be built into programs to guard against domestic violence. But this only raises doubts about how "healthy" will be defined, and by whom, and whether we even know how to help people create better relationships.

There also are some plainly foolish ideas in the marriage movement. West Virginia currently gives married families an extra $100 a month in welfare payments as a "marriage incentive." Robert Rector of the Heritage

---

[27] Ruth-Arlene W. Howe, "Legal Rights and Obligations: An Uneven Evolution," in *Young Unwed Fathers: Changing Roles and Emerging Policies*, eds. Robert I. Lerman and Theodora Ooms (Philadelphia: Temple UP, 1993), pp. 141–69.

[28] See, for example, Robin Toner, "Welfare Chief Is Hoping to Promote Marriage," *New York Times*, February 19, 2002, sec. A, p. 1.

Foundation has proposed giving a $4,000 government bounty to welfare recipients who marry before they have a child and stay married for two years.[29] Charles Murray wants to end public assistance altogether and has proposed eliminating all aid to *unmarried* mothers under 21 in one state to test the idea. This proposal is especially egregious and surely would harm children of single mothers.[30]

Progressives and others thus are placed in a quandary. They don't want to oppose marriage—which most Americans still value highly—but are skeptical of many pro-marriage initiatives. Given that healthy marriage is plainly good for children, however, one can envision a reasonable agenda—one that would gain broad support—that we might call marriage-plus. This approach puts the well-being of children first by helping more of them grow up in married, healthy, two-parent families. However, for many children, the reality is that marriage is not a feasible or even a desirable option for their parents. Thus, a secondary goal is to help these parents—whether unmarried, separated, divorced, or remarried—cooperate better in raising their children. These are not alternative strategies. Children need us to do both.

A marriage-plus agenda does not promote marriage just for marriage's sake. It acknowledges that married and unmarried parents, mothers and fathers, may need both economic resources and non-economic supports to increase the likelihood of stable, healthy marriages and better co-parenting relationships. In addition, a marriage-plus agenda focuses more on the front end—making marriage better to be in—rather than the back end—making marriage more difficult to get out of.

Here are some elements of this agenda.   15

Strengthen "fragile families" at the birth of a child. For many poor families, relationship-education programs may be helpful but not enough. A new national study finds that at the time of their child's birth, one-half of unmarried parents (so-called "fragile families") are living together, and another third are romantically attached but not cohabiting.[31] The majorities of these parents are committed to each other and to their child and have high hopes of eventual marriage and a future together—although these hopes too often are not realized. We should reach out to young parents to help them achieve their desire to remain together as a family. A

---

[29] Robert Rector, *A Plan to Reduce Illegitimacy*, memorandum handed out at a meeting on Capitol Hill in early 2001.

[30] Charles Murray, "Family Formation," in *The New World of Welfare*, eds. Rebecca M. Blank and Ron Haskins (Washington, DC: Brookings Institution Press, 2001), pp. 137–68.

[31] Sara McLanahan et al., *The Fragile Families and Child Wellbeing Study Baseline Report*, August 2001, http://crcw.princeton.edu/fragilefamilies/nationalreport.pdf; and Sara McLanahan, Irwin Garfinkel, and Ronald B. Mincy, "Fragile Families, Welfare Reform, and Marriage," *Welfare Reform and Beyond Policy Brief*, No. 10, November 2001. http://www.brookings.edu/dybdocroot/wrb/publications/pb/pb10.htm. For additional papers from the Fragile Families study, see http://crcw.princeton.edu/fragilefamilies/index.htm.

helpful package of services to offer these young families might include a combination of "soft" services—relationship-skills and marriage-education workshops, financial-management classes, and peer-support groups—and "hard" services, such as job training and placement, housing, medical coverage, and substance-abuse treatment, if necessary. At present, all we do is get the father to admit paternity and hound him for child support.

Reduce economic stress by reducing poverty. Poverty and unemployment can stress couples' relationships to their breaking point. Results of a welfare-to-work demonstration program in Minnesota suggest that enhancing the income of the working poor can indirectly promote marriage. The Minnesota Family Investment Program (MFIP), which subsidized the earnings of employed welfare families, found that marriage rates increased for both single-parent long-term recipients and two-parent families. Married two-parent families were significantly more likely to remain married. MFIP also reduced the reported incidence of domestic abuse.[32]

Provide better-paying jobs and job assistance for the poor. The inability of low-skilled, unemployed men to provide income to their families is a major reason for their failure to marry the mothers of their children. Better employment opportunities help low-income fathers, and men in general, to become responsible fathers and, perhaps, more attractive and economically stable marriage partners.[33] There is also growing support for making changes in the child-support system to ensure that more support paid by fathers goes to the children (rather than being used to recoup government program costs).[34]

Invest more in proven programs that reduce out-of-wedlock childbearing. Teen pregnancy and birth rates have fallen by over 20 percent since the early 1990s, and there is now strong evidence that a number of prevention programs are effective. A related strategy is enforcement of child support. States that have tough, effective child support systems have been found to have lower nonmarital birth rates, presumably because men are beginning to understand there are serious costs associated with fathering a child.[35]

[32] Virginia Knox, Cynthia Miller, and Lisa A. Gennetian, *Reforming Welfare and Rewarding Work: A Summary of the Final Report on the Minnesota Family Investment Program* (New York: Manpower Demonstration Research Corporation, September, 2000).

[33] See Chapter 4, "The Fading Inner-City Family," in William Julius Wilson, *When Work Disappears: The World of the New Urban Poor* (New York: Alfred A. Knopf, 1996), pp. 87–110; Kathy Edin, "Few Good Men: Why Poor Mothers Don't Marry or Remarry," *The American Prospect*, January 3, 2000.

[34] See Vicki Turetsky, Testimony Given to the Social Security and Family Policy Subcommittee of the U.S. Senate Finance Committee, October 11, 2001, and Vick Turetsky, *What If All the Money Came Home?* (Washington, DC: Center for Law and Social Policy, June, 2000). Both available online at www.clasp.org.

[35] Robert D. Plotnick, Inhoe Ku, Irwin Garfinkel, and Sara S. McLanahan, *The Impact of Child Support Enforcement Policy on Nonmarital Childbearing*. Paper presented at the Association for Public Policy Analysis and Management, Year 2000 Research Conference in Seattle, WA.

Institute workplace policies to reduce work/family conflict and stress on 20
couples. Stress in the workplace spills over into the home. Persistent
overtime, frequent travel, and inflexible leave policies place great strain
on couples at all income levels. Employers are increasingly demanding
nonstandard work schedules. A recent study found that married couples
with children who work night and rotating shifts are at higher risk of separation and divorce.[36] The absence of affordable and reliable child care
forces many parents who would prefer a normal workday to working split
shifts solely to make sure that a parent is home with the children.

Reduce tax penalties and other disincentives to marriage. There has always
been strong support for reducing marriage tax penalties for many two-
earner families. This is a complicated task because the majority of married
couples, in fact, receive tax bonuses rather than penalties.[37] A positive
step was taken in 2001 to reduce significantly the marriage penalty affecting low-income working families in the Earned Income Tax Credit program. While there is uncertainty about the extent to which these
tax-related marriage penalties affect marital behavior, there is broad general agreement that government has a responsibility to "first do no harm"
when it comes to marriage.

Similarly, there is near unanimous agreement that government
should not make it harder for eligible two-parent families to receive welfare benefits and assistance. In the past, the old welfare program, Aid to
Families with Dependent Children, was much criticized for offering incentives to break up families. At least 33 states already have removed the
stricter eligibility rules placed on two-parent families,[38] and the president's welfare reauthorization proposal encourages the other states to do
the same. In addition, it proposes to end the higher work participation
rate for two-parent families, a federal rule that has been criticized widely
by the states. Another needed reform would forgive accumulated child-
support debt owed by noncustodial fathers if they marry the mothers of
their children. (Currently, such debt is owed to the state if the mothers
and children are receiving welfare benefits.)[39]

*Educate those who want to marry and stay married about how to have
healthy relationships and good marriages.* A vast industry is devoted to helping couples plan a successful wedding day—wedding planners, 500-page

---

[36]Harriet B. Presser, "Nonstandard Work Schedules and Marital Instability," *Journal of
Marriage and the Family* (February 2000).

[37]Congressional Budget Office, *For Better or For Worse: Marriage and the Federal Income
Tax* (Washington, DC: Congress of the United States, Congressional Budget Office, June
1997).

[38]Gene Falk and Jill Tauber, *Welfare Reform: TANF Provisions Related to Marriage and
Two-Parent Families* (Washington, DC: Congressional Research Service, Library of Congress, October 30, 2001).

[39]Paul Roberts, *An Ounce of Prevention and a Pound of Cure: Developing State Policy on
the Payment of Child Support Arrears by Low Income Parents.* (Washington, DC: Center for
Law and Social Policy, May 2001). Available online at www.clasp.org.

bridal guides, specialty caterers, the list goes on. But where do young people go to learn about how to sustain good, lifelong marriages? In fact, we now know a lot about what makes contemporary marriages work. With the transformation of gender roles, there now are fewer fixed rules for couples to follow, meaning they have to negotiate daily about who does what and when. In the absence of the legal and social constraints that used to keep marriages together, there's now a premium on developing effective relationship skills. Building on three decades of research, there are a small but rapidly growing number of programs (both religious and secular) that help people from high school through adulthood understand the benefits of marriage for children and for themselves, develop realistic expectations for healthy relationships, understand the meaning of commitment, and learn the skills and attitudes needed to make marriage succeed.[40] Other programs help married couples survive the inevitable ups and downs that occur in most marriages, and remarried couples with the additional challenges of step-parenting. Oklahoma, Utah, and Michigan have begun using government funds to make these relationship- and marriage-education programs accessible to low-income couples. The Greater Grand Rapids Community Marriage Policy initiative is urging area businesses to include marriage education as an Employee Assistance Program benefit, arguing that it's more cost-effective to prevent marital distress than incur the costs of counseling and lost productivity involved when employees' marriages break up.[41]

A marriage-plus agenda that includes activities such as these is not just the responsibility of government. Some of the strategies proposed here are being implemented by private and religious groups, some by governments, and some by partnerships between these sectors. The approach adopted in Oklahoma, Greater Grand Rapids, and Chattanooga, for example, mobilizes the resources of many sectors of the community — government, education, legal, faith, business, and media — in a comprehensive effort to create a more marriage-supportive culture and to provide new services to promote, support, and strengthen couples and marriage and reduce out-of-wedlock childbearing and divorce. This "saturation model" seems particularly promising because it takes into account the many factors that influence individuals' decisions to marry, to divorce, or to remain unmarried. We should proceed cautiously, trying out and evaluating new ideas before applying them widely.

[40]See Scott Stanley, "Making a Case for Premarital Education," in *Family Relations* (July 2001). Also see *Directory of Couples and Marriage Education Programs* at www .smartmarriages.com.
[41]Personal communication with Mark Eastburg, Ph.D., director of Pine Rest Family Institute, Grand Rapids, Michigan. See Web site for the Greater Grand Rapids Community Marriage Initiative, www.ggrcmarriagepolicy.org.

Ironically, in the midst of this furor about government's role in mar- 25
riage, it's worth noting that the federal government recently has begun to
shirk a basic responsibility: counting the numbers of marriages and divorces in the United States. Since budget cuts in 1995, the government
has been unable to report on marriage and divorce rates in the states or
for the nation as a whole.[42] And, for the first time in the history of the
Census, Americans were not asked to give their marital status in the 2000
survey. What kind of pro-marriage message from the government is that?

If liberals and conservatives are serious about strengthening families
for the sake of helping children, liberals ought to acknowledge that non-
coercive and egalitarian approaches to bolstering marriage are sound policy. Conservatives, meanwhile, should admit that much of what it takes
to make marriage work for the benefit of spouses and children is not just
moral but economic.

READING AND DISCUSSION QUESTIONS

1. What does Ooms mean when she says in the first paragraph that in 1996
   "the federal government decided to get into the business of promoting
   marriage"?

2. How does Ooms support her belief that children are better off in a two-
   parent home?

3. What type of support does she use in the sixth paragraph to argue that
   "[m]arriage also brings benefits to husbands and wives"?

4. What are some of the problems that arise when government gets involved in promoting marriage?

5. What claim is Ooms supporting? How effective is she in supporting that
   claim? Are some types of support that she uses more effective than others, in your opinion?

WRITING SUGGESTIONS

6. Write an essay in which you oppose or support Ooms's marriage-plus
   plan.

7. Analyze the primary types of support that Ooms uses. If you wish, you
   may go a step further and evaluate the effectiveness of her support.

[42]Stephanie Ventura, "Vital Statistics from the National Center for Health Statistics,"
in *Data Needs for Measuring Family and Fertility Change after Welfare Reform,* ed. Douglas
Besharov (College Park, MD: Maryland School of Public Affairs, Welfare Reform
Academy).

Praise for Student's Footage of Virginia Tech Mass Killing

LILY YULIANTI

On a CNN Larry King Live special report of the student massacre at Virginia Tech that saw 33 people killed King praised Jamal Albarghouti, the Palestinian graduate student who took the eyewitness footage of the immediate aftermath on his cellphone.

At roughly 10 a.m. Albarghouti was at the Blacksburg, VA, campus to meet with his graduate adviser. He sensed that something terrible had just happened on campus, explaining, "Everyone [was] running and screaming. The situation was so frightening. I ran to a safe place and then decided to record the situation using my cellphone."

He then sent his video to CNN's I-Report, a citizen-reporter video blog site, which repeatedly used it to accompany its other reporting of the incident. This has been without doubt the worst mass shooting tragedy in U.S. history, and Albarghouti was the one to capture the incident for the world.

His footage, some of it shaky, set the scene inside the campus: an empty road outside a nearby building being approached by three police officers, then sounds of gunshots registering almost simultaneously, the last sounding like a bomb blast.

In the CNN interview with Larry King, Albarghouti explained how the 5 scene reminded him of his homeland of Palestine. King and another CNN news anchor tried to get at why Albarghouti decided not to dash for safety with other students and staffers, but chose to stand fast and record the incident. "Weren't you scared? What sort of cellphone did you use? Did you think you were really safe at that time?"

His response was to demonstrate the value of a citizen reporter in providing an on-the-spot report of a history-making, traumatic event, in having the gadget at the ready to take the footage, and in having the presence of mind and the passion to play his historical role. He was not the only eyewitness, but also stood his ground as a resourceful citizen reporter, taking the initiative to record the scene.

Lily Yulianti is a journalist and writer from Indonesia who works in Tokyo as an Indonesian language specialist and broadcaster for Radio Tokyo. As a citizen journalist herself, she posted this article on Korea's massive online outlet for citizen journalists, Ohmynews, on April 17, 2007.

We can understand how CNN's professional journalists and a famous TV personality like Larry King could be so taken with Albarghouti's "journalism skill." Tempted to discount the capability of ordinary citizens in their chosen field of journalism, there are many well-trained professional journalists, proud of their skill and experience, who become intrigued whenever an unsung citizen reporter performs such a heroic act of historical reportage.

Apart from the unevenness of the footage he provided, Albarghouti showed that being confident in the use of his cellphone and uploading the resulting footage could be taken as matters of course. Above all, he provided King a clear and firm account of the situation, exactly in the manner of a professional TV journalist making a live report. What added special depth and human interest to this live report was his being reminded of the grievous situation in his own country when hearing the gun shots on campus. "I am quite familiar with the sound of gunshots, because they remind me of the situation in the West Bank and Gaza. But when I saw it was happening here, in a peaceful place like this, it was hard to believe."

Such was the personal background of a citizen-reporter that made Larry King say later, "What an irony . . .".

Again, Albarghouti and his cellphone video have shown the power of 10 the ordinary citizen to capture a news event. Granted that the efforts of ordinary people as citizen journalists are a matter for debate, the traditional media still make a reflexively negative comparison between citizen journalism and that provided by their professionals. Interestingly, when presented with a citizen who sent an exclusive report to the mainstream media, as Albarghouti did to CNN's I-Report, they insist on wondering, in grudging amazement, "What made you record the event? How did you record it?"

Of course, the mainstream media should first of all be thankful, because there is a live video record from the site. The role of Albarghouti was not only that of eyewitness but also of a citizen reporter who in fact provided a high-quality report for CNN.

In raising questions like these, professionals in the media show a tendency to overlook the existence of many ordinary citizens out there who embrace the idea of participatory journalism, people who have shifted from being passive media consumers to active citizen reporters, believing they can create a better society if they get involved in conveying the news. They make videos, they write on various issues, and they raise their voices. As for the mainstream media, they have begun to open their doors to citizen reporters, seeing that their well-trained professionals cannot always respond quickly enough to reach the location of an epochal event.

Disaster Photos: Newsworthy or Irresponsible?

MARK MEMMOTT WITH ALAN LEVIN AND GREG LIVADAS

Photos taken by survivors of the London bombings[43] and Tuesday's plane crash in Toronto are prompting concerns by safety investigators and journalism scholars.

At issue: Whether as camera phones and digital cameras multiply, so do the odds that victims will put themselves and others at risk by pausing to snap pictures.

Questions are also being raised about whether the media may be encouraging risky behavior by broadcasting the images.

On the other side of the debate, such photos may aid investigators.

Within a few hours of the London attacks [on] July 7, photos taken 5 by survivors with camera phones were ricocheting around the world on the Internet and on television.

Four photos taken Tuesday by Air France Flight 358 passenger Eddie Ho were broadcast later on several outlets, including ABC's *Good Morning America*, CNN, and NBC's *Today*. One was snapped inside the jet moments after it skidded to a halt in Toronto. It shows passengers heading to an exit. The others were taken outside the jet and show passengers fleeing the crippled fuselage.

All 309 people aboard survived.

Ho, 19, a South African attending college in Canada, said Thursday in a telephone interview with USA TODAY that his digital camera was in his pocket during the flight. He is an "airline enthusiast" who often takes pictures while flying. Ho sold the photos to two syndicates, which are now reselling them to the media.

Ho said he doesn't think he delayed his exit or anyone else's. "I was running and taking pictures," he said. "I just kept pressing the button." He said he would not have tried to retrieve his camera if it had been in a bag.

Still, a top accident investigation official in the USA strongly advises 10 passengers not to do such things.

---

[43] On two different dates in July 2005, London's bus and subway system was the target of a synchronized cluster of bombs. On July 7, fifty-two people were killed and 770 injured. On July 21, four devices were planted on three subways and one bus, as in the previous incident, but this time all failed to go off.

Mark Memmott has worked for *USA Today* since 1984 as a reporter and editor, and he has been a blogger for *USA Today* since they launched its On Deadline blog in January 2006. He specializes in the media's coverage of politics and campaign advertising and Internet efforts. This article was published on August 4, 2005. Alan Levin is a reporter for *USA Today* and Greg Livadas is a reporter for the *Rochester Democrat and Chronicle* in New York.

Mark Rosenker, acting chairman of the National Transportation Safety Board, said, "Your business is to get off the airplane. Your business is to help anybody who needs help." Taking photos is "irresponsible," he said.

Helen Muir, aerospace psychology professor at Cranfield University in Great Britain, said in most crashes "you only have two minutes from the first spark to conditions not being survivable in the cabin." Pausing even for a second "is just what we don't want people to do." But, Muir said, the pictures could be "very valuable to accident investigators." They contain clues to the jet's condition after the crash.

More such photos are inevitable. There are digital cameras in about half of U.S. households and camera phones in about 40%, the market research firm IDC estimates. About 92 million camera phones have been sold in the USA, IDC says.

Kelly McBride, who lectures about media ethics at the Poynter Institute for professional journalists, said the media have a responsibility "to refuse to publish photos taken (by amateurs) when someone was obviously risking his life or the lives of others."

McBride said journalists must "talk to the person about the circum- 15 stances under which he took the photos and share that information with the public."

Ben Sherwood, executive producer at *Good Morning America*, said there was no reason to think Ho had caused any problems at the scene. "From what we could tell" from the photos, Sherwood said, "one was taken (in the jet) during what appeared to be an orderly evacuation. The others were taken from outside, looking back."

Sherwood said *Good Morning America* "welcomes contributions from people who find themselves in the middle of news stories [but] would never encourage anyone to take an unnecessary risk."

Jonathan Klein, president of CNN/US, said his network "urges folks, on the air, not to take foolish risks." He doubts many survivors are thinking about the media when they pull out their cameras.

"They're taking (pictures) in order to satisfy that primordial urge to record one's history," Klein said.

Mark Glaser, a columnist at the USC Annenberg School of Journalism's 20 *Online Journalism Review*, said, "Over time, people will recognize when it's the right time to use your camera in an emergency."

Unfortunately, he said, "it may take someone dying" because they stopped to take a picture before that "cultural norm" is reached.

DISCUSSION QUESTIONS

1. What, if any, events can you recall that had better or more complete coverage because of the presence of citizen journalists?

2. The South Korean online newspaper to which Yulianti submitted her article, Ohmynews, draws 80 percent of its content from reporters who are

not professional journalists. What sort of assumptions would you make about the quality of the reporting you would find in it?

3. What did Larry King mean when he said that Albarghouti's situation was ironic?

4. What is your opinion about what Albarghouti did during the massacre at Virginia Tech?

5. What is your opinion about what Ho did during the evacuation of Air France Flight 358?

6. In general, do you believe that Yulianti or Memmott builds a more compelling case?

ASSIGNMENTS FOR PROVIDING SUPPORT

READING AND DISCUSSION QUESTIONS

1. Consider what types of evidence you find most convincing in an argument. Is the best type of evidence dependent on the topic and the context? Explain.

2. Look for examples in the media of the misuse of evidence. Explain why the evidence is misleading.

3. Use examples to explain which news shows depend on factual evidence and which depend largely on opinion. Do both have a useful role to play in our society? Explain.

4. Consider what Claudius E. Watts's warrant is in "Single-Sex Education Benefits Men Too." Could the same warrant be used in other contexts to justify discrimination? Explain.

5. In the aftermath of the massacre at Virginia Tech, at least one state tried to pass a law allowing registered owners to carry their weapons on school and college campuses. What needs of the people were those who proposed the law appealing to? How could the opponents have used similar types of appeal to argue their case?

6. Consider presidential debates you have seen or other televised coverage of candidates during the months leading up to an election. What are some specific examples of how the candidates try to appeal to the voters' needs and values?

7. Bernard Goldberg argues in his essay, "Connecting the Dots . . . to Terrorism," that the average American citizen is usually ignorant of much of the reality of what goes on in the Arab world. When Americans take a stand on issues such as U.S. involvement in Iraq, to what extent do you believe they are basing that stand on solid supporting evidence?

WRITING ASSIGNMENTS

8. Using Bethany Royce's "The True Confusion about SUV Costs" as a model, write an essay evaluating the use of support in one of the Readings for Analysis.

9. Write an essay explaining the types of support used in one of the Readings for Analysis or comparing the use of support in two of them.

10. Write an essay explaining which of the two authors in the debate over citizen journalists you believe presents a more convincing argument, Lily Yulianti or Mark Memmott.

11. Analyze different television commercials for the same product or similar products. Write an essay supporting a conclusion you are able to draw about the types of appeal used in the commercials.

12. Write a letter about a problem on your campus to the person who is in a position to correct the problem. Provide convincing evidence that a problem exists and, in suggesting a solution to the problem, keep in mind the needs and values of your audience as well as those of others on campus.

CHAPTER 8

Analyzing Warrants

WHAT ARE WARRANTS?

We now come to the third element in the structure of the argument—the warrant. Claim and support, the other major elements we have discussed, are more familiar in ordinary discourse, but there is nothing mysterious or unusual about the warrant. All our claims, both formal and informal, are grounded in warrants or assumptions that the audience must share with us if our claims are to prove to be acceptable.

The following exercise provides a good starting point for this chapter. Do the assigned task by yourself or in a small group.

PRACTICE

A series of environmental catastrophic events has virtually wiped out human life on Earth. The only known survivors in your vicinity are the eleven listed below. There are resources to sustain only seven. Choose seven of the following people to survive. List them in the order in which you would choose them and be prepared to explain the reasons for your selection: that is, why you chose these particular persons and why you placed them in this certain order.

- Dr. D.—thirty-seven, Ph.D. in history, college professor, in good health (jogs daily), hobby is botany, enjoys politics, married with one child (Bobby).
- Mrs. D.—thirty-eight, rather obese, diabetic, M.A. in psychology, counselor in a mental health clinic, married to Dr. D., has one child.
- Bobby D.—ten, mentally retarded with IQ of 70, healthy and strong for his age.

- Mrs. G.—twenty-three, ninth-grade education, cocktail waitress, worked as a prostitute, married at age sixteen, divorced at age eighteen, one son (Joseph).
- Joseph G.—three months old, healthy.
- Mary E.—eighteen, trade school education, wears glasses, artistic.
- Mr. N.—twenty-five, starting last year of medical school, music as a hobby, physical fitness buff.
- Mrs. C.—twenty-eight, daughter of a minister, college graduate, electronics engineer, single now after a brief marriage, member of Zero Population Growth.
- Mr. B.—fifty-one, B.S. in mechanics, married with four children, enjoys outdoors, much experience in construction, quite handy.
- Father Frans—thirty-seven, Catholic priest, active in civil rights, former college athlete, farming background, often criticized for liberal views.
- Dr. L.—sixty-six, doctor in general practice, two heart attacks in the past five years, loves literature and quotes extensively.

There may have been a great deal of disagreement over which survivors to select. If so, the reason for that disagreement was that in making their choices, different members of your group or of your class as a whole were operating under different assumptions or basing their decisions on different warrants. Some of you may have chosen not to let Mrs. G. survive because she seemed to have nothing particularly vital to offer to the survival of the group as a whole. Others of you may have felt that she should be allowed to survive along with her child, the infant in the group. Some of you, whether you acknowledge it or not, may have opposed letting Mrs. G. survive because she was once a prostitute. Think about the warrant that would underlie the claim that Mrs. G. should not be one of the seven allowed to survive. What assumption—what generalized principle—would a person who made that claim be accepting about women who were once prostitutes? What assumption would underlie the claim that she should be allowed to survive? What assumption would underlie the claim that Bobby D. should be allowed to live (or die)?

Obviously this is an exercise with no right answer. What it can teach us, however, is to consider the assumptions on which our beliefs are based. There are reasons you might have chosen certain individuals to survive that could be stated as general principles: Those who are in the best physical condition should be allowed to survive. Those with the most useful skills should be allowed to survive. Those who are mentally deficient should not be allowed to survive. Those who are most likely to reproduce should be allowed to survive.

Fortunately, this is merely an intellectual exercise. Whenever you take a stand in a real-life situation, though, you do so on the basis of certain general principles that guide your choices. Those general principles that you feel most strongly about exist as part of your intellectual and moral being because of what you have experienced in your life thus far. They have been shaped by your observations, your personal experience, and your participation in a culture. But because these observations, experiences, and cultural associations will vary, the audience may not always agree with the warrants or assumptions of the writer.

What does this have to do with argumentation? Any time you support an argumentative claim, you have to analyze the assumptions behind the argument and consider whether the members of your audience share the same assumptions. Some warrants are so widely accepted that you do not need to state them or to offer any proof of their validity. If you argue that every new dorm on campus should have a sprinkler system, you probably do not even need to state your warrant. If you did, it would be something like this: Measures that would increase the likelihood that dorm residents would survive a fire should be implemented in all dorms.

What about claims that are more controversial? Why is it so difficult for those who oppose abortion, for example, to communicate with those who favor it and vice versa? Anyone who believes that abortion is the murder of an unborn child is basing that argument on the warrant that a fetus is a child from conception. Many on the other side of the debate do not accept that warrant and thus do not accept the claim. Obviously disagreements on such emotionally charged issues are very difficult to resolve because the underlying warrants are based on firmly held beliefs that are difficult to change. It is always better to be aware of your opponent's warrants, however, than to simply dismiss them as irrelevant.

The British philosopher Stephen Toulmin, who developed the concept of warrants, dismissed more traditional forms of logical reasoning in favor of a more audience-based, courtroom-derived approach to argumentation. He refers to warrants as "general, hypothetical statements, which can act as bridges" and "entitle one to draw conclusions or make claims."[1] The word *bridges* to denote the action of the warrant is crucial. One dictionary defines warrant as a "guarantee or justification." We use the word *warrant* to emphasize that in an argument it guarantees a connecting link—a bridge—between the claim and the support. This means that even if a reader agrees that the support is sound, the support cannot prove the validity of the claim unless the reader also agrees with the underlying warrant. Recall the sample argument outlined in Chapter 1 (p. 15):

CLAIM: Backscatter screening should be implemented in America's airports.

SUPPORT: Backscatter screening will make planes safer.

WARRANT: Any screening technique that will make planes safer should be implemented.

[1] Stephen Toulmin, *The Uses of Argument* (Cambridge: Cambridge University Press, 1958), p. 98.

Notice that the reader must agree with the assumption that safety is worth undergoing any screening technique, even one that some would consider an invasion of privacy. Simply providing evidence that a certain technique will make planes safer is not enough to convince all readers that backscatter screening should be implemented in America's airports.

The following dialogue offers another example of the relationship between the warrant and the other elements of the argument.

> *"I don't think that Larry can do the job. He's pretty dumb."*
> *"Really? I thought he was smart. What makes you say he's dumb?"*
> *"Did you know that he's illiterate — can't read above third-grade level? In my book that makes him dumb."*

If we put this into outline form, the warrant or assumption in the argument becomes clear.

CLAIM: Larry is pretty dumb.

EVIDENCE: He can't read above third-grade level.

WARRANT: Anybody who can't read above third-grade level must be dumb.

We can also represent the argument in diagram form, which shows the warrant as a bridge between the claim and the support.

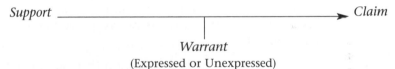

Support ————————————————————————→ *Claim*

Warrant
(Expressed or Unexpressed)

The argument above can then be written like this:

Support ————————————————————————→ *Claim*
Larry can't read above   He's pretty dumb.
third-grade level.

Warrant
Anybody who can't read above third-grade
level must be pretty dumb.

Is this warrant valid? We cannot answer this question until we consider the *backing*. Every warrant or assumption rests on something else that gives it authority; this is what we call backing. Backing or authority for the warrant in this example would consist of research data that prove a relationship between stupidity and low reading ability. This particular warrant, we would discover, lacks backing because we know that the failure to learn to read well may be due to a number of things unrelated to intelligence. So if the warrant is unprovable, the claim — that Larry is dumb — is also unprovable, even if the evidence is true. In this case, then, the evidence does not guarantee the soundness of the claim.

Now consider this example of a somewhat more complicated warrant: The beautiful and unspoiled Eastern Shore of Maryland is being discovered by thousands of tourists, vacationers, and developers who will, according to the residents, change the landscape and the way of life, which is now based largely on fishing and farming. In a few years the Eastern Shore may become a noisy, crowded string of resorts. Mrs. Walkup, the Kent County commissioner, says,

> Catering to the wealthy puts property back on the tax rolls, but it's going to make the Eastern Shore look like the rest of the country. Everything that made our way of life so special is being eroded. We are a fragile area. The Eastern Shore is still special, but it is feeling pressure from all directions. Lots of people don't seem to appreciate the fact that God made us to need a little peace and quiet now and then.[2]

In simplified form the argument of those opposed to development would be outlined this way:

CLAIM: Development will bring undesirable changes to the present way of life on the Eastern Shore, a life of farming and fishing, peace and quiet.

SUPPORT: Developers will build express highways, condominiums, casinos, and nightclubs.

WARRANT: A pastoral life of fishing and farming is superior to the way of life brought by expensive, fast-paced modern development.

Notice that the warrant is a broad generalization that can apply to a number of different situations, while the claim is about a specific place and time. It should be added that in other arguments the warrant may not be stated in such general terms. However, even in arguments in which the warrant makes a more specific reference to the claim, the reader can infer an extension of the warrant to other similar arguments. In the backscatter screening example outlined on page 274, the warrant mentions a specific screening technique. But it is clear that such warrants can be generalized to apply to other arguments in which we accept a claim based on an appeal to our very human need to feel secure.

To be convinced of the validity of Mrs. Walkup's claim, you must first find that the support is true, that the developers plan to introduce drastic changes that will destroy the pastoral life of the Eastern Shore. You may, however, believe that the support is not entirely sound, that the development will be much more modest than residents fear, and that the Eastern Shore will not be seriously altered. Next, you may want to see more justification for the warrant. Is pastoral life superior to the life that will result

[2]Michael Wright, "The Changing Chesapeake," *New York Times Magazine*, July 10, 1983, p. 27.

from large-scale development? Perhaps you have always thought that a life of fishing and farming means poverty and limited opportunities for the majority of the residents. Although the superiority of a way of life is largely a matter of taste and therefore difficult to prove, Mrs. Walkup may need to produce backing for her belief that the present way of life is more desirable than one based on developing the area for new residents and summer visitors. If you find either the support or the warrant unconvincing, you cannot accept the claim.

Remember that a claim is often modified by one or more qualifiers, which limit the claim. Mrs. Walkup might have said, "Development will *probably* destroy *some aspects of* the present way of life on the Eastern Shore." Warrants can also be modified or limited by *reservations*, which remind the reader that there are conditions under which the warrants will not be relevant. Mrs. Walkup might have added, "unless increased prosperity and exposure to the outside world brought by development improve some aspects of our lives."

A diagram of Mrs. Walkup's argument shows the additional elements:

Support ⎯⎯⎯⎯⎯⎯⎯⎯⎯⎯⎯⎯⎯▶ *Claim*

The developers will build highways, condos, casinos, nightclubs.	Development will bring undesirable changes to life on the Eastern Shore.
Warrant	*Qualifier*
A way of life devoted to farming and fishing is superior to a way of life brought by development.	Development will *most likely* bring undesirable changes.

Backing
We have experienced crowds, traffic, noise, rich strangers, and high-rises, and they destroy peace and quiet.

Reservation
But increased development might improve some aspects of our lives.

Claim and support (or lack of support) are relatively easy to uncover in most arguments. One thing that makes the warrant different is that it is often unexpressed and therefore unexamined by both writer and reader because they take it for granted. In the argument about Larry's intelligence, the warrant was stated. But in the argument about development on the Eastern Shore, Mrs. Walkup did not state her warrant directly, although her meaning is perfectly clear. She probably felt that it was not necessary to be more explicit because her readers would understand and supply the warrant.

We can make the discovery of warrants even clearer by examining another argument, in this case a policy claim. We've looked at a factual claim (that Larry is dumb) and a value claim (that Eastern Shore development is undesirable). Now we examine a policy claim that rests on one expressed and one unexpressed warrant. Policy claims are usually more complicated than other claims because the statement of policy is preceded by an array of facts and values. In addition, such claims may represent chains of reasoning in which one argument is dependent on another. These complicated arguments may be difficult or impossible to summarize in a simple diagram, but careful reading, asking the same kinds of questions that the author may have asked about his claim, can help you to find the warrant or chain of warrants that must be accepted before evidence and claim can be linked.

In a familiar argument that appeared a few years ago,[3] the author argues for a radical reform in college sports—the elimination of subprofessional intermural team sports, as practiced above all in football and basketball. The claim is clear, and evidence for the professional character of college sports not hard to find: the large salaries paid to coaches, the generous perquisites offered to players, the recruitment policies that ignore academic standing, the virtually full-time commitment of the players, the lucrative television contracts. But can this evidence support the author's claim that such sports do not belong on college campuses? Advocates of these sports may ask, Why not? In the conclusion of the article the author states one warrant or assumption underlying his claim.

> Even if the money to pay college athletes could be found, though, a larger question must be answered—namely, why should a system of professional athletics be affiliated with universities at all? For the truth is that the requirements of athletics and academics operate at cross purposes, and the attempt to play both games at once serves only to reduce the level of performance of each.

In other words, the author assumes that the goals of an academic education on the one hand and the goals of big-time college sports on the other hand are incompatible. In the article he develops the ways in which each enterprise harms the other.

But the argument clearly rests on another warrant that is not expressed because the author takes for granted that his readers will supply it: The academic goals of the university are primary and should take precedence over all other collegiate activities. This is an argument based on an authority warrant, the authority of those who define the goals of the university—scholars, public officials, university administrators, and others. (Types of warrants are discussed in the following section.)

This warrant makes clear that the evidence of the professional nature of college sports cited above supports the claim that they should be elim-

---

[3]D. G. Myers, "Why College Sports?" *Commentary*, December 1990, pp. 49–51.

inated. If quasiprofessional college sports are harmful to the primary educational function of the college or university, then they must go. In the author's words, "The two are separate enterprises, to be judged by separate criteria. . . . For college sports, the university is not an educational institution at all; it is merely a locus, a means of coordinating the different aspects of the sporting enterprise."

This argument may be summarized in outline form as follows:

CLAIM: Intermural college team sports should be abolished.

SUPPORT: College sports have become subprofessional.

WARRANT: The goals of an academic education and big-time college sports are incompatible.

BACKING FOR THE WARRANT: Academic education is the primary goal of the college and must take precedence over athletic activity.

PRACTICE

Read the following argument by Robert A. Sirico. Then summarize the argument in a paragraph. Next, explain what the claim is, what types of support are used, and what the warrant is. Is the warrant one that you agree with? Explain.

An Unjust Sacrifice

ROBERT A. SIRICO

An appeals court in London has made a Solomonic ruling, deciding that eight-week-old twins joined at the pelvis must be separated. In effect, one twin, known as Mary, is to be sacrificed to save the other, known as Jodie, in an operation the babies' parents oppose.

The judges invoked a utilitarian rationale, justified on the basis of medical testimony. The specialists agreed that there is an 80 to 90 percent chance that the strong and alert Jodie could not survive more than a few months if she continued to support the weak heart and lungs of Mary, whose brain is underdeveloped.

This is a heartbreaking case, and the decision of the court was not arrived at lightly. But even the best of intentions, on the part of the state or the parents, is no substitute for sound moral reasoning. Utilitarian considerations like Mary's quality of life are not the issue. Nor should doctors' expert testimony, which is subject to error, be considered decisive.

Here, as in the case of abortion, one simple principle applies: There is no justification for deliberately destroying innocent life. In this case, the court has turned its back on a tenet that the West has stood by: Life, no matter how limited, should be protected.

Robert A. Sirico, a Roman Catholic priest, is president of the Acton Institute for the Study of Religion and Liberty in Grand Rapids, Michigan. This article appeared in the September 28, 2000, *New York Times*.

While this case is so far unique, there are guidelines that must be fol-   5
lowed. No human being, for instance, can be coerced into donating an
organ—even if the individual donating the organ is unlikely to be harmed
and the individual receiving the organ could be saved. In principle, no
person should ever be forced to volunteer his own body to save another's
life, even if that individual is a newborn baby.

To understand the gravity of the court's error, consider the parents'
point of view. They are from Gozo, an island in Malta. After being told of
their daughters' condition, while the twins were in utero, they went to
Manchester, England, seeking out the best possible medical care. Yet, after
the birth on August 8, the parents were told that they needed to separate
the twins, which would be fatal for Mary.

They protested, telling the court: "We cannot begin to accept or contemplate that one of our children should die to enable the other one to survive. That is not God's will. Everyone has a right to life, so why should we
kill one of our daughters to enable the other one to survive?"

And yet, a court in a country in which they sought refuge has overruled
their wishes. This is a clear evil: coercion against the parents and coercion
against their child, justified in the name of a speculative medical calculus.

The parents' phrase "God's will" is easily caricatured, as if they believed
divine revelation were guiding them to ignore science. In fact, they believe
in the merit of science, or they would not have gone to Britain for help in
the first place.

But utilitarian rationality has overtaken their case. The lawyer appointed   10
by the court to represent Jodie insisted that Mary's was "a futile life." That
is a dangerous statement—sending us down a slippery slope where lives
can be measured for their supposed value and discarded if deemed not useful enough.

Some might argue that in thinking about the twins, we should apply
the philosophical principle known as "double effect," which, in some circumstances, permits the loss of a life when it is an unintended consequence
of saving another. But in this case, ending Mary's life would be a deliberate
decision, not an unintended effect.

Can we ever take one life in favor of another? No, not even in this case,
however fateful the consequences.

Arguers will often neglect to state their warrants for one of two reasons:
First, like Mrs. Walkup, they may believe that the warrant is obvious and
need not be expressed; second, they may want to conceal the warrant in the
hope that the reader will overlook its weakness.

What kinds of warrants are so obvious that they need not be expressed?
Here are a few that will probably sound familiar:

Mothers love their children.

The more expensive the product, the more satisfactory it will be.

A good harvest will result in lower prices for produce.

First come, first served.

These statements seem to embody beliefs that most of us would share and that might be unnecessary to make explicit in an argument. The last statement, for example, is taken as axiomatic, an article of faith that we seldom question in ordinary circumstances. Suppose you hear someone make the claim, "I deserve to get the last ticket to the concert." If you ask why he is entitled to a ticket that you also would like to have, he may answer in support of his claim, "Because I was here first." No doubt you accept his claim without further argument because you understand and agree with the warrant that is not expressed: "If you arrive first, you deserve to be served before those who come later." Your acceptance of the warrant probably also takes into account the unexpressed backing that is based on a belief in justice: "It is only fair that those who sacrifice time and comfort to be first in line should be rewarded for their trouble."

In this case it may not be necessary to expose the warrant and examine it. Indeed, as Stephen Toulmin tells us, "If we demanded the credentials of all warrants at sight and never let one pass unchallenged, argument could scarcely begin."[4]

But even those warrants that seem to express universal truths invite analysis if we can think of claims for which these warrants might not, after all, be relevant. "First in line," for example, may justify the claim of a person who wants a concert ticket, but it cannot in itself justify the claim of someone who wants a vital medication that is in short supply. Moreover, offering a rebuttal to a long-held but unexamined warrant can often produce an interesting and original argument. If someone exclaims, "All this buying of gifts! I think people have forgotten that Christmas celebrates the birth of Christ," she need not express the assumption—that the buying of gifts violates what ought to be a religious celebration. It goes unstated by the speaker because it has been uttered so often that she knows the hearer will supply it. But one writer, in an essay titled "God's Gift: A Commercial Christmas," argued that, contrary to popular belief, the purchase of gifts, which means the expenditure of time, money, and thought on others rather than oneself, is not a violation but an affirmation of the Christmas spirit.[5]

The second reason for refusal to state the warrant lies in the arguer's intention to disarm or deceive the reader, although the arguer may not be aware of this. For instance, failure to state the warrant is common in advertising and politics, where the desire to sell a product or an idea may outweigh the responsibility to argue explicitly. The following advertisement is famous not only for what it says but for what it does not say:

> In 1918 Leona Currie scandalized a New Jersey beach with a bathing suit cut above her knees. And to irk the establishment even more, she smoked a cigarette. Leona Currie was promptly arrested.
> Oh, how Leona would smile if she could see you today.

---

[4] *The Uses of Argument* (Cambridge: Cambridge University Press, 1958), p. 106.
[5] Robert A. Sirico, *Wall Street Journal*, December 21, 1993, sec. A, p. 12.

> You've come a long way, baby. *Virginia Slims*. The taste for today's woman.

What is the unstated warrant? The manufacturer of Virginia Slims hopes we will agree that being permitted to smoke cigarettes is a significant sign of female liberation. But many readers would insist that proving "You've come a long way, baby" requires more evidence than women's freedom to smoke (or wear short bathing suits). The shaky warrant weakens the claim.

Politicians, too, conceal warrants that may not survive close scrutiny. In the 1983 mayoral election in Chicago, one candidate revealed that his opponent had undergone psychiatric treatment. He did not have to state the warrant supporting his claim. He knew that many in his audience would assume that anyone who had undergone psychiatric treatment was unfit to hold public office. This same assumption contributed to the withdrawal of a vice-presidential candidate from the 1972 campaign.

TYPES OF WARRANTS

Arguments may be classified according to the types of warrants offered as proof. Because warrants represent the reasoning process by which we establish the relationship between support and claim, analysis of the major types of warrants enables us to see the whole argument as a sum of its parts.

Warrants may be organized into three categories: "*authoritative, substantive*, and *motivational*."[6] The *authoritative warrant* is based on the credibility or trustworthiness of the source. If we assume that the source of the data is authoritative, then we find that the support justifies the claim. A *substantive warrant* is based on beliefs about reliability of factual evidence. In the example on page 275 the speaker assumes, although mistakenly, that the relationship between low reading level and stupidity is a verifiable datum, one that can be proved by objective research. A *motivational warrant*, on the other hand, is based on the needs and values of the audience. For example, the warrant about backscatter screening reflects a concern for safety, a value that would cause a reader who held it to agree that more rigid screening techniques are a good idea.

Each type of warrant requires a different set of questions for testing its soundness. The following list of questions will help you to decide whether a particular warrant is valid and can justify a particular claim.

1. *Authoritative* (based on the credibility of the sources)

   Is the authority sufficiently respected to make a credible claim?

   Do other equally reputable authorities agree with the authority cited?

   Are there equally reputable authorities who disagree?

[6] D. Ehninger and W. Brockriede, *Decision by Debate* (New York: Dodd, Mead, 1953).

2. *Substantive* (based on beliefs about the reliability of factual evidence)

Are sufficient examples given to convince us that a general statement is justified? That is, are the examples given representative of the whole community?

If you have argued that one event or condition can bring about another (a cause-and-effect argument), does the cause given seem to account entirely for the effect? Are other possible causes equally important as explanations for the effect?

If you have used comparisons, are the similarities between the two situations greater than the differences?

If you have used analogies, does the analogy explain or merely describe? Are there sufficient similarities between the two elements to make the analogy appropriate?

3. *Motivational* (based on the values of the arguer and the audience)

Are the values ones that the audience will regard as important?

Are the values relevant to the claim?

SAMPLE ANNOTATED ESSAY

The Case for Torture

MICHAEL LEVIN

Introduction: statement of opposing view

I t is generally assumed that torture is impermissible, a throwback to a more brutal age. Enlightened societies reject it outright, and regimes suspected of using it risk the wrath of the United States.

Claim of policy: rebuttal of opposing view

I believe this attitude is unwise. There are situations in which torture is not merely permissible but morally mandatory. Moreover, these situations are moving from the realm of imagination to fact.

Support: hypothetical example to test the reader's belief

Suppose a terrorist has hidden an atomic bomb on Manhattan Island which will detonate at noon on July 4 unless . . . (here follow the usual demands for money and release of his friends from jail). Suppose, further, that he is caught at 10 A.M. of the fateful day, but—preferring death to failure—won't

Michael Levin is a professor of philosophy at the City University of New York. This essay is reprinted from the June 7, 1982, issue of *Newsweek*.

disclose where the bomb is. What do we do? If we follow due process—wait for his lawyer, arraign him—millions of people will die. If the only way to save those lives is to subject the terrorist to the most excruciating possible pain, what grounds can there be for not doing so? I suggest there are none. In any case, I ask you to face the question with an open mind.

Torturing the terrorist is unconstitutional? Probably. But millions of lives surely outweigh constitutionality. Torture is barbaric? Mass murder is far more barbaric. Indeed, letting millions of innocents die in deference to one who flaunts his guilt is moral cowardice, an unwillingness to dirty one's hands. If *you* caught the terrorist, could you sleep nights knowing that millions died because you couldn't bring yourself to apply the electrodes?

Once you concede that torture is justified in   5 extreme cases, you have admitted that the decision to use torture is a matter of balancing innocent lives against the means needed to save them. You must now face more realistic cases involving

Support: hypothetical example

more modest numbers. Someone plants a bomb on a jumbo jet. He alone can disarm it, and his demands cannot be met (or if they can, we refuse to set a precedent by yielding to his threats). Surely we can, we must, do anything to the extortionist to save the passengers. How can we tell 300, or 100, or 10 people who never asked to be put in danger, "I'm sorry, you'll have to die in agony, we just couldn't bring ourselves to . . ."

Support: informal poll

Here are the results of an informal poll about a third, hypothetical, case. Suppose a terrorist group kidnapped a newborn baby from a hospital. I asked four mothers if they would approve of torturing kidnappers if that were necessary to get their own newborns back. All said yes, the most "liberal" adding that she would administer it herself.

Defense of the claim a) Not punishment but protection of the innocent

I am not advocating torture as punishment. Punishment is addressed to deeds irrevocably past. Rather, I am advocating torture as an acceptable measure for preventing future evils. So understood, it is far less objectionable than many extant punishments. Opponents of the death penalty, for example, are forever insisting that executing a murderer will not bring back his victim (as if the purpose of capital punishment were supposed to be resurrection, not deterrence or retribution). But torture, in the cases described, is intended not to bring anyone back but to keep innocents from being dispatched. The most powerful argument against using torture as a punishment or to secure confessions is that such practices disregard the rights of the individual. Well, if the individual is all that important—and he is—it is correspondingly important to protect the rights of individuals threatened by terrorists. If life is so valuable that it must never be taken, the lives of the innocents must be saved even at the price of hurting the one who endangers them.

Hypothetical examples:
b) Analogies with World War II

Better precedents for torture are assassination and preemptive attack. No Allied leader would have flinched at assassinating Hitler, had that been possible. (The Allies did assassinate Heydrich.) Americans would be angered to learn that Roosevelt could have had Hitler killed in 1943—thereby shortening the war and saving millions of lives—but refused on moral grounds. Similarly, if nation A learns that nation B is about to launch an unprovoked attack, A has a right to save itself by destroying B's military capability first. In the same way, if the police can by torture save those who would otherwise die at the hands of kidnappers or terrorists, they must.

c) Denial that terrorists have rights

There is an important difference between terrorists and their victims that should mute talk of the terrorists' "rights." The terrorist's victims are at risk unintentionally, not having asked to be endangered. But the terrorist knowingly initiated his actions. Unlike his victims, he volunteered for the risks of his deed. By threatening to kill for profit or idealism, he renounces civilized standards, and he can have no complaint if civilization tries to thwart him by whatever means necessary.

Just as torture is justified only to save lives (not 10 extort confessions or recantations), it is justifiably administered only to those *known* to hold innocent lives in their hands. Ah, but how can the authorities ever be sure they have the right malefactor? Isn't there a danger of error and abuse? Won't We turn into Them?

d) Easy identification of terrorists

Questions like these are disingenuous in a world in which terrorists proclaim themselves and perform for television. The name of their game is public recognition. After all, you can't very well intimidate a government into releasing your freedom fighters unless you announce that it is your group that has seized its embassy. "Clear guilt" is difficult to define, but when 40 million people see a group of masked gunmen seize an airplane on the evening news, there is not much question about who the perpetrators are. There will be hard cases where the situation is murkier. Nonetheless, a line demarcating the legitimate use of torture can be drawn. Torture only the obviously guilty, and only for the sake of saving innocents, and the line between Us and Them will remain clear.

Conclusion warrant: "Paralysis in the face of evil is the greater danger."

There is little danger that the Western democracies will lose their way if they choose to inflict pain as one way of preserving order. Paralysis in the face of evil is the greater danger. Some day soon a terrorist will threaten tens of thousands of lives, and torture will be the only way to save them. We had better start thinking about this.

■ Analysis

Levin's controversial essay attacks a popular assumption that most people have never thought to question—that torture is impermissible under any circumstances. Levin argues that in extreme cases torture is morally justified to bring about a greater good than the rights of the individual who is tortured.

Against the initial resistance that most readers may feel, Levin makes a strong case. Its strength lies in the backing he provides for the warrant that torture is sometimes necessary. This backing consists in the use of two effective argumentative strategies. One is the anticipation of objections. Unprecedented? No. Unconstitutional? No. Barbaric? No. Second, and more important, are the hypothetical examples that compel readers to rethink their positions and possibly arrive at agreement with the author. Levin chooses extreme examples—kidnapping of a newborn child, planting a bomb on a jumbo jet, detonating an atomic bomb in Manhattan—that draw a line between clear and murky cases and make agreement easier. And he bolsters his moral position by insisting that torture is not to be used as punishment or revenge but only to save innocent lives.

To support such an unpopular assumption the writer must convey the impression that he is a reasonable man, and this Levin attempts to do by a searching definition of terms, the careful organization and development of his argument, including references to the opinions of other people, and the expression of compassion for innocent lives.

Another strength of the article is its readability—the use of contractions, informal questions, conversational locutions. This easy, familiar style is disarming; the reader doesn't feel threatened by heavy admonitions from a writer who affects a superior, moral attitude.

Writer's Guide: Recognizing Warrants

1. Locate in your essay the one sentence that best states your claim, or if there is no single sentence that does so, try to express your claim in a single sentence.

2. If you have not already done so, think about for what audience you are writing. How is that audience likely to respond to your claim? The most important question to ask about your audience regarding warrants is this one: What assumption or assumptions must my audience make to be able to accept my claim? The answer to that question will be the warrant or warrants on which your essay is based.

3. The support you offer will make it easier for your audience to accept your claim. Remember that the warrant is the link between claim and support. It may help to use the formula used in this chapter to think systematically through your argument. Ask yourself what the claim is, what support you are offering, and what warrant connects the two. Do that for each major supporting statement that you make.

4. You may not need to state your warrant directly if it is a universally accepted truth that most reasonable readers would agree with it. You should be able to do so, however, in order to check your own logic.

5. If you are asking the members of your audience to accept a warrant that they are not likely to accept, you must offer backing for that warrant or consider restating your claim in a way that does not ask them to agree to an assumption that they will not be willing to agree with.

We're All Celebrities in Post-Privacy Age

ERIC AUCHARD

Move over, Paris Hilton. We all have celebrity issues in an age when any-one can create an online profile, post confessional videos on YouTube, or make snarky online comments about other people.

The latest generation of Web sites—which attract tens of millions of users daily to share words, photos, and videos about themselves and their friends—make a virtue of openness at the expense of traditional notions of privacy.

"My grandparents would have had a different attitude about privacy," says Jeff Jarvis, a former critic for *TV Guide* turned top blogger and colum-nist for the *Guardian* in London.

"There is a different calculus now," he says.

Sites like Facebook, Photobucket, and Flickr are enjoying surging pop- 5 ularity for allowing people to control their online identities in ways that make the danger of revealing too much information a constant worry— and all part of the game.

"Within the Web realm there is no private self," argues David Wein-berger, author of a newly published book, "Everything Is Miscellaneous: The Power of the New Digital Disorder."

"The closest you can mean is that you are with a small group behind some password-protected mechanism," he says.

The danger of such exposure is that it could affect careers when stu-dents seek jobs in the real world or private citizens seek public office.

George W. Bush and Bill Clinton might never have been elected pres-ident had sites like Google Inc.'s YouTube or News Corp.'s MySpace, the world's biggest online meeting places, existed to record the events of their younger years.

But while policy makers ponder how to bolster online anonymity, so- 10 cial network users are more concerned about deciding what to reveal about themselves next.

Control, Community Trump Privacy

Most users of the new self-publishing tools report finding a stronger sense of community among friends, family, and random Web site visitors who share their interests.

Eric Auchard has worked for Reuters news service since 1992. In 1993 he switched to technology writing and now coordinates the technology news covered by 200 reporters and editors worldwide, working himself as both a reporter and an editor for Reuters. This article appeared online on June 21, 2007.

Facebook, a site started by a Harvard University undergraduate as a way for students to get to know one another, has exploded in popularity among professional users in Britain and the United States since the site took steps to open up to people of all ages over the past year. It now claims 25 million active users, who like the control Facebook gives them over who they let into their network of online acquaintances.

"What Facebook does is it allows me to control my identity and my society—my group of friends," Jarvis says. "You can call it privacy or you can call it publicness. I am controlling both sides of that equation, together—that's the secret."

Highlighting his own change of thinking on the subject of privacy, Jarvis revealed last year in a blog post, entitled "My cheatin' heart," that he was suffering from a medical condition that slowed work on his widely read media criticism blog, BuzzMachine (http://www.buzzmachine.com/). Supportive comments, and advice about potential treatments, poured in.

"Revealing a little bit of yourself is the only way to make connections 15 to other people and that is how the Internet works," Jarvis says. "I couldn't have gotten that benefit unless I revealed the condition."

Caterina Fake, co-founder of popular photo sharing site Flickr, said recently that the defining moment for her start-up was when it decided all photos on the site would be public. Previously, photo sites had assumed users' photos should be private, unless deliberately published for public consumption.

Mena Trott, who, with her husband, Ben, developed Movable Type, a software system for publishing blogs, says "control" is a better word than "privacy" for defining oneself in different situations on the Web.

"We think blogging is sharing the stuff you care about with the people you care about," Trott says. "It comes down to control. They may or may not use it. But people want control."

Trott's company, Six Apart, makes publishing tools used by everyone from Hollywood gossip reporters to moms who seek to document their everyday lives, in private or semi-public mode.

"The Internet is often accused of leading to uncivil behavior," Jarvis 20 says. "Identity will lead to civility because we are being watched. It's like living in a small town again."

READING AND DISCUSSION QUESTIONS

1. What experience, if any, have you had with the sort of sites to which Auchard refers: for example, Facebook, Photobucket, and Flickr?

2. What are the pros and cons of posting to such social networking sites?

3. The heading halfway through the article reads, "Control, Community Trump Privacy." Explain what Auchard means by that.

4. What is Auchard's claim?

5. What types of support does he use?

6. What is his warrant?

7. Explain whether or not you accept his warrant.

WRITING SUGGESTIONS

8. Attack or defend this statement made by Auchard: "The danger of such exposure [on the Web] is that it could affect careers when students seek jobs in the real world or private citizens seek public office."

9. Write an essay in which you explain whether or not you believe that it is possible to achieve, on the Web, a balance between publicness and privacy.

10. What are the dangers of exposing personal information on the Internet?

11. Explain why you believe that sites like Facebook and MySpace are so popular.

DISCUSSION QUESTIONS

1. What is the significance of the name of the product?

2. What assumptions underlie the remaining text in the ad?

3. How do the visual elements reinforce the text?

4. Can you think of other ads that make use of celebrities? What are some of the warrants that underlie the use of celebrities to sell products?

Do We Need the Census Race Question?

NATHAN GLAZER

A FEW years ago, when I was asked to comment on the controversy over how best to handle the demand of so-called multiracial advocacy groups for a "multiracial" category in the census, I made a brash and wildly unrealistic proposal.[1] Before describing my proposal, however, I should explain what concerned me about the existing questions on race, Hispanicity, and ancestry in the census. These questions had evolved by the 1980 and 1990 censuses in a way that was to my mind false to American racial and ethnic reality and incapable of getting coherent responses, to the degree that that is possible and that is normally expected in a census.

The census short form is the piece of official government paper that is probably seen by more Americans than any other, surpassing in the extent of its distribution the income tax forms. It is a message to the American people, and like any message it educates them to some reality: This is what the government needs, this what it wants, this is what it thinks is important. The census tells the American people that the government thinks the most important thing about them is to get them classified by race and ethnicity—ethnicity, that is, only if it qualifies as something called "Hispanic"; otherwise, the government is not interested. The census asks Americans first for the kinds of information that almost any form does, whether for a credit card or a driver's license—name, sex, age, family status—but then it turns out the main thing the government is interested in is their "race," described in the greatest detail, down to distinctions between Samoan and Guamanian and, if the respondent is Hispanic, between Argentinean, Colombian, Dominican, Nicaraguan, and even Spanish.

The government, in this message sent to all of us, apparently considers these matters more important than how educated we are, or whether we are citizens, or whether we are foreign born, or whether we voted in the last election. Scholars and researchers who follow the matter closely know why these questions are there, so prominently, so fully detailed. Do the American people in general know? If they do not—and it is hardly likely they are fully briefed on the legislation and regulations and politics and the pressures that have made the census form, with respect to race and Hispanicity, what it is today—what are they to conclude?

Nathan Glazer is a professor emeritus at the Graduate School of Education at Harvard University and past professor of sociology at the University of California at Berkeley. He is a former assistant editor for *Commentary* magazine and is a contributing editor of the *New Republic*. His books include *Beyond the Melting Pot* (with Daniel Patrick Moynihan; 1970), *We Are All Multiculturalists Now* (1997), and *The Lonely Crowd* (with David Riesman; rev. ed. 2001). He has served on presidential task forces on education and urban policy and on National Academy of Science committees on urban policy and minority issues.

The census is supposed to give us a portrait of America. Is this what America looks like? Is the matter of race so important that it deserves this prominence and degree of detail?

A further problem is evident: that these questions are trying to impose   5
on identities in flux—not all, of course, but many—a categorization scheme that will inevitably confuse many people. It is a scheme in which many cannot place themselves, and one that requires all sorts of manipulations by the census professionals to put the results into a form in which it can be presented to Congress, the press, and the American people. There is bound to be a substantial degree of error in these final figures, which are never rounded to indicate their uncertainty nor presented with any indication of their degree of error—in contrast with public opinion polls. Yet asking about race and ethnicity has many similarities to public opinion polls about attitudes, compared with questions about age, or amount of schooling, or a number of other topics on which respondents are pretty clear.

Finally, there is simply the irrationality of the categories. Why does Hispanicity include people from Argentina and Spain but not those from Brazil or Portugal? Are there really all those races in Asia, where each country seems to consist of a single and different race, compared with simply "white" for all of Europe and the Middle East? Why, indeed, do people of Spanish origin rate special treatment, as against people from Italy, Poland, or Greece?

All this is familiar. And so I made my proposal. I confess that underlying my proposal was an ideological or political position—just as ideological and political positions underlie the present census arrangements. My position was that it is necessary and desirable to recognize and encourage the ongoing assimilation of the many strands that make the American people into a common culture. It is, I realize, a delicate task to draw a line between "recognize"—which is what the census should do—and "encourage," which it should not see as part of its task. Any form of recognition or nonrecognition is also, however, a form of encouragement or dissuasion. One encourages what one recognizes and dissuades what one does not. My proposal also responded to my interest as a social scientist in recording the progress of this change, which has been continuous in American history, affecting all groups in different degree but tragically leaving aside, for most of our history, one major group.

So then, my brash and unrealistic proposal: I proposed reducing the mishmash of race, Hispanicity, and ancestry to basically two questions. One question would determine whether a person considered himself or herself black or African American. That would remain the only race for which the census requested information. A second question or group of questions would ask in which country the respondent was born and in which country his or her parents were born and could be extended to ask where that person's grandparents were born. These questions on the country of birth of parents and grandparents would be filled in by respondents rather than presented in a multiple-choice format with predetermined options.

Why the interest in only one race? The census has counted blacks, slave and free, since the first enumeration of 1790. History alone and the virtues of continuity would make a claim that that determination be continued. There are, of course, far more potent reasons. This is the group that has suffered from prejudice, discrimination, and a lower-caste status since the origins of the Republic. In law, all this is now overcome and does not exist, but African Americans, we know, despite their presence in large numbers from our origins as a group of British colonies on the Atlantic shore, are less integrated in American society than any other large group. They are more segregated residentially. The rate of intermarriage with others outside the group, even if rapidly increasing, is still the lowest for any large group. They have a clear sense of their identity. One can depend on a high degree of reliability in the answers they give to the race question, as census research has shown.

The second question or group of questions replaces the "ancestry" question because of the rapid rate of assimilation of all groups except blacks or African Americans. The limitation of these questions to the parental generation, and possibly the grandparental, is first a response to the reality that by the third generation and certainly by the fourth, the mix of ethnicities is extensive; second, it serves as an indication that the census and the government are not interested in group characteristics in the third generation and beyond.[2] With intermarriage rates in new nonblack immigrant groups of 30 percent or thereabouts, we assume that by the third generation assimilation has progressed to the point at which identity is mixed and fluctuating and its ethnic character has become largely symbolic. We leave the question of what that identity consists of to the excellent sociologists, such as Richard Alba and Mary Waters, who have studied the nature of ethnic identification in these later generations. The census thereby gets out of the business of trying to affix an ancestry to each American.

If one thinks that each of the peoples of Asia forms a distinct race, this question will be able to encompass all the immigrants from that country and their children. There are not many yet in the third generation. By the time there is a substantial third generation of the post-1960s wave of immigrants, many will be of mixed ancestry, and the question of their identity will be left to them. Intermarriage statistics suggest the same for Hispanics, the great majority of whom are now immigrants and the children of immigrants. The only distinct group for which the census will try to get statistics on all those identified with it is the black or African American, for historical reasons we all know but also because black or African American identity does not fade after a few generations in this country but maintains itself in a varying but full form generation after generation.

I realize that problems remain regarding American Indians, Alaska Natives, Hawaiians, and part-Hawaiians. All these groups have a legal status, and there are means for determining who does and does not belong to each of these groups. I can see the virtue of specific questions beyond those I have suggested for Hawaii and Alaska, but I do not think 280 million

Americans have to be troubled to determine the numbers of these very small groups.

Questions on birthplace and parental birthplace as posed today, as against the same questions during the last great wave of immigration, have one virtue: during that earlier wave, immigrants came from Europe, where many ethnic groups could be found within the boundaries of great multi-ethnic empires, and thus birthplace said little about ethnicity. In addition, the boundaries of eastern Europe have been radically recast three times in a century, and European immigrants and their children could be properly confused as to the country of their birth. What was the birthplace of a person born in Bukowina? If the census asks, "what country were you born in?" there are at least four reasonable candidates. Most of today's immigrants, in contrast, come from countries whose boundaries have been stable for a century or more, and their birthplaces and those of their parents permit us to make reasonable judgments as to their ethnic group.

This, I argued, was all that was needed in place of the present questions on race, Hispanicity, and ancestry. These two questions would provide less detailed data but more accurate data. They would also be more responsive to what America was like, and what it was becoming.

I knew the proposal was politically naive, but I was not aware of how 15 powerful and steady were the forces that created the present unsatisfactory situation until I went further into the history of the creation of the present categories (Skerry 2000; Nobles 2000; Anderson and Fienberg 1999; Bryant and Dunn 1995; Mitroff, Mason, and Barabba 1983). This research underlines the somewhat utopian character of my proposals today.

The experts seem to agree that when it comes to the census, the political outweighs the scientific, and this is a reality we have to live with. The word "political" can, of course, refer to many things, from the more to the less noble. What we have today in the census is political in all these senses. Some of it is, in part, the result of major civil rights legislation, which, to my mind, falls on the noble side. That legislation had to be interpreted by the courts and by the administrative agencies, however, under the pressure of ethnic groups. As we follow this process further into the details that shaped the form of the census questions, the element of nobility in the political process declines. I am not sure the legislation itself, which was concerned with the right to vote, required what the census has done in its effort to respond to the demand for small-area data on Hispanics and Asian Americans. One could make a case that questions on birthplace and parental birthplace alone and the language question could give us the data to satisfy the legislation. But it would not give us the data in a form that satisfies proponents of distinct group interests and activists.

There are also the less noble political interventions. The census questions, whatever we think of their incongruity and irrationality, are the direct result of powerful pressures from the ethnic groups concerned, from

Congress, and from the Executive Office of the President. These are political, alas, not only in the sense that political actors are involved but also in the narrower and less respectable sense that they are often motivated by narrow partisan political considerations.

Thus, Peter Skerry informs us, the unfortunate "ancestry" question was "criticized by social scientists for being vague and uninformative" in comparison with the question on birthplace of respondent's parents that it replaced. The Census Bureau also opposed it. "So why did the ancestry question end up on the questionnaire?" Skerry asks. "According to former deputy census director Louis Kincannon, who was working at the Statistical Policy Division of OMB when the decision was made, 'the ethnic desk' in the [Carter] White House insisted that the ancestry question go on the census. . . . It is evident that in the period leading up to the 1980 Presidential campaign, politics overrode the objections of both the OMB and the Census Bureau" (Skerry 2000, 37).

Democrats are understandably more responsive than Republicans to ethnic-group pressures, but Skerry tells us that Republican administrations have been no help, either. Concerning the origins of the Hispanic question, he notes that:

> the finalized questionnaires for the 1970 census were already at the printers when a Mexican American member of the U.S. Interagency Committee on Mexican American Affairs demanded that a specific Hispanic-origin question be included. . . . Over the opposition of Census Bureau officials, who argued against inclusion of an untested question so late in the process, Nixon ordered the secretary of commerce and the census director to add the question. . . . So it was hastily added to the long form. As former bureau official Conrad Taeuber recalls, "The order came down that we were to ask a direct question, have the people identify themselves as Hispanic." (Skerry 2000, 37–38)

The pressures initially come from the ethnic groups involved or their [20] leaders. Although there is only an uncertain relation between the numbers and the benefits that members of a group might get from one affirmative action program or another, undoubtedly the notion that one will in some way benefit from being counted as a distinct group plays a role in these pressures. At one time, Asian Indians were divided as to whether they should be "Caucasian" or yet another Asian race. Melissa Nobles reports on the discussion in the 1970s of the Federal Interagency Committee on Education on devising racial and ethnic categories for various federal programs. "The committee debated whether persons from India should be categorized under the 'Asian and Pacific Islander' category or under the 'White/ Caucasian' category. . . . In the trial directive, they were classified as Caucasian, but they were reclassified as Asian in the final version (most likely in response to Asian Indian lobbying to ensure racial minority status)" (Nobles 2000, 79).

At the time, many in the Asian Indian community, taking into account their relatively high educational and economic position in the United States, rejected the idea that they should be eligible for benefits. Alas, the possibility of getting preferences for Indians under affirmative action programs for government contracts outweighed other considerations, and Indians— or at least some leadership groups—decided it was best to join the Chinese, Japanese, Koreans, and the rest as an "Asian race." I recall a report in an Indian newspaper that President Ronald Reagan's Small Business Administration (SBA) director had announced to an Indian conference that the SBA had decided to include South Asians among the groups that were considered qualified for preference in bidding for government contracts—this despite the fact that President Reagan was publicly an opponent of affirmative action programs. No doubt the administration hoped to garner a few Indian contributions or votes.

Congressional intervention can go into a level of detail that boggles the mind. Congress intervened in the wording of the 1990 race question when the Census Bureau shortened it to include only seven categories. Representative Robert Matsui introduced legislation "in which the formatting of the . . . race question was spelled out, even to the point of stipulating that 'Taiwanese' be one of the subgroups." Both houses passed it. "It was only President Reagan's pocket veto that blocked this extraordinary degree of congressional involvement in what is ordinarily considered the technical side of questionnaire design" (Skerry 2000, 41).

Social scientists deal with levels of irrationality—irrationality, that is, from the point of view of social science—that cannot be much affected by reasoned argument. Stanley Lieberson describes what happened when he attended a conference preparatory to the 1990 census. "I naively suggested that there was no reason to have a Hispanic question separate from the ethnic ancestry question since the former—as far as I could tell—could be classified as a subpart of the latter. Several participants from prominent Hispanic organizations were furious with such a proposal. They were furious, by the way, not at me (just a naive academic), rather it was in the form of a warning to census personnel of the consequences that would follow were this proposal to be taken seriously" (Lieberson 1993, 30).

So, what else is new? Undoubtedly the degree of political intervention, however we understand the term "political," is now at a peak, and to propose changes in the race, Hispanicity, and ancestry questions is probably an exercise in futility. (I wonder whether Reynolds Farley's excellent suggestion that the three questions be combined into one—"What is this person's primary identity?"—followed by the five "official" group designations, with write-ins permitted under each, has ever gotten any public discussion.)

In the longer view, we know that politics has always played a signifi- 25 cant role in the census. Melissa Nobles tells us the fascinating history of the use of "mulatto" in the census—a term that was included in censuses from 1850 until 1920 (Nobles 2000). It was originally introduced to support slaveholders' arguments that freedom and intermixture was bad for blacks. The abolition of slavery did not end the use of the category—it could still be used, its proponents believed, to argue that races were best off separated and that intermixture produced an inferior human being. In 1888, a member of Congress from Alabama, having decided that it was necessary to go into more detail on this thesis, introduced legislation— which passed both houses and became law—directing the census to "take such steps as may be necessary to ascertain . . . the birth rate and death rate among pure whites, and among negroes, Chinamen, Indians, and half-breeds or hybrids of any description . . . as well as of mulattoes, quadroons, and octoroons" (quoted in Nobles 2000, 56). Indeed, so directed, the census did have categories for quadroons and octoroons in the 1890 census—however useless may have been the results.

The mulattoes, quadroons, and octoroons are gone. What are the long-term prospects for that astonishing list of races in the census and that equally astonishing list of "Hispanics"? Will the lists get longer in the future, or shorter, and what factors might affect their future?

This is an interesting exercise in forecasting and prediction. It is possible that the pressures that derive from affirmative action and the hope for benefits from it, for example, will decline as affirmative action itself is restricted. It has already been banned, by public referendum, judicial action, or administrative action, in the public colleges and universities of four states. One effect of this ban has been an increase in the number of students giving no racial or ethnic identity to university authorities. There has been a substantial increase in the number of such students at the University of California at Berkeley. Why identify oneself if there is no longer a benefit in doing so? Is there an incipient revolt one can detect against the degree of racial and ethnic categorization that has been institutionalized, a revolt that will reduce further the reliability of these questions?

Much of the institutionalization of these categories in the census can be traced to the Voting Rights Act, and the ill-advised extension of this act in 1975 to "language minorities," persons of Spanish heritage, American Indians, and Asian Americans. I do not know what evidence there was, even in 1975, that these groups were prevented from voting because of lack of knowledge of English. This act requires hundreds of jurisdictions to produce voting materials in various languages—itself an irritation in various parts of the country. I wonder whether there is any evidence this has increased voting among members of these groups. (I would guess there is not.) These provisions require the census to tabulate and distribute census small-area data on the groups protected in the Voting Rights Act very rapidly after a census has been taken.

There is an inherent contradiction between the assumptions of this act and the requirement that one know English to be naturalized as a citizen. When a large number of Jewish immigrants spoke Yiddish and read only Yiddish-language newspapers, they had no trouble voting in substantial numbers equivalent to their English-speaking neighbors—even electing Socialist legislators. Are matters very different for current immigrants speaking foreign languages? Will these provisions survive, even to the census of 2010? Note that whenever a measure to declare English the "official language" gets on the ballot, as it has in a number of states, it passes. This suggests a popular hostility to these Voting Rights Act provisions. How long would they survive if submitted to a popular vote? The original point of the act was to overcome barriers to voting by blacks in the South, which were indeed great, were enforced by white officials, and had little to do with knowledge of English. The bilingual voting assistance provisions come up for renewal in 2007. Is it possible that some bold member of Congress will suggest that they are no longer needed?

All this suggests that the present distribution of political forces is not 30 eternal, and the time may come when the questions now used for race and Hispanicity will seem as outlandish as the 1890 attempt to count quadroons and octoroons. The powerful assimilatory forces in American life are at work—working more slowly, it is true, for blacks than for other groups but still working to an end that will change how the census asks about race, Hispanicity, and ancestry. I hope that change comes about not because of some xenophobic revolt against this excessive census involvement in racial and ethnic categorization but because the members of the groups so marked out themselves no longer see any reason for the U.S. government to inquire officially into an ever murkier and indeterminate racial and ethnic identity.

Notes

1. My proposal is most easily found in Hartman 1997. It originally appeared in *Poverty and Race*, the newsletter of the Poverty and Race Research Action Council.

2. On the mix of ethnicities, see the impressive demonstration in Perlmann 2000. It is also evident in the analysis of responses to the ancestry question presented in Lieberson and Waters 1998.

References

Anderson, Margo J., & Fienberg, Stephen E. (1999). *Who Counts? The Politics of Census-Taking in Contemporary America*. New York: Russell Sage Foundation.

Bryant, Barbara Everitt, & Dunn, William. (1995). *Moving Power and Money: The Politics of Census Taking*. Ithaca: New Strategist Publications.

Hartman, Chester. (Ed.) (1997). *Double Exposure: Poverty and Race in America*. Armonk: M. E. Sharpe.

Lieberson, Stanley. (1993). "The Enumeration of Ethnic and Racial Groups in the Census: Some Devilish Principles." In *Challenges of Measuring an Ethnic World*. Proceedings of the Joint Canada-United States Conference on the Measurement of Ethnicity. Washington: U.S. Department of Commerce, U.S. Bureau of the Census.

Lieberson, Stanley, & Waters, Mary. (1988). *From Many Strands*. New York: Russell Sage Foundation.

Mitroff, Ian I., Mason, Richard O., & Barabba, Vincent P. (1983). *The 1980 Census: Policy-making Amid Turbulence*. Lexington: Lexington Books.

Nobles, Melissa. (2000). *Shades of Citizenship*. Stanford: Stanford University Press.

Perlmann, Joel. (2000). "Demographic Outcomes of Ethnic Intermarriage in American History: Italian-Americans Through Four Generations." Working Paper 312. Annandale-on-Hudson: Jerome Levy Economics Institute.

Skerry, Peter. (2000). *Counting on the Census: Race, Group Identity, and the Evasion of Politics*. Washington: Brookings Institution.

READING AND DISCUSSION QUESTIONS

1. Glazer is discussing a change in the census form that he suggested "a few years ago." (The article was published in 2002.) What was his proposal?

2. Why does he believe his proposal offers an improvement over the current census form's questions about race and ethnicity?

3. What warrant or warrants underlie his argument?

4. Does his proposal seem to be reasonable? Does it seem to be an improvement on the current form?

5. This article by Glazer appeared on the Web before it was published in print form in a collection of essays. In the online article, Glazer had no documentation. He did have a note, however, that explained that a version with documentation was forthcoming in print. Is there less need for documentation when a piece of writing appears in electronic form? Why add documentation only when the piece moves into print?

WRITING SUGGESTIONS

6. Write an essay in which you either agree or disagree with Glazer's proposed change.

7. Glazer argues that ethnic and racial lines become blurred quickly after a short time in America. Do you believe that is a positive or a negative result of immigration to America?

8. Why do so many forms that we fill out ask for our race or national origin? Are there some situations in which race and national origin are relevant and others in which they are not? Explain. (Can you think of situations in which it is unlawful to ask such a question?)

Civil Disobedience

HENRY DAVID THOREAU

I heartily accept the motto,—"That government is best which governs least"; and I should like to see it acted up to more rapidly and systematically. Carried out, it finally amounts to this, which also I believe,—"That government is best which governs not at all"; and when men are prepared for it, that will be the kind of government which they will have. Government is at best but an expedient; but most governments are usually, and all governments are sometimes, inexpedient. The objections which have been brought against a standing army, and they are many and weighty, and deserve to prevail, may also at last be brought against a standing government. The standing army is only an arm of the standing government. The government itself, which is only the mode which the people have chosen to execute their will, is equally liable to be abused and perverted before the people can act through it. Witness the present Mexican war, the work of comparatively a few individuals using the standing government as their tool; for, in the outset, the people would not have consented to this measure.

This American government,—what is it but a tradition, though a recent one, endeavoring to transmit itself unimpaired to posterity, but each instant losing some of its integrity? It has not the vitality and force of a single living man; for a single man can bend it to his will. It is a sort of wooden gun to the people themselves. But it is not the less necessary for this; for the people must have some complicated machinery or other, and hear its din, to satisfy that idea of government which they have. Governments show thus how successfully men can be imposed on, even impose on themselves, for their own advantage. It is excellent, we must all allow. Yet this government never of itself furthered any enterprise, but by the alacrity with which it got out of its way. *It* does not keep the country free. *It* does not settle the West. *It* does not educate. The character inherent in the American people has done all that has been accomplished; and it would have done somewhat more, if the government had not sometimes got in its way. For government is an expedient by which men would fain succeed in letting one another alone; and, as has been said, when it is most expedient, the governed are most let alone by it. Trade and commerce, if they were not made of India-rubber, would never manage to bounce over the

Henry David Thoreau (1817–1862), philosopher and writer, is best known for *Walden*, an account of his solitary retreat to Walden Pond, near Concord, Massachusetts. Here he remained for more than two years in an effort to "live deliberately, to front only the essential facts of life." "Civil Disobedience" was first given as a lecture in 1848 and published in 1849. It was widely read and influenced both Mahatma Gandhi in the passive-resistance campaign he led against the British in India and Martin Luther King Jr. in the U.S. civil rights movement.

obstacles which legislators are continually putting in their way; and, if one were to judge these men wholly by the effects of their actions, and not partly by their intentions, they would deserve to be classed and punished with those mischievous persons who put obstructions on the railroads.

But, to speak practically and as a citizen, unlike those who call themselves no-government men, I ask for, not at once no government, but *at once* a better government. Let every man make known what kind of government would command his respect, and that will be one step toward obtaining it.

After all, the practical reason why, when the power is once in the hands of the people, a majority are permitted, and for a long period continue, to rule, is not because they are most likely to be in the right, nor because this seems fairest to the minority, but because they are physically the strongest. But a government in which the majority rule in all cases cannot be based on justice, even as far as men understand it. Can there not be a government in which majorities do not virtually decide right and wrong, but conscience?—in which majorities decide only those questions to which the rule of expediency is applicable? Must the citizen ever for a moment, or in the least degree, resign his conscience to the legislator? Why has every man a conscience, then? I think that we should be men first, and subjects afterward. It is not desirable to cultivate a respect for the law, so much as for the right. The only obligation which I have a right to assume, is to do at any time what I think right. It is truly enough said, that a corporation has no conscience; but a corporation of conscientious men is a corporation *with* a conscience. Law never made men a whit more just; and, by means of their respect for it, even the well-disposed are daily made the agents of injustice. A common and natural result of an undue respect for law is, that you may see a file of soldiers, colonel, captain, corporal, privates, powder-monkeys, and all, marching in admirable order over hill and dale to the wars, against their wills, aye, against their common sense and consciences, which makes it very steep marching indeed, and produces a palpitation of the heart. They have no doubt that it is a damnable business in which they are concerned; they are all peaceably inclined. Now, what are they? Men at all? or small moveable forts and magazines, at the service of some unscrupulous man in power? Visit the Navy-Yard, and behold a marine, such a man as an American government can make, or such as it can make a man with its black arts,—a mere shadow and reminiscence of humanity, a man laid out alive and standing, and already, as one may say, buried under arms with funeral accompaniments, though it may be, —

Not a drum was heard, nor a funeral note,
As his corse to the rampart we hurried;
Not a soldier discharged his farewell shot
O'er the grave where our hero we buried.

The mass of men serve the state thus, not as men mainly, but as ma- 5
chines, with their bodies. They are the standing army, and the militia,
jailers, constables, posse comitatus, &c. In most cases there is no free exercise whatever of the judgment or of the moral sense; but they put themselves on a level with wood and earth and stones; and wooden men can
perhaps be manufactured that will serve the purpose as well. Such command no more respect than men of straw, or a lump of dirt. They have
the same sort of worth only as horses and dogs. Yet such as these even are
commonly esteemed good citizens. Others,—as most legislators, politicians, lawyers, ministers, and office-holders,—serve the State chiefly with
their heads; and, as they rarely make any moral distinctions, they are as
likely to serve the Devil, without *intending* it, as God. A very few, as heroes, patriots, martyrs, reformers in the great sense, and *men*, serve the
state with their consciences also, and so necessarily resist it for the most
part, and they are commonly treated as enemies by it. A wise man will
only be useful as a man, and will not submit to be "clay," and "stop a hole
to keep the wind away," but leave that office to his dust at least:—

> I am too high-born to be propertied,
> To be a secondary at control,
> Or useful serving-man and instrument
> To any sovereign state throughout the world.

He who gives himself entirely to his fellow-men appears to them useless and selfish; but he who gives himself partially to them is pronounced
a benefactor and philanthropist.

How does it become a man to behave toward this American government today? I answer that he cannot without disgrace be associated with
it. I cannot for an instant recognize that political organization as *my* government which is the *slave's* government also.

All men recognize the right of revolution; that is, the right to refuse
allegiance to, and to resist, the government, when its tyranny or its inef-
ficiency are great and unendurable. But almost all say that such is not the
case now. But such was the case, they think, in the Revolution of '75. If
one were to tell me that this was a bad government because it taxed certain foreign commodities brought to its ports, it is most probable that I
should not make an ado about it, for I can do without them. All machines
have their friction; and possibly this does enough good to counterbalance
the evil. At any rate, it is a great evil to make a stir about it. But when the
friction comes to have its machine, and oppression and robbery are organized, I say, let us not have such a machine any longer. In other words,
when a sixth of the population of a nation which has undertaken to be
the refuge of liberty are slaves, and a whole country is unjustly overrun
and conquered by a foreign army, and subjected to military law, I think
that it is not too soon for honest men to rebel and revolutionize. What

makes this duty the more urgent is the fact, that the country so overrun is not our own, but ours is the invading army.

Paley, a common authority with many on moral questions, in his chapter on the "Duty of Submission to Civil Government," resolves all civil obligation into expediency; and he proceeds to say, "that so long as the interest of the whole society requires it, that is, so long as the established government cannot be resisted or changed without public inconveniency, it is the will of God that the established government be obeyed, and no longer. . . . This principle being admitted, the justice of every particular case of resistance is reduced to a computation of the quantity of the danger and grievance on the one side, and of the probability and expense of redressing it on the other." Of this, he says, every man shall judge for himself. But Paley appears never to have contemplated those cases to which the rule of expediency does not apply, in which a people, as well as an individual, must do justice, cost what it may. If I have unjustly wrested a plank from a drowning man, I must restore it to him though I drown myself. This, according to Paley, would be inconvenient. But he that would save his life, in such a case, shall lose it. This people must cease to hold slaves, and to make war on Mexico, though it cost them their existence as a people.

In their practice, nations agree with Paley; but does any one think   10
that Massachusetts does exactly what is right at the present crisis?

> A drab of state, a cloth-'o-silver slut,
> To have her train borne up, and her soul trail in the dirt.

Practically speaking, the opponents to a reform in Massachusetts are not a hundred thousand politicians at the South, but a hundred thousand merchants and farmers here, who are more interested in commerce and agriculture than they are in humanity, and are not prepared to do justice to the slave and to Mexico, *cost what it may.* I quarrel not with far-off foes, but with those who, near at home, cooperate with, and do the bidding of, those far away, and without whom the latter would be harmless. We are accustomed to say, that the mass of men are unprepared; but improvement is slow, because the few are not materially wiser or better than the many. It is not so important that many should be as good as you, as that there be some absolute goodness somewhere; for that will leaven the whole lump. There are thousands who are *in opinion* opposed to slavery and to the war, who yet in effect do nothing to put an end to them; who, esteeming themselves children of Washington and Franklin, sit down with their hands in their pockets, and say that they know not what to do, and do nothing; who even postpone the question of freedom to the question of free-trade, and quietly read the prices-current along with the latest advice from Mexico, after dinner, and, it may be, fall asleep over them both. What is the price-current of an honest man and patriot today? They hesitate, and they regret, and sometimes they petition; but they do nothing in earnest and with effect. They will wait, well disposed, for others to remedy the evil, that they may no longer have it to regret. At most, they give only a cheap vote, and a feeble countenance and God-speed, to the right, as it goes by them. There are nine hundred and ninety-nine patrons of virtue to one virtuous man; but it is easier to deal with the real possessor of a thing than with the temporary guardian of it.

All voting is a sort of gaming, like checkers or backgammon, with a slight moral tinge to it, a playing with right and wrong, with moral questions; and betting naturally accompanies it. The character of the voters is not staked. I cast my vote, perchance, as I think right; but I am not vitally concerned that that right should prevail. I am willing to leave it to the majority. Its obligation, therefore, never exceeds that of expediency. Even voting *for the right* is *doing* nothing for it. It is only expressing to men feebly your desire that it should prevail. A wise man will not leave the right to the mercy of chance, nor wish it to prevail through the power of the majority. There is but little virtue in the action of masses of men. When the majority shall at length vote for the abolition of slavery, it will be because they are indifferent to slavery, or because there is but little slavery left to be abolished by their vote. *They* will then be the only slaves. Only *his* vote can hasten the abolition of slavery who asserts his own freedom by his vote.

I hear of a convention to be held at Baltimore, or elsewhere, for the selection of a candidate for the presidency, made up chiefly of editors, and men who are politicians by profession; but I think, what is it to any independent, intelligent, and respectable man what decision they may come to? Shall we not have the advantage of his wisdom and honesty, nevertheless? Can we not count upon some independent votes? Are there not many individuals in the country who do not attend conventions? But no: I find that the respectable man, so called, has immediately drifted from his position, and despairs of his country, when his country has more reason to despair of him. He forthwith adopts one of the candidates thus selected as the only *available* one, thus providing that he is himself *available* for any purposes of the demagogue. His vote is of no more worth than that of any unprincipled foreigner or hireling native, who may have been bought. O for a man who is *a man*, and, as my neighbor says, has a bone in his back which you cannot pass your hand through! Our statistics are at fault: The population has been returned too large. How many *men* are there to a square thousand miles in this country? Hardly one. Does not America offer any inducement for men to settle here? The American has dwindled into an Odd Fellow,—one who may be known by the development of his organ of gregariousness, and a manifest lack of intellect and cheerful self-reliance; whose first and chief concern, on coming into the world, is to see that the Almshouses are in good repair; and, before yet he has lawfully donned the virile garb, to collect a fund for the support of the widows and orphans that may be; who, in short, ventures to live only by the aid of the Mutual Insurance company, which has promised to bury him decently.

It is not a man's duty, as a matter of course, to devote himself to the eradication of any, even the most enormous wrong; he may still properly have other concerns to engage him; but it is his duty, at least, to wash his hands of it, and, if he gives it no thought longer, not to give it practically his support. If I devote myself to other pursuits and contemplations, I must first see, at least, that I do not pursue them sitting upon another man's shoulders. I must get off him first, that he may pursue his contemplations too. See what gross inconsistency is tolerated. I have heard some of my townsmen say, "I should like to have them order me out to help put down an insurrection of the slaves, or to march to Mexico; — see if I would go"; and yet these very men have each, directly by their allegiance, and so indirectly, at least, by their money, furnished a substitute. The soldier is applauded who refuses to serve in an unjust war by those who do not refuse to sustain the unjust government which makes the war; is applauded by those whose own act and authority he disregards and sets at nought; as if the State were penitent to that degree that it hired one to scourge it while it sinned, but not to that degree that it left off sinning for a moment. Thus, under the name of Order and Civil Government, we are all made at last to pay homage to and support our own meanness. After the first blush of sin, comes its indifference; and from immoral it becomes, as it were, *unmoral*, and not quite unnecessary to that life which we have made.

The broadest and most prevalent error requires the most disinterested virtue to sustain it. The slight reproach to which the virtue of patriotism is commonly liable, the noble are most likely to incur. Those who, while they disapprove of the character and measures of a government, yield to it their allegiance and support, are undoubtedly its most conscientious supporters, and so frequently the most serious obstacles to reform. Some are petitioning the State to dissolve the Union, to disregard the requisitions of the President. Why do they not dissolve it themselves, — the union between themselves and the State, — and refuse to pay their quota into its treasury? Do not they stand in the same relation to the State, that the State does to the Union? And have not the same reasons prevented the State from resisting the Union which have prevented them from resisting the State?

How can a man be satisfied to entertain an opinion merely, and enjoy 15 *it*? Is there any enjoyment in it, if his opinion is that he is aggrieved? If you are cheated out of a single dollar by your neighbor, you do not rest satisfied with knowing that you are cheated, or with saying that you are cheated, or even with petitioning him to pay you your due; but you take effectual steps at once to obtain the full amount, and see that you are never cheated again. Action from principle, the perception and the performance of right, changes things and relations; it is essentially revolutionary, and does not consist wholly with anything which was. It not only divides states and churches, it divides families; ay, it divides the *individual*, separating the diabolical in him from the divine.

Unjust laws exist: Shall we be content to obey them, or shall we endeavor to amend them, and obey them until we have succeeded, or shall we transgress them at once? Men generally, under such a government as this, think that they ought to wait until they have persuaded the majority to alter them. They think that, if they should resist, the remedy would be worse than the evil. But it is the fault of the government itself that the remedy *is* worse than the evil. *It* makes it worse. Why is it not more apt to anticipate and provide for reform? Why does it not cherish its wise minority? Why does it cry and resist before it is hurt? Why does it not encourage its citizens to be on the alert to point out its faults, and *do* better than it would have them? Why does it always crucify Christ, and excommunicate Copernicus and Luther, and pronounce Washington and Franklin rebels?

One would think, that a deliberate and practical denial of its authority was the only offence never contemplated by government; else, why has it not assigned its definite, its suitable and proportionate penalty? If a man who has no property refuses but once to earn nine shillings for the State, he is put in prison for a period unlimited by any law that I know, and determined only by the discretion of those who placed him there; but if he should steal ninety times nine shillings from the State, he is soon permitted to go at large again.

If the injustice is part of the necessary friction of the machine of government, let it go, let it go: Perchance it will wear smooth, — certainly the machine will wear out. If the injustice has a spring, or a pulley, or a rope, or a crank, exclusively for itself, then perhaps you may consider whether the remedy will not be worse than the evil; but if it is of such a nature that it requires you to be the agent of injustice to another, then, I say, break the law. Let your life be a counter friction to stop the machine. What I have to do is to see, at any rate, that I do not lend myself to the wrong which I condemn.

As for adopting the ways which the State has provided for remedying the evil, I know not of such ways. They take too much time, and a man's life will be gone. I have other affairs to attend to. I came into this world, not chiefly to make this a good place to live in, but to live in it, be it good or bad. A man has not everything to do, but something; and because he cannot do *everything*, it is not necessary that he should do *something* wrong. It is not my business to be petitioning the Governor or the Legislature any more than it is theirs to petition me; and, if they should not hear my petition, what should I do then? But in this case the State has provided no way: Its very Constitution is the evil. This may seem to be harsh and stubborn and unconciliatory; but it is to treat with the utmost kindness and consideration the only spirit that can appreciate or deserves it. So is all change for the better, like birth and death, which convulse the body.

I do not hesitate to say, that those who call themselves Abolitionists 20 should at once effectually withdraw their support, both in person and property, from the government of Massachusetts, and not wait till they constitute a majority of one, before they suffer the right to prevail through them. I think that it is enough if they have God on their side, without waiting for that other one. Moreover, any man more right than his neighbors, constitutes a majority of one already.

I meet this American government, or its representative, the State government, directly, and face to face, once a year—no more—in the person of its tax-gatherer; this is the only mode in which a man situated as I am necessarily meets it; and it then says distinctly, Recognize me; and the simplest, the most effectual, and, in the present posture of affairs, the indispensablest mode of treating with it on this head, of expressing your little satisfaction with and love for it, is to deny it then. My civil neighbor, the tax-gatherer, is the very man I have to deal with,—for it is, after all, with men and not with parchment that I quarrel,—and he has voluntarily chosen to be an agent of the government. How shall he ever know well what he is and does as an officer of the government, or as a man, until he is obliged to consider whether he shall treat me, his neighbor, for whom he has respect, as a neighbor and well-disposed man, or as a maniac and disturber of the peace, and see if he can get over this obstruction to his neighborliness without a ruder and more impetuous thought or speech corresponding with his action? I know this well, that if one thousand, if one hundred, if ten men whom I could name,—if ten *honest* men only,—aye, if *one* HONEST man, in this State of Massachusetts, *ceasing to hold slaves*, were actually to withdraw from this copartnership, and be locked up in the county jail therefor, it would be the abolition of slavery in America. For it matters not how small the beginning may seem to be: What is once well done is done forever. But we love better to talk about it: That we say is our mission. Reform keeps many scores of newspapers in its service, but not one man. If my esteemed neighbor, the State's ambassador, who will devote his days to the settlement of the question of human rights in the Council Chamber, instead of being threatened with the prisons of Carolina, were to sit down the prisoner of Massachusetts, that State which is so anxious to foist the sin of slavery upon her sister,—though at present she can discover only an act of inhospitality to be the ground of a quarrel with her,—the Legislature would not wholly waive the subject the following winter.

Under a government which imprisons any unjustly, the true place for a just man is also a prison. The proper place today, the only place which Massachusetts has provided for her freer and less desponding spirits, is in her prisons, to be put out and locked out of the State by her own act, as they have already put themselves out by their principles. It is there that the fugitive slave, and the Mexican prisoner on parole, and the Indian come to plead the wrongs of his race, should find them; on that separate, but more free and honorable ground, where the State places those who are not *with* her, but *against* her,—the only house in a slave State in which a free man can abide with honor. If any think that their influence would be lost there, and their voices no longer afflict the ear of the State, that they would not be as an enemy within its walls, they do not know by how much truth is stronger than error, nor how much more eloquently and effectively he can combat injustice who has experienced a little in his own person. Cast your whole vote, not a strip of paper merely, but your whole influence. A minority is powerless while it conforms to the majority; it is not even a minority then; but it is irresistible when it clogs by its whole weight. If the alternative is to keep all just men in prison, or give up war and slavery, the State will not hesitate which to choose. If a thousand men were not to pay their tax-bills this year, that would not be a violent and bloody measure, as it would be to pay them, and enable the State to commit violence and shed innocent blood. This is, in fact, the definition of a peaceable revolution, if any such is possible. If the tax-gatherer, or any other public officer, asks me, as one has done, "But what shall I do?" my answer is, "If you really wish to do any thing, resign your office." When the subject has refused allegiance, and the officer has resigned his office, then the revolution is accomplished. But even suppose blood should flow. Is there not a sort of blood shed when the conscience is wounded? Through this wound a man's real manhood and immortality flow out, and he bleeds to an everlasting death. I see this blood flowing now.

I have contemplated the imprisonment of the offender, rather than the seizure of his goods,—though both will serve the same purpose,—because they who assert the purest right, and consequently are most dangerous to a corrupt State, commonly have not spent much time in accumulating property. To such the State renders comparatively small service, and a slight tax is wont to appear exorbitant, particularly if they are obliged to earn it by special labor with their hands. If there were one who lived wholly without the use of money, the State itself would hesitate to demand it of him. But the rich man,—not to make any invidious comparison,—is always sold to the institution which makes him rich. Absolutely speaking, the more money, the less virtue; for money comes between a man and his objects, and obtains them for him; and it was certainly no great virtue to obtain it. It puts to rest many questions which he would otherwise be taxed to answer; while the only new question which it puts is the hard but superfluous one, how to spend it. Thus his moral ground is taken from under his feet. The opportunities of living are diminished in proportion as what are called the "means" are increased. The best thing a man can do for his culture when he is rich is to endeavor to carry out those schemes which he entertained when he was poor. Christ answered the Herodians according to their condition. "Show me the tribute-money," said he;—and one took a penny out of his pocket;— if you use money which has the image of Cæsar on it, and which he has made current and valuable, that is, *if you are men of the State*, and gladly enjoy the advantages of Cæsar's government, then pay him back some of his own when he demands it; "Render therefore to Cæsar that which is Cæsar's, and to God those things which are God's,"—leaving them no wiser than before as to which was which; for they did not wish to know.

When I converse with the freest of my neighbors, I perceive that, whatever they may say about the magnitude and seriousness of the question, and their regard for the public tranquility, the long and the short of the matter is, that they cannot spare the protection of the existing government, and they dread the consequences to their property and families of disobedience to it. For my own part, I should not like to think that I ever rely on the protection of the State. But, if I deny the authority of the State when it presents its tax-bill, it will soon take and waste all my property, and so harass me and my children without end. This is hard. This makes it impossible for a man to live honestly, and at the same time comfortably, in outward respects. It will not be worth the while to accumulate property; that would be sure to go again. You must hire or squat somewhere, and raise but a small crop, and eat that soon. You must live within yourself, and depend upon yourself always tucked up and ready for a start, and not have many affairs. A man may grow rich in Turkey even, if he will be in all respects a good subject of the Turkish government. Confucius said: "If a state is governed by the principles of reason, poverty and misery are subjects of shame; if a state is not governed by the principles of reason, riches and honors are the subjects of shame." No: Until I want the protection of Massachusetts to be extended to me in some distant southern port, where my liberty is endangered, or until I am bent solely on building up an estate at home by peaceful enterprise, I can afford to refuse allegiance to Massachusetts, and her right to my property and life. It costs me less in every sense to incur the penalty of disobedience to the State, than it would to obey. I should feel as if I were worth less in that case.

Some years ago, the State met me in behalf of the Church, and com- 25 manded me to pay a certain sum toward the support of a clergyman whose preaching my father attended, but never I myself. "Pay," it said, "or be locked up in the jail." I declined to pay. But, unfortunately, another man saw fit to pay it. I did not see why the schoolmaster should be taxed to support the priest, and not the priest the schoolmaster; for I was not the State's schoolmaster, but I supported myself by voluntary subscription. I did not see why the lyceum should not present its tax-bill, and have the State to back its demand, as well as the Church. However, at the request of the selectmen, I condescended to make some such statement as this in writing:—"Know all men by these presents, that I, Henry

Thoreau, do not wish to be regarded as a member of any incorporated society which I have not joined." This I gave to the town clerk; and he has it. The State, having thus learned that I did not wish to be regarded as a member of that church, has never made a like demand on me since; though it said that it must adhere to its original presumption that time. If I had known how to name them, I should then have signed off in detail from all the societies which I never signed on to; but I did not know where to find a complete list.

I have paid no poll-tax for six years. I was put into a jail once on this account, for one night; and, as I stood considering the walls of solid stone, two or three feet thick, the door of wood and iron, a foot thick, and the iron grating which strained the light, I could not help being struck with the foolishness of that institution which treated me as if I were mere flesh and blood and bones, to be locked up. I wondered that it should have concluded at length that this was the best use it could put me to, and had never thought to avail itself of my services in some way. I saw that, if there was a wall of stone between me and my townsmen, there was a still more difficult one to climb or break through, before they could get to be as free as I was. I did not for a moment feel confined, and the walls seemed a great waste of stone and mortar. I felt as if I alone of all my townsmen had paid my tax. They plainly did not know how to treat me, but behaved like persons who are underbred. In every threat and in every compliment there was a blunder; for they thought that my chief desire was to stand the other side of that stone wall. I could not but smile to see how industriously they locked the door on my meditations, which followed them out again without let or hindrance, and *they* were really all that was dangerous. As they could not reach me, they had resolved to punish my body; just as boys, if they cannot come at some person against whom they have a spite, will abuse his dog. I saw that the State was half-witted, and it was timid as a lone woman with her silver spoons, and that it did not know its friends from its foes, and I lost all my remaining respect for it, and pitied it.

Thus the State never intentionally confronts a man's sense, intellectual or moral, but only his body, his senses. It is not armed with superior wit or honesty, but with superior physical strength. I was not born to be forced. I will breathe after my own fashion. Let us see who is the strongest. What force has a multitude? They only can force me who obey a higher law than I. They force me to become like themselves. I do not hear of *men* being *forced* to live this way or that by masses of men. What sort of life were that to live? When I meet a government which says to me, "Your money or your life," why should I be in haste to give it my money? It may be in a great strait, and not know what to do: I cannot help that. It must help itself; do as I do. It is not worth the while to snivel about it. I am not responsible for the successful working of the machinery of society. I am not the son of the engineer. I perceive that, when an acorn and a chestnut fall side by side, the one does not remain inert to make way for the other, but both obey their own laws, and spring and grow and flourish as best they can, till one, perchance, overshadows and destroys the other. If a plant cannot live according to its nature, it dies; and so a man.

The night in prison was novel and interesting enough. The prisoners in their shirt-sleeves were enjoying a chat and the evening air in the doorway, when I entered. But the jailer said, "Come, boys, it is time to lock up"; and so they dispersed, and I heard the sound of their steps returning into the hollow apartments. My roommate was introduced to me by the jailer, as "a first-rate fellow and a clever man." When the door was locked, he showed me where to hang my hat, and how he managed matters there. The rooms were white-washed once a month; and this one, at least, was the whitest, most simply furnished, and probably the neatest apartment in the town. He naturally wanted to know where I came from, and what brought me there; and, when I had told him, I asked him in my turn how he came there, presuming him to be an honest man, of course; and, as the world goes, I believe he was. "Why," said he, "they accuse me of burning a barn; but I never did it." As near as I could discover, he had probably gone to bed in a barn when drunk, and smoked his pipe there; and so a barn was burnt. He had the reputation of being a clever man, had been there some three months waiting for his trial to come on, and would have to wait as much longer; but he was quite domesticated and contented, since he got his board for nothing, and thought that he was well-treated.

He occupied one window, and I the other; and I saw, that if one stayed there long, his principal business would be to look out the window. I had soon read all the tracts that were left there, and examined where former prisoners had broken out, and where a grate had been sawed off, and heard the history of the various occupants of that room; for I found that even here there was a history and a gossip which never circulated beyond the walls of the jail. Probably this is the only house in the town where verses are composed, which are afterward printed in a circular form, but not published. I was shown quite a long list of verses which were composed by some young men who had been detected in an attempt to escape, who avenged themselves by singing them.

I pumped my fellow-prisoner as dry as I could, for fear I should never 30 see him again; but at length he showed me which was my bed, and left me to blow out the lamp.

It was like travelling into a far country, such as I had never expected to behold, to lie there for one night. It seemed to me that I never had heard the town-clock strike before, nor the evening sounds of the village; for we slept with the windows open, which were inside the grating. It was to see my native village in the light of the Middle Ages, and our Concord was turned into a Rhine stream, and visions of knights and castles passed before me. They were the voices of old burghers that I heard in the streets. I was an involuntary spectator and auditor of whatever was done and said in the kitchen of the adjacent village-inn, — a wholly new and rare experience to me. It was a closer view of my native town. I was fairly inside of it. I never had seen its institutions before. This is one of its peculiar institutions; for it is a shire town. I began to comprehend what its inhabitants were about.

In the morning, our breakfasts were put through the hole in the door, in small oblong-square tin pans, made to fit, and holding a pint of chocolate, with brown bread, and an iron spoon. When they called for the vessels again, I was green enough to return what bread I had left; but my comrade seized it, and said that I should lay that up for lunch or dinner. Soon after, he was let out to work at haying in a neighboring field, whither he went every day, and would not be back till noon; so he bade me good-day, saying that he doubted if he should see me again.

When I came out of prison, — for some one interfered, and paid that tax, — I did not perceive that great changes had taken place on the common, such as he observed who went in a youth, and emerged a tottering and gray-headed man; and yet a change had to my eyes come over the scene, — the town, and State, and country, — greater than any that mere time could effect. I saw yet more distinctly the State in which I lived. I saw to what extent the people among whom I lived could be trusted as good neighbors and friends; that their friendship was for summer weather only; that they did not greatly propose to do right; that they were a distinct race from me by their prejudices and superstitions, as the Chinamen and Malays are; that, in their sacrifices to humanity, they ran no risks, not even to their property; that, after all, they were not so noble but they treated the thief as he had treated them, and hoped, by a certain outward observance and a few prayers, and by walking in a particular straight though useless path from time to time, to save their souls. This may be to judge my neighbors harshly; for I believe that many of them are not aware that they have such an institution as the jail in their village.

It was formerly the custom in our village, when a poor debtor came out of jail, for his acquaintances to salute him, looking through their fingers, which were crossed to represent the grating of a jail window, "How do ye do?" My neighbors did not thus salute me, but first looked at me, and then at one another, as if I had returned from a long journey. I was put into jail as I was going to the shoemaker's to get a shoe which was mended. When I was let out the next morning, I proceeded to finish my errand, and having put on my mended shoe, joined a huckleberry party, who were impatient to put themselves under my conduct; and in half an hour, — for the horse was soon tackled, — was in the midst of a huckleberry field, on one of our highest hills, two miles off, and then the State was nowhere to be seen.

This is the whole story of "My Prisons."   35

I have never declined paying the highway tax, because I am as desirous of being a good neighbor as I am of being a bad subject; and, as for supporting schools, I am doing my part to educate my fellow-countrymen now. It is for no particular item in the tax-bill that I refuse to pay it. I simply wish to refuse allegiance to the State, to withdraw and stand aloof from it effectually. I do not care to trace the course of my dollar, if I could, till it buys a man, or a musket to shoot one with, — the dollar is innocent, — but I am concerned to trace the effects of my allegiance. In fact, I quietly declare war with the State, after my fashion, though I will still make what use and get what advantage of her I can, as is usual in such cases.

If others pay the tax which is demanded of me, from a sympathy with the State, they do but what they have already done in their own case, or rather they abet injustice to a greater extent than the State requires. If they pay the tax from a mistaken interest in the individual taxed, to save his property or prevent his going to jail, it is because they have not considered wisely how far they let their private feelings interfere with the public good.

This, then, is my position at present. But one cannot be too much on his guard in such a case, lest his action be biased by obstinacy, or an undue regard for the opinions of men. Let him see that he does only what belongs to himself and to the hour.

I think sometimes, Why, this people mean well; they are only ignorant; they would do better if they knew how: why give your neighbors this pain to treat you as they are inclined to? But I think again, this is no reason why I should do as they do, or permit others to suffer much greater pain of a different kind. Again, I sometimes say to myself, When many millions of men, without heat, without ill will, without personal feelings of any kind, demand of you a few shillings only, without the possibility, such is their constitution, of retracing or altering their present demand, and without the possibility, on your side, of appeal to any other millions, why expose yourself to this overwhelming brute force? You do not resist cold and hunger, the winds and the waves, thus obstinately; you quietly submit to a thousand similar necessities. You do not put your head into the fire. But just in proportion as I regard this as not wholly a brute force, partly a human force, and consider that I have relations to those millions as to so many millions of men, and not of mere brute or inanimate things, I see that appeal is possible, first and instantaneously, from them to the Maker of them, and, secondly, from them to themselves. But, if I put my head deliberately into the fire, there is no appeal to fire or to the Maker of fire, and I have only myself to blame. If I could convince myself that I have any right to be satisfied with men as they are, and to treat them according, and not according, in some respects, to my requisitions and expectations of what they and I ought to be, then, like a good Mussulman and fatalist, I should endeavor to be satisfied with things as they are, and say it is the will of God. And, above all, there is this difference between resisting this and a purely brute or natural force, that I can resist this with some effect; but I cannot expect, like Orpheus, to change the nature of the rocks and trees and beasts.

I do not wish to quarrel with any man or nation. I do not wish to split 40 hairs, to make fine distinctions, or set myself up as better than my neighbors. I seek rather, I may say, even an excuse for conforming to the laws of the land. I am but too ready to conform to them. Indeed, I have reason to suspect myself on this head; and each year, as the tax-gatherer comes round, I find myself disposed to review the acts and position of the general and State governments, and the spirit of the people, to discover a pretext for conformity.

> We must affect our country as our parents;
> And if at any time we alienate
> Our love or industry from doing it honor,
> We must respect effects and teach the soul
> Matter of conscience and religion,
> And not desire of rule or benefit.

I believe that the State will soon be able to take all my work of this sort out of my hands, and then I shall be no better a patriot than my fellow-countrymen. Seen from a lower point of view, the Constitution, with all its faults, is very good; the law and the courts are very respectable; even this State and this American government are, in many respects, very admirable and rare things, to be thankful for, such as a great many have described them; but seen from a point of view a little higher, they are what I have described them; seen from a higher still, and the highest, who shall say what they are, or that they are worth looking at or thinking of at all?

However, the government does not concern me much, and I shall bestow the fewest possible thoughts on it. It is not many moments that I live under a government, even in this world. If a man is thought-free, fancy-free, imagination-free, that which *is not* never for a long time appearing *to be* to him, unwise rulers or reformers cannot fatally interrupt him.

I know that most men think differently from myself; but those whose lives are by profession devoted to the study of these or kindred subjects, content me as little as any. Statesmen and legislators, standing so completely within the institution, never distinctly and nakedly behold it. They speak of moving society, but have no resting-place without it. They may be men of a certain experience and discrimination, and have no doubt invented ingenious and even useful systems, for which we sincerely thank them; but all their wit and usefulness lie within certain not very wide limits. They are wont to forget that the world is not governed by policy and expediency. Webster never goes behind government, and so cannot speak with authority about it. His words are wisdom to those legislators who contemplate no essential reform in the existing government; but for thinkers, and those who legislate for all time, he never once glances at the subject. I know of those whose serene and wise speculations on this theme would soon reveal the limits of his mind's range and hospitality. Yet, compared with the cheap professions of most reformers, and the still cheaper wisdom and eloquence of politicians in general, his are almost the only sensible and valuable words, and we thank Heaven for him. Comparatively, he is always strong, original, and, above all, practical. Still his quality is not wisdom, but prudence. The lawyer's truth is not Truth, but consistency, or a consistent expediency. Truth is always in harmony with herself, and is not concerned chiefly to reveal the justice that may consist with wrong-doing. He well deserves to be called, as he has been called, the Defender of the Constitution. There are really no blows to be given by him but defensive ones. He is not a leader, but a follower. His leaders are the men of '87. "I have never made an effort," he says, "and never propose to make an effort; I have never countenanced an effort, and never mean to countenance an effort, to disturb the arrangement as originally made, by which the various States came into the Union." Still thinking of the sanction which the Constitution gives to slavery, he says, "Because it was a part of the original compact, — let it stand." Notwithstanding his special acuteness and ability, he is unable to take a fact out of its merely political relations, and behold it as it lies absolutely to be disposed of by the intellect, — what, for instance, it behooves a man to do here in America today with regard to slavery, but ventures, or is driven, to make some such desperate answer as the following, while professing to speak absolutely, and as a private man, — from which what new and singular code of social duties might be inferred? "The manner," says he, "in which the governments of those States where slavery exists are to regulate it, is for their own consideration, under their responsibility to their constituents, to the general laws of propriety, humanity, and justice, and to God. Associations formed elsewhere, springing from a feeling of humanity, or any other cause, have nothing whatever to do with it. They have never received any encouragement from me, and they never will."[1]

They who know of no purer sources of truth, who have traced up its stream no higher, stand, and wisely stand, by the Bible and the Constitution, and drink at it there with reverence and humility; but they who behold where it comes trickling into this lake or that pool, gird up their loins once more, and continue their pilgrimage toward its fountainhead.

No man with a genius for legislation has appeared in America. They are rare in the history of the world. There are orators, politicians, and eloquent men, by the thousand; but the speaker has not yet opened his

---

[1] These extracts have been inserted since the Lecture was read.

mouth to speak, who is capable of settling the much-vexed questions of the day. We love eloquence for its own sake, and not for any truth which it may utter, or any heroism it may inspire. Our legislators have not yet learned the comparative value of free-trade and of freedom, of union, and of rectitude, to a nation. They have no genius or talent for comparatively humble questions of taxation and finance, commerce and manufactures and agriculture. If we were left solely to the wordy wit of legislators in Congress for our guidance, uncorrected by the seasonable experience and the effectual complaints of the people, America would not long retain her rank among the nations. For eighteen hundred years, though perchance I have no right to say it, the New Testament has been written; yet where is the legislator who has wisdom and practical talent enough to avail himself of the light which it sheds on the science of legislation?

The authority of government, even such as I am willing to submit 45 to,—for I will cheerfully obey those who know and can do better than I, and in many things even those who neither know nor can do so well,— is still an impure one: To be strictly just, it must have the sanction and consent of the governed. It can have no pure right over my person and property but what I concede to it. The progress from an absolute to a limited monarchy, from a limited monarchy to a democracy, is a progress toward a true respect for the individual. Even the Chinese philosopher was wise enough to regard the individual as the basis of the empire. Is a democracy, such as we know it, the last improvement possible in government? Is it not possible to take a step further towards recognizing and organizing the rights of man? There will never be a really free and enlightened State, until the State comes to recognize the individual as a higher and independent power, from which all its own power and authority are derived, and treats him accordingly. I please myself with imagining a State at last which can afford to be just to all men, and to treat the individual with respect as a neighbor; which even would not think it inconsistent with its own repose, if a few were to live aloof from it, not meddling with it, nor embraced by it, who fulfilled all the duties of neighbors and fellowmen. A State which bore this kind of fruit, and suffered it to drop off as fast as it ripened, would prepare the way for a still more perfect and glorious State, which also I have imagined, but not yet anywhere seen.

DISCUSSION QUESTIONS

1. Summarize briefly Thoreau's reasons for arguing that civil disobedience is sometimes a *duty.*

2. Thoreau, like Martin Luther King Jr. in "Letter from Birmingham Jail" (p. 192), speaks of "unjust laws" (para. 16). Do they agree on the positions that citizens should take in response to these laws? Are Thoreau and King guided by the same principles?

3. What examples of government policy and action does Thoreau use to prove that civil disobedience is a duty? Explain why they are—or are not—effective.

4. Why do you think Thoreau provides such a detailed account of one day in prison? (Notice that King does not give a description of his confinement.) What observation about the community struck Thoreau when he emerged from jail?

5. What warrant or warrants must readers accept in order to accept Thoreau's argument?

WRITING SUGGESTIONS

6. Argue that civil disobedience to a school policy or action is justified. (Examples might include failure to establish an ethnic studies department, refusal to allow ROTC on campus, refusal to suspend a professor accused of sexual harassment.) Be specific about the injustice of the policy or action and the values that underlie the resistance.

7. Under what circumstances might civil disobedience prove to be dangerous and immoral? Can you think of cases of disobedience when *conscience*, as Thoreau uses the term, did not appear to be the guiding principle? Try to identify what you think is the true motivation for the resistance.

DEBATE: Are you responsible for your own weight?

Absolutely. Government Has No Business Interfering with What You Eat

RADLEY BALKO

Nutrition activists are agitating for a panoply of initiatives that would bring the government between you and your waistline. President Bush earmarked $125 million in his budget for the encouragement of healthy lifestyles. State legislatures and school boards have begun banning snacks and soda from school campuses and vending machines. Several state legislators and Oakland, California, Mayor Jerry Brown, among others, have called for a "fat tax" on high-calorie foods. Congress is considering menu-labeling legislation that would force chain restaurants to list fat, sodium and calories for each item.

Radley Balko is a senior editor for *Reason* magazine, a former policy analyst with the Cato Institute, and a columnist for FoxNews.com. This article first appeared in *Time* on June 7, 2004.

That is precisely the wrong way to fight obesity. Instead of intervening in the array of food options available to Americans, our government ought to be working to foster a personal sense of responsibility for our health and well-being.

We're doing just the opposite. For decades, America's health-care system has been migrating toward nationalized medicine. We have a law that requires some Americans to pay for other Americans' medicine, and several states bar health insurers from charging lower premiums to people who stay fit. That removes the financial incentive for making healthy decisions. Worse, socialized health care makes us troublingly tolerant of government trespasses on our personal freedom. If my neighbor's heart attack shows up on my tax bill, I'm more likely to support state regulation of what he eats—restrictions on what grocery stores can put on their shelves, for example, or what McDonald's can put between its sesame-seed buns.

The best way to combat the public-health threat of obesity is to remove obesity from the realm of "public health." It's difficult to think of a matter more private and less public than what we choose to put in our bodies. Give Americans moral, financial and personal responsibility for their own health, and obesity is no longer a public matter but a private one—with all the costs, concerns, and worries of being overweight borne only by those people who are actually overweight.

Let each of us take full responsibility for our diet and lifestyle. We're   5
likely to make better decisions when someone else isn't paying for the consequences.

Not If Blaming the Victim Is Just an Excuse to Let Industry Off the Hook

KELLY BROWNELL AND MARION NESTLE

The food industry, like any other, must grow to stay in business. One way it does so is by promoting unhealthy foods, particularly to children. Each year kids see more than 10,000 food ads on TV alone, almost all for items like soft drinks, fast foods and sugared cereals. In the same year that the government spent $2 million on its main nutrition-education program, McDonald's spent $500 million on its We Love to See You Smile campaign. It can be no surprise that teenagers consume nearly twice as much soda as milk (the reverse was true twenty years ago) and that 25 percent of all vegetables eaten in the United States are french fries.

To counter criticism, the food industry and pro-business groups use a public relations script focused on personal responsibility. The script has three elements: (1) if people are overweight, it is their own fault; (2) industry responds to consumer demand but does not create it; and (3) insisting that industry change—say, by not marketing to children or requiring restaurants to reveal calories—is an attack on freedom.

Why quarrel with the personal-responsibility argument?

First, it's wrong. The prevalence of obesity increases year after year. Were people less responsible in 2002 than in 2001? Obesity is a global problem. Is irresponsibility an epidemic around the world?

Second, it ignores biology. Humans are hardwired, as a survival strat- 5 egy, to like foods high in sugar, fat, and calories.

Third, the argument is not helpful. Imploring people to eat better and exercise more has been the default approach to obesity for years. That is a failed experiment.

Fourth, personal responsibility is a trap. The argument is startlingly similar to the tobacco industry's efforts to stave off legislative and regulatory

Kelly D. Brownell is professor and chair of psychology at Yale University and also serves as professor of epidemiology and public health and as director of the Yale Center for Eating and Weight Disorders. He has written numerous books, and one of his articles, "Understanding and Preventing Relapse," published in the *American Psychologist*, is one of the most frequently cited articles in the field of psychology.

Marion Nestle is Paulette Goddard Professor in the Department of Nutrition, Food Studies, and Public Health at New York University. Her degrees include a Ph.D. in molecular biology and an M.P.H. in public health nutrition, both from the University of California, at Berkeley. She is the author of *Food Politics: How the Food Industry Influences Nutrition and Health* (2002), *Safe Food: Bacteria, Biotechnology, and Bioterrorism* (2003), and *What to Eat* (2007).

interventions. The nation tolerated personal-responsibility arguments from Big Tobacco for decades, with disastrous results.

Governments collude with industry when they shift attention from conditions promoting poor diets to the individuals who consume them. Government should be doing everything it can to create conditions that lead to healthy eating, support parents in raising healthy children, and make decisions in the interests of public health rather than private profit.

DISCUSSION QUESTIONS

1. In his first paragraph, Balko mentions some specific initiatives that would involve some governmental control over Americans' eating habits. Which of them, if any, do you support?
2. What does Balko favor instead of such initiatives?
3. According to Balko, what mistakes have Americans made in the way they have tried to fight obesity?
4. Why do Brownell and Nestle believe that the government must bear some of the blame for obesity?
5. What does the food industry offer in its defense?
6. How did the practice of making health the personal responsibility of the consumer work when it came to smoking?
7. Whose argument do you find more convincing, and why?

ASSIGNMENTS FOR ANALYZING WARRANTS

READING AND DISCUSSION QUESTIONS

1. Should students be given a direct voice in the hiring of faculty members? On what warrants about education do you base your answer?
2. Discuss the validity of the warrant in this statement from the *Watch Tower* (a publication of the Jehovah's Witnesses) about genital herpes: "The sexually loose are indeed 'receiving in themselves the full recompense, which was due for their error' (Romans 1:27)."
3. Read the following passage about suicide by the Greek philosopher Aristotle (adapted from his *Ethics*). Then defend or attack his argument, being careful to make clear both Aristotle's and your own warrants.

   > Just as a murderer does not have the right to take a mother from her family or a child from her parents and simultaneously to deny society the use of a productive citizen, so the suicide, even though he or she freely chooses to be his or her own victim, does not possess the right to thus diminish the welfare of so many others.

4. In view of the increasing interest in health in general, and nutrition and exercise in particular, do you think that universities and colleges should impose physical education requirements? If so, what form should they take? If not, why not? What warrant underlies your position?

5. What are some of the assumptions underlying the preference for natural foods and medicines? Can *natural* be clearly defined? Is this preference part of a broader philosophy? Try to evaluate the validity of the assumption.

6. The author of the following passage, Katherine Butler Hathaway, became a hunchback as a result of a childhood illness. Here she writes about the relationship between love and beauty from the point of view of someone who is deformed. Discuss the warrants on which the author bases her conclusions.

> I could secretly pretend that I had a lover . . . but I could never risk showing that I thought such a thing was possible for me . . . with any man. Because of my repeated encounters with the mirror and my irrepressible tendency to forget what I had seen, I had begun to force myself to believe and to remember, and especially to remember, that I would never be chosen for what I imagined to be the supreme and most intimate of all experience. I thought of sexual love as an honor that was too great and too beautiful for the body in which I was doomed to live.

WRITING ASSIGNMENTS

7. In "An Unjust Sacrifice," Robert A. Sirico presents a case in which he finds no justification for letting one Siamese twin die in order to save the other. His belief in the sanctity of human life appears to be absolute, even when it will most likely lead to the death of both twins. Write an essay in which you give examples of how your value system underlies your political views.

8. Write an essay explaining why you think either Radley Balko or Kelly Brownell and Marion Nestle make a better argument.

9. Both state and federal governments have been embroiled in controversies concerning the rights of citizens to engage in harmful practices. In Massachusetts, for example, a mandatory seat-belt law was repealed by voters who considered the law an infringement of their freedom. (It was later reinstated.) Write an essay in which you explain what principles you believe should guide government regulation of dangerous practices.

10. Henry David Thoreau writes, "Unjust laws exist: Shall we be content to obey them, or shall we endeavor to amend them, and obey them until we have succeeded, or shall we transgress them at once?" Write an essay in which you explain under what circumstances you would feel compelled to break the law, or why you feel that you would never do so.

CHAPTER 9

Avoiding Flawed Logic

Throughout the book we have pointed out the weaknesses that cause arguments to break down. In the vast majority of cases these weaknesses represent breakdowns in logic or the reasoning process. We call such weaknesses *fallacies*, a term derived from Latin. Sometimes these false or erroneous arguments are deliberate; in fact, the Latin word *fallere* means "to deceive." But more often these arguments are either carelessly or unintentionally constructed. Thoughtful readers learn to recognize them; thoughtful writers learn to avoid them.

The reasoning process was first given formal expression by Aristotle, the Greek philosopher, almost 2,500 years ago. In his famous treatises, he described the way we try to discover the truth—observing the world, selecting impressions, making inferences, generalizing. In this process Aristotle identified two forms of reasoning: *induction* and *deduction*. Both forms, he realized, are subject to error. Our observations may be incorrect or insufficient, and our conclusions may be faulty because they have violated the rules governing the relationship between statements. The terms we've introduced may be unfamiliar, but the processes of reasoning, as well as the fallacies that violate these processes, are not. Induction and deduction are not reserved only for formal arguments about important problems; they also represent our everyday thinking about the most ordinary matters. As for the fallacies, they, too, unfortunately, may crop up anywhere, whenever we are careless in our use of the reasoning process.

In this chapter we examine some of the most common fallacies. First, however, a closer look at induction and deduction will make clear what happens when fallacies occur.

INDUCTION

Induction is the form of reasoning in which we come to conclusions about the whole on the basis of observations of particular instances. If you notice that prices on the four items you bought in the campus bookstore are higher than similar items in the bookstore in town, you may come to the conclusion that the campus store is a more expensive place to shop. If you also noticed that all three of the instructors you saw on the first day of school were wearing faded jeans and running shoes, you might say that your teachers are generally informal in their dress. In both cases you have made an *inductive leap*, reasoning from what you have learned about a few examples to what you think is true of a whole class of things.

How safe are you in coming to these conclusions? As we've noticed in discussing data and generalization warrants, the reliability of your conclusion depends on the quantity and quality of your observations. Were four items out of the thousands available in the campus store a sufficiently large sample? Would you come to the same conclusion if you chose fifty items? Might another selection have produced a different conclusion? As for the casually dressed instructors, perhaps further investigation would disclose that the teachers wearing jeans were all teaching assistants and that associate and full professors usually wore business clothes. Or the difference might lie in the academic discipline; anthropology teachers might turn out to dress less formally than business school teachers.

In these two situations, you could come closer to verifying your conclusions by further observation and experience—that is, by pricing more items at both stores over a longer period of time and by coming into contact with a greater number of teachers during a whole semester. Even without pricing every item in both stores or encountering every instructor on campus, you would be more confident of your generalization as the quality and quantity of your samples increased.

In some cases you can observe all the instances in a particular situation. For example, by acquiring information about the religious beliefs of all the residents of the dormitory, you can arrive at an accurate assessment of the number of Buddhists. But since our ability to make definitive observations about everything is limited, we must also make an inductive leap about categories of things that we ourselves can never encounter in their entirety. For some generalizations, as we have learned about evidence, we rely on the testimony of reliable witnesses who report that they have experienced or observed many more instances of the phenomenon. A television documentary may give us information about unwed teenage mothers in a city neighborhood; four girls are interviewed and followed for several days by the reporter. Are these girls typical of thousands of others? A sociologist on the program assures us that, in fact, they are. She herself has consulted with hundreds of other young mothers and can vouch for the fact that a conclusion about them, based on our observation of the four, will be sound. Obviously, though, our conclusion can only be probable, not certain. The sociologist's sample is large, but she can account only for hundreds, not thousands, and there may be unexamined cases that will seriously weaken our conclusions.

In other cases, we may rely on a principle known in science as "the uniformity of nature." We assume that certain conclusions about oak trees in the temperate zone of North America, for example, will also be true for oak trees growing elsewhere under similar climatic conditions. We also use this principle in attempting to explain the causes of behavior in human beings. If we discover that institutionalization of some children from infancy results in severe emotional retardation, we think it safe to conclude that under the same circumstances all children would suffer the same consequences. As in the previous example, we are aware that certainty about every case of institutionalization is impossible. With rare exceptions, the process of induction can offer only probability, not certain truth.

SAMPLE ESSAY: AN INDUCTIVE ARGUMENT

True or False: Schools Fail Immigrants

RICHARD ROTHSTEIN

A common indictment of public schools is that they no longer offer upward mobility to most immigrants. It is said that in the first half of the twentieth century, children learned English, went to college, and joined the middle class but that many of today's immigrants are more likely to drop out, take dead-end jobs, or end up in prison.

Many true accounts reinforce these beliefs. But less noticed are equally valid anecdotes pointing to an opposite claim.

Policy by anecdote is flawed because too often we notice only what confirms our preconceptions. California's recent experience with Mexican immigrants provides ample material for stories about school failure. But on a day to celebrate the American promise, we might also turn to anecdotes of another kind.

Recent college commencements across California featured many immigrants from impoverished families whose first language was Spanish, who came through much-maligned bilingual education programs, learned English, and now head for graduate schools or professions.

Richard Rothstein is a research associate of the Economic Policy Institute, a senior correspondent of the *American Prospect*, and the former national education columnist of the *New York Times*, where this article appeared on July 4, 2001. He is the author of *The Way We Were: Myths and Realities of America's Student Achievement* (1997), *All Else Equal: Are Public and Private Schools Different?* (2003), and *The Charter School Dust-up* (2005).

At California State University at Fresno, for example, about 700 of 4,000 5
graduates this spring were Latino, typically the first in their families to attend
college. Top-ranked were Pedro Nava and Maria Rocio Magaña, Mexican-
born children of farm laborers and cannery workers.

Mr. Nava did not settle in the United States until the third grade. Before that, he lived in migrant labor camps during harvests and in Mexico
the rest of the year. His California schooling was in Spanish until the fifth
grade, when he was moved to English instruction. Now, with a college
degree, he has enrolled in management and teacher training courses.

Ms. Magaña did not place into English classes until the second half of the
eleventh grade. Now fluent in both academic and conversational English, she
will soon begin a Ph.D. program in anthropology at the University of Chicago.

Their achievements are not unique. Both credit success to their mothers' emphasis on education. Both mothers enrolled in English and high
school equivalency courses at the local community college.

Across California, these two-year institutions play an especially important role for immigrants.

Lourdes Andrade just finished her junior year at Brown University, 10
having transferred there after getting associate of arts degrees in history
and liberal arts at Oxnard Community College, about forty miles northwest of Los Angeles.

Ms. Andrade arrived here at the age of four and all through elementary school worked with her mother making beds and cleaning bathrooms
in hotels. Ms. Andrade, too, attributes her success to her mother's strong
academic pressure and also to mentoring she received in a federally financed
program to give extra academic support to migrant children.

The program's director, Lorenzo Moraza, also grew up speaking only
Spanish. Now a school principal, Mr. Moraza estimates that about 30 percent of the immigrant children he has worked with acquired public school
records that led them to college. Those who receive bachelor's degrees are
many fewer, but Mr. Moraza says he thinks most drop out of college for
economic reasons, not academic ones.

At the Fresno campus, nearly two-thirds of the immigrants and children
of immigrants who enter as freshmen eventually graduate. The university
operates special support services to help them do so.

You cannot spend time in California without noticing an extensive
middle class of Latino schoolteachers, doctors, lawyers, and small-business
people. Not all are recent immigrants, but many are. Some attended Catholic
schools, but most are products of the public system. Many had bilingual
education in the 1970s, 80s, and 90s. California has now banned such instruction, assuming it failed.

There are plenty of anecdotes to support a claim that schools fail im- 15
migrant children or an equally persuasive claim that schools serve them
well. Getting better statistics should be a priority. Government numbers do
not distinguish between students who are immigrants (or whose parents
immigrated) from Hispanics with American roots for several generations.

To help interpret California's experience, the best federal data tell only that in 1996, there were 100,000 college students nationwide who were American citizens born in Mexico. This is less than 1 percent of all college students. But uncounted are even larger numbers of those born here to recent migrants.

Even a balanced collection of anecdotes that include successes as well as failures cannot determine whether California schools are less effective than we should expect, and whether wholesale change is needed to move more immigrants to the middle class. But the answer is certainly more complex than the stereotypes of systematic failure that pervade most accounts.

■ Analysis

An inductive argument proceeds by examining particulars and arriving at a generalization that represents a probable truth. The author of this article arrives at the truth he will defend—that public schools have been more successful than is often acknowledged in moving many immigrants into the middle class—by offering statistical data and a number of stories about immigrants from poor families who have entered graduate school or one of the professions.

Rothstein begins, as many arguers do, with a brief summary of the popular position with which he disagrees. At the end of the third paragraph, he announces that he will provide examples that point to a different conclusion.

The reader should ask three questions of an inductive argument: Is the evidence sufficient? Is it representative? Is it up-to-date? The evidence that Rothstein assembles consists of a series of anecdotes and statistical data about the performance of immigrant students. The success stories of five real persons are impressive, despite limitations imposed by the brevity of the essay, in part because they offer vivid examples of struggle that appeal to our emotions and bring to life an issue with which some of us may not be familiar. But five stories are hardly enough to prove a case; perhaps they are not representative. Rothstein, therefore, adds other data about the rate at which immigrant students graduate and the growing number of Latino professionals and businesspeople.

Although the essay was published in 2001, his numbers are drawn from the 1990s and are thus a bit dated. A look at more recent data would reveal whether his conclusions remain valid.

The reader has some reason to believe that the facts are accurate. At the time this article was published, Rothstein wrote a regular column for a prestigious daily newspaper whose readers would have been quick to find errors in arguments of which they were critical. At the same time, he does not claim that his argument is beyond debate, since the data are incomplete. Even the title suggests that the issue is still unsettled. Modesty in the arguer is always welcome and disposes the reader to view the argument more favorably.

PRACTICE

Read Goldberg's essay "Connecting the Dots . . . to Terrorism" (p. 246). Explain how Goldberg uses inductive reasoning in the essay while not structuring the whole essay around it. What larger purpose does he have in the essay, and how does inductive reasoning help him achieve that purpose?

DEDUCTION

While induction attempts to arrive at the truth, deduction guarantees sound relationships between statements. If each of a series of statements, called *premises*, is true, deductive logic tells us that the conclusion must also be true. Unlike the conclusions from induction, which are only probable, the conclusions from deduction are certain. The simplest deductive argument consists of two premises and a conclusion. In outline such an argument looks like this:

MAJOR PREMISE: All students with 3.5 averages and above for three years are invited to become members of Kappa Gamma Pi, the honor society.

MINOR PREMISE: George has had a 3.8 average for over three years.

CONCLUSION: Therefore, he will be invited to join Kappa Gamma Pi.

This deductive conclusion is *valid*, or logically consistent, because it follows necessarily from the premises. No other conclusion is possible. Validity, however, refers only to the form of the argument. The argument itself may not be satisfactory if the premises are not true—if Kappa Gamma Pi has imposed other conditions or if George has only a 3.4 average. The difference between truth and validity is important because it alerts us to the necessity for examining the truth of the premises before we decide that the conclusion is sound.

One way of discovering how the deductive process works is to look at the methods used by Sherlock Holmes, that most famous of literary detectives, in solving his mysteries. His reasoning process follows a familiar pattern. Through the inductive process—that is, observing the particulars of the world—he came to certain conclusions about those particulars. Then he applied deductive reasoning to come to a conclusion about a particular person or event.

On one occasion Holmes observed that a man sitting opposite him on a train had chalk dust on his fingers. From this observation Holmes deduced that the man was a schoolteacher. If his thinking were outlined, it would take the form of the syllogism, the classic form of deductive reasoning:

MAJOR PREMISE: All men with chalk dust on their fingers are
                   schoolteachers.

MINOR PREMISE: This man has chalk dust on his fingers.

CONCLUSION: Therefore, this man is a schoolteacher.

One dictionary defines *syllogism* as "a formula of argument consisting of three propositions." The first proposition is called the major premise and offers a generalization about a large group or class. This generalization has been arrived at through inductive reasoning or observation of particulars. The second proposition is called the minor premise, and it makes a statement about a member of that group or class. The third proposition is the conclusion, which links the other two propositions, in much the same way that the warrant links the support and the claim.

If we look back at the syllogism that summarizes Holmes's thinking, we see how it represents the deductive process. The major premise, the first statement, is an inductive generalization, a statement arrived at after observation of a number of men with chalk on their fingers. The minor premise, the second statement, assigns a particular member, the man on the train, to the general class of those who have dust on their fingers.

But although the argument may be logical, it is faulty. The deductive argument is only as strong as its premises. As Lionel Ruby pointed out, Sherlock Holmes was often wrong.[1] Holmes once deduced from the size of a large hat found in the street that the owner was intelligent. He obviously believed that a large head meant a large brain and that a large brain indicated intelligence. Had he lived one hundred years later, new information about the relationship of brain size to intelligence would have enabled him to come to a different and better conclusion.

In this case, we might first object to the major premise, the generalization that all men with chalk dust on their fingers are schoolteachers. Is it true? Perhaps all the men with dusty fingers whom Holmes had so far observed had turned out to be schoolteachers, but was his sample sufficiently large to allow him to conclude that all dust-fingered men, even those with whom he might never have contact, were teachers? Were there no other vocations or situations that might require the use of chalk? In Holmes's day draftsmen or carpenters or tailors might have had fingers just as white as those of schoolteachers. In other words, Holmes may have ascertained that all schoolteachers have chalk dust on their fingers, but he had not determined that *only* schoolteachers could be thus identified. Sometimes it is helpful to draw circles representing the various groups in their relation to the whole.

If a large circle (see the figure below) represents all those who have chalk dust on their fingers, we see that several different groups may be contained

---

[1] *The Art of Making Sense* (Philadelphia: Lippincott, 1954), ch. 17.

in this universe. To be safe, Holmes should have deduced that the man on the train *might* have been a schoolteacher; he was not safe in deducing more than that. Obviously, if the inductive generalization or major premise is false, the conclusion of the particular argument is also false or invalid.

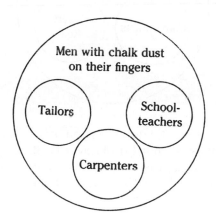

The deductive argument may also go wrong elsewhere. What if the minor premise is untrue? Could Holmes have mistaken the source of the white powder on the man's fingers? Suppose it was not chalk dust but flour or confectioner's sugar or talcum or heroin? Any of these possibilities would weaken or invalidate his conclusion.

Another example, closer to the kinds of arguments you will examine, reveals the flaw in the deductive process.

MAJOR PREMISE: All Communists oppose organized religion.

MINOR PREMISE: Robert Roe opposes organized religion.

CONCLUSION: Therefore, Robert Roe is a Communist.

The common name for this fallacy is "guilt by association." The fact that two things share an attribute does not mean that they are the same thing. The following diagram makes clear that Robert Roe and Communists do not necessarily share all attributes. Remembering that Holmes may have misinterpreted the signs of chalk on the traveler's fingers, we may also want to question whether Robert Roe's opposition to organized religion has been misinterpreted.

An example from history shows us how such an argument may be used. In a campaign speech during the summer of 1952, Senator Joseph McCarthy, who had made a reputation as a tireless enemy of communism, said, "I do not tell you that Schlesinger, Stevenson's number one man, number one braintrust, I don't tell you he's a Communist. I have no information on that point. But I do know that if he were a Communist he would also ridicule religion as Schlesinger has done."[2] This is an argument based on a sign warrant. Clearly the sign referred to by Senator McCarthy, ridicule of religion, would not be sufficient to characterize someone as a Communist.

Some deductive arguments give trouble because one of the premises, usually the major premise, is omitted. As in the warrants we examined in Chapter 8, a failure to evaluate the truth of the unexpressed premise may lead to an invalid conclusion. When only two parts of the syllogism appear, we call the resulting form an *enthymeme*. Suppose we overhear the following snatch of conversation:

> *"Did you hear about Jean's father? He had a heart attack last week."*
> *"That's too bad. But I'm not surprised. I know he always refused to go for his annual physical checkups."*

The second speaker has used an unexpressed major premise, the cause-and-effect warrant "If you have annual physical checkups, you can avoid heart attacks." He does not express it because he assumes that it is unnecessary to do so. The first speaker recognizes the unspoken warrant and may agree with it. Or the first speaker may produce evidence from reputable sources that such a generalization is by no means universally true, in which case the conclusion of the second speaker is suspect.

A knowledge of the deductive process can help guide you toward an evaluation of the soundness of your reasoning in an argument you are constructing. The syllogism is often clearer than an outline in establishing the relations between the different parts of an argument.

---

[2] Joseph R. McCarthy, "The Red-Tinted Washington Crowd," speech delivered to a Republican campaign meeting at Appleton, Wisconsin, November 3, 1952.

Suppose you wanted to argue that your former high school should introduce a dress code. You might begin by asking these questions: What would be the purpose of such a regulation? How would a dress code fulfill that purpose? What reasons could you provide to support your claim?

Then you might set down part of your argument like this:

> Dressing in different styles makes students more aware of social differences among themselves.
>
> The students in this school dress in many different styles.
>
> Therefore, they are more aware of differences in social status among the student body.

As you diagram this first part of the argument, you should ask two sets of questions:

1. Is the major premise true? Do differences in dress cause awareness of differences in social status? Has my experience confirmed this?
2. Is the minor premise true? Has my observation confirmed this?

The conclusion, of course, represents something that you don't have to observe. You can deduce with certainty that it is true if both the major and minor premises are true.

So far the testing of your argument has been relatively easy because you have been concerned with the testing of observation and experience. Now you must examine something that does not appear in the syllogism. You have determined certain facts about perceptions of social status, but you have not arrived at the policy you want to recommend: that a dress code should be mandated. Notice that the dress code argument is based on acceptance of a moral value.

> Reducing awareness of social differences is a desirable goal for the school.
>
> A uniform dress code would help to achieve that goal.
>
> Therefore, students should be required to dress uniformly.

The major premise in this syllogism is clearly different from the previous one. While the premise in the previous syllogism can be tested by examining sufficient examples to determine probability, this statement, about the desirability of the goal, is a value judgment and cannot be proved by counting examples. Whether equality of social status is a desirable goal depends on an appeal to other, more basic values.

Setting down your own or someone else's argument in this form will not necessarily give you the answers to questions about how to support your claim, but it should clearly indicate what your claims are and, above all, what logical connections exist between your statements.

It's All about Him

DAVID VON DREHLE

The author establishes his knowledge of mass murders, his "claim to authority."

My reporter's odyssey has taken me from the chill dawn outside the Florida prison in which serial killer Ted Bundy met his end, to the charred façade of a Bronx nightclub where Julio Gonzalez incinerated 87 people, to a muddy Colorado hillside overlooking the Columbine High School library, in which Eric Harris and Dylan Klebold wrought their mayhem. Along the way, I've come to believe that we're looking for why in all the wrong places.

I've lost interest in the cracks, chips, holes, and broken places in the lives of men like Cho Seung-Hui, the mass murderer of Virginia Tech. The pain, grievances, and self-pity of mass killers are only symptoms of the real explanation. Those who do these things share one common trait. They are raging narcissists. "I died—like Jesus Christ," Cho said in a video sent to NBC.

His thesis statement (and major premise): mass murderers are narcissists

Psychologists from South Africa to Chicago have begun to recognize that extreme self-centeredness is the forest in these stories, and all the other things—guns, games, lyrics, pornography—are just trees. To list the traits of the narcissist is enough to prove the point: grandiosity, numbness to the needs and pain of others, emotional isolation, resentment, and envy.

The traits of the narcissist

In interviews with Ted Bundy taped a quarter-century ago, journalists Stephen Michaud and Hugh Aynesworth captured the essence of homicidal narcissism. Through hour after tedious hour, a man who killed 30 or more young women and girls preened for his audience. He spoke of himself as an actor, of life as a series of roles, and of other people as props and scenery. His desires were simple: "control" and

Major premise applied to Ted Bundy

David von Drehle is a senior writer at the *Washington Post*, where he has also been national political writer, magazine staff writer, New York bureau chief, and assistant managing editor. His most recent book is *Triangle: The Fire That Changed America* (2003). This article appeared in *Time* on April 30, 2007.

"mastery." He took whatever he wanted, from shop-lifted tube socks to human lives, because nothing mattered beyond his desires. Bundy said he was always surprised that anyone noticed his victims had vanished. "I mean, there are so many people," he explained. The only death he regretted was his own.

Criminologists distinguish between serial killers 5 like Bundy, whose crimes occur one at a time and who try hard to avoid capture, and mass killers like Cho. But the central role of narcissism plainly connects them. Only a narcissist could decide that his alienation should be underlined in the blood of strangers. The flamboyant nature of these crimes is like a neon sign pointing to the truth. Charles Whitman playing God in his Texas clock tower, James Huberty spraying lead in a California restaurant, Harris and Klebold in their theatrical trench coats—they're all stars in the cinema of their self-absorbed minds.

Other examples of narcissistic mass murderers

Freud explained narcissism as a failure to grow up. All infants are narcissists, he pointed out, but as we grow, we ought to learn that other people have lives independent of our own. It's not their job to please us, applaud for us, or even notice us—let alone die because we're unhappy.

Freud said narcissists never grow up. They put their happiness over others' lives.

A generation ago, the social critic Christopher Lasch diagnosed narcissism as the signal disorder of contemporary American culture. The cult of celebrity, the marketing of instant gratification, skepticism toward moral codes, and the politics of victimhood were signs of a society regressing toward the infant stage. You don't have to buy Freud's explanation or Lasch's indictment, however, to see an immediate danger in the way we examine the lives of mass killers. Earnestly and honestly, detectives and journalists dig up apparent clues and weave them into a sort of explanation. In the days after Columbine, for example, Harris and Klebold emerged as alienated misfits in the jock culture of their suburban high school. We learned about their morbid taste in music and their violent video games. Largely missing, though, was the proper frame around the picture: the extreme narcissism that licensed these boys, in their minds, to murder their teachers and classmates.

Investigators have failed to recognize narcissism as the real motivation in mass murder cases.

Major premise applied to Cho

Something similar is now going on with Cho, whose florid writings and videos were an almanac of gripes. "I'm so lonely," he moped to a teacher, failing to mention that he often refused to answer even when people said hello. Of course he was lonely.

In Holocaust studies, there is a school of thought that says to explain is to forgive. I won't go that far. But we must stop explaining killers on their terms.

Outside the context of narcissism, the murderers' actions can seem too logical.

Minus the clear context of narcissism, the biographical details of these men can begin to look like a plausible chain of cause and effect—especially to other narcissists. And they don't need any more encouragement.

There's a telling moment in Michael Moore's 10 film *Bowling for Columbine*, in which singer Marilyn Manson dismisses the idea that listening to his lyrics contributed to the disintegration of Harris and Klebold. What the Columbine killers needed, Manson suggests, was for someone to listen to them. This is the narcissist's view of narcissism: everything would be fine if only he received more atten-

The author reiterates that the killer's problem is not lack of attention but how the killer sees himself.

tion. The real problem can be found in the killer's mirror.

■ Analysis

Von Drehle wrote "It's All about Him" shortly after the 2007 massacre at Virginia Tech. Although we cannot know exactly how he arrived at the thesis, we can reasonably assume he went through something of an inductive process on the way to writing this deductive essay. Perhaps he read and watched enough about Cho, the shooter at Virginia Tech, to start to hypothesize about Cho's motivation. His earlier observations of other mass murderers led him to notice similarities among them. Once he arrived at a theory about what they had in common, he had the major premise for a deductive argument that he could test out on other mass murderers. He was able to construct an argument that could be summarized in syllogistic form:

MAJOR PREMISE: Mass murderers are narcissistic.

MINOR PREMISE: Cho was a mass murderer.

CONCLUSION: Cho was narcissistic.

In his essay he presents his major premise early and then applies it to other U.S. mass murderers: Ted Bundy, Charles Whitman, James Huberty, Eric Harris, and Dylan Klebold.

Remember that there is a difference between a syllogism being valid or logically consistent and its conclusion being true. If von Drehle's major and minor premises are true, the conclusion, of necessity, must be true. That Cho was a mass murderer is an indisputable fact; thus the minor premise is true. But what of the major premise? If you applied the deduction that mass murderers are narcissistic to mass murderers not mentioned by von Drehle, would the conclusion be the same in each case? In other words, is it true that mass murderers are narcissistic?

Because it would be virtually impossible to apply von Drehle's deduction to all mass murderers, he would have built a more convincing case had he restricted his thesis statement with a word like *most* or *many*. That, however, would have invalidated the deductive logic that tells us that a syllogism's conclusion must be true. As it is, the examples he offers are not enough to convince all readers that his theory of narcissism is valid. Still, he offers a unique look at the motivation of mass murderers and one that makes it impossible for anyone else to be blamed for the crimes that these men and boys have committed. Behind his argument are his many years of journalistic experience and his opening revelation that he has been on the scene during the aftermath of many of the crimes to which he refers.

PRACTICE

Reread the Declaration of Independence (p. 33). Explain why it is an example of deductive reasoning.

A NOTE ON THE SYLLOGISM AND THE TOULMIN MODEL

In examining the classical deductive syllogism, you may have noticed the resemblance of its three-part outline to the three-part structure of claim, support, and warrant that we have used throughout the text to illustrate the elements of argument. We mentioned that the syllogism was articulated over two thousand years ago by the Greek philosopher Aristotle. By contrast, the claim-support-warrant structure is based on the model of argument proposed by the modern British philosopher Stephen Toulmin.

Now, there is every reason to think that all models of argument will share some similarities. Nevertheless, the differences between the formal syllogism and the informal Toulmin model suggest that the latter is a more effective instrument for writers who want to know which questions to ask, both before they begin and during the process of developing their arguments.

The syllogism is useful for laying out the basic elements of an argument, as we have seen in several examples. It lends itself more readily to simple arguments. The following syllogism summarizes a familiar argument.

MAJOR PREMISE: Advertising of things harmful to our health should be legally banned.

MINOR PREMISE: Cigarettes are harmful to our health.

CONCLUSION: Therefore, advertising of cigarettes should be legally banned.

Cast in the form of a Toulmin outline, the argument looks like this:

CLAIM: Advertising of cigarettes should be legally banned.

SUPPORT (EVIDENCE):   Cigarettes are harmful to our health.

WARRANT: Advertising of things harmful to our health should be legally banned.

Or in diagram form:

Support
Cigarettes are harmful to our health.

Claim
Advertising of cigarettes should be legally banned.

Warrant
Advertising of things harmful to our health should be legally banned.

In both the syllogism and the Toulmin model the principal elements of the argument are expressed in three statements. You can see that the claim in the Toulmin model is the conclusion in the syllogism—that is, the proposition that you are trying to prove. The evidence (support) in the Toulmin model corresponds to the minor premise in the syllogism. And the warrant in the Toulmin model resembles the major premise of the syllogism.

But the differences are significant. One difference is the use of language. The syllogism represents an argument "in which the validity of the assumption underlying the inference 'leap' is uncontested."[3] That is, the words "major premise" seem to suggest that the assumption has been proved. They do not emphasize that an analysis of the premise—"Advertising of things harmful to our health should be legally banned"—is necessary before we can decide that the conclusion is acceptable. Of course, a

[3] Wayne E. Brockenreide and Douglas Ehninger, "Toulmin on Argument: An Interpretation and Application," *Contemporary Theories of Rhetoric: Selected Readings,* ed. Richard L. Johannesen (New York: Harper and Row, 1971), p. 245. This comparative analysis is indebted to Brockenreide and Ehninger's influential article.

careful arguer will try to establish the truth and validity of all parts of the syllogism, but the terms in which the syllogism is framed do not encourage him or her to examine the real relationship among the three elements. Sometimes the enthymeme (see p. 330), which uses only two elements in the argument and suppresses the third, makes analyzing the relationship even more difficult.

In the Toulmin model, the use of the term *warrant* indicates that the validity of the proposition must be established to *guarantee* the claim or make the crossing from support to claim. It makes clear that the arguer must ask *why* such advertising must be banned.

Nor is the term *minor premise* as useful to the arguer as "support." The word *support* instructs the arguer that he or she must take steps to provide the claim with factual evidence or an appeal to values.

A second difference is that while the syllogism is essentially static, with all three parts logically locked into place, the Toulmin model suggests that an argument is a *movement* from support to claim by way of the warrant, which acts as a bridge. Toulmin introduced the concept of warrant by asking "How do you get there?" (His first two questions, introducing the claim and support, were, "What are you trying to prove?" and "What have you got to go on?")

Lastly, recall that in addition to the three basic elements, the Toulmin model offers supplementary elements of argument. The *qualifier*, in the form of words like "probably" or "more likely," shows that the claim is not absolute. The *backing* offers support for the validity of the warrant. The *reservation* suggests that the validity of the warrant may be limited. These additional elements, which refine and expand the argument itself, reflect the real flexibility and complexity of the argumentative process.

COMMON FALLACIES

In this necessarily brief review it would be impossible to discuss all the fallacies listed by logicians, but we can examine the ones most likely to be found in the arguments you will read and write. Fallacies are difficult to classify, first, because there are literally dozens of systems for classifying, and second, because under any system there is always a good deal of overlap. Our discussion of the reasoning process, however, tells us where faulty reasoning occurs.

Inductive fallacies, as we know, result from the wrong use of evidence: That is, the arguer leaps to a conclusion on the basis of an insufficient sample, ignoring evidence that might have altered his or her conclusion. Deductive fallacies, on the other hand, result from a failure to follow the logic of a series of statements. Here the arguer neglects to make a clear connection between the parts of his or her argument. One of the commonest strategies is the introduction of an irrelevant issue, one that has little or no direct bearing on the development of the claim and serves only to distract the reader.

It's helpful to remember that, even if you cannot name the particular fallacy, you can learn to recognize it and not only refute it in the arguments of others but avoid it in your own as well.

■ 1. Hasty Generalization

In Chapter 7 (see pp. 211–71) we discussed the dangers in drawing conclusions on the basis of insufficient evidence. Many of our prejudices are a result of hasty generalization. A prejudice is literally a judgment made before the facts are in. On the basis of experience with two or three members of an ethnic group, for example, we may form the prejudice that all members of the group share the characteristics that we have attributed to the two or three in our experience.

Superstitions are also based in part on hasty generalization. As a result of a very small number of experiences with black cats, broken mirrors, Friday the thirteenth, or spilled salt, some people will assume a cause-and-effect relation between these signs and misfortunes. *Superstition* has been defined as "a notion maintained despite evidence to the contrary." The evidence would certainly show that, contrary to the superstitious belief, in a lifetime hundreds of such "unlucky" signs are not followed by unfortunate events. To generalize about a connection is therefore unjustified.

■ 2. Faulty Use of Authority

The use of authority—the attempt to bolster claims by citing the opinions of experts—was discussed in Chapter 7. Experts are a valuable source of information on subjects we have no personal experience with or specialized knowledge about. Properly identified, they can provide essential support. The faulty use of authority occurs when individuals are presented as authorities in fields in which they are not. An actor who plays a doctor on television may be hired to advertise the latest sleep medicine but actually has no more expertise with medications than the average consumer. The role that he plays may make him appear to be an authority but does not make him one. No matter how impressive credentials sound, they are largely meaningless unless they establish relevant authority. Both writers and readers need to be especially aware of the testimony of authorities who may disagree with those cited. In circumstances where experts disagree, you are encouraged to undertake a careful evaluation and comparison of credentials.

■ 3. Post Hoc or Doubtful Cause

The entire Latin term for this fallacy is *post hoc, ergo propter hoc*, meaning, "After this, therefore because of this." The arguer infers that because one event follows another event, the first event must be the cause of the second. But proximity of events or conditions does not guarantee a causal relation. The rooster crows every morning at 5:00 and, seeing the sun rise immediately after, decides that his crowing has caused the sun to rise. A month after A-bomb tests are concluded, tornadoes damage the area where the tests were held, and residents decide that the tests caused the tornadoes. After the school principal suspends daily prayers in the classroom, acts of vandalism increase, and some parents are convinced that failure to conduct prayer is responsible for the rise in vandalism. In each of these cases, the fact that one event follows another does not prove a causal connection. The two events may be coincidental, or the first event may be only one, and an insignificant one, of many causes that have produced the second event. The reader or writer of causal arguments must determine whether another more plausible explanation exists and whether several causes have combined to produce the effect. Perhaps the suspension of prayer was only one of a number of related causes: a decline in disciplinary action, a relaxation of academic standards, a change in school administration, and changes in family structure in the school community.

In a previous section we saw that superstitions are the result not only of hasty generalization but also of the willingness to find a cause-and-effect connection in the juxtaposition of two events. A belief in astrological signs also derives from erroneous inferences about cause and effect. Only a very few of the millions of people who consult the astrology charts every day in newspapers and magazines have submitted the predictions to statistical analysis. A curious reader might try this strategy: Save the columns, usually at the beginning or end of the year, in which astrologers and clairvoyants make predictions for events in the coming year, allegedly based on their reading of the stars and other signs. At the end of the year evaluate the percentage of predictions that were fulfilled. The number will be very small. But even if some of the predictions prove true, there may be other less fanciful explanations for their accuracy.

In defending simple explanations against complex ones, philosophers and scientists often refer to a maxim called *Occam's razor*, a principle formulated by the medieval philosopher and theologian William of Occam. A modern science writer says this principle "urges a preference for the simplest hypothesis that does all we want it to do."[4] Bertrand Russell, the twentieth-century British philosopher, explained it this way:

> It is vain to do with more what can be done with fewer. That is to say, if everything in some science can be interpreted without assuming this or that hypothetical entity, there is no ground for assuming it. I have myself found this a most fruitful principle in logical analysis.[5]

In other words, choose the simpler, more credible explanation wherever possible.

---

[4]Martin Gardner, *The Whys of a Philosophical Scrivener* (New York: Quill, 1983), p. 174.
[5]*Dictionary of Mind, Matter and Morals* (New York: Philosophical Library, 1952), p. 166.

We all share the belief that scientific experimentation and research can answer questions about a wide range of natural and social phenomena: evolutionary development, hurricanes, disease, crime, poverty. It is true that repeated experiments in controlled situations can establish what seem to be solid relations suggesting cause and effect. But even scientists prefer to talk not about cause but about an extremely high probability that under controlled conditions one event will follow another.

In the social sciences cause-and-effect relations are especially susceptible to challenge. Human experiences can seldom be subjected to laboratory conditions. In addition, the complexity of the social environment makes it difficult, even impossible, to extract one cause from among the many that influence human behavior.

■ 4. False Analogy

Many analogies are merely descriptive and offer no proof of the connection between the two things being compared. In recent years a debate has emerged between weight-loss professionals about the wisdom of urging overweight people to lose weight for health reasons. Susan Wooley, director of the eating disorders clinic at the University of Cincinnati and a professor of psychiatry, offered the following analogy in defense of her view that dieting is dangerous.

> We know that overweight people have a higher mortality rate than thin people. We also know that black people have a higher mortality rate than white people. Do we subject black people to torturous treatments to bleach their skin? Of course not. We have enough sense to know skin-bleaching will not eliminate sickle-cell anemia. So why do we have blind faith that weight loss will cure the diseases associated with obesity?"[6]

But it is clear that the false analogy between black skin and excessive weight does not work. Bleaching one's skin does not eliminate sickle-cell anemia, but there is an abundance of proof that excess weight influences mortality.

Historians are fond of using analogical arguments to demonstrate that particular circumstances prevailing in the past are being reproduced in the present. They therefore feel safe in predicting that the present course of history will follow that of the past. British historian Arnold Toynbee argues by analogy that humans' tenure on earth may be limited.

> On the evidence of the past history of life on this planet, even the extinction of the human race is not entirely unlikely. After all, the reign of man on the Earth, if we are right in thinking that man established his present ascendancy in the middle paleolithic age, is so far only about 100,000 years old, and what is that compared to the 500 million or 900 million years during which life has been in existence on the sur-

[6]*New York Times,* April 12, 1992, sec. C, p. 43.

face of this planet? In the past, other forms of life have enjoyed reigns which have lasted for almost inconceivably longer periods—and which yet at last have come to an end.[7]

Toynbee finds similarities between the limited reigns of other animal species and the possible disappearance of the human race. For this analogy, however, we need to ask whether the conditions of the past, so far as we know them, at all resemble the conditions under which human existence on earth might be terminated. Is the fact that human beings are also members of the animal kingdom sufficient support for this comparison?

■ 5. Ad Hominem

The Latin term *ad hominem* means "against the man" and refers to an attack on the person rather than on the argument or the issue. The assumption in such a fallacy is that if the speaker proves to be unacceptable in some way, his or her statements must also be judged unacceptable. Attacking the author of the statement is a strategy of diversion that prevents the reader from giving attention where it is due—to the issue under discussion.

You might hear someone complain, "What can the priest tell us about marriage? He's never been married himself." This ad hominem accusation ignores the validity of the advice the priest might offer. In the same way an overweight patient might reject the advice on diet by an overweight physician. In politics it is not uncommon for antagonists to attack each other for personal characteristics that may not be relevant to the tasks they will be elected to perform. They may be accused of infidelity to their partners, homosexuality, atheism, or a flamboyant social life. Even if certain accusations should be proved true, voters should not ignore the substance of what politicians do and say in their public offices.

This confusion of private life with professional record also exists in literature and the other arts. According to their biographers, the American writers Thomas Wolfe, Robert Frost, and William Saroyan—to name only a few—and numbers of film stars, including Charlie Chaplin, Joan Crawford, and Bing Crosby, made life miserable for those closest to them. Having read about their unpleasant personal characteristics, some people find it hard to separate the artist from his or her creation, although the personality and character of the artist are often irrelevant to the content of the work.

Ad hominem accusations against the person do *not* constitute a fallacy if the characteristics under attack are relevant to the argument. If the politician is irresponsible and dishonest in the conduct of his or her personal life, we may be justified in thinking that the person will also behave irresponsibly and dishonestly in public office.

---

[7] *Civilization on Trial* (New York: Oxford University Press, 1948), pp. 162–63.

■ 6. False Dilemma

As the name tells us, the false dilemma, sometimes called the *black-white fallacy,* poses an either-or situation. The arguer suggests that only two alternatives exist, although there may be other explanations of or solutions to the problem under discussion. The false dilemma reflects the simplification of a complex problem. Sometimes it is offered out of ignorance or laziness, sometimes to divert attention from the real explanation or solution that the arguer rejects for doubtful reasons.

You may encounter the either-or situation in dilemmas about personal choices. "At the University of Georgia," says one writer, "the measure of a man was football. You either played it or worshiped those who did, and there was no middle ground."[8] Clearly this dilemma—playing football or worshiping those who do—ignores other measures of manhood.

Politics and government offer a wealth of examples. In an interview with the *New York Times* in 1975, the Shah of Iran was asked why he could not introduce into his authoritarian regime greater freedom for his subjects. His reply was, "What's wrong with authority? Is anarchy better?" Apparently he considered that only two paths were open to him—authoritarianism or anarchy. Of course, democracy was also an option, which, perhaps fatally, he declined to consider.

■ 7. Slippery Slope

If an arguer predicts that taking a first step will lead inevitably to a second, usually undesirable step, he or she must provide evidence that this will happen. Otherwise, the arguer is guilty of a slippery slope fallacy.

Asked by an inquiring photographer on the street how he felt about censorship of a pornographic magazine, a man replied, "I don't think any publication should be banned. It's a slippery slope when you start making decisions on what people should be permitted to read. . . . It's a dangerous precedent." Perhaps. But if questioned further, the man should have offered evidence that a ban on some things leads inevitably to a ban on everything.

Predictions based on the danger inherent in taking the first step are commonplace:

> Legalization of abortion will lead to murder of the old and the physically and mentally handicapped.
>
> The Connecticut law allowing sixteen-year-olds and their parents to divorce each other will mean the death of the family.
>
> If we ban handguns, we will end up banning rifles and other hunting weapons.

[8]Phil Gailey, "A Nonsports Fan," *New York Times Magazine,* December 18, 1983, sec. 6, p. 96.

Distinguishing between probable and improbable predictions—that is, recognizing the slippery-slope fallacy—poses special problems because only future developments can verify or refute predictions. For example, in 1941 the imposition of military conscription aroused some opponents to predict that the draft was a precursor of fascism in this country. Only after the war, when 10 million draftees were demobilized, did it become clear that the draft had been an insufficient sign for a prediction of fascism. In this case the slippery-slope prediction of fascism might have been avoided if closer attention had been paid to other influences pointing to the strength of democracy.

More recently, the debate about cloning has raised fears of creation of genetic copies of adults. The *New York Times* reported that

> Many lawmakers today warned that if therapeutic cloning went forward, scientists would step onto a slippery slope that would inevitably lead to cloning people.[9]

Most scientists, however, reject this possibility for the foreseeable future.

Slippery slope predictions are simplistic. They ignore not only the dissimilarities between first and last steps but also the complexity of the developments in any long chain of events.

■ 8. Begging the Question

If the writer makes a statement that assumes that the very question being argued has already been proved, the writer is guilty of begging the question. In a letter to the editor of a college newspaper protesting the failure of the majority of students to meet the writing requirement because they had failed an exemption test, the writer said, "Not exempting all students who honestly qualify for exemption is an insult." But whether the students are honestly qualified is precisely the question that the exemption test was supposed to resolve. The writer has not proved that the students who failed the writing test were qualified for exemption. She has only made an assertion *as if* she had already proved it.

Circular reasoning is an extreme example of begging the question: "Women should not be permitted to join men's clubs because the clubs are for men only." The question to be resolved first, of course, is whether clubs for men only should continue to exist.

■ 9. Straw Man

The straw-man fallacy consists of an attack on a view similar to but not the same as the one your opponent holds. It is a familiar diversionary tactic. The name probably derives from an old game in which a straw man was

[9] August 1, 2001, sec. A, p. 11.

set up to divert attention from the real target that a contestant was supposed to knock down.

One of the outstanding examples of the straw-man fallacy occurred in the famous Checkers speech of Senator Richard Nixon. In 1952 during his vice-presidential campaign, Nixon was accused of having appropriated $18,000 in campaign funds for his personal use. At one point in the radio and television speech in which he defended his reputation, he said:

> One other thing I probably should tell you, because if I don't they will probably be saying this about me, too. We did get something, a gift, after the election.
>
> A man down in Texas heard Pat on the radio mention the fact that our two youngsters would like to have a dog, and, believe it or not, the day before we left on this campaign trip we got a message from Union Station in Baltimore saying they had a package for us. We went down to get it. You know what it was?
>
> It was a little cocker spaniel dog, in a crate that he had sent all the way from Texas, black and white, spotted, and our little girl, Tricia, the six-year-old, named it Checkers.
>
> And, you know, the kids, like all kids, loved the dog, and I just want to say this, right now, that regardless of what they say about it, we are going to keep it.[10]

Of course, Nixon knew that the issue was the alleged misappropriation of funds, not the ownership of the dog, which no one had asked him to return.

■ 10. Two Wrongs Make a Right

The two-wrongs-make-a-right fallacy is another example of the way in which attention may be diverted from the question at issue.

After President Jimmy Carter in March 1977 attacked the human rights record of the Soviet Union, Russian officials responded:

> As for the present state of human rights in the United States, it is characterized by the following facts: millions of unemployed, racial discrimination, social inequality of women, infringement of citizens' personal freedom, the growth of crime, and so on.[11]

The Russians made no attempt to deny the failure of *their* human rights record; instead they attacked by pointing out that the Americans are not blameless either.

---

[10] Radio and television address of Senator Nixon from Los Angeles on September 23, 1952.

[11] *New York Times,* March 3, 1977, p. 1.

■ 11. Non Sequitur

The Latin term *non sequitur,* which means "it does not follow," is another fallacy of irrelevance. An advertisement for a book, *Worlds in Collision,* whose theories about the origin of the earth and evolutionary development have been challenged by almost all reputable scientists, states:

> Once rejected as "preposterous"! Critics called it an outrage! It aroused incredible antagonism in scientific and literary circles. Yet half a million copies were sold and for twenty-seven years it remained an outstanding bestseller.

We know, of course, that the popularity of a book does not bestow scientific respectability. The number of sales, therefore, is irrelevant to proof of the book's theoretical soundness—a non sequitur.

Other examples sometimes appear in the comments of political candidates. Donald Trump, the wealthy real-estate developer, in considering a run for president of the United States in 2000, told an interviewer:

> My entire life, I've watched politicians bragging about how poor they are, how they came from nothing, how poor their parents and grandparents were. And I said to myself, if they can stay so poor for so many generations, maybe this isn't the kind of person we want to be electing to higher office. How smart can they be? They're morons. . . . Do you want someone who gets to be president and that's literally the highest paying job he's ever had?[12]

As a brief glance at U.S. history shows, it does not follow that men of small success in the world of commerce are unfit to make sound decisions about matters of state.

■ 12. Ad Populum

Arguers guilty of the *ad populum* fallacy make an appeal to the prejudices of the people (*populum* in Latin). They assume that their claim can be adequately defended without further support if they emphasize a belief or attitude that the audience shares with them. One common form of ad populum is an appeal to patriotism, which may allow arguers to omit evidence that the audience needs for proper evaluation of the claim. In the following advertisement the makers of Zippo lighters made such an appeal in urging readers to buy their product.

> It's a grand old lighter. Zippo—the grand old lighter that's made right here in the good old U.S.A.
> We truly make an all-American product. The raw materials used in making a Zippo lighter are all right from this great land of ours.
> Zippo windproof lighters are proud to be Americans.

[12] *New York Times,* November 28, 1999, p. 11.

■ 13. Appeal to Tradition

In making an appeal to tradition, the arguer assumes that what has existed for a long time and has therefore become a tradition should continue to exist *because* it is a tradition. If the arguer avoids telling his or her reader *why* the tradition should be preserved, he or she may be accused of failing to meet the real issue.

The following statement appeared in a letter defending the membership policy of the Century Club, an all-male club established in New York City in 1847 that was under pressure to admit women. The writer was a Presbyterian minister who opposed the admission of women.

> I am totally opposed to a proposal which would radically change the nature of the Century. . . . A club creates an ethos of its own over the years, and I would deeply deplore a step that would inevitably create an entirely different kind of place.
>
> A club like the Century should surely be unaffected by fashionable whims. . . .[13]

■ 14. Faulty Emotional Appeals

In some discussions of fallacies, appeals to the emotions of the audience are treated as illegitimate or "counterfeit proofs." All such appeals, however, are *not* illegitimate. As we saw in Chapter 7 on support, appeals to the values and emotions of an audience are an appropriate form of persuasion. You can recognize fallacious emotional appeals if (1) they are irrelevant to the argument or draw attention from the issues being argued or (2) they appear to conceal another purpose. Here we treat two of the most popular appeals — to pity and to fear.

Appeals to pity, compassion, and natural willingness to help the unfortunate are particularly hard to resist. The requests for aid by most charitable organizations — for hungry children, victims of disaster, stray animals — offer examples of legitimate appeals. But these appeals to our sympathetic feelings should not divert us from considering other issues in a particular case. It would be wrong, for example, to allow a multiple murderer to escape punishment because he or she had experienced a wretched childhood. Likewise, if you are asked to contribute to a charitable cause, you should try to learn how many unfortunate people or animals are being helped and what percentage of the contribution will be allocated to maintaining the organization and its officers. In some cases the financial records are closed to public review, and only a small share of the contribution will reach the alleged beneficiaries.

Appeals to fear are likely to be even more effective. But they must be based on evidence that fear is an appropriate response to the issues and that

---

[13]David H. C. Read, letter to the *New York Times*, January 13, 1983, p. 14.

it can move an audience toward a solution to the problem. (Fear can also have the adverse effect of preventing people from taking a necessary action.) Insurance companies, for example, make appeals to our fears of destitution for ourselves and our families as a result of injury, unemployment, sickness, and death. These appeals are justified if the possibilities of such destitution are real and if the insurance will provide relief. It would also be legitimate to arouse fear of the consequences of drunk driving, provided, again, that the descriptions were accurate. On the other hand, it would be wrong to induce fear that fluoridation of public water supplies causes cancer without presenting sound evidence of the probability.

An emotional response by itself is not always the soundest basis for making decisions. Your own experience has probably taught you that in the grip of a strong emotion like love or hate or anger you often overlook good reasons for making different and better choices. Like you, your readers want to be given the opportunity to consider all the available kinds of support for an argument.

PRACTICE

Decide whether the reasoning in the following examples is faulty. Explain your answers.

1. The presiding judge of a revolutionary tribunal, being asked why people are being executed without trial, replies, "Why should we put them on trial when we know that they're guilty?"

Writer's Guide: Avoiding Logical Fallacies

1. If you are making use of induction, that is, drawing a conclusion based on a number of individual examples, do you have enough examples with variety to justify the conclusion? In other words, will your readers be able to make the inductive leap from examples to the conclusion you are asking them to make?

2. If you are making use of deduction, is your conclusion a logical one based on the premises underlying it? To be sure, write out your argument in the form of a syllogism. Also avoid wording your thesis in absolute terms like *all, every, everyone, everybody,* and *always.*

3. It is relatively easy—and sometimes humorous—to notice other writers' logical fallacies. It is harder to notice your own. Use the list of fallacies in this chapter as a checklist as you read the draft of each of your essays with a critical eye, looking for any breakdown in logic. It may be useful to read your essay aloud to someone because if that listener cannot follow your logic, you may need to clarify your points.

2. The government has the right to require the wearing of helmets while operating or riding on a motorcycle because of the high rate of head injuries incurred in motorcycle accidents.

3. Children who watch game shows rather than situation comedies receive higher grades in school. So it must be true that game shows are more educational than situation comedies.

4. The meteorologist predicted the wrong amount of rain for May. Obviously the meteorologist is unreliable.

5. Women ought to be permitted to serve in combat. Why should men be the only ones to face death and danger?

6. If Cher uses Equal, it must taste better than Sweet 'n Low.

7. People will gamble anyway, so why not legalize gambling in this state?

8. Because so much money was spent on public education in the last decade while educational achievement declined, more money to improve education can't be the answer to reversing the decline.

9. He's a columnist for a campus newspaper, so he must be a pretty good writer.

10. We tend to exaggerate the need for Standard English. You don't need much Standard English for most jobs in this country.

11. It's discriminatory to mandate that police officers must conform to a certain height and weight.

12. A doctor can consult books to make a diagnosis, so a medical student should be able to consult books when being tested.

13. Because this soft drink contains so many chemicals, it must be unsafe.

14. Core requirements should be eliminated. After all, students are paying for their education, so they should be able to earn a diploma by choosing the courses they want.

15. We should encourage a return to arranged marriages in this country since marriages based on romantic love haven't been very successful.

16. I know three redheads who have terrible tempers, and since Annabel has red hair, I'll bet she has a terrible temper, too.

17. Supreme Court Justice Byron White was an all-American football player while in college, so how can you say that athletes are dumb?

18. Benjamin H. Sasway, a student at Humboldt State University in California, was indicted for failure to register for possible conscription. Barry Lynn, president of Draft Action, an antidraft group, said, "It is disgraceful that this administration is embarking on an effort to fill the prisons with men of conscience and moral commitment."

19. James A. Harris, former president of the National Education Association: "Twenty-three percent of schoolchildren are failing to graduate and another large segment graduates as functional illiterates. If 23 percent of anything else failed—23 percent of automobiles didn't run, 23 percent of the buildings fell down, 23 percent of stuffed ham spoiled—we'd look at the producer."

20. A professor at Rutgers University: "The arrest rate for women is rising three times as fast as that of men. Women, inflamed by the doctrines of feminism, are pursuing criminal careers with the same zeal as business and the professions."

21. Physical education should be required because physical activity is healthful.

22. George Meany, former president of the AFL-CIO, in 1968: "To these people who constantly say you have got to listen to these younger people, they have got something to say, I just don't buy that at all. They smoke more pot than we do and if the younger generation are the hundred thousand kids that lay around a field up in Woodstock, New York, I am not going to trust the destiny of the country to that group."

23. That candidate was poor as a child, so he will certainly be sympathetic to the poor if he's elected.

24. When the federal government sent troops into Little Rock, Arkansas, to enforce integration of the public school system, the governor of Arkansas attacked the action, saying that it was as brutal an act of intervention as Russia's sending troops into Hungary to squelch the Hungarians' rebellion. In both cases, the governor said, the rights of a freedom-loving, independent people were being violated.

25. Governor Jones was elected two years ago. Since that time constant examples of corruption and subversion have been unearthed. It is time to get rid of the man responsible for this kind of corrupt government.

26. Are we going to vote a pay increase for our teachers, or are we going to allow our schools to deteriorate into substandard custodial institutions?

27. You see, the priests were right. After we threw those virgins into the volcano, it quit erupting.

28. The people of Rome lost their vitality and desire for freedom when their emperors decided that the way to keep them happy was to provide them with bread and circuses. What can we expect of our own country now that the government gives people free food and there is a constant round of entertainment provided by television?

29. From Mark Clifton, "The Dread Tomato Affliction" (proving that eating tomatoes is dangerous and even deadly): "Ninety-two point four percent of juvenile delinquents have eaten tomatoes. Fifty-seven point one percent of the adult criminals in penitentiaries throughout the United States have eaten tomatoes. Eighty-four percent of all people killed in automobile accidents during the year have eaten tomatoes."

30. From Galileo, *Dialogues Concerning Two New Sciences*: "But can you doubt that air has weight when you have the clear testimony of Aristotle affirming that all elements have weight, including air, and excepting only fire?"

31. Robert Brustein, artistic director of the American Repertory Theatre, commenting on a threat by Congress in 1989 to withhold funding from an offensive art show: "Once we allow lawmakers to become art critics, we take the first step into the world of Ayatollah Khomeini, whose murderous review of *The Satanic Verses* still chills the heart of everyone committed to

free expression." (The Ayatollah Khomeini called for the death of the author, Salman Rushdie, because Rushdie had allegedly committed blasphemy against Islam in his novel.)

Show Biz Encourages Looser Teen Sex Habits

SHERYL McCARTHY

As the high school prom season winds down, we are learning more than we ever wanted to know about the social and sexual mores of today's teenagers.

Such as how they're avoiding "dating," opting instead to attend the prom with groups of friends. Everybody has a blast without suffering the angst of waiting for some guy to ask you to be his date, or worrying that the girl you ask will reject you.

This seems a lot healthier than it was when I went to my high school prom. I was lucky enough to have a great date and a wonderful prom night. But I've heard countless women complain thirty years later about missing their prom because nobody invited them. Going as a group takes the power to decide who gets to go out of the boys' hands, and takes the pressure of having to find a date off everybody.

Some of the other recent trends aren't so hot. A newspaper reporter who attended several local proms this year was shocked by the highly sexualized dancing that went on. When I was in school, the occasional guy put you in a back-breaking full-body lock that lasted the duration of a song. But now, virtually all the males and females engage in "freaking" and "backing up"—which amounts to simulating sex on the dance floor.

And there's the growing phenomenon of "hooking up." Having steady   5
boyfriends or girlfriends has been replaced by kids who travel in packs, breaking away to have casual sexual encounters with friends or mere acquaintances. These encounters range from kissing to petting, masturbating each other to oral sex—all without emotional strings. And they say they like it that way.

I find this retreat from intimacy rather depressing. My classmates weren't into sex, by and large. But there was something nice about the boyfriend-

Sheryl McCarthy is on the faculty of the Graduate School of Journalism of Columbia University. She has been a reporter for the *Boston Globe*, the *Baltimore Evening Sun*, and the New York *Daily News* and a national correspondent for ABC News. She is now a columnist for *Newsday*, where this article appeared on June 24, 2004.

girlfriend thing. In endless phone calls or Sunday night sofa-sitting, we achieved a certain emotional intimacy, along with our sexual gropings. The guys may have been thinking mostly about sex, but there was at least an idealized notion of what it meant to be a couple.

The current teenage social scene strikes me as rather aimless. Those who work with teenagers attribute the surge in dirty dancing to the music videos in which young musical stars like Britney Spears, Christina Aguilera, and Beyonce Knowles provocatively shake their scantily-clad booties, and legions of gorgeous females swarming over ordinary-looking men seem to define what relations between males and females are supposed to be.

Tamar Rothenberg, editor of *New Youth Connections*, a newspaper put out by New York City high school students, says she worries about the message the videos give to teenagers trying to figure out what they're supposed to be doing in relationships.

"Hooking up" apparently results from teenagers wanting to avoid being tied down in relationships that can cause pain and disappointment. Teenage girls may also be rebelling against the old sexual double standard and wanting to have the same freedom as boys. But the girls are often on the giving end of the casual sex, and teens often don't realize that they can catch diseases from oral sex.

The moguls of MTV and BET and the video producers and the titans of 10 hip-hop deserve a lot of the blame for this, and deserve to be booed off any stage where they are hypocritical enough to lament the high rate of teen pregnancy and the social fallout from irresponsible male sexual behavior.

But so do the spineless politicians and educators and the squeamish parents who are far more obsessed with keeping teenagers chaste than with helping them to have responsible relationships.

That's why I applaud groups like Planned Parenthood and *New Youth Connections* that treat teenagers like the semi-adults they are, and try to be helpful instead of self-righteous.

"I'm cool with kids having sex if they're being careful," says Rothenberg. "But they have to understand the possible emotional consequences and the health consequences."

Yeah, it was nice having prom dates who made no sexual demands, and having boyfriends instead of sexual hookups. But times have changed, and, to be helpful to teens living in a more sexualized world, the adults have to change too.

READING AND DISCUSSION QUESTIONS

1. Did McCarthy choose to use an inductive or a deductive approach to her subject?
2. Do you find the conclusions that McCarthy has drawn about today's teens convincing? Are they discredited by your own observations of teens?
3. Do you believe that there are any logical fallacies in McCarthy's argument? If so, what type of fallacies are they?

WRITING SUGGESTIONS

4. Examine how teen dating and/or sex habits are characterized on at least one current television show.

5. How do you respond to McCarthy's indictment of teens' sexual mores?

Food for Thought (and for Credit)

JENNIFER GROSSMAN

Want to combat the epidemic of obesity? Bring back home economics. Before you choke on your 300-calorie, trans-fat-laden Krispy Kreme, consider: Teaching basic nutrition and food preparation is a far less radical remedy than gastric bypass surgery or fast-food lawsuits. And probably far more effective. Obesity tends to invite such drastic solutions because it is so frustratingly difficult to treat. This intractability, coupled with the sad fact that obese children commonly grow up to be obese adults, argues for a preventative approach. As the new school year begins, we need to equip kids with the skills and practical knowledge to take control of their dietary destinies.

Despite its bad rep as Wife Ed 101, home economics has progressive roots. At the turn of the century it "helped transform domesticity into a vehicle to expand women's political power," according to Sarah Stage in *Rethinking Home Economics: Women and the History of a Profession.* In time, focus shifted from social reform to the practical priorities of sanitation and electrification, and then again to an emphasis on homemaking after World War II — giving ammunition to later critics like Betty Friedan who charged home ec with having helped foster the "feminine mystique."

Banished by feminists, Becky Home-ecky was left to wander backwater school districts. For a while it seemed that mandating male participation might salvage the discipline while satisfying political correctness. By the late 1970s one-third of male high school graduates had some home-ec training, whereas they comprised a mere 3.5 percent of home-ec students in 1962. Since then, "home economics has moved from the mainstream to the margins of American high school," according to the United States De-

Jennifer Grossman is director of the Dole Nutrition Institute, which distributes health information to the public through lectures and publications. Formerly, she was director of Education Policy at the Cato Institute and a speechwriter for President George H. W. Bush. She appears frequently as a commentator on shows such as *Larry King Live,* the *O'Reilly Factor,* the *Today Show,* and *Politically Incorrect.* She has written editorials for the *New York Times,* where this column appeared on September 2, 2003; the *Wall Street Journal;* the *Los Angeles Times;* the *New York Post;* the *Weekly Standard;* the *National Review;* and the *Women's Quarterly.*

partment of Education, with even female participation—near universal in the 1950s—plummeting by 67 percent.

What has happened since? Ronald McDonald and Colonel Sanders stepped in as the new mascots of American food culture, while the number of meals consumed outside the home has doubled—from a quarter in 1970 to nearly half today. As a result, market economics has increasingly determined ingredients, nutrient content, and portion size. Agricultural surpluses and technological breakthroughs supplied the cheap sweeteners and hydrogenated oils necessary for food to survive indefinitely on store shelves or under fast-food heat lamps.

Unsurprisingly, the caloric density of such foods soared relative to those   5 consumed at home. Good value no longer meant taste, presentation, and proper nutrition—but merely more-for-less. Thus, the serving of McDonald's French fries that contained 200 calories in 1960 contains 610 today. The lure of large was not limited to fast-food, inflating everything from snack foods to cereal boxes.

But the hunger for home economics didn't die with its academic exile. Martha Stewart made millions filling the void, vexing home-ec haters like Erica Jong for having "earned her freedom by glorifying the slavery of home." Home and Garden TV, the Food Network, and countless publications thrive on topics once taught by home ec.

All of which begs the question: If the free market has done such a good job of picking up the slack, why bring home ec back? Because much of the D.I.Y. (do-it-yourself) culture is divorced from the exigencies of everyday life. It's more like home rec: catering to pampered chefs with maids to clean up the kitchen.

The new home economics should be both pragmatic and egalitarian. Traditional topics—food and nutrition, family studies, home management—should be retooled for the twenty-first century. Children should be able to decipher headlines about the dangers of dioxin or the benefits of antioxidants. Subjects like home finance might include domestic problem-solving: How would you spend $100 to feed a family of four, including a diabetic, a nursing mother, and infant, for one week?

While this kind of training might most benefit those low-income minority children at highest risk of obesity, all children will be better equipped to make smart choices in the face of the more than $33 billion that food companies spend annually to promote their products. And consumer education is just part of the larger purpose: to teach kids to think, make, fix, and generally fend for themselves.

Some detractors will doubtless smell a plot to turn women back into   10 stitching, stirring Stepford Wives. Others will argue that schools should focus on the basics. But what could be more basic than life, food, home and hearth? A generation has grown up since we swept home ec into the dust heap of history and hung up our brooms. It's time to reevaluate the domestic discipline, and recapture lost skills.

READING AND DISCUSSION QUESTIONS

1. How would the students at the high school you attended have responded to a course such as the one Grossman describes?

2. Do you think that offering such a course would be a good idea? Why, or why not?

3. How convincing is Grossman's argument that there is a need for consumer education? How convincing is her argument that it should be offered in school?

4. Do you find any logical fallacies in her argument? If so, what type of fallacies are they?

WRITING SUGGESTIONS

5. Write a claim of policy essay arguing that the sort of course Grossman describes should be required of high school students.

6. Write an essay refuting what Grossman suggests.

7. Write an essay in which you argue that the majority of teenagers are responsible consumers or that they are not.

A Modest Proposal

JONATHAN SWIFT

It is a melancholy object to those who walk through this great town[1] or travel in the country, when they see the streets, the roads, and cabin doors, crowded with beggars of the female sex, followed by three, four, or six children, all in rags and importuning every passenger for an alms. These mothers, instead of being able to work for their honest livelihood, are forced to employ all their time in strolling to beg sustenance for their helpless infants, who, as they grow up, either turn thieves for want of work, or leave their

---

[1] Dublin. — EDS. [All notes are the editors'.]

This essay is acknowledged by almost all critics to be the most powerful example of irony in the English language. (*Irony* means saying one thing but meaning another.) In 1729 Jonathan Swift (1667–1745), prolific satirist and dean of St. Patrick's Cathedral in Dublin, was moved to write in protest against the terrible poverty in which the Irish were living under British rule. Notice that the essay is organized according to one of the patterns outlined in Part Two of this book (see Presenting the Stock Issues, Chapter 12, p. 481). First, Swift establishes the need for a change, then he offers his proposal, and finally, he lists its advantages.

dear native country to fight for the Pretender in Spain, or sell themselves to the Barbados.[2]

I think it is agreed by all parties that this prodigious number of children in the arms, or on the backs, or at the heels of their mothers, and frequently of their fathers, is in the present deplorable state of the kingdom a very great additional grievance; and therefore whoever could find out a fair, cheap, and easy method of making these children sound, useful members of the commonwealth would deserve so well of the public as to have his statue set up for a preserver of the nation.

But my intention is very far from being confined to provide only for the children of professed beggars; it is of a much greater extent, and shall take in the whole number of infants at a certain age who are born of parents in effect as little able to support them as those who demand our charity in the streets.

As to my own part, having turned my thoughts for many years upon this important subject, and maturely weighed the several schemes of other projectors,[3] I have always found them grossly mistaken in their computation. It is true, a child just dropped from its dam may be supported by her milk for a solar year, with little other nourishment; at most not above the value of two shillings, which the mother may certainly get, or the value in scraps, by her lawful occupation of begging; and it is exactly at one year that I propose to provide for them in such a manner as instead of being a charge upon their parents or the parish, or wanting food and raiment for the rest of their lives, they shall on the contrary contribute to the feeding, and partly to the clothing, of many thousands.

There is likewise another great advantage in my scheme, that it will 5 prevent those voluntary abortions, and that horrid practice of women murdering their bastard children, alas, too frequent among us, sacrificing the poor innocent babes, I doubt, more to avoid the expense than the shame, which would move tears and pity in the most savage and inhuman breast.

The number of souls in this kingdom being usually reckoned one million and a half, of these I calculate there may be about two hundred thousand couples whose wives are breeders; from which number I subtract thirty thousand couples who are able to maintain their own children, although I apprehend there cannot be so many under the present distress of the kingdom; but this being granted, there will remain an hundred and seventy thousand breeders. I again subtract fifty thousand for those women who miscarry, or whose children die by accident or disease within the year. There

---

[2] The Pretender was James Stuart, who was exiled to Spain. Many Irish men had joined an army attempting to return him to the English throne in 1715. Others had become indentured servants, agreeing to work for a set number of years in Barbados or other British colonies in exchange for their transportation out of Ireland.
   [3] Planners.

only remain an hundred and twenty thousand children of poor parents annually born. The question therefore is, how this number shall be reared and provided for, which, as I have already said, under the present situation of affairs, is utterly impossible by all the methods hitherto proposed. For we can neither employ them in handicraft or agriculture; we neither build houses (I mean in the country) nor cultivate land. They can very seldom pick up a livelihood by stealing till they arrive at six years old, except where they are of towardly parts;[4] although I confess they learn the rudiments much earlier, during which time they can however be looked upon only as probationers, as I have been informed by a principal gentleman in the county of Cavan, who protested to me that he never knew above one or two instances under the age of six, even in a part of the kingdom so renowned for the quickest proficiency in that art.

I am assured by our merchants that a boy or a girl before twelve years old is no salable commodity; and even when they come to this age they will not yield above three pounds, or three pounds and a half a crown at most on the Exchange; which cannot turn to account either to the parents or the kingdom, the charge of nutriment and rags having been at least four times that value.

I shall now therefore humbly propose my own thoughts, which I hope will not be liable to the least objection.

I have been assured by a very knowing American of my acquaintance in London, that a young healthy child well nursed is at a year old a most delicious, nourishing, and wholesome food, whether stewed, roasted, baked, or boiled; and I make no doubt that it will equally serve in a fricassee or a ragout.[5]

I do therefore humbly offer it to public consideration that of the hundred and twenty thousand children, already computed, twenty thousand may be reserved for breed, whereof only one fourth part to be males, which is more than we allow to sheep, black cattle, or swine; and my reason is that these children are seldom the fruits of marriage, a circumstance not much regarded by our savages, therefore one male will be sufficient to serve four females. That the remaining hundred thousand may at a year old be offered in sale to the persons of quality and fortune through the kingdom, always advising the mother to let them suck plentifully in the last month, so as to render them plump and fat for a good table. A child will make two dishes at an entertainment for friends; and when the family dines alone, the fore or hind quarter will make a reasonable dish, and seasoned with a little pepper or salt will be very good boiled on the fourth day, especially in winter.

I have reckoned upon a medium that a child just born will weigh twelve pounds, and in a solar year if tolerably nursed increaseth to twenty-eight pounds.

---

[4] Innate talents.
[5] Stew.

I grant this food will be somewhat dear, and therefore very proper for landlords, who, as they have already devoured most of the parents, seem to have the best title to the children.

Infant's flesh will be in season throughout the year, but more plentiful in March, and a little before and after. For we are told by a grave author, an eminent French physician,[6] that fish being a prolific diet, there are more children born in Roman Catholic countries about nine months after Lent than at any other season; therefore, reckoning a year after Lent, the markets will be more glutted than usual, because the number of popish infants is at least three to one in this kingdom; and therefore it will have one other collateral advantage, by lessening the number of Papists among us.

I have already computed the charge of nursing a beggar's child (in which list I reckon all cottagers, laborers, and four-fifths of the farmers) to be about two shillings per annum, rags included; and I believe no gentleman would repine to give ten shillings for the carcass of a good fat child, which, as I have said, will make four dishes of excellent nutritive meat, when he hath only some particular friend or his own family to dine with him. Thus the squire will learn to be a good landlord, and grow popular among the tenants; the mother will have eight shillings net profit, and be fit for work till she produces another child.

Those who are more thrifty (as I must confess the times require) may 15 flay the carcass; the skin of which artificially[7] dressed will make admirable gloves for ladies, and summer boots for fine gentlemen.

As to our city of Dublin, shambles[8] may be appointed for this purpose in the most convenient parts of it, and butchers we may be assured will not be wanting; although I rather recommend buying the children alive, and dressing them hot from the knife as we do roasting pigs.

A very worthy person, a true lover of his country, and whose virtues I highly esteem, was lately pleased in discoursing on this matter to offer a refinement upon my scheme. He said that many gentlemen of his kingdom, having of late destroyed their deer, he conceived that the want of venison might be well supplied by the bodies of young lads and maidens, not exceeding fourteen years of age nor under twelve, so great a number of both sexes in every county being now ready to starve for want of work and service; and these to be disposed of by their parents, if alive, or otherwise by their nearest relations. But with due deference to so excellent a friend and so deserving a patriot, I cannot be altogether in his sentiments; for as to the males, my American acquaintance assured me from frequent experience that their flesh was generally tough and lean, like that of our schoolboys, by continual exercise, and their taste disagreeable; and to fatten them would

---

[6] A reference to Swift's favorite French writer, François Rabelais (1494?–1553), who was actually a broad satirist known for his coarse humor.

[7] With art or craft.

[8] Butcher shops or slaughterhouses.

not answer the charge. Then as to the females, it would, I think with humble submission, be a loss to the public, because they soon would become breeders themselves; and besides, it is not improbable that some scrupulous people might be apt to censure such a practice (although indeed very unjustly) as a little bordering upon cruelty; which, I confess, hath always been with me the strongest objection against any project, how well soever intended.

But in order to justify my friend, he confessed that this expedient was put into his head by the famous Psalmanazar,[9] a native of the island Formosa, who came from thence to London above twenty years ago, and in conversation told my friend that in his country when any young person happened to be put to death, the executioner sold the carcass to persons of quality as a prime dainty; and that in his time the body of a plump girl of fifteen, who was crucified for an attempt to poison the emperor, was sold to his Imperial Majesty's prime minister of state, and other great mandarins of the court, in joints from the gibbet, at four hundred crowns. Neither indeed can I deny that if the same use were made of several plump young girls in this town, who without one single groat to their fortunes cannot stir abroad without a chair, and appear at the playhouse and assemblies in foreign fineries which they never will pay for, the kingdom would not be the worse.

Some persons of a desponding spirit are in great concern about that vast number of poor people who are aged, diseased, or maimed, and I have been desired to employ my thoughts what course may be taken to ease the nation of so grievous an encumbrance. But I am not in the least pain upon that matter, because it is very well known that they are every day dying and rotting by cold and famine, and filth and vermin, as fast as can be reasonably expected. And as to the younger laborers, they are now in almost as hopeful a condition. They cannot get work, and consequently pine away for want of nourishment to a degree that if any time they are accidentally hired to common labor, they have not strength to perform it; and thus the country and themselves are happily delivered from the evils to come.

I have too long digressed, and therefore shall return to my subject. I   20 think the advantages by the proposal which I have made are obvious and many, as well as of the highest importance.

For first, as I have already observed, it would greatly lessen the number of Papists, with whom we are yearly overrun, being the principal breeders of the nation as well as our most dangerous enemies; and who stay at home on purpose to deliver the kingdom to the Pretender, hoping to take their advantage by the absence of so many good Protestants, who have chosen rather to leave their country than to stay at home and pay tithes against their conscience to an Episcopal curate.

[9] Georges Psalmanazar was a Frenchman who pretended to be Japanese and wrote an entirely imaginary *Description of the Isle Formosa*. He had become well known in gullible London society.

Secondly, the poorer tenants will have something valuable of their own, which by law may be made liable to distress,[10] and help to pay their landlord's rent, their corn and cattle being already seized and money a thing unknown.

Thirdly, whereas the maintenance of an hundred thousand children, from two years old and upwards, cannot be computed at less than ten shillings a piece per annum, the nation's stock will be thereby increased fifty thousand pounds per annum, besides the profit of a new dish introduced to the tables of all gentlemen of fortune in the kingdom who have any refinement in taste. And the money will circulate among ourselves, the goods being entirely of our own growth and manufacture.

Fourthly, the constant breeders, besides the gain of eight shillings sterling per annum by the sale of their children, will be rid of the charge of maintaining them after the first year.

Fifthly, this food would likewise bring great custom to taverns, where 25 the vintners will certainly be so prudent as to procure the best receipts for dressing it to perfection, and consequently have their houses frequented by all the fine gentlemen, who justly value themselves upon their knowledge in good eating; and a skillful cook, who understands how to oblige his guests, will contrive to make it as expensive as they please.

Sixthly, this would be a great inducement to marriage, which all wise nations have either encouraged by rewards or enforced by laws and penalties. It would increase the care and tenderness of mothers toward their children, when they were sure of a settlement for life to the poor babes, provided in some sort by the public, to their annual profit instead of expense. We should see an honest emulation among the married women, which of them could bring the fattest child to the market. Men would become as fond of their wives during the time of their pregnancy as they are now of their mares in foal, their cows in calf, or sows when they are ready to farrow; nor offer to beat or kick them (as is too frequent a practice) for fear of a miscarriage.

Many other advantages might be enumerated. For instance, the addition of some thousand carcasses in our exportation of barreled beef, the propagation of swine's flesh, and improvements in the art of making good bacon, so much wanted among us by the great destruction of pigs, too frequent at our tables, which are no way comparable in taste or magnificence to a well-grown, fat, yearling child, which roasted whole will make a considerable figure at a lord mayor's feast or any other public entertainment. But this and many others I omit, being studious of brevity.

Supposing that one thousand families in this city would be constant customers for infants' flesh, besides others who might have it at merry meetings, particularly weddings and christenings, I compute that Dublin would take off annually about twenty thousand carcasses, and the rest of

---

[10]Subject to possession by lenders.

the kingdom (where probably they will be sold somewhat cheaper) the remaining eighty thousand.

I can think of no one objection that will possibly be raised against this proposal, unless it should be urged that the number of people will be thereby much lessened in the kingdom. This I freely own, and it was indeed one principal design in offering it to the world. I desire the reader will observe, that I calculate my remedy for this one individual kingdom of Ireland and for no other that ever was, is, or I think ever can be upon earth. Therefore let no man talk to me of other expedients: of taxing our absentees at five shillings a pound: of using neither clothes nor household furniture except what is of our own growth and manufacture: of utterly rejecting the materials and instruments that promote foreign luxury: of curing the expensiveness of pride, vanity, idleness, and gaming in our women: of introducing a vein of parsimony, prudence, and temperance: of learning to love our country, in the want of which we differ even from Laplanders and the inhabitants of Topinamboo:[11] of quitting our animosities and factions, nor acting any longer like the Jews, who were murdering one another at the very moment their city was taken:[12] of being a little cautious not to sell our country and conscience for nothing: of teaching landlords to have at least one degree of mercy toward their tenants: lastly, of putting a spirit of honesty, industry, and skill into our shopkeepers; who, if a resolution could now be taken to buy only our native goods, would immediately unite to cheat and exact upon us in the price, the measure, and the goodness, nor could ever yet be brought to make one fair proposal of just dealing, though often and earnestly invited to it.

Therefore I repeat, let no man talk to me of these and the like expedients, till he hath at least some glimpse of hope that there will ever be some hearty and sincere attempt to put them in practice. 30

But as to myself, having been wearied out for many years with offering vain, idle, visionary thoughts, and at length utterly despairing of success, I fortunately fell upon this proposal, which, as it is wholly new, so it hath something solid and real, of no expense and little trouble, full in our own power, and whereby we can incur no danger in disobliging England. For this kind of commodity will not bear exportation, the flesh being of too tender a consistence to admit a long continuance in salt, although perhaps I could name a country which would be glad to eat up our whole nation without it.

After all, I am not so violently bent upon my own opinion as to reject any offer proposed by wise men, which shall be found equally innocent, cheap, easy, and effectual. But before something of that kind shall be advanced in contradiction to my scheme, and offering a better, I desire the author or authors will be pleased maturely to consider two points.

---

[11] District of Brazil.
[12] During the Roman siege of Jerusalem (A.D. 70), prominent Jews were charged with collaborating with the enemy and put to death.

First, as things now stand, how they will be able to find food and raiment for an hundred thousand useless mouths and backs. And secondly, there being a round million of creatures in human figure throughout this kingdom, whose sole subsistence put into a common stock would leave them in debt two millions of pounds sterling, adding those who are beggars by profession to the bulk of farmers, cottagers, and laborers, with their wives and children who are beggars in effect; I desire those politicians who dislike my overture, and may perhaps be so bold to attempt an answer, that they will first ask the parents of these mortals whether they would not at this day think it a great happiness to have been sold for food at a year old in this manner I prescribe, and thereby have avoided such a perpetual scene of misfortunes as they have since gone through by the oppression of landlords, the impossibility of paying rent without money or trade, the want of common sustenance, with neither house nor clothes to cover them from the inclemencies of the weather, and the most inevitable prospect of entailing the like of greater miseries upon their breed forever.

I profess, in the sincerity of my heart, that I have not the least personal interest in endeavoring to promote this necessary work, having no other motive than the public good of my country, by advancing our trade, providing for infants, relieving the poor, and giving some pleasure to the rich. I have no children by which I can propose to get a single penny; the youngest being nine years old, and my wife past childbearing.

DISCUSSION QUESTIONS

1. What implicit assumption about the treatment of the Irish underlies Swift's proposal? Do expressions such as "just dropped from its dam" (para. 4) and "whose wives are breeders" (para. 6) give the reader a clue?

2. In this essay Swift assumes a persona; that is, for the purposes of the proposal he makes, he pretends to be a different person. Describe the characteristics of that person. Point out the places in the essay that reveal them.

3. In several places, however, Swift reveals himself as the outraged witness of English cruelty and indifference. Note the language that seems to reflect his own feelings.

4. Throughout the essay Swift recites lists of facts, many of them in the form of statistics. How do these facts contribute to the persuasiveness of his argument? How do they affect the reader?

5. What social practices and attitudes of both the Irish and the English does Swift condemn?

6. Does Swift offer any solutions for the problems he attacks? How do you know?

7. When this essay first appeared in 1729, some readers took it seriously and accused Swift of monstrous cruelty. Can you think of reasons that these readers failed to recognize the ironic intent?

8. What logical fallacies do you find in the essay?

WRITING SUGGESTIONS

9. Try an ironical essay of your own. Choose a subject that clearly lends itself to such treatment. As Swift did, use logic and restraint in your language.

10. Choose a problem for which you think you have a solution. Defend your solution by using the stock issues as your pattern of organization.

DEBATE: Should the federal government fund embryonic stem-cell research?

Use the Body's "Repair Kit": We Must Pursue Research on Embryonic Stem Cells

CHRISTOPHER REEVE

With the life expectancy of average Americans heading as high as 75 to 80 years, it is our responsibility to do everything possible to protect the quality of life of the present and future generations. A critical factor will be what we do with human embryonic stem cells. These cells have the potential to cure diseases and conditions ranging from Parkinson's and multiple sclerosis to diabetes and heart disease, Alzheimer's, Lou Gehrig's disease, even spinal-cord injuries like my own. They have been called the body's self-repair kit.

Their extraordinary potential is a recent discovery. And much basic research needs to be done before they can be sent to the front lines in the battle against disease. But no obstacle should stand in the way of responsible investigation of their possibilities. To that end, the work should be funded and supervised by the federal government through the National Institutes of Health. That will avoid abuses by for-profit corporations, avoid secrecy and destructive competition between laboratories, and ensure the widest possible dissemination of scientific breakthroughs. Human trials

Christopher Reeve was a well-established actor when in 1995 he was paralyzed from the shoulders down in a riding accident. From that time until his death in 2004, he served as an outspoken and respected advocate for the sort of stem-cell research he believed would eventually help him and others like him. Through his personal example and his books *Still Me* (1999) and *Nothing Is Impossible: Reflections on a New Life* (2002), he offered hope and inspiration to the disabled and others. This article is from the May 1, 2000, edition of *Time*.

should be conducted either on the NIH campus or in carefully monitored clinical facilities.

Fortunately, stem cells are readily available and easily harvested. In fertility clinics, women are given a choice of what to do with unused fertilized embryos: they can be discarded, donated to research, or frozen for future use. Under NIH supervision, scientists should be allowed to take cells only from women who freely consent to their use for research. This process would not be open ended; within one to two years a sufficient number could be gathered and made available to investigators. For those reasons, the ban on federally funded human embryonic stem-cell research should be lifted as quickly as possible.

But why has the use of discarded embryos for research suddenly become such an issue? Is it more ethical for a woman to donate unused embryos that will never become human beings, or to let them be tossed away as so much garbage when they could help save thousands of lives?

Treatment with stem cells has already begun. They have been taken   5
from umbilical cords and become healthy red cells used as a potential cure for sickle-cell anemia. Stem-cell therapy is also being used against certain types of cancer. But those are cells that have significantly differentiated; that is, they are no longer pluripotent, or capable of transforming into other cell types. For the true biological miracles that researchers have only begun to foresee, medical science must turn to undifferentiated stem cells. We need to clear the path for them as rapidly as possible.

Controversy over the treatment of certain diseases is nothing new in this country: witness the overwhelming opposition to government funding of AIDS research in the early '80s. For years the issue was a political football—until a massive grass-roots effort forced legislators to respond. Today, the NIH is authorized to spend approximately $1.8 billion annually on new protocols, and the virus is largely under control in the United States.

While we prolong the stem-cell debate, millions continue to suffer. It is time to harness the power of government and go forward.

The Misleading Debate on Stem-Cell Research

MONA CHAREN

Addressing the Democratic National Convention, Ron Reagan told the delegates that in the debate over funding research on embryonic stem cells, we face a choice between "the future and the past; between reason and ignorance; between true compassion and mere ideology." Not satisfied with that contrast, he elaborated that "a few of these folks (who oppose funding this research) are just grinding a political axe, and they should be ashamed of themselves."

It is Reagan who ought to be ashamed. As the mother of a ten-year-old with juvenile diabetes, I yearn more than most for breakthroughs in scientific research. My son takes between four and six shots of insulin daily and must test his blood sugar by pricking his finger the same number of times. This disease affects every major organ system in the body and places him in the high-risk category for more problems than I care to name. When he settles down to sleep at night, I can never be entirely sure that he won't slip into a coma from a sudden low blood sugar. How happily I would take the disease upon myself if I could only spare him! So please don't lecture me about grinding a political axe.

But like millions of others, I am troubled by the idea of embryonic stem-cell research. It crosses a moral line that this society should be loath to cross—even for the best of motives. Taking the stem cells from human embryos kills them. Before turning to the arguments of the pro-research side, permit a word about the pro-life position. Too many pro-life activists, it seems to me, have argued this case on the wrong grounds. My inbox is full of missives about the scientific misfires that stem-cell research has led to, as well as breathless announcements that adult stem cells actually hold more promise.

This is neither an honest nor a productive line of argument. The reason pro-lifers oppose embryonic stem-cell research is because they hold life sacred at all stages of development. They ought not to deny this or dress it up in a lab coat to give it greater palatability. The moral case is an honorable one. Leave it at that.

Proponents of embryonic stem-cell research point out that some of the embryos currently sitting in freezers in fertility clinics around the world are going to be washed down the drain anyway—which surely kills them, and

Mona Charen is a syndicated columnist whose column appears in over two hundred newspapers nationwide and a political analyst who for six years was a regular on CNN's *Capital Gang* and *Capital Gang Sunday*. From 1984 to 1986, she worked at the White House as a speechwriter for Nancy Reagan and in the Public Affairs Office. This article appeared on townhall.com in August 2004.

5

without any benefit to mankind. This is true. There are several answers to this. The first is that a society that truly honored each human life would take a different approach. Fertility clinics and the couples who use them would understand the moral obligation not to create more embryos than they can reasonably expect to transfer to the mother's uterus. In cases where this was impossible, the embryos could be placed for adoption with other infertile couples (this is already a widespread practice).

Once you begin to pull apart a human embryo and use its parts, you have thoroughly dehumanized it. You have justified taking one life to (speculatively) save another. Despite the rosy future painted by Ron Reagan and others, those of us who follow the field with avid interest have been disappointed by avenues of research that have failed, thus far, to pan out. Still, opponents of stem-cell research should not argue that the research is going to be fruitless. No one knows. The problem is that this kind of research is morally problematic. Germany, Italy, Portugal, Luxembourg, and Austria ban it. (The United States does not. We simply withhold federal funding.)

There is something else, as well. While the idea of growing spare parts—say, spinal nerves for a paraplegic—in a Petri dish seems wonderful, it may not be possible to do so from embryonic stem cells. As the *Wall Street Journal* reported on August 12 [2004], scientists have been frustrated by their inability to get stem cells to grow into endoderm (the cells that make up the liver, stomach, and pancreas), whereas they can coax them to become heart and nerve tissue.

"Scientists speculate," the *Journal* explained, "that might be because the embryo early on needs blood and nerve tissue to grow, while endoderm-based organs aren't needed until later." If we can use the stem cells of normal human embryos for research, by what logic would we shrink from allowing an embryo to reach a later stage of development in order to study better how endoderm forms?

These are treacherous moral waters we're setting sail in, and those who hesitate ought not to be scorned as ignorant, uncompassionate, or blinkered.

DISCUSSION QUESTIONS

1. Do both of these authors use evidence and appeal to needs and values? Explain. How is your reading of each piece affected by the author's personal circumstances?

2. What is the effect of Reeve's choosing to call stem cells "the body's self-repair kit"? Give other examples of how his word choice either helps or hurts his argument.

3. Is the language that Reeve uses in discussing the embryos different from that used by Charen? How and why?

4. In what other ways does Charen's choice of words affect her argument?

5. Where does each author most directly state the claim of his or her piece?

ASSIGNMENTS FOR AVOIDING FLAWED LOGIC

READING AND DISCUSSION QUESTIONS

1. Read through the draft of an essay that you are writing, looking for and correcting any logical fallacies that you find.
2. Compare the argument made to Congress by President Roosevelt on the day after the attack on Pearl Harbor in 1941 and the one made by President Bush after the attacks on the World Trade Center and the Pentagon in 2001.

WRITING ASSIGNMENTS

3. Write an essay explaining the logical fallacies in one of the essays from the Readings for Analysis portion of this chapter.
4. Explain in an essay whether you find Christopher Reeve's or Mona Charen's argument on stem-cell research more convincing, and why.
5. Find the printed text of a major political speech such as a State of the Union Address, a major political convention speech, or an inaugural address and analyze its logic. Does it use an inductive approach, a deductive approach, a combination? What types of support are used? Do you detect any logical fallacies? Write an essay about the speech that supports either a claim of fact or a claim of value.

CHAPTER 10

Choosing Fair and Precise Language

THE POWER OF WORDS

Words play such a critical role in argument that they deserve special treatment. An important part of successful writers' equipment is a large and active vocabulary, but no single chapter in a book can give this to you; only reading and study can widen your range of word choices. Even in a brief chapter, however, we can point out how words influence the feelings and attitudes of an audience, both favorably and unfavorably.

One kind of language responsible for shaping attitudes and feelings is *emotive language,* language that expresses and arouses emotions. Understanding it and using it effectively are indispensable to the arguer who wants to move an audience to accept a point of view or undertake an action.

In one of the most memorable speeches in the history of America, President Franklin Delano Roosevelt asked the country both to accept a point of view and to prepare to take action. In his brief speech to Congress he captured some of the grief and the feeling of outrage Americans were experiencing. Except for the most famous phrase in the speech, in which he declares December 7, 1941, a "date which will live in infamy," most of the first portion of the speech establishes the facts. A turning point in the speech comes when he shifts from facts to implications. The speech then builds to its emotional climax in the next-to-last paragraph before he concludes with a declaration of war.

Address to Congress, December 8, 1941

FRANKLIN DELANO ROOSEVELT

Yesterday, December 7, 1941—a date which will live in infamy—the United States of America was suddenly and deliberately attacked by naval and air forces of the Empire of Japan.

The United States was at peace with that nation, and, at the solicitation of Japan, was still in conversation with its government and its Emperor looking toward the maintenance of peace in the Pacific.

Indeed, one hour after Japanese air squadrons had commenced bombing in the American island of Oahu, the Japanese Ambassador to the United States and his colleague delivered to our Secretary of State a formal reply to a recent American message. And, while this reply stated that it seemed useless to continue the existing diplomatic negotiations, it contained no threat or hint of war or of armed attack.

It will be recorded that the distance of Hawaii from Japan makes it obvious that the attack was deliberately planned many days or even weeks ago. During the intervening time the Japanese Government has deliberately sought to deceive the United States by false statements and expressions of hope for continued peace.

The attack yesterday on the Hawaiian Islands has caused severe dam- 5 age to American naval and military forces. I regret to tell you that very many American lives have been lost. In addition, American ships have been reported torpedoed on the high seas between San Francisco and Honolulu.

Yesterday the Japanese Government also launched an attack against Malaya. Last night Japanese forces attacked Hong Kong. Last night Japanese forces attacked Guam. Last night Japanese forces attacked the Philippine Islands. Last night the Japanese attacked Wake Island. And this morning the Japanese attacked Midway Island.

Japan has therefore undertaken a surprise offensive extending throughout the Pacific area. The facts of yesterday and today speak for themselves. The people of the United States have already formed their opinions and well understand the implications to the very life and safety of our nation.

As Commander-in-Chief of the Army and Navy I have directed that all measures be taken for our defense, that always will our whole nation remember the character of the onslaught against us.

No matter how long it may take us to overcome this premeditated invasion, the American people, in their righteous might, will win through to absolute victory.

I believe that I interpret the will of the Congress and of the people 10 when I assert that we will not only defend ourselves to the uttermost but will make it very certain that this form of treachery shall never again endanger us.

Hostilities exist. There is no blinking at the fact that our people, our territory, and our interests are in grave danger.

With confidence in our armed forces, with the unbounding determination of our people, we will gain the inevitable triumph, so help us God.

I ask that the Congress declare that since the unprovoked and dastardly attack by Japan on Sunday, December 7, 1941, a state of war has existed between the United States and the Japanese Empire.

Long before you thought about writing your first argument, you learned that words had the power to affect you. Endearments and affectionate and flattering nicknames evoked good feelings about the speaker and yourself. Insulting nicknames and slurs produced dislike for the speaker and bad feelings about yourself. Perhaps you were told, "Sticks and stones may break your bones, but words will never hurt you." But even to a small child it is clear that ugly words are as painful as sticks and stones and that the injuries are sometimes more lasting.

Nowhere is the power of words more obvious and more familiar than in advertising, where the success of a product may depend on the feelings that certain words produce in the prospective buyer. Even the names of products may have emotive significance. In recent years a new industry, composed of consultants who supply names for products, has emerged. Although most manufacturers agree that a good name won't save a poor product, they also recognize that the right name can catch the attention of the public and persuade people to buy a product at least once. According to an article in the *Wall Street Journal,* a product name not only should be memorable but also should "remind people of emotional or physical experiences."[1]

PRACTICE

Careful thought and extensive research go into the naming of automobiles, a "big ticket" item for most consumers. What reasoning might have gone into the naming of these models, old and new?

Aspen	Jaguar
Colorado	Liberty
Dart	Malibu
Eclipse	Matrix
Electra	Mustang
Grand Prix	Nova
Impala	Odyssey
Infinity	Quest

[1] *Wall Street Journal,* August 5, 1982, p. 19.

Rainier   Taurus
Regal   Trailblazer
Rendezvous   Viper
Sequoia

What response do the names Mercedes-Benz and Rolls-Royce evoke?

Even scientists recognize the power of words to attract the attention of other scientists and the public to discoveries and theories that might otherwise remain obscure. A good name can even enable the scientist to visualize a new concept. One scientist says that "a good name," such as "quark," "black hole," "big bang," "chaos," or "great attractor," "helps in communicating a theory and can have substantial impact on financing."

It is not hard to see the connection between the use of words in conversation and advertising and the use of emotive language in the more formal arguments you will be writing. Emotive language reveals your approval or disapproval, assigns praise or blame—in other words, makes a judgment about the subject. Keep in mind that unless you are writing purely factual statements, such as scientists write, you will find it hard to avoid expressing judgments. Neutrality does not come easily, even where it may be desirable, as in news stories or reports of historical events. For this reason you need to attend carefully to the statements in your argument, making sure that you have not disguised judgments as statements of fact. Of course, in attempting to prove a claim, you will not be neutral. You will be revealing your judgment about the subject, first in the selection of facts and opinions and the emphasis you give to them and second in the selection of words.

Like the choice of facts and opinions, the choice of words can be effective or ineffective in advancing your argument, moral or immoral in the honesty with which you exercise it. The following discussions offer some insights into recognizing and evaluating the use of emotive language in the arguments you read, as well as into using such language in your own arguments where it is appropriate and avoiding it where it is not.

CONNOTATION

The connotations of a word are the meanings we attach to it apart from its explicit definition. Because these added meanings derive from our feelings, connotations are one form of emotive language. For example, the word *rat* denotes or points to a kind of rodent, but the attached meanings of "selfish person," "evil-doer," "betrayer," and "traitor" reflect the feelings that have accumulated around the word.

In Chapter 5 we observed that definitions of controversial terms, such as *poverty* and *unemployment,* may vary so widely that writer and reader cannot always be sure that they are thinking of the same thing. A similar problem arises when a writer assumes that the reader shares his or her emotional response to a word. Emotive meanings originate partly in personal experience. The word *home,* defined merely as "a family's place of residence," may suggest love, warmth, and security to one person; it may suggest friction, violence, and alienation to another. The values of the groups to which we belong also influence meaning. Writers and speakers count on cultural associations when they refer to our country, our flag, and heroes and enemies we have never seen. The arguer must also be aware that some apparently neutral words trigger different responses from different groups—words such as *cult, revolution, police,* and *beauty contest.*

Various reform movements have recognized that words with unfavorable connotations have the power not only to reflect but also to shape our perceptions of things. In 2007, the NAACP went so far as to hold a "funeral for the N— word." The women's liberation movement also insisted on changes that would bring about improved attitudes toward women. The movement condemned the use of *girl* for a female over the age of eighteen and the use in news stories of descriptive adjectives that emphasized the physical appearance of women. And the homosexual community succeeded in reintroducing the word *gay,* a word current centuries ago, as a substitute for words they considered offensive. Now *queer,* a word long regarded as offensive, has been adopted as a substitute for *gay* by a new generation of gays and lesbians, although it is still considered unacceptable by many members of the homosexual community.

Members of certain occupations have invented terms to confer greater respectability on their work. The work does not change, but the workers hope that public perceptions will change if janitors are called custodians, if garbage collectors are called sanitation engineers, if undertakers are called morticians, if people who sell makeup are called cosmetologists. Events considered unpleasant or unmentionable are sometimes disguised by polite terms, called *euphemisms.* During the 1992 to 1993 recession new terms emerged that disguised, or tried to, the grim fact that thousands of people were being dismissed from their jobs: *skill-mix adjustment, workforce-imbalance correction, redundancy elimination, downsizing, indefinite idling,* even a daring *career-change opportunity.* Many people refuse to use the word *died* and choose *passed away* instead. Some psychologists and physicians use the phrase *negative patient care outcome* for what most of us would call *death.* Even when referring to their pets, some people cannot bring themselves to say *put to death* but substitute *put to sleep* or *put down.* In place of a term to describe an act of sexual intercourse, some people use *slept together* or *went to bed together* or *had an affair.*

Polite words are not always so harmless. If a euphemism disguises a shameful event or condition, it is morally irresponsible to use it to mislead the reader into believing that the shameful condition does not exist. In his powerful essay "Politics and the English Language" (p. 406) George Orwell pointed out that politicians and reporters have sometimes used terms like *pacification* or *rectification of frontiers* to conceal acts that result in torture and death for millions of people. An example of such usage was cited by a member of Amnesty International, a group monitoring human rights violations throughout the world. He objected to a news report describing camps in which the Chinese were promoting "reeducation through labor." This term, he wrote, "makes these institutions seem like a cross between Police Athletic League and Civilian Conservation Corps camps." On the contrary, he went on, the reality of "reeducation through labor" was that the victims were confined to "rather unpleasant prison camps." The details he offered about the conditions under which people lived and worked gave substance to his claim.[2]

Perhaps the most striking examples of the way that connotations influence our perceptions of reality occur when people are asked to respond to questions of poll-takers. Sociologists and students of poll-taking know that the phrasing of a question, or the choice of words, can affect the answers and even undermine the validity of the poll. In one case poll-takers first asked a selected group of people if they favored continuing the welfare system. The majority answered no. But when the poll-takers asked if they favored government aid to the poor, the majority answered yes. Although the terms *welfare* and *government aid to the poor* refer to essentially the same forms of government assistance, *welfare* has acquired for many people negative connotations of corruption and shiftless recipients.

In a *New York Times*/CBS poll conducted in January 1998, "a representative sample of Americans were asked which statement came nearer to their opinion: 'Is abortion the same thing as murdering a child, or is abortion not murder because the fetus really isn't a child?'" Thirty-eight percent chose "the fetus really isn't a child." But 58 percent, including a third of those who chose "abortion is the same thing as murdering a child," agreed that abortion "was sometimes the best course in a bad situation." The author of the report suggests an explanation of the fact that a majority of those polled seemed to have chosen "murder" as an acceptable solution to an unwanted pregnancy:

> These replies reveal, at least, a considerable moral confusion.
> Or maybe only verbal confusion? Should the question have asked whether abortion came closer, in the respondent's view, to "killing" rather than "murdering" a child? That would leave room for the explanation that Americans, while valuing life, are ultimately not pacifists: killing, they hold, may be justified in certain circumstances (self-defense, warfare, capital punishment).
> So one can challenge the wording of the question. Indeed, one can almost always challenge the wording of poll questions. . . . Poll takers

---

[2]Letter to the *New York Times*, August 30, 1982, p. 25.

themselves acknowledge the difficulty of wording questions and warn against relying too much on any single finding.[3]

This is also true in polls concerning rape, another highly charged subject. Dr. Neil Malamuth, a psychologist at the University of California at Los Angeles, says, "When men are asked if there is any likelihood they would force a woman to have sex against her will if they could get away with it, about half say they would. But if you ask them if they would rape a woman if they knew they could get away with it, only about 15 percent say they would." The men who change their answers aren't aware that "the only difference is in the words used to describe the same act."[4]

The wording of an argument is crucial. Because readers may interpret the words you use on the basis of feelings different from your own, you must support your word choices with definitions and with evidence that allows readers to determine how and why you made them.

SLANTING

Slanting, says one dictionary, is "interpreting or presenting in line with a special interest." The term is almost always used in a negative sense. It means that the arguer has selected facts and words with favorable or unfavorable connotations to create the impression that no alternative view exists or can be defended. For some questions it is true that no alternative view is worthy of presentation, and emotionally charged language to defend or attack a position that is clearly right or wrong would be entirely appropriate. We aren't neutral, nor should we be, about the tragic abuse of human rights anywhere in the world or even about infractions of the law such as drunk driving or vandalism, and we should use strong language to express our disapproval of these practices.

Most of your arguments, however, will concern controversial questions about which people of goodwill can argue on both sides. In such cases, your own judgments should be restrained. Slanting will suggest a prejudice — that is, a judgment made without regard to all the facts. Unfortunately, you may not always be aware of your bias or special interest; you may believe that your position is the only correct one. You may also feel the need to communicate a passionate belief about a serious problem. But if you are interested in persuading a reader to accept your belief and to act on it, you must also ask: If the reader is not sympathetic, how will he or she respond? Will he or she perceive my words as "loaded" — one-sided and prejudicial — and my view as slanted?

---

[3] Peter Steinfels, "Beliefs," *New York Times,* January 24, 1998, sec. A, p. 15.
[4] *New York Times,* August 29, 1989, sec. C, p. 1.

R. D. Laing, a Scottish psychiatrist, defined *prayer* in this way: "Someone is gibbering away on his knees, talking to someone who is not there."[5] This description probably reflects a sincerely held belief. Laing also clearly intended it for an audience that already agreed with him. But the phrases "gibbering away" and "someone who is not there" would be offensive to people for whom prayer is sacred.

The following remarks by one writer attacking another appeared in *Salon,* an online magazine:

> Urging the hyperbolic *Salon* columnist David Horowitz to calm down and cite facts instead of spewing insults seems as pointless as asking a dog not to defecate on the sidewalk. In either instance, the result is always and predictably the same: Somebody has to clean up a stinking pile.[6]

An audience, whether friendly or unfriendly, interested in a discussion of the issues, would probably be both embarrassed and repelled by this use of language in a serious argument.

In the mid-1980s an English environmental group, London Greenpeace, began to distribute leaflets accusing the McDonald's restaurants of a wide assortment of crimes. The leaflets said in part:

> McDollars, McGreedy, McCancer, McMurder, McDisease, McProfits, McDeadly, McHunger, McRipoff, McTorture, McWasteful, McGarbage.
> This leaflet is asking you to think for a moment about what lies behind McDonald's clean, bright image. It's got a lot to hide. . . .
> McDonald's and Burger King are two of the many U.S. corporations using lethal poisons to destroy vast areas of Central American rain forest to create grazing pastures for cattle to be sent back to the States as burgers and pet food. . . .
> What they don't make clear is that a diet high in fat, sugar, animal products and salt . . . and low in fiber, vitamins and minerals—which describes an average McDonald's meal—is linked with cancers of the breast and bowel, and heart disease. . . .[7]

Even readers who share the belief that McDonald's is not a reliable source of good nutrition might feel that London Greenpeace has gone too far, and that the name-calling, loaded words, and exaggeration have damaged the credibility of the attackers more than the reputation of McDonald's.

---

[5] "The Obvious," in David Cooper, ed., *The Dialectics of Liberation* (Penguin Books, 1968), p. 17.

[6] July 6, 2000.

[7] *New York Times,* August 6, 1995, sec. E, p. 7. In 1990 McDonald's sued the group for libel. In June 1997, after the longest libel trial in British history, the judge ruled in favor of the plaintiff, awarding McDonald's £60,000. In March 1999 an appeal partially overturned the verdict and reduced the damages awarded to McDonald's by approximately one-third.

Selection, Slanting, and Charged Language

NEWMAN P. BIRK AND GENEVIEVE B. BIRK

A. THE PRINCIPLE OF SELECTION

Before it is expressed in words, our knowledge, both inside and outside, is influenced by the principle of selection. What we know or observe depends on what we notice; that is, what we select, consciously or unconsciously, as worthy of notice or attention. As we observe, the principle of selection determines which facts we take in.

Suppose, for example, that three people, a lumberjack, an artist, and a tree surgeon, are examining a large tree in the forest. Since the tree itself is a complicated object, the number of particulars or facts about it that one could observe would be very great indeed. Which of these facts a particular observer will notice will be a matter of selection, a selection that is determined by his interests and purposes. A lumberjack might be interested in the best way to cut the tree down, cut it up, and transport it to the lumber mill. His interest would then determine his principle of selection in observing and thinking about the tree. The artist might consider painting a picture of the tree, and his purpose would furnish his principle of selection. The tree surgeon's professional interest in the physical health of the tree might establish a principle of selection for him. If each man were now required to write an exhaustive, detailed report on every thing he observed about the tree, the facts supplied by each would differ, for each would report those facts that his particular principle of selection led him to notice. . . .[1]

The principle of selection then serves as a kind of sieve or screen through which our knowledge passes before it becomes our knowledge. Since we can't notice everything about a complicated object or situation or action or state of our own consciousness, what we do notice is determined by whatever principle of selection is operating for us at the time we gain the knowledge. . . .

B. THE PRINCIPLE OF SLANTING

When we put our knowledge into words, a second process of selection, the process of slanting, takes place. Just as there is something, a rather mysterious principle of selection, which chooses for us what we will notice, and what will

[1]Of course, all three observers would probably report a good many facts in common — the height of the tree, for example, and the size of the trunk. The point we wish to make is that each observer would give us a different impression of the tree because of the different principle of selection that guided his observation. [All notes are the authors'.]

This selection first appeared in *Understanding and Using English* (1972). Together, the Birks also wrote *A Handbook of Grammar, Rhetoric, Mechanics, and Usage* (1976).

then become our knowledge, there is also a principle which operates, with or without our awareness, to select certain facts and feelings from our store of knowledge, and to choose the words and emphasis that we shall use to communicate our meaning.[2] Slanting may be defined as the process of selecting (1) knowledge—factual and attitudinal; (2) words; and (3) emphasis, to achieve the intention of the communicator. Slanting is present in some degree in all communication: one may *slant for* (favorable slanting), *slant against* (unfavorable slanting), or *slant both ways* (balanced shifting). . . .

C. SLANTING BY USE OF EMPHASIS

Slanting by use of the devices of emphasis is unavoidable,[3] for emphasis is   5
simply the giving of stress to subject matter, and so indicating what is important and what is less important. In speech, for example, if we say that Socrates was *a wise old man,* we can give several slightly different meanings, one by stressing *wise,* another by stressing *old,* another by giving equal stress to *wise* and *old,* and still another by giving chief stress to *man.* Each different stress gives a different slant (favorable or unfavorable or balanced) to the statement because it conveys a different attitude toward Socrates or a different judgment of him. Connectives and word order also slant by the emphasis they give: Consider the difference in slanting or emphasis produced by *old but wise, old and wise, wise but old.* In writing, we cannot indicate subtle stresses on words as clearly as in speech, but we can achieve our emphasis and so can slant by the use of more complex patterns of word order, [by choice of connectives, by underlining heavily stressed words, and] by marks of punctuation that indicate short or long pauses and so give light or heavy emphasis. Question marks, quotation marks, and exclamation points can also contribute to slanting.[4] It is impossible either in speech or in writing to put two facts together without giving some slight emphasis or slant. For example, if we have in mind only two facts about a man, his awkwardness and his strength, we subtly slant those facts favorably or unfavorably in whatever way we may choose to join them.

More Favorable Slanting	*Less Favorable Slanting*
He is awkward and strong.	He is strong and awkward.
He is awkward but strong.	He is strong but awkward.
Although he is somewhat awkward, he is very strong.	He may be strong, but he's very awkward.

[2] Notice that the "principle of selection" is at work as *we take in* knowledge, and that slanting occurs *as we express* our knowledge in words.

[3] When emphasis is present—and we can think of no instance in the use of language in which it is not—it necessarily influences the meaning by playing a part in the favorable, unfavorable, or balanced slant of the communicator. We are likely to emphasize by voice stress, even when we answer *yes* or *no* to simple questions.

[4] Consider the slanting achieved by punctuation in the following sentences: He called the Senator an honest man? *He* called the Senator an honest man? He called the Senator an honest man! He said one more such "honest" senator would corrupt the state.

With more facts and in longer passages it is possible to maintain a delicate balance by alternating favorable emphasis and so producing a balanced effect.

All communication, then, is in some degree slanted by the *emphasis* of the communicator.

D. SLANTING BY SELECTION OF FACTS

To illustrate the technique of slanting by selection of facts, we shall examine three passages of informative writing which achieve different effects simply by the selection and emphasis of material. Each passage is made up of true statements or facts about a dog, yet the reader is given three different impressions. The first passage is an example of objective writing or balanced slanting, the second is slanted unfavorably, and the third is slanted favorably.

1. Balanced Presentation

Our dog, Toddy, sold to us as a cocker, produces various reactions in various people. Those who come to the back door she usually growls and barks at (a milkman has said that he is afraid of her); those who come to the front door, she whines at and paws; also she tries to lick people's faces unless we have forestalled her by putting a newspaper in her mouth. (Some of our friends encourage these actions; others discourage them. Mrs. Firmly, one friend, slaps the dog with a newspaper and says, "I know how hard dogs are to train.") Toddy knows and responds to a number of words and phrases, and guests sometimes remark that she is a "very intelligent dog." She has fleas in the summer, and she sheds, at times copiously, the year round. Her blonde hairs are conspicuous when they are on people's clothing or on rugs or furniture. Her color and her large brown eyes frequently produce favorable comment. An expert on cockers would say that her ears are too short and set too high and that she is at least six pounds too heavy.

The passage above is made up of facts, verifiable facts,[5] deliberately selected and emphasized to produce a *balanced* impression. Of course not all the facts about the dog have been given — to supply *all* the facts on any subject, even such a comparatively simple one, would be an almost impossible task. Both favorable and unfavorable facts are used, however, and an effort has been made to alternate favorable and unfavorable details so that neither will receive greater emphasis by position, proportion, or grammatical structure.

---

[5] *Verifiable* facts are facts that can be checked and agreed upon and proved to be true by people who wish to verify them. That a particular theme received a failing grade is a verifiable fact; one needs merely to see the theme with the grade on it. That the instructor should have failed the theme is not, strictly speaking, a verifiable fact, but a matter of opinion. That women on the average live longer than men is a verifiable fact; that they live better is a matter of opinion, *a value judgment.*

2. Facts Slanted Against

That dog put her paws on my white dress as soon as I came in the door, and she made so much noise that it was two minutes before she had quieted down enough for us to talk and hear each other. Then the gas man came and she did a great deal of barking. And her hairs are on the rug and on the furniture. If you wear a dark dress they stick to it like lint. When Mrs. Firmly came in, she actually hit the dog with a newspaper to make it stay down, and she made some remark about training dogs. I wish the Birks would take the hint or get rid of that noisy, shorteared, overweight "cocker" of theirs.

This unfavorably slanted version is based on the same facts, but now these facts have been selected and given a new emphasis. The speaker, using her selected facts to give her impression of the dog, is quite possibly unaware of her negative slanting.

Now for a favorably slanted version:

3. Facts Slanted For

What a lively and responsible dog! When I walked in the door, there she was with a newspaper in her mouth, whining and standing on her hind legs and wagging her tail all at the same time. And what an intelligent dog. If you suggest going for a walk, she will get her collar from the kitchen and hand it to you, and she brings Mrs. Birk's slippers whenever Mrs. Birk says she is "tired" or mentions slippers. At a command she catches balls, rolls over, "speaks," or stands on her hind feet and twirls around. She sits up and balances a piece of bread on her nose until she is told to take it; then she tosses it up and catches it. If you are eating something, she sits up in front of you and "begs" with those big dark brown eyes set in that light, buff-colored face of hers. When I got up to go and told her I was leaving, she rolled her eyes at me and sat up like a squirrel. She certainly is a lively and intelligent dog.

Speaker 3, like Speaker 2, is selecting from the "facts" summarized in balanced version 1, and is emphasizing his facts to communicate his impression.

All three passages are examples of *reporting* (i.e., consist only of verifiable facts), yet they give three very different impressions of the same dog because of the different ways the speakers slanted the facts. Some people say that figures don't lie, and many people believe that if they have the "facts," they have the "truth." Yet if we carefully examine the ways of thought and language, we see that any knowledge that comes to us through words has been subjected to the double screening of the principle of selection and the slanting of language. . . .

Wise listeners and readers realize that the double screening that is produced by the principle of selection and by slanting takes place even when people honestly try to report the facts as they know them. (Speakers 2 and 3, for instance, probably thought of themselves as simply giving information about a dog and were not deliberately trying to mislead.)

Wise listeners and readers know too that deliberate manipulators of language, by mere selection and emphasis, can make their slanted facts appear to support almost any cause.

In arriving at opinions and values we cannot always be sure that the 15 facts that sift into our minds through language are representative and relevant and true. We need to remember that much of our information about politics, governmental activities, business conditions, and foreign affairs comes to us selected and slanted. More than we realize, our opinions on these matters may depend on what newspaper we read or what news commentator we listen to. Worthwhile opinions call for knowledge of reliable facts and reasonable arguments for and against—and such opinions include beliefs about morality and truth and religion as well as about public affairs. Because complex subjects involve knowing and dealing with many facts on both sides, reliable judgments are at best difficult to arrive at. If we want to be fairminded, we must be willing to subject our opinions to continual testing by new knowledge, and must realize that after all they *are* opinions, more or less trustworthy. Their trustworthiness will depend on the representativeness of our facts, on the quality of our reasoning, and on the standard of values that we choose to apply.

We shall not give here a passage illustrating the unscrupulous slanting of facts. Such a passage would also include irrelevant facts and false statements presented as facts, along with various subtle distortions of fact. Yet to the uninformed reader the passage would be indistinguishable from a passage intended to give a fair account. If two passages (2 and 3) of casual and unintentional slanting of facts about a dog can give such contradictory impressions of a simple subject, the reader can imagine what a skilled and designing manipulation of facts and statistics could do to mislead an uninformed reader about a really complex subject. An example of such manipulation might be the account of the United States that Soviet propaganda has supplied to the average Russian. Such propaganda, however, would go beyond the mere slanting of the facts: It would clothe the selected facts in charged words and would make use of the many other devices of slanting that appear in charged language.

E. SLANTING BY USE OF CHARGED WORDS

In the passages describing the dog Toddy, we were illustrating the technique of slanting by the selection and emphasis of facts. Though the facts selected had to be expressed in words, the words chosen were as factual as possible, and it was the selection and emphasis of facts and not of words that was mainly responsible for the two distinctly different impressions of the dog. In the passages below we are demonstrating another way of slanting—by the use of charged words. This time the accounts are very similar in the facts they contain; the different impressions of the subject, Corlyn, are produced not by different facts but by the subtle selection of charged words.

The passages were written by a clever student who was told to choose as his subject a person in action, and to write two descriptions, each using the "same facts." The instructions required that one description be slanted positively and the other negatively, so that the first would make the reader favorably inclined toward the person and the action, and the second would make him unfavorably inclined.

Here is the favorably charged description. Read it carefully and form your opinion of the person before you go on to read the second description.

Corlyn

Corlyn paused at the entrance to the room and glanced about. A well-cut black dress draped subtly about her slender form. Her long blonde hair gave her chiseled features the simple frame they required. She smiled an engaging smile as she accepted a cigarette from her escort. As he lit it for her she looked over the flame and into his eyes. Corlyn had that rare talent of making every male feel that he was the only man in the world.

She took his arm and they descended the steps into the room. She walked with an effortless grace and spoke with equal ease. They each took a cup of coffee and joined a group of friends near the fire. The flickering light danced across her face and lent an ethereal quality to her beauty. The good conversation, the crackling logs, and the stimulating coffee gave her a feeling of internal warmth. Her eyes danced with each leap of the flames.

Taken by itself this passage might seem just a description of an attrac- 20
tive girl. The favorable slanting by use of charged words has been done so skillfully that it is inconspicuous. Now we turn to the unfavorably slanted description of the "same" girl in the "same" actions:

Corlyn

Corlyn halted at the entrance to the room and looked around. A plain black dress hung on her thin frame. Her stringy bleached hair accentuated her harsh features. She smiled an inane smile as she took a cigarette from her escort. As he lit it for her she stared over the lighter and into his eyes. Corlyn had a habit of making every male feel that he was the last man on earth.

She grasped his arm and they walked down the steps and into the room. Her pace was fast and ungainly, as was her speed. They each reached for some coffee and broke into a group of acquaintances near the fire. The flickering light played across her face and revealed every flaw. The loud talk, the fire, and the coffee she had gulped down made her feel hot. Her eyes grew more red with each leap of the flames.

When the reader compares these two descriptions, he can see how charged words influence the reader's attitude. One needs to read the two descriptions several times to appreciate all the subtle differences between them. Words, some rather heavily charged, others innocent-looking but lightly charged, work together to carry to the reader a judgment of a person and a situation. If the reader had seen only the first description of Corlyn, he might well have thought that he had formed his "own judgment on the basis of the facts." And the examples just given only begin to suggest the techniques that may be used in heavily charged language. For one thing, the two descriptions of Corlyn contain no really good example of the use of charged abstractions; for another, the writer was obliged by the assignment to use the same set of facts and so could not slant by selecting his material.

F. SLANTING AND CHARGED LANGUAGE

. . . When slanting the facts, or words, or emphasis, or any combination of the three *significantly influences* feelings toward, or judgments about, a subject, the language used is charged language. . . .

Of course communications vary in the amount of charge they carry and in their effect on different people; what is very favorably charged for one person may have little or no charge, or may even be adversely charged, for others. It is sometimes hard to distinguish between charged and uncharged expression. But it is safe to say that whenever we wish to convey any kind of inner knowledge—feelings, attitudes, judgments, values—we are obliged to convey that attitudinal meaning through the medium of charged language; and when we wish to understand the inside knowledge of others, we have to interpret the charged language that they choose, or are obliged to use. Charged language, then, is the natural and necessary medium for the communication of charged or attitudinal meaning. At times we have difficulty in living with it, but we should have even greater difficulty in living without it.

Some of the difficulties in living with charged language are caused by its use in dishonest propaganda, in some editorials, in many political speeches, in most advertising, in certain kinds of effusive salesmanship, and in blatantly insincere, or exaggerated, or sentimental expressions of emotion. Other difficulties are caused by the misunderstandings and misinterpretations that charged language produces. A charged phrase misinterpreted in a love letter; a charged word spoken in haste or in anger; an acrimonious argument about religion or politics or athletics or fraternities; the frustrating uncertainty produced by the effort to understand the complex attitudinal meaning in a poem or play or a short story—these troubles, all growing out of the use of charged language, may give us the feeling that Robert Louis Stevenson expressed when he said, "The battle goes sore against us to the going down of the sun. . . ."

READING AND DISCUSSION QUESTIONS

1. How do the Birks distinguish between the process of selection and the process of slanting?
2. Explain the three types of slanting described by the Birks and illustrate each with examples from your own experience.
3. According to the Birks, why is charged language unavoidable—and ultimately desirable?

WRITING SUGGESTIONS

4. Choose a printed ad and analyze the use of language, applying the Birks' terminology.

5. Choose one or more editorials or letters to the editor and show how word choice reveals a writer's attitude toward a subject.

We find slanting everywhere, not only in advertising and propaganda, where we expect to find it, but in news stories, which should be strictly neutral in their recounting of events, and in textbooks. In the field of history, for example, it is often difficult for scholars to remain impartial about significant events. Like the rest of us, they may approve or disapprove, and their choice of words will reflect their judgments.

The following passage by a distinguished Catholic historian describes the events surrounding the momentous decision by Henry VIII, king of England, to break with the Roman Catholic Church in 1534, in part because of the Pope's refusal to grant him a divorce from the Catholic princess Catherine of Aragon so that he could marry Anne Boleyn.

> The *protracted* delay in receiving an annulment was very *irritating* to the *impulsive* English king. . . . Gradually Henry's former *effusive* loyalty to Rome gave way to a settled conviction of the tyranny of the papal power, and there *rushed* to his mind the recollections of efforts of earlier English rulers to restrict that power. A few *salutary* enactments against the Church might *compel* a favorable decision from the Pope.
>
> Henry seriously opened his campaign against the Roman Church in 1531, when he *frightened* the clergy into paying a fine of over half a million dollars for violating an *obsolete* statute . . . and in the same year he *forced* the clergy to recognize himself as supreme head of the Church. . . .
>
> His *subservient* Parliament then empowered him to stop the payments of annates to the Pope and to appoint bishops in England without recourse to the papacy. *Without waiting longer* for the decision from Rome, he had Cranmer, *one of his own creatures,* whom he had just named Archbishop of Canterbury, declare his marriage null and void. . . .
>
> Yet Henry VIII encountered considerable *opposition* from the *higher clergy,* from the monks, and from many *intellectual leaders.* . . . A *popular uprising*—the Pilgrimage of Grace—was *sternly* suppressed, and such men as the *brilliant* Sir Thomas More and John Fisher, the *aged* and *saintly* bishop of Rochester, were beheaded because they retained their former belief in papal supremacy.[8] [Italics added.]

---

[8] Carlton J. H. Hayes, *A Political and Cultural History of Modern Europe,* vol. 1 (New York: Macmillan, 1933), pp. 172–73.

In the first paragraph the italicized words help make the following points: that Henry was rash, impulsive, and insincere and that he was intent on punishing the church (the word *salutary* means healthful or beneficial and is used sarcastically). In the second paragraph the choice of words stresses Henry's use of force and the cowardly submission of his followers. In the third paragraph the adjectives describing the opposition to Henry's campaign and those who were executed emphasize Henry's cruelty and despotism. Within the limits of this brief passage the author has offered support for his strong indictment of Henry VIII's actions, both in defining the statute as obsolete and in describing the popular opposition. In a longer exposition you would expect to find a more elaborate justification with facts and authoritative opinion from other sources.

The advocate of a position in an argument, unlike the reporter or the historian, must express a judgment, but the preceding examples demonstrate how the arguer should use language to avoid or minimize slanting and to persuade readers that he or she has come to a conclusion after careful analysis. The careful arguer must not conceal his or her judgments by presenting them as if they were statements of fact, but must offer convincing support for his or her choice of words and respect the audience's feelings and attitudes by using temperate language.

Depending on the circumstances, *exaggeration* can be defined, in the words of one writer, as "a form of lying." An essay in *Time* magazine, "Watching Out for Loaded Words," points to the danger for the arguer in relying on exaggerated language as an essential part of the argument.

> The trouble with loaded words is they tend to short-circuit thought. While they may describe something, they simultaneously try to seduce the mind into accepting a prefabricated opinion about the something described.[9]

PRACTICE

Locate specific examples of slanted language in the first of these two excerpts from the debate later in the chapter. What effect does the word choice have in the first piece? How does it compare to the word choice in the second passage, on the same topic?

> 1. Grandstanding politicians love to rail against the gun. Inanimate objects are good targets to beat up on. That way, politicians do not have to address the real problems in our society. We pay a price for this craven misdirection, though, in thousands of murders, muggings, rapes, robberies, and burglaries.
> Yet that is not the greatest danger we face. The Founding Fathers knew that *governments* could turn criminal. That is the principal

[9] *Time*, May 24, 1982, p. 86.

reason they wanted every man armed: An armed citizenry militates against the development of tyranny. The Founding Fathers did not want every man armed in order to shoot a burglar, although they had nothing against doing so. The Founding Fathers did not want every man armed in order to shoot Bambi or Thumper, although they had nothing against doing so. The Founding Fathers wanted every man armed in order to shoot soldiers or police of tyrannical regimes who suppress the rights of free men. (McGrath 425)

2. Americans also have a right to defend their homes, and we need not challenge that. Nor does anyone seriously question that the Constitution protects the right of hunters to own and keep sporting guns for hunting game any more than anyone would challenge the right to own and keep fishing rods and other equipment for fishing—or to own automobiles. To "keep and bear arms" for hunting today is essentially a recreational activity and not an imperative of survival, as it was 200 years ago; "Saturday night specials" and machine guns are not recreational weapons and surely are as much in need of regulation as motor vehicles.

Americans should ask themselves a few questions. The Constitution does not mention automobiles or motorboats, but the right to keep and own an automobile is beyond question; equally beyond question is the power of the state to regulate the purchase or the transfer of such vehicle and the right to license the vehicle and the driver with reasonable standards. In some places, even a bicycle must be registered, as must some household dogs. (Burger 419)

PICTURESQUE LANGUAGE

Picturesque language consists of words that produce images in the mind of the reader. Students sometimes assume that vivid picture-making language is the exclusive instrument of novelists and poets, but writers of arguments can also avail themselves of such devices to heighten the impact of their messages.

Picturesque language can do more than render a scene. It shares with other kinds of emotive language the power to express and arouse deep feelings. Like a fine painting or photograph, it can draw readers into the picture where they partake of the writer's experience as if they were also present. Such power may be used to delight, to instruct, or to horrify. In 1741 the Puritan preacher Jonathan Edwards delivered his sermon "Sinners in the Hands of an Angry God," in which people were likened to repulsive spiders hanging over the flames of Hell to be dropped into the fire whenever a wrathful God was pleased to release them. The congregation's reaction to Edwards's picture of the everlasting horrors to be suffered in the netherworld included panic, fainting, hysteria, and convulsions. Subsequently Edwards lost his pulpit in Massachusetts, in part as a consequence of his success at provoking such uncontrollable terror among his congregation.

Language as intense and vivid as Edwards's emerges from very strong emotion about a deeply felt cause. In the following paragraph, Lavina Melwani uses picturesque language to call attention to some of the problems faced daily by undocumented workers.

> The rats—bold, tenacious, and totally fearless—are what bothered him the most. Prem, who requested his last name not be used, says the rodents have the run of the old apartment he shares in Baltimore City, Maryland, with five other Nepali men, most of them undocumented. "It is impossible to have beds for six people in two rooms," he says. "So we have small roll-out beds or mattresses on the floor. There are many rats running around the apartment and it's difficult to catch them. We can't complain. The landlord doesn't care. He knows we have to live here and have no choice."[10]

The rules governing the use of picturesque language are the same as those governing other kinds of emotive language. Is the language appropriate? Is it too strong, too colorful for the purpose of the message? Does it result in slanting or distortion? What will its impact be on a hostile or indifferent audience? Will they be angered, repelled? Will they cease to read or listen if the imagery is too disturbing?

CONCRETE AND ABSTRACT LANGUAGE

Writers of argument need to be aware of another use of language—the distinction between concrete and abstract. Concrete words point to real objects and real experiences. Abstract words express qualities apart from particular things and events. *Velvety, dark red roses* is concrete; we can see, touch, and smell them. *Beauty* in the eye of the beholder is abstract; we can speak of the quality of beauty without reference to a particular object or event. *Returning money found in the street to the owner, although no one has seen the discovery* is concrete. *Honesty* is abstract. In abstracting we separate a quality shared by a number of objects or events, however different from each other the individual objects or events may be.

Writing that describes or tells a story leans heavily on concrete language. Although arguments also rely on the vividness of concrete language, they use abstract terms far more extensively than other kinds of writing. Using abstractions effectively, especially in arguments of value and policy, is important for two reasons: (1) Abstractions represent the qualities,

---

[10] "No Roof No Roots No Rights." *Little India*, April 12, 2006, p. 42.

characteristics, and values that the writer is explaining, defending, or attacking; and (2) they enable the writer to make generalizations about his or her data. Equally important is knowing when to avoid abstractions that obscure the message.

You should not expect abstract terms alone to carry the emotional content of your message. The effect of even the most suggestive words can be enhanced by details, examples, and anecdotes. One mode of expression is not superior to the other; both abstractions and concrete detail work together to produce clear, persuasive argument. This is especially true when the meanings assigned to abstract terms vary from reader to reader.

In establishing claims based on the support of values, for example, you may use such abstract terms as *religion, duty, freedom, peace, progress, justice, equality, democracy,* and *pursuit of happiness.* You can assume that some of these words are associated with the same ideas and emotions for almost all readers; others require further explanation. Suppose you write, "We have made great progress in the last fifty years." One dictionary defines *progress* as "a gradual betterment," another abstraction. How will you define "gradual betterment" for your readers? Can you be sure that they have in mind the same references for progress that you do? If not, misunderstandings are inevitable. You may offer examples: supersonic planes, computers, shopping malls, nuclear energy. Many of your readers will react favorably to the mention of these innovations, which to them represent progress; others, for whom these inventions represent change but not progress, will react unfavorably. You may not be able to convince all of your readers that "we have made great progress," but all of them will now understand what you mean by "progress." And intelligent disagreement is preferable to misunderstanding.

Abstractions tell us what conclusions we have arrived at; details tell us how we got there. But there are dangers in either too many details or too many abstractions. For example, a writer may present only concrete data without telling readers what conclusions are to be drawn from them. Suppose you read the following:

> To Chinese road-users, traffic police are part of the grass . . . and neither they nor the rules they're supposed to enforce are paid the least attention. . . . Ignoring traffic-lights is only one peculiarity of Chinese traffic. It's normal for a pedestrian to walk straight out into a stream of cars without so much as lifting his head; and goodness knows how many Chinese cyclists I've almost killed as they have shot blindly in front of me across busy main roads.[11]

These details would constitute no more than interesting gossip until we read, "It's not so much a sign of ignorance or recklessness . . . but of fatalism." The details of specific behavior have now acquired a significance expressed in the abstraction *fatalism.*

---

[11] Philip Short, "The Chinese and the Russians," *The Listener,* April 8, 1982, p. 6.

A more common problem, however, in using abstractions is omission of details. Either the writer is not a skilled observer and cannot provide the details, or he or she believes that such details are too small and quiet compared to the grand sounds made by abstract terms. These grand sounds, unfortunately, cannot compensate for the lack of clarity and liveliness. Lacking detailed support, abstract words may be misinterpreted. They may also represent ideas that are so vague as to be meaningless. Sometimes they function illegitimately as short cuts (discussed on pp. 388–93), arousing emotions but unaccompanied by good reasons for their use. The following paragraph exhibits some of these common faults. How would you translate it into clear English?

> We respectively petition, request, and entreat that due and adequate provision be made, this day and the date hereinafter subscribed, for the satisfying of these petitioners' nutritional requirements and for the organizing of such methods of allocation and distribution as may be deemed necessary and proper to assure the reception by and for said petitioners of such quantities of baked cereal products as shall, in the judgment of the aforesaid petitioners, constitute a sufficient supply thereof.[12]

If you had trouble decoding this, it was because there were almost no concrete references—the homely words *baked* and *cereal* leap out of the paragraph like English signposts in a foreign country—and too many long words or words of Latin origin when simple words would do: *requirements* instead of *needs, petition* instead of *ask*. An absence of concrete references and an excess of long Latinate words can have a depressing effect on both writer and reader. The writer may be in danger of losing the thread of the argument, the reader at a loss to discover the message.

The paragraph above, according to James B. Minor, a lawyer who teaches courses in legal drafting, is "how a federal regulation writer would probably write, 'Give us this day our daily bread.'" This brief sentence with its short, familiar words and its origin in the Lord's Prayer has a deep emotional effect. The paragraph composed by Minor deadens any emotional impact because of its preponderance of abstract terms and its lack of connection with the world of our senses.

Finally, there are the moral implications of using abstractions that conceal a disagreeable reality. George Orwell pointed them out more than sixty years ago in "Politics and the English Language." Another essayist, Joseph Wood Krutch, in criticizing the attitude that cheating "doesn't really hurt anybody," observed, "'It really doesn't hurt anybody' means it doesn't do that abstraction called society any harm." The following news story reports a proposal with which Orwell and Krutch might have agreed. His intention, says the author, is to "slow the hand of any President who might be tempted to unleash a nuclear attack."

[12] *New York Times,* May 10, 1977, p. 35.

It has long been feared that a President could be making his fateful decision while at a "psychological distance" from the victims of a nuclear barrage; that he would be in a clean, air-conditioned room, surrounded by well-scrubbed aides, all talking in abstract terms about appropriate military responses in an international crisis, and that he might well push to the back of his mind the realization that hundreds of millions of people would be exterminated.

So Roger Fisher, professor of law at Harvard University, offers a simple suggestion to make the stakes more real. He would put the codes needed to fire nuclear weapons in a little capsule, and implant the capsule next to the heart of a volunteer, who would carry a big butcher knife as he accompanied the President everywhere. If the President ever wanted to fire nuclear weapons, he would first have to kill, with his own hands, that human being.

He has to look at someone and realize what death is—what an innocent death is. "It's reality brought home," says Professor Fisher.[13]

The moral lesson is clear: It is much easier to do harm if we convince ourselves that the object of the injury is only an abstraction.

SHORT CUTS

Short cuts are arguments that depend on readers' responses to words. Short cuts, like other devices we have discussed so far, are a common use of emotive language but are often mistaken for valid argument.

Although they have power to move us, these abbreviated substitutes for argument avoid the hard work necessary to provide facts, expert opinion, and analysis of warrants. Even experts, however, can be guilty of using short cuts, and the writer who consults an authority should be alert to that authority's use of language. Two of the most common uses of short cuts are clichés and slogans.

■ Clichés

A cliché is an expression or idea grown stale through overuse. Clichés in language are tired expressions that have faded like old photographs; readers no longer see anything when clichés are placed before them. Clichés include phrases like "cradle of civilization," "few and far between," "rude awakening," "follow in the footsteps of," "fly in the ointment."

But more important to recognize and avoid are clichés of thought. A cliché of thought may be likened to a formula, which one dictionary defines as "any conventional rule or method for doing something, especially when used, applied, or repeated without thought." Clichés of thought rep-

---

[13] *New York Times,* September 7, 1982, sec. C, p. 1.

resent ready-made answers to questions, stereotyped solutions to problems, "knee-jerk" reactions. Two writers who call these forms of expression "mass language" describe it this way: "Mass language is language which presents the reader with a response he is expected to make without giving him adequate reason for having this response."[14] These clichés of thought are often expressed in single words or phrases.

Certain cultural attitudes encourage the use of clichés. The liberal American tradition has been governed by hopeful assumptions about our ability to solve problems. A professor of communications says that "we tell our students that for every problem there must be a solution."[15] But real solutions are hard to come by. In our haste to provide them, to prove that we can be decisive, we may be tempted to produce familiar responses that resemble solutions. All reasonable solutions are worthy of consideration, but they must be defined and supported if they are to be used in a thoughtful, well-constructed argument.

Although formulas change with the times, some are unexpectedly hardy and survive long after critics have revealed their weaknesses. Overpopulation is often cited as the cause of poverty, disease, and war. It can be found in the writing of the ancient Greeks 2,500 years ago. "That perspective," says the editor of *Food Monitor,* a journal published by World Hunger Year, Inc., "is so pervasive that most Americans have simply stopped thinking about population and resort to inane clucking of tongues."[16] If the writer offering overpopulation as an explanation for poverty were to look further, he or she would discover that the explanation rested on shaky data. Singapore, the most densely populated country in the world (11,574 persons per square mile) is also one of the richest ($16,500 per capita income per year). Chad, one of the most sparsely populated (11 persons per square mile) is also one of the poorest ($190 per capita income per year).[17] Strictly defined, overpopulation may serve to explain some instances of poverty; obviously it cannot serve as a blanket to cover all or even most instances. "By repeating stock phrases," one columnist reminds us, "we lose the ability, finally, to hear what we are saying."

◼ Slogans

I have always been rather impressed by those people who wear badges stating where they stand on certain issues. The badges have to be small, and therefore the message has to be small, concise, and without elaboration. So

---

[14] Richard E. Hughes and P. Albert Duhamel, *Rhetoric: Principles and Usage* (Englewood Cliffs, N.J.: Prentice-Hall, 1962), p. 161.

[15] Malcolm O. Sillars, "The New Conservatism and the Teacher of Speech," *Southern Speech Journal* 21 (1956), p. 240.

[16] Letter to the *New York Times,* October 4, 1982, sec. A, p. 18.

[17] *World Almanac and Book of Facts,* 1995 (New York: World Almanac, 1995), pp. 754, 818.

it comes out as "I hate something" or "I love something," or ban this or ban that. There isn't space for argument, and I therefore envy the badge-wearer who is so clear-cut about his or her opinions.[18]

The word *slogan* has a picturesque origin. A slogan was the war cry or rallying cry of a Scottish or Irish clan. From that early use it has come to mean a "catchword or rallying motto distinctly associated with a political party or other group" as well as a "catch phrase used to advertise a product."

Slogans, like clichés, are short, undeveloped arguments. They represent abbreviated responses to often complex questions. As a reader you need to be aware that slogans merely call attention to a problem; they cannot offer persuasive proof for a claim in a dozen words or less. As a writer you should avoid the use of slogans that evoke an emotional response "without giving [the reader] adequate reason for having this response."

Advertising slogans are the most familiar. Some of them are probably better known than nursery rhymes: "Got milk?" "L'Oréal, because I'm worth it," "Nike, just do it." Advertisements may, of course, rely for their effectiveness on more than slogans. They may also give us interesting and valuable information about products, but most advertisements give us slogans that ignore proof—short cuts substituting for argument.

The persuasive appeal of advertising slogans heavily depends on the connotations associated with products. In Chapter 7 (see p. 227, under "Appeals to Needs and Values"), we discussed the way in which advertisements promise to satisfy our needs and protect our values. Wherever evidence is scarce or nonexistent, the advertiser must persuade us through skillful choice of words and phrases (as well as pictures), especially those that produce pleasurable feelings. "Let it inspire you" is the slogan of a popular liqueur. It suggests a desirable state of being but remains suitably vague about the nature of the inspiration. Another familiar slogan—"Noxzema, clean makeup"—also emphasizes a quality that we approve of, but what is "clean" makeup? Since the advertisers are silent, we are left with warm feelings about the word and not much more.

Advertising slogans are persuasive because their witty phrasing and punchy rhythms produce an automatic yes response. We react to them as we might react to the lyrics of popular songs, and we treat them far less critically than we treat more straightforward and elaborate arguments. Still, the consequences of failing to analyze the slogans of advertisers are usually not serious. You may be tempted to buy a product because you were fascinated by a brilliant slogan, but if the product doesn't satisfy, you can abandon it without much loss. However, ignoring ideological slogans coined by political parties or special-interest groups may carry an enormous price, and the results are not so easily undone.

Ideological slogans, like advertising slogans, depend on the power of connotation, the emotional associations aroused by a word or phrase. In the

---

[18] Anthony Smith, "Nuclear Power—Why Not?" *The Listener,* October 22, 1981, p. 463.

1960s and 1970s, a period of well-advertised social change, slogans flourished; they appeared by the hundreds of thousands on buttons, T-shirts, and
bumper stickers. One of them read, "Student Power!" To some readers of the
slogan, distrustful of young people and worried about student unrest on campuses and in the streets, the suggestion was frightening. To others, mostly
students, the idea of power, however undefined, was intoxicating. Notice that
"Student Power!" is not an argument; it is only a claim. (It might also represent a warrant.) As a claim, for example, it might take this form: Students at
this school should have the power to select the faculty. Of course, the arguer
would need to provide the kinds of proof that support his or her claim, something the slogan by itself cannot do. Many people, whether they accepted or
rejected the claim, supplied the rest of the argument without knowing exactly what the issues were and how a developed argument would proceed.
They were accepting or rejecting the slogan largely on the basis of emotional
reaction to words.

American political history is, in fact, a repository of slogans. Leaf
through a history of the United States and you will come across "Tippe-
canoe and Tyler, too," "manifest destiny," "fifty-four forty or fight," "make
the world safe for democracy," "the silent majority," "the domino theory,"
"the missile gap," "the window of vulnerability." Each administration tries
to capture the attention and allegiance of the public by coining catchy
phrases. Roosevelt's New Deal in 1932 was followed by the Square Deal
and the New Frontier. Today, slogans must be carefully selected to avoid
offending groups that are sensitive to the ways in which words affect their
interests. In 1983 Senator John Glenn, announcing his candidacy for president, talked about bringing "old values and new horizons" to the White
House. "New horizons" apparently carried positive connotations. His staff,
however, worried that "old values" might suggest racism and sexism to minorities and women.

Over a period of time slogans, like clichés, can acquire a life of their own
and, if they are repeated often enough, come to represent an unchanging
truth we no longer need to examine. "Dangerously," says the writer quoted
above, "policy makers become prisoners of the slogans they popularize."

Following are two examples. The first is part of the second inaugural
address of George C. Wallace, governor of Alabama, in 1971. The second
is taken from an article in the *Militia News,* the organ of a group that believed the U.S. government was engaged in a "satanic conspiracy" to disarm the American people and then enslave them. Timothy McVeigh, who
blew up the Oklahoma City federal building in 1995, was influenced by
the group.

> The people of the South and those who think like the South, represent
> the majority viewpoint within our constitutional democracy, but they are
> not organized and do not speak with a loud voice. Until the day arrives
> when the voice of the people of the South and those who think like us is,
> within the law, thrust into the face of the bureaucrats, only then can the

"people's power" express itself legally and ethically and get results. . . . Too long, oh, too long, has the voice of the people been silenced by their own disruptive government—by governmental bribery in quasi-governmental handouts such as H.E.W. and others that exist in America today! An aroused people can save this nation from those evil forces who seek our destruction. The choice is yours. The hour is growing late![19]

Every gun owner who is the least bit informed knows that those who are behind this conspiracy—who now have their people well placed in political office, in the courts, in the media, and in the schools, are working for the total disarming of the American people and the sur-render of our nation and our sovereignty. . . . The time is at hand when men and women must decide whether they are on the side of freedom and justice, the American republic, and Almighty God, or if they are on the side of tyranny and oppression, the New World Order, and Satan.[20]

Whatever power these recommendations might have if their propos-als were more clearly formulated, as they stand they are collections of slo-gans and loaded words. (Even the language falters: Can the voice of the people be thrust into the face of the bureaucrats?) We can visualize some of the slogans as brightly colored banners: "Dislodge Big Money!" "Power to the People!" "Save This Nation from Evil Forces!" "The Choice Is Yours!" Do all the groups mentioned share identical interests? If so, what are they? Given the vagueness of the terms, it is not surprising that arguers on opposite sides of the political spectrum—loosely characterized as lib-eral and conservative—sometimes resort to the same clichés and slogans: the language of populism, or a belief in conspiracies against God-fearing people, in these examples.

Slogans have numerous shortcomings as substitutes for the develop-ment of an argument. First, their brevity presents serious disadvantages. Slogans necessarily ignore exceptions or negative instances that might qualify a claim. They usually speak in absolute terms without describing the circumstances in which a principle or idea might not work. Their claims therefore seem shrill and exaggerated. In addition, brevity prevents the sloganeer from revealing how he or she arrived at conclusions.

Second, slogans may conceal unexamined warrants. When Japanese cars were beginning to compete with American cars, the slogan "Made in America by Americans" appeared on the bumpers of thousands of American-made cars. A thoughtful reader would have discovered in this slogan several implied warrants: American cars are better than Japanese cars; the American economy will improve if we buy American; patriotism can be expressed by buying American goods. If the reader were to ask a few probing questions, he or she might find these warrants unconvincing.

---

[19] Second Inaugural Address as governor of Alabama, January 18, 1971.
[20] Chip Berlet and Matthew N. Lyons, *Right-Wing Populism in America* (New York: Guildford Press, 2000), p. 301.

Silent warrants that express values hide in other popular and influential slogans. "Pro-life," the slogan of those who oppose abortion, assumes that the fetus is a living being entitled to the same rights as individuals already born. "Pro-choice," the slogan of those who favor abortion, suggests that the freedom of the pregnant woman to choose is the foremost or only consideration. The words *life* and *choice* have been carefully selected to reflect desirable qualities, but the words are only the beginning of the argument.

Third, although slogans may express admirable sentiments, they often fail to tell us how to achieve their objectives. They address us in the imperative mode, ordering us to take an action or refrain from it. But the means of achieving the objectives may be nonexistent or very costly. If the sloganeer cannot offer workable means for implementing his or her goals, he or she risks alienating the audience.

Sloganeering is one of the recognizable attributes of propaganda. Propaganda for both good and bad purposes is a form of slanting, of selecting language and facts to persuade an audience to take a certain action. Even a good cause may be weakened by an unsatisfactory slogan. The slogans of some organizations devoted to fundraising for people with physical handicaps have come under attack for depicting those with handicaps as helpless. According to one critic, the popular slogan "Jerry's kids" promotes the idea that Jerry Lewis is the sole support of children with muscular dystrophy. Perhaps increased sensitivity to the needs of people with disabilities will produce new words and new slogans. If you assume that your audience is sophisticated and alert, you will probably write your strongest arguments, devoid of clichés and slogans.

SAMPLE ANNOTATED ESSAY

President's Address to the Nation, September 11, 2006

GEORGE W. BUSH

Words like seared, barbarity, and murdered are examples of slanting used appropriately for the author's purpose.

Good evening. Five years ago, this date — September the 11th — was seared into America's memory. Nineteen men attacked us with a barbarity unequaled in our history. They murdered people of all colors, creeds, and nationalities — and made war upon the entire free world. Since that day, America and her allies have taken the offensive in a war unlike any we have fought before. Today, we are safer, but we are not yet safe. On this solemn night, I've asked for some of your time to discuss the nature of the threat still before us, what we are doing to protect our nation, and the building of a more hopeful Middle East that holds the key to peace for America and the world.

On 9/11, our nation saw the face of evil. Yet on that awful day, we also witnessed something distinctly American: ordinary citizens rising to the occasion, and responding with extraordinary acts of courage. We saw courage in office workers who were trapped on the high floors of burning skyscrapers— and called home so that their last words to their families would be of comfort and love. We saw courage in passengers aboard Flight 93, who recited the 23rd Psalm—and then charged the cockpit. And we saw courage in the Pentagon staff who made it out of the flames and smoke—and ran back in to answer cries for help. On this day, we remember the innocent who lost their lives—and we pay tribute to those who gave their lives so that others might live.

For many of our citizens, the wounds of that morning are still fresh. I've met firefighters and police officers who choke up at the memory of fallen comrades. I've stood with families gathered on a grassy field in Pennsylvania, who take bittersweet pride in loved ones who refused to be victims—and gave America our first victory in the war on terror. I've sat beside young mothers with children who are now five years old—and still long for the daddies who will never cradle them in their arms. Out of this suffering, we resolve to honor every man and woman lost. And we seek their lasting memorial in a safer and more hopeful world.

Since the horror of 9/11, we've learned a great deal about the enemy. We have learned that they are evil and kill without mercy—but not without purpose. We have learned that they form a global network of extremists who are driven by a perverted vision of Islam—a totalitarian ideology that hates freedom, rejects tolerance, and despises all dissent. And we have learned that their goal is to build a radical Islamic empire where women are prisoners in their homes, men are beaten for missing prayer meetings, and terrorists have a safe haven

---

It is exaggeration to say that the acts described in this paragraph are distinctly American, but the concrete examples are effective for the author's purpose.

More concrete examples, with the first person I making it clear that Bush has shared moments of grief with the victims' families.

For the second time Bush refers to a more hopeful world. If the rest of the essay does not provide further explanation, this will be a cliché of thought.

Two of the strongest slanted words here are perverted and, in contrast to the reference to civilized nations, the implication that America's enemies are uncivilized.

On the other hand, to have a calling carries a positive slant, suggesting a religious or at least honorable sense of duty.

The allusion to the Cold War will evoke negative memories for some, depending on their age.

The reference to the war in Iraq as one that America didn't ask for suggests that it was imposed on an unwilling nation.

Suggesting what a loss would mean for America's children is an appeal to emotion.

To be held to account for their actions is a cliché, one that may hide uncomfortable truths, given suspicions aroused about how the U.S. questions prisoners.

to plan and launch attacks on America and other civilized nations. The war against this enemy is more than a military conflict. It is the decisive ideological struggle of the 21st century, and the calling of our generation.

Our nation is being tested in a way that we have   5
not been since the start of the Cold War. We saw what a handful of our enemies can do with box-cutters and plane tickets. We hear their threats to launch even more terrible attacks on our people. And we know that if they were able to get their hands on weapons of mass destruction, they would use them against us. We face an enemy determined to bring death and suffering into our homes. America did not ask for this war, and every American wishes it were over. So do I. But the war is not over—and it will not be over until either we or the extremists emerge victorious. If we do not defeat these enemies now, we will leave our children to face a Middle East overrun by terrorist states and radical dictators armed with nuclear weapons. We are in a war that will set the course for this new century—and determine the destiny of millions across the world.

For America, 9/11 was more than a tragedy— it changed the way we look at the world. On September the 11th, we resolved that we would go on the offense against our enemies, and we would not distinguish between the terrorists and those who harbor or support them. So we helped drive the Taliban from power in Afghanistan. We put al Qaeda on the run, and killed or captured most of those who planned the 9/11 attacks, including the man believed to be the mastermind, Khalid Sheik Mohammed. He and other suspected terrorists have been questioned by the Central Intelligence Agency, and they provided valuable information that has helped stop attacks in America and across the world. Now these men have been transferred to Guantanamo Bay, so they can be held to account for their actions. Osama bin Laden and other terrorists are still in hiding. Our message to them is clear: No matter how long it takes, America will find you, and we will bring you to justice.

On September the 11th, we learned that America must confront threats before they reach our shores, whether those threats come from terrorist networks or terrorist states. I'm often asked why we're in Iraq when Saddam Hussein was not responsible for the 9/11 attacks. The answer is that the regime of Saddam Hussein was a clear threat. My administration, the Congress, and the United Nations saw the threat—and after 9/11, Saddam's regime posed a risk that the world could not afford to take. The world is safer because Saddam Hussein is no longer in power. And now the challenge is to help the Iraqi people build a democracy that fulfills the dreams of the nearly 12 million Iraqis who came out to vote in free elections last December.

Another cliché of thought: a risk that the world could not afford to take.

Al Qaeda and other extremists from across the world have come to Iraq to stop the rise of a free society in the heart of the Middle East. They have joined the remnants of Saddam's regime and other armed groups to foment sectarian violence and drive us out. Our enemies in Iraq are tough and they are committed—but so are Iraqi and coalition forces. We're adapting to stay ahead of the enemy, and we are carrying out a clear plan to ensure that a democratic Iraq succeeds.

References to democracy and free elections have positive connotations for most Americans.

We're training Iraqi troops so they can defend their nation. We're helping Iraq's unity government grow in strength and serve its people. We will not leave until this work is done. Whatever mistakes have been made in Iraq, the worst mistake would be to think that if we pulled out, the terrorists would leave us alone. They will not leave us alone. They will follow us. The safety of America depends on the outcome of the battle in the streets of Baghdad. Osama bin Laden calls this fight "the Third World War"—and he says that victory for the terrorists in Iraq will mean America's "defeat and disgrace forever." If we yield Iraq to men like bin Laden, our enemies will be emboldened; they will gain a new safe haven; they will use Iraq's resources to fuel their extremist movement. We will not allow this to happen. America will stay in the fight. Iraq will be a free nation, and a strong ally in the war on terror.

The allusion to World War I and World War II by alluding to a Third World War, like the allusion to the Cold War, evokes memories, mostly negative, for older Americans.

Osama bin Laden's reference to America's defeat and disgrace forever is a verbal assault on national pride.

The primary slogan for the war in Iraq: the war on terror.

The enemy is guilty of unspeakable violence. The Iraqi people are steadfast. Our Armed Forces have exhibited skill and resolve, made great sacrifices.

Appeals to Americans' need for security.

Slanted language: the enemy's ideology is hateful.

The use of the adjective legal to modify authority is loaded for those who believe Congress was rushed into passing laws that threaten Americans' right to privacy out of fear.

We can be confident that our coalition will suc- 10 ceed because the Iraqi people have been steadfast in the face of unspeakable violence. And we can be confident in victory because of the skill and resolve of America's Armed Forces. Every one of our troops is a volunteer, and since the attacks of September the 11th, more than 1.6 million Americans have stepped forward to put on our nation's uniform. In Iraq, Afghanistan, and other fronts in the war on terror, the men and women of our military are making great sacrifices to keep us safe. Some have suffered terrible injuries—and nearly 3,000 have given their lives. America cherishes their memory. We pray for their families. And we will never back down from the work they have begun.

We also honor those who toil day and night to keep our homeland safe, and we are giving them the tools they need to protect our people. We've created the Department of Homeland Security. We have torn down the wall that kept law enforcement and intelligence from sharing information. We've tightened security at our airports and seaports and borders, and we've created new programs to monitor enemy bank records and phone calls. Thanks to the hard work of our law enforcement and intelligence professionals, we have broken up terrorist cells in our midst and saved American lives.

Five years after 9/11, our enemies have not succeeded in launching another attack on our soil, but they've not been idle. Al Qaeda and those inspired by its hateful ideology have carried out terrorist attacks in more than two dozen nations. And just last month, they were foiled in a plot to blow up passenger planes headed for the United States. They remain determined to attack America and kill our citizens—and we are determined to stop them. We'll continue to give the men and women who protect us every resource and legal authority they need to do their jobs.

In the first days after the 9/11 attacks I promised to use every element of national power to fight the terrorists, wherever we find them. One of the strongest weapons in our arsenal is the power of freedom. The terrorists fear freedom as much as they

Many abstractions here that are clichés of thought if not supported: power of freedom, clash of civilization, struggle for civilization, way of life enjoyed by free nations.

do our firepower. They are thrown into panic at the sight of an old man pulling the election lever, girls enrolling in schools, or families worshiping God in their own traditions. They know that given a choice, people will choose freedom over their extremist ideology. So their answer is to deny people this choice by raging against the forces of freedom and moderation. This struggle has been called a clash of civilizations. In truth, it is a struggle for civilization. We are fighting to maintain the way of life enjoyed by free nations. And we're fighting for the possibility that good and decent people across the Middle East can raise up societies based on freedom and tolerance and personal dignity.

We are now in the early hours of this struggle between tyranny and freedom. Amid the violence, some question whether the people of the Middle East want their freedom, and whether the forces of moderation can prevail. For 60 years, these doubts guided our policies in the Middle East. And then, on a bright September morning, it became clear that the calm we saw in the Middle East was only a mirage. Years of pursuing stability to promote peace had left us with neither. So we changed our policies, and committed America's influence in the world to advancing freedom and democracy as the great alternatives to repression and radicalism.

With our help, the people of the Middle East are   15
now stepping forward to claim their freedom. From Kabul to Baghdad to Beirut, there are brave men and women risking their lives each day for the same freedoms that we enjoy. And they have one question for us: Do we have the confidence to do in the Middle East what our fathers and grandfathers accomplished in Europe and Asia? By standing with democratic leaders and reformers, by giving voice to the hopes of decent men and women, we're offering a path away from radicalism. And we are enlisting the most powerful force for peace and moderation in the Middle East: the desire of millions to be free.

The references to what our fathers and grandfathers *did in* Europe and Asia *is an additional appeal to American pride. Only those who agree with America deserve the label* decent.

Across the broader Middle East, the extremists are fighting to prevent such a future. Yet America has confronted evil before, and we have defeated it—sometimes at the cost of thousands of good

Allusions to previous American victories and former presidents who led the nation during World War II and the Cold War.

Desert of despotism and fertile ground of liberty — picturesque language used for contrast.

A specific example that carries emotional impact.

men in a single battle. When Franklin Roosevelt vowed to defeat two enemies across two oceans, he could not have foreseen D-Day and Iwo Jima — but he would not have been surprised at the outcome. When Harry Truman promised American support for free peoples resisting Soviet aggression, he could not have foreseen the rise of the Berlin Wall—but he would not have been surprised to see it brought down. Throughout our history, America has seen liberty challenged, and every time, we have seen liberty triumph with sacrifice and determination.

At the start of this young century, America looks to the day when the people of the Middle East leave the desert of despotism for the fertile gardens of liberty, and resume their rightful place in a world of peace and prosperity. We look to the day when the nations of that region recognize their greatest resource is not the oil in the ground, but the talent and creativity of their people. We look to the day when moms and dads throughout the Middle East see a future of hope and opportunity for their children. And when that good day comes, the clouds of war will part, the appeal of radicalism will decline, and we will leave our children with a better and safer world.

On this solemn anniversary, we rededicate ourselves to this cause. Our nation has endured trials, and we face a difficult road ahead. Winning this war will require the determined efforts of a unified country, and we must put aside our differences and work together to meet the test that history has given us. We will defeat our enemies. We will protect our people. And we will lead the 21st century into a shining age of human liberty.

Earlier this year, I traveled to the United States Military Academy. I was there to deliver the commencement address to the first class to arrive at West Point after the attacks of September the 11th. That day I met a proud mom named RoseEllen Dowdell. She was there to watch her son, Patrick, accept his commission in the finest Army the world has ever known. A few weeks earlier, RoseEllen had watched her other son, James, graduate from the Fire Academy in New York City. On both these days, her thoughts turned to someone who was not there to share the moment: her husband, Kevin Dowdell. Kevin was one of the 343 firefighters who rushed to the burning towers of the World Trade Center on September the 11th—and never came home. His sons lost their father that day, but not the passion for service he instilled in them. Here is what RoseEllen says about her boys: "As a mother, I cross my fingers and pray all the time for their safety—but as worried as I am, I'm also proud, and I know their dad would be, too."

A creative play on the two ways that people are brought to their knees.

Our nation is blessed to have young Americans 20 like these—and we will need them. Dangerous enemies have declared their intention to destroy our way of life. They're not the first to try, and their fate will be the same as those who tried before. Nine-Eleven showed us why. The attacks were meant to bring us to our knees, and they did, but not in the way the terrorists intended. Americans united in prayer, came to the aid of neighbors in need, and resolved that our enemies would not have the last word. The spirit of our people is the source of America's strength. And we go forward with trust in that spirit, confidence in our purpose, and faith in a loving God who made us to be free.

Thank you, and may God bless you.

Writer's Guide: Choosing Your Words Carefully

1. Be sure you have avoided language with connotations that might produce a negative reaction in your audience that would weaken your argument.
2. If you have used slanted language, consider whether it will advance your argument instead of weakening it.
3. Use picturesque language where appropriate for your purposes.
4. Replace abstract language with concrete language to be more effective.
5. Edit out any clichés or slogans from your early drafts.
6. Achieve a voice that is appropriate for your subject and audience.

Americans Entitled to Cheap Gas—Right?

JOAN RYAN

Over the years, Americans have taken a lot of vicious abuse for being self-ish and irresponsible. We are often portrayed as a nation that wants to have its cake and eat it too, which, as any American knows, is patently untrue. We also want our ice cream and maybe some Cool Whip.

I bring this up because, once again, we are the targets of international ridicule, this time for our anger over rising gas prices. Gas is up now to about $2 a gallon around the nation. It is averaging $2.31 in California. These prices are outrageous, as indicated by the newspaper and TV-news stories quoting motorists as saying, "These prices are outrageous."

The rest of the world, however, is not sympathetic. They think that because gas is $5.22 a gallon in England, $4.24 a gallon in Tokyo, and $4.92 a gallon in France, we are being piggy for complaining about per-gallon gas prices that, even with the recent spike, are still cheaper than a Starbucks Frappuccino.

Apparently the rest of the world doesn't understand the underlying sociological reasons we react as we do to increases in gas prices. Unlike them, we drive cars the size of Paris apartments. They obviously don't realize how much gas cars like these consume! It apparently has come as something of a surprise to many of us, too.

When asked to rank the importance of 56 characteristics they consid- 5
ered when buying a new car, Americans ranked fuel economy 44th. This explains why sport utility vehicles, minivans, and light trucks accounted for 54 percent of all new cars bought last year.

"It's still more important to have the right number of cup holders than high fuel economy," said Art Spinella, director of CNW Marketing Research, which conducted the survey.

Peter Rennert sells cars at John Irish Jeep in San Rafael. He showed a gray Grand Cherokee to a woman one morning earlier this week. She took the slow stroll around the vehicle, opened the doors, checked out the cargo space, took it for a test drive.

"What kind of gas mileage does it get?" she asked Rennert. He showed her the manufacturer's sticker on the window: 17 to 21 miles per gallon highway.

"That was the last I ever heard about it," Rennert said. "People bring it up mostly because they believe they're supposed to." (The woman loved the car and said she'd be back soon with her husband to hammer out a deal.)

Joan Ryan is a columnist for the *San Francisco Chronicle*, where this column appeared on May 20, 2004.

To understand Americans, it is essential for the rest of the world to re- 10
member that, underneath it all, we are socially responsible beings just like
they are, except we like big things and lots of them. In the United States,
there are now 204 million cars and 191 million drivers, more cars than we
have people to operate them. Blueberry muffins here are the size of our
heads. Soda cups are big enough to harbor small children. We build houses
designed on the well-known scientific practice of multiplying the number
of family members by pi to reach the appropriate number of bathrooms.

If the rest of the world wants to understand us better, I recommend
they see the new movie, *Supersize Me!* It's a documentary about a guy who
eats nothing but McDonald's food for a month. The movie reinforces
what we Americans already know and have known for years: Fast food
makes us fat and unhealthy. The movies shows, too, that this knowledge
makes no difference whatsoever in our behavior. We still pull up to the
golden arches, breathe in that great deep-fry aroma, and order a sack of
cholesterol to go.

Why? For the same reasons we buy big cars despite our heartfelt concerns
about saving the environment and weaning ourselves from Middle East oil:
because it makes us feel good, and because everybody else is doing it.

Across the bay in Richmond, at the ARCO station on Cutting Boule-
vard and Harbor Way, Sandra Currier filled up her 1998 Chevy Blazer for
$42 the other day. "This is the most I've ever paid," she said of the $2.29
regular unleaded. "It's got to come down."

She is a mobile notary public from Castro Valley who sometimes has
to travel as much as 200 miles in a day. She is considering charging more
for her services to cover the rising price of gas, but gas is not yet expensive enough to consider trading in her Blazer for something smaller and
more fuel-efficient. Maybe when it hits $2.75 a gallon, she said.

"I feel my daughter is safer in the SUV," Currier said. "I don't want to be 15
lower (than everybody else on the road), looking up and getting crunched."

In other words, if everybody else downsized, she would, too. Until then,
she's not going to put herself in harm's way by being the poodle on a free-
way of water buffalo.

How can the rest of the world blame her? They would do the same
under the same circumstances, according to another CNW survey. In Western Europe, respondents said if gas prices were low enough, they would
buy SUVs and big sedans, just like the Americans.

"It is kind of amusing," Spinella said. "When we do an international
wish list, it's remarkable how similar people are in the kinds of things they
would like to get their hands on."

See? There it is. We could be as responsible as the rest of the world if we
had the benefit they do of high gas prices. The low price of gas in the
United States enables our SUV indulgences. To put this complex social dynamic in the parlance of the latest psychological research: It is not our fault.

Therefore, since this situation is not of our own making, we should 20
not have to pay higher gas prices and give up the big-car life to which we
have become accustomed. That would not be right.

And if there is one thing Americans believe in, it is doing what's right.

READING AND DISCUSSION QUESTIONS

1. In the first paragraph, how does Ryan reveal her attitude toward Americans' spending habits?

2. Does Ryan offer any support for her opinion other than her own emotional response to the values of other Americans?

3. How does Ryan's choice of language help her to make her point?

4. Is Ryan's use of sarcasm and exaggeration effective?

WRITING SUGGESTIONS

5. Rewrite Ryan's article using objective language.

6. Choose another one of America's "passions" and write an essay poking gentle fun at it. (Consider, for example, Americans' consumption of fast food.)

7. Compare Ryan's use of language in this piece with that used by Varian in "The True Cost of SUVs" in Chapter 7.

$hotgun Weddings

KATHA POLLITT

W hat would the government have to do to convince you to get married when you otherwise wouldn't? More than pay you $80 a month, I'll bet, the amount Wisconsin's much-ballyhooed "Bridefare" pilot program offered unwed teen welfare mothers beginning in the early nineties, which is perhaps why then-Governor Tommy Thompson, now Health and Human Services Secretary,[1] was uninterested in having it properly evaluated and why you don't hear much about Bridefare today. OK, how about $100 a month? That's what West Virginia is currently offering to add to a couple's welfare benefits if they wed. But even though the state has simultaneously cut by 25 percent the checks of recipients living with adults to whom they are not married (including, in some cases, their own grown

---

[1]Thompson resigned on December 3, 2004.

Katha Pollitt has written about controversial moral and political issues for *The Nation*, *The New Yorker*, and the *New York Times*. This selection originally appeared in the February 4, 2002, edition of *The Nation*.

children, if you can believe that!), results have been modest: Only around 1,600 couples have applied for the bonus and presumably some of these would have married anyway. With the state's welfare budget expected to show a $90 million shortfall by 2003, the marriage bonus is likely to be quietly abolished.

Although welfare reform was sold to the public as promoting work, the Personal Responsibility and Work Opportunity Reconciliation Act of 1996 actually opens with the declaration that "marriage is the foundation of a successful society." According to Charles Murray, Robert Rector, and other right-wing ideologues, welfare enabled poor women to rely on the state instead of husbands; forcing them off the dole and into the rigors of low-wage employment would push them into marriage, restore "the family," and lift children out of poverty. That was always a silly idea. For one thing, as any single woman could have told them, it wrongly assumed that whether a woman married was only up to her; for another, it has been well documented that the men available to poor women are also poor and often (like the women) have other problems as well: In one study, 30 percent of poor single fathers were unemployed in the week before the survey and almost 40 percent had been incarcerated; drugs, drink, violence, poor health, and bad attitudes were not uncommon. Would Murray want *his* daughter to marry a guy with even one of those strikes against him? Not surprisingly, there has been no upsurge of marriage among former welfare recipients since 1996. Of all births, the proportion that are to unwed mothers has stayed roughly where it was, at 33 percent.

Since the stick of work and the carrot of cash have both proved ineffective in herding women to the altar, family values conservatives are calling for more lectures. Marriage promotion will be a hot item when welfare reform comes up for reauthorization later this year. At the federal level conservatives are calling for 10 percent of all TANF [Temporary Assistance for Needy Families] money to be set aside for promoting marriage; Utah, Arizona, and Oklahoma have already raided TANF to fund such ventures as a "healthy marriage" handbook for couples seeking a marriage license. And it's not just Republicans: Senator Joe Lieberman and Representative Ben Cardin, the ranking Democrat on the House Ways and Means Committee, are also interested in funding "family formation." In place of cash bonuses to individuals, which at least put money in the pockets of poor people, look for massive funding of faith-based marriage preparation courses (and never you mind that pesky separation of church and state), for fatherhood intervention programs, classes to instruct poor single moms in the benefits of marriage (as if they didn't know!), for self-help groups like Marriage Savers, abstinence education for kids and grownups alike and, of course, ingenious pilot projects by the dozen. There's even been a proposal to endow pro-marriage professorships at state universities— and don't forget millions of dollars for evaluation, follow-up, filing and forgetting.

There's nothing wrong with programs that aim to raise people's marital IQ—I love that journalistic evergreen about the engaged couple who take a quiz in order to qualify for a church wedding and call it off when they discover he wants seven kids and she wants to live in a tree. But remember when it was conservatives who argued against social engineering and micromanaging people's private lives and "throwing money at the problem"?

Domestic violence experts have warned that poor women may find 5 themselves pushed into marrying their abusers and staying with them— in a disturbing bit of Senate testimony, Mike McManus of Marriage Savers said domestic violence could usually be overcome with faith-based help. Is that the message women in danger should be getting? But there are even larger issues: Marriage is a deeply personal, intimate matter, involving our most private, barely articulated selves. Why should the government try to maneuver reluctant women into dubious choices just because they are poor? Even as a meal ticket wedlock is no panacea—that marriage is a cure for poverty is only true if you marry someone who isn't poor, who will share his income with you and your children, who won't divorce you later and leave you worse off than ever. The relation between poverty and marriage is virtually the opposite of what pro-marriage ideologues claim: It isn't that getting married gives feckless poor people middle-class values and stability; it's that stable middle-class people are the ones who can "afford" to be married. However marriage functioned a half-century ago, today it is a class marker. Instead of marketing marriage as a poverty program, how much better to invest in poor women—and poor men—as human beings in their own right: with education, training for high-paying jobs, housing, mental health services, really good childcare for their kids. Every TANF dollar spent on marital propaganda means a dollar less for programs that really help people.

The very fact that welfare reformers are reduced to bribing, cajoling, and guilt-tripping people into marriage should tell us something. Or have they just not hit on the right incentive? As a divorced single mother, I've given some thought to what it would take for me to marry against my own inclination in order to make America great again. Here's my offer: If the government brings Otis Redding back to life and books him to sing at my wedding, I will marry the Devil himself. And if the Devil is unavailable, my ex-husband says he's ready.

READING AND DISCUSSION QUESTIONS

1. What claim is Pollitt supporting in the essay?
2. What does Pollitt reveal about the history of welfare reform as it relates to marriage? Where does Pollitt say the money for welfare reform is going? Where should it go?
3. Where does Pollitt's word choice reveal her bias? Does her own opinion keep her from being fair?

WRITING SUGGESTIONS

4. Write an essay in which you either support or refute Pollitt's claim.

5. If a monetary marriage bonus is not enough to entice many unwed Americans to get married, what might be enough?

Politics and the English Language

GEORGE ORWELL

Most people who bother with the matter at all would admit that the English language is in a bad way, but it is generally assumed that we cannot by conscious action do anything about it. Our civilization is decadent and our language — so the argument runs — must inevitably share in the general collapse. It follows that any struggle against the abuse of language is a sentimental archaism, like preferring candles to electric light or hansom cabs to aeroplanes. Underneath this lies the half-conscious belief that language is a natural growth and not an instrument which we shape for our own purposes.

Now, it is clear that the decline of a language must ultimately have political and economic causes: It is not due simply to the bad influence of this or that individual writer. But an effect can become a cause, reinforcing the original cause and producing the same effect in an intensified form, and so on indefinitely. A man may take to drink because he feels himself to be a failure, and then fail all the more completely because he drinks. It is rather the same thing that is happening to the English language. It becomes ugly and inaccurate because our thoughts are foolish, but the slovenliness of our language makes it easier for us to have foolish thoughts. The point is that the process is reversible. Modern English, especially written English, is full of bad habits which spread by imitation and which can be avoided if one is willing to take the necessary trouble. If one gets rid of these habits one can think more clearly, and to think clearly is a necessary first step towards political regeneration: So that the fight against bad English is not frivolous and is not the exclusive concern of professional writers. I will come back to this presently, and I hope that by that time the meaning of what I have said here will have become clearer.

This essay, written shortly after World War II, develops George Orwell's claim that careless and dishonest use of language contributes to careless and dishonest thought and political corruption. Political language, he argues, is "largely the defense of the indefensible." But Orwell (1903–1950), novelist, critic, and political satirist — best known for his books *Animal Farm* (1945) and *1984* (1949) — believes that bad language habits can be reversed, and he lists rules for getting rid of some of the most offensive. This essay first appeared in *Horizon* in April 1946.

Meanwhile, here are five specimens of the English language as it is now habitually written.

These five passages have not been picked out because they are especially bad—I could have quoted far worse if I had chosen—but because they illustrate various of the mental vices from which we now suffer. They are a little below the average, but are fairly representative samples. I number them so that I can refer back to them when necessary:

(1) I am not, indeed, sure whether it is not true to say that the Milton who once seemed not unlike a seventeenth-century Shelley had not become out of an experience ever more bitter in each year, more alien *[sic]* to the founder of that Jesuit sect which nothing could induce him to tolerate.

> Professor Harold Laski (Essay in *Freedom of Expression*)

(2) Above all, we cannot play ducks and drakes with a native battery of idioms which prescribes such egregious collocations of vocables as the Basic *put up with* for *tolerate* or *put at a loss* for *bewilder*.

> Professor Lancelot Hogben (*Interglossa*)

(3) On the one side we have the free personality: By definition it is not neurotic, for it has neither conflict nor dream. Its desires, such as they are, are transparent, for they are just what institutional approval keeps in the forefront of consciousness; another institutional pattern would alter their number and intensity; there is little in them that is natural, irreducible, or culturally dangerous. But *on the other side*, the social bond itself is nothing but the mutual reflection of these self-secure integrities. Recall the definition of love. Is not this the very picture of a small academic? Where is there a place in this hall of mirrors for either personality or fraternity?

> Essay on psychology in *Politics* (New York)

(4) All the "best people" from the gentlemen's clubs, and all the frantic fascist captains, united in common hatred of Socialism and bestial horror of the rising tide of the mass revolutionary movement, have turned to acts of provocation, to foul incendiarism, to medieval legends of poisoned wells, to legalize their own destruction of proletarian organizations, and rouse the agitated petty-bourgeoisie to chauvinistic fervor on behalf of the fight against the revolutionary way out of the crisis.

> Communist pamphlet

(5) If a new spirit *is* to be infused into this old country, there is one thorny and contentious reform which must be tackled, and that is the humanization and galvanization of the BBC. Timidity here will bespeak cancer and atrophy of the soul. The heart of Britain may be sound and of strong beat, for instance, but the British lion's roar at present is like that of Bottom in Shakespeare's *Midsummer Night's Dream*—as gentle as any sucking dove. A virile new Britain cannot continue indefinitely to be traduced in the eyes or rather ears, of the world by the effete languors of Langham Place, brazenly masquerading as "standard English." When the Voice of Britain is heard at nine o'clock, better far and infinitely less ludicrous to hear aitches honestly dropped than the present

priggish, inflated, inhibited, school-ma'amish arch braying of blameless bashful mewing maidens!

Letter in *Tribune*

Each of these passages has faults of its own, but, quite apart from avoidable ugliness, two qualities are common to all of them. The first is staleness of imagery. The other is lack of precision. The writer either has a meaning and cannot express it, or he inadvertently says something else, or he is almost indifferent as to whether his words mean anything or not. The mixture of vagueness and sheer incompetence is the most marked characteristic of modern English prose, and especially of any kind of political writing. As soon as certain topics are raised, the concrete melts into the abstract and no one seems to think of turns of speech that are not hackneyed: Prose consists less and less of *words* chosen for the sake of their meaning, and more and more of *phrases* tacked together like the sections of a prefabricated hen-house. I list below, with notes and examples, various of the tricks by means of which the work of prose-construction is habitually dodged:

Dying metaphors. A newly invented metaphor assists thought by evoking a visual image, while on the other hand a metaphor which is technically "dead" (e.g., *iron resolution*) has in effect reverted to being an ordinary word and can generally be used without loss of vividness. But in between these two classes there is a huge dump of worn-out metaphors which have lost all evocative power and are merely used because they save people the trouble of inventing phrases for themselves. Examples are: *ring the changes on, take up the cudgels for, toe the line, ride roughshod over, stand shoulder to shoulder with, play into the hands of, no axe to grind, grist to the mill, fishing in troubled waters, rift within the lute, on the order of the day, Achilles' heel, swan song, hotbed.* Many of these are used without knowledge of their meaning (what is a "rift," for instance?), and incompatible metaphors are frequently mixed, a sure sign that the writer is not interested in what he is saying. Some metaphors now current have been twisted out of their original meaning without those who use them even being aware of the fact. For example, *toe the line* is sometimes written *tow the line*. Another example is *the hammer and the anvil*, now always used with the implication that the anvil gets the worst of it. In real life it is always the anvil that breaks the hammer, never the other way about: A writer who stopped to think what he was saying would be aware of this, and would avoid perverting the original phrase.

Operators or verbal false limbs. These save the trouble of picking out appropriate verbs and nouns, and at the same time pad each sentence with extra syllables which give it an appearance of symmetry. Characteristic phrases are: *render inoperative, militate against, make contact with, be sub-*

jected to, give rise to, give grounds for, have the effect of, play a leading part (role) in, make itself felt, take effect, exhibit a tendency to, serve the purpose of, etc., etc. The keynote is the elimination of simple verbs. Instead of being a single word, such as *break, stop, spoil, mend, kill*, a verb becomes a *phrase*, made up of a noun or adjective tacked on to some general-purpose verb such as *prove, serve, form, play, render*. In addition, the passive voice is wherever possible used in preference to the active, and noun constructions are used instead of gerunds (*by examination of* instead of *by examining*). The range of verbs is further cut down by means of the *-ize* and *de-* formation, and the banal statements are given an appearance of profundity by means of the *not un-* formation. Simple conjunctions and prepositions are replaced by such phrases as *with respect to, having regard to, the fact that, by dint of, in view of, in the interests of, on the hypothesis that;* and the ends of sentences are saved from anticlimax by such resounding commonplaces as *greatly to be desired, cannot be left out of account, a development to be expected in the near future, deserving of serious consideration, brought to a satisfactory conclusion*, and so on and so forth.

Pretentious diction.   Words like *phenomenon, element, individual* (as noun), *objective, categorical, effective, virtual, basic, primary, promote, constitute, exhibit, exploit, utilize, eliminate, liquidate*, are used to dress up simple statements and give an air of scientific impartiality to biased judgments. Adjectives like *epoch-making, epic, historic, unforgettable, triumphant, age-old, inevitable, inexorable, veritable*, are used to dignify the sordid processes of international politics, while writing that aims at glorifying war usually takes on an archaic color, its characteristic words being: *realm, throne, chariot, mailed fist, trident, sword, shield, buckler, banner, jackboot, clarion*. Foreign words and expressions such as *cul de sac, ancien régime, deus ex machina, mutatis mutandis, status quo, gleichshaltung, weltanschauung*, are used to give an air of culture and elegance. Except for the useful abbreviations *i.e., e.g.*, and *etc.*, there is no real need for any of the hundreds of foreign phrases now current in English. Bad writers, and especially scientific, political, and sociological writers, are nearly always haunted by the notion that Latin or Greek words are grander than Saxon ones, and unnecessary words like *expedite, ameliorate, predict, extraneous, deracinated, clandestine, subaqueous*, and hundreds of others constantly gain ground from their Anglo-Saxon opposite numbers.[1] The jargon peculiar to Marxist writing (*hyena, hangman, cannibal, petty bourgeois, these gentry, lackey, flunkey, mad dog, White Guard*, etc.) consists largely of words and phrases

---

[1] An interesting illustration of this is the way in which the English flower names which were in use till very recently are being ousted by Greek ones, *snapdragon* becoming *antirrhinum*, *forget-me-not* becoming *myosotis*, etc. It is hard to see any practical reason for this change of fashion: It is probably due to an instinctive turning-away from the more homely word and a vague feeling that the Greek word is scientific. [All notes are Orwell's.]

translated from Russian, German, or French; but the normal way of coining a new word is to use a Latin or Greek root with the appropriate affix and, where necessary, the -*ize* formation. It is often easier to make up words of this kind (*deregionalize, impermissible, extramarital, nonfragmentatory,* and so forth) than to think up the English words that will cover one's meaning. The result, in general, is an increase in slovenliness and vagueness.

Meaningless words.   In certain kinds of writing, particularly in art criticism and literary criticism, it is normal to come across long passages which are almost completely lacking in meaning.[2] Words like *romantic, plastic, values, human, dead, sentimental, natural, vitality,* as used in art criticism, are strictly meaningless in the sense that they not only do not point to any discoverable object, but are hardly ever expected to do so by the reader. When one critic writes, "The outstanding feature of Mr. X's work is its living quality," while another writes, "The immediately striking thing about Mr. X's work is its peculiar deadness," the reader accepts this as a simple difference of opinion. If words like *black* and *white* were involved, instead of the jargon words *dead* and *living,* he would see at once that language was being used in an improper way. Many political words are similarly abused. The word *fascism* has now no meaning except insofar as it signifies "something not desirable." The words *democracy, socialism, freedom, patriotic, realistic, justice,* have each of them several different meanings which cannot be reconciled with one another. In the case of a word like *democracy,* not only is there no agreed definition, but the attempt to make one is resisted from all sides. It is almost universally felt that when we call a country democratic we are praising it. Consequently the defenders of every kind of regime claim that it is a democracy, and fear that they might have to stop using the word if it were tied down to any one meaning. Words of this kind are often used in a consciously dishonest way. That is, the person who uses them has his own private definition, but allows his hearer to think he means something quite different. Statements like *Marshal Pétain was a true patriot, The Soviet Press is the freest in the world, The Catholic Church is opposed to persecution,* are almost always made with intent to deceive. Other words used in variable meanings, in most cases more or less dishonestly, are: *class, totalitarian, science, progressive, reactionary, bourgeois, equality.*

Now that I have made this catalog of swindles and perversions, let me give another example of the kind of writing that they lead to. This time

---

[2] Example: "Comfort's catholicity of perception and image, strangely Whitmanesque in range, almost the exact opposite in aesthetic compulsion, continues to evoke that trembling atmospheric accumulative hinting at a cruel, an inexorably serene timelessness. . . . Wrey Gardiner scores by aiming at simple bull's-eyes with precision. Only they are not so simple, and through this contended sadness runs more than the surface bittersweet of resignation" (*Poetry Quarterly*).

it must of its nature be an imaginary one. I am going to translate a passage of good English into modern English of the worst sort. Here is a well-known verse from Ecclesiastes:

> I returned and saw under the sun, that the race is not to the swift, nor the battle to the strong, neither yet bread to the wise, nor yet riches to men of understanding, nor yet favor to men of skill; but time and chance happeneth to them all.

Here it is in modern English:

> Objective consideration of contemporary phenomena compels the conclusion that success or failure in competitive activities exhibits no tendency to be commensurate with innate capacity, but that a considerable element of the unpredictable must invariably be taken into account.

This is a parody, but not a very gross one. Exhibit (3), above, for instance, contains several patches of the same kind of English. It will be seen that I have not made a full translation. The beginning and ending of the sentence follow the original meaning fairly closely, but in the middle the concrete illustrations—race, battle, bread—dissolve into the vague phrase "success or failure in competitive activities." This had to be so, because no modern writer of the kind I am discussing—no one capable of using phrases like "objective consideration of contemporary phenomena"— would ever tabulate his thoughts in that precise and detailed way. The whole tendency of modern prose is away from concreteness. Now analyze these two sentences a little more closely. The first contains forty-nine words but only sixty syllables, and all its words are those of everyday life. The second contains thirty-eight words of ninety syllables: Eighteen of its words are from Latin roots, and one from Greek. The first sentence contains six vivid images, and only one phrase ("time and chance") that could be called vague. The second contains not a single fresh, arresting phrase, and in spite of its ninety syllables it gives only a shortened version of the meaning contained in the first. Yet without a doubt it is the second kind of sentence that is gaining ground in modern English. I do not want to exaggerate. This kind of writing is not yet universal, and outcrops of simplicity will occur here and there in the worst-written page. Still, if you or I were told to write a few lines on the uncertainty of human fortunes, we should probably come much nearer to my imaginary sentence than to the one from Ecclesiastes.

As I have tried to show, modern writing at its worst does not consist in picking out words for the sake of their meaning and inventing images in order to make the meaning clearer. It consists in gumming together long strips of words which have already been set in order by someone else, and making the results presentable by sheer humbug. The attraction of this way of writing is that it is easy. It is easier—even quicker once you have the habit—to say *In my opinion it is a not unjustifiable assumption that* than to say *I think*. If you use ready-made phrases, you not only don't have to hunt about for words; you also don't have to bother with the rhythms of your sentences, since these phrases are generally so arranged as to be more or less euphonious. When you are composing in a hurry—when you are dictating to a stenographer, for instance, or making a public speech— it is natural to fall into a pretentious, Latinized style. Tags like *a considera- tion which we should do well to bear in mind* or *a conclusion to which all of us would readily assent* will save many a sentence from coming down with a bump. By using stale metaphors, similes, and idioms, you save much men- tal effort, at the cost of leaving your meaning vague, not only for your reader but for yourself. This is the significance of mixed metaphors. The sole aim of a metaphor is to call up a visual image. When these images clash—as in *The Fascist octopus has sung its swan song, the jackboot is thrown into the melting pot*—it can be taken as certain that the writer is not seeing a mental image of the objects he is naming; in other words he is not really thinking. Look again at the examples I gave at the beginning of this essay. Professor Laski (1) uses five negatives in fifty-three words. One of these is superfluous, making nonsense of the whole passage, and in addition there is the slip *alien* for akin, making further nonsense, and several avoidable pieces of clumsiness which increase the general vagueness. Professor Hog- ben (2) plays ducks and drakes with a battery which is able to write pre- scriptions, and, while disapproving of the everyday phrase *put up with*, is unwilling to look *egregious* up in the dictionary and see what it means. (3), if one takes an uncharitable attitude towards it, is simply meaningless: Probably one could work out its intended meaning by reading the whole of the article in which it occurs. In (4), the writer knows more or less what he wants to say, but an accumulation of stale phrases chokes him like tea leaves blocking a sink. In (5), words and meaning have almost parted com- pany. People who write in this manner usually have a general emotional meaning—they dislike one thing and want to express solidarity with an- other—but they are not interested in the detail of what they are saying. A scrupulous writer, in every sentence that he writes, will ask himself at least four questions, thus: What am I trying to say? What words will express it? What image or idiom will make it clearer? Is this image fresh enough to have an effect? And he will probably ask himself two more: Could I put it more shortly? Have I said anything that is avoidably ugly? But you are not obliged to go to all this trouble. You can shirk it by simply throwing your mind open and letting the ready-made phrases come crowding in. They will construct your sentences for you—even think your thoughts for you, to a certain extent—and at need they will perform the important service of partially concealing your meaning even from yourself. It is at this point that the special connection between politics and the debasement of lan- guage becomes clear.

In our time it is broadly true that political writing is bad writing. Where it is not true, it will generally be found that the writer is some kind of rebel, expressing his private opinions and not a "party line." Orthodoxy, of whatever color, seems to demand a lifeless, imitative style. The political dialects to be found in pamphlets, leading articles, manifestos, White Papers, and the speeches of undersecretaries do, of course, vary from party to party, but they are all alike in that one almost never finds in them a fresh, vivid, home-made turn of speech. When one watches some tired hack on the platform mechanically repeating the familiar phrases—*bestial atrocities, iron heel, bloodstained tyranny, free peoples of the world, stand shoulder to shoulder*—one often has a curious feeling that one is not watching a live human being but some kind of dummy; a feeling which suddenly becomes stronger at moments when the light catches the speaker's spectacles and turns them into blank discs which seem to have no eyes behind them. And this is not altogether fanciful. A speaker who uses that kind of phraseology has gone some distance towards turning himself into a machine. The appropriate noises are coming out of his larynx, but his brain is not involved as it would be if he were choosing his words for himself. If the speech he is making is one that he is accustomed to make over and over again, he may be almost unconscious of what he is saying, as one is when one utters the responses in church. And this reduced state of consciousness, if not indispensable, is at any rate favorable to political conformity.

In our time, political speech and writing are largely the defense of the indefensible. Things like the continuance of British rule in India, the Russian purges and deportations, the dropping of the atom bombs on Japan, can indeed be defended, but only by arguments which are too brutal for most people to face, and which do not square with the professed aims of political parties. Thus political language has to consist largely of euphemism, question-begging, and sheer cloudy vagueness. Defenseless villages are bombarded from the air, the inhabitants driven out into the countryside, the cattle machine-gunned, the huts set on fire with incendiary bullets: This is called *pacification*. Millions of peasants are robbed of their farms and sent trudging along the roads with no more than they can carry; this is called *transfer of population* or *rectification of frontiers*. People are imprisoned for years without trial, or shot in the back of the neck, or sent to die of scurvy in Arctic lumber camps: This is called *elimination of unreliable elements*. Such phraseology is needed if one wants to name things without calling up mental pictures of them. Consider for instance some comfortable English professor defending Russian totalitarianism. He cannot say outright, "I believe in killing off your opponents when you can get good results by doing so." Probably, therefore, he will say something like this:

> While freely conceding that the Soviet régime exhibits certain features which the humanitarian may be inclined to deplore, we must, I think, agree that a certain curtailment of the right to political opposition is an

unavoidable concomitant of transitional periods, and that the rigors which the Russian people have been called upon to undergo have been amply justified in the sphere of concrete achievement.

The inflated style is itself a kind of euphemism. A mass of Latin words fall upon the facts like soft snow, blurring the outlines and covering up all the details. The great enemy of clear language is insincerity. When there is a gap between one's real and one's declared aims, one turns as it were instinctively to long words and exhausted idioms, like a cuttlefish squirting out ink. In our age there is no such thing as "keeping out of politics." All issues are political issues, and politics itself is a mass of lies, evasions, folly, hatred, and schizophrenia. When the general atmosphere is bad, language must suffer. I should expect to find—this is a guess which I have not sufficient knowledge to verify—that the German, Russian, and Italian languages have all deteriorated in the last ten or fifteen years, as a result of dictatorship.

But if thought corrupts language, language can also corrupt thought.   15 A bad usage can spread by tradition and imitation, even among people who should and do know better. The debased language that I have been discussing is in some ways very convenient. Phrases like *a not unjustifiable assumption, leaves much to be desired, would serve no good purpose, a consideration which we should do well to bear in mind,* are a continuous temptation, a packet of aspirins always at one's elbow. Look back through this essay, and for certain you will find that I have again and again committed the very faults I am protesting against. By this morning's post I have received a pamphlet dealing with conditions in Germany. The author tells me that he "felt impelled" to write it. I open it at random, and here is almost the first sentence that I see: "(The Allies) have an opportunity not only of achieving a radical transformation of Germany's social and political structure in such a way as to avoid a nationalistic reaction in Germany itself, but at the same time of laying the foundations of a cooperative and unified Europe." You see, he "feels impelled" to write—feels, presumably, that he has something new to say—and yet his words, like cavalry horses answering the bugle, group themselves automatically into the familiar dreary pattern. This invasion of one's mind by ready-made phrases *(lay the foundations, achieve a radical transformation)* can only be prevented if one is constantly on guard against them, and every such phrase anesthetizes a portion of one's brain.

I said earlier that the decadence of our language is probably curable. Those who deny this would argue, if they produced an argument at all, that language merely reflects existing social conditions, and that we cannot influence its development by any direct tinkering with words and constructions. So far as the general tone or spirit of a language goes, this may be true, but it is not true in detail. Silly words and expressions have often disappeared, not through any evolutionary process but owing to the conscious action of a minority. Two recent examples were *explore every avenue* and *leave no stone unturned,* which were killed by the jeers of a few journalists. There is a long list of flyblown metaphors which could similarly be got rid of if enough people would interest themselves in the job; and it should also be possible to laugh the *not un-* formation out of existence,[3] to reduce the amount of Latin and Greek in the average sentence, to drive out foreign phrases and strayed scientific words, and, in general, to make pretentiousness unfashionable. But all these are minor points. The defense of the English language implies more than this, and perhaps it is best to start by saying what it does *not* imply.

To begin with it has nothing to do with archaism, with the salvaging of obsolete words and turns of speech, or with the setting up of a "standard English" which must never be departed from. On the contrary, it is especially concerned with the scrapping of every word or idiom which has outworn its usefulness. It has nothing to do with correct grammar and syntax, which are of no importance so long as one makes one's meaning clear, or with the avoidance of Americanisms, or with having what is called a "good prose style." On the other hand it is not concerned with fake simplicity and the attempt to make written English colloquial. Nor does it even imply in every case preferring the Saxon word to the Latin one, though it does imply using the fewest and shortest words that will cover one's meaning. What is above all needed is to let the meaning choose the word, and not the other way about. In prose, the worst thing one can do with words is to surrender to them. When you think of a concrete object, you think wordlessly, and then, if you want to describe the thing you have been visualizing you probably hunt about till you find the exact words that seem to fit. When you think of something abstract you are more inclined to use words from the start, and unless you make a conscious effort to prevent it, the existing dialect will come rushing in and do the job for you, at the expense of blurring or even changing your meaning. Probably it is better to put off using words as long as possible and get one's meaning as clear as one can through pictures or sensations. Afterwards one can choose — not simply *accept* — the phrases that will best cover the meaning, and then switch round and decide what impression one's words are likely to make on another person. This last effort of the mind cuts out all stale or mixed images, all prefabricated phrases, needless repetitions, and humbug and vagueness generally. But one can often be in doubt about the effect of a word or a phrase, and one needs rules that one can rely on when instinct fails. I think the following rules will cover most cases:

(i) Never use a metaphor, simile, or other figure of speech which you are used to seeing in print.

(ii) Never use a long word where a short one will do.

---

[3] One can cure oneself of the *not un-* formation by memorizing this sentence: *A not unblack dog was chasing a not unsmall rabbit across a not ungreen field.*

(iii) If it is possible to cut a word out, always cut it out.

(iv) Never use the passive where you can use the active.

(v) Never use a foreign phrase, a scientific word, or a jargon word if you can think of an everyday English equivalent.

(vi) Break any of these rules sooner than say anything outright barbarous.

These rules sound elementary, and so they are, but they demand a deep change in attitude in anyone who has grown used to writing in the style now fashionable. One could keep all of them and still write bad English, but one could not write the kind of stuff that I quoted in those five specimens at the beginning of this article.

I have not here been considering the literary use of language, but merely language as an instrument for expressing and not for concealing or preventing thought. Stuart Chase and others have come near to claiming that all abstract words are meaningless, and have used this as a pretext for advocating a kind of political quietism. Since you don't know what Fascism is, how can you struggle against Fascism? One need not swallow such absurdities as this, but one ought to recognize that the present political chaos is connected with the decay of language, and that one can probably bring about some improvement by starting at the verbal end. If you simplify your English, you are freed from the worst follies of orthodoxy. You cannot speak any of the necessary dialects, and when you make a stupid remark its stupidity will be obvious, even to yourself. Political language—and with variations this is true of all political parties, from Conservatives to Anarchists—is designed to make lies sound truthful and murder respectable, and to give an appearance of solidity to pure wind. One cannot change this all in a moment, but one can at least change one's own habits, and from time to time one can even, if one jeers loudly enough, send some worn-out and useless phrase—some *jackboot, Achilles' heel, hotbed, melting pot, acid test, veritable inferno,* or other lump of verbal refuse—into the dustbin where it belongs.

DISCUSSION QUESTIONS

1. Orwell disagrees with a common assumption about language. What is it? Where in the essay does he attack this assumption directly?

2. What faults do his five samples of bad language have in common? Select examples of these faults in each passage.

3. What "tricks" (para. 4) for avoiding good prose does Orwell list? Do you think that some are more dangerous or misleading than others? Explain the reasons for your answer.

4. What different reasons does Orwell suggest for the slovenliness of much political writing and speaking? What examples does he give to support these reasons? Are they persuasive?

5. How does Orwell propose that we get rid of our bad language habits? Do you think his recommendations are realistic? Can the teaching of writing in school assist in the remedy?

6. Why does Orwell urge the reader to "look back through this essay" to find "the very faults I am protesting against" (para. 15)? Can you, in fact, find any?

WRITING SUGGESTIONS

7. Choose a speech or an editorial whose meaning seems to be obscured by pretentious diction, meaningless words, euphemism, or "sheer cloudy vagueness." Point out the real meaning of the piece. If you think that its purpose is deceptive, expose the unpleasant truth that the author is concealing. Use Orwell's device, giving concrete meaning to any abstractions. (One source of speeches is a publication called *Vital Speeches of the Day.* Another is the *New York Times*, which often prints in full, or excerpts major portions of, speeches by leading figures in public life.)

8. Orwell's essay appeared before the widespread use of television. Do you think that TV makes it harder for politicians to be dishonest? Choose a particular public event—a war, a street riot, a terrorist activity, a campaign stop—and argue either for or against the claim that televised coverage makes it harder for a politician to engage in "sheer cloudy vagueness." Or does it make no difference at all? Be specific in your use of evidence.

DEBATE: Does the government have the right to regulate guns?

The Right to Bear Arms

WARREN E. BURGER

Our metropolitan centers, and some suburban communities of America, are setting new records for homicides by handguns. Many of our large centers have up to ten times the murder rate of all of Western Europe. In 1988, there were 9,000 handgun murders in America. Last year, Washington, D.C., alone had more than 400 homicides—setting a new record for our capital.

The Constitution of the United States, in its Second Amendment, guarantees a "right of the people to keep and bear arms." However, the meaning of this clause cannot be understood except by looking to the purpose,

---

Warren E. Burger (1907–1995) was chief justice of the United States from 1969 to 1986. This article is from the January 14, 1990, issue of *Parade* magazine.

the setting, and the objectives of the draftsmen. The first ten amendments—the Bill of Rights—were not drafted at Philadelphia in 1787; that document came two years later than the Constitution. Most of the states already had bills of rights, but the Constitution might not have been ratified in 1788 if the states had not had assurances that a national Bill of Rights would soon be added.

People of that day were apprehensive about the new "monster" national government presented to them, and this helps explain the language and purpose of the Second Amendment. A few lines after the First Amendment's guarantees—against "establishment of religion," "free exercise" of religion, free speech and free press—came a guarantee that grew out of the deep-seated fear of a "national" or "standing" army. The same First Congress that approved the right to keep and bear arms also limited the national army to 840 men; Congress in the Second Amendment then provided:

> A well regulated Militia, being necessary to the security of a free State, the right of the people to keep and bear Arms, shall not be infringed.

In the 1789 debate in Congress on James Madison's proposed Bill of Rights, Elbridge Gerry argued that a state militia was necessary:

> to prevent the establishment of a standing army, the bane of liberty. . . . Whenever governments mean to invade the rights and liberties of the people, they always attempt to destroy the militia in order to raise an army upon their ruins.

We see that the need for a state militia was the predicate of the "right"   5 guaranteed; in short, it was declared "necessary" in order to have a state military force to protect the security of the state. That Second Amendment clause must be read as though the word "because" was the opening word of the guarantee. Today, of course, the "state militia" serves a very different purpose. A huge national defense establishment has taken over the role of the militia of 200 years ago.

Some have exploited these ancient concerns, blurring sporting guns—rifles, shotguns, and even machine pistols—with all firearms, including what are now called "Saturday night specials." There is, of course, a great difference between sporting guns and handguns. Some regulation of handguns has long been accepted as imperative; laws relating to "concealed weapons" are common. That we may be "overregulated" in some areas of life has never held us back from more regulation of automobiles, airplanes, motorboats, and "concealed weapons."

Let's look at the history.

First, many of the 3.5 million people living in the thirteen original Colonies depended on wild game for food, and a good many of them required firearms for their defense from marauding Indians—and later from the French and English. Underlying all these needs was an important concept that each able-bodied man in each of the thirteen independent states had to help or defend his state.

The early opposition to the idea of national or standing armies was maintained under the Articles of Confederation; that confederation had no standing army and wanted none. The state militia—essentially a part-time citizen army, as in Switzerland today—was the only kind of "army" they wanted. From the time of the Declaration of Independence through the victory at Yorktown in 1781, George Washington, as the commander in chief of these volunteer-militia armies, had to depend upon the states to send those volunteers.

When a company of New Jersey militia volunteers reported for duty 10 to Washington at Valley Forge, the men initially declined to take an oath to "the United States," maintaining, "Our country is New Jersey." Massachusetts Bay men, Virginians, and others felt the same way. To the American of the eighteenth century, his state was his country, and his freedom was defended by his militia.

The victory at Yorktown—and the ratification of the Bill of Rights a decade later—did not change people's attitudes about a national army. They had lived for years under the notion that each state would maintain its own military establishment, and the seaboard states had their own navies as well. These people, and their fathers and grandfathers before them, remembered how monarchs had used standing armies to oppress their ancestors in Europe. Americans wanted no part of this. A state militia, like a rifle and powder horn, was as much a part of life as the automobile is today; pistols were largely for officers, aristocrats—and dueling.

Against this background, it was not surprising that the provision concerning firearms emerged in very simple terms with the significant predicate—basing the right on the *necessity* for a "well regulated militia," a state army.

In the two centuries since then—with two world wars and some lesser ones—it has become clear, sadly, that we have no choice but to maintain a standing national army while still maintaining a "militia" by way of the National Guard, which can be swiftly integrated into the national defense forces.

Americans also have a right to defend their homes, and we need not challenge that. Nor does anyone seriously question that the Constitution protects the right of hunters to own and keep sporting guns for hunting game any more than anyone would challenge the right to own and keep fishing rods and other equipment for fishing—or to own automobiles. To "keep and bear arms" for hunting today is essentially a recreational activity and not an imperative of survival, as it was 200 years ago; "Saturday night specials" and machine guns are not recreational weapons and surely are as much in need of regulation as motor vehicles.

Americans should ask themselves a few questions. The Constitution 15 does not mention automobiles or motorboats, but the right to keep and own an automobile is beyond question; equally beyond question is the power of the state to regulate the purchase or the transfer of such vehicle and the right to license the vehicle and the driver with reasonable standards. In some places, even a bicycle must be registered, as must some household dogs.

If we are to stop this mindless homicidal carnage, is it unreasonable:

1. to provide that, to acquire a firearm, an application be made reciting age, residence, employment, and any prior criminal convictions?

2. to require that this application lie on the table for ten days (absent a showing for urgent need) before the license would be issued?

3. that the transfer of a firearm be made essentially as that of a motor vehicle?

4. to have a "ballistic fingerprint" of the firearm made by the manufacturer and filed with the license record so that, if a bullet is found in a victim's body, law enforcement might be helped in finding the culprit?

These are the kinds of questions the American people must answer if we are to preserve the "domestic tranquility" promised in the Constitution.

A God-Given Natural Right

ROGER D. McGRATH

I do not believe in unilateral disarmament: not for the nation; not for our citizens. Neither did the Founding Fathers. They were students of history, especially of classical antiquity. They knew the history of the Greek city-states and Rome as well as they knew the history of the American colonies. This led them to conclude that an armed citizenry is essential to the preservation of freedom and democracy. Once disarmed, populations either submit meekly to tyrants or fight in vain.

The ancient Greeks knew this. The Greek city-state of Laconia had a population that was five percent Spartan (the warrior aristocracy), one percent *perioeci* (small merchants and craftsmen), and 94 percent *helots* (serfs bound to the soil). It is no mystery how five percent of the population kept 94 percent of the people enslaved. The *helots* were kept disarmed and, if found in possession of a weapon, were put to death.

For fifteen years, Roger McGrath taught courses in the history of the American West, California, and the United States at UCLA and has also taught at California State University, Northridge. He is a captain in the Naval Detachment of the California State Military Reserve. His articles have appeared in the *Wall Street Journal, American Guardian, Chronicles,* the *New York Times,* and *Harper's,* among others, and he appears extensively in documentaries about the West and has served as a consultant for television and movies. He is the author of *Gunfighters, Highwaymen, and Vigilantes* (1984) and coauthor of *Violence in America* (1989). This article appeared in the October 2003 issue of *Chronicles.*

Meanwhile, most of the Greek city-states were bastions of democracy because they had developed strong middle classes of armed citizens known as *hoplites*. Supplying their own weapons and equipment, the *hoplites* went into battle not out of fear of punishment or in hopes of plunder and booty, as did subject peoples of the Oriental empires, but to defend their liberties and to protect hearth and home. They fought side by side with neighbors, brothers, fathers, sons, uncles, and cousins. They did their utmost to demonstrate courage, side by side with their comrades in arms. If they lost a battle to the armies of an Oriental despot, they stood to lose everything—property, freedom, democracy. A defeat for subject peoples usually meant nothing more than a change of rulers.

The ancient Romans also knew this. When Tarquin, the Etruscan king of Rome, issued an order—for the public good, for safety and security—that the Romans be disarmed, they rose in rebellion. Tarquin was driven from the city, and the early Roman Republic was established. For several hundred years, Rome was defended not by a professional army of mercenaries or subject peoples but by armed citizen-soldiers who left the farm from time to time to serve the republic. Once the system broke down, the Roman Republic was transformed into an empire similar to the despotic regimes of the East.

Death and destruction commonly followed disarmament. England did it to the Gaels—the Irish and Scots—and the consequences beggar description. England had been fighting in Ireland for hundreds of years by the time the English got Irish leader Patrick Sarsfield to sign the Treaty of Limerick in 1691. The treaty guaranteed all Irish full civil, religious, and property rights. In return, it required that Sarsfield and more than 20,000 of his soldiers leave Ireland for the Continent.

With the armed defenders of Ireland overseas, England began to abrogate the rights supposedly guaranteed by the treaty. Beginning in 1709, England passed the statutes that collectively became known as the Penal Laws. One of the first of these laws declared that, for public safety, no Irish Catholic could keep and bear arms. Then the Irish Catholic was denied the right to an education, to enter a profession, to hold public office, to engage in trade or commerce, to own a horse of greater value than five pounds, to purchase or lease land, to vote, to attend the worship of his choice, to send his children abroad to receive an education. By the time the last of the Penal Laws was enacted, the Irish, although they were not chattel property, in many ways had fewer rights than black slaves in America. The Irish were kept on a near starvation diet, and their life expectancy was the lowest in the Western world.

Things were not much better in the Highlands of Scotland. England had subdued the Lowlands by the fourteenth century, but the Highlands, the truly Gaelic portion of Scotland, continued to be troublesome well into the eighteenth century. A major rebellion erupted in 1715; another, in 1745. The end for the Highlanders came at the Battle of Culloden in 1746. Following the battle, the English built a series of forts across the

Highlands and passed laws for the Highlanders—who were originally Irish, of course—similar to the Penal Laws. England made it a crime for the Highlanders to wear kilts, play bagpipes, and keep and bear arms. A Highlander found with a claymore or any other kind of sword or arm was put to death. The English army, understanding that it is easier to starve a fierce enemy into submission than to fight him, eagerly slaughtered the cattle herds of the Highlands, precipitating a great starvation. Thousands of Highlanders died or fled. The English later engaged in the infamous "clearances" in which thousands more were driven from the land. Without arms, the Highlanders were helpless.

What the English did to the Irish and Scots was not lost on our Founding Fathers or on the colonists in general. More than a quarter of the colonists were Irish or Scottish or Scotch-Irish. When England tried to disarm the American colonists, all under the guise of preserving public order and peace, the colonists reacted violently. While it is rarely taught in schools today, the reason the British army marched to Lexington and Concord was to confiscate the arms caches of the local citizenry.

It is not by accident, then, that the Framers of the Constitution ensured that the government could not infringe on "the right of the people to keep and bear arms." It is important to understand that the Second Amendment grants no right to the people to keep and bear arms. This is a point misunderstood by most Americans today, even by most of those who are interested in keeping their guns.

The Second Amendment, like the First, recognizes a God-given, natural right of the people and guarantees that the government not interfere with the exercise of that right. Note the wording of the amendment. Nowhere does it say, "This Constitution grants the people the right to . . ." Instead, it says "the right of the people . . . shall not be infringed." The right to keep and bear arms, like that of freedom of speech, is known, constitutionally, as an inherent right. By contrast, the Sixth Amendment right to be represented by an attorney in a criminal case is a derivative right—a right that comes from the Constitution.

To understand this is critical to all arguments about guns, or about freedom of speech, or religion, or the press. These freedoms were not given to us by the Founding Fathers. They were recognized by the Founding Fathers as God-given, natural rights that existed long before the establishment of our republic. These rights are not granted to men by a benevolent government but given to man by God. They are not to be destroyed, suppressed, or even compromised. When they are, it is the duty of the citizens to rise in revolt, overthrow the government, and establish a government that will protect these unalienable rights. Sound familiar? It should. This was the philosophy of our Founding Fathers.

The most basic of the natural rights of man is the right to self-preservation, the right to self-defense. No one would deny that we have such a right. In debates at universities and at other public forums, in debates on radio, in debates on television, I have never seen anyone deny that man has a natural right to self-defense. It follows that, if man has a natural right to self-defense, then he has a right to the arms necessary for that self-defense. The right to be armed is a logical and inescapable corollary of the right to self-defense. We cannot have one without the other.

If we do not have the right to the arms necessary for self-defense, then the right of self-defense is purely theoretical—something like having freedom of the press but not being allowed access to a printing press. Can you imagine the National Rifle Association telling the *New York Times* that it has freedom of the press but it may not have printing presses, or that the *Times* can purchase only one printing press per month, or that its writers must undergo background checks by the government, or that it cannot buy ink for the presses in New York City, or that its presses have limits on their speed and capacity, or that its presses must meet certain design requirements? If any of this were suggested, the *Times* would squeal like a stuck pig, and well it should.

Some people, presumably well intentioned, argue that the right to arms (and, thus, the right to self-defense) should be compromised—compromised further than it already has been—in an effort to make society safer. Such a position is ironic on two counts.

First, many of the same people who make gun-restriction arguments, such as the ACLU, would be apoplectic if it were suggested that freedom of speech be curtailed to ensure greater public safety. For example, we could have a two-week waiting period on expressing an opinion after the opinion was duly registered with a government agency. That way, the government could screen the opinion to ensure that it was politically correct.

The compromise-your-rights-for-safety argument is also ironic because the thousands of gun laws on the books—municipal, county, state, and federal—have done nothing to stop crime. In fact, they have done the opposite. The laws, for the most part, have disarmed, or made access to guns more difficult for, the law-abiding, peaceable citizen. Criminals do not turn in their guns. Murderers, rapists, and robbers do not obey gun laws. However, they do calculate the risks involved in committing crime. If they can assume that potential victims are unarmed, they are emboldened and are more likely to attack.

John Lott, in *More Guns Less Crime*, an exhaustive county-by-county study of rates of gun ownership and crime, concludes that the counties with the highest rates of gun ownership have the least crime and that those with the lowest rates of gun ownership have the most crime. For years, this has been obvious when looking at cities. Washington, D.C., and New York City, for example, with the most restrictive gun laws in the nation, have, for a generation, been cesspools of crime. Criminals there know that they can count on their victims being unarmed.

I suspect that even deeply disturbed killers, such as the teenage boys in Littleton, Colorado, understood that they could kill with impunity in the disarmed environment of the high school. The presence of a highly trained, armed security guard, with a reputation as an expert marksman, may have deterred them. If not, then the guard might have granted them their suicidal wish before they were able to commit mass murder. One or two key teachers, trained and armed, might also have made a difference. Certainly, gun laws did nothing to stop the killers. The two boys violated more than a dozen different gun laws, including one of the oldest on the books—possession of a sawed-off shotgun. Gun laws promise much and deliver little, because they affect only the law abiding, something like sheep passing resolutions requiring vegetarianism while wolves circle the flock.

I grew up in Los Angeles when gun laws were few and crime was low. Nearly everyone I knew had a 30.06, a couple of .22s, a shotgun, and a revolver or two sitting around their house. We could buy guns mail-order and pick up our ammunition at the local grocery store. A gun was a common companion to the road maps in the glove compartment of the car. Did this cause crime? In 1952, there were 81 murders in Los Angeles. In 1992, 40 years and many gun laws later, there were 1,092 murders. If the increase in murder had kept pace with the increase in population, there would have been 142 murders, a 75 percent increase. Instead, murder increased 1,350 percent. Other crimes had similar increases: robbery, 1,540 percent; auto theft, 1,100 percent.

The Los Angeles Police Department used to solve more than 90 per- 20 cent of the murders committed in the city. Today, the figure is 60 percent. Detectives complain that the caseload is too great to conduct the kind of thorough investigations that were common in the '40s and '50s. It is far worse for lesser crimes. Merchants complain that customers brazenly walk out of their stores without paying for merchandise because they know that the police will not respond (at least in a timely fashion) to a call reporting shoplifting. Cars are stolen so often, some 200 per day, that the LAPD does nothing more than list the vehicle on a "hot sheet" and wish the victim good luck.

In the '50s, if your bicycle were stolen, the police would come out to your house and take a report. Try calling the LAPD today and telling them that your bike has been stolen! The police are simply overwhelmed by the sheer volume of crime and are kept fully occupied by murder, armed robbery, and rape—occupied, that is, by the aftermath of murder, armed robbery, and rape. When police arrive at the scene of a crime, the crime has already taken place—the victim has already been murdered, robbed, or raped.

"Carjacking" has become quite common in Los Angeles, because the carjackers know that California drivers cannot legally carry loaded firearms and will nearly always be unarmed. Occasionally, carjackers make poor choices. Three such carjackers followed my friend's son, Justin, as he drove home in his new car late one night. Little did they know that Justin was a reserve police officer. They did not know that he was well armed and an expert marksman.

When Justin pulled into the family driveway and got out of his car, one of the carjackers jumped out of his own vehicle and yelled at Justin, whose back was turned, "Freeze, motherf—er!" It was exactly what Justin had expected. Justin spun about and emptied the contents of his .45 into the carjacker. The carjacker's partners sped away as fast as their car would take them, leaving their good buddy very dead on my friend's front lawn.

Not long after Justin had sent the carjacker to the great salvage yard in the sky, I read of an off-duty police officer who had a similar encounter. On his way home and wearing plainclothes, he stopped to make a phone call. While he stood talking to his wife on an outdoor public phone, two muggers rushed up to him. One of them brandished a gun and said: "Your wallet!" Instead of pulling out his wallet, the cop drew a gun and sent the mugger to the morgue.

The *Los Angeles Times* noted that the mugger certainly picked on the 25 wrong person. This is the same *Los Angeles Times* that regularly editorializes against an armed citizenry and has never seen a gun law that it did not like. Somehow, the newspaper thinks that disarming peaceable, law-abiding citizens will affect criminal behavior for the better. Disarming peaceable, law-abiding citizens *will* affect criminal behavior—but for the worse. Criminals will be emboldened because their chances of picking on the wrong person will be dramatically reduced. Shouldn't the opposite be the case? Shouldn't every person be the wrong person or, at least, potentially the wrong person?

Grandstanding politicians love to rail against the gun. Inanimate objects are good targets to beat up on. That way, politicians do not have to address the real problems in our society. We pay a price for this craven misdirection, though, in thousands of murders, muggings, rapes, robberies, and burglaries.

Yet that is not the greatest danger we face. The Founding Fathers knew that *governments* could turn criminal. That is the principal reason they wanted every man armed: An armed citizenry militates against the development of tyranny. The Founding Fathers did not want every man armed in order to shoot a burglar, although they had nothing against doing so. The Founding Fathers did not want every man armed in order to shoot Bambi or Thumper, although they had nothing against doing so. The Founding Fathers wanted every man armed in order to shoot soldiers or police of tyrannical regimes who suppress the rights of free men.

When governments become criminal, they disarm the populace. Then the numbers of deaths reach the tens of thousands, the hundreds of thousands, the millions. Can't happen? Ask the Irish and the Scots, or the Armenians, the Ukrainians, the Jews, the Chinese, the Cambodians.

In the Marine Corps, I was trained never to surrender my weapon. It was good advice then, and it is good advice now. I shall put my faith not in the goodwill of governments but in an armed citizenry—a band of brothers—steeped in the ideology of the Founding Fathers and the spirit of Patrick Henry, who said: "Is life so dear or peace so sweet as to be purchased at the price of slavery and chains? I know not what course others may take, but as for me, give me liberty or give me death."

DISCUSSION QUESTIONS

1. What does Burger understand the intent of the Second Amendment to have been, in context? How has history changed the way it should now be read?

2. What analogy does Burger make between guns and automobiles? Is his point a good one?

3. What questions does Burger believe Americans should be answering if we are to stop what he calls "this mindless homicidal carnage" (para. 15)?

4. Does McGrath make use of history in the same way and for the same purpose as Burger does? Explain.

5. What does McGrath mean when he says, "It is important to understand that the Second Amendment grants no right to the people to keep and bear arms" (para. 9)?

6. What is the warrant underlying Burger's essay? McGrath's?

7. What is McGrath's response to the claim that restrictions on guns would lead to a safer society?

8. Do you detect any logical fallacies in either essay?

9. Compare the authors' use of language. Do the authors use slanted or emotive language? Short cuts? Where in McGrath's essay is there a shift in the type of language used, and why?

ASSIGNMENTS FOR CHOOSING FAIR AND PRECISE LANGUAGE

READING AND DISCUSSION QUESTIONS

1. Select one or two related bumper stickers visible in your town or city. Examine the hidden warrants on which they are based, and assess their validity.

2. For a slogan found on a bumper sticker or elsewhere, supply the evidence to support the claim in the slogan. Or find evidence that disproves the claim.

3. Examine a few periodicals from fifty or more years ago. Select either an advertising or a political slogan in one of them, and relate it to beliefs or events of the period. Or tell why the slogan is no longer relevant.

4. Discuss the origin of a cliché or slogan. Describe, as far as possible, the backgrounds and motives of its users.

5. Make up your own slogan for a cause that you support. Explain and defend your slogan.

6. Choose a cliché, and find evidence to support or refute it. *Examples:* People were much happier in the past. Mother knows best. Life used to be simpler. Money can't buy happiness.

7. Select a passage, perhaps from a textbook, written largely in abstractions, and rewrite it using simpler and more concrete language.

8. In watching television dramas about law, medicine, or criminal or medical investigation, do you find that the professional language, some of which you may not fully understand, plays a positive or negative role in your enjoyment of the show? Explain your answer.

9. Listen to a radio or television report of a sports event. Do the announcers use a kind of language, especially jargon, that would not be used in print reports? One critic thinks that sports broadcasting has had a "destructive effect . . . on ordinary American English." Is he right or wrong?

10 Whose argument about the right to bear arms do you find more convincing, Burger's or McGrath's? Explain.

WRITING SUGGESTIONS

11. Choose a popular slogan from advertising or politics. Write an essay explaining how it appeals to needs and values.

12. Write an essay explaining which argument about the right to bear arms you find most convincing, Burger's or McGrath's.

13. Write an essay explaining how picturesque language is used to advance arguments. Be sure to provide specific examples.

14. Why are short cuts a natural result of ours being a technological age?

15. Analyze a presidential or other debate using some of the terms discussed in this chapter.

16. Locate a copy of President Bush's first speech after the attacks of 9/11 and compare it to Roosevelt's after the bombing of Pearl Harbor.

17. Write an essay explaining to what extent you believe that the points that Orwell makes in "Politics and the English Language" are still valid today.

Part Two

Researching, Writing, and Presenting Arguments

CHAPTER 11

Planning and Researching an Argumentative Paper

The person who understands how arguments are constructed has an important advantage in today's world. Television commercials, political speeches, newspaper editorials, and magazine advertisements, as well as many communications between individuals, all draw on the principles we have examined in the preceding chapters. By now you should be fairly adept at picking out claims, support, and warrants (explicit or unstated) in these presentations. The next step is to apply your skills to writing an argument of your own on a subject of your choice or for an assignment on a topic other than those covered in this text. The process of using what you have learned will enhance your ability to analyze critically the marketing efforts with which we are all bombarded every day. Mastering the writing of arguments also gives you a valuable tool for communicating with other people in school, on the job, and even at home.

In this chapter we move through the various stages involved in preparing to write an argumentative paper: choosing a topic, locating and evaluating sources, and taking notes. We also consider the more general question of how to use the principles already discussed in order to convince a real audience. The more carefully you follow the guidelines set out here and the more thought you give to your work at each point, the better you will be able to utilize the art of argument when this course is over.

FINDING AN APPROPRIATE TOPIC

An old British recipe for jugged hare is said to begin, "First, catch your hare." To write an argumentative paper, you first must choose your topic. This is a relatively easy task for someone writing an argument as part of his or her job—a lawyer defending a client, for example, or an advertising executive presenting a campaign. For a student, however, it can be daunting. Which of the many ideas in the world worth debating would make a good subject?

Several guidelines can help you evaluate the possibilities. Perhaps your assignment limits your choices. If you have been asked to write a research paper, you obviously must find a topic on which research is available. If your assignment is more open-ended, you need a topic that is worth the time and effort you expect to invest in it. In either case, your subject should be one that interests you. Don't feel you have to write about what you know—very often finding out what you don't know will turn out to be more satisfying. You should, however, choose a subject that is familiar enough for you to argue about without fearing you're in over your head.

■ Invention Strategies

As a starting point, think of conversations you've had in the past few days or weeks that have involved defending a position. Is there some current political issue you're concerned about? Some dispute with friends that would make a valid paper topic? One of the best sources is controversies in the media. Keep your project in mind as you watch TV, read print or online sources, or listen to the radio. You may even run into a potential subject in your course reading assignments or classroom discussions. Fortunately for the would-be writer, nearly every human activity includes its share of disagreement.

As you consider possible topics, write them down. One that looks unlikely at first glance may suggest others or may have more appeal when you come back to it later. Further, simply putting words on paper has a way of stimulating the thought processes involved in writing. Even if your ideas are tentative, the act of converting them into phrases or sentences can often help in developing them.

■ Evaluating Possible Topics

Besides interesting you, your topic must interest your audience. Who is the audience? For a lawyer it is usually a judge or jury; for a columnist, anyone who reads the newspaper in which his or her column appears. For the student writer, the audience is to some extent hypothetical. You should assume that your paper is directed at readers who are reasonably intelligent and well informed, but who have no specific knowledge of the subject. It may be useful to imagine you are writing for a local or school publication—this may be the case if your paper turns out well.

Be sure, too, that you choose a topic that can be seen from more than one perspective. The purpose of an argument is to defend or refute a thesis, which means the thesis must be debatable. In evaluating a subject that looks promising, ask yourself: Can a case be made for other views? If not, you have no workable ground for building your own case.

Finally, check the scope of your thesis. Consider how long your paper will be, and whether you can do justice to your topic in that amount of space. For example, suppose you want to argue in favor of worldwide nuclear disarmament. Is this a thesis you can support persuasively in a short paper? One way to find out is by listing the potential issues or points about which arguers might disagree. Consider the thesis: "The future of the world is in danger as long as nuclear weapons exist." Obviously this statement is too general. You would have to specify what you mean by the future of the world (the continuation of human life? of all life? of the earth itself?) and exactly how nuclear weapons endanger it before the claim would hold up. You could narrow it down: "Human beings are error-prone; therefore as long as nuclear weapons exist there is the chance that a large number of people will be killed accidentally." Though this statement is more specific and includes an important warrant, it still depends on other unstated warrants: that one human being (or a small group) is in the position to discharge a nuclear weapon capable of killing a large number of people; that such a weapon could, in fact, be discharged by mistake, given current safety systems. Can you expect to show sufficient evidence for these assumptions in the space available to you?

By now it should be apparent that arguing in favor of nuclear disarmament is too broad an undertaking. A more workable approach might be to defend or refute one of the disarmament proposals under consideration by the U.S. Congress, or to show that nuclear weapons pose some specific danger (such as long-term water pollution) that is sufficient reason to strive for disarmament.

Can a thesis be too narrow? Certainly. If this is true of the one you have chosen, you probably realized it when you asked yourself whether the topic was debatable. If you can prove your point convincingly in a paragraph, or even a page, you need a broader thesis.

At this preliminary stage, don't worry if you don't know exactly how to word your thesis. It's useful to write down a few possible phrasings to be sure your topic is one you can work with, but you need not be precise. The information you unearth as you do research will help you to formulate your ideas. Also, stating a thesis in final terms is premature until you know the organization and tone of your paper. If your topic or assignment does not require research, you may want to move ahead to Chapter 12.

INITIATING RESEARCH

The success of any argument, short or long, depends in large part on the quantity and quality of the support behind it. Research, therefore, can be crucial for any argument outside your own experience. Most papers will benefit from research in the library and elsewhere because development of the claim requires facts, examples, statistics, and informed opinions that are available only from primary and secondary research sources.

Writer's Guide: Keeping Your Research on Track

1. Focus your investigation on building your argument, not merely on collecting information about the topic. Do follow any promising leads that turn up from the sources you consult, but don't be diverted into general reading that has no direct bearing on your thesis.

2. Look for at least two pieces of evidence to support each point you want to make. If you cannot find sufficient evidence, you may need to revise or abandon the point.

3. Use a variety of sources. Seek evidence from different kinds of sources (books, magazines, Web sites, government reports, even personal interviews with experts) and from different fields.

4. Be sure your sources are authoritative. We have already pointed out in Chapter 7 the necessity for examining the credentials of sources. Although it may be difficult or impossible for those outside the field to conclude that one authority is more trustworthy than another, some guidelines are available. Articles and essays in scholarly journals are probably more authoritative than articles in college newspapers or in magazines. Authors whose credentials include many publications and years of study at reputable institutions are probably more reliable than newspaper columnists and the so-called man in the street. However, we can judge reliability much more easily if we are dealing with facts and inferences than with values and emotions.

5. Don't let your sources' opinions outweigh your own. Your paper should demonstrate that the thesis and ideas you present are yours, arrived at after careful reflection and supported by research. The thesis need not be original, but your paper should be more than a collection of quotations or a report of the facts and opinions you have been reading. It should be clear to the reader that the quotations and other materials support *your* claim and that *you* have been responsible for finding and emphasizing the important issues, examining the data, and choosing between strong and weak opinions.

6. Don't ignore information that opposes the position you plan to support. Your argument is not strengthened by pretending such information does not exist. You may find that you must revise or qualify your position based on what your research reveals. Your readers may be aware of other positions on the issue and may judge you to be unreliable, careless, or dishonest if you do not acknowledge them. It is far better to fairly summarize opposing arguments and refute them than to ignore them.

7. Prepare for research by identifying potential resources and learning how they work. Make sure you know how to use the library's catalog and

other databases available either in the library or through the campus network. For each database that looks useful, explore how to execute a subject search, how to refine a search, and how to print out or download results. Make sure you know how to find books, relevant reference materials, and journals. Find out whether interlibrary loan is an option and how long it takes. If you plan to use government publications, find out if your library is a depository for federal documents. Identify relevant organizations using the *Encyclopedia of Associations* and visit their Web sites. Finally, discuss your topic with a librarian at the reference desk to make sure you haven't overlooked anything.

Writer's Guide: Why Use Sources?

1. You cannot be an authority on every subject. That means that you must turn to those who are authorities on subjects you know little about.

2. Because you may not yet have a name or credentials that are recognized for their authority, you may need to use those who are considered experts as sources of information and prestige.

3. The use of sources shows that you have taken the time to do some research on the subject at hand, including researching positions other than your own.

4. As in a court of law, the more evidence you can provide for your position, the stronger your case will be.

MAPPING RESEARCH: A SAMPLE OUTLINE

To explore a range of research activities, let's suppose that you are preparing a research paper, six to ten pages long. You have chosen to defend the following thesis: *Even though thalidomide is infamous for causing birth defects in the 1960s, it has promise as a treatment for cancer and other diseases.* To keep your material under control and give direction to your reading, you would sketch a preliminary outline, which might look like this:

Thalidomide: Changing a Drug's Reputation

I. Thalidomide's history: a promising drug but a medical nightmare

   A. Explain how drug was developed

   B. Explain the medical disaster it caused

II. New look at thalidomide: its potential to effectively treat cancer and other diseases

   A. Discuss how it first worked to treat leprosy

        B. Support how it can treat cancer

        C. Support how it can treat other diseases

   III.   Conclusion

Now you need to begin the search for the materials that will support your argument. There are two principal ways of gathering the materials — primary research and secondary research. Most writers will not want to limit themselves to one kind of research, but one method may work better than another for a particular project.

USING SOURCES: PRIMARY RESEARCH

Primary research involves looking for firsthand information. By *firsthand* we mean information taken directly from the original source, including field research (interviews, surveys, personal observations, or experiments). If your topic relates to a local issue involving your school or community, or if it focuses on a story that has never been reported by others, field research may be more valuable than anything available in the library. However, the library can be a source of firsthand information. Memoirs and letters written by witnesses to past events, photographs, contemporary news reports of historical events, or expert testimony presented at congressional hearings are all primary sources that may be available in your library. The Internet, too, can be a source of primary data. A discussion list, newsgroup, or chat room focused on your topic may give you a means to converse with activists and contact experts. Web sites of certain organizations provide documentation of their views, unfiltered by others' opinions. The text of laws, court opinions, bills, debates in Congress, environmental impact statements, and even selected declassified FBI files can be found through government-sponsored Web sites. Other sites present statistical data or the text of historical or political documents.

One of the rewards of primary research is that it often generates new information, which in turn produces new interpretations of familiar conditions. It is a favored method for anthropologists and sociologists, and most physical and natural scientists use observation and experiment at some point as essential tools in their research.

Consider the sample thesis that *even though thalidomide is infamous for causing birth defects in the 1960s, it has promise as a treatment for cancer and other diseases.* It is possible to go to primary sources in addition to or instead of consulting books. For example:

- Interview one or more physicians about current or potential uses of thalidomide.

- Interview someone locally who has had a family member affected by thalidomide.

- Read a first-person account by someone negatively affected by thalidomide use.

- Read a first-person account by someone positively affected by thalidomide use.

- Research newspaper reports from the time period regarding the birth defects caused by thalidomide before its dangers were known.

- Search the Web for reputable sources of information about thalidomide and the uses for which it is currently approved.

The information gleaned from primary research can be used directly to support your claim, or can provide a starting point for secondary research.

USING SOURCES: SECONDARY RESEARCH

Secondary research involves locating commentary on and analysis of your topic. In addition to raw evidence found through primary research, secondary sources provide a sense of how others are examining the issues and can provide useful information and analysis. Secondary sources may be written for a popular audience, ranging from news coverage, to popular explanations of research findings, to social analysis, to opinion pieces. Or they may be scholarly publications—experts presenting their research and theories to other researchers. These sources might also come in the form of analytical reports written to untangle possible courses of action, such as a report written by staff members for a congressional committee or an analysis of an issue by a think tank that wants to use the evidence it has gathered to influence public opinion.

Whatever form it may take, be sure when you use a secondary source that you consider the author's purpose and the validity of the material presented to ensure that it is useful evidence for your argument. An opinion piece published in a small-town paper, for example, may be a less impressive source for your argument than an analysis written by a former cabinet member. A description of a scientific discovery published in a magazine will carry less weight as evidence than the article written by the scientists making the discovery, presenting their research findings in a scientific journal.

The nature of your topic will determine which route you follow to find good sources. If the topic is current, you may find it more important to use articles than books and might bypass the library catalog altogether. If the topic has to do with social policy or politics, government publications may be particularly useful, though they would be unhelpful for a literary paper. If the topic relates to popular culture, the Internet may provide more information than more traditional publications. Consider what kinds of sources will be most useful as you choose your strategy. If you aren't certain which approaches fit your topic best, consult with a librarian at the reference desk.

■ Selecting and Searching Databases

You will most likely use one or more *databases* (online catalogs of reference materials) to locate books and articles on your topic. The library catalog is a database of books and other materials owned by the library; other databases may cover articles in popular or specialized journals and may even provide the full text of articles. Some databases may be available only in the library; others may be accessible all over campus. Here are some common features that appear in many databases.

Keyword or Subject Searching.   You might have the option of searching a database by *keyword*—using the words that you think are most relevant to your search—or by subject. Typically, a keyword search will search for any occurrence of your search term in titles, notes, or the descriptive headings provided by database catalogers or indexers. The advantage to keyword searching is that you can use terms that come naturally to you to cast your net as widely as possible. The disadvantage is that there may be more than one way to express your topic and you may not capture all the relevant materials unless you use the right keywords.

With *subject searching*, you use search terms from a list of subject headings (sometimes called *descriptors*) established by the creators of the database. To make searching as efficient as possible, they choose one word or phrase to express a subject. Every time a new source is entered into the database, the indexers describe it using words from the list of subject headings: When you use the list to search the database, you retrieve every relevant source. You might find that a database lists these subject headings through a thesaurus feature. The sophisticated researcher will always pay attention to the subject headings or descriptors generally listed at the bottom of a record for clues to terms that might work best and for related terms that might be worth trying.

Searching for More Than One Concept.   Most database searches allow you to combine terms using the connectors *and*, *or*, and *not*. These connectors (also known as *Boolean operators*) group search terms in different ways. If you search for zoos *and* animal rights, for example, the resulting list of sources will include only those that deal with both zoos and animal rights, leaving out any that deal with only one subject and not the other. If you connect terms with *or*, your list will contain sources that deal with either concept: A search for dogs *or* cats will create a list of sources that cover either animal. *Not* excludes concepts from a search. A search for animal rights *not* furs will search for the concept animal rights and then cut out any sources that deal with furs.

Limiting a Search.   Most databases have some options for limiting a search by a number of variables, such as publication date, language, or format. If you find a large number of sources in a database search, you might limit your search to sources published in English in the past three years. If you need a visual aid for a presentation, you might limit a search of the library's catalog to videos, and so on.

Truncating Search Terms with Wild Cards. At times you will search for a word that has many possible endings. A wild card is a symbol that, placed at the end of a word root, allows for any possible ending for a word. For example, *animal** will allow a search for *animal* or *animals.*

Options for Saving Records. You may have the opportunity to print, download, or e-mail to yourself the citations you find in a database. Many databases have a feature for marking just the records you want so you save only those of interest.

Help Screens. Most databases offer some kind of online help that explains how to use the database effectively. If you invest five minutes getting familiar with the basics of a database, it may save you twenty minutes later.

■ Types of Databases

The Library Catalog. If you want to search for books, videos, or periodical publications, the library catalog is the database to search. Most libraries now have computerized catalogs, but some still have a card catalog. In either case, the type of information provided is the same. Every book in the library has an entry in the catalog that gives its author, title, publisher, date, length, and subject headings and perhaps some notes about its contents. It also gives the call number or location on the shelf and often some indication as to whether it is currently available. You can search the catalog for an author, title, subject, or keyword. Most online catalogs have ways of combining and limiting searches and for printing results. Remember when searching the catalog, though, that entries are created for whole books and not for specific parts of them. If you use too narrow search terms, you may not find a book that has a chapter that includes exactly what you are looking for. Use broad search terms, and check the subject headings for search terms that will work best. Plan to browse the shelves and examine the tables of contents of the books that you find through the catalog to see which, in fact, are most helpful for your topic.

General Periodical Databases. If you want to search for articles, you can find a number of options at your library. Most libraries have a generalized database of periodical articles that may include citations, citations with abstracts (brief summaries), or the entire text of articles. *EBSCOhost, Infotrac, Searchbank, Readers' Guide Abstracts,* and *ProQuest* are all online indexes of this type. Ask a librarian what is available in your library. These are particularly good for finding current information in fairly nonspecialized sources, though they may include some scholarly journals. If you are looking for articles published before the 1980s — say, for news accounts published when the atomic bomb was dropped on Hiroshima—you would most likely need to use a print index such as the *Readers' Guide to Periodical Literature,* which began publication in 1900.

Specialized Databases. In addition to these general databases, you may find you need to delve deeper into a particular subject area. Every academic discipline has some sort of in-depth index to its research, and though the materials they cover tend to be highly specialized, they can provide more substantial support for your claims because they tend to cover sources written by experts in their fields. These resources may be available in electronic or print form:

Art Index

Biological Abstracts (the online version is known as *Biosis*)

Business Periodicals Index

ERIC (focused on education research)

Index Medicus (*Medline* or *PubMed* online)

Modern Languages Association International Bibliography (*MLA Bibliography* online)

Psychological Abstracts (*PsychInfo* or *PsychLit* online)

Sociological Abstracts (*Sociofile* online)

Sample Online Catalog Record

You searched for the TITLE—animal rights movement

```
CALL #      Z7164.C45 M38 1994.
AUTHOR      Manzo, Bettina, 1943-
TITLE       The animal rights movement in the United States, 1975-
                1990 : an annotated bibliography / by Bettina Manzo.
IMPRINT     Metuchen, N.J. : Scarecrow Press, 1994.
PHYS DESCR  xi, 296 p. ; 23 cm.
NOTE        Includes indexes.
CONTENTS    Animal rights movement -- Activists and organizations --
                Philosophy, ethics, and religion -- Law and legislation
                -- Factory farming and vegetarianism -- Trapping and
                fur industry -- Companion animals -- Wildlife --
                Circuses, zoos, rodeos, dog
SUBJECT     Animal rights movement --United States --Bibliography.
            Animal rights --United States --Bibliography.
            Animal experimentation --United States --Bibliography.
OCLC #      30671149.
ISBN/ISSN   GB95-17241.
```

Check with a librarian to find out which specialized databases or indexes that relate to your topic are available in your library.

Database Services. In addition to individual databases, many libraries subscribe to database services that provide access to a number of databases from one search screen. *FirstSearch,* for example, provides access to a variety of subject-specific databases as well as *WorldCat,* a massive database of library catalogs. *Lexis/Nexis* is a collection of databases to over a billion texts, most of them available in full text; it is a strong source for news coverage, legal research, and business information. These may be available to you through the Web anywhere on campus. Again, a visit with a librarian will help you quickly identify what your library has available.

■ Encyclopedias

General and specialized encyclopedias offer quick overviews of topics and easy access to factual information. They also tend to have excellent selective bibliographies, pointing you toward useful sources. You will find a wide variety of encyclopedias in your library's reference collection; you may also have an online encyclopedia, such as *Britannica Online,* available through the Web anywhere on campus. Some specialized encyclopedias include the following:

> *Encyclopedia of African American History and Culture*
>
> *Encyclopedia of American Social History*
>
> *Encyclopedia of Bioethics*
>
> *Encyclopedia of Educational Research*
>
> *Encyclopedia of Hispanic Culture in the United States*
>
> *Encyclopedia of International Relations*
>
> *Encyclopedia of Philosophy*
>
> *Encyclopedia of Sociology*
>
> *Encyclopedia of the United States in the Twentieth Century*
>
> *Encyclopedia of World Cultures*
>
> *International Encyclopedia of Communications*
>
> *McGraw-Hill Encyclopedia of Science and Technology*
>
> *Political Handbook of the World*

■ Statistical Resources

Often statistics are used as evidence in an argument. If your argument depends on establishing that one category is bigger than another, that the majority of people hold a certain opinion, or that one group is more affected by something than another group, statistics can provide the evidence you need. Of course, as with any other source, you need to be sure that your statistics are as reliable as possible and that you are reporting them responsibly.

It isn't always easy to find things counted the way you want. If you embark on a search for numbers to support your argument, be prepared to spend some time locating and interpreting data. Always read the fine print that explains how and when the data were gathered. Some sources for statistics include these:

U.S. Bureau of the Census.   This government agency produces a wealth of statistical data, much of it available on CD-ROM or through the Web at www.census.gov. A handy compilation of their most useful tables is found in the one-volume annual handbook, *Statistical Abstract of the United States,* which also includes statistics from other government sources.

Other Federal Agencies. Numerous federal agencies gather statistical data. Among these are the National Center for Education Statistics, the National Center for Health Statistics, the National Bureau of Labor Statistics, and the Federal Bureau of Investigation, which annually compiles national crime statistics. One handy place to find a wide variety of federal statistics is a Web site called *FedStats* at www.fedstats.gov.

United Nations. Compilations of international data published by the United Nations include the *Demographic Yearbook* and *Statistical Yearbook.* Some statistics are also published by U.N. agencies such as the Food and Health Organization. Some are available from the U.N. Web site at www.un.org.

Opinion Polls. Several companies conduct opinion polls, and some of these are available in libraries. One such compilation is the Gallup Poll series, which summarizes public opinion polling from 1935 to the present. Other poll results are reported by the press. Search a database that covers news publications by using your topic and *polls* as keywords to help you locate some summaries of results.

■ Government Publications

Beyond statistics, government agencies compile and publish a wealth of information. For topics that concern public welfare, health, education, politics, foreign relations, earth sciences, the environment, or the economy, government documents may provide just the information you need.

The U.S. federal government is the largest publisher in the world. Its publications are distributed free to libraries designated as document depositories across the country. If your library is not a depository, chances are there is a regional depository somewhere nearby. Local, state, and foreign governments are also potential sources of information.

Federal documents distributed to depository libraries are indexed in *The Monthly Catalog of U.S. Government Documents,* available in many libraries as an electronic database. These include congressional documents such as hearings and committee reports, presidential papers, studies conducted by the Education Department or the Centers for Disease Control, and so on. Many government documents are available through the Internet. If you learn about a government publication through the news media, chances are you will be able to obtain a copy at the Web site of the sponsoring agency or congressional body. In fact, government publications are among the most valuable of resources available on the Web because they are rigorously controlled for content. You know you are looking at a U.S. federal government site when you see the domain suffix *.gov* in the URL.

■ Searching the Web

The World Wide Web is an increasingly important resource for researchers. It is particularly helpful if you are looking for information about organizations, current events, political debates, popular culture, or government-sponsored research and activities. It is not an especially good place to look for literary criticism, historical analysis, or scholarly research articles, which are still more likely to be published in traditional ways. Biologists reporting on an important experiment, for example, are more likely to submit an article about it to a prestigious journal in the field than simply post their results on the Web.

Because anyone can publish whatever they like on the Web, searching for good information can be frustrating. Search engines operate by means of automated programs that gather information about sites and match search terms to whatever is out there, regardless of quality. A search engine may locate thousands of Web documents on a topic, but most are of little relevance and dubious quality. The key is to know in advance what information you need and who might have produced it. For example, if your topic has to do with some aspect of free speech and you know that the American Civil Liberties Union is involved in the issue, a trip to the ACLU home page may provide you with a wealth of information, albeit from a particular perspective. If your state's pollution control agency just issued a report on water quality in the area, you may find the report published at their Web site or the e-mail address of someone who could send it to you. The more you know about your topic before you sit down to surf, the more likely you will use your time productively.

If you have a fairly broad topic and no specific clues about where it might be covered, you may want to start your search using a selective guide to good sites. For example, the University of Texas maintains an excellent directory to sites relating to Latin America. Subject guides that selectively list valuable sites can be found at the University of California's *Infomine* at http://infomine.ucr.edu and the *World Wide Web Virtual Library* project at www.vlib.org/Home.html. Reference librarians will also be able to point you to quality sites that relate to your topic.

If you have a fairly specific topic in mind or are looking for a particular organization or document on the Web, a search engine can help you find it. *Google* is one of the best. No matter what search engine you choose, find out how it works, how it ranks results, and how deeply it indexes Web pages. Some search engines will retrieve more results than others simply because of the way the program gathers information from sites. As with databases, there are usually ways to refine a search and improve your results. Many search engines offer an advanced search option that may provide some useful options for refining and limiting a search.

It is important to know what will not be retrieved by a search engine. Because publishing and transmitting texts on the Web is relatively easy, it is becoming more common for libraries to subscribe to databases and electronic journals that are accessed through a Web browser. You may have *Britannica Online* and *Lexis/Nexis* as options on your library's home page. However, the contents of those subscriptions will be available only to your campus community and will not be searched by general Web search engines.

EVALUATING SOURCES

When you begin studying your sources, read first to acquire general familiarity with your subject. Make sure that you are covering both sides of the question—in this case the negative as well as the positive aspects of the use of thalidomide—as well as facts and opinions from a variety of sources. In investigating this subject, you might examine data from doctors, victims of earlier thalidomide use, scientists studying the current uses of thalidomide, the manufacturer of the drug, and recent patients; their varied points of view will contribute to the strength of your claim.

As you read, look for what seem to be the major issues. They will probably be represented in all or most of your sources. Record questions as they occur to you in your reading. What went wrong when thalidomide was used in the 1960s? Why is it again receiving attention? What reasons are there for bringing back such a dangerous drug? Are there advantages that outweigh the dangers? What has changed that might make use of the drug safer today?

■ Evaluating Print Sources

The sources you find provide useful information that you need for your paper and help you support your claims. One key to supporting claims effectively is to make sure you have the best evidence available. It is tempting when searching a database or the Web to take the first sources that look good, print them or copy them, and not give them another thought until you are sitting down to compose your argument—only to discover that the sources aren't as valuable as they could be. Sources that looked pretty good at the beginning of your research may turn out to be less useful once you have learned more about the topic. And a source that seems interesting at first glance may turn out to be a rehash or digest of a much more valuable source, something you realize only when you sit down and look at it carefully.

To find the right stuff, be a critical thinker from the start of your research process. Scan and evaluate the references you encounter throughout your search. As you examine options in a database, choose sources that use relevant terms in their titles, seem directed to an appropriate audience, and are published in places that will look good in your Works Cited list. For example, a Senate Foreign Relations Committee report will be more impressive as a source than a comparable article in *Good Housekeeping*. An article from the scholarly journal *Foreign Affairs* will carry more clout than an article from *Reader's Digest,* even if they are on the same subject.

Skim and quickly evaluate each source that looks valuable.

- Is it relevant to your topic?

- Does it provide information you haven't found elsewhere?

- Can you learn anything about the author, and does what you learn inspire confidence?

As you begin to learn more about your topic and develop an outline, you can use sources to help direct your search. If a source mentions an organization, for example, you may use that clue to run a search on the Web for that organization's home page. If a newspaper story refers to a study published in a scientific journal, you may want to seek out that study to see the results of the research firsthand. And if you have a source that includes references to other publications, scan through them, and see which might also prove helpful to you. When you first started your research, chances are you weren't quite sure what you were looking for. Once you are familiar with your topic, you need to concentrate on finding sources that will best support the claims you want to make, and your increasing familiarity with the issue will make it easier to identify the best sources. That may mean a return trip to the library.

Once you have selected some useful sources to support your claims, make a more in-depth evaluation to be sure you have the best evidence available.

- Is it current enough? Have circumstances changed since this text was published?

- Is the author someone I want to call on as an expert witness? Does the author have the experience or credentials to make a solid argument that carries weight with my readers?

- Is it reliable information for my purposes? It may be highly opinionated, but are the basic facts it presents confirmed in other sources? Is the evidence presented in the text convincing?

These questions are not always easy to answer. In some cases, articles will include some information about the author, such as where he or she works. In other cases, no information or even an author's name is given. In that case, it may help to evaluate the publication and its reputation. If you aren't familiar with a publication and don't feel confident making your own judgment, see if it is described in Katz's *Magazines for Libraries,* which evaluates the reputation and quality of periodicals.

■ Evaluating Web Sources

Web sites pose challenges and offer unique opportunities for researchers, for one reason because they are part of a developing genre of writing. When evaluating a Web site, first examine what kind of site you are reading. Is the Web page selling or advertising goods or services (a business site)? Is it advocating a point of view (an advocacy site) or providing relatively neutral information, such as that found in the yellow pages (an informative or educational site)? Is the Web site addressing the interests of people in a particular organization or with common interests (an information-sharing site)? Is it reporting up-to-the-minute news (a news site) or appealing to some aspect of an individual's life and interests (a personal site)? Useful information for a research paper may be obtained from any of these kinds of Web pages, but it is helpful to know what the main purpose of the site is—and who its primary audience is—when determining how productive it will be for your research.

As you weigh the main purpose of the site, evaluate its original context. Does the site originate in a traditional medium, such as a print journal or an encyclopedia? Is the site part of an online journal, in which case its material had to go through a screening process? Or is the site the product of one individual's or organization's desire to create a Web page, which means the work may not have been screened or evaluated by any outside agency? In that case, the information may still be valuable, but you must be even more careful when evaluating it.

Answering preliminary questions like these helps you before you begin a more specific evaluation of the site's content. To find answers to many of these questions, make a brief overview of the site itself, by looking, for example, at the clues contained in the Web address. That is, *.com* in the address means a business or commercial site; *.edu,* a site sponsored by a university or college; *.k12* is a site associated with a primary or secondary school; *.gov* indicates that the federal government sponsored the site; and *.org* suggests that the site is part of a nonprofit or noncommercial group. Sites originating outside the United States have URLs that end with a two-letter country abbreviation, such as *.uk* for United Kingdom.

Although these address clues can reveal a great deal about the origins and purposes of a Web site, remember that personal Web sites may also contain some of these abbreviations. Institutions such as schools and businesses sometimes sponsor individuals' personal Web sites (which are often unscreened by the institution) as well as official institutional sites. One possible key to determining whether a Web site is a personal page, however, is to look for a tilde (~) plus a name or part of a name in the address. Finally, if you are unsure of the sponsoring organization of a page, try erasing all the information in the URL after the first slash (/) and pressing the "Enter" key. Doing so often brings you to the main page of the organization sponsoring the Web site.

Most Web sites include a way to contact the author or sponsoring organization of the site, usually through e-mail. This is often a quick and easy way to get answers to the preliminary questions. If the site contains an address or phone number as part of its contact information, this means the organization or individual is available and probably willing to stand behind the site's content. If you can't find contact information the site may not be suitable to use as a primary resource. The information is not necessarily invalid, but such clues should alert you that information found on that page needs to be verified.

For the next step—that of more closely evaluating the contents of any Web site—Web researchers generally agree on the importance of five criteria: the authority, accuracy, objectivity, currency, and coverage of the site.[1] These criteria are just as important in evaluating traditional print texts, but electronic texts require special care. To understand how these criteria work, let's look at a specific example.

■ Evaluating a Web Site: One Example

Assume that your observations have led you to conclude that high school students are largely apathetic about government and politics. As a likely future parent, you have decided to research ways of interesting teenagers in the political process. You hypothesize that students who take the whole cyberworld for granted as a part of everyday life might be attracted to an interactive Web site. You do a search on *Google* using different combinations of keywords, and one site you access looks promising. You want to be sure, however, that the site meets the tests of authority, accuracy, objectivity, currency, and coverage.

The site is Student Voices, designed to teach high school students about government and civic responsibility. Your first job is to evaluate the home page.

The home page design is simple but attractive, and the text is easy to read. There are a number of different features to explore, and the site is

[1] Wolfgram Memorial Library Web site.

The Student-voices.org home page

typical in that there is no set order for accessing the different links. It is clear from the buttons at the top of the page that the site is used in the context of classes because there are teacher resources as well as student ones.

Clicking on the Student Resources link leads to a useful video called *How to Use the Student Voices Web Site.* This ten-minute video introduces the resources the site offers students. The Teacher Resources page does the same for teachers. Teachers can get a password to the site that allows their students to interact with the material on the site.

The Student Resources page also includes links to a wealth of sources about government, including these:

- encyclopedia entries on the U.S. president, U.S. senators, the federal government, and state government
- official government sites, from the White House to the Library of Congress
- sources that can be used for general research and constitutional research, and for access to voting/elections information
- major newspapers from across the country and Web sites of the major television networks

The video also explains the different ways that students can use the site interactively. Going back to the home page, you can see its major divisions:

The Student-voices.org Student Resources page

- **Speak Out** is just that—a chance for students to speak out on current political issues. Every few weeks the topic on the home page changes, and the staff of Student Voices presents a brief summary of a "hot" issue such as eminent domain, illegal aliens, or wiretapping. Students can then respond to what they read, read Speak Out on other subjects, or read more on the topic.

- **Polls.** At any given time, there is one question on which students are being polled, plus access to previous polls.

- **What's New.** Clicking on this box takes students to information about what their representatives are voting on at the time.

- **Current News.** The national political news of the day.

- **Other Voices.** Additional news of the day from a half dozen links to specific states.

- **Go Local.** These links let the students discover who their local and federal elected representatives are, what their local newspapers are, and what the census reveals about their community.

- **Next Election.** This box is updated every day to reveal how many days until the next election, who is running, and how to register to vote.

- **Photos.** These show Student Voices and related events.

The navigation bar also provides a link to a glossary of political terms.

Now that you have an overview of the site, consider whether it meets the criteria for a good source.

Authority. You decide to investigate who is behind this site. At the bottom of the home page is the information that the site is copyrighted by the Annenberg Public Policy Center. A quick check on *Google* leads you to this center's site, where you discover that the APPC is a part of the University of Pennsylvania. This is the way the center describes its mission:

> The Annenberg Public Policy Center of the University of Pennsylvania has been the premier communication policy center in the country since its founding in 1993. By conducting and releasing research, staging conferences and hosting policy discussions, its scholars have addressed the role of communication in politics, adolescent behavior, child development, health care, civics and mental health, among other important arenas. The Center's researchers have drafted materials that helped policy-makers, journalists, scholars, constituent groups and the general public better understand the role that media play in their lives and the life of the nation. The Policy Center maintains offices in Philadelphia and Washington, D.C.
>
> APPC's work has informed the policy debates around campaign finance, children's television, internet privacy, tobacco advertising and the tone of discourse in Washington. Scholars at the Policy Center have offered guidance to journalists covering difficult stories, including terrorist threats, suicide and mental health. The Center's discussions of key public policy issues have brought together industry representatives, advocates, government officials and the scholarly community. Its research has examined what messages work best to reduce the spread of HIV and drug use, how to improve candidate discourse and specific strategies for parents to use to monitor their children's media exposure. APPC has developed materials to help educators and schools do a better job of teaching youth about civic responsibility, democracy and the Constitution.
>
> To further our mission, we are launching this new web site. It is designed to give scholars, the media and the general public expanded access to the work that we began in 1993. We intend to make that complete body of research, including extensive data sets and topline surveys, available as quickly as possible. If there are any questions about materials not yet posted on the site, please contact our Philadelphia office at the number listed at the bottom of this page, or send an email to [the address shown].

The fact that the Annenberg Public Policy Center is part of a reputable university tends to give the information it presents on the site credence. There also is an e-mail address by which to reach someone at Annenberg, which also suggests credibility. The biographies of the staff at Annenberg reveal that they are scholars and journalists with substantial experience in Washington D.C.

Accuracy. Much of the information on the site is factual. The site's affiliation with a major university and its well-qualified staff make a reader inclined to accept that the facts are accurately presented. Since the site is
updated daily, news does not get old, as it can with sites that are not well
maintained. Those parts of the site that elicit opinion are clearly that—an
invitation for students to express their opinions, right or wrong. No one
under the age of thirteen is allowed to participate in Speak Out, and those
between thirteen and eighteen must have parental permission to participate or to send any personally identifying information. In fact, one other
project of the APPC is FactCheck.org, a site that analyzes statements made
to the media and points out inaccuracies. There is a link from the home
page of Student Voices to FactCheck.org.

Objectivity. Again, it is easier to maintain objectivity when dealing with
facts like the outcome of a vote in the Senate or the name of a local representative. Most of the links that provide information about government
are linked directly to governmental sites—the House of Representatives,
the Library of Congress, and the White House, for example. They are not
to sites that present partisan views of the government. The links to broad
categories such as U.S. presidents are to MSN's *Encarta*. The links to newspapers are to ones that are well established and well respected, such as the
New York Times and the *Washington Post*, but they also show a range of
possible slants on controversial issues. Included in the list, for example, is
the *Christian Science Monitor*.

The factual nature of much of the information on the site increases
the odds that the site is objective. The purpose of the whole site is to encourage students to discuss current political issues and to form their own
opinions rather than to be presented with set notions as to what the
"right" answer is. For those who want to read others' views, the analyses
on FactCheck.org could be a starting point.

Currency. The site is updated every day. Although the Speak Out topic remains the same for a few weeks, that schedule allows students time to respond, and the national and state news is updated daily, as are the
countdown to the next election and the What's New section.

Coverage. The site covers thoroughly much of the information that students need to learn about the political process on the national, state, and
local levels. They can find in one place information that would be much
more difficult and time-consuming to locate without its having been
brought together in one place. Hypertext works well in such a context because the multiple links put masses of information at the students' fingertips. The Student Resources add great depth to the knowledge available
on the home page, where there is also a link to another project of the
APPC, Justice Learning, where students can go into more depth about
some of the major issues of the day, should they want or need to.

TAKING NOTES

While everyone has methods of taking notes, here are a few suggestions that should be useful to research writers who need to read materials quickly, comprehend and evaluate the sources, use them as part of a research paper assignment, and manage their time carefully. If you need more detailed help with quoting, paraphrasing, and summarizing, review pages 92–102 in Chapter 4.

When taking notes from a source, summarize instead of quoting long passages. Summarizing as you read saves time. If you feel that a direct quote is more effective than anything you could write and provides crucial support for your argument, copy the material word for word. Leave all punctuation exactly as it appears and insert ellipsis points ("...") if you delete material. Enclose all quotations in quotation marks and copy complete information about your source, including the author's name, the title of the book or article, the journal name if appropriate, page numbers, and publishing information. If you quote an article that appears in an anthology, record complete information about the book itself.

If you aren't sure whether you will use a piece of information later, don't copy the whole passage. Instead, make a note of its bibliographic information so that you can find it again if you need it. Taking too many notes, however, is preferable to taking too few, a problem that will force you to go back to the source for missing information.

Use the note-taking process as a prewriting activity. Often when you summarize an author's ideas or write down direct quotes, you see or understand the material in new ways. Freewrite about the importance of these quotes, paraphrases, or summaries, or at least about those that seem especially important. If nothing else, take a minute to justify in writing why you chose to record the notes. Doing so will help you clarify and develop your thoughts about your argument.

Taking this prewriting step seriously will help you analyze the ideas you record from outside sources. You will then be better prepared for the more formal (and inevitable) work of summarizing, paraphrasing, and composing involved in thinking critically about your topic and writing a research paper. Maybe most important, such work will help with that moment all writers face when they realize they "know what they want to say but can't find the words to say it." Overcoming such moments does not depend on finding inspiration while writing the final draft of a paper. Instead, successfully working through this common form of writer's block depends more on the amount of prewriting and thoughtful consideration of the notes done early in the research process.

As you take notes, also remember to refer to your outline to ensure that you are acquiring sufficient data to support all the points you intend to raise. Of course, you will be revising your outline during the course of your research as issues are clarified and new ideas emerge, but the outline will serve as a rough guide throughout the writing process. Keeping close track of your outline will also prevent you from recording material that is interesting but not relevant. It may help to label your notes with the heading from the outline to which they are most relevant.

Relying on the knowledge of others is an important part of doing research; expert opinions and eloquent arguments help support your claims when your own expertise is limited. But remember, this is *your* paper. Your ideas and insights into other people's ideas are just as important as the information you uncover at the library or through reputable online sources. When writing an argument, do not simply regurgitate the words and thoughts of others in your essay. Work to achieve a balance between providing solid information from expert sources and offering your own interpretation of the argument and the evidence that supports it. You are entering an ongoing conversation on your topic, not simply recording what others have already said.

Using word-processing software can invigorate the process of note taking and of outlining. Taking notes using a computer gives you more flexibility than using pen and paper alone. For example, you can save your computer-generated notes and your comments on them in numerous places (at home, school, or work, or on a disk); you can cut and paste the text into various documents; you can add to the notes or modify them and still revert to the originals with ease.

You can also link notes to background material on the Web that may be useful once you begin writing drafts of your paper. For example, you could create links to an author's Web page or to any of his or her other works published on the Web. You could create a link to a study or an additional source cited in your notes, or you could link to the work of other researchers who support or argue against the information you recorded.

Because you can record information in any number of ways on your computer, your notes act as tools in the writing process. One of the best ways to start is to open a file for each source; enter the bibliographic information; directly type into the file a series of potentially useful quotations, paraphrases, and summaries; and add your initial ideas about the source. (For each entry, note the correct page references as you go along and indicate clearly whether you are quoting, paraphrasing, or summarizing.) You can then use the capabilities of your computer to aid you in the later stages of the writing process. For example, you can collect all your research notes into one large file in which you group like sources, evaluate whether you have too much information about one issue or one side of an argument, or examine sources that conflict with one another. You can imagine various organizational schemes for your paper based on the central themes and issues of the notes you have taken, and you can more clearly determine which quotes and summaries are essential to your paper and which may not be needed.

When you're ready to begin your first draft, the computer allows you to readily integrate material from your source notes into your research

paper by cutting and pasting, thus eliminating the need to retype and reducing the chance of error. You can also combine all the bibliographic
materials you have saved in separate files and then use the computer to
alphabetize your sources for your final draft.

Although taking notes on the computer does not dramatically change
the research process, it does highlight the fact that taking notes, prewriting, drafting a paper, and creating a Works Cited page are integrated activities that should build from one another. When you take notes from a
journal, book, or Web site, you develop your note-taking abilities so that
they help with the entire writing process.

DOCUMENTING YOUR RESEARCH (MLA SYSTEM)

One of the most effective ways to save yourself time and trouble when
you are ready to write your research paper is to document your research
as you go along. That way, when the time comes to create your Works
Cited page, you will be ready to put the works you used in alphabetical
order—or let your computer do it for you—and provide a list of those
works at the end of your paper. Some instructors may require a bibliography, or a list of all of the works you consulted (sometimes called simply
Works Consulted), but at a minimum you will need a Works Cited page.
As that title indicates, the list will be only those works that you quote,
paraphrase, or summarize in your paper.

Once you are fairly certain that you will use a certain source, go ahead
and put it in proper bibliographic form. That way, if the citation form is
complicated, you can look it up or ask your instructor before the last
minute. Also, you will realize immediately if you are missing information
required by the citation and can record it while the source is still at hand.

Following are examples of the citation forms you are most likely to
need as you document your research. In general, for both books and magazines, information should appear in the following order: author, title,
and publication information. Each item should be followed by a period.
When using as a source an essay that appears in this book, follow the citation model for "Material reprinted from another source," unless your
instructor indicates otherwise. Consult the *MLA Handbook for Writers of
Research Papers*, Sixth Edition, by Joseph Gibaldi (New York: Modern Language Association of America, 2003) for other documentation models and
a list of acceptable shortened forms of publishers.

■ **Print Sources**

A BOOK BY A SINGLE AUTHOR

Gubar, Susan. Racechanges: White Skin, Black Face in American Culture. New York:
Oxford UP, 1997.

THE ELEMENTS OF CITATION: BOOK (MLA)

When you cite a book using MLA style, include the following:

1 Author
2 Title and subtitle
3 City of publication

4 Publisher
5 Date of publication

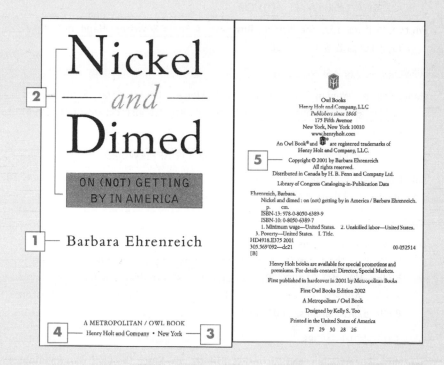

Works Cited entry for a book in MLA style

```
        1                         2
Ehrenreich, Barbara. Nickel and Dimed: On (Not) Getting by in America.
   3      4    5
New York: Holt, 2001.
```

AN ANTHOLOGY OR COMPILATION

Dark, Larry, ed. Prize Stories 1997: The O. Henry Awards. New York: Anchor, 1997.

A BOOK BY TWO AUTHORS

Alderman, Ellen, and Caroline Kennedy. The Right to Privacy. New York: Vintage, 1995.

Note: This form is followed even for two authors with the same last name.

Ehrlich, Paul, and Anne Ehrlich. Extinction: The Causes and Consequences of the Disappearance of Species. New York: Random, 1981.

A BOOK BY TWO OR MORE AUTHORS

Heffernan, William A., Mark Johnston, and Frank Hodgins. Literature: Art and
Artifact. San Diego: Harcourt, 1987.

If there are more than three authors, name only the first and add "et al."
(meaning "and others").

A BOOK BY A CORPORATE AUTHOR

Poets & Writers, Inc. The Writing Business: A Poets & Writers Handbook. New
York: Poets & Writers, 1985.

A WORK IN AN ANTHOLOGY

Head, Bessie. "Woman from America." Wild Women: Contemporary Short Stories
by Women Celebrating Women. Ed. Sue Thomas. Woodstock: Overlook, 1994.
45-51.

AN INTRODUCTION, PREFACE, FOREWORD, OR AFTERWORD

Callahan, John F. Introduction. Flying Home and Other Stories. By Ralph Ellison. Ed.
John F. Callahan. New York: Vintage, 1996. 1-9.

MATERIAL REPRINTED FROM ANOTHER SOURCE

Diffie, Whitfield, and Susan Landau. "Privacy: Protections and Threats."
Privacy on the Line: The Politics of Wiretapping and Encryption. Cam-
bridge, MA: MIT P, 1998. Rpt. in Elements of Argument: A Text and
Reader. Annette T. Rottenberg and Donna Haisty Winchell. 8th ed. Boston:
Bedford/St. Martin's, 2006. 601.

A MULTIVOLUME WORK

Skotheim, Robert Allen, and Michael McGiffert, eds. Since the Civil War. Reading: Ad-
dison, 1972. Vol. 2 of American Social Thought: Sources and Interpretations.
2 vols. 1972.

AN EDITION OTHER THAN THE FIRST

Charters, Ann, ed. The Story and Its Writer: An Introduction to Short Fiction,
7th ed. Boston: Bedford/St. Martin's, 2007.

A TRANSLATION

Allende, Isabel. The House of the Spirits. Trans. Magda Bogin. New York: Knopf,
1985.

A REPUBLISHED BOOK

Weesner, Theodore. The Car Thief. 1972. New York: Vintage-Random, 1987.

Note: The only information about original publication you need to provide is the publication date, which appears immediately after the title.

A BOOK IN A SERIES

Eady, Cornelius. Victims of the Latest Dance Craze. Omnation Press Dialogues on
   Dance Series 5. Chicago: Omnation, 1985.

AN ARTICLE FROM A DAILY NEWSPAPER

Doctorow, E. L. "Quick Cuts: The Novel Follows Film into a World of Fewer Words."
   New York Times 15 Mar. 1999, sec. B: 1+.

AN ARTICLE FROM A MAGAZINE

Schulhofer, Stephen. "Unwanted Sex." Atlantic Monthly Oct. 1998: 55–66.

AN UNSIGNED EDITORIAL

"Medium, Message." Editorial. Nation 28 Mar. 1987: 383–84.

ANONYMOUS WORKS

"The March Almanac." Atlantic Monthly Mar. 1995: 20.

Citation World Atlas. Maplewood: Hammond, 1999.

AN ARTICLE FROM A JOURNAL WITH SEPARATE PAGINATION FOR EACH ISSUE

Brewer, Derek. "The Battleground of Home: Versions of Fairy Tales." Encounter
   54.4 (1980): 52–61.

AN ARTICLE IN A JOURNAL WITH CONTINUOUS PAGINATION THROUGHOUT THE VOLUME

McCafferty, Janey. "The Shadders Go Away." New England Review and Bread Loaf
   Quarterly 9 (1987): 332–42.

Note that the issue number is not mentioned here; because the volume
has continuous pagination throughout the year, only the volume number 9 is needed.

A REVIEW

Walker, David. Rev. of A Wave, by John Ashbery. Field 32 (1985): 63–71.

AN ARTICLE IN A REFERENCE WORK

"Bylina." The New Princeton Encyclopedia of Poetry and Poetics. Ed. Alex Prem-
   inger and T. V. F. Brogan. Princeton: Princeton UP, 1993.

A GOVERNMENT DOCUMENT

United States. National Endowment for the Arts. 2006 Annual Report. Washington:
   Office of Public Affairs, 2007.

Frequently the Government Printing Office (GPO) is the publisher of federal government documents.

REPORTS

Gura, Mark. <u>The Gorgeous Mosaic Project: A Work of Art by the Schoolchildren of the World</u>. Teacher's packet. East Brunswick: Children's Atelier, 1990. ERIC ED 347 257.

Kassebaum, Peter. <u>Cultural Awareness Training Manual and Study Guide</u>. ERIC, 1992. ED 347 289.

The ERIC number at the end of the entry indicates that this source is available through ERIC (Educational Resource Information Center); some libraries have these available on microfiche. The number indicates which report to look for. Some ERIC documents were published elsewhere, as in the first example. If no other publishing information is given, treat ERIC (with no city given) as the publisher, as shown in the second entry. Reports are also published by NTIS (National Technical Information Service), state geological surveys, organizations, institutes within universities, and so on and may be called "technical reports," or "occasional papers." Be sure to include the source and the unique report number, if given.

AN UNPUBLISHED MANUSCRIPT

Leahy, Ellen. "An Investigation of the Computerization of Information Systems in a Family Planning Program." Unpublished master's degree project. Div. of Public Health, U of Massachusetts, Amherst, 1990.

A LETTER TO THE EDITOR

Flannery, James W. Letter. <u>New York Times Book Review</u> 28 Feb. 1993: 34.

PERSONAL CORRESPONDENCE

Bennett, David. Letter to the author. 3 Mar. 2007.

A CARTOON

Henley, Marian. "Maxine." Cartoon. <u>Valley Advocate</u> 25 Feb. 1993: 39.

■ Electronic Sources

A WEB SITE

<u>Fairy Tales: Origins and Evolution</u>. Ed. Christine Daaé. 12 Dec. 2007 <http://www.darkgoddess.com/fairy>.

Include the title if available; the author's name if available or, if not, a generic description such as "Home page"; the sponsoring organization or institution except in the case of commercial sponsorship; date of access; and URL in angle brackets.

THE ELEMENTS OF CITATION:
ARTICLE FROM A WEB SITE (MLA)

When you cite a brief article from a Web site using MLA style, include the following:

1 Author
2 Title of work
3 Title of Web site
4 Date of publication or latest update

5 Sponsor of site
6 Date of access
7 URL

Works Cited entry for a brief article from a Web site in MLA style

```
┌─── 1 ───┐ ┌──────── 2 ────────┐ ┌──── 3 ────┐
Zavis, Alexandra. "Women Assume Greater Roles." MilitaryCity.com.
┌─── 4 ───┐ ┌── 5 ──┐ ┌── 6 ──┐
17 Mar. 2003. Military Times. 23 Aug. 2007
┌────────────────── 7 ──────────────────┐
<http://www.militarycity.com/iraq/1670883.html>.
```

A PAGE WITHIN A WEB SITE

"Don't Zoos Contribute to the Saving of Species from Extinction?" Animal Rights
    Resource Site. Envirolink Network. 14 Dec. 2007 <http://arrs.envirolink
    .org/faqs+Ref/ar-faq/Q68.html>.

THE ELEMENTS OF CITATION:
ARTICLE FROM A DATABASE (MLA)

When you cite an article from a database using MLA style, include the following:

1 Author
2 Title of article
3 Title of periodical, volume and issue numbers
4 Date of publication
5 Inclusive pages

6 Name of database
7 Name of subscription service
8 Library at which you retrieved the source
9 Date of access
10 URL of service

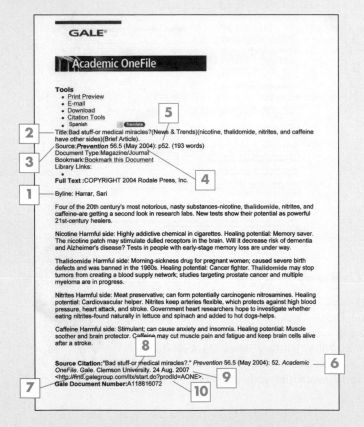

Works Cited entry for an article from a database in MLA style

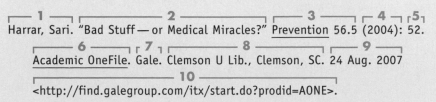

Harrar, Sari. "Bad Stuff — or Medical Miracles?" Prevention 56.5 (2004): 52. Academic OneFile. Gale. Clemson U Lib., Clemson, SC. 24 Aug. 2007 <http://find.galegroup.com/itx/start.do?prodid=AONE>.

A BOOK AVAILABLE ON THE WEB

Kramer, Heinrich, and James Sprenger. The Malleus Maleficarum. Trans.
Montague Summers. New York: Dover, 1971. 14 Dec. 2007 <http://www
.geocities.com/Athens/2962/witchcraze/malleus_2_ii_html>.

In this case the book had been previously published, and information
about its original publication was included at the site.

AN ARTICLE FROM AN ELECTRONIC JOURNAL

Minow, Mary. "Filters and the Public Library: A Legal and Policy Analysis."
First Monday 2.12 (1 Dec. 1997). 28 Nov. 2007 <http:www
.firstmonday.dk/issues/issue2_12/minow/index.html>.

MATERIAL ACCESSED THROUGH A COMPUTER SERVICE

Boynton, Robert S. "The New Intellectuals." Atlantic Monthly Mar. 1995.
Atlantic Unbound. America Online. 3 Mar. 2007. Keyword: Atlantic.

A CD-ROM

Corcoran, Mary B. "Fairy Tale." Grolier Multimedia Encyclopedia. CD-ROM. Dan-
bury: Grolier, 1995.

AN ARTICLE FROM A FULL-TEXT DATABASE AVAILABLE THROUGH THE WEB

Warner, Marina. "Pity the Stepmother." New York Times. 12 May 1991, late
ed.: D17. Lexis/Nexis Universe 12 Dec. 2007. <http://web.lexis-nexis.com/
universe/form/academic/univ_gennews.html>.

Include the original source information and the name of the database, access date, and URL.

AN ARTICLE FROM A CD-ROM FULL-TEXT DATABASE

"Tribal/DNC Donations." News from Indian Country. (Dec. 1997). Ethnic
Newswatch. CD-ROM. Softline. 12 Oct. 2007.

Include the original source information and the name of the database, the designation *CD-ROM,* the publisher of the CD-ROM, and
the electronic publication data, if available.

AN ARTICLE FROM AN ELECTRONIC REFERENCE WORK

"Folk Arts." Britannica Online. Encyclopaedia Britannica. 14 Dec. 2007.
<http://www.eb.com:180>.

A PERSONAL E-MAIL COMMUNICATION

Franz, Kenneth. "Re: Species Reintroduction." E-mail to the author. 12 Oct. 2007.

AN E-MAIL COMMUNICATION POSTED TO A DISCUSSION LIST

Lee, Constance. "Re: Mothers and Stepmothers." Online posting. 10 Sept. 2007.
Folklore Discussion List <mglazer@panam.edu>.

If the address of the discussion list archives is known, include that information in angle brackets; if not, place the moderator's e-mail address in angle brackets.

A POSTING TO A WEB FORUM

DeYoung, Chris. Online posting. 12 Dec. 2007. Issues: Gay Rights. 14 Dec. 2007
   <http://community.cnn.com/cgi-bin/WebX?14@52.7bmLaPoSc49^0@
   .ee7239c/12479>.

Include the author, header (if any) in quotation marks, the designation *Online posting*, the date of the posting, the name of the forum, the date of access, and the URL.

A NEWSGROUP POSTING

Vining, Philip. "Zoos and Infotainment." Online posting. 16 Oct. 2007. 12 Dec.
   2007. <news:alt.animals.ethics.vegetarian>.

Include the author, header in quotation marks, the designation *Online posting*, the date of posting, the date of access, and the name of the newsgroup.

A SYNCHRONOUS COMMUNICATION

Krishnamurthi, Ashok. Online discussion of cyberlaw and the media. "Reinventing
   Copyright in a Digital Environment." 25 Oct. 2007. MediaMOO. 25 Oct. 2007
   <telnet://purple-crayon.media.mit.edu:8888>.

To cite a synchronous communication from a MUD or a MOO, include the name of the speaker, a description of the event, the date, the forum, the date of access, and the electronic address.

■ Other Sources

A LECTURE

Calvino, Italo. "Right and Wrong Political Uses of Literature." Symposium on European Politics. Amherst College, Amherst. 25 Feb. 1976.

A FILM

The Voice of the Khalam. Prod. Loretta Pauker. Perf. Leopold Senghor, Okara, Bi-
   rago Diop, Rubadiri, and Francis Parkes. Contemporary Films/McGraw-Hill, 1971.
   16 mm, 29 min.

Other pertinent information to give in film references, if available, is the writer and director (see model for radio/television program for style).

A TELEVISION OR RADIO PROGRAM

The Shakers: Hands to Work, Hearts to God. Narr. David McCullough. Dir. Ken Burns
   and Amy Stechler Burns. Writ. Amy Stechler Burns, Wendy Tilghman, and Tom
   Lewis. PBS. WGBY, Springfield. 28 Dec. 1992.

A VIDEOTAPE

Style Wars! Videotape. Prod. Tony Silver and Henry Chalfont. New Day Films,
    1985. 69 min.

DVD

Harry Potter and the Order of the Phoenix. DVD. Prod. David Barron and David
    Heyman. Warner Bros., 2007. 139 min.

A PERFORMANCE

Quilters: A Musical Celebration. By Molly Newman and Barbara Damashek. Dir.
    Joyce Devlin. Musical dir. Faith Fung. Mt. Holyoke Laboratory Theatre, South
    Hadley, MA. 26 Apr. 1991. Based on The Quilters: Women and
    Domestic Art by Patricia Cooper and Norma Bradley Allen.

AN INTERVIEW

Hines, Gregory. Interview. With D. C. Denison. Boston Globe Magazine 29 Mar.
    1987: 2.

Note: An interview conducted by the author of the paper would be documented as follows:

Hines, Gregory. Personal interview. 29 Mar. 1987.

DOCUMENTING YOUR RESEARCH (APA SYSTEM)

Following are examples of the bibliographical forms you are most likely
to employ if you are using the American Psychological Association (APA)
system for documenting sources. If you need the format for a type of publication not listed here, consult the *Publication Manual of the American Psychological Association*, Fifth Edition (2001).

If you are used to the Modern Language Association (MLA) system for
documenting sources, take a moment to notice some of the key differences.
In APA style, authors and editors are listed by last name and initials(s) only,
and the year comes immediately after the author's or editor's name instead
of at or near the end of the entry. Titles of long works are italicized instead
of being underlined, and titles in general are not capitalized in the conventional way. The overall structure of each entry, however, will be familiar: author, title, publication information.

■ Print Sources

A BOOK BY A SINGLE AUTHOR

Briggs, J. (1988). *Fire in the crucible: The alchemy of creative genius*. New York:
    St. Martin's Press.

THE ELEMENTS OF CITATION:
BOOK (APA)

When you cite a book using APA style, include the following:

1 Author
2 Date of publication
3 Title and subtitle
4 City of publication
5 Publisher

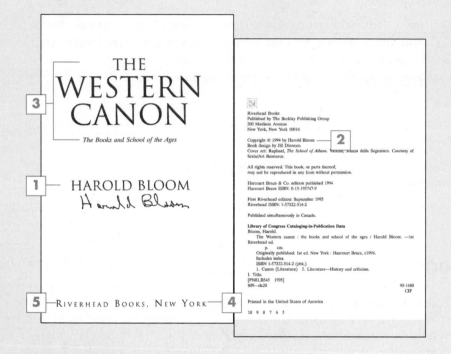

Reference list entry for a book in APA style

```
┌─ 1 ─┐ ┌─ 2 ─┐ ┌──────────────── 3 ─────────────────┐
```
Bloom, H. (1994). *The western canon: The books and school of the ages.*
```
┌── 4 ──┐ ┌──── 5 ────┐
```
New York: Riverhead Books.

MULTIPLE WORKS BY THE SAME AUTHOR IN THE SAME YEAR

Gardner, H. (1982a). *Art, mind, and brain: A cognitive approach to creativity.*
New York: Basic Books.

Gardner, H. (1982b). *Developmental psychology: An introduction* (2nd ed.).
Boston: Little, Brown.

AN ANTHOLOGY OR COMPILATION

Gioseffi, D. (Ed.). (1988). *Women on war*. New York: Simon & Schuster.

A BOOK BY TWO OR MORE AUTHORS OR EDITORS

Atwan, R., & Roberts, J. (Eds.). (1996). *Left, right, and center: Voices from across the political spectrum*. Boston: Bedford Books.

Note: List the names of *all* the authors or editors, no matter how many.

A BOOK BY A CORPORATE AUTHOR

International Advertising Association. (1977). *Controversy advertising: How advertisers present points of view on public affairs*. New York: Hastings House.

A WORK IN AN ANTHOLOGY

Mukherjee, B. (1988). The colonization of the mind. In D. Gioseffi (Ed.), *Women on war* (pp. 140–142). New York: Simon & Schuster.

AN INTRODUCTION, PREFACE, FOREWORD, OR AFTERWORD

Hemenway, R. (1984). Introduction. In Z. N. Hurston, *Dust tracks on a road*. Urbana: University of Illinois Press, ix–xxxix.

AN EDITION OTHER THAN THE FIRST

Gumpert, G., & Cathcart, R. (Eds.). (1986). *Inter/media: Interpersonal communication in a media world* (3rd ed.). New York: Oxford University Press.

A TRANSLATION

Sartre, J. P. (1962). *Literature and existentialism* (B. Frechtman, Trans.). New York: Citadel Press. (Original work published 1949)

A REPUBLISHED BOOK

James, W. (1969). *The varieties of religious experience: A study in human nature*. London: Collier Books. (Original work published 1902)

A BOOK IN A SERIES

Berthrong, D. J. (1976). *The Cheyenne and Arapaho ordeal: Reservation and agency life in the Indian territory, 1875-1907. Vol. 136. The civilization of the American Indian series*. Norman: University of Oklahoma Press.

A MULTIVOLUME WORK

Mussen, P. H. (Ed.). (1983). *Handbook of child psychology* (4th ed., Vols. 1–4). New York: Wiley.

AN ARTICLE FROM A DAILY NEWSPAPER

Hottelet, R. C. (1990, March 15). Germany: Why it can't happen again. *Christian Science Monitor*, p. 19.

AN ARTICLE FROM A PERIODICAL

Gorriti, G. A. (1989, July). How to fight the drug war. *Atlantic Monthly,* 70–76.

AN ARTICLE IN A JOURNAL WITH CONTINUOUS PAGINATION THROUGHOUT THE VOLUME

Cockburn, A. (1989). British justice, Irish victims. *The Nation, 249,* 554–555.

AN ARTICLE FROM A JOURNAL WITH SEPARATE PAGINATION FOR EACH ISSUE

Mukerji, C. (1984). Visual language in science and the exercise of power: The case of cartography in early modern Europe. *Studies in Visual Communication, 10*(3), 30–45.

AN ARTICLE IN A REFERENCE WORK

Frisby, J. P. (1990). Direct perception. In M. W. Eysenck (Ed.), *Blackwell dictionary of cognitive psychology* (pp. 95–100). Oxford: Basil Blackwell.

A GOVERNMENT PUBLICATION

United States Dept. of Health, Education, and Welfare. (1973). *Current ethical issues in mental health.* Washington, DC: U.S. Government Printing Office.

AN ABSTRACT

Fritz, M. (1990/1991). A comparison of social interactions using a friendship awareness activity. *Education and Training in Mental Retardation, 25,* 352–359. (From *Psychological Abstracts,* 1991, 78, Abstract No. 11474)

When the dates of the original publication and of the abstract differ, give both dates separated by a slash.

AN ANONYMOUS WORK

The status of women: Different but the same. (1992–1993). *Zontian, 73*(3), 5.

If the primary contributors to developing the program are known, begin the reference with those as the author(s) instead of the corporate author. If you are citing a documentation manual rather than the program itself, add the word "manual" before the closing bracket. If there is additional information needed for retrieving the program (such as report and/or acquisition numbers), add this at the end of the entry, in parentheses after the last period.

A REVIEW

Harris, I. M. (1991). [Review of the book *Rediscovering masculinity: Reason, language, and sexuality*]. *Gender and Society, 5,* 259–261.

Give the author of the review, not the author of the book being reviewed. Use this form for a film review also. If the review has a title, place it before the bracketed material, and treat it like an article title.

A LETTER TO THE EDITOR

Pritchett, J. T., & Kellner, C. H. (1993). Comment on spontaneous seizure activity [Letter to the editor]. *Journal of Nervous and Mental Disease, 181,* 138–139.

PERSONAL CORRESPONDENCE

B. Ehrenreich (personal communication, August 7, 2007).

(B. Ehrenreich, personal communication, August 7, 2007.)

Cite all personal communications to you (such as letters, memos, e-mails, and telephone conversations) in text only, *without* listing them among the references. The phrasing of your sentences will determine which of the two above forms to use.

AN UNPUBLISHED MANUSCRIPT

McIntosh, P. (1988). *White privilege and male privilege: A personal account of coming to see correspondences through work in women's studies.* Working Paper 189. Unpublished manuscript, Wellesley College, Center for Research on Women, Wellesley, MA.

PROCEEDINGS OF A MEETING, PUBLISHED

Guerrero, R. (1972/1973). Possible effects of the periodic abstinence method. In W. A. Uricchio & M. K. Williams (Eds.), *Proceedings of a Research Conference on Natural Family Planning* (pp. 96–105). Washington, DC: Human Life Foundation.

If the date of the symposium or conference is different from the date of publication, give both, separated by a slash. If the proceedings are published annually, treat the reference like a periodical article.

■ Electronic Sources

AN ARTICLE FROM AN ONLINE PERIODICAL

Palya, W., Walter, D., Kessel, R., & Lucke, R. (2001). Linear modeling of steady-state behavioral dynamics [Electronic version]. *Journal of the Experimental Analysis of Behavior, 77,* 3–27.

If the article duplicates the version which appeared in a print periodical, use the same basic primary journal reference. See "An Article from a Periodical." If you have viewed the article only in its electronic form, add in brackets [Electronic version].

Riordan, V. (2001, January 1). Verbal-performance IQ discrepancies in children attending a child and adolescent psychiatry clinic. *Child and Adolescent Psychiatry On-Line.* Retrieved August 9, 2007, from http://www.priory.com/psych/iq.htm

THE ELEMENTS OF CITATION:
ARTICLE FROM A WEB SITE (APA)

When you cite an article from a Web site using APA style, include the following:

1 Author

2 Date of publication or most recent update

3 Title of document on Web site

4 Date of access

5 URL of document

Reference list entry for a brief article from a Web site in APA style

┌─ 1 ─┐ ┌───── 2 ─────┐ ┌──────────────── 3 ────────────────┐
Marulli, C. (2007, March 1). *Woman gunner helps protect security detachment.*

┌──────── 4 ────────┐ ┌──────────── 5 ────────────┐
Retrieved November 5, 2007, from http://www.defenselink.mil/home/

faceofdefense/fod/2007-03/f20070301a.html

If the article does not have a corresponding print version, include the date of access and the URL.

A NONPERIODICAL WEB DOCUMENT

Munro, K. (2001, February). *Changing your body image*. Retrieved February 5, 2007, from http://www.kalimunro.com/article_changing_body_image.html

THE ELEMENTS OF CITATION:
ARTICLE FROM A DATABASE (APA)

When you cite an article from a database using APA style, include the following:

1 Author
2 Date of publication
3 Title of article
4 Name of periodical
5 Volume and issue numbers

6 Page numbers
7 Date of access
0 Name of database
9 Document number

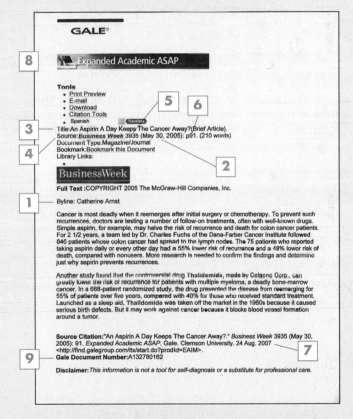

Reference list entry for an article from a database in APA style

┌ 1 ┐ ┌──── 2 ────┐ ┌──────── 3 ────────┐ ┌ 4 ─
Arnst, C. (2005, May 30). An aspirin a day keeps the cancer away? *Business*

┌ 5 ┐┌6┐ ┌──── 7 ────┐ ┌──── 8 ────
Week 3935, 91. Retrieved August 24, 2007, from Expanded Academic ASAP

┌── 9 ──┐
database (A132780162).

In general, follow this format: author's name, the date of publication (if no publication date is available, use "n.d."), the title of the document in italics, date of access, and the source's URL.

A CHAPTER OR SECTION IN A WEB DOCUMENT

National Council of Welfare, Canada. (1998). Other issues related to poverty lines. In *A new poverty line: Yes, no or maybe?* (chap. 5). Retrieved July 9, 2007, from http://www.ncwcnbes.net/htmdocument/reportnewpovline/ chap5.htm

AN E-MAIL

Do not include personal communications such as e-mails in your list of references. See "Personal Correspondence."

A MESSAGE POSTED TO A NEWSGROUP

Isaacs, K. (2008, January 20). Philosophical roots of psychology [Msg 1]. Message posted to news://sci.psychology.psychotherapy.moderated

Include an online posting in your reference list only if the posting is archived and is retrievable. Otherwise, cite an online posting as a personal communication and do not include it in the list of references. Care should be taken when citing electronic discussions. In general, they are not scholarly sources.

AN ARTICLE FROM A DATABASE

Lopez, F. G., Melendez, M. C., Sauer, E. M., Berger, E., & Wyssmann, J. (1998). Internal working models, self-reported problems, and help-seeking attitudes among college students. *Journal of Counseling Psychology, 45,* 79–83. Retrieved April 1, 2007, from PsycARTICLES database.

To cite material retrieved from a database, follow the format appropriate to the work retrieved and add the date of retrieval and the name of the database.

■ Other Sources

A FILM

Wachowski, A., & Wachowski, L. (Writers/Directors). Silver, J. (Producer). (1999). *The matrix* [Motion picture]. United States: Warner Bros.

Include the name and the function of the originator or primary contributor (director or producer). Identify the work as a motion picture. Include the country of origin and the studio. If the motion picture is of limited circulation, provide the name and address of the distributor in parentheses at the end of the reference.

A TELEVISION SERIES

Jones, R. (Producer). (1990). *Exploring consciousness* [Television series]. Boston: WGBH.

WRAPPING UP RESEARCH

■ Including Visuals in Your Paper

In this world of instantaneous Internet access to millions of documents and sites, it is easy to perceive knowledge as free for our use. The fact that information is easy to access does not relieve you of the responsibility of giving credit to those who originated the ideas expressed there. In fact, the ease with which material can be posted to the Internet makes it even more difficult to separate valid information from that which is questionable at best.

Since the Internet is a world of images as well as words, it may give you ideas for livening up your own work with all sorts of visuals. Don't forget, though, that you are obligated to give credit to the source of your visuals along with the ideas and words that you use. A graph or chart may provide just the sort of statistical support that will make a key point in your argument, and it can be easily cut and pasted or scanned into your electronic text, but you must document that graph or chart just as you would text. You should acknowledge the location where you found the visual and as much information as is provided about who produced it. If you use copyrighted graphs or charts in work that you publish either in print or electronic form, you should seek permission for their use. The same is true for photographs and other illustrations, although some books and Web sites offer images that you can use free of charge. You may be surprised to find that something as common as your school's logo is copyrighted and cannot be used on your Web page, for example, without permission.

■ Keeping Research under Control

How do you know when you have done enough research? If you have kept your outline updated, you have a visual record of your progress. Check this against the guidelines on pages 434–35. Is each point backed by at least two pieces of support? Do your sources represent a range of authors and of types of data? If a large proportion of your support comes from one book, or if most of your references are to newspaper articles, you probably need to keep working. On the other hand, if your notes cite five different authorities making essentially the same point, you may have collected more data than you need. It can be useful to point out that more than one authority holds a given view and to make notes of examples that are notably different from one another. But it is not necessary to take down all the passages or examples expressing the same idea.

■ To This Point

Before you leave the library or your primary sources and start writing, check to make sure your research is complete.

1. Does your working outline show any gaps in your argument?

2. Have you found adequate data to support your claim?

3. Have you identified the warrants linking your claim with data and ensured that these warrants too are adequately documented?

4. If you intend to quote or paraphrase sources in your paper, do your notes include exact copies of all statements you may want to use and complete references?

5. Have you answered all the relevant questions that have come up during your research?

6. Do you have enough information about your sources to document your paper?

■ Compiling an Annotated Bibliography

An annotated bibliography is a list of sources that includes the usual bibliographic information followed by a paragraph describing and evaluating each source. Its purpose is to provide information about each source in a bibliography so that the reader has an overview of the resources related to a given topic.

For each source in an annotated bibliography, the same bibliographic information included in a Works Cited or References list is provided, alphabetized by author. Each reference also has a short paragraph that describes the work, its main focus, and, if appropriate, the methodology used in or the style of the work. An annotation might note special features such as tables or illustrations. Usually an annotation evaluates the source by analyzing its usefulness, reliability, and overall significance for understanding the topic. An annotation might include some information on the credentials of the author or the organization that produced it.

A SAMPLE ANNOTATION USING THE MLA CITATION STYLE

Warner, Marina. "Pity the Stepmother." New York Times. 12 May 1991, late
    ed.: D17. Lexis/Nexis Universe 12 Dec. 2007 <http://web.lexis-nexis
    .com/universe/form/academic/univ_gennews.html>.

The author asserts that many fairy tales feature absent or cruel mothers, transformed by romantic editors such as the Grimm brothers into stepmothers because the idea of a wicked mother desecrated an ideal. She argues that figures in fairy tales should be viewed in their historical context and that social conditions often affected the way that motherhood figured in fairy tales. Warner, a novelist and author of books on the images of Joan of Arc and the Virgin Mary, writes persuasively about the social roots of a fairy-tale archetype.

A SAMPLE ANNOTATION USING THE APA CITATION STYLE

"Don't Zoos Contribute to the Saving of Species from Extinction?" *Animal*
   Rights Resource Site. Envirolink Network. 14 Dec. 2007 <http://arrs
   .envirolink.org/Faqs+Ref/ar-faq/Q68.html>.

This Web site provides arguments against the idea that zoos save species from extinction. Breeding in captivity doesn't always work, and the limited gene pool creates problems. Habitat restoration is difficult, and until the problems of poaching and pollution are solved, the habitat will be dangerous for reintroduced species. Meanwhile, the individual animals living in zoos lose their freedom because of an abstract and possibly faulty concept. This Web site, part of the Animal Rights Resource Site sponsored by the Envirolink organization, is brief but outlines the major arguments against zoos' role in preserving species.

CHAPTER 12

Writing an Argumentative Paper

Chapter 11 discusses the planning of an argumentative paper and the process involved in researching topics that require support beyond what the writer knows firsthand. This chapter discusses moving from the planning and researching stage into the actual writing of the paper.

Making a preliminary outline before you conduct any needed research gives direction to your research. If your topic requires no research, a preliminary outline helps you to organize your own thoughts on the subject. Preliminary outlines can change, however, in the process of researching and writing the paper. As you begin drafting the paper, you will need to finalize your decisions about what issues you want to raise.

Once you are satisfied that you have identified all the issues that will appear in your paper, you should begin to determine what kind of organization will be most effective for your argument. Now is the time to organize the results of your thinking into a logical and persuasive form. If you have read about your topic, answered questions, and acquired some evidence, you may already have decided on ways to approach your subject. If not, you should look closely at your outline now, recalling your purposes when you began your investigation, and develop a strategy for using the information you have gathered to achieve those purposes.

DEFINING THE ISSUES

■ Case Study: School Uniforms

To see how we raise and evaluate issues in a specific context, let's look at a controversy that has surfaced recently in many of our nation's public schools.

Some schools are considering requiring school uniforms, but that proposal has not been met with unanimous support from students or their parents.

In one particular school district, those in favor of school uniforms raised these issues:

1. Other schools that initiated a uniform requirement experienced an improvement in discipline.
2. Buying uniforms is economical for parents.
3. Wearing uniforms takes away undesirable distinctions based on social and economic class.
4. Students who wear uniforms are not distracted by what they or others are wearing.
5. A uniform requirement does away with the need for increasingly detailed dress codes.

On the other side, those who opposed school uniforms introduced the following issues:

1. Requiring uniforms does not guarantee improved discipline.
2. A uniform requirement prevents parents from buying inexpensive clothing alternatives.
3. Students have the right to express themselves through their choice of clothing.
4. A dress code can eliminate fashions that are distracting to other students without taking away the student's choice of clothing completely.
5. Some students' weight, body shape, etc., may make them uncomfortable and self-conscious in the style of uniform chosen.

You would have to understand these issues—understand the ongoing conversation—before you could argue successfully about the topic. Now let's analyze these issues, comparing their strengths and weaknesses.

1. It is clear that not all the issues in this dispute were equally important. The arguers decided, therefore, to give greater emphasis to the issues most likely to be persuasive to their audiences and less attention to those difficult to prove or narrower in their appeal. At this time in some of the communities in the district, massive layoffs had forced parents out of work. Therefore, the cost of switching to uniforms was a major concern. If parents did not have to spend money on uniforms, they could shop for the most economic alternatives or let their younger children wear clothes their older children had outgrown. Within the district, there had been few problems with fashions that were extreme enough to be a distraction to other students, and those few could be addressed with minor additions to the dress code, certainly an easy accommodation to make. To those opposed to the uniform requirement, the economic concerns seemed to outweigh the use of

uniforms as a means of establishing discipline, a goal they felt could be accomplished by other means.

2. It was also clear that, as in several of the other cases we have examined, the support on both sides consisted of both factual data and appeals to values. With regard to the factual data, each side reported evidence to prove that:

a. the wearing of uniforms leads or does not lead to a reduced number of discipline problems.

b. uniforms are or are not an economical alternative.

c. the majority of students favored or opposed wearing uniforms.

d. the majority of parents favored or opposed the uniform requirement.

The factual data were important. If opponents could prove that uniforms would place an increased financial burden on families already hurt by layoffs, the argument in favor of uniforms would be weakened. It would be weakened further if factual data from other similar districts showed no improvement in discipline.

Let us assume that the factual claims either were settled or remained in abeyance. We now turn our attention to a second set of issues, a contest over the values to be served.

3. Both sides in the dispute were concerned about the well-being of the students. Related to that, of course, was the well-being of their families. Improved discipline in the schools would benefit all students because the focus could be on education, not on policing student behavior. Beyond both of these concerns, however, were the issues of students' rights and their need to express themselves. If the majority of the students opposed uniforms, was that a strong enough concern to override the financial burden on their families? What about the minority who favored uniforms and perhaps had felt stigmatized by being unable to afford the clothes in style among their peers? In such a situation, should a vote by the students play a major role in policy decisions? Students are not allowed to hire their own teachers or to choose their manner of instruction, their courses of study, their grades, or the rules of admission. In the school community, administrators argued, the experienced are required to lead and instruct the inexperienced.

No controversy exists out of context. An outsider who entered this debate unaware of the recent layoffs, for example, would probably underestimate the weight that finances should receive in considering the uniform issue. In a different setting, a uniform requirement might raise questions about discrimination against those required by their religion to be veiled. In different cultures, students have gone to court to protect their right to wear clothing depicting the Confederate flag or making statements opposing the war in Iraq in spite of school rules against these types of displays.

Recently, a controversy over a billboard arose in a university town. An apartment complex near the university called The Reserve had designed an ad that played on its name. The left-hand side of the billboard pictured a demure young lady with the caption "Reserved." The right-hand side pictured a young lady smiling over her shoulder at the camera, dressed in low-cut jeans exposing a tattoo on her lower back. This picture, of course, was labeled "Unreserved." The billboard probably would have been accepted as a clever play on words and a catchy marketing ploy had a student not been murdered in the complex only months before, strangled with her bikini top. Members of the community were quick to judge the billboard inappropriate under the circumstances—so vocally that the billboard was taken down. The concern was that this visual might make young women at the complex the target for further sex crimes. The context influenced the response to this particular visual argument.

As you approach the writing of your argument, be mindful of the context in which the argument is taking place.

In making our way through the uniform debate, we have summarized a procedure for tackling the issues in any controversial problem.

1. Raise the relevant issues and arrange them in order of importance. Plan to devote more time and space to issues you regard as crucial.

2. Produce the strongest evidence you can to support your factual claims, knowing that the opposing side or critical readers may try to produce conflicting evidence.

3. Defend your value claims by finding support in the fundamental principles with which most people in your audience would agree.

4. Argue with yourself. Try to foresee what kinds of refutation are possible. Try to anticipate and meet the opposing arguments.

5. Consider the context in which your argument will be read and be sensitive to the concerns of your audience.

ORGANIZING THE MATERIAL

The first point to establish in organizing your material is what type of thesis you plan to present. Is your intention to make readers aware of some problem? To offer a solution to the problem? To defend a position? To refute a position held by others? The way you organize your material will depend to a great extent on your goal. With that goal in mind, look over your outline and reevaluate the relative importance of your issues. Which ones are most convincing? Which are backed up by the strongest support? Which ones relate to facts, and which concern values?

With these points in mind, let us look at various ways of organizing an argumentative paper. It would be foolish to decide in advance how many paragraphs a paper ought to have; however, you can and should choose a general strategy before you begin writing. If your thesis presents an opinion or recommends some course of action, you may choose simply to state your main idea and then defend it. If your thesis argues against an opposing view, you probably will want to mention that view and then refute it. Both these organizations introduce the thesis in the first or second paragraph (called the *thesis paragraph*). You may decide that two or more differing positions have merit and that you want to offer a compromise between or among positions. A fourth possibility is to start establishing that a problem exists and then introduce your thesis as the solution; this method is called *presenting the stock issues*. Although these four approaches sometimes overlap in practice, examining each one individually can help you structure your paper. Let's take a look at each arrangement.

■ Defending the Main Idea

All forms of organization will require you to defend your main idea, but one way of doing this is simple and direct. Early in the paper state the main idea that you will defend throughout your argument. You can also indicate here the two or three points you intend to develop in support of your claim; or you can raise these later as they come up. Suppose your thesis is that widespread vegetarianism would solve a number of problems. You could phrase it this way: "If the majority of people in this country adopted a vegetarian diet, we would see improvements in the economy, in the health of our people, and in moral sensitivity." You would then develop each of the claims in your list with appropriate data and warrants. Notice that the thesis statement in the first (thesis) paragraph has already outlined your organizational pattern. However, if you find that listing your two or three main ideas in the thesis leads to too much repetition later in the paper, you can introduce each one as it arises in your discussion of the topic.

Defending the main idea is effective for factual claims as well as policy claims, in which you urge the adoption of a certain policy and give the reasons for its adoption. It is most appropriate when your thesis is straightforward and can be readily supported by direct statements.

■ Refuting an Opposing View

Refuting an opposing view means to attack it in order to weaken, invalidate, or make it less credible to a reader. Since all arguments are dialogues or debates—even when the opponent is only imaginary—refutation of another point of view is always implicit in your arguments. As you write, keep in mind the issues that an opponent may raise. You will be looking at your own argument as an unsympathetic reader may look at it, asking yourself the same kinds of critical questions and trying to find its weaknesses in order to correct them. In this way every argument you write becomes a form of refutation.

How do you plan a refutation? Here are some general guidelines.

1. If you want to refute the argument in a specific essay or article, read the argument carefully, noting all the points with which you disagree. This advice may seem obvious, but it cannot be too strongly emphasized. If your refutation does not indicate scrupulous familiarity with your opponent's argument, he or she has the right to say, and often does, "You haven't really read what I wrote. You haven't really answered my argument."

2. If you think that your readers are sympathetic to an opposing view or are not familiar with it, summarize it at the beginning of your paper, providing enough information to give readers an understanding of exactly what you plan to refute. When you summarize, it's important to be respectful of the opposition's views. You don't want to alienate readers who might not agree with you at first.

3. If your argument is long and complex, choose only the most important points to refute. Otherwise the reader who does not have the original argument on hand may find a detailed refutation hard to follow. If the argument is short and relatively simple — a claim supported by only two or three points — you may decide to refute all of them, devoting more space to the most important ones.

4. Attack the principal elements in the argument of your opponent.

    a.   Question the evidence. (See pp. 220–22 in the text.) Question whether your opponent has proved that a problem exists.

    b.   Attack the warrants or assumptions that underlie the claim. (See pp. 282–83 in the text.)

    c.   Attack the logic or reasoning of the opposing view. (Refer to the discussion of fallacious reasoning on pp. 337–47 in the text.)

    d.   Attack the proposed solution to a problem, pointing out that it will not work.

5. Be prepared to do more than attack the opposing view. Supply evidence and good reasons in support of your own claim.

■ Finding the Middle Ground

Although an argument, by definition, assumes a difference of opinion, we know that opposing sides frequently find accommodation somewhere in the middle. As you mount your own argument about a controversial issue, you need not confine yourself to support of any of the differing positions. You may want to acknowledge that there is some justice on all sides and that you understand the difficulty of resolving the issue.

Consider these guidelines for an argument that offers a compromise between or among competing positions:

1. Early in your essay explain the differing positions. Make clear the major differences separating the two (or more) sides.

2. Point out, whenever possible, that the differing sides already agree to some exceptions to their stated positions. Such evidence may prove that the differences are not so extreme as their advocates insist. Several commentators, writing about the budget conflict between Democrats and Republicans in late 1998, adopted this strategy, suggesting that compromise was possible because the differences were narrower than the public believed.

3. Make clear your own moderation and sympathy, your own willingness to negotiate. An example of this attitude appears in an essay on abortion in which the author infers how Abraham Lincoln might have treated the question of abortion rights.

> In this debate I have made my own position clear. It is a pro-life position (though it may not please all pro-lifers), and its model is Lincoln's position on slavery from 1854 until well into the Civil War: tolerate, restrict, discourage. Like Lincoln's, its touchstone is the common good of the nation, not the sovereign self. Like Lincoln's position, it accepts the legality but not the moral legitimacy of the institution that it seeks to contain. It invites argument and negotiation; it is a gambit, not a gauntlet.[1]

4. If you favor one side of the controversy, acknowledge that opposing views deserve to be considered. For example, in another essay on abortion, the author, who supports abortion rights, says,

> Those of us who are pro-choice must come to terms with those thoughtful pro-lifers who believe that in elevating the right to privacy above all other values, the most helpless form of humanity is left unprotected and is, in fact, defined away. They deserve to have their views addressed with sympathy and moral clarity.[2]

5. Provide evidence that accepting a middle ground can offer marked advantages for the whole society. Wherever possible, show that continued polarization can result in violence, injustice, and suffering.

6. In offering a solution that finds a common ground, be as specific as possible, emphasizing the part that you are willing to play in reach-

---

[1] George McKenna, "On Abortion: A Lincolnian Position," *Atlantic Monthly,* September 1995, p. 68. (A gauntlet or glove is flung down in order to challenge an opponent to combat; a gambit is the opening move in a chess game, or in the words of one dictionary, "a concession that invites discussion." — EDS.)

[2] Benjamin C. Schwarz, "Judge Ginsburg's Moral Myopia," *New York Times,* July 30, 1993, sec. A, p. 27.

ing a settlement. In an essay titled "Pro-Life and Pro-Choice? Yes!" the author concludes with this:

> Must those of us who abhor abortion, then, reconcile ourselves to seeing it spread unchecked? By no means. We can refuse to practice it ourselves—or, if we are male, beseech the women who carry our children to let them be born, and promise to support them, and mean it and do it. We can counsel and preach to others; those of us who are religious can pray. . . . What we must not do is ask the state to impose our views on those who disagree.[3]

On a different subject, a debate on pornography, the author, who is opposed to free distribution of obscene material, nevertheless refuses to endorse censorship.

> I think that, by enlarging the First Amendment to protect, in effect, freedom of expression, rather than freedom of speech and of the press, the courts made a mistake. The courts have made other mistakes, but I do not know a better way of defining the interests of the community than through legislation and through the courts. So I am willing to put up with things I think are wrong in the hope that they will be corrected. I know of no alternative that would always make the right decisions.[4]

■ Presenting the Stock Issues

Presenting the stock issues, or stating the problem before the solution, is a type of organization borrowed from traditional debate format. It works for policy claims when an audience must be convinced that a need exists for changing the status quo (present conditions) and for introducing plans to solve the problem. You begin by establishing that a problem exists (need). You then propose a solution (plan), which is your thesis. Finally, you show reasons for adopting the plan (advantages). These three elements—need, plan, and advantages—are called the stock issues.

For example, suppose you wanted to argue that measures for reducing acid rain should be introduced at once. You would first have to establish a need for such measures by defining the problem and providing evidence of damage. Then you would produce your thesis, a means for improving conditions. Finally you would suggest the benefits that would follow from implementation of your plan. Notice that in this organization your thesis paragraph usually appears toward the middle of your paper, although it may also appear at the beginning.

[3]George Church, *Time,* March 6, 1995, p. 108.
[4]Ernest van den Haag, *Smashing Liberal Icons: A Collection of Debates* (Washington, D.C.: Heritage Foundation, 1981), p. 101.

■ Ordering Material for Emphasis

Whichever way you choose to work, you should revise your outline to reflect the order in which you intend to present your thesis and supporting ideas. Not only the placement of your thesis paragraph but also the wording and arrangement of your ideas will determine what points in your paper receive the most emphasis.

Suppose your purpose is to convince the reader that cigarette smoking is a bad habit. You might decide to concentrate on three unpleasant attributes of cigarette smoking: (1) it is unhealthy; (2) it is dirty; (3) it is expensive. Obviously, these are not equally important as possible deterrents. You would no doubt consider the first reason the most compelling, accompanied by evidence to prove the relationship between cigarette smoking and cancer, heart disease, emphysema, and other diseases. This issue, therefore, should be given greater emphasis than the others.

There are several ways to achieve emphasis. One is to make the explicit statement that you consider a certain issue the most important.

> Finally, and *most importantly,* human culture is often able to neutralize or reverse what might otherwise be genetically advantageous consequences of selfish behavior.[5]

This quotation also reveals a second way—placing the material to be emphasized in an emphatic position, either first or last in the paper. The end position, however, is generally more emphatic.

A third way to achieve emphasis is to elaborate on the material to be emphasized, treating it at greater length, offering more data and reasons for it than you give for the other issues.

■ Considering Scope and Audience

With a working outline in hand that indicates the order of your thesis and claims, you are almost ready to begin turning your notes into prose. First, however, it is useful to review the limits on your paper to be sure your writing time will be used to the best possible advantage.

The first limit involves scope. As mentioned earlier, your thesis should introduce a claim that can be adequately supported in the space available to you. If your research has opened up more aspects than you anticipated, you may want to narrow your thesis to one major subtopic. Or you could emphasize only the most persuasive arguments for your position (assuming these are sufficient to make your case) and omit the others. In a brief paper (three or four pages), three issues are probably all you have room to develop. On the other hand, if you suspect your thesis can be proved in one or two pages, look for ways to expand it. What additional issues might

---

[5] Peter Singer, *The Expanding Circle* (New York: New American Library, 1982), p. 171.

be brought in to bolster your argument? Alternatively, is there a larger issue for which your thesis could become a supporting idea?

Other limits on your paper are imposed by the need to make your points in a way that will be persuasive to an audience. The style and tone you choose depend not only on the nature of the subject but also on how you can best convince readers that you are a credible source. *Style* in this context refers to the elements of your prose—simple versus complex sentences, active versus passive verbs, metaphors, analogies, and other literary devices. *Tone* is the approach you take to your topic—solemn or humorous, detached or sympathetic. Style and tone together compose your voice as a writer.

Many students assume that every writer has only one voice. In fact, a writer typically adapts his or her voice to the material and the audience. Perhaps the easiest way to appreciate this is to think of two or three works by the same author that are written in different voices. Or compare the speeches of two different characters in the same story, novel, or film. Every writer has individual talents and inclinations that appear in most or all of his or her work. A good writer, however, is able to amplify some stylistic elements and diminish others, as well as to change tone, by choice.

It is usually appropriate in a short paper to choose an *expository* style, which emphasizes the elements of your argument rather than your personality. You may want to appeal to your readers' emotions as well as their intellects, but keep in mind that sympathy is most effectively gained when it is supported by believable evidence. If you press your point stridently, your audience is likely to be suspicious rather than receptive. If you sprinkle your prose with jokes or metaphors, you may diminish your credibility by detracting from the substance of your case. Both humor and analogy can be useful tools, but they should be used with discretion.

You can discover some helpful pointers on essay style by reading the editorials in newspapers such as the *New York Times,* the *Washington Post,* or the *Wall Street Journal.* The authors are typically addressing a mixed audience comparable to the hypothetical readers of your own paper. Though their approaches vary, each writer is attempting to portray himself or herself as an objective analyst whose argument deserves careful attention.

Again, remember your goals. You are trying to convince your audience of something; an argument is, by its nature, directed at people who may not initially agree with its thesis. Therefore, your voice as well as the claims you make must be convincing.

■ To This Point

The organizing steps that come between preparation and writing are often neglected. Careful planning at this stage, however, can save much time and effort later. As you prepare to start writing, you should be able to answer the following questions:

1. Is the purpose of my paper to persuade readers to accept a potentially controversial idea, to refute someone else's position, to find middle ground, or to propose a solution to a problem?

2. Can or should my solution also incorporate elements of compromise and negotiation?

3. Have I decided on an organization that is likely to accomplish this purpose?

4. Does my outline arrange my thesis and issues in an appropriate order to emphasize the most important issues?

5. Does my outline show an argument whose scope suits the needs of this paper?

6. What questions of style and tone do I need to keep in mind as I write to ensure that my argument will be persuasive?

WRITING

■ Beginning the Paper

Having found a claim you can defend and the voice you will adopt toward your audience, you must now think about how to begin. An introduction to your subject should consist of more than just the first paragraph of your paper. It should invite the reader to give attention to what you have to say. It should also point you in the direction you will take in developing your argument. You may want to begin the actual writing of your paper with the thesis paragraph. It is useful to consider the whole paragraph rather than simply the thesis statement for two reasons. First, not all theses are effectively expressed in a single sentence. Second, the rest of the paragraph will be closely related to your statement of the main idea. You may show why you have chosen this topic or why your audience will benefit from reading your paper. You may introduce your warrant, qualify your claim, and in other ways prepare for the body of your argument. Because readers will perceive the whole paragraph as a unit, it makes sense to approach it that way.

Consider first the kind of argument you intend to present. Does your paper make a factual claim? Does it address values? Does it recommend a policy or action? Is it a rebuttal of some current policy or belief? The answers to those questions will influence the way you introduce the subject.

If your thesis makes a factual claim, you may be able to summarize it in one or two opening sentences. "Whether we like it or not, money is obsolete. The currency of today is not paper or coin, but plastic." Refutations are easy to introduce in a brief statement: "Contrary to popular views on the subject, the institution of marriage is as sound today as it was a generation ago."

A thesis that defends a value is usually best preceded by an explanatory introduction. "Some wars are morally defensible" is a thesis that can be stated as a simple declarative opening sentence. However, readers who disagree may not read any further than the first line. Someone defending this claim is likely to be more persuasive if he or she first gives an example of a situation in which war is or was preferable to peace or presents the thesis less directly.

One way to keep such a thesis from alienating the audience is to phrase it as a question "Are all wars morally indefensible?" Still better would be to prepare for the question:

> Few if any of us favor war as a solution to international problems. We are too vividly aware of the human suffering imposed by armed conflict, as well as the political and financial turmoil that inevitably result. Yet can we honestly agree that no war is ever morally defensible?

Notice that this paragraph gains appeal from use of the first person *we*. The author implies that he or she shares the readers' feelings but has good reasons for believing those feelings are not sufficient grounds for condemning all wars. Even if readers are skeptical, the conciliatory phrasing of the thesis should encourage them to continue reading.

For any subject that is highly controversial or emotionally charged, especially one that strongly condemns an existing situation or belief, you may sometimes want to express your indignation directly. Of course, you must be sure that your indignation can be justified. The author of the following introduction, a physician and writer, openly admits that he is about to make a case that may offend readers.

> Is there any polite way to introduce today's subject? I'm afraid not. It must be said plainly that the media have done about as sorry and dishonest a job of covering health news as is humanly possible, and that when the media do not fail from bias and mendacity, they fail from ignorance and laziness.[6]

If your thesis advocates a policy or makes a recommendation, it may be a good idea, as in a value claim, to provide a short background. The following paragraph introduces an argument favoring relaxation of controls in high schools.

> "Free the New York City 275,000" read a button worn by many young New Yorkers some years ago. The number was roughly the total of students enrolled in the City's high schools.
>
> The condition of un-freedom which is described was not, however, unique to the schools of one city. According to the Carnegie Commission's comprehensive study of American public education, *Crisis in the Classroom,* public schools across the country share a common characteristic,

---

[6]Michael Halberstam, "TV's Unhealthy Approach to Health News," *TV Guide,* September 20–26, 1980, p. 24.

namely, "preoccupation with order and control." The result is that students find themselves the victims of "oppressive and petty rules which give their schools a repressive, almost prison-like atmosphere."[7]

There are also other ways to introduce your subject. One is to begin with an appropriate quotation.

"Reading makes a full man, conversation makes a ready man, and writing makes an exact man." So Francis Bacon told us around 1600. Recently I have been wondering how Bacon's formula might apply to present-day college students.[8]

Or you may begin with an anecdote. In the following introduction to an article about the relation between cancer and mental attitude, the author recounts a personal experience.

Shortly after I moved to California, a new acquaintance sat in my San Francisco living room drinking rose-hip tea and chainsmoking. Like so many residents of the Golden West, Cecil was "into" all things healthy, from jogging to *shiatsu* massage to kelp. Tobacco didn't seem to fit, but he told me confidently that there was no contradiction. "It all has to do with energy," he said. "Unless you have a lot of negative energy about smoking cigarettes, there's no way they can hurt you; you won't get cancer."[9]

Finally, you may introduce yourself as the author of the claim.

I wish to argue an unpopular cause: the cause of the old, free elective system in the academic world, or the untrammeled right of the undergraduate to make his own mistakes.[10]

My subject is the world of Hamlet. I do not of course mean Denmark, except as Denmark is given a body by the play; and I do not mean Elizabethan England, though this is necessarily close behind the scenes. I mean simply the imaginative environment that the play asks us to enter when we read it or go to see it.[11]

You should, however, use such introductions with care. They suggest an authority about the subject that you shouldn't attempt to assume unless you can demonstrate that you are entitled to it. Some instructors do

---

[7] Alan Levine and Eve Carey, *The Rights of Students* (New York: Avon Books, 1977), p. 11.

[8] William Aiken, "The Conversation on Campus Today Is, Uh . . . ," *Wall Street Journal*, May 4, 1982, p. 18.

[9] Joel Guerin, "Cancer and the Mind," *Harvard Magazine*, November–December 1978, p. 11.

[10] Howard Mumford Jones, "Undergraduates on Apron Strings," *Atlantic Monthly*, October 1955, p. 45.

[11] Maynard Mack, "The World of Hamlet," *Yale Review*, June 1952, p. 502.

not allow the use of first person in argumentative essays, so check the written guidelines for your assignments or ask your instructor.

■ Guidelines for Good Writing

In general, the writer of an argument follows the same rules that govern any form of expository writing. Your style should be clear and readable, your organization logical, your ideas connected by transitional phrases and sentences, your paragraphs coherent. The main difference between an argument and expository writing, as noted earlier, is the need to persuade an audience to adopt a belief or take an action. You should assume your readers will be critical rather than neutral or sympathetic. Therefore, you must be equally critical of your own work. Any apparent gap in reasoning or ambiguity in presentation is likely to weaken the argument.

As you read the essays in this book and elsewhere, you will discover that good style in argumentative writing shares several characteristics:

- variety in sentence structure: a mixture of both long and short sentences, different sentence beginnings
- rich but standard vocabulary: avoidance of specialized terms unless they are fully explained, word choice appropriate to a thoughtful argument
- use of details and examples to illustrate and clarify abstract terms, principles, and generalizations

You should take care to avoid the following:

- unnecessary repetition: making the same point without new data or interpretation
- exaggeration or stridency, which can create suspicion of your fairness and powers of observation
- short paragraphs of one or two sentences, which are common in advertising and newspaper writing to get the reader's attention but are inappropriate in a thoughtful essay

In addition to these stylistic principles, seven general points are worth keeping in mind:

1. Although *you*, like *I*, should be used judiciously, it can be found even in the treatment of weighty subjects. Here is an example from an essay by the distinguished British mathematician and philosopher, Bertrand Russell.

> Suppose you are a scientific pioneer and you make some discovery of great scientific importance and suppose you say to yourself, "I am afraid this discovery will do harm": you know that other people are likely to

make the same discovery if they are allowed suitable opportunities for research; you must therefore, if you do not wish the discovery to become public, either discourage your sort of research or control publication by a board of censors.[12]

2. Don't pad. This point should be obvious; the word *pad* suggests the addition of unnecessary material. Many writers find it tempting, however, to enlarge a discussion even when they have little more to say. It is never wise to introduce more words into a paper that has already made its point. If the paper turns out to be shorter than you had hoped, it may mean that you have not sufficiently developed the subject or that the subject was less substantial than you thought when you selected it. Padding, which is easy to detect in its repetition and sentences empty of content, weakens the writer's credibility.

3. For any absolute generalization—a statement containing words such as *all* or *every*—consider the possibility that there may be at least one example that will weaken the generalization. Such a precaution means that you won't have to backtrack and admit that your generalization is not, after all, universal. A student who was arguing against capital punishment for the reason that all killing was wrong suddenly paused in her presentation and added, "On the other hand, if given the chance, I'd probably have been willing to kill Hitler." This admission meant that she recognized important exceptions to her rule and that she would have to qualify her generalization in some significant way.

4. When offering an explanation, especially one that is complicated or extraordinary, look first for a cause that is easier to accept, one that doesn't strain credibility. For example, years ago a great many people were bemused by reports about the mysterious Bermuda Triangle, which had apparently swallowed up ships and planes since the mid-nineteenth century. The forces at work were variously described as space-time warps, UFOs that transported earthlings to other planets, and sea monsters seeking revenge. But a careful investigation revealed familiar, natural causes. A reasonable person interested in the truth would have searched for more conventional explanations before accepting the bizarre stories of extraterrestrial creatures. He or she would also exercise caution when confronted by conspiracy theories that try to account for controversial political events, such as the assassination of John F. Kennedy.

5. Check carefully for questionable warrants. Your outline should specify your warrants. When necessary, these should be included in your paper to link claims with support. Many an argument has failed because it depended on an unstated warrant with which the reader did not agree. If you were arguing for a physical education requirement at your school, you might make a good case for all the physical and psychological benefits of

---

[12]"Science and Human Life," in James R. Newman, ed., *What Is Science?* (New York: Simon and Schuster, 1955), p. 12.

such a requirement. But you would certainly need to introduce and develop the warrant on which your claim was based—that it is the proper function of a college or university to provide the benefits of a physical education. Many readers would agree that physical education is valuable, but they might question the assumption that an academic institution should introduce a nonintellectual enterprise into the curriculum. At any point where you draw a controversial or tenuous conclusion, be sure your reasoning is clear and logical.

6. Avoid conclusions that are merely summaries. Summaries may be needed in long technical papers, but in brief arguments they create endings that are without force or interest. In the closing paragraph you should find a new idea that emerges naturally from the development of the whole argument.

7. Strive for a paper that is unified, coherent, and emphatic where appropriate. A *unified* paper stays focused on its goal and directs each claim, warrant, and piece of evidence toward that goal. Extraneous information or unsupported claims impair unity. *Coherence* means that all ideas are fully explained and adequately connected by transitions. To ensure coherence, give especially close attention to the beginnings and ends of your paragraphs: Is each new concept introduced in a way that shows it following naturally from the one that preceded it? *Emphasis,* as we have mentioned, is a function partly of structure and partly of language. Your most important claims should be placed where they are certain of receiving the reader's attention: key sentences at the beginning or end of a paragraph, key paragraphs at the beginning or end of your paper. Sentence structure can also be used for emphasis. If you have used several long, complex sentences, you can emphasize a significant point by stating it briefly and simply. You can also create emphasis with verbal flags, such as "The primary issue to consider . . ." or "Finally, we cannot ignore. . . ."

All clear expository prose will exhibit the qualities of unity, coherence, and emphasis. But the success of an argumentative paper is especially dependent on these qualities because the reader may have to follow a line of reasoning that is both complicated and unfamiliar. Moreover, a paper that is unified, coherent, and properly emphatic will be more readable, the first requisite of an effective argument.

THE MLA SYSTEM FOR CITING SOURCES

As you write your paper, any time that you make use of the wording or ideas of one of your sources, you must document that use. One of the simplest methods of crediting sources is the Modern Language Association (MLA) in-text system, which is used in the research paper on thalidomide in this chapter. In the text of your paper, immediately after any quotation, paraphrase, or idea you need to document, simply insert a parenthetical mention of the author's last name and the page number on which the material appears. You don't need a comma after the author's name or an abbreviation of the word *page* or *p*. For example, the following sentence appears in the thalidomide paper:

> Some of the forms of cancer that researchers believe may be treated with thalidomide are breast cancer; prostate cancer; brain cancer; and Kaposi's sarcoma, which is cancer normally found in AIDS patients (Burkholz 12).

The parenthetical reference tells the reader that the information in this sentence came from page 12 of the book or article by Burkholz that appears in the Works Cited, at the end of the paper. The complete reference on the Works Cited page provides all of the information readers need to locate the original source:

> Burkholz, Herbert. "Giving Thalidomide a Second Chance." FDA Consumer
> Sept.-Oct. 1997: 12–14.

If the author's name is mentioned in the same sentence, it is also acceptable to place only the page numbers in parentheses; it is not necessary to repeat the author's name. For example,

> Burkholz reports that some of the forms of cancer that researchers believe may be treated with thalidomide are breast cancer; prostate cancer; brain cancer; and Kaposi's sarcoma, which is cancer normally found in AIDS patients (12).

Remember, though, that a major reason for using qualified sources is that they lend authority to the ideas expressed. The first time an author is cited in the paper, he should be identified by full name and by claim to authority:

> According to William A. Silverman, a specialist in neonatology who has served as professor of pediatrics at Columbia University in New York and head of intensive care at San Francisco's Children's Hospital, thalidomide was first developed in Germany back in 1954 as an antihistamine by a small, new pharmaceuticals firm, Chemie Grunenthal (404).

A last name and page number in parentheses do not carry nearly the same weight as a full name and credentials. You should save the former for subsequent citations once the author has been fully identified. If more than one sentence comes from the same source, you do not need to put parentheses after each sentence. One parenthetical citation at the end of the material from a source is enough if it is clear from the way you introduce the material where your ideas end and the source's begin.

If you are using more than one work by the same author, you will need to provide in the parentheses the title or a recognizable shortened form of the title of the particular work being cited. If the author's name is not mentioned in the sentence, you should include in parentheses the author's last name, the title, and the page number, with a comma between the author's name and the title. If both the author's name and the title of any work being cited are mentioned in the sentence, the parentheses will include only the page number. Had two works by Burkholz been listed in the Works Cited, the first example above would have looked like this:

> Some of the forms of cancer that researchers believe may be treated with thalidomide are breast cancer; prostate cancer; brain cancer; and Kaposi's sarcoma, which is cancer normally found in AIDS patients (Burkholz, "Giving" 1).

If there is more than one author, don't forget to give credit to all. Two or three authors are acknowledged by name in the parentheses if not in your own sentence: (Harmon, Livesy, and Jones 23). With four or more authors, use *et al.*, the Latin term for *and others*: (Braithwaite et al. 137).

Some sources do not name an author. To cite a work with an unknown author, give the title, or a recognizable shortened form, in the text of your paper. If the work does not have numbered pages, often the case in Web pages or nonprint sources, do not include page numbers. For example,

> In some cases Sephardic Jews, "converted" under duress, practiced Christianity openly and Judaism in secret until recently ("Search for the Buried Past").

Direct quotations should always be introduced or worked into the grammatical structure of your own sentences. If you need help introducing quotations, refer to the Writer's Guide in Chapter 4 (pp. 96–98). Remember, however, that you need to provide parenthetical documentation not only for every direct quotation but also for every paraphrase or summary. Document any words or ideas that are not your own.

As a general rule, you cannot make any changes in a quotation. Two exceptions are clearly marked when they occur. At times you may use brackets to make a slight change that does not change the meaning of the quotation. For example, a pronoun may need to be replaced by a noun in brackets to make its reference clear. Or a verb tense may be changed and bracketed to make the quotation fit more smoothly into your sentence. An ellipsis (. . .) is used when you omit a portion of the quotation that does not change the essential meaning of the quote. You do not need to use ellipses at the beginning or end of a direct quotation. If the omitted portion included the end of one sentence and the beginning of another, there should be a fourth period (. . . .).

If a quotation is more than four typed lines long, it needs to be handled as a block quotation. A block quotation is usually introduced by a sentence followed by a colon. The quotation itself is indented one inch or ten spaces from the left margin. No quotation marks are necessary since the placement on the page informs the reader that it is a quotation. The only quotation marks in a block quotation would be ones copied from the original, as in dialogue. A paragraph break within a block quotation is indented an additional five spaces. The parenthetical citation is the same as with a quotation run into your text, but the period appears before the parentheses.

With print sources in particular, you will often need to cite one work that is quoted in another or a work from an anthology. For the former, the parenthetical documentation provides name and page number of the source you actually used, preceded by the words "qtd. in":

> In the quest for evidence, Col. Patrick Toffler, Director of the United States Military Office of Institutional Research, reported that they had identified 120 physical differences. The female soldier "is, on the average, about five inches shorter than the male soldier, has half the upper body strength, lower aerobic capacity and 37 percent less muscle mass" (qtd. in Owens 35).

A work in an anthology is cited parenthetically by the name of the author of the work, not the editor of the anthology: (Simkovich 3).

The list of Works Cited includes all material you have used to write your research paper. This list appears at the end of your paper and always starts on a new page. Center the title Works Cited, double-space between the title and the first entry, and begin your list, which should be arranged alphabetically by author. Each entry should start at the left margin; indent all subsequent lines of the entry five spaces. Number each page, and double-space throughout.

Another method of documenting sources is to use notes, either foot-notes (at the foot of the page) or endnotes (on a separate page at the end of the paper). The note method is not as commonly used today as the in-text system because reference notes repeat almost all the information already given on the Works Cited page. If footnotes or endnotes are used, most word-processing programs have functions that make the insertion of these notes convenient.

Nevertheless, it is a valid method, so we illustrate it here. Superscript numbers go at the end of the sentence or phrase being referenced:

> Roman authors admit to borrowing frequently from earlier Greek writers for their jokes, although no joke books in the original Greek survive today.[1]

The reference note for this citation would be

> [1]Alexander Humez and Nicholas Humez, Alpha to Omega (Boston: Godine, 1981) 79.

On the Works Cited page this reference would be:

Humez, Alexander, and Nicholas Humez. Alpha to Omega. Boston: Godine, 1981.

Notice that the page number for a book citation is given in the note but not the reference and that the punctuation differs. Otherwise the information is the same. Number the notes consecutively throughout your paper.

One more point: *Content notes*, which provide additional information not readily worked into a research paper, are also indicated by superscript numbers. Content notes are included on a Notes page before the list of Works Cited.

REVISING

The final stage in writing an argumentative paper is revising. The first step is to read through what you have written for mistakes. Next, check your work against the guidelines listed under "Organizing the Material" and "Writing." Have you omitted any of the issues, warrants, or supporting evidence on your outline? Is each paragraph coherent in itself? Do your paragraphs work together to create a coherent paper? All the elements of the argument—the issues raised, the underlying assumptions, and the supporting material—should contribute to the development of the claim in your thesis statement. Any material that is interesting but irrelevant to that claim should be cut. Finally, does your paper reach a clear conclusion that reinforces your thesis?

Be sure, too, that the style and tone of your paper are appropriate for the topic and the audience. Remember that people choose to read an argument because they want the answer to a troubling question or the solution to a recurrent problem. Besides stating your thesis in a way that invites the reader to join you in your investigation, you must retain your audience's interest through a discussion that may be unfamiliar or contrary to their convictions. The outstanding qualities of argumentative prose style, therefore, are clarity and readability.

Style is obviously harder to evaluate in your own writing than organization. Your outline provides a map against which to check the structure of your paper. Clarity and readability, by comparison, are somewhat abstract qualities. Two procedures may be helpful. The first is to read two or three (or more) essays by authors whose style you admire and then turn back to your own writing. Awkward spots in your prose are sometimes easier to see if you get away from it and respond to someone else's perspective than if you simply keep rereading your own writing.

The second method is to read aloud. If you have never tried it, you are likely to be surprised at how valuable this can be. Again, start with someone else's work that you feel is clearly written, and practice until you achieve a smooth rhythmic delivery that satisfies you. And listen to what you are reading. Your objective is to absorb the patterns of English structure that characterize the clearest, most readable prose. Then read your paper aloud, and listen to the construction of your sentences. Are they also clear and readable? Do they say what you want them to say? How would they sound to a reader? According to one theory, you can learn the rhythm and phrasing of a language as you learn the rhythm and phrasing of a melody. And you will often *hear* a mistake or a clumsy construction in your writing that has escaped your eye in proofreading.

PREPARING THE MANUSCRIPT

Print your typed essay on one side of 8½-by-11-inch white computer paper, double-spacing throughout. Leave margins of 1 to 1½ inches on all sides, and indent each paragraph one-half inch or five spaces. Unless a formal outline is part of the paper, a separate title page is unnecessary. Instead, beginning about one inch from the top of the first page and flush with the left margin, type your name, the instructor's name, the course title, and the date, each on a separate line; then double-space and type the title, capitalizing the first letter of the words of the title except for articles, prepositions, and conjunctions. Double-space and type the body of the paper.

Number all pages at the top right corner, typing your last name before each page number in case pages are mislaid. If an outline is included, number its pages with lowercase roman numerals.

Writer's Guide: Checklist for Argumentative Papers

1. Present a thesis that interests both you and the audience, is debatable, and can be defended in the amount of space available.

2. Back up each statement offered in support of the thesis with enough evidence to give it credibility. Cite data from a variety of sources. Fully document all quotations and direct references to primary or secondary sources.

3. The warrants linking claims to support must be either specified or implicit in your data and line of reasoning. No claim should depend on an unstated warrant with which skeptical readers might disagree.

4. Present the thesis clearly and adequately introduce it in a thesis paragraph, indicating the purpose of the paper.

5. Organize supporting statements and data in a way that builds the argument, emphasizes your main ideas, and justifies the paper's conclusions.

6. Anticipate all possible opposing arguments and either refute or accommodate them.

7. Write in a style and tone appropriate for the topic and the intended audience. Your prose should be clear and readable.

8. Make sure your manuscript is clean, carefully proofed, and typed in an acceptable format.

Use the spell-check and grammar-check functions of your word-processing program, but keep in mind that correctness depends on context. A spell-check program will not flag a real word that is used incorrectly, such as the word *it's* used where the word *its* is needed. Also, a grammar-check function lacks the sophistication to interpret the meaning of a sentence and may flag as incorrect a group of words that is indeed correct while missing actual errors. It is ultimately up to you to proofread the paper carefully for other mistakes. Correct the errors, and reprint the pages in question.

SAMPLE RESEARCH PAPER (MLA STYLE)

The following paper, prepared in MLA style, was written for an argumentation class. A number of Suzanne's sources were articles that she accessed online via InfoTrac, so her Works Cited page offers several examples of how to document sources from databases. The Silverman article, which she accessed in the library in bound periodicals, illustrates how to cite an article from a journal. Although FDA Consumer, which contains Burkholz's article, is technically a government document, it is a magazine published by the FDA; thus articles from it are cited as magazine articles. The article from MayoClinic.com shows how to cite a short work from a Web site. Notice that there are a number of sources that do not have authors. These are cited parenthetically by shortened versions of the titles and alphabetized on the Works Cited page by title. The fact that online sources often have no page numbers explains why some parenthetical citations do not include page references. In some cases, there are no parentheses at all because the works are from online sources, and both authors and titles are named in the text sentences. Notice that in every case, there is enough information in the paper for a reader to find the proper source on the Works Cited page and enough information on the Works Cited page for a reader to locate the source.

Simkovich 1

Suzanne Simkovich
Ms. Carter
English 102-14
April 14, 2003

Thalidomide: Changing a Drug's Reputation

The Roman poet Ovid is commonly credited with having said, "Medicine sometimes snatches away health, sometimes gives it." He could have easily been talking about the medically controversial drug thalidomide, which has been known to do both. According to William A. Silverman, a specialist in neonatology who has served as professor of pediatrics at Columbia University in New York and head of intensive care at San Francisco's Children's Hospital, thalidomide was first developed in Germany back in 1954 as an antihistamine by a small, new pharmaceuticals firm, Chemie Grunenthal. Early hints of what was to come were ignored. Silverman gives one example:

> In the town of Stolberg, on Christmas Day in 1956, 10 months before thalidomide was placed on the market in Germany, a child was born without ears. The father, an employee of Chemie Grunenthal, had brought home samples of the new drug for his pregnant wife; years later, he learned that his daughter was the first living victim of the subsequent epidemic of thalidomide-induced infant deaths and malformations. (404)

When it was not shown to be effective as an antihistamine, doctors started to prescribe thalidomide as a sedative, and it was marketed worldwide. Many pregnant women were taking it to help with nausea and sleep. There was brief testing done on the drug, and it was proven to be safe (Silverman 404–05). Around this same time, there were an increasing number of malformed babies. Then in 1961, reports were published that linked thalidomide to these deformities (Silverman 405–06). The deformities were caused by a birth defect called phocomelia, which is one that causes deformed limbs and internal organs ("Good"). Randolph Warren, a victim of the thalidomide disaster himself

The saying is commonly attributed to Ovid, but without a source

Source's name and claim to authority used to introduce paraphrase

History of the drug

A block quotation from the same source

No quotation marks around the indented block quotation

Page number in parentheses follows period

Same source, but author not named in sentence

An article with no author listed and no page number because accessed through a subscription service

Simkovich 2

and founder and executive director of the Thalidomide Victims Association of Canada, reports that it is estimated 10,000 to 12,000 deformed babies were born to mothers who took thalidomide (40). Thalidomide was labeled a major medical disaster.

Although thalidomide was labeled a medical disaster, some researchers have been looking at more positive aspects of the drug, such as its ability to cure illnesses. Even though thalidomide created horrible birth defects when given to pregnant women in the sixties, it has potential to be an effective treatment in fighting cancer and other diseases since it restricts the growth of cells and lowers the production of some proteins in humans.

Many would want to know why researchers would still touch a drug that caused such horrible defects. Ricki Lewis, a contributing editor for The Scientist, explains that it all began in 1964, when a doctor in Israel began to use thalidomide to treat leprosy. The form of leprosy that was being treated was one which causes severe pain and eye and nerve damage, along with blindness (Elash). This doctor's success caused more research to begin into more uses of thalidomide. The Food and Drug Administration has now approved thalidomide for use in treating leprosy ("Thalidomide Maker"). This encouraged more experimentation in possible uses of the drug.

Thalidomide has properties that would make it an effective treatment for many types of cancer and other diseases. According to Karen Wright's article "Thalidomide Is Back," in the 1990s immunologist Gilla Kaplan found that thalidomide lowers TNF Alpha levels. Herbert Burkholz, a member of the Federal Drug Administration's public affairs staff, explains that when patients have cancer or a serious infection, their tumor necrosis factor (TNF) Alpha rises. It is believed that the high levels of TNF Alpha in cancer patients cause their condition to deteriorate (13). This protein, when found in moderate levels, fights infections and tumors, but in high levels causes fever, weight loss, and inflammation (Elash). Since thalidomide has the ability to lower this protein's levels, it can be an effective treatment for some illnesses (Elash). This property has made

A government document in magazine form accessed through a subscription service

Transition to positive effects of drug

A weekly magazine accessed online

Elash's article is from a weekly magazine accessed online

No author, so cited by title

The use of authors' names here clarifies where one author's ideas end and the other's begin

Use of thalidomide to fight cancer

Simkovich 3

thalidomide specifically effective in treating multiple myeloma, which is a malignancy of plasma cells (Lewis). In particular, thalidomide seems to be the only possible treatment for multiple myeloma. Those who were treated with thalidomide for multiple myeloma experienced an 82% success rate, with success rate meaning improvement (Lewis). Knowing this fact about thalidomide definitely will help in the fight against cancer.

In addition to its property of lowering the protein TNF Alpha, thalidomide has some other properties that are helpful in fighting cancer. The first is that thalidomide has been shown to restrict the growth of new blood vessels (Burkholz 13). In cancer patients, this would inhibit new cancer growth. Thalidomide specifically "inhibits vascular endothelial growth factor and basic fibroblast growth factor," which are factors that cause the proliferation of blood vessels that form in some types of cancer (Lewis). This property of thalidomide has also been shown effective in treating macular degeneration, which is when too many blood vessels form in the retina of the eye (Burkholz 13). Another effective quality that thalidomide has is its ability to "stimulate immune-system cells and other immunoregulators" (Wright). Thalidomide also has anti-angiogenic properties that make it effective in treating Crohn's disease ("Thalidomide: New"). These are all effective in stabilizing patients suffering from some types of cancer.

With these astounding properties that thalidomide has, there are a variety of different illnesses that it can be used to treat. It is being used in treating Erythema nodosum leprosum, Behcet's disease, inflammatory bowel diseases, rheumatoid arthritis, sarcoidosis, aphthous ulcers in HIV infections, and systemic lupus erythematosus (von Moos), along with helping against "a potentially deadly immune system reaction in bone marrow transplant patients" (Elash). Of this extensive list, the HIV patients are helped because thalidomide helps heal lesions in the mouth and esophagus. This is helpful because these lesions normally keep patients from being able to eat (Burkholz 13). Some of the forms of cancer that researchers believe may be treated with thalidomide are breast cancer; prostate cancer;

Other properties that help it fight cancer

An article from a Web site

Thalidomide's use with other diseases

Page numbers can be pinpointed with print sources

Simkovich 4

brain cancer; and Kaposi's sarcoma, which is cancer normally found in AIDS patients (Burkholz 12). Researchers are beginning to firmly believe that thalidomide can be a miracle cure for patients with some of these inoperable conditions.

Currently, the modern benefits of thalidomide keep on building. Now, thirty years after it was developed, it appears to be a miracle drug due to positive results it is showing when given to patients. There still are some common side effects such as sleepiness, constipation, rash, mood changes, dry mouth, nausea, headache, increased appetite, puffiness of face and limbs, dry skin, itching, slow heart rate, irregular menstrual periods, low white blood cell count, and thyroid problems ("Thalidomide: New"). Although this seems like an extensive list of side effects, the benefits of not dying of cancer or any other illness thalidomide might be prescribed for far outweigh the discomfort. At this point, the FDA has approved thalidomide for use in treating leprosy, and for experimental use only in treating cancer and AIDS ("Thalidomide Maker"). The drug manufacturer, Celgene, and the FDA have imposed strict policies to prevent birth defects, including a program called System for Thalidomide Education and Prescribing Safety (STEPS) ("Thalidomide Maker"). Since thalidomide has some FDA approval, the use of it has become safer because it has now been taken off the underground market ("Thalidomide Maker"). Overall, there is major promise in this new drug.

Many people are currently being helped by thalidomide. The fact that the drug has a terrible history does not mean that the future will repeat the past. Today we have much safer procedures for investigating new drugs, and we work harder in restricting the uses of drugs, by creating such programs as STEPS, for example. If thalidomide had been created today, the 12,000 that were harmed by the drug probably would not have been due to more safety in drug development and use. Since more research is currently being done on thalidomide, many more than 12,000 could be helped instead of harmed. Is it not worth attempting to help people who have no other chance at life, in spite of thalidomide's dark history?

Reasons thalidomide is not the risk it once was

The essay's thesis in question form

Simkovich 5

Works Cited

Burkholz, Herbert. "Giving Thalidomide a Second Chance." <u>FDA Consumer</u> 31.6 (Sept.-Oct. 1997): 12–14.

Elash, Anita. "Thalidomide Is Back: A Horror Drug from the '60s May Find New Cases." <u>MacLean's</u> 10 Mar. 1997: 48. <u>Expanded Academic ASAP</u>. InfoTrac. Clemson U Lib., Clemson, SC. 3 Mar. 2003 <http://infotrac.galegroup.com>.

"Good Stuff." <u>The Economist</u> 17 Mar. 2001. 87–88. <u>Expanded Academic ASAP</u>. InfoTrac. Clemson U Lib., Clemson, SC. 3 Mar. 2003 <http://infotrac.galegroup.com>.

Lewis, Ricki. "The Return of Thalidomide." <u>The Scientist</u> 22 Jan. 2001: 5. <u>Expanded Academic ASAP</u>. InfoTrac. Clemson U Lib., Clemson, SC. 3 Mar. 2003 <http://infotrac.galegroup.com>.

Silverman, William A. "The Schizophrenic Career of a 'Monster Drug.'" <u>Pediatrics</u> 110.2 (Aug. 2002): 404–06.

"Thalidomide Maker Hopes Safer Drugs Follow." <u>Cancer Weekly Plus</u> 7 Sept. 1998: 8–9. <u>Expanded Academic ASAP</u>. InfoTrac. Clemson U Lib., Clemson, SC. 3 Mar. 2003 <http://infotrac .galegroup.com>.

"Thalidomide: New Uses for Notorious Drug." <u>MayoClinic.com</u> 21 Aug. 2002. Mayo Foundation. 3 Apr. 2003 <http://www .mayoclinic.com/invke.cfm?objectid=8DFF08EE-3CD>.

von Moos, Roger, et al. "Thalidomide: From Tragedy to Promise." <u>Swiss Med. Wkly.</u> 133 (2003): 77–87. <u>Expanded Academic ASAP</u>. InfoTrac. Clemson U Lib., Clemson, SC. 3 Mar. 2003 <http://infotrac.galegroup.com>.

Warren, Randolph. "Living in a World with Thalidomide: A Dose of Reality." <u>FDA Consumer</u> 35.2 (Mar.–Apr. 2001): 40. <u>Expanded Academic ASAP</u>. InfoTrac. Clemson U Lib., Clemson, SC. 3 Mar. 2003 <http://infotrac.galegroup.com>.

Wright, Karen. "Thalidomide Is Back." <u>Discover</u> Apr. 2000: 31–33. <u>Expanded Academic ASAP</u>. InfoTrac. Clemson U Lib., Clemson, SC. 3 Mar. 2003 <http://infotrac.galegroup.com>.

THE APA SYSTEM FOR CITING SOURCES

Instructors in the social sciences might prefer the citation system of the American Psychological Association (APA), which is used in the paper on women in the military in this chapter. Like the MLA system, the APA system calls for a parenthetical citation in the text of the paper following any quotations from your sources. The APA only recommends that page numbers be included for paraphrases or summaries, but you should provide page numbers for these as well unless your instructor advises you that they are not necessary. In the text of your paper, immediately after any quotation, paraphrase, or idea you need to document, insert a parenthetical mention of the author's last name and the page number on which the material appears. Unlike the MLA system, the APA system also includes the year of publication in the parenthetical reference, using a comma to separate the items within the citation and using "p." or "pp." before the page number(s). Even if the source has a month of publication, only the year is included in the parenthetical citation. Here is an example:

> As of now, women are restricted from 30 percent of Army assignments and 1 percent of Air Force assignments (Baer, 2003, p. 1A).

The parenthetical reference tells the reader that the information in this sentence comes from page 1A of the 2003 work by Baer that appears on the References page at the end of the paper. The complete publication information that a reader would need to locate Baer's work will appear on the References page:

> Baer, S. (2003, March 3). In Iraq war, women would serve closer to front lines than in past. *The Baltimore Sun*, p. 1A.

If the author's name is mentioned in the same sentence in your text, the year in which the work was published follows it, in parentheses, and the page number only is placed in parentheses at the end of the sentence.

> According to Baer (2003) of the *Baltimore Sun*, as of now, women are restricted from 30 percent of Army assignments and 1 percent of Air Force assignments (p. 1A).

In the APA system, it is appropriate to include only the last name of the author unless you have more than one author with the same name in your list of references, in which case you would include the first initial of the author.

If your list of references includes more than one work written by the same author in the same year, cite the first work as "a" and the second as "b." For example, Baer's second article of 2003 would be cited in your paper like this: (Baer, 2003b).

If a work has two authors, list both in your sentence or in the parentheses, using "and" between them. In these examples from the women in combat paper, there is no page number because the source is a short work from a Web site:

> The fall 2000 suggestion from DACOWITS included a possible recruiting slogan: "A gynecologist on every aircraft carrier!" (Yoest & Yoest, 2001).

> Yoest and Yoest (2001) recall the fall 2000 suggestion from DACOWITS for a possible recruiting slogan: "A gynecologist on every aircraft carrier!"

If there are three to five authors, list them all by last name the first time they are referred to and, after that, by the last name of the first author and the term "et al." (meaning "and others"): (Sommers, Mylroie, Donnelly, & Hill, 2001); (Sommers et al., 2001). Also use the last name of the first author and "et al." when there are more than five authors, which is often the case in the sciences and social sciences.

If no author is given, use the name of the work where you would normally use the author's name, placing the names of short works in quotation marks and italicizing those of book-length works. Notice throughout citations and references, APA style uses italics for titles where MLA uses underlining.

When using electronic sources, follow as much as possible the rules for parenthetical documentation of print ones. If no author's name is given, cite by the title of the work. If no date is given, use the abbreviation "n.d." instead. For a long work, if there are no page numbers, as is often the case with electronic sources, give paragraph numbers if the work has numbered paragraphs, or, if the work is divided into sections, the paragraph number within that section:

> Jamison (1999) warned about the moral issues associated with stem cell research, particularly the guilt that some parents felt about letting their children's cells be used (Parental Guilt section, para. 2).

Remember that the purpose of parenthetical documentation is to help a reader locate the information that you are citing.

At times you will need to cite one work that is quoted in another or a work from an anthology. For the former, the parenthetical documentation provides author's name, year of publication, and page number of the source you actually used, preceded by the words "as qtd. in":

> The female soldier "is, on the average, about five inches shorter than the male soldier, has half the upper body strength, lower aerobic capacity and 37 percent less muscle mass" (as qtd. in Owens, 1997, Anatomy section, para. 2).

A work in an anthology is cited parenthetically by the name of the author of the work, not the editor of the anthology.

SAMPLE RESEARCH PAPER (APA STYLE)

The following paper shows APA citations in the context of an actual text and the format for several different entries on the References page. Allison has used quotations sparingly and has instead made extensive use of summary and paraphrase. Often there is no page number in her parenthetical citations. That is because she was drawing from short online sources in which the paragraphs are not numbered but in which it is easy to find the material she refers to.

The format of the title page illustrates APA guidelines, as does the running head that is on each page and the use of lowercase Roman numerals to number each page before the first page of actual text.

Notice that Allison's thesis appears as the last sentence in her first paragraph. She carefully documents the restrictions on women that still exist in the U.S. military and argues why those restrictions are appropriate.

Women in Combat   i

The Controversy over Women in Combat

Allison Mathews

English 103-13

Ms. Carter

April 7, 2003

Women in Combat   ii

Abstract

Women have served in the U.S. military since World War I. Although many barriers to their complete participation in all phases of military service have been broken, they are still appropriately restricted from direct ground combat assignments. Because women are held to a lower physical standard than men, men in their units cannot trust their ability to perform on the battlefield. One argument in favor of combat assignments for women has been that the lack of combat experience stands in the way of their progressing through the ranks. Such careerism, however, goes against a soldier's sworn duty, and there are ways to advance in the military other than combat service. The social and logistical problems created are an argument against women's serving in close quarters with men. Pregnancy among enlisted women is also inevitable and poses its own medical and logistical problems. Combat assignments for women would be a threat to the effectiveness and readiness of American troops.

Women in Combat   1

The Controversy over Women in Combat

Throughout the history of the military, the role of women has changed and adapted as the needs of the country have. From Molly Pitcher to Rosie the Riveter, women have always held a place in making the military what it is today. Issues have surfaced in the modern military about the current role of female service members with regard to combat assignments. Positions on submarines, small destroyers, specialized combat teams, and a handful of other assignments are restricted to men-only clubs. The factors determining why women are restricted from these assignments include physical ability, deployability, the cost effectiveness of providing the facilities that women need, and the effect on the overall readiness of the military. Women who desire these assignments, and other opponents of these restrictions, have retorted with reasons that they should be included, the foremost being women's rights and their desire to advance up the ranks of the military. However, women are rightly restricted from direct ground combat assignments to ensure the readiness of the military and the effectiveness of these combat units.

Women were first recruited, and began serving, in the military during World War I because they were needed to fill the clerical, technical, and health care jobs that were left vacant as more men were drafted. All these women, however, were discharged as soon as the war ended. The Women's Army Corps (WAC) was founded during World War II and gave women their own branch of the military. They served in the same jobs as they did in WWI but with the addition of non-combatant pilot assignments. Women did not get their permanent place in the ranks until 1948 when the Women Armed Services Integration Act was passed through Congress, allowing them to serve under the conditions that they were not to hold any rank above colonel, were limited mostly to clerical or health care jobs, and were not to make up more than 2 percent of the entire military. They were still limited to their own female only corps until 1978, when the military was fully integrated and women were

Overview of the controversy

Opposing view

Thesis

A history of women in the military from a source accessed through a subscription service

Women in Combat   2

allowed to hold any assignment that their male counterparts could except for combat roles. The rules have been relaxed over the years as women have proven themselves in combat support missions, especially in the Persian Gulf War in 1991 ("Women," 2000). They continue to push to be allowed into every job that men hold, and the effect this is having on the military is a fiery issue.

According to Baer (2003) of the *Baltimore Sun*, as of now, women are restricted from 30 percent of Army assignments, 38 percent of Marine assignments, and 1 percent of Air Force assignments. From the Navy, women are excluded from the special operations SEAL groups. These exclusions are from Military Occupational Specialities (MOS) "whose primary mission is ground combat" as defined by the Pentagon. They are also excluded from Navy submarines and small battleships that do not have the facilities to accommodate women (p. 1A).

There have been many advancements for combat seeking women since the Persian Gulf War. McDonough (2003), writing for the Associated Press, reports that females are now allowed to fly combat missions in fighter jets and bombers for the Air Force and Navy. They can serve in many combat support roles such as combat Military Police companies. They can also be assigned to chemical specialist units that clean up contaminated areas on the battlefield, and to engineering units who build and repair bridges and runways in high risk areas. Women can also pilot the Army's Apache assault helicopters over the battlefield during high risk conditions, and pilot troop carrying helicopters onto the battlefield to deliver troops for a rescue mission during an assault. However, none of these MOSs are in selective special operations units such as Marine Force Recon or Army Airborne Rangers who serve as the "tip of the spear" in ground combat for missions like Operation Enduring Freedom in Afghanistan or Operation Iraqi Freedom.

The federal government and military have been under pressure from several sides on the issue of women serving in combat roles in the military. There are those that believe that all

The parenthetical citation shows where paraphrase ends and her ideas begin

Source and year included in text

Page only in parentheses

Author and year in text; no page number because electronic version

APA

Women in Combat   3

assignments, no matter how demanding of time, body, talent, and mind should be open to women as well as men. According to Gerber (2002) of the James MacGregor Burns Academy of Leadership, this is the general consensus of the Defense Advisory Committee on Women in the Services (DACOWITS). It was established in 1951 by General George Marshall but was disbanded when Secretary of Defense Donald Rumsfeld let its charter run out when it came up for renewal in 2002. However, its motives could be called into question as to whether it is rallying for the good of the military and its purposes or pushing its own platform that women should be integrated in all parts just because they believe it is deserved. Former DACOWITS Chairperson Vickie McCall even told the U.S. Air Force in Europe News Service, "You have to understand. We don't report facts, we report perception" (as qtd. in Yoest & Yoest, 2001). DACOWITS has often teamed up with other private women's rights activist groups that believe that the military should be an "equal opportunity employer" along with all other private and public employers.

A Web site

One source quoted in another; source with two authors

One cause of concern over women's inclusion in combat units has been the rigorous physical standards these troops must meet in training and in turn on the battlefield. Many studies have been done to prove or disprove a distinction between men's and women's physical capabilities. In the quest for evidence, Col. Patrick Toffler, Director of the United States Military Office of Institutional Research, reported that it had identified 120 physical differences (Owens, 1997, p. 40). The female soldier "is, on the average, about five inches shorter than the male soldier, has half the upper body strength, lower aerobic capacity and 37 percent less muscle mass" (as qtd. in Owens, 1997, p. 38). Leo (1997) reports in *U.S. News and World Report* that the way that the military accommodates for these differences is called "gender norming" and works by lowering the standards that women have to reach to pass the physical fitness tests. For instance, in the Marines, men are required to climb the length of a rope and females are only required to climb to a point below that marked with a yellow line (p. 14). These stan-

A journal paginated by issue

A magazine

Women in Combat   4

dards are mostly for people to enlist in the services; so the bar is significantly raised for those that choose to compete for a MOS in special operations or combat units. Females enrolled in Army Jump School to be paratroopers are still not required to run as far or do as many pushups or sit-ups as their male counterparts. When this double standard is employed in the military, it blurs the distinction as to which soldiers actually have the physical ability to perform on the battlefield.

When there is a question as to the physical abilities of a fellow soldier in a unit, there can be no guarantee that everyone can cover your back as well as you could for them. When there is no trust in a unit, it breaks down. Take, for example, the Marine ideology that no one is left behind on the battlefield. Imagine an officer trying to motivate his troops to jump out of a helicopter in the heat of battle. Some of the soldiers may doubt a female comrade's capability to carry them to safety should they be injured, because she does not have to meet the same physical standards as her male counterparts do. The training is not only meant to prepare the troops for war combat and to show the officers that they meet the physical requirements. It is also a time to begin to build the trust that binds the troop's lives together and prove to each other they have the physical and mental toughness to accomplish the mission and bring each other back safely. How can this trust be established when male soldiers witness some female soldiers being excused from throwing live grenades in practice because they cannot throw the dummy ones far enough to keep from being blown to shreds? "The military should be the real world," said Jeanne Holm, retired two-star General of the Air Force. "The name of the game is putting together a team that fits and works together. That is the top priority, not social experimentation" (as qtd. in Yoest & Yoest, 2001). The military studies prove that a female body is not equipped to perform the same physical rigors as the male body; therefore, they should not be put in the position where impossible war fighting demands are put on them.

One source quoted in another

Women in Combat   5

When left out of selective combat positions, there is the possibility that women cannot advance up the ranks because they would not get ample opportunity to prove themselves on the battlefield and gain combat experience. This experience goes a long way because it stands to prove that an officer has the leadership ability to command troops under fire and accomplish the mission. Experience can be gained in many ways, though, since America is not always at war. All officer career fields are necessary to the overall success of the mission, and in order to be promoted every officer must pull his or her weight. Even though the proceedings of the promotion committees are supposed to be kept private, it is no secret that combat experience weighs heavily on promotion picks (Nath, 2002). In a military that is centered on the chain of command, seniority is the most valuable commodity for any member, especially officers. The practice of officers' jockeying for promotions to further their career, stature, and income is called "careerism" (Nath, 2002). This is supposedly prohibited under the Air Force's second core value of "Service Before Self," and similar pledges in the other branches. The argument lies in the conflict between the career ambition of female officers seeking a combat MOS and the needs of a ready military to support the mission.

No page number given

The truth is, however, that the United States Armed Forces is not an "equal opportunity employer" as many other public and private organizations are. The military is not out to make a profit, or provide a ladder to corporate success. Instead, military officers swear to "support and defend the Constitution of the United States against all enemies, foreign and domestic; that I will bear the true faith and allegiance to the same" (Oath of Office, 2003). This oath states they are to uphold the best interest of the mission that the Commander in Chief charges them with. Careerism is not an option under this oath because it is only serving the individual's ambition, and not the mission of the military. Elaine Donnelly, President of the Center for Military Readiness, says, "Equal opportunity is important, but the armed forces exist to defend the country. If there is a

Women in Combat   6

conflict between career opportunities and military necessity, the needs of the military must come first" (as qtd. in "Women," 2000).

Another concern with females in combat is their deployability, or their availability to be deployed. Because the very nature of combat units is being the "tip of the spear" in battle, they are deployed and away from home much of the year and are used for an indefinite period of time during the war. Donnelly explains that "if you have a pregnancy rate and it's constant, 10 or 15%, you know that out of 500 women on a carrier at least 50 are going to be unavailable before or during the six-month deployment" (Sommers, Mylroie, Donnelly, & Hill, 2001). This pregnancy issue is not just applicable for conception before the deployment, but during deployment, as is evident on Navy aircraft carriers and destroyers that house women. Even though fraternization, defined as "sexual relationships between service members" (Nath, 2002), is illegal, many ships such as the U.S.S. *Lincoln* "report a dozen [pregnancies] a month" (Layton, 2003). In a close quarters environment, where combat units are together every hour of the day, this kind of problem distracts from the mission. Also, sailors on submarines sleep in what they call "hot beds," which are rotating shifts for sleep in the few available beds, and changing this system to accommodate separate quarters for females would not be cost effective. Also, pregnant females aboard aircraft carriers are being taken from their duty, and they must be replaced, which is a costly endeavor for the military and throws off the working relationship between service members.

When men and women are put in close quarters, it is just human nature that sexual relationships will begin to develop. This fact has been proven all around the military from the pregnancies on board Naval ships all the way up to the Navy's "Tail Hook Convention," where in Las Vegas in 1991, dozens of female officers reported being openly sexually assaulted by male officers, both married and unmarried ("Women," 2000). If there was this kind of distraction within special operation ground

First reference to source with four authors

Different parts of the same sentence cited to different sources

Women in Combat   7

combat units, the mission would suffer greatly because fraternization would become a huge issue, for favoritism would ensue.
When the mission is not the first thing on these troops' minds,
the morale, and most importantly, the trust breaks down.

   Another very real barrier to the inclusion of women in
these units and on small battleships and submarines is the
medical needs of the female body. The fall 2000 suggestion
from DACOWITS included as a possible recruiting slogan "A gynecologist on every aircraft carrier! (Yoest & Yoest, 2001). This
is a possibility on every base and possibly on huge aircraft carriers, but these needs of women cannot be met in the field hospitals in the deserts of Iraq and Afghanistan where the only
goal is to keep soldiers from dying long enough to get them to
a base hospital. Another dilemma on 40–50 person submarines
is that if a woman were to get pregnant, as is the proven trend,
the vessel would have to make a risky surface to get her off to
be cared for and find a replacement for her job on board.
DACOWITS also suggested to "ensure an adequate supply of hygiene products during deployment" (Yoest & Yoest, 2001), which
is a far cry from reality when Marines who are currently in Iraq
already march with a 130-pound rucksack holding their bare living necessities. The military certainly does not have the money
to cover these hygiene and medical needs when in high risk areas
simply because the resources must go to fulfilling the mission.

   As the way word we do battle continues to change, so will
the roles of males and females; and the military will always
have to come up with the best solution to accommodate these
differences. As for now, the restrictions that are placed on
women's assignments are based in sound reasoning. For the military's purposes, women do not have the physical abilities to
fill combat oriented jobs, and the military does not have the
resources to make these assignments available to them. The
military needs to be aware of and most concerned with the effectiveness and readiness of its troops and figure out the best
way to accomplish its mission and preserve America's freedom
and sovereignty.

Women in Combat   8

References

Baer, S. (2003, March 3). In Iraq war, women would serve closer to front lines than in past. *The Baltimore Sun*, p. 1A. Retrieved March 25, 2007, from LexisNexis.

Dobbin, M. (2003, March 2). As war looms, women's role in U.S. military expands. *The Modesto Bee*, p. 3A. Retrieved March 25, 2003, from LexisNexis.

Gerber, R. (2002, September 23). Don't send military women to the back of the troop train. Retrieved March 25, 2003, from the James MacGregor Burns Academy of Leadership Web site: http://www.academy.umd.edu/AboutUs/news/articles/9-23-02.htm.

Layton, L. (2003, March 15). Navy women finding ways to adapt to a man's world. *The Washington Post*, p. A15. Retrieved April 1, 2003, from LexisNexis.

Leo, J. (1997, August 11). A kinder, gentler army. *U.S. News and World Report, 123*, 14.

McDonough, S. (2003, February 10). More U.S. military women edging closer to combat positions in preparation for Iraq war. The Associated Press. Retrieved April 1, 2003, from LexisNexis.

Nath, C. (2002). *United States Air Force Leadership Studies*. Washington, DC: Air Education and Training Command, United States Air Force.

Oath of office. Retrieved April 16, 2003, from http://www.apfn.org/apfn/oathofoffice.htm

Owens, M. (1997, Spring). Mothers in combat boots: Feminists call for women in the military. *Human Life Review*, 23(2), 35–45.

Sommers, C., Mylroie, L., Donnelly, E., & Hill, M. (2001, October 17). IWF panel: Women facing war. *Independent Women's Forum*. Retrieved April 1, 2003, from RDS Contemporary Women's Issues.

Warrior women. (2003, February 16). *New York Times*, sect. 6, p. 23. Retrieved March 25, 2003, from LexisNexis.

Women in the military. (2000, September 1). *Issues and Controversies*. Retrieved April 1, 2003, from http://www.2facts.com

Yoest, C. & Yoest, J. (2001, October 10). Booby traps at the Pentagon. *Independent Women's Forum*. Retrieved April 16, 2003, from RDS Contemporary Women's Issues.

CHAPTER 13

Presenting an Argument Orally

You already know a good deal about the power of persuasive speech. You've not only listened to it from parents, teachers, preachers, coaches, friends, and enemies; you've practiced it yourself with varying degrees of success.

A classics scholar points out that the oratorical techniques we use today were "invented in antiquity and have been used to great effect ever since."[1] But history is not our only guide to the principles of public speaking. Much of what we know about the power of persuasive speech is knowledge based on lifelong experience—things we learn in everyday discourse with different kinds of people who respond to different appeals. Early in life you learned that you did not use the same language or the same approach to argue with your mother or your teacher as you used with your sibling or your friend. You learned, or tried to learn, how to convince people to listen to you and to trust you because you were truthful and knew what you were talking about. And perhaps equally important, if you won the argument, you wanted to make it clear that your victory would not mean hardship for the loser (no obvious gloating). Although speeches to a larger, less familiar audience will require much more preparation, many of the rules of argument that guided you in your personal encounters can be made to work for you in more public arenas.

You will often be asked to make oral presentations in your college classes. Many jobs, both professional and nonprofessional, will call for speeches to groups of fellow employees or prospective customers, to community groups, and even government officials. Wherever you live, there

[1] Mary Lefkowitz, "Classic Oratory," *New York Times*, January 24, 1999, sec. W, p. 15.

will be controversies and public meetings about schooling and political candidates, about budgets for libraries and road repairs and pet control. The ability to rise and make your case before an audience is one that you will want to cultivate as a citizen of a democracy. Great oratory is probably no longer the most powerful influence in our society, and computer networks have usurped the role of oral communication in many areas of public life. But whether it's in person or on television there is still a significant role for a live presenter, a real human being to be seen and heard.

Some of your objectives as a writer will also be relevant to you as a speaker: making the appropriate appeal to an audience, establishing your credibility, finding adequate support for your claim. But other elements of argument will be different: language, organization, and the use of visual and other aids.

Before you begin a brief examination of these elements, keep in mind the larger objectives of the speechmaker. A good introduction to the process of influencing an audience is *the motivated sequence.*[2] This outline, created by a professor of speech communication, lists the five steps that must be taken in order to motivate an audience to adopt a policy, an action, or a belief.

1. Getting attention (attention step)
2. Showing the need: describing the problem (need step)
3. Satisfying the need: presenting the solution (satisfaction step)
4. Visualizing the results (visualization step)
5. Requesting action or approval (action step)

Perhaps you noticed that these steps resemble the steps taken by advertisers. The resemblance is not accidental. According to the author of the motivated sequence, this is a description of the way "people systematically think their way through to a decision."

As you read the following discussions of audience, credibility, language, organization, support, and visual and aural aids, try to think of occasions in your own experience when you were aware of these elements in spoken argument, formal or informal.

THE AUDIENCE

Most speakers who confront a live audience already know something about the members of that audience. They may know why the audience is assembled to hear the particular speaker, their vocations, their level of education, and their familiarity with the subject. They may know whether

[2] Bruce E. Gronbeck, et al., *Principles of Speech Communication*, 13th brief ed. (New York: Longman, 1998), pp. 243–47.

the audience is friendly, hostile, or neutral to the views that the speaker will express. Analyzing the audience is an essential part of speech preparation. If speakers neglect it, both audience and speaker will suffer. At some time all of us have been trapped as members of an audience, forced to listen to a lecture, a sermon, an appeal for action when it was clear that the speaker had little or no idea what we were interested in or capable of understanding. In such situations the speaker who seems indifferent to the needs of the audience will also suffer because the audience will either cease to listen or reject his claim outright.

In college classes students who make assigned speeches on controversial topics are often encouraged to first survey the class. Questionnaires and interviews can give the speaker important clues to the things he should emphasize or avoid: They will tell him whether he should give both sides of a debatable question, introduce humor, use simpler language, and bring in visual or other aids.

But even where such specific information is not immediately available, speakers are well advised to find out as much as they can about the beliefs and attitudes of their audience from other sources. They will then be better equipped to make the kinds of appeals—to reason and to emotion—that the audience is most responsive to. For example, two young evangelists for a religious group (not students at the university) were invited to visit a speech class and present an argument for joining their group. The visitors knew that the class was learning the principles of persuasive speaking; they had no other information about the listeners. After the speech, the students in the class asked questions about some practices of the religious group which had received unfavorable media attention, but the speakers turned aside all questions, saying they did not engage in argument but were instructed only to describe the rewards of joining their group. Before some other audience, such a strategy might have been emotionally satisfying and ultimately persuasive. For this class, however, which was prepared to look for hard evidence, logic, and valid assumptions, the refusal to answer questions suggested evasion and indifference to the interests of their audience. Class evaluations of the speech revealed, to no one's surprise, that the visitors had failed to motivate their listeners.

If you know something about your audience, ask yourself what impression your clothing, gestures and bodily movements, voice, and general demeanor might convey. It might be worth pointing out here that the visitors cited above arrived dressed in dress slacks, white shirts, and ties to confront an audience in T-shirts and jeans. The fact that both speakers and listeners were the same age was not quite enough to overcome an impression of real differences. Make sure, too, that you understand the nature of the occasion—is it too solemn for humor? too formal for personal anecdotes?—and the purpose of the meeting, which can influence your choice of language and the most effective appeal.

CREDIBILITY

The evaluation of audience and the presentation of your own credibility are closely related. In other words, what can you do to persuade this particular audience that you are a reliable exponent of the views you are expressing? Credibility, as you learned in Chapter 1, is another name for *ethos* (the Greek word from which the English word *ethics* is derived) and refers to the honesty, moral character, and intellectual competence of the speaker.

Public figures, whose speeches and actions are reported in the media, can acquire (or fail to acquire) reputations for being endowed with those characteristics. And there is little doubt that a reputation for competence and honesty can incline an audience to accept an argument that would be rejected if offered by a speaker who lacks such a reputation. One study, among many that report similar results, has shown that the same speech will be rated highly by an audience that thinks the Surgeon General of the United States has delivered it but treated with much less regard if they hear it delivered by a college sophomore.

How, then, does a speaker who is unknown to the audience or who boasts only modest credentials convince his listeners that he is a responsible advocate? From the moment the speaker appears before them, members of the audience begin to make an evaluation, based on external signs, such as clothing and mannerisms. But the most significant impression of the speaker's credibility will be based on what the speaker says and how he says it. Does the speaker give evidence that he knows the subject? Does he seem to be aware of the needs and values of the audience? Especially if he is arguing an unpopular claim, does he seem modest and conciliatory?

An unknown speaker is often advised to establish his credentials in the introduction to his speech, to summarize his background and experience as proof of his right to argue the subject he has chosen. A prize-winning and widely reprinted speech by a student begins with these words:

> When you look at me, it is easy to see several similarities between us. I have two arms, two legs, a brain, and a heart just like you. These are my hands, and they are just like yours. Like you, I also have wants and desires; I am capable of love and hate. I can laugh and I can cry. Yes, I'm just like you, except for one very important fact—I am an ex-con.[3]

This is a possibly risky beginning—not everybody in the audience will be friendly to an ex-con—but it signifies that the speaker brings some authority to his subject, which is prison reform. It also attests to the speaker's honesty and may rouse sympathy among certain listeners. (To some in the

---

[3]Richard M. Duesterbeck, "Man's Other Society," in Wil Linkugel, R. R. Allen, and Richard Johannesen, eds., *Contemporary American Speeches* (Belmont, Calif.: Wadsworth, 1965), p. 264.

audience, the speaker's allusions to his own humanity will recall another moving defense, the famous speech by Shylock, the Jewish moneylender, in Shakespeare's *The Merchant of Venice*.)

The speaker will often use an admission of modesty as proof of an honest and unassuming character. He presents himself not as an expert but as one well aware of his limitations. Such an appeal can generate sympathy in the audience (if they believe him) and a sense of identification with the speaker.

The professor of classics quoted earlier has analyzed the speech of a former senator who defended President Clinton at his impeachment trial. She found that the speaker "made sure his audience understood that he was one of them, a friend, on their level, not above them. He denied he was a great speaker and spoke of his friendship with Mr. Clinton." As the writer points out, this confession brings to mind the speech by Mark Antony in *Julius Caesar:*

> I am no orator, as Brutus is,
> But (as you know me all) a plain blunt man
> That loves my friend; (3.2.226–28)

The similarity of these attempts at credibility, separated by almost four hundred years (to say nothing of the fact that Aristotle wrote about *ethos* 2,500 years ago) tells us a good deal about the enduring influence of *ethos* or character on the speaker's message.

ORGANIZATION

Look at the student speech on page 527. The organization of this short speech—the usual length of speeches delivered in the classroom—is easily mastered and works for all kinds of claims.

At the end of the first paragraph the speaker states what he will try to prove, that a vegetarian diet contributes to prevention of chronic diseases. In the third paragraph the speaker gives the four points that he will develop in his argument for vegetarianism. Following the development of these four topics, the conclusion urges the audience to take action, in this case, to stop eating meat.

This basic method of organizing a short speech has several virtues. First, the claim or thesis statement that appears early in a short speech, if the subject is well chosen, can engage the interest of the audience at once. Second, the list of topics guides the speaker in planning and developing his speech. Moreover, it tells the audience what to listen for as they follow the argument.

A well-planned speech has a clearly defined beginning, middle, and end. The beginning, which offers the introduction, can take a number of forms, depending on the kind of speech and its subject. Above all, the introduction must win the attention of the audience, especially if they have been required to attend, and encourage them to look forward to the rest of the speech. The authors of the motivated sequence suggest seven basic attention-getters: (1) referring to the subject or occasion, (2) using a personal reference, (3) asking a rhetorical question, (4) making a startling statement of fact or opinion, (5) using a quotation, (6) telling a humorous anecdote, (7) using an illustration.[4]

The speeches by the ex-con and the vegetarian provide examples of two of the attention-getters cited above—using a personal reference and asking a rhetorical question. In another kind of argument, a claim of fact, the student speaker uses a combination of devices to introduce her claim that culturally deprived children are capable of learning:

> In Charles Schulz's popular cartoon depiction of happiness, one of his definitions has special significance for the American school system. The drawing shows Linus, with his eyes closed in a state of supreme bliss, a broad smile across two-thirds of his face and holding a report card upon which is a big bold "A." The caption reads: "Happiness is finding out you're not so dumb after all." For once, happiness is not defined as a function of material possessions, yet even this happiness is practically unattainable for the "unteachables" of the city slums. Are these children intellectually inferior? Are they unable to learn? Are they not worth the time and the effort to teach? Unfortunately, too many people have answered "yes" to these questions and promptly dismissed the issue.[5]

The middle or body of the speech is, of course, the longest part. It will be devoted to development of the claim that appeared at the beginning. The length of the speech and the complexity of the subject will determine how much support you provide. Some points will be more important than others and should therefore receive more extended treatment. Unless the order is chronological, it makes sense for the speaker to arrange the supporting points in emphatic order, that is, the most important at the end because this may be the one that listeners will remember.

The conclusion should be brief; some rhetoricians suggest that the ending should constitute 5 percent of the total length of the speech. For speeches that contain several main points with supporting data, you may need to summarize. Or you may return to one of the attention-getters mentioned earlier. One writer recommends this as "the most obvious method" of concluding speeches, "particularly appropriate when the introduction has included a quotation, an interesting anecdote, a reference to an occasion

---

[4]Gronbeck et al., pp. 134–38.

[5]Carolyn Kay Geiman, "Are They Really 'Unteachables'?" in Linkugel, Allen, and Johannesen, p. 123.

or a place, an appeal to the self-interest of the audience, or a reference to a recent incident."[6]

An example of such an ending appears in a speech given by Bruce Babbitt, Secretary of the Interior, in 1996. Speaking to an audience of scientists and theologians, the Secretary defended laws that protected the environment. This is how the speech began:

> A wolf's green eyes, a sacred blue mountain, the words from Genesis, and the answers of children all reveal the religious values manifest in the 1977 Endangered Species Act.

(The children Babbitt refers to had written answers to a question posed at an "eco-expo" fair, "Why Save the Environment?")

And this is the ending of the speech:

> I conclude here tonight by affirming that those religious values remain at the heart of the Endangered Species Act, that they make themselves manifest through the green eyes of the grey wolf, through the call of the whooping crane, through the splash of the Pacific salmon, through the voices of America's children.
>
> We are living between the flood and the rainbow: between the threats to creation on the one side and God's covenant to protect life on the other.
>
> Why should we save endangered species?
>
> Let us answer this question with one voice, the voice of the child at that expo, who scrawled her answer at the very bottom of the sheet: "Because we can."[7]

The speaker must also ensure the smooth flow of his argument throughout. Coherence, or the orderly connections between ideas, is even more important in speech than in writing because the listener cannot go back to uncover these connections. The audience listens for expressions that serve as guideposts — words, phrases, and sentences to indicate which direction the argument will take. The student speech on vegetarianism uses these words among others: *next, then, finally, here, first of all, whereas, in addition, secondly, in fact, now, in conclusion.* Other expressions can also help the listener to follow the development. Each of the following examples from real speeches makes a bridge from a previous idea to a new one: "Valid factual proof, right? No, wrong!" "Consider an illustration of this misinformation." "But there is another way." "Up to this point, I've spoken only of therapy." "And so we face this new challenge." "How do we make this clear?" "Now, why is this so important?"

---

[6]James C. McCroskey, *An Introduction to Rhetorical Communication* (Englewood Cliffs, N.J.: Prentice-Hall, 1968), p. 204.

[7]Calvin McLeod Logue and Jean DeHart, eds., *Representative American Speeches, 1995–1996* (New York: Wilson, 1996), p. 70ff.

LANGUAGE

> It should be observed that each kind of rhetoric has its own appropriate
> style. That of written prose is not the same as that of spoken oratory.
>
> —Aristotle

In the end, your speech depends on the language. No matter how accurate your analysis of the audience, how appealing your presentation of self, how deep your grasp of the material, if the language does not clearly and emphatically convey your argument, the speech will probably fail. Fortunately, the effectiveness of language does not depend on long words or complex sentence structure; quite the contrary. Most speeches, especially those given by beginners to small audiences, are distinguished by an oral style that respects the rhythms of ordinary speech and sounds spontaneous.

The vocabulary you choose, like the other elements of spoken discourse we have discussed, is influenced by the kind of audience you confront. A student audience may be entertained or moved to identification with you and your message if you use the slang of your generation; an assembly of elderly church members at a funeral may not be so generous. Use words that both you and your listeners are familiar with, language that convinces the audience you are sharing your knowledge and opinions, neither speaking down to them nor over their heads. As one writer puts it, "You never want to use language that makes the audience appear ignorant or stupid."

Make sure, too, that the words you use will not be considered offensive by some members of your audience. Today we are all sensitive, sometimes hypersensitive, to terms that were once used freely if not wisely. One word, improperly used, can cause some listeners to reject the whole speech.

The short speeches you give will probably not be devoted to elaborating grand abstractions, but it is not only abstract terms that need definition. When you know your subject very well, you forget that others can be ignorant of it. Think whether the subject is one that the particular audience you are addressing is not likely to be familiar with. If this is the case, then explain even the basic terms. In one class a student who had chosen to discuss a subject about which he was extremely knowledgeable, betting on horse races, neglected to define clearly the words *exacta, subfecta, trifecta, parimutuel,* and others, leaving his audience fairly befuddled.

Wherever it is appropriate, use concrete language with details and examples that create images and cause the listener to feel as well as think. One student speaker used strong words to good effect in providing some unappetizing facts about hot dogs: "In fact, the hot dog is so adulterated with chemicals, so contaminated with bacteria, so puffy with gristle, fat, water, and lacking in protein, that it is nutritionally worthless."[8]

---

[8] Donovan Ochs and Anthony Winkler, *A Brief Introduction to Speech* (New York: Harcourt, Brace, Jovanovich, 1979), p. 74.

Another speech on a far more serious subject offered a personal experience with vivid details. The student speaker was a hemophiliac making a plea for blood donations.

> I remember the three long years when I couldn't even walk because repeated hemorrhages had twisted my ankles and knees to pretzel-like forms. I remember being pulled to school in a wagon while other boys rode their bikes and pushed to my table. I remember sitting in the dark empty classroom by myself during recess while the others went out in the sun to run and play. And I remember the first terrible day at the big high school when I came on crutches and built-up shoes carrying my books in a sack around my neck.[9]

As a rule, the oral style demands simpler sentences. That is because the listener must grasp the grammatical construction without the visual clues of punctuation available on the printed page. Simpler means shorter and more direct. Use subject-verb constructions without a string of phrases or clauses preceding the subject or interrupting the natural flow of the sentence. Use the active voice frequently. In addition to assuring clarity for the audience, such sentences are easier for the speaker to remember and to say. (The sentences in the paragraph above are long, but notice that the sentence elements of subject, verb, and subordinate clause are arranged in the order dictated by natural speech.)

Simpler, however, does not mean less impressive. A speech before any audience may be simply expressed without loss of emotional or intellectual power. One of the most eloquent short speeches ever delivered in this country is the surrender speech in 1877 by Chief Joseph of the Nez Percé Tribe, which clearly demonstrates the power of simple words and sentences.

> I am tired of fighting. Our chiefs are killed. Looking Glass is dead. Toohulsote is dead. The old men are all dead. It is the young men who say no and yes. He who led the young men is dead. It is cold and we have no blankets. The little children are freezing to death. My people, some of them, have run away to the hills and have no blankets, no food. No one knows where they are—perhaps they are freezing to death. I want to have time to look for my children and see how many of them I can find. Maybe I shall find them among the dead. Hear me, my chiefs. I am tired. My heart is sad and sick. From where the sun now stands I will fight no more forever.[10]

If you are in doubt about the kind of language in which you should express yourself, you might follow Lincoln's advice: "Speak so that the most lowly can understand you, and the rest will have no difficulty."

---

[9] Ralph Zimmerman, "Mingled Blood," in Linkugel, Allen, and Johannesen, p. 200.
[10] M. Gidley, *Kopet: A Documentary Narrative of Chief Joseph's Last Years* (Chicago: Contemporary Books, 1981), p. 31.

A popular stylistic device—repetition and balance or parallel structure—can emphasize and enrich parts of your message. Look back to the balanced sentences of the passage from the student speaker on hemophilia, sentences beginning with "I remember." Almost all inspirational speeches, including religious exhortation and political oratory, take advantage of such constructions, whose rhythms evoke an immediate emotional response. It is one of the strengths of Martin Luther King Jr.'s "I Have a Dream." (See p. 529.) Keep in mind that the ideas in parallel structures must be similar and that, for maximum effectiveness, they should be used sparingly in a short speech. Not least, the subject should be weighty enough to carry this imposing construction.

SUPPORT

The support for a claim is essentially the same for both spoken and written arguments. Factual evidence, including statistics and expert opinion, as well as appeals to needs and values, are equally important in oral presentations. But time constraints will make a difference. In a speech the amount of support that you provide will be limited to the capacity of listeners to digest and remember information that they cannot review. This means that you must choose subjects that can be supported adequately in the time allotted. The speech by Secretary Babbitt, for example, on saving the environmental protection laws, developed material on animals, national lands, water, his own history, religious tradition, and the history of environmental legislation, to name only the most important. It would have been impossible to defend his proposition in a half-hour speech. Although his subject was far more limited, the author of the argument for vegetarianism could not do full justice to his claim for lack of time. Meat-eaters would find that some of their questions remain unanswered, and even those listeners friendly to the author's claim might ask for more evidence from authoritative sources.

While both speakers and writers use logical, ethical, and emotional appeals in support of their arguments, the forms of presentation can make a significant difference. The reasoning process demanded of listeners must be relatively brief and straightforward, and the supporting evidence readily assimilated. The ethical appeal or credibility of the speaker is affected not only by what he says but by his appearance, bodily movements, and vocal expressions. And the appeal to the sympathy of the audience can be greatly enhanced by the presence of the speaker. Take the excerpt from the speech of the hemophiliac. The written descriptions of pain and heartbreak are very moving, but place yourself in the audience, looking at the victim and imagining the suffering experienced by the human body standing in front of you. No doubt the effect would be deep and long-lasting, perhaps more memorable even than the written word.

Because the human instrument is so powerful, it must be used with care. You have probably listened to speakers who used gestures and voice inflections that had been dutifully rehearsed but were obviously contrived and worked, unfortunately, to undermine rather than support the speaker's message and credibility. If you are not a gifted actor, avoid gestures, body language, and vocal expressions that are not truly felt.

Some speech theorists treat support or proofs as *nonartistic* and *artistic*. The nonartistic support—factual data, expert opinion, examples—is considered objective and verifiable. Its acceptability should not depend on the character and personality of the speaker. It is plainly different from the artistic proof, which is subjective, based on the values and attitudes of the listener, and therefore more difficult for the speaker to control. This form of support is called artistic because it includes creative strategies within the power of the speaker to manipulate. In earlier parts of this chapter we have discussed the artistic proofs, ways of establishing credibility, and recognizing the values of the audience.

PRESENTATION AIDS

■ Charts, Graphs, Handouts

Some speeches, though not all, will be enhanced by visual and other aids: charts, graphs, maps, models, objects, handouts, recordings, and computerized images. These aids, however, no matter how visually or aurally exciting, should not overwhelm your own oral presentation. The objects are not the stars of the show. They exist to make your spoken argument more persuasive.

Charts and graphs, large enough and clear enough to be seen and understood, can illuminate speeches that contain numbers of any kind, especially statistical comparisons. You can make a simple chart yourself, on paper for use with an easel or a transparency for use with a slide projector. Enlarged illustrations or a model of a complicated machine—say, the space shuttle—would help a speaker to explain its function. You already know that photographs or videos are powerful instruments of persuasion, above all in support of appeals for humanitarian aid, for both people and animals.

Court cases have been won or lost on the basis of diagrams or charts that purport to prove the innocence or guilt of a defendant. Such aids do not always speak for themselves. No matter how clear they are to the designer, they may be misinterpreted or misunderstood by a viewer. Some critics have argued that the jury in the O. J. Simpson case failed to understand the graphs of DNA relationships that experts for the prosecution displayed during the trial. Before you show any diagrams or charts of any complexity to your audience, ask friends if they find them easy to understand.

The use of a handout also requires planning. It's probably unwise to put your speech on hold while the audience reads or studies a handout that requires time and concentration. Confine the subject matter of handouts to material that can be easily grasped as you discuss or explain it.

■ Audio

Audio aids may also enliven a speech or even be indispensable to its success. One student played a recording of a scene from *Romeo and Juliet*, spoken by a cast of professional actors, to make a point about the relationship between the two lovers. Another student chose to define several types of popular music, including rap, goth, heavy metal, and techno. But he used only words, and the lack of any musical demonstration meant that the distinctions remained unclear.

■ Video

With sight, sound, and movement, a video can illustrate or reinforce the main points of a speech. A speech warning people not to drink and drive will have a much greater effect if enhanced by a video showing the tragic and often gruesome outcome of car accidents caused by drunk driving. Schools that teach driver's education frequently rely on these bone-chilling videos to show their students that getting behind the wheel is a serious responsibility, not a game. If you want to use video, check to make sure that a VCR or a DVD player and television are available to you. Most schools have an audio-visual department that manages the delivery, setup, and return of all equipment.

■ Multimedia

Multimedia presentation software programs enable you to combine several different media such as text, charts, sound, and still or moving pictures into one unit. In the business world, multimedia presentations are commonly used in situations where you have a limited amount of time to persuade or teach a fairly large audience. For instance, the promotion director of a leading teen magazine is trying to persuade skeptical executives that a magazine Web site would increase sales and advertising revenue. Since the magazine is sold through newsstand and subscription, some executives question whether the cost of creating and maintaining a Web site outweighs the benefits. Using multimedia presentation software, the promotion director can integrate demographic charts and graphs showing that steadily increasing numbers of teenagers surf the Web, a segment from a television news program reporting that many teens shop online (an attraction for advertisers), and downloaded pages from a competitor's Web site to demonstrate that others are already reaping the benefits of the Internet. People today are increasingly "visual" in their learning styles, and multimedia software may be the most effective aid for an important presentation.

Though effective when done well, technically complicated presentations require large amounts of time and careful planning. First you must ensure that your computer is powerful enough to adeptly handle presentation software. Then you need to familiarize yourself with the program. Most presentation software programs come equipped with helpful tutorials. If the task of creating your own presentation from scratch seems overwhelming, you can use one of the many preformatted presentation templates: You will simply need to customize the content. Robert Stephens, the founder of the Geek Squad, a Minneapolis-based business that provides on-site emergency response to computer problems, gives the following tips for multimedia presentations:

1. In case of equipment failure, always bring two of everything.

2. Back up your presentation on CD-ROM or a Zip drive.

3. Avoid live visits to the Internet. Because connections can fail or be painfully slow, and sites can move or disappear, if you must visit the Internet in your presentation, download the appropriate pages onto your hard drive ahead of time. It will still look like a live visit.

4. In the end, technology cannot replace creativity. Make sure that you are using multimedia to reinforce not replace your main points.[11]

Make sure that any necessary apparatus will be available at the right time. If you have never used the devices you need for your presentation, practice using them before the speech. Few things are more disconcerting for the speechmaker and the audience than a speaker who is fumbling with his materials, unable to find the right picture or to make a machine work.

SAMPLE PERSUASIVE SPEECH

The following speech was delivered by C. Renzi Stone to his public speaking class at the University of Oklahoma. Told to prepare a persuasive speech, Stone chose to speak about the health benefits of vegetarianism. Note his attention-grabbing introduction.

---

[11] Robert Stephens as paraphrased in "When Your Presentation Crashes . . . Who You Gonna Call?" by Eric Matson, *Fast Company*, February/March 1997, p. 130.

Live Longer and Healthier: Stop Eating Meat!

C. RENZI STONE

What do Steve Martin, Dustin Hoffman, Albert Einstein, Jerry Garcia, Michael Stipe, Eddie Vedder, Martina Navratilova, Carl Lewis, and 12 million other Americans all have in common? All of these well-known people were or are vegetarians. What do they know that we don't? Consuming a regimen of high-fat, high-protein flesh foods is a sure-fire prescription for disaster, like running diesel fuel through your car's gasoline engine. In the book *Why Do Vegetarians Eat Like That?* David Gabbe asserts that millions of people today are afflicted with chronic diseases that can be directly linked to the consumption of meat. Eating a vegetarian diet can help prevent many of those diseases.

In 1996, 12 million Americans identified themselves as vegetarians. That number is twice as many as in the decade before. According to a recent National Restaurant Association poll found in *Health* magazine, one in five diners say they now go out of their way to choose restaurants that serve at least a few meatless entrees. Obviously, the traditionally American trait of a meat-dominated society has subsided in recent years.

In discussing vegetarianism today, first I will tell how vegetarians are perceived in society. Next, I will introduce several studies validating my claim that a meatless diet is extraordinarily healthy. I will then show how a veggie diet can strengthen the immune system and make the meatless body a shield from unwanted diseases such as cancer and heart disease. Maintaining a strict vegetarian diet can also lead to a longer life. Finally, I will put an image into the audience's mind of a meatless society that relies on vegetables for the main course at breakfast, lunch, and dinner.

Moving to my first point, society generally holds two major misperceptions about vegetarians. First of all, society often perceives vegetarians as a radical group of people with extreme principles. In this view, vegetarians are seen as a monolithic group of people who choose to eat vegetables because they are opposed to the killing of animals for food. The second major misconception is that because vegetarians do not eat meat, they do not get the proper amounts of essential vitamins and minerals often found in meat.

Here is my response to these misconceived notions. First of all, vegetar-   5
ians are not a homogeneous group of radicals. Whereas many vegetarians in the past did join the movement on the principle that killing animals is wrong, many join the movement today mainly for its health benefits. In addition, there are many different levels of vegetarianism. Some vegetarians eat nothing but vegetables. Others don't eat red meat but do occasionally eat chicken and fish.

Secondly, contrary to popular opinion, vegetarians get more than enough vitamins and minerals in their diet and generally receive healthier nourishment than meat eaters. In fact, in an article for *Health* magazine, Peter Jaret states that vegetarians actually get larger amounts of amino acids due to the elimination of saturated fats which are often found in meat products. Studies show that the health benefits of a veggie lifestyle contribute to increased life expectancy and overall productivity.

Hopefully you now see that society's perceptions of vegetarians are outdated and just plain wrong. You are familiar with many of the problems associated with a meat-based diet, and you have heard many of the benefits of a vegetarian diet. Now try to imagine how you personally can improve your life by becoming a vegetarian.

Can you imagine a world where people retire at age eighty and lead productive lives into their early 100s? Close your eyes and think about celebrating your seventieth wedding anniversary, seeing your great-grandchildren get married, and witnessing 100 years of world events and technological innovations. David Gabbe's book refers to studies that have shown a vegetarian diet can increase your life expectancy up to fifteen years. A longer life is within your reach, and the diet you eat has a direct impact on your health and how you age.

In conclusion, vegetarianism is a healthy life choice, not a radical cult. By eliminating meat from their diet, vegetarians reap the benefits of a vegetable-based diet that helps prevent disease and increase life expectancy. People, take heed of my advice. There are many more sources of information available for those who want to take a few hours to research the benefits of the veggie lifestyle. If you don't believe my comments, discover the whole truth for yourself.

Twelve million Americans know the health benefits that come with   10 being a vegetarian. Changing your eating habits can be just as easy as making your bed in the morning. Sure, it takes a few extra minutes and some thought, but your body will thank you in the long run.

You only live once. Why not make it a long stay?

I Have a Dream

MARTIN LUTHER KING JR.

F ive score years ago, a great American, in whose symbolic shadow we
stand, signed the Emancipation Proclamation. This momentous decree
came as a great beacon light of hope to millions of Negro slaves who had
been seared in the flames of withering injustice. It came as a joyous day-
break to end the long night of captivity.

But one hundred years later, we must face the tragic fact that the
Negro is still not free. One hundred years later, the life of the Negro is still
sadly crippled by the manacles of segregation and the chains of discrimination. One hundred years later, the Negro lives on a lonely island of
poverty in the midst of a vast ocean of material prosperity. One hundred
years later, the Negro is still languishing in the corners of American society and finds himself an exile in his own land. So we have come here
today to dramatize an appalling condition.

In a sense we have come to our nation's capital to cash a check. When
the architects of our republic wrote the magnificent words of the Constitution and the Declaration of Independence, they were signing a promissory note to which every American was to fall heir. This note was a promise
that all men would be guaranteed the unalienable rights of life, liberty, and
the pursuit of happiness.

It is obvious today that America has defaulted on this promissory note
insofar as her citizens of color are concerned. Instead of honoring this sacred obligation, America has given the Negro people a bad check; a check
which has come back marked "insufficient funds." But we refuse to believe that the bank of justice is bankrupt. We refuse to believe that there
are insufficient funds in the great vaults of opportunity of this nation. So
we have come to cash this check—a check that will give us upon demand
the riches of freedom and the security of justice. We have also come to
this hallowed spot to remind America of the fierce urgency of *now*. This is
no time to engage in the luxury of cooling off or to take the tranquilizing
drugs of gradualism. *Now* is the time to make real the promises of Democracy. *Now* is the time to rise from the dark and desolate valley of segregation to the sunlit path of racial justice. *Now* is the time to open the doors
of opportunity to all of God's children. *Now* is the time to lift our nation
from the quicksands of racial injustice to the solid rock of brotherhood.

In the widely reprinted "I Have a Dream" speech, Martin Luther King Jr. appears as the
charismatic leader of the civil rights movement. This inspirational address was delivered on August 28, 1963, in Washington, D.C., at a demonstration by two hundred
thousand people for civil rights for African Americans. From *A Testament of Hope* (1986).

It would be fatal for the nation to overlook the urgency of the mo-   5
ment and to underestimate the determination of the Negro. This sweltering summer of the Negro's legitimate discontent will not pass until there is
an invigorating autumn of freedom and equality. Nineteen sixty-three is
not an end, but a beginning. Those who hope that the Negro needed to
blow off steam and will now be content will have a rude awakening if the
nation returns to business as usual. There will be neither rest nor tranquil-
lity in America until the Negro is granted his citizenship rights. The whirl-
winds of revolt will continue to shake the foundations of our nation until
the bright day of justice emerges.

But there is something that I must say to my people who stand on the
warm threshold which leads into the palace of justice. In the process of
gaining our rightful place we must not be guilty of wrongful deeds. Let us
not seek to satisfy our thirst for freedom by drinking from the cup of bitterness and hatred. We must forever conduct our struggle on the high
plane of dignity and discipline. We must not allow our creative protest to
degenerate into physical violence. Again and again we must rise to the
majestic heights of meeting physical force with soul force. The marvelous
new militancy which has engulfed the Negro community must not lead
us to a distrust of all white people, for many of our white brothers, as evidenced by their presence here today, have come to realize that their destiny is tied up with our destiny and their freedom is inextricably bound
to our freedom. We cannot walk alone.

And as we walk, we must make the pledge that we shall march ahead.
We cannot turn back. There are those who are asking the devotees of civil
rights, "When will you be satisfied?" We can never be satisfied as long as
the Negro is the victim of the unspeakable horrors of police brutality. We
can never be satisfied as long as our bodies, heavy with the fatigue of
travel, cannot gain lodging in the motels of the highways and the hotels
of the cities. We cannot be satisfied as long as the Negro's basic mobility
is from a smaller ghetto to a larger one. We can never be satisfied as long
as a Negro in Mississippi cannot vote and a Negro in New York believes
he has nothing for which to vote. No, no, we are not satisfied, and we will
not be satisfied until justice rolls down like waters and righteousness like
a mighty stream.

I am not unmindful that some of you have come here out of great trials and tribulations. Some of you have come fresh from narrow jail cells.
Some of you have come from areas where your quest for freedom left you
battered by the storms of persecution and staggered by the winds of police brutality. You have been the veterans of creative suffering. Continue
to work with the faith that unearned suffering is redemptive.

Go back to Mississippi, go back to Alabama, go back to South Carolina, go back to Georgia, go back to Louisiana, go back to the slums and
ghettos of our northern cities, knowing that somehow this situation can
and will be changed. Let us not wallow in the valley of despair.

I say to you today, my friends, that in spite of the difficulties and frus- 10
trations of the moment I still have a dream. It is a dream deeply rooted in
the American dream.

I have a dream that one day this nation will rise up and live out the
true meaning of its creed: "We hold these truths to be self-evident; that
all men are created equal."

I have a dream that one day on the red hills of Georgia the sons of
former slaves and the sons of former slaveowners will be able to sit down
together at the table of brotherhood.

I have a dream that one day even the state of Mississippi, a desert
state sweltering with the heat of injustice and oppression, will be transformed into an oasis of freedom and justice.

I have a dream that my four little children will one day live in a nation where they will not be judged by the color of their skin but by the
content of their character.

I have a dream today.   15

I have a dream that one day the state of Alabama, whose governor's
lips are presently dripping with the words of interposition and nullification, will be transformed into a situation where little black boys and black
girls will be able to join hands with little white boys and white girls and
walk together as sisters and brothers.

I have a dream today.

I have a dream that one day every valley shall be exalted, every hill
and mountain shall be made low, the rough places will be made plain,
and the crooked places will be made straight, and the glory of the Lord
shall be revealed, and all flesh shall see it together.

This is our hope. This is the faith with which I return to the South.
With this faith we will be able to hew out of the mountain of despair a
stone of hope. With this faith we will be able to transform the jangling
discords of our nation into a beautiful symphony of brotherhood. With
this faith we will be able to work together, to pray together, to struggle together, to go to jail together, to stand up for freedom together, knowing
that we will be free one day.

This will be the day when all of God's children will be able to sing 20
with new meaning

My country, 'tis of thee,
Sweet land of liberty,
   Of thee I sing:
Land where my fathers died,
Land of the pilgrims' pride,
From every mountain-side
   Let freedom ring.

And if America is to be a great nation this must become true. So let
freedom ring from the prodigious hilltops of New Hampshire. Let freedom

ring from the mighty mountains of New York. Let freedom ring from the heightening Alleghenies of Pennsylvania!

Let freedom ring from the snowcapped Rockies of Colorado!

Let freedom ring from the curvaceous peaks of California!

But not only that; let freedom ring from Stone Mountain of Georgia!

Let freedom ring from Lookout Mountain of Tennessee!   25

Let freedom ring from every hill and molehill of Mississippi. From every mountainside, let freedom ring.

When we let freedom ring, when we let it ring from every village and every hamlet, from every state and every city, we will be able to speed up that day when all of God's children, black men and white men, Jews and Gentiles, Protestants and Catholics, will be able to join hands and sing in the words of the old Negro spiritual, "Free at last! free at last! thank God almighty, we are free at last!"

READING AND DISCUSSION QUESTIONS

1. What were the circumstances in which King delivered this speech? Of whom did the audience consist? How might the circumstances and the audience have affected decisions King made in composing the speech? Where in the speech does he most directly refer to his audience?

2. What sort of reputation had King established by the time he gave this speech in 1963? Are there ways in which he establishes his credibility through the speech itself? Explain.

3. How would you describe the organization of the speech?

4. Explain the metaphor of the check. Where else does King make use of metaphorical language?

5. How else does King's use of language lend power to his speech?

6. What allusions do you find in the speech?

WRITING SUGGESTIONS

7. Write an essay analyzing King's speech according to the elements of oral argument discussed in this chapter.

8. Write an essay analyzing King's language as a major source of the effectiveness of this historic speech.

Part Three

Multiple Viewpoints

The following section contains a variety of viewpoints on eight controversial questions. These questions generate conflict among experts and laypeople alike for two principal reasons. First, even when the facts are not in dispute, they may be interpreted differently by opposing sides. Second, and certainly more difficult to resolve, equally worthwhile values may be in conflict.

Multiple Viewpoints lends itself to classroom debates, both formal and informal. It can also serve as a useful source of informed opinions, which can lead to further research. First, read all the articles in one chapter of a Multiple Viewpoints section. You may wish to begin further research by choosing material to support your claim from two or three articles in the text or by exploring sources on the Web.

Ask the following questions about each controversy:

1. Are there two — or more — different points of view on the subject? Do all sides make clear what they are trying to prove? Summarize their claims.
2. Do all sides share the same goals? If not, how are they different?
3. How important is definition of key terms? Do all sides agree on the definitions? If so, what are they? If not, how do they differ? Does definition become a significant issue in the controversy?
4. How important is evidence in support of the claims? Does the support fulfill the appropriate criteria? If not, what are its weaknesses? Do the authorities have convincing credentials?
5. Do the arguers base any part of their arguments on needs and values that their readers are expected to share? What are they? Do the arguers provide examples of the ways these values function? Is there a conflict of values? If so, which seem more important?
6. What warrants or assumptions underlie the claims? Are they implicit or explicit? Do the arguers examine them for the reader? Are the warrants acceptable? If not, point out their weaknesses.
7. What are the main issues? Is there a genuine debate — that is, does each side try to respond to arguments on the other side?
8. Do the arguers propose solutions to a problem? Are the advantages of their proposals clear? Are there obvious disadvantages?
9. Does each argument follow a clear and orderly organization, one that lends itself to a good outline? If not, what are the weaknesses?
10. Does language play a part in the argument? Are there any examples of misuse of language — slanted or loaded words, clichés, slogans?
11. Do the arguers show an awareness of audience? How would you describe the audience(s) for whom the various arguments are presented?
12. Do you think that one side won the argument? Can you find examples of negotiation and compromise, of attempts to establish a common ground? Explain your answer in detail.

CHAPTER 14

How Far Will We Go to Change Our Body Image?

We live in a society where appearance matters. How much it matters is clear from magazines, television shows, movies, and advertisements. It is clear from the number of diets hyped on talk shows and in bookstores. It is clear from the alarming number of young women—and, increasingly, young men—with anorexia and bulimia, from the celebrities that our youth, male and female, choose to idolize and emulate, and from the drastic increase in recent years in the amount of plastic surgery being performed. We exercise, count our carbs, and are acutely aware of the face that stares back at us in the mirror.

Cosmetic surgery has changed countless lives by correcting birth defects and other abnormalities. It does not save lives, although at times cosmetic surgery may be closely linked to corrective surgery, as when a cleft lip is corrected in conjunction with correcting a cleft palate or when plastic surgery repairs the ravages of severe burns once the burns themselves are no longer life threatening. A cleft palate interferes with one's health. A cleft lip is repaired primarily for aesthetic reasons. The scars left on a burn victim may require plastic surgery to help heal the psychological damage left after the body has healed.

Having a nose job or a breast enlargement purely for aesthetic reasons was once the sort of thing only movie stars and the extremely wealthy would have considered. Today many average citizens are enhancing or reshaping their bodies. For some, changing each imperfection becomes an obsession. Women are generally accused of being the most conscious of body image. The steroids that men take, though, improve physique as well as athletic performance—and increase the chances of lasting damage to the body.

The dangers associated with the use of drugs, diets, and plastic surgery to enhance body image are the frequent focus of argumentative speech or writing. The psychological dangers may be as grave as the physical ones. We must question why so many are willing to tamper with their physical appearance and wonder how they feel once the changes are made. To whose model of physical perfection are we aspiring? Is it right, for example, to seek to remove physical signs of ethnicity? Some regard such changes as a betrayal of the race. In changing what makes each of us distinct, are we giving in, as one author included here suggests, to "the tyranny of the normal"? How much are we willing to spend—how much money and how much pain or discomfort—to look good?

From *Body Image and Adolescents*

JILLIAN CROLL

> **BEFORE READING:** What forces shaped your feelings about your size and shape during early adolescence? Did they have a positive or negative effect on the way you perceived your own body?

B ody image is the dynamic perception of one's body—how it looks, feels, and moves. It is shaped by perception, emotions, physical sensations, and is not static, but can change in relation to mood, physical experience, and environment. Because adolescents experience significant physical changes in their bodies during puberty, they are likely to experience highly dynamic perceptions of body image. Body image is influenced strongly by self-esteem and self-evaluation, more so than by external evaluation by others. It can, however, be powerfully influenced and affected by cultural messages and societal standards of appearance and attractiveness. Given the overwhelming prevalence of thin and lean female images and strong and lean male images common to all westernized societies, body image concerns have become widespread among adolescents.

- 50–88% of adolescent girls feel negatively about their body shape or size.[1,2]

- 49% of teenage girls say they know someone with an eating disorders.[1]

- Only 33% of girls say they are at the "right weight for their body," while 58% want to lose weight. Just 9% want to gain weight.[3]

Jillian Croll is a registered licensed dietician who specializes in eating disorders. She is the director of the Eating Disorders Institute in St. Louis Park, Minnesota, and 2005–2007 cochair of the Nutrition Special Interest Group of the Academy of Eating Disorders.

- Females are much more likely than males to think their current size is too large (66% vs. 21%).[4]

- Over one-third of males think their current size is too small, while only 10% of women consider their size too small.[4]

- Strikingly, while only 30% of older adolescents surveyed consider their current size acceptable to *them*, 85% of females and 95% of males considered their current size socially acceptable for *others*.[4]

- 85% of young women worry "a lot" about how they look and twice as many males as females say they are satisfied with their appearance.[5]

- A report by the American Association of University Women indicated that for girls, "the way I look" is the most important indicator of self-worth, while for boys, self-worth is based on abilities, rather than looks.[6]

Going through puberty can amplify body image concerns. Puberty for boys brings characteristics typically admired by society—height, speed, broadness, and strength. Puberty for girls brings with it characteristics often perceived as less laudable, as girls generally get rounder and have increased body fat. These changes can serve to further enhance dissatisfaction among girls.[7] Going through puberty later or earlier than peers can have an impact on body image as well as psychological health. Generally, early development for girls and late development for boys present the greatest challenges to healthy body image.[8]

ETIOLOGY/CONTRIBUTING FACTORS

Media Messages Strong social and cultural forces influence body image in young people. From childhood to adulthood, television, billboards, movies, music videos, video games, computer games, toys, the Internet, and magazines convey images of ideal attractiveness, beauty, shape, size, strength, and weight. Consider these statistics from the TV-Turnoff Network.[9]

- Adolescents watch an average of 28 hours of television per week.

- American youth spend, on average, 900 hours a year in school and an average of 1,023 hours a year watching television.

- The average American consumes 11.8 hours per day of media of all kinds.

- Children view more than 20,000 commercials per year.

- 75% of all adolescents spend at least 6 hours a week watching music videos.[10]

Eight million children at 12,000 schools across the country watch television at school each day via Channel One, an in-school broadcast current events program provided (including TV and VCR equipment) free of charge to schools. The program includes ten minutes of broadcast news and current events coverage and two minutes of advertisements for products such as chips, candy, and beauty-aids. These advertisements promote poor body image through their "beauty" ads and provide mixed messages regarding adolescent lifestyle.[11]

In childhood, popular toys such as action figures and dolls have sim-   5 ilar body shapes: tall and slender for female figures and tall, slender, and muscular for male figures. The body shapes advertised by these toys, dolls and media sources are not realistic (see Table 1). If Barbie were real, her neck would be too long and thin to support the weight of her head, and her upper body proportions would make it difficult for her to walk upright. If Ken were real, his huge barrel chest and enormously thick neck would nearly preclude him from wearing a shirt.

Magazines targeted at female adolescents are full of images of young, slim, attractive, blemish-free females with small waists, large chests and only ever-so-slightly-rounded hips, while magazines produced for males are full of strong, lean, attractive, blemish-free males, frequently displayed with the aforementioned females in close proximity. Beauty pageants continue to be a popular and avidly watched showcase of ideal societal beauty.

- The average female model is 5'10" and weighs 110 pounds. The average American female is 5'4" and weighs 144 pounds. That makes the average model at least 30 pounds lighter and 6 inches taller than the average female looking at her.

- Over 800 million Barbie dolls have been sold and annual sales amount to more than 1 billion dollars.[12] If Barbie were real, given her proportions, she would barely be able to stand upright.

TABLE 1 If Barbie and Ken Were Real				
	If Barbie was a real female	Real female	If Ken was a real male	Real male
Height (ft, in)	7'2"	5'2"	7'8"	6"
Chest (in)	40	35	50	40
Waist (in)	22	28	43	33
Neck Circumference (in)	12	12.2	23.4	15.5
Neck Length (in)	6.2	3.0	6.35	5.5

Source: Statistics from Brownell KD, Napolitano MA. Distorting reality for children: body size proportions of Barbie and Ken dolls. Int J Eat Disord 1995;18(3):295–298.

- Miss America contestants have become increasingly thinner over the past 75 years. In the 1920s, contestants had BMIs in the normal range of 20–25. Since then, pageant winners' body weights have decreased steadily to a level about 12% below levels from the mid-1900s. Since 1970, nearly all of the winners have had BMIs below the healthy range, with some as low as 16.9, a BMI that would meet part of the diagnostic criteria for anorexia nervosa.[13]

- Even educational materials have messages regarding body size. Textbook images of girls have gotten more slender every decade since 1900, while images of boys have not changed significantly.[14]

- Adolescent females watching the most media idealizing thin body types, such as soap operas and movies, report the highest body dissatisfaction and those watching music videos report a strong drive for thinness.[15]

- Young women surveyed before and after being shown fashion and beauty magazines have decreased self-image and increased desire to lose weight as compared to young women shown news magazines. Females report they exercise and diet more in response to fashion magazine images.[2,16]

- Drive to attain the ideal standard of attractiveness for males (bigger, bulkier, and more muscular) has been associated with poor self-esteem and depression.[17]

- While most body image research has been done with white youth, research does indicate that African-American adolescents, particularly females, tend to have healthier body images than their white counterparts. However, even among African-American females, as their body shapes and sizes get further from the cultural idealized shape and size, body dissatisfaction increases.[8]

- Asian Americans may have healthier body images than their white, African-American, or Hispanic peers due to cultural norms influencing modesty and are the only group in which boys and girls have similarly high body satisfaction.[8] However, as more acculturation in American society occurs, body satisfaction decreases and body image concerns arise, particularly among males.[8]

Familial Messages Familial concerns and pressures may also contribute to increased body dissatisfaction and body image concerns. Socialization encourages males to strive to become stronger and more developed, while females are to make their bodies more beautiful. Parents tend to become less positive and more critical regarding their children's appearance, eating and physical activity as they move into and through adolescence. Adolescents receive the most criticism regarding their physical appearance and the most efforts to change their appearance.[18] Parental overconcern with children being thin or encouragement to avoid being fat can influence young people to become constant dieters and use unhealthy weight control methods.[16] Health professionals should work with parents to help them encourage their children to be healthy in a manner that supports healthy body image development.

CONSEQUENCES

While the contributing factors may vary, the outcomes are similar. Overconcern with body image and shape can lead to restrictive dieting and unhealthy weight control methods which may lead to potentially dangerous disordered eating behaviors. Societal reinforcement of body image concern, in the form of a multibillion-dollar diet and weight loss industry, aids in maintenance of body dissatisfaction and the elusive search for the perfect body. Societal promotion of the thin ideal may also lead to prejudicial treatment of overweight individuals or teasing based on weight and shape, especially among youth. Overconcern with body image can have damaging effects.

- In large-scale studies, approximately 30% of boys and over 55% of girls report using unhealthy weight control methods such as vomiting, laxatives, diet pills, cigarette smoking, and diuretics in an effort to lose weight.[19,20]

- At 8 years old, girls believe that weight control is strongly associated with self-worth and view dieting as a means of improving self-worth.[21]

- Poor body image often leads to dieting, which can lead to unhealthy weight control behaviors, disordered eating, and ultimately eating disorders.

- Poor body image is strongly associated with low self-esteem and low self-worth, both of which can severely limit the potential for youth to succeed.

- Teasing related to weight and shape is implicated as contributing to disordered eating.[22]

SCREENING/ASSESSMENT

Given the ubiquitous nature of body image concerns and socio-cultural messages regarding body shape and size, as well as the complexity of the nature of body image, it is prudent to screen all adolescents for body image issues and work to foster a healthy body image among all youth. . . .

REFERENCES

1. EPM Communications. Youth Markets Alert 2000;12:8.
2. Field AE, Cheung L, Wolf AM, Herzog DB, Gortmaker SL, Colditz GA. Exposure to the mass media and weight concerns among girls. Pediatrics 1999;103(3):E36.
3. SmartGirl Speaks. Eating disorder quick poll reports. SmartGirl.org, University of Michigan. http://www.smartgirl.org/. Accessed 07/14/04.
4. Rand CS, Resnick JL, Seldman RS. Assessment of socially acceptable body sizes by university students. Obes Res 1997;5(5):425–429.

5. A cappella: A report on the realities, concerns, expectations, and barriers experienced by adolescent women in Canada. Ottawa: Canadian Teacher's Federation, 1990.

6. How schools shortchange girls: The AAUW report. A study of major findings in education. Washington, DC: American Association of University Women Educational Foundation, 1992.

7. O'Dea JA, Abraham S. Onset of disordered eating attitudes and behaviors in early adolescence: interplay of pubertal status, gender, weight, and age. Adolescence 1999;34 (136):671–679.

8. Siegel JM, Yancey AK, Aneshensel CS, Schuler R. Body image, perceived pubertal timing, and adolescent mental health. J Adolesc Health 1999,25(2). 155–165.

9. Facts and figures about our TV habits. TV-Turnoff Network. http://www.tvturnoff .org/. Accessed 7/14/04.

10. Television Viewing Study. Teenage Research Unlimited, 1996.

11. Reid LGA, Gedissman A. Required TV program in school encourages poor lifestyle choices. AAP News. November 2000. American Academy of Pediatrics. http://www.aap .org/advocacy/reidll00.htm. Accessed 7/14/04.

12. Billion Dollar Barbie. New York Times Magazine 1994;27:22.

13. Rubinstein S, Caballero B. Is Miss America an undernourished role model? JAMA 2000;283(12):1569.

14. Davis J, Oswalt R. Societal influences on a thinner body size in children. Percept Mot Skills 1992;74(3 Pt 1):697–698.

15. Tiggemann M, Pickering AS. Role of television in adolescent women's body dissatisfaction and drive for thinness. Int J Eat Disord 1996;20(2):199–203.

16. Field AE, Camargo CA, Jr., Taylor CB, Berkey CS, Roberts SB, Colditz GA. Peer, parent, and media influences on the development of weight concerns and frequent dieting among preadolescent and adolescent girls and boys. Pediatrics 2001;107(1):54–60.

17. McCreary DR, Sasse DK. An exploration of the drive for muscularity in adolescent boys and girls. J Am Coll Health 2000;48(6):297–304.

18. Striegel-Moore RH, Kearney-Cooke A. Exploring parents' attitudes and behaviors about their children's physical appearance. Int J Eat Disord 1994;15(4):377–385.

19. Emmons L. Dieting and purging behavior in black and white high school students. J Am Diet Assoc 1992;92(3):306–312.

20. Neumark-Sztainer D, Story M, Falkner NH, Behuring T, Resnick MD. Sociodemographic and personal characteristics of adolescents engaged in weight loss and weight/ muscle gain behaviors: who is doing what? Prev Med 1999;28(1):4–5.

21. Hill AJ, Pallin V. Dieting awareness and low self-worth: Related issues in 8-year-old girls. Int J Eat Disord 1998;24:405–413.

22. Taylor CB, Sharpe T, Shisslak C, Bryson S, Estes LS, Gray N, McKnight KM, Crago M, Kraemer HC, Killen JD. Factors associated with weight concerns in adolescent girls. Int J Eat Disord 1998;24(1):31–42.

When Is Thin Too Thin?

ERIC WILSON

BEFORE READING: Do you believe that the media present unrealistic models of body shape and size? Of physical attractiveness? Explain and provide examples.

They were alarmingly thin. Snejana Onopka, Natasha Poly, and Hana Soukupova, models in demand among the fashion designers who showed their collections in New York last week, appeared so gaunt and thin that their knees and elbows were larger than their concave thighs and pipe cleaner arms, and their bobbling heads looked as if a slight breeze could detach them from their frail bodies.

Linda Wells, the editor of the beauty magazine *Allure*, said there were moments during the shows when she could hear gasps in the audience at their appearance.

"What becomes alarming is when you see bones and start counting ribs," Ms. Wells said.

At a *Vogue* party on Monday for a young designer competition, the model Jessica Stam expressed similar dismay. "There are a lot of girls doing the shows who are very thin and frail," she said. "I don't know if they are healthy or not, but I don't think the frail, fragile look is very feminine, and I don't think it's attractive."

Yet there remains an ideal among designers who seem to prize an ever 5 thinner frame to display their clothes. Some who attended the New York shows question whether acceptable boundaries have been crossed, as when fashion glamorized images of heroin abuse in the early 1990's. Despite perennial complaints that models are too thin, there is a new sense of concern that designers are contributing to unhealthy and potentially life-threatening behavior among models vying to appear in their shows.

"We are minutes away from a catastrophe," said David Bonnouvrier, the chief executive of DNA Models, which represents many of the top faces in the business. In an interview, Mr. Bonnouvrier said designers and model bookers were encouraging extreme thinness, so much so that several of the models he represents, when asked about their weight, have refused to seek medical attention for what are probable eating disorders.

"This goes against everything we stand for as an industry," Mr. Bonnouvrier said. "I am kicking and screaming about it now because this should be an industry of beauty and luxury, not famished-looking people that look pale and sick."

Eric Wilson is a fashion reporter for the *New York Times*, where this article appeared on September 21, 2006.

Over the last decade fashion magazines have responded to such criticism by including a range of body types in their layouts, but when designers first show their collections at runway shows, they tend to use models who are little more than spectral wisps, expressionless hangers for their clothes.

Last week the organizers of Madrid fashion week, usually an overlooked event in comparison with the major shows in New York, London (this week), Milan, and Paris, said they were banning models with a height-to-weight ratio below what the World Health Organization considered normal. In effect, models who weigh less than 125 pounds are prohibited from working the runways. Organizers of the event said they wanted to project "an image of beauty and health."

Complaints about the idolization of role models who suggest unhealthy 10 lifestyles are culturally endemic. Celebrities like Nicole Richie, Lindsay Lohan, Paris Hilton, and Mischa Barton have all been subjects of tabloid headlines asking, "Are they too thin?" In all likelihood, the answer is yes, but that does not stop magazines from displaying their pictures or, likewise, designers from casting thin models in their shows.

"What's happening right now is an extreme," Ms. Wells said. "Some of the models really are too thin, but that is such a tricky thing to say."

The news media squall about underweight models, which is engulfing the fashion events in Madrid and now in London, centers largely on whether fashion shows perpetuate an unhealthy image of beauty, encouraging eating disorders among young women.

The producers of these fashion events have largely dismissed the concerns. On Saturday a British cabinet member, Culture Secretary Tessa Jowell, called for London designers to follow the example of Madrid by banning underweight models. But the British Fashion Council, led by Stuart Rose, the chief executive of Marks & Spencer, said it would not interfere with the designers' aesthetic. And some designers said it was misleading to equate thinness with being unhealthy and that the standard cited by the organizers in Madrid did not take into account age and puberty, which may cause a model who is unusually tall to appear frighteningly thin.

"We're talking about this because Madrid chose to do something now," said Katie Ford, the chief executive of Ford Models. "Do I think because you're thin that you're anorexic? No. The runway represents a very small segment of the entire fashion business. On the runway, model size has been frequently a representation of the designers' image at that point of time."

But that debate has overshadowed the likelihood that some of these 15 models, who have thus far been limited to runway shows but who aspire to more lucrative magazine work, are suffering from real eating disorders.

"I feel that people are taking the wrong angle on this whole issue," Mr. Bonnouvrier said. "These models look sick."

Although it would seem reasonable that the agencies that represent the models have a responsibility to monitor their health, Mr. Bonnouvrier and other agents described an environment that is dictated by the designers. A model's success depends on fitting an ideal image. He said that many of the models come from broken homes or poor countries, speak little English, and are conforming to those demands as a means of survival. If he complains, he said, they will simply switch to another agency.

"I want to really emphasize the point that we have very little leverage over our clients should they have such problems when they continue to be confirmed by the most important designers, photographers, and magazines in this industry," Mr. Bonnouvrier said. "A young model suffering from eating disorders is an ancient topic. What is new, however, is the alarming number of young models that are suffering and yet still work."

There has been some resistance among designers. Amanda Brooks, who assists Bryan Bradley of Tuleh with model castings, said a top runway model was turned down because she looked too thin. "You could see her hip bones," Ms. Brooks said. "We couldn't imagine putting her in a dress."

Some designers dispute that they are solely to blame for models' 20 weight issues. "I think we're all to blame," said Michael Vollbracht, the designer of Bill Blass. "I'm very aware of these girls who look too thin or unhealthy, and at one point during the casting I had to walk out of the room. We called a model's agency and said, 'Do you even watch these girls?'"

Milla Jovovich, the model and designer of a fashion collection called Jovovich-Hawk, said that dangerously thin models have been around since she was modeling as a child, as have the complaints, though little has ever been done in terms of prevention.

"There need to be more rules and regulations within the modeling industry," Ms. Jovovich said. "A lot of problems that are very gray areas need to be put in black and white."

All to Be Tall

JOE KITA

BEFORE READING: Should any restrictions be placed on unnecessary plastic surgery? Where would you draw the line?

Vertically challenged men are paying up to $80,000 to have their legs broken, caged, and then lengthened.

The gain: 3 inches.

The pain: extraordinary.

The cages surround Jim Conran's legs like little scaffolds. Each has eleven metal pins that screw into his broken bones. Every six hours, he must turn these pins ever so slightly in order to tighten wires that pull the bones apart and align them correctly. He has been doing this now for sixty-eight days. And all the time, the pain has been intensifying.

"It's like tuning a violin," he explains. "With each turn of the knobs, 5 the ligaments and muscles and skin come under more tension. Each day everything gets tighter. It's incredibly painful." So much so that Conran[1] won't allow himself to sleep for longer than three hours. "I'm frightened I'll miss a dose of medication, and the pain will get ahead of me," he says. Recently, he was given morphine, and that's helped somewhat. But he's still confined to a wheelchair and can stagger only short distances around his Manhattan apartment.

Before you start pitying Conran, you should know that he was not in a horrible accident that shattered his legs, nor does he suffer from a birth defect that's finally being corrected. No, he is an otherwise healthy, forty-five-year-old, single attorney who is paying $70,000 for this voluntary procedure. In fact, he's been looking forward to this for much of his life. Despite how it seems, he is living his dream.

You see, Jim Conran is $5'5\frac{3}{4}$ tall. Or rather, he was $5'5\frac{3}{4}$ tall. In the past few months, he has "grown" 1 millimeter per day (about$\frac{1}{25}$") by turning his 22 pins ever so precisely. And as he's done so, new bone has been steadily forming in the gaps where the segments of tibia and fibula are being pulled

---

[1] The name has been changed for privacy. — EDS.

Joe Kita is a writer and editor at *Men's Health*. His book *GuyQ* (2003) is a compilation of the 1,305 best tips on men's health and fitness published in the fifteen years of the magazine's existence. When at forty he hit a mid-life crisis, he looked back at his biggest regrets and decided to do something about them. The result was the humorous *Another Shot: How I Relived My Life in Less Than a Year* (2001). Another year was devoted to systematically confronting each of his fears. Those experiences are recounted in *Accidental Courage: Finding Out I'm a Bit Brave After All* (2002). This article appeared in the January/February 2004 issue of *Men's Health*.

apart. When he last checked—and he checks daily—he was $5'8\frac{1}{4}''$. When he (hopefully) reaches his goal height of $5'9''$ and this violin tuning ends, he's confident his life will finally be in harmony.

Short. It's a five-letter word that carries four-letter connotations for men below the national average of $5'9''$. Unless you're one of them, you don't know how much it hurts to be called that.

Imagine this scenario. You've been accepted at Harvard, West Point, and Annapolis. You're an A student. You've won seven varsity letters, and you nearly qualified for the Olympics. Yet to get into West Point (your first choice), you must meet a height requirement of $5'6''$. You're slightly below that. So the night before your admittance physical, you have your father repeatedly whack you on top of the head with a textbook in order to raise a bump. Next day, you officially measure in at $5'6\frac{1}{16}''$. You go on to graduate with honors, serve your country overseas, and eventually end up as an aide to the president of the United States. And you know, your whole life long, that you might have missed all of this—by a quarter inch.

"From a very early age, you start getting clear, institutionalized mes- 10 sages that you're less desirable," says George Holdt, the soldier in question, who, like Conran, is now undergoing limb lengthening. "From the violence you experience in school to the behavior you encounter throughout your social and professional life, the discrimination is always there."

Today, height requirements in any workplace are largely a thing of the past (the military's cutoff is now $5'$). But it's an example of the frustration that is the legacy of the diminutive man. And no, it isn't his imagination. Numerous scientific studies have verified the advantages of height. For example, taller men . . .

. . . Are more likely to be hired. When recruiters in one study from Eastern Michigan University were asked to choose between two equally qualified candidates who differed in height, 72 percent chose the taller applicant.

. . . Make more money. Graduating seniors at the University of Pittsburgh who were $6'2''$ or taller enjoyed starting salaries $4,000 higher than counterparts $5'5''$ or under. Economists at the University of Pennsylvania even estimate that added height is worth nearly 2 percent in additional income per inch per annum.

. . . Are chosen as leaders. Nancy Etcoff, Ph.D., a professor of psychology at Harvard Medical School, points out in her book *Survival of the Prettiest*, "the easiest way to predict the winner in a United States election is to bet on the taller man." Of 43 American presidents, only five have been significantly below average height. What's more, Etcoff cites a study of *Fortune* 500 CEOs that found that more than half were taller than 6 feet, and just 3 percent were shorter than $5'7''$.

. . . Make better first impressions. Surveys by Henry Biller, Ph.D., a 15 professor of psychology at the University of Rhode Island and coauthor of *Stature and Stigma*, show that compared with shorter men, guys of average and above-average height are seen as "more mature, uninhibited, positive, secure, masculine, active, complete, successful, optimistic, dominant, capable, confident, and outgoing."

While all of this pisses off short guys, what really bothers them is how they're viewed by women. Walter W. Windisch, Ph.D., is a psychologist in Towson, Maryland, who evaluates short men who are considering limb lengthening. "The average patient," he notes, "is 28 years old, male, college educated, professional, of some financial means, the product of parents who expressed concern about height, and, in every case, single."

Indeed, if you read the personals section of your local newspaper or log onto any online dating service, you'll find lots of ads from women listing height preferences. Why are they so particular, especially when they're paying by the letter? Certainly a portion of it stems from the statistics cited earlier—that taller men earn more and enjoy a higher social status. Some of it also comes from Hollywood, where leading ladies routinely look up into the eyes of the tall, dark, and handsome man. It's the romantic ideal. But a good chunk is also based on an almost primitive assessment. Is he a good provider, a worthy protector, a gifted procreator? And on some anthropological level, it's as if she ultimately decides the short man is not. Less than one-half of 1 percent of women marry men who are shorter than they are, according to Etcoff.

"Someone once asked Sigmund Freud, 'What is the goal of life?' and his answer was, 'To love and to work,'" says Windisch. "That's a fairly good summary of what's bugging these guys. They're looking to love and be loved, to work and be valued. It's just that their stature, something totally beyond their control, is keeping them from it."

About 2,500 kilometers east of Moscow, at the western edge of Siberia, is the Ilizarov Scientific Center for Restorative Traumatology and Orthopedics. Located in the Russian city of Kurgan, in the shadow of the Ural Mountains, it was founded in 1971 by Professor Gavriil Abramovich Ilizarov. Decades earlier, faced with treating a large number of World War II veterans with complicated limb fractures, he began experimenting with "circular external fixators" to keep bones aligned and to speed healing. Their use as limb-lengthening tools, however, was discovered by accident. While Ilizarov was on vacation, a nurse adjusted a fixator in the wrong direction. When he returned and examined the patient's X-ray, he noticed new bone forming in the gap. This set the stage for a variety of new applications, including the correction of leg-length deformities, bow legs, anchondroplasia (dwarfism), and, lately, short stature. More than a half century later, the Ilizarov method— as it's come to be known—is still being used in a surprisingly unevolved form throughout the world.

Here's how it works: After taking a series of X-rays to map out the precise dimensions of the bones, the surgeon orders a regional anesthetic and makes two half-inch-long incisions in each leg (usually below the knee). Using a surgical chisel, he then cracks the tibias and fibulas, being careful 20 to disrupt as little of the surrounding tissue as possible. (Note: When a doctor breaks your legs, it's called an "osteotomy.") Next, he attaches the circular aluminum frames. This requires piercing each leg with eleven arrow-sharp carbide pins and pushing them in until they bottom out against bone. The pins are of varying lengths and diameters, with the thicker ones being positioned closer to the breaks for added stability. Once the pins are in position, the surgeon slowly screws them into the hard calcium-and-collagen shell that surrounds the marrow. The rest is comparatively straightforward: Affix the adjustment wires to the pins, sew the two osteotomy incisions shut, treat and bandage the pin wounds. For all that's involved, the entire operation takes just $2\frac{1}{2}$ hours. Patients typically remain in the hospital for two to three days, after which they can take a dozen or so steps.

But this is the easy part. The frames usually stay on for three to six months, during which time the bones are gradually separated. This is called the "distraction phase." All but one of the men we spoke with said that, even with heavy doses of narcotics, such as Vicodin, the resulting pain was just on the edge of bearable.

"It will reduce the toughest man to a crying little girl in a matter of weeks," says Jack Turner, a 39-year-old salesman who "grew" $2\frac{1}{2}$ inches as a result of this surgery.

"It's an act of aggression against your own body," adds Conran.

Just as difficult is the helplessness that results. Patients are dependent on wheelchairs, walkers, and the supportive arms of friends and relatives to get around. Most are bedridden except for periodic doctor visits and daily physical therapy. Work is out of the question. This is true not only during the distraction phase but also for three months or more after the frames come off and the new bone is hardening. "You need somebody to take care of you virtually all the time," says Rick Morgan, another patient. "Sometimes you can't even reach the bathroom."

Although some doctors make lofty promises, most legs won't tolerate 25 being stretched past three inches. It's not the bones that balk but rather the muscles and tendons that surround them. Overall, there's a 25 percent complication rate from this surgery, with the most frequent problem being pin-site infection. That's why patients are given a prescription for oral antibiotics, which they're told to begin taking at the first sign of redness, tenderness, or discolored drainage at the pin entry points. If an infection goes unnoticed, it will spread into the deep leg tissue and then the bone.

A less common but still serious complication is nerve damage. In one study review of 814 limb lengthenings, approximately 10 percent of patients had experienced some form of temporary nerve damage, characterized by chronic pain or impaired motor skills.

But the most catastrophic possibility doesn't present itself until the frames are removed. Even though the doctor will have taken X-rays to gauge structural integrity (the whiter the area, the stronger the bone), there's still a chance that what took months of agonizing pain and tens of thousands of dollars to build will, at the moment of truth, snap. Or the new bone will hold, only to buckle and break weeks later. Either way, doctors call this a re-fracture; there's a one-in-twelve chance of its happening.

If you're a short man seeking salvation through surgery, you've prob-ably heard of the International Center for Limb Lengthening, in Balti-more. An affiliate of Sinai Hospital, the ICLL was the first facility of its kind in North America and remains the largest — half of all the limb lengthenings for height are performed here. The bulk of its business, how-ever, deals with correcting functional deformities. "I'm very strict when it comes to doing this surgery on otherwise healthy people," says forty-seven-year-old chief surgeon Dror Paley, M.D., himself 6'. "In fact, I try to discourage it. The magnitude of what you have to go through is so large, it's not in the realm of having your nose done or your tummy tucked."

Dr. Paley generally will not operate on men over 5'6" (or women over 5'2"), and he requires that all prospective patients first undergo an inten-sive, ten-hour psychological exam by Windisch. Only about 10 percent go on to have the operation. "You must be careful," says Dr. Paley. "I've had some real nutcases—people who were willing to sell their houses, steal their wives' money, do unbelievable things for a few extra inches."

Depending on the facility and the specifics of the case, those inches 30 typically run between $50,000 and $80,000. When limb lengthening is done on a healthy person, medical insurance won't pay for it. However, if done to correct a leg-length discrepancy, bow legs, or any other limb de-formity, it is usually covered.

Some of those people who can't raise the necessary funds or who don't pass the screening process go elsewhere—like Jack Turner, who ended up in Italy after being "dumped," as he calls it, by Dr. Paley. "The cost turned out to be one-eighth what it was in America," he explains, "and I felt I got better care."

And yet, even though it's been almost three years since Turner had his operation, he says he's still at only 80 percent of his former physical ability. "I don't think anyone can break both legs and come back 100 per-cent," he says. "For instance, I can't run as fast, and I have pain when the weather is damp."

The long-term effects are unknown. Although some doctors insist that dwarves who were lengthened as much as a foot decades ago show no traces of bone weakening or arthritis, other experts remain skeptical. "There's an enormous risk," says Michael Ain, M.D., a 4'3" orthopedic surgeon at Johns Hopkins Hospital in Baltimore. "Nobody really knows what's going to happen to people getting this surgery."

Neither the American Society for Aesthetic Plastic Surgery nor the American Academy of Orthopedic Surgeons (AAOS) endorses cosmetic limb lengthening. Others condemn it outright. "I'm appalled that our so-ciety has become so imbued with self-image that patients are willing to put their necks on the line like this. There are just too many risks," says

William Tipton, M.D., director of medical affairs for the AAOS. "And the surgeons who are doing these operations on otherwise healthy people should remember this: *Primum non nocere.* That's Latin for 'First, no injury.'"

One of those surgeons is S. Robert Rozbruch, M.D., director of the Insti- 35 tute for Limb Lengthening and Reconstruction at the Hospital for Special Surgery, in New York City. He counters: "Seeing the profound impact this surgery can have on someone has convinced me that, for a very select group of people, it should be brought out of the closet and done more freely."

Paul Steven Miller, for one, thinks limb lengthening is unnecessary. Miller is an attorney and the commissioner of the U.S. Equal Employment Opportunity Commission. He also happens to be a 4'5" dwarf, who has experienced height discrimination firsthand. "One law firm told me they feared their clients would think they were running a circus freak show if they hired me," he recounts. Nonetheless, Miller says cosmetic limb lengthening is "silly." "I have a hard time believing it really makes a difference in these people's lives."

With predicted advances in limb lengthening, combined with the recent FDA approval of growth-hormone therapy for short children, will Diminutive Man soon take his place next to Cro-Magnon in the Museum of Natural History? Are we entering an era of stature cleansing?

"The way we need to judge this," says David Sandberg, Ph.D., an associate professor of psychiatry at the University of Buffalo's School of Medicine, "is not by what's happening physically to these patients. Rather, what must be demonstrated is that increased height is actually translating into a better quality of life."

And only the patients themselves can assess that. Among the men we spoke with, sentiments are mixed. "It's kind of like the old P. T. Barnum thing," says Turner, "where you pay a quarter to go look at something that isn't very good. But when you come out, you have to basically say it was great. Not getting 3+ inches was disappointing, but on the other hand, I'm much more comfortable being 5'7" than 5'4+". I can only surmise that it's making subtle differences in my life. Overall, I think it's a great way for men with a height issue to increase their rank in the pecking order, but you're not going to suddenly be dating supermodels."

"Before I had this surgery, I was depressed and very self-conscious," 40 says Mark Pace, DO, an osteopath in South Florida who was 4'11". "I was afraid to walk into a roomful of children because they would make fun of me, and I could barely talk to women. I had zero confidence. Now, I'm just under 5'3", and the difference is unbelievable. I'm seeing eye-to-eye with people, and I'm actually dating."

"I've gained about $2\frac{1}{2}$ inches," says Conran, "and it feels great. In fact, I'm reluctant to let the thrill wear off. I'm almost 5'9". Now, I sure don't consider that tall, but it's not short. It's average, and that's all I ever wanted to be. I wanted to be accepted on my own merits without having my height held against me."

"I can't wait to walk down the streets of New York City, visit my old neighborhood, and see things from a slightly different perspective," adds Jose Rodriguez, who recently got his frames removed and is $2\frac{3}{4}$ inches taller. "Those extra inches make you a little more confident, a little more happy, and the day a little brighter."

If you're still skeptical, Rodriguez suggests an experiment. "Take a few books, set them on the floor, and stand on top of them," he says. "You don't think a couple of inches can make a difference, but it's amazing."

Smooth Operations

ALLISON SAMUELS

> BEFORE READING: Why do you think few African Americans elected to have cosmetic surgery until quite recently?

Long before Janet Jackson revealed a little too much of her body, Tanisha Rollins was obsessed with having one just like it. After watching the singer strut in a 1993 video, Rollins embarked on a quest for washboard abs. For the next decade she stuck to a rigorous regimen. But her abs pretty much stayed the same. Then a friend skipped all the hard work and got a tummy tuck. "I was just like, 'What magazines have you been reading?!'" says Rollins, twenty-nine, an administrative assistant in Dayton, Ohio. She thought nipping and tucking was only for "rich white people and Michael Jackson," not African American women like her, making $30,000 a year.

Last year Rollins shelled out $5,000 for a tummy tuck of her own, joining the small but growing ranks of African Americans opting for cosmetic surgery. The number of blacks seeking facial or reconstructive surgery more than tripled between 1997 and 2002, reflecting both the growing affluence of African Americans and the subtle easing of some long-held cultural taboos against such procedures. Except for the Jacksons (or perhaps because of them), even black celebrities, whose looks are essential to their livelihood, have been loath to go under the knife. "I was just so worried about looking crazy or looking like Jennifer Grey, who no one recognized after she had her nose job," says one forty-year-old black actress, who decided last year to have her nose and breasts done after being inspired by singer Patti LaBelle. (Though LaBelle, sixty, talks about her nose job, the actress requested anonymity.)

Allison Samuels is a correspondent in *Newsweek*'s Los Angeles bureau, covering sports and entertainment. Earlier she worked as a researcher at Quincy Jones Entertainment and as a reporter for the *Los Angeles Times*. She is on the UCLA Black Studies Department Board of Directors. This article is from the July 5, 2004, issue of *Newsweek*.

In an age when plastic surgeons advertise their services on the subway, it may come as a surprise that cosmetic surgery is frowned upon in the black community. "People want to look good," says Dr. Karen Low, who is African American and a plastic surgeon in Greensboro, North Carolina, "but they also want to avoid any criticism that might come from the community, which has for years supported larger frames, wider noses, and not-so-perfect features. Changing those things is sometimes seen as an insult to our ancestors and to the culture." Rollins experienced that backlash when she told her family she was having a tummy tuck. Not only did they think it was risky and expensive, they couldn't understand why she wanted to tinker with "God's work." "It's hard telling your mother that you don't want to look like her when you're fifty," Rollins says. "I think my mother resented that and felt hurt, but I had to be honest."

There's a lot more at work here than simple vanity. "I think African American women have finally just decided that it's time to love ourselves," says *Essence* magazine beauty editor Miki Taylor. African Americans have become the biggest consumers of beauty products in the United States, spending at least $20 billion a year, as companies like L'Oreal, which opened its Institute for Ethnic Hair and Skin Research in 2003, are well aware. The increase in plastic surgery is in many ways an extension of that trend.

Blacks accounted for nearly 5 percent of the 8.7 million cosmetic-surgery 5 procedures done last year. As the numbers have grown, doctors have had to adapt to their clientele. For starters, black women and white women tend to want to tune up different areas of their bodies. While the nose is Job No. 1 for whites, black women's top request is the tummy tuck. Breast enhancement? More black women want reductions. "Let's be clear that I did it for my health," says rapper-actress Queen Latifah, who went from a double-E bra cup to a D. Facelifts are not as popular as they are among white women, a testament, perhaps, to a long-held belief in the African American community: "Black don't crack."

But black skin does scar, much more easily than white skin, and that has been a big deterrent to African Americans considering elective surgery. Doctors try to be as minimally invasive as possible, using lasers and making smaller incisions, hiding scars in inconspicuous places, and using electron-beam radiation to diminish the appearance of scars. Dermatologist Marcia Glenn, who opened Odyssey Medispa in Marina del Rey, California, with an eye toward African American women like herself, encourages patients to try less-invasive procedures like Botox before choosing surgery.

Like many women who have cosmetic surgery, Patti LaBelle was hoping to cut away at her insecurities in the process. Looking at childhood pictures, "I realized I wasn't a very good-looking girl," says the singer, who was teased mercilessly about her broad nose. "I didn't like the way that made me feel." As middle age sank in, she hoped surgery would make her feel better about herself. Rather than go for a button nose, LaBelle was sensitive about keeping her features looking African American. "Nothing drastic, just enough to make me feel and look as good as I could," she says. "If, in a few years, I want to get some more work done on my chin or my neck, I will."

How Men Really Feel about Their Bodies

TED SPIKER

BEFORE READING: Are men and women equally concerned about body image? Explain.

Dressed only in my underwear, I'm eight years old and sitting on the pediatrician's exam table, waiting for my checkup. My mother points to the two mounds of fatty flesh between my chest and belly. She asks the doctor, "Could they be tumors?"

"No," he says, "it's just fat."

Since that day, my fat has absorbed more darts than the back wall of a bar.

When I turned fourteen, my new doctor asked me, "Do you get embarrassed on the beach because of your femininely shaped hips and chest?" . . . In high school, locker-room jokesters composed a song about my love handles. And in college, a friend analyzed my body shape by explaining that I have "a low center of gravity and those childbearing hips."

At 6'2" and 215 pounds, I'm not huge. I just carry my weight where 5 women do — in my hips, butt, and thighs. And I hate it. I hate the way clothes fit. I hate that friends say I use the "big-butt defense" in basketball.

But I'm not the only man who wishes his body looked more like Michael Jordan's and less like a vat of pudding. A recent survey showed that only 18 percent of men are happy enough with their physiques that they wouldn't change them. "Men used to see their bodies as functional objects — to lift things, to play sports, to do something," says Roberto Olivardia, Ph.D., a clinical psychologist at Harvard Medical School and coauthor of *The Adonis Complex*. "Over the past 20 years, the tide has changed. The idea of men's bodies as sexual objects has intensified."

So while women got there first, they don't have a monopoly on stressing over looks. Here, eight fundamental truths about men:

Ted Spiker, an associate professor of journalism at the University of Florida, is a contributing editor to *Men's Health* and collaborated with David Zinczenko on *The Abs Diet: The Six-Week Plan to Flatten Your Stomach and Keep You Lean for Life* (2004). This article appeared in the August 2003 *O: The Oprah Magazine*.

1. We have more body angst than you realize, but we'll never have a serious conversation with you about it.

Look at the standards we have to measure up to: If we're fat, we're labeled as beer-guzzling couch potatoes. Too thin, and we're deemed wimpy. Too short, and we're ruled out for a date. We can have too little hair on our heads or too much on our backs. And maybe worst of all, we can be too big in the backside of our pants yet too small in the front.

Now add the fact that our mental struggle has two layers. "A man 10 thinks, Not only does it bother me that I'm fat and my hair is thinning. It bothers me that it bothers me, because I'm not supposed to feel this way," says Thomas Cash, Ph.D., a professor of psychology at Old Dominion University in Norfolk, Virginia. "The thinking is that it's like a woman to worry about looks."

So we won't talk to you about our insecurities. Nor will you ever catch us asking a friend for advice: "Hey Bill, do these pants slim my beer gut? Do I need to trim my chest hair? Which accentuates my triceps, the blue shirt or the red?"

2. Instead, we'll joke about our bodies.

When a friend recently saw the size of the pizza I was about to eat, he said, "Ted, that pizza should have its own zip code." I responded, "So should my ass." We make fun of ourselves to cover up what we're really feeling—frustration, embarrassment, and anger that we're not perfect.

But other people's jokes sting. Mark Meador, thirty-seven, of Westerville, Ohio, returned from a trip to Disney World with photos of himself. "Man, you look like Big Pun," Meador's friend said, referring to the obese rapper who died of a heart attack. Meador laughed off the comment, not letting on that it hurt. That same weekend, his daughter said, "Dad, you look like you're having a baby." Fortunately for Meador, the gentle pokes inspired him to change. He dropped junk food, started Tae Bo, and lost more than forty pounds.

3. We're worried about our bodies because we're competing for 15 you—and against you.

With more people both marrying later and getting divorced, it's a competitive environment for finding mates. And since this generation of women can support themselves, they're freer to pick a man for his cute butt. Lynne Luciano, Ph.D., who has researched body-image issues at California State University at Dominguez Hills, says women are tired of being objectified and have turned the tables on men. "They don't like a man to be overly vain," she says. "He shouldn't care too much about the way he looks, but on the other hand, he should look good."

At the same time, men are also shaping up because they're seeing that people who are fit are more successful at work. "Women are very good at using their looks for competition," Cash says. "So men think, I'd better clean up my act."

4. We're not just checking you out.

We're a visual gender. We like the way you look. A lot. But that doesn't mean we don't compare ourselves to other men the way women compare themselves to other women. I notice the way men look on the beach, at work, or simply walking by. Maybe it's male competitiveness or primal instincts, but we don't just want to have better bodies to attract you. We want better bodies to improve our position among ourselves. A scary thought that proves the point: When Luciano interviewed doctors who perform penis enlargements, they reported that the main reason men undergo the surgery isn't to improve their relationships but to be more impressive in the locker room.

5. We want to look like we're twenty-five. 20

It used to be that our mythical heroes had wisdom, experience, and maturity. Think Harrison Ford as Indiana Jones. Now our heroes are baby faced with six-pack abs. Think Tobey Maguire as Spider-Man. "The youth movement has been cruel to men," says Luciano. "The Cary Grants have fallen though the cracks. Today's ideal is younger, buffer, more muscular. A lot of men in their 40s and 50s have trouble trying to emulate that." So men, like women, are swimming against the age current. That might explain why from 1997 to 2001, the number of men who had cosmetic surgery increased 256 percent. (Last year more than 800,000 men—and north of six million women—went under the knife.)

Fear of aging also explains why going bald is so painful. We can try to stop it (Rogaine, Propecia), hide it (hats, comb-overs), or live with it (doing nothing, shaving our heads), but hair loss signifies a loss of vitality and control. "If a man's not in a relationship, if he hasn't fallen in love, he figures that's it, that's the end of romance," Cash says. "He thinks no one will ever want to be with him."

6. Desperation makes us do desperate things. Delusion makes us do nothing.

I can't remember the last pair of pants that fit me well. If I buy size 38s, they fit around the waist but suffocate my hips and butt. If I go to a 40, they're roomy where I need it but gaping in the waist. Several years ago, I tried on my wife's post-pregnancy size-20 jeans to see if they were cut differently. Did I just admit that? Trying on women's jeans—this is about as low as it gets, I thought. Then I realized it could get lower: The jeans fit me perfectly.

I wore those jeans for six months, and I felt leaner every day I wore 25 them. My wife asked me why I didn't just buy a big pair of men's jeans and have a tailor alter them. My answer: Why pay for alterations when I know that tomorrow I'm going to start an exercise routine that will change my body shape forever? It's been my mantra for two decades.

7. Men's body-image problems can be just as dangerous as women's.

For some men, poor body image can lead to anger, anxiety, depression, sexual dysfunction, and steroid abuse. Doctors may fail to recognize eating disorders or muscle dysmorphia (the need to constantly bulk up), even though it's estimated that eating disorders affect one million men. Olivardia, the Harvard psychologist, says secrecy reinforces the patients' sense of shame. "I've treated men who would tell people they were alcoholics, but they'd never admit they were bulimic," he says.

Cody Swann, a twenty-one-year-old graduate student from Stuart, Florida, was so obsessed with being thin that he measured himself on a body-fat scale every day. "I remember how happy I was when I stood on the thing and it came back 'error' because I didn't have enough body fat for it to read," he says. "It wouldn't read below 2 percent, which is what I was. Woohoo, can't do much better than that." It took Swann one year to realize he was anorexic. At six feet tall, Swann is now a muscular 205 pounds and feels he has overcome the disorder. But he still obsesses about his appearance. He exercises three to four hours every day and has eaten in a restaurant only twice in the past two years. If he can't weigh his food, he won't eat it. Swann watches every last morsel. "My rule is that I have to chew a piece of gum for thirty minutes so I burn off the calories in it."

8. We don't blame anyone (except maybe Tiger Woods and Taco Bell). But we'll be grateful to anyone who makes us feel good about shaping up.

We know what it's like to be bombarded with images of perfect bod- 30 ies. We see the men in commercials and on magazine covers, the bigger-stronger-better mentality that dominates our culture. "Look at Tiger Woods. The best golfer in the world has an outstanding physique. Golfers used to be everyday men," says J. Kevin Thompson, Ph.D., professor of psychology at the University of South Florida. "Basketball players used to be skinny. They're all muscular now." Hell, even our president runs sub-seven-minute miles.

As much as I'd like to, I won't blame my shape on genetics or the media. I'd love to blame stress or lack of time. But the real culprit is my elephantine appetite and a four-times-a-week Taco Bell habit.

Nine years ago, though, I'd had enough. I took a 150-mile charity bike ride and gained weight rather than lost it because of all the cookies I ate at the pit stops. That was my epiphany. Four months later, I dropped from my all-time high of 231 pounds to 191. My wife dubbed me "Little" as I started to lose weight. That encouragement kept me on my program. But now I'm back around 215 and want desperately to drop to 180—for my health, for my looks, for my confidence, for the quest to find a perfect-fitting pair of pants.

It's not that I can't change my body; it's just that I haven't. All I do know is that I'll never stop trying to shrink my hips, tighten my gut, and deflate my rear tire. Because if there's one thing I believe in, it's that every love-handle story should have a happy ending.

Not Too Rich or Too Thin

LISA TAKEUCHI CULLEN

> BEFORE READING: There is an old saying that "you can never be too rich or too thin."
> Do you tend to associate images of slender bodies with the wealthy? Why, or
> why not?

One of the first things that strike foreigners visiting the United States is that the rich tend to be skinny and the poor fat. Studies bear this out. The less money you have in America, the likelier you are to be overweight. One in four adults below the poverty level is obese, compared with 1 in 6 in households with an income of $67,000 or more. For minorities, poverty has an even heavier effect: Obesity strikes one in three poor African Americans.

On the surface, this makes little sense. If the poor must struggle to buy groceries, how can they pack away enough to gain all that weight? The assumption used to be that the poor were making bad food and lifestyle choices—Krispy Kremes instead of crispy greens. But now researchers have begun to suspect that the blame lies elsewhere.

The cost of food—quality food—is perhaps the best place to start. Calorically speaking, the best bang for the buck tends to be packed with sugar, fat, and refined grains (think cookies and candy bars). In general, processed foods hog ever larger portions of all Americans' diets—one reason we spend just a tenth of our incomes on food today, compared with a fifth in 1950. But a pound of lean steak costs a lot more than a pound of hot dogs. "The stomach is a dumb organ," says J. Larry Brown, director of the Center on Hunger and Poverty in Waltham, Massachusetts. "It doesn't know anything about quality. It knows only when it's full."

Processed foods aren't just cheap, tasty, and filling. They're also more accessible. One study found that 28 percent of Americans live in what nutritionists call "food deserts," places where big supermarkets are at least ten miles, or a twenty-minute drive, away. People who live in these places wind up buying much of their daily groceries from convenience stores or gas stations, where they can find Chef Boyardee but not baby carrots. Some communities are trying to remedy this. Philadelphia, for instance, recently announced a $100 million effort to open ten supermarkets in urban neighborhoods. But for much of the country, says Troy Blanchard, a sociology professor at Mississippi State University who studies this issue, "you have people who are literally distanced out of healthy diets."

Lisa Takeuchi Cullen writes for *Time* magazine. This article appeared in the June 7, 2004, issue.

Children of the poor face especially steep odds in fighting obesity. The 5
cash-strapped schools many of them attend are more likely than others to
cut physical-education classes and strike franchise deals with snack-food
and beverage makers. After school, working parents would rather their kids
stay inside watching TV than play outside in unsafe streets. Those hours
in front of the tube, meanwhile, feed them a diet of ads heavy on sugary
cereals and greasy burgers. No wonder obese adolescents are twice as likely
to come from low-income families.

Though the ballooning obesity problem among the poor is finally
getting the attention of academics and the government, nobody has yet
come up with an easy fix. "Our remedies are very middle class," says
Adam Drewnowski, director of the Center for Public Health Nutrition at
the University of Washington. "They tell you, Seek a healthy diet and exercise. Well, if you're working two jobs and living in a trailer, you're in no
mood to get home and make a salad." In the end, fitness may have less
to do with genetics than with tax brackets.

"Now that we're old and covered with wrinkles,
they come out with the camera phone."

The Tyranny of the Normal

LESLIE FIEDLER

BEFORE READING: How do you define the term *normal* as it applies to physical appearance? Is the ability to be physically "normal" related to social class?

I am not a doctor or a nurse or a social worker, confronted in my daily rounds with the problem of physical disability; not even a lawyer, philosopher, or theologian trained to deal with its moral and legal implications. I am only a poet, novelist, critic—more at home in the world of words and metaphor than fact, which is to say, an expert, if at all, in reality once removed. Yet despite this, I have been asked on numerous occasions to address groups of health-care professionals about this subject—no doubt because I once published a book called *Freaks: Myths and Images of the Secret Self.* In that book, I was primarily interested in exploring (as the subtitle declares) the fascination of "normals" with the sort of congenital malformations traditionally displayed at Fairs and Sideshows, and especially the way in which such freaks are simultaneously understood as symbols of the absolute Other and the essential Self. Yet in the long and difficult process of putting that study together (it took almost six years of my life and led me into dark places in my own psyche I was reluctant to enter), I stumbled inadvertently into dealing also with the subject of "the care of imperiled newborns."

How difficult and dangerous a topic this was I did not realize, however, until just before my book was due to appear. I was at a party celebrating the imminent event when I mentioned offhand to one of my fellow-celebrants, a young man who turned out to be an M.D., one of the discoveries I had made in the course of my research: that in all probability more "abnormal" babies were being allowed to die (in effect, being killed) in modern hospitals than had been in the Bad Old Days when they were exposed and left to perish by their fathers. And I went on to declare that in my opinion, at least, this was not good; at which point, my interlocutor screamed at me (rather contradictorily, I thought) that what I asserted was simply not true— and that, in any case, it was perfectly all right to do so. Then he hurled his Martini glass at the wall behind me and stalked out of the room.

He did not stay long enough for me to explain that our disagreement was more than merely personal, based on more than the traditional mutual distrust of the scientist and the humanist. Both of our attitudes, I

Leslie Fiedler (1917–2003) was best known as a literary critic and theorist. Until his death, he for many years was on the American literature faculty at the State University of New York at Buffalo. His interest in variations on the "normal" was spurred by research and interviews he did for his book *Freaks: Myths and Images of the Secret Self* (1978). This essay is from his book of the same title: *The Tyranny of the Normal* (1996).

wanted to tell him, had deep primordial roots: sources far below the level of our fully conscious values and the facile rationalizations by which we customarily defend them. It is, therefore, to certain ancient myths and legends that we must turn—and here my literary expertise stands me in good stead—to understand the roots of our deep ambivalence toward fellow creatures who are perceived at any given moment as disturbingly deviant, outside currently acceptable physiological norms. That ambivalence has traditionally impelled us toward two quite different responses to the "monsters" we beget. On the one hand, we have throughout the course of history killed them—ritually at the beginning, as befits divinely sent omens of disaster, portents of doom. On the other hand, we have sometimes worshiped them as if they were themselves divine, though never without overtones of fear and repulsion. In either case, what prompted our response was a sense of wonder and awe: a feeling that such "unnatural" products of the natural process by which we continue the species are mysterious, uncanny, finally "taboo."

Though it may not be immediately evident, the most cursory analysis reveals that not only have that primitive wonder and awe persisted into our "scientific," secular age, but so also have the two most archaic ways of expressing it. In the first place, we continue to kill, or at least allow to die, monstrously malformed neonates. We euphemize the procedure, however, disguise the superstitious horror at its roots, by calling what we do "the removal of life supports from nonviable *terata*" (*terata* being Greek for "monster"). Moreover, thanks to advanced medical techniques, we can do better these days than merely fail to give malformed preemies a fair chance to prove whether or not they are really "viable." We can detect and destroy before birth, babies likely to be born deformed; even abort them wholesale when the occasion arises, as in the infamous case of the Thalidomide babies of the sixties. That was a particularly unsavory episode (which we in this country were spared), since the phocomelic infants,[1] carried by mothers dosed with an antidote prescribed for morning sickness, were in the full sense of the word "iatrogenic[2] freaks." And the doctors who urged their wholesale abortion (aware that less than half of them would prove to be deformed, but why take chances?) were in many cases the very ones who had actually prescribed the medication.

To be sure, those responsible for such pre-infanticide did not confess— 5 were not even aware, though any poet could have told them—that they were motivated by vestigial primitive fears of abnormality, exacerbated by their guilt at having caused it. They sought only, they assured themselves and the rest of the world, to spare years of suffering to the doomed children and their parents; as well as to alleviate the financial burden on those

---

[1] *Phocomelic infants*: Children born with extremely short limbs. [All notes are the editors'.]

[2] *Iatrogenic*: A condition inadvertently caused by a doctor or by medical treatment.

parents and the larger community, which would have to support them through what promised to be a nonproductive lifetime. We do, however, have at this point records of the subsequent lives of some of the Thalidomide babies whose parents insisted on sparing them (a wide-ranging study was made some years later in Canada), which turned out to have been, from their own point of view, at least, neither notably nonproductive, nor especially miserable. None of them, at any rate, were willing to confess that they would have wished themselves dead.

But such disconcerting facts do not faze apologists for such drastic procedures. Nor does the even more dismaying fact that the most wholehearted, full-scale attempt at teratacide occurred in Hitler's Germany, with the collaboration, by the way, of not a few quite respectable doctors and teratologists, most notably a certain Etienne Wolff of the University of Strasbourg. Not only were dwarfs and other "useless people" sent to Nazi extermination camps and parents adjudged "likely" to beget anomalous children sterilized; but other unfortunate human beings regarded—at that time and in that society—as undesirable deviations from the Norm were also destroyed: Jews and Gypsies first of all, with Blacks, Slavs, and Mediterraneans presumably next in line. It is a development which should make us aware of just how dangerous enforced physiological normality is when the definition of its parameters falls into the hands of politicians and bureaucrats. And into what other hands can we reasonably expect it to fall in any society we know or can imagine in the foreseeable future?

Similarly, even as the responsibility for the ritual slaughter of Freaks was passing from the family to the State, the terrified adoration of Freaks was passing from the realm of worship to that of entertainment and art. To be sure, the adoration of Freaks in the Western world was never a recognized religion but at best an underground Cult. Think, for instance, of the scene in Fellini's *Satyricon*,[3] in which a Hermaphrodite is ritually displayed to a group of awestricken onlookers, who regard him as more than a curiosity, though not quite a god: after all, the two reigning myth-systems of our culture, the Hellenic and the Judaeo-Christian, both disavowed the portrayal of the divine in freakish guise, regarding as barbarous or pagan the presentation of theriomorphic, two-headed, or multilimbed divinities.

Yet there would seem always to have been a hunger in all of us, a need to behold in quasi-religious wonder our mysteriously anomalous brothers and sisters. For a long time, this need was satisfied in Courts for the privileged few, at fairs and sideshows for the general populace, by collecting and exhibiting Giants, Dwarfs, Intersexes, Joined Twins, Fat Ladies, and Living Skeletons. Consequently, even in a world that grew ever more secular and rational, we could still continue to be baffled, horrified, and moved by Freaks, as we were able to be by fewer and fewer other things once considered most

---

[3] Fellini's *Satyricon*: Federico Fellini (1920–1993) was an Italian film director known for bizarre and colorful films, including *Satyricon* (1969).

sacred and terrifying. Finally though, the Sideshow began to die, even as the rulers of the world learned to be ashamed of their taste for human "curiosities." By then, however, their images had been preserved in works of art, in which their implicit meanings are made manifest.

Walk through the picture galleries of any museum in the western world and you will find side by side with the portraits of Kings and Courtesans depictions of the Freaks they once kept to amuse them, by painters as distinguished as Goya and Velasquez. Nor has the practice died out in more recent times, carried on by artists as different as Currier and Ives (who immortalized such stars of P. T. Barnum's sideshow as General Tom Thumb) and Pablo Picasso (who once spent more than a year painting over and over in ever shifting perspectives the dwarfs who first appeared in Velasquez's *Las Meninas*). Nor did other popular forms of representation abandon that intriguing subject. Not only have photographers captured on film the freaks of their time, but after a while they were portrayed in fiction as well. No sooner, in fact, had the novel been invented, than it too began to portray the monstrous and malformed as objects of pity and fear and—however secularized—wonder, always wonder. Some authors of the nineteenth century, indeed, seem so freak-haunted that remembering them, we remember first of all the monsters they created. We can scarcely think of Victor Hugo, for instance, without recalling his grotesque Hunchback of Notre Dame, any more than we can recall Charles Dickens without thinking of his monstrous dwarf, Quilp, or our own Mark Twain without remembering "Those Incredible Twins." And the tradition has been continued by postmodernists like John Barth and Donald Barthelme and Vladimir Nabokov, who, turning their backs on almost all the other trappings of the conventional novel, still reflect its obsession with Freaks.

In the twentieth century, the images of congenital malformations are, 10 as we might expect, chiefly preserved in the artform it invented, the cinema: on the one hand, in Art Films intended for a select audience of connoisseurs, like the surreal fantasies of Fellini and Ingmar Bergman; and on the other, in a series of popular movies from Todd Browning's thirties' masterpiece, *Freaks*, to the more recent *Elephant Man*, in its various versions. Browning's extraordinary film was by no means an immediate success; in fact, it horrified its earliest audience and first critics, who drove it from the screen and its director into early retirement. But it was revived in the sixties and has since continued to be replayed all over the world, particularly in colleges and universities. And this seems especially appropriate, since in the course of filming his fable of the Freaks' revenge on their "normal" exploiters, Browning gathered together the largest collection of showfreaks ever assembled in a single place: an immortal Super-Sideshow, memorializing a popular artform on the verge of disappearing along with certain congenital malformations it once "starred" (but that are now routinely "repaired"), like Siamese Twins.

For this reason, perhaps, we are these days particularly freak-obsessed, as attested also by the recent success of *The Elephant Man* on stage and TV and at the neighborhood movie theatre. The central fable of that parabolic tale, in which a Doctor, a Showman, the Press, and the Public contend for the soul of a freak, though the events on which it is based happened in Victorian times, seems especially opposite to our present ambivalent response to human abnormality, reminding us of what we now otherwise find it difficult to confess except in our REM sleep: that those wretched caricatures of our idealized body image, which at first appear to represent the absolutely "Other" (thus reassuring us who come to gape that we are "normal") are really a revelation of what in our deepest psyches we recognize as the Secret Self. After all, not only do we know that each of us is a freak to someone else; but in the depths of our unconscious (where the insecurities of childhood and adolescence never die) we seem forever freaks to ourselves.

Perhaps it is especially important for us to realize that *there are no normals,* at a moment when we are striving desperately to eliminate freaks, to normalize the world. This misguided impulse represents a third, an utterly new response to the mystery of human anomalies—made possible for the first time by modern medical technology and sophisticated laboratory techniques. Oddly enough (and to me terrifyingly), it proved possible for such experimental scientists to produce monsters long before they learned to prevent or cure them. To my mind, therefore, the whole therapeutic enterprise is haunted by the ghosts of those two-headed, three-legged, one-eyed chicks and piglets that the first scientific teratologists of the eighteenth century created and destroyed in their laboratories.

Nonetheless, I do not consider those first experimenters with genetic mutation my enemies, for all their deliberate profanation of a mystery dear to the hearts of the artists with whom I identify. Nor would I be presumptuous, heartless enough to argue—on esthetic or even moral grounds— that congenital malformations under no circumstances be "repaired," or if need be, denied birth, to spare suffering to themselves or others. I am, however, deeply ambivalent on this score for various reasons, some of which I have already made clear, and others of which I will now try to elucidate. I simply do not assume (indeed, the burden of evidence indicates the contrary) that being born a freak is per se an unendurable fate. As I learned reading scores of biographies of such creatures in the course of writing my book about them, the most grotesque among them have managed to live lives neither notably worse nor better than that of most humans. They have managed to support themselves at work which they enjoyed (including displaying themselves to the public); they have loved and been loved, married and begot children—sometimes in their own images, sometimes not.

More often than not, they have survived and coped; sometimes, indeed, with special pride and satisfaction because of their presumed "handicaps," which not a few of them have resisted attempts to "cure." Dwarfs in particular have joined together to fight for their "rights," one of which they consider to be *not* having their size brought up by chemotherapy and endocrine injections to a height we others call "normal," but that they refer to, less honorifically, as "average." And I must say I sympathize with their stand, insofar as the war against "abnormality" implies a dangerous kind of politics, which beginning with a fear of difference, eventuates in a tyranny of the Normal. That tyranny, moreover, is sustained by creating in those outside the Norm shame and self-hatred—particularly if they happen to suffer from those "deformities" (which are still the vast majority) that we cannot prevent or cure.

Reflecting on these matters, I cannot help remembering not only the 15 plight of the Jews and Blacks under Hitler but the situation of the same ethnic groups—more pathetic-comic than tragic, but deplorable all the same—here in supposedly non-totalitarian America merely a generation or two ago. At that point, many Blacks went scurrying off to their corner pharmacy in quest of skin bleaches and hair straighteners; and Jewish women with proud semitic beaks turned to cosmetic surgeons for nose jobs. To be sure, as the example of Barbra Streisand makes clear, we have begun to deliver ourselves from the tyranny of such ethnocentric Norms in the last decades of the twentieth century; so that looking Niggerish or Kike-ish no longer seems as freakish as it once did, and the children of "lesser breeds" no longer eat their hearts out because they do not look like Dick and Jane, the WASP-lets portrayed in their Primers.

But the Cult of Slimness, that aberration of Anglo-Saxon taste (no African or Slav or Mediterranean ever believed in his homeland that "no one can be too rich or too thin") still prevails. And joined with the Cult of Eternal Youth, it has driven a population growing ever older and fatter to absurd excesses of jogging, dieting, and popping amphetamines—or removing with the aid of plastic surgery those stigmata of time and experience once considered worthy of reverence. Nor do things stop there; since the skills of the surgeon are now capable of recreating our bodies in whatever shape whim and fashion may decree as esthetically or sexually desirable: large breasts and buttocks at one moment, meagre ones at another. But why *not*, after all? If in the not-so-distant future, the grosser physiological abnormalities that have for so long haunted us disappear forever—prevented, repaired, aborted, or permitted to die at birth—those of us allowed to survive by the official enforcers of the Norm will be free to become ever more homogeneously, monotonously beautiful; which is to say, supernormal, however that ideal may be defined. And who except some nostalgic poet, in love with difference for its own sake, would yearn for a world where ugliness is still possible? Is it not better to envision and work for one where all humans are at last *really* equal—physiologically as well as socially and politically?

But, alas (and this is what finally gives me pause), it is impossible for all of us to achieve this dubious democratic goal—certainly not in the context of our society as it is now and promises to remain in the foreseeable future: a place in which supernormality is to be had not for the asking but only for the buying (cosmetic surgery, after all, is not included in Medicare). What seems probable, therefore, as a score of science-fiction novels have already prophesied, is that we are approaching with alarming speed a future in which the rich and privileged will have as one more, ultimate privilege the hope of a surgically, chemically, hormonally induced and preserved normality—with the promise of immortality by organ transplant just over the horizon. And the poor (who, we are assured on good authority, we always have with us) will be our sole remaining Freaks.

THINKING AND WRITING ABOUT BODY IMAGE

QUESTIONS FOR DISCUSSION AND WRITING

1. Charles Cooley once wrote: "Our sense of ourselves . . . is formed by our imagination of the way we appear in the eyes of others. Other people are a looking glass in which we see not merely our own reflection but a judgment about the value of that reflection." Use your own experience, your research, or a combination of both to agree or disagree.

2. Jot down some of the conclusions about cosmetic surgery that you have reached after having read some or all of the selections in this unit. Use those conclusions to write one example of a claim of fact, one of a claim of value, and one of a claim of policy about cosmetic surgery. Develop one of those claims as the thesis for an essay, using one or more of the readings to support it.

3. Do the research necessary to find out what percentage of those having cosmetic surgery are men, what percentage are women, and what types of surgery are most frequent for each gender. Present the results of your research in an essay based on a claim of fact.

4. Write an essay in which you explain to what extent Croll's observations about body image and adolescents are consistent with your own observations.

5. Explain in an essay to what extent you believe Americans' views of what is attractive are shaped by television, movies, and advertisements.

6. Which of the essays in this unit do you believe makes most effective use of support? Explain.

7. Write an essay in which you explain what point Fiedler is making when he uses the term "the tyranny of the normal" and discuss whether you agree with him or not.

TOPICS FOR RESEARCH

Images of women in advertising

Anorexia nervosa

Physical education requirements in public schools

Vending machines in schools

How gender affects frequency and types of cosmetic surgery

The search for the perfect body: an addiction?

The costs of cosmetic surgery

Medical malpractice and cosmetic surgery

CHAPTER 15

Is Academic Integrity on Our College Campuses under Assault?

Consider the irony captured in the opening of a 2003 essay on academic integrity from the *New York Times*:

> "Academic cheating is a major problem and has negative results on everyone involved."
>
> So goes the first sentence of a recently composed essay on cheating in academia. To get the whole essay, though, you'll need to pay for a membership at DirectEssays.com, an Internet operation that promises access to "over 101,000 high-quality term papers and essays."[1]

Some students may have been guilty of cheating since the first school opened, but no one can deny that the Internet has made it much easier. With dozens of sites offering term papers and essays for a price, the temptation is hard to resist when pressure builds and deadlines loom. It is so much easier to cut and paste others' words and ideas together than to come up with original ones. Add to that the fact that some students have used their cell phones to text answers during exams and have hacked into computers to change their grades and those of their friends, and it seems the more we progress technologically the more we regress morally.

There are varying opinions on why students cheat and on what might be done to prevent cheating. Central to most theories, though, is the belief that the academic community in which the students live and write makes a difference as to whether or not they give in to the temptation to

---

[1] Mark Edmundson, "How Teachers Can Stop Cheaters," *New York Times*, September 9, 2003, p. A29.

buy a term paper or to download an assignment from their roommate's computer and what sort of approach to the issue of academic integrity might compel them to say no. Are students less likely to cheat on a campus that has an honor code? Are they willing to sign an honor code that requires them to turn in any other student observed cheating? And what about the mixed message sent to students on those campuses that require an honor code yet also submit those same students' papers to an online plagiarism detection service?

Term papers and essays are not all that is being downloaded on our college campuses. Students download so much illegal music that universities in some cases are being criticized for allowing the activity to go unchecked. Numbers of students have settled by paying $3,000 rather than be charged with illegal downloads.

The most recent site that caters exclusively to college students is *PlayboyU*. Now they can attend parties at Hugh Hefner's Playboy Mansion — online, of course — and can enjoy all that the online universe of *Playboy* has to offer — minus the total nudity. All it takes is an .edu e-mail address, but any faculty or staff caught using the site will be blocked.

Thus the question: Is academic integrity under assault on our college campuses? Is integrity in general under assault?

Expect, but Respect, Original Work by Students

BILL WALSH

> BEFORE READING: Was cheating a common occurrence at the high school you attended? What sort of attitude did those who did not cheat have toward those who did?

P oetic justice can be sweet, like when a thief gets something stolen from him or when an anti-plagiarism company gets sued for . . . copyright infringement.

Do you remember ever copying phrases, sentences, or even whole passages from the book for some school assignment? Well, today's students do the same thing — with the Internet. Only with literally billions of Web sites out there in cyberspace, it's getting harder for teachers to see (or prove) that a student copied something or used words that were not his own.

Enter a company called Turnitin.com. They tout themselves as a "plagiarism prevention" service. Student assignments are fed into the company's Web site, and a powerful search engine compares each student paper

Bill Walsh is a columnist for the *Billerica Minute Minuteman*. The article appeared there on May 24, 2007.

with (according to the company) over 12 billion Web pages, more than 10,000 newspapers, magazines and journals, thousands of books, and in excess of 40 million student papers. The teacher and/or student gets the paper back electronically, with portions that seem to have been copied from other sources highlighted. The report presents a "similarity index" and a copy of the original material which it thinks was copied. Turnitin stresses that they do not accuse or punish students for plagiarism—that's up to the teachers and professors. Turnitin merely points out passages which seem to have a lot in common.

Actually, the service can be used in many ways. Some schools or teachers feed kids' papers into the service to detect plagiarism, and if any is found, the student fails. Other disciplinary action may follow, based on the school's rules and academic honesty policy.

Other schools (including the one where I teach) try to avoid the 5 "gotcha" approach and attempt instead to use Turnitin as a learning tool. It's the student who submits the paper and gets the report back. What follows are timely lessons and examples on proper citation, paraphrasing, and how to quote another source. The student can rewrite and resubmit the paper numerous times, fixing himself any possible plagiarism (conscious or subconscious).

Thousands of colleges, universities, and high schools subscribe to Turnitin, at about 87 cents per student per year. The company's revenue is in the tens of millions of dollars annually. Approximately 100,000 papers are submitted to the company every day. It's a very big—and successful—business.

But there's a problem, and it involves the archiving and use of student papers. Turnitin says that over half of all unoriginal work comes from students copying other kids' papers, and so it's very proud of its growing collection of papers from more than 10 million students. Each paper that a student submits is added to millions of papers Turnitin already has in its database, and against which all new papers are compared.

Students claim that the company is using their work without permission as part of its business. Adding each new paper to the company's database, the students claim, is actually infringing on the students' intellectual property, making money from it, and violating the very copyright laws Turnitin is supposed to be protecting. Students do not submit their work voluntarily they claim; they're forced to do so by their schools or teachers.

Some high school students in Virginia found a sympathetic attorney who agreed to handle their case for free. He then advised them to register the copyright of their papers ($45 each) and to explicitly tell both their teacher and Turnitin that the papers were now protected intellectual property and not to be added to Turnitin's database. When the company ignored their request, the students sued for $900,000 ($150,000 per copyright violation). *Time* magazine reports that the case will probably go to court this fall.

For their part, Turnitin has engaged its own attorneys, who have re- 10 portedly examined copyright law and contend that the kids have no case.

Computers and the Internet have certainly revolutionized writing in general and research in particular. To get the facts for just this column, for instance, I checked dozens of Web sites, downloaded news stories, and read Turnitin's own promotional literature—right here in my den.

All new technology has its price, and the ease of plagiarism is one of the prices we pay for the wealth of information at our fingertips through the Internet. And while one company has tried to use that same wealth of information and computer technology to catch those who would steal it, they in turn have been accused of violating the very precepts they say they're protecting.

Some lawyers say that the students have an excellent chance of prevailing in their lawsuit.

Sometimes there are no easy answers, no computer-driven solutions to our moral quagmires. Once again those who try to insure honesty and morality run afoul of basic tenets of right and wrong themselves.

You can't steal stuff. That's something students need to learn, but not 15 from the hands of those who expropriate student work to teach them that very important lesson.

Battling Term-Paper Cheats

JULIE RAWE

> BEFORE READING: Do you believe that faculty should submit all of their students' essays to a plagiarism detection site in order to catch any student who might have used sources without giving them credit? Explain why or why not.

Affordabletermpapers.com charges a minimum of $9.95 per page for a custom-written essay. Rush jobs cost $24.95 a page. The site, which dutifully states that its papers should be used for "assistance purposes only"—uh-huh—guarantees that customers won't run into trouble with plagiarism or they'll get their money back and a free rewrite. There are hundreds of online paper mills like this one, catering to all the stressed-out, disaffected, or just plain lazy students with Internet access and a credit card or money order. But just as the Internet has made it easier for kids to cheat, it's also helping high schools and colleges ferret out the flimflammers. Every day more than 100,000 papers are fed into Turnitin .com a plagiarism-detection site that compares each submission with billions of Web pages, tens of thousands of journals and periodicals, and a

---

Julie Rawe is a correspondent for *Time* magazine, in which this article appeared on May 17, 2007.

growing archive of some 40 million student papers. More than 7,000 educational institutions use the system, including Harvard and Oxford. But while Turnitin lets faculty level the playing field, many students—even the straight arrows—see its use as a breach of trust.

Amid startling data on the prevalence of cheating—in an undergraduate survey conducted this academic year at a dozen colleges by Rutgers professor Donald McCabe, 67% of the 13,248 respondents admitted to having cheated at least once on a paper or test—some students are getting administrators to rethink their use of gotcha tools. Nova Scotia's Mount St. Vincent University went as far as banning Turnitin after the student-union president complained that it created "a culture of mistrust, a culture of guilt."

Aside from the guilty-until-proved-innocent argument, many students are apoplectic that a for-profit entity—which charges 87¢ per student per year for plagiarism detection—is making money off their homework. As soon as a paper is vetted for cut-and-paste plagiarism, it joins a database against which every new submission will be compared. Thus, argues a recent Op-Ed in the Texas A&M newspaper, the company should have to pay to use these works, "without which their service would be crippled." Concerns about intellectual-property rights as well as cost led the University of Kansas to announce last fall that it was turning off Turnitin. Faculty protested so vehemently, however, that the school quickly signed up again.

But many teachers are torn when it comes to Turnitin. "How do you reconcile this [service] with a place that's trying to presume honor?" asks Bob Thompson, Duke University's vice provost for undergraduate education. Duke, which recently endured a cheating scandal at its business school, no longer uses Turnitin—in part because it did not like adding to the company's database—and this spring expanded its honor code by obligating students to take action if they observe or hear about cheating. "We will truly lose the battle if we think we're going to fight technology with technology," says Tim Dodd, executive director of the Duke-affiliated Center for Academic Integrity. "Kids will always be two generations ahead of us."

Meanwhile, students at a high school in McLean, Virginia, are trying 5 to bring down Turnitin by suing its parent company, iParadigms, for alleged copyright infringement. To file such a lawsuit, a writer has to pay $45 to register a copyright, be it for a Pulitzer prize–winning novel or a ninth-grader's meanderings on *Animal Farm*, and the penalty per copyright violation can be as much as $150,000. So if the McLean High School students prevail with their copyrighted essays—a trial will probably begin this fall—ambulance-chasing lawyers will start tailing school buses, and Turnitin may have to close up shop.

"We've got to come back to reality," iParadigms CEO John Barrie says of the copyright suit. "These aren't nuclear-missile secrets." Papers are being archived at the same time as testing sites install cell-phone detectors to keep students from text-messaging answers or finding them online. One result of the high-tech cheating wars: paranoia. McCabe says fewer students are filling out his anonymous surveys. "Students started accusing me of getting their IP address," he says.

But given how easy it is to pluck a term paper off the Web, it's hard to argue against using Turnitin to curb academic dishonesty. That's why some schools, including McLean, rely on both honor codes and plagiarism-detection software to keep students on the up-and-up—without seeing these methods as being at odds with each other. The Air Force Academy, which expelled 15 first-year cadets this month for cheating, takes great pride in its honor code but also checks for plagiarism. Says Joey Smith, 22, chairman of the cadets' honor committee: "It's the whole idea of trust but verify."

Which is why it would be a shame if the McLean Committee for Student Rights succeeds in dismantling Turnitin. Yes, it is important to trust students. But an equally important lesson is that cheating shouldn't be rewarded. What's so terrible about making students think long and hard when an affordable term paper is just a click away?

It Takes a Village: Academic Dishonesty and Educational Opportunity

DONALD L. McCABE

BEFORE READING: What might McCabe have been suggesting about the link between community and cheating by calling his piece "It Takes a Village"?

For the last fifteen years, I have researched questions of academic integrity. My initial interest in these questions was driven by my own experience as an undergraduate at Princeton University in the mid-1960s. Graduating from a high school where cheating was common, I was particularly intrigued by one item I received among the blizzard of forms and papers Princeton sent me as I prepared to matriculate: information about the Princeton honor code. I was informed that exams would be unproctored; that, on every exam, I would have to affirm that I had not cheated or seen anyone else cheat by signing a pledge (which I can still recite verbatim almost forty years after my graduation); and that all alleged violations of the code would be addressed by a student honor committee. Although

Donald L. McCabe is professor of management and global business at Rutgers University and founding president of the Center for Academic Integrity. His article appeared in *Liberal Education* in Summer–Fall 2005.

somewhat skeptical in light of my high school experience, I headed off to Princeton confident I would do my part to uphold this seventy-year-old tradition. Apparently, the overwhelming majority of my classmates felt the same way. During my four years at Princeton, I never observed, suspected, or heard of anyone cheating, although surely there were at least some minor transgressions of the code.

When I returned to academia after more than twenty years in the corporate world, where I witnessed firsthand the continuous erosion in the ethical values of recent college graduates, I was intrigued by the opportunity to conduct meaningful research on academic integrity. I was particularly curious to see whether campus honor codes were still a viable strategy and to explore the impact they were having on a new generation of students. While I remain a strong advocate of honor codes, my thinking about academic integrity has evolved over the last fifteen years—often in surprising ways.

The problem

In the fall of 1990, I surveyed students at thirty-one of the country's most competitive colleges and universities (McCabe and Trevino 1993). Fourteen institutions had traditional academic honor codes, and seventeen did not, having chosen instead to "control" student dishonesty through such strategies as the careful proctoring of exams. From the more than six thousand students who responded, I learned several important lessons.

The incidence of cheating was higher than I expected, and many students were quite willing to admit their transgressions. For example, 47 percent of students attending a school with no honor code reported one or more serious incidents of test or exam cheating during the past year, as did 24 percent of students at schools with honor codes. While such comparisons would seem to support the power of honor codes, it was not the code itself that was the most critical factor. Rather, the student culture that existed on campus concerning the question of academic integrity was more important. The existence of a code did not always result in lower levels of cheating. More importantly, the converse was also true: some campuses achieved high levels of integrity without an honor code. While these campuses were doing many of the same things as campuses with codes—e.g., making academic integrity a clear campus priority and placing much of the responsibility for student integrity on the students themselves—they did not use a pledge and they did not mandate unproctored exams. What was important was the culture of academic integrity to which incoming students were exposed.

Many of the students I surveyed were troubled by the failure of their 5 institution, and often its faculty, to address the issue of cheating. Because they believed that weak institutional policies and unobservant or unconcerned faculty were "allowing" others to cheat and, thereby, to gain an unfair advantage, students viewed cheating as a way to level the playing field. This was a particular problem on large campuses and in courses with large enrollments—environments where, arguably, it is harder to establish a strong, positive community culture.

In 1993 (McCabe and Trevino 1996), I surveyed nine medium to large universities that, thirty years earlier, had participated in the landmark study of college cheating conducted by William Bowers (1964). Bowers's project surveyed over five thousand students on ninety-nine campuses across the country and provided considerable insight on how often students were cheating and why. Two outcomes of my 1993 project are particularly noteworthy in comparison to Bowers's results. First, there were substantial increases in self-reported test and exam cheating at these nine schools. For example, 39 percent of students completing the 1963 survey acknowledged one or more incidents of serious test or exam cheating; by 1993, this had grown to 64 percent. Based on student responses to the 1993 survey, however, it was difficult to tell how much of this change represented an actual increase in cheating, and how much was simply a reflection of changing student attitudes about cheating. In 1993, many students simply did not see cheating as a big deal, so it was easier to acknowledge—especially in an anonymous survey.

Second, there was no change in the incidence of serious cheating on written work; 65 percent of students in 1963 acknowledged such behavior, and 66 percent did so in 1993. However, student comments in the 1993 survey suggested that this younger generation of students was more lenient in defining what constitutes plagiarism. Although survey questions were worded to ask students about a specific behavior, without labeling it as cheating, more than a trivial number of students in 1993 said they had not engaged in a particular behavior, while providing an explanation of why the instances in which they actually had done so were not cheating. The ethics of cheating is very situational for many students.

Just as technology has enabled new forms of cheating that are becoming popular with students, that same technology has made it easier to reach large numbers of students in surveys. Since 2001, I have been conducting Web-based surveys that make it possible to reach an entire campus population with relative ease. However, many students are concerned that it is easier to identify the source of electronically submitted surveys, so they elect either not to participate or to do so while being cautious about what they say. While it is hard to get people to be honest about their dishonesty in any circumstances, it is even harder to get them to do so when they are concerned about the anonymity of their responses. This is reflected in notably lower rates of self-reported cheating in Web surveys and lower levels of participation (as low as 10–15 percent on average compared to 25–35 percent for written surveys in this project).

Nonetheless, in these Web surveys of over forty thousand undergraduates on sixty-eight campuses in the United States and Canada, conducted over the last two academic years, 21 percent of respondents have acknowledged at least one incident of serious test or exam cheating, and 51 percent have acknowledged at least one incident of serious cheating on written work. Although most had engaged in other cheating behaviors as well, four out of every five students who reported they had cheated on a written assignment acknowledged that they had engaged in some form of Internet-related cheating—either cut-and-paste plagiarism from Internet sources or submitting a paper downloaded or purchased from a term-paper mill or Web site. Although the self-reported rates of cheating found in these Web surveys are lower than in earlier surveys, they clearly are still of concern. In addition, the difference may relate more to research methodology than to any real change.

Of concern to whom?

Each campus constituency tends to shift the "blame" for cheating else-   10
where. This is a major problem. Many students argue, with some justification, that campus integrity policies are ill-defined, outdated, biased against students, and rarely discussed by faculty. They also fault faculty who look the other way in the face of obvious cheating. They are even more critical of faculty who, taking "the law" into their own hands when they suspect cheating, punish students without affording them their "rights" under the campus integrity policy. Many faculty believe that these campus policies are overly bureaucratic and legalistic and that they often find "guilty" students innocent. Some faculty argue that they are paid to be teachers, not police, and that, if students have not learned the difference between right and wrong by the time they get to college, it's not their job to teach them—especially in a publish-or-perish world. Although the evidence suggests otherwise, many also believe it's too late to change student behavior at this point.

Faculty also complain about administrators who fail to support them in the face of what they perceive as obvious cases of cheating. They complain about administrators who, at least in the minds of some faculty, are more concerned with whether the student is a star athlete, the child of a major donor, or has achieved some other favored status. Of course, many administrators can detail a litany of the ways in which they think faculty shirk their responsibilities in the area of academic integrity. Still others complain that students are only concerned with grades; how they obtain those grades is less important for many.

The most appropriate response to student cheating depends in large part on the goals of the institution. If the primary goal is simply to reduce cheating, then there are a variety of strategies to consider, including increased proctoring, encouraging faculty to use multiple versions of exams and not to recycle old tests and exams, aggressively using plagiarism detection software, and employing stronger sanctions to punish offenders. But while such strategies are likely to reduce cheating, I can't imagine many people would want to learn in such an environment. As educators, we owe our students more than this, especially when cheating may reflect cynicism about what they perceive as eroding moral standards in the academy and in society.

Today's students seem to be less concerned with what administrators and/or faculty consider appropriate behavior and much more concerned with the views and behavior of their peers. Students do expect to hear the president, the provost, a dean, or some other official tell them during orientation how they are about to become academic "adults," adults who respect the learning process and who, among other things, don't cheat. And many students want to hear this message. But it's clear from student comments in my surveys that the real "proof" for students is in the behavior of their peers and the faculty. Regardless of the campus integrity policy, if students see others cheating, and faculty who fail to see it or choose to ignore it, they are likely to conclude that cheating is necessary to remain competitive. Many students ask, "If faculty members aren't concerned about cheating, why should I be?"

It takes a village

I have always been intrigued by the African tribal maxim that it takes a village to raise a child. In a similar sense, I would argue it takes the whole campus community—students, faculty, and administrators—to effectively educate a student. If our only goal is to reduce cheating, there are far simpler strategies we can employ, as I have suggested earlier. But if we have the courage to set our sights higher, and strive to achieve the goals of a liberal education, the challenge is much greater. Among other things, it is a challenge to develop students who accept responsibility for the ethical consequences of their ideas and actions. Our goal should not simply be to reduce cheating; rather, our goal should be to find innovative and creative ways to use academic integrity as a building block in our efforts to develop more responsible students and, ultimately, more responsible citizens. Our campuses must become places where the entire "village"— the community of students, faculty, and administrators—actively works together to achieve this goal. As Ernest Boyer observed almost two decades ago (Boyer 1987,184), "integrity cannot be divided. If high standards of conduct are expected of students, colleges must have impeccable integrity themselves. Otherwise the lessons of the 'hidden curriculum' will shape the undergraduate experience. Colleges teach values to students by the standards they set for themselves."

In setting standards, faculty have a particularly important role to play; 15 students look to them for guidance in academic matters—not just to their peers. In particular, to help students appropriately orient themselves and develop an appropriate mental framework as they try to make sense of their college experience, faculty must recognize and affirm academic integrity as a core institutional value. Without such guidance, cheating makes sense for many students as they fall back on strategies they used in high school to negotiate heavy work loads and to achieve good grades.

One of the most important ways faculty can help is by clarifying their expectations for appropriate behavior in their courses. Although faculty certainly have the primary responsibility here, they should share this responsibility with students. Not only does such "consultation" result in policies in which students feel a greater degree of ownership and responsibility, but it also helps to convince students they truly are partners in their own education. Nonetheless, faculty do have a unique and primary role to play in the classroom, and it is incumbent upon them not only to minimize opportunities to engage in academic dishonesty (even if only out of fairness to honest students) but also to respond in some way when cheating is suspected. While some may argue over the most appropriate response, it is essential that there be some response. As noted earlier, students suggest that faculty who do nothing about what appears to be obvious cheating simply invite more of the same from an ever-increasing number of students who feel they are being "cheated" by such faculty reluctance.

While faculty can do much to improve the climate of academic integrity in their campus "villages," they should not be expected to shoulder this burden alone. University administrators need to look more carefully at the role they play. The Center for Academic Integrity at Duke has encouraged, and helped, many campuses to examine their academic integrity policies, yet there are still many schools that have not reviewed their policies in decades. Instead of reacting to an increasing number of faculty complaints about Internet plagiarism by simply subscribing to a plagiarism detection service, for example, perhaps these schools should take a more comprehensive look at their integrity policies. While some may decide that plagiarism detection software is an appropriate component of their integrity policy, I trust many more will conclude that it's time to abandon their almost exclusive reliance on deterrence and punishment and to look at the issue of academic dishonesty as an educational opportunity as well.

Over the last fifteen years, I have become convinced that a primary reliance on deterrence is unreasonable and that, if we truly believe in our role as educators, we would do better to view most instances of cheating as educational opportunities. While strong sanctions clearly are appropriate for more serious forms of cheating, it's also clear that most student cheating is far less egregious. What, for example, is an appropriate sanction for a student who cuts and pastes a few sentences from a Web site on the Internet without citation? In some cases, this behavior occurs out of ignorance of the rules of citation or is motivated by a student's failure to properly budget his or her time. In a last minute effort to complete the two papers s/he has due that week, as well as study for a test on Friday, s/he panics. If the student is a first-time "offender," what's the educational value of a strong sanction?

Having decided that sanctions do little more than to permanently mar a student's record, an increasing number of schools are taking a more educational approach to academic dishonesty. They are striving to implement strategies that will help offending students understand the ethical consequences of their behavior. These strategies seem often to be win-win situations. Faculty are more willing to report suspected cheating, or to address it themselves, when they understand that educational rather than punitive sanctions are likely to result. A common choice now is to do nothing or to punish the student privately, which makes it almost impossible to identify repeat offenders. On a growing number of campuses, however, faculty are being encouraged to address issues of cheating directly with students. As long as the student acknowledges the cheating and accepts the faculty member's proposed remedy, the faculty member simply sends a notation to a designated party and never gets involved with what many consider the unnecessary bureaucracy and legalisms of campus judicial systems.

When more faculty take such actions, students who cheat sense they 20 are more likely to be caught, and the overall level of cheating on campus is likely to decline. Administrators, especially student and judicial affairs personnel, can then devote more of their time and resources to proactive strategies. For example, several schools have developed mini-courses that are commonly part of the sanction given to first-time violators of campus integrity policies; others have devoted resources to promoting integrity on campus, rather than investing further in detection and punishment strategies. A common outcome on campuses implementing such strategies is a greater willingness on the part of faculty to report suspected cheating. They view sanctions as more reasonable, designed to change behavior in positive ways, demonstrating to students that inappropriate behavior does have ethical consequences. As students quickly learn that second offenses will be dealt with much more strongly, increased reporting also serves as an effective deterrent to continued cheating.

Of course, the most effective solution to student cheating is likely to vary from campus to campus, depending on the unique campus culture that has developed over the course of a school's history. Indeed, no campus is likely to reach the ideal state where the proactive strategies I have described are sufficient in and of themselves. Rather, some balance of punishment and proactive strategies will be optimal on each campus and, although that optimum will vary from campus to campus, punishment will always have some role. The stakes are high for most college students today, who think their entire future—their chances of gaining admission to professional school, getting job interviews with the best companies recruiting on campus, etc.—depends on a few key grades. It is, therefore, unrealistic to think that none will succumb to the temptation to cheat.

Students, even the most ethical, want to know that offenders will be punished so that other students will be deterred from engaging in similar behaviors. In fact, I am often surprised by the comments many students offer in my surveys calling for stronger punishments for students who engage in serious cheating. While they are willing to look the other way when someone engages in more trivial forms of cheating to manage a heavy workload, for example, they are far less forgiving of students who cheat in more explicit ways on major tests or assignments. The difficult task for every school is to find the appropriate balance between punishment and proactive strategies that deters students who would otherwise cheat when the opportunity arises yet that also works to build a community of trust among students and between students and faculty, a campus community that values ethical behavior and where academic integrity is the norm.

The need to achieve some balance between punishment and proactive strategies was well summarized for me this spring when I made a presentation at the Coast Guard Academy in New London, Connecticut. A second classman who was listening to my emphasis on proactive strategies suggested that, since students see so much cheating in high school and in the larger society, deterrence probably plays an important role in reducing cheating in college. In his own case, he suggested that during his first two years at the academy the biggest factor in his decision not to cheat was fear of the strong sanctions that existed and were often used. But during those two years, he was also exposed to many proactive messages about why integrity matters, especially in an occupation where the lives of so many may depend on doing one's job with integrity. He observed that he has now reached the point where he wouldn't think of cheating—no longer for fear of punishment, but because he understands the importance of integrity. However, for him, and perhaps for many other students, those strong rules helped him learn behaviors that he could later understand and value for more idealistic reasons. No campus may ever reach a truly ideal combination, but deterrence and proactive strategies both should play an important role in any academic integrity policy.

Do something

It is impossible to know whether such proposals will work on every campus. But to those campuses that have doubts about the effectiveness of such strategies, I offer the same advice I give students when they express concern about reporting peers they suspect of cheating because of the fear of reprisal or because they believe sanctions on their campus are too severe. Do something! While I'm sure there are some campuses where the modest suggestions offered here may not work as well as other possible choices, I'm even more convinced that any campus that has not reviewed its integrity policies for some time is derelict in its responsibilities to its students and likely has a degree of discontent among its faculty. Perhaps even more important, it is depriving its students of an important learning opportunity in the true liberal arts tradition.

REFERENCES

Bowers, W. J. 1964. Student dishonesty and its control in college. New York: Bureau of Applied Social Research, Columbia University.
Boyer, E. L. 1987, *College: The undergraduate experience in America*. New York: Harper & Row.

McCabe, D. L., and L. K. Trevino. 1996. What we know about cheating in college: Longitudinal trends and recent developments. Change 28, 28–33.

_____. 1993. Academic dishonesty: Honor codes and other contextual influences. Journal of Higher Education 64, 522–38.

Bulletproof Assessment, War Stories, and Tactics: Avoiding Cybercheating

SUSAN STONEY AND MARK McMAHON

BEFORE READING: What are some ways that college faculty might fight against plagiarism?

Cybercheating

The advent of the Internet has brought academics a surfeit of information, broadened their research, and generally improved the accessibility of courses. However, it has also increased the opportunities for students to cheat by various means. Cybercheating has become so prevalent in Australian universities that the Federal Education Minister, Dr. Brendan Nelson, has stated that the higher education industry is at risk (ABC, 2003).

Cybercheating covers a wide range of academic misconduct, from cutting and pasting from the Web, to buying papers from papermills and even eBay. This "Napsterization" of knowledge (Boynton, 2001) is an inevitable outcome of the e-society in which we live. Students are so used to finding anything they want from the Internet, from music and movies to product information, that they automatically turn to this source when asked to produce an assignment, and believe that information on the Internet is free for appropriation as they wish (Stoney & Stoney, 2001). There are myriad statistics on the prevalence of cybercheating in its various forms. In 2002 it was estimated that up to 14% of Australian university students were plagiarizing from the Web (Foster, 2002b), and a review of the statistics collected by www.plagiarism.org shows that almost 80% of students admit to cheating at least once, with 12% of students reporting themselves as serial cheaters. University of California–Berkley officials believe that cheating has increased an estimated 744% from 1993 to 1997 (Overbeck, 2000). This, of course, coincides with the advent of the Internet into common usage in Universities. Interestingly, www.plagiarism.org reports that 90% of students believe that cheaters are never caught, or if they are, are not appropriately

Susan Stoney is a member of the Faculty of Business and Law at Edith Cowan University in Perth, Australia, and Mark McMahon is a lecturer in Interactive Multimedia and coordinator of the Digital Media program there. The paper was presented at the Twenty-first Australian Society for Computers in Learning in Tertiary Education conference in 2004.

disciplined. Furthermore, a survey conducted by Aaron and Georgia (1994) cited in (Bricault, 1998), shows that university student affairs officers believe that the problem of cheating has not been addressed adequately.

These statistics show that cybercheating is endemic in Universities around the world, and that academics and administrators have to wage a war to both stop and prevent such cheating. When students are caught cheating, they can become litigious. A recent case at the University of Kent has highlighted this when a student, who plagiarized in his third year of study and was excluded from his course, is now suing the university for not catching him sooner. The student admits to downloading information from the Internet, but claims that he did not realize there was a problem as it was not detected earlier in his course. The student is demanding a refund of his course fees as he cannot complete the course in which he was enrolled (Sherriff, 2004).

There have also been cases where students failed for plagiarizing have had their marks reinstated. A large Australian university was recently embroiled in such an incident where 15 students received pass marks when they had previously failed. The incident was referred to the NSW Independent Commission against Corruption, with the university claiming that there had been a misunderstanding of their policy (ABC, 2003).

In such a climate, the issue of plagiarism can rightly be described as a 5 battleground, where a war is waged between students and institutions, and played out using all of the means afforded by contemporary digital technologies. In this contemporary scenario, three main strategies dominate. The war can be fought through intelligence, where knowledge afforded by Internet technologies is the primary weapon. This war is also a propaganda war, as policies and litigation compete for supremacy. Finally this paper argues that the best offense is good defense—bulletproof approaches need to be developed to protect against the onslaught of cybercheating.

Fighting with intelligence

Since the cold war, intelligence has been one of the primary tools for war. However, as recent events have shown, decisions made on the basis of intelligence are only as good as the availability, accuracy, and ability to use the intelligence itself.

One of the major intelligence tools for plagiarism in the digital age is the World Wide Web. It is an easy task for the educator to use a web search engine with a sample of a student's work to identify whether it already exists on the web. This is probably the most common strategy used by educators to "trap" plagiarized work. However, when the enemy has the same access to the intelligence that you do, you can end up in a war of digital "brinkmanship" with each party trying to outplay the other.

One tool provided to institutions is a web based repository of copyright materials that can be used as a benchmark to check students' work. One example of this is Turnitin.com (http://www.turnitin.com/). This self proclaimed "standard in on-line plagiarism prevention" (Turnitin.com, 2004) contains a database of existing publications from a variety of sources. Each time a subscriber submits an article to check for plagiarism that article is added to the database. Plagiarism.org reports that 30% of a large sampling of Berkeley students were caught plagiarizing directly from the Internet when their assignments were run through a Turnitin.com test (http://www.plagiarism.org/).

While an effective digital solution on some levels, the Turnitin approach raises a number of issues. Firstly, its database, while large, is still limited. Secondly, the automatic storage of articles raises its own intellectual property issues, as student work is being "published" to the database, often without their permission (Foster, 2002a). An interesting weakness of this type of software has been highlighted by (Dehnart, 1999) who ran his own thesis through a plagiarism testing service and was told that it was plagiarized. After an examination of the detailed analysis, he found that the company had found a copy of his thesis online and was comparing the two. The worrying aspect of this is that a busy academic may not examine the detailed analysis to pick up such anomalies, and graduate students, in particular, may be falsely accused of plagiarism.

Another issue, that of whether it is ethically appropriate for students 10 to be forcefully contributing to the value of an external commercial entity, is yet to be resolved.

Such approaches are also only useful where plagiarized content takes the form of written articles. In technology based courses, the work may take the form of a digital graphic, audio, animation, or computer software product. Solutions to identify plagiarism in these newer digital forms are not so well developed.

It is here where the student has the intelligence advantage. Firstly, they have access to the same digital resources as their lecturers, which already levels the battlefield. Secondly, they are usually much more adept at using digital technologies to source information. In being able to source a broader variety of copyright material than the lecturer may be able to access they can often remain undetected. Add to that the now instant availability of services that offer to complete university assessments for you, and the problem appears insurmountable. These on-line "paper mills" offer expertise in many areas and provide written work that is often unique and undetectable by plagiarism software.

War story: When intelligence fails

Although lecturers may be highly skilled in their areas of expertise, they may lack the digital "savvy" to identify cybercheating. One lecturer describes how he got lucky: I was running a unit in 3 Dimensional Modeling and Animation. One of the assignments was for students to create a 3D model from a physical toy and create several rendered images of their toy in different settings. On the whole the assignment was completed quite well.

It was only several weeks later when I was browsing one of the 3D web communities that I noticed a forum post by a guy, "Count Zero," who claimed to have produced a toy in 3D and asking for feedback. I downloaded the files and was amazed to see a 3D scene containing a fully realized toy as well as 6 rendered images that were instantly recognizable as an assignment submitted by one of my students.

I e-mailed "Count Zero" and found out that he was not my student, but had received a request from someone on a different community asking for help with modeling a toy. He directed me to the original community and thread. When I got there I was stunned to see a post by my student requesting help and submitting scanned photos of his toy. Count Zero, being the community minded 3D artist that he was, had gone to the extent of completing the toy for the student and posting the files to the forum.

15

I was fuming. The whole time, my student had claimed this was all his own work, didn't provide any reference to the forum, and hadn't even bothered to re-render or modify the work in any way. I went into the files for both my student and Locust and found that they were exactly the same right down to the smallest polygon.

If it wasn't for the fact that I'm a 3D nut and was a regular lurker on the 3D communites I'd never have caught him! (Extract from interview with Seamus.)

Fighting with propaganda

In *Manufacturing Consent*, Noam Chomsky (1988) argued the intrinsicness of propaganda to democracy. When you cannot control people's actions directly, you have to control the way people think. While directed primarily at the media, universities, too, rely on propaganda as their primary tool of control. In the university system, we call it "education" but while we try to phrase our policies in terms of student centered and constructivist principles, the fact remains that universities are large institutions that communicate ideas in value laden ways:

> Universities . . . are not independent institutions. There may be independent people scattered around in them but that is true of the media as well. And it's generally true of corporations. It's true of Fascist states, for that matter. But the institution itself is parasitic. It's dependent on outside sources of support and those sources of support, such as private wealth, big corporations with grants, and the government (which is so closely interlinked with corporate power you can barely distinguish them). (Chomsky, 1997)

A section of one large university's strategic plan includes the notion of "professionalism," which is described as "demonstrating the highest standard of professional behavior in relationships with students, staff, and the community."

While professionalism is a somewhat loose depiction of the university's traditional roles, the equal emphasis placed upon seeking new markets and a view of the student as a customer, makes it difficult to argue against the contention that rather than educating students, universities are now in the business of trading in degrees. This raises concerns with regard to the relationship between universities and students over issues such as plagiarism.

Most universities have policies and procedures that are designed to 20 ensure the student is aware of his or her responsibilities regarding plagiarism. This "propaganda" model seeks to ensure compliance through education. It is a "carrot and stick" approach to communication.

The carrot is offered in the form of activities and assessments that are designed to teach students about the dangers of plagiarism. Forms that these can take include:

- Providing plagiarism information at orientation sessions.

- Providing courses in referencing and study skills.

- Incorporating the "Intelligence Model" by using tools such as "www.turnitin.com" as a means of educating students about what plagiarism is.

- Incorporating the notion of "honor" as part of the university ethos. (Boynton, 2001)

The stick comes in the form of procedures designed to regulate over transgressions of the plagiarism policy. Students attach assignment cover sheets to their work that require them to sign off on it being free of plagiarism. Some courses have students agree to terms and conditions before submitting electronic assignments. There are also warnings about penalties defined for transgressions permanently available from the student home page.

But the student is your customer and isn't the customer always right? When concerns over issues such as plagiarism are balanced with competing market driven concerns, propaganda starts to become an increasingly ineffectual weapon. After all, threats and persuasion can only do so much.

War story: Negotiating lies

Although Universities have policies that require staff to make every effort to detect plagiarism, there are many staff who believe that it is simply not worth the effort. The following extract from a staff interview highlights some of these issues:

> My story involves a postgraduate student ("Edwin") who was working on a major paper. He was able to pick his own topic, but it had to revolve around a particular theme.
>
> When the paper was submitted to me, I was immediately suspicious due to the fact that it talked about a study, which was not described in the paper, and the fact that the paper did not hang together. I decided to "Google" sections of the paper to see whether any of it had been plagiarized.
>
> I found every part of the paper, which had been "mosaiced" together from 6 websites. None of these websites were cited in the paper, all the

cited references being those from the original papers from which this one had been drawn.

I immediately notified the administration of the plagiarism, and Edwin was advised that he had failed the paper (and the unit), and he was supplied with the evidence. I checked some of the work he had done prior to this, and found that he had used some of this same material in another paper without it being recognized as plagiarism, although he failed this unit as well. Because he had failed these units, he automatically failed his course. He finished up suing the University for breach of contract. In the end the University refunded his fees with interest. He was also allowed back to the University to finish his course. This has left me feeling powerless, and makes me wonder why I would bother to spend time and effort checking to see whether students are doing the right thing. I also feel for the students who do put in the effort as they finish up with an identical degree to the ones who are academically dishonest. (Extract from interview with Amelia.)

Fighting with armor

A study by two faculty members from Harvard University and University of Illinois has shown that it is almost impossible to deter students from plagiarizing through warnings, instead they found that demonstrating to students the efficacy of plagiarizing detection algorithms had a far greater effect (Braumoeller & Gains, 2001), although they do discuss the intellectual property issues outlined earlier in this paper.

This is the failure of propaganda and intelligence approaches. Their ultimate reliance on counteractive measures or a misplaced faith in the intentions of others weakens their value as tactics. If education fails, then an ineffectual counter strike is going to do little to alter the course of the war. What this paper proposes is a pre-emptive measure referred to [as] bulletproof assessment. By building assessment items that are armored against the possibility of cybercheating, the war itself may be averted. This does not mean that propaganda and intelligence do not have their place; rather they need to be combined with a clear battle strategy to prevent the opportunity of plagiarism in the first place.

Such measures can be built into course outlines before the semester begins. Forms of armor can include:

- Giving the students the resources yourself and requiring them to use only those. Thus students may not be engaging heavily in research but still need to synthesize information in their own ways.

- Getting the students to provide the resources as part of their assessment. Making students provide the original artifacts, such as photocopies of articles, and printouts of web pages brings the intelligence battle down to a level field. Lecturers can easily crosscheck assignments against the references used.

- Making assignments highly contemporary. There are several approaches here. Students can be required to provide very up to date references, which immediately outdates paper mill products, or they can be required to contextualize their responses to an up to date medium. An example of this is where students respond to a provided news or journal article using their research as a basis for this response, but requiring them to transform their understandings to critique a specific product.

- Setting a series of developmental steps for the paper. Students then are required to respond to formative feedback; they may need to provide oral reports justifying a position and explaining the terms they have used.

None of these approaches is an instant fix to the problem of cybercheating. Oral reporting can be time consuming, for example, and the affordances of digital technologies in accessing up to date information place constraints upon the tactic of contemporizing assignments. To be fully effective, bulletproof assessments require multiple layers of armor and may still involve tactics aligned to intelligence and propaganda. With information being so easily shared through synchronous communication technologies, cyber "copying" between students is endemic in large units of study, where duplicate assignments are hard to distinguish. Using tools such as turnitin.com combined with assessment strategies that ensure submissions are up to date, adapted to a specific and unique context, and involve formative verification such as staged submission, and oral reporting, many of the current examples of cybercheating can be beaten.

Best of all, bulletproof assessment can make students better learners. Students engage in a process that requires multiple forms of evidence, and a reflection on their performance. A final layer of armor may be the requirement of a metalearning essay where students write an overview of their paper or product, explaining how they went about writing it, describing major obstacles and issues, and outlining what they learned (Harris, 2002). Such self monitoring activities can involve connecting new information to former knowledge, selecting thinking strategies deliberately, and planning, monitoring, and evaluating thinking processes, and are associated with the promotion of student metacognitive skills (Nelson & Narens, 1994).

The war against plagiarism is an on-going one. Digital technologies 30 make it an evolving battle of shifting powers and political intrigue, in which maintaining the edge in knowledge and policy is a continual struggle. The best approach is to combine these with preventative tactics that effectively armor you against the possibility of cybercheating. Bulletproof assessment is the ultimate aim, where the very possibility of plagiarism is limited, and where the inherent limitations of waging the war with propaganda and intelligence are overcome.

REFERENCES

Chomsky, N. (1997). What makes mainstream media mainstream. *Z Magazine, October.* [verified 26 Oct. 2004] http://www.chomsky.info/articles/19ff710—.htm

Chomsky, N. & Herman, E. S. (1988). *Manufacturing Consent.* Pantheon Books.

ABC (2003). *Watchdog to probe uni plagiarism scandal.* Sunday, 3 August. [23 Jun. 2004, verified 26 Oct. 2004] http://www.abc.net.au/newcastle/news/200308/s916119.htm

Boynton, R. (2001). *Is honor up for grabs? Education isn't about surveillance.* Washington Post, 27 May. [verified 26 Oct. 2004] http://www.washingtonpost.com/ac2/wp-dyn/A80312-2001May26?language=printer

Braumoeller, B. F. & Gains, B. J. (2001). Actions do speak louder than words: Deterring plagiarism with the use of plagiarism detection software. *PS: Political Science and Politics,* 34(4, Dec.), [verified 26 Oct. 2004] http://www.apsanet.org/PS/dec01/braumoeller.cfm

Bricault, D. (1998). *Legal Aspects of Academic Dishonesty: Policies, Perceptions, and Realities.* [2 Jul. 2004, verified 26 Oct. 2004] http://campus.northpark.edu/esl/dishnst.html#legal

Dehnart, A. (1999). The Web's plagiarism police. *Salon Technology.* [4 Jun. 2004, verified 26 Oct. 2004] http://www.salon.com/tech/feature/1999/06/14/plagiarism/

Foster, A. L. (2002a). Plagiarism-detection tool creates legal quandary. *The Chronicle of Higher Education,* 48(36). [verified 26 Oct. 2004] http://chronicle.com/free/v48/i36/36a03701.htm

Foster, A. L. (2002b). Up to 14% of Australian university students may be plagiarising from web, study suggests. *The Chronicle of Higher Education,* 20 November [verified 26 Oct. 2004] http://chronicle.com/free/2002/11/2002112001t.htm

Harris, R. (2002). Anti-plagiarism strategies for research papers. *VirtualSalt.* [verified 26 Oct. 2004] http://www.virtualsalt.com/antiplag.htm

Nelson, T. O. & Narens, L. (1994). The role of metacognition in problem solving. In J. Metcalfe & A. Shiminura (Eds), *Metacognition* (pp. 207–226). Cambridge: MIT Press.

Overbeck, B. K. (2000). *Plagiarism statistics.* [23 Jun. 2004, verified 26 Oct. 2004] http://iml.jou.ufl.edu/projects/Spring2000/Overbeck/stats.html

Plagiarism.org (n.d.). http://www.plagiarism.org/

Seamus. (2004). Interview on plagiarism. By M. McMahon. Perth.

Sherriff, L. (2004). Web-cheat student to sue university. *The Register,* 28 May.

Stoney, M. & Stoney, S. (2001). Copyright law for using the Internet in Teaching and Learning. Paper presented at the *8th International Conference on Information & Literacy,* Spetses, Greece.

Turnitin.com (2004). *Turnitin.* http://www.turnitin.com/

Universities Strike Back in Battle over Illegal Downloads

AMY BRITTAIN

BEFORE READING: Why do you think college students will steal music by downloading it from the Internet when they would not think of stealing a CD from a music store?

In addition to paying hefty tuition and footing the bill for costly textbooks, university students may also need to pay prominent record labels a chunk of change if they choose to illegally download music on the Internet.

The 2006–07 academic year was an aggressive one for the Recording Industry Association of America's crackdown on illegal downloads by college students. RIAA sent three times more copyright violation notices to universities than it did the previous academic year. Hundreds of prelitigation letters offered to settle for about $3,000.

Statistics show that college students illegally obtained two-thirds of their music and accounted for 1.3 billion illegal downloads in 2006 alone — in what the RIAA estimates as millions of dollars in losses directly attributed to college students. Now, Congress is taking action and pressuring universities to tighten network security and ethical standards — even comparing digital piracy to plagiarizing term papers in an effort to change the mind-set of students and administrators. Result: Universities are getting new software, and students are getting the message.

"If you're on a college campus, that's where they're looking," says Kent State University student Dave Bachman, who in April settled for $3,000 with RIAA.

Students now have more options than ever for obtaining music legally 5 with the introduction of free or inexpensive programs that cater to the college crowd. Many universities have seen a reduction in copyright violation notices after promoting such legal programs. One such program, the Ruckus Network, reworked its format in January to provide free, legal music downloads to all US college students with a valid ".edu" e-mail address. Though it won't release hard figures, Ruckus says that since it opened the floodgates to all college students, it has experienced a 60 percent increase in users and now serves "hundreds of thousands."

The accelerating adoption of digital music has contributed to a 13 percent drop in physical music sales in 2006 (and down more than 30 percent

---

When she wrote this essay, Amy Brittain was a student in the Manship School of Mass Communication at Louisiana State University, and she has served as in-depth editor for the online edition of LSU's *Daily Reveille*. The essay was published in the online version of the *Christian Science Monitor* (www.csmonitor.com) on June 18, 2007.

from its 1999 peak) and a nearly 75 percent increase in digital sales that same year, according to RIAA year-end charts.

The online music industry has evolved dramatically since Northeastern University student Shawn "Napster" Fanning introduced a peer-to-peer (P2P) file-sharing service in 1999 known as Napster. The RIAA sued soon after, and in 2001 the Ninth Circuit Court of Appeals ruled that Napster could not facilitate the trade of copyrighted music. Napster shut down and partially settled in an agreement to pay copyright holders millions.

Since then, other services have provided free, but illegal, methods for P2P file sharing. In P2P sharing, a user establishes an account, downloads music or video files, and lets other users download his or her files in turn. The problem: Copyrighted music changes hands for free, and record labels don't get the licensing control guaranteed under 1998's Digital Millennium Copyright Act.

Many Napster copycats, including Kazaa, iMesh, BearShare, and Grokster, have settled with record labels for damages. Kazaa—once the premier P2P service, with 4.2 million users—settled in July, agreeing to copyright filters.

LimeWire is the last P2P giant standing, but several major record labels have a joint lawsuit pending to shut it down. According to the NPD Group, an entertainment research firm, LimeWire accounted for 62 percent of P2P downloads in 2006. 10

The free and easy access to P2P services has long plagued university administrators. Not only do such downloads take up a lot of "bandwidth," costing campuses thousands of dollars, the downloads themselves are more likely to contain viruses and spyware that can infest the university's system. Spyware, which can transmit a user's Web-browsing habits to advertisers, may even be bundled with P2P software—and linger after the P2P program is uninstalled.

In March, US Rep. Ric Keller (R) of Florida introduced a bill to increase funds for antipiracy.

"For every one Justin Timberlake, there are hundreds of sound technicians, back-up singers, and retail workers who are hurt by illegal downloading," Representative Keller said in a phone interview. "It costs our economy billions of dollars, thousands of jobs, and we lose a great deal of tax revenue."

An immunity clause in the Digital Millennium Copyright Act of 1998 protects universities from lawsuits related to illegal file sharing on campus networks.

But that immunity could be reconsidered, Keller says pointedly, "if we find that we continue to have a situation where over half of the college students continue to illegally download and the colleges do nothing about it." 15

Many universities are enlisting technology to deter piracy. Software programs like Audible Magic installs a campuswide filter to stop the flow of copyrighted material.

Charles Wright, an associate vice president at the University of Utah in Salt Lake City, testified to Congress that RIAA copyright violation notices to his campus declined more than 90 percent since the software was installed two years ago. The University of Florida saved hundreds of thousands of dollars in bandwidth costs after implementing Red Lambda, a program that blocks P2P systems.

While Napster, iTunes, and Rhapsody Music now have subscription-based services for the general public, Ruckus uses an ad-supported model. (A Rensselaer Polytechnic Institute student who uses Ruckus and LimeWire says Ruckus is "not very user friendly" because "there are way too many advertisements on it.")

According to Ruckus spokesman Chris Lawson, schools with Ruckus contracts get extra benefits, such as a local server that reduces bandwidth consumption, and a movie and TV library that students can subscribe to for about $15 per semester. Mr. Lawson says students from 900 universities have registered with the service, and some 120 universities have Ruckus contracts.

The music is free to students to download and play, but if a user wants 20 to transfer files to a portable music player, he or she must pay about $20 per semester. Note: Ruckus uses Microsoft Digital Rights Management software; it won't work with Apple computers or iPods.

The Top 10 campuses for illegal file downloads

The Recording Industry Association of America recently released a list of schools it says most frequently violated the Digital Millennium Copyright Act from September 2006 to mid-February 2007. The Top 10:

1. Ohio University (1,287 violations)
2. Purdue University (1,068)
3. University of Nebraska, Lincoln (1,002)
4. University of Tennessee, Knoxville (959)
5. University of South Carolina (914)
6. University of Massachusetts at Amherst (897)
7. Michigan State University (753)
8. Howard University (572)
9. North Carolina State University (550)
10. University of Wisconsin, Madison (513)

Since the list was published in February, the RIAA has noted progress:

- University of South Carolina has had no notices since the list was published.
- Ohio University received only about seven notices in May after it installed network-protection tools.

- Michigan State University has only received 14 notices.
- Howard University has gotten just three notices.

RateMyProfessors: Hidden Camera Edition

SCOTT JASCHIK

> BEFORE READING: What are the pros and cons of the relatively new ability to take pictures with cell phones?

There's a new reason to worry about students with cell phones in your classes. RateMyProfessors.com, the Web site whose popularity with students is matched by the grief it gives professors, has launched a new feature, encouraging students to shoot photographs of their faculty members and to post them along with the anonymous ratings of professors.

Think RateMyProfessors is going to ask your permission to post a photograph that you may not even know was taken (camera phones are being recommended to students)? Of course not, although RateMyProfessor asserts that it has other quality control mechanisms in place.

In the 48 hours since RateMyProfessors posted information about this new service on its site, it has received more than 1,200 photographs of professors and it is in the process of reviewing and uploading them.

"Camera phones in the classroom have a new meaning," exulted Patrick Nagle, president of the company, in a press release.

In an interview, he said that site administrators would "look into" 5 whether photographs submitted are in fact of the professors named. He said, for example, that the site would check the submitted pictures against photographs professors post of themselves online. He also said photographs that are clearly pornographic or that have been altered will not be posted. He did not indicate how the site would determine the veracity of photographs when a professor doesn't have public online photographs, but Nagle said professors could inform the site of errors.

One of the criticisms of RateMyProfessors has been that there is no way to tell if a comment is from a student angry at failing a class, a student happy about an A in a gut course—or a professor's mother.

Nagle said that the new photo feature was actually part of a plan to "give the professors a voice on our site." Professors will now be offered the chance to sign up for an RSS feed so that they can be notified whenever one of their students (or someone claiming to be) posts something about them (photographs or comments). Professors who sign up for the service

---

Scott Jaschik, former editor of the *Chronicle of Higher Education*, is now editor of *Inside Higher Ed*. This article was published online at www.insidehighered.com on November 2, 2006.

can then notify RateMyProfessors if they object to a photograph or want to replace it with a new photograph.

Such requests will "very likely" be honored, Nagle said. He declined to answer why they might not be honored.

Requests to correct inaccurate statements in student comments will probably not be honored, he said, "because students are protected by the First Amendment."

As to how this all gives professors more voice, Nagle said that the site 10 would soon be adding a blog feature for professors so they could regularly comment on comments posted about them or communicate with one another.

The new photo feature of RateMyProfessors comes at a time that many professors have already been expressing concern about having their lectures taped without their permission for posting (and mocking) on YouTube. At least one professor is already in danger of losing his job because of video posted of one of his lectures.

Will professors be happy to have their photos posted on the site? If general reaction to RateMyProfessors is any indication, that seems unlikely—and opposition won't only come from those who are camera-shy or worried about how the site will rate their "hotness" (RateMyProfessors lets students award chili peppers to hot professors and maintains a list of the 50 hottest—a disproportionate number of whom teach at Canadian colleges and universities).

Hugo Schwyzer might seem like just the kind of professor who would like RateMyProfessors. A historian at Pasadena City College, he's on the hottest list, has great ratings on RateMyProfessors, and has no hesitation about sharing life details or photographs—along with his philosophy and ruminations—online, at his blog.

Indeed Schwyzer said that he had high hopes for RateMyProfessors and thought it might provide a good source of anonymous feedback for him so he could improve his teaching. But he said that by asking students to send in photographs of professors, without a system to check first on whether the photos were taken with permission, it was clear that "the primary function is to humiliate."

Schwyzer said he's seen "the speciousness of the whole system" in re- 15 cent weeks. He offended some men's rights activists on his blog, and they responded by posting numerous critical comments on RateMyProfessors to bring down his scores. While some of those comments have been removed, Schwyzer said he witnessed "a remarkably detailed discussion of my appearance."

To the extent RateMyProfessors could have served a valuable purpose, he said, it would have been about teaching and classroom performance. The non-scientific approach to those subjects and the increasing emphasis on physical appearance take away that potential, he added. By going with the photo feature, Schwyzer said, RateMyProfessors "loses whatever shreds of legitimacy it had."

Playboy Launches Social-Networking Site

BEFORE READING: What is your initial response to the fact that *Playboy* has started a Web site specifically for college students?

Playboy is heading back to school to boost the bottom line. Riding a wave of renewed popularity among consumers around the globe, Hugh Hefner's Playboy empire is set to launch a sexy social networking site dedicated solely to college students, its latest online venture as it tries to reinvigorate its stagnant finances.

The launch of Playboy U, which has similar features to those found on Facebook, comes as Playboy's 54-year-old magazine continues to lose money and readers. To compensate, Chicago-based Playboy Enterprises Inc. (PLA) is embarking on one of its biggest expansion efforts in years. "This is one brand that is relevant to 18 through 81-year-olds," said Scott Stephen, executive vice president of operations for Playboy's entertainment division. "We're looking at this as a way to introduce and escort someone through their adult life."

Playboy has cozied up to collegians before, featuring parties, promotional events, and pictorials of student bodies from across the country. Now executives hope Playboy U will help build brand loyalty among young consumers. Backed by a hit cable TV show featuring Hefner's three girlfriends, a Sirius radio channel, and the adoration of young Hollywood stars who are again flocking to parties at the Playboy mansion, the company is trying to grow its licensing business and online presence and build an international fan base that includes a surprising legion of female fans.

Thanks in part to those initiatives, Playboy is gradually returning to profitability after years of operating in the red. Last year the company eked out a $2.3 million profit, its second-best since posting a $47.6 million loss in 2000. So far this year, Playboy has earned $5.7 million. But growth has been slow as Playboy wrestles with other struggling units, like its domestic television business that is facing increasing competition and losing favor to other video-on-demand offerings. (Playboy executives said they're working to stabilize the TV unit by offering their own on-demand lineup.)

"They definitely haven't had the blowout kind of success that you 5 would expect a big brand like Playboy to have," said Rick Munarriz, a senior analyst with the investment advisory service The Motley Fool. "The brand seems to be having some kind of renaissance around the world yet, financially speaking, it's not really contributing to the top and bottom line."

The latest statistics compiled by the Audit Bureau of Circulations show the magazine's average paid circulation has fallen to just under 2.9

This unsigned article appeared on FoxNews.com on August 24, 2007.

million readers, less than half of the 6.25 million readers who bought the magazine during its heyday in 1974. During the first six months of the fiscal year, the magazine unit lost $4.7 million, 15 percent more than it lost during the same period last year.

Playboy executives said there are no plans to eliminate the publication, even as the company turns its attention to other parts of the bunny empire that include Playboy-themed casinos, clubs, and apparel. Next month, Playboy will open its ninth retail store, stocking jeans, jewelry, T-shirts, and cosmetics.

After resurrecting its night clubs last fall with the Playboy Club at The Palms Casino in Las Vegas, the company is building "location-based entertainment venues." A 40,000-square-foot Playboy Mansion in Macau will open in late 2009 and Playboy is eyeing similar projects in London, Atlantic City, Eastern Europe, Mexico, and the Caribbean.

Executives declined to say how much they've invested in Playboy U, saying only that the effort is "sizable" and that the advertising-supported online community may ultimately bring in revenue. But when and how long that will take is anyone's guess, especially as more companies flock to compete with industry heavyweights Facebook and MySpace for the attention of fickle young people. The Web site has managed to get 2,000 members from 500 colleges during early beta tests.

"It's a very lucrative market," said Michael Kelman, senior media an-   10
alyst at Susquehanna Financial Group. "The college kids, they're going to be better-educated and have higher disposable incomes. [But] it's been a very, very tough audience to grab."

The site bars nudity but leaves little to the imagination with pictures from the mansion's "Midsummer Night's Dream" party and message topics such as "What Do You Think About Penis Enlargement" and "How Many People Have You Slept With? To Lie or Not to Lie."

The site has instituted a college-only policy, which bars anyone without an e-mail address ending in .edu from joining. And Playboy U says it will boot any university faculty, staff, or alumni or other non-students that it discovers on the site.

In many ways its format is similar to Facebook and MySpace—people choose to "friend" each other, can post videos and photos, or leave messages on a "wall." But users can also access university-specific pages that list campus events while viewing individual profiles of Playboy U members throughout the Web site.

"Your little brother can't get in. Your little sister can't get in. Nor can your mother and father," Stephen said. It's that exclusivity coupled with the Playboy cachet personified by Hefner that Adam Gibson, a 24-year-old public relations major at West Virginia University, likes most about the site.

"They do a really good job at blending in the Playboy lifestyle with   15
the student," said Gibson, who promotes the Web site to his classmates. "There's a level of exclusivity to it. And I think that keeps it cool."

THINKING AND WRITING ABOUT ACADEMIC INTEGRITY

QUESTIONS FOR DISCUSSION AND WRITING

1. Explain whether or not you believe that students should be required to sign a statement on exams indicating that they have neither received nor given help on the test.

2. What is your opinion of honor codes? What if that code includes the statement that the student will report any instances of cheating that he or she observes?

3. Walsh and Rawe express different views about the use of Turnitin.com to detect plagiarism. Which do you agree with, and why?

4. Do you agree with the students who brought a lawsuit against Turnitin.com that the company has no right to add students' essays to its database—and make money from their use—without the students' consent?

5. Explain whether or not you believe that McCabe offers a realistic solution for dealing with plagiarism.

6. Do you agree with McCabe that "it takes a village" to educate a student? Does it "take a village" to provide that student with character education, or is that something that the individual or the individual and his or her family should be responsible for?

7. How closely do McCabe's figures on the frequency of cheating match your observations?

8. Analyze Stoney and McMahon's tactics that universities can use to fight plagiarism.

9. Do any of the authors represented in this chapter present tactics that you believe would be successful in discouraging plagiarism? Can you suggest tactics that you believe would be more effective?

10. Why do you think so many college students are willing to break the law by downloading music illegally?

TOPICS FOR RESEARCH

Cheating in sports

Your school's honor code

How cheating in a relationship is defined today

Movie and music downloading

Integrity and politicians

Playboy U

CHAPTER 16

Have We Become Too Reliant on Standardized Testing?

If you attended typical American public schools—and most likely, even if you attended private ones—you arrived at college already something of an expert on standardized testing. The very fact that you are taking a college course suggests that you probably took at least one standardized test for admission. You may also have taken Advanced Placement exams and almost certainly took statewide exams required for you to graduate or for your school to receive funding. Some of you probably started taking preliminary forms of the SAT as early as seventh grade. You may have been placed in or excluded from honors or gifted programs on the basis of a test you took in second grade. As one of the authors represented here reminds us, even some preschools and kindergartens have admissions exams. Whether or not you can use scissors well at the age of three can literally shape your future.

Today more voices than ever before are arguing that our educational system has gone too far in its dependence on standardized testing. Standardized tests are above and beyond any quizzes, tests, or exams that students take in individual courses. One of the primary criticisms of standardized testing is that it ignores all of the grades and other evaluations that students get from the teachers who know them best in favor of a single test that is not necessarily linked in any clear way to a school's curriculum. But because schools depend on state and federal funding, too often the curriculum is reshaped to prepare students for the test. Those on the other side of the debate argue that there is no other way to compare students from different schools since the easy A from one school is not equivalent to the challenging B from another.

The emphasis on standardized testing only increased with the No Child Left Behind Act of 2001, signed into law on January 8, 2002, by President George W. Bush, reauthorizing the Elementary and Secondary Education Act of 1965. The goal is simple: to have every child working at grade level in math and reading by the year 2014. The solution is far from simple, as is the means of proving the "adequate yearly progress" required by the legislation. Educators and parents alike are questioning what schools are giving up in their attempt to satisfy the new requirements.

Even the most firmly established test for college admissions, the SAT, is under fire, with some states threatening to stop using it in admissions decisions at state colleges and universities. The test has long been suspected of bias against minorities, and it has little value as a tool for helping students discover what they might do differently to improve their scores and thus their chances of admission into the college of their choice.

One reason that standardized testing remains a topic ripe for argument is that no one has yet discovered a viable alternative that serves the purpose it now serves.

Why Can't We Let Boys Be Boys?

MARCIA VICKERS

> BEFORE READING: What are some of your earliest memories of taking tests? How did you feel about the tests? How did taking them make you feel?

In the fall of 2001, my husband and I were bursting with enthusiasm, anticipating our first-ever parent-teacher conference. We couldn't wait to hear glowing remarks about Christopher, our three-year-old genius. How he could sing the words from almost every Wiggles song and had been reciting the alphabet since he was a year and a half—only leaving out the occasional "t" or "y."

We eagerly walked into his classroom and sat down in midget-size wooden chairs as his two teachers brought out a long manila envelope. Then came the usual "how nice it is to have your son in our class" patter.

Not far into the discussion came the zinger. "Christopher is having a difficult time with stickers," said one teacher, holding up a sheet of green and purple dinosaurs. "What do you mean?" my husband and I asked in unison. "Well, he hasn't figured out that he needs to scratch the edge with his fingernail and lift and peel," said the teacher. It turns out, at least

---

Marcia Vickers is a writer for *BusinessWeek* magazine, where this article originally appeared on May 26, 2003.

according to his teachers, whom we genuinely liked, that he was having trouble with his fine motor skills—grasping and manipulating things with his fingers.

Looking back, the sticker incident was the precise point of liftoff into a world of which I was previously unaware: evaluations with child-development experts, the screening and eventual hiring of occupational and physical therapists (OTs and PTs), and trips to sensory gyms, which supposedly help the brain process sensory information though activities like touching different textures. Like most parents, I wanted to make sure Christopher had every possible advantage to overcome any weakness— however far-fetched it might sound. After all, we're no experts.

But some two years later, I've come to suspect the diagnosis is often 5
flawed. It turns out that it's not uncommon for young boys to have a so-called problem with fine motor skills.

In Manhattan, where we live, this phenomenon has become the status quo. One reason is that four-year-olds must score well on a standardized test to gain acceptance to the city's elite private kindergartens. This test has a section that emphasizes fine motor skills. So multitudes of young boys are in OT or PT. A cottage industry, in fact, has sprung up around it— most private OTs charge upwards of $135 per 45-minute session. There are waiting lists to get kids —mostly boys—into these therapy sessions.

All this for a simple biological fact: Boys typically develop fine motor skills up to six years later than girls. And in the early years, boys tend to be unfairly compared with girls on that score. This can have a devastating effect, say experts. If boys can't draw and color a bunny rabbit or cut simple shapes with scissors, they are subtly made to feel inferior. And a growing number of professionals believe that pressuring boys early only creates a sense of helplessness on their part. That can extend to how they feel about themselves and how they view school for many years.

Educators should be careful not to single out boys as "developmentally delayed" because they can't color in a sunflower as well as a girl. Now that a few experts are focusing on boys' learning gaps, the danger is to address the problem in the wrong way.

Some schools emphasize teaching methods that allow boys to brandish spatial mechanical skills as well as channel their energy. Says Dr. Leonard Sax, executive director of the National Association for Single-Sex Public Education: "Especially in the early years, schools should be playing to boys' strengths, such as playing games, building forts out of blocks, kicking a soccer ball, rather than emphasizing their weaknesses."

Christopher, who will soon turn five, suddenly loves writing his name 10
and drawing things from his incredibly vivid imagination, like space monsters and magic men. Last week, he wrote and illustrated a construction-paper book about a little boy whose hair turns into green beans. I think the therapy he has had has given him more confidence with crayons and scissors. But I'm not convinced he wouldn't have come around on his own.

Recently, he got one of the highest scores possible in vocabulary and general knowledge on that standardized test—though on the part that called for drawing shapes, he fell into the "average" category. Is he still our little genius? More than ever. He has even aced dinosaur stickers. Now, if only he wouldn't put the darned things on the furniture.

Standardized Testing and Its Victims

ALFIE KOHN

BEFORE READING: Speculate as to why Kohn refers to those who take standardized tests as victims.

S tandardized testing has swelled and mutated, like a creature in one of those old horror movies, to the point that it now threatens to swallow our schools whole. (Of course, on "The Late, Late Show," no one ever insists that the monster is really doing us a favor by making its victims more "accountable.") But let's put aside metaphors and even opinions for a moment so that we can review some indisputable facts on the subject.

Fact 1. Our children are tested to an extent that is unprecedented in our history and unparalleled anywhere else in the world. While previous generations of American students have had to sit through tests, never have the tests been given so frequently, and never have they played such a prominent role in schooling. The current situation is also unusual from an international perspective: Few countries use standardized tests for children below high school age—or multiple-choice tests for students of any age.

Fact 2. Noninstructional factors explain most of the variance among test scores when schools or districts are compared. A study of math results on the 1992 National Assessment of Educational Progress found that the combination of four such variables (number of parents living at home, parents' educational background, type of community, and poverty rate) accounted for a whopping 89 percent of the differences in state scores. To the best of my knowledge, all such analyses of state tests have found comparable results,

---

Alfie Kohn writes on educational and parenting issues and is an outspoken critic of standardized testing who is frequently invited to speak at professional meetings and to parent groups. His eleven books include *The Homework Myth: Why Our Kids Get Too Much Out of a Bad Thing* (2006), *Unconditional Parenting: Moving from Rewards and Punishments to Love and Reason* (2005), and, most relevant here, *The Case against Standardized Testing: Raising the Scores, Ruining the Schools* (2000). This article appeared in *Education Week* on September 27, 2000.

with the numbers varying only slightly as a function of which socioeconomic variables were considered.

Fact 3. *Norm-referenced tests were never intended to measure the quality of learning or teaching.* The Stanford, Metropolitan, and California Achievement Tests (SAT, MAT, and CAT), as well as the Iowa and Comprehensive Tests of Basic Skills (ITBS and CTBS), are designed so that only about half the test-takers will respond correctly to most items. The main objective of these tests is to rank, not to rate; to spread out the scores, not to gauge the quality of a given student or school.

Fact 4. *Standardized-test scores often measure superficial thinking.* In a study 5 published in the *Journal of Educational Psychology*, elementary school students were classified as "actively" engaged in learning if they asked questions of themselves while they read and tried to connect what they were doing to past learning; and as "superficially" engaged if they just copied down answers, guessed a lot, and skipped the hard parts. It turned out that high scores on both the CTBS and the MAT were more likely to be found among students who exhibited the superficial approach to learning. Similar findings have emerged from studies of middle school students (also using the CTBS) and high school students (using the other SAT, the college-admission exam). To be sure, there are plenty of students who think deeply and score well on tests—and plenty of students who do neither. But, as a rule, it appears that standardized-test results are positively correlated with a shallow approach to learning.

Fact 5. *Virtually all specialists condemn the practice of giving standardized tests to children younger than 8 or 9 years old.* I say "virtually" to cover myself here, but, in fact, I have yet to find a single reputable scholar in the field of early-childhood education who endorses such testing for young children.

Fact 6. *Virtually all relevant experts and organizations condemn the practice of basing important decisions, such as graduation or promotion, on the results of a single test.* The National Research Council takes this position, as do most other professional groups (such as the American Educational Research Association and the American Psychological Association), the generally pro-testing American Federation of Teachers, and even the companies that manufacture and sell the exams. Yet just such high-stakes testing is currently taking place, or scheduled to be introduced soon, in more than half the states.

Fact 7. *The time, energy, and money that are being devoted to preparing students for standardized tests have to come from somewhere.* Schools across the country are cutting back or even eliminating programs in the arts, recess for young children, electives for high schoolers, class meetings (and other activities intended to promote social and moral learning), discussions about current events (since that material will not appear on the test), the use of literature in the early grades (if the tests are focused narrowly on decoding skills), and entire subject areas such as science (if the tests cover only language arts and math). Anyone who doubts the scope and significance of what is being sacrificed in the desperate quest to raise scores has not been inside a school lately.

Fact 8. Many educators are leaving the field because of what is being done to schools in the name of "accountability" and "tougher standards." I have no hard numbers here, but there is more than enough anecdotal evidence— corroborated by administrators, teacher-educators, and other observers across the country, and supported by several state surveys that quantify the extent of disenchantment with testing—to warrant classifying this as a fact. Prospective teachers are rethinking whether they want to begin a career in which high test scores matter most, and in which they will be pressured to produce these scores. Similarly, as the *New York Times* reported in its lead story of September 3, 2000, "a growing number of schools are rudderless, struggling to replace a graying corps of principals at a time when the pressure to raise test scores and other new demands have made an already difficult job an increasingly thankless one." It also seems clear that most of the people who are quitting, or seriously thinking about doing so, are not mediocre performers who are afraid of being held accountable. Rather, they are among the very best educators, frustrated by the difficulty of doing high-quality teaching in the current climate.

Faced with inconvenient facts such as these, the leading fall-back position 10 for defenders of standardized testing runs as follows: Even if it's true that suburban schools are being dumbed down by the tests, inner-city schools are often horrendous to begin with. There, at least, standards are finally being raised as a result of high-stakes testing.

Let's assume this argument is made in good faith, rather than as a cover for pursuing a standards-and-testing agenda for other reasons. Moreover, let's immediately concede the major premise here, that low-income minority students have been badly served for years. The problem is that the cure is in many ways worse than the disease—and not only because of the preceding eight facts, which remain both stubbornly true and painfully relevant to testing in the inner city. As Sen. Paul Wellstone, D-Minn., put it in a speech delivered last spring: "Making students accountable for test scores works well on a bumper sticker, and it allows many politicians to look good by saying that they will not tolerate failure. But it represents a hollow promise. Far from improving education, high-stakes testing marks a major retreat from fairness, from accuracy, from quality, and from equity." Here's why.

The tests may be biased. For decades, critics have complained that many standardized tests are unfair because the questions require a set of knowledge and skills more likely to be possessed by children from a privileged background. The discriminatory effect is particularly pronounced with norm-referenced tests, where the imperative to spread out the scores often produces questions that tap knowledge gained outside of school. This, as W. James Popham argues, provides a powerful advantage to students whose parents are affluent and well-educated. It's more than a little ironic to rely on biased tests to "close the gap" between rich and poor.

Guess who can afford better test preparation. When the stakes rise, people seek help anywhere they can find it, and companies eager to profit from this desperation by selling test-prep materials and services have begun to appear on the scene, most recently tailoring their products to state exams. Naturally, affluent families, schools, and districts are better able to afford such products, and the most effective versions of such products, thereby exacerbating the inequity of such testing. Moreover, when poorer schools do manage to scrape together the money to buy these materials, it's often at the expense of books and other educational resources that they really need.

The quality of instruction declines most for those who have least. Standardized tests tend to measure the temporary acquisition of facts and skills, including the skill of test-taking itself, more than genuine understanding. To that extent, the fact that such tests are more likely to be used and emphasized in schools with higher percentages of minority students (a fact that has been empirically verified) predictably results in poorer-quality teaching in such schools. The use of a high-stakes strategy only underscores the preoccupation with these tests and, as a result, accelerates a reliance on direct-instruction techniques and endless practice tests. "Skills-based instruction, the type to which most children of color are subjected, tends to foster low-level uniformity and subvert academic potential," as Dorothy Strickland, an African-American professor at Rutgers University, has remarked.

Again, there's no denying that many schools serving low-income chil- 15 dren of color were second-rate to begin with. Now, however, some of these schools, in Chicago, Houston, Baltimore, and elsewhere, are arguably becoming third-rate as testing pressures lead to a more systematic use of low-level, drill-and-skill teaching, often in the context of packaged programs purchased by school districts. Thus, when someone emphasizes the importance of "higher expectations" for minority children, we might reply, "Higher expectations to do what? Bubble-in more ovals correctly on a bad test—or pursue engaging projects that promote sophisticated thinking?" The movement driven by "tougher standards," "accountability," and similar slogans arguably lowers meaningful expectations insofar as it relies on standardized testing as the primary measure of achievement. The more that poor children fill in worksheets on command (in an effort to raise their test scores), the further they fall behind affluent kids who are more likely to get lessons that help them understand ideas. If the drilling does result in higher scores, the proper response is not celebration, but outrage: The test results may well have improved at the expense of real learning.

Standards aren't the main ingredient that's in low supply. Anyone who is serious about addressing the inequities of American education would naturally want to investigate differences in available resources. A good argument could be made that the fairest allocation strategy, which is only common sense in some countries, is to provide not merely equal amounts across schools and districts, but more for the most challenging student populations. This does happen in some states—by no means all—but, even when it does, the money is commonly offered as a short-term grant (hardly sufficient to compensate for years of inadequate funding) and is often earmarked for test preparation rather than for higher-quality teaching. Worse, high-stakes testing systems may provide more money to those already successful (for example, in the form of bonuses for good scores) and less to those whose need is greatest.

Many public officials, along with like-minded journalists and other observers, are apt to minimize the matter of resources and assume that everything deficient about education for poor and minority children can be remedied by more forceful demands that we "raise the bar." The implication here would seem to be that teachers and students could be doing a better job but have, for some reason, chosen not to do so and need only be bribed or threatened into improvement. (In fact, this is the tacit assumption behind all incentive systems.) The focus among policymakers has been on standards of outcome rather than standards of opportunity.

To make matters worse, some supporters of high-stakes testing have not just ignored, but contemptuously dismissed, the relevance of barriers to achievement in certain neighborhoods. Explanations about very real obstacles such as racism, poverty, fear of crime, low teacher salaries, inadequate facilities, and language barriers are sometimes written off as mere "excuses." This is at once naive and callous, and, like any other example of minimizing the relevance of structural constraints, ultimately serves the interests of those fortunate enough not to face them.

Those allegedly being helped will be driven out. When rewards and punishments are applied to educators, those who teach low-scoring populations are the most likely to be branded as failures and may decide to leave the profession. Minority and low-income students are disproportionately affected by the incessant pressure on teachers to raise scores. But when high stakes are applied to the students themselves, there is little doubt about who is most likely to be denied diplomas as a consequence of failing an exit exam—or who will simply give up and drop out in anticipation of such an outcome. If states persist in making a student's fate rest on a single test, the likely result over the next few years will be nothing short of catastrophic. Unless we act to stop this, we will be facing a scenario that might be described without exaggeration as an educational ethnic cleansing.

Let's be charitable and assume that the ethnic aspect of this perfectly 20 predictable consequence is unintentional. Still, it is hard to deny that high-stakes testing, even when the tests aren't norm-referenced, is ultimately about sorting. Someone unfamiliar with the relevant psychological research (and with reality) might insist that raising the bar will "motivate" more students to succeed. But perform the following thought experiment:

Imagine that almost all the students in a given state met the standards and passed the tests. What would be the reaction from most politicians, businesspeople, and pundits? Would they now concede that our public schools are terrific—or would they take this result as prima facie evidence that the standards were too low and the tests were too easy? As Deborah Meier and others have observed, the phrase "high standards" by definition means standards that everyone won't be able to meet.

The tests are just the means by which this game is played. It is a game that a lot of kids—predominantly kids of color—simply cannot win. In voking these very kids to justify a top-down, heavy-handed, corporate-style, test-driven version of school reform requires a stunning degree of audacity. To take the cause of equity seriously is to work for the elimination of tracking, for more equitable funding, and for the universal implementation of more sophisticated approaches to pedagogy (as opposed to heavily scripted direct-instruction programs). But standardized testing, while bad news across the board, is especially hurtful to students who need our help the most.

Standardized Students: The Problems with Writing for Tests Instead of People

BRONWYN T. WILLIAMS

BEFORE READING: How effective do you believe the writing samples done on standardized tests are in assessing writing ability? Refer to your own experience if it is relevant.

I'm not usually a huge fan of bumper stickers, even the ones I agree with, because of the way they shout out simplistic positions on complex issues. I still remember, though, when I saw the one that read "Standardized Testing Produces Standardized Students." I smiled and nodded my head a bit in agreement. Simplistic as that phrase may be, over the years it comes back to me when I am involved in conversations about testing that seem bound in reductive and simplistic arguments about standards, rigor, and accountability. I don't use the phrase because I don't think using a bumper-sticker argument I agree with makes it superior to my opponents' bumper-sticker arguments. But I do try my best to nudge arguments about

Bronwyn T. Williams is an associate professor of English and director of composition at the University of Louisville, where his specialties are literacy, popular culture, and pedagogy. He recently edited *Identity Papers: Literacy and Power in Higher Education* (2006). This article appeared in the October 2005 issue of the *Journal of Adolescent and Adult Literacy*.

testing toward a more complex consideration of the myriad implications of the concept of standardization.

Some levels of standardization I rely on. I take great comfort that there are identifiable standards for inspecting elevators, for example. I also appreciate that most medical doctors go through some kind of standard training in human anatomy. And I believe that we teachers have a responsibility to assess whether students are learning the concepts, ideas, and ways of thinking that we believe are important and also to hold ourselves and our pedagogies accountable if we are failing to reach most of our students.

Like many of my colleagues, however, I am not convinced that literacy assessment is best achieved through standardized tests given to huge groups of students in high-stakes situations. More and more, it seems as if the point of literacy education—of all education—is becoming standardized assessment and rankings rather than learning. Standardized assessment differs from assessment that attempts to determine whether students are learning what we are trying to teach. No one I know is against the latter. What recent trends in standardized assessment emphasize, however, is not learning but the comparison and ranking of failure. Incessant testing regimes, such as the infamous No Child Left Behind (2002) law in the United States (known ruefully among many teachers as No Teacher Left Standing), focus on broad comparisons of students, with little regard to their differences, and severe punishments for schools and teachers who fail to meet the "standards." As long as students meet the standards, what they may actually be learning seems to be beside the point.

The fervor for this kind of standardized testing reinforces the kind of ranking games that are a particular enthusiasm of Americans and are certainly not unknown in other countries. We're willing and eager to rank anything—from the 100 greatest movies to the 250 best cities in which to raise children. Never mind that the criteria for such rankings are hazy at best; if we can't put a number on it and rank it, then what good is it? Numbers seem scientific and technological. So we test and test and test, oblivious or resistant to the possibility that standardized literacy testing often produces numbers with about as much utility or connection to reality as ranking songs on the old American Bandstand television program. "It sounds good, has a good beat, and I can dance to it. I give it an 87."

Testing as punishment

My concerns about the increasingly pervasive reliance on standardized 5 testing in literacy education are about more than questionable methods of assessment and measurement, however. I am also deeply troubled about the implications for issues of literacy and identity. What effect does the unrelenting emphasis on standardized literacy testing have on students' perception of the purposes and possibilities of literacy? By extension, what effect does such testing have on their perception of the possibilities for themselves as readers and writers?

Many concerns about identity and standardized testing have been framed in terms of race and social class and have been well documented and well argued by others (McNeil, 2000; Murphy, 1997; Ohanian, 1999; Orfield & Kornhaber, 2001). These teachers and researchers have argued that standardized testing works not from a set of objective standards somehow as constant as the North Star but from a set of cultural conceptions about literacy that are neither objective nor static. Students whose race or social class is not part of the dominant culture often face challenges in meeting the standards of that dominant culture. Much of the impulse behind standardized tests and their illusion of objectivity seems to be a drive to punish, ridicule, and marginalize those who already feel punished, ridiculed, and marginalized by the institutions of education. At the same time the standardized tests from the dominant culture reassure its members about the quality of their educational institutions as well as their children. Using literacy tests to reinforce dominant privileges and exclude others is nothing new; all we have to do is remember the literacy tests used to reject immigrants to the United States or to keep African Americans off U.S. voting rolls in the last century. The standardized testing movement today is just better able to cloak such motives within the rationale of "not leaving children behind."

I do have another concern about these methods of literacy assessment in terms of student identity. Most teachers have stories of bright students who "don't test well." I've seen such students at every level, from middle school to university, and all of them could do innovative, creative, fascinating work on a project or a paper. But for reasons stretching from learning disabilities to personality traits and cognitive ways of processing and communicating information, they could not score well on timed, standardized tests. Nevertheless, there are students who blossom in such test-taking situations—students who understand the rhetorical demands and structures of standardized exams, and whose minds organize and recall certain kinds of information quickly and efficiently.

I see one of each kind of student when I look at my twin adolescent sons, who were born just 15 minutes apart and raised in the same circumstances. One son excels at taking standardized tests of all kinds by understanding the rhetorical structure of the questions and the institutional demands of the exam. The other, though in some ways a more powerful writer and just as strong a student in school, has always found standardized tests rigid and bewildering. If all I knew about them were the results of their annual standardized tests, I would no doubt rejoice in how the school system was succeeding to educate one while worrying over its failure to reach the other. Their wildly divergent test scores tell me nothing about their abilities and nothing about the quality of teaching they receive.

Yet U.S. culture clings to standardized literacy tests as a means of providing meaningful information about students, teachers, and schools because such tests offer the illusion of scientific rigor (as well as those all-important quantifiable numbers) to an endeavor that ultimately can't be measured in a lab and for which numbers are meaningless. This infuriating numbers game allows politicians and media pundits to make facile judgments, and cynical proclamations, about education that they turn into a relentless cycle of testing, criticism, and punishment. From the administrators to the teachers and students, testing drives the curriculum, and the curriculum shapes student identities in terms of literacy practices.

Writing as a human endeavor

Standardized testing, to be standardized, must create questions and answers   10
that leave no room for interpretation. Such rigid questions and answers remove the importance of context from literacy practices and allow for no independent meaning making from students. Yet it is in that moment when an individual makes meaning in writing and reading in a specific cultural context that identity and literacy come together. When literacy education becomes more about standardized assessment, it becomes less about writing and reading by individuals who make meaning and have something to say. In the drive to assess and quantify, what is forgotten is why we want students to read and write in the first place. Reading and writing is about communicating with other human beings—about being part of a society and its ongoing conversations. I think most literacy teachers dream that students, once their days of school are over, will be inspired and educated to read and write about what matters to them. That is the kind of literate identity we want for our students.

However, the increasing pressure of standardized testing disconnects literacy education from human concerns. Students face writing prompts and reading tests that have no connection to their lives, communities, or interests. The tests are created and then read by disconnected, uninvested, anonymous readers—and now perhaps even computers. Literacy practices become less about communicating with people and more about communicating with a faceless system or a machine. What students, like administrators and teachers, learn from this system is that only the numbers matter, not the meaning or the communication.

Students and teachers have also learned that, like any system, standardized tests can be "gamed." When work is written only to be assessed rather than to communicate ideas, the activity becomes more about ensuring that certain qualities are present (e.g., the use of examples, the complexity of sentences, transition devices, vocabulary) regardless of the overall effect of the piece of writing. In the United States, one example of such an activity is the brief writing section recently added to the Scholastic Aptitude Test (SAT)—the test taken by thousands of university-bound students that is supposed to indicate their abilities to succeed in higher education. Using a 25-minute writing sample to determine a student's ability to write the kind of extended critical prose required in university is like using a person's ability to back a car down a driveway to determine whether the driver can make it through rush-hour traffic. The writing samples on the SAT are apparently scored on such generalizable characteristics of writing as smooth transitions and varied sentences rather than on content or overall effect (Klein, 2005).

So let's say specific examples are highly prized, particularly those that are not about personal experiences. Now, it doesn't matter if the specific examples are made up, as long as they are specific, and so pretty soon we'll find students sprinkling their essays with impressively "specific" examples. What the students will know, and what we as teachers will have to admit, is that writing as a means of communicating ideas does not matter in this situation; it's racking up the right number of smooth transitions and specific examples that does. It is difficult to imagine such a situation creating the conditions to inspire students to think of themselves as writers and readers and to engage in writing with any sense of ownership or passion.

Gaming the testing machines

Even more troubling is the recent trend toward evaluating student writing through computer software. No longer is the student writing for any person, even an anonymous person; instead it is writing done to be judged by a series of algorithms that look for quantifiable characteristics such as transitional phrases and complex syntax. But any of these programs can be easily "fooled." Give one an essay that is gibberish but includes the proper characteristics of syntax and vocabulary, and you receive high marks.

In fact, computer assessment software can be gamed by other computer software. Hesse (2005) pointed this out in a recent presentation. First he used the online Essay Generator (www.EssayGenerator.com) to create an essay. If you've never used this website, it is great fun. You enter any word or phrase and are immediately rewarded with an essay on that topic with complete sentences; sections on social, economic, and political factors; and even important-looking citations and a graph. But reading the essay more closely reveals its delightful ridiculousness. For example, I just entered the phrase "standardized testing" and received an essay with the following opening sentences:

> The issues involving standardized testing has been a popular topic amongst scholars for many years. In depth analysis of standardized testing can be an enriching experience. Though standardized testing is a favorite topic of discussion amongst monarchs presidents and dictators, there are just not enough blues songs written about standardized testing.

The essay continues with complex and syntactically correct sentences that make little or no sense at all. Hesse (2005) took his randomly generated essay, full of similar nonsense, and then submitted it to "intelligent" essay assessing software and received a report that praised the high quality of the writing, including the mature command of language and the effective use of examples and transitional devices. I replicated Hesse's experiment with similar results (and it's worth trying yourself if you want to be simultaneously amused and horrified). Perhaps this is the wave of the future: We can have computers write essays to be read and evaluated by other computers and leave students out of the process altogether.

Even so, the important concern in the use of computer assessment, as well as standardized testing, is not whether such systems can be fooled. Those advocating the development of such software maintain that some-day computer software may be able to read student essays for content as well as for syntactic characteristics. They may be right. But the sophisti-cation of the software is not the point. The more disturbing question is about what writing becomes when it is produced to be read and evaluated by a computer. What is the point of writing for a computer? Will there be writers who will care as deeply about what a computer thinks about their writing in the way that they care about pleasing a human audience? Will anyone take writing for a computer seriously? Students may care whether they pass a test, but what will they learn about literacy and identity when there is no human connection to what they write?

I'm a die-hard humanist on this issue. Writing and reading are about touching the mind of another person, whether in a proposal, a poem, or a polemic. When advocates of computer software or standardized testing argue that their systems will be more objective, it is an argument that again strikes me as beside the point. Writing for other human beings—even when they are teachers—is by nature subjective. Everything about writing depends on context, culture, and the occasional unpredictability of human response. Such is the challenge and joy of writing, along with its intermit-tent frustration. Even as I write this column, thinking I have some sense of my audience and the context of this journal, I know that I cannot predict all the possible responses. I can't think of a writer who doesn't know in her or his bones that writing will always be responded to and judged subjec-tively. Yet standardized literacy testing and evaluation would have us pre-tend to students and their parents that such subjective responses can be overcome with scientific methods and better technology, and that such methods can generate a set of numbers that are meaningful about the qual-ity of that writing. And we forget that even standardized test readers and computer software programmers are people with their own biases and pref-erences. We do these same students a significant disservice by acquiescing to this pretense of objectivity and by not talking to them about how real humans in real contexts read and how best we can try to identify and re-spond to such real people and situations.

In conversations with students about how real audiences in real situa-tions respond to writing is where meaningful assessment can happen. If I want to know if students are learning to write, I first want to see those stu-dents write about subjects that matter to them for an interested audience and reflect on the reasons for their writing choices. Once students get a real response from an audience, I want them to reflect again on that response and what it might teach them about what they wrote and why. I always talk with students about assessment and how their work could be assessed. Then

I discuss my choices during assessment and how I evaluate both their writing and their reflections on it. I'm not against assessing writing. I tell students that every piece of writing read by another person is assessed in some way, even if only in the reader's choice to read all the way to the end. I'm just against thinking that we can assess writing through some pseudoscientific, technology-driven, one-size-fits-all, a-contextual test.

Making a difference with human response

Sommers and Saltz (2004), in their longitudinal study of more than 400 university student writers, found that the students who made the most progress in terms of writing shared two characteristics. First, these students, even if they began their university careers as relatively weak writers, were the ones who brought ideas and issues that mattered to them to their choice of courses and their responses to assignments. Equally important for these students was the ability to see writing assignments as something more than just fulfilling a requirement for a grade:

> When students begin to see writing as a transaction, an exchange in which they can "get and give," they begin to see a larger purpose for their writing. They have their first glimmerings of audience; they begin to understand that they are writing for flesh-and-blood human beings, readers who want them to bring their interests into a course, not simply teachers who are poised with red pens ready to evaluate what they don't know. (p. 139)

In addition, Sommers (2005) found that the responses from teachers that resulted in the most substantial improvement in student writers took the work and the ideas of the writers seriously and, along with constructive criticism, provided comments and questions that pointed the students toward what they might improve in future pieces of writing. Writing for a real audience about ideas that engage individual interests and intellects and having that audience provide thoughtful individualized responses not only helps students become better writers, it also helps them create their identities as writers. Such an approach to writing is the antithesis of standardized testing.

Of course, the sad fact is that there are people in and out of education 20 who are not concerned about whether writing with passion for real readers will inspire students and help them develop identities as confident writers. This camp wants to ensure that students attain a functional literacy that makes them productive in the workplace—in clerical and service industry jobs. As I've argued before in this column, the way literacy instruction is conceived and enacted is often connected to issues of social class, and it's the same with standardized tests as well. One benefit of standardized testing as assessment is that it is much cheaper than the kind of individualized assessment I advocated earlier. Affluent students will be taught to "game" the standardized testing system. But these same students will also have abundant opportunities in small classes in elite schools to write for real readers and to read for meaning, pleasure, and enrichment. By contrast, it is working class and poor students, for whom pleasure and the construction of literate identities is deemed unimportant, who will encounter a curriculum driven by the fear of standardized testing. The administrators and teachers of those students, facing large classes, few resources, and the threat of punishments over low scores, will be forced to create a curriculum in which students will be taught to write only for the anonymous readers and machines that evaluate such tests. Certainly that will be cheaper than providing the resources and trust in poorer schools that would allow teachers to face the same class sizes and use the same approaches for teaching writing that affluent schools enjoy. But students from poorer schools will encounter fewer and fewer opportunities to think of themselves as writers communicating their interests and passions for real readers.

What is to be done?

Many teachers, even when facing the pressure of standardized testing, continue to design assignments that fulfill the needs of assessment while providing students with places to do writing and reading that matters. And systems of assessment that are not bound up in concerns about time and technology, such as writing portfolios, can provide responsible assessment that is valuable for students, teachers, and institutions. However, writing portfolios can become as rigid and impersonal as any approach to assessment if the focus of the writing becomes the assessment itself rather than the communication of ideas.

The pressure toward standardized testing is such that more must be done than just designing good pedagogy around the margins of a test-driven curriculum. It is time for individual teachers at every level to take back the debate about assessment from the people who say the only valid evaluation of writing is timed, standardized, and faceless. It is time to take back the debate that maintains that only assessment that results in quantifiable numbers is valid. Engaging in this debate does not happen on a grand stage, it happens as a persistent, continuing conversation with the people in our communities. It is the responsibility of teachers to keep explaining to students, parents, administrators, neighbors, and newspaper editors that writing and reading that matters for real audiences is what creates literate citizens. It is the responsibility of teachers to explain how such writing can be assessed, that such instruction can be responsible and accountable, but that assessment and instruction happen differently in literacy education than in other fields. Finally, it is the responsibility of teachers not only to keep talking about what the best practices and outcomes for student literacy education should be but also to publicize our successes.

Reading and writing matter, and we teachers care deeply about them. If we want students to think of themselves as readers and writers, then those activities have to matter to students beyond learning how to game the test to avoid being punished. It is time we reclaimed the idea that having standards does not necessarily mean accepting or aspiring to standardization.

REFERENCES

Hesse, D. (2005, March). *Who owns writing?* Keynote address at the Conference on College Composition and Communication, San Francisco.
Klein, K. (2005, April 3). How I gamed the SAT. *The Los Angeles Times*, p. A20.
McNeil, L. (2000). *Contradictions of reform: Educational costs of standardized testing.* London: Routledge.
Murphy, S. (1997). Literacy assessment and the politics of identities. *Reading and Writing Quarterly, 13*, 261–278.
No Child Left Behind Act of 2001, Pub. L. No. 107–110, 115 Stat. 1425 (2002).
Ohanian, S. (1999). *One size fits few. The folly of educational standards.* Portsmouth, NH: Heinemann.
Orfield, G., & Kornhaber, M. L. (2001). *Raising standards or raising barriers? Inequality and high-stakes testing in public education.* New York: Century Foundation Press.
Sommers, N. (2005, March). *Across the drafts: Responding to writings longitudinal perspective.* Paper presented at the Conference on College Composition and Communication, San Francisco.
Sommers, N., & Saltz, L. (2004). The novice as expert: Writing the freshman year. *College Composition and Communication, 56*, 124–149.

Testing Has Raised Students' Expectations, and Progress in Learning Is Evident Nationwide

ROD PAIGE

BEFORE READING: Should standardized test scores be used as a measure to determine how much funding schools receive? Explain.

Testing is a part of life. In fact, testing starts at the beginning stages of life: The moment we are born, neonatologists measure our reflexes and responses and give us what is called an Apgar score on a scale of one to ten. As we grow up, our teachers test us in school and we take other standardized tests that compare us with the rest of the nation's students. We are tested if we want to practice a trade—whether it be to get a cosmetology license, a driver's permit, or pilot training. And often we are retested and retested again to show that our skills remain at peak level.

Former U.S. Secretary of Education Rod Paige has been a teacher, coach, college dean, schoolboard member, and superintendent of one of the largest school districts in the United States, in Houston. This article first appeared, paired with Reg Weaver's (p. 615), in a symposium titled "Are the tests required by No Child Left Behind making schools more accountable?" in *Insight* magazine, May 11–24, 2004.

In short, tests exist for a reason. In the case of a doctor, they certify that he or she is capable of practicing medicine. In the case of a teacher, they show that he or she has the knowledge to help children learn a given subject. And in the case of a student, they demonstrate whether a child has indeed learned and understood the lesson or the subject.

At their core, tests are simply tools—they subjectively measure things. In education, they are particularly important because they pinpoint where students are doing well and where they need help. In fact, testing has been a part of education since the first child sat behind the first desk. Assessments are an important component of educational accountability; in other words, they tell us whether the system is performing as it should. They diagnose, for the teacher, the parent and the student, any problems so that they can be fixed.

Educational accountability is the cornerstone of the No Child Left Behind Act, President George W. Bush's historic initiative that is designed to raise student performance across America. The law embraces a number of commonsense ways to reach that goal: accountability for results, empowering parents with information about school performance and giving them options, more local control, and flexibility to tailor the law to local circumstances.

No Child Left Behind is a revolutionary change, challenging the cur- 5 rent educational system and helping it to improve. It aims to challenge the status quo by pushing the educational system into the twenty-first century so that American students leave school better prepared for higher education or the workforce.

Educational accountability is not a new concept—several states have been instituting accountability reforms for years. No Child Left Behind builds on the good work of some of these states that were at the forefront of the reform movement. The truth is that this law has one goal: to get all children reading and doing math at grade level. It's that simple. The law itself is a federal law, but it is nothing more than a framework. Elementary and secondary education are the traditional province of state and local governments, which is why the specific standards, tests and most of the other major tenets of the law are designed and implemented by the state departments of education, because they are in the best position to assess local expectations and parental demands.

The federal role in education also is not a new concept. There is a compelling national interest in education, which is why the federal government is involved and has been for some time. The federal government has stepped in to correct overt unfairness or inequality, starting with measures to enforce civil rights and dismantle segregation in the wake of the *Brown v. Board of Education* case (a Supreme Court decision that is now fifty years old). The federal government's first major legislative involvement in education goes back to 1965 with the Elementary and Secondary Education Act, which marked the first federal aid given to school districts with large percentages of children living in poverty. In 2001 the law was reauthorized as the No Child Left Behind Act (NCLB), which preserves the states' traditional role but asks them to set standards for accountability and teacher quality, thereby improving the quality, inclusivity, fairness, and justice of American education.

NCLB focuses on facts, not just feelings and hunches. It is no longer acceptable simply to believe schools are improving without knowing for certain whether they are. As Robert F. Kennedy asked back in 1965 when this federal education law was first debated, "What happened to the children? [How do we know] whether they can read or not?" With new state-accountability systems—and tests—we will have the full picture.

Let's examine what we do know. According to the nation's report card (the National Assessment of Educational Progress, or NAEP), only one in six African Americans and one in five Hispanics are proficient in reading by the time they are high-school seniors. NAEP math scores are even worse: Only 3 percent of blacks and 4 percent of Hispanics are testing at the proficient level. This is the status quo result of a decades-old education system before the NCLB.

Of the ten fastest-growing occupations in the United States, the top five 10 are computer-related, which are jobs that require high-level skills. High-school dropouts need not apply. We are all concerned about outsourcing jobs overseas, and we should note that the unemployment rate for high-school dropouts is almost twice that of those with high-school diplomas (7.3 percent compared with 4.2 percent) and nearly four times that of college graduates (7.3 percent vs. 2.3 percent). For young black men the unemployment rate is a staggering 26 percent. Even a high-school diploma isn't the cure: A vast majority of employers sadly expect that a high-school graduate will not write clearly or have even fair math skills. No wonder a recent study claimed a high-school diploma has become nothing more than a "certificate of attendance." For millions of children, they were given a seat in the school but not an education of the mind.

It is clear that our system as a whole is not preparing the next generation of workers for the global economy ahead of them. As Federal Reserve Chairman Alan Greenspan noted recently: "We need to be forward looking in order to adapt our educational system to the evolving needs of the economy and the realities of our changing society. . . . It is an effort that should not be postponed." That's why I am so passionate about making these historic reforms and drawing attention to the issue.

The old system—the status quo—is one that we must fight to change. That's why the president and both parties in Congress understood the urgency of the situation and put NCLB into law. They also ensured that the money would be there to get the job done, providing the means to states fully to implement the law; indeed, there's been 41 percent more federal support for education since President Bush took office.

But some defenders of the status quo have aired complaints about the law, saying its requirements are unreasonable and the tests are arbitrary. The bottom line is, these cynics do not believe in the worth of all children—they have written some of them off. You can guess which ones fall into that category. This pessimism relegates these children to failure. The president aptly refers to this phenomenon as the "soft bigotry of low expectations." But NCLB says the excuses must stop—all children must be given a chance.

NCLB helps us zero in on student needs. With little information about individual students' abilities with different skills, most teachers must rely on a "buckshot" approach to teaching their classes, aiming for the middle and hoping to produce a decent average. With an emphasis on scientifically based research techniques and effective use of information, NCLB helps fund programs that teachers can use to identify specific areas of weakness among their students.

For example, the Granite School District in Utah used Title I funds   15 (support for economically disadvantaged students) to procure the "Yearly Progress Pro" computer program. Now a fourth-grade class at Stansbury Elementary School visits the computer lab for a quick 15-minute test each week; the teacher walks out with a printout identifying changes in performance in specific skill areas over the week.

Child by child, the improvements add up. For example, a study by the Council of Great City Schools examined the recent gains in large metropolitan school systems. The Beating the Odds IV report showed that since NCLB has been implemented, public-school students across the country have shown a marked improvement in reading. The report found that the achievement gap in reading and math between African Americans and whites, and Hispanics and whites in large cities, is narrowing for fourth- and eighth-grade students. And it appears, according to the report, that our big-city schools are closing the gap at a faster rate than the statewide rate. Not only are the achievement gaps closing, the report states, but also math and reading achievement are improving.

For a concrete example of how the law is working, look at the Cheltenham School District in Pennsylvania, where leaders are disaggregating data to find the cracks they must fill. Drawing on test results, the district provides schools with specific information about each student's abilities and weaknesses in specific academic areas. Schools receive this data in easily accessible electronic formats in July, before the students arrive, giving them time to plan for the year. Now teachers can account for the effectiveness of their strategies and, if they are not working for some students, adapt to alternatives.

These findings are especially significant because research shows that it is often the students in the large-city schools who need the most help and face the greatest odds. Clearly, this report demonstrates that if you challenge students, they will rise to the occasion. This concept is at the fundamental core of NCLB because we can no longer mask our challenges in the aggregate of our successes. We must make sure that all children, regardless of their skin color and Zip codes, have the opportunity to receive a high-quality education.

While the press focuses on the complaints of the unwilling, whole communities are taking on the challenge of accountability and achieving great results. Perhaps my favorite example is in the Peck School in rural Michigan, where I visited in late March and found that the school culture had embraced the accountability treatment. A huge poster hangs in the hallway of the school emblazoned with No Child Left Behind! Showing creativity and commitment, the school launched a tutoring program, began intervening sooner with low-performing students, and even created a peer-counseling program to address the conflicts that often spill into the classroom and distract from learning. Everyone in the Peck School is taking responsibility for the students' education, truly fostering the character of good citizenship.

It is time to think of the children and to give them what they need. It 20 is time to work to make the law successful. We need to create an American public educational system that matches the vision of this law, where we strive for excellence without exclusion, where our children achieve greatness rather than greatly underachieving, and where 10 or 20 years from now a new generation of adults realize that we gave them a better life because we had courage and conviction now.

NCLB's Excessive Reliance on Testing Is Unrealistic, Arbitrary, and Frequently Unfair

REG WEAVER

BEFORE READING: Should standardized test scores be used as a measure to determine how much funding schools receive? Explain.

As I travel around the country visiting schools and talking with National Education Association (NEA) members, I sense a growing concern among teachers and parents about the overwhelming emphasis given to standardized testing in America's schools. This concern is heightened when high stakes are attached to the outcomes of such tests. Teachers and parents worry that more and more of the important things

Reg Weaver is president of the National Education Association. He has thirty years of teaching experience and serves on the executive board of the National Council for the Accreditation of Teacher Education as well as the National Board for Professional Teaching Standards. His article first appeared, in conjunction with Rod Paige's (p. 611), in a symposium titled "Are the tests required by No Child Left Behind making schools more accountable?" in the May 11–24, 2004, issue of *Insight* magazine.

that prepare us for life will be pushed off the curriculum plate to make room for test preparation.

According to a recent poll by Public Agenda, 88 percent of teachers say the amount of attention their school pays to standardized test results has increased during the last several years. And 61 percent agreed that teaching to the test "inevitably stifles real teaching and learning."

As any good teacher knows, there is no one-size-fits-all approach to either teaching or learning. In fact, we now have a solid body of research about cognition and learning styles that provides ample confirmation of this. Any good teacher also knows that proper assessment of learning is both complex and multifaceted. Tests—particularly paper and pencil tests that are standardized—are only one type of assessment. Good teachers make judgments about what has been learned on the basis of a variety of assessments. Finally, we know that what constitutes spectacular achievement for a child who suffers serious challenges may not equal the progress of his or her peers, but we honor this progress nonetheless.

The NEA has a proud history of supporting and nurturing our system of public education. When we are critical of the so-called No Child Left Behind (NCLB) Act, our interest is to fix those elements of the law that we see as destructive to public education and, ultimately, to the children we serve.

A consensus is emerging from coast to coast and across the political   5
spectrum that this is a law in need of repair. And the present definition of adequate yearly progress is at the heart of what is wrong with the law.

The concept of adequate yearly progress is relatively simple: Set a lofty goal, establish a time frame for accomplishing the goal, establish incremental targets or steps toward achieving the goal, and hold schools accountable for meeting the targets and, ultimately, the goal. The goal is 100 percent proficiency in reading and math, and all schools must meet it by 2014.

Wouldn't life, and particularly parenting and teaching, be simple if progress in learning were linear and time-sensitive? Parents, teachers and cognitive psychologists alike know that learning is anything but linear. And yet we now have a federal law that not only violates what we know to be true about human learning but says that unless schools achieve linear progress, the federal government will punish you.

Do we have a problem with this? You bet we do. Can it be fixed? We think so.

One of our state affiliates, the Connecticut Education Association (CEA), is a leader in recognizing and studying the problems with the federal definition of "adequate yearly progress" (AYP). Shortly after the law was adopted, the CEA had an independent economist develop a scenario based on existing test data in Connecticut in an attempt to visualize the impact of AYP in one of the highest achieving states in the nation. The initial results were shocking; however, because the law had yet to be implemented, the results were still hypothetical. Nonetheless, the prediction became reality last summer when nearly 25 percent of schools in Connecticut were identified as having failed to make AYP. An astonishing 155 elementary and middle schools and 88 high schools were identified as "in need of improvement" under the federal law.

More recently, armed with two years of test data, the CEA asked its 10 economist, Ed Moscovitch of Massachusetts, to update the scenarios. This time the CEA asked what failure rates might look like over the full 12 years of implementation. The new scenario, based on a model that allows for the rate of growth that students actually achieved in the last two years of testing, is very revealing. At the end of 12 years, 744 of 802 elementary and middle schools in Connecticut will have failed to make adequate yearly progress — that's 93 percent of its elementary and middle schools.

In the first year none of the schools identified had the white non-Hispanic subgroup failing to make AYP. In the final year 585 of the 744 schools will have the white subgroup failing to do so. Even the powerful combination of social capital and great schools in a state that is regarded nationally as a high performer is not adequate to meet the statistical demands of this law.

Only in Lake Wobegon, perhaps, where all the students are above average, is there a chance of meeting the requirements set forth in the so-called No Child Left Behind law.

The current formula for AYP fails to consider the difference between where you start and how quickly you must reach the goal. That is, in my opinion, irresponsible. It is particularly irresponsible as it applies to English-language learners and special-education subgroups. While the Department of Education (DOE) finally has acknowledged that students whose first language is not English may not perform well when given a test in English, it does not go far enough to correct the problem. With respect to special-education students, the DOE has granted some leeway for the small percentage of severely cognitively disabled students, but there are thousands of other students in this subgroup for whom the test is totally inappropriate and emotionally injurious.

What's more, while the department has acknowledged the unfairness of how English-language learners and students with disabilities were tested, it has refused to go back and reconsider schools labeled "in need of improvement" under the old procedures.

Is this all the law of unintended consequences? Or is there, as many 15 believe, an insidious intent to discredit public education, paving the way for a breakup of the current system — an opening of the door to a boutique system with increased privatization and government vouchers?

We believe that for every ideologue who wants to subject public education to market forces, there are scores of policymakers and political officials who supported this law based solely on its stated, laudable intent. Many of them still do not understand the full import of what they supported. So what do we believe needs to be done?

First, we need to ask whether the measurement of AYP is an accurate barometer of a student's progress or a school's effectiveness. We have urged the adoption of multiple indicators. Measuring this year's fourth-graders against next year's fourth-graders tells us little that we need to know about the improvement of individual students. Wouldn't it make more sense to follow the progress of individual children? We have called for this kind of cohort analysis, and recently 14 state superintendents asked for the same change in a meeting with President George W. Bush.

Second, is it fair to have the same starting point for all groups? We need to find a more rational way to acknowledge the dramatic gaps in performance among subgroups. As an example, high-achieving students in Connecticut wait for years for targeted low-achieving subgroups to catch up with their performance, while other groups are asked to fill an unachievable gap in one year just to get to the starting gate. Yet the race begins at the same time and at the same pace for all. For certain subgroups, even dramatic increases in performance relative to their prior performance will only lead to failure. We need to acknowledge and honor progress.

Third, if we really have a goal of improving student achievement, shouldn't we offer tutoring to struggling students first? Right now NCLB adopts an "abandon ship" philosophy of allowing parents to change schools. The focus should be on helping the individual student in the subgroup in need of attention. And by the way, why is it less important to have a highly qualified tutor, or supplemental service provider, than it is to have a highly qualified teacher? Academic tutors should be certified, as well. Current law prohibits states from requiring that tutors be certified.

So in answer to the question "Does AYP increase school accountability?" our answer is no. But it could with serious and thoughtful revision.   20

The NEA and its state affiliates have always supported high standards and accountability. And we believe that no child should be left behind. We believe that every child in a public school should be taught by a highly qualified teacher in an atmosphere that is safe and conducive to learning, and all students should have access to a rich and deep curriculum. We also believe that each child is unique and brings to the classroom a variety of gifts and challenges. We have built a system in the United States that has struggled to honor this notion of gifts and challenges — our doors are open to all — and we have huge systemic challenges in meeting this philosophical ideal. There's much more that the federal government must do to guarantee that No Child Left Behind is more than just an empty promise.

Are We Fixing the Wrong Things?

YONG ZHAO

BEFORE READING: What stereotypes are you aware of regarding Asian students? What do you think the sources of those stereotypes might be?

*O*ur *Nation is at risk. Our once unchallenged preeminence in commerce, in-dustry, science, and technological innovation is being overtaken by com-petitors throughout the world.*

So opens the influential report *A Nation at Risk*. The report goes on to identify what put the nation at risk:

> The educational foundations of our society are presently being eroded by a rising tide of mediocrity that threatens our very future as a Nation and a people. . . . Others are matching and surpassing our educational attainments.

The writers feared that the United States would lose out to its com-petitors, such as Japan and South Korea, because "we are raising a new generation of Americans that is scientifically and technologically illiter-ate" (National Commission on Excellence in Education, 1983).

More than two decades later, the United States remains a superpower, dominating the world as the most scientifically and technologically ad-vanced nation. The core innovations that drove the global digital revolu-tion were created in the United States; the leaders of the computer and Internet industries are from the United States. Moreover, nearly two-thirds of the 300,000 patents issued in 2002 went to Americans (Florida, 2005). In the meantime, the countries that spurred the alarm, Japan and South Korea, have been in an economic recession for more than a decade.

How could "a nation at risk" and a "generation of Americans that is sci- 5 entifically and technologically illiterate" accomplish this? Did the report-induced reforms lift U.S. education out of mediocrity and save the nation from the crisis?

Apparently not. Although the report received tremendous attention and ushered in an era of education reform, "its goals have not yet been re-alized," wrote Diane Ravitch, former U.S. assistant secretary of education and professor at New York University (2003). Many would agree. Educa-tion reforms have generally not changed, let alone improved, U.S. schools.

Yong Zhao is University Distinguished Professor of Technology in Education and Edu-cational Psychology and director of the Center of Teaching and Technology in the Col-lege of Education at Michigan State University. He also directs the U.S.–China Center for Research on Educational Excellence. This article appeared in *Educational Leadership* in May 2006.

According to Bill Gates, U.S. schools are not only in trouble—they're "obsolete" (2005).

Did imported foreign talents, then, save the United States, as some would believe? Not according to records kept by the U.S. Department of Labor. In 2004, of the nearly 49 million people who had jobs in the category titled "Management, Professional, and Related Occupations," which includes the professions most related to science and technology, only 9 percent were foreign-born. Moreover, in the subcategory of "Computer and Mathematics Occupations," only 5 percent of workers were foreign-born. In "Architecture and Engineering Occupations," 6.5 percent of workers were foreign-born (Bureau of Labor Statistics, 2005). It is difficult to imagine that these small percentages of foreign-born workers had such a decisive impact on U.S. scientific and technological advances.

Is it possible that U.S. schools were *not* in trouble after all? Or were they in a different kind of trouble? Did reforms overlook the real problem and try to fix something that wasn't really broken?

Déjà Vu Reform

We are currently experiencing a wave of education reform similar to that which followed *A Nation at Risk*, with similar justification. "Clearly, we're no longer the only economic kid on the block," said Margaret Spellings, U.S. secretary of education (2005a). At the National Education Summit on High Schools, Spellings added,

> This is reaching crisis stages in the fields of science and engineering. . . .
> China now graduates six times as many engineering majors as the U.S.;
> South Korea and Japan, four times as many. This type of performance
> has serious implications for the future. (2005b)

A day earlier, Bill Gates had told the same audience, "In the interna- 10 tional competition to have the biggest and best supply of knowledge workers, America is falling behind" (Gates, 2005). Why? Because U.S. students don't test as well as their peers in Asian countries, and the United States doesn't graduate as many engineers as India and China do. Recommendations for dealing with this new crisis are almost identical to those made in *A Nation at Risk*, except this time the reformers vow to implement them with greater force.

Our Secret Weapon

The world has changed; social commentators have observed that it has become a "global village" and "flat." The reformers are therefore correct in pointing out that the United States can no longer isolate itself and that the country needs to be able to effectively compete with other nations. The reformers are also right about the problematic state of U.S. education. But they could be wrong about two things: what it takes to compete internationally and what the real problems in U.S. education are.

As indicators of crisis, the reformers often cite the lower performance of U.S. students in math and science, especially in international comparison studies; the declining interest and enrollment in math and science courses; and the growing number of college graduates in other nations. But the secret weapon that has helped the United States remain an economic leader and innovation powerhouse is the creative, risk-taking, can-do spirit of its people. This spirit is not normally measured in standardized tests or compared in international studies.

Sim Wong Hoo, founder and CEO of Singapore-based Creative Technology, pointed out this very fact. When asked in an interview with *Newsweek* about the advantages and disadvantages of having his company based in Singapore, Hoo answered,

> The advantage is we come from a very conscientious culture. You tell our people what to do, they'll follow the rules, they'll do it. The downside is they are not as creative. We fixed that by having a U.S.-based R&D team that's doing more advanced research. (Levy, 2005)

Singapore, by the way, has repeatedly been the top-performing nation in the Trends in International Mathematics and Science Study (TIMSS).

Whereas U.S. schools are now encouraged, even forced, to chase after 15 test scores, China, Singapore, South Korea, and Japan—all named as major competitors—have started education reforms aimed at fostering more creativity and innovative thinking among their citizens. China, for example, has taken drastic measures to reform its curriculum. As the United States raised the status of standardized testing to a record high in 2001 with No Child Left Behind, the Chinese Ministry of Education issued an executive order to significantly minimize the consequences of testing (2002). As the United States pushes for more centralized curriculum standards, China is abandoning its one nation–one syllabus tradition. As the United States moves toward a required program of study for high schools, China is working hard to implement a flexible system with more electives and choices for students. As the United States calls for more homework and more study time, China has launched a battle to reduce such burdens on its students.

The Real Problems to Tackle

Creativity cannot be taught, but it can be killed. What fosters creativity in the United States is the whole multifaceted experience of growing up: the soccer games, the orchestra performances, the opportunities to pick and choose courses, even the much criticized mile-wide–inch-deep curriculum standards, which give students the flexibility to pursue topics that interest them and to progress differently than other students in the same school, district, or state. The current or proposed reform initiatives—centralized curriculum, standardized testing, accountability, required course of study— could kill creativity, the United States' real competitive edge.

The reform initiatives also neglect two pressing problems in U.S. education: (1) the lack of a curriculum that focuses on international issues and prepares students to actively engage in global affairs, and (2) the lack of opportunities for impoverished children to participate in the globalization discourse. We urgently need to learn how to work with our neighbors in the global village and help schools and children in poverty.

This "flat" world demands individuals who can market innovations to other countries without being perceived as arrogant or imperialistic. For this, we need people who can speak other languages, who understand and respect other cultures, and who realize that globalization and economic development in other nations do not necessarily mean job losses, lower wages, and a trade deficit in the United States. We need to realize that these developments can also result in expanded markets for U.S. inventions, a new workforce for U.S. companies, and a safer world for everyone.

REFERENCES

Bureau of Labor Statistics. (2005). *Labor force characteristics of foreign-born workers in 2004*. Washington, DC: U.S. Department of Labor. Available: www.bls.gov/news.release/forbrn.toc.htm

Chinese Ministry of Education. (2002). *Ministry of Education's notice regarding furthering the reform of evaluation and assessment systems in elementary and secondary schools*. Beijing, China: Author. Available: www.moe.edu.cn/edoas/website18/info405.htm

Florida, R. (2005, October). The world is spiky. *The Atlantic*, 48–51.

Gates, W. (2005). *Prepared remarks at the National Education Summit on High Schools*. Available: www.gatesfoundation.org/MediaCenter/Speeches/BillgSpeeches/BGSpeechNGA-050226.htm

Levy, S. (2005, March 7). The Zen of fighting iPod. *Newsweek International*. Available: www.msnbc.msn.com/id/7037971/site/newsweek

National Commission on Excellence in Education. (1983). *A nation at risk: The imperative for educational reform*. Available: www.ed.gov/pubs/NatAtRisk

Ravitch, D. (2003). A nation at risk: Twenty years later. *Weekly Essay: Hoover Institution*. Available: www-hoover.stanford.edu/pubaffairs/we/2003/ravitch04.html

Spellings, M. (2005a). *Prepared testimony of Secretary Spellings before the Senate Committee on Health, Education, Labor, and Pensions: Lifelong learning*. Available: www.ed.gov/news/speeches/2005/04/04142005.html

Spellings, M. (2005b). *Ahead of the curve: Prepared remarks for Secretary Spellings at the National Governors Association's National Education Summit on High Schools*. Available: www.ed.gov/news/speeches/2005/02/02272005.html

The SAT's Greatest Test: Social, Legal, and Demographic Forces Threaten to Dethrone the Most Widely Used College-Entrance Exam

BEN GOSE AND JEFFREY SELINGO

BEFORE READING: How accurately do you believe the SAT (or ACT) predicts a student's success in college? Do you believe it is weighed too heavily in admissions? If so, what other factors should receive more emphasis?

The SAT is to criticism as a halfback is to a football—always on the receiving end.

For most of the past two decades, the College Board, which owns the test, has done a good job holding onto the ball, fending off critics who maintain that the test discriminates against female and minority students.

The board has sponsored several studies that show, for example, that the test usually gives black and Hispanic students a helping hand in the admissions process— it predicts that they will perform *better* in college than they actually do. And the board is scrupulously careful about material that appears on the SAT so that there will be no more embarrassments about questions that would seem to favor students familiar with yachts.

It's hardly surprising, then, that faced with an unprecedented assault from a wholly different quarter, the test's keepers resort to the standard defense.

"This is not a biased test," says Gaston Caperton, the College Board's president, from his office here near Lincoln Center. "What we have is an unequal educational system. It's not the kids. It's not the test." 5

What Mr. Caperton seems to have missed is that today the battle has shifted drastically, from accusations of bias to questions that undermine the very basis for the test and may, in the end, lead to its demise. Today's critics have opened an assault on the use of what is essentially an IQ test to measure students' ability to learn. The outcome of the debate will affect how colleges with competitive admissions pick students, how racially diverse those students will be, and how high-school students prepare for college.

The College Board has for years tried to distance the SAT from its roots in IQ tests, but the perception remains that the most widely administered college-entrance examination measures intelligence, not a mastery of learning. Many education leaders—most notably, Richard C. Atkinson,

Ben Gose is senior editor and Jeffrey Selingo assistant editor of the Government and Politics section of the *Chronicle of Higher Education*, the section that covers state and federal policies and their effects on colleges, students, and researchers. Their article appeared in the *Chronicle* on October 26, 2001.

president of the University of California system—say that legacy creates perverse incentives, as students waste time and money "prepping" for the SAT's idiosyncratic questions, such as the analogies section of the verbal exam.

If college-entrance exams were tied more closely to the curriculum, the critics say, students would have a clear idea of what standards they must meet, and high schools could more easily be held accountable when students fail.

Last February, Mr. Atkinson stunned college leaders by calling on his nine-campus, 170,000-student system to become the first public university with competitive admissions to drop the requirement that applicants take the SAT. The system's size and prominence immediately led to speculation about whether others would dump the SAT; the University of Texas at Austin and North Carolina's public colleges are studying the issue.

Mr. Atkinson's announcement "was by far the most important single 10 anti-SAT effort ever in the history of the test," says Nicholas Lemann, author of *The Big Test: The Secret History of the American Meritocracy* (Farrar, Straus & Giroux), a recent book about the SAT.

In the 1940s, the University of California was the first major public system to require the test. "That was the key to making the SAT the dominant test," says Robert A. Schaeffer, public-education director at the National Center for Fair and Open Testing, also known as Fair Test. "If you follow that historical analogy, you'll find that the key to ending the dominance of the SAT also lies in California."

Other threats also loom. Thirteen top colleges, including Harvard University, the Massachusetts Institute of Technology, and the University of Michigan at Ann Arbor, are participating in a study to determine if state exams already given to high-school students may one day be used in college admissions. And recent court decisions and referendums may lead many colleges seeking a diverse student body to lower the weight they place on the SAT—or to ignore it altogether.

To be sure, the College Board and the Educational Testing Service, which engineers the test, aren't exactly on the ropes. The obsession with identifying—and getting into—the best colleges has been as good for the SAT as it has been for college-guide publishers like *U.S. News & World Report*. Roughly 1.3 million high-school seniors per year take the test, and more than half take it at least twice, yielding an annual revenue stream of more than $200 million. For now, many admissions officers continue to rely on SAT scores to compare students who come from high schools of widely varying quality. Many colleges also feel they must report high average SAT scores to the guidebooks, in order to earn top rankings and keep applications flowing their way.

The SAT also may continue to thrive because the alternatives to the test are embryonic, too expensive, or lacking in political support. Mr. Lemann champions a national curriculum, with a national exam that matches it, but when the topic comes up on Capitol Hill, "everyone runs and hides," he says. The state-based exams, which for now merely test whether a student has mastered the basic skills needed to graduate from high school, aren't of much use to a college with competitive admissions. Some large state institutions want to de-emphasize the SAT by considering a variety of subjective factors in admissions, such as overcoming adversity, but first they must find money to hire additional people to handle those reviews.

And while much has been made of the correlation between SAT scores 15 and family income—the wealthier you are, the better your score, on average—that connection is even stronger on the standardized subject tests now known as SAT II, formerly called the Achievement Tests, one of Mr. Atkinson's proposed alternatives to the SAT.

"I hear a lot of people criticize the SAT," says Kurt M. Landgraf, president of the Educational Testing Service. "I've yet to hear what should be put in its place."

First administered in 1926, the SAT was designed to measure aptitude, or innate mental ability. It became widely used in the 1940s and 1950s, thanks in large part to James B. Conant, president of Harvard, who believed that subject-based achievement tests favored privileged students, whose families could afford to send them to boarding schools. The SAT, with its multiple-choice questions and systematic scoring, was seen as the great equalizer, a test that would allow the country's future leaders to be tapped based on intelligence rather than family connections. "The new elite's essential quality, the factor that would make its power deserved where the old elite's had been merely inherited, would be brains," Mr. Lemann writes in *The Big Test.*

Today, the enthusiasm for intelligence tests has plummeted, and most colleges claim to put more emphasis on high-school grades than on either the SAT or its primary competitor, the ACT.

Still, the SAT, whose two parts, verbal and mathematics, are each scored on a 200-to-800-point scale, has no shortage of fans. "The test is the one unchanging benchmark that can differentiate between those students who get B's at a tough school and those who coast with A's from an easy school," says John Maguire, an admissions consultant and former admissions director at Boston College.

Enrollment managers also know that recruiting students with high SAT 20 scores is an easy way to improve an institution's reputation. Dan Lundquist, vice president and dean of admissions at New York's Union College, says he uses the SAT as a "scale tipper" with students who are similarly qualified.

But he acknowledges that there's another good reason to do the tipping. "If you get enough [students] with 50 points higher than the rest, you can bring your mean SAT score up," he says.

Mr. Maguire concedes that there's a certain hypocrisy at work. "In public, people will say the SAT's aren't worth a bucket of warm spit," Mr. Maguire says. "Nonetheless, the boards of trustees and the college leadership are looking at [them] as badges similar to the rankings, that indicate that they are improving."

However, critics of the test—and many students who take it—view the SAT as a black box. "When you say someone has 1100, what does that communicate to a high-school student who wants to do better?" asks David T. Conley, an associate professor of education policy at the University of Oregon, who is directing a project on the use of state tests in college admissions. "It doesn't communicate anything but to tell the high-school student to get smarter."

Nor is it clear how to prepare for the exam, which leads many students to Kaplan and Princeton Review, companies seen as possessing "tricks" that help students raise their scores. Even some high-school teachers are taking time away from basic reading and writing instruction to prepare students for the SAT—a practice that Mr. Atkinson criticized.

Bill Wetzel, a freshman at New York University, says the SAT made   25
some courses during his junior and senior years at New Jersey's Red Bank Regional High School downright boring. "I noticed the difference between some classes, where the teachers and the students were trying to get the highest scores possible, and classes that emphasized curiosity and real critical thinking," he says.

Mr. Wetzel, founder of a group called Students Against Testing, notes somewhat sheepishly that his 1420 score helped land him at NYU, although he says that if he had to do it all over again he would attend an SAT-optional college. Now, he hopes to organize creative protests against the SAT and other standardized tests. He cites a recent "testfest" in Colorado in which students read books and played music while their peers took the SAT in a nearby building.

Using state examinations or subject tests would be an improvement, Mr. Wetzel says, but he isn't sure they would solve the core problem. "Both ideas have the potential for high schools to become factories for a different kind of test prep," he says.

Mr. Atkinson believes that his proposal, which would require students to take three SAT II tests (in writing, math, and a subject of each student's choice), would help students better understand the relevance of their high-school courses. There are more than a dozen SAT II exams, each covering a different subject area.

Some educators want to go even further, by using state examinations rather than the SAT. Every state requires its high-school students to undergo some form of statewide assessment, either at the end of their course work in core subjects or as a requirement for graduation. Advocates say the tests could provide a good snapshot of a student's readiness for college.

Last summer, a North Carolina legislator proposed a bill that would   30
make public colleges there drop the SAT requirement in favor of the state's assessment exam. When college officials balked, saying the tests don't do a good-enough job of measuring high-level skills, the sides compromised

by ordering a study of the issue by college officials. "If we're going to require students to take state tests, then we should use them for college entrance," says State Representative Gene G. Arnold, a Republican, who sponsored the bill. "It's unfair to use the SAT when our standard course of study is not geared toward preparing students for the test."

College officials elsewhere expect similar pressure from lawmakers who seek a better return on the hundreds of millions of dollars spent annually on the state exams. While those tests were intended to increase the accountability of public schools, some lawmakers say students have little at stake, once they realize how easy it is to pass, and thus have failed to take the tests seriously.

Because admissions officers would need the tests to provide meaningful information, college officials want a role in the development of future state tests. Thirteen research universities are sponsoring a study that aims to help states design better tests by agreeing on a set of skills needed by freshmen at their institutions. In addition, the project will create a database of current state tests, so that colleges can compare scores on tests in different states if they choose to use them in admissions decisions. The Association of American Universities, a group of 61 research institutions, is coordinating the project.

Without such a database, admissions directors say they will face a logistical nightmare in trying to make sense of scores from different states. John Katzman, founder and chief executive officer of *Princeton Review* and a supporter of state tests, says the College Board should take on the role of comparing state tests, by developing a chart similar to one that provides equivalencies for SAT and ACT scores.

"If the College Board won't do it, because they're too committed to saving the SAT, then other people will spring up that will, among them me," says Mr. Katzman, who favors the elimination of the SAT. Already, 100 Princeton Review employees are working on products to prepare students for state tests.

Wayne Camara, the College Board's vice president for research and de- 35 velopment, says the group has no intention of assuming that role. He cites a 1999 study by the National Academy of Sciences that said such efforts were destined to fail. "Comparing the full array of currently administered commercial and state achievement tests to one another, through the development of a single equivalency or linking scale, is not feasible," the study said.

Mr. Camara notes that any effort to correlate the scores would be incredibly complex, because some groups—such as Hispanic students or women—may score lower on certain state tests than they do on others.

College officials say it may come down to how well the state tests predict freshman grades, which is what the SAT claims to do. In April, the University of Minnesota-Twin Cities released a study, financed by the College Board, that found that the SAT reliably predicts students' academic performance, not only as freshmen but throughout college.

"We may find that the end-of-course tests are great predictors, or we may find that they are consistent with everything else we're doing, in which case why would we have to add yet another measure that schools have to collect and send on to colleges?" asks Gretchen Bataille, senior vice president for academic affairs at the University of North Carolina system.

Mr. Caperton, the College Board president, says that when states learn how much it costs to develop fair questions and ensure security for an admissions test, they will use that money instead for other priorities, like paying teachers more. "Could you turn a statewide test into an admissions test?" he asks rhetorically. "Absolutely. But when you compare what it costs to what you get, nobody is going to spend their money that way."

Mr. Conley, the Oregon researcher who is heading up the Association 40 of American Universities' project on state tests, says the money is worth spending to give students and high schools better measures of where they need to improve.

"The SAT is limited in its ability to provide diagnostic information to schools," Mr. Conley says. "It was never conceived as a means to bring about systemic improvement or to close an achievement gap between groups."

University of California officials agree. They acknowledge that students of different races will probably show the same performance gaps on the SAT II and even state tests. But those exams are better suited to closing the gaps and identifying poor schools, they say. "By having curriculum-based tests, we can relate [students' scores to] the quality of instruction in schools," says Patrick Hayashi, associate president of the University of California system.

The point differential between white and minority students is also leading to a diminished role for the SAT, simply because it lays bare the use of racial preferences in college admissions. In the 2000–2001 academic year, white students scored an average of 1060 on the test, compared with 859 for black students and 925 for Hispanic students.

Asian American students were on top, with an average score of 1095.

Many large public colleges, which generally make admissions decisions 45 based on a formula rather than a subjective "reading" of each application, have sought to preserve enrollments of black and Hispanic students by giving them an explicit bonus in the process. But in several high-profile legal decisions—including a ruling by a federal appeals court in August that struck down the admissions process at the University of Georgia—such mechanical awarding of racial preferences has been successfully challenged as unconstitutional by white students who were denied admission.

As a result, admissions directors say that colleges may be forced to gravitate toward a more holistic set of criteria that recognize a wider range of achievement, such as leadership and overcoming adversity.

"Frankly, even those schools that are not highly selective are going to have to put in place procedures that allow for the reading of all applicants," says Jerome A. Lucido, associate provost and director of admissions at the University of North Carolina at Chapel Hill. "The days of looking solely at students' grades and SAT scores and saying 'they're in' are coming to an end."

Some very selective public institutions, like North Carolina and the University of Virginia, have been reading every admissions folder for decades. Combined, the two universities receive 32,000 applications annually, and both hire temporary staff members to read them all. Officials at both universities admit that taking essays and other written material into consideration is more subjective than using only grades and test scores, but they say that each application is reviewed by two or more readers to ensure consistency.

The Board of Regents at the University of California will vote on whether to establish a similar process, called "comprehensive review," next month. (The board won't decide whether to drop the SAT requirement until next spring.)

The proposed review process would require admissions officers at the 50 university system's nine campuses to evaluate every student on a broad array of criteria, including initiative and hardship.

The super-competitive Berkeley campus has already curtailed the influence of the SAT. In 1998, two years after the state's voters approved a referendum banning affirmative action in public-college admissions, Berkeley officials started reading every application, some 36,000 last year. Before then, the first half of available slots for freshmen, about 4,400 seats, were allocated solely on the basis of SAT scores and high-school grade-point averages.

Now, those coveted first seats are given out based on a much broader and less rigid formula. It still includes an applicant's SAT score and GPA, but adds other academic factors, such as the strength of the curriculum and pattern of grades throughout high school. In the first year that Berkeley relied less on SAT scores, officials found that 25 percent of the admissions decisions were different than if the old procedure had been in place. (The remaining half of the university's freshmen are accepted using the expanded academic criteria and other personal factors.)

Although the changes in the admissions process at Berkeley were aimed in part to capture underrepresented minority students in the wake of the state ban on affirmative action, the number of black and Hispanic students accepted at Berkeley has actually fallen since the new procedures were put in place. University officials say they expected the minority numbers to drop. But "we didn't have the degree of loss that we would have had if we didn't put this extra care and effort into reading every application," says Pamela Burnett, the university's director of undergraduate admissions.

The College Board, which has long urged colleges not to rely too heavily on the SAT, supports the UC system's proposed move to a fuller review — for reasons that are not entirely altruistic. "If UC goes for comprehensive review, there's less pressure to do away with the SAT," says the board's Mr. Camara. The SAT would become just one of many tools in evaluating applicants, he says.

But Robert Laird, a former undergraduate-admissions director at Berke- 55 ley, wonders whether the practice of reading every application will become widespread at large public institutions, given the cost involved.

"As state budgets across the country shrink sharply, it's going to be difficult to generate the legislative and institutional financial support to put significantly more money into the undergraduate admissions process," he says.

In the late 1990s, some states facing bans on affirmative action discovered a cheaper way to ensure that their public campuses remained racially diverse. California, Florida, and Texas now automatically admit large numbers of students based solely on class rank, essentially making SAT scores irrelevant. Texas' public colleges began guaranteeing spots for the top 10 percent of the state's high-school classes in 1997, and California and Florida followed in 1999, holding slots for the top 4 percent and 20 percent, respectively. The policies take advantage of the many high schools that are predominantly black or Hispanic.

Now, the University of Texas at Austin is considering whether the SAT is even worth requiring for the half of the freshman class not automatically admitted under the state's 10-percent policy. A faculty committee convened by the university's president, Larry R. Faulkner, started meeting last month to study the fairness of standardized tests in Austin's admissions process.

The trend toward "x-percent plans" and more-subjective admissions policies hasn't escaped the gaze of those who uphold high standards or oppose racial preferences. Michael McIntyre, a professor of organizational and industrial psychology at the University of Tennessee at Knoxville who has studied the SAT, says that if the goal at the University of California is to maintain diversity, officials should be honest about their motives. "A change in policy is very likely to change the demographic mix," Mr. McIntyre says. "If that's the goal of the the change, then let's be upfront about it. Let's admit it if we are trying to achieve some social end, rather than an academic end."

Mr. Lemann, the author, supports affirmative action, but cautions that 60 college officials may be fooling themselves if they think a subjective admissions process will shield them from lawsuits. He says that legal groups leading the fight against racial preferences, like the Center for Individual Rights, would have a more difficult time proving that such policies discriminate against white students, but in some cases would still be able to do so. "The Center for Individual Rights has gone after the low-hanging fruit," Mr. Lemann says, "and there's a lot of it."

The College Board and ETS, meanwhile, occupy a strange position in the affirmative-action debate. Both are firmly within the academic establishment, which strongly defends the use of racial preferences in admissions. The College Board is a membership organization that represents colleges and schools. ETS, meanwhile, lures top researchers, in part, by providing college-like surroundings on its verdant 360-acre campus outside Princeton, New Jersey. Partly because of the scrutiny of affirmative action, both groups have counseled colleges to avoid relying too heavily on test scores.

But now that some colleges are not even considering the SAT in admitting large portions of their students, the traditional alliances may be breaking down. Mr. Landgraf, the ETS president, for example, views the "x-percent plans" as a blow to high standards, even though they are a handy tool for maintaining black and Hispanic enrollments. "Are the interests of the states best served by silencing the debate," Mr. Landgraf asks, "or by doing what's right?"

Mr. Landgraf and nearly everyone else agree that the best way to end the debate would be to eliminate the performance gap between students of different races. Most of those who use the x-percent plans admit privately that they would go back to the SAT in a minute, were it not for those racial gaps. But despite considerable hand-wringing, and efforts at outreach, the gaps between white, black, and Hispanic students have barely budged in more than a decade.

The College Board sponsors a good deal of research aimed at broadening the scope of skills measured by the SAT, and much of that work has the secondary goal of finding measurements upon which black and Hispanic students will score well.

Robert Sternberg, a Yale University psychology professor who believes the SAT should be expanded to measure creative and practical skills, is among the most prominent scholars receiving funds from the board. To measure creativity, Mr. Sternberg suggests showing students a single-frame cartoon and asking them to write a caption for it. To measure practical ability or common sense, he would include a reading about a real-life dilemma that teenagers might face, and ask students to identify the best way to handle the situation. 65

Mr. Sternberg acknowledges that grading the answers would be more expensive than it is now; particularly on the creative questions, a machine would not be able to do the job. But the College Board could hire readers, as it does to grade essays on Advanced Placement tests. The readers would use examples that would illustrate what types of captions might earn top scores for creativity.

"By measuring a broader range of abilities, you would no longer need affirmative action," Mr. Sternberg says. "Some of the kids who grow up in culturally different environments have to develop creative and practical skills to survive. If you grow up in a white, upper-middle-class environment, you don't need those skills as much."

He and a team of researchers are conducting a study that involves roughly 1,000 college students at 16 sites. "So far, our results are in line with our hypothesis—that we can find better ways of predicting success," he says.

Those sorts of measures generally draw howls of protest from critics of affirmative action, and many of the psychometricians involved in creating the SAT are equally dubious.

"I'd be a little concerned that you could coach someone to pretend to 70 be creative," says Thomas Van Essen, who develops verbal tests at ETS. "Think of those kids you knew in high school who were 'creative'—they all acted the same."

The testing giant's own efforts to narrow the gap in test scores have elicited similar skepticism. In 1999, ETS officials revealed that they were working on a project that would help admissions officers measure disadvantage, by identifying as a "striver" any student who scored more than 200 points above the average score of students from a similar background. The scale took into account 14 variables, such as family income and parents' education, but its developers noted that the only way to achieve "a student body that mirrors the racial composition of the U.S. population" was to use race in the process.

The effort was excoriated by opponents of affirmative action, and quickly condemned by Mr. Caperton. Last month in Princeton, a table of six ETS officials briefly fell silent when the topic was broached.

"We didn't feel there was sufficient technical quality behind it," says Drew H. Gitomer, senior vice president for statistics and research. "While the intent of the study was noble, we didn't feel there was a whole lot there."

Meanwhile, the College Board's efforts to deal with its other problem— the perception that the SAT has no link to the curriculum—can best be described as modest. For years, it reacted mainly with semantics. In 1994, it changed the name "Scholastic Aptitude Test" to "Scholastic Assessment Test," to suggest a measurement of educational accomplishment rather than innate ability. A few years later, it shortened the name to just "SAT."

College Board officials insist that the test has responded to changes in 75 the curriculum over time. They note that they began permitting calculators on the math exam in 1994, to reflect the practice of many schools. The same year, they killed a section of questions on antonyms, to answer critics who suggested that it was encouraging schools to spend too much time on vocabulary devoid of context.

Similar criticisms are now being leveled at the analogies section, and the College Board is studying whether it would be feasible to replace that part with questions on a short, high-level reading passage.

"The notion that this test hasn't changed in 50 years is completely untrue," says Amy Schmidt, the College Board's director of higher-education research and educational evaluation.

Somewhat belatedly, the board is also beginning to help test takers figure out what skills they need to improve to raise their scores. This fall, for the first time, the board is sending score reports to students who have taken the PSAT, which high-school sophomores and juniors take as a warm-up to the SAT.

The reports list specific skills that each student needs to work on— such as understanding the main ideas of a reading passage, or applying the rules of algebra and geometry. There are no immediate plans to provide such reports to students who take the SAT.

"Maybe we could have done a little better job over the years of com- 80 municating what these questions do measure," concedes Mr. Gitomer.

Whether those efforts will be enough to save the SAT remains to be seen. The best hope for the test may be that it's so entrenched in the admissions process.

Mr. Conley, the advocate for state tests, doesn't expect them to be required on college applications anytime soon. "The college-admissions process is a conservative system, and we're talking about a brand-new infrastructure that doesn't exist," he says. "It's like setting a massive ship off in a different direction, and that's never easy or quick."

When a committee studying whether to eliminate the SAT requirement at the University of Texas first met last month, several professors wondered what would replace the test if its use were abolished. They feared that a process without standardized tests would lead to inconsistent admissions decisions.

The SAT is still required at the highly selective public colleges that give every application a thorough read. John A. Blackburn, Virginia's dean of admissions, says the university does not plan to drop the requirement.

"In a major system, where you have to make decisions about a lot of 85 people and where you're responsible to the public, you must have some norm that cuts across high schools," Mr. Blackburn says. "Until we have something better, the SAT is really the only instrument that achieves that."

Are SAT Scores "Worse Than Meaningless"?

BEFORE READING: How does the state in which you attended high school compare with other states when it comes to the perceived quality of education students get in the public schools? Did you believe that you were getting a good education? Did your perception match any published reports about the quality of your state's schools?

R anking states according to their SAT averages is "worse than meaningless," warn Greg Marchant and Sharon Paulson, education experts at Ball State University, Muncie, Indiana. "The state SAT rankings are worthless in determining the quality of the schools in a state, and the potential for basing perceptions and policies on the rankings is even worse," argues Marchant.

Research by Marchant and Paulson determined that the rankings say more about the nature of the students taking the test than about the states' educational systems. Their study examined the characteristics of individuals taking the SAT and compared the ten highest-scoring states with the ten lowest. They found the larger the percentage of students taking the SAT in a state, the lower the average score.

In the ten states with the highest SAT scores, an average of eight percent of their high school students took the SAT, while 69 percent of students took the test in the ten lowest-scoring states. Moreover, the lowest ten states had twice as many high school juniors taking the test and 14 times as many SAT takers overall.

"The states with the highest SAT scores and lowest percentage of SAT takers tend to be testing mostly their best and brightest," Marchant explains. "There is more diversity in the ability of test takers that come from the lower-scoring states. In the top-scoring states, twice as many test takers come from the top 10 percent of their class. Test takers from lower-scoring states represent a far greater range of both class rank and grade-point average." The more a state's education system works to increase college attendance for students who have traditionally not pursued higher education, the lower the state's average SAT scores are likely to be, he points out.

Differences in parent income and parent education of the test takers ac- 5 counted for 92 percent of the difference among states' average SAT scores. The ten bottom-scoring states had more than 41 times as many test takers from families with incomes less than $10,000. "This is a major issue for high school students attempting to be first-generation college students," Marchant notes. Compared to the ten highest-scoring states, the bottom ten states had more than 31 times as many test takers with parents holding only a

---

This unsigned article appeared in the December 1, 2001, issue of *USA Today Magazine*.

high school diploma and more than 60 times as many test takers with parents who did not graduate from high school.

"Policymakers and the general public are likely to be misled about the relative quality of a state's education system," he warns. "They do not understand that the rankings reflect the characteristics of the students taking the test. This confusion can lead to erroneous policy decisions and false perceptions."

THINKING AND WRITING ABOUT RELIANCE ON STANDARDIZED TESTING

QUESTIONS FOR DISCUSSION AND WRITING

1. Do you agree with Vickers that today's children are pressured too much too early by parents who want them to succeed academically? Is the same true in other areas of the children's lives, such as sports or music?

2. Do you believe that children and teenagers are "pigeonholed" in school because of their performance on standardized tests? Or are there other reasons that some students are assumed, for example, to be "college material" while others are not?

3. Whose argument do you find more convincing, Paige's or Weaver's? Why?

4. Do you believe that schools are guilty of teaching to the test too much? What should be emphasized instead?

5. Argue for or against keeping the SAT as a factor in college admissions. If you favor doing away with the SAT as an admissions tool, what should be used in its place?

6. A part of the accountability movement is the publishing of test results by state, by district, and by school. Does the article from *USA Today* convince you that those published results may not be as straightforward as they seem? Explain.

7. Write an argument of fact essay explaining the current status of the movement to do away with the SAT as a college admission requirement.

8. Write an essay arguing whether or not American students would be better served by the creative approach to education toward which China is now moving.

TOPICS FOR RESEARCH

Bias against minorities in standardized testing

What the SAT really tests

Individual states' success stories with standardized testing

The SAT as a predictor of success in college

What statistics on standardized testing really reveal

CHAPTER 17

What Is the Role of Sex and Violence in Popular Culture?

The ongoing controversy about explicit sex and violence in movies, television shows, rap music, and computer and video games does not seem likely to subside soon. Depictions of sex and violence become increasingly graphic and increasingly accessible each year. In one of the essays in this unit, Ron Kaufman quotes William F. Baker and George Dessart, who in their book *Down the Tube* (1998) write, "In its simplest terms, the business of television in this country is the buying and selling of eyeballs." The same might be said of the business of making movies or producing computer and video games, and the success of rap music and rap music videos that openly celebrate violence and sexism reinforces the notion that if sex and violence sell, no shortage of entrepreneurs will be ready to cash in.

Are some forms of popular entertainment necessarily dangerous and immoral? How much are viewers affected by continued exposure to depictions of explicit sex and violence? Researchers have argued the point for years, but today a majority believe that long-term viewing does, in fact, alter the behavior of certain audiences. In recent years, what appear to be copycat crimes have followed the release of particularly violent films. Experts also debate the relative effects of fictional and real-life images: Which are more disturbing and potentially more corrupting—the graphic creations in movies or the daily reports of real-life horrors in the news? And do children recognize the difference?

Not surprisingly, even where agreement exists on the nature of the problem, there is disagreement about solutions. However strongly some critics feel about the dangers of exposure, they argue that the dangers of government censorship may, in the long run, be greater. But if government intervention is rejected, can other solutions—a rating system for television shows and music albums, a V-chip in the TV set allowing parents to block undesirable programs, respect by producers for the so-called family hour, and above all, closer monitoring by parents—guarantee that young people will be insulated from exposure to sex and violence in the media? Most Americans are not optimistic.

Of course, popular culture is not the only source of exposure. Movies, television, music, and games reflect the activities, tastes, fantasies, and prejudices of a larger society. Reducing the amount of sex and violence in the media is certainly easier than reforming a whole society. Still, questions remain: Why are some of the most popular forms of entertainment those with the highest body count and the most grisly depiction of carnage and suffering? To what extent can any reform in popular entertainment successfully address the problems of crime and immorality?

Does Watching Sex on Television Influence Teens' Sexual Activity?

REBECCA L. COLLINS ET AL.

BEFORE READING: How would you answer the question posed in the title of this essay?

The average American teenager watches three hours of television a day. Typical teen fare contains heavy doses of sexual content, ranging from touching, kissing, jokes, and innuendo to conversations about sexual activity and portrayals of intercourse. Sex is often presented as a casual activity without risk or consequences. Conventional wisdom holds that the messages young viewers absorb from television promote sexual activity in this group. Yet, despite the prevalence of this view, there has been little empirical study to date of how watching sex on television influences teenagers' sexual behavior.

Two recent studies led by RAND Health behavioral scientist Rebecca Collins examined the impact of TV sex on teenagers' sexual beliefs and

This Highlight summarizes RAND Health research reported in the following publications: Collins, Rebecca L., Marc N. Elliott, Sandra H. Berry, David E. Kanouse, Dale Kunkel, Sarah B. Hunter, and Angela Miu, "Watching Sex on Television Predicts Adolescent Initiation of Sexual Behavior," *Pediatrics*, Vol. 114, No. 3, September 2004.
Collins, Rebecca L., Marc N. Elliott, Sandra H. Berry, David E. Kanouse, and Sarah B. Hunter, "Entertainment Television as a Healthy Sex Educator: The Impact of Condom-Efficacy Information in an Episode of *Friends*," *Pediatrics*, Vol. 112, No. 5, November 2003.

activities. The results supported the view that watching shows with sexual content may influence teen sexual behavior, but also found that some viewing effects can be positive.

- Watching TV shows with sexual content apparently hastens the initiation of teen sexual activity.

- Sexual talk on TV has the same effect on teens as depictions of sex.

- Shows with content about contraception and pregnancy can help to educate teens about the risks and consequences of sex—and can also foster beneficial dialogue between teens and parents.

Exposure to TV Sex May Hasten the Initiation of Sexual Activity among Teens

Unplanned pregnancies and sexually transmitted diseases (STDs) are more common among youth who begin sexual activity at earlier ages. Thus, early initiation of intercourse is an important public health issue. It is widely believed that TV plays a role in hastening the initiation of sexual activity in teens. The first RAND study, funded by the National Institute of Child Health and Human Development, examined this issue. Analysts surveyed a national sample of households containing an adolescent from 12 to 17 years old. A total of 1,762 adolescents were asked about their sexual experiences and also their television-viewing habits and, one year later, were surveyed again.

The researchers measured levels of exposure to three kinds of sexual content on television: (1) sexual behavior, such as kissing, intimate touching, and implied or depicted intercourse, (2) talk about sexual plans or desires or about sex that has occurred, and expert advice, and (3) talk about or behavior showing the risks of or the need for safety in regard to sexual activity: abstinence, waiting to have sex, portrayals mentioning or showing contraceptives, and portrayals related to consequences, such as AIDS, STDs, pregnancy, and abortion.

The results showed that heavy exposure to sexual content on television related strongly to teens' initiation of intercourse or their progression to more advanced sexual activities (such as "making out" or oral sex) apart from intercourse in the following year. Youths who viewed the greatest amounts of sexual content were two times more likely than those who viewed the smallest amount to initiate sexual intercourse during the following year (see figure) or to progress to more-advanced levels of other sexual activity. In effect, youths who watched the most sexual content "acted older": a 12-year-old at the highest levels of exposure behaved like a 14- or 15-year-old at the lowest levels.

The study also identified other factors that increased the likelihood that teens would initiate intercourse, including being older, having older friends, getting lower grades, engaging in rule-breaking such as skipping class, and sensation-seeking.

Across All Age Groups, Teens Who Saw the Most Sex on Television Were Twice as Likely to Initiate Intercourse Within the Next Year as Were Those Who Saw the Least

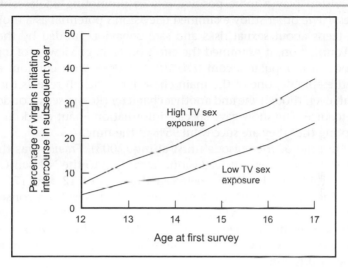

A different set of factors was found to decrease the likelihood of first intercourse. Many of these factors centered on parent characteristics, including having parents who monitored teens' activities, having parents who were more educated or who were clearly disapproving of teens' having sexual relations, and living with both parents. Other factors that reduced the likelihood of having sex included being more religious and feeling less depressed or anxious than other youths. Most of these characteristics were also related to how much sex teens saw on television; however, viewing sexual content on TV was related to advances in sexual behavior even after these other factors were taken into account.

The results also showed that talk about sex on TV had virtually the same effect on teen behavior as depictions of sexual activity. This finding runs counter to the widespread belief that portrayals of action have a more powerful impact than talk.

The study found no strong connection between delays in sexual behavior and TV content that dealt with risks, except among African-American youths, indicating that this group may be more strongly affected by portrayals of the negative consequences of sex. However, given the rarity of such programming, the study did not conclude that there is no effect on youth from other ethnic groups. Rather, it concluded that more-effective tests of such material are needed. One way to test such effects is to examine the impact of particular shows or episodes that deal with sexual risk. The second study, described on the following page, took this approach.

TV Can Also Inform Teens about Risks and Foster Communication with Parents

Can television play a more positive role in promoting adolescent sexual 10 awareness? The other study examined television's potential as a tool for educating teens about sexual risks and safe behavior. Funded by the Kaiser Family Foundation, it examined the effect on teenage viewers of a particular episode of a popular sitcom (*Friends*) that dealt with condom efficacy. During the episode, one of the main characters (Rachel) reveals that she is pregnant, even though she and another character (Ross) used a condom during intercourse. The show gave specific information about condom-efficacy rates, noting that they are successful 95% of the time.

At the time of the episode's first airing (2003), *Friends* was the most popular show on American television. According to the Nielsen Corporation, 1.67 million adolescents between the ages of 12 and 17 saw this episode. The possibility of condom failure and the resulting consequence of pregnancy were thus vividly communicated to a very large adolescent audience, as was the message that condoms almost always work. Given the size of the audience, the episode's potential to influence large numbers of teens was enormous.

To gauge the episode's impact, RAND used information from its earlier study to identify adolescents who watch *Friends* regularly, and phoned them to ask about the *Friends* condom episode and assess its impact on their perceptions of condom use and failure. The results showed that

- the majority of teens (65%) whose viewing of the episode could be confirmed recalled the show's specific information about condom-efficacy rates.

- the majority of teen viewers continued to perceive condoms as somewhat or very effective, as in the earlier survey, though the episode caused about equal amounts of positive and negative change in that perception.

- as a result of watching the episode, many teens (10% of viewers) talked with a parent or another adult about the effectiveness of condoms.

- teens' reactions to the episode were changed by viewing or discussing the episode with an adult. These teens were more than twice as likely to recall information about condom efficacy.

The study did not find dramatic changes in teens' sexual knowledge or belief. However, it looked at only a single episode of television, and one that included the somewhat complicated message that condoms almost always work, but sometimes fail, and with huge consequences. The researchers concluded that entertainment shows that include portrayals of sexual risks and consequences can potentially have two beneficial effects on teen sexual awareness: They can teach accurate messages about sexual risks, and they can stimulate a conversation with adults that can reinforce those messages.

Implications

Taken together, the two studies suggest the need to reduce teens' exposure to sexual content on television and to explore greater use of entertainment shows to inform teens about risk. Reducing the amount of sexual talk and behavior on television, or the amount of time that adolescents are exposed to them, could appreciably delay the onset of sexual activity. At the same time, increasing the percentage of portrayals of sexual risk and safety relative to other sexual content might also inhibit early sexual activity, increase knowledge of sexual risks and how to be safe, and stimulate dialogue with parents.

Reducing teens' exposure to portrayals of sex on television poses challenges, however. An alternative approach that has worked with violent content may also work with sexual content: having parents view programs with their children and discuss their own beliefs regarding the behavior depicted. Doing so can reinforce the benefits of accurate risk information and positive messages and may help to limit the negative effects of sexual portrayals that do not contain risk information. 15

Filling Their Minds with Death: TV Violence and Children

RON KAUFMAN

> BEFORE READING: Do you believe that television shows and movies have gone too far in the depiction of sex and violence? Is the exposure of such explicit programming to children a legitimate concern?

> We do not believe there is anything sexist or violent about the World Wrestling Federation. I think it's unfair of you to insinuate it when there are so many shows and so many different movies, and so many different social problems that really do contribute to violence in this country. —UPN president Dean Valentine in 1999 after a seven-year-old child in Dallas killed his little brother with a "clothesline" maneuver he had seen on a wrestling show.

One fact should not be in dispute: TV is violent! Guns, shootings, murders, hitting, punching, slapping, screaming, kicking, stabbing, explosions, car chases, car smashes, disasters, and death are shown daily

---

Ron Kaufman, a journalist and teacher, is the creator of TurnOffYourTV.com, where this article originally appeared. In the online original, he provided links directly to most of his sources.

throughout TV programming. Most violence is not even in nightly news programs and nearly all of the violence on television is fake. TV presents violent acts through acting—with fake guns and fake blood. For adults, televised violence is probably not a big deal. When a character is killed off a TV show one week, we know the same actor will reappear the next week on another show on a different network.

A study by the Parents Television Council (PTC) entitled "TV Bloodbath: Violence on Prime Time Broadcast TV" looked at changes in the levels of violence on television from 1998 to 2002. The report notes that on the major noncable broadcast networks, "In 2002, depictions of violence were 41 percent more frequent during the 8:00 P.M. Family Hour, and 134.4 percent more frequent during the 9:00 P.M. hour than in 1998." The study also noted that while CBS was the least violent network, Fox was the most violent, followed closely by UPN and NBC.

The PTC study, though limited, did see increases in certain types of violence such as an increase in blood, guns, deaths, and torture:

8:00–9:00 P.M.	1998 %	2002 %
Fight	44	32
Blood	0	9
Guns and other weapons	29	38
Crashes, explosions, fire	6	5
Threats of violence	7	5
Graphic depictions	10	1
Deaths depicted	4	5
Deaths implied	0	3
Torture	0	2

The Center for Media Literacy presents three common themes with respect to TV violence:

1. Violence Drives the Storyline

Violence is always involved. The fictional programs on television require a crime, murder, or fist-fight to develop plot and story. For example, in January 2004 CBS ran three straight hours of violent shows on Thursday nights starting with *Cold Case:* "Churchgoing People," "Lilly investigates the 1990 murder of a church organist who was found in an alley surrounded by crack vials and racy magazines." This was followed by *CSI:* "Fur and Loathing," "A team explores the world of fetishes after finding a dead man dressed in a raccoon costume; the corpse of a convenience-store employee turns up in an industrial freezer." CBS finished off with *Without a Trace:* "Prodigy," "A fourteen-year-old Russian violinist disappears after a rehearsal for a concert appearance."

5

Figure 1. Overall Industry Averages: Three-Year Comparisons
(National Television Violence Study, p. 27.)

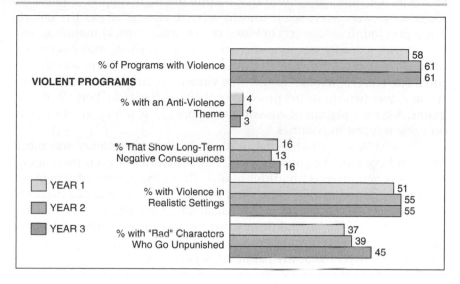

Not to be outdone, the Fox network ran *Tru Calling:* "Reunion," "Tru attends her high-school reunion and finds the most popular girl from school dead in a swimming pool." This program was then followed by *The World's Worst Drivers Caught on Tape 3,* "Cameras record motorists creating havoc on the roadways."

The National Cable Television Association's National Television Violence Study (Report 3 released in 1998) states that "across the three years of this study, a steady 60 percent of TV programs contain violence . . . [and] much of the violence is glamorized, sanitized, and trivialized." (See Fig. 1.)

2. Violence Has No Consequences

C'mon now—the hero *always* wins. The hero of TV shows never gets in trouble for his/her violent actions. The hero is always "justified" in one way or another when committing violent acts. "TV rarely shows the consequences of violence. Guardians of law and order whether it's Maxwell Smart, Kojak, or the *Miami Vice* squad emerge from their conflicts with little more than a scrape. Occasionally, unlucky characters (but never the hero!) end up in a nice clean hospital bed," explains the Center for Media Literacy (*Media & Values,* Issue no. 62, Spring 1993, by Barbara Osborn).

Television will never show a main character lose an arm or leg or get killed on screen. In reality, with as much gunplay that appears on TV, main characters should also get shot. The "bad guy" can get shot, killed, burned, or maimed, but never the hero. In fact, the hero can really be as violent has he/she wants.

A study released by the Center for Media and Public Affairs (CMPA)   10
in June 1999 states that though television shows a lot of violence, it rarely
shows its outcome. "We found that despite the high volume of televised
violence, viewers rarely see it causing adverse effects," states the report.
The report found serious acts of violence—murder, rape, kidnapping, and
assault with a deadly weapon—occurred once every four minutes on the
major TV networks. However, it notes that "no physical harm was shown
three quarters (75 percent) of the time violence occurred on broadcast series and over two-thirds (68 percent) of the time it occurred on cable programs. A mere 7 percent of violent acts on broadcast shows and 4 percent
on cable resulted in fatalities."

The CMPA report notes that in its study, "serious violence was more
likely to have tangible consequences, but a majority of even these more
brutal acts had no direct harmful results. Fifty-nine percent of acts of serious violence on broadcast series and 54 percent on cable lacked negative
consequences." Only in rare instances, about 10 percent, did violence result in some type of mental distress for the victim or another character.
"Thus, fully 90 percent of violent acts on broadcast and 87 percent on
cable proved psychologically painless," says the report.

The current trend in TV programs is to permit not only the police to
commit justifiable violence but criminals as well. "HBO's *The Sopranos* [is]
the beginning of a new trend celebrating what's called the 'criminal pro-

Context of Violence in TV Series (percent)
(Center for Media and Public Affairs: "Merchandising Mayhem: Violence
in Popular Entertainment, 1998–1999.")

	Broadcast		Cable	
	All	Serious Only	All	Serious Only
Presentation				
Shown	98	82	98	67
Aftermath	2	18	2	33
Physical harm				
None	75	59	68	54
Fatal injury	7	14	4	8
Other injury	11	18	20	32
Property damage	7	8	8	6
Psychological harm				
None	90	84	87	84
Victim	8	8	11	10
Others	2	8	2	6

tagonist,' in this case a murderous crime boss we can learn to love," says L. Brent Bozell III, president of the Parents Television Council. "Entertainment producers and critics alike love 'moral complexity,' but what they're sowing is moral confusion. They think good and evil, black and white, is so old hat. Let's coat everyone and everything with a lovely shade of gray —as the red blood flows."

Bozell's group is not against TV but has serious problems with the amount of violence currently shown on the networks. The PTC has also led many campaigns against advertisers to try and reduce the revenue streams to violent programs. "Imagine my shock—and the shock of millions of others—coming across FX's wicked-cop series *The Shield . . .* the show ended with 'criminal protagonist' Vic Mackey gratuitously shoving a man's face into an electric burner. Watch the melting flesh as Fox counts the advertising dollars."

On TV today, it's not even that "bad" characters go unpunished but that "good" characters are *justified* in being bad. Sure, the cops on *Miami Vice* had to be violent to get the criminals, the *A-Team* was always "wrongly accused," and Buck Rogers didn't ever do a bad thing with a laser gun. The idea of *justifiable violence* is something that should have parents really consider what their children are watching.

3. TV Is a World of Good and Bad

Even though both criminals and cops can commit justifiable violence— television is still a simple medium. TV presents "good guys" and "bad guys." On average, there are fifteen minutes of commercials for every one hour of TV programming, so producers only have a short amount of time in which to establish plot, story, characters, and resolution. Good characters and bad characters must be quickly and simply established.

"Deeper, more realistic, more ambiguous characterizations make it hard for viewers to know who to root for. It also requires more screen time that takes away from on screen action," states the Center for Media Literacy. "As a result, TV and film criminals are reduced to caricatures. They are 100 percent bad. No one could care about them. They have no families. Many of them don't even have full names, only nicknames. They deserve no sympathy and they get what they deserve."

The bad guys, whether they are cops or robbers, have to be 100 percent bad to justify the violence against them. Television violence is the struggle of good versus evil. It's OK to shoot the bad guy—after all, he's the "bad guy."

According to the study by the Center for Media and Public Affairs, the most violent show observed in 1999 was CBS's *Walker, Texas Ranger*. This show "took the top spot for overall violence with a rate of 112 acts per show, over two-thirds of them (82) serious. Almost every episode of this long-running Chuck Norris cop show includes several martial arts fight scenes and some gunplay," says the report. "The fall season's first episode was especially violent. It opened with a combination gun battle/fight

15

scene that ran approximately ten minutes, resulting in several characters being shot and beaten. This episode also featured a montage of violent scenes, including police raids to catch the bad guys as well as another major gun battle."

There have been many studies about the effects of television violence on children. Research shows a number of facts:

1. Children in the United States Watch Many Hours of TV

According to the ACT Against Violence Project, on average, young chil- 20 dren spend two to four hours per day watching television. They also spend thirty-five hours per week of screen time with TV or video games. The Kaiser Foundation reports that nearly all children in the United States (99 percent) live in homes with a TV set and one-third have a TV in their bedroom. "The vast majority of children are growing up in homes where television is a near-constant presence," writes the Kaiser Foundation in a report entitled "Zero to Six: Electronic Media in the Lives of Infants, Toddlers, and Preschoolers." (See Fig. 2.)

Figure 2.
(The Henry J. Kaiser Family Foundation, "Zero to Six: Electronic Media in the Lives of Infants, Toddlers, and Preschoolers," Fall 2003, p. 4.)

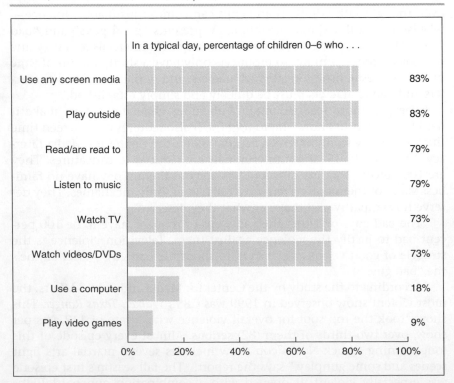

In a typical day, percentage of children 0–6 who . . .

Use any screen media	83%
Play outside	83%
Read/are read to	79%
Listen to music	79%
Watch TV	73%
Watch videos/DVDs	73%
Use a computer	18%
Play video games	9%

0%   20%   40%   60%   80%   100%

Two-thirds of zero-to-six-year-olds (65 percent) live in a home where the TV is on at least half the time or more, even if no one is watching and one-third (36 percent) live in "heavy" TV households, where the television is left on "always" or "most of the time."

2. Violent Behavior Is a Learned Trait

Most psychologists agree that experiences children have during their early years will have a longstanding impact in their lives. "What a child learns about violence, a child learns for life," states ACT Against Violence. The organization breaks down the early years of TV viewing development this way:

INFANTS (0–18 MONTHS)

From birth to 18 months, infants are interested in TV only for brief periods of time because they are attracted to the light and sound.

TODDLERS (18–36 MONTHS)

They pay much more attention to what is on TV and are able to get meaning from programs they watch. They react equally to animated violence and real violence because their link between fantasy and reality is not strong.

PRESCHOOLERS (3–5 YEARS)

Children look forward to shows. They understand what they are viewing but cannot give it a context. They cannot judge reality versus fantasy or commercials versus regular programs. They are attracted to highly vivid scenes, rapid movement, sound, and color. In other words, most children pay the most attention to the most violent scenes on the screen.

ELEMENTARY SCHOOL AGE (6–11 YEARS)

Children believe that TV reflects real life and will become more active and show more aggressive behavior after viewing violent scenes. High viewing levels have been shown to interfere with reading development.

The Kaiser Foundation report states that 81 percent of parents have seen their children imitate either positive (e.g., sharing, helping) or aggressive (e.g., hitting, kicking) behaviors from TV. The report notes that overall, by the time children are six years old, nearly half (47 percent) the parents studied reported that their children imitated aggressive behaviors from TV.

A child's cognitive development during the early years is extremely important. ACT Against Violence explains that "young infants can imitate live models as well as what they see on TV, even without full understanding of their actions; they learn by watching and imitating others." Over the course of a child's first three years, the brain continues to grow and expand at a rapid pace. New nerve connections (called synapses) permit more complex methods of thinking, moving, and talking. Children learn a great deal about the world when they are young and base their future cognitive, motor, and emotional development by "mimicking" adults.

Children exposed to large doses of violent programming will give them violent heroes to imitate (and it doesn't matter if the TV character was *justified* to use violence). It will also show children that violence is the right way to handle conflicts and may also whet their appetite for viewing more violence. Violence usually begets more extreme forms of violence.

The American Psychological Association (APA) notes that research 25 shows that babies as young as twelve months will read and react to actors' emotions on television. The American Association of Pediatrics (AAP) recommends that children under two years old do not watch TV at all. An AAP policy statement asks pediatricians to "encourage more interactive activities [for infants] that will promote proper brain development, such as talking, playing, singing, and reading together."

3. Children Who Watch a Lot of Television Become Aggressive Adults

The most influential research released to date on this subject was published in March 2003. Researchers from the University of Michigan published their findings from a fifteen-year longitudinal study of 329 youths. It showed that men and women who watched violent TV programming as children were more inclined to show violent tendencies as adults.

"Results show that men who were high TV-violence viewers as children were significantly more likely to have pushed, grabbed, or shoved their spouses, to have responded to an insult by shoving a person, to have been convicted of a crime, and to have committed a moving traffic violation. Such men, for example, had been convicted of crimes at over three times the rate of other men," says the study entitled "Longitudinal Relations Between Children's Exposure to TV Violence and Their Aggressive and Violent Behavior in Young Adulthood: 1977–1992."

"Women who were high TV-violence viewers as children were more likely to have thrown something at their spouses, to have responded to someone who made them mad by shoving, punching, beating, or choking the person, to have committed some type of criminal act, and to have committed a moving traffic violation. Such women, for example, reported having punched, beaten, or choked another adult at over four times the rate of other women," says the report.

The report also proves that violent programs that probably have the most detrimental effects on a child's cognitive development are the ones where the hero is *justified* in being violent. "Violent scenes that children are most likely to model their behavior after are ones in which they identify with the perpetrator of the violence, the perpetrator is rewarded for the violence, and in which children perceive the scene as telling about life like it really is," according to the researchers. "Thus, a violent act by someone like Dirty Harry that results in a criminal being eliminated and brings glory to Harry is of more concern than a bloodier murder by a despicable criminal who is brought to justice."

The National Institute of Mental Health has identified three major effects of seeing violence on television: 30

- Children may become less sensitive to the pain and suffering of others.

- Children may be more fearful of the world around them.

- Children may be more likely to behave in aggressive or harmful ways toward others.

The extent to which these behaviors manifest themselves in a child can depend on other factors—environmental and parental. However, there is a lot of research showing a strong link between televised violence and its effect on children.

The APA notes that children exposed to a large dose of TV violence when they are young will be less aroused by violent scenes as teenagers. In general, the group notes that "they're less bothered by violence in general, and less likely to see anything wrong with it. One example: In several studies, those who watched a violent program instead of a nonviolent one were slower to intervene or to call for help when, a little later, they saw younger children fighting or playing destructively."

"Children who watch the violent shows, even 'just funny' cartoons, were more likely to hit out at their playmates, argue, disobey class rules, and leave tasks unfinished and were less willing to wait for things than those who watched the nonviolent programs," says a researcher commenting on a study done at the University of Pennsylvania.

The question for parents is *not* "Shouldn't entertainment media be less violent?" Whether for good or for bad, violent programming is popular and is here to stay. For adults, TV shows such as *The Sopranos, The Shield, 24,* or *Walker: Texas Ranger* are usually no big deal. Most adults can deal with fake televised violence in a mature manner.

The real question is how the *children* of today's world deal with being bombarded from nearly every entertainment outlet with an array of violent acts, situations, and language? What lessons are children learning about the world? Children are impressionable and look at TV and movies differently than adults. What is TV teaching?

"The amount and influence of violence on television has long been 35 the topic of study and national debate. For close to thirty years, dating from the 1960s to the Surgeon General's report in 1972, the National Institute of Mental Health report in 1982, and the American Psychological Association's report in 1992, more than 1,000 scientific studies have validated the premise that TV violence influences aggressive behavior in some children," writes a doctor from the American Association of Pediatrics.

Because television is our children's No. 1 leisure activity, we should not minimize the ongoing impact of its thousands of visual messages on children, especially those at risk for behavioral problems.

Modern television violence is so much more vivid than a play by William Shakespeare. Families must put limits on the amount of TV young children watch. "Children have fewer checks on primal violent urges than adults. As parents and pediatricians, we hope to contain and rechannel those urges. Unprotected use of media can warp psychological development that allows awareness of human suffering to control violent desires. Knowing media and how they work will allow children to recognize and direct their effects, to use them wisely, and to learn of human suffering through ways that allow them to grow up healthy and safe," says the AAP.

Though cable has its share of violent programming, the CMPA study found that of the 3,381 acts of violence in 284 series episodes it counted during its two week study period, 80 percent of the violence occurred on over-the-air broadcast TV (ABC, CBS, NBC, Fox, UPN, and the WB). "The simple fact . . . is that people watch programs. If the program is something they want to see, they will watch," said William F. Baker and George Dessart in their book *Down the Tube*. "Nothing can make people watch a television program they don't want to see."

Violent programming is obviously popular and commercial television is entirely based on gaining audience. "Commercial television is not in the business of presenting programs; commercial television is not in the business of selling advertising," write Baker and Dessart. "Nor is it in the business of selling time to advertisers. Commercial television is, quite simply, in the business of aggregating and then selling audiences. In its simplest terms, the business of television in this country is the buying and selling of eyeballs."

To a broadcaster, viewers are only numbers. Those numbers are then used to charge a sponsor and adjust advertising revenue. Television watchers, say the authors, only matter in respect to "how much the sponsor is willing to pay to reach any single viewer. Thus, in the marketplace model, programming has only one function: Each program must attract as many viewers as possible." It should go without saying, that television is not about performing a public service. TV networks are only concerned with making money.

The most important task for television networks is the creation and cul- 40
tivation of viewers. Violent shows are the most popular shows on television. For example, one of the consistently top rated shows on TV is the CBS crime drama *CSI (Crime Scene Investigation)*. This program, ranked as the #1 worst show on television for families by the Parents Television Council, almost completely revolves around violence. "*CSI* [provides] graphic depictions of decaying bodies, grisly crime scenes, brutal murders, and themes of incest and sadomasochism," says the PTC. The group notes that during the 2002–2003 season, "episodes of *CSI* have included story lines about cannibalism, S&M sex clubs, and pornographic snuff films. Episodes this season

have also contained scenes depicting a man receiving oral sex in an alley, the mutilated victims of a deranged killer, and a man in bed with two women." *CSI* and its spinoff show *CSI: Miami* are two of the top-rated shows on television. They regularly get Nielsen ratings between 13 and 14 which converts to around 15 million households.

Another ultraviolent show on television is NBC's *Kingpin*. Though only on the air for one season, *Kingpin's* violence was almost unmatched. "*Kingpin* is centered on the criminal protagonist Miguel Cadena, a Mexican drug lord and troubled family man," explains the PTC. "In the six episodes that aired [in 2003], the PTC counted 16 raunchy depictions of sex, 23 murders, 8 depictions of torture, and 16 instances of drug use. In one particularly gruesome episode, a man is shown tossing a human leg to his pet tiger. . . . In yet another episode, a man is brutally beaten and then sodomized by a police officer."

Another popular but extremely violent show is Fox's *24*. Throughout the show's third season (2002–2003), *24* was regularly getting Nielsen ratings of 4.9 (5.1 among adults 18–49) which converts to around 5.3 million households. *New York Daily News* TV critic David Bianculli, who watches a lot of television, was shocked at the brutality on the program. "Kiefer Sutherland's Jack Bauer died at the end of Fox's *24* Tuesday, which may have shocked a lot of people (even though he could be revived). What shocked me was the way he died," explains Bianculli. "He was tortured for most of the show's hour, in some of the most disturbing and graphic depictions of violence I've ever seen on a broadcast network entertainment program. Bauer was hung naked from his wrists, with his mouth forced open by a bit gag. His skin was sliced with a scalpel, he was shocked with electrical current and Tasers, and his flesh was burned until parts of his body emitted smoke." Bianculli also notes that *24* plays on the old "good guys versus bad guys" theme which plagues most TV violence. "Those scenes were so disturbing to me precisely because the characters and the conflicts were credible enough to suck me in. These encounters with evil let us know just how bad the bad guys are in these cases, and how high the stakes can be."

Another TV critic, Matt Feeney, writes that *24* is a show entirely focused on graphic violence. He writes that *24* shows pain in the form of "brute physical agonies of gunshot wounds, heroin withdrawal, and radiation sickness." (In its real-time, single-day format, the show was poised to allow the daylong radiation death of one character to take an entire *24*-show season, but this hideous, closely observed demise was cut short two-thirds of the way through—in an irony of almost comic massiveness—by a nuclear explosion.) Then there is the torture, which occurs with astonishing regularity.

> On *24*, torture is less an unfortunate last resort than an epistemology. Whenever an urgent or sticky question of fact arises, someone—bad guy or good guy, terrorist or counterterror agent; it doesn't matter—automatically sparks up the electrodes or starts filling syringes with seizure juice.

Fox scores another violent hit program with *The Shield*. Shown on the FX network, *The Shield* is another program whose entire plot is based on violence. The main character is a TV antihero similar to the Mafia-with-a-heart characters on HBO's *The Sopranos*. *The Shield*'s main character is Vic Mackey, "a crooked, bullying, and bigoted cop who is running his own drug operation within the Los Angeles Police Department," explains *Washington Post* TV critic Tom Shales. "Virtually every episode . . . [includes] scenes of extremely gory, graphic violence. During the opening credits of last week's season premiere, gang members murdered a police informant by putting a gasoline-soaked tire around his neck and lighting it. The screams of agony were chilling, as were shots of the body being consumed by flames," he explains.

> On tonight's show, a cocaine addict vomits blood copiously and, later in the show, the reckless Mackey mercilessly brutalizes a suspected gang leader—first by beating him so furiously that Mackey himself gets splattered in blood, then by forcing the man's face down, repeatedly, on a scalding hot plate.

Though some advertisers have pulled their spots from *The Shield* because of the intense violence, actor Michael Chiklis won an Emmy in 2002 for his work in the principal role.

Shales explains how *justifiable violence* is used in *The Shield* for dra- 45 matic effect. "Viewers are likely to find themselves rooting for the 'bad guy,' Mackey, who for all his contemptible traits often seems sympathetic. . . . Chiklis is skillful enough to show a trace of pathos behind the vindictiveness. . . . The good and honest cops, meanwhile, often come off as prudes, stuffed shirts, or spoilsports. CCH Pounder plays a cop who is diligent and tough, but Mackey's slick effectiveness, which includes beating confessions out of suspects, makes humane tactics seem naive or even quaint. Another 'good' cop in the precinct, played by Jay Karnes, comes across as a WASPy dork," writes Shales.

Of course, any discussion of violent TV must include the World Wrestling Federation. The WWF (now called WWE for World Wrestling Entertainment) has been around for decades. It is not a sport—it is not real. WWE wrestling is fake with outrageous acts of physical punishment. The WWE could be called comical or silly or even "mindless television entertainment." However, to say it is *not* violent is quite naive. The WWF is entirely based on physical violence, *machismo,* and blood. As with other violent programming, the WWE gets extremely high ratings: Primetime showings of *WWE Raw* on the Spike Network are some of the highest rated cable programs with around 3.5 million households watching (during the week of April 12, 2004, *WWE Raw Zone* tied for first place in ratings with the George W. Bush presidential news conference concerning the war in Iraq).

The National Institute on Media and the Family quotes a year long study (50 episodes, from 2/12/98 to 2/1/99) by Indiana University's Department of Telecommunication of the World Wrestling Federation's *Raw Is War* program. The study recorded instances of sexual and violent interactions:

- crotch grabbing or pointing: 1,658 instances
- garbage cans, chairs, tables, and brooms used in wrestling: 609
- kicks to the groin: 273
- profane descriptions of people: 158
- obscene finger gesture: 157
- simulated sexual activity: 128
- scantily clad women: 70
- urinating (talking about/appearing to): 21

This is really only significant when one considers that 15 percent of the audience for wrestling shows (more than 1 million viewers) is eleven years old or younger.

Overall, only 10 percent of children's viewing time is spent watching TV designed for kids. The other 90 percent of the time is spent watching programs designed for adults (Iowa State University, "Getting Along: Taming the TV," Oct. 1999).

Violent television is popular and high ratings means more advertising revenue. However, a new study actually shows that ad recall is diminished when placed between a program with intense violence or sexual content. In a report called "Violence and Sex Impair Memory for Television Ads," researchers from Iowa State University found that both men and women had problems recalling a particular advertised brand when the content of the TV program showed graphic violence or sex. Their findings were consistent regardless of whether the viewer liked the program or not. "We suggest that sex and violence impair commercial memory because they consume attention and prompt sexual and violent thoughts, thus reducing the likelihood that the commercial message is encoded into long-term memory," says the report.

The study notes that because viewers have a limited amount of atten- 50 tion to direct toward TV shows, if they are thinking about violence they are not absorbing commercials. Because violent programs are more engaging and "attention grabbing," advertising will get lost. "The more attentive individuals are toward a TV program, the less attentive capacity they have for the commercials embedded in the program," states the report.

Clearly, the violence shown in TV programs of today is far more graphic and disturbing than in the past. Television of today is gruesome and shocking—gone are the days of *The Lone Ranger, The Untouchables, Gunsmoke, The A-Team,* or *Battlestar Galactica.* TV of the past is tame by comparison to today's programs. Part of the reason is that TV networks have been free to become as violent as possible, without any government oversight.

The United States Federal Communications Commission (FCC) is supposed to be the governmental body which holds networks accountable for their programming. The FCC is supposed to enforce the ban on violent programs during the prime time "Family Hour." However, currently there are no laws on the books prohibiting or restricting depictions of violence on television. The only types of broadcasts the FCC chooses to control are those which, in the words of the FCC, display "in a patently offensive way, sexual conduct specifically defined by applicable law." In the eyes of the FCC, breasts, genitalia, or one utterance of the word *fuck* will get maximum fines imposed on a TV network or station. However, murder and torture in a graphic manner can pass over the airwaves without comment.

In the end, however, even if the FCC took a responsible attitude toward televised violence, censorship is not the answer. Censorship is *never* the answer. TurnOffYourTV.com advocates choosing to not watch television — Turn Off *Your* TV and Kill *Your* TV. People should stop watching television because of its effects on the human body and its troubling content. The bottom line is that television is violent, and parents must use discretion to get control over the medium and not allow children to watch inappropriate programming. Only parental involvement, not the government, not a special computer chip, and certainly not the networks themselves will help the situation. The issue of TV violence is a matter of content and parental control.

So for your children . . . Turn Off Your TV!

Television More Oversexed Than Ever, Study Finds

LISA DE MORAES

> BEFORE READING: Do you believe that television networks today go too far in the amount of sexual content they air?

Teenagers watching television are bombarded with nearly twice as many sex scenes as seven years ago, according to a new study by the Kaiser Family Foundation. Sex, lots of sex. Sex, sex, sex. Casual sex, dirty sex. Hot, sweaty, recreational sex with desperate housewives on expensive, carved, imported-from-Italy dining tables. Adolescent girls perform-

---

Lisa de Moraes writes "The TV Column," which appears regularly in the *Washington Post*. Before assuming that position in 1998, she served for almost ten years as the TV editor for the *Hollywood Reporter*. This column appeared in the *Washington Post* on November 10, 2005.

ing oral sex on middle-aged managers of expensive clothing stores in backrooms jammed with nekkid mannequins in exchange for some of that expensive clothing—plus accessories!

In the slightly more than 1,000 shows scrutinized in the study, nearly 4,000 scenes had sexual content, compared with fewer than 2,000 in 1998, when the foundation started studying TV sex. And yet the rate of teen pregnancy in this country has plunged by about one-third during approximately the same time. Clearly, the television networks are doing something wrong. Especially since, of the TV programs pregnant with sexual content (70 percent of all shows, averaging about five sex scenes per hour), only a very small percentage included a message about the risks and responsibilities of sex.

Only about 14 percent discussed contraception, abstinence, or other "safe sex" messages, the study found, though Kaiser veep Vicky Rideout, who oversaw the study, admitted during its unveiling yesterday that a first good-night kiss at the door between two television characters probably does not call for an on-screen discussion between the guy and chick as to whether they should use a condom. Yes, the Kaiser study includes a first good-night kiss at the door in its definition of "sexual behavior." And "sexual content" includes any discussion about sex. Given that, it's a wonder they found only 4,000 scenes in those 1,000 shows over the course of the study. Maybe they didn't get some of the jokes in those *Sex and the City* reruns on TNT.

TNT is, in fact, among the networks scrutinized for the study, along with HBO, Lifetime, and USA cable networks, though why they chose those particular networks over ones that, say, teens actually were watching, like MTV, remains a mystery to the TV Column.

Last year, for instance, 6 percent of HBO's viewers were teens, compared   5
with nearly 30 percent ages 50 and older. Lifetime, the Men Are Pigs and the Women Who Love Them network, had an audience of only 4 percent teens and more than half age 50 and older. More than 40 percent of the audience for USA Network and TNT was 50 or older and about 5 percent were teens. MTV had nearly 30 percent teens in its audience, 3 percent viewers 50-plus.

But, as with most studies, it's best not to ponder these things too closely lest the top of one's head start to come off. Back to the study:

ABC, CBS, NBC, Fox, and WB shows also were included, though not UPN. Again, out of consideration for the top of our head, we'll think about that tomorrow.

"Given how high the stakes are, the messages TV sends teens about sex are important," Rideout said in the news release handed out yesterday and, in slightly different form, live to those attending the unveiling of the study at the Kaiser Family Foundation digs at 13th and G (which, by the way—very plush). Why, we wondered, given that, despite TV's best effort, teen pregnancy rates had plunged, fewer teens are having sex, and more of those who are having intercourse are using protection.

University of Arizona at Tucson communications professor Dale Kunkel, who worked on the study, noted sourly that just because there has been a decline doesn't mean that all groups are working toward that end. He said he worries that the media are working against groups trying to remedy the problem. He's comforted, no doubt, by the fact that teen pregnancy numbers are still higher in this country than elsewhere.

That's even though many of those countries with lower teen pregnancy 10 rates don't regulate TV content nearly as much, noted Tony Vinciquerra, president and CEO of Fox Network Group, who, along with Kunkel, was part of a panel discussion during the unveiling ceremony. Also participating were FCC Commissioner Kathleen Abernathy, *Law & Order: SVU* executive producer Neal Baer, National Campaign to Prevent Teen Pregnancy Executive Director Sarah Brown, and Rand Corp. behavioral scientist Rebecca Collins.

Vinciquerra noted that his Fox Reality cable network can't rerun much reality programming from overseas because it's too risque for this market. Based on our observations yesterday, Vinciquerra has risen to great heights at Fox because of his almost superhuman ability to attend the Mad Hatter's tea party and not grab the Dormouse by the shoulders and shake it until its teeth rattle when it suggests that things are just different in this country because television has become our religion, in a way. The Dormouse in this case being FCC Commissioner Abernathy.

There was nobody on the panel to speak up for the 65 percent of the country's homes in which no one under 18 resides and some of whose favorite TV shows were under discussion, and not in a good way. Very little discussion also about the fact that nearly 70 percent of kids have TVs in their bedrooms, bought for them by parents—83 percent of whom, the Kaiser foundation says, firmly believe that exposure to sex on TV contributed to children becoming involved in sexual situations before they're ready.

Sen. Barack Obama, fresh from his brilliant overshadowing of Jon Stewart on Comedy Central's *Daily Show* earlier in the week, continued his "I'm So Over-Hyped" tour with an appearance at the debut of the "Sex on TV" study, addressing a conference room packed with what appeared to be a handful of reporters, some lobbyists from networks monitoring the situation, and—judging by the knicker-knottedness of the questions directed to the Illinois Democrat after his speech—members of TV watchdog and other special-interest groups.

Obama killed. Yes, he quoted Newton Minow's famous "vast wasteland" speech. Politicians always do. But he had some other material. Like how, when he watches TV with his young daughters and they're in the middle of a family program and a commercial for Cialis comes on, "It's more than troubling to find yourself wondering how you'll explain certain medical conditions that last longer than three hours to a 4-year-old and a 7-year-old."

Not terribly original, but good stuff! More talk about how the adult 15 content on *Schindler's List* is good while the adult content on *Desperate*

Housewives is "far different." And "we don't teach our children that healthy relationships involve drunken naked parties in a hot tub with strangers — but that's what they see when they turn on *The Real World*." Undeniable facts, all.

"What do we do when bad television becomes the enemy of good parenting?" Obama asked. We steeled ourselves for the worst. "I think, as parents, we have an obligation to our children to turn off the TV," he suggested. Revolutionary!

Cultural Studies and "Forensic Noir"

THOMAS DOHERTY

> **BEFORE READING:** Why are some of the most popular television shows graphic in their portrayal of the victims of crime? Do you personally like to watch the "forensic" dramas that focus on crime scene investigations and autopsies? Why, or why not?

"Apparently, people will watch forensics seven nights a week," shrugs David Caruso, star of the hit show *CSI: Miami*, a spinoff of the hit show *CSI: Crime Scene Investigation*. Shilling for the series on Fox's *Pat Sajak Weekend* earlier this year, he cited a CBS survey indicating that autopsy-driven entertainment is the hottest trend in American popular culture. Indeed, avid morgue attendants may also tally up the body count on HBO's *Autopsy*, NBC's *Law & Order: Criminal Intent*, Court TV's *Forensic Files*, A&E's *Cold Case Files*, and, in a more mordant vein, HBO's *Six Feet Under*. As the current season gets under way, CBS also gives us the scientific and forensically flavored *Cold Case* and *Navy NCIS*.

All over television, it seems rigor mortis has become de rigueur.

The purest form of the genre has been dubbed "forensic noir," and already its conventions have hardened like a plaster mold on a femur. A phalanx of experts bearing tweezers and baggies mills around yellow police tape and scours the site for bits of evidence. Back at headquarters, men and women in white lab coats collate data and conduct microscopic analysis on blood, drugs, wood, paint, insects, dirt, metal, and anything else known to the periodic table of elements. The recurring close-ups show investigators sniffing the tips of their white-gloved fingers. Could this be dextromethorphan? Blindsided by science, the culprit is nailed, the case closed.

Thomas Doherty is an associate professor of film studies at Brandeis University and author of *Hollywood's Censor: Joseph I. Breen and the Production Code Administration* (2007); *Pre-Code Hollywood: Sex, Immorality, and Insurrection in American Cinema, 1930–1934* (1999); *Projections of War: Hollywood, American Culture, and World War II* (1993); and *Teenagers & Teenpics: The Juvenilization of American Movies in the 1950s* (1988). This article appeared in the October 24, 2003, issue of *The Chronicle of Higher Education*.

With such tantalizing roadkill littering the media landscape, one might have expected circling scholars to have already descended for a hermeneutical feast. However, forensic noir is not yet one of the dominant intellectual categories of early twenty-first-century scholarship. In fact, even the last meeting of the ultrahip Society for Cinema and Media Studies failed to devote a panel to the topic (although wait till next year), and the genre is still too new a phenomenon to inspire the title of a university-press book (heads up, Ph.D. students).

Still, forensic noir has been anticipated and mapped by another kind of CSI   5 team: Cultural-Studies Intellectuals, a dauntless band of scholars committed to digging into the symbolic meanings of the corporeal body. Their preliminary findings are likely to inform and guide future inquiries into a genre that has single-handedly revitalized both the flat-lined formula of the detective series and the flat ratings of prime-time network television.

Of course, the latest academic foray into criminal territory also partakes of a rich literary and cinematic tradition. From Victor Hugo to Mario Puzo, the sordid denizens of the underworld have been rehabilitated as merely refracted images of mainstream values, figures whose deviant ways illuminate the greater deviance of a soul-destroying culture: the Corleone family as the moral equivalents of the Rockefellers, only with better cuisine. Like the televisual CSI teams, however, the agents of cultural studies take the corpus delicti for their main text. The criminal himself is interesting only insofar as he produces the body.

Any examination of the body-as-text within the groves of academe begins with the high priest of high theory, Michel Foucault, the French philosopher who died in 1984 but who lives on as the animating footnote of the field. In his 1975 study *Discipline and Punish: The Birth of the Prison,* Foucault cast a cold eye on "the power and knowledge relations that invest human bodies and subjugate them by turning them into objects of knowledge." Brandishing the inevitable pun on the "body politic," he inspected bodies docile and tortured, under surveillance and under the knife. Soon humanities scholars who were once enchanted by the sensuous pulchritude of Renaissance nudes or the chiseled features of Hollywood stars embraced an altogether different body of scholarship. Now their patients were not just etherized but embalmed upon a table.

Foucault's timing was dead-on for stateside consumption.

Just as his work was being translated and taught in graduate seminars, a new criminal avatar was stalking the back roads of American culture, pushing aside drug dealers, gang bangers, and rogue CIA agents as the villain of choice for popular entertainment: the serial killer. Unlike the outlaw of the Old West or the gangster of the urban frontier, the serial killer struck at random, committed murder for no financial gain, and racked up a double-digit body count with absolutely no remorse. Yet, as a product of the mobility and anonymity of late twentieth-century life, he was a peculiarly American figure, cruising the two-lane blacktops of the prairie, picking up lone hitchhikers, and befriending truck-stop waitresses. No ordinary murderer, he seemed an almost supernatural creature of the night.

Although popular culture understood the new modus operandi immediately, the flummoxed forces of law enforcement were slower on the uptake. A predator who crossed state lines and murdered for reasons of his own, the serial killer operated under the radar of traditional police practices. The cops turned to the statistics and science of national databanks, criminal profilers, and crime labs with the forensic expertise to link bodies to each other, and the killer to the bodies. 10

Using Foucault as a desk reference, an eclectic array of scholarship on pornography, horror, homicide, violent spectacle, and the delights of observing the same also looked anew at those bodies dead or alive. Linda Williams's pioneering *Hard Core: Power, Pleasure, and the "Frenzy of the Visible"* (University of California Press, 1989) and Carol J. Clover's *Men, Women, and Chain Saws: Gender in the Modern Horror Film* (Princeton University Press, 1992) scoped out the scene early; more recent entries include Mark I. Seltzer's *Serial Killers: Death and Life in America's Wound Culture* (Routledge, 1998), Philip L. Simpson's *Psycho Paths: Tracking the Serial Killer Through Contemporary American Film and Fiction* (Southern Illinois University Press, 2000), and Joel Black's *The Reality Effect: Film Culture and the Graphic Imperative* (Routledge, 2002).

By common consent, the famous curtain opener to Foucault's *Discipline and Punish*— an excruciating, play-by-play account of an execution by torture in eighteenth-century France—laid out the preferred method for surgical exegesis. However, it was Williams, a professor of film studies and rhetoric at the University of California at Berkeley, who introduced the elastic term "body genre" into the conversation, detecting an impulse at once voyeuristic and scientific behind cinematic spectatorship. "The desire to see and know more about the human body," she noted, "underlies the very invention of cinema." Although Williams's own lens was focused mainly on gender and pornography, her outlook suggests why the naked exposure of human organs, gushing fluids, and bodily penetration— scenes that comprise what might be called the "money shots" of forensic noir—are so ubiquitous.

This energetic body work is a far better test kit for tracing the tropes of forensic noir than the criticism on what may seem to be the TV fare's parent genre, film noir. Any kinship between the two noirs is only skin-deep. A moody mesh of German expressionism and French existentialism, film noir languishes in a cloud of smoky atmospherics and moral ambiguities, a lush dream world that, for all its dark tone and mean streets, has proved extraordinarily popular, even beloved. To take a classic example: In Robert Siodmak's fluorescent version of Ernest Hemingway's *The Killers* (1946), the investigator is obsessed with the *why* of a mysterious murder, not the how or even the who, when he seeks the motive for a contract hit, and the reason the victim accepted his own execution with such stoic resignation. More a mutant offspring than a direct descendent, forensic noir retains the mystery and murder but rejects the hopeless surrender to the forces of fate that waft through film noir.

Besides, bio-labs and operating rooms require bright lighting, high-tech implements, and smoke-free conditions. Film noir is hard-boiled, resigned, and romantic; forensic noir is air-conditioned, tenacious, and scientific. Film noir is body heat; forensic noir is body stiff. Quoting the film critic André Bazin, Indiana University's James Naremore, in his elegant study *More Than Night: Film Noir and its Contexts* (University of California Press, 1998), reminds us that, for the French critics who first embraced Hollywood's "black" films — a generation woozy on Sartre, unfiltered Gitanes, and postwar angst — Humphrey Bogart was an existential icon because the alcoholic lines visible on his face revealed "the corpse on reprieve within all of us." The icon of forensic noir gets his philosophy from the *Physician's Desk Reference,* cuts into too many charcoal-filled lungs to think smoking is cool, and succumbs to existential angst only when a rookie cop contaminates the crime scene.

Similarly, though rooted in vintage police procedurals such as Jack 15 Webb's just-the-facts-ma'am *Dragnet* (1951–59, 1967–70) and Quinn Martin's *The F.B.I.* (1965–74), and glimpsed in sanitized form in *Quincy* (1976–83), forensic noir can be readily distinguished from its generic ancestors. It is marked by two obsessions: a superstitious faith in better detecting through chemistry and a ghoulish relish in the rituals of medical dissection. Unlike the hero of the classic police shows, the rule-breaking maverick who played hunches and infuriated the by-the-book captain, the forensic cop is a clinical practitioner of the scientific method, at home amid the sinks, slabs, and scalpels of the morgue. The *locus classicus* for the genre is the scene in *The Silence of the Lambs* (1991), when the FBI profiler Jack Crawford and the trainee Clarice Starling spread Vicks VapoRub under their nostrils to examine a decomposed corpse, the victim of a serial killer. On television, the model was *The X Files* (1993–2002), where another pair of FBI agents — he an excitable agent provocateur, she a level-headed pathologist — spent almost a decade probing and being probed by swarms of extraterrestrial species.

In addition to the usual comforts of serial narrative soothingly resolved in a fixed time frame, forensic noir provides a crash course in the genetic ingenuity of real-life crime fighting, a vocation that is increasingly a matter of fibers, microbes, and DNA. Whether at the FBI or on *CSI*, the emblematic clue is no longer the matchbook cover but saliva or semen, a telltale trace that cracks the case once the results come back from the lab. Significantly, though, the boundless faith in forensic experts is confined to matters after the fact: So resourceful during the crime-scene sweep, the new FBI-*CSI* team has little predictive ability. Quite literally, their skill is all postmortem.

However, once the body is bagged and tagged, forensic noir lives up to its name. Corpses on slabs appear as featured players while body parts and bone fragments serve as set design. The trademark gag shows the coroner digging into his work while munching a slice of pizza. The rookie agent chokes; the home audience smirks. In *The Reality Effect,* Black, a professor of comparative literature at the University of Georgia, finds it unsurprising that a mass-mediated audience awash in spectacles of virtual reality should seek a jolt of flesh-and-blood reality in a "return to art's primitive, ritual originals—to 'regress' from a sublimated aesthetic of ideas and contemplation to an aesthetic of cruelty and sensation."

Innovations in special-effects technology have heightened the impact of the anatomy lessons. CGI (computer generated imagery) and grisly makeup mock-ups can now render the most grotesque eviscerations with stomach-churning verisimilitude. To enhance the mood, the dissections are accompanied by the buzz of a surgical saw cutting through bone and the whoosh of blood splattering onto a face mask. The camera then zooms in for a traveling shot through the corridors of a human orifice— ears, nose, mouth, you get the picture.

The fixation on the body of the victim represents a telling shift away from the former site of detective work, the mind of the murderer. As with university budget lines, the sure payoffs from the hard sciences have channeled investments away from the uncertain returns of the soft sciences. Preferring pathology to psychology, forensic detectives admit that human motives are beyond their ken.

Where once crime dramas confidently dragged out sociologists and psychologists to offer reassuring explanations for criminal deviance— think of the shrink in the coda to Alfred Hitchcock's *Psycho* (1960) — even liberal Hollywood has given up the quest for a Freudian magic bullet to help comprehend the killer. Unable either to prevent crime, or to understand the criminal, the heroes of forensic noir settle for matching up DNA. They seek closure more than justice; catching the killer is a bonus.

Another even darker cultural impulse may also account for the proliferation of forensic noir. "This knowledge and this mastery constitute what might be called the political technology of the body," declared the chief coroner himself in *Discipline and Punish.* The intrusions of a surveillance society find an apt metaphor in violations of the body conducted by curious technicians. In probing, prying, and cutting into the citizen's no-longer-private parts, the state asserts its ultimate power over the individual, a kind of unanswerable last tag.

How much more can viewers stomach? How much further can television test the limits of forensic noir? In London last year, a doctor conducted a public autopsy for the delectation of a crowd of paying spectators. In the United States, a television producer may already be pitching a high-concept show that will combine the current obsession with a more traditional fixation: *Celebrity Autopsy.*

By permission of Mike Luckovich and Creators Syndicate, Inc.

Hollow Claims about Fantasy Violence

RICHARD RHODES

BEFORE READING: As you grow older, does violence in the media appeal to you more — or less? Can you account for your reactions?

The moral entrepreneurs are at it again, pounding the entertainment industry for advertising its Grand Guignolesque[1] confections to children. If exposure to this mock violence contributes to the development of violent behavior, then our political leadership is justified in its indignation at what the Federal Trade Commission has reported about the

---

[1] Grand Guignol, a popular theater founded in Paris in 1897 to present graphic performances of crimes — EDS.

Richard Rhodes is the author of more than two dozen books, including *The Making of the Atomic Bomb* (1986), which won a Pulitzer Prize for nonfiction, and *Why They Kill: The Discoveries of a Maverick Criminologist* (1999). The *New York Times* printed this article on September 17, 2000.

marketing of violent fare to children. Senators John McCain and Joseph Lieberman have been especially quick to fasten on the FTC report as they make an issue of violent offerings to children.

But is there really a link between entertainment and violent behavior?

The American Medical Association, the American Psychological Association, the American Academy of Pediatrics, and the National Institutes of Mental Health all say yes. They base their claims on social science research that has been sharply criticized and disputed within the social science profession, especially outside the United States. In fact, no direct, causal link between exposure to mock violence in the media and subsequent violent behavior has ever been demonstrated, and the few claims of modest correlation have been contradicted by other findings, sometimes in the same studies.

History alone should call such a link into question. Private violence has been declining in the West since the media-barren late Middle Ages, when homicide rates are estimated to have been ten times what they are in Western nations today. Historians attribute the decline to improving social controls over violence—police forces and common access to courts of law—and to a shift away from brutal physical punishment in child-rearing (a practice that still appears as a common factor in the background of violent criminals today).

The American Medical Association has based its endorsement of the   5 media violence theory in major part on the studies of Brandon Centerwall, a psychiatrist in Seattle. Dr. Centerwall compared the murder rates for whites in three countries from 1945 to 1974 with numbers for television set ownership. Until 1975, television broadcasting was banned in South Africa, and "white homicide rates remained stable" there, Dr. Centerwall found, while corresponding rates in Canada and the United States doubled after television was introduced.

A spectacular finding, but it is meaningless. As Franklin E. Zimring and Gordon Hawkins of the University of California at Berkeley subsequently pointed out, homicide rates in France, Germany, Italy, and Japan either failed to change with increasing television ownership in the same period or actually declined, and American homicide rates have more recently been sharply declining despite a proliferation of popular media outlets—not only movies and television, but also video games and the Internet.

Other social science that supposedly undergirds the theory, too, is marginal and problematic. Laboratory studies that expose children to selected incidents of televised mock violence and then assess changes in the children's behavior have sometimes found more "aggressive" behavior after the exposure—usually verbal, occasionally physical.

But sometimes the control group, shown incidents judged not to be violent, behaves more aggressively afterward than the test group; sometimes comedy produces the more aggressive behavior; and sometimes there's no change. The only obvious conclusion is that sitting and watching television stimulates subsequent physical activity. Any kid could tell you that.

As to those who claim that entertainment promotes violent behavior by desensitizing people to violence, the British scholar Martin Barker offers this critique: "Their claim is that the materials they judge to be harmful can only influence us by trying to make us be the same as them. So horrible things will make us horrible—not horrified. Terrifying things will make us terrifying—not terrified. To see something aggressive makes us feel aggressive—not aggressed against. This idea is so odd, it is hard to know where to begin in challenging it."

Even more influential on national policy has been a twenty-two year   10 study by two University of Michigan psychologists, Leonard D. Eron and L. Rowell Huesmann, of boys exposed to so-called violent media. The Telecommunications Act of 1996, which mandated the television V-chip, allowing parents to screen out unwanted programming, invoked these findings, asserting, "Studies have shown that children exposed to violent video programming at a young age have a higher tendency for violent and aggressive behavior later in life than children not so exposed."

Well, not exactly. Following 875 children in upstate New York from third grade through high school, the psychologists found a correlation between a preference for violent television at age eight and aggressiveness at age eighteen. The correlation—0.31—would mean television accounted for about 10 percent of the influences that led to this behavior. But the correlation only turned up in one of three measures of aggression: the assessment of students by their peers. It didn't show up in students' reports about themselves or in psychological testing. And for girls, there was no correlation at all.

Despite the lack of evidence, politicians can't resist blaming the media for violence. They can stake out the moral high ground confident that the First Amendment will protect them from having to actually write legislation that would be likely to alienate the entertainment industry. Some use the issue as a smokescreen to avoid having to confront gun control.

But violence isn't learned from mock violence. There is good evidence—causal evidence, not correlational—that it's learned in personal violent encounters, beginning with the brutalization of children by their parents or their peers.

The money spent on all the social science research I've described was diverted from the National Institute of Mental Health budget by reducing support for the construction of community mental health centers. To this day there is no standardized reporting system for emergency-room findings of physical child abuse. Violence is on the decline in America, but if we want to reduce it even further, protecting children from real violence in their real lives—not the pale shadow of mock violence—is the place to begin.

A Desensitized Society Drenched in Sleaze

JEFF JACOBY

BEFORE READING: What's the difference between the violence depicted in popular movies and described in the lyrics of some rap songs and the violence portrayed in *Macbeth* or a classic Greek play like *Oedipus Rex?*

I was seventeen years old when I first saw an X-rated movie. It was Thanksgiving in Washington, D.C. My college dorm had all but emptied out for the holiday weekend. With no classes, no tests, and nobody around, I decided to scratch an itch that had long been tormenting me.

I used to see these movies advertised in the old *Washington Star,* and—like any seventeen-year-old boy whose sex life is mostly theoretical—I burned with curiosity. I wondered what such films might be like, what awful, thrilling secrets they might expose.

And so that weekend I took myself to see one. Full of anticipation, nervous and embarrassed, I walked to the Casino Royale at 14th Street and New York Avenue. At the top of a long flight of stairs, a cashier sat behind a cage. "Five dollars," he demanded—steep for my budget, especially since a ticket to the movies in the late seventies usually cost $3.50. But I'd come this far and couldn't turn back. I paid, I entered, I watched.

For about twenty minutes. The movie, I still remember, was called *Cry for Cindy,* and what I saw on the screen I'd never seen—I'd never even imagined—before. A man and a woman, oral sex, extreme closeups. The sheer gynecological explicitness of it jolted me. Was *this* the forbidden delight hinted at by those ads? This wasn't arousing, it was repellent. I was shocked. More than that: I was ashamed.

I literally couldn't take it. I bolted the theater and tumbled down the steps. My heart was pounding and my face was burning. I felt dirty. Guilty. I was conscience-stricken. 5

All that—over a dirty movie.

Well, I was an innocent at seventeen. I was naive and inexperienced, shy with girls, the product of a parochial-school education and a strict upbringing. Explicit sex—in the movies, music, my social life—was foreign to me. Coming from such an environment, who *wouldn't* recoil from *Cry for Cindy* or feel repelled by what it put up on that screen?

But here's the rub: Dirty movies don't have that effect on me anymore. I don't make a practice of seeking out skin flicks or films with explicit nudity, but in the years since I was seventeen, I've certainly seen my share. Today another sex scene is just another sex scene. Not shocking,

---

Jeff Jacoby is a columnist for the *Boston Globe,* where this essay appeared on June 8, 1995.

not appalling, nothing I feel ashamed to look at. Writhing bodies on the screen? Raunchy lyrics in a song? They may entertain me or they may bore me, but one thing they no longer do is make me blush.

I've become jaded. And if a decade and a half of being exposed to this stuff can leave *me* jaded—with my background, my religious schooling, my disciplined origins—what impact does it have on kids and young adults who have never been sheltered from anything? What impact does it have on a generation growing up amid dysfunctional families, broken-down schools, and a culture of values-free secularism?

If sex- and violence-drenched entertainment can desensitize me, it   10 can desensitize anyone. It can desensitize a whole society. It can drag us to the point where nothing is revolting. Where nothing makes us blush.

And what happens to an unblushing society? Why, everything. Central Park joggers get raped and beaten into comas. Sixth-graders sleep around. Los Angeles rioters burn down their neighborhood and murder dozens of their neighbors. The Menendez boys blow off their parents' heads. Lorena Bobbitt mutilates her husband in his sleep. "Artists" sell photographs of crucifixes dunked in urine. Prolife fanatics open fire on abortion clinics. Daytime TV fills up with deviants. The U.S. Naval Academy fills up with cheaters. The teen suicide rate goes through the roof.

And we get used to all of it. We don't blush.

The point isn't that moviegoers walk out of Oliver Stone's latest grotesquerie primed to kill. Or that Geto Boys' sociopathic lyrics ("Leavin'

Rob Rogers: © The Pittsburgh Post-Gazette/Dist. by United Features Syndicate, Inc.

out her house, grabbed the bitch by her mouth / Drug her back in, slam her down on the couch. / Whipped out my knife, said, 'If you scream I'm cutting,' / Open her legs and . . .") cause rape. The point is that when blood and mayhem and sleazy sex drench our popular culture, we get accustomed to blood and mayhem and sleazy sex. We grow jaded. Depravity becomes more and more tolerable because less and less scandalizes us.

Of course, the entertainment industry accepts no responsibility for any of this. Time Warner and Hollywood indignantly reject the criticisms heaped on them in recent days. We don't cause society's ills, they say, we only reflect them. "If an artist wants to deal with violence or sexuality or images of darkness and horror," said film director Clive Barker, "those are legitimate subjects for artists."

They are, true. Artists have dealt with violence and sexuality and   15
horror since time immemorial. But debauchery is not art. There is nothing ennobling about a two-hour paean to bloodlust. To suggest that Snoop Doggy Dogg's barbaric gang-rape fantasies somehow follow in the tradition of Sophocles' tragic drama, Chaucer's romantic poetry, or Solzhenitsyn's moral testimony is to suggest that there is no difference between meaning and meaninglessness.

For Hollywood and Time Warner, perhaps there no longer is. The question before the house is, what about the rest of us?

Gore for Sale

EVAN GAHR

BEFORE READING: Did you enjoy violent video games when you were younger? Can you explain why they did or did not appeal to you?

F resh corpses litter the ground. Blood is everywhere. Victims moan and beg for mercy. Others scream for help.

This may sound like a horrific scene from the Littleton, Colorado, shooting. But players of the computer game Postal just call it fun. They assume the role of Postal Dude, who snaps one day and mows down everyone in sight. For added realism, as the Web site of the developer (Running with Scissors) proudly states: "Corpses stay where they fall for the duration of the game — no mysterious disappearing bodies." But they do not fall right away. First "watch your victims run around on fire."

Evan Gahr is the Washington correspondent for *Jewish World Review* and an adjunct scholar at the Washington-based Center for Equal Opportunity. This article appeared in the *Wall Street Journal* on April 30, 1999.

If you have a perverse fascination with violence, it's no longer necessary to skulk around in search of underground entertainments. Just visit your neighborhood electronics store. At the Wiz on Manhattan's Upper East Side, the notorious game Grand Theft Auto is smack in the middle of a display rack behind the cashier. The game's story line: As either a "gansta" or "psycho bitch" you will be "running over innocent pedestrians, shooting cops, and evading the long arm of the law."

In another game, Duke Nukem (manufactured by GT Interactive), sex and violence combine. Determined to expel from Los Angeles the aliens who are kidnapping scantily clad women, Duke Nukem trolls the seedy quarters of the city and shoots anyone who gets in his way. He even kicks his victims' decapitated heads through goalposts to celebrate.

In Doom, one of the most popular among violent video games and a 5 favorite of one of the Littleton murderers, the player wanders through a maze of rooms, corridors, and halls killing everything in sight. Survive and you make it to the next level. For lethal power you can choose among a pistol, shot gun, rocket launcher, and chainsaw. The aliens and monsters don't go down easily. Bodily fluid spurts all over the walls; aliens are left to lie in pools of blood, their limbs sometimes dangling in the air.

The manufacturer of Doom, id Software, advises that you should "prepare for the most intense mutant-laden, blood-spattered action ever. You don't just play Doom—you live it." You certainly do.

A more advanced version of Doom, called Quake, is an "ultra-violent gorefest," as one online reviewer called it. Players wander through a maze and use every weapon imaginable to slay aliens. (The nail gun is a big hit.) There's heightened realism because you can view any part of the game from an endless number of angles. For example, it's possible to bounce a grenade off a wall to hit someone around the corner. Lucky you.

What is going on here? Well, for one thing entrepreneurship. Violent computer games are a small but influential part of the $6.2 billion video- and computer-game market. They have proliferated in recent years and are now deeply embedded in youth culture. They are played either on play stations (Nintendo or Sony), PCs, or the Internet, where you battle it out with other players.

With each new release players are promised seemingly endless amounts of blood and gore. The more people you kill and maim the better. It is an entire subculture that uses 3D graphics, spectacular sound effects, and other computer-driven bells and whistles to blur the distinction between reality and fantasy—and to celebrate criminality. The game titles speak for themselves: Blood, Bedlam, Death Rally, and Redneck Rampage.

The idea is not just to kill but to kill with glee. Last year, a new joy- 10 stick system promised: "You get better accuracy and control, but what are you going to do with all the extra bodies? Be the first on your block to make your neighbors say, 'What's that smell?'" Another manufacturer,

Interplay Productions, celebrates "the sheer ecstasy of crunching bones against their bumper" in its game Carmageddon. "Drive whatever you want, wherever you want, and over whoever you want. You make the rules. Your motto. Just kill, baby." And watch the blood spatter on the windshield.

Video-game violence is not new. As Eric Rozenman noted in a recent *Washington Times* article, one of the earlier games, Death Race, caused quite a commotion in the mid-1970s: "The game involved an automobile driver running down pedestrians. The latter expired with unconvincing moans, the skilled motorists recording a tally of crucifixes."

Even Space Invaders was considered too violent when it was released in the late 1970s. But the games have become progressively more violent ever since—and vivid. The most remarkable breakthrough came in 1992, when a first-person shooter game called Wolfenstein 3-D hit the market.

Previously, players looked at the screen as if from above. With Wolfenstein 3-D, however, you see the action from the on-screen character's point of view. You become the character. The following year Doom was introduced. A deluge of first-person shooter games followed.

These caught the attention of Senator Joseph Lieberman (Democrat, Connecticut). He and Senator Herb Kohl (Democrat, Wisconsin) held hearings on the games in 1993. Prodded by the senators, the industry adopted a voluntary rating system. Yet the ratings are not even enforced by stores, and incredibly violent games are often rated suitable for kids. More important, parents don't seem to realize what their kids are playing.

Should they be concerned? What message, for example, does Grand 15 Theft Auto send? Jayson Bernstein, spokesman for the manufacturer, American Softworks Corp., says, "It's just a game." Industry spokesmen also defend their products by contending that there are no studies that conclusively link computer games to violence.

Some academics, too, say the games get a bum rap. The real problem is—big surprise here—social injustice. Henry Jenkins, director of Comparative Media Studies at MIT, recently argued that the focus on video-game violence seems to be the most recent strategy of our culture to shift focus away from the obvious root causes of violence: urban conditions, poverty and the ready availability of guns.

And so on. Luckily, for those who worry about a culture in which these games thrive, a small backlash is evident. In January, the city of Stanton, California, allowed a new arcade to open only after it promised not to use violent or sexually charged games. The Minnesota Legislature is considering banning the sale of violent games to children under eighteen. In Chicago, about fifty people recently demanded that Toys " Я " Us stop selling violent video games and toys. The protesters, from a partnership of several churches, held a mock funeral outside the store. The store ignored them. In the wake of Littleton, how will such protests play?

Like other refuse that litters the cultural landscape, these computer games didn't just magically appear one day. They have flourished in a cultural milieu in which most anything goes. These days, to paraphrase FDR, it sometimes seems that we have nothing left to stigmatize but stigma itself. When parents and community members try to fight such garbage, or even quarantine it, they are derided in certain quarters as intolerant zealots or enemies of the First Amendment.

But if twelve-year-olds wake up one day and discover they no longer have such easy access to Redneck Rampage, free speech will survive. And everyone else might even be a bit safer.

THINKING AND WRITING ABOUT SEX AND VIOLENCE IN POPULAR CULTURE

QUESTIONS FOR DISCUSSION AND WRITING

1. De Moraes uses sarcasm and a light tone in her essay, but does she have valid points to make about the weaknesses in the study done by the Kaiser Family Foundation? Explain.

2. Explain to what extent the RAND studies accurately reflect the effect that watching sex on television has on teenagers, according to your observations of teenagers.

3. The RAND studies focus on televised sex. Are teenagers more influenced by the sex in movies than that on television? Why, or why not? What other influences determine a teen's level of sexual activity?

4. Some schools have organizations that stress abstinence. If you are aware of such organizations, how would you describe the attitude that other students have toward those who advocate abstinence?

5. Evaluate the effectiveness of the support that Kaufman offers for his claim. His essay was originally published online at TurnOffYourTV.com. What is the effect of using links to Web sites as one of his primary means of support?

6. Doherty makes this statement: "The fixation on the body of the victim represents a telling shift away from the former site of detective work, the mind of the murderer" (para. 19). Do you agree? Explain.

7. How would you explain the popularity of forensic shows such as *CSI: Crime Scene Investigation*?

8. What evidence do you find in these essays that establishes a cause-and-effect relationship between TV violence and actual crimes?

9. Rhodes provides evidence from several studies to prove that TV and movie violence does not influence the behavior of young viewers. How convincing is it?

10. Several authors contend that TV or movie violence is not to blame for the high crime rate among young people. What causes do you suggest?

11. You are probably familiar with some of the games Gahr describes or others like them. Do you agree with the manufacturers that they are harmless? How does Gahr answer objections about violations of "freedom of speech"?

TOPICS FOR RESEARCH

Violence in selected TV shows, justified or unjustified?

Sex on TV: what message?

The significance of gangsta rap

Survey of studies on the effect of TV and movie violence

Influence of music videos or sports events on youthful behavior

CHAPTER 18

Are Limits on Freedom of Speech Ever Justified?

The First Amendment to the Constitution of the United States reads, "Congress shall make no laws respecting an establishment of religion, or prohibiting the free expression thereof; or abridging the freedom of speech, or of the press; or the right of the people peaceably to assemble, and to petition the Government for a redress of grievances." (The first ten amendments were ratified on December 15, 1791, and form what is known as the Bill of Rights.) The arguments in this section will consider primarily the issue of "abridging the freedom of speech."

The limits of free speech in the United States are constantly being adjusted as social values change and new cases testing those limits emerge. Several prominent areas of controversy are emphasized in the following selection of essays.

In 1969, the U.S. Supreme Court ruled that neither students nor teachers "shed their constitutional right to freedom of speech or expression at the schoolhouse gate" (*Tinker v. Des Moines Independent School District*). High schools, colleges, and universities are places where the exchange of ideas is generally welcome. The controversy arises over whether or not there are some ideas—some language, some symbols—that are not welcome. The First Amendment has been at the heart of court cases over everything from racist and sexist speech to the words or symbols printed on a T-shirt.

Those same students and teachers step outside the "schoolhouse gate" to confront a world in which many feel even the news is not fit for children, let alone prime-time television or even many movies rated G or PG, which one parent claims now stands for "profanity guaranteed." Rap music enrages those who find its attitude toward women and its call to violence offensive while others defend it as art protected by the First Amendment. The Federal Communications Commission has tightened its enforcement of rules against language or actions that go against the "public interest," but many consumers argue that it has not done enough. One of the authors included here even argues that the very existence of the FCC is unconstitutional.

Times of crisis resurrect old concerns about freedom of speech in times of crisis. Do American citizens have the right to speak out against a war in which Americans are fighting and dying? Should they? In some of these selections you will hear a sincere expression of concern that even in our patriotism we must not sacrifice our First Amendment right to freedom of speech.

TOLES © 1986 The Buffalo News. Reprinted with permission of UNIVERSAL PRESS SYNDICATE. All rights reserved.

Student Sues School District for Banning Anti-War T-Shirt

ALANA KEYNES

BEFORE READING: What restrictions, if any, did your high school have on what words, pictures, or symbols could be displayed on students' clothing? How did you feel about that policy? Was it necessary, in your opinion? Why, or why not?

A case addressing students' right to protest the Iraqi war in school has landed in the courts, with the American Civil Liberties Union (ACLU) suing a Michigan school district on behalf of a student sent home for wearing a T-shirt calling President Bush an "International Terrorist."

The suit, filed March 27 at the U.S. Eastern District Court of Michigan, alleges that Dearborn, Michigan, school officials violated the free-speech rights of Bretton Barber, a junior at Dearborn High School, since there was no evidence the T-shirt caused any disruption at school.

"There are strong indications in this case that the reaction of Dearborn High School officials to Barber's T-shirt was prompted by their disagreement with the message," the complaint states. "The only rationale given when Barber pressed for one was that the shirt would promote terrorism, which plainly could not have been a serious contention."

School administrators' claim that the shirt was disruptive is a "ludicrous charge," said Wendy Wagenheim, spokeswoman for the ACLU of Michigan. "They don't want to rock the boat in any way." There have been no instances of students causing problems by fighting with each other or teachers over the message conveyed in the T-shirt, she said. The complaint cites *Castorina v. Madison County School Board* (246 F.2d 536), the 6th Circuit Court of Appeals' decision that school officials could not ban two Kentucky students from wearing T-shirts with a picture of the Confederate flag to school (*ED*, March 12, 2001). Michigan is one of four states governed by the 6th Circuit.

Administrators also did not have a right to send Barber home, accord- 5 ing to the complaint, because legal precedent only permits schools to discipline students who are violating a written rule, and the Dearborn district does not have a policy banning political speech.

But the 11th Circuit Court of Appeals ruled last month that a Florida school district could suspend students who brought Confederate flags to school, though there was no written policy prohibiting them on campus (*ED*, March 26).

Alana Keynes is on the editorial staff at both *Education Daily*, where this article appeared on April 4, 2003, and *Federal Grants and Contracts Weekly*.

Wagenheim said she is not concerned that the 11th Circuit ruling will affect the ACLU's case, since federal appellate courts often issue conflicting rulings.

A spokesman from the Dearborn school district refused to comment on the suit. The district's superintendent issued a statement saying "this is now an issue for the courts to decide. The school district has no further remarks at this time."

Students' and teachers' right to express their views about the war has become a major issue in schools nationwide, as administrators continue to grapple with the appropriate limits of free speech in school (*ED*, March 21).

This is the first case the ACLU has taken on students' free-speech   10 rights in response to the Iraqi war, Wagenheim said, but many of its offices nationwide have received calls from students inquiring about their right to demonstrate against the war during school hours.

"Those inquiries are common occurrences at this point," she said.

The "Bong Hits 4 Jesus" Student Speech Case: With Kenneth Starr Seeking High Court Review of the Ninth Circuit Decision, Is Someone Blowing Smoke?

JULIE HILDEN

> BEFORE READING: What limitations are there currently on the language used by public school students? What cases can you recall from your own experience or the media that involved censorship of student speech?

L ast Monday, September 11, former Independent Counsel Kenneth Starr — now a lawyer at Kirkland & Ellis — asked the Supreme Court to review a March 10 decision by the U.S. Court of Appeals for the Ninth Circuit, in the case of *Frederick v. Morse*. The decision upheld a public high school student's First Amendment right to display a banner off campus. Starr represents the school district on a pro bono basis. . . .

Julie Hilden is both an attorney and a novelist. After graduating from Yale Law School, she worked for several years as a litigation associate for a Washington, D.C., law firm, specializing in First Amendment issues. Since 1999, she has been a columnist for Find-Law, an online source for legal news and commentary where this article appeared on September 18, 2006.

The Facts of the *Frederick* Case

The *Frederick* case grew out of an incident in which Juneau, Alaska, high school senior Joseph Frederick unfurled a banner reading "Bong Hits 4 Jesus" on a public sidewalk. He did so during a privately sponsored rally where townspeople watched the Olympic torch pass by. Students were released from school to attend the rally. The high school's "pep band" and cheerleaders performed there, but the court found that teacher supervision of other students at the rally was "minimal or nonexistent."

Frederick and his friends made sure they unfurled their banner when TV cameras were passing by—but the school's principal, Deborah Morse, who was also attending the rally, went up to Frederick, grabbed the banner, crumpled it up, and suspended him for ten days.

Frederick later sued, invoking the federal civil rights statute that allows plaintiffs to seek money damages for government infringements of their constitutional rights, including First Amendment rights.

In my view, the principal's conduct was appalling. She didn't just tell 5 Frederick to put his sign away, or that it was inappropriate, nor did she warn him that he could be suspended. Rather, she actually went right up to him on a public street and destroyed his banner.

This is the kind of thing that we believe cannot happen in this country. Is it suddenly acceptable simply because the victim is eighteen? What happened to school officials' duty to try to convince students—first, by setting the right example—to solve their differences with reason, not violence? Ironically, if Frederick had ripped up another student's poster on school grounds, he surely would have been suspended for doing so.

In short, the example this principal is setting is a very ugly one. No wonder the Ninth Circuit held—on the separate question of the principal's claim to immunity under the federal civil rights statute—that "it would be clear to a reasonable [principal] that [her] conduct was unlawful in the situation [she] confronted." (As a result, the principal herself may face liability for damages; she is a co-defendant in the case, along with the school board.)

How could this kind of behavior strike Starr, or Kirkland & Ellis, as so worthy of protecting, that it was worth taking this case on for the school district as a pro bono project?

The Legal Standards for Public School Students' Speech

There are three Supreme Court cases setting forth standards for public school students' speech—which were considered by the Ninth Circuit—but only one is relevant here.

One of the cases, *Hazelwood School Dist. v. Kuhlmeier*—addressing 10 school-sponsored speech—doesn't apply because neither Frederick's banner (nor the rally itself) was school-sponsored in the sense that, for instance, a school-funded student newspaper is.

A second case, *Bethel School Dist. No. 3 v. Fraser*—which was relied on by the district court, but distinguished by the Ninth Circuit—doesn't apply because it addresses only vulgar, lewd, obscene, and otherwise "plainly offensive" speech, and because the Ninth Circuit has interpreted that to mean, in essence, obscenity or, at least, speech involving four-letter words or similarly profane language.

Finally, there is *Tinker v. Des Moines Independent Community School Dist.* Its rule is simple: Student speech—other than speech that falls under the precedents noted above—can only be punished or otherwise regulated if it "materially disrupts classwork or involves substantial disorder or invasion of the rights of others." Moreover, to support the punishment or regulation, school districts must cite "evidence that [the punishment] is necessary to avoid material or substantial interference with schoolwork or discipline."

Applying the Legal Standard in the *Frederick* Case

The Juneau School District had an exceptionally weak case under *Tinker*.

In support of its case that Frederick's banner was disruptive, the District claimed that the banner would be read by many at the rally as "advocating or condoning illegal drug use."

Similarly, School Superintendent Peggy Cowan recently told CNN that 15 this case is appropriate for Supreme Court review because it raises "an important question about how the First Amendment applies to pro-drug messages in an educational setting."

But even if this was, to some extent, a pro-drug message, that wasn't all it was. The district itself acknowledged that Frederick could have been not just responding to, but parodying the school's anti-drug message (and parody is strongly protected by the First Amendment). Moreover the "for Jesus" part shouldn't be left out of the analysis; juxtaposing "Bong Hits," the informal "4" for "for," and "Jesus" may also send a message that religion shouldn't be taken so seriously, and a message that Jesus was more laid-back, and would have been more sympathetic to the counterculture, than some authoritarians would admit.

I'm not, of course, claiming that this message was well-thought out. To the contrary, it reads like a spur-of-the-moment lark, a prank. But I do think that it meant something different and more complicated, than just, say, a "Smoke Pot" banner would have. (Frederick himself said the banner was intended to be meaningless and funny, and he just wanted to get it on television. However, as many First Amendment cases have shown, words often have an impact beyond their intended meaning.)

The District also claimed that if the principal had done nothing, the district would have been seen by many as giving its imprimatur to Frederick's pro-drug message. But that claim seems ridiculous: If the District was as avid about spreading its anti-drug message as it claims that it was, no one would believe that it had suddenly changed its policy by merely deciding not to rip up Frederick's poster. If anything, onlookers might believe the District tolerated Frederick's poster out of a healthy respect for the First Amendment, or that the school district simply wasn't worried about its own message being undermined by a poorly-thought-out sophomoric sign.

Why the Ninth Circuit Is Right, and Starr Is Wrong, in This Case

Because this case is such a clear First Amendment violation, and because the Ninth Circuit rightly sided with the student, there's no good reason here for Supreme Court review.

In explaining why review was sought, Eric Hagen, an attorney from 20 Starr's office who also worked on the Supreme Court petition, told a reporter, "It makes it a little harder when teachers and principals in their daily duties might be subject to a damages lawsuit and be held personally liable." But it's only harder for teachers and principals to perform their daily duties when the lines for liability are unclear.

As noted above, there are few First Amendment violations clearer than a government employee's crumpling up someone's banner at a privately sponsored rally on a public street. That's censorship with a capital "C." If the Supreme Court does want to make the line between permissible disciplinary action and impermissible First Amendment violation clearer, perhaps it should wait for a subtler, closer case.

Ironically, I think most schoolchildren, if taught a bit about the First Amendment, could easily identify this as an obvious violation. Their teachers and principals ought at least to be able to do the same. . . .

The Case against School Prayer

ANNIE LAURIE GAYLOR

BEFORE READING: Did your school(s) observe a moment of silence or have daily school prayer? Do you believe that such practices violate the policy of separation of church and state? Explain.

"I pledge allegiance to the flag of the United States of America, and to the republic for which it stands, one nation indivisible, with liberty and justice for all." —The "godless" Pledge of Allegiance, as it was recited by generations of school children, before Congress inserted a religious phrase, "under God," in 1954.

Keep the Church and State Forever Separate

Should Students Pray in Public Schools? Public schools exist to educate, not to proselytize. Children in public schools are a captive audience. Making prayer an official part of the school day is coercive and invasive. What 5-, 8-, or 10-year-old could view prayers recited as part of class routine as "voluntary"? Religion is private, and schools are public, so it is appropriate that the two should not mix. To introduce religion in our public schools builds walls between children who may not have been aware of religious difference before.

Why Should Schools Be Neutral? Our public schools are for *all* children, whether Catholic, Baptist, Quaker, atheist, Buddhist, Jewish, agnostic. The schools are supported by *all* taxpayers, and therefore should be free of religious observances and coercion. It is the sacred duty of parents and churches to instill religious beliefs, free from government dictation. Institutionalizing prayers in public schools usurps the rights of parents.

School prayer proponents mistake government *neutrality* toward religion as *hostility*. The record shows that religious beliefs have flourished in this country not in spite of but because of the constitutional separation of church and state.

What Happens When Worship Enters Public Schools? When religion has invaded our public school system, it has singled out the lone Jewish student,

---

In 1978 Annie Laurie Gaylor was cofounder, with her mother, of the Freedom from Religion Foundation, described on the organization's Web site as "the largest group of atheists and agnostics in North America," founded "to promote freethought and defend the constitutional principle of the separation of state and church." With her husband, Gaylor is co-president of the organization, and she also edits *Freethought Today* and frequently publishes and makes presentations on the separation of church and state. This article is from the organization's Web site.

The original pre-1955 Pledge, without "under God."

The PLEDGE *to the* FLAG

I PLEDGE ALLEGIANCE
to the FLAG *of the*
UNITED STATES *of* AMERICA
and to the REPUBLIC *for which*
IT STANDS
ONE NATION INDIVISIBLE
with LIBERTY *and* JUSTICE
for ALL

the class Unitarian or agnostic, the children in the minority. Families who protest state/church violations in our public schools invariably experience persecution. It was commonplace prior to the court decision against school prayer to put non-religious or nonorthodox children in places of detention during bible-reading or prayer recitation. The children of Supreme Court plaintiffs against religion in schools, such as Vashti McCollum, Ed Schempp, and Ishmael Jaffree, were beaten up on the way to and from school, their families subjected to community harassment and death threats for speaking out in defense of a constitutional principle. We know from history how harmful and destructive religion is in our public schools. In those school districts that do not abide by the law, school children continue to be persecuted today.

Can't Students Pray in Public Schools Now? Individual, silent, personal prayer 5 never has and never could be outlawed in public schools. The courts have declared *government-fostered* prayers unconstitutional—those led, required, sanctioned, scheduled, or suggested by officials.

It is dishonest to call any prayer "voluntary" that is encouraged or required by a public official or legislature. By definition, if the government suggests that students pray, whether by penning the prayer, asking them to vote whether to pray, or setting aside time to pray, it is endorsing and promoting that prayer. It is coercive for schools to schedule worship as an official part of the school day, school sports or activities, or to use prayer to formalize graduation ceremonies. Such prayers are more "mandatory" than "voluntary."

What's Wrong with a "Voluntary" Prayer Amendment? Proponents of so-called "voluntary" school prayer amendment (such as the one proposed in 1995) are admitting that our secular Constitution prohibits organized prayers in public schools. Otherwise, why would an amendment to our U.S. Constitution be required? The nation must ask whether politically-motivated Newt Gingrich & Co. are wiser than James Madison, principal author of the Constitution, and the other founders who engineered the World's oldest and most successful constitution!

The radical school prayer amendment would negate the First Amendment's guarantee against government establishment of religion. Most distressing, it would be at the expense of the civil rights of children, America's most vulnerable class. It would attack the heart of the Bill of Rights, which safeguards the rights of the individual from the tyranny of the majority.

What Would the Prayer Amendment Permit? The text of the proposed federal amendment (as of January, 1995) reads:

> *"Nothing in this Constitution shall be construed to prohibit individual or group prayer in public schools or other public institutions. No person shall be required by the United States or by any State to participate in prayer. Neither the United States or any State shall compose the words of any prayer to be said in public schools."*

Since the right to "individual prayer" already exists, the real motive is to instill "group prayer."

No wording in this amendment would prevent the government from 10 *selecting* the prayer, or the particular version of the bible it should be taken from. Nothing restricts prayers to "nondenominational" or "nonsectarian" (not that such a restriction would make it acceptable). Nothing would prevent a school from selecting the Lord's Prayer or other prayers to Jesus, and blasting it over the intercom. For that matter, nothing would prevent the school from sponsoring prayers to Allah or Zoroaster. Nothing would prevent principals, teachers, or clergy from leading the students. Nothing would prevent nonparticipating students from being singled out The proposal also seeks to institutionalize group prayer in other public settings, presumably public-supported senior centers, courthouses, etc.

School prayer supporters envision organized, vocal, group recitations of prayer, daily classroom displays of belief in a deity or religion, dictated by the majority. Those in the minority would be compelled to conform to a religion or ritual in which they disbelieve, to suffer the humiliation and imposition of submitting to a daily religious exercise against their will, or be singled out by orthodox classmates and teachers as "heretics" or "sinners" for not participating.

Haven't Public Schools Always Had Prayer? At the time the U.S. Supreme Court issued its 1962 and 1963 decrees against school-sponsored prayers and bible-reading, it is estimated religious observances were unknown in about half of the nation's public schools.

Horace Mann, the father of our public school system, championed the elimination of sectarianism from American schools, largely accomplished by the 1840's. Bible reading, prayers, or hymns in public schools were absent from most public schools by the end of the 19th century, after Catholic or minority-religion immigrants objected to Protestant bias in public schools.

Until the 20th century, only Massachusetts required bible-reading in the schools, in a statute passed by the virulently anti-Catholic Know Nothing Party in the 1850's. Only after 1913 did eleven other states make prayers or bible-reading compulsory. A number of other states outlawed such practices by judicial or administrative decree, and half a dozen state supreme courts overruled devotionals in public schools.

As early as the 1850's, the Superintendent of Schools of New York State 15 ordered that prayers could no longer be required as part of public school activities. The Cincinnati Board of Education resolved in 1869 that "religious instruction and the reading of religious books, including the Holy Bible, was prohibited in the common schools of Cincinnati."

Presidents Ulysses S. Grant and Theodore Roosevelt spoke up for what Roosevelt called "absolutely nonsectarian public schools." Roosevelt added that it is "not our business to have the Protestant Bible or the Catholic Vulgate or the Talmud read in these schools."

For nearly half a century, the United States Supreme Court, consistent with this nation's history of secular schools, has ruled against religious indoctrination through schools (*McCollum v. Board of Education*, 1948), prayers and devotionals in public schools (*Engel v. Vitale*, 1962), and prayers and bible-reading (*Abington School District v. Schempp*, 1963), right up through the 1992 *Weisman* decision against prayers at public school commencements and *Santa Fe v. Doe* (2000) barring student-led prayers at public school events.

How Can Prayer Be Harmful? Contrary to right-wing claims, piety is not synonymous with virtue. People should be judged by their actions, not by what religion they believe in or how publicly or loudly they pray.

Some Americans believe in the power of prayer; others believe nothing fails like prayer. Some citizens say prayer makes them feel better, but others contend that prayer is counterproductive to personal responsibility. Such a diversity of views is constitutionally protected; our secular government simply is not permitted to pick a side in religious debates.

"The hands that help are better far than lips that pray," wrote Robert 20 G. Ingersoll. Who could disagree?

Should Government Become "Prayer Police"? How ironic that those campaigning on an anti-Big Government theme, who contend that government should get out of our private lives, would seek to tell our children who to pray to in our public schools! As many editorials across the country have pointed out, the school prayer debate seems calculated to deflect attention away from the more pressing economic questions facing our nation. As one conservative governor put it: "If we don't deal with the economic issues, we'll need more than prayer to solve our problems."

Can't Moral Decline Be Traced to the Prayer Decisions? Some politicians like to blame everything bad in America upon the absence of school prayer. Get real! Entire generations of Americans have grown up to be law-abiding citizens without ever once reciting a prayer in school! If prayer is the answer, why are our jails and prisons bulging with born-agains! Japan, where no one prays at school, has the lowest crime rate of any developed nation.

Institutionalizing school prayer cannot raise the SAT scores (only more studying and less praying can do that). It is irrational to charge that the complicated sociological problems facing our everchanging population stem from a lack of prayer in schools.

One might just as well credit the lack of prayer with the great advances that have taken place since the 1962 and 1963 decisions on prayer. Look at the leap in civil liberties, equality, environmental awareness, women's rights, science, technology, and medicine! The polio scare is over. Fountains, buses, schools are no longer segregated by law. We've made great strides in medical treatment. We have VCRs and the computer chip. The Cold War has ended! Who would turn the clock back?

What about the Rights of the Majority? Our political system is a democratic 25 republic in which we use majority vote to elect certain officials or pass referenda. But we do not use majority vote to decide what religion, if any, our neighbors must observe! The "majority" is free to worship at home, at tax-exempt churches, on the way to and from school, or privately in school. There are 16 school-less hours a day when children can pray, not to mention weekends.

Many in the "majority" do not support school prayers. And if the majority religion gets to choose which prayers are said in schools, that would mean a lot of Protestant kids will be reciting Catholic prayers! The Roman Catholic Church is the single largest denomination in our country. Should Protestant minorities be excused so the classroom can pray in unison to the Virgin Mary? In a few school districts, Muslims outnumber other religions. Should Christian minorities march into the hall with their ears covered while the principal prays to Allah over the intercom?

What's Wrong with a Moment of Silence? Given the regimentation of school children, it would make more sense to have a "moment of bedlam" than a "moment of silence"! Obviously, the impetus for "moments of silence or meditation" is to circumvent the rulings against religion in schools. The legislative history of such state laws reveals the religious motives behind the legislation, as in the Alabama law struck down by the U.S. Supreme Court in 1985 calling for a "moment of silence for meditation or prayer."

When a "moment of silence" law was enacted in Arkansas at the suggestion of then-Gov. Bill Clinton, the law mandating this meaningless ritual was later repealed following popular indifference. We know from experience that many teachers and principals would regard a "moment of silence" mandate as a green light to introduce prayers, causing more legal challenges at the expense of taxpayers.

Should Commencements Start with Prayers? In 1992, the Court ruled in *Lee v. Weisman* that prayers at public school commencements are an impermissible establishment of religion: "The lessons of the First Amendment are as urgent in the modern world as the 18th Century when it was written. One timeless lesson is that if citizens are subjected to state-sponsored religious exercises, the State disavows its own duty to guard and respect that sphere of inviolable conscience and belief which is the mark of a free people," wrote Justice Kennedy for the majority. He dismissed as unacceptable the cruel idea that a student should forfeit her own graduation in order to be free from such an establishment of religion.

What About "Student-Initiated" Prayer? This is a ruse proposed by extremist 30 Christian legal groups such as the Rutherford Institute, and the American Center for Law and Justice run by televangelist Pat Robertson. Religious coercion is even worse at the hands of another student, subjecting students to peer pressure, pitting students in the majority against students in the minority, treating them as outsiders with school complicity.

Imposing prayer-by-majority-vote is flagrant and insensitive abuse of school authority. Such schools should be teaching students about the purpose of the Bill of Rights, instead of teaching them to be religious bullies. Some principals or school boards have even made seniors hold open class votes on whether to pray at graduation, leading to hostility and reprisal against those students brave enough to stand up for the First Amendment.

"The notion that a person's constitutional rights may be subject to a majority vote is itself anathema," wrote Judge Albert V. Bryan, Jr. in a 1993 ruling in Virginia, one of several similar district court rulings around the nation banning any prayer, whether student- or clergy-led.

We cannot put liberties protected by our Bill of Rights up to a vote of school children! Should kindergartners be forced to vote about whether to pray before their milk and cookies? Under such reasoning, what would make it wrong for students to vote to segregate schools or otherwise violate the civil liberties of minorities?

Keep the State and Church Forever Separate Our founders wisely adopted a secular, godless constitution, the first to derive its powers from "We, the People" and the consent of the governed, rather than claiming divine authority. They knew from the experience of religious persecution, witchhunts, and religious discrimination in the Thirteen Colonies, and from the bloody history left behind in Europe, that the surest path to tyranny was to entangle church and state. That is why they adopted a secular constitution whose only references to religion are exclusionary, such as that there shall be no religious test for public office (Art. VI). There were no prayers offered at the Constitutional Convention, which shows their intent to separate religion from secular affairs.

Prayers in schools and religion in government are no panacea for so- 35
cial ills—they are an invitation to divisiveness. More people have been killed in the name of religion than for any other cause. As Thomas Paine pointed out, "Persecution is not an original feature in any religion; but it is always the strongly marked feature of all religions established by law."

Even Jesus Was against School Prayer "Thou shalt not be as the hypocrites are: for they love to pray standing in the synagogues and in the corners of the streets, that they may be seen of men. . . . But thou, when thou prayest, enter into thy closet, and when thou hast shut thy door, pray to thy Father which is in secret." —*Matt.* 6:5–6.

> "There is no such source and cause of strife, quarrel, fights, malignant opposition, persecution, and war, and all evil in the state, as religion. Let it once enter our civil affairs, our government would soon be destroyed. Let it once enter our common schools, they would be destroyed."
> —Supreme Court of Wisconsin, *Weiss v. District Board*, March 18, 1890

> "Leave the matter of religion to the family altar, the church, and the private school, supported entirely by private contributions. Keep the church and state forever separate."
> —Ulysses S. Grant, "The President's Speech at Des Moines" (1875)

> "Congress shall make no law respecting an establishment of religion, or prohibiting the free exercise thereof."
> —First Amendment, Bill of Rights, U.S. Constitution

> Thomas Jefferson, author of the sweeping Virginia Statute of Religious Freedom, stating that no citizen "shall be compelled to frequent or support any religious worship, place, or ministry whatsoever . . ." and that to "compel a man to furnish contributions of money for the propagation of [religious] opinions which he disbelieves is sinful and tyrannical."

> "I contemplate with sovereign reverence that act of the whole American people which declared that their legislature should make no law 're-specting an establishment of religion, or prohibiting the free exercise thereof,' thus building a wall of separation between church and state."
> —President Thomas Jefferson, 1802 letter to the Baptists of Danbury, Connecticut

Supreme Court Cases Opposing Religious Worship in Schools

McCollum v. Board of Education, 333 U.S. 203, 212 (1948).
  Struck down religious instruction in public schools. The case involved school-sponsored religious instruction in which the sole nonreligious

student, Jim McCollum, was placed in detention and persecuted by schoolmates in Champaign, Illinois.

Tudor v. Board of Education of Rutherford, 14 N.J. 31 (1953), cert. denied, 348 U.S. 816 (1954).

Let stand a lower court ruling that the practice of allowing volunteers to distribute Gideon Bibles at public school was unconstitutional.

Engel v. Vitale, 370 U.S. 421 (1962).

Declared prayers in public school unconstitutional.

Abington Township School District v. Schempp, 374 U.S. 203 (1963).

Declared unconstitutional devotional bible-reading and recitation of the Lord's Prayer in public schools.

Epperson v. Arkansas, 393 U.S., 97, 104 (1968).

Struck down state law forbidding schools to teach the science of evolution.

Stone v. Graham, 449 U.S. 39 (1980).

Declared unconstitutional the posting of the Ten Commandments in classrooms.

Wallace v. Jaffree, 472 U.S. 38, 72 (1985).

Overturned law requiring daily "period of silence not to exceed one minute . . . for meditation or daily prayer."

Jager v. Douglas County School District, 862 F.2d 824 (11th Cir.), cert. denied, 490 U.S. 1090 (1989).

Let stand a lower court ruling in Georgia that pre-game invocations at high school football games are unconstitutional.

Lee v. Weisman, 120 L. Ed. 2d 467 (1992).

Ruled prayers at public school graduations an impermissible establishment of religion.

Berger v. Rensselaer, 982 F.2d 1160 (7th Cir.), cert. denied, 124 L. Ed. 254 (1993).

Let stand ruling barring access to Gideons to pass out bibles in Indiana schools.

Santa Fe Independent School District v. Doe, 530 U.S. 290 (2000).

Barred student-led prayers at public school functions.

Why We Need to Abolish the FCC

ROBERT GARMONG

BEFORE READING: The Federal Communications Commission regulates what can be said on the air. Do you believe that the FCC is too restrictive, not restrictive enough, or generally right on target in deciding what should be allowed on the broadcast media?

Since the infamous "wardrobe malfunction" at the Super Bowl, there have been strident demands for a crackdown by a tougher, stricter Federal Communications Commission. The FCC's various commissioners now call for the power to regulate cable TV in addition to broadcast media.

In June, Congress voted to increase the maximum fine the FCC can impose tenfold, from $27,500 to $275,000. Commissioner Michael Copps has vowed that he will not be satisfied until "I see us send one or two . . . cases for license revocation."

In this headlong rush to expand the government's authority over the media, no one has paused to consider whether the government should have such authority in the first place. No one has noticed that the very existence of the FCC is a flagrant violation of the right to free speech.

Central Premise of the United States

Throughout history, the norm was tyranny over the mind. Men were allowed to speak only by government imprimatur, until America's First Amendment established freedom of speech as a central premise of our nation.

The First Amendment declares that "Congress shall pass no law . . .   5
abridging the freedom of speech, or of the press." This language could not be clearer, or more absolute: no matter who disagrees with you or considers your speech offensive, the government may not abridge your right to say it.

Free speech is the protection of the rational mind and its literary, intellectual, and scientific products. It means the absolute right to express one's views, so long as one does not violate the rights of others.

Free speech means no American should fear the fate of Galileo, persecuted for daring to assert scientific truths that contradicted the official Church's doctrines, nor that of Socrates, put to death for offending the state.

Yet the FCC exists to dictate what can be said on-air. Each year since the early days of radio, every broadcast station must apply to the FCC for permission to use the airwaves. In exchange for their licenses, broadcasters

---

Robert Garmong holds a Ph.D. in philosophy and is a writer for the Ayn Rand Institute in Irvine, California. This article originally appeared in the *San Diego Business Journal* on August 9, 2004.

must promise to serve the "public interest." Stations that the FCC regards as having failed to do so can be fined, or even shut down, at the FCC's sole discretion.

The putative justification for the FCC's regulation of broadcasters is that the airwaves are public property. But just as the government does not own—and so has no legitimate control over—the presses of the *New York Times*, so it has no business regulating what may be broadcast over airwaves.

The airwaves, which would be useless without the transmission net- 10 works created by radio and TV stations, belong to the individuals and companies that developed them. Broadcasters should not have to plead to the authorities for annual licenses, any more than a homeowner should have to beg for an annual license to use the patch of land he has developed.

No other media in America is subjected to such persecution. If the *New York Times* or Barnes & Noble publishes and distributes content some members of the public disapprove of, the government cannot threaten them with fines or penalties. But let Howard Stern offend a listener, and Clear Channel is hammered with more than a million dollars in fines.

"Indecency" Crackdown

So far, only "indecency" has been targeted by the FCC's crackdown—but politicians on both sides of the aisle have begun whispering demands to censor PBS or the Fox News Channel on the grounds that their alleged biases violate the "public interest."

Both the liberals, with their political correctness, and the conservatives, with their puritanical religious ethic, claim to speak for the "public interest." Can it be long before the two sides begin the battle over which ideas and values Americans are allowed to see and hear on-air?

As the FCC wields its club ever more fiercely, broadcasters are running scared. Clear Channel has canceled its "shock-jock" programs. Skittish station managers have bleeped out words such as "urinate," "damn," and "orgy" from the Rush Limbaugh program. Most ominous, the National Association of Broadcasters convened a "Summit on Responsible Programming" to define industrywide standards of self-censorship.

America was founded on the freedom of speech—on the right and re- 15 sponsibility of the individual to decide what to say, and what to listen to. Yet in the name of protecting ourselves from being offended—and almost without noticing it—we are well on the way to surrendering that crucial right to the control of the omnipotent state.

Freedom of Speech and My Right to Silence at Bath Time

PATTI WALDMEIR

BEFORE READING: What is your opinion of the do-not-call registry designed to keep citizens from receiving calls from telemarketers? Are there two sides to the argument?

It is funny how the U.S. Constitution intrudes into one's daily life in America. Some countries do not even have one; ours dictates the smallest details of mundane life—such as whether I can bathe my children in peace or catch a catnap on a Sunday without an invasion of the telemarketers.

Today a federal appeals court in Oklahoma will address the pressing national question of whether I have a constitutional right to silence at bath time.

The case before the court tests the constitutionality of the federal do-not-call registry, which allows Americans to assert their right to silence by banning commercial telemarketing calls. The registry is wildly popular—the single most popular thing the federal government has done in years. But that does not make it constitutional; and the fate of do-not-call efforts could well foretell the future of do-not-spam.

Either way, it is a question of commercial free speech: advertisers have a right to broadcast their wares, but consumers have a right to refuse to listen. This case will test the role of government in helping consumers block their ears. It could have big implications, not just for junk calls and junk e-mail but also for the future of corporate free speech in America.

Eventually, one of the new generation of do-not-advertise cases will 5 probably end up before the U.S. Supreme Court, but that may take a while. Until then, proponents of a crackdown can brandish powerful quotes from former Supreme Court justices that appear to condemn the invasion of the advertisers: Justice Louis Brandeis said the right to be let alone was "the right most valued by civilized men"; Justice William O. Douglas said it was "the beginning of all freedoms." They were not talking about telemarketing. But their views are a powerful rhetorical tool for those who think a man's home should be more than a spam receptacle.

So what happens when a man's right to preserve the privacy of his castle collides with the free speech rights of advertisers? That is the issue before the 10th circuit court of appeals in Tulsa today: Can the government help consumers place a gag order on telemarketers by enforcing a

---

Patti Waldmeir writes a column about law and society for the *Financial Times* in London. Before her move to London, she was the U.S. editor for the *Financial Times*, based in Washington, D.C.

national do-not-call list? Or does the first amendment to the U.S. Constitution prohibit the registry as a free speech violation?

Judge Edward Nottingham became one of the most despised men in America when he struck down the registry as unconstitutional in September. And the grounds for his ruling made it seem all the more absurd: He objected because the registry would block only commercial calls and not charitable solicitations. Judge Nottingham argued that the government had no right to discriminate between a sales pitch from AT&T and one from the Policemen's Benevolent Association. Ironically, he struck down the registry not because it banned too much speech but because it banned too little.

But although his decision enraged the 50 million American households that had already signed up for the registry, that does not make it wrong. Judge Nottingham insisted the government had failed to show why the registry should apply to one kind of call and not the other. Charitable calls disrupt my nap and bother my bath time just as surely as any other solicitation. In fact, I find charity calls from the police even more upsetting than offers of double-glazing and cheap credit. I do not feel threatened by window salesmen; but when policemen ask me for funds, I feel I have been hit for protection money. Both kinds of call are annoying and upsetting. Should one be allowed and not the other?

There is no satisfactory answer to that question, says Stuart Banner of UCLA law school, who argues that every do-not-advertise effort will encounter first amendment problems. If government enforces a ban against all solicitation, commercial and noncommercial, it may be restricting speech that is essentially political and that enjoys the highest form of first amendment protection. Commercial speech gets less protection; but the government still needs a good reason to hinder it unless it is fraudulent. So there is no way, he argues, to write a do-not-call or do-not-spam rule that does not end up in the courts.

Still, he predicts most such efforts will survive because most judges 10 are pragmatic rather than purist: "Judges don't usually pursue constitutional doctrines to their logical end if doing so would require dashing the hopes of tens of millions of Americans (especially if some of those Americans are judges, as I imagine they are)," he wrote recently in the *Washington Post*. In a world where judges get spam too, do-not-spam efforts probably have a guaranteed future.

As Michael Powell, chairman of the Federal Communications Commission, said when the FCC do-not-call registry was first challenged: "I refuse to believe that the Constitution of the United States shuts down the ability of consumers to protect the sanctity of their homes." He is probably right, which is good news for the sanctity of bath time. But it could be seriously bad news for commercial speech in the United States: Telemarketers have rights too. We all share the same constitution; somehow, it must protect us all.

TOO MUCH COFFEE MAN
BY SHANNON WHEELER

Dare Call It Treason

ERIC FONER

BEFORE READING: Do you believe that Americans should be able to speak out against a war their country is involved in? Brainstorm what you know about the history of such dissent in the United States.

Few traditions are more American than freedom of speech and the right to dissent. But an equally powerful American tradition has been the effort by government and private "patriots" to suppress free expression in times of crisis. During the fighting in Iraq, former military leaders who criticized planning for the war were denounced for endangering troops in the field and warned to remain silent. A number of scholars, including myself, were branded "Traitor Professors" on a television talk show. If criticism of a war while it is in progress makes one a traitor, that category will have to include Abraham Lincoln, who denounced the Mexican War while serving in Congress in 1847; Mark Twain, who vehemently attacked government policy in the Spanish-American and Philippine wars at the turn of the last century; and Martin Luther King Jr., who eloquently called for an end to the war in Vietnam.

With the exception of World War II, every significant war in American history has inspired vigorous dissent. Many colonists remained loyal to Britain during the American Revolution. Most New Englanders opposed the War of 1812. Numerous Americans considered the Mexican War an effort to extend the territory of slavery. Both North and South were internally divided during the Civil War. World War I and Vietnam produced massive antiwar movements. This is part of our democratic tradition.

Equally persistent, however, have been efforts to suppress wartime dissent. The Alien and Sedition Acts during the "quasi-war" with France in 1798 allowed the president to deport aliens and made it illegal to criticize the government. Both Union and Confederate governments suppressed opposition newspapers and jailed critics. World War I witnessed a massive repression of freedom of speech, with critics of the war, socialists, and labor leaders jailed or deported; those suspected of disloyalty rounded up

---

Eric Foner is the DeWitt Clinton Professor of History at Columbia University and has also taught at Oxford, Cambridge, and Moscow state universities. He is an elected fellow of the American Academy of Arts and Sciences and the British Academy and has served as president of both the Organization of American Historians and the American Historical Association. Foner has written a number of books about American history, including the 2004 textbook *Give Me Liberty! An American History*. He was invited to revise the presentation of American history at the Hall of Presidents at Disney World and Meet Mr. Lincoln at Disneyland and has served as consultant to several National Parks Service historical sites and historical museums.

by private vigilantes; and the speaking of German banned in some places. Universities, including my own, fired professors who opposed American involvement.

Self-proclaimed patriots not only seek to determine the boundaries of acceptable speech about the present but rewrite history to create a more politically useful past. During World War I, the Committee on Public Information, a government propaganda agency, published pamphlets demonstrating the "common principles" of Oliver Cromwell, Jean-Jacques Rousseau, and Thomas Jefferson in order to create a historical lineage for the Anglo-French-American military alliance. Today, statements about history that in normal times would seem uncontroversial have been labeled treasonous. Daniel Pipes said in his syndicated newspaper column that I "hate America" because I noted that Japan invoked the idea of preemptive war to justify its attack on Pearl Harbor (a point also made by that well-known anti-American, Arthur Schlesinger Jr.). My comment to a reporter that the United States has frequently embarked on military ventures without being attacked, as in Haiti, the Dominican Republic, and Vietnam, prompted accusations of treason in the media.

In the aftermath of the Civil War, a far greater crisis than the war on 5 Iraq, the Supreme Court in the *Milligan* case invalidated the use of military tribunals to try civilians. The Court proclaimed that the Constitution is not suspended in wartime: "It is a law for rulers and people, equally in war and in peace." Alas, we have not always lived up to this ideal. The history of civil liberties in the United States is not a straight-line trajectory toward ever-greater freedom. It is a complex story in which victories can prove temporary and regression can follow progress.

Our civil liberties are neither self-enforcing nor self-correcting. Historians today view past suppressions of free speech as shameful episodes. But we are now living through another moment when many commentators, both in and out of government, seem to view freedom of expression as at best an inconvenience and at worst unpatriotic. The incessant attacks on dissenters as traitors are intended to create an atmosphere of shock and awe within the United States, so that those tempted to speak their mind become too intimidated to do so.

George W. Bush has claimed that America's enemies wish to destroy our freedoms. If we surrender freedom of speech in the hope that this will bring swifter victory on current and future battlefields, who then will have won the war?

The Imus Fallout: Who Can Say What?

JAMES PONIEWOZIK

BEFORE READING: What restrictions, if any, are there on what language can be used on the radio? Are those restrictions the same as for television? Should they be?

S ay this for Don Imus: the man knows how to turn an economical phrase. When the radio shock jock described the Rutgers women's basketball team, on the April 4 *Imus in the Morning*, as "nappy-headed hos," he packed so many layers of offense into the statement that it was like a perfect little diamond of insult. There was a racial element, a gender element, and even a class element (the joke implied that the Scarlet Knights were thuggish and ghetto compared with the Tennessee Lady Vols).

Imus was a famous, rich, old white man picking on a bunch of young, mostly black college women. So it seemed pretty cut-and-dried that his bosses at CBS Radio would suspend his show—half frat party, half political salon for the Beltway elite—for two weeks, and that MSNBC would cancel the TV simulcast. And that Imus would plan to meet with the students he offended. Case closed, justice served, lesson—possibly—learned. Move on.

But a reasonable person could ask, What was the big deal? And I don't mean the lots-of-black-rappers-say- "hos" argument, though we'll get to that. Rather, I mean, what celebrity isn't slurring some group nowadays?

I exaggerate slightly. But our culture has experienced an almost psychotic outburst of -isms in the past year. Michael Richards and "nigger." Isaiah Washington and "faggot." Senator George Allen and "macaca." Mel Gibson and "f__ing Jews."

But we also live in a culture in which racially and sexually edgy mate- 5 rial is often—legitimately—considered brilliant comment, even art. Last year's most critically praised comedy, *Borat: Cultural Learnings of America for Make Benefit Glorious Nation of Kazakhstan*, won Sacha Baron Cohen a Golden Globe for playing a Kazakh journalist who calls Alan Keyes a "genuine chocolate face" and asks a gun-shop owner to suggest a good piece for killing a Jew. Quentin Tarantino has made a career borrowing tropes from blaxploitation movies. In the critics-favorite sitcom *The Sarah Silverman Program*, the star sleeps with God, who is African American and who she assumes is "God's black friend." And the current season of *South Park* opened with an episode about a Michael Richards-esque controversy erupting when a character blurts the word *niggers* on *Wheel of Fortune*. (He

---

James Poniewozik worked as the media critic and media section leader for the online magazine Salon.com before he joined *Time* in 1999 as media and television critic. He is also a commentator for National Public Radio's *All Things Considered* and *On the Media*. This article was published on April 12, 2007.

answers a puzzle—N-GGERS—for which the clue is "People who annoy you"; the correct answer is "naggers.")

This is not to say that *Borat* made Imus do it or to make excuses for Imus. Even in the midst of his apology tour last week, Imus did enough of that for himself, citing his charity work, his support of black Senate candidate Harold Ford Jr., even his booking the black singing group Blind Boys of Alabama on his show. (He didn't mention how, last fall, he groused about persuading the "money grubbing" "Jewish management" to okay the booking.)

But in the middle of his stunning medley of sneer, apology, and rationalization, Imus asked a pretty good question: "This phrase that I use, it originated in the black community. That didn't give me a right to use it, but that's where it originated. Who calls who that and why? We need to know that. I need to know that."

So let's ask.

Imus crossed a line, boorishly, creepily, paleolithically. But where is that line nowadays? In a way, the question is an outgrowth of something healthy in our society: the assumption that there is a diverse audience that is willing to talk about previously taboo social distinctions more openly, frankly, and daringly than before. It used to be assumed that people were free to joke about their own kind (with some license for black comedians to talk about how white people dance). Crossing those lines was the province of the occasional "socially conscious artist," like Dick Gregory or Lenny Bruce, who was explicit about his goals: in Bruce's words, to repeat "'niggerniggernigger' until the word [didn't] mean anything anymore."

Now, however, we live in a mash-up world, where people—especially 10 young people—feel free to borrow one another's cultural signifiers. In a now classic episode of *Chappelle's Show*, comic Dave Chappelle plays a blind, black white supremacist who inadvertently calls a carload of rap-listening white boys "niggers." The kids' reaction: "Did he just call us niggers? Awesome!" The country is, at least, more pop-culturally integrated—one nation under Jessica Alba, J. Lo and Harold & Kumar—and with that comes greater comfort in talking about differences.

But that's a harder attitude for older people—who grew up with more cultural and actual segregation—to accept or to mimic. Part of the problem with Imus' joke was that it was so tone-deaf. "That's some rough girls from Rutgers," he said. "Man, they got tattoos . . . That's some nappy-headed hos there." The joke played badly in every community, raising memories of beauty bias (against darker skin and kinkier hair) that dates back to slavery. Tracy Riley, 37, of Des Moines, Iowa, who is of mixed race, said the incident was among her four kids' first exposures to overt racism. "Our kids don't see color the way we do," she said. "They don't see it as much. 'You're my friend or not,' but it's not about race."

The line was as damning as anything for what it suggested about Imus's thought process: a 66-year-old white male country-music fan rummaging in his subconscious for something to suggest that some young black women looked scary, and coming up with a reference to African-American hair and a random piece of rap slang. (Maybe because older, male media honchos are more conscious of—and thus fixated on—race than gender, much of the coverage of Imus ignored the sexual part of the slur on a show with a locker-room vibe and a mostly male guest list. If Imus had said "niggas" rather than "hos," would his bosses have waited as long to act?)

So who gets to say "ho," in an age when *Pimp My Ride* is an innocent car show and *It's Hard Out Here for a Pimp* is an Oscar-winning song? As even Essence Carlson, one of the Rutgers students Imus insulted, acknowledged at a press conference, black rap artists labeled young black women as "hos" long before Imus did. And while straight people may not be able to say "faggot," *Queer Eye for the Straight Guy* and *Will & Grace* helped mainstream the nonhostile gay joke for straight people. But all this reappropriation and blurring—distinguishing a good-natured "That's so gay!" from a homophobic one—has created a situation in which, when Richards went off on his Laugh Factory rant, it was possible to wonder if he was playing a character.

The license to borrow terms other people have taken back can worry even edgy comics. A few months ago, I interviewed Silverman, who argued that her material was not racist but about racism (and I agree). But she added something that surprised me, coming from her: "I'm not saying 'I can say nigger because I'm liberal.' There is a certain aspect of that that I'm starting to get grossed out by. 'Oh, we're not racist. We can say it.'"

Comedians work through these danger zones in the presence of other 15 comics. In a comedians' get-together or a TV writers' room, nothing is off-limits: without airing the joke that goes too far, you can never get to the joke that flies in front of an audience. Trouble might come if material meant for that smaller audience went public, as in 1993, when Ted Danson got in trouble after word got out of a Friars Club routine he did in blackface, though his jokes were defended—and reportedly written by—his then girlfriend Whoopi Goldberg.

Today, because of cable and YouTube, because of a media culture that rewards the fastest, least censoring mouth, we are all in the writers' room. (Friars Club roasts are now televised on Comedy Central.) Punditry and gonzo comedy have become less and less distinguishable. (And I'm not talking here about *The Daily Show*, whose host Jon Stewart is, ironically, one of the most conservative defenders of the idea of sober, evenhanded news—see his 2004 tirade against Tucker Carlson.) Got something on your mind? Say it! Don't think about it! If you don't, the next guy in the greenroom will! C'mon, it'll kill!

Right-wing pundit Ann Coulter is probably the best example of this, playing a constant game of "Can you top this?" with herself, as in March, when she told the Conservative Political Action Conference that she would have a comment on Senator John Edwards, "but it turns out that you have to go into rehab if you use the word faggot." Coulter is only the most egregious example—from Bill O'Reilly on Fox to Glenn Beck on CNN, offense is the coin of the cable realm.

The flip side of the instant-attention era is the gotcha era. We may be more inured to shock than ever, but when someone manages to find and cross a line, we're better able to generate, spread, and sustain offense. You get eaten by the same tiger that you train. Imus got special love from the media over the years because his show was such a media hangout. But when the controversy erupted, it snowballed in part because the media love to cover the media.

Every public figure—athlete, pundit, actor—now has two audiences: the one he or she is addressing and the one that will eventually read the blogs or see the viral video. A few have adapted, like Stephen Colbert, whose routine at last year's White House Correspondents' Association dinner was decried by attendees as rude and shrill—but made him a hero to his YouTube audience. Imus, a 30-plus-year veteran of radio shock, seemed to underestimate the power of the modern umbrage-amplification machine. The day after his remarks, Imus said dismissively on air that people needed to relax about "some idiot comment meant to be amusing." Shockingly, they did not, and by the next day, Imus had tapped an inner wellspring of deepest regret.

As in so many scandals, the first response may have been the most 20 authentic—at least we're inclined to take it that way because the contrition cycle has become so familiar. You blurt. You deny. You apologize. You visit the rehab center or speak with the Official Minority Spokesperson of your choice and go on with your life. Although—or maybe because—it's so easy to get caught today, it's also easier to get forgiven. In 1988 Jimmy (the Greek) Snyder was fired by CBS for saying black athletes were "bred" to be better than whites. In 1996 CBS golf analyst Ben Wright was suspended indefinitely after he was quoted as saying that lesbians had hurt the sport.

To his credit, Imus never played the "I'm sick" card. Perhaps he felt confident because he had been legitimized by his high-profile guests. Imus could have made a remark just as bad years ago and suffered few if any consequences. Scratch that: Imus did make remarks as bad or worse for years. Speaking about Gwen Ifill, the African-American PBS anchor who was then White House correspondent for the *New York Times*, he said, "Isn't the *Times* wonderful? It lets the cleaning lady cover the White House." He called a *Washington Post* writer a "boner-nosed, beanie-wearing Jewboy" and Arabs "towelheads."

Yet politicians and journalists (including *Time* writers) still went on his show to plug their candidacies and books because Imus knew how to sell. "If Don Imus likes a book," says Katie Wainwright, executive director of publicity at publisher Hyperion, "not only does he have the author on, he will talk about it before, during and after, often for weeks afterwards." The price: implicitly telling America that the mostly white male Beltway elite is cool with looking the other way at racism. They compartmentalized the lengthy interviews he did with them from the "bad" parts of the show, though the boundary was always a little porous. And evidently many still do. "Solidarity forever," pledged *Boston Globe* columnist Tom Oliphant in a phone interview with Imus on April 9. Senator John McCain and Rudolph Giuliani said they would return to the show. "I called him a little while ago to talk to him about it personally," Giuliani told the *New York Times*. "And I believe that he understands that he made a very big mistake." (Senator Barack Obama, who appeared on the show once, has said he will not go back; other politicians have hedged.)

In fact, while there might be more media and blogger scrutiny of Imus' future guests, his suspension may have inoculated them—if his radio show survives. The show draws 2 million daily listeners, and it's a more valuable property on radio than it was on TV. (It brings in about $15 million annually for CBS Radio compared with several million for MSNBC.) But the show has already lost advertisers, including American Express, Staples, and Procter & Gamble.

Imus argued repeatedly that his critics should consider the "context" of his larger life, including the formidable work for sick children he does through his Imus Ranch charity. But it's not Imus Ranch he broadcasts from 20 hours a week. You can't totally separate the lives of celebrities from their work—it didn't excuse Gibson that he attacked the Jews in his free time—but finally what determines who can make what jokes is the context of their work: the tone of their acts, the personas they present, the vehicles they create for their work.

That context is not as kind to Imus. He comes out of the shock jock 25 tradition, but all shock jocks are not created equal. If Opie & Anthony or Mancow had made the "nappy-headed" comment, it wouldn't have been a blip because future presidents do not do cable-news interviews with Opie & Anthony and Mancow.

Then there's personality, or at least persona. Compared with Imus, for instance, his rival Howard Stern may be offensive, but he's also self-deprecating, making fun of his own satyrism, looks, and even manly endowment. Imus doesn't take it nearly as well as he dishes it out. His shtick is all cowboy-hatted swagger, and his insults set him up as superior to his targets and the alpha dog to his supplicant guests.

Imus uses jokes to establish his power, in other words. He's hardly the only humorist to do that. But making jokes about difference—race, gender, sexual orientation, the whole list—is ultimately about power. You need to purchase the right to do it through some form of vulnerability, especially if you happen to be a rich, famous white man. But the I-Man—his radio persona, anyway—is not about vulnerability. (The nickname, for Pete's sake: I, Man!) That's creepy enough when he's having a big-name columnist kiss his ring; when he hurled his tinfoil thunderbolts at a team of college kids, it was too much. "Some people have said, 'Well, he says this all the time,'" Rutgers' team captain Carson told *Time*. "But does that justify the remarks he's made about anyone?"

Of course, assessing Imus' show is a subjective judgment, and setting these boundaries is as much an aesthetic call as a moral one. It's arbitrary, nebulous and, yes, unfair. Who doesn't have a list of artists or leaders whose sins they rationalize: Elvis Costello for calling Ray Charles a "blind, ignorant nigger," Eminem for peppering his lyrics with "faggot," Jesse Jackson for "Hymietown," D. W. Griffith for lionizing the Klan, or T. S. Eliot for maligning Jews?

You might say that there's no excuse and that I'm as big a hypocrite as Imus's defenders for suggesting that there is one. Which may be true. That's finally why "Where's the line?" is a misleading question. There are as many lines as there are people. We draw and redraw them by constantly arguing them. This is how we avoid throwing out the brilliance of a Sacha Baron Cohen—who offends us to point out absurdities in our society, not just to make "idiot comments meant to be amusing"—with a shock jock's dirty bathwater. It's a draining, polarizing but necessary process.

Which may be why it was such a catharsis to see the Rutgers players 30 respond to Imus at their press conference in their own words. "I'm a woman, and I'm someone's child," said Kia Vaughn. "I achieve a lot. And unless they've given this name, a 'ho,' a new definition, then that is not what I am." She stood with her teammates, a row of unbowed, confident women. For a few minutes, anyway, they drew a line we could all agree on and formed a line we could all get behind.

A Case the Scouts Had to Win

STEFFEN N. JOHNSON

> **BEFORE READING:** Should college fraternities and sororities be permitted to limit their membership to certain races and religions? Are these practices an example of free association guaranteed by the First Amendment?

To the dismay of gay rights groups and some civil libertarians, the Supreme Court ruled on Wednesday that it is unconstitutional for the state to require a Boy Scout troop to admit a gay scoutmaster. The court's

---

Steffen N. Johnson is a lawyer and a lecturer at the University of Chicago Law School. His article was published in the June 30, 2000, edition of the *New York Times*.

decision, however, goes to the heart of the First Amendment's guarantee of free association. It may be a civil right to have access to employment, or to transportation, or to hotels and restaurants. But it is not a civil right to assist in raising other people's children.

In the past, the court had understandably ruled that society's interest in ensuring access to certain opportunities like jobs, school, and other basic necessities must sometimes override the right to associate with whomever one pleases. Everyone needs to make a living. Everyone needs an education. Thus, the court ruled that businesses or commercial gatherings like the Rotary Club cannot exclude women from their ranks.

But serving as a role model for young children whose parents share common values is not the same sort of privilege as a job or an education. It is a service, and one entrusted to few people.

To extend the reach of anti-discrimination laws to private groups whose purpose is not to make a profit but to bring together people with similar values, would destroy the nation's diverse tradition of voluntary collaboration for common causes. And a world in which the government could declare which causes and which moral positions benefit society, and which do not, could only be described as Orwellian.

The case arose when the Scouts informed James Dale that he could   5
not serve as a leader of a troop in Monmouth County, New Jersey. Mr. Dale sued, claiming that the Scouts had unlawfully discriminated against him because he was gay, and the New Jersey courts agreed. But the Supreme Court, in a five to four ruling, said that forcing a group to accept certain members may impair its ability to "express those views, and only those views, that it intends to express."

Exercising the right to exclude others may seem intolerant, but such a right is indispensable to private groups seeking to define themselves, to chart their own moral course, and to work together for common ends. If the Boy Scouts were required to admit leaders who advocated a position contrary to its own, then men could assert the right to lead the Girl Scouts, gentiles could assert the right to head Jewish groups, and heterosexuals could assert the right to lead gay groups.

Mr. Dale's supporters said that the case was about status-based discrimination and that enforcing anti-discrimination laws against voluntary groups like the Scouts was valid because antigay beliefs are not what brought the Scouts together. But a group should not need to have an antigay agenda to hold the view that homosexual behavior is wrong. Many churches, for example, teach that homosexual activity is immoral while affirming that gay people should be treated with equal dignity and respect. That does not mean that they have given up their right not to appoint homosexuals to leadership.

Like many Americans, the Boy Scouts attempt to walk the line between tolerance of everyone and disapproval of certain types of conduct. That they wish to express their view by example or by quiet persuasion, rather than an outspoken campaign, does not diminish their right to take a position on moral issues.

As the court's majority understood, people's rights to hold moral positions, to associate with others who share the same views, and to instill those views in their children without threat of outside interference are liberties that belong as much to gay men and lesbians as to the Boy Scouts, as much to those who advocate alternative lifestyles as to those who advocate traditional morality.

THINKING AND WRITING ABOUT THE LIMITS ON FREEDOM OF SPEECH

QUESTIONS FOR DISCUSSION AND WRITING

1. How do you believe the court should decide in the case of the student who wore the anti-war T-shirt?
2. Can you think of circumstances in which creative freedom should bow to social responsibility? Explain.
3. Explain your position on how much control there should be on what is broadcast over the air waves—and who should control it.
4. Although the majority of Americans seem to celebrate the do-not-call registry, Waldmeir explains that there are two sides to the controversy. Write an essay in which you make clear why this is not a clear-cut case of one group being right and the other wrong.
5. Do you believe there should be any restrictions on Americans' right to speak out against a war they believe is wrong? Explain.
6. What distinction does Johnson make between the right to a job or an education and the right to associate with particular people? Explain why Johnson believes that the Scouts are protected by the First Amendment.
7. Don Imus was fired as a result of his remark on the air about the Rutgers women's basketball team. Explain in an essay whether you think his firing was an appropriate response.
8. Many believe that rap music goes too far in its demeaning of women and its championing of violence (an argument that was used often in defending Imus's remark). Defend rap as an artistic expression of a culture or argue that it does indeed go too far.
9. Explain to what extent you agree with Gaylor's arguments against school prayer.
10. The introduction to this chapter quotes a Supreme Court justice who wrote that neither students nor teachers "shed their constitutional right to freedom of speech or expression at the schoolhouse gate." Do the examples in the readings support that statement or argue against it?

TOPICS FOR RESEARCH

Lyrics in rock music: How dangerous are they?

Codes of speech conduct at some colleges and universities: goals and effects

Religious displays on public land

Freedom of speech on the Internet

Prayer in public schools

Free speech issues in school newspapers

CHAPTER 19

Why and How Should Immigration Be Controlled?

U.S. immigration has become a hot topic during the early years of the twenty-first century. This is not the first time in U.S. history that such attention has been focused on the number of foreigners entering the country. U.S. history has been through cycles of rigid quotas alternating with more liberal immigration policies. Now, however, the number of Mexicans and others crossing our southern border has raised the number of illegal aliens to unprecedented heights and has made both legislators and their constituents aware that something must be done to control the flood of immigrants from the south. There is no simple solution, however, as evidenced by the difficulty in passing immigration legislation.

Part of what makes the current situation so complex is that the United States now depends on the labor done by illegal aliens—or undocumented workers, as they are called by those more sympathetic to their cause. As native-born Americans have become better educated, they have increasingly sought higher paying skilled positions, leaving certain unskilled or physical labor jobs unfilled. Undocumented workers from Mexico and other countries, however, receive far more pay for these unskilled jobs in the United States than for any work they can find in their home countries. Because U.S. businesses and consumers experience a benefit from having these jobs filled, legislation that fines employers for hiring undocumented workers has largely been ignored. On the negative side, however, is that the number of illegal immigrants strains public school systems and medical institutions in parts of the country, especially because often these immigrants do not pay taxes to support public institutions. Another concern to many is how the ease with which thousands cross the border illegally each year highlights for terror-ists an easy route into the United States.

At the other end of the spectrum are skilled foreigners from countries such as India and China, often educated at U.S. colleges and universities, who cannot gain visas to work in high-tech industries where they are needed.

The proposed solutions to the "invasion" from the south have ranged from building a wall along the entire U.S. southern border to granting amnesty to those illegal aliens already here to deporting all of them. The proposals to bring in skilled workers from abroad have included new guest worker programs and more temporary visas.

Some Americans will always have a bias against foreigners that, trag-ically, can sometimes erupt into violence against them. Others are more willing to see the human side of immigration, such as the special prob-lems endured by children who immigrate or who are born to illegal aliens in America and the tragedy of thousands of Mexicans who have died in the border crossing while seeking the American Dream.

The Hard Truth of Immigration

ROBERT J. SAMUELSON

BEFORE READING: Why is immigration currently such a complex and controversial issue in the United States?

Immigration is crawling its way back onto the national agenda—and not just as a footnote to keeping terrorists out. Earlier this year, Congress en-acted a law intended to prevent illegal aliens from getting state drivers' li-censes, the volunteer "minutemen" who recently patrolled the porous Arizona border with Mexico attracted huge attention, and members of Congress from both parties are now crafting proposals to deal with illegal immigration. All this is good. But unless we're brutally candid with our-selves, it won't amount to much. Being brutally candid means recognizing that the huge and largely uncontrolled inflow of unskilled Latino workers into the United States is increasingly sabotaging the assimilation process.

Americans rightly glorify our heritage of absorbing immigrants. Over time, they move into the economic, political, and social mainstream; over time, they become American rather than whatever they were—even though immigrants themselves constantly refashion the American iden-

Robert J. Samuelson, a contributing editor at *Newsweek*, has written a column for the *Washington Post* since 1977. This essay appeared in the June 13, 2005, issue of *Newsweek*.

tity. But no society has a boundless capacity to accept newcomers, especially when many are poor and unskilled. There are now an estimated 34 million immigrants in the United States, about a third of them illegal. About 35 percent lack health insurance and 26 percent receive some sort of federal benefit, reports Steven Camarota of the Center for Immigration Studies. To make immigration succeed, we need (paradoxically) to control immigration.

Although this is common sense, it's common sense that fits uneasily inside our adversarial political culture. You're supposed to be either pro immigrant or anti-immigrant—it's hard to be pro-immigrant and pro tougher immigration restrictions. But that's the sensible position, as any examination of immigration trends suggests.

Consider a new study of Mexican immigrants by Harvard economists George Borjas and Lawrence Katz. Mexicans are now the single largest group of U.S. immigrants, 30 percent of the total in 2000. Indeed, the present Mexican immigration "is historically unprecedented, being both numerically and proportionately larger than any other immigrant influx in the past century," note Borjas and Katz. In 1920, for example, the two largest immigrant groups—Germans and Italians—totaled only 24 percent of the immigrant population.

Some Mexican-Americans have made spectacular gains, but the overall 5 picture is dispiriting. Among men, about one in 20 U.S. workers is now a Mexican immigrant; in 1970, that was less than one in 100. The vast majority of Mexican workers lacked a high-school diploma in 2000 (63 percent for men, 57 percent for women). Only a tiny share had college degrees (3 percent for men, 5 percent for women). By contrast, only 7 percent of native-born U.S. workers were high-school dropouts and 28 percent were college graduates in 2000. Mexican workers are inevitably crammed into low-wage jobs: food workers, janitors, gardeners, laborers, farm workers. In 2000, their average wages were 41 percent lower than average U.S. wages for men and 33 percent lower for women.

What's particularly disturbing about the Borjas-Katz study is that children of Mexican immigrants don't advance quickly. In 2000, Americans of Mexican ancestry still had lower levels of educational achievement and wages than most native-born workers. Among men, the wage gap was 27 percent; about 21 percent were high-school dropouts and only 11 percent were college graduates. Borjas and Katz can't explain the lags. "What's the role of culture vs. lousy [U.S.] schools?" asks Katz. "It's hard to say." Borjas doubts that the cause is discrimination. Low skills seem to explain most of the gap, he says. Indeed, after correcting for education and age, most of the wage gap disappears. Otherwise, says Borjas, "I don't know."

But some things we do know—or can infer. For today's Mexican immigrants (legal or illegal), the closest competitors are tomorrow's Mexican immigrants (legal or illegal). The more who arrive, the harder it will be for existing low-skilled workers to advance. Despite the recession, immigration did not much slow after 2000, says Camarota. Not surprisingly, a study by the Pew Hispanic Center found that inflation-adjusted weekly earnings for all Hispanics (foreign and American-born) dropped by 2.2 percent in 2003 and 2.6 percent in 2004. "Latinos are the only major group of workers whose wages have fallen for two consecutive years," said the study. Similarly, the more poor immigrants, the harder it will be for schools to improve the skills of their children. The schools will be overwhelmed; the same goes for social services.

We could do a better job of stopping illegal immigration on our southern border and of policing employers who hire illegal immigrants. At the same time, we could provide legal status to illegal immigrants already here. We could also make more sensible decisions about legal immigrants—favoring the skilled over the unskilled. But the necessary steps are much tougher than most politicians have so far embraced, and their timidity reflects a lack of candor about the seriousness of the problem. The stakes are simple: will immigration continue to foster national pride and strength or will it cause more and more weakness and anger?

A Legacy of the Unforeseen

CAROLYN LOCHHEAD

> **BEFORE READING:** Immigration expert Daniel Tichenor writes, "One lesson from the past is that Americans have tended to celebrate their immigrant past but dread the immigrant present." Explain what you think he means by that.

Many of the most radical changes in the origins and numbers of America's vast flow of immigrants were accidentally set in motion by politicians who expected an entirely different result. As Congress consider yet another round of immigration reform, the lesson from history is to beware of unintended consequences.

An estimated 12 million immigrants are living illegally in the United States. Another 1 million gain legal residence each year. Millions more are expected to seek entry in coming decades. No one can accurately predict how they might respond to the harsh border crackdown endorsed by the House or the Senate's plan to offer a path to citizenship for those here illegally and a guest worker program for new arrivals.

Carolyn Lochhead is the Washington correspondent for the *San Francisco Chronicle* and a contributing editor at *Reason* magazine, which "provides a refreshing alternative to right-wing and left-wing opinion magazines by making a principled case for liberty and individual choice in all areas of human activity." This article appeared in the August/September 2006 issue of *Reason*.

"Human behavior has often defied the best-laid plans," says Daniel Tichenor, an immigration expert at Rutgers University. The past is seldom consulted during today's debates, but previous attempts at reform suggest how quickly things can go off course.

It was a freshly minted young Massachusetts senator named Edward Kennedy who 40 years ago, in what he called "my maiden effort in the Senate," managed the landmark Immigration Act of 1965, at the time a minor coda to the Civil Rights Act. (Today, Kennedy is the lead Democratic sponsor of the Senate's bipartisan immigration bill) The 1965 act eliminated the national origins quotas of the 1920s that favored Northern Europe. It established visa preferences, still in place today, based on family unification and labor skills. It imposed the first numeric limits on Latin American immigration. And it forever changed the face of the United States.

"Arguments against the bill were chiefly based on unsubstantiated fears ᵅ that the bill would greatly increase annual immigration" and permit "excessive entry" of Asians and Africans, Kennedy wrote in 1966. The Johnson administration declared that "immigration will not be predominantly from Asia and Africa . . . indeed very few people from certain areas could even pay the cost of tickets to come here."

New migrants were expected to come from Italy, Greece, and other countries in Southern and Eastern Europe that had been subject to national origins quotas, in addition to the British, Germans and Scandinavians who had dominated immigration under the quotas. Members of Congress asserted that hordes from other, darker continents would be unable to use family unification because they had no relatives in the United States.

Oddly, the national origins quotas had ignored Mexico, leaving the southern border all but open before 1965. By blocking Southern and Eastern Europeans, the quotas allowed Mexican laborers (and black farmers migrating from the South) to fill their shoes. Lawmakers considered Mexicans, unlike Poles or Italians, to be "returnable," Tichenor says. "If you want to look at the very early origins of illegal immigration as an issue in America, there it is."

"This bill that we will sign today is not a revolutionary bill," President Lyndon Johnson said on Liberty Island, October 1965. "It does not affect the lives of millions." Within five years, Asian immigration had quadrupled. The first new entrants came through occupational visas, then brought their families, beginning unanticipated network migrations, notes the New York University historian David Reimers. Within a decade, the proportion of European to Asian and Latin American immigrants had reversed. "The way we teach students is we say, in general, the unintended consequences of immigration reforms are more important than the intended consequences," says Philip Martin, a farm immigration expert at U.C.- Davis.

Two decades later, on November 7, 1986, President Ronald Reagan signed another major immigration reform. It was intended to stop illegal immigration, then seen as a burgeoning problem, by providing a one-time amnesty and banning employers from knowingly hiring illegal workers. "Future generations of Americans will be thankful for our efforts to humanely regain control of our borders and thereby preserve the value of one of the most sacred possessions of our people, American citizenship," Reagan said.

Sen. Alan Simpson, (R-Wyo.), a chief sponsor of the bill, predicted employers would voluntarily comply with the new sanctions. Employer sanctions quickly collapsed under widespread document fraud. Enforcement, never vigorous, has dropped to negligible levels. "People following it at the time knew that employer sanctions would be a joke without secure means of identification," says Peter Skerry, a political scientist at Boston College. "Everyone was sort of holding their nose, blocking their eyes, doing the best that could get cobbled together."

Many experts believe the current pattern of illegal immigration from Mexico and Central America was a consequence of the 1986 law's border tightening, followed by a tougher crackdown in 1996 that built fences in San Diego and El Paso. "The perverse effect has been to dramatically lower return migration out of the country," says Douglas S. Massey, a Princeton sociologist and co-director of the Mexican Migration Project, a longitudinal survey of more than 18,000 migrants, the largest of its kind. "So we've transformed what was before 1986 a circular flow of workers into an increasingly settled population of families. We have actually accelerated the rate of undocumented population growth in the United States and shifted it from a less costly population of male workers into a much more costly population of families."

The problem, Massey says, is that by making border crossing "very risky and unpleasant and increasingly expensive, you prolong the length of the trips, you reduce the probability of return migration, and you make it more likely that migrants . . . just hunker down and stay." The rate of migration from Mexico has actually stayed constant for the last two decades, Massey found. But the rate of return has fallen by half, from 50 percent to 25 percent.

Ever since Ben Franklin expressed alarm that growing enclaves of Germans in Pennsylvania showed no signs of learning English, Americans have feared new immigrants and waxed sentimental about the previous stock. "One lesson from the past is that Americans have tended to celebrate their immigrant past but dread the immigrant present," says Tichenor. "They have often viewed the newest arrivals as menacing or as threats to the national identity or economy. What's intriguing is they've usually made snap judgments in very short time horizons."

U.S. policy has lurched between bouts of expansion and restriction, often accompanied by strong racial animus. Borders were open until the late 1800s, when Congress passed the Chinese Exclusion Act in 1882. The 1907 "Gentlemen's Agreement" barred Japanese laborers—a deal made after the San Francisco school board ordered Japanese children to segregated Chinese schools. The *San Francisco Chronicle* warned of an invasion of vagrant Japanese workers it deemed "bumptious, disagreeable and unreliable."

The government conducted mass deportations of Mexicans during the 15 Great Depression and in a program labeled Operation Wetback in 1954, deporting an estimated 1.4 million people in all. Bad economic times, backlashes against new immigrants, or worries about national security often brought new restrictions. The national origins quotas of 1924 and 1928 followed the Great Migration at the turn of the century and the isolationism and fear of Bolshevik influences that followed World War I. Not even the Holocaust moved Congress to ease the restrictions.

Immigration often expanded after wars. The 1954 War Brides Act admitted 100,000 spouses after World War II and the Korean War. After the Vietnam War, more than 1 million Vietnamese, Laotians, and Cambodians were admitted.

Expansions of immigration often occured over public objection. "I don't know a single poll going back to the 1930s that's indicated the public wants more immigrants to come in as opposed to fewer," says Reimers, the historian. Defiance of public opinion is a striking constant of immigration policy, long fascinating political scientists. Major expansions were often achieved through unorthodox alliances joining businesses, ethnic groups, free-market think tanks and churches.

Because immigration has often divided both political parties, interest groups wield extraordinary influence in the debates, says the Stanford political scientist Carolyn Wong, author of *Lobbying for Inclusion*. Business lobbies wanting more labor visas and ethnic groups wanting more family visas often form powerful alliances.

California growers have long been key players. Congress created its first major guest worker plan in 1942, the Bracero ("strong-armed one") program for unskilled Mexicans to relieve temporary labor shortages during World War II. The program lasted 22 years, admitting 4.5 million workers. Rife with abuses, it was dropped around the time the 1964 Civil Rights Act was passed.

Many scholars believe the Bracero program laid the groundwork for 20 today's illegal immigration by setting up labor networks in Mexico and distorting the U.S. farm economy. The program was plagued by red tape and graft on both sides of the border, inducing many Mexicans to cross illegally. By providing an ample labor force of often-abused workers, it induced growers to plant high-profit, labor-intensive crops. California growers were able to undercut Southern growers, producing California's vibrant fruit and vegetable industry which to this day relies on illegal migrants.

Because wages for migrant farm workers hardly rose, those who could leave for better-paying jobs in cities fled the farms, requiring a constant flow of workers.

Growers warned that California's canned tomato industry would die and food prices would rise if the Bracero program ended. At its height in

1960, 45,000 farm workers harvested 2.2 million tons of processing tomatoes, according to U.C.-Davis' Martin. Six years after the program ended, a new oblong tomato was developed that could be machine harvested. By 1999, just 5,000 farm workers harvested 12 million tons of tomatoes and costs fell 54 percent, Martin found. The United Farm Workers union soon won a wage increase. "I think they honestly didn't think change could happen near as quickly as it actually happened," says Martin.

Another expansion came in the 1990 immigration reform, including an obscure provision known as the "diversity visa" to fix perceived problems created by the 1965 act, then referred to by some as the "Irish Exclusion Act," according to a study by DePaul University political scientist Anna O. Law. Sponsored by Kennedy, the diversity visa was supposed to redress the 1965 law's unforeseen restrictions on immigration from "old seed sources of our heritage." But the diversity visa today admits 50,000 people a year and is used heavily by Egyptians, Moroccans, Nigerians and other Africans. "In about 10 years," says Reimers, "the country may not be so hysterical about Hispanics and may be more hysterical about Africans."

Don't Bad-Mouth Unskilled Immigrants

TYLER COWEN AND DANIEL M. ROTHSCHILD

BEFORE READING: In what ways do recent immigrants affect the American economy?

G oogle, Yahoo!, and Sun Microsystems were all founded by immigrants— from Russia, Taiwan and India, respectively. There is nearly universal agreement that skilled immigrants are an enormous boon to the American economy.

But what about the millions of unskilled laborers who arrive in this country every year? Recent public discourse would have us believe they poach American jobs, lower wages, and sponge off welfare. Yet economic research suggests a different picture: Unskilled immigrants are good for the U.S., and the U.S. is good for them.

Until the late 1990s, when a boom in native-born self-employment occurred, immigrants were more likely than natives to work for themselves. Immigrant small businesses, from the Korean corner market to the Mexi-

Tyler Cowen is a professor of economics at George Mason University and at the Center for the Study of Public Choice. He is the director of George Mason's Mercatus Center, which tries to bridge the gap between economic theory and real-world policymaking. Daniel M. Rothschild is associate director of the Global Prosperity Initiative at the Mercatus Center. This article appeared in the August/September 2006 issue of *Reason* magazine.

can landscaping service, are, well, as American as apple pie. The labor market is not a zero-sum game with a finite number of jobs; immigrants create their own work.

A key question for economists has been whether the influx raises or lowers "native" American wages. U.C.- Berkeley's David Card, who studied patterns in different U.S. cities, concludes that immigration has not lowered wages for American workers. George Borjas of Harvard counters that immigration reduced the wages of high school dropouts by 7.4 percent between 1980 and 2000.

Most economists have sided with Card. For one thing, his studies bet-   5
ter capture the notion that immigrant labor makes work easier for all of us and brings new skills to the table. Additionally, as Card points out, the percentage of native-born high school dropouts has fallen sharply during the last few decades, creating a shortage of unskilled laborers that immigrants fill. In 1980, one out of three American adults had less than a high school education; by 2000, this figure had fallen to less than one in five.

Gianmarco Ottaviano of the University of Bologna and Giovanni Peri of the National Bureau of Economic Research have shown that immigrants and low-skilled American workers fill very different roles in the economy. For instance, 54 percent of tailors in the U.S. are foreign-born, compared with less than 1 percent of crane operators. A similar discrepancy exists between plaster-stucco masons (44 percent immigrant) and sewer-pipe cleaners (less than 1 percent foreign-born). Immigrants come to the United States with different skills, inclinations and ideas; they are not looking to simply copy the behavior of American workers.

New arrivals, by producing more goods and services, also keep prices down across the economy. Even Borjas, the favorite economist of immigration restrictionists, admits the net gain to the U.S. from immigration is about $7 billion annually.

During the coming decades, the need for immigrant labor will increase, according to demographers. The baby boom generation will need more health care and more nursing homes. The upcoming Medicare fiscal crunch will require more and younger laborers to finance the program.

Some argue that we should employ a more restrictive policy that allows in only immigrants with "needed" skills. But this assumes that the government can read the economic tea leaves. Most bureaucrats in 1980 did not foresee the building or biomedical booms of the 1990s, or the decline of auto manufacturing. We should not trust government to know what kind of laborers we will need 20 years from now. The ready presence of immigrant workers, including the unskilled, makes *all* businesses easier to start, and thus spurs American creativity.

We should not forget that immigration is good for the immigrants   10
themselves. It often means the difference between extreme poverty and the good life.

Card finds that post-1965 immigrants, according to U.S. census data, have a good record of assimilation. Second-generation children have, on average, higher education and wages than the children of natives. Of the 39 largest country-of-origin groups, the sons of 33 and the daughters of 32 of those groups have surpassed the educational levels of natives' children.

Finally, it is fitting that both Card and Borjas are themselves immigrants. Borjas emigrated from Cuba when he was 12, and Card came from Canada to earn his doctorate at Princeton. Their very debate shows how immigrants have become central to the American enterprise.

Yes, immigration brings some real costs. But most of these problems are concentrated in a few border and urban areas; federal policy can help correct the imbalances.

Americans have heard from politicians for more than 200 years that immigration will cause the sky to fall. Yet each time it has only made us stronger.

Living with Illegals?

MICHAEL BARONE

> BEFORE READING: Immigrants usually see America as a land of opportunity. In what ways is the presence of so many immigrants an opportunity for America?

This week the Senate is expected to take up immigration, almost 20 years after passage of the last major immigration bill. Immigration is in some ways an American success story—half of all immigrants in the world head to the United States. But it's also a story of failure—we have an estimated 12 million illegal immigrants within our borders. The House in December passed a border security bill. The Senate Judiciary Committee spent three weeks hashing over border security and illegal immigrant and guest workers' provisions. Senate Majority Leader Bill Frist nudged it toward a decision by announcing that he'd bring up a border security bill this Monday. Judiciary seems headed to a bipartisan majority on all three issues, which could go to the floor.

So the Senate may take action—after which its bill would have to be reconciled with the House bill in conference, and then the result would have to be jammed through a House where a lot of Republicans hate anything that smacks of amnesty. George W. Bush has set out principles—border security, a path to legalization, a guest worker program—and seems likely to sign anything Congress can pass.

Michael Barone is a senior writer for *U.S. News and World Report*. He has written for such publications as the *Economist* and the *New York Times* and is the principal coauthor of *The Almanac of American Politics*. This essay appeared in the April 3, 2006, issue of *U.S. News and World Report*.

The immigration issue shows us to be an attractive country with a vibrant economy and a government that seems on the verge of breakdown. Why can't we protect our borders, many immigration critics, justifiably, ask. Increased enforcement in El Paso, Texas, and the fence built south of San Diego have reduced crossings at those choke points. But thousands of illegal immigrants walk across the border in the Arizona desert—and some of them die of thirst in the sun. Some Republicans want to build a fence along the whole 2,000-plus-mile border. But that would be very expensive, and it's not clear that people wouldn't be able to scale the fence in unpopulated areas—and most of the border is unpopulated. The United States was able to control its borders when most immigrants arrived by ship and could be processed at places like Ellis Island. Now it seems that immigrants can keep coming by land illegally, unless we can establish a way that they can come legally. Then at least we'd be able to keep tabs on them for homeland security purposes.

The 1986 immigration law included an amnesty on illegals and sanctions on employers of illegals. But the sanctions have proved toothless, since employers can escape liability by accepting pieces of paper that can easily be forged. The obvious solution is some kind of electronic verification. Visa and MasterCard transfer billions of dollars a day via plastic cards, with high reliability. But government has trouble with information technology: The FBI and the Federal Aviation Administration both had to abandon massive IT programs as unfeasible, despite years of effort and millions of dollars. The answer most likely is subcontracting the verification technology to the private sector.

Labor pool. Capitalism "laughs at frontiers," wrote the French historian 5 Fernand Braudel. The dynamic American economy has attracted illegal immigrants from Mexico and other Latin countries to work in construction, hotels and restaurants, meatpacking, and gardening and landscaping. We talk as if our immigration laws can structure our labor markets, but in practice Congress's task now is to get our immigration laws working in tandem with labor markets. We are not going to expel a population the size of the state of Ohio. But we shouldn't simply acquiesce in violation of the law. We need to legalize and regularize the flow of immigrants the labor market demands.

And we need to encourage their assimilation into America. Opponents of immigration often express distaste with the growing Latino neighborhoods increasingly visible across the country. One hundred years ago, Henry James expressed similar distaste when he visited the Lower East Side of New York. But in time, those immigrants or their children were assimilated, and today their descendants seem as American as anyone else. Assimilation then had the wholehearted support of leaders like Theodore Roosevelt; today many of our elites have transnational (Samuel Huntington's word) attitudes and regard assimilation as oppressive. The vast majority of ordinary Americans have better sense. Congress, while rewriting the immigration law, ought to take care to encourage assimilation—Americanization, as TR put it. For immigration is not just a challenge; it's an opportunity.

The Invasion

PATRICK J. BUCHANAN

BEFORE READING: In what ways do immigrants pose a threat to native-born Americans?

> The American Southwest seems to be slowly returning to the jurisdiction of Mexico without a shot being fired.[1]
>
> —*Excelsior*, July 20, 1982, Mexico's national newspaper

> Demographically, socially, and culturally, the *reconquista* of the Southwest United States . . . is well underway.[2]
>
> —Samuel Huntington, Harvard University, 2004

On August 12, 2005, Governor Bill Richardson of New Mexico declared a state of emergency on the Mexican border, claiming the region had been "devastated by the ravages and terror of human smuggling, drug smuggling, kidnapping, murder, destruction of property and the death of livestock."[3]

Three days later, Governor Janet Napolitano of Arizona declared a state of emergency on her southern border. By March 2006, Napolitano was moving National Guard to the border while assuring the people of Arizona, "We are not at war with Mexico."[4]

But the state of emergency is not confined to the Southwest. Our state of emergency is a national one. America is being invaded, and if this is not stopped, it will mean the end of the United States.

The Southwest is being overrun by illegal aliens who cross in the thousands every day in an endless trek north as they repopulate America. The trafficking in narcotics and people is a human rights outrage and a national disgrace. Even more so is the failure of the government of the United States to enforce our laws and protect our borders, stretches of which have become a hell on earth. On September 20, 2004, *Time* magazine described what is happening on the Mexican border:

> When the crowds cross the ranches along and near the border, they discard backpacks, empty Gatorade and water bottles and soiled clothes. . . . They turn the land into a vast latrine, leaving behind revolting mounds

Patrick J. Buchanan is a well-known conservative who served as senior advisor to three presidents, ran for the Republican presidential nomination in 1992 and 1996, and was the candidate for the Reform Party in 2000. He is a syndicated columnist and helped found some of America's best-known public affairs shows: *The McLaughlin Group, The Capitol Gang*, and *Crossfire*. This excerpt is from his eighth book, *State of Emergency: The Third World Invasion and Conquest of America* (2006).

of personal refuse and enough discarded plastic bags to stock a Wal-Mart. Night after night, they cut fences intended to hold in cattle and horses. Cows that eat the bags must often be killed because the plastic becomes lodged between the first and second stomachs. The immigrants steal vehicles and saddles. They poison dogs to quiet them. The illegal traffic is so heavy that some ranchers, because of the disruptions and noise, get very little sleep at night.[5]

It testifies to the moral rot in both parties that our leaders are so ter-   5 rified of being called "nativist," "xenophobic," or even "racist" that they blind themselves to the rampant criminality along our southern frontier.

Who Are the Invaders?

On November 28, 2005, President Bush, speaking in Tucson, conceded that in five years 4.5 million aliens had been caught attempting to break into the United States. Among that 4.5 million, Bush admitted, were "more than 350,000 with criminal records."[6] One in every twelve illegal aliens the U.S. Border Patrol had apprehended was a criminal.

That is 70,000 felons apprehended each year, 200 felons every single day for five years, trying to break into our country to rob, rape, and murder Americans. Of the millions who succeeded on Bush's watch, how many came for just such purposes? How many Americans have been robbed, assaulted, or murdered because the president failed in his duty to defend the borders of the United States?

Nearly 8 million foreigners did enter during those five years, 3.7 million of them illegally. If one in twelve was a criminal, 300,000 felons slipped in during Bush's tenure. This is an historic dereliction of presidential duty.

There are today 36 million foreign-born in the United States, almost three times as many people as the 13.5 million here at the peak of the Great Wave in 1910. And it is among these tens of millions of foreign-born that illegal aliens find sanctuary. As James Edwards of the Hudson Institute writes, legal and illegal immigration are two sides of the same coin. If we fail to control the one, we cannot control the other. As a rule, he notes, when legal immigration rises, illegal immigration soars. Mexicans account for perhaps 30 percent of all the foreign-born population in the United States today, and more than half are here illegally. And while illegals made up only 21 percent of the foreign-born in 1980, they constitute 28 percent today.[7]

To measure the immensity of the immigrant cohort, let us go back to   10 John F. Kennedy's *A Nation of Immigrants*, published in the run-up to the 1960 election. In it, the future president marvels at how many had come to these shores:

> The gates were now flung open, and men and women in search of a new life came to these shores in ever-increasing numbers—150,000 in the 1820's, 1.7 million in the 1840's, 2.8 million in the 1870's, 5.2 million in the 1880's, 8.8 million in the first decade of the 20th century. . . .

> Between 1830 and 1930, the period of the greatest migration from Europe to the United States, Germany sent six million people to the United States—more than any other nation. . . .
>
> Italy has contributed more immigrants to the United States than any other country except Germany. Over five million Italians came to this country between 1820 and 1963.[8]

Using Kennedy's numbers, there are as many illegal aliens in the United States today as all the German and Italian immigrants who ever came, the two largest immigrant groups in our history. Our foreign-born population today is almost equal to the 42 million who came over the three and a half centuries from 1607 to 1965.[9] The Border Patrol catches as many illegal aliens *every month* as all the legal immigrants who came to America in the 1820s. Today's numbers are of a different order of magnitude.

No nation has ever attempted to assimilate 36 million foreigners in a generation. Yet, each year, 1.5 million more are added to the number, half of them illegals, 90 percent of them from Third World countries whose people have never before been assimilated into our population. In the New York and San Francisco metropolitan areas, immigrants account for more than 25 percent of the population. In the Los Angeles and Miami-Dade metro areas, the respective figures are 32 percent and 36 percent.

The *Time* magazine investigation, "Who Left the Door Open?," concluded: "It's fair to estimate . . . . that the number of illegal aliens flooding into the U.S. this year will total 3 million—enough to fill 22,000 Boeing 737-700 aircraft, or 60 flights every day for a year."[10]

In January 2005, a Bear Stearns study maintained: "The number of illegal immigrants in the United States may be as high as 20 million people."[11] If near the mark, we have millions more illegal aliens in the United States today than the sum total of all the Germans, Italians, Irish, and Jews who ever came to America in the four hundred years of our history on this continent.

In a January 2006 *New Republic* essay, "Border War," John Judis writes 15 that "over the course of a year, almost two million will make it, sometimes after several tries, and enter the underworld of undocumented migrants. . . ."[12]

In *Whatever it Takes*, Congressman J. D. Hayworth notes: "At *minimum*, almost 4,500 people cross into Arizona illegally *each day* without getting caught. . . ."[13] By Hayworth's estimates, 1.6 million illegals come through Arizona alone, every year. And as Professor Glynn Gustred, cofounder of the California Civil Rights Initiative, writes, the attitude and the character of the intruders crossing the California desert has changed radically.

> Eventually the temper of the illegal aliens changed. They became more aggressive, more brazen, more dangerous. In some cases, instead of asking for food or water, they would kick down doors to get it. Meanwhile, dogs are poisoned or their throats cut; property is damaged and goods are stolen, cars are hijacked and residents threatened. One lady on her way to look after her neighbors' pets was waylaid by passing illegal

aliens and murdered for her car. People in east San Diego County now often go armed as they do along the Arizona border.[14]

In 2005, 687 assaults on U.S. Border Patrol agents were recorded, near double the number of the previous year. In the San Diego and Tucson sectors, Border Patrol agents reported being fired upon forty-three times, more than twice the number of shooting incidents as in the previous year.[15]

America faces an existential crisis. If we do not get control of our borders, by 2050 Americans of European descent will be a minority in the nation their ancestors created and built. No nation has ever undergone so radical a demographic transformation and survived.

By 2050, the Hispanic population will have tripled to 102 million, or 24 percent of the nation. Most will be of Mexican ancestry and concentrated in a Southwest that Mexican children are taught was stolen from their country by American aggressors a century and a half ago.

As early as 2010, it is estimated that in the regions surrounding the 20 cities of Miami, Houston, Los Angeles, San Francisco, and Washington, D.C., Americans of European descent will have become a minority. In the Washington metro area between 2000 and 2005, the white population grew by 2.5 percent, the black population by 5.3 percent. But the Asian population shot up 21.5 percent and the Hispanic population grew by almost 28 percent.[16]

In California and Texas, Americans of European descent are already a minority and their share of our population falls every year. Hispanics account for 34 percent of our two most populous states and their numbers are surging. During the 1990s, for the first time since it came into the Union, California's white population fell by 2 million as its native-born sons and daughters packed and left for Nevada, Idaho, Arizona, and Colorado to live out their lives in places more like the Golden State they grew up in. The *reconquista* of Alta California by Mexico is well advanced and the great question is now on the table.

Will the American Southwest become a giant Kosovo, a part of the nation separated from the rest by language, ethnicity, history, and culture, to be reabsorbed in all but name by Mexico from whom we took these lands in the time of Jackson and Polk? Chicano chauvinists and Mexican agents have made clear their intent to take back through demography and culture what their ancestors lost through war. . . .

Notes

1. Patrick J. Buchanan, *The Death of the West: How Dying Populations and Immigrant Invasions Imperil Our Country and Civilization* (New York: St. Martin's Press, 2002), p. 123.

2. Huntington quoted in Yeh Ling-Ling, "Mexican Immigration and Its Potential Impact on the Political Future of the United States," *Journal of Social, Political and Economic Studies*, vol. 29, no. 4 (Winter 2004); www.diversity.alliance.org/docs/article/_2004winter.htm.

3. "Border Emergency Declared in New Mexico," *CNN.com*, Aug, 13, 2005; www.cnn.com/2005/US/08/12/newmexico.

4. Jacques Billeaud, "Ariz. Governor Orders Troops to Border," Associated Press, Man 8, 2006.

5. Donald L. Barlett and James B. Steele, "Who Left the Door Open?" *Time* magazine, Sept. 20, 2004; www.time-proxy.yaga.com/time/archive.

6. "President Discusses Border Security and Immigration Reform in America," Tucson, Arizona, Office of the Press Secretary, The White House, Nov. 28, 2005; www/whitehouse.gov/news/releases/2005/11.

7. James R. Edwards, Jr., "Two Sides of the Same Coin: The Connection Between Legal and Illegal Immigration," Center for Immigration Studies; www/cis.org/articles/2006/back106.html.

8. John F. Kennedy, *A Nation of Immigrants*. Revised and enlarged edition with an Introduction by Robert F. Kennedy (New York: Harper & Row, 1965), pp. 17, 51, 58.

9. Ibid., pp. 2, 3.

10. Barlett and Steele, op. cit.

11. Robert Justich and Betty Ng, "The Underground Labor Force Is Rising to the Surface," Bear Stearns Asset Management, Jan. 3, 2005.

12. John Judis, "Border War," *New Republic*, Jan. 16, 2006, p. 15.

13. J. D. Hayworth, with Joseph J. Eule, *Whatever It Takes: Illegal Immigration, Border Security, and the War on Terror* (Washington, DC: Regnery Publishing, 2006), p. 1 (italics in the original).

14. Glynn Custred, "Friends and Elites, Chickens and Coyotes," *American Spectator* (Nov. 2005), p. 28.

15. "Violent Clashes at Mexican Border Double," *Newsmax.com Wires*, Oct. 31, 2005.

16. D'Vera Cohn, "Area Soon to Be Mostly Minority," *Washington Post*, Mar. 25, 2006, p. A1.

Alien Nation

MICHAEL MAIELLO AND NICOLE RIDGWAY

BEFORE READING: What solutions to the problem of illegal immigration have you heard or read about?

Where do you get your workers? We ask a certain highly successful roofing contractor in Washington, D.C. Technically speaking, he allows, his employees are all legal. They have papers, and it's not his responsibility to determine if the papers are forged. But he lives on the edge. That's why he recently declined to bid on a lucrative deal offered by the National Security Agency. The spy agency didn't want foreigners working on its premises and could be expected to do a much better job than Immigration & Customs Enforcement does of enforcing the law against employing illegals.

This entrepreneur won't admit that he has hired illegals. But, he concedes, "[If] I need five or ten additional men, I let it be known amongst a certain circle of guys. And I have access to those people immediately."

It's not easy finding American citizens willing to push shingles around on a hot roof during 100-degree weather. It's not easy finding engineers, either. James Goodnight, chief executive of SAS, the world's largest privately held software company, recently went looking for Ph.D. engineers. He needed them for a project to help companies increase profits by getting a handle on their suppliers. Plenty of willing and able foreigners could have done the work, but landing the H-1B visas, which allow foreigners with special skills to work in the U.S. for up to six years, would be next to impossible. As a result, Goodnight came close to opening an R&D center in Poland. "I wish I had done it," he laments.

America's immigration policy is a shambles. "The current situation can only be described as untenable," says Craig Barrett, chairman of Intel Corp., which has a voracious appetite for chip designers. The U.S. does a brilliant job educating foreigners in our engineering schools, and then, during the recruiting season, chases this human capital away. Australia and the U.K. have a much better system. They come pretty close to stapling a visa to an engineer's diploma. "If we had purposefully set out to design a system that would cripple our ability to be competitive, we could hardly do better than what we have today," says Barrett.

Michael Maiello is a senior reporter and writer for *Forbes* and also contributes to several newspapers. He appears frequently on *Journalist's Roundtable* and *Money Weekend*. He is the author of *Buy the Rumor, Sell the Fact: 85 Maxims of Wall Street and What They Really Mean* (2007). Nicole Ridgway is a senior editor for SmartMoney.com and oversees all of that Web site's personal finance coverage. Prior to joining SmartMoney.com, she worked at *Forbes*, where this article appeared April 10, 2006.

We've been here before. Twenty years ago Congress passed the Simpson-   5
Rodino immigration reform, a bill four years in the making. The law was
supposed to halt the flood of illegal immigrants swarming in to take low-
paying jobs. It granted a one-year amnesty to aliens who had been living
in the U.S. since before 1982 and let them apply for legal status; it also
slapped businesses with criminal penalties for knowingly hiring illegals.
But the government did not enforce the law. The public, it seems, does not
have the appetite for chasing millions of workers back to Mexico. And so
the government has settled on a half-hearted enforcement scheme that com-
bines a game of tag played out in the Arizona desert with very few raids on
employers. Every now and then some meatpacker or night cleaning firm
is scolded and fined. The penalty for individuals caught employing an undocumented nanny is loss of a cabinet appointment.

Illegals keep cascading in, recently at the rate of 700,000 a year, and
businesses and families keep hiring them. The Pew Hispanic Center estimates that in the last decade the number of undocumented aliens living in
the U.S. has doubled to 12 million. This despite a growth in spending on
domestic security averaging 13.4% a year. President Bush recently requested
$42.7 billion for the Department of Homeland Security and $2.6 billion for
guarding the border with Mexico, the source of no known terrorist.

Adding to this morass of ambivalence about foreigners doing our dirty
work: the fear and xenophobia that grew out of September 11. The resulting crackdown did nothing to stop the unskilled workers walking across
the border, but it did choke off the engineers from India and China. Since
2001 Congress has whacked the number of H-1B visas from 195,000 to
65,000 a year. Separately, green cards — permanent resident visas that allow
for work, among other things, and granted to noncitizens — are handed
out at the rate of 140,000 a year. Rationing of these precious documents is
done not by setting employment priorities but by trying applicants' patience
and forcing them to spend money on lawyers. For employment visas the
waiting period for an initial interview with the U.S. consulate in the home
country can be up to 149 days. Homeland Security says it does 35 million
security checks a year before issuing visas to workers, tourists, visiting lecturers and the like.

Chipmaker Texas Instruments was trying to secure 65 visas last summer when the federal limit ran out and was told it would have to wait for
many of them until April, when applications for 2007 are accepted, to
begin the process all over again. That means advertising the jobs for 30
days to find "minimally qualified" U.S. workers, sifting through résumés,
submitting paperwork to the Labor Department, and trying again to lure
talented recruits from abroad, a process that can cost up to $30,000 for
each employee — and increases the risk that a company will lose foreign
candidates it has its eye on, as Texas Instruments did. "The more barriers
we have in place and more process steps we have to take, the more we're
going to see these things happen," says Steve W. Lyle, TI's director of worldwide staffing.

How to fix the mess? Herewith, a few proposals from the Beltway and the academic braintrust—and their chances of being adopted.

Compassionate compromise

President Bush has a plan that he claims "serves the American economy and reflects the American dream." Those illegals already in the U.S. would receive temporary worker cards that allow them to stay for up to three years and renew once for an unspecified period — then, vamoose. The same offer would apply to new aliens once a U.S. employer identifies a job and certifies that no American is qualified for or wants to take it. This isn't an amnesty program, the administration has been at pains to point out to avoid torpedoes from the hard right. (A bill introduced by John McCain and Edward Kennedy last May would let illegals apply for citizenship, once they pay a fine, clear up tax problems and learn English.) "I oppose amnesty — placing undocumented workers on the automatic path to citizenship," the President has said. Nor would he give them a leg up on foreigners who come legally and apply for a green card, which offers permanent resident status. He also supports lifting the ceiling on H-1Bs, but his plan doesn't say by how much.

On the tough side, Bush's proposal would turn the screws on businesses that wittingly break the law but doesn't spell out the penalties. Enforcement would fall under the Department of Homeland Security, working with the Labor Department and other federal agencies. "Our homeland will be more secure when we can better account for those who enter our country," said Bush. Hard to disagree with that nostrum.

What's the likelihood we'll see some version of the plan? Not high, considering that no one in Congress has run with it — and the President introduced the idea on January 7, 2004.

Build up that wall

Last December, by 260–159, the House passed an amendment that would mandate the construction of a 700-mile fence along the 1,952-mile border with Mexico. Calling for a series of steel barriers armed with motion detectors, floodlights and surveillance equipment, the plan has been the pet project of Representative Duncan Hunter (R-Calif.) for the past 20 years. He finally got it on the radar as part of a get-tough immigration bill that would beef up security and tighten enforcement. Construction costs: $2.2 billion by Hunter's estimate; proponents of the idea, like Colin Hanna, president of Weneedafence.com, think it could easily reach $8 billion.

Good fences don't always make good neighbors, as Israel's recent attempt to wall itself off from the Palestinians most vividly illustrates. The House amendment drew immediate fire from Mexican President Vicente Fox, who complained that Congress had given into "xenophobic groups that impose the law at will." It would be hard for Mexico to swallow any reform plan that threatens the flow of dollars from Mexican expats to their families back home. Chance of success: iffy; there isn't much support in the Administration.

Caps off

Some people argue the best way to deal with illegals is to create so many   15
opportunities for legal immigration that no rational migrant would risk a
deadly trek through the desert. (Last year, 460 people died trying to get
into the U.S., up from 61 in 1995.) Daniel Griswold, director of the Cato
Institute's Center for Trade Policy Studies, suggests letting in at least
300,000 temporary workers on three-year, renewable visas each year. Undocumented workers here could receive the same visa. But unlike Bush's
proposal, this one does not force illegal residents to go home; they could
pursue citizenship, as long as they pay an unspecified fine ("not chump
change," Griswold says) and have clean records. Douglas S. Massey, a
Princeton University professor of sociology and public affairs and author
of *Beyond Smoke and Mirrors: Mexican Immigration in an Era of Economic Integration* (Russell Sage, 2002), would also let in 300,000 temporary workers every year. Each of them would pay $400 or so, about one-third what
a "coyote" charges to smuggle people across the border, giving immigrants a financial incentive to play by the rules. Griswold agrees, adding
that such reform would "drain the swamp of human smuggling and document fraud that facilitates illegal immigration."

As for the illegals already in place, Massey would allow anyone who
arrived as a minor to apply for permanent legal status right away. Their
parents would have the option to apply for temporary status. But, in any
event, Massey wants the U.S. to allow far more than the current 20,000
green cards for Mexicans each year. That would swell their contributions
to the U.S. Treasury. Massey's surveys have shown that a surprising 62% of
illegal workers have taxes withheld from their paychecks and 66% pay
Social Security. In 2004, illegal workers contributed $7 billion to Social
Security and $1.5 billion to Medicare. Yet these workers seldom use social
services because they fear getting busted. Massey found that only 10% of
illegal Mexicans have sent a child to a U.S. public school, and just 5% have
received food stamps or unemployment.

Chances for any legislative action? Maybe some tidbit from the guest-
worker program. So far, it hasn't caught fire with feds or Joe Six-Pack. A
recent Zogby International poll says 56% of likely voters oppose giving illegals any chance at citizenship.

Selling the American dream—for a price

Nobel laureate Gary Becker, who teaches economics at the University of
Chicago, thinks the U.S. should welcome anyone who's not a criminal, a
terrorist, or a carrier of a communicable disease—for a fee of $50,000. That
buys permanent status. Becker says the plan would lure skilled workers
since they have more to gain. For those who can't afford a ticket, Becker
would encourage commercial banks to make high-interest immigration
loans.

Becker is tempted to push his own proposal a bit further. Why not
auction off guest-worker visas—and the chance of citizenship—to the

highest bidders? At a minimum, Becker thinks, such auctions could bring in $50 billion a year—enough to pay for the entire budget of the Department of Homeland Security.

Sound weird? There's a version already in place, known as the EB-5 20 visa, introduced in 1990. It's available to 10,000 foreigners a year who are willing to invest at least $500,000 (in some cases, $1 million) to create a new business or expand an existing one, creating ten or more jobs. But does the government really want to be in the business of marketing U.S. citizenship abroad?

Bring on Big Brother

What if we could open our borders and safeguard the country? Technology is a ministep in that direction. Last summer Homeland Security began a $100 million pilot program that embedded radio-frequency identification on the entry documents of those coming in from Canada and Mexico, tracking their arrival and departure, as Wal-Mart does pallets of toothpaste. The test didn't sit well with civil liberties groups or with Senator Patrick Leahy (D.–Vt.), who pointed out that the so-called pass card used an RFID chip that was incompatible with the one the State Department was using in passports. Could bad guys jam the systems or hack into them? That would make our borders less secure.

More plausible is an extension of a new practice that already exists. All foreign applicants for visas must schedule an interview with the U.S. consulate in their host country, where they submit to biometric fingerprint scans of their left and right index fingers and a digital photo. Such high-tech ID is also in 105 U.S. airports, as well as in all American seaports and border crossings. Draft legislation by Arlen Specter (R.–Pa.), the chairman of the Senate Judiciary Committee, would require the same kind of whiz-bang identification on the visas of all immigrants already in the States by 2007 and, by that time, would force compatibility between systems used by the FBI and Homeland Security. To curtail fraud, Specter would require companies to enter a social security number on an online government database for each prospective employee—and if it's bounced, the employer is responsible for reporting the culprit to the Immigration & Customs Enforcement agency.

The Specter bill is a melting pot of competing proposals that draw from the right and the left. Illegals already in the States could stay here indefinitely, as long as they have been employed since January 2004 and passed a background investigation by Homeland Security; whether they could become American citizens is still murky. Newly arrived aliens don't get quite as good a deal. Citizenship is off the table. But as guest workers, they would receive visas and have a chance to stay in the U.S., as long as they had jobs, for up to six years, when they would have to leave. However, they could apply for green cards from their home country. (A competing proposal by Senators John Cornyn [R.–Tex.] and Jon Kyl [R.–Ariz.] would allow temporary workers six years of employment in U.S., so long

Protesters voice their opinions on immigration. Consider each photograph as an argument. What assumptions are at play in each?

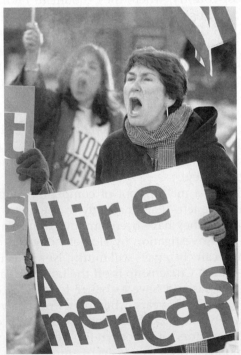

as they go home for a year every two years, with little chance to gain citizenship.) Specter would also almost triple H-1Bs to 180,000 the first year and thereafter adjust the number to market demand. Anyone with an advanced degree in science, technology, engineering, or math is exempt from a visa cap.

Business has warmed to his proposals. "We have talented people we want to hire, whom we've offered a job to—and we can't bring them into the country," says Pamela Passman, vice president of global corporate affairs for Microsoft. "We think Specter's bill does address the [H-1B] crisis."

So what are its chances? It's a complex, omnibus package with many wiggling parts. Nothing will be enacted quickly. The 1986 reform took four years, and that was before September 11. Xenophobia and protectionism combined to defeat an honest airing about whether an Arab ally should operate U.S. ports. Immigration probably won't fare any better.

25

Waiting in Limbo, Their Childhood Lost

DANIELLE KNIGHT

BEFORE READING: What are some of the special problems faced by children who immigrate into the United States or who are born here to illegal aliens?

I sau Flores Portillo was 10 years old when he left his home in Honduras, fleeing the beatings of his abusive stepfather to live on the streets. But gangs beat him, he says, and murderous police security forces threatened his life. In 1999, desperate for a safe haven, he packed his few belongings and began a 1,200-mile journey north to the United States. He walked, hopped trains, and thumbed rides. Early the next year, he crossed the border into Laredo, Texas, but a better life did not await him.

U.S. immigration agents detained him. He was kept in a juvenile jail in Texas for six months, alongside young criminals convicted of rape and assault. Later, he was mistakenly deported back to Honduras. He returned to the United States, only to be taken back into custody. Four years have passed since he first set foot in Texas. "It is too much time," says Isau, now 16, in an interview with *U.S. News* at a detention center in Pennsylvania.

Up to 80,000 children and teenagers, unaccompanied by parents or other legal guardians, come from all over the world—but mostly from Mexico and Central America—fleeing persecution, traffickers, poverty, and abuse.

Danielle Knight worked as a freelance print and radio journalist before becoming a reporter for *U.S. News and World Report* in 2003 as a member of its investigations team. In the same year, she was the winner of the Columbia University James A. Wechsler Award for International Reporting. This essay appeared in *U.S. News* on March 15, 2004.

Most are deported within 72 hours, but the relatively few who are allowed to stay—about 4,800 in fiscal year 2003, up from 3,150 in 1997—must wait for their turn in the docket before a federal immigration judge. Some, like Isau, wait for years. Without laws to protect them, these children are ignored by an immigration bureaucracy hell bent on avoiding another September 11. "There is an inherent conflict of interest between law enforcement and the best interests of these children," says Chris Nugent, a Washington, D.C., attorney who represents children seeking asylum.

Shackled

While they wait, the children are supposed to be held in the least restrictive setting possible, usually one of 40 detention facilities nationwide. Despite recent reforms, however, many children have been held in juvenile jails, adult prisons, and locked hotel rooms with armed guards stationed outside. Children described to *U.S. News* how they have been shackled and handcuffed. Others have been placed in solitary confinement.

More than half of the children in custody do not have lawyers, say child advocates, and the results can sometimes be bizarre. In June 2000, an 18-month-old Jamaican girl appeared before an immigration judge in Miami in the arms of a deportation officer. No one was there to defend her. She was later deported with a relative. "These children have not been adequately protected and have been forced to endure hardship at the hands of federal immigration authorities, instead of receiving the appropriate care they deserve," says Sen. Dianne Feinstein, a Democrat from California, who is pressing reform legislation.

The hardships include being jailed with criminals. Malik Jarno, a mentally retarded asylum seeker from Guinea, was detained in adult prisons for three years after he arrived in this country in 2001 at age 16. He sued the Piedmont Regional Jail in Farmville, Virginia, claiming that guards, while trying to subdue a prisoner, beat him and blinded him with pepper spray. Another time, he was confined to a cell for almost two weeks, say his lawyers. He lost the civil suit. Jail officials say that he was confined because he had fought with inmates and guards. Malik claims that he is the son of a religious leader who died after a politically motivated arrest—and that he is fleeing political persecution. Last fall, 35 members of Congress joined human-rights and disability-rights groups to call for Malik's release from prison. He now lives in a refugee shelter in York, Pennsylvania; his case is pending, and he could yet be deported.

Broken promise

Malik, Isau, and others weren't supposed to be housed with criminals. A 1996 immigration reform law requires detention of all asylum seekers who don't have proper travel documents. But under a 1997 legal settlement, the Immigration and Naturalization Service was required to separate child immigrants from juvenile criminals and adult inmates—and to release them to family residing in the United States, when possible.

That deal isn't always kept. Eldin Escobar, a 15-year-old from Honduras, was detained with juvenile offenders for six months in 2003 at a detention center in Berks County, Pennsylvania. Eldin says he feared his guards, who he says would often try to provoke him into breaking rules. They made him "gobble like a turkey" before a meal, he says. If he didn't, they threatened to have him sit with his head down all day. Eric Ruth, assistant superintendent at the Berks center, said he had not heard the accusation. "Such conduct on the part of our staff would not be condoned and would be met with immediate disciplinary action," he says. Still, after visiting the facility with a *U.S. News* reporter, an official of the federal Office of Refugee Resettlement—which had custody of Eldin—says it will not renew its contract with Berks County. "It is too institutional and prisonlike," says Maureen Dunn of ORR. Dunn had Isau, Eldin, and other children transferred from the Berks County center to other facilities.

In 2001, the inspector general of the Justice Department found that 34 of 57 secure juvenile detention facilities did not have procedures or facilities to segregate nondelinquent youths from juvenile offenders. Last year, Amnesty International reported that one third of children seeking asylum in the United States were detained in juvenile jails and in some cases were shackled and handcuffed, isolated, and physically abused.

Congress tried to improve the treatment of these minors. In 2003, the Homeland Security Act reorganized the immigration bureaucracy and shifted custody of children to child welfare experts at the Office of Refugee Resettlement in the Department of Health and Human Services. The immigration service, critics charged, couldn't simultaneously act as police officer, jailer, and guardian. Since the switch, contracts with facilities are being reviewed to ensure that juveniles who haven't committed crimes are not held with youth offenders or with adult inmates. HHS also tracks where kids have been detained, something immigration authorities don't do. "I am confident that we are running this properly," says Wade Horn, a senior official at HHS. Pro bono attorneys for children concede that more children have been released to relatives or foster families while they wait for their immigration status to be resolved. But they argue that some minors are still mistreated, either because they remain under the authority of immigration officials or because they are classified as adults.

No one tracks how many young asylum seekers are wrongfully held as adults. Richemond Joseph arrived in Florida from Haiti in February 2003 by ship and was immediately detained. His birth certificate, which authorities couldn't be sure was authentic, says he was 16. Medical tests suggested that he was older. But immigration officials rely on a technique to determine age—using dental and wrist X-rays—that many medical experts consider inaccurate. He is now incarcerated in a New Orleans prison. "I'm not a criminal," says Joseph, through his attorney.

Joseph is lucky to have a lawyer. There is no official procedure to ensure that children in custody get an attorney. Children with little formal education who do not speak English are often pitted against government

10

attorneys. "The whole deck is stacked against them," says Wendy Young, an official of a New York–based refugee organization.

Asylum seekers who have a lawyer are up to six times as likely to be granted asylum as those who don't, according to a study by Georgetown University's Institute for the Study of International Migration. The Department of Health and Human Services is trying to establish a formal network of pro bono lawyers who would be contacted automatically if a minor needs counsel.

HHS is charged with looking out for the best interests of children—but the agency doesn't have jurisdiction over all of them. When a deportation order is issued, the Department of Homeland Security detains or deports the youngsters. Where precisely one agency's mission ends and the other's begins is still being worked out. "It's as clear as mud," says David Venturella, an official at the U.S. Immigration and Customs Enforcement office, or ICE. Meanwhile, children find themselves caught in the middle.

Rose Thermitus, a 10th grader at Roosevelt High School on Long Is- 15 land, found herself at the center of the turf battle between the two federal bureaucracies. In October 2002, Rose and her brother fled Haiti after government supporters burned her family's home in Cap Haitien. The boat carrying Rose and 200 other Haitians ran aground near Miami. Rose was detained in a hotel room for six months and then for 10 more months at the Boystown juvenile detention shelter in Florida.

Immigration officials want to deport Rose, but the Haitian Consulate won't let her return without her parents' consent. She says her parents have disappeared. Horn of HHS took an interest in the case after human-rights groups protested her detention. His department recommended she be released to an aunt who is a legal resident in New York State. "We worked aggressively to resolve this issue," says Horn. "I asked about it every other day." Rose was released in January, but she's still in legal limbo. Her request for asylum was rejected, and she may be deported when she turns 18 in October. "I knew that if I was caught in the United States, I would go to prison," Rose says, "but I never thought it would be for so long."

Terrorized

A new emphasis on security is one reason for the delay in Rose's case. "9/11 slowed Rose's release and the release of other Haitian children," says Lisa Frydman, Rose's lawyer. Following the terrorist attacks, new government rules required that asylum seekers from Haiti and some other countries be taken into custody. That meant Rose had to be detained. The Justice Department also changed the immigration appeals process. Asylum seekers who would have won in immigration courts must now turn to federal courts, says Eleanor Acer of Human Rights First, an advocacy group.

That can add years to their time in custody. Children in detention do not know how long they will be held or when their next hearing will take place, says Jacqueline Bhabha of Harvard University's Committee on Human Rights Studies. "Most children awaiting decisions on their cases are trapped in a stressful, seemingly endless limbo of uncertainty," she says. Venturella says it takes time for immigration officials to review each case. "They perceive this as foot dragging," he says, "but we are just doing our job thoroughly."

Meanwhile, Isau Flores Portillo is now in his 43rd month in federal custody. "It has been just one frustrating event after another," says Laura Bachman, his Houston lawyer. But, she adds, things could always be worse. If the Department of Homeland Security gets its way, Isau will be deported back to Honduras, where he could end up back where his odyssey began four years ago: on the streets, homeless and alone.

In Limbo

Thousands of children under 18 without parents or guardians try to enter 20 the United States each year. Here's what happens to them:

About 80,000 unaccompanied minors seek asylum in the U.S.

About 75,000 are sent back.

About 5,000 are detained and sent to:

Juvenile detention

Adult prisons

Foster care

Group homes

Relatives

Source: Rod Little—*USN&WR*

Where They Come From

Most children in federal custody come from Central America:

Honduras 29.5 pct.

El Salvador 27.7 pct.

Guatemala 21.5 pct.

Mexico 6.7 pct.

Haiti 2.3 pct.

Brazil 1.9 pct.

China 1.6 pct.

Nicaragua 1.2 pct.

Other 7.6 pct.

Sources: U.S. Department of Health and Human Services; *USN&WR*

Lining Up for Citizenship

ARIAN CAMPO-FLORES WITH RICHARD WOLFFE

BEFORE READING: Why do so many immigrants from Mexico never seek citizenship? What changes might there be in America if large numbers of them did?

M anuel Ortega didn't like what he was hearing. Though the Mexican native has been a legal permanent resident in the United States for 15 years, he grew jittery at all the talk of deportation amid the rancorous national debate on illegal immigration. "Residency can be taken away from one moment to the next," he says. "With citizenship, you can protect yourself." So on a crisp Saturday morning last month, he headed to a citizenship workshop at Saint Pius Church in Chicago. By the time he arrived at 7:30 a.m., the line already stretched for two blocks. Event planners had expected several hundred people to show up; instead, about 1,000 came, forcing organizers to shut the doors at noon. Ortega, 40, finally filed his paperwork after a six-hour wait. It was a first step, he says, "to get more rights and to get the vote."

While the furor over illegal immigration has galvanized the undocumented, it also appears to have stirred up longtime legal residents like Ortega. They're applying in greater numbers to naturalize, or become citizens — an option for people who have had green cards for at least five years. According to U.S. Citizenship and Immigration Services, naturalization applications in the first three months of the year increased 19 percent over the same period last year. And in March, visitors to the USCIS Web site downloaded a record 162,000 citizenship applications. Some immigrants may be driven by fear, others by a desire for full political participation, and still others by a wish to petition for relatives living abroad. The immigration debate that has mobilized them will once again seize center stage this week. Senate leaders have agreed to bring an immigration bill to the floor, and on Monday night President George W. Bush will address the nation on the subject. Aides say he'll continue to plug his favored guest-worker program, but will also emphasize border security and raise the possibility of deploying the National Guard — a proposal that will likely play well with his conservative base.

Arian Campo-Flores began his career as an English teacher in Buenos Aires and from there moved to reporting for a monthly magazine, *The American Lawyer*. He next worked as a New York correspondent for *Newsweek* and served as *Newsweek*'s Miami Bureau chief. He covered Florida's crucial presidential voting in 2004 and most recently covered the war in Iraq as an embedded journalist. Richard Wolffe is *Newsweek*'s senior White House correspondent. This article appeared in the May 22, 2006, issue of *Newsweek*.

While immigrant advocates continue to push for reform, they're increasingly trying to energize legal residents, many of whom joined the recent marches. The pool of green-card holders who are eligible for citizenship exceeds 8 million by some estimates—all of them potential voters. "We want to capitalize on that movement energy and translate it into a real political voice for immigrants," says Deepak Bhargava of the Center for Community Change. So last week the newly formed "We Are America Alliance," comprised of Bhargava's group and scores more, announced an initiative to produce 1 million new citizens and voters by Election Day 2006. As part of a so-called Democracy Summer, citizenship schools nationwide will help immigrants with their paperwork, offer civics classes, and promote political participation. To kick it all off, U.S. Rep. Luis Gutierrez of Chicago has proposed a National Citizenship Day on July 1, when he hopes to draw as many as 30,000 applicants across the country.

But enrolling new citizens is no easy task. Many eligible permanent residents choose not to apply, whether because of the cost ($400), lack of English skills, or plans to head home someday. To help prod them, some pro-immigrant groups are highlighting the safeguards of citizenship. In new ads by the Illinois Coalition for Immigrant and Refugee Rights—which oversaw the workshop Ortega attended—an announcer intones darkly, "Immigrants are being attacked daily. Protect your family. Become a citizen today." ICIRR also notes that application costs will continue to rise and argues that a revamped citizenship test due to be completed next year will be more difficult (a USCIS spokesman denies that). Fear has motivated immigrants in the past: in the wake of a 1994 ballot initiative in California that stripped away benefits for the undocumented, naturalization surged, reaching a peak of 1 million two years later.

If organizers manage to enlist hundreds of thousands of new citizens 5 who go on to vote, the political impact could be far-reaching. Eligible permanent residents make up sizeable portions of the population in many key swing states—numbering about 600,000 in Florida, for instance. And naturalized citizens—537,000 of whom were minted in 2004—vote at higher rates than the U.S.-born, according to studies by the National Association of Latino Elected and Appointed Officials. Still, advocacy groups have repeatedly been disappointed by immigrants who have often failed to flex their political muscle. "Our mission is to make good on the slogan, 'Today we march, tomorrow we vote,'" says Chung-Wha Hong of the New York Immigration Coalition. If that happens, maybe the next line Ortega stands in will be the one for the ballot box.

Rousing the Zealots

JEFFREY RESSNER

BEFORE READING: What dangers might immigrants face from those individuals and groups most vehemently opposed to illegal immigration?

Pugnacious anthems and racist diatribes have never been in short supply at Nordic Fest, an annual white-power Woodstock held over the Memorial Day break near the former mining town of Dawson Springs, Kentucky. And this past weekend was no exception. On the agenda were a *Triumph of the Will*–themed running event and a cross "lighting" sponsored by the Imperial Klans of America. But something new did arise at Nordic Fest this year: bellicose talk and plans of action against illegal immigrants. Among the scheduled guest speakers was Hal Turner, a New Jersey Internet radio talk-show host who recently instructed his audience to "clean your guns, have plenty of ammunition . . . and then do what has to be done" to undocumented workers.

With immigration perhaps America's most volatile issue, a troubling backlash has erupted among its most fervent foes. There are, of course, the Minutemen, the self-appointed border vigilantes who operate in several states. And now groups of militiamen, white supremacists, and neo-Nazis are using resentment over the estimated 11 million illegal immigrants in the U.S. as a potent rallying cry. "The immigration furor has been critical to the growth we've seen" in hate groups, says Mark Potok, head of the Intelligence Project at the Southern Poverty Law Center. The center counts some 800 racist groups operating in the U.S. today, a 5% spurt in the past year and a 33% jump from 2000. "They think they've found an issue with racial overtones and a real resonance with the American public," says Potok, "and they are exploiting it as effectively as they can."

Both Potok's group and the Anti-Defamation League (ADL) are worried that extremists are burrowing their way into the anti-immigration mainstream. Mark Martin, 43, of Covington, Ohio, is a chef at a French restaurant and tends his backyard organic garden. But he also dons the black and brown uniform of western Ohio's National Socialist (read: Nazi) Movement. "There's nothing neo about us," he says. Martin admits he frequently harasses day laborers and threatens them with deportation. "As Americans, we have the right to make a citizen's arrest and detain them," he insists. "And if they try to get away, we have the right to get physical with them." Martin gleefully boasts about leading eight fellow storm troopers in disrupting a May 1 pro-immigrant rally in Dayton by taunting protesters. Although police

---

Jeffrey Ressner is a reporter for *Time*, in which this article appeared on June 5, 2006.

ultimately restrained him, Martin believes his agitation was worthwhile because it attracted new recruits. "After the rally, the Klan called us," he says.
"Now we've started working together more often."

In addition to white supremacists, the immigration debate seems to
have reinvigorated members of the antigovernment militias of the 1990s.
Those groups largely disbanded after the Oklahoma City bombing orches-
trated by militia groupie Timothy McVeigh and, later, the failure of a Y2K
bug to trigger the mass chaos some militia members expected. "We've seen
people from Missouri and Kentucky militias involved in border-vigilante
activity, especially with the gung-ho Arizona group Ranch Rescue that
used face paint, military uniforms, and weapons," says Mark Pitcavage,
fact-finding director of the ADL. "It's a natural shift. Militias fell on hard
times, and this anti-immigration movement is new and fresh."

One leader who has morphed from militiaman to Minuteman is Mike   5
Vanderboegh, 53, of Pinson, Alabama. Once the "commander" of what he
called the First Alabama Cavalry Regiment Constitutional Militia, which
published anti-terrorism screeds, Vanderboegh is the past Alabama state director of the Minutemen. He has advocated hurling bricks through the windows of Congress members who support giving illegal immigrants the same
rights as U.S. citizens. Those bricks, he says, should be used to build a wall
sealing the U.S. off from Mexico. He argues that the open borders facilitate
drug trafficking and the sexual exploitation of immigrant women.

Vanderboegh says he is not a racist, and he has taken pains to distance
himself from neo-Nazis. He acknowledges that anti-immigrant sentiment
is giving the Klan "fertile ground for recruiting," whereas a few years ago
"they could have held a convention in a phone booth." "Illegal immigration and the destruction of the rule of law is social napalm, and people are
running around with matches," he warns. "One day it will go off."

THINKING AND WRITING ABOUT IMMIGRATION

QUESTIONS FOR DISCUSSION AND WRITING

1. More than one author mentions that, as Americans, we feel a conflict between wanting to stay true to our heritage as a nation of immigrants and
   wanting to keep out some immigrants. How do you personally reconcile
   those two desires?

2. In her opening paragraph, Lochhead argues about immigration that "the
   lesson from history is to beware of unintended consequences." If all Mexicans now in America illegally were given the chance to apply for citizenship, what would you predict some of the consequences would be?

3. Using at least two of the readings in this chapter as sources, explain what
   effect the current immigration situation in the United States is having on
   the U.S. economy.

4. Are you convinced that immigrants illegally crossing the United States's southern border are not a threat to jobs held by native-born Americans? Explain.

5. Which do you believe builds a more convincing case about the employment opportunities in the United States for immigrants from Mexico, Cowen and Rothschild's article or Samuelson's? Explain why.

6. How effective do you believe Buchanan is in supporting his contention that "America is being invaded, and if this is not stopped, it will mean the end of the United States"?

7. Evaluate the proposals that Maiello and Ridgway offer for solving immigration problems.

8. Any children born to illegal aliens in America are automatically American citizens. How does this complicate any attempts to solve the immigration problem?

RESEARCH TOPICS

The effect illegal immigrants currently have on the U.S. economy

The dangers of illegally crossing the Mexican–U.S. border

Asylum cities

Medical care for undocumented aliens

Education for undocumented aliens

Driver's licenses for illegal immigrants

Effect of the immigration issue on the 2008 presidential campaign

CHAPTER 20

In the World of Medicine, Who Decides What Is Ethical?

With virtually every advance in medical science come new questions about medical ethics. "First, do no harm" sounds simple, but it doesn't help a doctor decide which of two patients should receive a donor heart. A donor registry exists, but amid suspicions that donor organs might go to the highest bidder or that those with no insurance might never even make it to the list. In desperation, some potential recipients have even started advertising for directed donations of organs.

It has become necessary to look closely at the definition of life itself—and of death. When is a potential donor legally dead so that his organs can be harvested? How long should donors be kept alive artificially waiting for the harvesting? Well-publicized cases have focused national attention on the issue of who has the right to decide to terminate life support.

The ability to freeze and store embryos has been a godsend to many families. Now a decision must be made as to what should be done with leftover frozen embryos, and heated debate continues over what use should be made of embryonic stem cells. Is it ethical to use them at all, even if they show promise in treating conditions such as Parkinson's, diabetes, and spinal cord injuries? Should research into their use be postponed in light of promising new research into the possibility of growing stem cells from other body cells?

Doctors are human beings too, with their own value systems. Does a doctor have the right to refuse to treat a patient because to do so would violate that doctor's own moral code? What if the doctor neglects to inform the patient of all viable options for treatment because some violate the doctor's personal code of ethics?

Complex as the science is that makes possible brave new worlds of medicine, equally complex are the accompanying moral issues.

Need an Organ? It Helps to Be Rich

JOY VICTORY

> BEFORE READING: When there is a waiting list for donor organs, how is the decision made as to who will get them? Do you think that our country's system for deciding which patients get donor organs is fair? Explain why or why not.

B rian Shane Regions is dying.

Medications sustain the 34-year-old for now, but a heart transplant is his only hope of a cure for his congestive heart failure — as is the case for the thousands of others who suffer from irreversible heart damage. But Regions lacks health insurance and receives inconsistent care for his condition. He said some of his doctors have casually suggested that he should be on the waiting list for a new heart, but not one has helped him pursue it.

"There's really nothing I can do," said Regions, a freelance photographer in Campti, Louisiana. "I don't have the insurance to do it right now. They are treating the symptoms. I'm managing, but I know I'm slowly getting worse and it's not going to get any better."

It's the harsh reality of the organ transplant field: Patients who are uninsured or unable to pay are sometimes denied lifesaving treatment because hospitals can't afford to foot the bill for the surgery or the extensive recovery. And while inadequate health care is a big problem in general for uninsured Americans, organ transplants raise unique ethical issues, said the authors of a report in the *Journal of the American College of Cardiology*. While the uninsured or poor can't easily receive organs, they do donate them: As many as 25 percent of organs come from the uninsured, according to estimates by the authors of "Health Insurance and Cardiac Transplantation: A Call for Reform." Or, in other words, as the report states: "Individuals donate their hearts, although they themselves would not have been eligible to receive a transplant had they needed one." But whether the organ transplant system is fair or not depends on whom you ask.

Most bioethicists say the organ transplant system should be "equal opportunity" — that anyone who is willing to donate should be eligible for a transplant themselves, regardless of the ability to pay. But some say the   5

Joy Victory is the online health editor at About.com and has written about health issues for newspapers and for ABC News. This article appeared on ABC News online on January 20, 2006.

health care system is full of similar examples in which either the poor or the rich (but mostly the rich) are at an advantage and transplants are just a small part of a bigger problem.

The "Wallet Biopsy"

To find matching donor organs, transplant centers rely on the United Network for Organ Sharing, or UNOS, a nonprofit organization that maintains a nationwide patient waiting list. Organs are then typically dispensed to the sickest patients or to those who have been waiting a long time. UNOS maintains the list, but it's left up to 256 organ transplant centers across the United States to decide who *gets* on the list. Each center sets its own criteria, which often include the patient's ability to pay. Laura Siminoff, a bioethicist, called this the "wallet biopsy," during which a person's financial standing comes under scrutiny.

"Every transplant center can do what they want," said Siminoff, who directs the bioethics program at Case Western University and is a board member of the Minority Organ Tissue and Transplant Education Program in Cleveland. "Centers have different practices. And if you're a well-to-do patient, you can shop around to centers. But if you don't have any money, you will go wherever is closest, and their policies are what you are stuck with."

Trying to Help the Poor

Thankfully, not all transplant centers turn away uninsured patients, pointed out Mary Simmerling, a bioethics fellow at the MacLean Center for Clinical Medical Ethics at the University of Chicago. She also runs a regional ethics consortium on organ transplants. "Some [centers] have the luxury of really helping their transplant candidates to pay for the medications," she said, referring to the anti-rejection drugs that must be taken post-transplant and can sometimes cost more than the surgery itself.

The staff at the University of Michigan Transplant Center tries to help uninsured patients find a way to pay, said Dr. Jeffrey Punch, director of the transplant center. For some patients, financial assistance through Medicare or Medicaid can be arranged, although there are income limits. "At our transplant center we have evaluated thousands of patients for liver transplantation, and we virtually never do a transplant without a plan for how it will be paid for," he said. "But we have only very rarely turned down a patient because of lack of insurance. In virtually all circumstances, the patient can arrange coverage of some sort." However, because there is little governance over the transplant centers, it is not known how many people receive care like that at UMich or are turned away because of a lack of money, said Dr. Mark Drazner, a cardiologist at the University of Texas Southwestern Medical Center.

A Lack of Data

To get a clearer picture of the problem, Drazner and the other authors of   10 "Health Insurance and Cardiac Transplantation" set out to compile data on organ transplant recipients and donors to see how many were uninsured. But they didn't find any nationwide data, so they relied primarily upon a database of 420 families of organ donors, known as the National Study of Family Consent to Organ Donation. Siminoff conducted it. In her survey of hundreds of Pennsylvania and Ohio families, 23 percent of organ donors were uninsured. She believes that a national survey would produce a number similar to that. But her database is not enough to make that assertion, Punch said. "The article . . . merely assumes that everyone without health insurance cannot get a transplant. They quote four references to this point, none of which offer empirical evidence to their assertion," Punch said of the paper. Also, he said it is not fair to compare the ability to donate organs with the ability to receive organs. "Donating organs has no risk, damages no party, and causes no problem with any large-scale religious communities. I agree entirely that the uninsured people in our country are a huge public problem, but I disagree that this can be used to indict the practice of organ donation as unfair."

Siminoff feels a bit differently. "From a very clinical point of view, you can ask what is the difference if the donor is dead? Except as a society we don't view dead people as garbage. People have very definite feelings about how dead bodies should be treated and what they represent," she said. "Families [of donors] can be harmed if they felt the person was desecrated or not treated with respect. It could have irreparable damage."

Looking at the Decisions

For patients like Regions, these are nominal concerns. His failing heart, and lack of health care, takes precedent. At the moment, he's not sure what he's going to do. He visits online support groups and works as a photographer when he has the energy. But after researching what it would take to have a transplant, he said that any measure taken to help the uninsured should include the enormous cost of immunosuppressant medications that people have to take for the rest of their lives after a transplant. "The aftermath of the heart transplant, or any transplant, would cost more than the actual surgery itself," Regions said, adding that people who have reasonably good health insurance are still burdened by the cost of medication. Plus, Siminoff noted, even having private health insurance doesn't make this issue go away. "Health insurance comes and goes in this country, and some of the people [who receive transplants] are never able to go back to work full time and [they] lose health insurance," Siminoff said. This sometimes forces people to stop taking the medication, putting them in the same poor health they were in before the transplant, Simmerling, the bioethicist, said.

"We really tend to think of transplants [and the organ transplant list] as different—it's held up as this oasis of fairness and neutrality," Simmerling said. "But when you really start to look at how decisions are made it has a lot to do with socioeconomic status."

No Quick Solutions

While this is probably correct, some said the organ transplant system is no less fair than other areas of medicine or life in general. Put another way: Being poor is not easy.

"The primary source of inequity here is the failure to provide univer- 15 sal insurance coverage for all citizens or residents," said Norman Daniels, a professor of population ethics at the Harvard School of Public Health. "Remember, we are the only industrialized country to fail to do that."

Family law professor Timothy Jost agreed. "It is unethical not to provide heart transplants for the poor, but only because it is unethical to deny the poor health care generally," said Jost, at the Washington and Lee University School of Law in Lexington, Virginia.

Drazner and the other study authors do not disagree with this notion. But they hope that the report at least spurs interest in the creation of a national registry that tracks that and other important information about donors and recipients. "It's good to have all the players involved to address the situation and be aware of the financial aspects that need to be considered," he said.

Tom Mayo, a Southern Methodist University bioethicist who helped write the report, said the enormous cost of organ transplants means they can't be excluded from any debate on national health care. At the very least, he hopes the report will raise that concern among policymakers. "How much of a health care budget should go into a transplant budget?" he said. "This opens the door to a much broader debate. This is an area where line drawing has been done and will continue for the indefinite future."

Ethics of Organ Donation

LAWRENCE A. HOWARDS

BEFORE READING: Why is the decision to harvest organs from one patient to try to save the life of another difficult both ethically and medically?

M any of us have signed the backs of our driver's license allowing the harvesting and donation of body organs such as corneas, kidneys, liver, lungs, and heart if we are hopelessly brain injured and on life support.[1] What

[1] Gail Van Norman, M.D. University of Washington, Seattle, WA. Presented at the Midwest Anesthesia Conference, May 1, 1999.

Dr. Lawrence A. Howards is co–medical director of the Sinai Samaritan Pain Clinic at Sinai Samaritan Hospital.

may then happen to us could range from the gift of life to murder. The problem is deciding the difference between dead and nearly dead.

The difference is important and can be illustrated by a character in the movie *The Princess Bride*. In this movie, a prince has most, but not all life extracted from him. "Is he dead?" a character asks. "No, only nearly dead. We can revive him," is the answer. That perfectly illustrates the problem in organ donation.

It is very hard to define death in a person with a heartbeat and some intact vital functions, supported by a ventilator and intravenous drugs. Defining death was easier when the definition of death was, simply, no heartbeat and no effort to breathe. Three actual case histories not only should make physicians uncomfortable, but also describe how hard it is to make a decision.

- A 32-year-old man is totally unresponsive to pain and makes no effort to breathe on his own following a traffic accident. He is brought to the operating room for removal of his liver and kidneys. The anesthesiologist in charge of keeping his heart beating to preserve the organs before their removal gives an antidote to muscle relaxants that were given when the accident victim was first hospitalized. The dead man begins to breathe and grimaces in pain as the surgeons cut. "Stop!" calls out the anesthesiologist. "This man is still alive!" "Too late," answers a member of the surgical team. "We have already removed his liver."

- An 18-year-old man with a massive brain injury is being wheeled to the operating room. On the way, he seems to make some twitching movements. The anesthesiologist points this out to the harvesting team. They tell the anesthesiologist that there is no brain wave activity, and the man will not breathe on his own. The donation continues.

- A young woman has lapsed into a coma during childbirth from a rare complication. She has been on a ventilator for three days and is totally unresponsive. On the way to the operating room, the anesthesiologist notes that the ventilator has been set to give too much inflation. After correcting this problem, the patient began to breathe on her own. The transplant team wants to go ahead because everything is set up for an organ transplant. The anesthesiologist refuses to assist in the operation. The surgeons tell him that they will continue without his help. He calls an administrator to stop the procedure. Several days later, the woman is able to sit up in bed and can talk to her husband.

I am certain you find these case histories just as disturbing as I have found them. In an examination of these three patients, the first and third patients were only nearly dead. The second patient was really dead by definition.[2] All 50 states use the same definition of brain death, an isoelectric (flat) EEG, no ventilatory effort, and an absence of reflexes originating in the brain. Reflexes originating in the spinal cord, as in the second example, are not considered a sign of life. In Europe, an isoelectric EEG is considered brain death.

We are bound to protect individuals until the moment of death in order to prevent what could be interpreted as murder. However, there are some special circumstances when live humans may be used for donor organs as in the case of anencephalic newborns.[3] The law considers babies born without brains *non persons*. This allows the legal use of their organs.

The problem with the use of *non persons* is just who fits into this definition. In Nazi Germany, the term *unter menchen*, which basically means the same thing, was applied eventually to cripples, the mentally retarded, the insane, and later, Gypsies and Jews in a slippery slope of unethical behavior. This is not the only slippery slope that we must avoid. As two of the three case histories illustrate, an eagerness to harvest donor organs may result in poorly diagnosed death accidentally, or possibly, deliberately.

In Medieval times, noblemen were buried with a bell they could ring if revived in their caskets. Being buried alive in that medically unenlightened era was a distinct possibility. Today, we use medical tests, some of which are dependent on the perfect functioning of complicated electronic devices. Clearly, this is wrong. Most, but not all, doctors use more than just an EEG showing no brain wave activity because the brain may recover after showing no activity, and a loose connection or malfunctioning transistor can give a false result.

It is now recommended that several things are needed before declaring a person with a beating heart a corpse.

- No brain wave activity.
- Fully reversed sedation, anesthetics, and muscle relaxants that may mimic a death-like condition by causing reduced brain wave activity and lack of responsiveness or coma.
- No attempt to breathe in the presence of normal blood gases during ventilator support.
- No cranial reflexes.
- Brain stem evoked potentials are absent. (This test is not always available.)
- No blood flow to the brain. (This test is not always available.)

---

[2] *Ad Hoc* Committee of Harvard Medical School, definition of brain death and irreversible coma. JAMA 1968: Vol. 205, pp. 85–90.

[3] Council on Ethical and Judicial Affairs, AMA. JAMA 1995: Vol. 273: pp. 1614–1618.

You will notice I did not include coma as criteria, although a person with the above conditions certainly would be in a coma.

The problem with declaring a person dead because [he or she appears] to be in a hopeless coma is a controversial problem, especially in a young person. Miraculous recoveries from coma are well recorded. Further, recent evidence indicates that the victim of coma may be aware of what is going on.

A coma victim may not fit into the definition of death as I have described it. I don't believe these people should be considered organ donors until their coma condition has been diagnosed as hopeless. This is particularly hard to do on a person who is breathing without life support and is a task that should not be undertaken lightly.

Living wills can help caregivers make a decision between life and death. Anyone making the decision between life and death must follow strict guidelines to avoid murder. Organ harvesting teams must practice with scrupulous ethics and avoid "for profit" motivation.

Equally, people should not act unethically and arrange to be paid for their organs while they are alive. The definition of a *non person* must be very clear and not subject to interpretation. Anesthesiologists must always act as a patient advocate before participating in organ harvesting.

Cancer and the Constitution — Choice at Life's End

GEORGE J. ANNAS

> **BEFORE READING:** Do you believe that patients who have exhausted all approved treatments for cancer should be allowed to take experimental drugs? What are the pros and cons?

J. M. Coetzee's violent, anti-apartheid *Age of Iron*, a novel the *Wall Street Journal* termed "a fierce pageant of modern South Africa," is written as a letter by a retired classics professor, Mrs. Curren, to her daughter, who lives in the United States. Mrs. Curren is dying of cancer, and her daughter advises her to come to the United States for treatment. She replies, "I can't afford to die in America. . . . No one can, except Americans."[1] Dying of cancer

George J. Annas is the Edward R. Utley Professor and chair of the Department of Health Law, Bioethics, and Human Rights at the Boston University School of Public Health, as well as a professor in the university's schools of medicine and law. He is cofounder of Global Lawyers and Physicians, a transnational professional association that promotes human rights and health, and is the author of twelve books on health law and bioethics. The article was published in the *New England Journal of Medicine* on July 26, 2007.

has been considered a "hard death" for at least a century, unproven and even quack remedies have been common, and price has been a secondary consideration. Efforts sponsored by the federal government to find cures for cancer date from the establishment of the National Cancer Institute (NCI) in 1937. Cancer research was intensified after President Richard Nixon's declaration of a "war on cancer" and passage of the National Cancer Act of 1971.[2] Most recently, calls for more cancer research have followed the announcement by Elizabeth Edwards, wife of presidential candidate John Edwards, that her cancer is no longer considered curable.

Frustration with the methods and slow progress of mainstream medical research has helped fuel a resistance movement that distrusts both conventional medicine and government and that has called for the recognition of a right for terminally ill patients with cancer to have access to any drugs they want to take. Prominent examples include the popularity of Krebiozen in the 1950s and of laetrile in the 1970s. As an NCI spokesperson put it more than 20 years ago, when thousands of people were calling the NCI hotline pleading for access to interleukin-2, "What the callers are saying is, 'Our mother, our brother, our sister is dying at this very moment. We have nothing to lose.' "[2] Today, families search the Internet for clinical trials, and even untested chemicals such as dichloroacetate, that seem to offer them some hope. In addition, basing advocacy on their personal experiences with cancer, many families have focused their frustrations on the Food and Drug Administration (FDA), which they see as a government agency denying them access to treatments they need.

In May 2006 these families won an apparent major victory when the Court of Appeals for the District of Columbia, in the case of *Abigail Alliance v. Von Eschenbach* (hereafter referred to as *Abigail Alliance*),[3] agreed with their argument that patients with cancer have a constitutional right of access to investigational cancer drugs. In reaction, the FDA began the process of rewriting its own regulations to make it easier for terminally ill patients not enrolled in clinical trials to have access to investigational drugs.[4] In November 2006, the full bench of the Court of Appeals vacated the May 2006 opinion, and the case was reheard in March 2007.[5] The decision of the full bench, expected by the fall, will hinge on the answer to a central question: Do terminally ill adult patients with cancer for whom there are no effective treatments have a constitutional right of access to investigational drugs their physicians think might be beneficial?[1]

The Constitutional Controversy

The Abigail Alliance for Better Access to Developmental Drugs (hereafter called the Abigail Alliance) sued the FDA to prevent it from enforcing its

---

[1] EDS. Note: On August 7, 2007, the District of Columbia Circuit Court of Appeals voted 8-2 against the Abigail Alliance, and on January 14, 2008, the Supreme Court declined to take up the issue.

policy of prohibiting the sale of drugs that had not been proved safe and effective to competent adult patients who are terminally ill and have no alternative treatment options. The Abigail Alliance is named after Abigail Burroughs, whose squamous-cell carcinoma of the head and neck was diagnosed when she was only 19 years old. Two years later, in 2001, she died. Before her death she had tried unsuccessfully to obtain investigational drugs on a compassionate use basis from ImClone and AstraZeneca and was accepted for a clinical trial only shortly before her death. Her father founded the Abigail Alliance in her memory.[6]

The district court dismissed the Abigail Alliance lawsuit. The appeals 5 court, in a two-to-one opinion written by Judge Judith Rogers, who was joined by Judge Douglas Ginsburg, reversed the decision. It concluded that competent, terminally ill adult patients have a constitutional "right to access to potentially life-saving post-Phase I investigational new drugs, upon a doctor's advice, even where that medicine carries risks for the patient," and remanded the case to the district court to determine whether the FDA's current policy violated that right.[3]

The Right to Life

The appeals court found that the relevant constitutional right was determined by the due-process clause of the Fifth Amendment: "no person shall be . . . deprived of life, liberty, or property without due process of law." In the court's words, the narrow question presented by *Abigail Alliance* is whether the due-process clause "protects the right of terminally ill patients to make an informed decision that may prolong life, specifically by use of potentially life-saving new drugs that the FDA has yet to approve for commercial marketing but that the FDA has determined, after Phase I clinical human trials, are safe enough for further testing on a substantial number of human beings."[3]

The court answered yes, finding that this right has deep legal roots in the right to self-defense, and that "Barring a terminally ill patient from the use of a potentially life-saving treatment impinges on this right of self-preservation."[3] In a footnote, the court restated this proposition: "The fundamental right to take action, even risky action, free from government interference, in order to save one's own life undergirds the court's decision."[3] The court relied primarily on the *Cruzan* case,[7] in which the Supreme Court recognized the right of a competent adult to refuse life-sustaining treatment, including a feeding tube:

> The logical corollary is that an individual must also be free to decide for
> herself whether to assume any known or unknown risks of taking a
> medication that might prolong her life. Like the right claimed in *Cruzan*,
> the right claimed by the [Abigail] Alliance to be free of FDA imposition
> does not involve treatment by the government or a government sub-
> sidy. Rather, much as the guardians of the comatose [sic] patient in

Cruzan did, the Alliance seeks to have the government step aside by changing its policy so the individual right of self-determination is not violated.[3]

The appeals court concluded that the Supreme Court's 1979 unanimous decision on laetrile,[8] in which the Court concluded that Congress had made no exceptions in the FDA law for terminally ill cancer patients, was not relevant because laetrile had never been studied in a phase 1 trial and because the Court did not address the question of whether terminally ill cancer patients have a constitutional right to take whatever drugs their physicians prescribe.

The Dissent

Judge Thomas Griffith, the dissenting judge, argued that the suggested constitutional right simply does not exist. He noted, for example, that the self-defense cases relied on are examples of "abstract concepts of personal autonomy," and cannot be used to craft new rights. As to the nation's history and traditions, he concluded that the FDA's drug-regulatory efforts have been reasonable responses "to new risks as they are presented."[3] Accepting his argument leaves the majority resting squarely on *Cruzan* and the laetrile case. As to *Cruzan*, the dissent argued that "A tradition of protecting individual *freedom* from life-saving, but forced, medical treatment does not evidence a constitutional tradition of providing affirmative *access* to a potentially harmful, even fatal, commercial good."[3] As to the laetrile case, the judge noted simply that the Court had agreed with the FDA that, "For the terminally ill, as for anyone else, a drug is unsafe if its potential for inflicting death or physical injury is not offset by the possibility of therapeutic benefit."[3,8]

Finally, the dissenting judge argued that if the new constitutional right [10] were accepted, it was too vague to be applied only to terminally ill patients seeking drugs that had been tested in phase 1 trials. Specifically, the judge asked, must the right also apply to patients with "serious medical conditions," to patients who "cannot afford potentially life-saving treatment," or to patients whose physicians believe "marijuana for medicinal purposes . . . is potentially life saving?"[3] In other words, there is no principled reason to restrict the constitutional right the majority created to either terminally ill patients or to post–phase 1 drugs.

Discussion

The facts as illustrated by stories of patients dying of cancer while trying unsuccessfully to enroll in clinical trials are compelling, and our current system of ad hoc exceptions is deeply flawed. The central constitutional issue, however, rests primarily on determining whether this case is or is not like the right-to-refuse-treatment case of Nancy Cruzan, a woman in a permanent vegetative state whose family wanted tube feeding discontinued because they believed that discontinuation was what she would have wanted. I do not think *Abigail Alliance* is like *Cruzan*. Rather, it is substantially identical to cases involving physician-assisted suicide, in which a terminally ill patient claims a constitutional right of access to physician-prescribed drugs to commit suicide.

The Supreme Court has decided, unanimously, that no right to physician-prescribed drugs for suicide exists.[9,10] There is no historical tradition of support for this right. And although the right seems to be narrowly defined, it is unclear to whom it should apply — why only to terminally ill patients? Don't patients in chronic pain have even a stronger interest in suicide? Why is the physician necessary, and why are physician-prescribed drugs the only acceptable method of suicide? None of these questions can be answered by examining the Constitution.[11]

Similarly, in *Abigail Alliance*, the new constitutional right proposed has no tradition in the United States, and it cannot be narrowly applied. For example, why should a constitutional right apply only to people who have a particular medical status? And why should a physician be involved at all? If patients have a right to autonomy, why isn't the requirement of a government-licensed physician's recommendation at least as burdensome as the requirement of the FDA's approval of the investigational drug? And why would the Constitution apply only to investigational drugs for which phase 1 trials have been completed? Why not include access to investigational medical devices, like the artificial heart, or even to Schedule I controlled substances, like marijuana or lysergic acid diethylamide (LSD)? If it is a constitutional right, these should be available too, at least unless the state can demonstrate a "compelling interest" in regulating them.

My prediction is that after rehearing this case en banc, the full Circuit Court will reject the position of the Abigail Alliance for the same reasons that the Supreme Court rejected the "right" of terminally ill patients to have access to physician-prescribed drugs they could use to end their lives.[9,10,11] To decide otherwise would entirely undermine the legitimacy of the FDA. Patients in the United States have always had a right to refuse any medical treatment, but we have never had a right to demand mistreatment, inappropriate treatment, or even investigational or experimental interventions. This will not, however, be the end of the matter. After the physician-assisted–suicide cases, the fight appropriately shifted to the states, although so far only one, Oregon, has provided its physicians with immunity for prescribing life-ending drugs to their competent, terminally ill patients.[12] In the *Abigail Alliance* case, the debate will continue in the forum in which it began — the FDA — and in Congress.

Congress

Congressional action also had its birth with the story of one patient with cancer and was also heavily influenced by another individual patient involved in a controversy over removal of a feeding tube. "Terri's Law" was enacted in Florida in 2003 to try to prevent the removal of a feeding tube from Terri Schiavo; the case was substantially similar to *Cruzan*. Terri's case gained national attention 2 years later.[13] In the midst of it, in March 2005, the *Wall Street Journal* asserted, in an editorial titled "How About a 'Kianna's Law'?," "If Terri Schiavo deserves emergency federal intervention to save her life, people like Kianna Karnes deserve it even more."[14] At the time, Kianna Karnes was a 44-year-old mother of four who was dying of kidney cancer. Her only hope of survival, according to the editorial, was to gain access to one of two experimental drugs in clinical trials, but neither of the two companies running the trials (Bayer and Pfizer) would make the drugs available to her on a compassionate-use basis. This was because, according to the *Wall Street Journal*, the FDA "makes it all but impossible" for the manufacturers "to provide [drugs] to terminal patients on a 'compassionate use' basis."[14]

Almost immediately after the editorial was published, both drug manufacturers contacted Kianna's physicians to discuss releasing the drugs to her. But within 2 days after publication, she was dead. The *Wall Street Journal* editorialized, "Isn't it a national scandal that cancer sufferers should have to be written about in the *Wall Street Journal* to be offered legal access to emerging therapies once they've run out of other options?"[15] It noted that Mrs. Karnes' father, John Rowe—himself a survivor of leukemia—was working with the Abigail Alliance on a "Kianna's Law." That law, formally titled the "Access, Compassion, Care, and Ethics for Seriously Ill Patients Act" or the "ACCESS Act," was introduced in November 2005 and is an attempt to make it much easier for seriously ill patients to gain access to experimental drugs.[16,17]

The act begins with a series of congressional findings, including that "Seriously ill patients have a right to access available investigational drugs, biological products, and devices." The act permits the sponsor to apply for approval to make an investigational drug, biologic product, or device available on the basis of data from a completed phase 1 trial, "preliminary evidence that the product may be effective against a serious or life-threatening condition or disease," and an assurance that the clinical trial will continue.[17] The patient, who must have exhausted all approved treatments, must provide written informed consent and must also sign "a written waiver of the right to sue the manufacturer or sponsor of the drug, biological product, or device, or the physicians who prescribed the product or the institution where it was administered, for an adverse event caused by the product, which shall be binding in every State and Federal court."[17]

Although Congress is the proper forum to address this issue, this initial attempt has some of the same problems as the *Abigail Alliance* decision: the patients to whom it applies are ambiguously classified, and clinical research seems to be equated with clinical care. Also troubling is that the patients (and would-be subjects) are asked to assume all of the risks of the uncontrolled experiments, and current rules of research—which protect subjects by prohibiting mandatory waivers of rights—are jettisoned, with the requirement of such waivers becoming the price of obtaining the investigational agent from an otherwise reluctant drug company.

FDA Proposal

In direct response to *Abigail Alliance*, the FDA proposed amending its rules to encourage more drug companies to offer their investigational drugs through compassionate-use programs.[4] These programs first came into prominence during the early days of infection with the human immunodeficiency virus (HIV) and AIDS, when there were no effective treatments and AIDS activists insisted that they have early access to investigational drugs because, in the words of their inaccurate slogan, "A Research Trial Is Treatment Too."[18] Because the FDA could not stand the political pressure generated by the activists, the compassionate-use program was developed as a kind of political safety valve to provide enough exceptions to save their basic research rules. In early December 2006, the FDA continued this political-safety-valve approach by issuing new proposed regulations with a title that could have been taken directly from the AIDS Coalition to Unleash Power (ACT-UP): "Expanded Access to Investigational Drugs for Treatment Use."[19]

The FDA's expanded-access proposal applies to "seriously ill patients 20 when there is no comparable or satisfactory alternative therapy to diagnose, monitor, or treat the patient's disease or condition."[4] Manufacturers are required to file an "expanded access submission," and the product must be administered or dispensed by a licensed physician who will be considered an "investigator," with all the reporting requirements that role entails.[3]

Whether or not the proposal is adopted, it will do little to increase access, since the major bottleneck in the compassionate-use program has never been the FDA. The manufacturers have no incentives to make their investigational products available outside clinical trials. This is because direct access to investigational drugs by individuals may make it more difficult to recruit research subjects, and thus to conduct the clinical trials necessary for drug approval, and could also subject the drug manufacturer to liability for serious adverse reactions. Even without a lawsuit, a serious reaction to a drug outside a trial could adversely affect the trial itself.[4,16,20] The drug companies are right to worry that the approaches of the judiciary, Congress, and the FDA will probably make clinical trials more difficult to conduct, because few seriously ill patients who have exhausted conventional treatments would rather be randomly assigned to an investigational drug than have a guarantee that they will receive the investigational drug their physician recommends for them. This could result in significant delays in the approval and overall availability of drugs that demonstrate effectiveness—a result no one favors. Even if patients with cancer are willing buyers, drug manufacturers are not willing sellers.

Physicians and Patients

The cover story for all the proposed changes is patients' choice. But without scientific evidence of the risks and benefits of a drug, choice cannot be informed, and for seriously ill patients, fear of death will predictably overcome fear of unknown risks. This is understandable. As psychiatrist Jay Katz, the leading scholar on informed consent, has noted, when medical science seems impotent to fight nature, "all kinds of senseless interventions are tried in an unconscious effort to cure the incurable magically through a 'wonder drug,' a novel surgical procedure, or a penetrating psychological interpretation."[21] Another *Wall Street Journal* article, entitled "Saying No to Penelope,"[22] illustrates the impossibility of limiting access to unproven cancer drugs to competent adults. The article tells the story of 4-year-old Penelope, who is dying from neuroblastoma that has proved resistant to all conventional treatments. Her parents seek "anything [that] has a prayer of saving her." In her father's words, "The chance of anything bringing her back from the abyss now is very low. But the only thing I know for sure is if we don't treat her, she will die." With Penelope hospitalized and in pain, her parents continue "searching Penelope's big brown eyes for clues as to how long she wants to continue to battle for life."

It is suggested that the requirement of a physician's recommendation can safeguard against "magical thinking" and help make informed consent real.[23] But as Katz has noted, although physicians (and, he could have added, drug companies) often justify such last-ditch interventions as simply being responsive to patient needs, the interventions "may turn out to be a projection of their own needs onto patients."[21]

Government and the Market

Another recurrent theme is the belief that government regulation is evil, a central tenet of the laetrile litigation of the 1970s. The court hearing *Abigail Alliance* was correct to note that laetrile never underwent a phase 1 trial, but every indication was that the drug, also known as vitamin B_{17}, was harmless, albeit also ineffective against cancer. Laetrile became a legal cause celebre in 1972, when California physician John A. Richardson was prosecuted for promoting laetrile. Richardson was a member of the John Birch Society, which quickly formed the Committee for Freedom of Choice in Cancer Therapy, with more than 100 committees nationwide.[24] It took another 7 years before the FDA prevailed in its case against laetrile before the Supreme Court.[8] The basic arguments against FDA regulation remain the same today: the FDA follows a "paternalistic public policy that prevents individuals from exercising their own judgment about risks and benefits. If the FDA must err, it should be on the side of patients' freedom to choose."[25]

Public Policy

The FDA will prevail again today, not only because there is no constitutional right of access to unapproved drugs but also because even if there were, the state has the same compelling interest in approving drugs as it has in licensing physicians. From a public policy view, the *Abigail Alliance* court, the Congress, and the FDA all seem to be suffering from the "therapeutic illusion" in which research, designed to test a hypothesis for society, is confused with treatment, administered in the best interests of individual patients.[21,26,27] Of course there is a continuum, and it is perfectly understandable that many patients with cancer, told that there is nothing conventional medicine can do for them, will want access to whatever is available in or outside the context of clinical trials. But this is a problem for patients, physicians, the FDA, and drug manufacturers. First, because terminally ill patients can be harmed and exploited, there are better and worse ways to die.[21,26] Second, it is only through research, not "treatment," that cancer may become a chronic illness that is treated with a complex array of drugs, given either together or in a progression.[28,29] The right to choose in medicine is a central right of patients, but the choices can and should be limited to reasonable medical alternatives, which themselves are based on evidence.

This is, I believe, good public policy. But it is also much easier said than done.[30] Death is feared and even dreaded in our culture, and few Americans are able to die at home, at peace, with our loved ones in attendance, without seeking the "latest new treatment." There always seems to be something new to try, and there is almost always anecdotal evidence that it could help. This is one reason that even extremely high prices do not affect demand for cancer drugs, even ones that add little or no survival time.[31,32] When does caring for the patient demand primary attention to palliation rather than to long-shot, high-risk, investigational interventions? Coetzee's Mrs. Curren, who rejected new medical treatment for her cancer and insisted on dying at home, told her physician, whom she saw as "withdrawing" from her after giving her a terminal prognosis—"His allegiance to the living, not the dying"— "I have no illusions about my condition, doctor. It is not [experimental] care I need, just help with the pain."[1]

REFERENCES

1. Coetzee JM. Age of iron. London: Seeker & Warburg, 1990.
2. Patterson JT. The dread disease: cancer and modern American culture. Cambridge, MA: Harvard University Press, 1987.
3. Abigail Alliance v. Von Eschenbach, 445 F.3d 470 (DC Cir 2006). Vacated 469 F.3d 129 (DC Cir 2006).
4. Proposed rules for charging for investigational drugs and expanded access to investigational drugs for treatment use. Rockville, MD: Food and Drug Administration, 2006. (Accessed July 6, 2007, at http://www.fda.gov/cder/regulatory/applications/IND_PR.htm.)
5. Abigail Alliance v. Von Eschenbach, 429 F.3d 129 (DC Cir 2006).
6. Jacobson PD, Parmet WE. A new era of unapproved drugs: the case of Abigail Alliance v. Von Eschenbach. JAMA 2007;297:205–208. [Free Full Text]
7. Cruzan v. Director, Missouri Dept. of Health, 497 U.S. 261 (1990).
8. United States v. Rutherford, 442 U.S. 544 (1979).
9. Washington v. Glucksberg, 521 U.S. 702 (1997).

10. Vacco v. Quill, 521 U.S. 793 (1997).

11. Annas GJ. The bell tolls for a constitutional right to assisted suicide. N Engl J Med 1997;337:1098–1103. [Free Full Text]

12. Gonzales v. Oregon, 546 U.S. 243 (2006).

13. Annas GJ. "I want to live": medicine betrayed by ideology in the political debate over Terri Schiavo. Stetson Law Rev 2005;35:49–80. [Medline]

14. How about a "Kianna's Law"? Wall Street Journal. March 24, 2005:A14.

15. Kianna's legacy. Wall Street Journal. March 29, 2005:Al4.

16. Groopman J. The right to a trial: should dying patients have access to experimental drugs? The New Yorker. December 18, 2006:40–7.

17. ACCESS Act (Access, Compassion, Care, and Ethics for Seriously Ill Patients), S. 1956, 109th Cong (2005).

18. Annas GJ. Faith (healing), hope and charity at the FDA: the politics of AIDS drug trials Villanova Law Rev 1989;34:771–797. [Medline]

19. FDA proposes rules overhaul to expand availability of experimental drugs: the agency also clarifies permissible charges to patients. Rockville, MD: Food and Drug Administration, December 11, 2006. (Accessed July 6, 2007, at http://www.fda.gov/bbs/topics/NEWS/2006/NEW01520.html.)

20. Prud'homme A. The cell game: Sam Waksal's fast money and false promises—and the fate of ImClone's cancer drug. New York: Harper Business, 2004.

21. Katz J. The silent world of doctor and patient. New Haven, CT: Yale University Press, 1984:151.

22. Anand G. Saying no to Penelope: father seeks experimental cancer drug, but a biotech firm says risk is too high. Wall Street Journal. May 1, 2007:A1.

23. Robertson J. Controversial medical treatment and the right to health care. Hastings Cent Rep 2006;36:15–20. [CrossRef][ISI][Medline]

24. Culbert ML. Vitamin B17: Forbidden weapon against cancer. New Rochelle, NY: Arlington House, 1974.

25. Miller HI. Paternalism costs lives. Wall Street Journal. March 2, 2006:A15.

26. Annas GJ. The changing landscape of human experimentation: Nuremberg, Helsinki, and beyond. Health Matrix J Law Med 1992;2:119–40.

27. Appelbaum PS, Lidz CW. Re-evaluating the therapeutic misconception: response to Miller and Joffe. Kennedy Inst Ethics J 2006;16:367–373. [CrossRef][ISI]

28. Nathan D. The cancer treatment revolution: How smart drugs and other therapies are renewing our hope and changing the face of medicine. New York: John Wiley, 2007.

29. Brugarolas J. Renal-cell carcinoma—molecular pathways and therapies. N Engl J Med 2007;356:185–186. [Free Full Text]

30. Callahan D. False hopes: why America's quest for perfect health is a recipe for failure. New York: Simon and Schuster, 1998.

31. Berenson A. Hope, at $4,200 a dose: Why a cancer drug's cost doesn't hurt demand. New York Times. October 1, 2006:BU1.

32. Anand G. From Wall Street, a warning about cancer drug prices. Wall Street Journal. March 15, 2007:A1.

Pillow Angel Ethics

NANCY GIBBS

BEFORE READING: What are some circumstances in which what is medically possible is not ethical?

What kind of doctors would agree to intentionally shorten and sterilize a disabled six-year-old girl to make it easier for her parents to take care of her? The question has had message boards steaming for days, but the answers are in no way easy.

Dr. Daniel Gunther and Dr. Douglas Diekema, who first revealed the details of "The Ashley Case" in the *Archives of Pediatric and Adolescent Medicine*, think that many of their critics don't understand the nature of this case. Talk to them, and you confront every modern challenge in weighing what medicine can do, versus what it should.

The case: Ashley is a brain-damaged girl whose parents feared that as she got bigger, it would be much harder to care for her; so they set out to keep her small. Through high-dose estrogen treatment over the past two years, her growth plates were closed and her prospective height reduced by about 13 inches, to 4'5". "Ashley's smaller and lighter size," her parents write on their blog "makes it more possible to include her in the typical family life and activities that provide her with needed comfort, closeness, security, and love: meal time, car trips, touch, snuggles, etc." They stress that the treatment's goal was "to improve our daughter's quality of life and not to convenience her caregivers."

But the treatment went further: doctors removed her uterus to prevent potential discomfort from menstrual cramps or pregnancy in the event of rape; and also her breast tissue, because of a family history of cancer and fibrocystic disease. Not having breasts would also make the harness straps that hold her upright more comfortable. "Ashley has no need for developed breasts since she will not breast feed," her parents argue, "and their presence would only be a source of discomfort to her."

The parents say that the decision to proceed with "The Ashley Treatment" was not a hard one for them, but the same cannot be said for the doctors. "This was something people hadn't thought about being a possibility, much less being done," says Diekema, who chairs the bioethics committee of the American Academy of Pediatrics and was brought in to consult on this case. For the ethics committee of Seattle Children's Hospital, which reviewed the proposed treatment, "it took time to get past

Nancy Gibbs was named a senior editor of *Time* magazine in October 1991, chief political writer in 1996, and editor at large in 2002.

the initial response—'wow, this is bizarre'—and think seriously about the reasons for the parents' request," says Diekema.

First they had to be sure there would be no medical harm: removing breast buds, Gunther says, is a much less invasive procedure than a mastectomy. The hormone treatment was commonly used 40 years ago on lanky teenage girls who didn't want to get any taller. "The main risk," Gunther says, "is of thrombosis or blood clot, which is a risk in anybody taking estrogen. It's hard to assess in a young child because no one this young has been treated with estrogen." There were very few reports of thrombosis among the teenage patients, he says, "So I suspect the risk is fairly low. After treatment is finished, I don't see any long-term risk, and we've eliminated the risk of uterine and breast cancer."

The ethics committee essentially did a cost-benefit analysis and concluded that the rewards outweighed the risks. Keeping Ashley smaller and more portable, the doctors argue, has medical as well as emotional benefits: more movement means better circulation, digestion and muscle condition, and fewer sores and infections. "If you're going to be against this," Gunther says, "you have to argue why the benefits are not worth pursuing."

They knew that the treatment would be controversial, though they did not quite foresee the media storm that would erupt when they decided to publish the case and invite their peers to weigh in. "I felt we were doing the right thing for this little girl—but that didn't keep me from feeling a bit of unease," admits Diekema. "And that's as it should be. Humility is important in a case like this."

Gunther also understands why the case has inspired such intense feelings—but notes that "visceral reactions are not an argument for or against." This was not a girl who was ever going to grow up, he says. She was only going to grow bigger. "Some disability advocates have suggested that this course of treatment is an abuse of Ashley's 'rights' and an affront to her 'dignity.' This is a mystery to me. Is there more dignity in having to hoist a full-grown body in harness and chains from bed to bath to wheelchair? Ashley will always have the mind of an infant, and now she will be able to stay where she belongs—in the arms of the family that loves her."

But how far would Drs. Gunther and Diekema take this argument? 10 Would they agree to amputate a child's legs to keep her lighter and more portable? Hormone treatment is nowhere near as risky and disfiguring as amputation, Diekema retorts; it just accelerates a natural process by which the body stops growing. Parents of short children give them growth hormones for social more than medical reasons, he notes. How can it be O.K. to make someone "unnaturally" taller but not smaller? To warnings of a slippery slope, Gunther tilts the logic the other way: "The argument that a beneficial treatment should not be used because it might be misused is itself a slippery slope," he says. "If we did not use therapies available because they could be misused, we'd be practicing very little medicine."

"Adoption" of Frozen Embryos A Loaded Term

JEFFREY P. KAHN

BEFORE READING: Below, Kahn quotes estimates that "over 200,000 embryos are left over from in vitro fertilization (IVF) attempts to help couples have children." What do you think should be done with these "leftover" frozen embryos?

The estimates are striking: over 200,000 embryos are left over from in vitro fertilization (IVF) attempts to help couples have children. The unused embryos are frozen in labs all over the United States, waiting for a decision about what will be done with them.

Unlike other countries, most notably Britain, the United States has no rules about how long human embryos can remain frozen before a decision about their fate must be made. This has led to a growing number of unused frozen embryos, with many suggestions but little consensus about what should happen to them. As it stands, couples can leave the embryos frozen for later use, donate them to other couples, donate them for research uses, or discard them.

In late July, the Bush administration's Department of Health and Human Services announced it was making funds available to "support development and delivery of public awareness campaigns on embryo adoption." The goal is to help couples better understand their options, or to advocate for a particular option—depending on political perspective. What's interesting is the focus on "adoption" of embryos, especially to the exclusion of the other legitimate options available to couples. What does such a funding program mean for how we should think of human embryos, and for the future of reproductive technologies in the wake of stem cell research?

Can embryos be "adopted"?

The use of the term "embryo adoption" puts a particular spin on the difficult issues surrounding what should happen to frozen embryos. It makes the obvious parallel between donating embryos and adopting children. In the process, the funding program implicitly grants embryos particular moral status without argument or discussion.

Up to now, the more general term "embryo donation" has been used 5 to describe both giving embryos to other couples and donating embryos for research purposes, such as stem cell research. Both are legitimate decisions for dealing with frozen embryos, but the new focus on "adoption"

Jeffrey P. Kahn, Ph.D., M.P.H., is director and professor, Maas Family Endowed Chair in Bioethics at the Center for Bioethics at the University of Minnesota; and professor, Department of Medicine, University of Minnesota Medical School. His column "Ethics Matters" is a biweekly feature from the Center for Bioethics and CNN Interactive.

effectively narrows embryo donation to couples who will try to create pregnancies with them—research labs won't "adopt" embryos. This perspective has implications not only for reproductive medicine, but for the abortion debate as well. If embryos created by IVF deserve an emphasis on their adoption, what about those embryos created the "regular" way inside a woman's womb?

Who gets to decide?

There is nothing wrong with government efforts to inform the public about available programs. But reproductive liberty demands that individuals be free to decide whether, when, and how they will reproduce, and it remains to be seen whether the government's plan unjustifiably limits that freedom. In the end, individuals should be free to determine what should happen to the embryos that are created for them, and donating embryos to other couples is only one option.

For the federal government to fund programs to exclusively encourage donation to other couples is to use public money to endorse a particular view about the status of embryos and what should be done with them.

Most important, it is a step away from couples controlling the fate of their embryos, and toward viewing embryos as needing government protection and the help of groups that seek to "place" them with caring families. The way we're heading, it's a short step to lab freezers being called orphanages, and social workers assigned to look after the interests of their frozen charges. Is it cold in here, or is it just me?

Doctors' Beliefs Hinder Patient Care

SABRINA RUBIN ERDELY

> **BEFORE READING:** What are some situations in which a doctor's personal beliefs might interfere with his or her ability to prescribe a certain medication or perform a certain procedure?

Lori Boyer couldn't stop trembling as she sat on the examining table, hugging her hospital gown around her. Her mind was reeling. She'd been raped hours earlier by a man she knew—a man who had assured Boyer, 35, that he only wanted to hang out at his place and talk. Instead, he had thrown her onto his bed and assaulted her. "I'm done with you," he'd tonelessly told her afterward. Boyer had grabbed her clothes and

Sabrina Rubin Erdely is a writer at large for *Philadelphia* magazine who writes frequently about health issues. She is also a contributing editor at *Self* magazine. This article, in its updated form, was posted on MSNBC.com on June 22, 2007.

dashed for her car in the freezing predawn darkness. Yet she'd had the clarity to drive straight to the nearest emergency room—Good Samaritan Hospital in Lebanon, Pennsylvania—to ask for a rape kit and talk to a sexual assault counselor. Bruised and in pain, she grimaced through the pelvic exam. Now, as Boyer watched Martin Gish, M.D., jot some final notes into her chart, she thought of something the rape counselor had mentioned earlier.

"I'll need the morning-after pill," she told him.

Dr. Gish looked up. He was a trim, middle-aged man with graying hair and, Boyer thought, an aloof manner. "No," Boyer says he replied abruptly. "I can't do that." He turned back to his writing.

Boyer stared in disbelief. *No?* She tried vainly to hold back tears as she reasoned with the doctor: She was midcycle, putting her in danger of getting pregnant. Emergency contraception is most effective within a short time frame, ideally 72 hours. If he wasn't willing to write an EC prescription, she'd be glad to see a different doctor. Dr. Gish simply shook his head. "It's against my religion," he said, according to Boyer. (When contacted, the doctor declined to comment for this article.)

Boyer left the emergency room empty-handed. "I was so vulnerable," 5 she says. "I felt victimized all over again. First the rape, and then the doctor making me feel powerless." Later that day, her rape counselor found Boyer a physician who would prescribe her EC. But Boyer remained haunted by the ER doctor's refusal—so profoundly, she hasn't been to see a gynecologist in the two and a half years since. "I haven't gotten the nerve up to go, for fear of being judged again," she says.

Doctors refusing treatment

Even under less dire circumstances than Boyer's, it's not always easy talking to your doctor about sex. Whether you're asking about birth control, STDs, or infertility, these discussions can be tinged with self-consciousness, even embarrassment. Now imagine those same conversations, but supercharged by the anxiety that your doctor might respond with moral condemnation— and actually refuse your requests.

That's exactly what's happening in medical offices and hospitals around the country: Catholic and conservative Christian health care providers are denying women a range of standard, legal medical care. Planned Parenthood M.D.s report patients coming to them because other gynecologists would not dole out birth control prescriptions or abortion referrals. Infertility clinics have turned away lesbians and unmarried women; anesthesiologists and obstetricians are refusing to do sterilizations; Catholic hospitals have delayed ending doomed pregnancies because abortions are only allowed to save the life of the mother. In a survey published this year in the *New England Journal of Medicine*, 63 percent of doctors said it is acceptable to tell patients they have moral objections to treatments, and 18 percent felt no obligation to refer patients elsewhere. And in a recent SELF.com poll, nearly 1 in 20 respondents said their doctors had refused to treat them for moral, ethical, or religious reasons. "It's obscene," says Jamie D. Brooks, a former staff attorney for the National Health Law Program who continues to work on projects with the Los Angeles advocacy group. "Doctors swear an oath to serve their patients. But instead, they are allowing their religious beliefs to compromise patient care. And too often, the victims of this practice are women."

Compared with the highly publicized issue of pharmacists who refuse to dispense birth control and emergency contraception, physician refusals are a little-discussed topic. Patients denied treatment rarely complain— the situation tends to feel so humiliatingly personal. And when patients do make noise, the case is usually resolved quietly. "The whole situation was traumatizing and embarrassing, and I just wanted to put it behind me," Boyer says. She came forward only after a local newspaper reported an almost identical story: In July 2006, retail clerk Tara Harnish visited the same ER after being sexually assaulted by a stranger, was examined by the same Dr. Gish—and when her mother called Dr. Gish's office the next day to get EC for Harnish, she was refused. "Then I knew it wasn't just me, that this was a larger problem and it could happen to anybody," Boyer says.

Harnish, 21, was shocked by the way the doctor treated her. "He seemed more concerned with saving the (potential) pregnancy than he was with my health," she says. "He turned me away when I needed medical help. That's not what a doctor is supposed to do." Harnish was too shaken by her rape to pursue the matter; her mother called Harnish's gynecologist for a prescription. Then she called the newspaper. Despite the attention the story attracted, Dr. Gish continues to work at Good Samaritan Hospital. Spokesman Bill Carpenter will only say that "the issue has been resolved internally, and we're going to move forward."

In many cases, women don't even know a doctor is withholding treatment. Boyer and Harnish, for example, wouldn't have realized they'd been denied care if they'd been among the estimated one in three women who don't know about EC. In the *New England Journal of Medicine* survey, 8 percent of physicians said they felt no obligation to present all options to their patients. "When you see a doctor, you presume you're getting all the information you need to make a decision," notes Jill Morrison, senior counsel for health and reproductive rights at the National Women's Law Center in Washington, D.C. "Especially in a crisis situation, like a rape, you often don't think to question your care. But unfortunately, now we can't even trust doctors to tell us what we need to know." 10

An ethical dilemma

To many doctors, however, the issue represents a genuine ethical dilemma. "The physician's number-one creed is 'First, do no harm,'" says Sandy Christiansen, M.D., an ob/gyn in Frederick, Maryland, who is active in the Christian Medical and Dental Associations, a 16,000-member group for health care professionals based in Bristol, Tennessee. "I know that life begins at conception, and that each person has inherent value. That includes the life of the unborn." Dr. Christiansen says she will not give abortion referrals, opposes EC, and, while she has prescribed birth control, is reconsidering the morality of that position. "Doctors are people, too," she adds. "We have to be able to leave the hospital and live with ourselves. If you feel in your heart an action would cause harm to somebody—born or unborn—it's legitimate to decline to participate."

The American Medical Association in Chicago, the nation's largest physician group, effectively agrees with her; its policy allows a doctor to decline a procedure if it conflicts with her moral ideology. The law also favors medical professionals. In 1973, following *Roe v. Wade*, Congress passed the so-called Church Amendment, allowing federally funded health care providers to refuse to do abortions. In the years since, 46 states have adopted their own abortion refusal clauses—or, as proponents call them, conscience clauses—allowing doctors to opt out. Now many states have gone further. Sixteen legislatures have given doctors the right to refuse to perform sterilizations; eight states say doctors don't have to prescribe contraception. "This is about the rights of the individual, about our constitutional right to freedom of religion," says Frank Manion, an attorney with the American Center for Law and Justice, a legal group in Washington, D.C. Founded by minister Pat Robertson, the organization has represented health care providers and lobbied for laws that protect them. "We're not trying to deny anybody access to treatment," Manion adds. "We're saying, 'Don't make your choice my choice.'"

When Elizabeth Dotts walked into her new doctor's office for a gynecologic exam and checkup, she didn't realize she was treading into the front lines of a culture war. "I was just going for my annual visit, nothing out of the ordinary," says the 26-year-old YWCA grant coordinator. Dotts, who was single, had recently moved to Birmingham, Alabama, and was seeing an M.D. recommended by a coworker. The visit was unremarkable until she asked for a refill of her birth control prescription. That's when the doctor informed her that he was Catholic and the pills were against his religion.

"The look he gave me actually made me feel ashamed," Dotts says. "Like I had this wild and crazy sex life. Like he was trying to protect me from myself." Her bewilderment quickly turned to anger—"I thought, 'Wait, what in the world? Where am I?'"—especially when she remembered that her insurance covered only one annual gynecology checkup. Dotts, who'd majored in religion in college, got tough with the doctor.

"I'm glad for you that you're faithful," she told him. "But don't push   15
it on me. I'm here for my treatment, and I expect you to give it to me." Five minutes of verbal sparring later, the doctor relented with a six-month prescription—but only after Dotts told him she had been put on the Pill to relieve menstrual cramping, not to prevent pregnancy. Dotts grabbed the prescription and left, resolving to find herself a new gynecologist. "Before, walking into a doctor's office, I assumed we were on the same side," she says. "I don't make that assumption now. I ask a million questions and advocate for myself."

Bills to protect patients

This tug-of-war between physicians and patients is playing out in state legislatures, where a handful of bills aim to protect women. A Pennsylvania proposal, for example, would compel ER doctors to provide rape victims with information about emergency contraception and to dispense it on request—a law already on the books in California, Massachusetts, New Jersey, New Mexico, New York, Ohio, and Washington. A federal version of the bill is under consideration by a House subcommittee.

But such efforts have been more than matched by those of conscience-clause activists. Since 2005, 27 states introduced bills to widen refusal clauses. Four states are considering granting carte blanche refusal rights—much like the law adopted by Mississippi in 2004, which allows any health care provider to refuse practically anything on moral grounds. "It's written so broadly, there's virtually no protection for patients," says Adam Sonfield, senior public policy associate for the Washington, D.C., office of the Guttmacher Institute, a reproductive-health research group. Sonfield notes that many refusal clauses do not require providers to warn women about restrictions on services or to refer them elsewhere. "You have to balance doctors' rights with their responsibilities to patients, employers, and communities," he adds. "Doctors shouldn't be forced to provide services, but they can't just abandon patients."

In theory, the laws aren't aimed solely at women's health—a bill in New Jersey lists eye doctors and prosthetics technicians as examples of providers who'd be allowed to refuse care based on their beliefs. But Morrison warns women not to be fooled. "I ask you, what belief would keep someone from fitting a patient with a prosthetic limb?" she asks. "What they're really after is limiting access to women's health care. Reproductive health is seen as something other than regular health care"—not a straightforward matter of treating and healing, but something laden with morality—"and if you treat it that way, it becomes something providers can say yes or no to." Men, for the most part, escape such scrutiny: It's pretty hard to imagine someone being made to feel he's going straight to hell for choosing to take Viagra or get a vasectomy. And if women come to fear their doctors' judgments, a new set of problems can develop. "Then you have women who don't communicate with their doctors or avoid getting care," Morrison warns. "Any way you look at it, it's dangerous for women."

Complaint filed, but case closed

The stakes were high for Realtor Cheryl Bray when she visited a physician in Encinitas, California, two and a half years ago. Though she was there for a routine physical, the reason for the exam was anything but routine: Then a single 41-year-old, Bray had decided to adopt a baby in Mexico and needed to prove to authorities there that she was healthy. "I was under a tight deadline," Bray remembers; she had been matched with a birth mother who was less than two months from delivering. Bray had already passed a daunting number of tests—having her taxes certified, multiple background checks, home inspections by a social worker, psychological evaluations. When she showed up at the office of Fred Salley, M.D., a new doctor a friend had recommended, she was looking forward to crossing another task off her list. Instead, 10 minutes into the appointment, Dr. Salley asked, "So, your husband is in agreement with your decision to adopt?"

"I'm not married," Bray told him.   20

"You're not?" He calmly put down his pen. "Then I'm not comfortable continuing this exam."

Bray says she tried to reason with Dr. Salley but received only an offer for a referral at some future date. Dr. Salley disputes this, telling SELF that he offered to send Bray to another doctor in his group that day. "My decision to refer Ms. Bray was not because she was unmarried; rather, it was based on my moral belief that a child should have two parental units," he adds. "Such religious beliefs are a fundamental right guaranteed by the Constitution of the United States."

Bray sobbed in her parked car for another 45 minutes before she could collect herself for the drive home. "I had a lot of pent-up emotions," she remembers. "When you are going through an adoption, you have to prove that you are a fit parent at every stage. I really felt put through the ringer, and the doctor compounded that feeling."

Bray managed to get an appointment with another physician about a month later and was approved for the adoption two weeks before her daughter, Paolina, was born. But she remained furious enough that she filed a complaint against Dr. Salley with the Medical Board of California—and then was shocked when, in April 2006, the board closed the case without taking any action. When she complained to Dr. Salley's employer, a clinic official wrote back that "based on personally held conscience and moral principles" her doctor had been within his rights to refuse her as a patient. "Apparently," she says, "it's OK to discriminate against somebody, as long as it's for religious reasons."

Providers often prevail

It's true that several lawsuits have favored health providers who refuse 25
services based on their principles. In a 2002 wrongful-termination case in Riverside County, California, for example, a born-again Christian nurse was fired for refusing to give out emergency contraception—but she was vindicated when the jury agreed that her rights had been violated, awarding her $19,000 in back pay and $28,000 for emotional distress. And in a recent case in San Diego, an appeals court ruled against 35-year-old Guadalupe Benitez. Hoping to start a family with her lesbian partner, Benitez received fertility treatments for nearly a year at North Coast Women's Care Medical Group in Encinitas. But when drugs and home inseminations failed, two doctors and a nurse all bowed out of doing an intrauterine insemination, saying their religion would not allow it.

Their reasoning is in dispute: Benitez has claimed both doctors told her they objected to her sexual orientation. Carlo Coppo, a lawyer for the doctors, says they refused because she was unmarried. Benitez, who went on to have three children with the help of another clinic, has appealed to the California Supreme Court and is awaiting its decision.

Her attorney, Jennifer C. Pizer of Lambda Legal in Los Angeles, says she's heard from numerous lesbians denied access to fertility treatments. "Reproductive medicine has given human beings choices that didn't exist in previous generations, but the rules about how we exercise those choices should be the same for all groups of people," she argues. Allowing doctors to refer a patient to someone else, she adds, is the equivalent of a restaurant telling a black person, "Go next door. We don't serve your kind here."

In the end, the women in all of the incidents above were able to get the treatment they wanted, even if they had to go elsewhere. So one could see doctor refusals as a mere inconvenience. "In 99.9 percent of these cases, the patients walk away with what they came for, and everyone's satisfied," Manion asserts. "I know there's the horror story of the lonely person in the middle of nowhere who meets one of my clients. But those cases are so rare." Access to reproductive health care, however, is already a challenge in some areas. "Out here, it's a very real issue," says Stacey Anderson of Planned Parenthood of Montana in Helena. "We have some really gigantic counties where if you're refused a service by a primary care physician or a gynecologist, you might have to drive two, three hours to find another."

Moreover, you don't need to be in a rural area to have limited access, points out attorney Brooks; all you need to be is poor. "Lower-income people who are refused health care are trapped," Brooks says. "They can't pay out of pocket for these services. And they may not have transportation to go elsewhere. So they really don't have options."

What's best for the patient

If there's one thing both sides can agree on, it's this: In an emergency, 30 doctors need to put aside personal beliefs to do what's best for the patient. But in a world guided by religious directives, even this can be a slippery proposition.

Ob/gyn Wayne Goldner, M.D., learned this lesson a few years back when a patient named Kathleen Hutchins came to his office in Manchester, New Hampshire. She was only 14 weeks pregnant, but her water had broken. Dr. Goldner delivered the bad news: Because there wasn't enough amniotic fluid left and it was too early for the fetus to survive on its own, the pregnancy was hopeless. Hutchins would likely miscarry in a matter of weeks. But in the meanwhile, she stood at risk for serious infection, which could lead to infertility or death. Dr. Goldner says his devastated patient chose to get an abortion at local Elliot Hospital. But there was a problem. Elliot had recently merged with nearby Catholic Medical Center—and as a result, the hospital forbade abortions.

"I was told I could not admit her unless there was a risk to her life," Dr. Goldner remembers. "They said, 'Why don't you wait until she has an infection or she gets a fever?' They were asking me to do something other than the standard of care. They wanted me to put her health in jeopardy." He tried admitting Hutchins elsewhere, only to discover that the nearest abortion provider was nearly 80 miles away in Lebanon, New Hampshire— and that she had no car. Ultimately, Dr. Goldner paid a taxi to drive her the hour and a half to the procedure. (The hospital merger has since dissolved, and Elliot is secular once again.)

"Unfortunately, her story is the tip of the iceberg," Dr. Goldner says. Since the early 1990s, hospitals have been steadily consolidating operations to save money; so many secular community hospitals have been bought up that, today, nearly one in five hospital beds is in a religiously owned institution, according to the nonprofit group MergerWatch in New York City.

What is standard of care?

Every Catholic hospital is bound by the ethical directives of the U.S. Conference of Catholic Bishops, which forbid abortion and sterilization (unless they are lifesaving), in vitro fertilization, surrogate motherhood, some prenatal genetic testing, all artificial forms of birth control, and the use of condoms for HIV prevention. Baptist and Seventh Day Adventist hospitals may also restrict abortions. Which means that if your local hospital has been taken over—or if you're ever rushed to the nearest hospital in an emergency—you could be in for a surprise at the services you can't get.

You wouldn't necessarily know a hospital's affiliation upon your arrival. "The name of the hospital may not change after a merger, even if its philosophy has," Morrison notes. "The community is often in the dark that changes have taken place at all." The burden to know falls entirely on the patient, who can either search the Catholic Health Association's directory of member hospitals (at CHAUSA.org) or ask her doctor outright. Either way, says Morrison, "it requires you to be an extremely educated consumer." 35

Family physician Debra Stulberg, M.D., was completing her residency in 2004 when West Suburban Medical Center in Oak Park, Illinois, was acquired by the large Catholic system Resurrection Health Care. "They assured us that patient care would be unaffected," Dr. Stulberg says. "But then I got to see the reality." The doctor was struck by the hoops women had to jump through to get basic care. "One of my patients was a mother of four who had wanted a tubal ligation at delivery but was turned down," she says. "When I saw her not long afterward, she was pregnant with unwanted twins."

And in emergency scenarios, Dr. Stulberg says, the newly merged hospital did not offer standard-of-care treatments. In one case that made the local paper, a patient came in with an ectopic pregnancy: an embryo had implanted in her fallopian tube. Such an embryo has zero chance of survival and is a serious threat to the mother, as its growth can rupture the tube. The more invasive way to treat an ectopic is to surgically remove the tube. An alternative, generally less risky way is to administer methotrexate, a drug also used for cancer. It dissolves the pregnancy but spares the tube, preserving the women's fertility. "The doctor thought the noninvasive treatment was best," Dr. Stulberg recounts. But Catholic directives specify that even in an ectopic pregnancy, doctors cannot perform "a direct abortion"—which, the on-call ob/gyn reasoned, would nix the drug option. (Surgery, on the other hand, could be considered a lifesaving measure that indirectly kills the embryo, and may be permitted.) The doctor didn't wait to take it up with the hospital's ethical committee; she told the patient to check out and head to another ER. (Citing patient confidentiality, West Suburban declined to comment, confirming only that as a Catholic hospital, it adheres to religious directives "in every instance.")

Turns out, the definition of *emergency* depends on whom you ask. Dr. Christiansen, the pro-life ob/gyn, says she would not object to either method of ending an ectopic pregnancy. "I do feel that the one indication for abortion is to save the mother's life—that's clear in my mind," she says. "But the reality is, the vast majority of abortions are elective. There are very, very few instances where the mother's life is truly in jeopardy." She can recall having seen only one such situation: During Dr. Christiansen's residency, a patient in the second trimester of pregnancy had a detached placenta; the attending physician performed an abortion to save the woman from bleeding to death. "That was a legitimate situation," Dr. Christiansen says. But in general, "it's a pure judgment call. A doctor would have to be in the situation and decide whether it constitutes a life-threatening emergency or not."

Raise your hand if you'd like to be the test case.

Does Stem Cell Advance Provide an Ethical Out?

ARTHUR CAPLAN

> **BEFORE READING:** Do you believe that it is ethical to use human embryonic stem cells to try to find cures for conditions such as diabetes, spinal cord injuries, and Parkinson's? Explain.

J ust as Congress is about to vote on a bill that would require federal funding for embryonic stem cell research, something has me tempted to join the ranks of those loony tunes who see conspiracies lurking around every corner.

Arthur Caplan, Ph.D., is the Emanuel and Robert Hart Professor of Bioethics, chair of the Department of Medical Ethics, and the Director of the Center for Bioethics at the University of Pennsylvania in Philadelphia. Caplan has authored or edited twenty-five books and over five hundred papers in medicine, science, philosophy, bioethics, and health policy journals. His most recent book is *Smart Mice, Not-So-Smart People* (2006).

The bill, the Stem Cell Research Enhancement Act of 2007, passed the Senate by a big margin in April. But just as the House prepares to vote later this week, news breaks that scientists have made progress in finding alternative ways to generate cells from other types of cells that can mimic the special powers of embryonic stem cells.

Convenient timing for those who oppose embryonic stem cell research, isn't it?

It's certainly not the first time a scientific "breakthrough" has promised an alternative to embryonic stem cells just as funding issues were under debate. It has happened so often that even the wolf is no longer listening to the boy crying out, "there are alternatives!" Except this time, there is a big difference. There really has been a breakthrough.

Today's news about other ways to create embryonic-like stem cells, 5 published in the journals *Nature* and *Stem Cell*, comes from mainstream, cutting-edge, world-class scientists. This is news worth listening to.

Rudi Jaenisch, a leading expert on cloning, and teams of scientists at the Whitehead Institute for Biomedical Research and the Massachusetts Institute of Technology were able to do some elegant engineering in which they genetically tweaked skin cells in mice to reprogram themselves and act like embryonic cells. They used artificial viruses to carry genetic information into a large batch of mice skin cells to turn on certain regulatory genes in the cells that normally only work in embryos. By injecting the reprogrammed cells with markers into early-stage mouse embryos, researchers were able to show that these reprogrammed cells turned into all manner of cells in the adult mice that grew from the embryos. That is exactly what stem cell researchers are seeking—cells that could be manipulated to turn into other types of cells to repair diseased ones in our bodies.

This is very big news indeed. So why bother with a vote in Congress on funding human embryonic stem cell research? Shouldn't we simply put all of our federal funds into this type of reprogramming research?

End to ethical quandary?

That would make President Bush and others who oppose the destruction of human embryos happy. And those who want to see progress made in trying to cure conditions such as diabetes, spinal cord injuries, and Parkinson's disease should be pleased as well. Ethical dilemma solved!

Well, not so fast. I'm afraid that ditching embryos and jumping to fund alternatives is not the right response to this fascinating news about mouse cells.

This research is promising, but it's in *mice*. Many technical hurdles re- 10 main for translating this work to human cells. Some of the techniques used by the MIT scientists to isolate embryonic mouse cells are known not to work in human cells. Also, using cells that have been changed by means of viral vectors can pose health risks. This form of gene therapy has proven very difficult to do safely in human beings.

It is certainly true that the reprogramming option in both animal and human cells deserves funding, but so does human embryonic stem cell research.

As much as critics of this field of research would like to have you believe that human embryos in dishes are people, that moral argument is not compelling.

Human embryos in dishes are not people or even potential people. They are, at best, *possible* potential people.

Frozen embryos in infertility clinics face a fate of certain destruction anyway. The moral case against using them, or cloned embryos, which have almost zero chance of becoming people, is no less compelling because progress has been made in another area of research.

The existence of a new way to perhaps make embryonic-like stem   15 cells is not enough to make frozen embryos and cloned embryos off-limits for American scientists or for research relying on federal funds.

Those in favor of human embryonic stem cell research, and that is the majority of Americans according to most polls, including one done by CNN just last month, do not have to change their minds about the morality of such research even when another avenue for creating embryonic-like cells is found in mice.

Explore all possible avenues

If you are an Iraq War veteran stuck in a wheelchair, if you are taking care of your father who is losing his ability to walk due to Parkinson's, if your child suffers from juvenile diabetes, or if you need new skin as a result of terrible burns, you want scientists to pursue all the ethical options available for stem cell research. No one knows for sure whether any of them will work. But it is certain that if they are not all aggressively pursued with generous federal support, then the chance of any line of research ever turning into a therapy is greatly reduced.

The House should pass the Stem Cell Research Enhancement Act of 2007. President Bush will surely veto it, undoubtedly invoking this latest work on reprogramming adult cells as one of his reasons. Congress should then override that veto.

On the frontiers of science, good news about one promising route should not cause anyone to abandon other possible roads until someone actually gets to where they are trying to go—in this case, the goal is new cures for the sick, the dying, and the severely disabled.

Too many lives are riding on this to be fooled into taking the wrong   20 detour.

THINKING AND WRITING ABOUT MEDICAL ETHICS

QUESTIONS FOR DISCUSSION AND WRITING

1. Why do advances in medicine so often bring ethical complications? What examples come to mind?

2. If you were a doctor, are there situations in which your personal beliefs might preclude your prescribing a certain medication or performing a certain procedure? How would you justify this to your patients?

3. Sometimes parents will not allow their children to have certain types of medical care (such as blood transfusions) because of their religious beliefs. Doctors have on occasion gone to court to win the right to go against the parents' wishes. Could you ever support such a move? Why, or why not? Under what circumstances?

4. If the choice were yours, would you be willing to permit the harvesting of a loved one's organs? On what would you base your decision?

5. What factors should enter into the decision as to who should receive donor organs? Should a patient who receives a donor organ be expected to donate his or her organs at death?

6. Do you believe that patients who receive donor organs should meet the living donors who donated them? What are the pros and cons?

7. Summarize the main points in Annas's argument. How convincing is his argument?

8. How convincing did you find Ashley's parents' argument in "Pillow Angel Ethics"?

9. Explain why Kahn's argument in " 'Adoption' of Frozen Embryos a Loaded Term" is based largely on definition. Or do the same for Howards's "Ethics of Organ Donation."

10. Explain why, to you, the use of human embryonic stem cells in research is an ethical problem or not.

11. Speculate as to some ethical dilemmas in the field of medicine that are likely to arise in the future.

12. Explain how both Victory's and Howards's arguments are strengthened by the use of examples. Which other author or authors here use examples as a major type of support?

13. Do you find Victory's argument convincing support for national health care? Explain.

14. Research and report the outcome of the case of *Abigail Alliance v. Von Eschenbach*.

15. Write a defense of your position on human embryonic stem-cell research.

TOPICS FOR RESEARCH

Ethics of cloning

Use of human embryos

Organ harvesting

Use of animals for medical testing

Euthanasia

Concept of "informed consent"

CHAPTER 21

How Has Terrorism Affected the American Idea of Justice?

September 11, 2001, has been called a day that changed America. Some of the changes were immediate, horrifying, and painful. Thousands of families mourned the loss of loved ones. Thousands more mourned the loss of friends and coworkers. Almost all mourned the loss of a sense of security that our nation may never experience again.

The changes in America that followed the attacks of September 11 are felt in small ways like having to go through increased security at airports. We have our backpacks and purses searched to enter football games, museums, and even those national monuments that are still open to the public. And the changes that followed those attacks are felt in large ways like losing thousands of soldiers in Iraq or wondering if it could be one of our schools next that is taken over by armed foreigners.

Just as the aftermath of September 11 has threatened the American way of life, it has also threatened the American system of justice. Abuse at Abu Ghraib Prison in Iraq brought before us vivid and startling pictures of Americans caught in the act at the very site where Saddam Hussein became notorious for the mistreatment and torture of his people. Americans were supposed to offer something better to a nation we had gone to war to help. Newspapers worldwide carried front-page stories that questioned whether America was any longer in a position to boast about justice.

As accusations about who was responsible for what happened at Abu Ghraib worked their way up the chain of command, it became increasingly clear that questions had earlier been passed up along the same chain of command about how far interrogators could go in their attempt to elicit from prisoners information that might foil future terrorist attacks.

There were also hard-to-answer questions about how terrorists should be tried in our country. Our court system is designed to give the accused the greatest possible protection under the law. But what if the accused is suspected of having plotted the bombing of the World Trade Center and the Pentagon? What if the accused just doesn't look "American" enough? Ironically, those who participated in the atrocities at Abu Ghraib looked surprisingly like the kids next door.

The USA PATRIOT Act:
Preserving Life and Liberty

WWW.LIFEANDLIBERTY.GOV

> **BEFORE READING:** In what ways, large or small, has your life been affected by the increased security that followed the terrorist attacks of September 11, 2001?

*C*ongress *enacted the Patriot Act by overwhelming, bipartisan margins, arming law enforcement with new tools to detect and prevent terrorism:* The USA Patriot Act was passed nearly unanimously by the Senate 98–1, and 357–66 in the House, with the support of members from across the political spectrum.

The Act Improves Our Counterterrorism Efforts in Several Significant Ways:

1. *The Patriot Act allows investigators to use the tools that were already available to investigate organized crime and drug trafficking.* Many of the tools the act provides to law enforcement to fight terrorism have been used for decades to fight organized crime and drug dealers, and have been reviewed and approved by the courts. As Senator Joseph Biden (D-Delaware) explained during the floor debate about the act, "the FBI could get a wiretap to investigate the Mafia, but they could not get one to investigate terrorists. To put it bluntly, that was crazy! What's good for the mob should be good for terrorists." (*Congressional Record*, 10/25/01)

- *Allows law enforcement to use surveillance against more crimes of terror.* Before the Patriot Act, courts could permit law enforcement to conduct electronic surveillance to investigate many ordinary, non-terrorism crimes, such as drug crimes, mail fraud, and passport fraud.

This explanation of the effects of the USA Patriot Act (Uniting and Strengthening America by Providing Appropriate Tools Required to Intercept and Obstruct Terrorism) is found on the Department of Justice Web site at www.lifeandliberty.gov.

Agents also could obtain wiretaps to investigate some, but not all, of the crimes that terrorists often commit. The act enabled investigators to gather information when looking into the full range of terrorism-related crimes, including chemical-weapons offenses, the use of weapons of mass destruction, killing Americans abroad, and terrorism financing.

- *Allows federal agents to follow sophisticated terrorists trained to evade detection.* For years, law enforcement has been able to use "roving wiretaps" to investigate ordinary crimes, including drug offenses and racketeering. A roving wiretap can be authorized by a federal judge to apply to a particular suspect rather than a particular phone or communications device. Because international terrorists are sophisticated and trained to thwart surveillance by rapidly changing locations and communication devices such as cell phones, the act authorized agents to seek court permission to use the same techniques in national security investigations to track terrorists.

- *Allows law enforcement to conduct investigations without tipping off terrorists.* In some cases if criminals are tipped off too early to an investigation, they might flee, destroy evidence, intimidate or kill witnesses, cut off contact with associates, or take other action to evade arrest. Therefore, federal courts in narrow circumstances long have allowed law enforcement to delay for a limited time when the subject is told that a judicially approved search warrant has been executed. Notice is always provided, but the reasonable delay gives law enforcement time to identify the criminal's associates, eliminate immediate threats to our communities, and coordinate the arrests of multiple individuals without tipping them off beforehand. These delayed notification search warrants have been used for decades, have proven crucial in drug and organized crime cases, and have been upheld by courts as fully constitutional.

- *Allows federal agents to ask a court for an order to obtain business records in national security terrorism cases.* Examining business records often provides the key that investigators are looking for to solve a wide range of crimes. Investigators might seek select records from hardware stores or chemical plants, for example, to find out who bought materials to make a bomb, or bank records to see who's sending money to terrorists. Law enforcement authorities have always been able to obtain business records in criminal cases through grand jury subpoenas and continue to do so in national security cases where appropriate. These records were sought in criminal cases such as the investigation of the Zodiac gunman, where police suspected the gunman was inspired by a Scottish occult poet and wanted to learn who had checked the poet's books out of the library. In national security cases where use of the grand jury process was not appropriate, investigators previously had limited tools at their disposal to obtain certain business records. Under the Patriot Act, the government can now ask a federal court (the Foreign Intelligence Surveillance Court), if needed to aid an investigation, to order production of the same type of records available through grand jury subpoenas. This federal court, however, can issue these orders only after the government demonstrates the records concerned are sought for an authorized investigation to obtain foreign intelligence information not concerning a U.S. person or to protect against international terrorism or clandestine intelligence activities, provided that such investigation of a U.S. person is not conducted solely on the basis of activities protected by the First Amendment.

2. The Patriot Act facilitated information sharing and cooperation among government agencies so that they can better "connect the dots." The act removed the major legal barriers that prevented the law enforcement, intelligence, and national defense communities from talking and coordinating their work to protect the American people and our national security. The government's prevention efforts should not be restricted by boxes on an organizational chart. Now police officers, FBI agents, federal prosecutors, and intelligence officials can protect our communities by "connecting the dots" to uncover terrorist plots before they are completed. As Senator John Edwards (D-North Carolina) said about the Patriot Act, "we simply cannot prevail in the battle against terrorism if the right hand of our government has no idea what the left hand is doing." (Press release, 10/26/01)

- Prosecutors can now share evidence obtained through grand juries with intelligence officials — and intelligence information can now be shared more easily with federal prosecutors. Such sharing of information leads to concrete results. For example, a federal grand jury recently indicted an individual in Florida, Sami al-Arian, for allegedly being the U.S. leader of the Palestinian Islamic Jihad, one of the world's most violent terrorist outfits. Palestinian Islamic Jihad is responsible for murdering more than one hundred innocent people, including a young American named Alisa Flatow who was killed in a tragic bus bombing in Gaza. The Patriot Act assisted us in obtaining the indictment by enabling the full sharing of information and advice about the case among prosecutors and investigators. Alisa's father, Steven Flatow, has said, "When you know the resources of your government are committed to right the wrongs committed against your daughter, that instills you with a sense of awe. As a father, you can't ask for anything more."

3. The Patriot Act updated the law to reflect new technologies and new threats. The act brought the law up to date with current technology, so we no longer have to fight a digital-age battle with antique weapons — legal authorities left over from the era of rotary telephones. When investigating the murder of *Wall Street Journal* reporter Daniel Pearl, for example, law enforcement used one of the act's new authorities to use high-tech means to identify and locate some of the killers.

- *Allows law enforcement officials to obtain a search warrant anywhere a terrorist-related activity occurred.* Before the Patriot Act, law enforcement personnel were required to obtain a search warrant in the district where they intended to conduct a search. However, modern terrorism investigations often span a number of districts, and officers therefore had to obtain multiple warrants in multiple jurisdictions, creating unnecessary delays. The act provides that warrants can be obtained in any district in which terrorism-related activities occurred, regardless of where they will be executed. This provision does not change the standards governing the availability of a search warrant but streamlines the search-warrant process.

- *Allows victims of computer hacking to request law enforcement assistance in monitoring the "trespassers" on their computers.* This change made the law technology-neutral; it placed electronic trespassers on the same footing as physical trespassers. Now, hacking victims can seek law enforcement assistance to combat hackers, just as burglary victims have been able to invite officers into their homes to catch burglars.

4. *The Patriot Act increased the penalties for those who commit terrorist crimes.* Americans are threatened as much by the terrorist who pays for a bomb as by the one who pushes the button. That's why the Patriot Act imposed tough new penalties on those who commit and support terrorist operations, both at home and abroad. In particular, the act:

- *Prohibits the harboring of terrorists.* The act created a new offense that prohibits knowingly harboring persons who have committed or are about to commit a variety of terrorist offenses, such as destruction of aircraft; use of nuclear, chemical, or biological weapons; use of weapons of mass destruction; bombing of government property; sabotage of nuclear facilities; and aircraft piracy.

- *Enhanced the inadequate maximum penalties for various crimes likely to be committed by terrorists,* including arson, destruction of energy facilities, material support to terrorists and terrorist organizations, and destruction of national-defense materials.

- *Enhanced a number of conspiracy penalties,* including for arson, killings in federal facilities, attacking communications systems, material support to terrorists, sabotage of nuclear facilities, and interference with flight crew members. Under previous law, many terrorism statutes did not specifically prohibit engaging in conspiracies to commit the underlying offenses. In such cases, the government could only bring prosecutions under the general federal conspiracy provision, which carries a maximum penalty of only five years in prison.

• *Punishes terrorist attacks on mass transit systems.*

• *Punishes bioterrorists.*

• *Eliminates the statutes of limitations for certain terrorism crimes and lengthens them for other terrorist crimes.*

The government's success in preventing another catastrophic attack on the American homeland since September 11, 2001, would have been much more difficult, if not impossible, without the USA Patriot Act. The authorities Congress provided have substantially enhanced our ability to prevent, investigate, and prosecute acts of terror.

Surveillance under the USA PATRIOT Act

AMERICAN CIVIL LIBERTIES UNION

> BEFORE READING: Do you ever feel that our nation has too many laws designed to protect the rights of those accused of wrongdoing? Explain.

What Is the USA PATRIOT Act?

Just six weeks after the September 11 attacks, a panicked Congress passed the "USA Patriot Act," an overnight revision of the nation's surveillance laws that vastly expanded the government's authority to spy on its own citizens, while simultaneously reducing checks and balances on those powers like judicial oversight, public accountability, and the ability to challenge government searches in court.

Why Congress Passed the Patriot Act

Most of the changes to surveillance law made by the Patriot Act were part of a long-standing law enforcement wish list that had been previously rejected by Congress, in some cases repeatedly. Congress reversed course because it was bullied into it by the Bush administration in the frightening weeks after the September 11 attack.

The Senate version of the Patriot Act, which closely resembled the legislation requested by Attorney General John Ashcroft, was sent straight to the floor with no discussion, debate, or hearings. Many senators complained

---

This article is from the Web site of the American Civil Liberties Union and the ACLU Foundation, www.aclu.org.

that they had little chance to read it, much less analyze it, before having to vote. In the House, hearings were held, and a carefully constructed compromise bill emerged from the Judiciary Committee. But then, with no debate or consultation with rank-and-file members, the House leadership threw out the compromise bill and replaced it with legislation that mirrored the Senate version. Neither discussion nor amendments were permitted, and once again members barely had time to read the thick bill before they were forced to cast an up-or-down vote on it. The Bush administration implied that members who voted against it would be blamed for any further attacks — a powerful threat at a time when the nation was expecting a second attack to come any moment and when reports of new anthrax letters were appearing daily.

Congress and the administration acted without any careful or systematic effort to determine whether weaknesses in our surveillance laws had contributed to the attacks, or whether the changes they were making would help prevent further attacks. Indeed, many of the act's provisions have nothing at all to do with terrorism.

The Patriot Act increases the government's surveillance powers in four   5
areas:

1. Records searches. It expands the government's ability to look at records on an individual's activity being held by third parties. (Section 215)

2. Secret searches. It expands the government's ability to search private property without notice to the owner. (Section 213)

3. Intelligence searches. It expands a narrow exception to the Fourth Amendment that had been created for the collection of foreign intelligence information. (Section 218)

4. "Trap and trace" searches. It expands another Fourth Amendment exception for spying that collects "addressing" information about the origin and destination of communications, as opposed to the content. (Section 214)

1. Expanded Access to Personal Records Held by Third Parties

One of the most significant provisions of the Patriot Act makes it far easier for the authorities to gain access to records of citizens' activities being held by a third party. At a time when computerization is leading to the creation of more and more such records, Section 215 of the Patriot Act allows the FBI to force anyone at all — including doctors, libraries, bookstores, universities, and Internet service providers — to turn over records on their clients or customers.

The result is unchecked government power to rifle through individuals' financial records, medical histories, Internet usage, bookstore purchases, library usage, travel patterns, or any other activity that leaves a record. Making matters worse:

- The government no longer has to show evidence that the subjects of search orders are an "agent of a foreign power," a requirement that previously protected Americans against abuse of this authority.

- The FBI does not even have to show a reasonable suspicion that the records are related to criminal activity, much less the requirement for "probable cause" that is listed in the Fourth Amendment to the Constitution. All the government needs to do is make the broad assertion that the request is related to an ongoing terrorism or foreign intelligence investigation.

- Judicial oversight of these new powers is essentially nonexistent. The government must only certify to a judge—with no need for evidence or proof—that such a search meets the statute's broad criteria, and the judge does not even have the authority to reject the application.

- Surveillance orders can be based in part on a person's First Amendment activities, such as the books they read, the Web sites they visit, or a letter to the editor they have written.

- A person or organization forced to turn over records is prohibited from disclosing the search to anyone. As a result of this gag order, the subjects of surveillance never even find out that their personal records have been examined by the government. That undercuts an important check and balance on this power: the ability of individuals to challenge illegitimate searches.

Section 215 of the Patriot Act violates the Constitution in several ways. It:

- Violates the Fourth Amendment, which says the government cannot conduct a search without obtaining a warrant and showing probable cause to believe that the person has committed or will commit a crime.

- Violates the First Amendment's guarantee of free speech by prohibiting the recipients of search orders from telling others about those orders, even where there is no real need for secrecy.

- Violates the First Amendment by effectively authorizing the FBI to launch investigations of American citizens in part for exercising their freedom of speech.

- Violates the Fourth Amendment by failing to provide notice—even after the fact—to persons whose privacy has been compromised. Notice is also a key element of due process, which is guaranteed by the Fifth Amendment.

2. More Secret Searches

For centuries, common law has required that the government can't go into your property without telling you, and must therefore give you notice before it executes a search. That "knock and announce" principle has long been recognized as a part of the Fourth Amendment to the Constitution.

The Patriot Act, however, unconstitutionally amends the Federal Rules 10 of Criminal Procedure to allow the government to conduct searches without notifying the subjects, at least until long after the search has been executed. This means that the government can enter a house, apartment, or office with a search warrant when the occupants are away, search through their property, take photographs, and in some cases even seize property — and not tell them until later.

Notice is a crucial check on the government's power because it forces the authorities to operate in the open, and allows the subjects of searches to protect their Fourth Amendment rights. For example, it allows them to point out irregularities in a warrant, such as the fact that the police are at the wrong address, or that the scope of the warrant is being exceeded (for example, by rifling through dresser drawers in a search for a stolen car). Search warrants often contain limits on what may be searched, but when the searching officers have complete and unsupervised discretion over a search, a property owner cannot defend his or her rights.

Finally, this new "sneak and peek" power can be applied as part of normal criminal investigations; it has nothing to do with fighting terrorism or collecting foreign intelligence.

3. Expansion of the Intelligence Exception in Wiretap Law

Under the Patriot Act, the FBI can secretly conduct a physical search or wiretap on American citizens to obtain evidence of crime without proving probable cause, as the Fourth Amendment explicitly requires.

A 1978 law called the Foreign Intelligence Surveillance Act (FISA) created an exception to the Fourth Amendment's requirement for probable cause when the purpose of a wiretap or search was to gather foreign intelligence. The rationale was that since the search was not conducted for the purpose of gathering evidence to put someone on trial, the standards could be loosened. In a stark demonstration of why it can be dangerous to create exceptions to fundamental rights, however, the Patriot Act expanded this once-narrow exception to cover wiretaps and searches that DO collect evidence for regular domestic criminal cases. FISA previously allowed searches only if the primary purpose was to gather foreign intelligence. But the Patriot Act changes the law to allow searches when "a significant purpose" is intelligence. That lets the government circumvent the Constitution's probable cause requirement even when its main goal is ordinary law enforcement.

The eagerness of many in law enforcement to dispense with the re- 15 quirements of the Fourth Amendment was revealed in August 2002 by the secret court that oversees domestic intelligence spying (the "FISA Court"). Making public one of its opinions for the first time in history, the court revealed that it had rejected an attempt by the Bush administration to allow criminal prosecutors to use intelligence warrants to evade the Fourth

Amendment entirely. The court also noted that agents applying for warrants had regularly filed false and misleading information. That opinion is now on appeal.

4. Expansion of the "Pen Register" Exception in Wiretap Law

Another exception to the normal requirement for probable cause in wiretap law is also expanded by the Patriot Act. Years ago, when the law governing telephone wiretaps was written, a distinction was created between two types of surveillance. The first allows surveillance of the content or meaning of a communication, and the second only allows monitoring of the transactional or addressing information attached to a communication. It is like the difference between reading the address printed on the outside of a letter, and reading the letter inside, or listening to a phone conversation and merely recording the phone numbers dialed and received.

Wiretaps limited to transactional or addressing information are known as "Pen register/trap and trace" searches (for the devices that were used on telephones to collect telephone numbers). The requirements for getting a PR/TT warrant are essentially nonexistent: the FBI need not show probable cause or even reasonable suspicion of criminal activity. It must only certify to a judge—without having to prove it—that such a warrant would be "relevant" to an ongoing criminal investigation. And the judge does not even have the authority to reject the application.

The Patriot Act broadens the pen register exception in two ways:

"Nationwide" pen register warrants. Under the Patriot Act PR/TT orders issued by a judge are no longer valid only in that judge's jurisdiction but can be made valid anywhere in the United States. This "nationwide service" further marginalizes the role of the judiciary because a judge cannot meaningfully monitor the extent to which his or her order is being used. In addition, this provision authorizes the equivalent of a blank warrant: The court issues the order, and the law enforcement agent fills in the places to be searched. That is a direct violation of the Fourth Amendment's explicit requirement that warrants be written "particularly describing the place to be searched."

Pen register searches applied to the Internet. The Patriot Act applies the distinction between transactional and content-oriented wiretaps to the Internet. The problem is that it takes the weak standards for access to transactional data and applies them to communications that are far more than addresses. On an e-mail message, for example, law enforcement has interpreted the "header" of a message to be transactional information accessible with a PR/TT warrant. But in addition to routing information, e-mail headers include the subject line, which is part of the substance of a communication— on a letter, for example, it would clearly be inside the envelope.

The government also argues that the transactional data for Web surfing is a list of the URLs or Web site addresses that a person visits. For example, it might record the fact that they visited <www.aclu.org> at 1:15 in the afternoon and then skipped over to <www.fbi.gov> at 1:30. This claim that URLs are just addressing data breaks down in two different ways:

- Web addresses are rich and revealing content. The URLs or "addresses" of the Web pages we read are not really addresses, they are the titles of documents that we download from the Internet. When we "visit" a Web page, what we are really doing is downloading that page from the Internet onto our computer, where it is displayed. Therefore, the list of URLs that we visit during a Web session is really a list of the documents we have downloaded—no different from a list of electronic books we might have purchased online. That is much richer information than a simple list of the people we have communicated with; it is intimate information that reveals who we are and what we are thinking about—much more like the content of a phone call than the number dialed. After all, it is often said that reading is a "conversation" with the author.

- Web addresses contain communications sent by a surfer. URLs themselves often have content embedded within them. A search on the Google search engine, for example, creates a page with a custom-generated URL that contains material that is clearly private content, such as <www.google.com/search?hl=en&lr=&ie=UTF-8&oe=UTF-8&q=sexual+orientation>.

Similarly, if I fill out an online form—to purchase goods or register my preferences, for example—those products and preferences will often be identified in the resulting URL.

The Erosion of Accountability

Attempts to find out how the new surveillance powers created by the Patriot Act were implemented during their first year were in vain. In June 2002 the House Judiciary Committee demanded that the Department of Justice answer questions about how it was using its new authority. The Bush/Ashcroft Justice Department essentially refused to describe how it was implementing the law; it left numerous substantial questions unanswered and classified others without justification. In short, not only has the Bush administration undermined judicial oversight of government spying on citizens by pushing the Patriot Act into law, but it is also undermining another crucial check and balance on surveillance powers: accountability to Congress and the public.

Nonsurveillance Provisions

Although this fact sheet focuses on the direct surveillance provisions of the Patriot Act, citizens should be aware that the act also contains a number of other provisions. The act:

- Puts CIA back in the business of spying on Americans. The Patriot Act gives the director of Central Intelligence the power to identify domestic intelligence requirements. That opens the door to the same abuses that took place in the 1970s and before, when the CIA engaged in widespread spying on protest groups and other Americans.

- Creates a new crime of "domestic terrorism." The Patriot Act transforms protesters into terrorists if they engage in conduct that "involves acts dangerous to human life" to "influence the policy of a government by intimidation or coercion." How long will it be before an ambitious or politically motivated prosecutor uses the statute to charge members of controversial activist groups like Operation Rescue or Greenpeace with terrorism? Under the Patriot Act, providing lodging or assistance to such "terrorists" exposes a person to surveillance or prosecution. Furthermore, the law gives the attorney general and the secretary of state the power to detain or deport any noncitizen who belongs to or donates money to one of these broadly defined "domestic terrorist" groups.

- Allows for the indefinite detention of noncitizens. The Patriot Act gives the attorney general unprecedented new power to determine the fate of immigrants. The attorney general can order detention based on a certification that he or she has "reasonable grounds to believe" a noncitizen endangers national security. Worse, if the foreigner does not have a country that will accept them, they can be detained indefinitely without trial.

From *The USA PATRIOT Act: H.R. 3162, Sections 213 and 215*

BEFORE READING: How would you differentiate between acts of terrorism and any other illegal activity?

Sec. 213. Authority for Delaying Notice of the Execution of a Warrant.

Section 3103a of title 18, United States Code, is amended—

1. by inserting "a. IN GENERAL—" before "In addition"; and

2. by adding at the end the following:

"b. DELAY—With respect to the issuance of any warrant or court order under this section, or any other rule of law, to search for and seize any property or material that constitutes evidence of a criminal offense in violation of the laws of the United States, any notice required, or that may be required, to be given may be delayed if —

"1. the court finds reasonable cause to believe that providing immediate notification of the execution of the warrant may have an adverse result (as defined in section 2705);

"2. the warrant prohibits the seizure of any tangible property, any wire or electronic communication (as defined in section 2510), or, except as expressly provided in chapter 121, any stored wire or electronic information, except where the court finds reasonable necessity for the seizure; and

"3. the warrant provides for the giving of such notice within a reasonable period of its execution, which period may thereafter be extended by the court for good cause shown."

Sec. 215. Access to Records and Other Items under the Foreign Intelligence Surveillance Act.

Title V of the Foreign Intelligence Surveillance Act of 1978 (50 U.S.C. 1861 et seq.) is amended by striking sections 501 through 503 and inserting the following:

"Sec. 501. Access to Certain Business Records for Foreign Intelligence and International Terrorism Investigations.

"a.1. The Director of the Federal Bureau of Investigation or a designee of the Director (whose rank shall be no lower than Assistant Special Agent in Charge) may make an application for an order requiring the production of any tangible things (including books, records, papers, documents, and other items) for an investigation to protect against international terrorism or clandestine intelligence activities, provided that such investigation of a United States person is not conducted solely upon the basis of activities protected by the first amendment to the Constitution.
    "a.2. An investigation conducted under the section shall—

"A. be conducted under guidelines approved by the Attorney General under Executive Order 12333 (or a successor order); and

"B. not be conducted of a United States person solely upon the basis of activities protected by the first amendment to the Constitution of the United States.

    "b. each application under this section—
    "b.1. shall be made to—

"A. a judge of the court established by section 103(a); or

"B. a United States Magistrate Judge under chapter 43 of title 28, United States Code, who is publicly designated by the Chief Justice of the United States to have the power to hear applications and grant orders for the production of tangible things under this section on behalf of a judge of that court; and "b.2. shall specify that the records concerned are sought for an authorized investigation conducted in accordance with subsection a.2. to protect against international terrorism or clandestine intelligence activities.

"c.1. Upon an application made pursuant to this section, the judge shall enter an ex parte order as requested, or as modified, approving the release of records if the judge finds that the application meets the requirements of this section.

"c.2. An order under this subsection shall not disclose that it is issued for purposes of an investigation described in subsection a.

"d. No person shall disclose to any other person (other than those persons necessary to produce the tangible things under this section) that the Federal Bureau of Investigation has sought or obtained tangible things under this section.

"e. A person who, in good faith, produces tangible things under an order pursuant to this section shall not be liable to any other person for such production. Such production shall not be deemed to constitute a waiver of any privilege in any other proceeding or context.

"Sec. 502. Congressional Oversight.

"a. On a semiannual basis, the Attorney General shall fully inform the Permanent Select Committee on Intelligence of the House of Representatives and the Select Committee on Intelligence of the Senate concerning all requests for the production of tangible things under section 402.

"b. On a semiannual basis, the Attorney General shall provide to the Committees on the Judiciary of the House of Representatives and the Senate a report setting forth with respect to the preceding six-month period—

"1. the total number of applications made for orders approving requests for the production of tangible things under section 402; and

"2. the total number of such orders either granted, modified, or denied."

The Patriot Act and You

JENNIFER HAHN AND WASIM SALFITI

BEFORE READING: How could the USA Patriot Act pose a threat to your personal privacy?

The Patriot Act and You

George W. Bush calls it "vital legislation" that protects us from the threat of terrorism; John Kerry says "there are good parts to it and bad parts to it"; the ACLU claims it threatens "the very rights and freedoms that we are struggling to protect." The Patriot Act has been condemned by librarians and by city councils from Los Angeles to Philadelphia. But how does the law affect you? Below, a visual survey of how a (particularly unlucky) U.S. citizen might run afoul of the "Uniting and Strengthening America by Providing Appropriate Tools Required to Intercept and Obstruct Terrorism (USA PATRIOT) Act of 2001."

SECTION 213: Changes standards for search warrants to allow "sneak and peek" searches in any investigation. Instead of serving the warrant in person, a federal agent can now snoop first and let you know later—often much later. **SECTION 218:** Expands an exception to the Fourth Amendment, allowing secret U.S. courts to authorize secret searches if the government can allege a foreign-intelligence rationale. Any evidence discovered can now be used in court.

SECTION 206: Permits "roving wiretaps," which allow the government to tap all phones or computers a suspect *might* use—including, say, those at a neighborhood pool hall or Internet café. Unconnected third parties can easily be swept into this wider net. Along with **SECTION 220**, it curtails judicial oversight of such wiretaps.

SECTION 214: By claiming relevance to a terrorism investigation, the government can track your incoming and outgoing calls without a warrant or probable cause.

SECTION 216: Allows, with a judge's approval, Internet wiretaps to be used in any criminal investigation. Authorities are supposed to be limited to collecting address information, not "content." But privacy advocates note that web addresses provide a direct path to content.

SECTION 215: Without demonstrating probable cause, the FBI can obtain a subpoena to search your personal records held by a library, bookstore, church, bank, video store, etc. The subpoena cannot be challenged in court, and it includes a "gag order" to keep you from even knowing it was served. **SECTION 505:** Just like 215, but there's no judge required. Anyone from John Ashcroft down to an FBI field officer can demand the same kinds of records simply by issuing a "national security letter." The agent has only to satisfy himself that the information might be "relevant" to an ongoing terror investigation.

Declared Unconstitutional:
SECTION 805(a)(2)(B): Banned giving "expert advice or assistance" to government-designated "foreign terrorist organizations." A federal judge tossed out this provision, noting that its "impermissibly vague" language could encompass "pure speech and advocacy protected by the First Amendment."

SECTION 802: Defines the new crime of "domestic terrorism" as illegal acts "dangerous to human life" that "appear to be intended" to influence government policy by "intimidation or coercion." The vague wording has activists ranging from environmentalists to anti-abortionists worried that their civil disobedience might be reclassified as terror. **SECTION 806:** Allows the Justice Department—without a hearing—to seize the assets of alleged domestic terrorists and their supporters.

Research by Jennifer Hahn and Wasim Salfiti.

Name Withheld: Harsh Justice for a September 11 Detainee

ELIZABETH AMON

BEFORE READING: Do you recall witnessing, reading about, or hearing about any change in Americans' attitude toward those of other nationalities living in this country in the aftermath of September 11?

In its investigation of the September 11 attacks, the U.S. government rounded up hundreds of Middle Eastern, South Asian, and Muslim immigrants. The precise number is unknown. In November 2001, the Department of Justice reported that 1,182 people had been arrested, but it has refused to supply a total since then. This June, a report from its Office of the Inspector General (OIG) chronicled the detention of 762 of the arrestees for violating immigration laws—typically, for overstaying visas. Almost all the September 11 detainees were men, and most remained in custody for months. Many were eventually deported, while others, like M., the man who is interviewed in this document, were released but are too anxious about their immigration status to talk openly to the press. The government has refused to give out the names of the detainees, whom it has labeled "special-interest." In fact, there was little more reason to arrest them than to arrest any of the eight million other out-of-status immigrants living on U.S. soil. Neither M. nor any of the other detainees was shown to have had any connection to terrorism.

1

M. lives in a brick home in a neat, middle-class subdivision. When I visited him this spring, a half-melted snowman, complete with carrot nose and coal eyes, was sinking into his front yard. A soft-spoken, middle-aged man with a slight accent, M. is cautious in conversation, and his anger at what has happened to him is apparent only occasionally in his words and never in his manner. In November 2001, he was at home with his young son and his wife, who suffers from lupus, when an FBI agent and multiple INS agents appeared at the door. A coworker at the medical clinic where M. worked had called the FBI; M., she contended, wore a surgical mask "more than necessary." The INS brought M. to their headquarters for further questioning. Despite the fact that his immigration papers, which had been pending at the time of his arrest, were approved six weeks later, M. spent the next five months in a New Jersey jail.

2

Beginning in December 2001, lawyers from the American Civil Liberties Union visited several of the New York–area facilities where the detainees were being held. Despite Attorney General John Ashcroft's assurances to the Senate that "all persons being detained have the right to contact their lawyers and families," the attorneys at first had tremendous difficulty gaining access. In some cases, the prisons claimed that they were unable to "prepare" the men for questioning; in others, they were told that the INS had not given approval for the visit. When the lawyers were able to meet with the detained, they wrote up a brief report on each. The notes from M.'s interview, portions of which the ACLU released and all of which was approved for release by M., are at right.

3

Elizabeth Amon writes for *The National Law Journal* and was a 2003 Soros Justice Media Fellow. This article appeared in the August 2003 issue of *Harper's Magazine*.

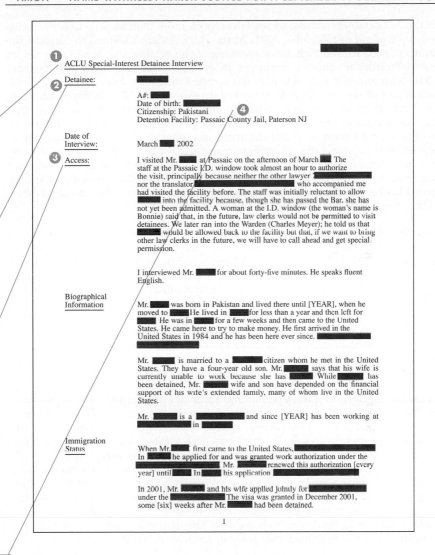

④ A third of the detainees were, like M., from Pakistan, by far the most common country of origin; the next most common were Egypt, Turkey, Jordan, and Yemen. All the detainees were immigrants, and after September 11, at the attorney general's request, the chief U.S. immigration judge allowed their hearings to be closed to the public and even to family members. At least 611 of the detainees were subjected to secret hearings, a practice that the Supreme Court this May allowed to stand as constitutional. The Department of Justice has argued that releasing even the detainees' names would compromise its terrorism investigations, despite the fact that the names of other terrorism suspects—e.g., Ernest James Ujaama in Seattle, Jeffrey Leon Battle in Portland, Sahim Alwan and Yahya Goba in Buffalo—have been trumpeted in the press by Ashcroft himself.

Of the 762 detainees covered by the OIG report, more than 80 percent were in custody by the end of November 2001. At the time, Ashcroft seemed to consider the numbers good P.R., and whenever speaking of the detainees he would take care to invoke "terrorism" once or, better yet, twice. (A typical statement, from October 2001: "Our anti-terrorism offensive has arrested or detained nearly 1,000 individuals as part of the September 11 terrorism investigation.") To this day Ashcroft, in his public statements, continues to imply a link between the detainees and terrorism. But the director of the Center for National Security Studies, which filed a lawsuit to obtain information about the detainees, says that in court papers, government officials never connect the detainees to terrorism. A General Accounting Office report from January 2003 found that nearly half of the DOJ's "terrorism" convictions had been misclassified as such. In New Jersey, 60 of the 62 terrorism indictments touted by the U.S. Attorney's Office involved foreign students who had hired others to take English proficiency tests on their behalf.

At 3:30 A.M. on the morning after his arrest, M. was taken to the Passaic jail and charged with having overstayed his visa—a civil, not a criminal, offense. On September 17, 2001, the INS changed its long-standing policy on immigrant detention, extending the time period that an immigrant could be held without charges from 24 to 48 hours and adding that, in "extraordinary circumstances," arrestees could be held uncharged for "an additional reasonable period of time." The DOJ's definition of "reasonable" has proved quite spacious. Of the special-interest detainees, 317 are known to have been held for more than 48 hours without charges, 36 for four weeks or more, 13 for more than 40 days, and nine for more than 50. Such arbitrary practices of detention contradict even the USA Patriot Act, which required that detainees be charged within seven days.

In December 2001, M.'s work permit and residency application were approved by the INS, and yet he was not released. The following month, the FBI cleared him of having any connection to terrorism, and yet still he was not released. Many detainees spent months in jail after they had been cleared; some had even received orders of deportation, or had volunteered to leave the country. Others were deported so quickly after September 11 that they weren't able to pursue any legal strategies for remaining. In many cases, men were sent to home countries where they had not lived or even visited for decades. The INS deported one Pakistani man, detained for having missed an immigration hearing more than five years earlier, without informing his American-born wife. The man was deposited, penniless, in Islamabad, even though his family lived in Karachi, more than 1,000 miles away.

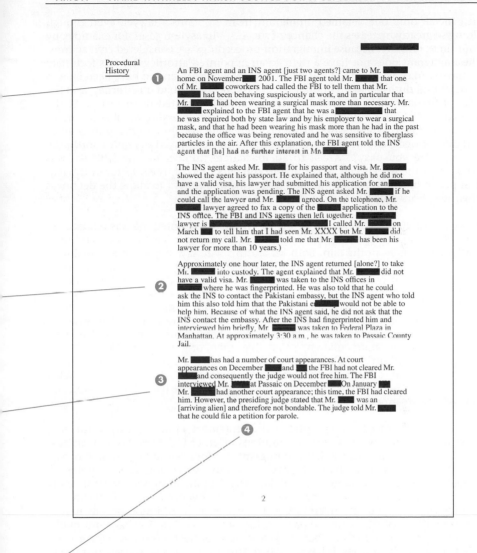

Procedural History

1 An FBI agent and an INS agent [just two agents?] came to Mr. ███ home on November███ 2001. The FBI agent told Mr. ████ that one of Mr. ████ coworkers had called the FBI to tell them that Mr. ████ had been behaving suspiciously at work, and in particular that Mr. ████ had been wearing a surgical mask more than necessary. Mr. ████ explained to the FBI agent that he was a ████████ that he was required both by state law and by his employer to wear a surgical mask, and that he had been wearing his mask more than he had in the past because the office was being renovated and he was sensitive to fiberglass particles in the air. After this explanation, the FBI agent told the INS agent that [he] had no further interest in Mr. ████

The INS agent asked Mr. ████ for his passport and visa. Mr. ████ showed the agent his passport. He explained that, although he did not have a valid visa, his lawyer had submitted his application for an ████ and the application was pending. The INS agent asked Mr. ████ if he could call the lawyer and Mr. ████ agreed. On the telephone, Mr. ████ lawyer agreed to fax a copy of the ████ application to the INS office. The FBI and INS agents then left together. ████ lawyer is ████████ I called Mr. ████ on March ██ to tell him that I had seen Mr. XXXX but Mr. ████ did not return my call. Mr. ████ told me that Mr. ████ has been his lawyer for more than 10 years.)

2 Approximately one hour later, the INS agent returned [alone?] to take Mr. ████ into custody. The agent explained that Mr. ████ did not have a valid visa. Mr. ████ was taken to the INS offices in ████ where he was fingerprinted. He was also told that he could ask the INS to contact the Pakistani embassy, but the INS agent who told him this also told him that the Pakistani e████would not be able to help him. Because of what the INS agent said, he did not ask that the INS contact the embassy. After the INS had fingerprinted him and interviewed him briefly, Mr. ████ was taken to Federal Plaza in Manhattan. At approximately 3:30 a.m., he was taken to Passaic County Jail.

3 Mr. ████ has had a number of court appearances. At court appearances on December ██ and ██ the FBI had not cleared Mr. ████ and consequently the judge would not free him. The FBI interviewed Mr. ████ at Passaic on December ██ On January ██ Mr. ████ had another court appearance; this time, the FBI had cleared him. However, the presiding judge stated that Mr. ████ was an [arriving alien] and therefore not bondable. The judge told Mr. ████ that he could file a petition for parole.

4

2

4 Requests by M.'s lawyer to have him released on bond were repeatedly rebuffed, even after he had been cleared by the FBI. Most people detained on minor immigration violations, such as M.'s, have traditionally been released on bond until their court hearings. But, as revealed in the OIG report, the Department of Justice in September 2001 ordered a "no bond" policy for all the special-interest detainees, even in cases in which there was no evidence that bond should be denied. Soon thereafter, a new regulation allowed the immigration service to overrule an immigration judge about whether *any* detainee is released on bond, even if he is not suspected of a crime or of terrorist activity. Thus the government trial attorney, who essentially is the prosecutor in an immigration proceeding, is allowed to take on a crucial judicial role as well.

In general, only one detained immigrant in five obtains a lawyer, even though doing so greatly increases the chance of success—in asylum cases, for example, by four times or more. Because immigration proceedings are considered civil actions, the immigrant does not have a right to an appointed attorney. M. was fortunate to have worked with the same attorney for sixteen years, and to have been able to contact him during his detention. Many of the detainees had no attorney, and the lists of free attorneys at the jails were invariably outdated or incorrect. At the Brooklyn MDC, not a single number on the list was a working number for an attorney willing to take on cases. Prisoners there were not always offered their allotted call per week, and when guards did offer it they employed a cryptic shorthand, asking, "Are you okay?" A call to an inaccurate number on the jail's list was counted as the weekly call. According to the OIG's report, the director of the federal prison bureau was told she should "not be in a hurry" to allow the detainees their telephone calls.

In late April 2002, M.'s request for parole was finally granted; he was released on a $5,000 bond, and had to get himself home by taking a bus to a train and then walking two miles in the rain. Both M. and his wife say they often are unable to sleep as a result of his experience, but they worry more about the impact on their five-year-old son (who sometimes asks, when M. leaves the house for work, "Is Daddy coming home?"). Moreover, M.'s five months of incarceration left his family $30,000 in debt. Despite these emotional and fiscal scars, M. is fortunate in how his case was resolved. Other of the detainees have not come home at all: An Egyptian man was deported and forced to leave behind his American-citizen wife and two American-born children; a Canadian man, originally from Syria, was deported to Syria—in violation of international law—where he disappeared for weeks. For others, detention was literally a physical trial. Two detainees contracted tuberculosis in the Brooklyn MDC. Another detainee there had a broken hand and was refused treatment.

Perhaps the most frightening aspect of the September 11 arrests was, in the end, how arbitrary they were. As a result, millions of other U.S. Muslims and Arabs— many of whom came here, as have immigrants for four centuries, in search of asylum from repression or hardship overseas—now see themselves as potential targets. Most of the detainees did violate U.S. immigration law, and for many Americans this fact seems to have absolved the government for its harsh and capricious justice. But in undermining the presumption of innocence, as well as the constitutional rights to due process, to counsel, and to a speedy and public trial, the Bush administration has weakened these protections for all, citizens and aliens alike. In the process, it has tarnished American democracy, even as it hopes to export this democracy to the very nations from which these men arrived.

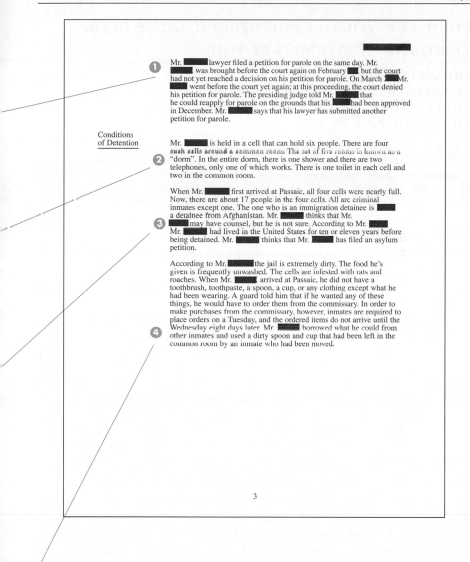

Mr. ████ lawyer filed a petition for parole on the same day. Mr. ████ was brought before the court again on February ██ but the court had not yet reached a decision on his petition for parole. On March ██ Mr. ████ went before the court yet again; at this proceeding, the court denied his petition for parole. The presiding judge told Mr. ████ that he could reapply for parole on the grounds that his ████ had been approved in December. Mr. ████ says that his lawyer has submitted another petition for parole.

Conditions
of Detention

Mr. ████ is held in a cell that can hold six people. There are four such cells around a common room. The set of five rooms is known as a "dorm". In the entire dorm, there is one shower and there are two telephones, only one of which works. There is one toilet in each cell and two in the common room.

When Mr. ████ first arrived at Passaic, all four cells were nearly full. Now, there are about 17 people in the four cells. All are criminal inmates except one. The one who is an immigration detainee is ████ a detainee from Afghanistan. Mr. ████ thinks that Mr. ████ may have counsel, but he is not sure. According to Mr. ████ Mr. ████ had lived in the United States for ten or eleven years before being detained. Mr. ████ thinks that Mr. ████ has filed an asylum petition.

According to Mr. ████ the jail is extremely dirty. The food he's given is frequently unwashed. The cells are infested with rats and roaches. When Mr. ████ arrived at Passaic, he did not have a toothbrush, toothpaste, a spoon, a cup, or any clothing except what he had been wearing. A guard told him that if he wanted any of these things, he would have to order them from the commissary. In order to make purchases from the commissary, however, inmates are required to place orders on a Tuesday, and the ordered items do not arrive until the Wednesday eight days later. Mr. ████ borrowed what he could from other inmates and used a dirty spoon and cup that had been left in the common room by an inmate who had been moved.

3

"My wife laughs at me," says M., "because I don't like my shoelace to touch the ground." The dirtiness of jail was an ordeal for M., who saw rats and roaches in his cell every day. More disturbing, the detainees—few of whom were guilty of anything more than having overstayed a visa—were forced to share cells with violent criminals. At the Metropolitan Detention Center (MDC) in Brooklyn, where many of the other detainees were held, conditions were even more brutal. The men were locked down for 23 hours a day and imprisoned in perpetual light. Ostensibly the lights were for videotaping—to ensure that the prisoners were not abused—but when the OIG tried to examine the tapes for evidence of abuse it found that those more than 30 days old had been destroyed. Prisoners at the MDC were routinely slammed against walls by guards and were allegedly taunted with anti-Arab slurs. The OIG's report notes that supervisors had told the facility's staff that the detainees were "suspected terrorists."

From *The Geneva Convention Relative to the Treatment of Prisoners of War*

THE DIPLOMATIC CONFERENCE FOR THE ESTABLISHMENT OF INTERNATIONAL CONVENTIONS FOR THE PROTECTION OF VICTIMS OF WAR

BEFORE READING: Brainstorm anything you know about the Geneva Convention. In what context or contexts have you heard that term?

Part II. General Protection of Prisoners of War

A rticle 12. Prisoners of war are in the hands of the enemy Power, but not of the individuals or military units who have captured them. Irrespective of the individual responsibilities that may exist, the Detaining Power is responsible for the treatment given them.

Prisoners of war may only be transferred by the Detaining Power to a Power which is a party to the Convention and after the Detaining Power has satisfied itself of the willingness and ability of such transferee Power to apply the Convention. When prisoners of war are transferred under such circumstances, responsibility for the application of the Convention rests on the Power accepting them while they are in its custody.

Nevertheless if that Power fails to carry out the provisions of the Convention in any important respect, the Power by whom the prisoners of war were transferred shall, upon being notified by the Protecting Power, take effective measures to correct the situation or shall request the return of the prisoners of war. Such requests must be complied with.

Article 13. Prisoners of war must at all times be humanely treated. Any unlawful act or omission by the Detaining Power causing death or seriously endangering the health of a prisoner of war in its custody is prohibited, and will be regarded as a serious breach of the present Convention. In particular, no prisoner of war may be subjected to physical mutilation or to medical or scientific experiments of any kind which are not justified by the medical, dental, or hospital treatment of the prisoner concerned and carried out in his interest.

Likewise, prisoners of war must at all times be protected, particularly 5 against acts of violence or intimidation and against insults and public curiosity.

This agreement was the revision of one signed at Geneva, Switzerland, in 1864 establishing a code for the treatment of the sick and wounded, those killed in battle, and prisoners of war. It was also the code that provided for the protection of buildings and vehicles having the emblem of the Red Cross. It was adopted on August 12, 1949.

Measures of reprisal against prisoners of war are prohibited.

Article 14. Prisoners of war are entitled in all circumstances to respect for their persons and their honor. Women shall be treated with all the regard due to their sex and shall in all cases benefit by treatment as favorable as that granted to men. Prisoners of war shall retain the full civil capacity which they enjoyed at the time of their capture. The Detaining Power may not restrict the exercise, either within or without its own territory, of the rights such capacity confers except in so far as the captivity requires.

Article 15. The Power detaining prisoners of war shall be bound to provide free of charge for their maintenance and for the medical attention required by their state of health.

Article 16. Taking into consideration the provisions of the present Convention relating to rank and sex, and subject to any privileged treatment which may be accorded to them by reason of their state of health, age, or professional qualifications, all prisoners of war shall be treated alike by the Detaining Power, without any adverse distinction based on race, nationality, religious belief, or political opinions, or any other distinction founded on similar criteria.

From *Prepared Remarks of Attorney General Alberto R. Gonzales at the JAG Corps Leadership Summit*

BEFORE READING: In what ways is our justice system not suitable for trying enemy combatants captured during the War on Terror?

. . . The President has made clear that our mission in Iraq and Afghanistan is nothing less than the establishment of the rule of law. The stakes are the highest, and your role is vital.

But the atrocities of September 11th made clear that we must use every instrument of national power to wage the War on Terror. The tools of law enforcement are often critical in protecting our citizens. But any thought that al Qaeda's campaign of global terrorism presented merely a law enforcement dilemma was laid to rest five years ago.

Alberto R. Gonzales became U.S. attorney general in 2005. Earlier he served as then Governor George W. Bush's general counsel and as both secretary of state and a justice of the Supreme Court of Texas. He has been a leader of the State Bar of Texas and the Houston Hispanic Bar Association. This excerpt is from a speech he delivered in October 2006 to a Leadership Summit of the Judge Advocate Generals (JAG) Corps.

When our enemies are willing to sacrifice their own lives to attack us, when their cause is nothing less than a return to the Dark Ages, and when the cost of each tactical success for the enemy is measured in the hundreds and thousands of innocent lives lost, then we face something fundamentally different from crime—we are at war. Every resource of our Nation, including the military and the intelligence services, must be directed at preventing future attacks before they occur.

Over the past five years, the United States and its allies can point to a number of successes on that front. Our intelligence-gathering efforts were instrumental in capturing dozens of Osama bin Laden's closest henchmen, including the mastermind of the 9/11 attacks, Khalid Sheikh Mohammed, as well as Abu Zubaydah and Ramzi bin al Shibh. And the capture of those terrorists has led to actionable intelligence that has disrupted many other terrorist plots.

These successes, and the vigorous prosecution of the War on Terror, have 5 undoubtedly made us safer, but we are not yet safe. Our enemy is patient and smart. While our successes have weakened and fractured al Qaeda, they have also forced our enemies to adapt. And so we continue to work with our allies around the globe to identify new ways to contain and combat the ever-changing threat of terrorism.

Because we are at war, we must govern our conduct by the law of war. And we must acknowledge that some of the limitations of the civilian justice system simply do not hold.

In order to defend the security of our citizens, we must have the ability

- to detain terrorists and remove them from the battlefield;

- to collect from them the vital intelligence that enables us to capture their associates and break up future plots;

- and to create effective and fair procedures that will allow us to prosecute and punish captured terrorists for their war crimes.

The legal doctrines directed at achieving these ends are not the same as those we would employ during peacetime. The Supreme Court has recognized this in several of its decisions, including its recent *Hamdan* decision. And Congress has endorsed this view with the Military Commissions Act of 2006, which the President signed into law last week. The successful implementation of this Act is one of the most important challenges we will face together going forward.

As you know, the military commissions created by this legislation have been the subject of extensive debate, inside and outside the Administration. I personally met with the service Judge Advocate Generals twice on this topic to get the benefit of their input and expertise. Members of my Department also consulted with the JAG Corps on many occasions. The input of the JAGs was important in creating an effective system of justice for terrorists, and much of what I heard was incorporated into the final product, such as the decision to use the Uniform Code of Military Justice as a model for the military commissions.

This new law provides for full and fair military trials of captured ter-   10
rorists; reinforces and clarifies our obligations under the Geneva Conventions; and buttresses our ability to gather vital intelligence to disrupt future terrorist attacks.

For hundreds of years, the United States and other nations have used military commissions—not civilian courts and not courts-martial—to try unlawful enemy combatants. Military necessity does not permit the strict application of all court-martial procedures, and of course, there are important differences between the procedures appropriate for trying our service members and those appropriate for trying the terrorists they fight against.

For instance, courts-martial, like the civilian justice system, provide for strict rules governing the use of hearsay and the collection of evidence. But many witnesses before the commissions are likely to be foreign nationals not amenable to process, and others may be unavailable because of military necessity, injury, or death. And the United States military cannot be expected to leave the battlefield to gather evidence like police officers in the course of fighting the enemy.

Military commissions are both necessary and appropriate in prosecuting unlawful enemy combatants. Let me emphasize, however, that they are also venues in which the accused will receive a full and fair trial. The procedures for these commissions, like those of international war crimes tribunals, are adapted to wartime circumstances. But they contain all of the procedural protections that we regard as fundamental:

- trial before an impartial military judge
- with a defense counsel drawn from the JAG Corps
- and the presumption of innocence unless proven guilty by competent evidence beyond a reasonable doubt.

The Military Commissions Act entrusts the JAG Corps with serving as the principal prosecution and defense counsel in these critically important trials. And, as your partner, the Department of Justice will continue to rely upon your professionalism and expertise in these terror trials.

Though our enemy shows nothing but contempt for the law of war, and   15
the standards of civilized nations, we provide him with these protections because they are consistent with the values of the United States. These values are among the many hallmarks of civilization that separate us from them.

While it is rooted in the traditions of the law of war, the Military Commissions Act gives individuals detained as enemy combatants at Guantanamo Bay greater legal rights than are provided to lawful prisoners of war under the Geneva Conventions. The new law, consistent with history, makes clear that alien enemy combatants may not file habeas corpus petitions in the civilian courts. Yet the United States provides every detainee at Guantanamo

Bay the opportunity to challenge his detention not merely before a military tribunal, but also with an unprecedented appeal to our own domestic courts.

The Act also contains important provisions to reinforce our compliance with the Geneva Conventions, and to clarify for U.S. personnel their international obligations. For instance, interrogations of prisoners have proven to be among the most vital sources of intelligence in the War on Terror, and they have saved the lives of innocent civilians in the United States and around the world. These interrogations employ tough techniques, but the techniques are safe, consistent with our values, and have been carefully reviewed to ensure compliance with the law.

The Act buttresses the President's authority under our Constitution to interpret the meaning and applicability of the Geneva Conventions for the United States. It empowers the President to provide our personnel, and particularly our interrogators, with clear and authoritative guidelines for what they must do to comply with the Geneva Conventions.

Panel Hears about Falsehoods in Two Wartime Incidents

MICHAEL LUO

BEFORE READING: Why is there a need for heroes during time of war?

House Democrats burrowed into the histories of Pfc. Jessica D. Lynch and Cpl. Pat Tillman in a hearing on Tuesday, holding up the episodes as egregious examples of officials' twisting the truth for public relations in wartime.

They received help in making their case from witnesses who have mostly shied from the spotlight, Ms. Lynch and Corporal Tillman's mother, Mary, and brother, Kevin, who enlisted in the Army along with him after the attacks on September 11, 2001.

"I am still confused as to why they chose to lie and tried to make me a legend when the real heroics of my fellow soldiers that day were, in fact, legendary," said Ms. Lynch, speaking softly but firmly into the microphone as more than 12 photographers clicked away in front of her.

Michael Luo is a reporter for the *New York Times*, having earlier worked on feature stories and projects around the country as a national writer for the Associated Press. The article appeared in the *Times* on April 25, 2007.

Accounts from officials of Ms. Lynch's bravery held the nation in thrall in the early stages of the Iraq invasion in 2003 after her maintenance convoy went astray near Nasiriya and she was taken prisoner. After her rescue, which was made into a television movie, she disputed those who said she fought off Iraqi soldiers until she was captured. She never fired a shot, she restated on Tuesday.

The "story of the little girl Rambo from the hills who went down fight-   5
ing" was untrue, she said.

Kevin Tillman was scathing in his assessment of how his brother's death in Afghanistan in 2004, which was later determined to be a result of American fire, was initially portrayed by the military as an act of heroism in the face of enemy fire.

"A terrible tragedy that might have further undermined support for the war in Iraq was transformed into an inspirational message that served instead to support the nation's foreign policy wars in Iraq and Afghanistan," Mr. Tillman said.

Representative Henry A. Waxman, Democrat of California and chairman of the House Committee on Oversight and Government Reform, promised to take his quest for answers in the case, which drew most of the questions from lawmakers, to the highest levels of the Bush administration.

"We don't know what the secretary of defense knew," said Mr. Waxman, who has made himself a thorn in the administration's side since Democrats took over control of the House in January. "We don't know what the White House knew. These are questions this committee seeks answers to."

Mr. Tillman, who was posthumously promoted to corporal and awarded   10
the Silver Star for valor, inspired legions after he quit his spot as a star defensive back for the Arizona Cardinals professional football team to be an Army Ranger.

The Army recently completed two inquiries into his death. The investigations found that even though soldiers and commanders suspected almost immediately after the death that it was accidental fratricide, Corporal Tillman's family was not notified about the true circumstances until more than a month later, a violation of Army rules.

The report from the inspector general's office in the Defense Department singled out four generals and five other officers for potential discipline but said that they had done nothing criminal and that there was no broader cover-up.

The report was especially critical, however, of Lt. Gen. Philip R. Kensinger Jr., head of the Army Special Operations Command at the time of Corporal Tillman's death. The document said General Kensinger most likely knew of the suspected fratricide before a nationally televised memorial service on May 3 that he and the Tillman family attended.

The oversight committee had requested that General Kensinger testify on Tuesday, but he declined through a lawyer, citing his constitutional right to avoid compelled self-incrimination.

Committee members heard from Specialist Bryan O'Neal, who was 15 with Corporal Tillman when he died. Specialist O'Neal said he knew immediately that it was American troops that had killed his comrade and that he wanted to tell Kevin Tillman, who was a specialist in the same platoon, right away. But he was barred from doing so, he said, by his battalion commander, Lt. Col. Jeff Bailey.

"I was ordered not to tell him what happened," he said, explaining that it was made clear that he "would get in trouble."

Specialist O'Neal also said he did not write statements attributed to him in the recommendation for Corporal Tillman's Silver Star about "engaging the enemy."

Thomas F. Gimble, acting inspector general at the Pentagon, said his investigators were unable to determine who had altered the statement.

"Somewhere in the approval chain, it got edited," Mr. Gimble said.

Democratic members of the committee devoted much time to an ur- 20 gent memorandum sent by a top special operations commander, Maj. Gen. Stanley McChrystal, to other high-ranking commanders a week after Corporal Tillman's death. General McChrystal is now a lieutenant general.

The memorandum said a preliminary investigation was likely to find that American fire caused the death. The message urged them to pass on the information to President Bush, the secretary of the army, and others.

The Tillmans said they believed that Defense Secretary Donald H. Rumsfeld must have known the truth early, a contention that Army investigators said they had failed to establish. "It's a bit disingenuous to think that the administration did not know about what was going on, something so politically sensitive," Kevin Tillman said. "So that's, kind of, what we were hoping you guys could get involved with and take a look."

What Abu Ghraib Taught Me

BARBARA EHRENREICH

> **BEFORE READING:** What is your position on women's role in combat? Has America's war in Iraq changed your position? Explain.

E ven those people we might have thought were impervious to shame, like the Secretary of Defense, admit that the photos of abuse in Iraq's Abu Ghraib prison turned their stomachs.

Barbara Ehrenreich is the author of *Nickel and Dimed: On (Not) Getting By in America* (2001) and *Bait and Switch: The (Futile) Pursuit of the American Dream* (2006). This article was first published in the Sunday Opinion section of the *Los Angeles Times*, on July 24, 2004.

The photos did something else to me, as a feminist: They broke my heart. I had no illusions about the U.S. mission in Iraq—whatever exactly it is—but it turns out that I did have some illusions about women.

Of the seven U.S. soldiers now charged with sickening forms of abuse in Abu Ghraib, three are women: Specialist Megan Ambuhl, Private First Class Lynndie England, and Specialist Sabrina Harman.

It was Harman we saw smiling an impish little smile and giving the thumbs-up sign from behind a pile of hooded, naked Iraqi men—as if to say, "Hi Mom, here I am in Abu Ghraib!" It was England we saw with a naked Iraqi man on a leash. If you were doing PR for Al Qaeda, you couldn't have staged a better picture to galvanize misogynist Islamic fundamentalists around the world.

Here, in these photos from Abu Ghraib, you have everything that the 5 Islamic fundamentalists believe characterizes Western culture, all nicely arranged in one hideous image—imperial arrogance, sexual depravity . . . and gender equality.

Maybe I shouldn't have been so shocked. We know that good people can do terrible things under the right circumstances. This is what psychologist Stanley Milgram found in his famous experiments in the 1960s. In all likelihood, Ambuhl, England, and Harman are not congenitally evil people. They are working-class women who wanted an education and knew that the military could be a stepping-stone in that direction. Once they had joined, they wanted to fit in.

And I also shouldn't be surprised because I never believed that women were innately gentler and less aggressive than men. Like most feminists, I have supported full opportunity for women within the military—(1) because I knew women could fight, and (2) because the military is one of the few options around for low-income young people.

Although I opposed the 1991 Persian Gulf War, I was proud of our servicewomen and delighted that their presence irked their Saudi hosts. Secretly, I hoped that the presence of women would over time change the military, making it more respectful of other people and cultures, more capable of genuine peacekeeping. That's what I thought, but I don't think that anymore.

A certain kind of feminism, or perhaps I should say a certain kind of feminist naiveté, died in Abu Ghraib. It was a feminism that saw men as the perpetual perpetrators, women as the perpetual victims, and male sexual violence against women as the root of all injustice. Rape has repeatedly been an instrument of war and, to some feminists, it was beginning to look as if war was an extension of rape. There seemed to be at least some evidence that male sexual sadism was connected to our species' tragic propensity for violence. That was before we had seen female sexual sadism in action.

But it's not just the theory of this naive feminism that was wrong. So 10 was its strategy and vision for change. That strategy and vision rested on the assumption, implicit or stated outright, that women were morally superior to men. We had a lot of debates over whether it was biology or conditioning that gave women the moral edge—or simply the experience of being a woman in a sexist culture. But the assumption of superiority, or at least a lesser inclination toward cruelty and violence, was more or less beyond debate. After all, women do most of the caring work in our culture, and in polls are consistently less inclined toward war than men.

I'm not the only one wrestling with that assumption today. Mary Jo Melone, a columnist for the *St. Petersburg* (Florida) *Times*, wrote on May 7: "I can't get that picture of England [pointing at a hooded Iraqi man's genitals] out of my head because this is not how women are expected to behave. Feminism taught me thirty years ago that not only had women gotten a raw deal from men, we were morally superior to them."

If that assumption had been accurate, then all we would have had to do to make the world a better place—kinder, less violent, more just—would have been to assimilate into what had been, for so many centuries, the world of men. We would fight so that women could become the generals, CEOs, senators, professors, and opinion-makers—and that was really the only fight we had to undertake. Because once they gained power and authority, once they had achieved a critical mass within the institutions of society, women would naturally work for change. That's what we thought, even if we thought it unconsciously—and it's just not true. Women can do the unthinkable.

You can't even argue, in the case of Abu Ghraib, that the problem was that there just weren't enough women in the military hierarchy to stop the abuses. The prison was directed by a woman, General Janis Karpinski. The top U.S. intelligence officer in Iraq, who also was responsible for reviewing the status of detainees before their release, was Major General Barbara Fast. And the U.S. official ultimately responsible for managing the occupation of Iraq since October was Condoleezza Rice. Like Donald H. Rumsfeld, she ignored repeated reports of abuse and torture until the undeniable photographic evidence emerged.

What we have learned from Abu Ghraib, once and for all, is that a uterus is not a substitute for a conscience. This doesn't mean gender equality isn't worth fighting for for its own sake. It is. If we believe in democracy, then we believe in a woman's right to do and achieve whatever men can do and achieve, even the bad things. It's just that gender equality cannot, all alone, bring about a just and peaceful world.

In fact, we have to realize, in all humility, that the kind of feminism 15 based on an assumption of female moral superiority is not only naive; it also is a lazy and self-indulgent form of feminism. Self-indulgent because it assumes that a victory for a woman—a promotion, a college degree, the right to serve alongside men in the military—is by its very nature a victory for all of humanity. And lazy because it assumes that we have only one struggle—the struggle for gender equality—when in fact we have many more.

The struggles for peace and social justice and against imperialist and racist arrogance, cannot, I am truly sorry to say, be folded into the struggle for gender equality.

What we need is a tough new kind of feminism with no illusions. Women do not change institutions simply by assimilating into them, only by consciously deciding to fight for change. We need a feminism that teaches a woman to say no — not just to the date rapist or overly insistent boyfriend but, when necessary, to the military or corporate hierarchy within which she finds herself.

In short, we need a kind of feminism that aims not just to assimilate into the institutions that men have created over the centuries but to infiltrate and subvert them.

To cite an old, and far from naive, feminist saying: "If you think equality is the goal, your standards are too low." It is not enough to be equal to men, when the men are acting like beasts. It is not enough to assimilate. We need to create a world worth assimilating into.

THINKING AND WRITING ABOUT THE EFFECT OF TERRORISM ON THE AMERICAN IDEA OF JUSTICE

QUESTIONS FOR DISCUSSION AND WRITING

1. Look at the essay "The Case for Torture" in Chapter 8. Does Levin's argument seem more relevant after the attacks of September 11? Why, or why not?

2. Do you believe that the use of torture is ever justified? Explain.

3. Do you believe that your rights have in any way been threatened by the increased security since September 11? Refer to at least one of the readings in this chapter in your response.

4. What do you consider to be the greatest threat to Americans' rights posed by the USA Patriot Act?

5. One group opposed to the Patriot Act have been librarians. Why would that group be concerned about this piece of legislation? Are their concerns justified?

6. Do you ever think that our nation has too many laws designed to protect the rights of those accused of wrongdoing? Could the Patriot Act help change that, even in cases where the suspected crime is not terrorism?

7. "Name Withheld" tells the story of one unidentified man held for five months largely because his nationality made him suspect. Are such cases the unavoidable price we pay for national security? Explain. (Had the man referred to as "M." done anything wrong?)

8. The case of Jessica Lynch, combined with the deaths of American women serving in Iraq, made very real for those back home what it means for women to serve in combat. Should the United States reconsider whether

American women who want to serve in combat should be allowed to do so? Explain.

9. In his remarks to the JAG Corps, Attorney General Gonzales made this statement: "Because we are at war, we must govern our conduct by the law of war. And we must acknowledge that some of the limitations of the civilian justice system simply do not hold." (para. 6). Explain to what extent you believe that Gonzales in his remarks presents convincing support for this statement.

10. To what extent do you believe that Gonzales's statement in question 9 above is valid?

11. Watch the movie *Flags of Our Fathers* and explain how the concept of hero is politicized in the film.

TOPICS FOR RESEARCH

The effect the Patriot Act has had on libraries

Military tribunals

The internment of Japanese Americans during World War II

The outcome of the Abu Ghraib trials

Acknowledgments (continued from page iv)

Charles Adams. "Lincoln's Logic." From *When in the Course of Human Events*, pp. 193–211. Copyright © 2000 by Rowman & Littlefield Publishing. Reprinted by permission of the publisher

Advocates for Youth. "Will the Politics of Teen Sex Stop a Cancer Vaccine?" From *Advocatesforyouth.org*. Reprinted by permission.

Kevin Alexander. "MySpace Not Responsible for Predators." From the *Battalion*, June 28, 2006. Reprinted by permission.

Elizabeth Amon. "Name Withheld: Harsh Justice for a September 11 Detainee." From *Harper's* magazine, August 2003, pp. 56–59. Copyright © 2003 by Harper's magazine. All rights reserved. Reproduced from the August issue by special permission.

George J. Annas, "Cancer and the Constitution: Choice at Life's End." From the *New England Journal of Medicine: Health, Law, Ethics and Human Rights*, Volume 357: 408–413, July 26, 2007, Number 4. Copyright © 2007 Massachusetts Medical Society. All rights reserved.

Eric Auchard. "We're All Celebrities in Post-Privacy Age." From *Reuters.com*, June 21, 2007. Reprinted by permission of FosteReprints.

Radley Balko. "Absolutely, Government Has No Business Interfering with What You Eat." From *Time* magazine, June 7, 2004. Copyright © 2004 by Radley Balko. Reprinted by permission of the author.

Michael Barone. "Living With Illegals?" From *U.S. News & World Report*, March 26, 2006. Copyright © 2007 U.S. News & World Report, LP. All rights reserved.

Newman P. Birk and Genevieve B. Birk. "Selection, Slanting, and Charged Learning." From *Understanding and Using English*. Copyright © 1959 Newman P. Birk and Genevieve Birk. Reprinted by permission of the authors' estate.

Birmingham Post-Herald. "Eight Clergymen's Statemtent." From the *Birmingham Post-Herald*, 13 April 1963, p. 10. Copyright 1963 Martin Luther King Jr.; Copyright renewed 1991 Coretta Scott King. Reprinted by arrangement with The Heirs to the Estate of Martin Luther King Jr., c/o Writer's House as agent for the proprietor New York, NY.

Donald J. Borut. "Vital Tool of Last Resort: Opposing View: Uproar Obscures Eminent Domain's Crucial Role in Revitalizing Areas." From *USA Today*, July 10, 2006. Reprinted by permission.

Amy Brittain. "Universities Strike Back in Battle Over Illegal Downloads." From *Christian Science Monitor*, June 18, 2007. Copyright © 2007.

Patrick J. Buchanan. "The Invasion." From *State of Emergency: The Third World Invasion*. Copyright © 2006 by Patrick J. Buchanan. All rights reserved.

Warren Burger. "The Right to Bear Arms." From *Parade* magazine, January 14, 1990. Reprinted by permission of the Estate of Warren Burger.

Arian Campo-Flores. "Lining Up for Citizenship." From *Newsweek*, May 22, 2006. Copyright © 2006 Newsweek. Reprinted by permission of PARS International.

Arthur Capian. "Does Stem Cell Advance Provide an Ethical Out?" From *MSNBC.com*, June 6, 2007.

Mona Charen. "The Misleading Debate on Stem Cell Research." From *Townhall.com*, August 20, 2004. Copyright © 2004 by News America Syndicate. Reprinted by permission of Mona Charen and Creator's Syndicate, Inc.

Jo Ann Citron. "Will it be Marriage or Civil Union?" From the *Gay & Lesbian Review Worldwide*, March/April 2004, v. 11 i2, p. 10(2). Copyright © 2004 Jo Ann Citron. Reprinted by permission of the author and the Gay & Lesbian Review Worldwide.

Tyler Cowen and Daniel M. Rothschild. "Don't Bad-Mouth Unskilled Immigrants." From the *Los Angeles Times*, May 15, 2006. Copyright © 2006 Tyler Cowen. Reprinted by permission of the author.

Jillian Croll. "Body Image and Adolescents." From Stang J, Story M. (Eds), *Guidelines for Adolescent Nutrition Services*. Copyright © 2005 Center for Leadership, Education, and Training in Maternal and Child Nutrition, Division of Epidemiology and Community Health, School of Public Health, University of Minnesota. Reprinted by permission.

Lisa Takeuchi Cullen. "Not Too Rich or Too Thin." From *Time* magazine, June 7, 2004. Copyright © 2004 Time Inc. Reprinted by permission. Time is a registered trademark of Time Inc. All rights reserved.

Lisa de Moraes. "Television More Oversexed Than Ever, Study Finds." From *Washingtonpost.com*, November 10, 2005. Reprinted by permission.

Alan M. Dershowitz. "Is There a Torturous Road to Justice?" From the *Los Angeles*

Times, Commentary, November 8, 2001. Reprinted by permission of the author.

Alan M. Dershowitz. "Should We Fight Terror with Torture?" From the *Independent*, July 3, 2006. Copyright © 2007 Independent News and Media Limited. Reprinted by permission.

Thomas Doherty. Cultural Studies and Forensic Noir. From *Chronicle of Higher Education*, October 24, 2003. Copyright © 2003 by Thomas Doherty. Reprinted by permission of the author.

Roger Ebert. "Crash." From *rogerebert.com*, May 5, 2005. Reprinted by permission of Universal Press Syndicate.

Barbara Ehrenreich. "What Abu Ghraib Taught Me." From *AlterNet: The Mix is the Message*, May 20, 2004. Copyright © 2004 Barbara Ehrenreich. Reprinted by permission of International Creative Management

Edward Jay Epstein. "Sex and the Cinema." From *Slate.com*, August 15, 2005. Reprinted by permission.

Sabrina Rubin Erdely. "Doctors' Beliefs Hinder Patient Care." From *MSNBC.com*, June 22, 2007.

Leslie Fiedler. "Tyranny of the Normal." From *Tyranny of the Normal: Essays on Bioethics, Theology & Myth* by Leslie Fiedler. Reprinted by permission of David R. Godine, Publisher, Inc. Copyright © 1996 by Leslie Fiedler.

Seth Finkelstein. "Alan Dershowitz's Tortuous Torturous Argument." From *Ethical Spectacle*, February 2002. Reprinted by permission of the author.

Eric Foner. "Dare Call it Treason." Reprinted with permission from the June 2, 2003 issue of the *Nation*. For subscription information, call 1-800-333-8536. Portions of each week's Nation magazine can be accessed at http://www.thenation.com.

Fox News. "Playboy Launches Social-Networking Site." From *FoxNews.com*, August 24, 2007. Copyright © 2007 by the Associated Press. Reprinted by permission.

Evan Gahr. "Gore for Sale." From the *Wall Street Journal*, April 30, 1999. Copyright © 1999 by Evan Gahr. Reprinted by permission of the author.

Robert Garmong. "Why We Need to Abolish the FCC." From *San Diego Business Journal*, August 9, 2004, v. 25, i.32, p. 39 (1). Copyright © 2004 San Diego Business Journal. Reprinted with permission.

Annie Laurie Gaylor. "The Case Against School Prayer." Copyright © 1995 by the Freedom From Religion Foundation, Inc. Reprinted by permission of the author.

Nancy Gibbs. "Pillow Angel Ethics." From *Time* magazine, Jan. 7, 2007. Copyright © 2007 Time Inc. Reprinted by permission. Time is a registered trademark of Time Inc. All rights reserved.

Nathan Glazer. "Do We Need the Census Race Question?" From the *Public Interest*. Copyright © 2000. Reprinted by permission of the Public Interest.

Bernard Goldberg. "Connecting the Dots to Terrorists." From *Bias* by Bernard Goldberg. Copyright © 2002. Published by Regnery Publishing, Inc. All rights reserved. Reprinted by special permission of Regnery Publishing Inc., Washington, D.C.

Ben Gose & Jeffrey Selingo. "The SAT's Greatest Test: social, legal, and demographic forces threaten to dethrone the most widely used college-entrance exam." From *Chronicle of Higher Education*, October 26, 2001. Copyright © 2001, the Chronicle of Higher Education. Reprinted with permission.

Jennifer Grossman. "Food for Thought (and for Credit)." From the *New York Times*, Sept. 2, 2003, p. 23, col. 1. Copyright © 2003 by Jennifer Grossman. Reprinted by permission of the author.

Elisha Dov Hack. "College Life Versus My Moral Code." From the *New York Times*, September 9, 1997. Reprinted by permission.

Richard Hayes. "Supersize Your Child?" Originally entitled "Selective Science." From *Tompaine.com*, February 12, 2004. Copyright © 2004 by Tompaine.com. Reprinted by permission.

Julie Hilden. "The 'Bong Hits 4 Jesus' Student Speech Case: With Kenneth Starr Seeking High Court Review of the Ninth Circuit Decision, Is Someone Blowing Smoke?" This material originally appeared on *Findlaw.com*, September 18, 2006. Copyright © 2006 Findlaw.

Lawrence A. Howards, M.D. "Ethics of Organ Donation." From *Milwaukee Journal Sentinel Online*, June 20, 1999. Reprinted by permission.

Jeff Jacoby. "A Desensitized Society Drenched in Sleaze." From the *Boston Globe*. Copyright © 1995 by Jeff Jacoby. Reprinted by permission of the author.

Scott Jaschik. "RateMyProfessors: Hidden Camera Edition." From *Inside Higher Ed*, November 2, 2006. Copyright © 2007 Inside Higher Ed. Reprinted by permission of the publisher.

Steffen N. Johnson. "A Case the Scouts Had to Win." From the *New York Times*, June 30, 2000. Copyright © 2000. Reprinted by permission of the New York Times Syndicate Inc.

Jeffrey Kahn. " 'Adoption' of Frozen Embryos a Loaded Term." From *CNN.com*. Reprinted by permission of the author.

Chris Kapper. "Freedom to Live Trumps All!" From *Cnet.com*. Reprinted by permission of YGS Group.

Ron Kaufman. "Filling Their Minds With Death: TV Violence and Children." From *www.turnoffyourtv.com*, 2004. Copyright © 2004 by Ron Kaufman. Reprinted by permission of the author.

Alana Keynes. "Student Sues District for Banning Anti-War T-Shirt." From *Education Daily*, April 4, 2003. Copyright © 2003 by LRP Publications, PO Box 24668, West Palm Beach, FL 33416-4668. All rights reserved.

Martin Luther King Jr. "Letter from Birmingham Jail" and "I Have a Dream." From *A Testament of Hope*. Copyright © 1963 by Martin Luther King Jr. Copyright renewed 1991 by Coretta Scott King. Reprinted by arrangement with the Estate of Martin Luther King Jr., c/o Writer's House, as agent for the proprietor.

Joe Kita. "All to be Tall." From *Men's Health®* magazine, Jan-Feb 2004,v19, i1 p. 130. Reprinted by permission of Men's Health® magazine. Copyright © 2004 Joe Kita. All rights reserved.

Danielle Knight. "Waiting in Limbo, Their Childhood Lost." From *U.S. News & World Report*. March 7, 2004. Copyright © 2004 U.S. News & World Report, LP. Reprinted with permission.

Alfie Kohn. "No-Win Situations." From *Women's Sports and Fitness* magazine (July–August 1990). Copyright © 1990. Reprinted with the author's permission. For more information, please see www.alfiekohn.org.

Alfie Kohn. "Standardized Testing and Its Victims." From *Education Week*, September 27, 2000. Copyright © 2000 by Alfie Kohn.

William Severini Kowinski. "Kids in the Mall: Growing up Controlled." From *The Malling of America* by William Severini Kowinski (Morrow, 1985). Copyright © 1985 by William Severini Kowinski. Reprinted by permission of the author.

Charles Krauthammer. "Let's Have No More Monkey Trials." From *Time* magazine, August 8, 2005. Reprinted by permission of the publisher.

Michael Levin. "The Case for Torture." Originally published in *Newsweek*, June 7, 1982. Copyright © 1982 by Michael Levin. Reprinted by permission of the author.

Abraham Lincoln. "The Gettysburg Address." Reprinted courtesy of the Abraham Lincoln Association.

Carolyn Lochhead. "A Legacy of the Unforeseen." From the *San Francisco Chronicle*, May 7, 2006.

Michael Luo. "Panel Hears about Falsehoods in 2 Wartime Incidents." From the *New York Times*, April 25, 2007 Copyright © 2007 by the New York Times Company. Reprinted by permission.

Michael Maiello and Nicole Ridgway. "Alien Nation." From *Forbes*, April 10, 2006. Copyright © 2006 Forbes, Inc. Reprinted with permission.

Donald L. McCabe. "It Takes a Village: Academic Dishonesty & Educational Opportunity." From *Liberal Education* 91.3 (Summer–Fall 2005): P. 26 (6). Copyright © 2005 Association of American Colleges and Universities. Reprinted by permission of Thomson-Gale.

Sheryl McCarthy. "Showbiz Encourages Looser Teen Sex Habits." From *Newsday*, June 24, 2004. Copyright © 2004 by Newsday. Reprinted by permission of the publisher.

Roger D. McGrath. "A God Given Natural Right 'Shall Not Be Infringed.' " From *Chronicles*, October 2003. Copyright © 2003. Reprinted by permission of the author.

Margaret Mead. "Warfare: An Invention—Not a Biological Necessity." From *Asia*, 1940. Reprinted by permission of the Institute for Intercultural Studies.

Mark Memmott. "Disaster Photos: Newsworthy or Irresponsible?" From *USAToday.com*, August 4, 2005. Reprinted by permission of USA Today and the authors.

Howard Moody. "Gay Marriage Shows Why We Need to Separate Church and State." From the *Nation*, July 2004. Reprinted by permission of the publisher.

Charles Morris. "Why U.S. Health Costs Aren't Too High." From *Harvard Business Review*, February, 2007. Reprinted by permission of the Harvard Business Review.

Wesley Morris. " 'Saw' Good at Tying Things in Knots." From *Boston Globe*, October 29, 2004. Reprinted by permission of the author.

Desda Moss. " 'Freak Dancing': If Only It Stopped There." From *USA Today* online April 7, 2005. Reprinted by permission of the author.

Geoffrey Nunberg. "Don't Torture English to Soft-Pedal Abuse." From *www.Newsday.com*, May 24, 2004. Copyright © 2004 by Newsday, Inc. Reprinted by permission of the author.

Theodora Ooms. "Marriage-Plus." Annotated and excerpted from a special issue of the *American Prospect* on "The Politics of the American Family," April 8, 2002.

Phillips (Eds), *Beyond the Comfort Zone: Proceedings of the 21st ASCILITE Conference* (pp. 881–886). Perth, 5–8 December. Copyright © 2004 Susan Stoney & Mark McMahon

Bob Sullivan. "MySpace and Sex Offenders: What's the Problem?" From *The Red Tape Chronicles*, MSNBC.com, May 29, 2007. Reprinted by permission of MSNBC.com via the Copyright Clearance Center.

Frank Thomas. "X-ray Tests Both Security, Privacy." From *USA Today*, December 26, 2006. Reprinted by permission of the publisher

USA Today. "One Year Later, Power to Seize Property Ripe for Abuse." From *USA Today*, July 10, 2006. Reprinted by permission of the publisher.

USA Today. "Are SAT Scores 'worse than meaningless'?" Reprinted from *USA Today*, December 2001. Copyright © 2001 by the Society for the Advancement of Education, Inc.

Hal Varian. "Economic Scene: Are Bigger Vehicles Safer? It Depends." From the *New York Times*, December 18, 2003. Copyright © 2003 by the New York Times Inc. Reprinted by permission.

Marcia Vickers. "Why Can't We Let Boys Be Boys." Reprinted from *Business Week*, May 26, 2003 by special permission. Copyright © 2003 by the McGraw-Hill Companies.

Joy Victory. "Need An Organ? It Helps to Be Rich." From *ABC News* January 20, 2006. Copyright © 2007 ABC News Internet Ventures. Reprinted by permission.

David Von Drehle. "It's All About Him: We Should Stop Explaining Killers on Their Terms. It's Not About Guns or culture. It's Narcissism." From *Time* magazine, Thursday, April 19, 2007. Copyright © 2007 Time Inc. Reprinted by permission. Time is a registered trademark of Time Inc. All rights reserved.

Patti Waldmeier. "Freedom of Speech and My Right to Silence at Bath Time." From *Financial Times*, Nov 10, 2003, p. 12. Copyright © 2003 by Financial Times. Reprinted by permission of the publisher.

Claudius E. Watts, III. "Single-Sex Education Benefits Men Too." From the *Wall Street Journal*, May 3, 1995. Reprinted by permission of the author.

Reg Weaver. "NCLB's excessive reliance on testing is unrealistic, arbitrary and frequently unfair." From *Insight*, May 11–12, 2004. Copyright © 2004 by Insight Online. Reprinted by permission.

Michael M. Weinstein. "A Reassuring Scorecard for Affirmative Action." From the *New York Times*, October 17, 2000. Reprinted by permission of PARS International.

Brian Whitaker. "The Definition of Terrorism." From the *Guardian Unlimited*, May 7, 2001. Copyright Guardian News & Media Ltd 2001. Reprinted by permission.

Barbara Dafoe Whitehead. "Parents Need Help: Restricting Access to Video Games." From *Commonweal*, January 28, 2005.

Bronwyn T. Williams. "Standardized Students: The Problems With Writing for Tests Instead of People." From *Journal of Adolescent and Adult Literacy*, 49.2 (Oct 2005): 152 (7). Copyright © 2005 International Reading Association, Inc.

Eric Wilson. "When is Thin Too Thin?" From the *New York Times*, September 21, 2006. Copyright © 2006 by the *New York Times* Company. Reprinted by permission.

Lily Yulianti. "Praise for Student's Footage of Virginia Tech Mass Killing." From *Ohmynews.com*, April 17, 2007. Copyright © 2007 Ohmynews. Reprinted by permission of the author.

Yong Zhao. "Are We Fixing the Wrong Things?" From *Educational Leadership*, May 2006, vol. 63, no. 8. Reprinted by permission of the American Society for Educational Leadership.

Eric Zorn. "Family a Symbol of Love and Life, but Not Politics." From the *Chicago Tribune*, May 23, 2004. Reprinted by permission.

PICTURE CREDITS

38 Photofest; **63** (top) AP Images/Dave Martin; (bottom) Chris Graythen/Getty Images; **65** AP Images/Eric Gay; **66** (top) Margaret Bourke-White/Getty Images; (bottom) Bruce Chambers/The Orange County Register; **75, 76** ©CharityUSA.com, LLC, www.thehungersite.com; **239** G. Paul Burnett/The New York Times/Redux; **448, 449** Student-Voices is a project of the Annenberg Public Policy Center; **455** Title page and copyright page from *Nickel and Dimed: On (Not) Getting By in America* written by Barbara Ehrenreich. Copyright, ©2001 by Henry Holt and Company. Reprinted by permission of Henry Holt and Company, LLC. **459** Reprinted by permission of Army Times Publishing Company; **464** Title and copyright page from *The Western Cannon: The Books and*

School of the Ages, copyright ©1994 by Harold Bloom, reprinted by permission of Harcourt, Inc. **468** From www.defenselink.mil. Article by Spc. Courtney Marulli, 2nd Brigade Combat Team, 2nd Infantry Division Public Affairs. **469** From Gale. *Screen shot from Thomson/Galegroup.com Expanded Academic ASAP.* ©Gale, a part of Cengage Learning, Inc. Reproduced by permission. www.cengage.com/permissions. Article reprinted from the May 30, 2005 issue of *BusinessWeek* by permission. Copyright 2005 by The McGraw-Hill Companies. **662** By permission of Mike Luckovich and Creators Syndicate, Inc. **666** Rob Rogers: © The Pittsburgh Post-Gazette/Dist. By United Features Syndicate, Inc. **673** TOLES ©1986 The Buffalo News. Reprinted with permission of UNIVERSAL PRESS SYNDICATE. All rights reserved. **680** ©Bettmann/Corbis; **724** (top) AP Images/ Nick Ut; (bottom) AP Images/Fred Beckham; **781** From *Mother Jones*, May/June 2004. ©2004, Foundation for National Progress

Glossary

Abstract language: language expressing a quality apart from a specific object or event; opposite of *concrete language*

Ad hominem: "against the man"; attacking the arguer rather than the *argument* or issue

Ad populum: "to the people"; playing on the prejudices of the *audience*

Anecdotal evidence: stories or examples used to illustrate a *claim* but that do not prove it with scientific certainty

Appeal to tradition: a proposal that something should continue because it has traditionally existed or been done that way

Argument: a process of reasoning and advancing proof about issues on which conflicting views may be held; also, a statement or statements providing *support* for a *claim*

Audience: those who will hear an *argument;* more generally, those to whom a communication is addressed

Authoritative warrant: a *warrant* based on the credibility or trustworthiness of the source

Backing: the assurances on which a *warrant* or assumption is based

Begging the question: making a statement that assumes that the issue being argued has already been decided

Claim: the conclusion of an argument; what the arguer is trying to prove

Claim of fact: a *claim* that asserts something exists, has existed, or will exist, based on data that the *audience* will accept as objectively verifiable

Claim of policy: a *claim* asserting that specific courses of action should be instituted as solutions to problems

Claim of value: a *claim* that asserts some things are more or less desirable than others

Cliché: a worn-out expression or idea, no longer capable of producing a visual image or provoking thought about a subject

Concrete language: language that describes specific, generally observable, persons, places, or things; in contrast to *abstract language*

Connotation: the overtones that adhere to a word through long usage

Credibility: the audience's belief in the arguer's trustworthiness; see also *ethos*

Data: facts or figures from which a conclusion may be inferred; see *evidence*

Deduction: reasoning by which we establish that a conclusion must be true because the statements on which it is based are true; see also *syllogism*

Definition: an explanation of the meaning of a term, concept, or experience; may be used for clarification, especially of a *claim,* or as a means of developing an *argument*

Definition by negation: defining a thing by saying what it is not

Empirical evidence: *support* verifiable by experience or experiment

Enthymeme: a *syllogism* in which one of the premises is implicit

Ethos: the qualities of character, intelligence, and goodwill in an arguer that contribute to an *audience's* acceptance of the *claim*

Euphemism: a pleasant or flattering expression used in place of one that is less agreeable but possibly more accurate

Evidence: *facts* or opinions that support an issue or *claim;* may consist of *statistics,* reports of personal experience, or views of experts

Extended definition: a *definition* that uses several different methods of development

Fact: something that is believed to have objective reality; a piece of information regarded as verifiable

Factual evidence: *support* consisting of *data* that are considered objectively verifiable by the audience

Fallacy: an error of reasoning based on faulty use of *evidence* or incorrect *inference*

False analogy: assuming without sufficient proof that if objects or processes are similar in some ways, then they are similar in other ways as well

False dilemma: simplifying a complex problem into an either/or dichotomy

Faulty emotional appeals: basing an argument on feelings, especially pity or fear—often to draw attention away from the real issues or conceal another purpose

Faulty use of authority: failing to acknowledge disagreement among experts or otherwise misrepresenting the trustworthiness of sources

Hasty generalization: drawing conclusions from insufficient evidence

Induction: reasoning by which a general statement is reached on the basis of particular examples

Inference: an interpretation of the *facts*

Major premise: see *syllogism*

Minor premise: see *syllogism*

MLA: the Modern Language Association, a professional organization for college teachers of English and foreign languages

Motivational appeal: an attempt to reach an *audience* by recognizing their *needs* and *values* and how these contribute to their decision making

Motivational warrant: a type of *warrant* based on the *needs* and *values* of an *audience*

Need: in the hierarchy of Abraham Maslow, whatever is required, whether psychological, or physiological, for the survival and welfare of a human being

Non sequitur: "it does not follow"; using irrelevant proof to buttress a *claim*

Paraphrase: to restate the content of an original source in your own words

Picturesque language: words that produce images in the minds of the *audience*

Plagiarism: the use of someone else's words or ideas without adequate acknowledgment

Policy: a course of action recommended or taken to solve a problem or guide decisions

Post hoc: mistakenly inferring that because one event follows another they have a causal relation; from *post hoc ergo propter hoc* ("after this, therefore because of this"); also called "doubtful cause"

Proposition: see *claim*

Qualifier: a restriction placed on the *claim* may not always be true as stated

Quote: to repeat exactly words from a printed, electronic, or spoken source

Refutation: an attack on an opposing view to weaken it, invalidate it, or make it less credible

Reservation: a restriction placed on the *warrant* to indicate that unless certain conditions are met, the warrant may not establish a connection between the *support* and the *claim*

Slanting: selecting *facts* or words with *connotations* that favor the arguer's bias and discredit alternatives

Slippery slope: predicting without justification that one step in a process will lead unavoidably to a second, generally undesirable step

Slogan: an attention-getting expression used largely in politics or advertising to promote support of a cause or product

Statistics: information expressed in numerical form

Stipulative definition: a *definition* that makes clear that it will explore a particular area of meaning of a term or issue

Straw man: disputing a view similar to, but not the same as, that of the arguer's opponent

Style: choices in words and sentence structure that make a writer's language distinctive

Substantive warrant: a *warrant* based on beliefs about the reliability of *factual evidence*

Support: any material that serves to prove an issue or *claim;* in addition to *evidence,* it includes appeals to the *needs* and *values* of the *audience*

Syllogism: a formula of deductive *argument* consisting of three propositions: a major premise, a minor premise, and a conclusion

Thesis: the main idea of an essay

Toulmin model: a conceptual system of argument devised by the philosopher Stephen Toulmin; the terms *claim, support, warrant, backing, qualifier,* and *reservation* are adapted from this system

Two wrongs make a right: diverting attention from the issue by introducing a new point, e.g., by responding to an accusation with a counteraccusation that makes no attempt to refute the first accusation

Values: conceptions or ideas that act as standards for judging what is right or wrong, worthwhile or worthless, beautiful or ugly, good or bad

Warrant: a general principle or assumption that establishes a connection between the *support* and the *claim*

Index of Subjects

Index of Authors and Titles

Need more help with writing and research?

Re:Writing is designed to help you with important writing concerns. You'll find advice from experts, models you can rely on, and exercises that will tell you right away how you're doing. And it's all free and available any hour of the day. All of these can be accessed at bedfordstmartins.com/rewriting.

Need help with grammar problems?
> *Exercise Central*
> (bedfordstmartins.com/exercisecentral)

Want to see what papers for your other courses look like?
> *Model Documents Gallery*
> (bedfordstmartins.com/modeldocs)

Stuck somewhere in the research process? (Maybe at the beginning?)
> *The Bedford Research Room*
> (bedfordstmartins.com/researchroom)

Wondering whether a Web site is good enough to use in your paper?
> *Tutorial for Evaluating Online Sources*
> (bedfordstmartins.com/onlinesourcetutorial)

Having trouble figuring out how to cite a source?
> *Research and Documentation Online*
> (bedfordstmartins.com/resdoc)

Confused about plagiarism?
> *The St. Martin's Tutorial on Avoiding Plagiarism*
> (bedfordstmartins.com/plagiarismtutorial)

Want to get more out of your word processor?
> *Using Your Word Processor*
> (bedfordstmartins.com/wordprocessor)

Trying to improve the look of your paper?
> *Using Your Word Processor to Design Documents*
> (bedfordstmartins.com/docdesigntutorial)

Need to create slides for a presentation?
> *Preparing Presentation Slides Tutorial*
> (bedfordstmartins.com/presentationslidetutorial)

Interested in creating a Web site?
> *Web Design Tutorial*
> (bedfordstmartins.com/webdesigntutorial)

Resources *for* Teaching

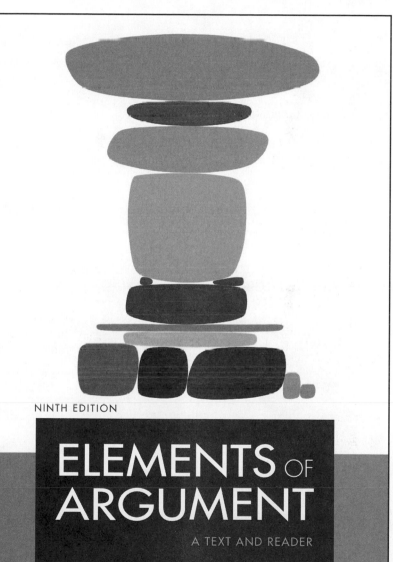

NINTH EDITION

ELEMENTS OF ARGUMENT

A TEXT AND READER

Annette T. Rottenberg | Donna Haisty Winchell

RESOURCES FOR TEACHING

ELEMENTS OF ARGUMENT

A Text and Reader

NINTH EDITION

PREPARED BY

Annette T. Rottenberg

Donna Haisty Winchell
Clemson University

With an essay by
Gail Stygall
University of Washington

BEDFORD/ST. MARTIN'S   BOSTON ◆ NEW YORK

3   2   1   0   9   8
f   e   d   c   b   a

For information, write: Bedford/St. Martin's
75 Arlington Street, Boston, MA 02116

ISBN-10: 0–312–48071–7

ISBN-13: 978–0–312–48071–4

Instructors who have adopted *Elements of Argument: A Text and Reader*, Ninth Edition, as a textbook for a course are authorized to duplicate portions of this manual for their students.

Preface

In these notes we have assembled some of the assignments and classroom activities that have proved successful over the years in illuminating the elements of argument and eliciting thoughtful student response. Every teacher will have a collection of favorite devices, and we claim no superiority for ours. If some of the materials are not suitable for some classes, they may, however, suggest other kinds that are. Together with the writing suggestions in the text they should provide an ample repertory of things to do for every day of the course. Clearly there will be more material than any single class can profitably use.

The text is flexible. Students usually need or want more practice in some areas than others. If the use of support, for example, is one element in which the majority of students are weak, you may want to spend more time on the material in Chapter 7 and omit an extended discussion of language and fallacies. The heart of the text is, of course, Chapters 4, 6, 7, and 8. Chapters 9 and 10 can be handled less intensively.

Part Two treats the writing process itself, analyzing its parts and providing guidelines for organizing, developing, and researching. Chapter 13 focuses on the presentation of oral argument, an increasingly important instrument for both laypeople and professionals. We hope to enable students to become not only more proficient public speakers but more knowledgeable members of an audience.

Part Three, "Multiple Viewpoints," lends itself to formal and informal classroom debate and longer papers that incorporate research. A short unit on debate is included in the *Resources for Teaching*. This chapter-by-chapter section can also be used throughout the course as a reference guide for papers that fulfill different kinds of writing assignments, especially those that call for in-depth analysis of opposing arguments.

The most ambitious use of "Multiple Viewpoints" is as a source of information and opinion for the research paper. A section on research and use of the library and two documented research papers appear in Chapters 11 and 12. Suggestions for research paper subjects appear at the end of each section in "Multiple Viewpoints." For shorter papers students can limit their reading to material in the text. For longer papers they can look for additional material in the library or on the Internet. We have included an appendix on Rogerian argument for instructors who would like to introduce the theories of Carl Rogers to their students.

The linear organization of the course should pose no problems. It is true that from the first assignment students will be writing arguments — before they have completed the study of the elements of argument. This practice, however, is the same as that of any other composition course where the process is one of deepening, widening, and enriching a first draft or a series of undeveloped generalizations. Many teachers of composition believe that students should begin to write whole essays from the beginning of the course. Attention to the components of argument follows when students attempt to make their essays stronger by concentrating on the particular areas that need development and revision.

Gail Stygall's essay at the beginning of this manual provides an overview of some of the special concerns and problems instructors should anticipate when teaching a course in argument, as well as practical general suggestions that might be useful in dealing with these concerns and problems.

Finally, teachers and students will find additional resources, including exercises, links, syllabi, assignment ideas, and online debates, at the book's Web site: <bedfordstmartins.com/rottenberg>.

Contents

Strategies for
Teaching Argumentation:
An Overview

INTRODUCTION

One of the joys we experience in teaching argumentation is seeing our students take a step into the real world of rhetoric and argument. Instructors who have taught many semesters of introductory freshman composition without including argument notice an immediate difference in the papers they read and evaluate when they do opt for a semester of argumentation. After a semester in the argumentation classroom, students often find they now have a means for articulating the opinions, views, and knowledge that they feel belong in the public discussion. Moreover, the informal logic model, once understood, may be taken into other classrooms as a means for analyzing readings and writing. With the flexibility of *Elements of Argument* and with the dialogue of argument in the classroom, students have access to a practical, everyday logic, so often missing in public discussions of issues.

Although teaching argument is different from teaching the purely expository freshman writing course, it is, in many ways, easier for the instructor. Many freshman composition instructors have struggled to create a real purpose for students when the students have to produce brief explanatory or illustrative essays. Not yet knowledgeable enough to join the essayists who populate their readers, students may not see the point of practicing consistency within forms. Even in the studio classroom, with a peer audience available, students in the expository course may reason that writing is just another form of exercise, not something they might ever need to do in the real world. Argument, on the other hand, diminishes the instructor's struggle to create a real audience. Students may participate immediately, whether the forum is the classroom, campuswide issues, or national elections, and they can see that their writing can make a difference with a real audience.

If you are new to teaching written argumentation, this shift into active argument need not mean you have to reject what you already know. Many of us now teaching English were ourselves taught composition by the modes approach. The various ways in which we articulate arguments make use of those very same patternings — process, cause and effect, classification, comparison, definition. What changes is that we teach our students how to use those structures to serve as support for their arguments.

STUDENTS' EXPERIENCE WITH ARGUMENT

Students arriving in the freshman composition classroom that is focused on argument have rarely been asked to take a stand before in writing contexts. Although many aspects of a process writing curriculum have been developed in the elementary and secondary schools, we still may not take it for granted that our students have had prior practice in argument. A related problem is that students doubt that we really want their opinions; in high school, they probably experienced institutional constraints on their views. Even if they offered their opinions, they may have had those opinions rejected and may now hesitate to trust us. Moreover, prior to college their basic belief systems have probably gone unchallenged. They may offer what appears to them to be the wisdom of a community, but they have not yet had to maintain that wisdom in the face of a decidedly different community, such as the college classroom.

SETTING THE TONE FOR THE CLASSROOM

Because students have often had so little practice in oral or written argument, we must try to maintain a classroom in which open discussion and debate are the standard procedure. Many instructors use intercollegiate debate as a model to set the necessary atmosphere. Instructors may tape sessions of *Face the Nation, Meet the Press*, or *The McLaughlin Group* for classroom discussion. Other instructors arrange for their classes to hear a full intercollegiate debate.

Setting the tone, however, goes beyond having students observe impersonal or distanced third-person demonstrations of debate and argumentation. Students need to hear one another assert and defend arguments, and they must have the opportunity to respond to one another face to face. Scheduling discussion time is a useful strategy, following selected reading assignments. Students may be asked to come to class with brief responses to a particular essay, responses that include the students' own arguments about the topic at issue. Arranging for these reaction discussions places tolerance at a premium in the argumentative writing classroom, and the instructor often becomes the immediate arbiter of conflicting views and opinions. You should expect students to ask for your opinion on the various topics, as they invariably will, and prepare your own reactions and responses accordingly.

MAINTAINING THE FORUM: DEBATES ON PAPER

Many instructors continue the open forum by shifting their focus to actual writing assignments, arranging assignments so that one student is graded for responding directly to another student's paper. Argument becomes quite real when a student sees that his or her reasoning does not convince a classmate. Even a skilled writer learns from this assignment that a good argument acknowledges alternative views. Students who quote out of context, don't order their arguments well, or use logical fallacies without understanding what they represent often see during the refutation process what effect these practices have on the audience. Some instructors extend the dialogue even further by requiring a rebuttal paper in response to the refutation paper. For instructors who have been using a process approach to writing, this paper exchange is a means of helping students recognize the value of audience. In a direct exchange of papers, students cannot help being reminded of the dialogic nature of argumentation.

USING PEER RESPONSES

Process approaches can be further adapted for the argumentation classroom through the use of the audience questionnaire, as suggested in Chapter 1 of this manual. Instructors, instead of distributing generic peer-response forms, may ask students to evaluate one another's work in terms of the results of class opinions, requiring students to write briefly about which segments of the class a particular essay will convince, harden, or fail to move. These same peer responders can explore in writing why they think the paper will succeed or fail by pointing to specific parts of the argument and evaluating the strategies informing its delivery. Peer responders may also list and develop counterarguments and offer counterevidence, keeping the focus on the dialogue between writer and reader.

Peer-response exercises can also be used effectively with Part One of *The Structure of Argument*. In conjunction with specific chapters, instructors can design peer-response forms for assigned student essays that direct the student responders to the important aspects of argument covered in those chapters. Instructors need to know that students who are inexperienced at focused response may need support in the form of a guided response sheet. Early in the semester, an instructor might ask both the student writer and the peer responder to answer the following questions about the student's essay:

What is the claim being made here? Write several sentences explaining your answer. You may want to quote from the text of the essay.

Is this an argument? Use evidence from Chapter 1 of your text to support your answer.

What type of claim is being made? Explain your answer based on what is said about claims in Chapter 6.

As writer, describe the purpose or the effect you believe your claim will have on the reader.

As reader, describe the actual effect of the claim. Do you agree? Did you agree before you started reading? Did your opinion change? Why, or why not?

Describe the representative person who you believe would be convinced by this essay. Include several characteristics such as age, sex, education, and family background.

Later in the semester, instructors can include further questions that ask students to evaluate the writer's use of definitions or to provide counterdefinitions in response to inadequately developed definitions. Chapter 7 on support and Chapter 8 on warrants also provide opportunities for students to integrate the material of the text with what they are attempting in their own writing.

PROVIDING BACKGROUND INFORMATION TO AID CRITICAL READING

Although peer-response exercises, discussion, and debate can promote critical reading, instructors should expect students to lack knowledge about the issues presented in the readings in the text. Instructors should anticipate that some or all of the students will know little about the issues involved. This cannot be attributed, in our view, to cultural "illiteracy," but rather to reasons of age or development. An issue may simply be one that we do not seek out until it affects us. That is not to say, however, that in an argumentation class we exempt our students from that issue because of their lack of experience. Instead, we simply need to be prepared to support their reading. For example, students may need contextual information to understand how an incident at Abu Ghraib prison in Iraq made Americans rethink the definition of torture.

If you have chosen to make "Multiple Viewpoints" the core of your course, you may find it useful before you begin assigning the sections to survey your students on the knowledge they have about the particular issue. Often gaps in knowledge revealed by the survey can be filled with very little discussion. But without the knowledge necessary to evaluate fully the arguments in question, students can have more difficulty than is necessary in discerning even the structure or main points of the essays.

TEACHING WARRANTS AND ASSUMPTIONS

At least partly because our students have had so little practice in argument, they may have problems understanding what we mean by warrants and assumptions. Conflating the terms *warrant* and *assumption* for the purposes of an introductory class, you may want to illustrate the terms by beginning with the exercise that opens Chapter 8. A further step in that exercise would be to ask students to rank survivors in order of their correspondence with students' value systems. Invariably, students are unable to reach a consensus, revealing underlying assumptions that they hold about human behavior.

Instructors can also begin teaching warrants by asking students to complete statements beginning with the following leads: All lawyers . . . ; All English teachers . . . ; All students. . . . Such statements allow students to begin to see the kinds of assumptions they use implicitly every day. What they say in a discussion about what all lawyers do often reveals what they believe about the criminal justice system or about the civil recovery system. The beliefs about English teachers are interesting and sometimes disheartening. Students report that they speak more carefully in front of an off-duty English teacher, reveal less about whether they read "popular" fiction, think we value grammar above everything, or believe we are the classic ivory tower type of teacher. Inevitably, students begin to recognize warrants and assumptions. Students realize that they have operating warrants about English teachers; that English teachers are always and on every occasion English teachers; that English teachers read only canonical literature; that grammar is all that counts in an English class; and that English classes have little to do with real life.

These discussions, however time-consuming, are a necessary part of introducing warrants to students. While the terminology may be foreign to students, the process of using warrants is not, and with very little practice students can learn the appropriate questions to ask themselves as they try to discern warrants in their own work and the work of others.

Students can also practice adding a series of "because" clauses to the main points of their papers as a way of clarifying their assumptions. For example, a student writing a paper about how television viewing negatively affects children cited passivity, exposure to violence, and fear as her main points. When in an in-class exercise she was asked to identify her warrants with a "because" clause for each, she wrote, "because interaction, not passivity, is a better learning experience" in response to her first point and "because violence and fear are poor standards for society" to the second and third. Not only did the student gain valuable experience in identifying the warrants behind her claims, she also learned a powerful revision strategy. As her peers pointed out to her, she had grouped two of the points together, with the third being entirely separate. In revising her paper, she concentrated on the last two points, eliminated the first, and turned in a more coherent paper, which included a now-explicit discussion of her warrant.

DIFFERENT WORDINGS OF CLAIMS AND WARRANTS

Students will often propose several versions of claim and warrant for the same essay. Often one group of students will select as claim a very narrow assertion, while another group will select a generalization, perhaps an inference from the text. Likewise, students will show variation in their wording of warrants. As long as students do not go beyond what claims and warrants a particular author might make, some variation in wording not only is acceptable, but also is helpful to students working in an argumentative setting. They will learn that the rhetorical effect of different wording is intrinsic to assessing and addressing their audience.

TEACHING FALLACIES:
THE EDITORIAL JOURNAL

Another tool for generating material for argument is the editorial journal. Instructors can require students to maintain a weekly folder containing several examples of what they think are successful and unsuccessful editorials and letters from local or campus newspapers and to record their responses to those editorials and letters in an editorial journal. Students assigned this exercise soon develop a standard against which they judge effective and ineffective arguments. It is then often useful to have students use their developing standard in combination with logical fallacies from Chapter 9. Students can submit for group discussion the most effective and least effective examples they've culled from editorial pages. Asking students to respond to the most troubling and fallacious letters and editorials often bridges the gap between classroom writing and the "real world" of discourse. Many students take the additional step of sending their responses to the local or campus newspaper and sometimes experience the delight of seeing their names in print in those pages.

A variation on this same exercise is an in-class letter-writing task in which students select the most troubling problem on campus and attempt to persuade the appropriate administrator to respond. The instructor may ask different groups to vary their approaches by assigning, for example, one group to argue a claim of fact, another a claim of value. Groups may assess the effectiveness of the arguments of other groups, with the entire class selecting the best letter for the particular audience.

DISTINGUISHING BETWEEN INDUCTION
AND DEDUCTION: RESEARCH ASSIGNMENTS

One other aspect of teaching an informal logic model in the writing classroom bears discussion. Many traditional argumentative writing courses have assigned induction and deduction separately. In teaching with an informal Toulmin model, the differences between the traditional and informal approaches often become blurred. Students who have become adept in using the informal model complain vigorously that there is no such thing as a truly inductive paper. Arguing that the Toulmin model requires that warrants be acknowledged, whether the paper is inductive or deductive, students assert that the differences are minimal. For the standard student paper, in which a thesis appears early in the essay, students are indeed correct, and the distinction is difficult to make. A so-called inductive paper with a thesis indicates that the writer has already drawn a conclusion, thus making it less than purely inductive in nature.

If the course you are teaching requires separate inductive and deductive papers, consider making the distinction on the basis of the style of research supporting the paper. For example, assign one essay that focuses on an inductive style of research as a primary research project. These projects, chosen in collaborative groups, may include student-designed surveys of their classmates; observations of behavior on campus, in parking lots, and in shopping malls; and interviews. Essays can be developed from student observations of people's behavior while standing in line, from student interviews with hard-core video game players, and from student surveys addressing the necessity of improving the food available in campus vending machines. Because inferencing and the "inductive leap" are highlighted with this approach, students can more easily see the differences between induction and deduction. For a deductive paper, on the other hand, you can stress a secondary research approach, having students begin from basic assumptions about a subject and then examine a particular instance.

Many philosophers and historians of science have made the same point: that observations are always guided by a particular framework. The informal Toulmin model makes this point quite clear to students. What counts as a fact or as an observation is already warranted before the search for facts and observations begins.

We hope our suggestions will be useful for planning a forum on issues in your writing classroom. It is probable that many of your students will have only the composition classroom in which to engage in written debates on public policy issues. Becoming engaged in the consideration, analysis, and argument of various positions, students truly prepare to take their place in civic discussions. As instructors of written argument, we hold a unique position by virtue of our providing the forum in which this process takes place. Few students leave the argumentation classroom without having experienced a change of some kind, and few teachers can resist that kind of opportunity. By providing a model of analysis of argument useful both inside and outside the classroom and by providing the forum for an exchange of views, we can emphasize the uses of writing in unexpectedly productive ways.

— Gail Stygall
University of Washington

MULTIMEDIA STRATEGIES: I•CLAIM VISUALIZING ARGUMENT CD-ROM

Why i•claim?

Mixed media and everyday arguments can be both more accessible and more challenging for students to examine. These arguments — commercials, comics, speeches, advertisements, and so on — are more recognizable for students, but students are not used to analyzing these types of texts. Nevertheless, a more contemporary, multimedia introduction to argumentation helps students think more critically about the world around them, and the arguments they encounter every day about what to think, what to do, and who to be.

There are also limitations inherent to any textbook's discussion of argument. Arguments use more than words, and exist beyond the printed page. In a book, students can't listen to a speech by Jesse Jackson, watch a presidential campaign commercial, change a greeting card's appeal, or drag and drop images to create their own personal ad. The i•claim CD-ROM offers a new way to visualize argument — because there are things you just can't do in a book.

The i•claim CD-ROM features six tutorials on fundamental qualities good arguments share. Arguments make *claims*. They come from a specific *context*. They are driven by clear *goals*. They need careful *support*. They consider multiple *viewpoints*. And they use *logic*. An illustrated glossary defines 50 key terms from argument theory and classical rhetoric, tying each abstract term to a contemporary visual example. Finally, the arguments section provides direct access to all of the multimedia arguments on the CD-ROM — over 70 in all. This flexible visual index allows you to browse the arguments in multiple ways: by genre and medium (posters, video clips, commercials), by type of appeal (ethos, pathos, logos), and by purpose (definition, evaluation, proposal).

How do I get i•claim?

The i•claim CD-ROM can be packaged for free with *Elements of Argument* and *The Structure of Argument*. To see a sample tutorial, visit <bedfordstmartins .com/iclaim>. For ordering information, contact your local sales representative or e-mail us at sales_support@bfwpub.com.

How does i•claim work?

Launching the i•claim CD-ROM:

Windows

1. Insert the CD-ROM into your CD-ROM drive.

2. Double-click on the "My Computer" icon on your desktop.

3. Double-click on the "i•claim" CD-ROM icon in the "My Computer" window. (For most computers, the CD-ROM drive is designated the "D" drive.)

Macintosh

1. Insert the CD-ROM into the CD-ROM drive.

2. Double-click on the "i•claim" CD-ROM icon that appears on your desktop.

Note: When you use i•claim, the CD-ROM must be in the CD ROM drive.

Navigating through i•claim

From the main screen, you may start with any of the six tutorials (click on one of the colored circles in the center to select a tutorial), or you may go to the glossary or the arguments index by clicking on the appropriate title. Once you have entered a section of the CD-ROM, you can navigate to any other section by using the top menu bar. If you are within a tutorial, you can go to any other tutorial by clicking on the numbered circles.

Responding to the read and compose assignment questions in the i•claim tutorials:

1. Click on the notebook paper icon in the introductory text for the assignment section of the tutorial.

2. In the pop-up window that appears, click in the desired question's text box. Type in your answer.

3. When you are finished responding to the questions, click on either "Print" to print out your answers or "E-mail" to e-mail your answers. If you choose to e-mail your answers, you will need to fill out the "To" and "From" e-mail address forms.

Who can I contact for technical assistance?

For technical support, please contact us at <http://bfwpub.com/techsupport>, techsupport@bfwpub.com, or 800-936-6899.

How do I incorporate i•claim into my course?

1. If you follow this book's structure in organizing your course, try directing your students to go through the first tutorial at home after you have introduced the chapter on claims. Similarly, you can assign them the fourth tutorial when you cover the chapter on support; the sixth tutorial when you cover the chapter on induction, deduction, and logical fallacies; and the fifth tutorial when you cover Part Three on multiple viewpoints.

2. If you have access to a computer classroom, try using the arguments index to present to your students some multimedia examples of different types of

arguments as you introduce them in class. Supplement your discussion of the logical fallacies with some of the examples on the CD-ROM, for instance.

3. If your students are having difficulty with the argument terminology you are introducing in class, they can use i•claim's glossary as a handy illustrated reference.

4. If you use the thematically organized chapters in the book, try pairing your discussion of these topics with topically relevant arguments on i•claim:

How Far Will We Go to Change Our Body Image?

Sims Online Video Game Trailer (tutorial 03, assignment)

Details "Gay or L.A." feature (glossary, "definition")

Cover of *The Low-Carb Baking and Dessert Cookbook* (glossary, "god (and devil) terms")

How Has Terrorism Affected the American Idea of Justice?

Gulf Wars Poster (tutorial 02, analysis)

Kerry Windsurfing Campaign Commercial (tutorial 06, overview)

Cover of *The Case for Democracy: The Power of Freedom to Overcome Tyranny and Terror* (glossary, "god (and devil) terms")

Are Limits on Freedom of Speech Ever Justified?

Adbusters Big Mac TV Spot (tutorial 02, assignment)

Careless Talk WPA Poster (tutorial 06, overview)

What Is the Role of Sex and Violence in Popular Culture?

"Are You Popular" Coronet Instructional Film (tutorial 06, analysis)

Sims Online Video Game Trailer (tutorial 03, assignment)

Bibliography on the Toulmin Model

Listed below are articles by teachers of composition, rhetoric, speech, and debate that explain and apply the Toulmin model for use in the classroom.

Brockriede, Wayne, and Douglas Ehninger. "Toulmin on Argument: An Interpretation and Application." *The Quarterly Journal of Speech* 46 (1960): 44–53. The authors interpret the Toulmin model as presented in Toulmin's *The Uses of Argument.* They clearly define each element of the model and explain its advantages over traditional systems of logic.

Christenson, Thomas, and Paul R. Nelson. "The Toulmin Model: Asset and Millstone." *Advanced Debate: Readings in Theory, Practice and Teaching.* Ed. David A. Thomas. Skokie, IL: National Textbook, 1975. 228–34. The authors provide a clear summary of Toulmin, distinguishing between the "basic" model — claim, data, and warrant — and the "expanded" model, which introduces the other elements of backing, reservation, and qualifier.

Kaufer, David S., and Christine M. Neuwirth. "Integrating Formal Logic and the New Rhetoric: A Four-Stage Heuristic." *College English* 45 (1983): 380–89. The authors argue that formal logic can be used to supplement insights from the new rhetoric (as put forth by Toulmin and others), believing that an argument should be tested for its deductive certainty as well as for the plausibility of its premises. They provide a four-stage model for teaching students how to integrate logical and probabilistic reasoning in arguments.

Kneupper, Charles W. "Teaching Argument: An Introduction to the Toulmin Model." *College Composition and Communication* 29 (1978): 237–41. Kneupper begins with an attack on the use of logic and fallacies as a means of teaching argumentative composition. He offers a brief summary of Toulmin's model as a superior method, then applies the model to the first paragraph of Thoreau's *Civil Disobedience,* diagramming the argument in simplified form. He emphasizes that for students "how they are arguing will be clearer," and they will be able to see relationships between parts of the argument.

Lunsford, Karen J. "Contextualizing Toulmin's Model in the Writing Classroom: A Case Study." *Written Communication* 19.1 (Jan. 2002): 109–75.

Stratman, James F. "Teaching Written Argument: The Significance of Toulmin's Layout for Sentence-Combining." *College English* 48 (1982): 718–33. The author believes that in using Toulmin's "layout" for argument in sentence-combining, students can learn new syntactic patterns. They can learn "skills appropriate to argument — estimating the relevance of acts, assessing validity, and planning refutations based on premises shared with an opponent." For example, one way of helping students to learn the function and importance of warrants is to have them adapt such warrants explicitly in a sentence-combining exercise. "Toulmin's layout can reveal how syntactic transformations strengthen or weaken the structure implicit in argumentative exercises by revealing changes in the underlying relations between 'claim' and 'evidence' that these transformations may entail." A complicated analysis but thought-provoking.

Trent, Jimmie D. "Toulmin's Model of an Argument: An Examination and Extension." *The Quarterly Journal of Speech* 54 (1968): 252–59. Trent views Toulmin's model as a supplement to syllogistic reasoning. He nevertheless argues that Toulmin presents arguments more clearly and accurately than the classical syllogism.

PART ONE

UNDERSTANDING ARGUMENT

CHAPTER 1
Understanding the Structure of Argument
(text pages 3–30)

After discussion of the chapter, assign a brief search through newspapers and magazines (beginning perhaps with the school newspaper) for arguments about current affairs. Such a search enables students to arrive at several important conclusions.

a. The most obvious one is that arguments of the kind they will be reading and writing in class are to be found everywhere and that they are the foundation of the democratic process. Students will also discover that a good deal of the factual reporting about political events is reporting of controversies or arguments.

b. Without much familiarity with formal arguments, students may at first regard them all as vehicles of reasoned analysis. As they reflect on their examples, they will recognize that passion and ideology are formidable — sometimes the only — components of many arguments.

c. Many, perhaps most, freshman students believe that hard-core problems in our society remain unsolved because at best we lack the will to solve them, or at worst evil people conspire to frustrate attempts at solution. One other explanation of our failures may not readily occur to them: lack of knowledge. We may ask: What kind of knowledge — that is, data and interpretation of data — do we need in order to solve apparently intractable problems of poverty, war, prejudice, crime, mental illness? When we introduce this question, we may find that some students think that these problems are new and peculiar to American society. Much of the information needed will turn out to be psychological, the kind most difficult to discover or verify. You can use this discussion to encourage a reflective caution when evaluating and advocating solutions.

d. Not all arguments have two equally valid sides. Some have multiple sides. Others may be said to have only one morally acceptable side. Ask students to suggest subjects that exemplify these conclusions.

Students may be asked to keep informal journals that list controversial subjects appearing in newspapers and magazines, on TV and radio, on the campus and in town. For each subject they may set down some of the important facts, values, and general principles underlying the claims. The journal entries can then serve as a source of subjects for assignments or discussion in class and in conferences with the instructor. A worthwhile dividend of such journal keeping is an increase in the practice of reading and listening, of becoming familiar with the sources and subjects of public controversies.

We suggest leaving discussion and analysis of the three major elements of argument — claim, support, and warrant — to the subsequent chapters. At this point we would require only that students show understanding of the definitions.

In speech classes students sometimes analyze their audience, i.e., their classmates, before making a proposal that might be unpopular. They distribute questionnaires that they themselves have constructed in an effort to discover the social and political preferences of their classmates. The results of the questionnaire help them to choose an argumentative strategy that will persuade this audience to look more favorably on the proposition being argued.

An application of this procedure for a writing class might work as follows: At the beginning of the semester, after having read about audience, a small group of students, perhaps four or five, makes up an informal questionnaire that is filled out by the members of the class. The results of the questionnaire are tabulated and distributed to the class. Later in the semester, for selected papers (for example, arguments of policy) the writers are encouraged to examine the results and add a note describing how and why they have adapted their arguments to the values of this particular audience.

CHAPTER 2
Reading and Listening Critically
(text pages 31–60)

This chapter emphasizes that critical reading and listening are essential to the mastery of the elements of argument. Most of us are familiar with the problems encountered by students in reading and responding to a difficult text. The problems are multiple: unfamiliarity with the subject, limited vocabulary, weak sense of metaphor, inability to recognize clues of organization and development. Many of these problems are clearly the result of too little practice — not enough careful attention to hard texts, not enough instruction in the mechanics of reading such material. It's also possible, as Sven Birkerts suggests in *The Gutenberg Elegies* (Faber and Faber, 1994), that reading is becoming more tedious as electronic communication effects a radical change in consciousness and literacy. But so far, there is no real substitute for reading in the print media. (Even Bill Gates and Nicholas Negroponte write books to tell us about computers.) Diagnosing the reading difficulties at the beginning of the course — through short quizzes and discussions — can tell us where to offer help.

If the amount of reading many of us do has declined, the amount of listening has greatly increased. But instruction in listening has not kept pace. Jay Heinrichs, author of "How Harvard Destroyed Rhetoric" (*Harvard Magazine*, July–August 1995), deplores the scarcity of serious academic interest in public speech. Rhetoric at Harvard was once, of course, the study of persuasive oratory. And rhetorical theory, whether or not we use the vocabulary of Aristotle or the Sophists, still animates any study of formal argument. Today the proliferation of "undisciplined argument" has convinced Heinrichs that the study of public speech should be restored. "Too few citizens," he says, "know how to listen critically."

Elsewhere in this manual we've suggested calling attention to the vocabulary of an assigned reading *before* students read it. Pointing out the clues that reveal the organization and development of a long, complex argument, again before students read the whole piece, can help them read it more effectively and with greater confidence. Most students find outlining tiresome and unenlightening, partly because they don't do it well, partly because many long articles defy conventional outlining. But early in the course, outlining one or two pieces on the board as students follow the text of an assigned essay can give a sense of what organization means and how it controls the development of the argument. Whether or not they outline their assignments, almost all students will find it useful to write a brief summary of an argument as a means of review.

The primary goals of critical reading, of course, are, first, understanding the argument and, then, determining how effectively the arguer supported his or her claim. But there are additional benefits to be derived from careful reading, benefits that can directly affect the student's writing. Critical reading, which often means over-reading, invites an appreciation of language. Winston Churchill spoke of the advantages of having been a relatively slow learner who had to repeat his lessons: "I got into my bones the essential structure of the ordinary British sentence — which is a noble thing."

This is where annotation pays off for the prospective writer. Students who must respond physically as well as mentally, by writing in the margins, should become more careful readers — more sensitive to diction and to the rhythms of a variety of styles and modes of organization that can be adapted for their own papers.

If you have asked students to write marginal notes while doing a critical reading of a piece, you may want to ask them to go back to the same piece and annotate it from the perspective of a writer. (It may help if they do so in a different colored ink to see the difference.) This time they will be noticing the writer's techniques more than the ideas, although the two necessarily overlap.

It can also be useful to have students do two different types of summaries. You may even want to have them summarize the same essay, with the point of one summary being to summarize the main ideas and the purpose of the other being to summarize the tactics. One summary could start, for instance, "In 'No-Win Situations,' Alfie Kohn argues that just as competition can have destructive effects in the workplace, it can also be destructive when it controls our recreational activities." The other might begin, "In 'No-Win situations,' Alfie Kohn begins with an example of the well-known childhood game of musical chairs to point out the destructive effects of competition in recreational activities."

Remind students that the summary is not yet the place to express an opinion.

Many school libraries have collections of recorded speeches and debates. Tapes allow replay of portions for class analysis. Just as students gloss a written text, they can annotate an oral presentation, expressing approval or disapproval, asking questions when they hear a doubtful statement. The instructor can model critical listening by stopping the tape at relevant intervals and offering a running commentary. She explains the reasons for her judgments and encourages additional response from the class. Students can listen for examples of logical argument and persuasive language. They can also learn to recognize clichés, slogans, short cuts, and other departures from clear thinking. (See Chapter 10.) With relatively little practice, students can become adept at the art of listening.

Deborah Tannen, professor of linguistics at Georgetown University, has written several books that interpret the conversational styles of different cultures as well as of men and women, among them *You Just Don't Understand: Women and Men in Conversation* (Ballantine, 1991) and *The Argument Culture: Moving from Debate to Dialogue* (Random House, 1998). Tannen's discussions emphasize the failure to listen attentively and with a will to understand as a major impediment to fruitful communication.

Careful listening plays a significant role in jury trials and formal investigations. In some celebrated cases, jurors seemed to have listened selectively. Students may be surprised to learn that jurors are not permitted to take notes during a trial or to ask questions of witnesses. A lawyer who has proposed changes in the jury system says, "Jurors often ignore the instructions or misapply them." We can ask students to be alert to televised trials or congressional committee hearings as sources of exercises in careful listening. Courtrooms, as Toulmin observed, are model venues of argumentation.

In learning to listen with attention to the speech of others, students may also improve their ability to hear their own language in writing. Because many students are able to hear errors in grammar and usage that escape the eye, we often ask them to read their papers aloud before submitting them.

Bibliography

Atwan, Robert, Donald McQuade, and John W. Wright. *Edsels, Luckies, and Frigidaires.* New York: Delta, 1979.

"The Content of Television Talk Shows: Topics, Guests, and Interactions." Michigan State U study, 1995. Commissioned by the Henry J. Kaiser Family Foundation.

Corbett, Edward P. J., and Robert J. Connors. *Classical Rhetoric for the Modern Student.* 4th ed. New York: Oxford UP, 1971.

Kurtz, Howard. *Hot Air: All Talk All the Time. An Inside Look at the Performers and the Pundits.* New York: New York Times Book, 1996.

CHAPTER 3
Reading Visual Texts Critically
(text pages 61–79)

This chapter examines the visual arguments in commercial advertisements, cartoons, photojournalism, and Web sites. Students are often unaware of the messages that even the simplest landscape or interior is capable of delivering —claims of fact, value, and policy. The great Hungarian photographer André Kertész, whose reception in New York was less than friendly, was told, "Your pictures talk too much." And, in fact, his photographs of people reading (*On Reading*, Penguin, 1982) are exquisite examples of value claims.

The pictures on TV and in newspapers and magazines that document the damage wrought by terrorist attacks on September 11, 2001, are powerful arguments that seem to need no verbal text. Several publications, including *Newsweek: America Under Attack* (Extra Edition, 2000), *New York Times Magazine* 23 Sept. 2001, and *The Day That Changed America* (American Media, Inc.) offered searing photographs of destruction and suffering. See also "The Expression of Grief and the Power of Art," *New York Times* 13 Sept. 2001: F1, a collection of comments on the subject by art, movie, television, and theatre critics.

Students in the class who know something about photography can be asked to explain the way in which composition, color, and other attributes work to convey a point of view. Or a member of the school art department can be invited to speak on the subject of visual argumentation in ads and photojournalism. Explaining the implicit argument in an ad that relies largely on visual imagery is an obvious subject for oral presentation in which visual aids can be used to good effect.

14

Some students may be interested in examining the implied claims in movie posters, such as those they see at the video store. Several critics have suggested interpretations that are not so obvious to the untrained eye. They are entertainingly summarized in *Civilization* Apr./May 1999: 35+.

Another accessible subject is fashion advertising, which has come under fire in recent years. Some of the most provocative ads, by Calvin Klein, are directed at young people of college age who will probably recognize the implied claims.

Bibliography

"Defining Moments: How Photography Changed Our World." *U.S. News & World Report* 9–16 July 2001.

Most writing done in the industrialized world is done on computers, and an increasing amount of that writing is being done over computer networks. One of the well-documented benefits of online responding is that students write much more than they do in non-networked classrooms.

Using computer networks for peer online responding to student drafts encourages students to develop greater critical reading and revising skills independently of the kind of continual teacher monitoring found in the traditional writing classroom. But occasions arise that require the specific guidance and intervention of the instructor. Generally, there are two kinds of these requirements for intervention: pedagogical and behavioral.

a. The instructor intervenes pedagogically online when review of the students' drafting or online responding indicates a need for information or advice.
b. The instructor intervenes for behavioral reasons when students take advantage of the freedoms of online writing to check e-mail, surf the Web, or engage in disruptive or illegal behavior. Such behavior may include harassment of various kinds, provocative statements that extend beyond the boundaries of academic discourse, or illegal use of electronic resources. Occasionally (but very rarely) students will engage in "flame wars," or heated verbal exchanges serving no academic purpose.

In these cases, the instructor sends mail to one or more parties emphasizing that online communication within the classroom context must remain within the terms of the class's policies and that otherwise sanctions may be imposed.

CHAPTER 4

Writing about Argument

(text pages 80–121)

While students are still workin through the chapters that introduce the elements of argument, they can practice applying those terms to the arguments of others. The claim for an essay about an argument can be either a claim of fact or a claim of value. It would be rare for an analysis of an argument to support a claim of policy. After reading an essay like Krauthammer's "Let's Have No More Monkey Trials," students can practice writing claims of fact and claims of value about the essay, understanding that a claim of fact objectively analyzes one or more elements of the essay while a claim of value evaluates one or more elements. One would explain the types of support used in the essay, for example, while the other would evaluate the effectiveness of the support.

The Seth Finkelstein essay is an example of an essay about an argument. It is an evaluation of the preceding article about toture by Alan Dershowitz. It will be immediately clear to students that Finkelstein is far from objective in the piece. By providing two essays by Dershowitz on the same topic, we offer students the opportunity to compare the use of support in the two, one of which is a much more fully developed treatment of the subject of torture.

This chapter is a good place to introduce the use of paraphrase, summary, and direct quotation as a means of supporting a thesis. Later, in writing a research paper, your students will most likely all be drawing on different sources — but for now, they can write about a limited number of sources, and the instructor can easily check their use of sources while they are all drawing on the same ones. The ability to work source material into one's own text is a learned skill and one that many students need to practice in order to master. In teaching the use of sources the instructor can also stress the importance of identifying the author of the source and some ways of expressing that author's authority on the subject. Students tend to include the author's name and a page number in parentheses and feel that is adequate documentation. Technically, it may be, but most often much of the impact of quoted or paraphrased material is due to who wrote it. While writing about the arguments of others, students can practice identifying the authors of the quoted or paraphrased material and using their authority as a means of strengthening an argument.

A good beginning exercise on the use of sources is to ask students to summarize an essay and, in doing so, to correctly incorproate at least one direct quotation. The first sentence can identify the author and his or her claim to authoirty.

This is also a good place to bring in the results of a survey, such as the brief ones reported frequently in magazines such as *Time* and *Newsweek*. Students can be asked to draw a conclusion from the data in the survey and then to write a paragraph supporting that conclusion and drawing on the survey for support.

Barbara Datoe Whitehead's essay "Parents Need Help" is a good one to ask students to evaluate because there is likely to be a good bit of disagreement. Whether stuents agree with Whitehead's argument or not, they have to understand her argument well enough to either support or attack it, and they must be able to argue why they evaluate it in the way that they do.

DEBATE: HOW SERIOUS IS THE PROBLEM OF ONLINE PREDATORS?

As usual, the two essays in the debate can be contrasted because they offer different perspectives on the same topic, in this case online predators.

1. You might start with a poll surveying your students about their online presence. How many of them have a profile on MySpace, Facebook, or other social networking sites? How many of them include personal information such as their addresses, class schedules, or photos of themselves in their profile?

2. According to Kimberly Mitchell, a psychology professor at the University of New Hampshire's Crimes Against Children Research Center, one out of every 25 children online is asked at some point during a year to transmit a sexual picture of themselves. What are your students' reactions to that statistic?

3. To what extent are your students familiar with the NBC show "To Catch a Predator," in which online solicitations to what men believe are teenage girls

result in arrest and public exposure? Do your students agree with the methods employed in the show?

CHAPTER 5
Defining Key Terms
(text pages 122–156)

You might want to begin this unit by dividing the class into four or five groups and assigning to each group the definition of a common object —book, bed, chair, cup, shoe. The definitions that emerge from the group are then compared to those in the dictionary. (The definitions by students are often remarkably close.)

After this exercise, ask students to describe the process of definition they have just engaged in. As the discussion proceeds, students discover, first of all, that in matters of definition we know more than we can tell. (See Michael Polanyi's fascinating examination of this in *The Tacit Dimension*, Routledge & K. Paul, 1967.) Apart from this philosophical dilemma, the attempt to define these familiar objects gives practice in distinguishing the properties that separate similar objects or objects belonging to the same genres. Equally important, students must think of examples if they are to make useful distinctions — between a shoe and a boot, between a chair and a stool, between a book and a magazine. The same necessity to resort to examples will become even clearer when they define abstract terms.

You may assign a single vague or ambiguous term, on which there is sure to be disagreement, for an extended discussion by each member of the class: success; the good life; normal sexuality; maturity; heroism; necessities, comforts, and luxuries. Some or all of the completed papers may be duplicated and distributed to the whole class or made available online. Through a discussion or written assignment the class may examine the criteria governing the different definitions. Can we reach a consensus? Why, or why not? What are the implications of success or failure in reaching consensus about these particular terms?

Students can also tackle the definitions of words that have acquired several, sometimes contradictory, meanings. *Example: discrimination.* For most students, this word carries a negative connotation. You might also offer the following example:

> A young woman who knows nothing about the mechanics of a car finds herself stranded in a parking lot because the engine of her car will not start. Passing near her are two people — a young man and a young woman. The car owner ignores the young woman and turns to the young man, asking him if he can identify and perhaps solve the problem of the stalled car.

Does this action represent *discrimination* in the negative sense? Students must explain their answers in such a way as to make clear how they define the term.

They might also be directed to examine the use of the word in aesthetic criticism. Why has the word taken on negative connotations in other areas of discourse?

Students can find examples of implicit definitions even in their popular songs. *Example:* Pink Floyd in "The Wall": "We don't need no education. We don't need no thought control. . . . Teachers, leave us kids alone." How is education defined in this song?

Stereotype has suffered the same fate as *discrimination.* We've discussed with students a different perception of a word almost always treated nowadays as a reflection of prejudice. From *The Biosexual Factor* by Richard Hagen:

> Stereotypes are the stuff of prediction. Used correctly, they can save us a great deal of grief. If ignored, they may exact a price. The teenage girl who hitchhikes alone because she doesn't accept stereotypic warnings about male sexual behavior is likely to learn a lot about stereotypes.

In recent years the definition of *disability* has received critical attention from the medical and legal professions. The American Psychiatric Association lists more than three hundred illnesses, among them "road rage" and "jury duty disorder." (Week In Review, *New York Times* 28 Sept. 1997.) Students can look up rulings on the Americans with Disabilities Act in *Facts on File* for June 27, 1998. More recent cases include the rights of near sighted pilots and tournament golfers who cannot walk, among others. See "What Is Golf? What Is a Disability?" *New York Times* 3 June 2001: Wk. 18.

Bibliography

Rosenbaum, Ron. "Degrees of Evil." The *Atlantic Monthly* Feb. 2001: 63–68. "Some thoughts on Hitler, bin Laden, and the hierarchy of wickedness."

DEBATE: IS THE DEFINITION OF MARRIAGE CHANGING?

A good starting point for the discussion of the essays by Moody and Citron is to review with students the doctrine of separation of church and state as established in the First Amendment to the Constitution: "Congress shall make no law respecting an establishment of religion, or prohibiting the exercise thereof. . . ." Understanding Moody's argument depends on understanding why he sees the issue of same-sex marriage as a constitutional issue. You might want to give students the assignment of finding for themselves in the Constitution the wording about separation of church and state (and perhaps the assignment of knowing where to find a copy of the Constitution), since many students draw on this historical document without knowing what it really says (as they do with the proposed Equal Rights Amendment).

The topic of same-sex marriage was a logical choice for this chapter because of the heated discussion of the definition of marriage that has arisen with the move to allow same-sex marriage in some states. Citron's essay introduces the possibility that using a term other than *marriage* for a same-sex union might be in the best interests of those who champion gay rights. You might ask your students to consider before they read the two essays how they define *marriage* and on what basis. Who has the right to define the term? Should every state have the right to define the term? What complications are created if the definition varies from state to state?

This pair of essays also provides an opportunity to consider the assumptions on which the two authors base their arguments. (If you want to delay that discussion until after studying warrants in more detail in Chapter 8, you can return to these essays later for more practice in identifying warrants.)

Bibliography

Bork, Robert H. "The Necessary Amendment." *First Things: A Monthly Journal of Religion and Public Life* Aug.–Sept. 2004: 17–21.

DeMarco, Donald. "The Abolition of Marriage." *Catholic Insight* Oct. 2004: 24–25.

Detweiler, George. "How to Protect Marriage." *New American* 20.16 (2004): 28–31.

Hope, Melanie. "To Have and to Hold." *Essence* Aug. 2004: 34.

Hudson, Mike. "Marriage Gets Real: Newly Married Same-Sex Couples in Massachusetts Are Fitting In — As Long As They Stay Local and Don't Ask the Feds for Recognition." *Advocate* 12 Oct. 2004: 33–34.

Mohr, Richard D. "Equal Dignity under the Law." *Gay and Lesbian Review Worldwide* Sept.–Oct. 2004: 30–35.

CHAPTER 6

Defending Claims

(text pages 157-210)

CLAIMS OF FACT

1. Students have little difficulty understanding claims of fact. But before giving an assignment, you may want to offer a dozen or more examples of such claims to make clear what kinds of arguments they produce. These are in addition to examples in the book.

2. If students have already elected a major or are about to do so, they can find subjects in their areas of specialization. At this point library research need not be emphasized. Students are often able to find sufficient factual data in their memories or their notes. (Wherever possible, they should, of course, give credit to their sources, even to a lecturer in an academic course.)

   The reports they may be asked to make on the job are often claims of fact, in which they will have to provide proof that a condition exists or that something has been found to be true as a result of research. The claims, or thesis statements of their essays, correspond to the conclusions of their reports, which, like the claims, may appear first. *Example* (in an article about food colorants): "The development of organic chemistry produced a series of compounds that are well suited to coloring food. Today most of the food colorants are chemicals produced by synthesis from simple basic materials." (*A Progress Report*, Massachusetts Agricultural Station, July–Aug. 1974.)

   Such straightforward factual reports are not likely to be models of creativity, but they emphasize other important qualities of good writing: adequate support, a direct, unadorned style, and clear transitions between ideas. They offer practice in the kind of clear exposition that all writers are well advised to master before they go further.

3. More challenging are factual claims that are clearly controversial. Some will require only reflection on personal observation as support; others will need objective data. *Examples*: "The students on this campus are increasingly conservative." "Teaching writing on computers will not produce better writers." "Children are now judged to be reliable witnesses in child-abuse cases." "Attractive people are regarded by others as more intelligent and sensitive than unattractive people."

   Encourage students to stick to the facts and avoid direct expression of value judgments (although, of course, these may be implicit).

4.   Another source of assignments may be the materials in Part One's short debates and Part Three's "Multiple Viewpoints." Ask students to choose one of the subjects and, after reading all or most of the selections, derive a limited factual claim. *Example:* "Human stem cells are readily available and easily harvested."

The supporting materials will not be original. This assignment tests the writer's ability to extract relevant data in suport of a thesis, express the facts in his or her own language, and organize them logically.

5.   In this edition we continue to include advertisements that represent all the elements of argument. In our culture ads are the most prominent examples of abbreviated arguments that often conceal as much as they reveal, and students enjoy uncovering the missing elements. One caution: Although students may have studied ads in high school and can analyze them with some sophistication, they are disposed to treat all advertisement as untruthful. Ads that conceal or distort are usually the most interesting to examine, but try to get students to make careful distinctions between the ads that support their claims, or seem to, and those that don't.

6.   Inevitably, controversial claims will move student writers to ascribe causes.

A number of tragic school shootings occurred in 1998 and 1999, both in the United States — Arkansas, Kentucky, Colorado — and abroad, in Scotland and Canada. They occasioned an outpouring of analyses, impassioned attempts to discover the *causes* of such aberrant behavior in children.

Students probably have discussed these events in their high school classes. They have also expressed their opinions about the causes to newspaper and television viewers. The social and psychological conditions that may have contributed to these tragedies are subjects for written assignments. So are suggested solutions as claims of policy.

7.   Students must be cautioned to avoid assuming that explanations imply justification. For example, according to psychology professor Erwin Staub, the atrocities that occurred in Kosovo province can be explained: "[E]ven violent leaders often express and even share needs of their people. The needs of the Serbs for a feeling of security and for identity as a people are intense." But, he goes on to say, although these needs help to explain Serb behavior, "they cannot justify it."[1]

Bibliography

Bok, Derek, and William G. Bowen. *The Shape of the River: Long-Term Consequences of Considering Race in College and University Admissions.* Princeton, NJ: Princeton UP, 1998. Evidence that affirmative action has contributed to an emergent middle class.

Chavez, Linda. "Colleges and Quotas." *Wall Street Journal* 22 Feb. 2001: 19. "A new study finds evidence that American universities are guilty of pervasive racial discrimination."

Traub, James. "The Class of Prop. 209." *New York Times Magazine* 2 May 1999: 44+. "In the wake of affirmative action, campuses in California are managing to maintain diversity without racial set-asides. This will satisfy neither liberals nor conservatives, but it's looking a lot like the future."

[1]*The Campus Chronicle* [University of Massachusetts, Amherst] 23 Apr. 1999: 1.

CLAIMS OF VALUE

1. As they begin to write, students will discover that the line between claims of fact and claims of value is often blurred, but in real-life arguments outside the classroom, these distinctions are not crucial. We make them in the classroom largely because they allow us to examine the elements more closely. Before beginning to write a claim of value, students should consult the "Writer's Guide: Defending a Claim of Value," which summarizes the process.

2. Claims of value are more demanding than claims of fact. Facts remain important, but now students must express an attitude toward them. Despite the fact that values are a part of almost every argument — even in claims of fact they may be implicit in the choices of subjects and data —students are sometimes unclear about how to uncover and express them. These approaches may be helpful:

    a. *Ask personal questions.* What do you want out of life? Do you dislike anything about yourself? Do you have religious beliefs? If so, how do they influence your behavior? What are the good things about your family? What are the most valuable things you own? What kind of country do you want the United States to be? And so on. (Of course, for purposes of the exercise the answers need not be true, and it should be clear to students that they are under no obligation to bare their souls. On the other hand, most students, like the rest of us, enjoy talking about themselves.)

        The answers that emerge can be written on the board, listed as positive and negative values. You will probably have to change the language, finding more precise terms than the ones that the students offer. This exercise defines values and value systems in a readily understandable way. Values as a form of support will be discussed more fully in Chapter 7, but this discussion should assist students to find the values that can be defended in their value claims.

    b. *Analyze one or two essays in the text to discover the values of the author.* What values seem to underlie, for example, Charles Krauthammer's argument in "Let's Have No More Monkey Trials." How do the values of Don Sullivan and Kevin Alexander seem to differ in the debate on online predators.

        Students can be asked to answer such questions in short, in-class assignments — fifteen minutes — for which they must produce a well-organized paragraph: clear topic sentence and sufficient supporting material. Because they stress economy and directness, such assignments are useful for teaching some elements of style.

3. As with claims of fact, students can draw on campus experience for subjects that lend themselves to class discussion, outlining, and reinforcing the ways in which claims of value differ from claims of fact. *Examples*: "Student evaluations of teachers are worthless." "Funds for Gay Awareness Week are unjustified."

4. In this unit, too, you might want to point out that claims of value are often required on the job in the form of personnel reports or reports that evaluate marketing strategies and campaigns. If students are interested, topics for such papers can be obtained from books on technical writing or from the business departments of the school.

5. A ready-to-use anthology of material for claims of value appears in a special supplement of the *Wall Street Journal* 5 Mar. 1998, called "Divining the American Character." It includes more than a dozen articles on how "the bedrock morals co-exist uneasily with a desire 'to live and let live.'" Needless

to say, several of the articles deal with then-President Clinton and public approval/disapproval of his public and private performance.

CLAIMS OF POLICY

1. Since claims of policy assert that something should or should not be done, they presuppose the existence of a problem needing solution. Both facts and values are indispensable to defense of a policy claim, because in many arguments students will first have to establish that a problem exists, then underscore how the desired values will be served by adoption of the proposed solution.

2. As an introduction to this unit, short problems, either real or hypothetical, can test the ability of students to find solutions — that is, to defend claims of policy. The facts are clearly laid out in the summary of the problem. In order to justify the solution, students will need to expose the values that underlie their claims. *Example of a real problem*:

The Plagiarism Problem

John Jones, a senior at U____ M____, was enrolled in a writing course, *Writing about Film*. A few weeks before the end of the semester he suffered a crisis in his love life. The woman who had been his inseparable companion suddenly informed him that she was no longer interested in continuing their friendship. John lost control of himself for a few weeks; he stayed in his room brooding, drank heavily every night, and stopped going to classes. Three days before the end of the semester, he found out that in order to pass the film course and then to graduate, he had to fulfill a final assignment — attend a film and write a review of it. Frantic, John went to the library, copied out a review of a film by a professional critic, and submitted it to the instructor. The instructor recognized the plagiarism and failed John for the course. The failure meant that John could not graduate despite the fact that he had a job waiting for him in Seattle. He argued with the instructor to no avail. The instructor said that he had made it very clear from the beginning of the semester that any plagiarism would result in a failure for the course. John appealed to the provost, who had the authority to grant a Pass for the course.

Question: Should the provost rule that John need not do anything more to fulfill the writing course and allow him to graduate?

3. We have called attention to this problem in the text, but perhaps it bears repeating. In defending claims of policy, students must guard against offering solutions for enormous problems that have defied solution for decades or even centuries. Their ambitions may be laudable, but nevertheless they should be urged to confine themselves to solutions that can be defended in 750 words.

4. "Multiple Viewpoints" is a collection of problems in search of solutions. Assign readings in any of the subjects and ask students to propose solutions based on their evaluations of the arguments.

In defending their claims of policy students should try to use the pattern of organization we call *defending the stock issues* — need, plan, and advantage (see Chapter 12, "Writing an Argumentative Paper"). This pattern permits them to be exhaustive without becoming confused by a multitude of details and a variety of possible approaches.

5. Policy claims are, of course, inherent in any business or professional activity. Ask students who have job experience to write out short summaries of specific problems they remember having encountered on the job, either their own or someone else's. The problems should be substantive, and the facts should be clearly stated. Then ask other students to suggest solutions. Students may also ask for examples of problems from the business departments of the school.

    These short writing exercises emphasize clarity, accuracy, and a sensitivity to the audience — the employer, supervisor, or other employees —who will act on the decision.

    If the solutions differ, students may discuss the differences and try to uncover the reasons for them. Do the differences derive from lack of sufficient data or from conflicting values? Can the differences be reconciled?

6. Since the imprisonment of Dr. Jack Kevorkian, "the suicide doctor," the press has paid little attention to cases of euthanasia, although it is widely acknowledged that physicians and family members continue to practice "mercy killings." The Netherlands has long tolerated euthanasia, but not many people are aware that only in 2001 did the practice become legal. The legalization aroused intense condemnation in other countries but especially in Germany. Students working toward an evaluation of euthanasia should inform themselves about its use by the Nazis, who put to death about 100,000 "men, women, and children who were physically and mentally handicapped. The aim was to improve what they called the Aryan race by eradicating those who doctors decided had congenital defects." ("Horror Expressed in Germany over Dutch Euthanasia," *New York Times* 11 Apr. 2001: A15.)

    Students may also be interested to know that under Dutch law, when their children reach the ages of sixteen and seventeen, "parents must be informed but no longer have the right to decide." Do students think that doctors and others should be able to assist teenagers to commit suicide? If not, why not? If yes, under what circumstances?

7. Should mentally unstable people be allowed to own guns? A state appeals court in Alaska has ruled that a mentally ill man — who claims that he has a computer chip in his head — need not surrender his gun. "Gun owners argue that state laws safeguard this Second Amendment right."

Bibliography

Humphry, Derek. *Let Me Die before I Wake*. Eugene, OR: Hemlock Soc., 1991.

McHugh, Paul R. "Dying Made Easy." *Commentary* Feb. 1999: 13–17.

Miniter, Richard. "The Dutch Way of Death." *Wall Street Journal* 25 Apr. 2001: A20.

DEBATE: UNDER WHAT CIRCUMSTANCES DOES THE GOVERNMENT HAVE THE RIGHT TO SEIZE PERSONAL PROPERTY?

1. Most of your students will have had any direct experience with property seizures made under the policy of eminent domain. Some may know of cases that they can summarize for the class. It is useful to review the definition of eminent domain and its history, considering why it came into existence in the first place. Students can also research other cases in which private citizens have taken on developers who have tried to seize their land for uses other than public purposes.

2. The *USA Today* article cites victories won by opponents of eminent domain. Students can research what other victories — or defeats — they have had in the time since the articles were published.

3. Borut concludes, "The prudent use of eminent domain has brought hope and opportunity — through good jobs and better housing — to thousands of Americans. That story deserves to be told." What evidence can students find that the story is true?

CHAPTER 7

Providing Support

(text pages 211–271)

EVIDENCE

1. Students seem to subscribe to the belief that a knowledge of the facts is sufficient to induce a change in our habits and attitudes, but there is plenty of expert evidence that the plain truth is not enough. Robert Sternberg, a Yale University psychologist, says, "People will go to great lengths to avoid information that contradicts their original stories. There's a lot of research that shows that people seek to confirm what they think, rather than disconfirm what they think" (*Boston Globe*, 21 Aug. 1993: 7).

   An interesting area for research by students is the relationship between facts about food and the choices people make. Several studies over the years suggest that the facts don't cause most people to alter their eating habits. Students can survey classmates to determine if their behavior confirms the results of these studies.

2. Assign reading of the following passage. Ask students to write either a short or a long essay that summarizes some of the inferences we draw from observing what people wear. Since the subject is so large (this excerpt is part of a book about clothing), this exercise gives students practice in narrowing the subject of discussion and choosing a thesis statement or paragraph that can be adequately developed in the number of words assigned.

   > For thousands of years human beings have communicated with one another first in the language of dress. Long before I am near enough to talk to you on the street, in a meeting, or at a party, you announce your sex, age, and class to me through what you are wearing — and possibly give me important information (or disinformation) as to your occupation, origin, personality, opinions, tastes, sexual desires, and current mood. I may not be able to put what I observe into words, but I register the information unconsciously, and you simultaneously do the same for me.
   > By the time we meet and converse we have already spoken to each other in an older and more universal tongue.
   >
   > — Alison Lurie
   > *The Language of Clothes*
   > (Random House, 1981)

3. On September 15, 1995, the *New York Times* published a report giving several different versions of an alleged crime: the shooting of a black police officer by a white police officer (p. B1). The white officer argued that he had mistaken the victim for a criminal. The *Times* summarized the disputed accounts in a

chart labeled "Sorting It Out." The chart included three different views of the shooting by witnesses and participants and three different opinions of the wound by medical examiners.

A written assignment on this story calls for a clear thesis statement or paragraph, extraction of the most important data, and arrangement of materials, in an orderly and emphatic way. Above all, it calls for an acknowledgment of the distinctions between facts and inferences in the testimony reported in the article and in the students' interpretations of the testimony. Not least, the students find this assignment interesting and provocative.

4. Ask students to look up information by advocates on both sides of the controversies surrounding one of the popular natural mysteries: the Loch Ness monster, the Bermuda Triangle, Findhorn, Bigfoot, or Sasquatch, etc. Then assign a paper, short or long, that reviews the data on both sides and tries to come to a conclusion regarding the validity of the respective claims. Have students justify their conclusions by defending the evidence. If students find that they cannot make up their minds, this is also a conclusion, but they should be prepared to say why the evidence on both sides proved equally strong or equally weak.

5. From the first paper students have been required to use evidence. Having now read the more elaborate explanations of both factual and opinion evidence in Chapter 7, students can return to their claims of fact, value, and policy and reevaluate the facts and opinions in their essays. Would more data strengthen their claim? If so, what kind? Where can it be found? Would additional expert opinion make their arguments more convincing? If so, whose opinions? Where can they be found?

If the students show some interest in revising their papers to include more data, encourage them to do so.

6. A popular exercise calls on students to look up the *New York Times* edition that appeared on their birthdays and write a paper that emphasizes straightforward presentation of data to support their claims. Students must find a thesis around which the information can be organized — about the kinds of films being shown, the nature of women's fashion, advertisements for jobs, scientific discoveries of the day, crimes, etc.

7. Advertisements again. This time students choose ads that offer information about the products. They then evaluate the data. In some cases, of course, they will be unequipped to decide whether the data are accurate or sufficient, but if the ads are directed to a lay audience, readers have a right to ask questions about the sufficiency, relevance, and recency of the data. In other words, if readers think that evidence for the virtues of the product is inadequate, what else would they want to know?

8. Students sometimes approach the subject of information in ads with the preconception that ads do not offer information — only slogans. Students may therefore be asked to contrast two or more ads that offer different amounts and qualities of information. Is information more important in some kinds of ads than others — for example, in automobile advertisements, which are often dense with facts?

9. If there is time for lengthier papers, ask students to examine the evidence in the following cases (or any others that remain controversial):

   a.   the Sacco–Vanzetti case, 1921
   b.   the kidnapping and murder of the Lindbergh baby, 1932
   c.   the kidnapping of Patty Hearst, 1974

d. the Bernhard Goetz case, 1987
e. the Rodney King case, 1991
f. the O. J. Simpson case, 1994
g. the Louise Woodward case, 1998
h. the Scott Peterson case, 2004
i. the assassination of Benazir Bhutto, 2007

10. In leading students to examine the credentials of experts, ask them to consider the authors in the text and the "Multiple Viewpoints" as "experts." It will be easy enough to identify Marion Nestle, a nutritionist, as an authority in her field. Even in more problematic disciplines, such as education, we recognize the authority of Rod Paige, for example, who, as a former U.S. Secretary of Education, has been a teacher, coach, college dean, schoolboard member, and superintendent of one of the largest school districts in the U.S.

But what are we to say of writers who reflect on their personal experience or expound their philosophies? Why do we think Elisha Dov Hack's views are worth reading? After all, he is no more an "expert" on sexual mores than many of his readers. It might come as a small revelation to students, and pertinent to their participation in a writing course, to recognize that the credibility of Hack and other nonprofessional "experts" is based largely on their excellence as writers. They can discover interesting propositions, and organize, develop, and express them in spirited and highly readable prose. They are intelligent, of course, but also curious about most subjects and well informed about many.

11. *The Science of Conjecture* by James Franklin (Johns Hopkins UP, 2001) "provides a history of the rational techniques that mankind has developed to acquire knowledge when certainty is not available — which is most of the time."

12. Students usually need practice in reporting statistics — extracting them from news stories and arranging them in interesting and readable form. Students can research the following subjects and report the information as data that might support a claim. They should, of course, limit the time period for the data. Have them submit their prose summaries to their classmates. Are the data clear and accessible to these readers?

a. world population growth
b. teenage pregnancies
c. women in the labor market
d. growth of ethnic populations in the United States
e. American marriage patterns
f. dimensions of poverty
g. voting patterns in the 2008 elections

13. The three books and one article mentioned below are entertaining and informative references for both teachers and students. They are full of useful examples that should help students avoid some of the common pitfalls in interpreting and reporting statistical evidence.

Campbell, Stephen K., *Flaws and Fallacies in Statistical Thinking*. Englewood Cliffs, NJ: Prentice-Hall, 1974.

Huff, Darrell. *How to Lie with Statistics*. New York: Norton, 1954.

Paulos, John Allen. *Innumeracy: Mathematical Illiteracy and Its Consequences*. New York: Hill, 1988. Students will discover that six degrees of Kevin Bacon is not so fanciful after all.

"Fright by the Numbers: Alarming Disease Data Are Frequently Flawed." *Wall Street Journal*, 12 Apr. 1996: B1. Calls attention to the need for caution in reading medical statistics.

Most of the numbers are extrapolations or estimates — at best. Yet as the media report them, often uncritically and without context, these conjectures assume the mantle of quantifiable fact.

14. Some students may be interested in and sufficiently informed about polling techniques to evaluate some of the famous polling gaffes: the *Literary Digest* poll of 1936 that predicted that Alfred Landon would defeat Franklin D. Roosevelt or the 1948 Gallup poll that predicted Thomas E. Dewey would defeat Harry S. Truman. Students might want to infer the reasons that such mistakes probably will not recur.

APPEALS TO NEEDS AND VALUES

1. A lively and immediate source of appeals to needs and values is found in speeches — students may be directed to *Vital Speeches of the Day*, which publishes speeches from a variety of speechmakers.

   Martin Luther King Jr.'s "I Have a Dream" is an outstanding example of spoken discourse that makes a profoundly emotional appeal. Other famous speeches for the purposes of this unit include:

   a. Clarence Darrow's "Address to the Prisoners of Cook County Jail" in 1902
   b. Vice President Richard Nixon's "Checkers" speech in 1952
   c. President John F. Kennedy's Inaugural Address in 1961
   d. Senator Edward Kennedy's TV address explaining to the people of Massachusetts his behavior during and after the accident at Chappaquiddick in 1969

   For example, Darrow's speech is remarkable for the inconsistency of his argument and its numerous fallacies, both of which have been overlooked by textbooks that reprint the address. Edward Kennedy's speech makes a personal appeal, arousing sympathy for his suffering and inducing guilt in the listener for having accused him unjustly.

   Since 1980, the *New York Times* has published "Basic Speeches," delivered by the major candidates in presidential campaigns. These appear in October of the campaign year. All the speeches contain copious and specific references to the values held by the candidates and, presumably, their audiences. The inaugural speeches are also revealing of the attention to values. In his inaugural speech on January 20, 2001, President George W. Bush spoke of America's commitment to "civility, courage, compassion, and character." "Our public interest," he said, depends on "private character, on civic duty and family bonds and basic fairness, on uncounted, unhonored acts of decency. . . ."

2. Advertisements by large corporations (GE, Microsoft, Wal-Mart) appearing frequently in newspapers and magazines comment on political and social issues rather than the merits of the companies' products. As short essays they can be useful for examination of values based on what is perceived to be common consent.

   a. What values do the advertisers assume that we share?
   b. What evidence (examples, facts, statistics) do they offer to convince the reader that their proposals will support our values?
   c. What tones are used in the essays (reasonable, generous, angry, sarcastic, humorous)?

3. Also useful are the ads that promise power, riches, great beauty, etc. Many of the most outrageous ones appear in *The National Enquirer* and similar publications.

   a. Can you infer to what audience they make a strong appeal?
   b. What fears, needs, desires do they appeal to?
   c. What attempts are made to provide credibility?

4. Quindlen's argument leads to a discussion of problems that depend on information unfamiliar to most students. As citizens and voters, however, they will be increasingly concerned with questions generated by advances in biology. For learners there is plenty of information available. An introduction to the stem-cell debate appears in an issue of *The Science Times* (18 Dec. 2000: sec. D), an eight-page summary of the facts that underlie the controversy. It contains clear definitions, diagrams, photographs, and expert opinion.

5. It is not surprising that the decision of the government to fund stem-cell research, however limited, should have roused some religious organizations to respond. Perhaps some students can speak or write on the positions taken by their churches or temples.

Bibliography

Fox, Cynthia. "Why Stem Cells Will Transform Medicine." *Fortune* 11 June 2001: 159–62.

"The New Animal Farm." *Newsweek* 2 Apr. 2001: 42–45.

DEBATE: IS ASSUMING THE ROLE OF CITIZEN JOURNALIST WORTH THE RISK?

1. Have any of your students used their cell phone cameras to document breaking news? What was the situation and the result?

2. The preamble to the Society of Professional Journalists reads in part:

   > Members of the Society of Professional Journalists believe that public enlightenment is the forerunner of justice and the foundation of democracy. The duty of the journalist is to further those ends by seeking truth and providing a fair and comprehensive account of events and issues.

   To what extent can and should non-journalists strive to provide accounts of events and issues? To what extent is there an obligation on the part of citizens to provide such accounts? What factors might limit such an obligation?

3. Cell phone cameras and blogs have allowed non-professionals to create accounts of newsworthy events as they unfold. What other new or emerging technologies allow for the recording and dissemination of news? What are the ethical constraints that accompany or should accompany the use of these technologies?

CHAPTER 8
Analyzing Warrants
(text pages 272–321)

1. Although the definition of the warrant in Toulmin's *The Uses of Argument* is more complicated than we have made it appear, for the purposes of an undergraduate composition course, those of us who have used the Toulmin model with some success believe that the model works best if we define the warrant as synonymous with assumption, a belief we take for granted, or a general principle underlying other beliefs and attitudes. If students raise questions, we can always widen the definition.

   For obvious reasons the concept of the warrant is more difficult for students to assimilate than that of support, in part because they have seldom been required to make their assumptions explicit. Fortunately for teaching purposes, the examples that we can use are so numerous and so varied that we may call attention to the warrant repeatedly without losing student interest.

2. Advertisements offer a rich and accessible source of material. Students may choose their own ads for analysis and write or speak about them to the class. The exercise should emphasize discussion of a controversial warrant. For an oral presentation, an ad that contains more than a paragraph of text can be duplicated for distribution, and the whole class can participate in a discussion of the validity of the warrant.

3. Subjects for examination of warrants appear almost every day in school newspapers. Sometimes the subjects are about education or other matters relevant to the function and management of the school; sometimes they respond to the world outside. Below are some current issues on college campuses today:

   a. A proposal to introduce a core diversity requirement designed to change attitudes on race and sex. (What assumptions about education underlie this proposal?)

   b. A demand that faculty appointments reflect the percentage of women and minorities in the general population. (What assumptions about education and the social and political functions of the university are at work in this affirmative action proposal?)

   c. A demand that Native Americans be allowed to live in a separate dormitory and be given their own student center. (What warrants about ethnic diversity and the goals of an academic institution can be uncovered?)

4. Other sources of analysis of warrants:

   a. *Etiquette books.* An interesting assignment would compare etiquette books of a generation or more ago with contemporary ones. (Judith Martin's books are valuable and amusing sources of comment about present-day manners.) Have there been large changes? Small changes? In what areas? On what assumptions about social relationships and freedom have these changes been based?

      Multicultural Manners: New Rules for a Changing Society by Norine Dresser (Wiley, 1996) gives rules of etiquette that recognize cultural and ethnic differences in this country. One reviewer of the book said, "For all its value, this book can push cultural tolerance to the breaking point."

   b. *Advice columns in newspapers and magazines.* What assumptions about marriage, sexual problems, child rearing, religion, etc. underlie the advice of the columnists?

c. *Magazines for teenagers.* Have they changed in the last fifteen or twenty years? On what assumptions about the lives and values of teenagers have the publishers based their changes?

d. *Arguments in magazines and newspapers that make a controversial or unpopular claim.* The views of Peter Singer, a professor of philosophy at Princeton University, are always good for an argument and the unearthing of warrants held by a very small minority. "The Singer Solution to World Poverty" (*New York Times Magazine* 5 Sept. 1999) explores Singer's claim that Americans are obligated to help support the world's poor: "Whatever money you're spending on luxuries, not necessities, should be given away." If students don't agree, they should try to defend the warrants that underlie their claims. And how do students define luxuries and necessities?

5. Go back to the earlier papers of definition and defense of value and policy claims and examine the warrants, expressed or unexpressed. *Example*: In defending his decision never to marry, a student writes that he values his freedom. What does he assume about marriage, love, individuality, commitment, etc.?

ADDITIONAL TYPES OF WARRANTS

In Chapter 8 we discuss three main categories of warrants, derived from Ehninger and Brockriede (1953): *authoritative, substantive,* and *motivational* warrants. If you would like to introduce your students to a more complex range of warrants, all of which are subtypes of the three main categories, we have provided discussions of each of seven types below: *authority, generalization, sign, cause and effect, comparison, analogy,* and *values.* A warrants chart on pages 34–35 shows in schematic form the types of warrants, with examples and critical questions that may help students detect them in arguments. If you do choose to teach these additional types of warrants to your students, you may wish to photocopy and distribute the chart.

Authority

Arguments from authority depend on the credibility of their sources, as in this example.

> [Benjamin] Bloom maintains that most children can learn everything that is taught them with complete competence.[1]

Because Benjamin Bloom was a professor of education at the University of Chicago and a widely respected authority on educational psychology, his statement about the educability of children carried considerable weight. Notice that Professor Bloom has qualified his claim by asserting that "most" children, but not all, can learn everything. The reader might also recognize the limits of the warrant — the authority could be mistaken, or there could be disagreement among authorities.

CLAIM: Most children can learn everything that is taught them with complete competence.

SUPPORT: Professor Bloom attests that this is so.

WARRANT: Professor Bloom's testimony is sufficient because he is an accepted authority on educational achievement.

RESERVATIONS: Unless the data for his studies were inaccurate, unless his criteria for evaluation were flawed, and so on.

[1]Michael Alper, "All Our Children Can Learn," *University of Chicago Magazine* Summer 1982: 3.

Generalization

Arguments from generalization are based on the belief that a general principle can be derived from a series of examples. But these warrants are credible only if the examples are representative of the whole group being described and not too many contradictory examples have been ignored. In the following excerpt the author documents the tragic effects for children born "unnaturally" (outside the mother's womb) or without knowledge of their fathers.

> For years I've collected bits of data about certain unfortunate people in the news: Son of Sam, the Hillside strangler, the Pennsylvania shoemaker who raped and brutalized several women, a Florida man who killed at least thirty-four women, the man sought in connection with the Tylenol scare. All of them grew up not knowing at least one of their natural parents; most knew neither.[2]

In outline the argument takes this form:

CLAIM:	People brought up without a sense of identity with their natural parents will respond to the world with rage and violence.
SUPPORT:	Son of Sam, the Hillside strangler, the Pennsylvania shoemaker, the Florida murderer, the man in the Tylenol scare responded to the world with rage and violence.
WARRANT:	What is true of this sample is true for others in this class.
RESERVATIONS:	Unless this sample is too small or exceptions have been ignored.

Sign

As the name suggests, in arguments based on sign the arguer offers an observable datum as an indicator of a condition. The warrant that a sign is convincing can be accepted only if the sign is appropriate, if it is sufficient, and if other indicators do not dispute it (for example, an argument in which the enjoyment of Virginia Slims is presented as a sign of female liberation). In the following example the warrant is stated:

> There are other signs of a gradual demoting of the professions to the level of ordinary trades and businesses. The right of lawyers and physicians to advertise, so as to reintroduce money competition and break down the "standard practices," is being granted. Architects are being allowed to act as contractors. Teachers have been unionized.[3]

Here, too, a reservation is in order.

CLAIM:	Professions are being demoted to the level of ordinary trades and businesses.
SUPPORT:	Lawyers and physicians advertise, architects act as contractors, teachers have been unionized.
WARRANT:	These business practices are signs of the demotion of the professions.
RESERVATION:	Unless these practices are not widespread.

---

[2]Lorraine Dusky, "Brave New Babies?" *Newsweek* 6 Dec. 1982: 30.
[3]Jacques Barzun, "The Professions under Siege," *Harper's* Oct. 1978: 66.

Cause and Effect

Causal reasoning assumes that one event or condition can bring about another. One can reason from the cause to the effect or from the effect to the cause. The following is an example of reasoning from effect (the claim) to cause (the warrant). The quotation is taken from the famous Supreme Court decision of 1954, *Brown v. Board of Education*, which mandated the desegregation of public schools throughout the United States.

> Segregation of white and colored children in public schools has a detrimental effect upon the colored children. The impact is greater when it has the sanction of the law; for the policy of separating the races is usually interpreted as denoting the inferiority of the Negro group. A sense of inferiority affects the motivation of a child to learn. Segregation with the sanction of law, therefore, has a tendency to [retard] the educational and mental development of Negro children and to deprive them of some of the benefits they would receive in a racial[ly] integrated school system.[4]

The outline of the argument would take this form:

CLAIM: (EFFECT):	Colored children have suffered mental and emotional damage in legally segregated schools.
SUPPORT:	They suffer from feelings of inferiority, which retard their ability to learn. They are being deprived of important social and educational benefits.
WARRANT: (CAUSE):	Legal segregation has a tendency to retard the emotional and mental development of Negro children.

In cause-effect arguments the reasoning may be more complicated than an outline suggests. For one thing, events and conditions in the world are not always the result of single causes, nor does a cause necessarily produce a single result. It is probably more realistic to speak of chains of causes as well as chains of effects. A recent headline emphasizes this form of reasoning: "Experts Fear That Unpredictable Chain of Events Could Bring Nuclear War." The article points to the assassination of Archduke Francis Ferdinand of Austria-Hungary in the Bosnian city of Sarajevo in 1914, which "set in motion a series of events that the world's most powerful leaders could not stop" — that is, World War I.

Or, as another example, opinion polls a few years ago indicated Americans' unwillingness to "approve any bellicose activity, unless US interests are seen as truly vital and are clearly defined."[5] The immediate cause of this isolationism is usually attributed to the "Vietnam syndrome," the relic of a bitter experience in an unpopular war. But this single cause, according to some students of the problem, is insufficient to explain the current mood. History, they say, reveals "decades of similar American resistance to foreign involvements." Needless to say, the "Vietnam syndrome" no longer prevails in the wake of the attacks on September 11, 2001, and the very real possibility of further attacks in the future. Some students may want to examine the causes of the furious hatred of the United States that triggered the September 11 attacks and to evaluate the plausibility of those causes.

Causes can also be either *necessary* or *sufficient*. That is, to contract tuberculosis, it is necessary to be exposed to the bacillus, but this exposure in itself may not be sufficient to bring on the disease. However, if the victim's immune system is depressed for some reason, exposure to the bacillus will be sufficient to cause the illness. Or, to make an example from law and politics: To reduce the incidence of drunk driving, it would be necessary to enact legislation that penalized the drunk

---

[4]*Brown v. Board of Education of Topeka*, 347 U.S. 487–96 (May 17, 1954).
[5]*Public Opinion*, Apr.–May 1982: 16.

driver. But that would not be sufficient unless the police and the courts were diligent in making arrests and imposing sentences.

Comparison

In some arguments characteristics and circumstances in two or more cases are compared to prove that what is true in one case ought to be true in another. Unlike the elements in analogies the things being matched in comparison belong to the same class. The following is a familiar argument based on a comparison of similar activities in different countries at different times. On the basis of these apparent similarities the author makes a judgment about America's future.

> Perhaps I'm wrong, but the auguries seem to me threatening. Like the bourgeoisie of pre–World War I in Europe, we are retreating into our well-furnished houses, hoping the storm, when it comes, will strike someone else, preferably the poor. Our narcissistic passion for sports and fitness reminds me of Germany in the twenties and early thirties, when the entire nation turned to hiking, sun-bathing, and the worship of the body beautiful, in part so as not to see what was happening to German politics — not to speak of the family next door. The belief that gold in the garden is more important than government helped to bring France to defeat in 1940 and near civil war in the 1950s. When the middle class stops believing in government or in the future, it's all over, time truly to sew the diamonds in the lining of your coat and make a run for it.[6]

This is the argument in outline form:

CLAIM:	The behavior of many middle-class Americans today threatens our future.
SUPPORT:	The same kind of behavior by the Germans in the twenties and thirties and by the French in the thirties and forties led to disaster.
WARRANT:	Because such behavior brought disaster to Germany and France, it will bring disaster to America.

But is this warrant believable? Are the dissimilarities between the United States now and these European countries in earlier decades greater than the similarities? For example, if the present American passion for sports and fitness is caused by very different social forces than those that operated in Germany in the twenties and thirties, then the comparison warrant is too weak to support the author's claim.

Analogy

An analogy warrant assumes a resemblance in some characteristics between dissimilar things. Analogies differ in their power to persuade. Some are explanatory; others are merely descriptive. Those that describe are less likely to be useful in a serious argument. In conversation human beings are often likened to other animals — cows, pigs, rats, chickens. Or life and happiness are compared to a variety of objects: "Life is a cabaret," "Life is just a bowl of cherries," "Happiness is a warm puppy." But such metaphorical uses are more colorful than precise. In those examples one quality is abstracted from all the others, leaving us with two objects that remain essentially dissimilar. Descriptive analogies promise immediate access to the reader, as do paintings or photographs. Such short cuts are tempting, but

---

[6]Michael Korda, "The New Pessimism," *Newsweek* 14 June 1982: 10.

descriptive analogies are seldom enough to support a claim. Consider the following example, which appears in a speech by Malcolm X, the black civil rights leader, criticizing the participation by whites in the march on Washington in 1962 for black rights and employment:

It's just like when you've got some coffee that's too black, which means it's too strong. What do you do? You integrate it with cream, you make it weak. But if you pour too much cream in it, you won't even know you ever had coffee.[7]

This is the outline of the argument:

CLAIM: Integration of black and white people in the march on Washington weakened the black movement for rights and jobs.

SUPPORT: Putting white cream into black coffee weakens the coffee.

WARRANT: Weakening coffee with cream is analogous to weakening the black rights movement by allowing white people to participate.

The imagery is vivid, but the analogy does not represent convincing proof. The dissimilarities between whitening coffee with cream and integrating a political movement are too great to convince the reader of the damaging effects of integration. Moreover, words like *strong* and *weak* as they apply to a civil rights movement need careful definition. To make a convincing case, the author would have to offer not imagery but facts and authoritative opinion.

The following analogy is more successful because it is explanatory rather than descriptive. The elements on both sides of the analogy are failing or sick human beings and less than productive tests. This excerpt appears in an article by Albert Shanker, late president of the American Federation of Teachers, deploring the low scores of American students in national tests.

It's not the first time we've heard about the dismal performance of US students in math: NAEP [National Assessment of Educational Progress] has been giving us the same bad news for twenty years. So it should come as no surprise that our kids are nowhere near "first in the world." What can we expect now? Only, I'm afraid, that another test will be administered two years from now to see if we're doing any better.

Suppose you were feeling terrible and went to a doctor who tested you, said you had a fever, and asked you to come back in two weeks. And suppose you returned every couple of weeks for a year or so to be tested, and every time, you got the same bad news but still no diagnosis and no advice. Few of us would think much of a doctor who did nothing but test us and give us bad news. But that's what's been going on in education for twenty years.[8]

Shanker's argument may be outlined like this:

CLAIM: Testing students in math year after year without proposing remedies is fruitless.

SUPPORT: Testing a sick person again and again without offering a diagnosis or treatment would be considered unacceptable medical practice.

WARRANT: Math tests which fail to diagnose the problem and propose remedies are analogous to medical tests which offer no diagnosis or treatment for the patient.

[7]"Message to the Grass Roots," *Roots of Rebellion*, ed. Richard P. Young (New York: Harper, 1970) 357.
[8]"Testing Is Not Enough," *New York Times* 20 Oct. 1991: E7.

WARRANTS CHART

Type of Warrant	Subtype	Example
Authoritative Warrants are based on the credibility of a source		CLAIM: Cigarette smoking is harmful.
Substantive Warrants are based on beliefs about the reliability of factual evidence	A **Generalization Warrant** is a substantive warrant based on the belief that it is possible to derive a general principle from a series of examples.	CLAIM: Marijuana is a potent medicine for relief of pain in seriously ill patients.
	A **Sign Warrant** is a substantive warrant based on the belief that an observable datum is an indicator of a particular condition.	CLAIM: Press reports and TV news programs deal in lies and deception.
	A **Cause-and-Effect Warrant** is a substantive warrant that assumes that one event or condition can bring about another.	CLAIM: Giving free food to poor countries can be counter-productive.
	A **Comparison Warrant** is a substantive warrant that assumes that what is true in one case ought to be true in another.	CLAIM: The United States should set an annual budget for physician spending, then let doctors do their work.
	An **Analogy Warrant** is a substantive warrant that assumes a resemblance in some characteristics between dissimilar things.	CLAIM: Sports have become the secular religion of America. (Harry Edwards)
Motivational Warrants are based on the values of the arguer and the audience.		CLAIM: People in this country work too hard to enjoy God and family.

SUPPORT:	WARRANT:	
The surgeon general has determined that cigarette smoking is hazardous to your health.	The surgeon general is a reliable medical authority.	Could the authority be mistaken in this case? Do other reputable authorities disagree?
SUPPORT: In controlled experiments marijuana has reduced severe side effects and pain of illness and cancer therapy in several patients.	WARRANT: What was true for the patients in the experiments will undoubtedly be true for many more.	Are the examples representative of the whole group being described? Have contradictory examples been ignored?
SUPPORT: In 1992, NBC faked exploding gas tanks in an exposé of GM trucks. In the past journalists greatly exaggerated the dangers of dioxin and radon.	WARRANT: Such fakery is a sign of the deceptive practices of the media.	Is the sign appropriate? Is the sign sufficient? Do other indicators dispute the sign?
SUPPORT: Poor farmers plant fewer crops if farming becomes unprofitable.	WARRANT: People will lack incentive to provide for themselves if others provide for them.	Is the cited cause sufficient to bring about the effect? Have other possible causes been overlooked?
SUPPORT: This practice has enabled Canada to save money without reducing the pay of doctors.	WARRANT: Because this practice is successful in Canada, it should be successful in the United States.	Are the dissimilarities between the things being compared greater than the similarities? Have all or only a few of the important characteristics been compared?
SUPPORT: Both sports and religion have gods, saints, houses of worship, and "true believers."	WARRANT: The feelings of veneration for the spectacle and values of sports are analogous to the feelings of adherents of formal religion.	Is the analogy explanatory or merely descriptive? Are there sufficient similarities between the two elements to make the analogy appropriate?
SUPPORT: Americans work 20 percent more today than in 1973 and have 32 percent less free time per week.	WARRANT: Work should not be an end in itself but a means to enjoyment of "mental culture, moral and social progress, and the Arts of Living." (J. S. Mill)	Might some people disagree with the arguer's values? Is the value relevant to the claim?

This analogy, however, suffers from the weakness of all analogies — dissimilarities between the objects being compared. Many physical illnesses may be easier to diagnose and cure than deficiencies in math. The latter are certainly due to a variety of social, economic, and personal problems that are difficult or impossible for the educational system to treat.

Values

Warrants may also reflect needs and values, and readers accept or reject the claim to the extent that they find the warrants relevant to their own goals and standards. In Chapter 8 Mrs. Walkup and others based their opposition to development of the Eastern Shore on a value warrant: Rural life is superior to the way of life being introduced by developers. Clearly, numbers of outsiders who valued a more sophisticated way of life did not agree.

The persuasive appeal of advertisements, as we know, leans heavily on value warrants, which are often unstated. Sometimes they include almost no printed message except the name of the product accompanied by a picture. The advertisers expect us to assume that if we use their product, we can acquire the desirable characteristics of the attractive people shown using it.

Value warrants are indispensable in arguments on public policy. In the following excerpt from a radio debate, a professor of statistics at Berkeley argues in favor of affirmative action policies to promote the hiring of women faculty. Her claim has been made earlier, but her warrant and any reservations remain unstated. This is her supporting material.

> 6.9 percent is [a] very tiny proportion of the faculty. You still have to go a long ways to see a woman teaching in this university. Most all of the students go to this university and never, ever have a woman professor, a woman associate professor, even a woman assistant professor teaching them. There's a lack of role models, there's a lack of teaching, and it brings a lack of breadth into the teaching.[9]

The Berkeley professor's argument may be outlined like this:

CLAIM: The proportion of women on the Berkeley faculty should be increased.

SUPPORT: Because women are only 6.9 percent of the faculty, most students never have a woman teacher.

WARRANT: Exposure of students to women faculty is a desirable educational goal.

RESERVATION: Unless individual women faculty members are significantly less competent than men.

DEBATE: ARE YOU RESPONSIBLE FOR YOUR OWN WEIGHT?

1. A good prewriting question to introduce this topic is whether your students believe there exists an epidemic of obesity in this country. A second question is what has caused a concern about obesity. A third is whether the government could or should take any action to fight that epidemic, if it exists. The two essayists represent the opposite sides in the controversy over the third question.

[9]Elizabeth Scott, quoted in "Affirmative Action: Not a Black and White Issue," National Public Radio, week of 25 Apr. 1977: 7.

2. Your students will also be able to follow through on this subject by discussing the ways in which the fast-food industry has responded to charges that their food is contributing to Americans' obesity. How have they justified changing their menus if they do not accept that they have been contributing to the problem? How is their position comparable to — and different from — that of tobacco companies?

3. Now that the students have read a detailed discussion of warrants and practiced identifying them, they should be ready to compare the warrants underlying these two arguments that defend opposite positions in a debate. How do the warrants affect the persuasiveness of each piece?

Bibliography

"Changing the Menu: Convenience Food." *Economist* 22 May 2004: 57.

Devaney, Polly. "Making a Meal of Couch Potatoes and Doughnuts." *Marketing Week* 25 Mar. 2004: 28–29.

"Fast-Food Density in Poor, Black Areas May Contribute to Obesity Epidemic." *Health and Medicine Week* 27 Sept. 2004: 889.

Healy, Melissa. "War on Fat Gets Serious." *Los Angeles Times* 3 Jan. 2004: 1.

Lennon, Robert. "They're Hatin' It." *Corporate Counsel* Apr. 2004: n. pag.

Shreve, Meg. "States Trying to Trim Obesity Litigation." *Business Insurance* 26 July 2004: 4.

"Study Links Fast Food to Overall Poor Nutrition, Obesity Risk." *AScribe Medicine News Service* 5 Jan. 2004: n. pag.

CHAPTER 9
Avoiding Flawed Logic
(text pages 322–366)

1. The teaching of fallacies poses special, though not insuperable, problems. Some fallacious statements by public figures are obvious, like those in the list of exercises in the text. But arguments by professional writers often contain concealed fallacies or fallacies that uninformed students are unable to identify. One example that comes immediately to mind is Ashley Montagu's "Man, the Ignoble Savage?" (from *The Nature of Human Aggression*). This essay, reprinted in several readers, purports to be an attack on the use of examples by others, but Montagu offers only one example in rebuttal, and this example is a scarcely credible rumor that remains unsubstantiated. (An interesting assignment would ask students to look for more convincing research to support Montagu's claim.)

    The rule for all of us — teachers and students alike — is to cultivate fearlessness in our criticism of articles by putative experts. Since freshman students are naturally disinclined to be critical of their mentors (publicly, at least), we may risk overzealousness in uncovering faulty arguments in textbooks, newspapers, and magazines. Advertisers are not the only arguers guilty of concealment or distorted reasoning.

2. Students should be on the alert for dubious arguments in what they read and hear and bring them in for examination by the class. If they are keeping

journals, they may record these fallacies or what they interpret as fallacies in their journals. The nomenclature is not important. Some of their entries will turn out to be examples of sound reasoning after all, but no matter. The objective of the exercise is increased alertness. Sensitive discrimination will, we hope, come later.

In some cases, students will be lucky to find explicit references to fallacies, as in the beginning of this letter (*Wall Street Journal* 15 Nov. 1983): "Your editorial is an illustration of the slippery slope argument." Less explicitly, the writer will say (*Wall Street Journal* 7 Dec. 1983): "Your editorial was critical of Surgeon General C. Everett Koop for 'citing particularly egregious magazine articles and medical cases as proof that the United States could easily slip into some Nazi-like approval of general euthanasia.' I, for one, would not dismiss Dr. Koop's concern quite so readily."

3. Some school newspapers are rife with weak and fallacious arguments in the editorials and letters to the editor. As a source of fallacies, they have two advantages: They are easily available, and students probably feel fewer inhibitions in attacking their peers.

EXERCISES FOR CRITICAL THINKING: ANSWERS

Students generally have no difficulty recognizing and explaining these fallacies even when they cannot find the names for them.

1. *Begging the question.* The judge is assuming the answer to the very question that a trial is supposed to answer.

2. *Non sequitur.* It doesn't follow that because something is good for us the government should enforce compliance.

3. *Post hoc fallacy.* There is no proof that watching these particular TV shows is the cause of high or low school grades. It's more reasonable to suppose that children who do well or poorly in school select one show or the other because of its appeal to their level of intelligence and achievement.

4. *Hasty generalization or small sample.* A faulty prediction for one month is not enough for an accusation of unreliability.

5. *Two wrongs don't make a right.* The writer thinks that death and danger are unacceptable for men in combat, but subjecting women to death and danger doesn't make these "wrongs" more acceptable.

6. *Faulty use of authority.* Taste is a matter of individual preference. It would be hard to prove that Cher, however gifted an actress, is superior to anybody else in her choice of a sweetener. (Of course, we also know that she is only posing for a paid advertisement.)

7. *Two wrongs don't make a right.* The arguer seems to infer that gambling is wrong, but legalizing it won't make it morally right. (This is what Norman Cousins calls "cop-out realism," or "If you can't beat 'em, join 'em.")

8. *Unknown fact or faulty comparison.* What was money spent for in the past? Have conditions changed that may make the expenditure of more money appropriate now?

9. *Non sequitur.* It doesn't follow that campus newspapers select the best or even good writers. They usually have to settle for those who make themselves available.

10. *Begging the question.* The arguer assumes that standard English is necessary only for certain kinds of employment, but that remains to be proved. Standard English has other uses unrelated to employment.

11. *Faulty definition.* In this case discrimination means making judicious choices. It should not be considered pejorative. To perform their duties, which may involve physical exertion, police officers should be required to fulfill certain physical standards.

12. *Faulty comparison or begging the question.* Qualified doctors and medical students are different. By definition a medical student is still being tested, and access to information in books during the testing process may defeat the purposes of testing.

13. *Faulty definition.* Chemicals are the building blocks of nature. Some may be unsafe, but they are not all synonymous with poisons by any means.

14. *Begging the question.* The arguer assumes that the only relevant criterion for choosing courses is payment of tuition. But a student enters into an implicit contract when he or she enrolls in the college or university and accepts the criteria laid down by the institution for the granting of a diploma.

15. *False dilemma.* The writer assumes that there are only two alternatives available to those who want to marry. But there is at least one more —marriages freely chosen that are not based on romantic love. Besides, we have no way of knowing how well arranged marriages worked. Staying married when divorce is difficult or unavailable doesn't prove the success of the marriage.

16. *Hasty generalization or small sample.* Three examples are not sufficient to support a generalization about a population of hundreds of thousands or millions.

17. *Hasty generalization or small sample.* One example of a highly intelligent athlete is not enough to prove the intelligence of a large population.

18. *Unknown fact.* There is insufficient evidence in this quotation to prove the reasons for Sasway's failure to register, which may or may not be based on moral principles. Also *begging the question.* One indictment does not lead to filling the prisons.

19. *False analogy.* Harris is making an analogy between inanimate objects —buildings, cars, ham — and animate objects or students. Students, after all, have choices and some control over their education.

20. *Post hoc fallacy.* There is no evidence here that doctrines of feminism have caused women to turn to crime. Anyway, crime is usually the result of many factors that are difficult to separate.

21. *Non sequitur.* It doesn't follow that just because an activity is healthful the university should require it. (There are a number of things that are good for us that a center of academic learning does not choose to introduce into its curriculum.)

22. *Ad hominem.* Meany is attacking the habits of the younger generation, not their views, which remain unknown.

23. *Non sequitur.* It doesn't follow that early poverty makes a candidate sympathetic to the problems of the poor. In fact, the opposite may be true.

24. *False analogy.* In the European cases troops were engaged in crushing freedom; in the Little Rock case they were engaged in extending it.

25. *Post hoc fallacy.* There is no evidence that the election of Governor Jones is the cause of the corruption. His election and government corruption may be

coincidental. In fact, he may be uncovering — and ending — corruption that existed before he took office.

26. *False dilemma.* These may not be the only alternatives for the voters. There may be ways to improve education without a pay increase.

27. *Post hoc fallacy.* It would be hard to prove a cause-effect relation.

28. *False analysis.* The dissimilarities between the two states are probably much greater than the similarities.

29. *Post hoc fallacy.* Self-explanatory.

30. *Faulty use of authority.* Even Galileo should have asked for stricter evidence than the great Aristotle could provide on the subject of natural science.

31. *Slippery slope fallacy.* The progression projected by Brustein — from Congress curtailing grants to artists whose work is controversial to Congress ordering the execution of artists whose work is deemed blasphemous — is hardly inevitable.

DEBATE: SHOULD THE FEDERAL GOVERNMENT FUND EMBRYONIC STEM-CELL RESEARCH?

1. Because of the speed with which both scientific advances and public policy are being made in this area, this is a good topic to approach by having the students research the most recent developments in the ongoing debate. This topic works well for instructors who like to have their students do two or more papers using the same basic research to better understand the different types of claims. Students could be asked to write a claim-of-fact paper on the issue of embryonic stem-cell research and then follow up with a second one supporting a claim of policy regarding such research. The first would be objective and the second, subjective.

2. The Reeve essay will inevitably lead to a discussion of the role that movie stars can or should play in politics. There is no question that Reeve had power as an advocate for stem-cell research in a way the thousands of average Americans who have suffered similar tragic accidents have not had. His loss of mobility was particularly ironic since millions had come to think of him as the Man of Steel. The faith and hope that he openly expressed after his accident revealed a very different type of strength. The emotional appeal of his essay is undeniable. Students can readily think of cases in which the Hollywood factor was not so positive, however. Is a movie star any better qualified than the average citizen to judge who is the better presidential candidate? Is a candidate preferable because of the band that plays at his fund-raiser? And did it really matter that much what Jane Fonda had to say about the Vietnam War or Susan Sarandon about the war in Iraq? (See the related articles in the bibliography below.)

3. Although Charen is not as well known as Reeve was, she is also a public figure. Students can discuss to what extent her essay makes use of emotional appeal. How is her appeal different from that used by Reeve?

Bibliography

"Center for Bioethics and Human Dignity: Ron Reagan Misguided on Embryonic Stem Cell Research, Cloning." *US Newswire* 29 July 2004: n. pag.

"Christian Coalition Commends Mel Gibson for His Strong Stance against Prop. 71 — The $3 Billion Human Embryonic Stem Cell Research Initiative on California Ballot." *US Newswire* 28 Oct. 2004: n. pag.

Daley, George Q. "Missed Opportunities in Embryonic Stem-Cell Research." *New England Journal of Medicine* 351.7 (2004): 627–28.

Friedrich, M. J. "Researchers Make the Case for Human Embryonic Stem Cell Research." *JAMA* 292.7 (2004): 791–92.

"New Study Shows Most Americans Support Embryonic Stem Cell Research." *Stem Cell Week* 8 Nov. 2004: 35.

"Reagan's Son Calls for Support for Embryonic Stem Cell Research." *America's Intelligence Wire* 28 July 2004: n. pag.

"Science Magazine Hosts Discussion of Debate on Embryonic Stem Cell Research." *Gene Therapy Weekly* 4 Nov. 2004: 69.

"'Snowflakes' Bring an Early Winter to Washington, D.C.: Meet the 'Faces' of Embryonic Stem-Cell Research." *US Newswire* 22 Sept. 2004: n. pag.

CHAPTER 10
Choosing Fair and Precise Language
(text pages 367–430)

1. Again we turn to advertisements for their use of slogans, clichés, and emotive language. Advertising claims in airline ads, we are told by a national advertising group, "promise great buys and then dissolve into airline jargon filled with restrictions." Ask students to examine some airline ads for jargon and code words that are meaningless or slippery.

   A paperback entitled *I Can Sell You Anything* by Carl P. Wrighter (Ballantine, 1972) offers a popular attack on techniques of advertising. Wrighter supports his claims by offering dozens of examples of "weasel words" in specific commercial advertisements. The claims of each ad are clearly stated. Often the argument is exaggerated, and some of the ads will no longer be familiar to students, but they can use Wrighter's formulas as a model, choosing their own ads and substituting their own weasel words.

   An article in the *New York Times* 26 Nov. 1998, "A Name So Smooth, the Product Glides In," by J. C. Herz, describes in fascinating detail how products are named, that is, how the sounds of letters like z, "one of the fastest sounds in the alphabet," can influence the choice of name for the product. "Orwell was dead wrong," says the author. "The language isn't being crushed under the weight of oppression. It is experiencing an algal bloom of new vocabulary." Students need not be linguists to try to uncover — or imagine — the origins of product names which seem to come out of nowhere — Advil, Nuon, Zima.

2. Have students collect literature from various politically active groups on campus. Assign a study of the language based on some of the categories in the text: connotations, euphemisms, clichés, slogans, slanted language, picturesque language.

   a. Is the message persuasive? How much of the persuasive effect is due to the way that language is used?

   b. Identify terms that you consider effective and tell why.

   c. Identify terms that you consider ineffective and tell why.

3. Students can find slogans everywhere. The slogans, of course, will differ from year to year and from place to place, depending on the emergence of new issues. In 2004, an election year, some slogans were generated, though not so many as we might have expected. Ask students to compose their own political slogans and defend them. To whom does the slogan appeal? What short cuts have been taken; that is, what questions about your abbreviated argument might be asked by an unfriendly reader?

4. There are clichés — statements of obvious ideas — everywhere. Students can examine the "Basic Speeches" referred to in assignments for Chapter 7. They might consider answers to the following questions: Can the use of clichés be justified? What would be the effect of substituting unusual ideas, even a surprising and perhaps unpleasant truth?

5. Have students examine some of the classic speeches of the past: Patrick Henry's *Speech before the Virginia Convention of 1775*, Abraham Lincoln's *Gettysburg Address*, Winston Churchill's address to the Congress of the United States of America on December 26, 1941. Students will notice that all of these speeches contain memorable phrases. Ask whether they think that the language in these speeches differs in any significant way from the language of the "Basic Speeches" of 2004. Have them explain any differences and describe how they contribute to the success or failure of particular speeches.

6. We have used an excerpt describing the actions of Henry VIII to demonstrate the use of partisan language by a Catholic historian. Below is a passage from a Protestant historian, G. M. Trevelyan, about the same events of the English Reformation, but exhibiting, through the use of selective language, an entirely different point of view. Students may be asked to pick out the words and phrases that indicate slanting.

> It is often falsely asserted that the [Protestant] Reformation was a plunder of the poor; that it dispossessed them of their heritage in favor of a squirearchy [landed proprietor class]. The fact is that the medieval Church, on its financial side, was a squirearchy richer and more jealous of its possessions than any which had existed since the Reformation. What the revolution did was to transfer enormous wealth from one squirearchy to another; from a squirearchy which, in its very nature, was intensely conservative and seldom let go of anything in its possessions, to another which lived far more among the people, and whose extravagances often led to the division of the land, so that there grew up in Elizabethan and Jacobean times a whole class of small yeoman farmers.
>
> The medieval Church was, no doubt, more friendly to the poor than any State Institution of those days would have been. But it was far from that Christian fraternity and generous beneficence which is often claimed for it, and which the earliest Christianity had actually displaced. It was deeply feudalized; it was no longer a really democratic institution in any strict sense of the word. Popes were the most absolute sovereigns of their day, and sometimes the most luxurious and most directly responsible for those wars which were chronic in Christendom.

We have tried to encourage students to uncover other examples in their own texts, but they find this difficult to do. The exercise above will at least induce a healthy caution about the objectivity of textbook writers, even distinguished historians.

7. An Internet marketer says that people expect informality on the Web, including "an editorial hook" which catches them right away. "People have it in their minds that a computer is more like a television than a magazine — it's a

screen, and that puts them in speed mode." Ask students if they feel that composing essays on their computers is qualitatively different from composing on the typewriter or with pen and pencil. If they have never tried the typewriter or the pen, have them experiment with an assigned essay. Does the computer encourage more informality of language? If so, how do they account for it?

8. Ask students to distinguish between the terms *terrorist* and *freedom fighter*. Their definitions should be based on specific examples that clarify and exclude.

9. The use of computers has clearly influenced language, perhaps in ways that are not so benign. "When the Geeks Get Snide, Computer Slang Scoffs at Wetware (the Humans)" by Michiko Kakutani (*New York Times* 27 June 2000: C1) argues that "geek-speak is flush with disparaging or defensive references to the real world and flesh-and-blood human beings." Students can probably provide examples of her thesis and argue for or against it.

10. One writer yearns for the return of "proper letter-writing" (Tunku Varadarjan, "Spilling Words and Hitting 'Send' — Not Letter-Perfect," *Wall Street Journal* 21 Sept. 2000: A19) as opposed to instantaneous and casual e-mail. Do students feel that the language of e-mail has drawbacks as a mode of communication? Does "proper" letter-writing have a place in their lives?

11. What about names of military operations? We are mostly unaware of the importance that leaders of government attach to the naming of wartime activities. The name first suggested for the war against the Taliban was *Infinite Justice*; then, after criticism, it became *Enduring Freedom*. Churchill said names should not have "an air of despondency, they should not be frivolous and ordinary, and they should not be a target for fun." The decisions about naming offer fascinating excursions into psychology and language. See "Operation Moniker: Military Name Game," *New York Times* 13 Oct. 2001: A15.

DEBATE: DOES THE GOVERNMENT HAVE THE RIGHT TO REGULATE GUNS?

1. This pair of essays can be used to discuss all of the elements of argument, but we chose them for this unit on language because they raise important issues of definition and word choice. Burger does an excellent job of putting the Second Amendment in context. In fact, one of his points is that a portion of the wording of the amendment is often taken out of context. Burger explains the historical context in which the amendment was written and explains how different those circumstances were from the world in which Americans now try to divine the intent of the men who drafted it. McGrath has a different, but interesting, read on the wording of the amendment. One of his main points is that with the reference to the right of the people to keep and bear arms, the members of the First Congress were assuming that such a right existed and did not need to be established through legislation. They were concerned only that a God-given right not be infringed. The significance of the wording of the amendment, in context, is rich subject matter for discussion in a chapter on language and thought.

You might also ask your students to consider the voice being used in each essay. They might be surprised that a judge could write in language so clear and free of jargon that it can be readily understood by average citizens. Burger lays out his case clearly and objectively. Students can be asked to consider the voice they hear speaking in the McGrath piece. In fact, most students, if pressed, will start to see that there is a shift in voice as the piece progresses. One way of pointing this out is to have them read the first few paragraphs and the last few and consider how the two are different.

2. If you want to go one step farther in the analysis of language in relation to this subject, you can ask your students to look for other essays on the subject and compare the voices in those essays. Are all of those essayists as reasonable as the two represented in the text? What sorts of warrants underlie some Americans' defense of their right to own guns? What warrants underlie arguments in favor of government regulation of guns? To what extent does emotional appeal enter into the arguments? (The ad that appears immediately before the debate is a good starting point for discussion.)

3. A possible research topic is governmental control (or lack of control) of guns in other countries. How is governmental control related to the homicide rate in this country and elsewhere?

Bibliography

"Add Gun Control to Litany of Misbegotten Government Plans." *Investor's Business Daily* 29 June 2004: A15.

Etzioni, Amitai. "Reasonable Regulation." *National Law Journal* 26.31 (2004): n. pag.

Jacobs, James B., and Kimberly A. Potter. "Keeping Guns Out of the Wrong Hands: The Brady Law and the Limits of Regulation." *Journal of Criminal Law and Criminology* 86.1 (1995): 93–120.

Mondics, Chris. "Outlook for Significant Government Regulations of Guns Clouded." *Knight-Ridder/Tribune News Service* 16 May 1999: K3329.

Stell, Lance K. "The Production of Criminal Violence in America: Is Strict Gun Control the Solution? *Journal of Law, Medicine and Ethics* 32.1 (2004): 38–46.

Zimring, Franklin E. "Firearms, Violence, and the Potential Impact of Firearms Control." *Journal of Law, Medicine and Ethics* 32.1 (2004): 34–37.

PART TWO

RESEARCHING, WRITING, AND PRESENTING ARGUMENTS

INTRODUCTION

Part Two is meant to complement all writing assignments throughout the semester. It is one thing for students to grasp the concept of a claim of fact, for example, but writing an essay in which they demonstrate their ability to communicate that understanding is quite another. Chapter 11, then, instructs students in the processes of planning and researching an argumentative paper. The discussion of each step is illuminated with examples from good writers.

Chapter 12 presents writing the research paper as a culmination of a course in argumentative writing. Although students in all their papers so far have been demonstrating their mastery of the elements of argument and the process of composition, the research paper will put their skills to a more demanding test. In this chapter we discuss the purposes of the research paper and the procedures for helping students to produce interesting and authoritative documents. In this chapter we've also provided two student research papers. They have been annotated to show students exactly how the authors proceed in defending a claim.

Chapter 13 provides guidelines for oral argument. In a course that emphasizes written discourse, defending a claim before a live audience encourages awareness of the differences between speech and writing. Students must learn to accommodate both language and organization to the differing needs of listeners and readers. They already know the importance of acquiring proficiency in speech, and, despite some initial misgivings, find the speech assignments a useful and enlightening experience.

CHAPTER 11

Planning and Researching
an Argumentative Paper

(text pages 431–473)

Unlike many courses in the upper classes, in which the only writing may be an examination and a research paper, our course requires writing from the very first week of class, and students practice research skills at some level throughout the semester. The research paper serves not to introduce but to bring together in a more ambitious exercise the principal elements of argument. But it is only one among many papers.

The purposes of the research paper are twofold: (1) mastering a long paper — perhaps three times longer than any of the weekly writing students have done so far — with its special and more demanding problems of organization; (2) learning how to substantiate more extensive claims of fact, value, and policy that require the data and authoritative opinion the writer cannot supply — in other words, more practice in organization and development.

New teachers who are introducing the research paper for the first time may find suggestions in the following outline that can be adapted to their particular programs.

1. Assign a fast reading of Chapter 11. Take ten or fifteen minutes to turn pages with students, pointing out what they will find and which parts deserve a slightly longer glance. For example, they should read the sample papers with care; for this reading, however, they can skip the MLA and APA style sheets.

    At the next class go over the important parts of the chapter. Concentrate on the tasks that must be accomplished first. Encourage questions. Reassure students that the assignment is not so daunting as they think it is. It might even be fun, and you are ready to help.

2. In class discuss finding a topic. The commonly quoted advice to graduate students about to embark on a dissertation still holds good: Choose something that really interests you, because you'll have to live with it for a while.

    The first and most obvious source of subjects will be in "Multiple Viewpoints," Part Three of the text. Topics are suggested for each chapter, but students may think of others that interest them more. Other subjects may be found in personal experience, at home and at school, and in the neighborhood, in town, or on campus.

3. Work out a schedule for the project. Freshman students need help in managing time, and they are grateful for a structure that defines their responsibilities. We favor making the time available for the research paper no longer than a month. (We've found that allowing more time for research and writing doesn't produce better papers.) Set deadlines for specific stages of the project:

    a. The choice of topic
    b. A briefly annotated list of five sources examined in the first week or ten days. Two of the items may be taken from "Multiple Viewpoints," the other three from other sources. (All of these may not appear in the final bibliography, but they represent a start.)
    c. The final paper

4. Announce the availability of conferences with the instructor at any point during the research and writing. Early in the project we schedule one conference with each student. Later conferences can be based on individual need. Some students will have trouble refining and narrowing the topic. Others will need help finding sources. And still others will encounter problems in organizing and in using the sources appropriately.

5. While students work on their research papers outside of class, you can ask for short papers, sometimes in class, which introduce an idea or present a piece of evidence that is part of the longer paper. Some papers will suggest the need for conference. If not, papers should be returned promptly with comments relevant to the research paper. Needless to say, attention to the ongoing process of the paper should also make plagiarism more difficult.

6. Unless you anticipate and address the problem, some students, drunk with their newly acquired knowledge of the research tool, will produce a series of quotations, sometimes as many as twenty in a six-page paper, tightly strung together like a well-made necklace, with nothing visible between the pearls.

This is *not* a research paper. We need to make clear to students that *they* are the authors and that the materials derived from other sources must be used *only* to support their claims. We should emphasize that too much research material can be as fatal as too little. The two sample research papers give students models for the intelligent use of quotations.

USE OF THE LIBRARY

At schools with large libraries it's not uncommon to discover that even by the end of the first semester, freshman students will not have visited the library unless assigned to do so. Big libraries can be intimidating, but a guided tour can reinforce the idea that the library is a friend, not an enemy. *The library tour should take place early in the semester, not at research paper time.* In this course students should begin to use the resources of the library at once, as they tackle the very first paper on defending a claim of fact.

Librarians are usually more than willing to cooperate in helping students to become familiar with library resources, and they can offer helpful experience to new instructors. Try turning to the librarians first and trying to accommodate their recommendations to the purposes of the course. Here are a few suggestions based on trial and error with our own classes.

1. A tour in which twenty students follow the librarian as he or she points out library services seldom works. The students in the back can't hear, and they lose interest. Even those near the speaker will not remember a couple of weeks later exactly what they learned. At most the librarian or the instructor can walk the students through some of the areas where they are likely to be busiest — the card catalog or computerized catalog, the indexes, the major reference works, the microfiche collection.

2. Prepare students for the visit. Go over the material in the book, offering additional information about the sources. Anecdotes about your own experience with research can enliven an apparently lifeless subject.

3. Students will remember much more about the library if they arrive with specific questions. One way to produce questions that will lead to a wide range of answers is to divide the class into three sections: humanities, social sciences, and natural and physical sciences. Each section meets and arrives at a research paper topic in its field; each student in that section then prepares a specific question on the topic. (Some of the questions will be weak, but the librarian can often ask the right questions of the student and elicit a nice rephrasing.) The students assemble with the librarian in a room with a blackboard or a computer where he or she can answer students' questions by writing down or calling up the names of the materials and their locations.

4. Use student resources. Some students in the class will be more proficient than others in unraveling the mysteries of the library, and they are often pleased and proud to be asked to accompany the others and point out how and where to look.

CHAPTER 12

Writing an Argumentative Paper

(text pages 474–513)

Success in teaching composition, like success in parenting, has its mysteries. Good writers and good children emerge from all kinds of environments —authoritarian, permissive, and unlikely combinations of the two. The suggestions that follow have been tested in a wide variety of programs — from some in which an activity and an assignment were designated for each day of the semester to others in which no structure was provided and floundering was a rite of passage.

When we supervise new teaching assistants, we always advise them to teach from their strengths, which might not be the same as ours, and if necessary to adapt any suggestions for assignments and classroom management to ones with which they feel more secure. New teachers who read these ideas will, we hope, be able to make similar adjustments.

COMPOSITION: STYLE, ORGANIZATION, AND DEVELOPMENT

Not surprisingly, these are the three elements of composition where student arguments are most likely to falter. Weaknesses here can, of course, cripple the most promising ideas. The bad news is that in one semester we can do little to produce polished stylists. The good news, however, is that we *can* teach organization and development.

Precision and grace in writing almost always depend on a good ear, long familiarity with good writing, and association with family and friends who know how to use language — conditions over which teachers of college freshmen have little control. We have tried and sometimes seen an improvement in style as a result of sentence-combining exercises, imitation of accessible prose stylists like George Orwell, and rewriting of clumsy passages by the instructor. Our goals should be modest — clarity would be enough — but our successes will also be modest.

One of the obstacles for some students on the way to clear and straightforward expression is their adoption of an artificial written style that has little resemblance to their own voices. The style is inflated and slightly pompous, but it seems to these writers that a language closer to colloquial speech would be inappropriate and even frivolous. Encourage these students to look closely at the prose of writers who often use one-syllable words and short sentences with strong rhetorical effect. Explain to students that simple prose is not merely an instructor's idiosyncratic preference.

A limited vocabulary, needless to say, is a serious impediment to the reading and writing of arguments. We can encourage use of a full-size desk dictionary; many college students have never consulted anything but a small paperback dictionary and are at a loss to interpret the symbols in a larger one. We can ask questions about the words in the assigned essays and insist that students look them up. We can emphasize words that student writers can usefully introduce into their own essays.

Unlike the arrangement of ideas in description, which may be spatial, or in narration, which may be chronological, the arrangement of ideas in argument is logical, and has, therefore, wide application. We can try to make clear to students that the modes of organization outlined in the text are exactly the same as those they will be expected to use in their writing in the workplace or in any activities which call for reports, evaluations, and recommendations.

If students have trouble arranging the materials of an argument, we can ask them first to establish the nature of their claims, and then to examine essays in the book that exemplify an appropriate organization. Often the first paragraph of an essay serves as an introduction to the kind of organization. Most beginning writers are glad to learn that these forms exist and are ready for use in any argument. As they gain power in using these conventional forms, they will be free to modify them — for example, withholding the main idea until the end.

As for development and support, we can stress this throughout the semester in every piece students read and write, pointing out varied strategies that good writers use to convince readers of the soundness of their claims.

In introducing or summarizing the concepts of organization and development, you may want to use the blackboard, smartboard, or computer. You can write down the claim or thesis statement for an argument suggested by a student — for example, "Schools should remove vending machines of unhealthful snack food" — and then ask students to suggest topic sentences for three paragraphs and the means of supporting the ideas summarized in the topic sentences. You can use this device for the three ways of organizing a claim and can make ample reference to the forms of support that are treated in Chapter 7.

From time to time you may want to duplicate good student papers, sometimes from a previous semester, for distribution to the class and discuss the successful use of the different ways of organizing and supporting a particular argument. Duplication of less successful papers — without names — can also work if the problems are not severe and the instructor can call attention to some strengths as well.

AVOIDING PLAGIARISM

There is no foolproof way of preventing plagiarism. But a few precautions can reduce the number of incidents.

1. Make sure that students understand the nature of the offense. Many students are genuinely ignorant of the necessity for crediting sources. Review the examples in the text. Some instructors warn students at the beginning of the semester that a finding of plagiarism will result in an F for the course. Urge students to ask questions about citation if they are in doubt.

2. Keep an impromptu paper, one written on the first or second day of class, as a sample of the student's style and thinking. (We assign a short essay in class on a subject that allows students to develop a simple argument.) This paper serves primarily as a test of the skills — or lack of skills — that students bring with them. However, if a subsequent paper exhibits a radical departure in vocabulary, syntax, and development of ideas, the instructor should inquire about the differences. A few judicious questions, starting perhaps with vocabulary, will lead to an acknowledgment of help. This works best, of course, when the source is a professional writer with clearly superior skills.

3. Avoid "free" assignments. Whatever their merits, they may tempt students who have difficulty finding subjects to "borrow" papers from friends or the library.

4. Vary assignments from year to year. It's time-consuming to think of variations on previous assignments, but it should go without saying that if the same assignment is peddled year after year, some student papers will also make the rounds.

5. If your program calls for reviewing several drafts of a paper, you should be able to notice any abrupt changes in the final draft. But be prepared to find that some ambitious plagiarists aren't daunted and will manufacture drafts of another student's essay.

EVALUATION AND GRADING

1. Before assigning the first paper, it is a good idea to discuss with students the criteria for grading. As an introduction, ask them to list in order of importance the elements of composition which ought to enter into an evaluation. In some classes half of the students will head their lists with spelling, punctuation, or grammar. What is probably already obvious to them but what they are afraid to say, knowing how perverse English teachers can be, usually comes as a relief — that nobody reads an essay merely for spelling or punctuation. The criteria ought to be (1) an interesting and important idea; (2) clarity of expression; (3) adequate development; (4) clear organization; (5) correct spelling, grammar, and punctuation. In class discussion you can try to elicit the reasons for this list and the order in which the items appear. Students need to see how these criteria are justified by their claims on the reader. (If the reader of an essay can't understand what the writer is trying to say, a good outline and lots of data will be powerless to save the argument.)

2. Although the emphasis in evaluation rests on the elements of argument, we don't ignore grammar and mechanics in considering the grade. For many students, accuracy will be a hallmark of their professions. In a class of mechanical engineers to whom one of us taught writing, students were told by the engineer who directed the course that sloppy letters of application were routinely discarded by most companies. Employers would infer that an engineer who was careless about spelling and punctuation might also be careless about specifications for a machine. In a real sense, then, matters of spelling, grammar, and punctuation are an integral part of the argument, and not only for engineers.

3. What students do read with high interest is the paragraph or two that instructors write in summing up their evaluation of the whole paper. Comments and questions in the margin are helpful but no substitute for this final evaluation, which for students represents part of the ongoing dialogue initiated by their arguments.

As an example, we reproduce here a student paper followed by the sort of evaluation one of us would write. The essay is above average in style, freedom from mechanical errors, organization, and attention to development. But it is weakened by flaws that are typical of many good student arguments. Here is the essay:

The New Drinking Laws: A Sour Taste

All I wanted was an Amaretto sour. To get it, I had to have the little black stamp on the back of my hand that told the bartender I was at least twenty-one. I was only twenty and a half. So there I sat at a North Carolina nightspot with my brother and his girlfriend Debbie, sipping a soda. Six months made the difference between a watery Coke and a taste of liquor.

Debbie had a solution. She led me back to the ladies' room, licked the black stamp on the back of her hand, and pressed it onto my hand. It was light, so I darkened it with black eyeliner.

"It's backwards, but they won't notice," Debbie assured me. "It's dark in here."

Well, the bartender did notice, and I didn't get the Amaretto sour. "This is a fake," he said. "You have to come with me." He walked around to my side of the bar, grabbed my arm, and led me to a small office at the front of the bar. There, he took a bottle of rubbing alcohol out of the desk, wet a piece of cotton with it, and wiped the stamp from my hand. "Now get out of here," he said.

At first, I wanted to cry. But as I walked to the car with Debbie and Grant, I became angry. I was a responsible person, and I had never taken a drink and gotten behind the wheel. I rarely had more than two drinks at a time. Sure, I had skirted the law, but the law was unfair.

Now young people across the country are getting a taste of that unfairness.

Under pressure from special-interest groups and a federal government that has threatened to take away their highway funds, every state in the country has raised the legal age for buying and drinking alcohol to twenty-one. I argue that, in raising the drinking age, states have violated the rights of a large group of people. Further, I believe that increasing the age is not the best way to deter drunken driving and reduce traffic fatalities.

Supporters of the current drinking laws question the ability of eighteen-year-olds to drink responsibly. These people need to take a look at the other responsibilities that rest with eighteen-year-olds now. Under United States law, an eighteen-year-old can vote, go to war, get married, and have a family, but cannot legally enjoy a beer. The implication is that people who are under the age of twenty-one are mature enough to assume the responsibilities of adulthood but are not responsible enough to enjoy its pleasures. I find this judgment arbitrary and unfair. Once we have decided what the age of majority should be (and we seem to have decided on the age of eighteen for most activities) we should apply that standard uniformly.

Other supporters of new laws argue that when drinking ages go up, traffic fatalities go down. In fact, studies have indicated that in states where the drinking age has been increased, fatalities have dropped by as much as 10 percent. This is good news, but it does not prove that the new drinking laws are entirely responsible for the drop in traffic fatalities. Tougher drunk driving laws and stepped-up efforts to educate the public about the dangers of drinking and driving could also have been major factors in the drop in fatalities.

In the last several years, drunk driving laws and penalties have been made tougher throughout the nation. That is good: Rigorous enforcement of these laws is what we need. Also, education is always a positive force. The better the general public understands the damage that irresponsible drinking can do to individuals and society, the better off everyone will be. There are problem drinkers in all age groups. The law should go after them instead of using an arbitrary age limit that restricts the rights of citizens.

Finally, I do not believe that the higher drinking age will deter people under the age of twenty-one from drinking. Those under the legal age have always found ways to skirt the law and get their hands on alcohol, and they will continue to do so. The quest for the pleasure of intoxication is part of our nature. Restricting the supply of alcohol might make it harder for eighteen-year-olds to get, but it will not make it less desirable.

I wasn't deterred from drinking the night that I got kicked out of that bar in North Carolina. After leaving there, we drove a few miles down the road to another bar, and my brother bought me my Amaretto sour. It might have been more satisfying had it been legal.

The written evaluation would say:

I think this is a hard claim to defend, but you've handled several things very well. The organization is tight, and you make excellent transitions between ideas. I liked the introduction; it's a lively, well-told personal anecdote, and your reference to it at the end makes clear that it was an integral part of your argument. Even more important, in the body of your argument you offer other kinds of support: an appeal to fairness and data about drinking and driving.

But some changes and additions might have made your argument even stronger. (1) You are probably right that the laws alone have not been responsible for the big drop in alcohol-related deaths — among fifteen- to nineteen-year-olds they have plunged from a peak of 6,281 in 1982 to 2,170 in 1988 — but most experts agree that the laws are at least partly responsible. So you would have to argue that the death rate won't rise if the drinking age is lowered. Can you find data and expert opinion to support that view? You say you are a responsible driver — good point — but are you typical? (2) The analogy with other rights granted to eighteen-year-olds is somewhat shaky. Couldn't someone argue that granting those rights to teenagers was a mistake and that we should raise the ages for all the activities you cite? There's nothing special about age eighteen that guarantees maturity. After all, most eighteen-year-olds don't vote, most marriages at eighteen aren't notably successful, and as soldiers in the army, eighteen-year-olds are under strict supervision. (3) Finally, I wonder who your audience is. Are you writing for adults who might be persuaded to change the laws? I'm not sure that your attempts to evade the law would convince them that you are mature and responsible, or that pleading for the "pleasure of intoxication" — at a time when drinking by young people is declining, for good reasons — will be very persuasive. If you like, we can talk more about this in conference, and I can show you the sources of my data.

PEER EVALUATION

Peer review is less useful in argumentation courses than in courses that emphasize other modes of discourse. That is because the student reviewer often lacks sufficient knowledge of the subject of the argument to make informed comment. An example: A student writing about prisons had taken all his data from a *Time* magazine article of about fifteen years ago. The paper was well written, but the student reading it had no way of knowing that the data had changed so greatly that the claims were no longer valid. If instructors want to give students practice in evaluating arguments of classmates — a potentially valuable exercise — they are well advised, I think, to limit the areas on which the critic is asked to comment.

It's true, of course, that instructors can also be ignorant of areas of knowledge investigated by a student writer. But most of us have sufficient experience as laborers in various fields of scholarship to know which questions to ask.

CONFERENCES

Some programs mandate a specific number of conferences during the semester. Some even prescribe the amount of time to be spent. One guide for teachers calls for an initial conference of two minutes! Other syllabi leave the number of conferences to the instructor. But why conferences at all?

1. One teacher of composition in a prestigious university says frankly that his function in a conference is to rewrite the student's paper, explaining the point of his revision as he goes. In fact, such an extreme strategy may work in some cases — if the student is alive to nuances of vocabulary and tone and can understand and accept the changes, if he or she learns by imitation, and if he

or she has sufficient confidence to take issue with some of the teacher's revisions. Most of us, however, see the conference at its best as a dialogue or a conversation which either the teacher or the student may initiate.

Arguments, we have told our students, are implicit dialogues, and a conference represents not only our opportunity to respond at greater length to the student's argument but the student's opportunity to respond to *us* —to the written comments, for example — and to talk about the process of composition. As the students articulate their theses, answering our questions and explaining what they tried to do and why they chose to do it this way, some things may become clear that remained opaque when they were engaged in a monologue. Conferences can also function as mini-workshops for two, three, or four students who share a composition problem or have argued the same subject with varying degrees of success.

2. In part, conferences also function as a kinder, gentler substitute for written comments. One instructor wrote, "Think More!" across the top of a student paper. It might be harder to give such peremptory and humiliating advice in person.

Poor writers, although they may come reluctantly to conference, may profit most from these sessions. They may be unwilling to pay the necessary attention to largely negative written comments, but in conference they must confront them, and the comments can be prefaced, softened, and modified to accommodate a vulnerable human presence. These students may also be more articulate in speech than in writing and better able to assist the instructor by giving a clearer sense of what they really wanted to argue.

3. Finally, conferences allow student and teacher to look at mechanical errors and their corrections in a different way. Corrections on the student essay of spelling, grammar, and punctuation errors don't always produce improvement; many students won't — or can't — read them. And a multitude of correction results in a trail of red ink that signifies a disaster. A conference has the virtue of allowing you to ask questions, listen to answers, offer explanations, and, most of all, point out with pencil and finger the things that need change. For such problems a small physical demonstration has an impact that the written correction does not.

CHAPTER 13

Presenting an Argument Orally

(text pages 514–532)

1. An introduction to speeches by the class might include a student guest speaker whose argument can be evaluated in a class discussion following the speech. Criticism should be based on criteria laid out in Chapter 11. The speaker need not be perfect but should demonstrate abilities against which students in the class can measure their own. An outside speaker allows students to offer a frank evaluation, which they are sometimes reluctant to do openly for a classmate. In many schools with debate clubs and speech or drama departments, instructors can find willing candidates for the role of guest speaker. The instructor should suggest the kind of speech that fulfills the objectives of the speech unit, preferably a claim of policy that will include both facts and values.

2. Students can fill out an evaluation form for each speech, briefly commenting on the main elements. (You can make copies of a simple form with

spaces for comment.) Before turning the evaluations over to the speakers, you can read them to make sure that they are serious and respectful and then remove the names of the critics.

3. When guest speakers appear to address either the whole school or an organization on campus, you can sometimes assign attendance for the class. As with the speeches in their own class, students can fill out evaluation forms. The objectives of any speech unit should, of course, include not only proficiency in delivering a speech, but the critical ability to evaluate an oral argument.

4. "Words Go Right to the Brain, But Can They Stir the Heart?: Some Say Popular Software Debases Public Speaking" discusses the influence of software on oral presentation, especially in business. (*New York Times* 17 Apr. 1999: A17.) Some critics think that PowerPoint and other software presentation aids "contribute to the debasement of rhetoric." A professor of communication asks us to imagine Martin Luther King Jr.'s "I Have a Dream" speech with PowerPoint.

   But Stephen Pinker, professor of cognitive science and the author of *The Language Instinct* (Morrow, 1994), argues that human beings are visual creatures. "If anything," he says, "PowerPoint, if used well, would ideally reflect the way we think." Pinker served on a committee at Massachusetts Institute of Technology that "updat[ed] the traditional writing requirement to include both speech and graphic communication."

PART THREE

MULTIPLE VIEWPOINTS

INTRODUCTION (text page 534)

1. The debates, articles, and letters in this section represent the argumentative process in its clearest and most understandable form. If throughout the semester we have emphasized that arguments are dialogues, the selections given here will show students how the dialogues work, that is, how people on opposing sides actually respond to each other, whether well or poorly. Where it is clear that the response is not direct, that there is no clash, the debates can be equally instructive.

2. "Multiple Viewpoints" may be used as a discrete unit or as a source of materials for assignments in the text.

   a. If it is used as a self-contained unit, the introduction and the questions that precede it suggest a number of ways of examining the material and writing about it.

   b. "Multiple Viewpoints" also lends itself to use as a source of data, expert opinion, motivational appeals, warrants, and ethical and unethical use of language. In fulfilling assignments that call for supporting materials, students may find material here, either as a substitute for or in addition to library research. In several places in these notes we have suggested assignments that give students the opportunity to look for support for their claims among the selections in "Multiple Viewpoints."

   c. In addition, as pointed out earlier, "Multiple Viewpoints" can furnish the material for a research paper. Longer papers may require supplementary library research, but there is probably sufficient material in each section for a paper of six to seven pages.

3. Some of these subjects will be more effective than others for a given group of students, depending on their experience with and knowledge of the subject. "Are Limits on Freedom of Speech Ever Justified?," for example, may be more interesting for students in schools where a speech code is being debated or where it has resulted in punishment for infraction. When time does not permit using all the subjects, we choose the most provocative ones, those that will produce, as far as we can tell, the liveliest feelings, both for and against.

4. Given the timeliness of these subjects, research to discover whether changes have occurred since the articles and letters in the book were written will be indispensable. Students must be encouraged to read at least one full-coverage daily newspaper, watch TV newscasts and special reports, and listen to radio programs like *Talk of the Nation* (NPR). *Talk of the Nation* has covered every topic in Part Three of this book and a good many other subjects as well. Surveys show that most college students don't read newspapers or listen to TV newscasts. Some of them do, however, read *Time* or *Newsweek* or *U.S. News & World Report*. These students can be asked to report to the class on the ways in which the same stories are treated in different news magazines.

5. An enormously productive unit may be organized around formal classroom debate. Although debate is almost always an oral exercise, there is plenty of opportunity in a writing class for students to commit their outlines to paper, develop major points that cannot be adequately treated in the five minutes allotted to oral presentation, and make extended critiques of the debates of their classmates.

    Each debate usually requires four people, two on the affirmative side, two on the negative, although the Lincoln–Douglas format — one debater on each side — is also possible. If time does not permit a round of formal debates, the class may choose four or five debate subjects, with each team producing an argument that will be duplicated or read aloud for consideration by the whole class. This organization reduces the arguments to one on each side and eliminates rebuttal time. After reading or hearing the arguments, the class may write evaluations based on answers to the questions on the debate sheet.

    For supporting materials students should confine themselves to the data in this section. Their efforts will involve extracting the relevant issues and organizing them in a succinct and understandable way. They may also, of course, need to do further research for more recent data.

DEBATE

Debate may be considered an extension of the problem-solving analysis. The debaters are considering the merits of a solution to some problem, for example, a plan to restrict government agencies in their investigations of private citizens.

The debate proposition is always a two-sided question; it can be answered yes or no.

The proposition is worded so that the affirmative (yes) side will be arguing for a change in policy, or, in the case of value questions, a new idea. (The argument that violence is justified in civil rights cases is an example of the latter.) Because the affirmative is arguing for a change, they are said to have the *burden of proof*, while the negative has only to defend the status quo.

The affirmative argument usually centers around three *stock issues* that grow out of the problem-solving analysis. The affirmative will argue

1. that there is a need for a change;
2. that their proposal will meet the need;
3. that their proposal is the best solution to the problem. These stock issues are referred to as need, plan, and advantages.

The negative may answer the affirmative case in a number of ways.

1. They may *debate* every issue. "There is no problem, and even if there were, your plan is expensive, inefficient, and undesirable."
2. They may *waive* an issue. "Yes, indeed, we agree there is a serious problem, but your proposed solution is useless."
3. They may propose a *counterplan*. "Things are bad all right, but I have a better idea for improving them than yours." Tournament debaters do not do this too often for strategic reasons: It means the negative must assume part of the burden of proof.

Following are some questions you might consider as you listen to a debate:

1. How important is definition of terms? Does it become an issue in the debate?

2. Does the negative attack the affirmative argument on every point, or does the debate narrow to one or two issues?

3. Do the speakers base their arguments on any generally accepted principles or values, such as justice, individual freedom, constitutional guarantees?

4. Do you find examples of causal argument, argument from example, or argument from analogy?

5. How important is evidence in the debate? Do the speakers question the credibility of each other's sources? To what extent, if any, does the argument center around evidence?

6. What comments would you make on the speakers' oral presentation (delivery)?

7. Which side do you think won, and why?

CHAPTER 14

How Far Will We Go to Change Our Body Image?

(text pages 535–565)

1. One way to begin the discussion of body image is to ask students to bring in advertisements that suggest how our society perceives the human body. How are images of the body used to sell products? What sorts of products? What audiences are the ads appealing to? What do the ads suggest about what our society values?

2. Many of your students will know someone who has or may have an eating disorder. Some may have eating disorders themselves. Ask your students to consider the relationships between and among the images of the human body presented in ads, on television, and in the movies and the average human body. There is also recent evidence that your students could find that suggests that more men are developing eating disorders. Kita's and Spiker's essays support the idea that it is not only women who are concerned about body image. Samuels points out that African Americans are starting to overcome an earlier taboo against plastic surgery that could be seen as an attempt to remove ethnic markers. That notion can be contrasted with the attempt of some of the famous to do exactly that.

3. Students could also look in magazines or online for pictures that support Cullen's claim that it is the poor in America who are overweight because of the unhealthy diet they eat. The evidence students find could be presented in the form of a collage or a PowerPoint presentation.

4. A fascinating topic for research is how advertisements have changed over the years to reflect how body image has been perceived differently in different time periods. (Savacool's article in the bibliography below could be a starting point.) The same is true in the world of fine arts. How have artists defined beauty differently over the centuries?

5. The emphasis in the readings is on *changing* body image through surgery and other means. A rash of television shows in the opening years of the twenty-first century have promised to remake the ugly ducklings of the world. One show's producers even chose to draw on the story of the ugly duckling by calling it *The Swan*. Another interesting topic for research is how those people's

lives were changed as a result of their makeovers. A search of a database such as *InfoTrac* or a search engine such as Google will lead to articles about their lives after their appearance on these shows. What does a willingness to undergo such change suggest about values?

6. If you are interested in incorporating brief literary pieces on the subject of body image, two excellent choices are "Barbie Doll," a poem by Marge Piercy, and "Barbie-Q," a short story by Sandra Cisneros.

7. With each new advance in the manipulation of human genes, we come closer to the day when parents may be able to predetermine their children's appearance. Possible essay topics on this issue range from a claim-of-fact paper explaining what is now possible and how close scientists are to controlling physical appearance to a claim-of-policy paper on whether such tampering with human development should be allowed.

Bibliography

Kuther, Tara L., and Erin McDonald. "Early Adolescents' Experiences with, and Views of, Barbie." *Adolescence* 39.153 (2004): 39–52.

"Male Eating Disorders Rise amid More Focus on Body Image, Experts Say." *America's Intelligence Wire* 11 May 2004: n. pag.

Pleasant, Lesley. Rev. of *Looking Good: College Women and Body Image*, *1875–1930*, by Margaret A. Lowe. *Iris: A Journal About Women* Spring–Summer 2004: 86.

Savacool, Julia. "Women's Ideal Bodies Then and Now." *Marie Claire* Apr. 2004: 102–07.

Wulff, Jennifer. "Pressure To Be Perfect." *People Weekly* 26 July 2004: 72.

CHAPTER 15

Is Academic Integrity on Our College Campuses under Assault?

(text pages 566–594)

Students should know whether or not their college or university has an honor code. Some schools stress the honor code to the point that there is no question that all students are aware of it. They may have to sign it upon enrolling in classes or every time they take a test. Students at other schools may have to do some digging to locate an honor code or may discover that there isn't one. A quick search on Google reveals cases in which students have sued their universities for harm caused to them as a result of having been penalized for honor code violations. Such cases could make an interesting subject for research. So can the history of the institutional honor code, which was first suggested by Thomas Jefferson.

The explosion of technological advances has made cheating easier than ever before. (It has also made some legitimate research easier as well.) You might ask your students to write about or discuss the ways computers, cell phones, and credit cards have made cheating more tempting and less time consuming than for earlier generations of students. You might also ask them to write about or discuss their perceptions of how college students view cheating.

Some students might be given the task of investigating whether their school has a formal means of educating students about academic integrity. All schools in their catalogs and some schools in presentations or educational CDs define academic dishonesty and explain the penalties for it. You might consider having your students write and possibly videotape vignettes designed to show examples of academic dishonesty. They may not realize that academic dishonesty includes more than turning in work written by someone else. Even more challenging would be drafting their own version of an honor code.

The use of Turnitin.com promises to be in the news for some time to come. The most recent challenges to its use can be investigated. The essays in this chapter also go beyond the matter of academic integrity to discuss the legal and moral implications of downloading music and entering the world of the Playboy Mansion via the Web. All of these topics could be subjects for research and writing.

CHAPTER 16

Have We Become Too Reliant on Standardized Testing?

(text pages 595–635)

1. Standardized testing is a subject that almost all college students have had extensive experience with. Tests most likely helped determine the college they are attending and have been factored in to many other decisions affecting them throughout their education. You might ask your students to do some freewriting on their experiences with standardized testing. What have those experiences been, and how did they feel about them? Some students these days start taking the SAT as early as age twelve. Placement in gifted and talented programs may be made as early as second grade. And as Vickers points out, testing may start influencing children even earlier than that.

2. A major concern is how much the tests affect what goes on in classrooms. As the essays by Paige and Weaver make clear, there is disagreement about whether testing has had a negative effect on education. Sometimes the negative effect may be hard to prove because of the results of the very tests that opponents are fighting against. If test scores look good, the school, the district, and the state look good. Relatively few ever see what goes on in the affected classrooms. Critics point out that there is too much "teaching to the test" and too little room for teachers to make decisions based on what is best for their students. A good topic for research is how teachers feel about the standardized tests that their students are required to take.

3. No Child Left Behind is an initiative of the Bush administration designed to bring all children up to a minimum level of proficiency in reading and math. The number of both supporters and opponents makes this a rich subject for discussion and research. What does this initiative offer the weakest students? What does it offer the best? How have teachers and school districts gone about meeting this mandate? Is what supporters of the bill would like to see happen even possible?

4. The last two essays in the chapter can be a starting point for discussion of and research on the values and the limitations of the SAT.

Bibliography

Boaler, Jo. "When Learning No Longer Matters: Standardized Testing and the Creation of Inequality." *Phi Delta Kappan* 84.7 (2003): 502.

Brady, Marion. "Not-Yet-Answered Questions about Standardized Testing." *Knight Ridder/Tribune Service* 28 Jan. 2003: K1854.

Cardman, Michael. "Study: Human Error Rife in Standardized Testing: Board Outlines Scenarios by Which Faulty Scores Penalized Thousands." *Education Daily* 2 July 2003: 1–2.

Mathews, Jay. "Seeking Alternatives to Standardized Testing." *Washingtonpost.com* 18 Feb. 2004: n. pag.

Winkler, Amber. "Division in the Ranks: Standardized Testing Draws Lines Between New and Veteran Teachers." *Phi Delta Kappan* 84.3 (2002): 219.

CHAPTER 17

What Is the Role of Sex and Violence in Popular Culture?

(text pages 636–671)

1   Students can serve as expert witnesses in cases for or against the censorship of sex and violence. Many of them have been immersed in television culture since early childhood. This doesn't mean, however, that they can be certain of general conclusions based only on personal experience. An analysis of this subject rests on all the important elements of argument.

a.   *Definition.* What constitutes "too much" attention to sex in TV, movies, and music? Can we distinguish "good" and "bad" violence?

b.   *Support.* Students should notice that in many discussions about this subject — including several articles in the text — evidence to support a point of view is selective. Students can probably uncover other examples that encourage questions about the strength of an author's conclusions.

c.   *Warrants.* Perhaps the most important issue is the cause-effect relationship between viewing and behavior. Although most experts seem to agree that a relationship exists, one prominent skeptic, Jonathan Freedman of the University of Toronto, continues to argue the weakness of causality: The fact that aggressive children like to watch violent shows hardly proves that the violent shows *cause* aggression. An English study found that it was "the chaos and change that [juvenile offenders] were living in" that promoted violent behavior and that "TV and movies played a relatively small part in their lives."

It's often been pointed out that Japanese movies, TV programs, and cartoons are at least as violent and pornographic as ours. Yet the rate of crime in Japan is far lower than in the United States. Ask students to find reasons that might account for the difference.

d.   From *The Economist* (13 Aug. 1994: 74):

Ron Slaby of Harvard University identifies four ways in which media violence can lay itself out in a child's personality: the aggressor effect, an increase in meanness; the victim effect, an increase in fearfulness and mistrust; the bystander effect, an increase in callousness; and the appetite effect, an increase in the desire to see or commit violence. Simple imitation may also play a part.

2. TV violence has been a target for criticism almost from the inception of television itself. The first congressional hearings on this issue took place in 1954. To date, there have been more than three thousand studies of the effects of TV violence. Students might consult some of these earlier attacks and try to determine first, if the violence on TV has changed, and second, if the nature of the criticism has changed. (A special issue of *TV Guide* on June 14, 1975, was titled "Violence! On TV —Does It Affect Our Society?")

   A high school teacher claims that movies and books that portray violence are different in their effects on the viewer or reader. "While movies can desensitize us to violence, I think reading can make us more sensitive to it. We understand in a much deeper sense, the impact of violence on a victim's life." Do our students think this is true?

3. Biblical stories, fairy tales, even nursery rhymes and lullabies — think of "London Bridge" and "Rockabye Baby" — contain images of cruelty and violence. Students can look for the ways, if any, in which those images are different from the representations in popular culture.

4. Someone has said, only half in jest, that liberals are worried about too much violence, conservatives about too much sex. If students agree that this judgment is true, ask them to examine the cultural assumptions that govern these preferences.

5. Do students agree with the following assessment of sexual content in TV shows and movies?

   The down side is that however much good the entertainment media's sexual liberation has done or may do, it also burdens the audience with additional anxiety by holding up images, over and over, of beauty, nonstop pleasure and excitement that most lives cannot match. (*New York Times* 29 Oct. 1995: H40.)

6. Ann Powers's "The Stresses of Youth, the Strains of Its Music" interprets the massacre in Littleton, Colorado, as an example of "the meanings and effects of youth culture." (*New York Times* 25 Apr. 1999: W18.) The author offers a penetrating analysis, with abundant support, of the violent extremes of music, fashion, and lifestyle which the murderers embraced. "Teachers," she says, "have long showed students how to grasp the nuances of literature and history. But instead of actually exploring youth culture in the company of young people, many adults debate its legality among themselves."

   How would students respond to explorations of youth culture in class with their teachers? Would they resent it as an intrusion — or a joke? Could students speak frankly about its appeal? After all, as the author points out, "Popular art aimed at adolescents often trades on alienation."

   "The hatemongers have gone global, aided by the Internet and the unmistakable drawing power of white power music." In "High-Decibel Hate" (*New York Times* 20 Aug. 2001: A21), Bob Herbert chronicles the rise of neo-Nazi and skinhead musical groups whose vicious lyrics target blacks, Jews, and gays. It is the music, say observers, that has been instrumental in attracting recruits into a movement that celebrates Hitler and condones violence. Perhaps students who have heard the music and the lyrics can analyze the nature of the appeal. From what youthful population are the recruits drawn?

7. What about comic books and video games? Believe it or not, there is a Comics Code Authority. It was created in 1954 to control the violence content in

comic books after Frederick Wertham's celebrated attack on comic and horror books in Seduction of the Innocent (Rinehart, 1954). Obviously, the code has relaxed its rules in recent years.

The video games Doom and Quake were mentioned as favorites of the Littleton killers. Can students find research proving that the influence of violent games and books can also be benign? Has their own experience with such entertainment suggested that there are valuable lessons about life to be learned from those contacts?

Bibliography

Allen, Steve. *Vulgarians at the Gate.* New York: Prometheus, 2001. Skewers Madonna, Howard Stern, Eminem, and Sex and the City as purveyors of "moral disorder and tastelessness."

Bok, Sisela. *Mayhem: Violence as Public Entertainment.* Cambridge, MA: Merloyd Lawrence/Perseus, 1998.

Edelstein, David. "Vigilante Vengeance, Hollywood's Response to Primal Fantasies." *New York Times* 10 Feb. 2002: AR15. "Do avengers in films encourage violence in real life? Or do they offer a safe outlet for venting?"

Heins, Marjorie. *Not in Front of the Children: Indecency, Censorship, and the Innocence of Youth.* New York: Hill, 2000. Dismisses the concern that sex and violence in the media can harm children.

Leland, John. "Bring the Noise." *New York Times Magazine* 27 Aug. 2000: 3. "As strident as it may be, the anger in popular music is only a faint reflection of larger forces — isolation, dislocation, fear — and fighting it, instead of them, won't solve much."

Morgenthal, David. "Counterpunch: Time to Rethink This Media Theory?" *Los Angeles Times* 1 Oct. 2001: 3. "Where are the antiviolence talking heads to explain to us why the banning of violent media from Afghani culture didn't lead to a peaceful utopia?"

CHAPTER 18

Are Limits on Freedom of Speech Ever Justified?

(text pages 672–702)

1. Freedom of speech on campus and on the Internet may be of most relevance to students, especially if there have been incidents of abusive language at their own schools and censorship of material on school-based Web sites. Students ought to examine any policy statements on their own campuses that define *racism, sexism,* or *homophobia* and threaten punishment for their expression. If examples don't exist or are difficult to find, students can be encouraged to supply them. As they do so, they should keep in mind that some schools have been forced to modify their guidelines after courts have ruled that strict speech codes violated the First Amendment.

Arguers may find themselves walking a narrow line between truth and offense. Students should consider this question: If the truth is offensive to some groups, should it nevertheless be expressed? The issue is complicated by the very nature of the academic purpose, which is usually defined as freedom in the search for truth. And there is another question: Do people have a right to express their feelings even if the expression is morally repugnant? Overtly racist speech or arguments that attempt to prove the superiority of the white race and the inferiority of all others can still be encountered in books and on the Internet. See J. Philippe Rushton, *Race, Evolution, and Behavior: A Life History Perspective* (Port Huron, MI, Charles Darwin Research Institute, 2000). This book, by a professor of psychology at the University of Western Ontario, argues for the superiority of "Orientals" and "whites" in intelligence and other vaguely defined characteristics, such as personality. Ask students to defend or attack the proposition that Rushton, who lectures widely, should be allowed to expound his views at a school assembly.

At the University of Massachusetts a new speech code proposal ensured freedom from harassment based on race, color, national or ethnic origin, gender, sexual orientation, age, religion, marital status, military service status, and disability. The Graduate Employees Organization wanted the policy extended to include citizenship, culture, HIV status, language, parental status, political affiliation or belief, and pregnancy status. A number of faculty members protested the expansion of "protected categories" as a serious impediment to free discussion of social issues in the classroom.

2. Is freedom of speech on campus different from freedom of speech on the street? The president of Emory University argues that free speech doesn't protect "vicious epithets," because universities are places where "the habits and manners of our civil society" are passed on to the next generation. But on the street there may be different rules. In New York State the highest court ruled that abusive speech was protected under federal and state constitutional guarantees of free speech. The case arose when a woman and her son, both mentally retarded, were verbally harassed by a neighbor.

In February 1998 nine teenagers in a Miami high school went to jail for publishing and circulating a pamphlet, "First Amendment Rights," which included a veiled death threat to the black principal, racist comments, and obscene cartoons. (*New York Times*, 4 March, 1998: A25.) The Miami American Civil Liberties Union defended the students, terming the pamphlet "a satire . . . in terms you hear on late-night stand-up comedy." The deputy superintendent of schools argued that "free speech doesn't give anyone the right to use a word that would inflame."

The newspaper article points out: "While the US Supreme Court has upheld students' right to political expression, it has also permitted school officials to censor student newspapers and to discipline a student who made suggestive comments in a speech."

Discuss with the class the limits to free speech in publications written and distributed by students.

Revisionist history has emerged as a new and troubling issue. It expresses itself not only in denial of the Holocaust but in new interpretations of ancient history. Students, of course, will not find it easy to marshal and examine all the facts in these debates, but they can attempt to assess the advantages and disadvantages of an academic freedom which gives college instructors the right to espouse any theory. (This freedom might also encompass the right to teach creationism.) Are there just and reasonable limits to such freedom?

In January 2001 an appeals court in Pennsylvania ruled that a school district's antiharassment policy violated First Amendment rights of free speech. The policy prohibited "jokes, name-calling, graffiti, innuendo, making fun of a student's clothing, social skills, or surname." The ruling was a response to a lawsuit by two students who feared they would be punished for expressing their religious belief that homosexuality is a sin. If asked to defend or attack the appeals court ruling, how would students define the kind of speech that should be punished?

3. The reference to lyrics in popular music should be of special interest to students. They will almost certainly know some of the offensive lyrics that have provoked their parents. Is labeling of albums a denial of free speech, a form of censorship? A distinction can be made between censure and censorship, a distinction often ignored in the debate over works of art considered offensive. Students can offer examples that clarify the definitions of these terms.

In the wake of the terrorist attack on September 11, 2001, some radio executives asked program directors not to broadcast certain songs which might be "taken the wrong way," for example, "When You're Falling" by Peter Gabriel. Other executives feared that such action heralded the suppression of free speech in popular music. Is the decision to honor the request a dangerous precedent or a responsible action demanded by a nation at war?

4. In 1996 Congress passed the Communications Decency Act, which forbade distribution of indecent material to minors on the Internet. But in 1999 the ban was ruled unconstitutional by the Supreme Court. Senator John McCain sponsored a bill to require antipornography filters on computers in schools and libraries that might receive federal funds for Internet hookups.

Ask students how they would respond to this kind of censorship. Is it feasible? Is there a better way to control children's access to obscene material on the Internet?

Thousands of underground high school newspapers are now on the Web. To what extent should school authorities be permitted to control or censor them? "Of greater concern," says a newspaper report, "are the Web sites created by students at home to post threats against or mock the teachers." A problem arises, says the deputy chief counsel for the Pennsylvania School Boards Administration, "if students are openly spilling hatred or contemplating violence against the staff." (*New York Times* 7 June 2001: E6.)

5. What about terrorists on the Web? Guerrilla groups now use the Internet to disseminate propaganda and plan attacks. Should they be controlled or censored? Or would this violate their rights to freedom of speech? See "Terrorists on the Web: Electronic 'Safe Haven,'" U.S. News & World Report 22 June 1998: 46.

Bibliography

Coles, Robert. "Safety Lessons for the Internet." *New York Times* 11 Oct. 1997: A23. Asks for some legal protection for children from pornography on the Internet.

Hanna, Judith Lynne, "Wrapping Nudity in a Cloak of Law." *New York Times* 29 July 2001: E14.

Hentoff, Nat. *Living the Bill of Rights: How to Be an Authentic American.* New York: HarperCollins, 1998.

Tribe, Laurence H. "The Internet vs. The First Amendment." *New York Times* 28 Apr. 1999: A27. The lessons of Littleton, Colorado: "It would be a mistake to think that good surveillance or control [of the Internet] can play an important role in preventing violent crimes."

CHAPTER 19

Why and How Should Immigration Be Controlled?

(text pages 703–734)

Immigration promises to be a source of controversy for the foreseeable future. Students from different regions of the U.S. may have very different views of the issue, and even those in the same community may see the situation differently and may respond with various levels of emotional intensity. You might ask students from different states and different towns and cities to what extent their communities have been affected by illegal immigration. The United States was founded as a nation of immigrants, so the prospect of sending back to their native country those who have established successful lives in America easily leads to the charge of hypocrisy. The situation is further complicated when children are born to immigrants who are in the U.S. illegally. Among the highly charged questions related to immigration concern whether those who entered the U.S. illegally should have access to health care, free public education, or even driver's licenses.

A good starting point for discussion is definition. Does the term "illegal alien" have the same connotations as the term "resident alien" or "undocumented worker"? In his novel *Migrant Souls*, Arturo Islas has the Mexican-American father tell his daughter why he is so offended when one of her classmates calls them resident aliens: "When people call Mexicans those words, it makes it easier for them to deport or kill them. Aliens come from outer space."[1]

Another question to consider with your students is the stereotypes that people have of those in the country illegally. You might ask your students to find evidence that those stereotypes are just that — hasty generalizations based on little data. Cowen and Rothschild's essay "Don't Bad-Mouth Unskilled Immigrants" points out significant contributions made by immigrants. On the other hand, you might ask them to look at Samuelson's essay "The Hard Truth of Immigration" for evidence that successive generations of immigrants continue to find it hard to break out of the cycle of poverty that comes with low paying jobs.

You might want to ask your students to chart the pros and cons of illegal immigration. To tie this prewriting activity more closely to the readings, you might ask them to base that chart on the arguments made by the writers in the chapter. They can also investigate the different proposals for stemming the flood of illegals across the southern border of the U.S. and for dealing with illegals already in the country.

An informal writing assignment based on Lochhead's "A Legacy of the Unforeseen" might ask students to speculate about what some of the unexpected consequences of immigration reform might be.

The excerpt from Pat Buchanan's book *State of Emergency*, "The Invasion," can profitably be analyzed for slanted language and logical fallacies. On the other hand, the same excerpt can be used to illustrate the power of statistics.

Because the picture on immigration is changing, the readings in the text can be supplemented and brought up to date with articles from recent newspapers and magazines.

---

[1]HarperCollins, 1990

CHAPTER 20

In the World of Medicine, Who Decides What Is Ethical?

(text pages 735–766)

As advances in the fields of medicine make possible things once thought impossible, questions arise about where to draw the line between what is possible and what is right. Should parents be able to choose the gender of their children? Should they undergo medical tests that might reveal abnormalities and thus might lead to an abortion? Should parents have a child in order to save the life of an older sibling? Should adopted children have the right to their birth parents' medical records? Students can readily add to this list. The list grows with every advance in medicine, so television, online, and print news sources should be watched for the latest in issues of medical ethics.

It is difficult to discuss medical ethics without discussing students' personal belief systems. The most devoutly religious students will want to turn to biblical authority as their primary or most significant source on such issues. Nowhere is it more important to discuss audience than where students most strongly feel their value systems are under attack or where they feel so strongly about their value system that they are not even willing to listen to other points of view. In teaching argument, you have probably stressed that there is little point in writing for those who agree with you. Assuming that their audience is at least mildly hostile to their point of view forces them to consider their opponent's side of the argument and to try to counter that opponent with the best support possible. This is a place where the results from a poll done at the beginning of the term or a more focused one given at this point in the term can be used to find out what the students in the class feel about medical ethics.

Writers and movie makers have long realized the attraction of speculating about science out of control. A classic like *Frankenstein* (the book and the movie) illustrates the danger of a scientist's playing God. A movie as recent as *I Am Legend* (2007) is based on the premise that a virus touted as the cure for cancer has gone out of control and has destroyed most of the inhabitants of the U.S. A subject that students enjoy discussing but that can also make them aware of some of the ethics involved in medical research is how close we have come to doing some of the things that were once possible only in novels or movies. Endless numbers of identical twins, for example, were a staple of society in Aldous Huxley's *Brave New World* (1932). Now we have clones.

Nancy Gibbs's article "Pillow Angel Ethics" clearly illustrates how what is medically possible is not necessarily ethical. Students can be asked to analyze the warrants implicit in the two sides of the debate over stunting the growth of a disabled individual.

George Annas's article "Cancer and the Constitution — Choice at Life's End" considers whether terminal patients should be allowed to try, as a last resort, drugs that are not yet known to be medically safe. This article also can lead to a fruitful discussion of warrants and thus of the ethical complexity of the field of medicine. **Note:** This article follows the citation style of the Council of Science Editors.

In his article "Does Stem Cell Advance Provide an Ethical Out," Arthur Caplan asks if it is more than a coincidence that a major advance in stem cell research was announced just as Congress was about to vote on a bill requiring federal funding of embryonic stem cell research. Students might research whether such "coincidences" have also occurred in the past. They can also discuss or investigate the extent to which medical research is dependent on federal funding and to what an extent, as a result, research is controlled by the government.

Students can also research the unethical use of human test subjects from the Nazi experiments during the Holocaust to the case of the Tuskegee airmen. The final essay in the chapter raises the question of when -or if -it is justified for a doctor to refuse treatment because that treatment violates his or her own ethics. Students can be asked to consider "what if." If they were doctors, are there treatments or procedures that their consciences would not let them provide (or withhold)?

CHAPTER 21
How Has Terrorism Affected the American Idea of Justice?
(text pages 767–798)

1. We include in this chapter all or part of two documents that your students almost certainly have heard of but probably have never read: the Geneva Convention and the Patriot Act. Reading the primary sources will aid them in understanding the arguments being made in the essays about the effects that terrorism has had on our justice system and our concept of justice in the broadest sense. The rules for the treatment of prisoners of war that grew out of the Geneva Convention have long been the accepted standard. We like to think that we as Americans are among those who follow the rules, that we are above the sort of atrocities carried out under Adolf Hitler or Saddam Hussein. A small number of the military personnel who represented us in Iraq were clearly not, and the whole Abu Ghraib prisoner abuse scandal brought into question how many others, high up in the chain of command, were willing to consider rewriting the rule book on the treatment of prisoners when those prisoners might be linked to terrorist attacks on American soil.

2. If your students have read Michael Levin's "A Case for Torture" in Chapter 8, they may have already considered whether torture is ever justified as a means of gaining information that could save lives. If not, you might want to link it to this unit. One defense offered by those who abused prisoners at Abu Ghraib was that their superiors encouraged them to do whatever was necessary to get information out of the prisoners.

3. Ehrenreich's essay "What Abu Ghraib Taught Me" expresses a feminist's disappointment that after women fought so hard for the right to serve in the military, some few dishonored other women in uniform. You might ask your students to consider Ehrenreich's piece in conjunction with the sample research paper "Women in Combat" in Chapter 12.

4. The pieces related to the Patriot Act are designed to let your students see multiple viewpoints on the issue. One way to begin the unit is by having students read the passage from the act themselves and speculate on what impact it could have on their lives. You might then have them consider the same question again after having read the other three pieces related to the act. By then they might be ready to support a claim of value or claim of policy regarding the potential threat the act poses to the rights of Americans and how that threat compares to the potential threat of terrorism.

5. The piece by Amon looks at how justice at home in America has been affected
    by terrorism. Your students could synthesize what they learn from this essay
    and what they learn from other sources that they find to draw some conclu-
    sions about how terrorism has affected our American system of justice.

Bibliography

Goldstone, Richard J. "International Law and Justice and America's War on
    Terrorism." *Social Research* 6.4 (2002): 1045–55.

Ignatieff, Michael. "What Geneva Conventions?" Rev. of *Chain of Command:
    The Road from 9/11 to Abu Ghraib*, by Seymour M. Hersh. New York Times
    Book Review 17 Oct. 2004: 13.

Neumeister, Larry. "At Close of Prosecution Case in New York Terrorism Trial,
    References to bin Laden, Sept. 11." *America's Intelligence Wire* 8 Oct. 2004:
    n. pag.

Slaughter, Anne-Marie. "Terrorism and Justice." *Financial Times* 12 Oct. 2001:
    23.

"Terrorism and Justice." *New York Times* 12 Dec. 2001: A30.

Appendix:
Rogerian Argument

Several instructors have expressed an interest in teaching the theories of Carl Rogers as an adjunct to Toulmin's theory of argument. Since Rogers emphasizes the importance of establishing common ground between two or more parties, his theories can be introduced with discussion of "Finding the Middle Ground" in Chapter 9. In addition to the information for instructors, this appendix includes a brief introduction on Carl Rogers that can be distributed to students as a handout along with an excerpt from his book *A Way of Being* (Houghton Mifflin, 1980).

For the Student

Carl Rogers (1902–1987) was one of the founders of humanistic psychology. Of himself as therapist he wrote: "I enter the relation [with the patient] not as a scientist, not as a physician who can accurately diagnose and cure, but as a person, entering into a personal relationship." He believed that the experience of two people meeting and speaking truly to each other without assuming other roles would have a healing effect.

In later years he became convinced that the same principles of nondirective, nonconfrontational therapy that emphasized attentive listening could work, not only for couples and small groups but also for large groups, even nations, to create more harmonious relationships.

Rogers was not, of course, the only psychologist who thought that a knowledge of psychological principles could offer insight into the causes and resolution of public controversies, even the violent confrontations in war, terrorism, and the taking of hostages. The passage below summarizes another humanistic psychologist's view of the causes of war, a view influenced by Rogers's belief that the failure to understand the "reality" of the enemy was a major cause of war.

> One theory holds that people's misperceptions about their enemies act as hindrances to peace. Possible distortions include an image of the enemy as diabolical, a virile self-image, an overconfident military, lack of empathy for the enemy, selective inattention to facts, and a moral self-image.[1]

Because Rogers was resolutely optimistic about the essential goodness of human nature, a study of Rogerian psychology inevitably provokes the question: Does human nature contain evil? This is the subject of a minidebate between Carl Rogers and Rollo May, a prominent psychoanalyst and author of *Man's Search for Himself* (Norton, 1953). Rollo May answered Yes. Carl Rogers answered No.[2] The excerpt below emphasizes the warrant on which Rogers based his claim.

Rollo May: Yes

> The culture admittedly has powerful effects upon us. But it could not have these effects were these tendencies not already present. Who makes up the culture except persons like you and me? The culture is evil as well as good because we, the human beings who constitute it, are evil as well

---

[1]Robert S. Feldman, *Understanding Psychology* (New York: McGraw, 1990) 734. Feldman is summarizing the view of Ralph K. White, editor o a guidebook on the ways that psychology can help to prevent a nuclear disaster.

[2]David Myers, *Psychology* (New York: worth, 1989) 428.

as good. . . . We are bundles of both evil and good potentialities. . . . Life, to me, is not a requirement to live out a pre-ordained pattern of goodness, but a challenge coming down through the centuries out of the fact that each of us can throw the lever toward good or toward evil. This seems to me to require the age-old religious truths of mercy and forgiveness, and it leaves no place for self-righteousness.

Carl Rogers: No

Though I am very well aware of the incredible amount of destructive, cruel, malevolent behavior in today's world — from the threats of war to the senseless violence in the streets — I do not find that this evil is inherent in human nature. In a psychological climate which is nurturant of growth and choice, I have never known an individual to choose the cruel or destructive path. . . . [So] my experience leads me to believe that it is cultural influences which are the major factor in our evil behaviors. . . . I see members of the human species . . . as essentially constructive in their fundamental nature, but damaged by their experience.

In the following passage from one of his books, Rogers reveals his intellectual and emotional journey from contemplation of his own reality to recognition of the realities of others. After reading his argument, you should try to find examples of public controversies — in this book and in the media where they are reported every day — which you think lend themselves to compromise or a middle ground. Try to be specific about the strategies you would suggest for achieving the compromise. Do you think there are controversies in which agreement is not possible or desirable? Be specific here, too, about the basic principles that might limit acceptance of a different point of view. Finally, can you point to a connection between Rogers's views of human nature in the minidebate and the proposals for educational reform that he offers in his book?

From A Way of Being

CARL ROGERS

I, and many others, have come to a new realization. It is this: The only reality I can possibly know is the world as I perceive and experience it at this moment. The only reality you can possibly know is the world as you perceive and experience it at this moment. And the only certainty is that those perceived realities are different. There are as many "real worlds" as there are people! This creates a most burdensome dilemma, one never before experienced in history.

From time immemorial, the tribe or the community or the nation or the culture has agreed upon what constitutes the real world. To be sure, different tribes or different cultures might have held sharply different world views, but at least there was a large, relatively unified group which felt assured in its knowledge of the world and the universe, and knew that this perception was true. So the community frowned upon, condemned, persecuted, even killed those who did not agree, who perceived reality differently. Copernicus, even though he kept his findings secret for many years, was eventually declared a heretic. Galileo established proof of Copernicus's views, but in his seventies he was forced to recant his teachings. Giordano Bruno was burned at the stake in 1600 for teaching that there were many worlds in our universe.

Individuals who deviated in their perception of religious reality were tortured and killed. In the mid-1800s, Ignaz Semmelweis, an intense young Hungarian physician-scientist, was driven insane by his persecutors because he made the then absurd claim that childbed fever, that dread scourge of the maternity room, was carried from one woman to another by invisible germs on the hands and instruments of the doctors. Obvious nonsense, in terms of the reality of his day. In our own American Colonies, those who were even suspected of having psychic powers were considered witches and were hanged or crushed under great stones. History offers a continuing series of examples of the awful price paid by those who perceive a reality different from the agreed-upon real world. Although society has often come around eventually to agree with its dissidents, as in the instances I have mentioned, there is no doubt that this insistence upon a known and certain universe has been part of the cement that holds a culture together.

Today we face a different situation. The ease and rapidity of worldwide communication means that every one of us is aware of a dozen "realities"; even though we may think some of them absurd (like reincarnation) or dangerous (like communism), we cannot help but be aware of them. No longer can we exist in a secure cocoon, knowing that we all see the world in the same way.

Because of this change, I want to raise a very serious question: Can we today afford the luxury of having "*a*" reality? Can we still preserve the belief that there is a "real world" upon whose definition we all agree? I am convinced that this is a luxury we *cannot* afford, a myth we dare not maintain. Only once in recent history has this been fully and successfully achieved. Millions of people were in complete agreement as to the nature of social and cultural reality — an agreement brought about by the mesmerizing influence of Hitler. This agreement about reality nearly marked the destruction of Western culture. I do not see it as something to be emulated.

In Western culture during this century — especially in the United States — there has also been an agreed-upon reality of values. This gospel can be stated very briefly: "More is better, bigger is better, faster is better, and modern technology will achieve all three of these eminently desirable goals." But now that credo is a crumbling disaster in which few believe. It is dissolving in the smog of pollution, the famine of overpopulation, the Damocles' sword of the nuclear bomb. We have so successfully achieved the goal of "a bigger bang for a buck" that we are in danger of destroying all life on this planet.

Our attempts, then, to live in the "real world" which all perceive in the same way have, in my opinion, led us to the brink of annihilation as a species. I will be so bold as to suggest an alternative.

It appears to me that the way of the future must be to base our lives and our education on the assumption that there are as many realities as there are persons, and that our highest priority is to accept that hypothesis and proceed from there. Proceed where? Proceed, each of us, to explore openmindedly the many, many perceptions of reality that exist. We would, I believe, enrich our own lives in the process. We would also become more able to cope with the reality in which each one of us exists, because we would be aware of many more options. This might well be a life full of perplexity and difficult choices, demanding greater maturity, but it would be an exciting and adventurous life.

The question may well be raised, however, whether we could have a community or a society based on this hypothesis of multiple realities. Might not such a society be a completely individualistic anarchy? That is not my opinion. Suppose my grudging tolerance of your separate world view became a full acceptance of you and your right to have such a view. Suppose that instead of shutting out the realities of others as absurd or dangerous or heretical or stupid, I was willing to explore and learn about those realities? Suppose you were willing to do the same. What would be the social result? I think that our society would be based not on a blind commitment to a cause or creed or view of reality, but on a common commitment to each other as rightfully separate persons, with separate realities. The natural human tendency to care for another would no longer be "I care for you because you are the same as I," but, instead, "I prize and treasure you because you are different from me."

Idealistic, you say? It surely is. How can I be so utterly naive and "unrealistic" as to have any hope that such a drastic change could conceivably come about? I base my hope partly on the view of world history so aptly stated by Charles Beard: "When the skies grow dark, the stars begin to shine." So we may see the emergence of leaders who are moving in this new direction.

I base my hope, even more solidly, on the view enunciated by Lancelot Whyte, the historian of ideas, in his final book before his death. It is his theory, in which he is not alone, that great steps in human history are anticipated, and probably brought about, by changes in the unconscious thinking of thousands and millions of individuals during the period preceding the change. Then, in a relatively short space of time, a new idea, a new perspective, seems to burst upon the world scene, and change occurs. He gives the example that before 1914, patriotism and nationalism were unquestioned virtues. Then began the faint unconscious questioning which built an unconscious tradition reversing a whole pattern of thought. This new perspective burst into the open between 1950 and 1970. "My country, right or wrong" is no longer a belief to live by. Nationalistic wars are out of date and out of favor, and even though they continue, world opinion is deeply opposed. Whyte (1974) points out that "at any moment the *unconscious levels are ahead of the conscious* in the task of unifying emotion, thought and action!" [*The Universe of Experience*, Harper Torchbooks, p. 107.]

For me, this line of thought is entirely congenial. I have stated that we are wiser than our intellects, that our organisms as a whole have a wisdom and purposiveness which goes well beyond our conscious thought. I believe that this idea applies to the concepts I have been presenting in this chapter. I think that men and women, individually and collectively, are inwardly and organismically rejecting the view of one single, culture-approved reality. I believe they are moving inevitably toward the acceptance of millions of separate, challenging, exciting, informative, *individual* perceptions of reality. I regard it as possible that this view — like the sudden and separate discovery of the principles of quantum mechanics by scientists in different countries — may begin to come into effective existence in many parts of the world at once. If so, we will be living in a totally new universe, different from any in history. Is it conceivable that such a change can come about?

Here lies the challenge to educators — probably the most insecure and frightened among any of the professions — battered by public pressures, limited by legislative restrictions, essentially conservative in their reactions. Can they possibly espouse such a view of multiple realities as I have been describing? Can they begin to bring into being the changes in attitudes, behaviors, and values that such a world view would demand? Certainly, by themselves they cannot. But with the underlying change in what Whyte calls "the unconscious tradition," and with the aid of the new person whom I and many others see emerging in our culture, it is just conceivable that they might succeed.

I conclude that if nations follow their past ways, then, because of the speed of world communication of separate views, each society will have to exert more and more coercion to bring about a forced agreement as to what constitutes the real world and its values. Those coerced agreements will differ from nation to nation, from culture to culture. The coercion will destroy individual freedom. We will bring about our own destruction through the clashes caused by differing world views.

But I have suggested an alternative. If we accept as a basic fact of all human life that we live in separate realities; if we can see those differing realities as the most promising resource for learning in all the history of the world; if we can live together in order to learn from one another without fear; if we can do all this, then a new age could be dawning. And perhaps — just perhaps — humankind's deep organic sensings are paving the way for just such a change.

To the Instructor

Most students will respond wholeheartedly to Rogers's summons, since it elicits our most generous impulses and promises a kinder, gentler world for all of us. In addition, his emphasis on education can encourage students to reflect on their own experience with multiculturalism and diversity as they have observed them, or not, at school.

Rogers was not without his critics and his contradictions. However welcome his essentially optimistic view of the human capacity for change and growth, his theories can also invite a lively dialogue. Before considering Rogers's policy recommendations, students should be familiar with the history on which Rogers bases his conclusions. They should be prepared to discuss the values that underlie his claims. (See the reference to Rogers in Chapter 7's "Divorce and Our National Values.") And, of course, they should be encouraged to ask hard questions.

We would begin by asking students to consider answers to these questions: Can you think of other examples of separate realities? Do you think that all realities are equally deserving of respect and accommodation? (Be specific.) Does Rogers try to prove that they are? Does recent history — since the publication of *A Way of Being* in 1980 — confirm or deny Rogers's hopes and convictions? Do you think Rogers and King in "I Have a Dream" agree about the shape of a future world?

Some students may want to know whether the analogy between private and public reconciliations can hold. Not everyone agrees that the therapies which are successful in solving problems between individuals can be called on to resolve the profound differences in the public arena. "In the context of a marriage, say, it does seem plausible that a husband and wife may have common goals. But is this also true in public life? [I]n many cases we don't share first principles at all — just think of the fights over abortion." (Larissa MacFarquhar, "Thank You for Not Fighting," rev. of *The Argument Culture*, by Deborah Tannen, *New York Times Book Review* 5 Apr. 1998: 38.)

Students may want to consult Tannen's book, which offers a Rogerian perspective. From the review quoted above, "Tannen's is a communitarian view of the world, in which we share enough first principles that we should in theory be able to agree on the right thing to do."

Need more help with writing and research?

Re:Writing is designed to help you with important writing concerns. You'll find advice from experts, models you can rely on, and exercises that will tell you right away how you're doing. And it's all free and available any hour of the day. All of these can be accessed at bedfordstmartins.com/rewriting.

Need help with grammar problems?
Exercise Central
(bedfordstmartins.com/exercisecentral)

Want to see what papers for your other courses look like?
Model Documents Gallery
(bedfordstmartins.com/modeldocs)

Stuck somewhere in the research process? (Maybe at the beginning?)
The Bedford Research Room
(bedfordstmartins.com/researchroom)

Wondering whether a Web site is good enough to use in your paper?
Tutorial for Evaluating Online Sources
(bedfordstmartins.com/onlinesourcestutorial)

Having trouble figuring out how to cite a source?
Research and Documentation Online
(bedfordstmartins.com/resdoc)

Confused about plagiarism?
The St. Martin's Tutorial on Avoiding Plagiarism
(bedfordstmartins.com/plagiarismtutorial)

Want to get more out of your word processor?
Using Your Word Processor
(bedfordstmartins.com/wordprocessor)

Trying to improve the look of your paper?
Using Your Word Processor to Design Documents
(bedfordstmartins.com/docdesigntutorial)

Need to create slides for a presentation?
Preparing Presentation Slides Tutorial
(bedfordstmartins.com/presentationslidetutorial)

Interested in creating a Web site?
Web Design Tutorial
(bedfordstmartins.com/webdesigntutorial)